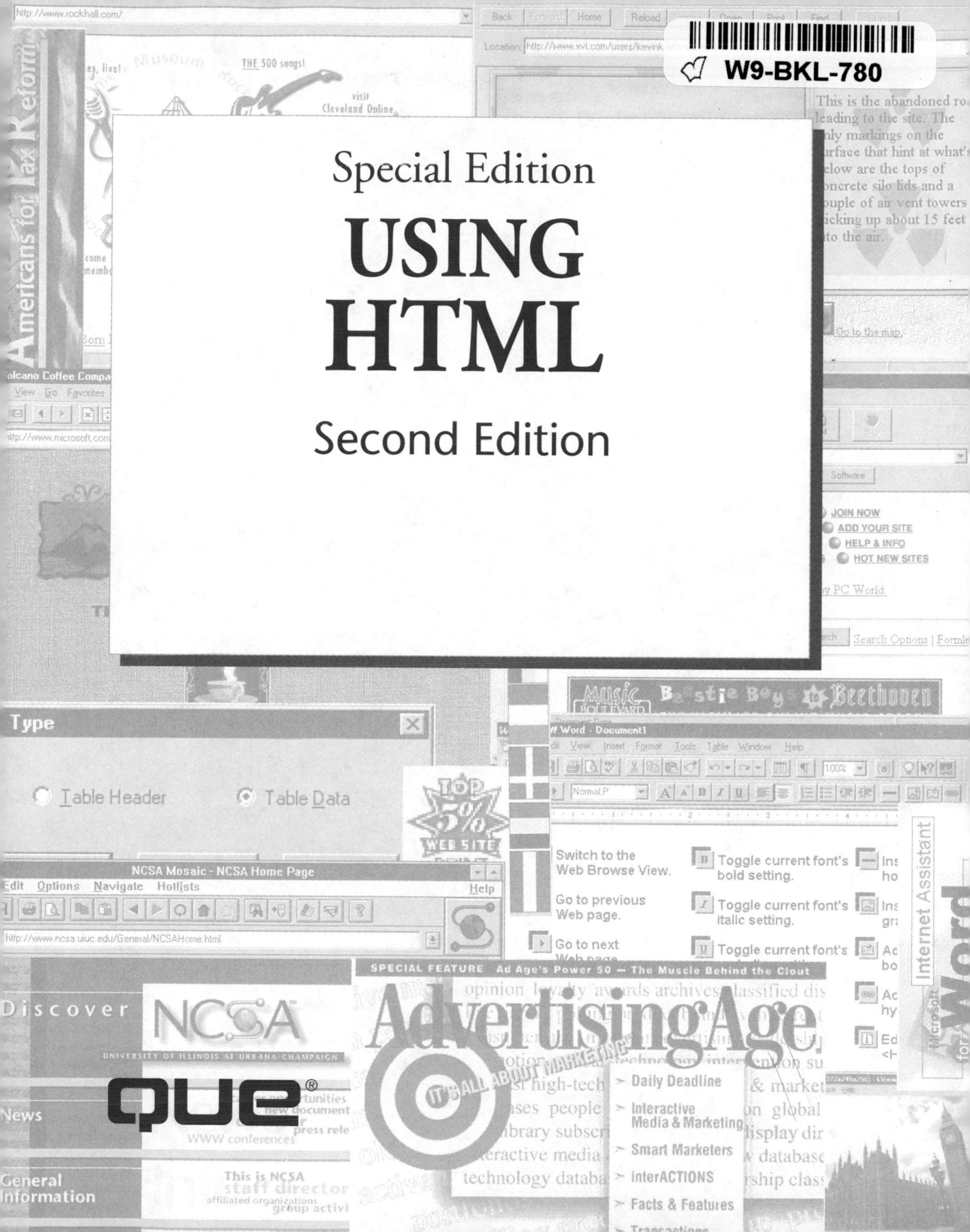

Special Edition

USING HTML

Second Edition

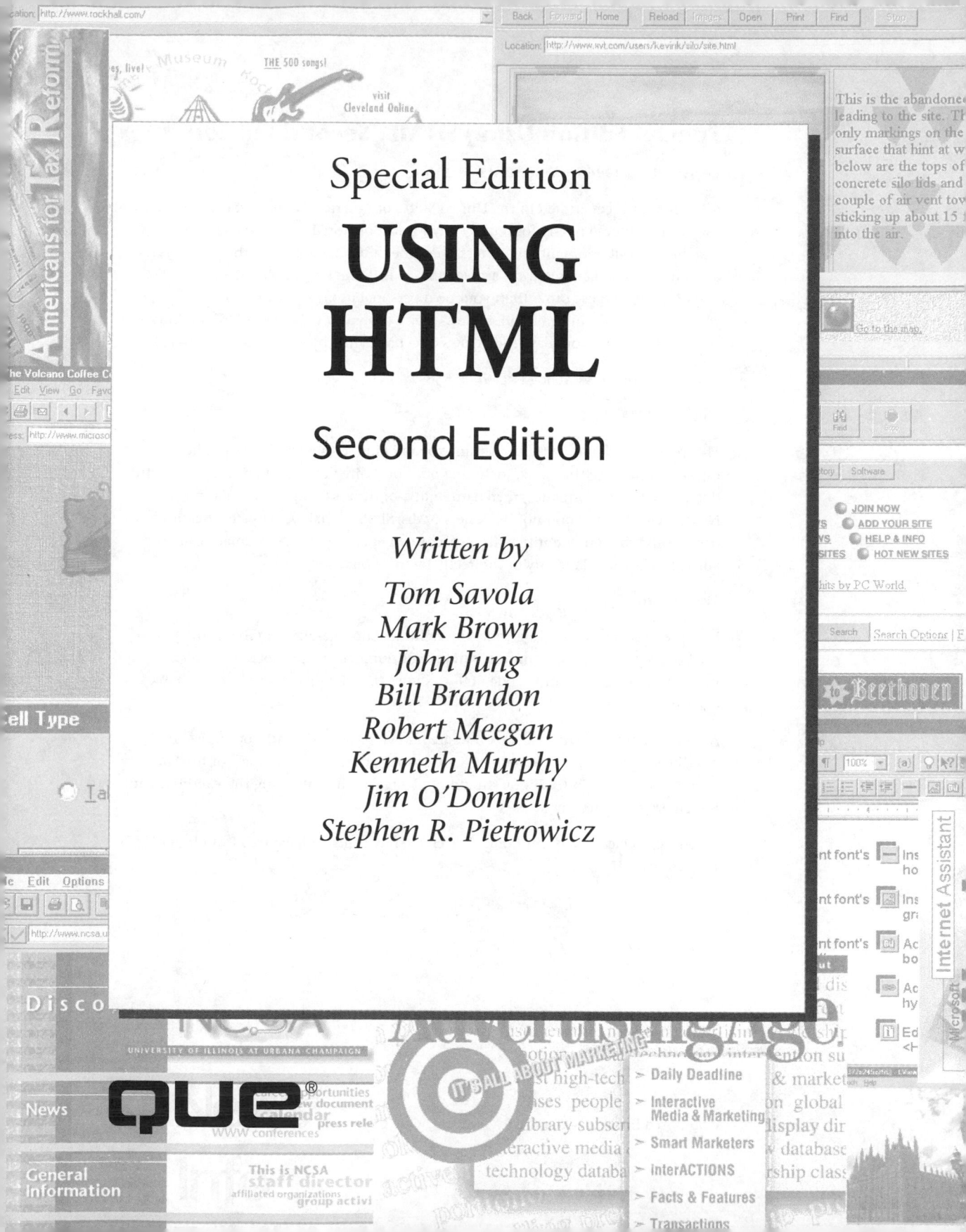

Special Edition

USING HTML

Second Edition

Written by

Tom Savola
Mark Brown
John Jung
Bill Brandon
Robert Meegan
Kenneth Murphy
Jim O'Donnell
Stephen R. Pietrowicz

que®

Special Edition Using HTML, Second Edition

Library of Congress Catalog No.: 96-67558

ISBN: 0-7897-0758-6

98 97 96   4 3 2 1

Interpretation of the printing code: the rightmost double-digit number is the year of the book's printing; the rightmost single-digit number, the number of the book's printing. For example, a printing code of 96-1 shows that the first printing of the book occurred in 1996.

Screen reproductions in this book were created by using Collage Plus from Inner Media, Inc., Hollis, NH.

Composed in *Stone Serif* and *MCPdigital* by Que Corporation

Credits

President
Roland Elgey

Vice President and Publisher
Marie Butler-Knight

Editorial Services Director
Elizabeth Keaffaber

Publishing Manager
Jim Minatel

Managing Editor
Sandy Doell

Acquisitions Editor
Doshia Stewart

Development Editor
Mark Cierzniak

Senior Editors
Nancy Sixsmith
Mike La Bonne

Copy Editors
Kelli Brooks
Tom Cirtin
Noelle Gasco
Chuck Hutchinson
Kelly Oliver

Technical Editor
Garrett Pease (Discovery Computing)

Technical Specialist
Nadeem Muhammed

Book Designer
Ruth Harvey

Cover Designer
Dan Armstrong

Production Team
Stephen Adams
Brian Buschkill
John Carroll
Chad Dressler
Jenny Earhart
Joan Evan
Bryan Flores
Trey Frank
Amy Gornik
Jason Hand
Sonja Hart
Damon Jordan
Clint Lahnen
Bob LaRoche
Stephanie Layton
Michelle Lee
Julie Quinn
Kaylene Riemen
Laura Robbins
Bobbi Satterfield
Linda Seifert
Todd Wente
Paul Wilson
Jody York

Indexer
Tom Dinse

To my wife, Carol, and my daughter, Jenny, who have always been my inspiration, my foundation, and my best friends.

Mark R. Brown

To my mom, dad, and brother. Thanks guys, for all your support in this endeavor.

John Jung

About the Authors

Tom Savola is the online technical director for Z. M. Interactive, a leading commercial Web developer (**http://www.zmiweb.com/**) whose recent sites include Universal City (**http://www.mca.com/unicity**), WaterWorld: Quest for the Mariner (**http://www.mca.com/unicity/waterworld/**), Jurassic Park—The Ride (**http://www.mca.com/unicity/attractions/jp.html**), and CityWalk on the Web (**http://www.mca.com/citywalk**). He is the author of *Special Edition Using HTML* (First Edition) and coauthor of *Using HTML*, both from Que Corporation. He teaches The Internet Workshop for Design Professionals, a four-day, hands-on workshop for media design specialists sponsored by Internet Solutions, Inc. (**http://intersolutions.com/workshop/**). Tom lives in Mill Creek, WA, with his wife, Laura, and cats, Cecil and Zoe. He can be reached by e-mail at **savola@haywire.com**, or via the Haywire Web site (**http://www.haywire.com/**).

John Jung has been a contributing author for almost half a dozen books. When he's not working on books, he has a day job that he thoroughly enjoys. As a professional systems administrator for a worldwide information services company, he's around computers all day. He takes a break from writing and working by watching TV, surfing the Net, and generally goofing off. You can reach John at his e-mail address: **jjung@netcom.com**.

Mark R. Brown has been writing computer magazine articles, books, and manuals for over 13 years. He was managing editor of *.info* magazine when it was named one of the six best computer magazines of 1991 by the Computer Press Association, and was nominated by the Software Publisher's Association for the 1988 Software Reviewer of the Year award. He is currently the manager of technical publications for Neural Applications Corporation, a major player in applying cutting-edge artificial intelligence techniques to industrial control applications, such as steel making and food processing. A bona fide personal computing pioneer, he hand-built his first PC in 1977, taught himself to program it in hexadecimal, and has since dabbled in dozens of different programming languages. He has been telecomputing since 1983, and is currently Webmaster of two World Wide Web sites: **http://www.neural.com**, and a personal Web site on the topic of airships which will have moved to a new URL by the time this is published. Mark is a life-long resident of Iowa. He enjoys reading and writing, gaming, Iowa Hawkeye Big 10 football, walks in the park with his dog, Bosco, and day trips through the Iowa countryside with his wife, Carol.

Bill Brandon is a human performance technologist: a designer of human systems to support mission-critical business outcomes. Many of these systems have as much to do with good design as with high technology. He has pursued this career in line and staff jobs since 1968. Along the way, Bill has been a manager of business units, classroom instructor and facilitator, author of computer-based training, and designer of World Wide Web sites and pages. He has coauthored four Que books since 1995, including *Building Multimedia Applications with Visual Basic 4* and *The Computer Trainer's Personal Training Guide*. Bill is a frequent speaker at local, national, and international conferences. His leadership accomplishments include operating a forum for computer training and support professionals on CompuServe and serving as president of the Dallas-Fort Worth Chapter of the International Society for Performance Improvement. Bill received his B.A. in History from the University of Texas at Austin, where he first learned to program (FORTRAN I on an IBM 1620-II). He did postgraduate work in Human Behavior at the U.S. International University in San Diego, and has completed extensive training in neurolinguistic programming. Bill owns Accomplishment Technology Unlimited, and is carrying out projects in multimedia, training, and performance support for clients in a number of industries. He lives near Dallas with his wife of 25 years; they have two daughters. Bill's e-mail address is **bill_brandon@msn.com.** You can also reach him at **71316,516** on CompuServe.

Robert Meegan makes his living designing industrial control systems. He has been working with computers for a very long time. Robert can be reached at **rmeegan@ia.net**.

Kenneth Murphy is a freelance PERL programmer living in the beautiful city of Columbia, Mo. In his free time, you can usually find him reading up on the latest programming languages or working out at the gym. Somehow, in the midst of everything, he also finds time to work slowly toward a master's in computer science.

Jim O'Donnell was born on Oct. 17, 1963 (you may forward birthday greetings to **odonnj@rpi.edu**), in Pittsburgh, PA. After a number of unproductive years, he began his studies in electrical engineering at Rensselaer Polytechnic Institute. He liked it so much that he spent 11 years there getting three degrees, graduating for the third (and final) time in the summer of 1992. He can now be found plying his trade at the NASA Goddard Space Flight Center (which takes a tolerant, though hardly enthusiastic view, of his writing endeavors). He's not a rocket scientist, but he's close. O'Donnell's first experience with a "personal" computer was in high school with a Southwest Technical Products computer using a paper tape storage device, quickly graduating to a TRS-80 Model II with cassette tape storage. His fate as a computer geek was sealed when Rensselaer gave him an Atari 800 as part of a scholarship. O'Donnell doesn't actually own a Windows PC, but expects to take the plunge, soon. Wish him luck.

Stephen R. Pietrowicz lives with his wife, Mary, and his daughter, Sarah, in Champaign, IL. For the past 10 years he has worked as a UNIX programmer in a variety of different areas including security, networking, Motif/X Window, and real-time operating systems. Most recently, he was part of the Mosaic for X Window team at the National Center for Supercomputing Applications (NCSA), home of the Mosaic web browser. He is now developing new Internet tools using Java at NCSA.

Acknowledgments

This book is made possible by more than a bunch of knowledgeable writers. First and foremost, we would like extend our deepest thanks to everybody at Que. In particular, we'd like to thank Doshia Stewart and Mark Cierzniak— Doshia for her patience, guidance, and encouragement, and Mark for his sharp eye in spotting when our writing wandered. These two people were the ones most responsible for making this book the best it possibly could be.

Mark Brown would like to personally thank Oran Sands for bringing him in the door at Que; Jim Oldfield for giving him his first chance (many, many years ago) to write professionally; Benn Dunnington for an intense eight-year apprenticeship that taught him to write as well as humanly possible under impossible deadlines; and Mr. Buxton, his seventh grade English teacher, who told him that he could be a writer if he only put his mind to it.

John Jung would like to personally thank a few of his friends. He'd like to thank Warren Ernst for his support and encouragement, for getting him started in book writing. If it weren't for him, John might not have tried his hand at writing one more time. Also thanks go out to Steve Ma and Argelia and Alex Osorio, for being his unwitting target audience. Whenever he needed to think about who he was writing for, one of them came to mind. Finally, John's deepest and most heartfelt thanks go to April Dean, for always reminding him about the important things in life. Her presence was always felt to let him know just why he was putting all those words to paper.

Finally, we would like to thank each of our families for their support. The writing sometimes got hectic and pressured, and their putting up with us didn't go unnoticed.

— John Jung & Mark R. Brown

We'd Like to Hear from You!

As part of our continuing effort to produce books of the highest possible quality, Que would like to hear your comments. To stay competitive, we *really* want you, as a computer book reader and user, to let us know what you like or dislike most about this book or other Que products.

You can mail comments, ideas, or suggestions for improving future editions to the address below, or send us a fax at (317) 581-4663. For the on-line inclined, Macmillan Computer Publishing now has a forum on CompuServe (type **GO QUEBOOKS** at any prompt) through which our staff and authors are available for questions and comments. The address of our Internet site is **http://www.mcp.com** (World Wide Web).

In addition to exploring our forum, please feel free to contact me personally to discuss your opinions of this book. You can reach me on CompuServe at **102521,3562**.

Thanks in advance—your comments will help us to continue publishing the best books available on computer topics in today's market.

Doshia Stewart
Product Development Specialist
Que Corporation
201 W. 103rd Street
Indianapolis, Indiana 46290
USA

Contents at a Glance

Contents

9 Displaying Text in Lists   173

10 Adding Graphics to Your Home Page   191

11 Handling Images 209

III Advanced HTML Presentation 227

12 Graphics Navigation with Imagemaps 229

13 Tables and Math Equations   251

14 HTML Style Sheets   277

18 Multimedia and Animation on the Web   397

23 All About CGI Scripts   **525**

24 Sample Code and CGI Scripts   **557**

V Developing Interactive Web Pages   597

25 Adding Live Chat Pages to Your Site   599

26 Java and JavaScript   621

VI HTML Authoring Tools 641

VII Sample HTML Applications   741

31 Online Visitor's Guide to Jubilee Falls State Park   743

D WWW Bibliography   867

Index   873

Introduction

by Mark Brown

You can't build a monument without bricks, and you can't make bricks without straw—everyone who has seen the film *The Ten Commandments* knows that.

The World Wide Web is built of Web pages, and those pages are themselves created with HyperText Markup Language, or HTML. Without HTML, there would be no Web pages, and without Web pages, there would be no World Wide Web.

If you plan to establish your own monumental presence on the World Wide Web, you have to start with the straw, and that's HTML.

Though many people speak of "HTML Programming" with a capital *P*, HTML is really not a programming language at all. HTML is exactly what it claims to be: a *markup language*. You use HTML to mark up a text document, just as you would if you were an editor using a red pencil. The marks you use indicate which format (or presentation style) should be used when displaying the marked text.

If you have ever used an old word processing program, you already know how a markup language works. In these old programs, if you wanted text to appear in italics, you surrounded it with control characters like this:

```
/Ithis is in italics/i
```

When you printed the document, the first /I kicked your line printer into italics mode, the following text was printed in italics, and the /i then turned off italics. The printer didn't actually print the /I or /i. They were just codes to tell it what to do. But the "marked up" text in between appeared in italics.

HTML works exactly the same way. If you want text to appear on a Web page in italics, you mark it like this:

```
<I>this is in italics</I>
```

The <I> turns on italics; the </I> turns it off. The <I> and </I> tags don't appear on-screen, but the text in between is displayed in italics.

Everything you create in HTML relies on marks, or *tags*, like these. To be a whiz-bang HTML programmer, all you need to learn is which tags do what. Fortunately, that's what this entire book is about.

A few other topics are covered along the way: page design techniques, the extensions to HTML supported by browsers such as Netscape Navigator and Internet Explorer, graphics creation, and even multimedia content for your Web site. You take a look at HTML and graphics editing tools, HTML code verification, and how to promote your site on the Web. You even take short side trips into Java applets, CGI programming, and Virtual Reality Modeling Language (VRML).

But you explore these topics only as they relate to the main theme: creating your own Web pages by using HTML. The major goal of this book is to help you learn as much as possible about HTML itself.

Who Should Use This Book?

Special Edition Using HTML, Second Edition, is intended for anyone and everyone who wants to create his or her own presence on the World Wide Web.

Novices will find information on what other people are doing on the Web, what is appropriate to put on the Web, and how to use basic HTML tags to begin to create their own Web pages.

Intermediate users will discover tips, tricks, and techniques for creating Web pages that exploit the full potential of HTML.

And advanced users will learn how to use powerful extensions to HTML and additional elements such as CGI-bin programs and Java applets to make their World Wide Web pages truly world class.

How This Book Is Organized

Special Edition Using HTML, Second Edition, is organized into six parts.

Part I, "Overview of the World Wide Web," gives a short history of the Internet and how the Web came to be. This part explores the relationships between the Web and earlier Internet services such as e-mail, FTP, Gopher, and UseNet news. A glossary of terms necessary for discussing Web-related topics is included, as is a chapter that explains how Web server computers and Web browser programs work together.

Part II, "Basic HTML Presentation," jumps into the basics of HTML page creation. First, you find out what kinds of information do and don't belong on the Web; in other words, you learn how to make sure that your Web pages present you as a good *netizen* (Net citizen). Then you learn about the HEAD and BODY sections of an HTML document, how to mark up text so that it appears on the screen in various styles, and how to link your pages gracefully to other Internet services such as Gopher, FTP, UseNet news, and e-mail. You find information on standard HTML page design practices such as signing and dating pages, and how to provide text-only pages for non-graphic browsers. An entire chapter is devoted to the topic of making HTML lists, and three chapters describe how to create and implement Web page graphics, including tricky topics such as transparent GIF images and progressive JPEGs.

Part III, "Advanced HTML Presentation," delves into tougher material like designing clickable image maps for easier Web site navigation and the subtleties of HTML tables. Chapter 14 provides a break by stepping you through the creation of two real home pages, one personal and one for business. Two chapters cover the extensions to HTML that are supported by Netscape and other Web browser programs. You also get a peek at the proposed HTML 3.0 standard. This part progresses to discuss VRML and multimedia, including MPEG, AVI, and MOV movies. The last two chapters in this part tell you how to verify your HTML code and how to promote your site on the Web.

Part IV, "Forms and CGI," tackles two of the most versatile and most challenging Web page-creation tools. Forms are HTML elements that allow your site to obtain information from your viewers. CGI programs (or scripts) let you use that information to create customized responses "on the fly."

Part V, "Developing Interactive Web Pages," goes beyond what you learned in Part IV with a chapter that explains how you can use forms to implement live chat pages. This part then moves on to discuss Java applets and what they can do for your pages, as well as how to use Netscape's new LiveWire product to implement Java on your site.

Part VI, "HTML Authoring Tools," fills you in on the latest HTML accessories for Web page creation, including Netscape Gold, Microsoft Internet Assistant for Word, and Quarterdeck WebAuthor. Stand-alone HTML editors such as HotDog, WebEdit, and Arachnid are also discussed.

Part VII, "Sample HTML Applications," gives you an insider's view of two fictitious Web sites where you can observe the process that two entities go through in developing their Web pages.

Finally, the appendixes include a full reference to HTML elements, an HTML quick reference guide, a list of what's on the book CD, and a World Wide Web bibliography.

The CD-ROM

Inside the back cover of this book, you'll find a CD-ROM containing multi-megabytes of links, tips, and programs to help you get the most out of HTML.

When you see a program mentioned in this book that is included on the book CD, an icon appears in the left margin. Keep an eye out for it.

Conventions Used in This Book

This book uses various stylistic and typographic conventions to make it easier to use.

Shortcut key combinations are joined by + (plus) signs; for example, Ctrl+X means to hold down the Ctrl key, press the X key, and then release both.

Menu items and dialog box selections often have a mnemonic key associated with them. This key is indicated by an underline on the item on-screen. To use these mnemonic keys, you press the Alt key and then the shortcut key. In this book, mnemonic keys are underlined, like this: File.

This book uses the following typeface conventions:

Typeface	Meaning
Italic	Variables in commands or addresses, or terms used for the first time
Bold	Text you type in, as well as addresses of Internet sites, newsgroups, mailing lists, and Web sites
`Computer type`	Commands

Note

Notes provide additional information related to the topic at hand.

Tip

Tips provide quick and helpful information to assist you along the way.

Caution

Cautions alert you to potential pitfalls or dangers in the operations discussed.

Troubleshooting

What are Troubleshooting notes?

Troubleshooting notes answer questions that might arise while following the procedures in this book.

Special Edition Using HTML, Second Edition, uses marginal references like the following to point you to other places in the book with additional information relevant to the topic. Right-pointing arrows guide you forward, and left-pointing arrows refer you to previous chapters. ❖

▶ See "Introducing the World Wide Web," p. 9

Part I

Overview of the World Wide Web

## CHAPTER 1

Introducing the World Wide Web

by Mark Brown

Contrary to what the media would have you believe, the World Wide Web did not spring into being overnight. Though relatively new in human terms, the Web has a venerable genealogy for a computing technology. It can trace its roots back over 25 years, which is more than half the distance back to the primordial dawn of the electronic computing age.

However, the media is right in noting that the Web's phenomenal growth has so far outstripped that of any of its predecessors that, like a prize hog, it has left almost no room at the trough for any of them anymore. But like that prize hog, the Web is so much bigger and better and so much more valuable than the network technologies that preceded it, there is little reason to mourn the fact that they've been superseded.

In this chapter I'll discuss the history, development, and characteristics of the Web. You'll find out where it came from and what it's good for. If you're the impatient type and you just want to start using HTML to develop Web pages as quickly as possible, you can certainly skip this chapter and jump right in. However, as with all things, a little understanding of the background and underlying structure of the Web will not only enhance your enjoyment of and appreciation for what it is and what it can do, but it might even give you some insights into how to approach the development of your own Web sites.

The Web came out of the Internet, and it is both empowered and limited by the structure of the Internet. Today, most Web browsers include the capability to access other Internet technologies, such as Gopher, e-mail, and Usenet news, as well as the World Wide Web. So the more you know about the Internet as a whole, as well as the Web's place in it, the better you'll understand how to exploit the entire Net to its fullest potential.

Then, too, the Web and the Internet are more than just technology: they are an environment in which the members of an entire cyberculture communicate, trade, and interact. If you hope to establish your own Web site and make yourself a part of that culture, you'd better know what you're getting into. In a way, it's like moving to another country and trying to set up shop; if you don't speak the lingo and learn the customs, you'll never become a part of the community.

In this chapter, you learn about the following:

- A short history of the Internet, the home of the Web
- What Net technologies existed before the Web, and how they work alongside the Web today
- How to decipher Internet e-mail addresses and domain names
- How and why the Web sprang so suddenly into being
- How the Web has quickly grown to reign supreme on the Net
- What's on the Web and why you'll want to develop a presence there

The Genealogy of the Web

In the late 1950s, at the height of the Cold War, the Department of Defense began to worry about what would happen to the nation's communications systems in the event of an atomic war. It was obvious that maintaining communications would be vital to the waging of a worldwide war, but it was also obvious that the very nature of an all-out nuclear conflict would practically guarantee that the nation's existing communications systems would be knocked out.

In 1962, Paul Baran, a researcher at the government's RAND think tank, described a solution to the problem in a paper titled "On Distributed Communications Networks." He proposed a nationwide system of computers connected together using a decentralized network so that if one or more major nodes were destroyed, the rest could dynamically adjust their connections to maintain communications.

If, for example, a computer in Washington, D.C., needed to communicate with one in Los Angeles, it might normally pass the information first to a computer in Kansas City, then on to L.A. But if Kansas City was destroyed or knocked out by an A-bomb blast, the Washington computer could reroute its communications through, say, Chicago instead, and the data would still arrive safely in L.A. (though too late to help the unfortunate citizens of Kansas City).

The proposal was discussed, developed, and expanded by various members of the computing community. In 1969, the first packet-switching network was funded by the Pentagon's Advanced Research Projects Agency (ARPA).

So What's Packet Switching?

Packet switching is a method of breaking up data files into small pieces—usually only a couple of kilobytes or less—called packets, which can then be transmitted to another location. There, the packets are reassembled to re-create the original file. Packets don't have to be transmitted in order or even by the same route. In fact, the same packet can be transmitted by several different routes just in case some don't come through. The receiving software at the other end throws away duplicate packets, checks to see if others haven't come through (and asks the originating computer to try to send them again), sorts them into their original order, and puts them back together again into a duplicate of the original data file. Although this isn't the fastest way to transmit data, it is certainly one of the most reliable.

Packet switching also enables several users to send data over the same connection by interleaving packets from each data stream, routing each to its own particular destination.

Besides the original file data, data packets may include information about where they came from, the places they've visited in transit, and where they're going. The data they contain may be compressed and/or encrypted. Packets almost always also include some kind of information to indicate whether the data that arrives at the destination is the same data that was sent in the first place.

ARPAnet, as it was called, linked four research facilities: the University of California at Los Angeles (UCLA), the Stanford Research Institute (SRI), the University of California at Santa Barbara (UCSB), and the University of Utah. By 1971, ARPAnet had grown to include 15 nodes; there were a grand total of 40 by 1972. That year also marked the creation of the InterNetworking Working Group (INWG), which was needed to establish common protocols for the rapidly growing system.

Tip

For more on the history of the Internet, consult Bruce Sterling's excellent article on the topic at **gopher://oak.zilker.net:70/00/bruces/F_SF_Science_Column/ F_SF_Five_**.

Because ARPAnet was decentralized, it was easy for computer administrators to add their machines to the network. All they needed was a phone line, a little hardware, and some free NCP (*Network Control Protocol*) software. Within just a few years, there were over a hundred mainframe computers connected to ARPAnet, including some overseas.

Electronic Mail: The First Application

ARPAnet immediately became a forum for the exchange of information and ideas. Collaboration among scientists and educators was the number one use of the system, and the main incentive for new sites to want to be connected. Thus, it is not surprising that the first major application developed for use on the ARPAnet was electronic mail.

With the advent of Ray Tomlinson's e-mail system in 1972, researchers connected to the Net could establish one-on-one communication links with colleagues all over the world and could exchange ideas and research at a pace never before imagined. With the eventual addition of the ability to send mail to multiple recipients, mailing lists were born and users began open discussions on a multitude of topics, including "frivolous" topics, such as science fiction.

> **Tip**
>
> There are thousands of mailing lists you can subscribe to on the Internet today, covering topics as diverse as PERL programming and dog breeding. For a list of some of the many mailing lists available on the Net, check out Stephanie de Silva's list of Publicly Accessible Mailing Lists, updated monthly, at **http://www.neosoft.com/internet/paml/**, the list of LISTSERV lists at **http://tile.net/listserv/**, or the forms-searchable Liszt database of 25,000 mailing lists at **http://www.liszt.com/**.

▶ See "Linking HTML Documents," p. 143

E-mail has proven its value over time and has remained one of the major uses of the Net. In fact, e-mail is now handled internally by many World Wide Web browsers, such as Netscape 2.0 (see fig. 1.1), so a separate e-mail program is not required.

> **Tip**
>
> You can find answers to most of your questions about Internet e-mail in the directory of e-mail FAQs at **ftp://ftp.uu.net/usenet/news.answers/mail/**.

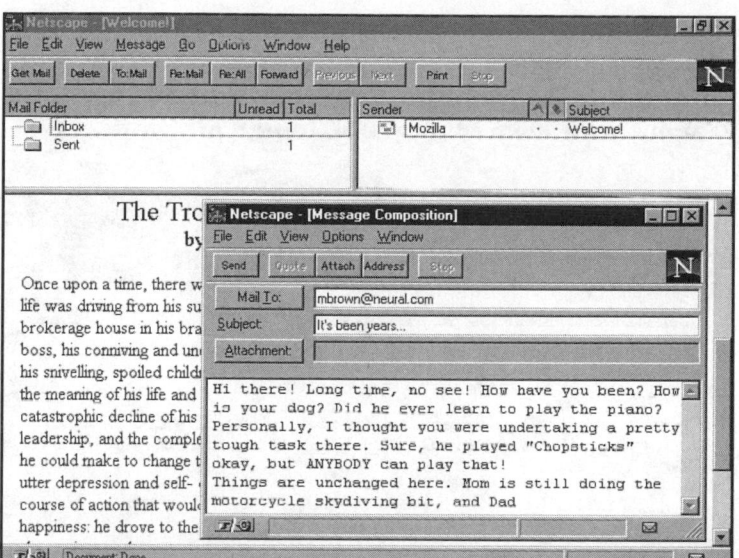

Fig. 1.1
Reading or sending e-mail with Netscape Navigator 2.0 brings up a separate e-mail window, shown here.

Deciphering Internet e-mail addresses can be a bit challenging. Like a letter sent through the mail, an electronic mail message must be sent to a specific address (or list of addresses). The format for an e-mail address is *name@site* (which is verbalized as "name at site").

The *name* portion of the address is the recipient's personal e-mail account name. At many sites, this may be the user's first initial and last name. For example, my e-mail account name is *mbrown*. However, e-mail names consist of anything from an obscure set of numbers and/or letters (*70215.1034*) to a funky nickname (*spanky*). (One nearly ubiquitous e-mail name is *webmaster*. This generic name is used by Webmasters at most of the Web sites in the world.)

The site portion of an e-mail address is the domain name of the server that the account is on. For example, all America Online users are at **aol.com**, and all CompuServe users are at **compuserve.com**. I'm at neural.com, so my complete e-mail address is **mbrown@neural.com**.

If you don't know someone's e-mail address, there are a variety of "white pages" services available on the Web for looking them up. As always, a good list of such services can be found on Yahoo! at **http://www.yahoo.com/ Reference/White_Pages/**. My current favorite is the Internet Address Finder at **http://www.iaf.net/** (see fig. 1.2).

For more information on Internet e-mail addresses, including lists of domain names for many popular online services, see John J. Chew's and Scott Yanoff's interactive forms-based "Inter-Network Mail Guide" at **http://alpha.acast.nova.edu/cgi-bin/inmgq.pl**.

Fig. 1.2
The Internet Address Finder can be used to find the e-mail addresses of over 3.5 million Internet users.

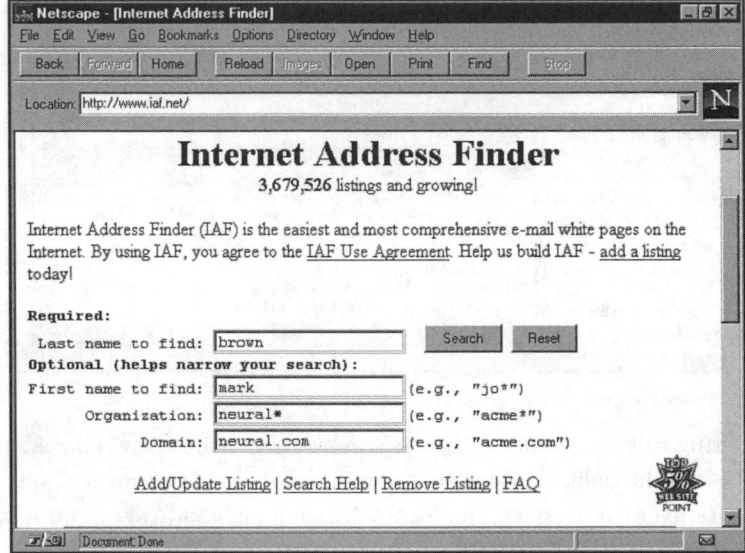

Usenet News

A logical extension of the mailing list is the interactive conference, or *newsgroup*. The concept of interactive conferencing actually predates the existence of the computers to do it on; it was first proposed by Vannevar Bush in an article titled "As We May Think" in the *Atlantic Monthly* in 1945 (v196(1), pp. 101–108).

The first actual online conferencing system was called *Delphi* (after the Greek oracle), and it debuted in 1970. Though slow, it did enable hundreds of researchers at multiple locations to participate in an organized, ongoing, international discussion group. It is not an exaggeration to say that it revolutionized the way research is done.

In 1976, AT&T Bell Labs added *UUCP* (UNIX-to-UNIX CoPy) to the UNIX V7 operating system. Tom Truscott and Jim Ellis of Duke University and Steve Bellovin at the University of North Carolina developed the first version of Usenet, the UNIX User Network, using UUCP and UNIX shell scripts, and connected the two sites in 1979. Usenet quickly became the online conferencing system of choice on the Net. In 1986, the Network News Transfer Protocol (NNTP) was created to improve Usenet news performance over TCP/IP networks. Since then, it has grown to accommodate more than 2.5 million people a month and is available to over ten million users at over 200,000 sites.

Note

Another important online conferencing system, *BITNET* (the "Because It's Time NETwork"), was started two years after Usenet at the City University of New York (CUNY). BITNET uses e-mail and a group mailing list server (*listserv*) to distribute more than 4,000 discussion groups to thousands of users daily.

Although BITNET traffic has peaked and is likely to be superseded completely by Usenet at some time in the future, it still plays an important role in online conferencing.

Usenet Newsgroups

There are over 10,000 active Usenet newsgroups, all of which are organized into hierarchies by subject matter The seven major categories are as follows:

comp.   Computer-related subjects, such as programming, PC hardware and software, and database management.

sci.   Scientific studies, research, and applications.

soc.   Social issues, socializing, world cultures, and other social and socio-logical topics.

talk.   Debates and discussions mostly concerned with opinions or *chat*. Some cynics have suggested that the subjects in these topic groups are essentially "content-free."

news.   Groups concerned with Usenet, its administration, organization, and development.

rec.   Hobbies and recreation.

misc.   Everything else. Subjects include fitness, job hunting, law, and investments.

There are also additional, less-official groups that may not be carried by all Usenet sites. The following are the three most popular:

alt.   For *alternative.* This category tends to attract the fringe elements, and topics range from sex and drugs to conspiracy theories, UFOs, and political anarchy.

gnu.   Discussions of the GNU Project of the Free Software Foundation.

biz.   Business-related groups.

(continues)

(continued)

If you have a question about what a newsgroup is all about or what is appropriate to post, you can usually find a *Frequently Asked Questions* (FAQ) list that will give you the answer. Most of the Usenet newsgroup FAQs are posted every month to the newsgroup news.answers. Many Web sites archive the most current Usenet FAQs. **ftp://ftp.uu.net/usenet/news.answers/** is a good place to start.

In some Usenet groups, it's more important to stay on topic than it is in others. For example, you really don't want the messages in a scientific research group to degenerate into *flame wars* over which personal computer is best. To make sure this doesn't happen, many of the more serious Usenet groups are moderated.

In a moderated group, all posted articles are first mailed to a human moderator who combs through the messages to make sure they're on topic. Appropriate messages are then posted for everyone to see, while inappropriate messages are deleted. The moderator may even e-mail posters of inappropriate messages to warn them not to repeat their indiscretions, or may lock them out of the newsgroup altogether.

Usenet is *not* the Internet or even a part of the Internet; it may be thought of as operating parallel to and in conjunction with the Internet. While most Internet sites carry Usenet newsfeeds, there is no direct or official relationship between the two. However, Usenet news has become such an important part of computer internetworking that a newsreader is now built into many Web browsers (see fig. 1.3).

Fig. 1.3
Many browsers, such as Netscape 2.0, now incorporate an integral newsreader for reading and posting to Usenet newsgroups.

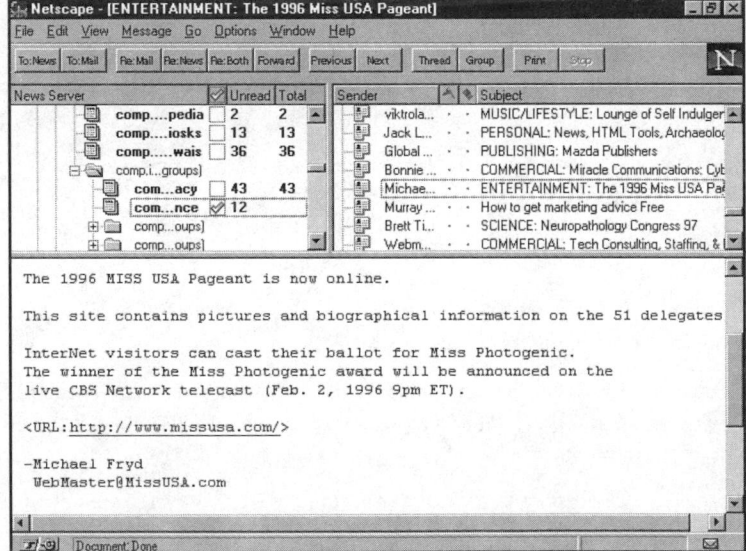

> **Tip**
>
> The definitive online guide to Usenet is the comprehensive list of Usenet FAQs archived at **http://www.cis.ohio-state.edu/hypertext/faq/usenet/usenet/ top.html**.

You can find Usenet newsgroups of interest using the search form at **http:// www.cen.uiuc.edu/cgi-bin/find-news**. The Usenet Info Center Launch Pad at **http://sunsite.unc.edu/usenet-i/** also offers a wealth of information on Usenet, including lists and indexes of available Usenet discussion groups.

TCP/IP

By the mid-1970s, many government agencies were on the ARPAnet, but each was running on a network developed by the lowest bidder for their specific project. For example, the Army's system was built by DEC, the Air Force's by IBM, and the Navy's by Unisys. All were capable networks, but all spoke different languages. What was clearly needed to make things work smoothly was a set of networking *protocols* that would tie together disparate networks and enable them to communicate with each other.

In 1974, Vint Cerf and Bob Kahn published a paper titled "A Protocol for Packet Network Internetworking" that detailed a design that would solve the problem. In 1982, this solution was implemented as *TCP/IP*. TCP stands for *Transmission Control Protocol;* IP is the abbreviation for *Internet Protocol*. With the advent of TCP/IP, the word *Internet*—which is a portmanteau word for *interconnected networks*—entered the language.

The TCP portion of the TCP/IP provides data transmission verification between client and server: If data is lost or scrambled, TCP triggers retransmission until the errors are corrected.

> **Note**
>
> You've probably heard the term *socket* mentioned in conjunction with TCP/IP. A socket is a package of subroutines that provide access to TCP/IP protocols. For example, most Windows systems have a file called *winsock.dll* in the windows/system directory that is required for a Web browser or other communications program to hook up to the Internet.

The IP portion of TCP/IP moves data packets from node to node. It decodes addresses and routes data to designated destinations. The Internet Protocol (IP) is what creates the network of networks, or *Internet,* by linking systems at different levels. It can be used by small computers to communicate across a LAN (Local Area Network) in the same room or with computer networks around the world. Individual computers connected via a LAN (either Ethernet or token ring) can share the LAN setup with both TCP/IP and other network protocols, such as Novell or Windows for Workgroups. One computer on the LAN then provides the TCP/IP connection to the outside world.

The Department of Defense quickly declared the TCP/IP suite as the standard protocol for internetworking military computers. TCP/IP has been ported to most computer systems, including personal computers, and has become the new standard in internetworking. It is the protocol set that provides the infrastructure for the Internet today.

TCP/IP comprises over 100 different protocols. It includes services for remote logon, file transfers, and data indexing and retrieval, among others.

Tip

An excellent source of additional information on TCP/IP is the Introduction to TCP/IP Gopher site at the University of California at Davis. Check it out at **gopher:// gopher-chem.ucdavis.edu/11/Index/Internet_aw/Intro_the_Internet/ intro.to.ip/**.

Telnet

One of the driving forces behind the development of ARPAnet was the desire to afford researchers at various locations the ability to log on to remote computers and run programs. At the time, there were very few computers in existence and only a handful of powerful supercomputers (though the supercomputers of the early 1970s were nowhere near as powerful as the desktop machines of today).

Along with e-mail, remote logon was one of the very first capabilities built into the ARPAnet.

Today, there is less reason for logging on to a remote system and running programs there. Most major government agencies, colleges, and research facilities have their own computers, each of which is as powerful as the computers at other sites.

TCP/IP provides a remote logon capability through the *Telnet* protocol. Users generally log in to a UNIX shell account on the remote system using a text-based or graphics-based terminal program. With Telnet, the user can list and navigate through directories on the remote system and run programs.

The most popular programs run on shell accounts are probably e-mail programs, such as PINE; Usenet news readers, such as *nn* or *rn*; and text editors, such as *vi* or *Emacs*. Students are the most common users of Telnet these days; professors, scientists, and administrators are more likely to have a more direct means of access to powerful computers, such as an X Windows terminal.

Most Web browsers don't include built-in Telnet capabilities. Telnet connections are usually established using a stand-alone terminal program, such as that shown in figure 1.4. These programs can also be used by those who want Telnet capabilities on the Web by configuring them as browser helper applications.

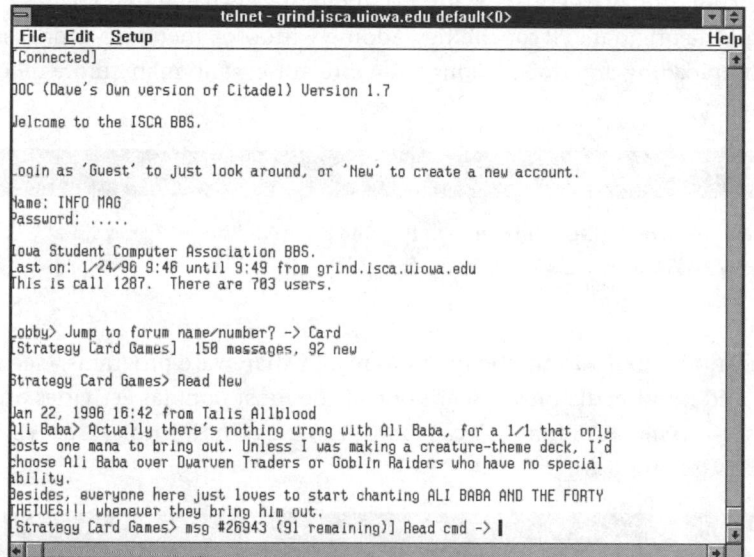

Fig. 1.4
A Telnet session can be initiated with an Internet computer using a stand-alone terminal program, such as QVTNET on Windows shown here.

Tip

An excellent online guide to Telnet is located on the University of Washington Library's site at **http://www.lib.washington.edu/libinfo/inetguides/ inet6.html**.

FTP

The ability to transfer data between computers is central to the inter-networking concept. TCP/IP implements computer-to-computer data transfers thorough *FTP* (File Transfer Protocol).

An FTP session involves first connecting to and signing on to an FTP server somewhere on the Net. Most public FTP sites allow *anonymous FTP*. This means you can sign in with the user name *anonymous* and use your e-mail address as your password. However, some sites are restricted and require the use of an assigned user name and password.

Once in, you can list the files available on the site and move around through the directory structure just as though you were on your own system. When you've found a file of interest, you can transfer it to your computer using the get command (or mget for multiple files). You can also upload files to an FTP site using the put command.

The FTP process was originally designed for text-only UNIX shell style systems. But today, there are many FTP programs available that go way beyond the original FTP capabilities, adding windows, menus, buttons, automated uploading and downloading, site directories, and many more modern amenities.

Tip

One of the biggest lists of FTP sites on the Web is the Monster FTP Sites List at **http://hoohoo.ncsa.uiuc.edu/ftp/**.

Using Anonymous FTP to obtain freeware and shareware programs, electronic texts, and multimedia files remains one of the most popular activities on the Internet—so much so that FTP capabilities are now built into most Web browsers (see fig. 1.5).

Tip

When accessing an FTP site using a Web browser, the URL will be preceded by *ftp://* rather than the *http://* shown when you're viewing a Web site.

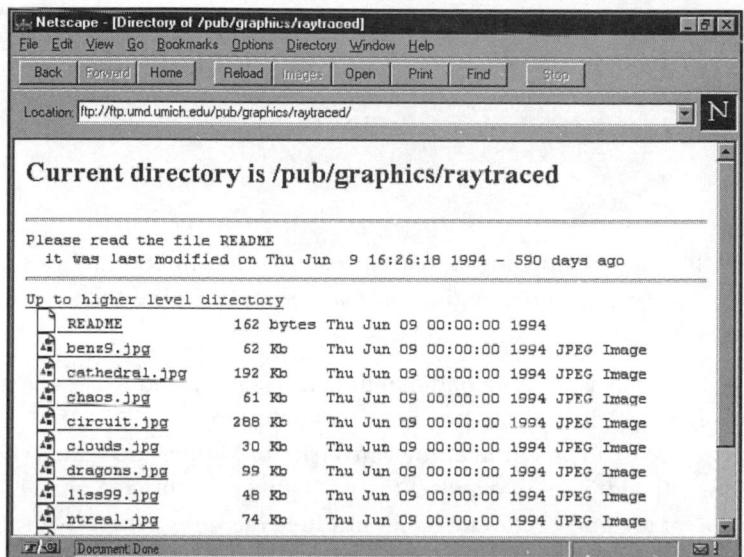

Fig. 1.5
Web browsers, such as Netscape 2.0, generally handle anonymous FTP too, automatically creating an on-screen directory file with icons and clickable links.

Individual files on an FTP site are handled according to the way they are defined in your browser's configuration setup, just as though you were browsing a Web site. For example, if you're exploring an FTP site and click the link for a .gif picture file, it will be displayed in the browser window. Text files and HTML encoded files will be displayed too. If you have configured helper applications for sound or video, clicking these types of files will display them using the configured helper applications. Clicking an unconfigured file type will generally bring up a requester asking you to configure a viewer or save the file to disk.

Since you most often want to save files to disk from an FTP site, not view them, you can generally get around all this by using the browser's interactive option to save a file rather than display it. For example, in Netscape you can choose to save a file rather than view it by simply holding down the Shift key before clicking the file's link.

You might wonder, with hundreds of FTP sites on the Net and millions of files stored at those sites, how in the world you can ever hope to find the file you're looking for? *Archie* is the answer. Archie is a program for finding files stored on any anonymous FTP site on the Internet. SURANET's Guide to the Archie Service at **http://www.sura.net/archie/Archie-Usage.html** provides an excellent overview of Archie, including instructions on how to find and hook up to Archie servers on the Net.

Tip

The complete list of FTP-related FAQs is located online at **http://www.cis.ohio-state.edu/hypertext/faq/usenet/ftp-list/faq/faq.html**.

Gopher

Along with e-mail, remote logon, and file transfer, information indexing and retrieval was one of the original *big four* concepts behind the idea of internetworking.

Though there were a plethora of different data indexing and retrieval experiments in the early days of the Net, none was ubiquitous until, in 1991, Paul Lindner and Mark P. McCahill at the University of Minnesota created *Gopher*. Though it suffered from an overly cute (but highly descriptive) name, its technique for organizing files under an intuitive menuing system won it instant acceptance on the Net.

Gopher treats all data as a menu, a document, an index, or a Telnet connection. Through Telnet, one Gopher site can access others, making it a true internetwork application capable of delivering data to a user from a multitude of sites via a single interface.

The direct precursor in both concept and function to the World Wide Web, Gopher lacks hypertext links or graphic elements. Its function on the Net is being taken over by the Web, though there are currently still several thousand Gopher sites on the Net, and it will probably be years before Gopher disappears completely. Because so much information is still contained in Gopher databases, the ability to navigate and view *Gopherspace* is now built into most Web browsers (see fig. 1.6).

Tip

When accessing a Gopher site using a Web browser, the URL will be preceded by *gopher://* rather than the *http://* shown when you're viewing a Web site.

As Archie is to FTP, *Veronica* is to Gopher. That is, if you want to know where something is on any Gopher site on the Net, the Veronica program can tell you. For a connection to Veronica via the Web, go to **http://www.scs.unr.edu/veronica.html**.

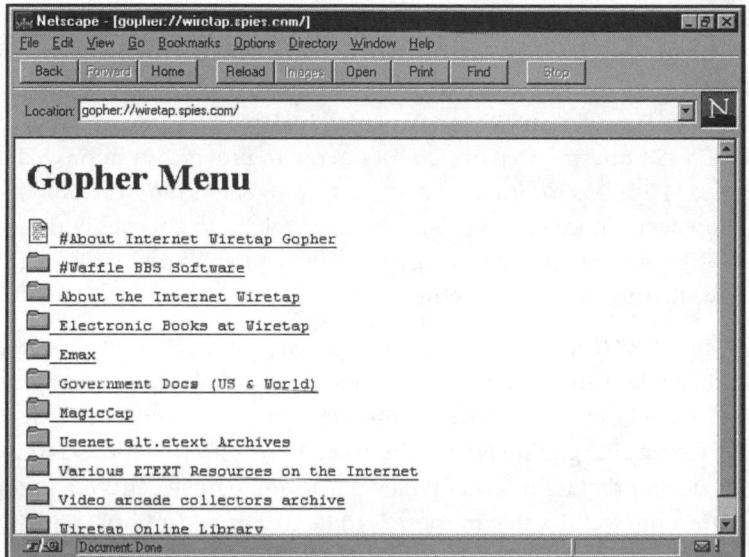

Fig. 1.6
Gopher sites
like this one are
displayed just fine
by most Web
browsers.

Although I'm slightly embarrassed to do so, I know that I must pass along to you the information that Veronica is actually an acronym, though it is almost never capitalized as one should be. What does it stand for? Would you believe *Very Easy Rodent Oriented Net-wide Index to Computerized Archives?*

Tip

The Net's best Gopher sites are on the Gopher Jewels list at **http://galaxy.einet. net/GJ/**.

Tip

For more about Gopher, consult the Gopher FAQ at **http://www.cis.ohio-state.edu/hypertext/faq/usenet/gopher-faq/faq.html**.

The Internet

With the near-universal changeover to TCP/IP protocols in the years following 1982, the word *Internet* became the common term for referring to the worldwide network of research, military, and university computers.

In 1983, ARPAnet was divided into ARPAnet and MILNET. MILNET was soon integrated into the Defense Data Network, which had been created in 1982. ARPAnet's role as the network backbone was taken over by NSFNET (the National Science Foundation NETwork), which had been created in 1986 with the aid of NASA and the Department of Energy to provide an improved backbone speed of 56Kbps for interconnecting a new generation of research supercomputers. Connections proliferated, especially to colleges, when in 1989 NSFNET was overhauled for faster T1 line connectivity by IBM, Merit, and MCI. ARPAnet was finally retired in 1990.

In 1993, InterNIC (the Internet Network Information Center) was created by the National Science Foundation to provide information, a directory and database, and registration services to the Internet community. InterNIC is, thus, the closest thing there is to an Internet administrative center. However, InterNIC doesn't dictate Internet policy or run some huge central computer that controls the Net. Its sole purpose is to handle organizational and "bookkeeping" functions, such as assigning Internet addresses (see the sidebar, "Domain Names").

Domain Names

Computers on the Internet are referenced using *IP addresses*, which are comprised of a series of four numbers separated by periods (always called *dots*). Each number is an 8-bit integer (a number from 0–255). For example, the IP address of my Web server at Neural Applications is 198.137.221.9 (verbalized as "one-ninety-eight dot one-thirty-seven dot two-twenty-one dot nine").

However, because addresses composed of nothing but numbers are difficult for humans to remember, in 1983 the University of Wisconsin developed the *Domain Name Server* (DNS), which was then introduced to the Net during the following year. DNS automatically and invisibly translates names composed of real words into their numeric IP addresses, which makes the Net *a lot* more user-friendly. To use the same example cited above, the DNS address of Neural's Web server is **www.neural.com** (pronounced "double-u double-u double-u dot neural dot cahm").

There is no formula for calculating an IP address from a domain name—the correlation must be established by looking one or the other up in a table.

Domain names consist of two or more parts, separated by periods (always, in Internet parlance, pronounced dot). Generally speaking, the leftmost part of the name is the most specific, with sections further to the right more general. A computer may have more than one domain name assigned to it, but any given domain name will "resolve" into only one specific IP address (which is unique for each machine).

Usually, all the machines on one network will share a right-hand and middle domain name portion. For example, you might see computers at one site with the names:

server.grizzly.com

mars.grizzly.com

www.grizzly.com

The leftmost portion of a domain name may indicate its purpose; for example, *www.* for a Web server or *mail.* for a mail server.

The rightmost portion of a domain name often indicates the type of site it lives on. The most common domain name extensions are:

.com	Commercial site
.edu	Educational site
.gov	Government site
.mil	Military site
.net	Network service provider
.org	Organization

Other (generally two-letter) extensions indicate a site's country of origin, such as *.ca* for Canada, *.de* for Germany, or *.fr* for France.

Tip

The topic of domain names is covered to the point of exhaustion in the Usenet FAQ on the topic, which can be downloaded from **ftp://ftp.uu.net/usenet/news. answers/internet/tcp-ip/domains-faq/**.

Your organization can get an IP address assigned by sending electronic mail to *Hostmaster@INTERNIC.NET*. This service used to be free, but there is now a reasonable charge because of the tremendous growth of the Internet and the privatization of the process. For more information, point your browser to InterNIC's Web site at **http://rs.internic.net/rs-internic.html**.

Tip

One of the best online guides to the Internet as a whole is the Electronic Freedom Foundation's Extended Guide to the Internet at **http://www.eff.org/papers/ bdgtti/eegtti.html**.

The Web Explosion

By 1990, the European High-Energy Particle Physics Lab (CERN) had become the largest Internet site in Europe and was the driving force in getting the rest of Europe connected to the Net. To help promote and facilitate the concept of distributed computing via the Internet, Tim Berners-Lee created the World Wide Web in 1992.

The Web was an extension of the Gopher idea, but with many, many improvements. Inspired by Ted Nelson's work on Xanadu and the hypertext concept, the World Wide Web incorporated graphics, typographic text styles, and—most importantly—hypertext links.

Note

The hypertext concept predates personal computers. It was first proposed by computer visionary Ted Nelson in his ground-breaking, self-published book *Computer Lib/ Dream Machines* in 1974.

In a nutshell, electronic hypertext involves adding links to words or phrases. When selected, these links jump you to associated text in the same document or in another document altogether. For example, you could click an unfamiliar term and jump to a definition, or add your own notes that would be optionally displayed when you or someone else selected the note's hyperlink.

The hypertext concept has since been expanded to incorporate the idea of *hypermedia,* in which links can also be added to and from graphics, video, and audio clips.

The Web uses three new technologies: HTML, or HyperText Markup Language, is used to write Web pages; a Web server computer uses HTTP (HyperText Transfer Protocol) to transmit those pages; and a Web browser client program receives the data, interprets it, and displays the results.

Using HTML, almost anyone with a text editor and an Internet site can build visually interesting pages that organize and present information in a way seldom seen in other online venues. In fact, Web sites are said to be composed of *pages* because the information on them looks more like magazine pages than traditional computer screens.

Note

HTML is, itself, a subset of the much more complex SGML, or Standard Generalized Markup Language. SGML is also used for creating pages on the Web, though it takes a different browser to be able to view SGML pages. SGML is discussed further in chapter 4, "Building Blocks of HTML," p. 87.

HTML is a markup language, which means that Web pages can only be viewed by using a specialized Internet terminal program called a *Web browser*. In the beginning, the potential was there for the typical computing "chicken and the egg problem": no one would create Web pages because no one owned a browser program to view them with, and no one would get a browser program because there were no Web pages to view.

Fortunately, this did not happen because shortly after the Web was invented, a killer browser program was released to the Internet community—free of charge!

In 1993, the National Center for Supercomputing Applications (NCSA) at the University of Illinois at Champaign-Urbana released Mosaic, a Web browser designed by Marc Andreessen and developed by a team of students and staff at the University of Illinois (see fig. 1.7). It spread like wildfire though the Internet community; within a year, an estimated two million users were on the Web with Mosaic. Suddenly, everyone was browsing the Web, and everyone else was creating Web pages. Nothing in the history of computing had grown so fast.

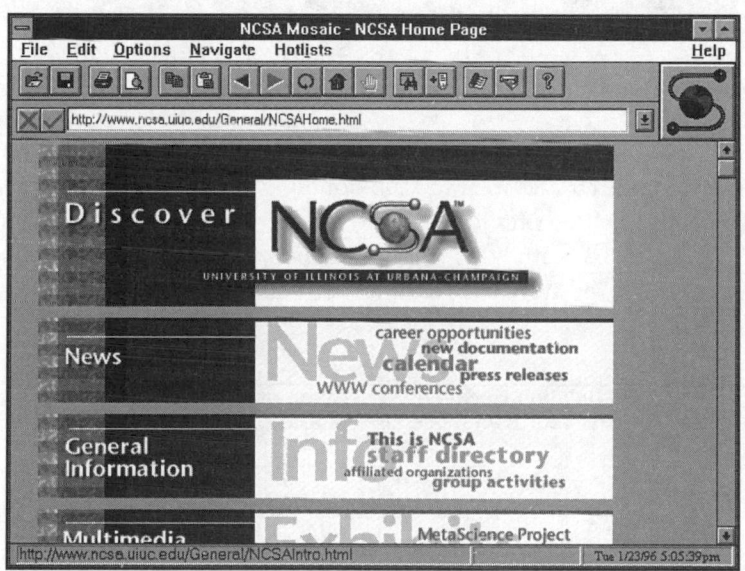

Fig. 1.7
NSCA Mosaic, the browser that drove the phenomenal growth of the World Wide Web, is still available free of charge for Windows, Windows NT, Windows 95, UNIX, and Macintosh.

By mid-1993, there were 130 sites on the World Wide Web. Six months later, there were over 600. Today, there are almost 100,000 Web sites in the world (some sources say there may be twice that many). For the first few months of its existence, the Web was doubling in size every three months. Even now, its doubling rate is (depending on whom you believe) less than five months. Table 1.1 shows just how quickly the Web has grown over its three-year history.

Table 1.1 Growth of the World Wide Web	
Date	**Web Sites**
6/93	130
12/93	623
6/94	2,738
12/94	10,022
6/95	23,500
1/96	90,000

Source: "Measuring the Growth of the Web," Copyright 1995, Matthew Gray, **http://www.netgen.com**.

Tip

For more information on NCSA Mosaic, check out the NCSA Web site at **http://www.ncsa.uiuc.edu/SDG/Software/Mosaic/**.

If the number of Web sites were to keep doubling at the current rate, there would be over 300 Web sites in the world for every man, woman, and child by the end of 1998. Clearly, this will not happen, but it does serve to illustrate just how fast the Web is expanding! See figure 1.8 for a graphical perspective.

Fig. 1.8
The Internet is growing at a phenomenal rate as a whole, but the Web is growing so much faster that it almost seems destined to take over the whole Net.

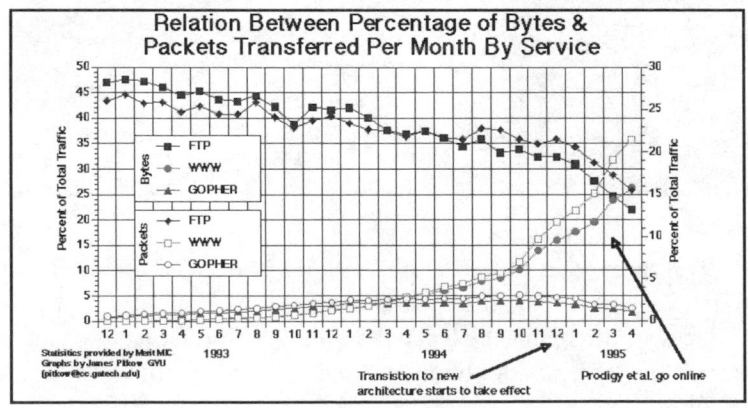

> **Note**
>
> For a wealth of both more and less accurate demographic information on the growth of the Internet in general and the World Wide Web in particular, begin with Yahoo!'s list of sites at **http://www.yahoo.com/Computers_and_Internet/Internet/ Statistics_and_Demographics/**. One good site to try is the GVU WWW User Survey at **http://www.cc.gatech.edu/gvu/user_surveys/ User_Survey_Home.html**.

Mosaic's success—and the fact that its source code was distributed for free!—spawned a wave of new browser introductions. Each topped the previous by adding new HTML commands and features. Marc Andreessen moved on from NCSA and joined with Jim Clark of Silicon Graphics to found Netscape Communications Corporation. They took along most of the NCSA Mosaic development team, which quickly turned out the first version of Netscape Navigator for Windows, Macintosh, and UNIX platforms. Because of its many new features and free trial preview offer, Netscape (as it is usually called) quickly became the most popular browser on the Web. The Web's incredible growth even attracted Microsoft's attention, and in 1995, it introduced its Internet Explorer Web browser to coincide with the launch of its new WWW service, the Microsoft Network (MSN).

▶ See "How Web Browsers and Servers Work Together," p. 37

▶ See chapter 15 "Netscape-Specific Extensions to HTML," p. 311

▶ See chapter 16 "HTML Extensions in Internet Explorer, Mosaic, and HTML 3.0," p. 347

Established online services like CompuServe, America Online, and Prodigy scrambled to meet their users' demands to add Web access to their systems. Most of them quickly developed their own version of Mosaic, customized to work in conjunction with their proprietary online services. This enabled millions of established commercial service subscribers to spill over onto the Web virtually overnight; "old-timers" who had been on the Web since its beginning (only a year and a half or so before) suddenly found themselves overtaken by a tidal wave of Web-surfing *newbies*. Even television discovered the Web, and it seemed that every other news report featured a story about surfing the Net.

The Web: What Is It Good For?

"All that growth is impressive," you say, "but...just what exactly is the Web good for?" Good question, and one with hundreds of good answers.

People are on the Web to conduct business, to exchange information, to express their creativity, to collaborate, and to just plain have fun.

Who Uses the Web and for What?

Today, there are over 37 million adults in North America with access to the Internet. 24 million of them actually use their access, and 18 million use their Internet access time to browse the World Wide Web. The total amount of time spent cruising the Web is greater than the time spent using all other Internet services combined, and is roughly equivalent to the time North Americans spend watching rented videotapes.

> *Some of the survey information used in this section is Copyright© 1995 CommerceNet Consortium/Nielsen Media Research.*

The number of people using the Internet is increasing so rapidly that if the growth rate were to continue at the current rate, by 2003 every person in the world would be on the Web!

Increasingly, people are using the Web to conduct business. Today, over 50 percent of the sites on the Web are commercial (with a *.com* domain name). Over half of the users of the Web look for products at least occasionally and—since Web users are predominantly upscale, well educated, and afflu-ent—business is paying attention. Expect Web growth in the near future to continue to be driven and driven hard by business expansion into cyberspace.

But Web surfers also use the Net for more traditional telecommunications purposes. Three-fourths browse the Web. Two-thirds exchange e-mail. One-third download software by FTP. One in three takes part in discussion groups, and one in five is active in multimedia.

Content

The World Wide Web didn't get its name by accident. It truly is a web that encompasses just about every topic in the world. A quick look at the premier topic index on the Web, Yahoo! (**http://www.yahoo.com**), lists topics as diverse as art, world news, sports, business, libraries, classified advertising, education, TV, science, fitness, and politics (see fig. 1.9). You can't get much more diverse than that! There are literally thousands of sites listed on Yahoo! under each of these topics and many more.

Fig. 1.9
If you really want
to know what's on
the Web, you need
look no further
than Yahoo!

Presentation

But mere mass isn't the main draw of the Web. It's the way in which all that information is presented. The best Web sites integrate graphics, hypertext links, and even video and audio. They make finding information interesting, fun, and intuitive.

Marshall McLuhan asserted that the medium is the message, and this is certainly true with the Web. Because its hypermedia presentation style can overwhelm its content if done poorly, the Web is a real challenge to developers. But when done well, the results are fantastic, such as the tour of an abandoned U.S. missile silo shown in figure 1.10 (**http://www.xvt.com/ users/kevink/silo/site.html**).

Tip

For more information about the World Wide Web, consult the WWW FAQ at **http:// sunsite.unc.edu/boutell/index.html**.

Fig. 1.10
A really cool Web
site integrates user
interface and
content seamlessly.

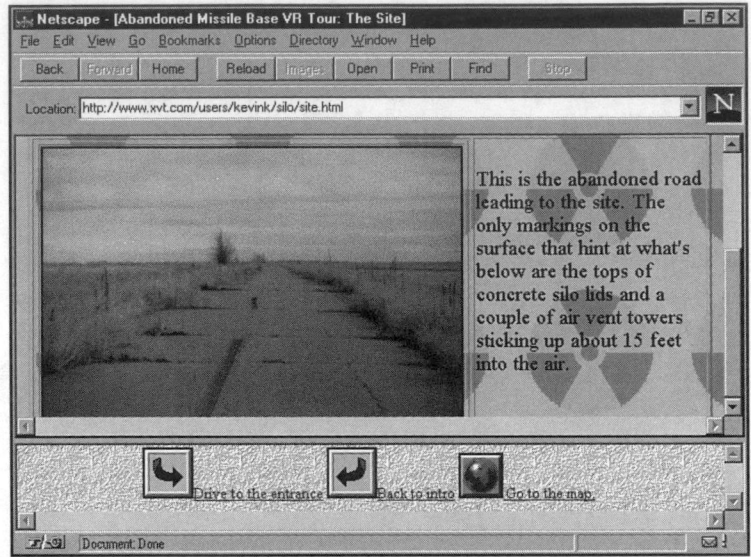

HTML: The Bricks and Mortar of the Web

▶ See "Distributing Information with HTML," p. 63

Now that you know where the Web came from, it's time to jump into the whole melange feet first—but with your eyes open. HTML (HyperText Markup Language) is what you use to create Web pages, and it's the topic of this book.

HTML is relatively simple in both concept and execution. In fact, if you have ever used a very old word processor, you are already familiar with the concept of a markup language.

In the "good old days" of word processing, if you wanted text to appear in, say, italics, you might surround it with control characters like this:

/Ithis is in italics/I

The "/I" at the beginning would indicate to the word processor that, when printed, the text following should be italicized. The "/I" would turn off italics so that any text afterward would be printed in a normal font. You literally *marked up* the text for printing just as you would if you were making editing marks on a printed copy with an editor's red pencil.

HTML works in much the same way. If, for example, you want text to appear on a Web page in italics, you mark it like this:

<I>this is in italics</I>

Almost everything you create in HTML relies on marks, or *tags*, like these.

The rest of this book elaborates on that simple fact.

► See "How Web Browsers and Servers Work Together," p. 37

A Short Internet Glossary

Although you don't need to know every term that's bantered about on the Internet to be able to work, play, and develop on the Web, an understanding of a few key terms will help you to better understand what's going on there. Here's a short glossary of Internet and Web terms to help you get started.

Backbone A high-speed network for internetworking computer networks.

Browse To navigate the World Wide Web. Synonyms: *cruise, surf.*

Browser A client program for viewing HTML documents sent by a server over an HTTP connection.

Client An application or computer that receives and interprets data sent by a matching server computer/application.

CGI Common Gateway Interface; the way in which Web CGI-BIN scripts are run.

CGI-BIN Script CGI Binary script; a server-side program that accomplishes a task that cannot be done using HTML. A means of extending the usefulness and versatility of the Web.

Domain Name The unique name that identifies each Internet site.

E-mail Electronic Mail; addressed messages sent over a computer network, either automatically or by a human user, to one or more recipients.

FAQ Frequently Asked Questions list, which attempts to answer the most-asked questions on a given topic. Many are transmitted on a monthly basis over Usenet, and are archived on the Net.

FORM A subset of HTML tags that can be used to create fields on a Web page to accept input from a user.

FTP File Transfer Protocol; the TCP/IP protocol for transferring files on the Internet.

GIF Graphics Interchange Format image, often used on Web pages because of its ability to render a background color as transparent.

Gopher A client/server application for indexing and retrieving information on the Internet. The predecessor to the World Wide Web.

Hit   An instance of someone (or something, such as a Webcrawler robot indexing program) accessing a Web page.

Hostname   The DNS name for a single computer on the Internet, e.g., www.yahoo.com.

HTML   HyperText Markup Language; the language used to create Web pages.

HTTP   HyperText Transfer Protocol; the client/server protocol for moving hypertext files on the Internet.

Hypertext   Text containing links that, when chosen by a user, will "jump" to another block of text, either in the same document or in another.

Internet   The worldwide network of computers connected by TCP/IP and other internetworking protocols.

IP Address   Internet Protocol address, which is composed of four numbers separated by periods ("dots"), e.g., 198.137.221.9.

ISP   Internet Service Provider; an institution that provides access to the Internet.

JAVA   An interpreted script language developed by Sun Microsystems that resembles C++. It was created to extend the capabilities of the Web by allowing programs to be associated with Web pages that can run on a Web client computer when the page is accessed.

JPEG   Joint Photographic Experts Group; compressed graphics images, often used on Web pages.

LAN   Local Area Network; a computer network limited in scope to a single group of locally interconnected computers.

Link   A user-selectable hypertext or hypermedia jump point, that, when selected, will "jump" to another text or multimedia object.

MIME   Multipurpose Internet Mail Extensions; a means of identifying content in e-mail files and on Web pages. Used by Web browser programs to identify Web page content for proper display.

MPEG   Moving Picture Experts Group; compression algorithm for video and audio files, often used on the Web.

Multimedia   Generic term for integrated, interactive video, audio, text, graphics, database, and other content.

Netscape   Shorthand for the Netscape Communications Corporation's Netscape Navigator WWW browser, generally acknowledged to be the most popular Web browser program today.

Network   A collection of computers connected by LAN, WAN, or Internet.

Newsgroup   A Usenet conference or discussion group.

Node   A single computer connected to a network.

NRE   National Research and Education Network; the entity that will form the backbone for the U.S. potion of the Internet for the near future.

Page   A single HTML document on the Web.

PERL   Practical Extraction Reporting Language; many CGI-BIN scripts on the Web are written in PERL.

POP   Post Office Protocol; the method whereby e-mail is generally transmitted.

Post   To send a message for public display in a Usenet newsgroup.

PPP   Point-to-Point Protocol; one of the protocols that enables a user to create a TCP/IP dialup connection to the Internet via modem.

RFC   Request For Comments; the process of writing a document proposing a new standard for the Internet and then asking for the Net community to comment on it. The standard method for establishing rules and methods on the Internet.

Server   A computer/application that sends data over the network to a matching client computer/program that is capable of properly interpreting that data.

SGML   Standard Generalized Markup Language; the precursor to and a superset of HTML.

SLIP   Serial Line Internet Protocol; an alternative to PPP.

T1   A leased-line Internet connection that operates at 1.5 megabits per second.

T3   A 45 megabit-per-second leased line Internet connection.

Tag   An HTML markup element.

TCP/IP   Transmission Control Protocol/Internet Protocol; the suite of protocols that provides the infrastructure for the Internet.

Telnet   A remote logon program that is part of the TCP/IP protocols.

URL   Uniform Resource Locator; the standard World Wide Web address format, e.g., **http://www.yahoo.com**.

Usenet   A worldwide system of discussion groups.

VRML   Virtual Reality Modeling Language for creating 3D sites on the Web.

WAIS   Wide Area Information Server, for indexing and accessing great quantities of information on the Net. Often an adjunct to Gopher.

WAN   Wide Area Network; an internetwork of LANs. The Internet is a huge WAN.

WWW   World Wide Web; the portion of the Internet that consists of linked HTML pages.

Note

For more on computer terminology, check out the Free Online Dictionary of Computing at **http://wfn-shop.princeton.edu/cgi-bin/foldoc**. If computer abbreviations and acronyms have you confused, seek enlightenment at BABEL, a dictionary of such alphabet soup at **http://www.access.digex.net/~ikind/ babel96a.html**. But if you want to become a *real* Net insider, you'll have to learn the slang; for that, check out the latest version of the legendary Jargon File at **http://www.ccil.org/jargon/jargon.html**.

## CHAPTER 2

How Web Browsers and Servers Work Together

by Mark Brown

They say that the camera never lies. A photograph is a record of a real scene as it was captured by the camera's lens.

On the other hand, two artists never paint the same scene the same way. Every element is subject to the artist's interpretation. One artist might paint a photo-realistic image that's almost sharper than reality; another might render an abstract smear that communicates mood more accurately than it portrays the scene. They might move, add, remove, or alter objects or change lighting to suit their depictions of the scene.

The World Wide Web works more like painting than it does like taking photographs. A Web server "serves up" a page over the Internet, and a Web browser program interprets it. The results may be almost as different as the two painting styles described above. This is the central, surprising truth about the World Wide Web: what you see on a Web page is *described*, not *defined*, by its HTML code. It is up to the user's browser program to render it in its final form.

Many new Web developers are shocked to discover that they have so little control over the final appearance of their pages. But, for better or worse, that's how the Web works. If you want to create Web pages that can be viewed accurately by a wide range of WWW users, you're going to have to be aware of the different server and browser programs that are out there and how they work together.

In this chapter, you learn about the following:

- The steps that occur when you view a Web page
- The difference between HTTP and HTML
- What a URL is
- How browser programs differ in the way they display Web pages
- Which server and browser programs are the most popular

How the Web Works

The World Wide Web has a *client/server* architecture. This means that a client program running on your computer (your Web browser) requests information from a server program running on another computer somewhere on the Internet. That server then sends the requested data back over the Net to your browser program, which interprets and displays the data on your screen. Figure 2.1 shows the whole process graphically. The following steps explain the process:

1. You run a Web browser client program on your computer.

2. You connect to the Internet—at work or school via a direct T1 or T3 line; at home via a modem dial-up connection to an Internet service provider (ISP).

3. You request a page from a site on the Web. Your browser sends a message over the Internet that includes the following:

   - The transfer protocol (http://)

   - The address, or *Uniform Resource Locator* (URL), e.g., www.somesite.net

4. The server receives your request and retrieves the requested Web page, which is composed in HTML (HyperText Markup Language).

5. The server then transmits the requested page back across the Internet to your computer.

6. Your browser program receives the HTML text and displays its interpretation of the page you requested.

Fig. 2.1
This is what happens when you view a page on the World Wide Web.

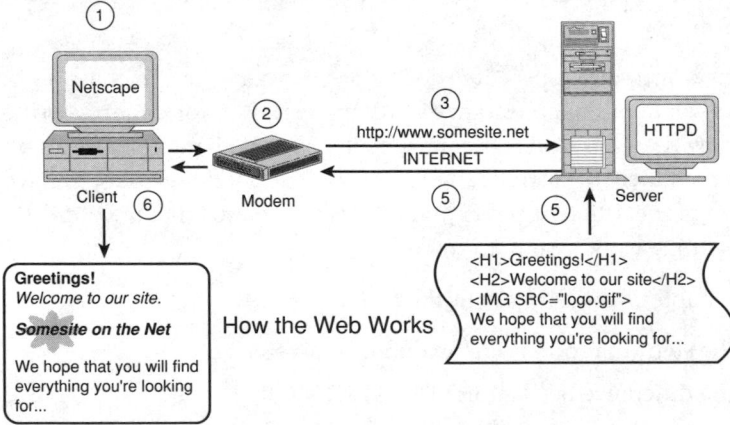

> **Note**
>
> Many computer networks include a security mechanism called a *firewall*. A firewall is software (often combined with specialized hardware) that creates a barrier to keep unauthorized outside users from accessing a site. If a system is equipped with a firewall, inside users must use proxy programs to access the Internet. Although this adds a couple of steps, the fundamental process of transferring data back and forth between client and server is essentially unchanged.

> **Note**
>
> You can also set up a server to run a Web site over a LAN (local area network) without connecting it to the outside world at all. This is sometimes referred to as an *Intranet.* In this scenario, only those connected directly to the LAN are able to access the pages on the server. Many companies use a setup like this for distributing internal information to their employees.

The Client Computer

To browse the Web, you need a client computer. There are two basic requirements for this machine: it must have a connection to the Internet and must be capable of running a Web browser program.

The Internet connection can be hard-wired, or it can be a dial-up phone connection via modem to an Internet service provider (ISP). You're most likely to have the former at work or school and the latter at home. The only difference you will notice between the two is speed; otherwise, they work identically.

There are Web browser programs for just about any computer you can name, from dumb text-only terminals running on mainframes to off-brand personal computers, such as the Amiga. (I'll list and discuss the most popular browser programs later in this chapter.)

The Server Computer

On the content-provider side of things, you need a server computer. This machine has requirements similar to those of the client computer: it must be connected to the Internet and must be able to run a Web server program.

Tip

A Web server program is often called an *HTTPD,* for HyperText Transfer Protocol Daemon. *Daemon* is computerese for a program that runs unseen in the background.

However, a Web server needs a more robust Internet connection than a Web client does. A server should ideally be hooked up to the Internet via a fast dedicated T1 or T3 line that remains connected all the time. Otherwise, people trying to access your Web site will often find that it just isn't there.

It is possible (though excruciatingly slow) to run a Web site on a dial-up line, especially if you can find an Internet service provider who will let you stay dialed in 24 hours a day without disconnecting you. However, you must make sure that your ISP can assign a permanent IP address to your machine—not a new IP address each time you connect. Otherwise, people won't even be able to find your site.

Note

A good intermediate solution to the direct vs. dial-up problem is an ISDN line. A sort of super fast digital phone line, an ISDN line costs more than a regular phone line but much, much less than a dedicated T1 or T3 line. It also requires a special interface card for your computer. ISDN lines are offered by most phone companies in urban areas and university towns, but you'll need to find an ISP that can provide an ISDN connection too. Contact the business office of your local phone company for details.

HTTPD server software is available for a wide variety of computers (see fig. 2.2). Surprisingly, server computers don't have to be very powerful; serving up Web content is simply not that demanding. More of a concern is having a multithreaded, multitasking operating system so that the server can handle several tasks at once without bogging down. Storage is a concern, however, because Web sites are notorious for growing without limit.

Communication: Requesting Information via URLs

An HTTP connection is said to be *stateless*. That is, no permanent connection is maintained between the server and the client. A request is made, and the connection is broken. Then a response is sent back, and the connection is broken again. This process is repeated for every request and often even for parts of a request. Programmers refer to this as a *query-response model* of interaction. It's the reason your browser program always seems to be saying "Waiting for reply..." in its status display line. (See the message at the bottom of fig. 2.3.)

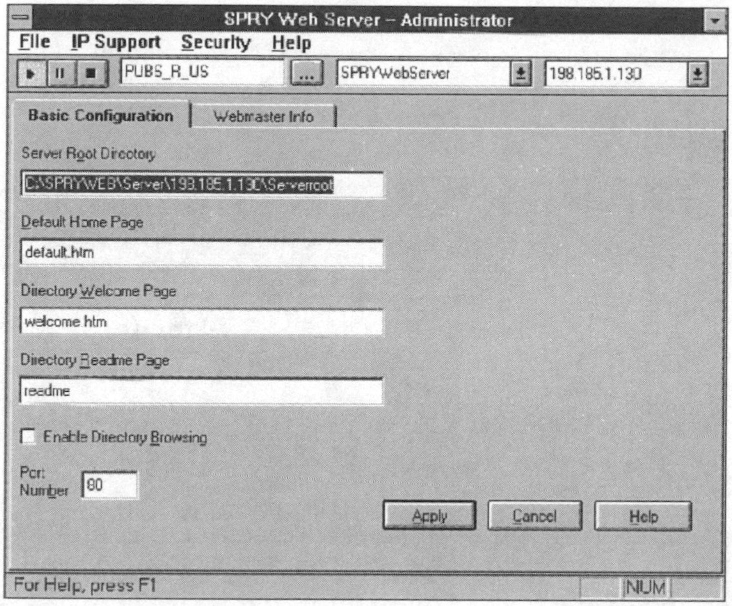

Fig. 2.2
The Spry Web
Server for UNIX X
Windows has a
rich GUI for
configuration and
maintenance tasks.

A browser's request for information takes the form of a URL (Uniform Resource Locator), which is also referred to as a page's *address* or *location*. URLs almost always look something like this:

http://www.somesite.nct/path/webpage.html

> **Tip**
>
> A URL is always a single, unbroken line of text with no spaces.

Web browsers generally display the URL of the Web page currently being viewed near the top of the window (see fig. 2.3).

Here's a real world example of a URL, taken from figure 2.3:

**http://www.microsoft.com/msoffice/freestuf/msword/
download/ia/default.htm**

The "http://" portion of the URL indicates that the browser has requested a transfer via HTTP protocol; that is, it wants a Web page. "www.microsoft.com" is the domain name of the server being queried; in this case, it's the Web server at Microsoft. The "msoffice/freestuf/msword/download/ia/" portion of the URL is the path name on the server's hard

◄ See "Domain
Names," p. 24

drive for the file you want. (Fortunately, this example is of one of the longer path names you're likely to run into on the Web.) "default.htm" is the name of the actual HTML file on the server; it's what is being displayed on the screen in figure 2.3.

Fig. 2.3
Web browsers let you know where you are on the Web by displaying the page's URL. Netscape shows this near the top of the display window and labels it "Location."

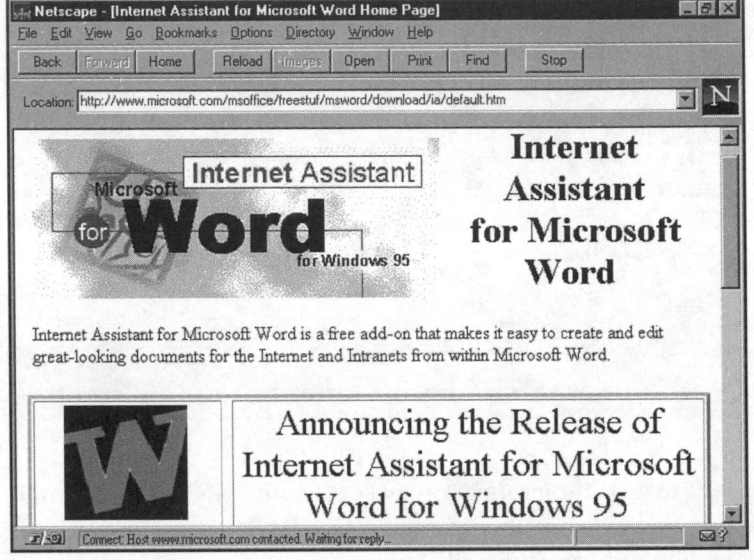

> **Tip**
>
> If the protocol portion of a URL is **https:// or snews://**, it means that the connection is secure. In Netscape, this will be confirmed by the presence of an unbroken security key in the lower left-hand corner of the screen.

▶ See "Linking HTML Documents," p. 143

URLs can reference not only Web pages, but also just about any service on the Internet, including FTP, Gopher, WAIS, Usenet, and Telnet. You can even load in a file from your own computer! Table 2.1 shows the syntax for the various types of sites that can be accessed via a Web browser.

Table 2.1   URL Syntax for Addressing Various Types of Internet Sites

URL Syntax	Type of Access
file://	a file on your local computer
ftp://	an FTP server

URL Syntax	Type of Access
gopher://	a Gopher server
http://	a Web page
news://	a Usenet newsgroup
telnet://	a connection to a Telnet site
WAIS://	a WAIS server

The domain name portion of a URL may include a colon followed by a port number, like this:

http://www.somesite.net:80/path/webpage.htm

This tells the server to access the site via a specific assigned port.

Tip

Port 80 is the default port defined in the HTTP specification. If not given, it is assumed.

Web page file names usually end in .htm or .html to indicate that they are HTML content files. Many home pages don't have path names or file names at all. Their URLs are in a very abbreviated format:

http://www.somesite.net

These addresses access a page that is stored in the server's root directory; that is, they don't need a path name because they aren't stored in a subdirectory. Most servers also assume a default file name for the home page, such as hompage.html or index.htm. If no page file name is specified, the server will automatically serve up the default page.

URLs can point to other types of files than HTML Web pages, of course. For example, the URL **http://www.somesite.net/logo.gif** would display a GIF image file. **http://www.somesite.net/path/program.zip** would, depending on how your browser is configured, prompt you to save the specified ZIP file to disk or would decompress the file and store the resulting program files to disk.

Sometimes you may see a URL that looks something like this:

http://www.somesite.net/cgi-bin/findit&toad+frog

Servers can include *gateways,* which enable them to run application programs called *CGI* (Common Gateway Interface) scripts or programs. These are, in most ways, just like any other programs run by a computer. Depending on

▶ See "All About CGI Scripts," p. 525

▶ See "Sample Code and CGI Scripts," p. 557

the machine and the gateway, CGI-bin (*bin* for *binary*) programs might be written in C, C++, BASIC, or the PERL scripting language. An URL like the one above instructs the server to run the CGI program called findit using the data toad and frog as inputs. In this example, it would be a fair guess that the server program, findit, was some sort of indexing program and that the user had instructed it to find references in its database to toads and frogs.

Some hyperlinks may reference a relative URL; that is, one in the same path name on the same server as the page currently being viewed. For example, if the current page is **http://www.somesite.net/path/thispage.html**, a relative link to **thatpage.html** would load in the page whose absolute address is **http://www.somesite.net/path/thatpage.html**. This technique not only saves page creation time and space on the server, but it also makes it very easy to move all of the files associated with a Web site to a new directory or even to a new machine. Only the references to the home page need to be changed; relative URLs remain the same.

Servers and HTTP

A Web server computer runs an HTTPD (HyperText Transfer Protocol Daemon) program (see fig. 2.4). The history behind the development of HTTP is told in chapter 1, "Introducing the World Wide Web." This section will concentrate on how Web servers use HTTP to communicate with browser clients.

Fig. 2.4
NetPublisher is an HTTPD server program for Windows NT. Unlike many bare-bones UNIX servers, NetPublisher sports an intuitive GUI.

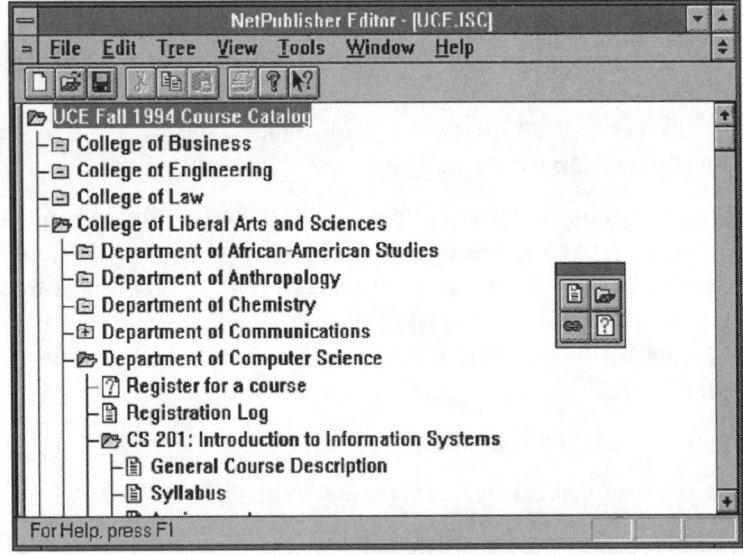

What Servers Do

When you analyze what a server does, you begin to fully realize just how much of the look and feel of the World Wide Web is in the browser program.

The browser client strips an URL down to its component parts: protocol, address, path name, and file name. From the protocol portion, it determines how it is going to interact with the server that it's addressing and how to display the data it will receive. It then *calls* the address contained in the URL and waits for a response from the server.

Once the server realizes that a request is coming through, it likewise checks the URL for the connection protocol (e.g., http:// for a Web page). It takes the path name and file name that it has been given, finds them on its hard drive, and sends the data off to the browser using the correct protocol.

Then it's the browser's turn again. This time it gathers in, interprets, and properly displays the data it has received.

It probably seems as if there is a lot more for the browser to do in this process than there is for the server, and in the case of a simple transaction, such as viewing a Web page, that's probably true. But there's much more than that going on in the background.

For example, if there's an error somewhere along the way—such as a request for a page that doesn't exist—the server has to send back the proper error message. If the user has requested an action that requires running a CGI program, the server has to load and run the program. This process usually means creating a custom HTML page "on the fly" that contains the results of the program's action, then sending that back to the browser.

Then, too, every data file transmitted by the server has to be properly identified by type and tagged with the appropriate *MIME* (Multipurpose Internet Mail Extension) data type header so the browser will know what to do with it. Most Web pages include a mix of HTML formatted text, GIF and JPEG graphics, and maybe even audio and video clips; each must be properly tagged, or the browser won't know how to interpret the pieces when they arrive.

Today's Web servers also include all kinds of esoterica—for example, data encryption and client authentication. These take up a great deal of the server's time, too.

◄ See "Introducing the World Wide Web," p. 9

Factor in the fact that a server is often handling requests from hundreds of clients at any one time, and you'll see that there's more than enough going on to keep it busy.

> **Tip**
>
> For more information on servers, check out the Usenet newsgroups **comp.infosystems.www.servers.misc**, **.mac**, **.ms-windows**, and **.unix**.

HTTP

The HyperText Transfer Protocol (HTTP) was designed to be quick, simple, and nonintrusive. The connection between a server and a client program (or *agent*) is temporary and must be reestablished for every data transfer.

The HTTP specification incorporates a whole set of methods that are used to perform the tasks associated with servicing a Web site, including information retrieval, searching, front-end updating, and annotation. The specification is open-ended, so additional functionality can be added without making the whole Web obsolete.

As discussed previously, messages are passed in a format that is similar to Internet Mail and the Multipurpose Internet Mail Extensions (MIME); gateways enable browsers to request the execution of CGI applications on the server hardware; and communication is possible with other Internet protocols, such as SMTP, NNTP, FTP, Gopher, and WAIS.

HTTP is, like these earlier protocols, a TCP/IP protocol. However, it can be implemented on top of any other protocol implementation that can communicate over the Internet or on other networks, including LANs.

> **Tip**
>
> The current version of the HTTP protocol specification can be found at the site maintained by the HTTP Working Group at **http://www.ics.uci.edu/pub/ietf/http/**.

An Overview of Popular HTTPD Server Programs

Almost any computer platform that you can name (and some you probably can't) can act as a Web server. There are HTTPD server programs for systems as varied as multimillion-dollar mainframes and PCs costing under $1000.

Which one is best? That's a question that is highly subjective, and it's certainly beyond the scope of this book. A more important question might be, "Do I need an HTTPD server program at all?"

If you usually hook up to the Web through an Internet service provider (ISP) and are thinking about setting up a personal Web site, the answer is almost certainly *no!* What you need is an account on somebody else's Web server, probably that of your ISP. Most ISPs offer a place for your own home page for little or nothing if you're already using their dial-up services. For example, my local ISP charges me $30 a month for unlimited Internet access and includes a 10 megabyte UNIX account on which I can keep my own World Wide Web pages.

If you think about it, this is an incredible bargain. For $1 a day—which is less than I pay for cable TV—I maintain a Web site that can be seen by anyone in the world, 24 hours a day! And they take care of all the headaches of setting up and configuring the server, maintaining the site, and handling glitches and bugs. It's great. All I have to do is develop the content for my site, write it in HTML, and upload it to my provider.

Tip

For an example of what kind of site you can set up using somebody else's Web server, check out my personal Web site at **http://www2.giant.net/people/mbrown**.

Even small- to medium-sized companies might want to consider having an ISP host their sites rather than setting up their own Web server. It can mean a major investment of both time and money to set up a server computer, hook it up via a permanent T1 or T3 land line, install the HTTPD software, and maintain all of that hardware and software over time. If your needs are moderate, having an ISP take care of all that for you can be a major headache reliever.

Tip

You can find a searchable list of Internet service providers on the ISP Yellow Pages site at **http://www.index.org/**.

However, if you are developing Web pages for a college or major corporation, you'll probably want to run your own site. This is the best way to go if your site:

- Is already hard wired to the Internet
- Will contain a great number of pages

- Needs to run custom CGI applications
- Will require frequent updating
- Needs to be secure

If any of these criteria describe the site you want to set up, then pick a computer platform and HTTPD server software that match your requirements.

It is beyond the scope of this book to review all of the many HTTPD servers that are currently available; nonetheless, I can discuss the ones that are the most popular. Although popularity is not exclusively determined by quality—price and compatibility are certainly major issues as well—it can serve as a good measure of which server programs are already working for a large number of sites.

> **Note**
>
> The server use statistics in this section were taken from the server survey data at **http://www.mirai.com/survey** and from the Spry Webcrawler statistics at **http://www.webcrawler.com/WebCrawler/Facts/WebFacts.html**.

Accurate statistical data about Web server usage is hard to come by. Most is based on random samplings of sites or on *volunteer* surveys, which can be highly skewed by inaccurate survey samples. But a comparison of the best data currently available on the Web seems to lead to the following conclusions about which computer platforms are probably the most popular Web servers:

- A little less than one-third of all Web servers run on Sun workstations.
- About one-third of all Web sites are running on Macintoshes or on IBM-compatible personal computers with some version of the Windows operating system. These are about evenly split between the two platforms. Twice as many of the IBM-compatible sites run NT as run Windows.
- The remaining one-third of all Web sites run on UNIX systems.
- Only about 4 percent of Web sites run on OS/2 or other operating systems.

This breakdown is shown graphically in the pie chart in figure 2.5.

A little over a year ago, more than 80 percent of the servers on the Web were UNIX-based. The shift shown in figure 2.5 certainly reflects two current trends: The rapid growth of the World Wide Web has moved it beyond the confines of academia and corporate America, where UNIX is most popular, and there has been, in the last year, a proliferation of HTTPD software for platforms other than UNIX.

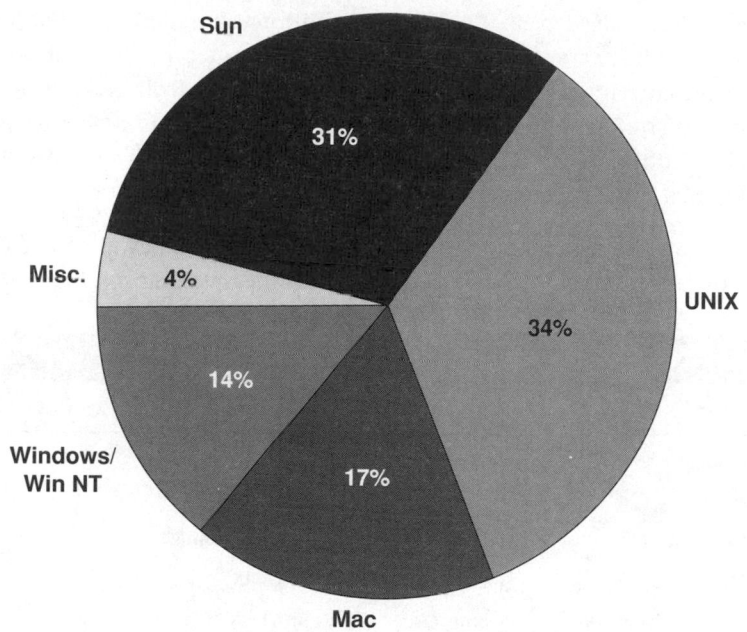

Server Market Share by Platform

Fig. 2.5
Sun workstations, personal computers, and UNIX systems split the server market into nearly equal thirds.

Overview of the Web

Let's take a look at specific servers.

One of the major reasons for UNIX's predominance has been the number of freely distributable HTTPD server programs available for it. CERN HTTPD and NCSA HTTPD have historically been the two most popular server programs on the Web, and they remain at or near the top of the list.

However, a plethora of new server programs has been introduced in the past year, and some of them are gaining market share quickly. Although there are a few new freebies—Apache, for instance—many of the fastest-growing servers are commercial packages from such companies as Netscape, Quarterdeck, and Open Market.

There are many good reasons for the fast growth of commercial Web server programs. For the price, those buying commercial servers get the peace of mind that comes with knowing that the product is fully supported, not freeware with a nebulous cloud of hobbyist developers working on it in their spare time. Then, too, these products are finished goods; they don't need to be compiled to run and are packaged with complete documentation and a full set of additional Web development software tools.

Further, commercial servers usually offer additional functionality that just isn't found in freeware servers, such as encryption and security. And finally, most of the current growth of the Web can be directly attributed to the addition of many new commercial sites. Unlike the personal and academic sites that preceded them, commercial sites aren't scared off by the $400–$5,000 price tag that commercial server software carries.

Table 2.2 lists the most popular servers on the Web, as nearly as can be determined by current data.* Figure 2.6 shows the same data graphically.

Table 2.2 The Most Popular HTTPD Server Software			
Server	**Availability**	**Platform(s)**	**Pct**
NCSA	Free	UNIX/Win	41
Apache	Free	UNIX	17
Netscape	Commercial	UNIX/WinNT	13
CERN HTTPD	Free	UNIX	11
WebSTAR/MacHTTP	Comm/Free	Macintosh	17
Others	Comm/Free	Varied	1

* *Source: Web Servers Survey Version 2.0, January 1996, by Paul E. Hoffman, Proper Publishing,* **http://www.proper.com/**.

There are, of course, a great many more HTTPD server programs available than those shown in table 2.2. Table 2.3 lists HTTPD server programs for a variety of platforms. To find out more about any of these servers, check out Paul Hoffman's Server Comparison Chart on the Web. This site contains a wealth of data for anyone who is thinking about establishing a presence on the World Wide Web, including hypertext links to the publishers of most of the Web server programs listed in table 2.3. Its location is **http://www.proper.com/www/servers-chart.html**.

Table 2.3 HTTPD Server Programs by Platform	
Platform	**Server**
Amiga	Amiga Web Server
AS/400	Server/400

Platform	Server
Macintosh	CL-HTTP, FTPd, httpd4Mac, MacHTTP, WebSTAR
Novell	SiteBuilder, Webware
OS/2	GoServe
UNIX	Apache, Boa, CERN, CL-HTTP, GN, NaviServer, NCSA, Netscape Commerce, Netscape Communications, Open Market Secure WS, Open Market WebServer, Phttpd, SafetyWEB UNIX, Spinner, Spry Web UNIX, TEAMate, WN
VM/CMS	Webshare
VMS	CERN, Purveyor, Region 6
Windows 3.1	FrontPage, Quarterdeck
Windows 95	Alibaba, Commerce Builder, Communications Builder, FolkWeb, FrontPage, Purveyor, Quarterdeck WebServer, SAIC, WebQuest, WebSite
Windows NT	Alibaba, Commerce Builder, Communications Builder, FolkWeb, FrontPage, HTTPS, Microsoft's Internet Information Server, NaviServer, NetPublisher, Netscape Commerce, Netscape Communications, Purveyor, Quarterdeck, SafetyWEB NT, SAIC, Spry Web NT, WebQuest, WebSite

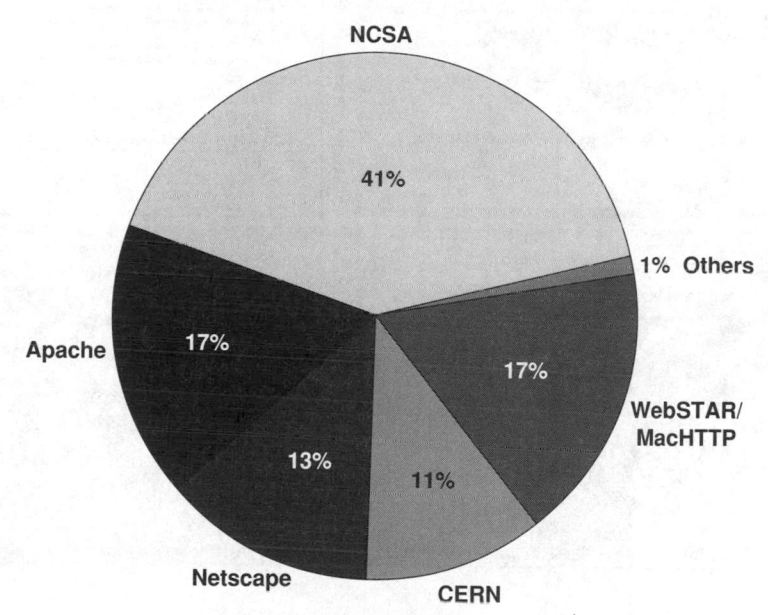

The Most Popular Web ServerSoftware

Fig. 2.6
Many of the most popular Web server software in use today are freeware, but commercial servers are gaining ground.

Overview of the Web

Browsers and HTML

To a large degree, the Web is what your Web browser makes it. Because Web pages are written in HTML and because HTML is subject to interpretation, your browser profoundly affects the appearance of Web pages and, consequently, your impression of the World Wide Web as a whole.

What Browsers Do

Figure 2.7 shows the same Web page as viewed by three different browser programs: the all-text UNIX Lynx browser (upper left), an older Windows browser called Cello (upper right), and Netscape Navigator 2.0 (lower right). The fourth image (lower left) is the same page displayed by Netscape 2.0 with customized color and font settings. You can see how differently various browsers can interpret the same page and how significant user settings are in the outcome.

Fig. 2.7
The same Web page can be displayed in very different ways by different browser programs.

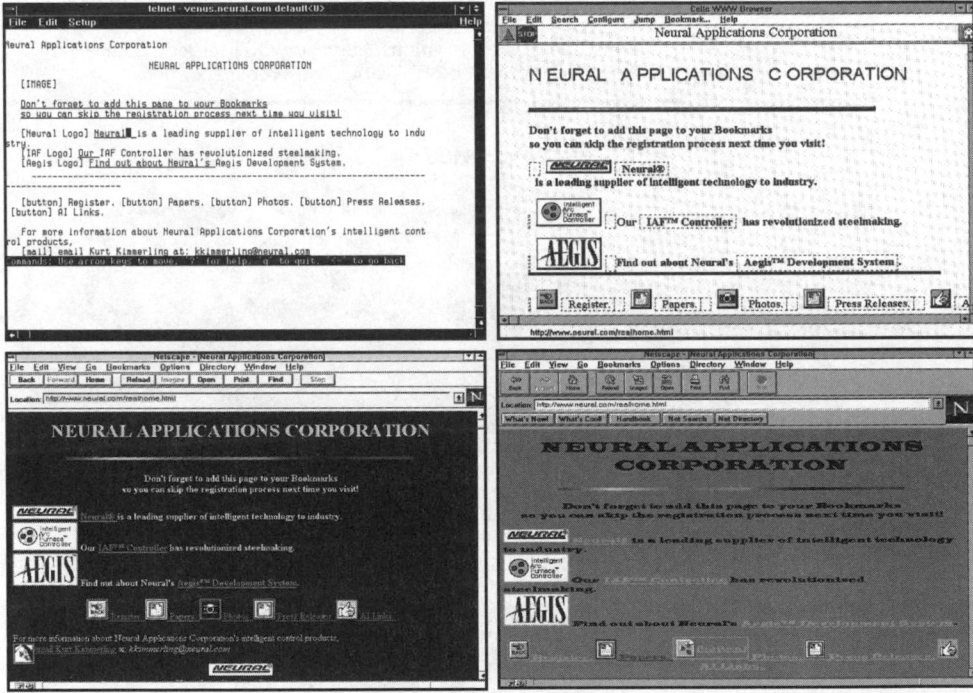

That's why it's important to make sure you have a good browser program (see fig. 2.8) if you're going to develop HTML documents for the World Wide Web. You want to make sure that your viewers are seeing the same pages you are.

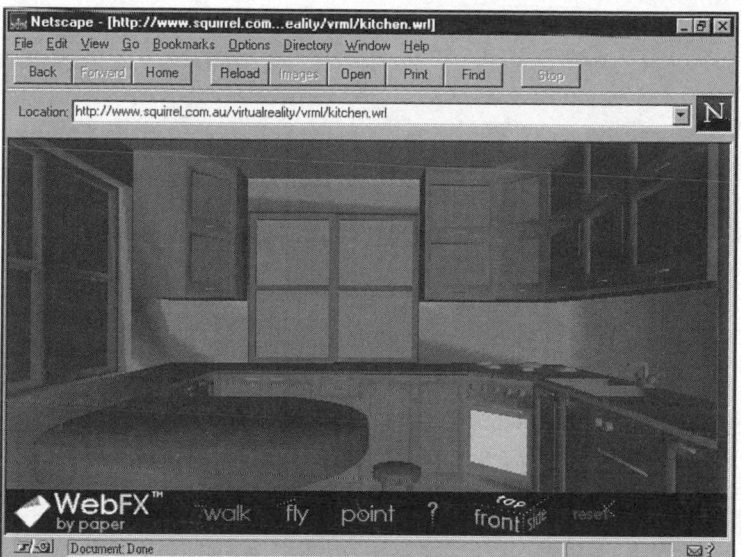

Fig. 2.8
Netscape Naviga-
tor, shown here in
version 2.0 for
Windows 95, is
the most popular
browser program
in use on the Web
today. In this
screen shot,
Netscape displays a
3-D VRML (Virtual
Reality Modeling
Language) virtual
world using the
WebFX plug-in.

Note

As a sort of experiment, you can simulate a Web browser program by Telneting
into a Web site and executing the same command by hand that a browser would.
Perform the following steps:

1. Run a Telnet application and log into a Web site. For most sites, you'll want to
   specify port 80. For example, access the Yahoo! Web site via Telnet at
   www.yahoo.com 0080.

2. Type **GET index.html**.

3. The ASCII HTML file that is Yahoo!'s home page will scroll by on your monitor.

4. Because HTTP is stateless, the connection is closed automatically when the
   document (or error message if you mistyped Step 2) is done transmitting.

Tip

For more information on Web browser programs, check out the Usenet newsgroups
comp.infosystems.www.browsers.misc, **.mac**, **.ms-windows**, and **.X**.

HTML

▶ See "Netscape-Specific Extensions to HTML," p. 311

▶ See "HTML Extensions in Internet Explorer, Mosaic, and HTML 3.0," p. 347

HTML is not intended to be an all-encompassing, all-powerful page layout environment. HTML describes a page's look by using markup tags to indicate the relative position of elements on the page. For example, you can specify which lines of text are headings and their level of importance. You can show where in the text an in-line image should appear and whether certain blocks of text should appear with a particular type of formatting. You can even create tables and forms. With some of the most recent versions of HTML, you can create frames in which different parts of pages are displayed, put up graphic background *wallpaper,* and change the color of text on the fly.

HTML cannot, however, determine which font, font size, or color will be used to display text; what the screen background color will be; how the colors in graphics will be interpreted; or any of a wide variety of other variables that are at the mercy of browser programs or the users' settings of various options in their browser programs.

"Why doesn't HTML give a page creator more control?" you ask.

HTML's main appeal is that it is easy to learn and easy to use. Ease of implementation was, in fact, the major design criterion for HTML, and it worked. A recent survey of Web page creators found that over half of them learned the basics of HTML in under three hours, and another quarter took only six hours. Most said that a good book (like this one!) and the Web itself were the only tools they needed to begin creating Web pages.

HTML was also designed to be compatible across a wide range of machines, from text-only UNIX terminals to the flashiest Silicon Graphics workstation. To a large degree, that goal has been met, too. Although there will certainly be some differences in the same Web page viewed on different machines with different browsers, the results will likely be similar enough and acceptable enough to convey the information presented in the manner intended by the page's creator.

The responsibility for making sure this happens rests squarely on the shoulders of the Web developer—you! Properly applied, HTML can make your pages look good on a wide variety of platforms. The more aware you are of the differences in Web browsers, the better you'll be able to make sure your pages look good on all (or at least most) of them.

> **Note**
>
> If you really want the pages you put on the Web to retain their original look and feel, you might want to consider making them available as *PDF* (Portable Document Format) files. A lot of companies and organizations do, from Adobe Systems to the IRS.
>
> A PDF file can't be read by a Web browser though—it needs an external viewer program. Adobe Acrobat is the most popular PDF format on the Web today. You can get information about Acrobat (and download a free viewer) from the Adobe Web site at **http://www.adobe.com**.

An Overview of a Few Popular Web Browser Programs

So which Web browser clients are the most popular? That's one with an easy answer. The most popular Web browser today is Netscape Navigator, which is used by over 80 percent of those cruising the Web. Other browsers don't account for over four percent of the market each.

Does this mean that you can, with impunity, develop only for Netscape and ignore the rest? In a word, no. First of all, there are several different versions of Netscape Navigator out there, running on UNIX, Windows, Windows 95, and Macintosh platforms. If you want to use some of the latest and greatest Netscape features—such as frames —you'll leave behind the three-quarters or more of your Netscape audience who are, as of this writing, still using Netscape 1.1. (See chapter 15, "Netscape-Specific Extensions to HTML.") And the 20 percent of Web users who don't use Netscape Navigator are a sizable chunk of your audience too. You don't want to leave them out in the cold, do you?

Table 2.4 should give you some idea of the wide variety of client programs that are out there browsing the Web.

Table 2.4   Web Browser Programs for Various Platforms

Platform	Browser	Comments
AMIGA	Amosaic	Based on NCSA Mosaic. FTP from aminet sites in **/pub/aminet/comm/net**. Home page at **http://insti.physics. sunysb.edu/AMosaic/home.html**. FAQ at **http://www. phone.net/ ATCPFAQ/amosaic.html**.

(continues)

Table 2.4 Continued

Platform	Browser	Comments
AMIGA	Amiga Lynx	Home page at **http://www.fhi-berlin.mpg.de/amiga/alynx.html**.
	EMACS w3-mode	Multi-platform browser for EMACS editor. Runs under Gnu EMACS on the Amiga. FTP from **ftp.cs.indiana.edu/pub/elisp/w3**.
MACINTOSH	Enhanced	From Spyglass. Multi-platform.
	Mosaic	Commercial version of NCSA Mosaic. Can only be licensed by OEMs. Home page at **http://www.spyglass.com**.
	MacWeb	From EINet. FTP from **ftp.einet.net/einet/mac/macweb**.
	NCSA Mosaic	Multi-platform and still free (see fig. 2.9). FTP from **ftp.ncsa.uiuc.edu/Mac/Mosaic**.
	Netscape Navigator	Tables, HTML extensions. Free to nonprofit and educational institutions; free 90-day evaluation for individuals. Home page at **http://home.netscape.com/info/index.html**. FTP from **ftp.netscape.com**.

Fig. 2.9
NCSA Mosaic was the original Web browser program. It has kept up well and is still available for Macintosh, Windows 3.1, Windows NT, Windows 95 (shown here), and X Windows systems. Many other browsers are derived from the original NCSA Mosaic source code.

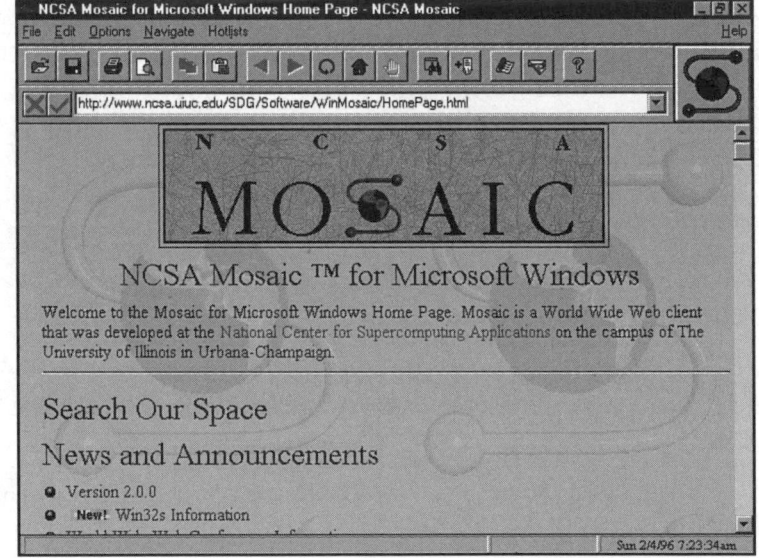

Platform	Browser	Comments
MS/DOS	DOSLynx	Can view GIFs, but not in-line. FTP from **ftp2.cc.ukans.edu/pub/WWW/DosLynx**.
	Minuet	Both text-mode and graphics-mode display. FTP from **minuet.micro.umn.edu/pub/minuet/latest/minuarc.exe**.
NEXTSTEP	CERN WorldWideWeb	Out of date; editor not operational. Requires NeXTStep 3.0. FTP from **ftp.w3.org/pub/www/src**.
	EMACS w3-mode Netsurfer	(See Amiga listing) FTP from **ftp.thoughtport.com/pub/next/netsurfer**. Home page at **http://www.netsurfer.com**.
	OmniWeb	Home page at **http://www.omnigroup.com/**. FTP from **ftp.omnigroup.com/pub/software/**.
	SpiderWoman	Multithreaded, graphical. FTP from **sente.epfl.ch/pub/software**. Home page at **http://sente.epfl.ch/**.
TEXT-MODE UNIX/VMS	EMACS w3-mode Line Mode Browser Lynx PERLWWW	(See Amiga listing) For dumb terminals. FTP from **www.w3.org/pub/www/src**. For VT100. FTP from **ftp2.cc.ukans.edu**. By Tom Fine. TTY-based, written in PERL. FTP from **archive.cis.ohiostate.edu/pub/w3browser/w3browser0.1.shar**.
	VMS	By Dudu Rashty. FTP from **vms.huji.ac.il/www/www_client**.
VM/CMS	Albert	FTP from **ftp.nerdc.ufl.edu/pub/vm/www/**.
	Charlotte	Written in REXX, runs on any CMS from v5 to v11. Gopher at **gopher:/p370.bcsc.gov.bc.ca**.
WINDOWS 3.1/ NT/95	Cello	From Cornell. Outdated. FTP from **ftp.law.cornell.edu/pub/ LII/cello**.
	CompuServe Mosaic EMACS w3-mode Emissary	From CompuServe. Comes with CompuServe subscription. (See Amiga listing) From Wollongong. Home page at **http://www.twg.com**.
	Enhanced Mosaic I-COMM	(See Macintosh listing) Operates without a TCP/IP connection. Requires UNIX or VMS shell account. Home page at **http://www.best.com/~icomm/icomm.htm**.
	Internet Explorer	From Microsoft (see fig. 2.10). Many HTML extensions. Home page at **http://www.microsoft.com**.

(continues)

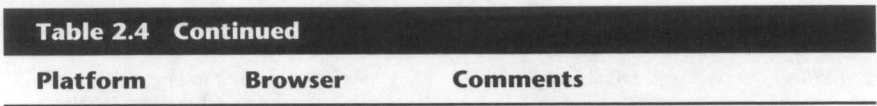

Table 2.4 Continued		
Platform	**Browser**	**Comments**

Fig. 2.10
Microsoft's
Internet Explorer
(shown here in its
v2.0 release for
Windows 95) is
one of the most
recent and one of
the most powerful
Web browser
programs cur-
rently available.

Platform	Browser	Comments
WINDOWS 3.1/ NT/95	InternetWorks	Now a part of Global Network Navigator and America Online. For information, contact **http://www.gnn.com**.
	Netscape Navigator NetShark	(See Macintosh listing) From InterCon Systems. Home page at **http://netshark.inter.net**. Supports HTML extensions. FTP Lite version from **netshark.inter.net/pub/ netshark/**.
	Quarterdeck Mosaic	From Quarterdeck. HTML extensions. 30-day evaluation copy downloadable from **http://www.qdeck.com/ qdeck/ demosoft/QMosaic**.
	SlipKnot	Operates without SLIP or PPP connection. Requires UNIX shell account. FTP from **oak.oakland.edu/ SimTel/win3/ internet**. Home page at **http:// www.interport.net/slipknot/ slipknot.html**.
	UdiWWW	Supports most of proposed HTML 3.0 plus Netscape extensions. Home page at **http://www.uni-ulm.de/~richter/ udiwww/index.htm**.
	WinMosaic	From NCSA. FTP from **ftp.ncsa.uiuc.edu/ PC/Windows/Mosaic**. Home page at **http://www.w3.org/hypertext/ WWW/MosaicForWindows/ Status.html**.

Platform	Browser	Comments
WINDOWS 3.1/ NT/95	WinWeb	From EINet. FTP from **ftp.einet.net/ einet/pc/winweb/winweb.zip**.
IBM OS/2	WebExplorer	Multithreaded with visual map of session. FTP from **ftp01.ny.us.ibm. net/pub/WebExplorer**.
	WebSurfer	From Netmanage. Included with Chameleon TCP/IP software package.
X/DECWINDOWS	Arena	Test bed for HTML Level 3. FTP from **ftp.w3.org/pub/www/arena**.
	Chimera	Uses Athena (doesn't require Motif). FTP from **ftp.cs.unlv.edu/pub/chimera**.
	EMACS w3-mode Enhanced Mosaic MMM	(See Amiga listing) (See Macintosh listing) Tcl/Tk user interface. Supports plug-in *applets* written in Caml Special Light. Home page at **http://pauillac.inria.fr/ ~rouaix/mmm**.
	NCSA Mosaic for VMS	(See Macintosh listing)
	NCSA Mosaic for X	(See Macintosh listing)
	Netscape Navigator	(See Macintosh listing)
	Quadralay Mosaic	From Quadralay. Commercial Mosaic for UNIX (Windows and Macintosh versions planned). Home page at **http:// www.quadralay.com/products/ products.html#gwhis**.
	TkWWW	UNIX Browser/Editor for X11. Supports WSYIWYG HTML editing. Home page at **http://www.w3.org/hypertext/ WWW/TkWWW/Status.html**.
	Viola for X	Two versions: one using Motif, one using Xlib. HTML Level 3 forms and tables. FTP from **ora.com/pub/ www/viola**. Home page at **http:// xcf.berkeley.edu/ht/projects/viola/ README**.

The information in this table came from the World Wide Web Frequently Asked Questions (FAQ) list, which is maintained by Thomas Boutell. You can download the latest version at **http://www.boutell.com/faq/** or **http://www.shu.edu/about/WWWFaq/**.

> **Note**
>
> Batch-mode browsers retrieve the contents of a URL specified on the UNIX shell command line and are intended for use in scripts. (Most of the text-based UNIX browsers can also do this.) One is available at **ftp.cc.utexas.edu/pub/zippy/url_get.tar.Z**. Another, written in extended Tcl (tclX), is available at **http://hplyot.obspm.fr/~dl/wwwtools.html**.

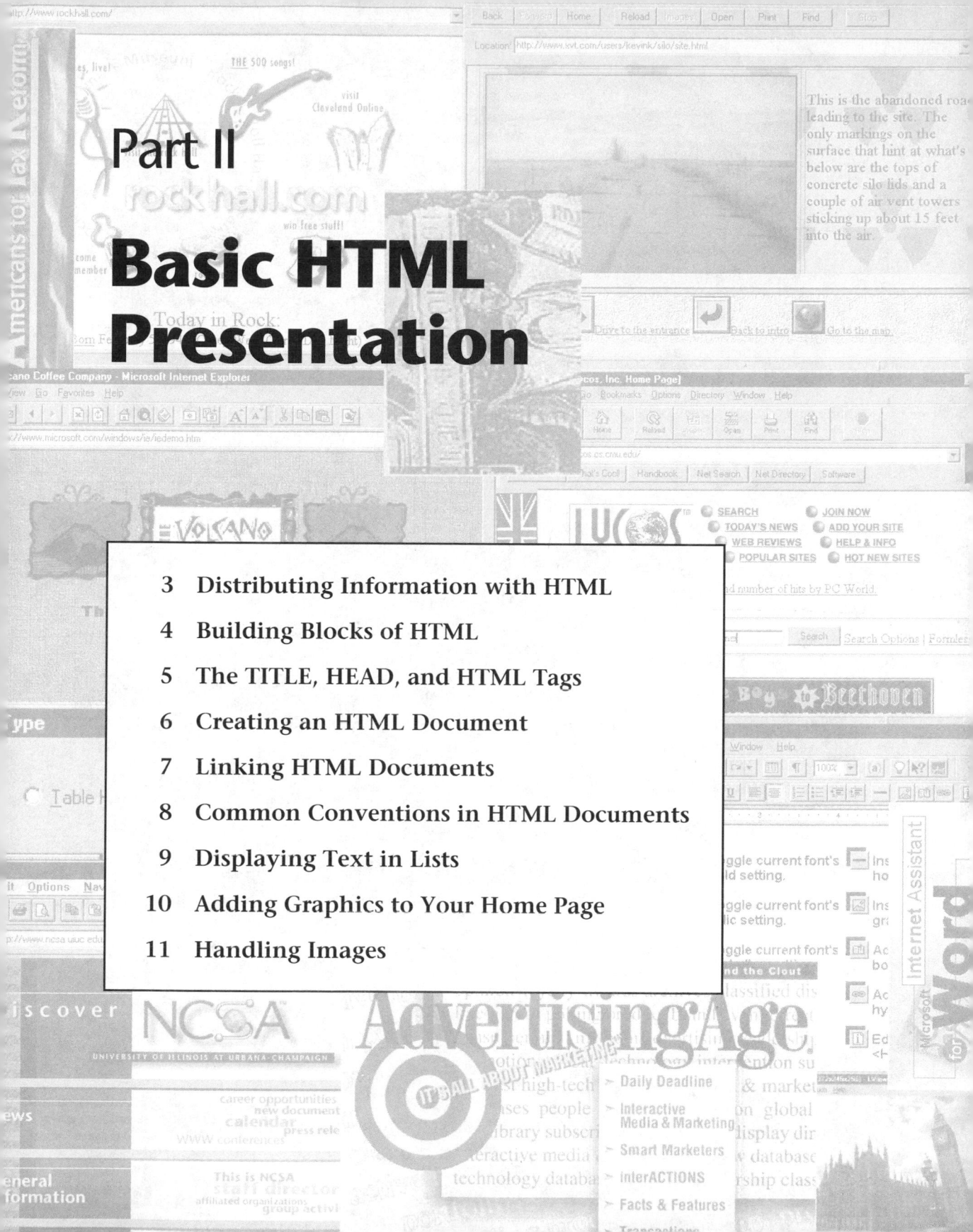

Part II

Basic HTML Presentation

## CHAPTER 3

Distributing Information with HTML

by Mark Brown

"Freedom of the press belongs to those who own one," wrote journalist and critic A.J. Liebling. But with the World Wide Web, almost anyone can own a "press," which can be used to disseminate the owner's views. What's more, that press reaches a much larger audience (the world) at a much lower cost (practically free) than any other form of information distribution that has preceded it.

But once you own a press, what do you print with it? Or to put it in Internet terms, now that you've decided to put up a World Wide Web site, what do you put on it?

There are really two issues here: content and presentation. Because the Web is such a visual medium (or *multimedium*, to coin a new term), the way in which information is presented can sometimes seem to almost bury the information itself.

In this chapter, you learn about the following:

- How presentation relates to content
- What to put on the Web
- What *not* to put on the Web
- Your legal and moral obligations
- How to translate existing documents for Web presentation

Image Is *Not* Everything

Billy Crystal's Fernando character on *Saturday Night Live* used to say, "As we all know, it is better to look good than to feel good...and you look *mahvelous!*" Unfortunately, it seems that many Web developers have a similar attitude: they believe that it is more important for Web pages to look good than to actually *be* good. You can find plenty of sites that are loaded with colorful graphics and that have a multitude of links to click, but they often lack good, solid content.

Good looks might draw people into your site, but good content will keep them coming back. If your site uses all the latest and greatest Web design techniques but has no solid content to keep your visitors' attention, they'll just move on (see fig. 3.1). And they'll never come back—not even if you learn your lesson and add good content later.

Why? Because the Web is so huge, no single site will ever have a chance to be the nine-day wonder type of attraction that drew people's attention in the last century. It won't even have the "fifteen minutes of fame" that Andy Warhol granted everyone in the 1960s. With hundreds of thousands of sites on the Web, the odds are good that visitors will only stop by your site once and make up their minds about it in a hurry—and for good. If you don't grab their attention when they surf in the first time, you probably won't get another chance!

Fig. 3.1
The designer of this site used some of the latest flashy Web design techniques— including frames. It looks pretty good, but there's no significant content here to keep people coming back.

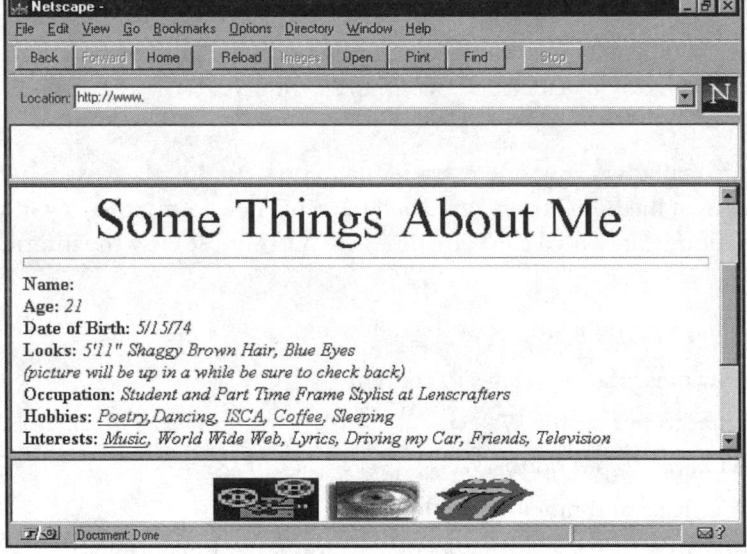

The flip side of this is, of course, that if your site has excellent content but isn't visually appealing, people aren't likely to stay around long enough to find out just how good it is. People have a tendency to judge a book by its cover, and with so many well-done, visually attractive sites out there on the Web, you're up against some stiff competition.

A case in point, chosen at random, is Rutgers University Libraries site of resources on American and British history at **http://info.rutgers.edu/ rulib/artshum/amhist.html** (see fig. 3.2). Everything is here from the autobiography of St. Patrick to the North American Free Trade Agreement (NAFTA). Unfortunately, this unadorned list of links is unlikely to be discovered by anyone except academics doing scholarly research. There's a lot of excellent information here, but it's hidden by unspectacular presentation. It's not even that the index is badly done; in fact, the information is very well organized. It's just not presented in an appealing manner.

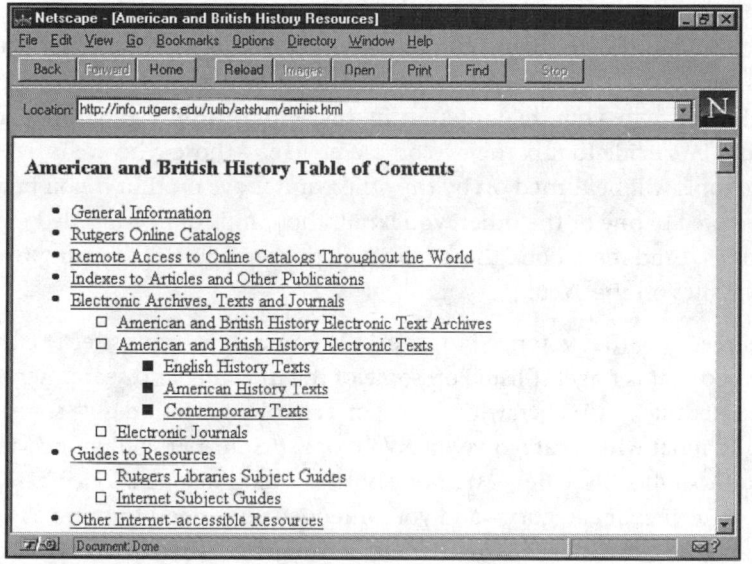

Fig. 3.2
This list of American and British history resources at Rutgers contains good information and is well organized, but the site suffers from bland presentation.

▶ See chapter 14, "HTML Style Sheets," p. 277, for instruction in Web page design.

If you're going to draw people in, you have to present your site the way a politician campaigns: you've only got the public's attention for a quick *sound bite*, so you must make your impression up front. Like it or not, Marshall McLuhan's statement about TV, "The Medium Is the Message," applies even more so to the Web.

> **Note**
>
> Though you want to strive for good Web page design, don't just shove a whole bunch of extra elements down your viewers' throats—give them a choice! If you want to add Java applications, animations, sound files, video clips, and even background graphics to your site, make most of them optional. Don't make your visitors automatically load a home page that is overloaded with lots of noncritical elements. Your viewers with slow modem connections will appreciate the opportunity to *not* view everything on your site.

Basic HTML Presentation

II

The Right Stuff: What to Put on the Web

I've established that looks aren't everything, but that without looks you'll never get your message across. Now it's time to think about what that message will be.

Here's your new motto: "Keep in focus!"

Your Web pages should focus on a single topic or, at most, a cluster of closely associated topics. There are millions of different Web surfers out there, and most of them won't even slow down for a generic, generalized site. They want to find information and entertainment that suits their personal needs, wants, and tastes. The odds are that you'll never find even a handful of individuals who share your dual interests in, say, windsurfing and Baroque music. It would be suicide to mix the two on a Web page—those who are interested in one topic will be turned off by the other, and move on. But if you put up a site devoted to one or the other, you'll pull thousands of like-minded individuals in. (And remember, there's nothing to keep you from putting two *separate* sites on the Web!)

▶ The entirety of chapter 20, "Make Yourself Known," p. 461, is devoted to the topic of advertising your site on the Web.

Remember, too, that you need to let people know about your site. The best way to do that is to get it listed on some of the indexing and search services on the Net, such as Webcrawler, Lycos, or Yahoo! You should give some thought about which category your Web topic fits into. If you're uncertain, check into Yahoo! (see fig. 3.3) or one of the other indexing services so that you can keep your category—and your intended audience—in mind as you develop your site. Table 3.1 lists the major categories and subcategories indexed by Yahoo!

Table 3.1 Subject Categories of Yahoo!	
Category	**Subcategories**
Arts	Humanities, Photography, Architecture,
Business and Economy	Directory, Investments, Classifieds
Computers and Internet	Internet, WWW, Software, Multimedia
Education	Universities, K–12, Courses
Entertainment	TV, Movies, Music, Magazines
Government	Politics, Agencies, Law, Military
Health	Medicine, Drugs, Diseases, Fitness
News	World, Daily, Current Events

Category	Subcategories
Recreation	Sports, Games, Travel, Autos
Reference	Libraries, Dictionaries, Phone Numbers
Regional	States, Countries, Regions, U.S.
Science	Computer Science, Biology, Astronomy, Engineering
Social Science	Anthropology, Sociology, Economics
Society and Culture	People, Environment, Religion

Fig. 3.3
Yahoo! is a good place to go for information about subject categories on the Web.

II

Basic HTML Presentation

Keep Focused

Above all, your site should be *interesting*. It should appeal to the audience you have identified for it. The topic should be focused—the tighter, the better. There are a million sites devoted to music, for example, or farming. The odds of drawing much of a crowd with such generic topics are slim—you're sure to be overwhelmed by other bigger and better established sites with more resources to devote to the project.

However, if *your* site is focused on something specific, such as Lithuanian folk music or llama raising, you're sure to pull in a devoted following of true, die-hard advocates of the topic. Figure 3.4 is a perfect example of a Web site with a tightly defined subject matter. The St. Augustine page at the University of Pennsylvania (**http://ccat.sas.upenn.edu/jod/augustine.html**) is a scholarly site devoted completely to the study of St. Augustine. There are complete texts (including some in Latin), images, commentaries, and essays, all presented in a well-organized and appealing way. And it's not stuffy—you'll even find the lyrics to Sting's rock-and-roll ballad, "St. Augustine in Hell"! Though this site won't draw many punk rockers or rocket scientists, its intended audience—philosophers and theologians, both amateur and professional—are sure to not only find it, but to keep coming back.

Fig. 3.4
This page, devoted to the study of St. Augustine, is a perfect example of a Web site that is focused, well-presented, and rich in content.

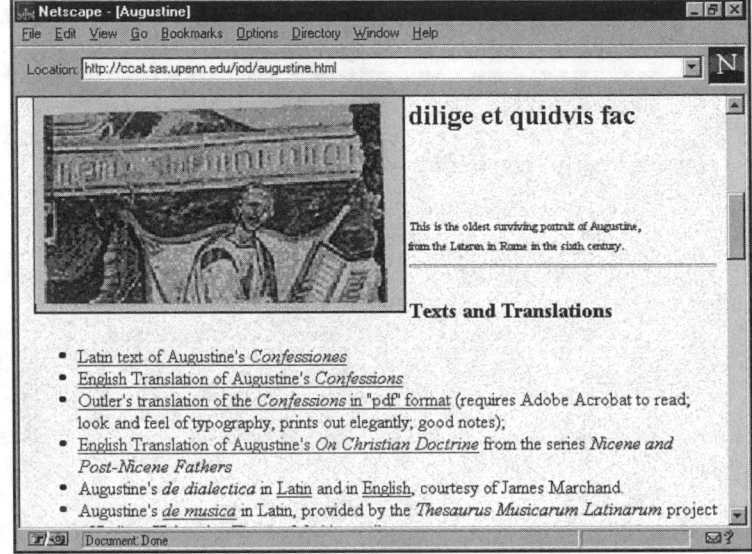

On the Links

Here's another motto for you: Think *hyper!*

Every site features hypertext links; they're what make the Web the Web. Unfortunately, many sites throw up a huge, unorganized list of links, some of which are more relevant to the topic at hand than others. A well-organized list of links is a valuable asset to a Web page. Even if your site isn't immediately appealing to every Web surfer who browses through, a killer list of links will enhance the odds that they'll bookmark your site as a reference point. And the more often they log on to your pages, the better the chance that you'll hit them with your message.

Scott Yanoff began his list of must-see sites on the Net back before the World Wide Web existed. People would FTP his list of informative Gopher, FTP, and Telnet sites every month or grab it off their Usenet feed when it was updated. With the advent of the Web, Yanoff added Web sites and set up a site of his own to host the list (**http://www.uwm.edu/Mirror/inet.services. html**). It is, and always has been, one of the best topically organized lists of resources on the Net (see fig. 3.5). Take a look at his site, and try to do as good a job of organizing your own hypertext link lists.

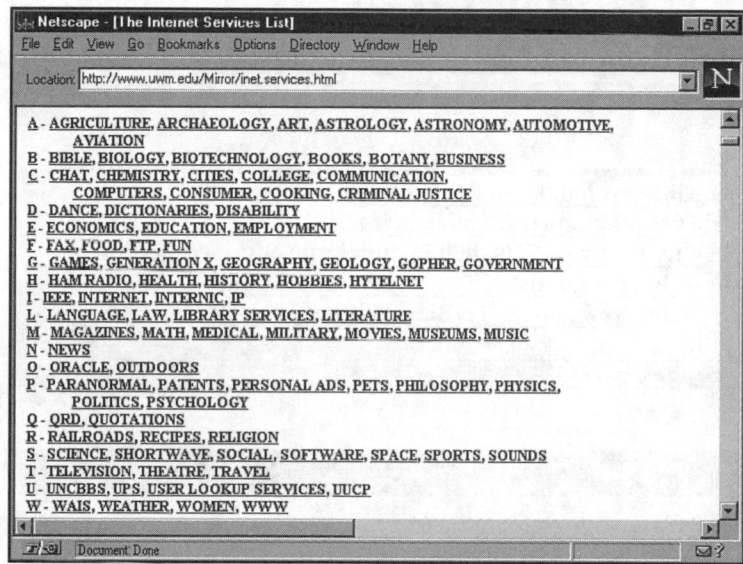

Fig. 3.5
Scott Yanoff's topical list of Internet services is one of the most comprehensive and well-organized lists of resources on the Web.

Timeliness

One of the reasons that people love the Web is because of its capability to deliver new information with an immediacy that can only be matched by other broadcast media, such as TV and radio. Whenever news breaks—whether it is a major world event, or just the release of the latest new software product—you can bet that the Web will have the information first. If you can keep the information on your site up-to-the-minute fresh, you're sure to attract loyal viewers.

Don't let your site lag behind. Keep it up-to-date. Always be on the lookout for new information and new links. Make sure to delete or update older information so that your site never, ever presents outdated or stale information.

There are hundreds of daily news sites that do an amazing job of posting the latest news items every day. Even if your site isn't news-oriented, you can learn a few things by checking out how these sites keep up the pace. Figure 3.6 shows the Web site of the Beloit Daily News, one of the smaller newspapers keeping a daily presence on the Web—and doing an excellent job of it. Check out its site at **http://www.bossnt.com/bdn.html**.

Fig. 3.6

The Beloit Daily News is just one of hundreds of sites that presents the latest news stories on the Web daily—or even hourly!

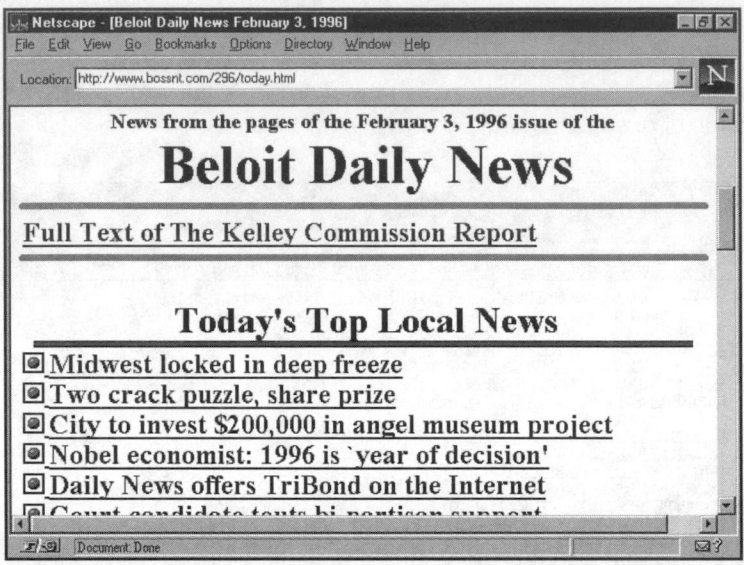

> **Tip**
>
> Add a "Last Date Modified:" line at the bottom of your home page, and change the date when you change the page. That way, your audience will know when your page was last updated—and you'll have the motivation to change it often!

Create a Vortex

So your site should be appealing, focused, organized, and up-to-date. That's not too much to ask, is it? The whole idea is to create an information vortex that draws in your audience like a spider draws in flies.

You've got to strike a careful balance between form and content, between innovation and familiarity. People long for the new, innovative, and unique—but, conversely, they are more comfortable with the recognizable and familiar. Everything must work together to make your site appealing.

Everything on your Web pages should be directed towards delivering your message. All should point to the center: your focus topic. Graphics should illustrate, links should be relevant, and design should set a mood.

There are people accomplishing this every day on the Web. For example, take a look at figure 3.7, the Web site for the Rock and Roll Hall of Fame at **http://www.rockhall.com**. The home page features a big, colorful, playful, clickable graphic menu that leads to fun and relevant areas of interest—from a tour of the museum itself to a list of the 500 top rock songs of all time. There's even a thoughtful link to the Cleveland home page. (This is a good tie-in because the Rock Hall is a tourist attraction, and potential visitors want to know about travel, hotels, restaurants, and other tourist sites in the area).

Right up front are two very timely items: a link to Rock News and an item right below the menu showing what happened in rock-and-roll history on this date. The first thing you think when you check into this site is *awesome!* But all of the information is relevant and up-front, so the site accomplishes its real goal: to entice people to visit the Rock and Roll Hall of Fame.

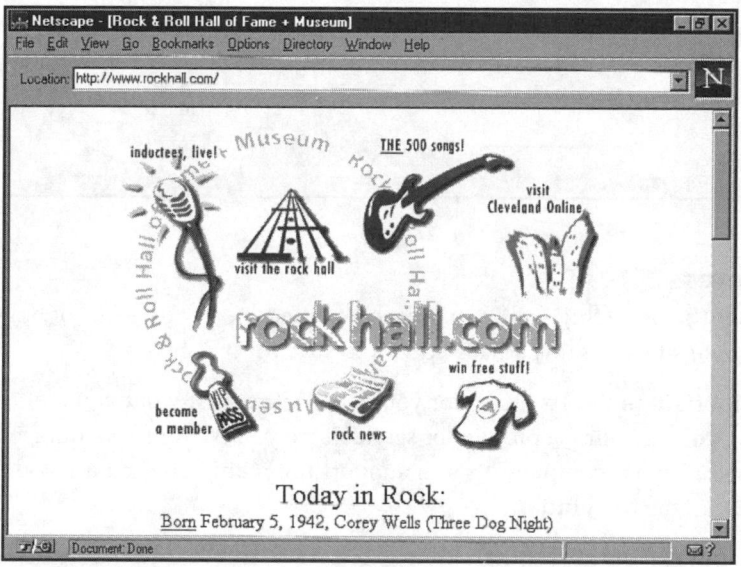

Fig. 3.7
The Rock and Roll Hall of Fame Web site is the perfect example of what a Web site should be: entertaining, appealing, and focused with a clear goal in mind.

How can you tell when you've done as good a job as the Rock and Roll Hall of Fame? Why, when your site is chosen to be listed in the Point survey of the top five percent of all sites on the Web, of course!

The Point survey is the biggest and most well-established of all the organizations that award *best of* status to sites on the Web. If a site is included on Point's list of the top five percent, you can bet it features a good combination of content, presentation, and expertise. If you really want a short course on how to do your own Web site, log on to the Point site at **http://www.pointcom.com** (see fig. 3.8) and check out some of the sites listed there. They're all indexed by category, so it's easy to survey your competition.

Fig. 3.8
The Point survey lists the best five percent of all the sites on the Web. Maybe someday your site will sport that blue logo!

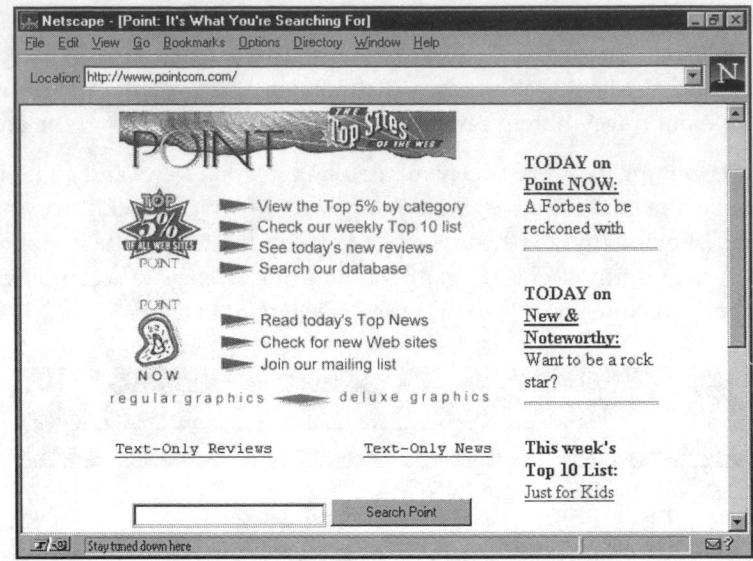

Business Sites

Though the preceding section has been couched mostly in terms of building a personal site, the same advice applies to sites for business.

It's important to have a *reason* for your site. Define first what you are trying to do. Are you selling a product or service? Are you trying to encourage investment in your company? Is user support the main issue? Or are you trying to build name recognition?

You can do all of these things at once, but it's best to create clearly delineated areas for each purpose. Many of the most successful corporations on the Web start with "maps" of their sites on their home pages, much like the Rock and Roll Hall of Fame shown in figure 3.7.

If you have the budget, consider hiring a public relations firm to help, just as you would when launching an ad campaign. There are, after all, millions of potential customers out there on the Web. Grabbing their attention would certainly be worth the investment. However, if you do hire a PR agency, make sure you find one with Web savvy. The Web is a whole different ball game than any other medium. You might want to check out some Web sites of companies that are about your size and already on the Web (those that are *not* your competitors). Most Web pages designed by agencies have a tag line somewhere that indicates who did the page design work. Clicking their link will take you right to the responsible party.

Keep in mind when designing your site that the customers you're likely to draw from the Web do *not* have the same demographics as your normal customer mix. They are much more likely to be upscale, young, and technically oriented, though this may change as the Web matures.

◀ For some Web demographics, see "Who Uses the Web and for What?" in chapter 1, "Introducing the World Wide Web," p. 30

No matter what kind of company you are putting on the Web, the following are a few surefire items that always draw attention:

- Provide news of cutting-edge research your company is conducting. Make sure you emphasize the *latest* developments, and keep it up-to-date.

- Announcements of interesting new products are always hot ticket items on the Web. Tag new features with "NEW!" markers.

- Remember that your audience on the Web is insatiably curious about nearly everything. If your company makes wieners, a "Multimedia History of Wieners" is guaranteed to make your site a hit!

- If you've got imprinted items, sell them on the Web. Even if you're a local brew pub in Maine, you'll be astounded at how many beer aficionados in Oregon will order your "Lobster Brew" sweatshirts.

- Provide links to related sites—even your competitors! Nothing sells a Web site like a well-organized set of relevant links. It's the surest way to get someone to bookmark your site, and once you're bookmarked, you've got your customer hooked for life! (Always make sure you've got something new and fascinating on your link page to grab their attention and keep them around when they use that bookmark in the future.)

Make sure that everything you put on the Web brings you closer to your goals for being there.

Do you need an example of an excellent corporate site? You'd expect the premier magazine of the advertising industry to host a good Web site, and *Advertising Age* does at **http://www.adage.com** (see fig. 3.9). It's flashy, fun, entertaining, and informative, and it never loses sight of why its on the Web. Check it out, if for no other reason than to read its reviews of other corporate Web sites.

Fig. 3.9

Advertising Age hosts a Web site that is a model of a corporate site.

Note

Do you want more? McQueen & Associates hosts an excellent online seminar for businesses wanting to get on the Web. It covers all aspects of getting on the Web, from why to do it in the first place to how to advertise your presence once you're online. The seminar is titled *Developing a Quality Presence on the Internet,* and it's at **http://www.training.com/315**. A longer version is also available on CD-ROM.

Organization Sites

Much of what I've said above about corporations also applies to nonprofit organizations. But for organizations, the Web offers one additional advantage—it's the most effective and least expensive means ever invented for getting your message to the people.

Whether your organization wants to clean up the environment or clean up Washington; whether you want to raise the whole world's awareness of hungry children or just round up a few hundred kindred spirits who might want to join the Emily Dickinson Appreciation Society, you'll find plenty of sympathetic listeners on the Web.

Of course, an organization's site should be more serious (unless your topic is decidedly nonserious, of course) than a commercial site. It should certainly be heavier on information. Think of your site as more of a resource than a selling tool.

The following are some items you'll definitely want to have online:

- Information about your organization: its history, membership, growth, awards, etc.

- Information about your cause: statistics, reports, digitized images, historical data, and news items

- Study guides and introductory material to ease people into the subject matter

- Links to related sites

- Testimonials from those whom your organization has helped and from celebrities who support your cause

- Information about how to join or support your organization and your cause

There are hundreds of nonprofit organizations on the Web, from the Red Cross to the Boy Scouts. Yahoo! and other index sites provide links to them, and you can learn a great deal by studying what they've done. Figure 3.10 shows what one small site has done on the Web to support its membership and advance the cause of the WOMBATS. No, not the animal—the WOmens' Mountain Bike And Tea Society. (I am not making this up.) This Fairfax, California, women's biking group has been together since 1984, but these days it's posting its newsletter (and lots of other entertaining stuff) on the World Wide Web. Its site is at **http://www.wombats.org**; check it out to see what even a small organization can do with a Web presence.

Fig. 3.10
The WOMBATS Web site is a shining example of what a small organization's Web site can and should be.

Personal Sites

All of this brings us full circle, back to the subject of personal Web sites. What should you put on yours?

Again, remember to focus. A personal hobby or interest is best, preferably one you know a *lot* about. The real challenge is to be able to draw in others who are interested in, say, airships, and show them something they didn't know before.

Airships? Yep! It's one of my passions. When I first got on the Web, I was disappointed to find that there were hardly any sites with any information on them at all. (Step One: Find a niche and fill it.)

So I lined up an ISP (Internet Service Provider) who would host my site for free, then I scanned in 30 or so airship images from a portfolio that was printed in the 1930s. (Step Two: Gather unique subject matter—not the same stuff everyone has already seen.)

Then I searched the Library of Congress's site and built up a bibliography of the hundreds of books in its collection on the subject of airships, including volumes in German and French. (Step Three: Go the extra mile, and remember your audience is international.)

Finally, I spent several hours accessing all the index sites I could find on the Web, tracking down obscure links to Web sites that had any information at all about airships. I turned this into a concise but complete list of links to those sites. (Step Four: Provide a well-organized list of links to other sites of interest to your defined audience.)

I put it all on the Web in as well-designed a manner as I could (see fig. 3.11). Then I advertised my site on several of the online indexing services. It didn't take long for other airship fans to find my site. Now I get over 300 hits a month and have struck up many good online friendships with people who share my interest. (And believe me, it was hard finding anyone locally who had any appreciation at all for the subject!)

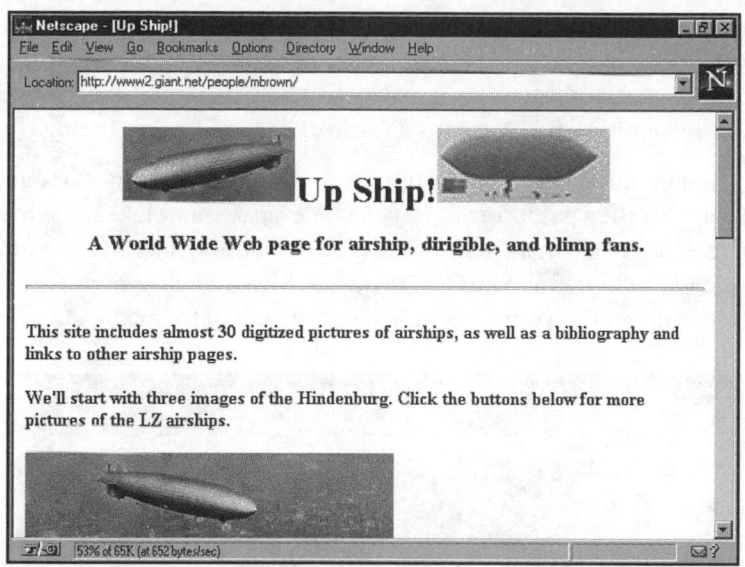

Fig. 3.11
My Web site, Up Ship! (**http://www2.giant.net/people/mbrown/**), is focused, factual, fun, and informative—and consequently, is visited by hundreds of airship fans each month.

The Wrong Stuff: What *Not* to Put on the Web

So what shouldn't you put on the Web? That's easy—just turn everything I've said so far around.

The Bad

Remember to focus. Don't try to be everything to everybody. This is the number two problem of personal sites. They haven't defined who or what they are there for. They spew out whatever pops up in whatever areas interest them at the moment. You might see graphics of motorcycles, rock bands, comic book characters, and computer screens all mixed up like a nightmare collage.

"Wait a minute," you protest, "you said that's the number *two* problem of personal Web sites. What's number one?"

Even worse than a site that's burdened down with everything is one that contains nothing of interest at all. Many personal sites contain next to nothing: lists of CDs or comic books the person owns; pictures of his dog, gerbil, or fish; fuzzy photos of the site's owner goofing around with friends; and so on. Let's face it; except for a small circle of your very closest friends, nobody but nobody (not even your significant other) wants to know that much about you. So why put it on the Web? It's a waste of bandwidth. It's boring.

What astounds me is that many people are aware that it's mind-numbingly boring, and yet they put it up anyway! Some even seem to take pride in how boring they can make their sites, as shown by examples like Greg's Wonderful World of Really Boring Stuff (see fig. 3.12). Please don't ever put another site like this up on the Web. There are far too many of them already.

Fig. 3.12
There are already too many boring sites on the Web. Make sure yours isn't one of them.

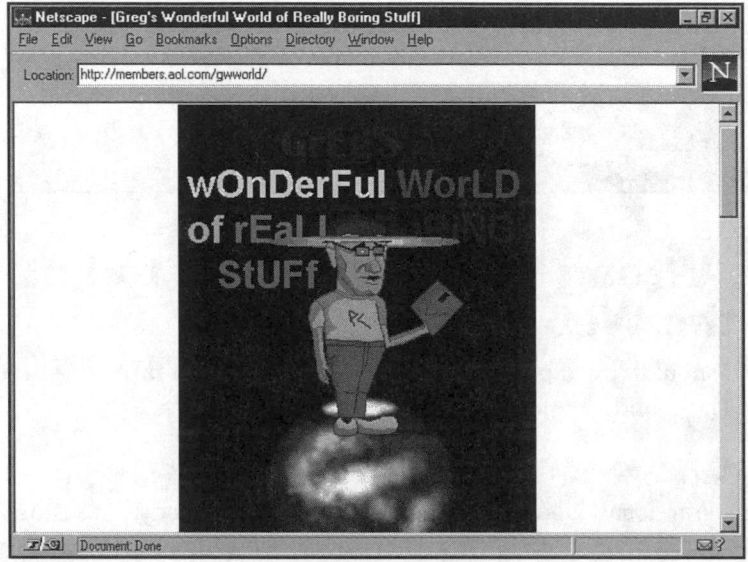

> **Tip**
>
> The number one rule of writing is this: Have something to say. If a writer has a message, or a story, or a cause, she never gets "writer's block." Apply the same rule to your Web site, and you'll never have to worry about what you should put online.

Another thing you definitely don't want to do is to put up a site that consists of nothing but huge wads of unedited, unorganized links, such as the site shown in figure 3.13. (And don't mistake alphabetical order for organization!) This site is like a library where the books are all stacked at random. It's almost worse than having none at all. People want useful links, but they also want to be able to find them easily.

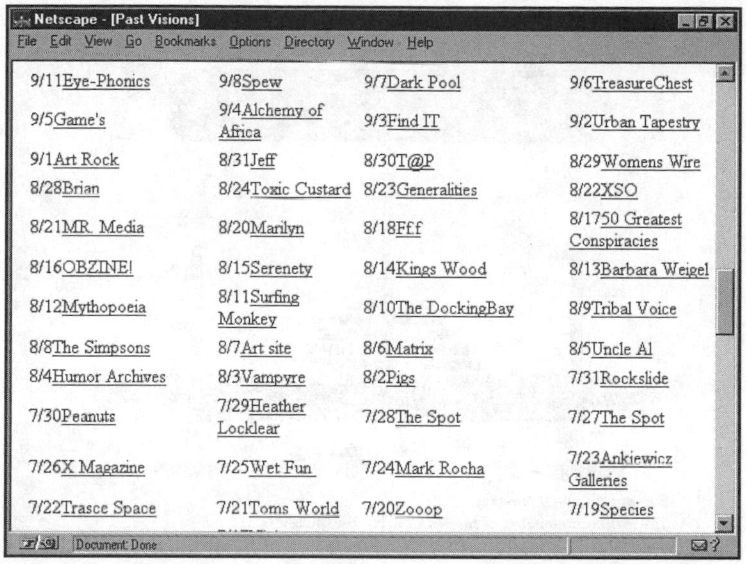

Fig. 3.13
An unorganized
list of random
links is of no use
to anyone.

Another problem is the proliferation of useless applications that are on the Web just to be on the Web. I'm talking here about forms-based or Java-based programs that would make better stand-alone programs than Web applications. A Web application should be there because it makes sense for it to be on the Web. If it makes more sense as a stand-alone program, then write it as such and offer it for downloading. Figure 3.14 is a perfect example. This is a Web-based version of the old Towers of Hanoi game; it's a complete waste of Internet bandwidth. Please don't clutter the Web with this stuff. People won't bother with it anyway.

The Web is a dynamic place, and everyone expects data to be up-to-date and accurate. The worst thing you can do to your viewers is to put up some purportedly useful data only to have it go stale. It's better to take your site down completely than to let it sit there with outdated, useless information.

Figure 3.15 is an example of a site past its prime. It features graphs of card prices for the collectable trading card game Magic: The Gathering. Prices for these cards fluctuate wildly, and when the data was current, this was a valuable service for card collectors. Unfortunately, the site is still up, and, as of this writing, the information is over nine months out-of-date. This is worse than useless, as someone is likely to consult these graphs and not notice that the information is outdated. They could make some bad decisions based on this old data. Don't ever do this to those who visit your site. If you can't keep it current, then take it down.

Fig. 3.14
Why is this application on the Web?

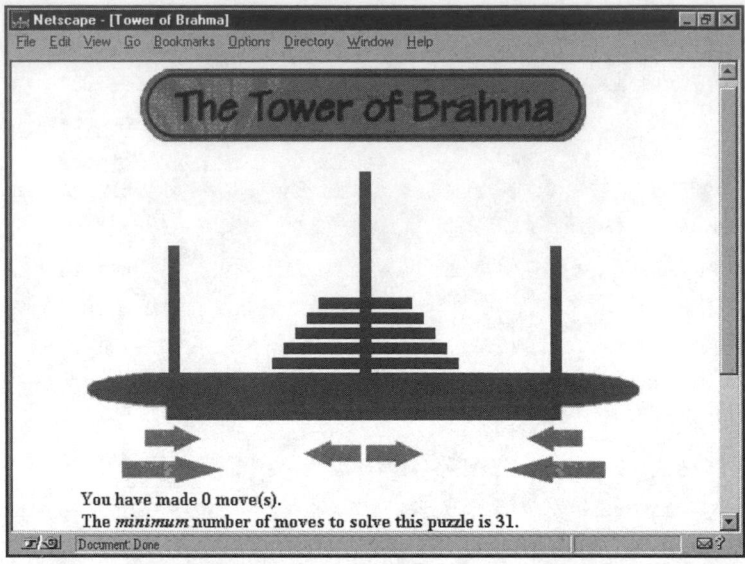

Fig. 3.15
The data in these graphs is outdated and useless. Visitors to this site are going to be disappointed.

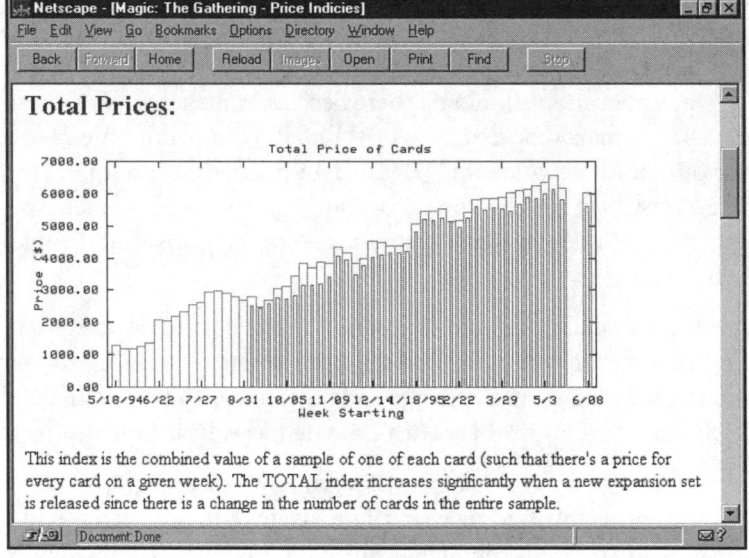

The following are some other items you definitely shouldn't put on your site:

- Lists or information repeated from another site (just add a link to them instead)
- Disorganized, meaningless ramblings

- Pictures of yourself and your friends
- Endless bragging about your site (let your viewers decide!)
- A site counter (nobody but you cares whether someone is the tenth visitor to your site or the ten millionth)

> **Note**
>
> Bad grammar and poor spelling are rampant on the Web. If a site is worth doing, it's worth doing well. No one is too hurried to use a spell checker or grammar checker. People who visit your site will assume that bad English usage and misspellings mean that you don't know what you're talking about, and they'll move on.

Just as there is a shrine for the top five percent of all sites on the Web (the Point survey shown in fig. 3.8), there is also a repository for the worst. It's called Mirsky's Worst of the Web, and it lives at **http://mirsky.turnpike.net/wow/Worst.html** (see fig. 3.16). Mirsky's picks the worst Web sites every couple of days and posts them with links. If you want a short course on what *not* to do on your site, a quick visit to Mirsky's will provide you with a lot of good examples of bad sites.

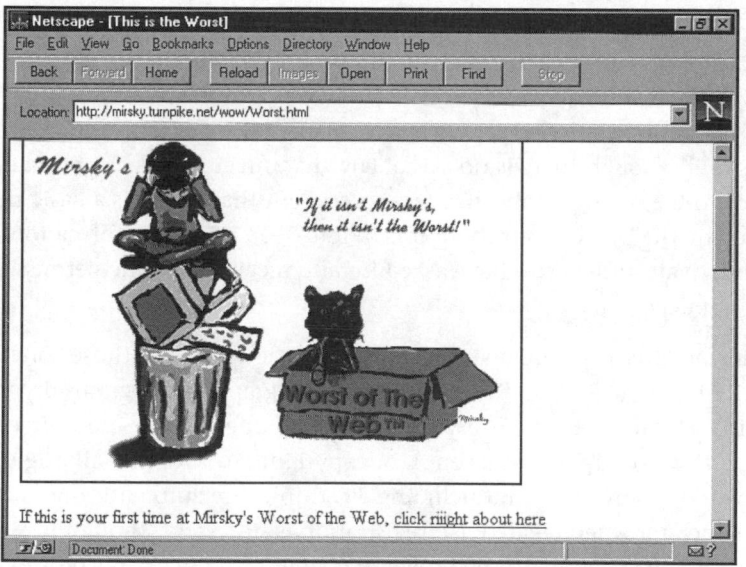

Fig. 3.16
Mirsky's Worst of the Web enshrines only truly awful Web sites.

Legal Issues

> **Note**
>
> I am not a lawyer, and this section is not a legal guide. It is, rather, an overview of some of the legal issues to keep in mind when you are developing a Web site. For advice on legal matters, consult an attorney.

The first amendment to the U.S. Constitution guarantees every American the right of free speech. This does not guarantee you the right to say anything you want with impunity. People who feel that you have treated them unfairly have legal recourse. You can be sued for libel and/or slander for anything you say online, just as you could if you had printed it on paper. And in this litigious society, it is probably better to err on the side of caution than to strike out boldly and without forethought.

Controversy and debate online are fine, but if you're diplomatic and noninflammatory you'll not only avoid legal battles, you'll attract more sympathizers. After all, you're on the Web to share your ideas, not to entice someone to sue you. Before you post something questionable, consider the following: Even if you're sure you'd win, do you really want to spend your time sitting in court for months on end?

The right to privacy ties in closely with libel and slander issues. If you receive private information about any of your users—through a registration form, for example—you must be very, very careful about how it is used and who has access to it. Though there is no actual law guaranteeing U.S. citizens a right to privacy, there is long-established legal precedent that says it is a basic right implied by the U.S. Constitution. It is best to keep all such information completely private, unless you have asked for and received specific permission to use it publicly.

Perhaps no laws are more openly flaunted on the Web than those concerning copyright and plagiarism. Everyone steals text, graphics, programs, hypertext link lists, HTML code, and everything else from one another pretty freely and openly. However, the most recent U.S. copyright law says that all original creative works in any medium (including electronic) are automatically assigned to their creator when created. No registration is necessary (though it is a good idea, so that ownership can be proven if challenged). Again, it's best to not "borrow" anything at all from anyone else's site, unless you have written permission to do so.

Perhaps no Web-related topic has gotten more press than the issue of adult material on the Web and its accessibility by minors. It is such a hot topic that Congress recently included tough anti-pornography language directed at the Internet in the Telecommunications Act of 1996. Although this law is certain to be challenged in the courts, it has made many ISPs very, very nervous about the content of pages posted through their sites. If you plan to post adult material on your site, you certainly should at least make people enter through a *disclaimer* page. And make sure you have the permission of your ISP beforehand, or you could be kicked unceremoniously offline at the first hint of controversy.

Got you scared, now? You say you need advice? The Electronic Freedom Foundation is the champion of the rights of those online. If you have questions about copyrights, pornography, libel, or other legal issues online, the odds are good that you can find the answers on the EFF site at **http://www.eff.org** (see fig. 3.17).

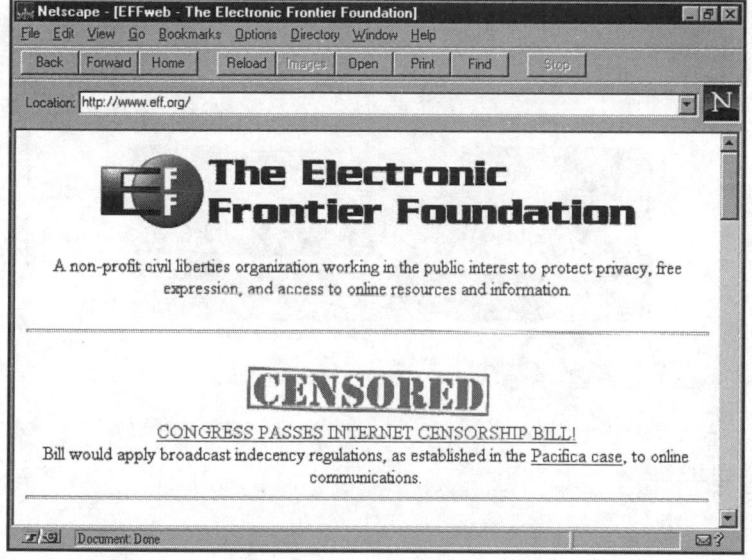

Fig. 3.17
The Electronic Freedom Foundation home page features full coverage of the topic of legal issues online, including a lively discussion of the Telecommunications Act of 1996.

Electronic Morality

Once past the legal issues, you might want to stop a moment and ponder the fine line between *rights* and *responsibilities*. Are you the guardian of society's mores? Is it up to you to try to bolster a civilization that is sagging under its own decaying weight? I happen to think that the answer to that question is a resounding "Yes!"

I've always considered it better to be positive than negative, to build up rather than to tear down. With a forum as wide-ranging as the World Wide Web, anyone putting up a Web site has a huge potential audience, and therefore a potential to do great good or great harm.

Nonetheless, there are legitimate issues, worthy of open discussion, that are the subjects of controversial Web sites. Take the flat tax, for instance. Both sides of the issue are represented in force on the Web (see fig. 3.18), and both sides draw their share of criticism, harassment, and hate mail. I'm sure those who have chosen to establish these sites consider the controversy all part of the territory. There are religious denominations, environmentalists, pro-choice and pro-life organizations, neo-Nazis, and other controversial groups on the Web who are constantly drawing fire from others. Before you establish a site that's destined to become the center of controversy, you should answer just one question: Can you take the heat? If the answer is *yes,* then by all means go online with your views.

Fig. 3.18
All sorts of controversial sites, such as this tax reform page, exist on the Web. Before you set one up, make sure you're willing to do battle for your cause.

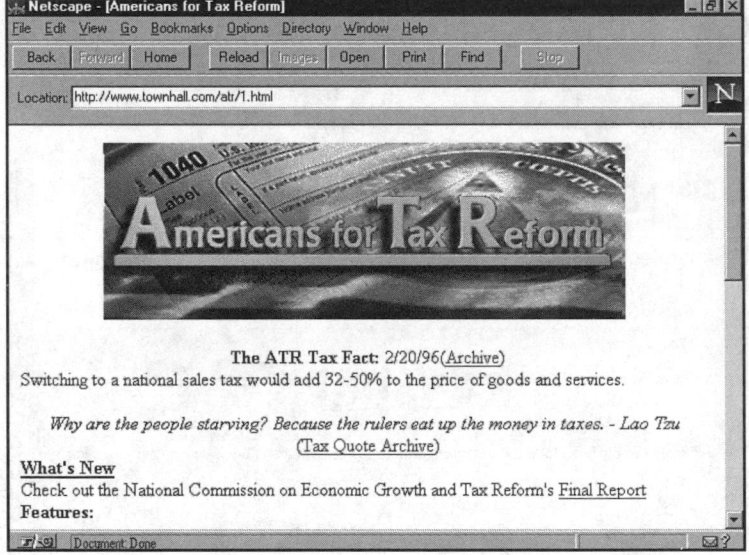

Putting Existing Documents on the Web

Almost anyone setting up a Web site is faced with one overwhelming problem: now that you've decided what should go on the Web, how do you get it from its original form onto your Web pages?

There are really four issues at work here, not one. Because the Web is a different medium than that for which your original information (brochures, videos, etc.) was prepared, you need to do some soul searching first to determine the following:

- What you should definitely put on the Web
- What you should definitely omit
- How it should be organized
- How to physically get the job done

What to Include

Your brochures, newsletters, and videos are a rich source of material about your company, your organization, or your personal interests. You can certainly glean a great many text blurbs, graphics, and clips that will help you communicate your message on the Web.

Just make sure the information you keep is targeted and focused on helping you meet the needs of your viewers. Keep in mind what I've said so far in this chapter, and you should be all right.

What to Omit

You should certainly throw away anything that is of use only to insiders. Remember that you are speaking to a worldwide audience, not preaching to the choir. Make especially certain that you do not post anything of a private or proprietary nature.

Keep all irrelevant or off-topic information off of your Web pages. Old annual reports, staff photos and biographies, and other irrelevant (read *boring*) information should be disposed of too.

How to Reorganize

Remember to think multimedia. Break text into short blocks and mix liberally with relevant graphics. Put the essentials up front; then provide hypertext links to the rest.

> **Note**
>
> Don't forget the "multi" in "multimedia!" Multimedia means more than just a few extra eye-catching graphic elements. It means video, audio, animation, and interactivite applications all integrated into a presentation that draws your viewers into your material. The more involved your audience gets with your Web pages, the better they will remember your message.

Build a good table of contents so that people will have no problem finding things on your site. Give them a clear, concise, topically oriented menu on your home page so that navigation will be easy.

Where possible, organize data into tables, or present information as charts and graphs. Make it friendly.

The Mechanics

If you have huge scanned-in graphics, redo them so that they load in a reasonable amount of time. Remember the lowest common denominator. Scale them down in both size and number of colors so that they will look good on a 640×480, 256-color screen.

If you have huge amounts of text as word processor files, first carve them down to a manageable size. Then feed them through a word processor-to-HTML converter.

Now that you know what to put on the Web and how you want it to look, you're ready to learn the HTML markup tags that will make your pages look and act the way you want. Press on. ❖

## CHAPTER 4

Building Blocks of HTML

by Jim O'Donnell

HTML pages are like annotated bibliographies: they give you the opportunity to expand on an endless variety of topics and present additional factual or thematic resources to further explore a subject.

Of course, HTML pages are also like gossip magazines: sooner or later you'll see just about everything on them.

But regardless of how anyone perceives HTML, everyone who uses it speaks the same language. Elements, tags, anchors, hyperlinks, URLs, and attributes: they're all part of the lexicon of the Web's documents. To create inspired Web pages (and to cast a critical eye on those already on the Web), you need to have an intimate familiarity with the building blocks of HTML.

This chapter answers the following questions:

- How is HTML related to SGML?
- What is a DTD?
- What's the difference between empty and container elements?
- What are the basic components of HTML?

HTML and SGML: A Parent-Child Relationship

HTML is a subset of SGML (Standardized General Markup Language). SGML documents are more complex and programming-like than HTML. Figure 4.1 shows how an SGML document describes the HTML standard (the figure is, in fact, the SGML declaration for HTML—the SGML document that defines HTML).

Fig. 4.1
SGML coding
provides machine-
level display
format and
function com-
mands.

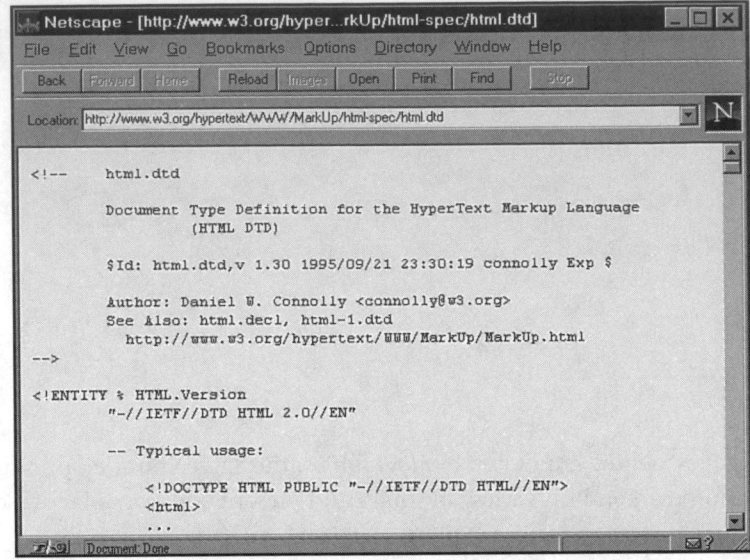

▶ See "Common
Conventions
in HTML
Documents,"
p. 157

HTML resembles simplified SGML. The observation that SGML is to HTML as
HTML is to plain text seems reasonable on the surface. When you take a look
under the hood, though, it's easy to see how HTML shares the advantages of
both systems of marking text.

Troubleshooting

SGML seems very complicated. How do I find out more about it?

SGML is not for the faint of heart, as the code in figure 4.1 suggests. SGML code
constructs are not based as much in "plain English" as HTML is. The following text is
written in SGML, describing how the HTML element BLOCKQUOTE is used:

```
<!ELEMENT (%blockquote) - - %body.content>

<!ATTLIST (%blockquote)

    %attrs;

    %needs; — for control of text flow —

    >
```

How would that read in English? The BLOCKQUOTE element is a container for text in
the BODY section (%body.content); it does not have any defined arguments that
affect its use or how its contents are displayed (no options are listed under the
%attrs; or %needs; categories).

SGML is a full-bodied language for defining text function and formatting that
many users have remained loyal to with the arrival of HTML. HTML's use of English

> language editing markup elements is a key reason for the popularity and success of the World Wide Web.
>
> A good way to learn a little more about SGML might be the "Gentle Introduction to SGML," available at
>
> ```
> ftp://www.ucc.ie/pub/sgml/p2sg.ps
> ```
>
> This is a PostScript file and can be read by printing it on a PostScript printer.

Advantages and Disadvantages

In his World Wide Web Research Notebook

```
http://www.w3.org/hypertext/WWW/People/Connolly/drafts/webresearch.html
```

Daniel Connolly outlines the advantages and disadvantages to carrying over SGML practices and constructs into the current HTML standard.

These are the benefits of using SGML to define HTML:

- Basing HTML on SGML makes it easy to test whether or not an HTML document conforms to the current standard. Document authors can have confidence in their documents that pass automatic verification processes.

- The SGML definition for HTML defined a document called the Entity Structure Information Set. This form allows a standard interpretation of all HTML documents.

- Like HTML, SGML provides a clear and widely supported standard for creating interchangeable documents.

These are the disadvantages of using SGML to define HTML:

- SGML coding is meant to be interpreted at the machine-level, and SGML documents are difficult for people to read and understand. This makes an HTML standard based on SGML difficult to understand by reading it.

- Due to its structural complexity, it's possible to read related SGML documents and come to incorrect assumptions about SGML usage and the standards they define.

- SGML is defined at a level of complexity beyond the function and purpose of HTML, and certain modular capabilities that use SGML are too complex for the level of author manageability HTML strives to provide.

II

Basic HTML Presentation

The Strength of the HTML Standard

HTML's strength comes from its combination of SGML machine-level constructs (the tags and elements that tell a viewer the purpose of document text) and standard English text markup notation.

For example, the <B> container tag is mnemonically correct (it stands for bold), and it signals a format change to the document's viewing software, which changes the display format of the following text. When the viewer comes across the </B> closing tag, which tells it to turn off the bold attribute, it returns to the previous text formatting.

The versatility of SGML and HTML is becoming widely acknowledged as they are adopted as hypertext document standards by more content managers, including the federal and many state governments.

Creating the Standards

The HTML standard is constantly under development. Users and developers from around the world contribute to the on-going discourse and testing of new ideas, concepts, and uses for HTML and its component elements. One user who provided an enormous amount of time and energy in this process is Daniel Connolly (connolly@w3.org) of the W3 Consortium at MIT. He outlined standards for the standards; he provided the following guidelines for the HTML development team to assist them in writing the current and upcoming specifications for HTML.

The goal of any HTML specification should be to promote confidence in the fidelity of communications using HTML. This means specifications need to adhere to the following standards:

- Make it clear to authors what idioms are available to express their ideas.

- Make it clear to implementers how to interpret the HTML format so that authors' ideas will be represented faithfully.

- Keep HTML simple enough that it can be implemented using readily available technology, and then processed interactively.

- Make HTML expressive enough that it can represent a useful majority of the contemporary communications idioms in the WWW community.

- Make some allowance for expressing idioms not captured by the specifications.

- Address relevant interoperability issues with other applications and technologies.

You can get more information about the ongoing HTML standards process from Daniel Connolly's Web page:

```
http://www.w3.org/hypertext/WWW/People/Connolly/
```

or by reading chapter 8, "Common Conventions in HTML Documents."

HTML's DTD

It's debatable who has contributed more to the "acronymization" of our culture. In a world where ATM can have two totally different meanings (one's great for convenience banking and the other for high-speed data networking), you might expect a language like HTML (itself an acronym) to continue the tradition.

And it does. From its elements—UL stands for, appropriately enough, unordered list—to its parent language SGML, HTML is defined by acronyms. An acronym defines HTML as well—HTML's DTD.

Levels of HTML Conformance

DTD stands for Document Type Definition. It's a document that describes the HTML language, its elements, and their legal uses. The HTML DTD has many levels that pertain to different categories of use or compatibility with the HTML standard. These levels are:

- Level 0. Minimal conformance to or use of HTML elements.
- Level 1. HTML compatibility with (or use of) HTML with Level 1 extensions.
- Level 2. HTML compatibility with (or use of) HTML with Level 2 extensions.

The HTML DTD is written in SGML and can be difficult to interpret. Figure 4.2 shows a portion of the HTML DTD for Level 0 (for the complete DTD, see appendix A, "HTML Tags"). The document coding is complex and difficult to read; it's not meant entirely to be read by people, but by SGML interpreters. Don't be surprised if it makes no sense to you—it doesn't to the vast majority of people.

Annotated versions of the HTML DTD make it easier for developers and end users to verify conformity issues. Daniel Connolly maintains one popular version, and you can find it at:

▶ See "HTML Tags," p. 787

```
http://www.w3.org/hypertext/WWW/People/Connolly/
```

The Web sites listed in appendix D, "WWW Bibliography," collect other descriptions of the various HTML standards.

▶ See "WWW Bibliography," p. 867

Checking Conformance of Documents with HTML Standards

It is possible to check your HTML documents for conformance with HTML standards. The Webtechs HTML Validation Service can be found at:

```
http://www.webtechs.com/html-val/svc/
```

As shown in figures 4.3 and 4.4, you can check for conformance at different levels, and supply the HTML document either as a URL to an existing document (see figure 4.3) or by directly inputting the HTML (see fig. 4.4).

Fig. 4.2
The document for each level defines a measure of compatibility to the HTML specification.

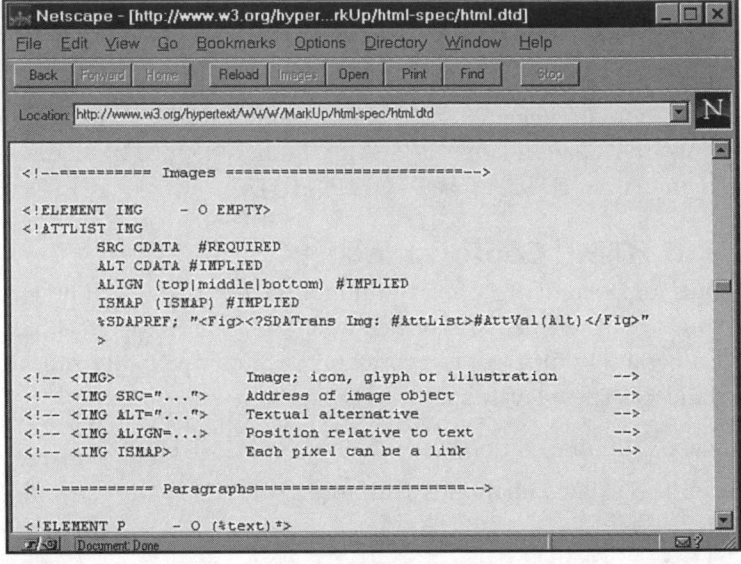

Fig. 4.3
The Webtechs HTML Validation Service allows you to check your HTML documents for conformance to a variety of levels.

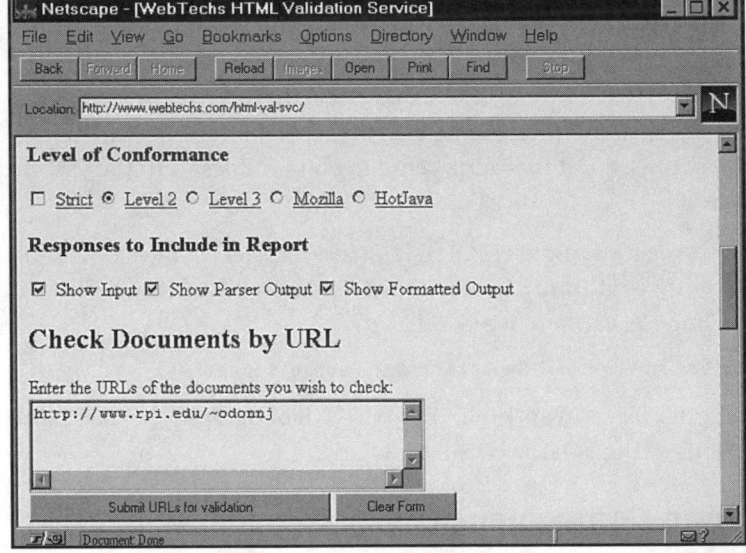

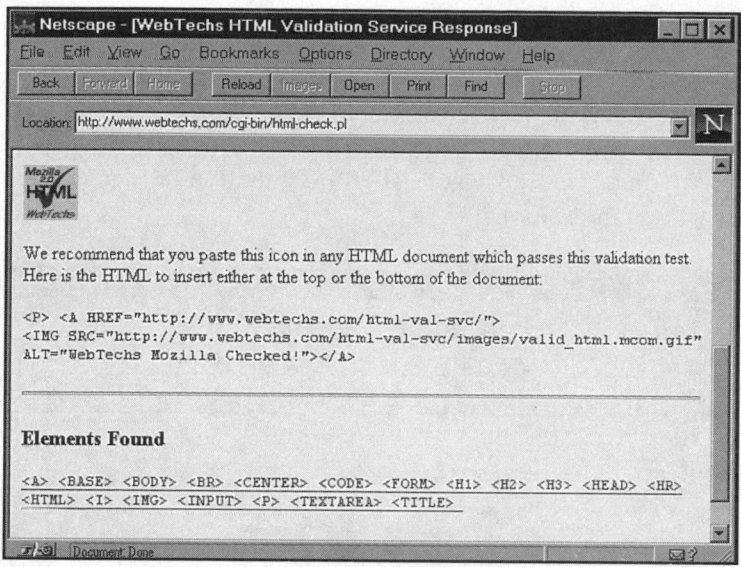

Fig. 4.4
If you want to check out a small amount of HTML, you can enter it directly, rather than building a separate web page.

After you submit your URL or HTML code, the Webtechs service will analyze it and return a report such as that shown in figure 4.5. If it conforms to the HTML 2.0 standard, you are invited to include the validation icon on your web pages.

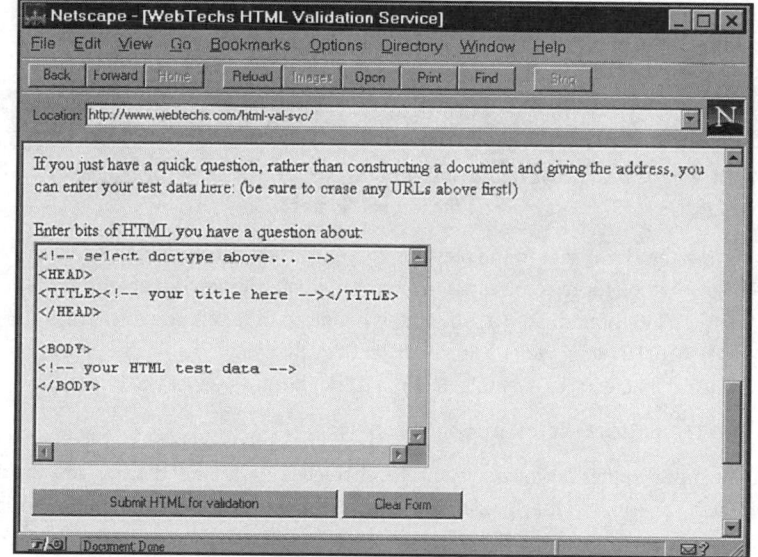

Fig. 4.5
Successfully passing the HTML Validation check can be indicated on your web pages by including a link to the validation icon.

Basic HTML Presentation

II

The Elements of HTML

HTML is composed of elements, or instructions, to WWW viewers to perform a defined task (make text bold, insert a paragraph break, or format and number a list in a predetermined manner). HTML tags consist of individual elements inside angle brackets. Figure 4.6 shows a few typical elements and how they are written in tag format.

Fig. 4.6
HTML tags are "invisible" when the WWW viewer displays the document.

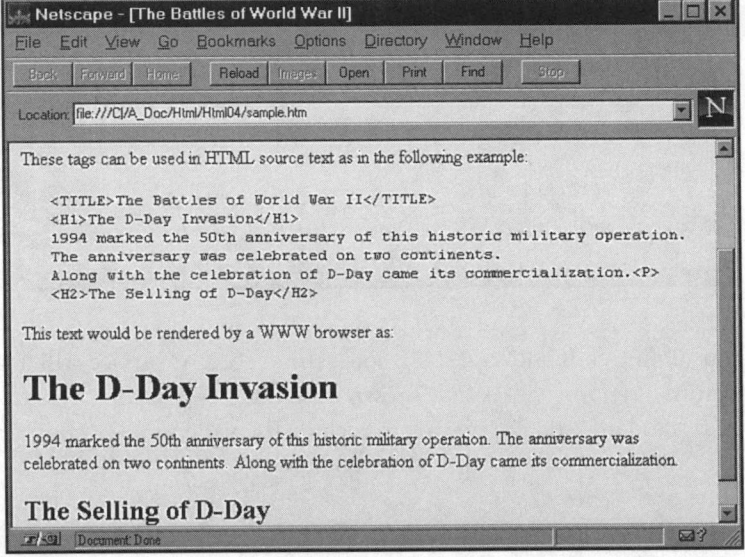

Troubleshooting

If WWW viewers read HTML tags as instructions, how did you show them in figure 4.6? Why didn't the viewer just mark up the text in the tags?

Displaying the HTML tags in the previous figure was not as easy as it looks. Because Web viewers look for tags as signals to format text, all occurrences of tags are supposed to be interpreted. To get around this handicap (after all, the software is just doing its job), HTML provides a list of text entities that viewers will interpret as certain ASCII characters. For example, to write a line that the viewer will display as

```
<TITLE>The Battles of World War Two</TITLE>
```

you must use entities for the angle bracket characters. HTML defines the "less than" bracket (<) as < and the "greater than" bracket (>) as >. Therefore, the previous line would be written in the HTML document as

```
&lt;TITLE&gt;The Battles of World War Two&lt;/TITLE&gt;
```

As the name implies, HTML marks up text in a document by defining the specific formatting for sections of the document. HTML is a hybrid, using some elements to define the abstract value of text (such as "emphasized") and others to define the actual on-screen representation in the WWW viewer's window (such as "italicized"). This "split personality" created quite a controversy in the authoring community, spawning two camps of thought that support the different uses of HTML markup.

Unlike the file systems of some operating systems, HTML element names are case independent. You can write tags with any mixture of upper and lowercase characters. For example, you can write one tag that defines the formatting of a section of text as <BLOCKQUOTE>, <blockquote>, <BlockQuote>, or any capitalization combination. Some authors use unorthodox capitalization schemes, such as <bLocKquOtE>, but that doesn't make for easy-to-read HTML, and your site administrator probably discourages this brand of "net.hipness."

> **Note**
>
> This book's convention of using all uppercase characters in HTML tags is for legibility only; feel free to use whatever scheme you're most comfortable with in your own documents, or whatever conforms to your Web site's HTML document style sheet—if there is one.

Empty and Container Tags

HTML uses two types of elements: empty (or open) and container tags. These tags differ because of what they represent. Empty tags represent formatting constructs, such as line breaks and horizontal rules. These tags indicate "one time" instructions that WWW viewers can read and execute without concern for any other HTML construction or document text.

Container tags define a section of text (or of the document itself) and specify the formatting or construction for all of the selected text. A container tag has both a beginning and an ending: the ending tag is identical to the beginning tag, with the addition of a forward slash. Most containers can overlap and hold other containers or empty tags (see fig. 4.7).

Fig. 4.7
Containers can hold other elements—the entire HTML document is actually one large container, defined by the tag <HTML>.

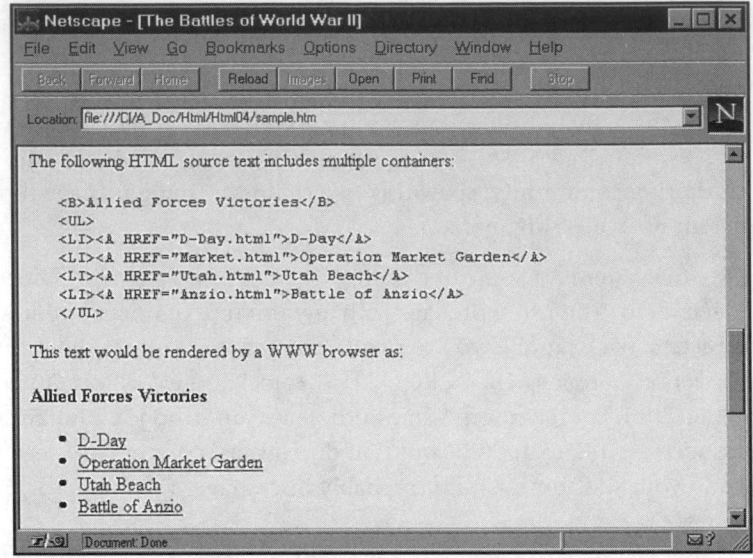

HTML Tag Arguments

I'm not talking about disagreements between tags in HTML documents. Like command-line applications, many HTML elements use additional parameters (known as arguments or attributes) to increase their functionality. These arguments are passed on to the client software and affect the way the element is applied to the section of text (or, with empty tags, how the tag's construct is displayed in the viewing software's window).

For example, the anchor element uses arguments to define the function of the anchor (whether it's a marker or a hypertext link to another document or anchor). So, a document can contain links to specific sections of text and named anchors at those text locations (see fig. 4.8). Notice that the parameters are contained in the tag's angle brackets.

In this example, the last line in the list

```
<LI><A HREF="#Anzio">Battle of AnzioD-Day</A>
```

is an anchor that points to a named anchor somewhere else in the document. The named anchor it points to would be found in a line such as

```
<A NAME="Anzio"><H1>The Battle of Anzio</H1></A>
```

When the user clicks the list item D-Day in the viewed document, the WWW browser would jump immediately to the associated named anchor.

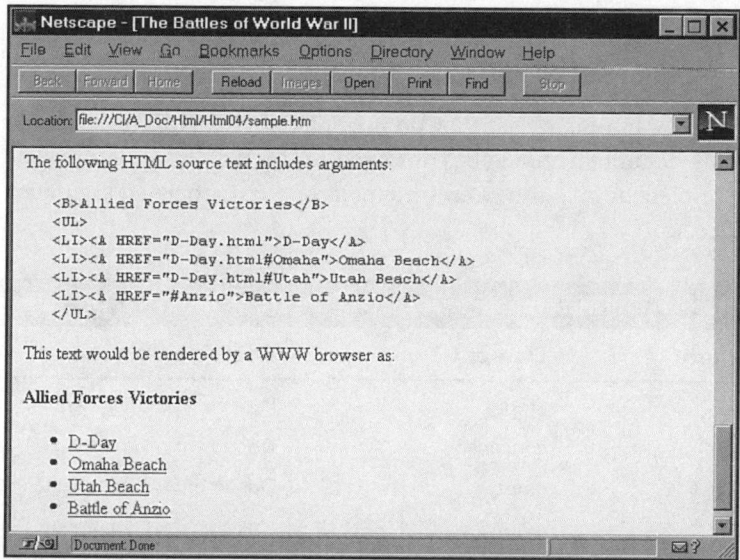

Fig. 4.8
You use anchors as
both the starting
and ending points
of hypertext
links in HTML
documents.

Caution

Underlining and colored borders (such as red or green) are used in some Web pages
to indicate hyperlink text and graphics, but these don't print well.

Some WWW viewers, notably Netscape Navigator and Microsoft Internet Explorer, provide support for non-standard arguments that primarily affect the
display of the HTML text in the viewer's window. WWW viewers that don't
support non-standard elements or arguments just ignore them. Non-standard
usage is noted in chapters 15 and 16.

▶ See "Netscape-
Specific Exten-
sions to
HTML," p. 311

▶ See "HTML
Extensions
in Internet
Explorer,
Mosaic, and
HTML 3.0,"
p. 347

Note

If you incorporate non-standard HTML in your own documents, let users know with
a simple statement at the head of your "entry-point" document (usually the "Welcome" or introduction page). This way, they know that a given browser displays your
Web pages as you intended them to be seen. Both Netscape and Microsoft have
programs that allow you to include special messages and icons on your web pages
indicating that they are best viewed with their browsers.

II

Basic HTML Presentation

An Overview of HTML Elements

Tables 4.1, 4.2, and 4.3 provide a brief overview of some of more common HTML elements found in different sections of HTML documents. These tables don't include arguments but they do include the element's tag type. The entire HTML document should be contained in the HTML container element. For a complete description of each element and its associated arguments, see appendix A.

Table 4.1 HTML Elements for Head Sections in HTML Documents

Element	Element Type	Description
BASE	empty	Base context document
HEAD	container	Document head
ISINDEX	empty	Document is a searchable index
LINK	empty	Link from this document
META	container	Generic meta-information
NEXTID	empty	Next ID to use for link name
TITLE	container	Title of document

Table 4.2 HTML Elements for Body Sections in HTML Documents

Element	Element Type	Description
A	container	Anchor: source and/or destination of a link
ADDRESS	container	Address, signature, or byline for a document or passage
B	container	Bold text
BLOCKQUOTE	container	Quoted passage
BODY	container	Document body
BR	empty	Line break
CITE	container	Name or title of cited work
CODE	container	Source code phrase
DD	empty	Definition of term
DIR	container	Directory list
DL	container	Definition list, or glossary
DT	empty	Term in definition list
EM	container	Emphasized phrase

Element	Element Type	Description
H1	container	Heading, level 1
H2	container	Heading, level 2
H3	container	Heading, level 3
H4	container	Heading, level 4
H5	container	Heading, level 5
H6	container	Heading, level 6
HR	empty	Horizontal rule
I	container	Italic text
IMG	empty	Image; icon, glyph, or illustration
KBD	container	Keyboard phrase, such as user input
LI	empty	List item
LISTING	container	Computer listing
MENU	container	Menu list
OL	container	Ordered or numbered list
P	empty	Paragraph
PRE	container	Preformatted text
SAMP	container	Sample text or characters
SELECT	empty	Selection of option(s)
STRONG	container	Strong emphasis
TT	container	Typewriter text
UL	container	Unordered list
VAR	container	Variable phrase or substitutable
XMP	container	Example section

II

Basic HTML Presentation

Note

As the HTML standard changes, elements will be deprecated, or replaced by new elements with greater functionality. Deprecated elements will still be supported by existing WWW viewers but may not be in the future. Be prepared to review your older HTML documents for deprecated elements that may no longer be useful.

Table 4.3	HTML Elements for Forms in HTML Documents	
Element	**Element Type**	**Description**
FORM	container	Fill-out or data-entry form
INPUT	empty	Form input datum
TEXTAREA	empty	Area for text input
OPTION	empty	Selection option

## CHAPTER 5

The TITLE, HEAD, and HTML Tags

by Jim O'Donnell

Creating an accurate document head is the first step to writing good HTML. Fortunately, it's also the easiest. The *head* section of an HTML document precedes the main content of the document. Similar to the banner page of a magazine, the head provides information for both the viewer software and the end user.

This chapter answers the following questions:

- How do you use the HTML element?
- What is the function of the head section in an HTML document?
- How does the TITLE element function?
- How can you create relationships between HTML documents?
- Can you simplify using relative URLs?
- How can you provide text searches in your documents?

The <HTML> Tag

HTML documents are *platform-independent,* meaning that they don't conform to any one system standard. If they are created properly, you can move home pages to any server platform, or you can access them with any compliant WWW viewer. One way to indicate this independence is the <HTML> tag. Because HTML documents are not compiled (or processed) for execution, some applications need a hint to know how to interpret the plain text in a home page. That's where the <HTML> tag comes into play.

Remember that the <HTML> and </HTML> tags should be the first and last elements of your HTML document. Although most viewers can handle a home page without the <HTML> tag, it is recommended that all your HTML documents use it (see fig. 5.1). The end of the HTML container is defined with the end tag </HTML>.

Fig. 5.1
Using the
<HTML> and
</HTML> tags to
open and close
your HTML
documents is a
good idea.

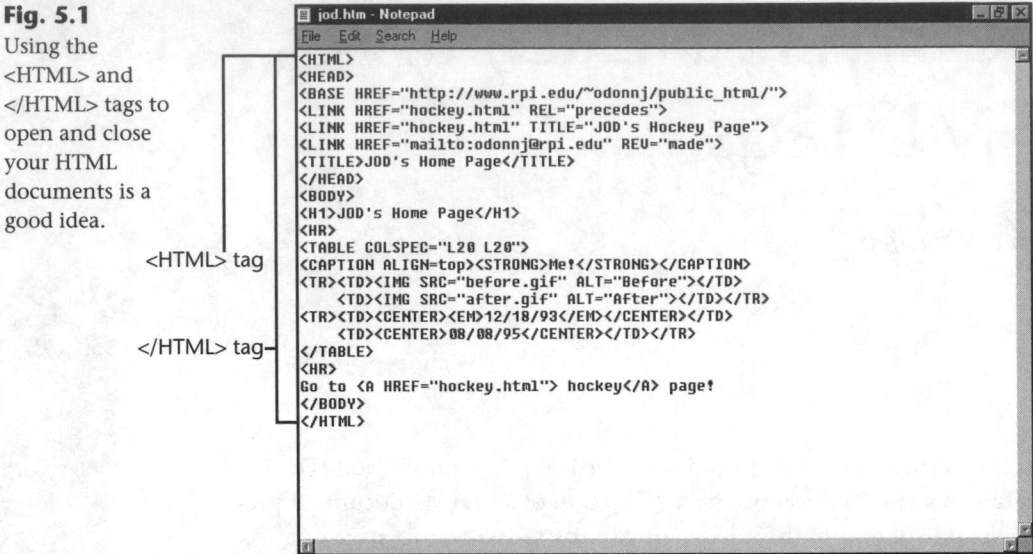

```
jod.htm - Notepad
File  Edit  Search  Help
<HTML>
<HEAD>
<BASE HREF="http://www.rpi.edu/~odonnj/public_html/">
<LINK HREF="hockey.html" REL="precedes">
<LINK HREF="hockey.html" TITLE="JOD's Hockey Page">
<LINK HREF="mailto:odonnj@rpi.edu" REV="made">
<TITLE>JOD's Home Page</TITLE>
</HEAD>
<BODY>
<H1>JOD's Home Page</H1>
<HR>
<TABLE COLSPEC="L20 L20">
<CAPTION ALIGN=top><STRONG>Me!</STRONG></CAPTION>
<TR><TD><IMG SRC="before.gif" ALT="Before"></TD>
    <TD><IMG SRC="after.gif" ALT="After"></TD></TR>
<TR><TD><CENTER><EM>12/18/93</EM></CENTER></TD>
    <TD><CENTER>08/08/95</CENTER></TD></TR>
</TABLE>
<HR>
Go to <A HREF="hockey.html"> hockey</A> page!
</BODY>
</HTML>
```

<HTML> tag

</HTML> tag

Note

Technically, the <HTML> tag is not part of the head section, as it contains all the HTML portions of the current document, including the head section. But, for purposes of clarity, the tag is presented here, where users begin to write their HTML code. The tag's closing component, </HTML>, comes at the very end of the document, like the traditional "The End" at the end of a book or movie. Logically, the closing is unnecessary (after all, if the file contains no more text, the document is ended). But, as a matter of good usage, take the extra second or two to include the </HTML> line.

Files without the <HTML> tag can be misinterpreted as text-only documents, and the markup tags as just more text on the page. This fact is particularly relevant as other applications increasingly access existing HTML documents without the presumption that the document is HTML and not a plain text file (mail and news readers, for instance).

The Head Section: Using the HEAD Element

The head section is like a quick reference for WWW viewers and other applications that access HTML files. The head supplies the document title and establishes relationships between HTML documents and file directories.

The document head can signal the WWW viewer to use its search capabilities to index the current document.

HTML provides the HEAD element to define the head section in a document. The <HEAD> tag encloses or contains the head section (which is enclosed by the <HTML> tag). The closing </HEAD> tag sets the bounds for the head section. The only element in the head section displayed by the end user's viewer is the value of the TITLE element. Figure 5.2 shows a typical document head.

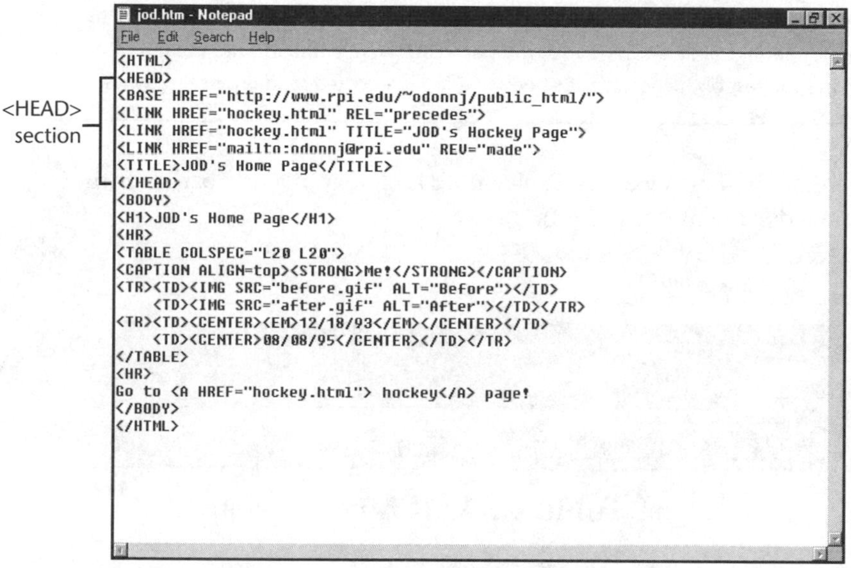

Fig. 5.2
The elements in a document head define its function and clearly show the relationships between the document and other files.

```
jod.htm - Notepad
File  Edit  Search  Help
<HTML>
<HEAD>
<BASE HREF="http://www.rpi.edu/~odonnj/public_html/">
<LINK HREF="hockey.html" REL="precedes">
<LINK HREF="hockey.html" TITLE="JOD's Hockey Page">
<LINK HREF="mailto:odonnj@rpi.edu" REV="made">
<TITLE>JOD's Home Page</TITLE>
</HEAD>
<BODY>
<H1>JOD's Home Page</H1>
<HR>
<TABLE COLSPEC="L20 L20">
<CAPTION ALIGN=top><STRONG>Me!</STRONG></CAPTION>
<TR><TD><IMG SRC="before.gif" ALT="Before"></TD>
    <TD><IMG SRC="after.gif" ALT="After"></TD></TR>
<TR><TD><CENTER><EM>12/18/93</EM></CENTER></TD>
    <TD><CENTER>08/08/95</CENTER></TD></TR>
</TABLE>
<HR>
Go to <A HREF="hockey.html"> hockey</A> page!
</BODY>
</HTML>
```

<HEAD> section

Writing proper document heads is not only good HTML, it also prepares your documents to be used by additional applications (such as WAIS searches) and other future, undefined uses.

> **Tip**
>
> It's not a head element, but it's a good idea to include a comment, enclosed in "<!—" "—>" to explain, describing the document in the head section.

How to Use the TITLE Element

Using the TITLE element is as simple as it sounds—the TITLE element "names" your document. The title doesn't assign a file name to a document; it defines a text string that is interpreted as the HTML title of the document.

II

Basic HTML Presentation

The actual file name is incidental (thankfully); most file systems either limit the number of characters in a file name or limit the use of "special" characters that are required by the system (such as the / character). In HTML titles, any character can be displayed.

> ### Caution
>
> The HTML character set does reserve some characters for special uses, such as the "less than" and "greater than" angle brackets. However, you can display these characters in your software viewer by using their HTML "entity" equivalents. If you try to use the special characters as normal, the viewer software either ignores them or displays the rest of the document's body text in unexpected (and unwanted) ways.

Many Windows-based viewers display the TITLE text in a title bar, or at the top of the document (see fig. 5.3).

Document title

Fig. 5.3
Windows viewers display the text in the viewer's interface.

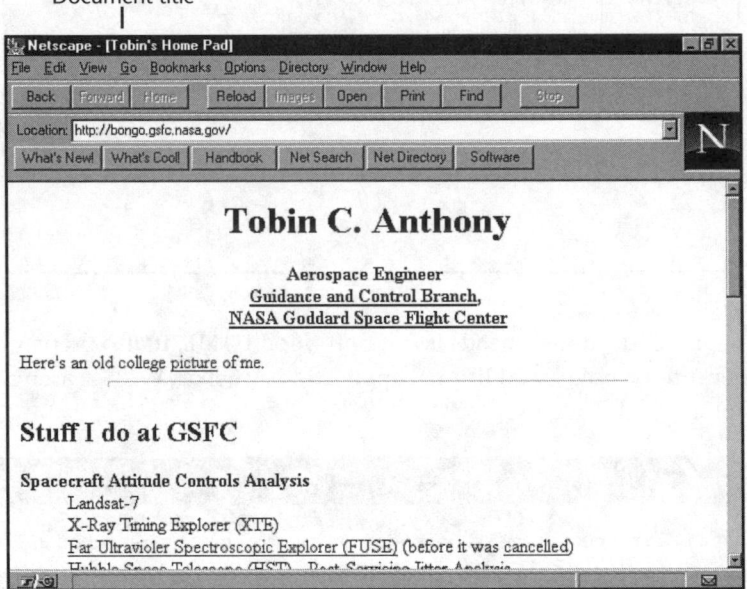

HTML doesn't limit the length of the TITLE element. However, before you rush off to give your documents voluminous and wonderfully expository titles, consider the space where the title is displayed (the viewer's title bar or window label). A good rule of thumb for the length of a title is no more than a single phrase or no longer than 60 characters. See figure 5.4 for an incorrect use of TITLE.

Title too long

Fig. 5.4
TITLE values that are too long might get cut off by the viewer's title bar or window, decreasing the effectiveness of the home page.

II

Basic HTML Presentation

Note

When a user adds your document to his or her viewer's "hot list" or bookmark list, the TITLE value is saved as the name of your document. Avoid nondescript TITLE values, such as "Page 1," for documents likely to be linked to. Or play with your audience's expectations by providing a tantalizing TITLE for the link.

Troubleshooting

I put a TITLE statement in the head section, but some people complain that their viewers display something else. What's happening?

You probably made a mistake in your document's head section, either leaving off an angle bracket or forgetting the closing tag </TITLE>. Although some viewers try to catch these errors and display what they think the author intended, others don't. Viewers can display all sorts of nasty text with a TITLE error. Go back and double-check your code, or use an HTML validation service, such as the WebTechs HTML Validation Service, at one of the following URLs:

```
http://www.webtechs.com/html-val-svc/index.html

http://cq-pan.cqu.edu.au/validate/

http://www.hensa.ac.uk/html-val-svc/

http://www.austria.eu.net/html-val-svc/
```

Although viewers have a limited capability to display a document's TITLE value, by combining the TITLE text with a lead heading statement, you can effectively create a "1–2" punch with your introductory text. This approach can provide a way of including a longer title for your document, including the longer title within the document as the lead heading and a shorter version as the actual title (see fig. 5.5.)

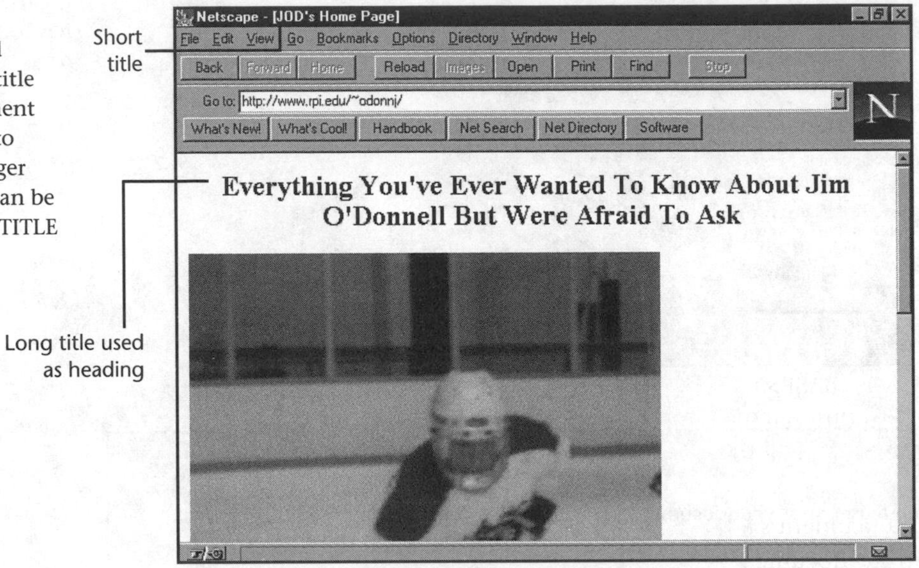

Fig. 5.5
Using a lead heading to title your document allows you to include longer titles than can be used in the TITLE element.

Short title

Long title used as heading

Creating Relationships between HTML Documents

Computer files are glorious things: small, lightweight, easily transportable. With a few keystrokes, you can relocate entire directories of files, or files with similar names or extensions. Reorganizing a hard disk of files or creating copies on a different system doesn't take a great deal of work (or knowledge). And making havoc of an orderly file system doesn't take any effort at all.

As the volume of HTML files under your management increases, you'll be thankful for two elements HTML uses for document heads. These tags serve to connect HTML documents to each other and to their authors.

Using <BASE> to Simplify URLs

HTML documents often rely on the physical locations of other HTML files. A document might include a pointer to another document, for instance (see fig. 5.6).

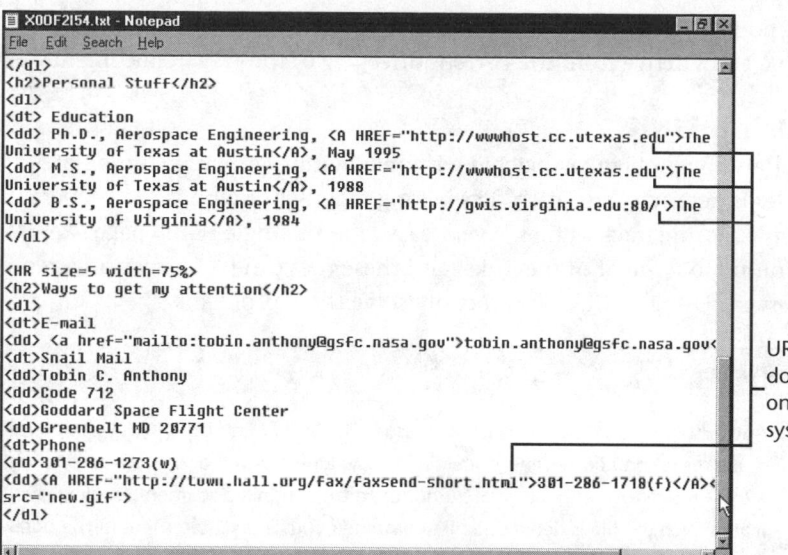

Fig. 5.6
Pointers in HTML documents can point to other documents (as shown here), or to other locations in the same document.

URLs to documents on other systems

The HTML <BASE> tag acts somewhat like the DOS PATH statement; it provides an additional file directory location for the WWW viewer to refer to when looking up a document link. By specifying a value for <BASE> in your document head, you can shorten the URL statements by using relative URLs in your document's anchor and image links. <BASE> protects relative URL links in the document from "breaking" should the file be physically moved. Figure 5.7 demonstrates a proper BASE statement.

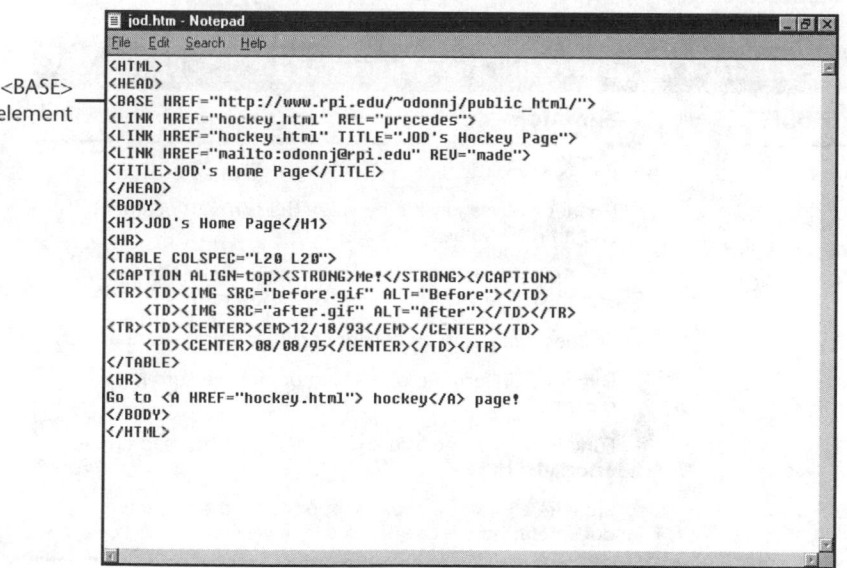

<BASE> element

Fig. 5.7
The value of <BASE> is a link to the document's absolute URL location written in the form of an anchor link.

Basic HTML Presentation

If no BASE value exists in a document, the WWW viewer assumes that relative URLs derive from the current directory of the HTML document.

Using LINK

Often one problem associated with managing a growing volume of HTML files is determining which files belong together or who is the proper author of a file. Losing track of files is very easy when a single home page can use an unlimited number of file links (and these files can be local or on a remote server). Using LINK, you can easily solve these problems.

Note

Authorship on the Internet is a sticky issue. The WWW and other Internet applications make retrieving and reusing documents easy. One manner of protection is to include a LINK reference to the original author or to the original document (or documents) from which the file is derived. LINK, combined with a text statement in the document's body, provides as much copyright protection as the Internet currently allows.

LINK statements define relationships between the current document and other documents, the author, or Web clients. They generally include a hypertext reference in the form of a URL and an attribute value that explains what the document's relationship with this URL is. Refer to appendix A, "HTML Tags," for more information about LINK attributes.

A document can include multiple LINK statements using as many attributes as necessary (see fig. 5.8). These attributes are shown in table 5.1.

Table 5.1   LINK Attributes and Their Functions

Attribute	Function
HREF	Points to a URL
REL	Defines the relationship between the current document and an HREF value
REV	Like REL, defines the relationship between the HREF value and the document (the opposite association)
NAME	Defines a link from an anchor or URL to this document
URN	Defines a Uniform Resource Number for the current document
TITLE	Functions the same as the <TITLE> tag in the head of the associated HREF
METHODS	Provides a list of functions supported by the current document; how it can be used by a viewer

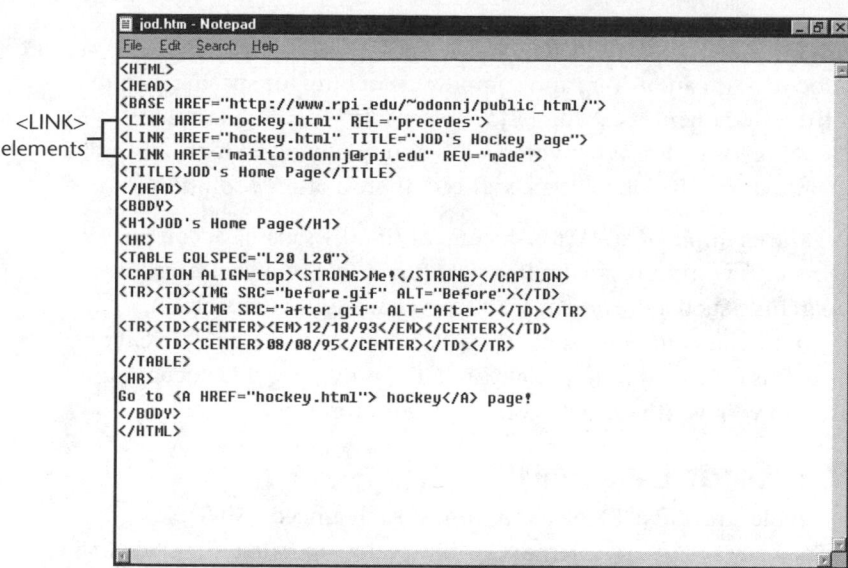

<LINK>
elements

Fig. 5.8
LINK options and attributes apply to the entire HTML document.

In this example, the LINK statements are performing three tasks. The first statement

```
<LINK HREF="hockey.html" REL="precedes">
```

tells the Web viewer that the current document (index.html) comes before the identified URL document (hockey.html).

The second statement

```
<LINK HREF="hockey.html" TITLE="Hockey Stuff">
```

identifies the title (Hockey Stuff) for the specified document (hockey.html).

The third statement

```
<LINK HREF="mailto:odonnj@rpi.edu" REV="made">
```

says that the author of this document (REV="made") is described at the following hypertext reference—in this case, an e-mail window that allows you to send a message to the author, odonnj@rpi.edu.

Of the attributes listed in table 5.1, HREF, NAME, REL, and REV are most often used. As HTML documents begin to be used by more applications, these values and attributes will become important to assist programs in using HTML documents.

II

Basic HTML Presentation

Indexing a Document

HTML documents can be long and complex. Searching for specific information in these documents is a tedious job, especially when the terminology you're looking for varies. What you need is a simple method for doing a difficult job, and in HTML, where there's a need, there's often a solution (or two).

Consider the example of an HTML document that lists classical composers and their works with associated music data files and a brief synopsis for each work. Searching such a document for a specific musical composition, or an obscure composer, could take some time. What you want is an efficient way to retrieve this information (especially if you're providing this document for wide use and you want people to come back for more).

HTML's ISINDEX Element

HTML provides the ISINDEX element for just such a need. ISINDEX signals the WWW viewer to use its internal capabilities to generate a simple search form, where the user enters one or more search variables (separated by commas) in a blank line and clicks the Search button. (The viewer can still view and read the document normally if a user doesn't want to perform a keyword search.) The viewer passes the search information to the document's server, which performs the search.

> **Note**
>
> Having the ISINDEX element in a document doesn't guarantee that the document can be searched. WWW viewers don't have the means to perform their own searches, so they rely on the document's server to have a "search engine" program. For this reason, most Web sites prefer to run a script that appends the ISINDEX element automatically to its HTML documents if a search engine is available.

ISINDEX requires no additional information or attributes—just add it to the head section of a document you want to make searchable.

Figure 5.9 shows how ISINDEX is included in the head of an HTML document used for searching a long HTML document of classical music. Figure 5.10 shows the resulting search form at the bottom of the Web page; entering text into the form and pressing Enter (or clicking the Submit button that some viewers provide) begins a search for the next occurrence of the text string.

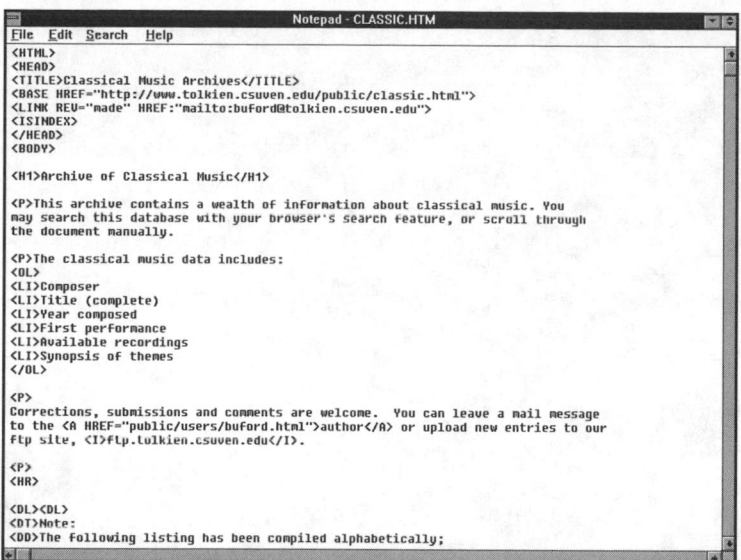

Fig. 5.9
The ISINDEX element requires no attributes or document information; it signals the viewer to provide a search form.

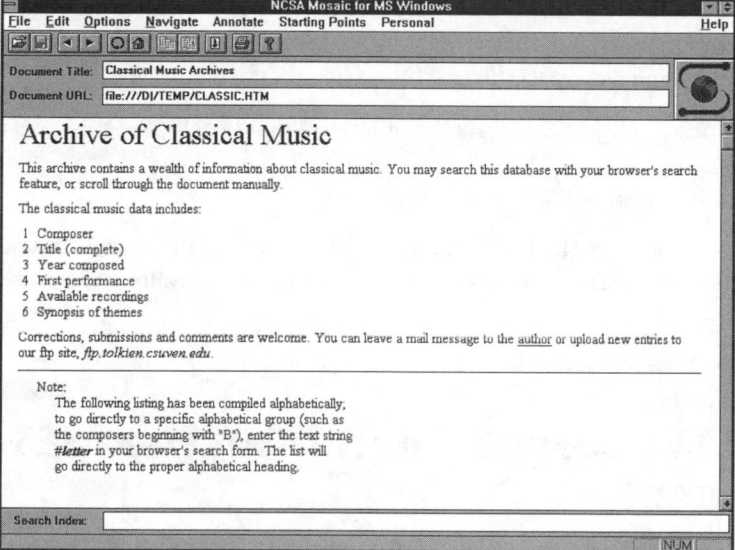

Fig. 5.10
The WWW viewer displays a search field when it finds the ISINDEX element in the document head; press Enter to start a search based on the text string in the search field.

Using an Alternate Indexing Method

Your Web server may not have a search engine to make ISINDEX a useful tool. An HTML document author, with sufficient time and desperation (and a Web site administrator who can't provide the necessary search program), can create a "rolodex" or "organizer" effect in a document. This effect is possible using anchors. Figure 5.11 shows an anchored index in a document.

Fig. 5.11
An HTML document can incorporate a rolodex-type search feature using named anchors; click an alphabetical category to jump to that point in the Web page.

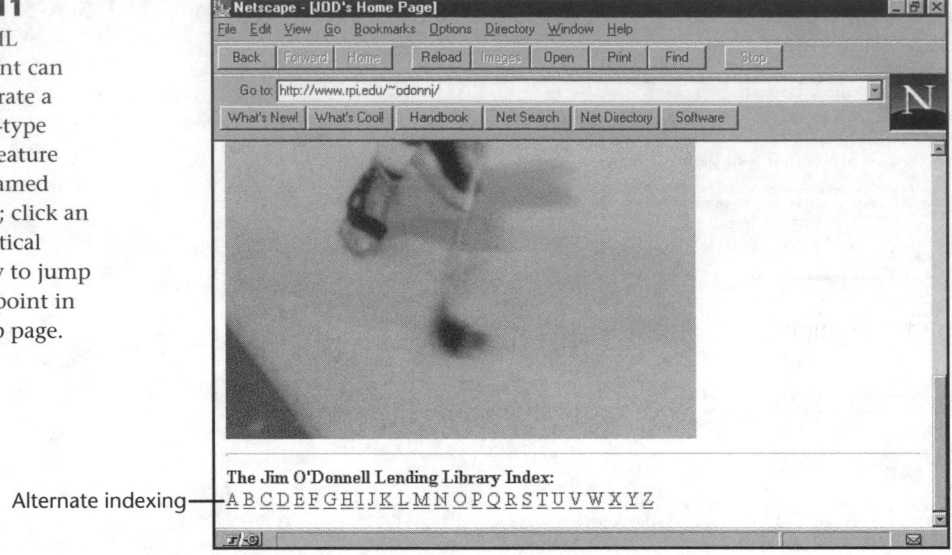

Alternate indexing ——

This search function works using the HTML ANCHOR element; by defining each letter as an anchor link to a named anchor, the user can click that letter and jump immediately to the specified point in the document.

For example, in figure 5.11, the list of letters would begin like this in HTML:

```
<A HREF="#A">A</A>
<A HREF="#B">B</A>
```

And so on. Clicking the highlighted B in the viewer window would jump to the line of HTML in the document that includes the following named anchor:

```
<A NAME="B">BACH</A>
```

Did We Forget Anything? The META Element

The HTML specification includes a mechanism to include other *meta-information*, information about the document, beyond the things such as title and base that have defined head section elements. This mechanism is the META element, which you can use to embed specialized information into the document header. The <META> element has the three attributes shown in table 5.2.

Table 5.2 **META Attributes and Their Functions**	
Attribute	**Function**
HTTP-EQUIV	Binds the META element to an HTTP response header
NAME	Names a property such as author, publication date, or similar. If the NAME element is not specified, it is assumed to be the same as HTTP-EQUIV
CONTENT	Supplies a value for a named property

Suppose, for example, that the document contains the following META elements:

```
<META HTTP-EQUIV="Expires" CONTENT="Thu, 01 Feb 1996 00:00:00 GMT">
<META HTTP-EQUIV="Reply-To" CONTENT="odonnj@rpi.edu (Jim O'Donnell)">
<META HTTP-EQUIV="Keywords" CONTENT="before, after">
```

Then if you view it and display the document information, you see the information shown in figure 5.12 (notice that the HTTP server converted the expired time from GMT to local time). The HTTP server on which I have my home page supports the Expires HTTP-EQUIV attribute of the META element but not the Keywords or Reply-To attributes. Unsupported attributes are ignored by the server.

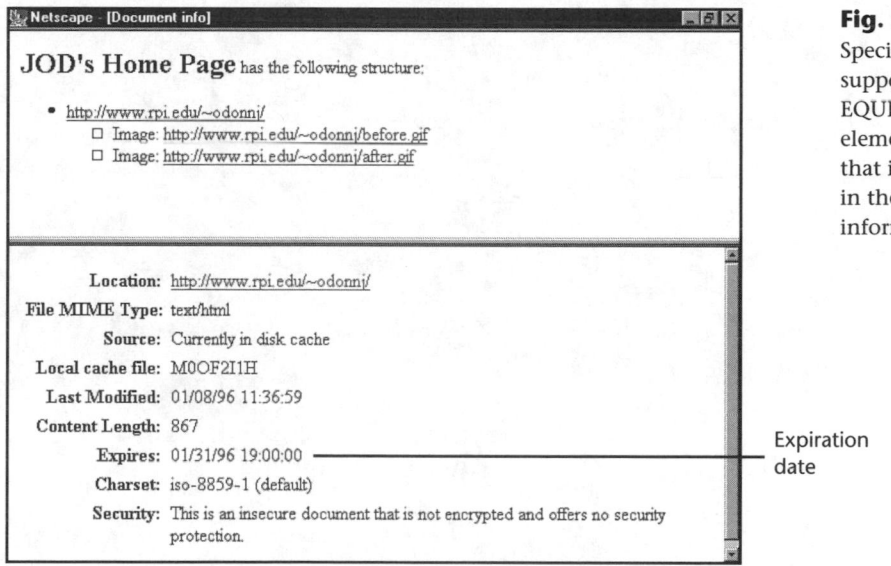

Fig. 5.12
Specifying supported HTTP-EQUIV META elements includes that information in the document information view.

Expiration date

II

Basic HTML Presentation

When no equivalent HTTP response headers are available, you should use the NAME attribute instead of HTTP-EQUIV. Examples of this use of the META element are as follows:

```
<META NAME="Last Validated" CONTENT="Mon, 01 Jan 1996 09:23:12 GMT">
<META NAME="Web Page Type" CONTENT="Personal">
<META NAME="Special Features" CONTENT="None">
```

## CHAPTER 6

Creating an HTML Document

by Robert Meegan

When you first venture out onto the Web, it all seems very much like a big cloud of gas with no form or structure. Later, as you develop some experience, you can begin to see the structure that constitutes the Web. At the top are the links that connect pages together, while at the bottom are the HTML documents that form the foundation.

Documents provide most of the content and a great deal of the form for the Web. It's your job as an author to create HTML documents that are informative and interesting about the subjects of which you are knowledgeable. The largest part of these documents will be the body element, where you will put the text and images that make up the content.

In this chapter, you will learn how to create the body element for your own HTML documents and you'll learn about the following:

- How to add body text to your HTML document
- How to use headers to add structure to your document
- The use of horizontal lines to divide the document
- How to format portions of your text to add emphasis
- How to add special characters to your document
- The new HTML body features coming in HTML 3.0

The Basics of the Body Element

Despite the graphical nature of the Web, the vast majority of its information is in the form of text documents. Most people who view your documents will be interested in what you have to say. Because of this, whether you are converting existing documents or creating new ones, you will spend much of your time working in the body.

Starting with the Required Elements

Before you can fill in your document, you need to lay out a basic working framework. As you saw in chapter 4, "Building Blocks of HTML," HTML documents must follow a defined pattern of elements if they are to be interpreted correctly. It is a good idea for you to create a template to use for each of your pages so that you are less likely to leave out an important detail. Listing 6.1 is an example of a basic template.

Listing 6.1   A Basic Document Template

```
<HTML>
<HEAD>
<TITLE> A Basic Document Template </TITLE>
<HEAD>
<BODY>
Put the body text in here.
</BODY>
</HTML>
```

This template begins with the <HTML> tag (see fig. 6.1), which is necessary for every HTML document. Next is the <HEAD> tag, which opens up the heading part of the document. This contains the <TITLE> element, which is used for adding a title to your document. This element is not required, but using it represents good practice as it helps readers of your document to know what they are reading. The heading is closed with the </HEAD> tag. Finally, the <BODY> element follows. This will be where you place the bulk of the material in your document. Remember to close the body element with the </BODY> tag and to finish the page with the </HTML> tag.

Because HTML is a markup language, the body of your document is turned on with the start tag, <BODY>. Everything that follows this tag is interpreted according to a strict set of rules that tell the browser about the contents. The body element is closed with the end tag, </BODY>.

Note

Strictly speaking, it isn't absolutely necessary to use the <BODY> start and end tags, as HTML allows you to skip a tag if it is obvious from the context. It's still a good idea to use them. Some older browsers and other HTML programs may become confused without them.

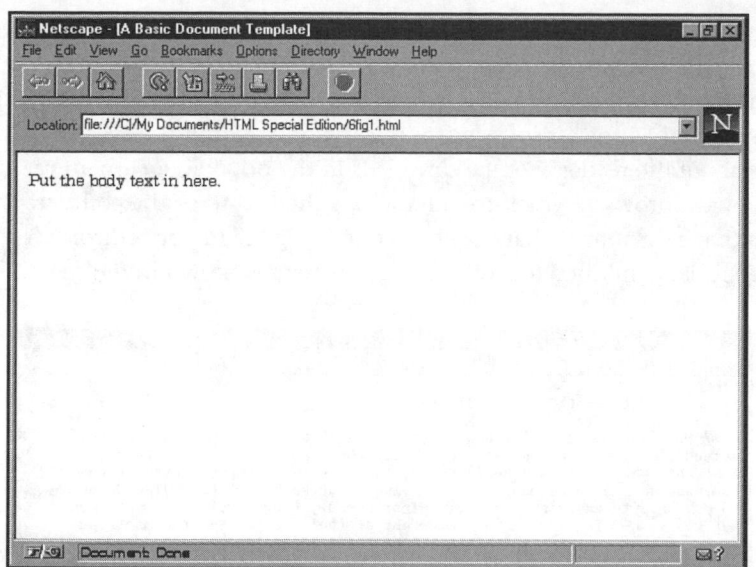

Fig. 6.1
The basic frame-
work creates a
document with a
title and a single
line of text.

In the basic template shown above, the body text is a single line. In your
document, you will replace this line with the main text of your document.
Unless you are using a special HTML editor, you must enter your text using
a strict ASCII format. This limits you to a common set of characters that can
be interpreted by computers throughout the world. The text that you enter
here—whether for the first time or from an existing document—must be
completely free of any special formatting. Note that some ASCII characters
can only be added to the document by using a special coding scheme.
This will be discussed later in this chapter.

> **Note**
>
> Most browsers consider all non-blank white space (tabs, end-of-line characters, etc.)
> as a single blank. Multiple white spaces are normally condensed to a single blank.

The body element in the template shown in listing 6.1 also includes an
address element. I'll tell you more about this later.

Breaking Text into Paragraphs

Your old English teacher taught you to break your writing up into paragraphs
that expressed complete thoughts, and an HTML document shouldn't be an
exception. Unfortunately, line and paragraph breaks are a little more complicated in HTML than you might expect.

As a markup language, HTML requires that you make no assumptions about your reader's machine. The readers of your document can set whatever margins and fonts they want to use. This means that text wrapping must be determined by the browser software, as it is the only part of the system that knows about the reader's setup. Line feeds in the original document are ignored by the browser, which then reformats the text to fit the context. This means that a document that may be perfectly legible in your editor (see fig. 6.2) is badly mashed together in the browser, as shown in figure 6.3.

Fig. 6.2

Line feeds separate the paragraphs in the editor.

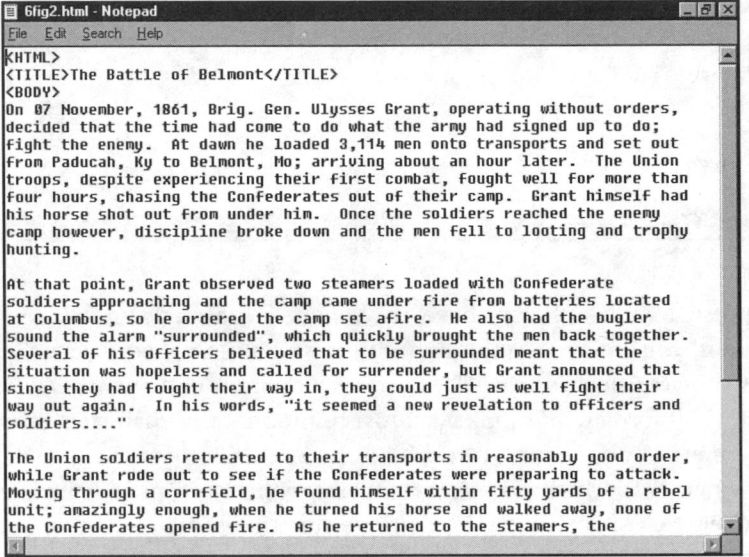

The proper way to break text into paragraphs is by using paragraph elements. Place a paragraph start tag, <P>, at the beginning of each new paragraph, and the browser will know to separate the paragraphs. Adding a paragraph end tag, </P>, is optional, as it is normally implied by the next start tag that comes along. Still, adding the </P> tag at the end of your text can help to protect your documents against browsers that don't precisely follow the HTML 2.0 standard. HTML 1.0 did use the paragraph tag as a container and documents created to that standard have all their text between paragraph start and end tags.

Figure 6.4 shows what the document looks like in the editor after the paragraph tags have been added. You can see that the tags were added to the start of each paragraph and that the line feeds are still in the document. Because the browser ignores the line feeds anyway, it is best to keep them in the source document to make it easier to edit later.

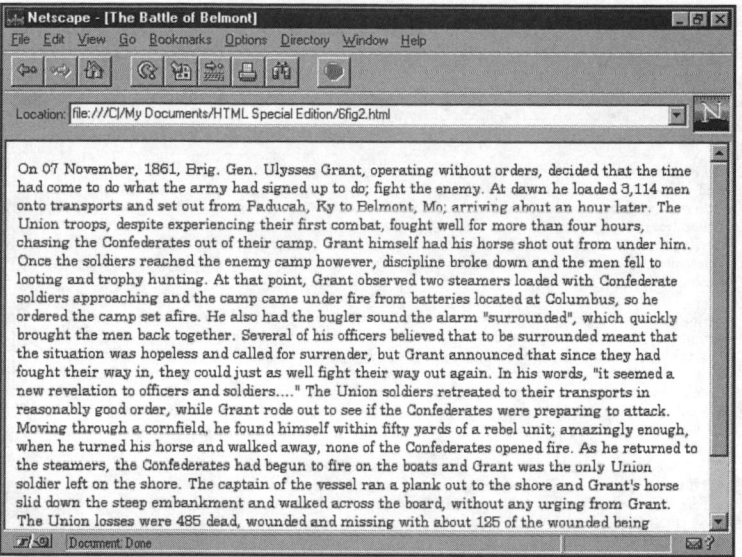

Fig. 6.3
The browser ignores the line feeds and runs the text together.

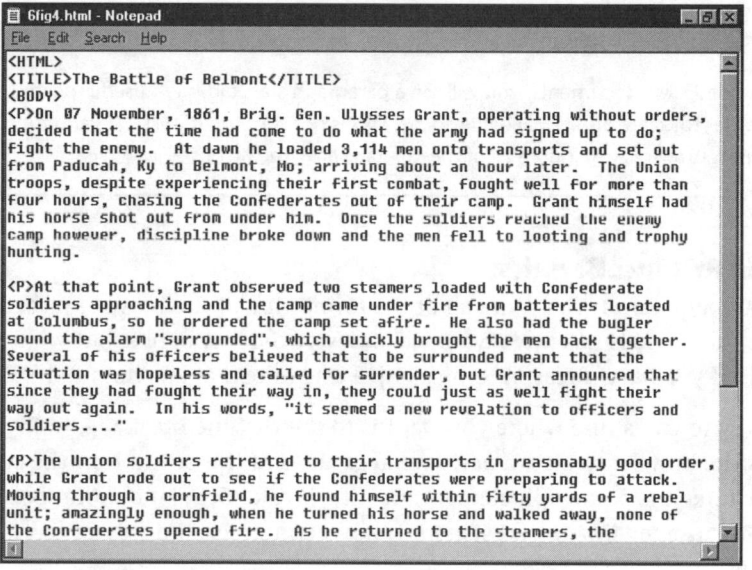

Fig. 6.4
You must begin each paragraph with the <P> tag.

When you look at the document in figure 6.5, you can see that the browser separated the paragraphs correctly by adding a double-spaced line between them.

Fig. 6.5
With paragraph elements, the text becomes much easier to read in the browser.

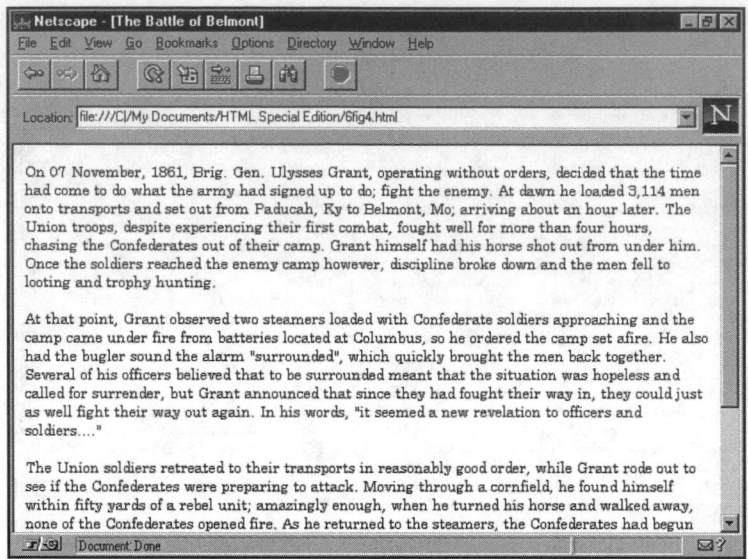

> On 07 November, 1861, Brig. Gen. Ulysses Grant, operating without orders, decided that the time had come to do what the army had signed up to do; fight the enemy. At dawn he loaded 3,114 men onto transports and set out from Paducah, Ky to Belmont, Mo; arriving about an hour later. The Union troops, despite experiencing their first combat, fought well for more than four hours, chasing the Confederates out of their camp. Grant himself had his horse shot out from under him. Once the soldiers reached the enemy camp however, discipline broke down and the men fell to looting and trophy hunting.
>
> At that point, Grant observed two steamers loaded with Confederate soldiers approaching and the camp came under fire from batteries located at Columbus, so he ordered the camp set afire. He also had the bugler sound the alarm "surrounded", which quickly brought the men back together. Several of his officers believed that to be surrounded meant that the situation was hopeless and called for surrender, but Grant announced that since they had fought their way in, they could just as well fight their way out again. In his words, "it seemed a new revelation to officers and soldiers...."
>
> The Union soldiers retreated to their transports in reasonably good order, while Grant rode out to see if the Confederates were preparing to attack. Moving through a cornfield, he found himself within fifty yards of a rebel unit; amazingly enough, when he turned his horse and walked away, none of the Confederates opened fire. As he returned to the steamers, the Confederates had begun

---

Note

In some HTML documents, you will see a paragraph start tag, <P>, used repeatedly in order to create additional white space. This is not supported in HTML, and most current browsers will ignore all of the <P> tags after the first one.

Adding Line Breaks

As you have seen, HTML does all of the formatting at the browser rather than at the source. This has the advantage of device independence. But what do you do if you have a reason to break up a line of text at a certain point?

The way to end a line where you want is to use the line break tag, <BR>. This forces the browser to start a new line, regardless of the position in the current line. Unlike the paragraph element, the line break does not double-space the text. Because the line break element is not a container, it does not have an end tag.

One reason you might want to force line breaks is to show off your poetic muse, as shown in listing 6.2.

**Listing 6.2   A Limerick Showing the Use of the
 Tag**

```
<HTML>
<HEAD>
<TITLE>Creating an HTML Document</TITLE>
</HEAD>
<BODY>
<P>A very intelligent turtle<BR>
Found programming UNIX a hurdle<BR>
The system, you see,<BR>
Ran as slow as did he,<BR>
And that's not saying much for the turtle.<BR>
<CITE>Mercifully anonymous</CITE>
</BODY>
</HTML>
```

When this source is viewed in figure 6.6, you can see how the line break element works.

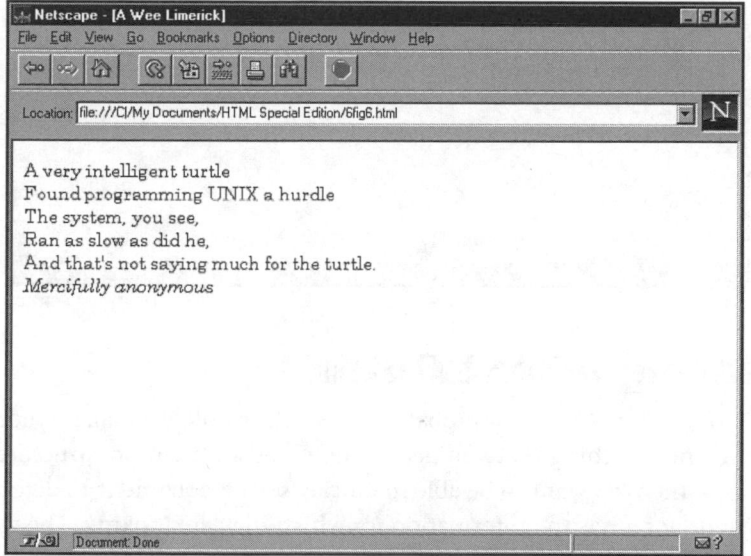

Fig. 6.6
Use line breaks to force a new line in the browser.

II

Basic HTML Presentation

Tip

Multiple line breaks can be used to provide extra white space in your document. The problem is that some browsers will condense multiple line breaks (multiple <BR> or <P> tags) to a single line break.

You need to be careful when using line breaks; if the line has already wrapped in the browser, your break may appear after only a couple of words in the next line. This is particularly the case if the browser that you test your documents on has wider margins than your reader's browser. Figure 6.7 shows an example where the author saw that the break was occurring in the middle of the quotation, so she added a <BR>. Unfortunately, when displayed on a screen with different margins, the word "actually" ends up on a line by itself.

Fig. 6.7
Careless use of line breaks can produce an unexpected result.

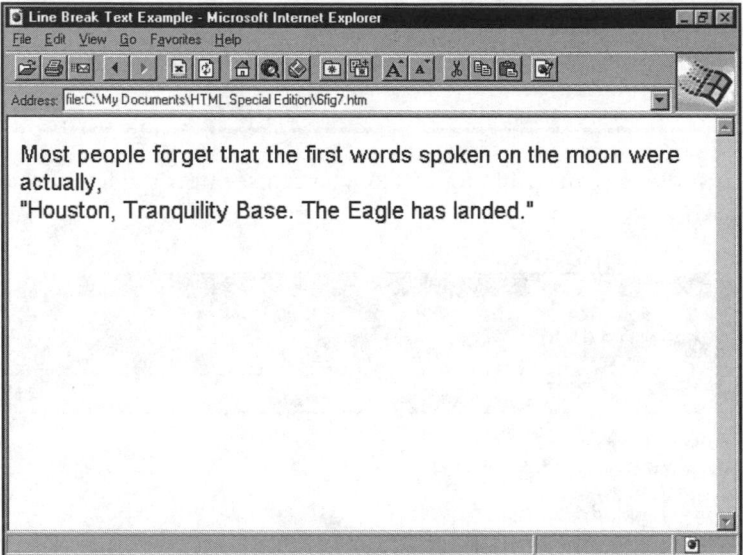

Creating a Text Outline

So far, your HTML document probably looks a little dull. To make it more interesting, the first thing that you need to do is add a little more structure to it. Users of the Web want to be able to quickly scan a document to determine whether or not it has the information for which they are looking. The way to make this scanning easier is to break the document up into logical sections, each covering a single topic.

After you have broken up the document, the next step is to add meaningful headers to each section, which enables your reader to quickly jump to the material of interest.

Adding Headings

Headings in HTML provide an outline of the text that forms the body of the document. As such, they direct the reader through the document and make your information more interesting and usable. They are probably the most commonly used formatting tag that you will find in HTML documents.

The heading element is a container and must have a start tag (<H1>) and an end tag (</H1>). HTML has six levels of headings: H1 (the most important), H2, H3, H4, H5, and H6 (the least important). Each of these levels will have its own appearance in the viewer's browser, but you have no direct control over what that appearance will be. This is part of the HTML philosophy: you, as the document writer, have the responsibility for the content, while the browser has the responsibility for the appearance. See the example in listing 6.3.

Listing 6.3   An HTML Document Showing the Use of Headings

```
<HTML>
<HEAD>
<TITLE>Creating an HTML Document</TITLE>
</HEAD>
<BODY>
<H1>Level 1 Heading</H1>
<H2>Level 2 Heading</H2>
<H3>Level 3 Heading</H3>
<H4>Level 4 Heading</H4>
<H5>Level 5 Heading</H5>
<H6>Level 6 Heading</H6>
</BODY>
</HTML>
```

Note

Although it is not absolutely necessary to use each of the heading levels, as a matter of good practice you should not skip levels because it may cause problems with automatic document converters. In particular, as new Web indexes come online, they will be able to search Web documents and create retrievable outlines. These may become confused if heading levels are missing.

Figures 6.8 and 6.9 show how these headings look when they are displayed in Netscape Navigator and Microsoft Internet Explorer. You can see that not only do they use different fonts, but the sizes of the headings are different.

Fig. 6.8
Here are the six
heading levels as
they appear in
Netscape.

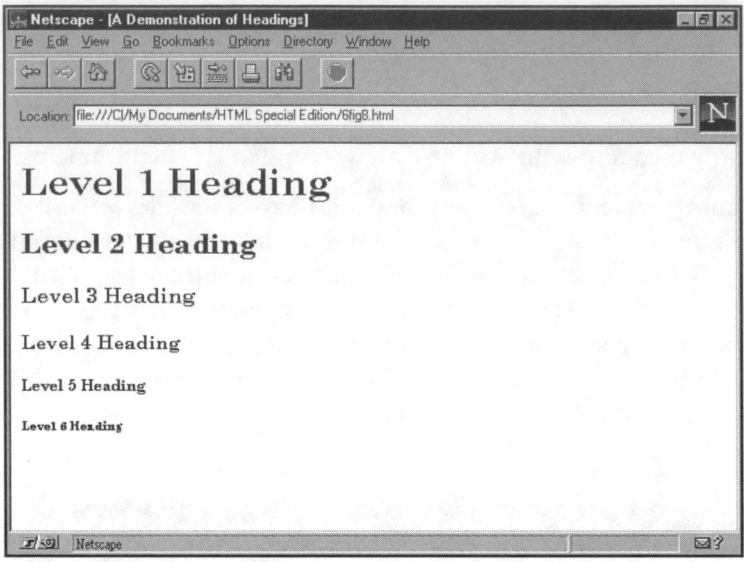

Fig. 6.9
Here are the six
heading levels as
they appear in the
Internet Explorer.

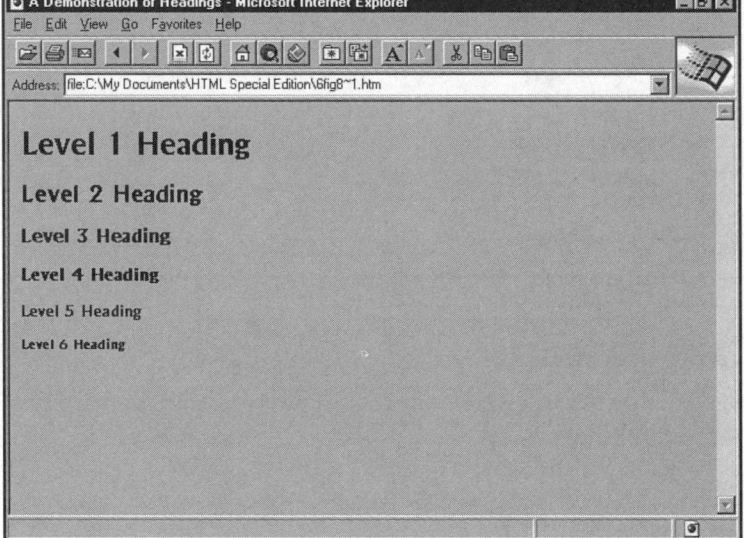

> **Note**
>
> Remember that forgetting to add an end tag will definitely mess up the appearance
> of your document. Headings are containers and require both start and end tags.
> Another thing to remember is that headings also have an implied paragraph break

before and after each one. You can't apply a heading to text in the middle of a paragraph to change the size or font. The result will be a paragraph broken into three separate pieces, and the middle one will have a heading format.

The best way to use headings is to consider them the outline for your document. Figure 6.10 shows a document in which each level of heading represents a new level of detail. Generally, it is good practice to use a new level whenever you have two to four items of equal importance. If more than four items are of the same importance under a parent heading, however, try breaking them into two different parent headings.

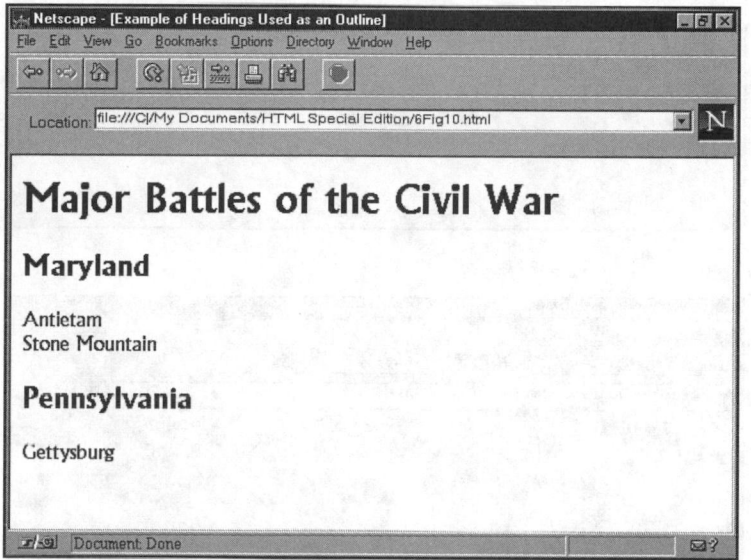

Fig. 6.10
Headings provide an outline of the document.

Adding Horizontal Lines

Another method for adding divisions to your documents is the use of horizontal lines. These provide a strong visual break between sections and are especially useful for separating the various parts of your document. Many browsers use an "etched" line that presents a crisp look and adds visual depth to the document.

You can create a horizontal line using the horizontal rule element, <HR>. This tag draws a shaded horizontal line across the browser's display. The <HR> tag is not a container and does not require an end tag. There is an implied paragraph break before and after a horizontal rule.

Figure 6.11 shows how horizontal rule tags are used, and figure 6.12 demonstrates their appearance in the Internet Explorer browser.

Fig. 6.11
Horizontal rules divide major sections.

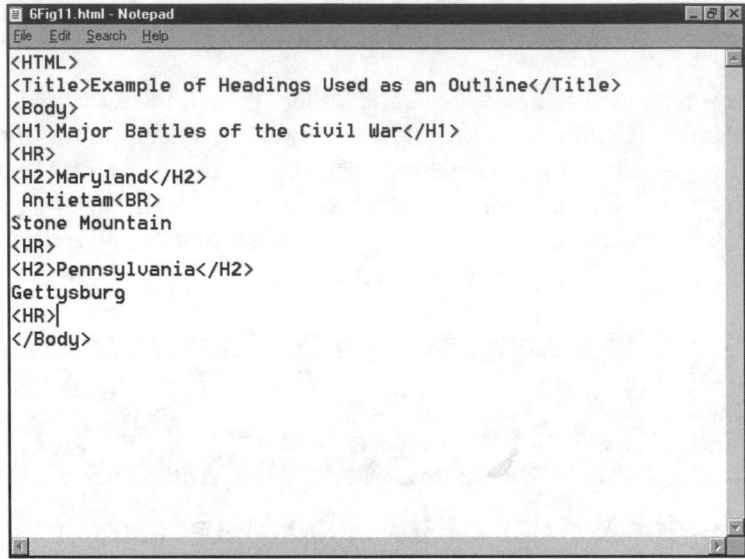

Fig. 6.12
Most browsers interpret the <HR> tag as an etched line.

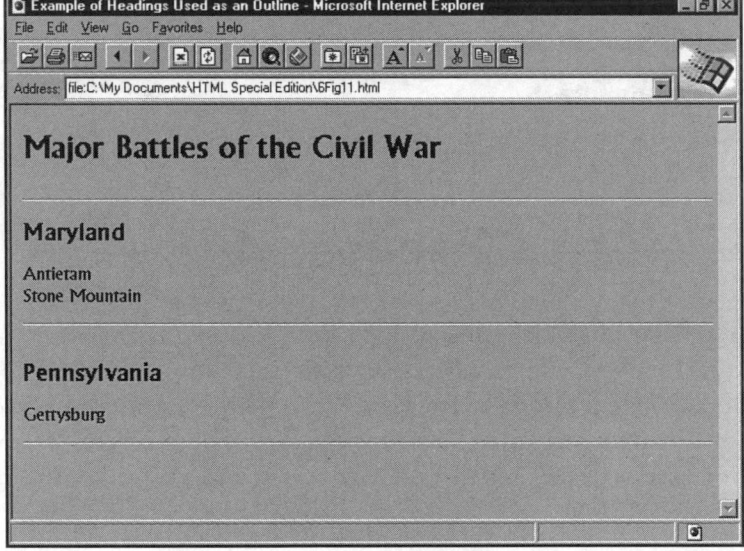

Horizontal rules should be reserved for instances when you want to represent a strong break in the flow of the text. Some basic guidelines for adding rules are that they should never come between a heading and the text that follows the heading and that they should not be used to create "white-space" in your document.

Formatting Your Text

Your readers are used to seeing sophisticated media presentations. The books, magazines, and even newspapers that they read are created with a variety of text styles designed to catch the eye and enable the reader to identify the significant elements quickly. This formatting makes up for the lack of voice inflection that would normally exist if the author were actually speaking.

Even with the addition of headings, the documents that you have created so far still lack interest. You are speaking to your readers in a monotone voice that displays none of the enthusiasm you have for your topic. This section covers methods that you can use to bring life to your documents.

> **Caution**
>
> Just as in any other form of computer publishing, it is possible to overuse any of these elements. Remember that attractive and informative documents will use these techniques sparingly.

Logical Format Elements

One of the ideas behind HTML is that documents should be laid out in a logical and structured manner. This gives the users of the documents as much flexibility as possible. With this in mind, the designers of HTML created a number of formatting elements that are labeled according to the purpose they serve rather than by their appearance. The advantage of this approach is that documents are not limited to a certain platform. Although they may look different on various platforms, the content and context will remain the same.

These logical format elements are as follows:

- <CITE>—The citation element is used to indicate the citation of a quotation. It can also be used to indicate the title of a book or article. An italic font is normally used to display citations.

  ```
  <CITE>Tom Sawyer</CITE> remains one of the classics of American literature.
  ```

- <CODE>—The code element is used to indicate a small amount of computer code. It is generally reserved for short sections, with longer sections noted using the <PRE> tag described later. Code normally appears in a monospaced font.

    ```
    One of the first lines that every C programmer learns is:
    <CODE>puts("Hello World!");</CODE>
    ```

- <EM>—The emphasis element is used to indicate a section of text that the author wants to identify as significant. Emphasis is generally shown in an italic font.

    ```
    The actual line reads, "Alas, poor Yorick. I knew him,
    ➥<EM>Horatio</EM>."
    ```

- <KBD>—The keyboard element is used to indicate a user entry response. A monospaced typewriter font is normally used to display keyboard text.

    ```
    To run the decoder, type <KBD>Restore</KBD> followed by your
    ➥password.
    ```

- <SAMP>—The sample element is used to indicate literal characters. These normally are a few characters that are intended to be precisely identified. Sample element text normally is shown in a monospaced font.

    ```
    The letters <SAMP>AEIOU</SAMP> are the vowels of the English
    ➥language.
    ```

- <STRONG>—The strong element is used to emphasize a particularly important section of text. Text using strong emphasis is normally set in a bold font.

    ```
    The most important rule to remember is <STRONG>Don't panic
    ➥</STRONG>!
    ```

- <VAR>—The variable element is used to indicate a dummy variable name. Variables are normally viewed in an italic font.

    ```
    The sort routine rotates on the <VAR>I</VAR>th element.
    ```

Note that all of these elements are containers, and as such, they require an end tag. Figure 6.13 shows how these logical elements look when seen in the Netscape browser.

You have probably noticed that a lot of these format styles use the same rendering. The most obvious question to ask is, why use them if they all look alike?

The answer is that these elements are logical styles. They indicate what the intention of the author was, not how the material should look. This is important because future uses of HTML may include programs that search the Web to find citations, for example, or the next generation of Web browsers may be able to read a document aloud. A program that can identify emphasis would be able to avoid the deadly monotone of current text-to-speech processors.

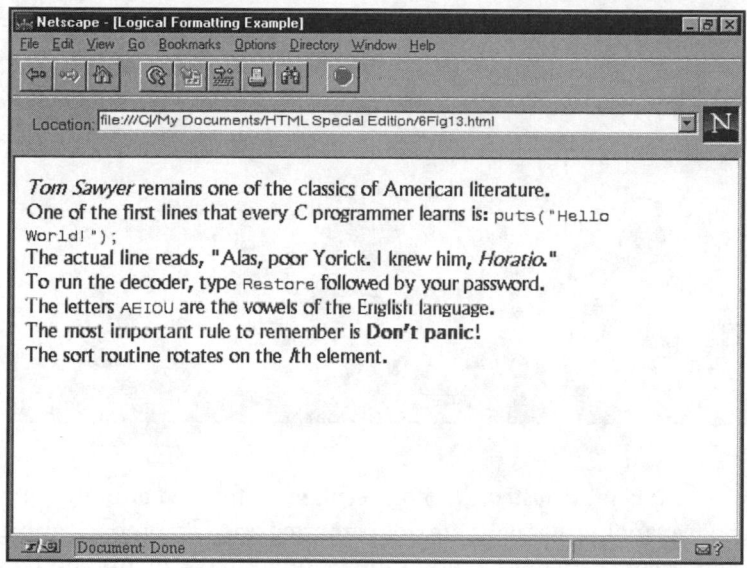

Fig. 6.13
Samples of the logical format elements are displayed in Netscape.

Physical Format Elements

Having said that HTML is intended to leave the appearance of the document up to the browser, I will now show you how you can have limited control over what the reader sees. In addition to the logical formatting elements, it is possible to use physical formatting elements that will change the appearance of the text in the browser. These physical elements are as follows:

- <B>—The bold element uses a bold font to display the text.

    ```
    This is in <B>bold</B> text.
    ```

- <I>—The italic element renders text using an italic font.

    ```
    This is in <I>italic</I> text.
    ```

- <TT>—The teletype element displays the contents with a monospaced typewriter font.

    ```
    This is in <TT>teletype</TT> text.
    ```

If the proper font isn't available, the viewer's browser must render the text in the closest possible manner. Once again, each of these is a container element and requires the use of an end tag. Figure 6.14 shows how these elements look in the Internet Explorer.

Fig. 6.14
Samples of the
physical format
elements are
shown in the
Internet Explorer.

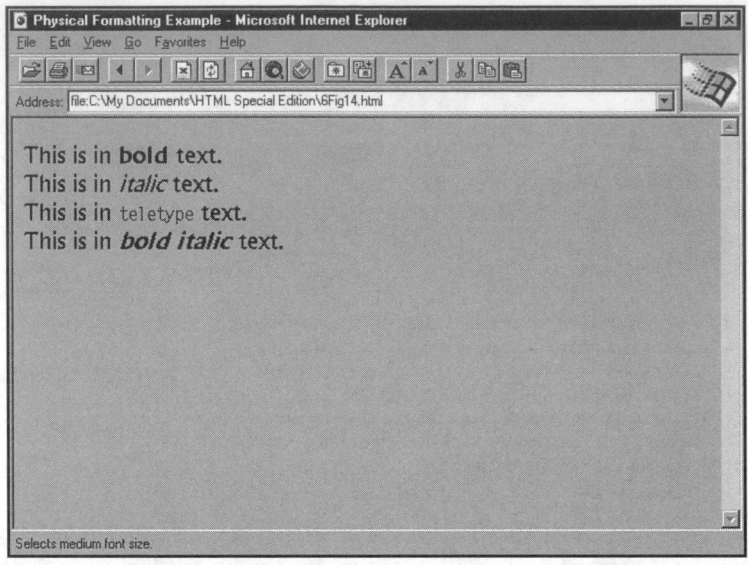

These elements can be nested, with one element contained entirely within another. Overlapping elements are not permitted and can produce unpredictable results. Figure 6.15 gives some examples of nested elements and how they can be used to create special effects.

Fig. 6.15
Logical and
physical format
elements can be
nested to create
additional format
styles.

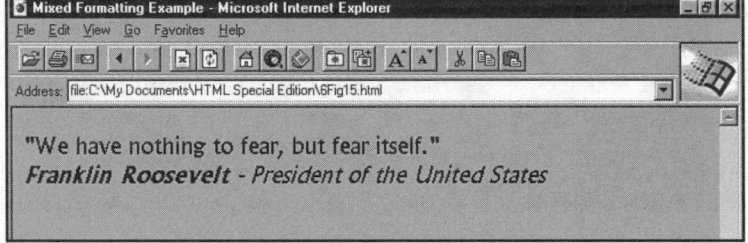

Additional Text Elements

Not everything that is in the body of your document is strictly paragraph text. There are other text elements that you might want to use in your documents. These are more specialized and should be reserved for cases that can't be handled any other way.

Special Characters

There are a number of special characters that are not found in the basic ASCII set. These include letters and characters used by other European languages, some mathematical symbols, and an assortment of other characters. These can be added to your document using the special character entity. The format of this entity is an ampersand (&) followed by the name of the character. The example in listing 6.4 shows how you can use the special characters.

Listing 6.4   Using Special Characters

```
<H3>The Use of Character Format Elements</H3>
This is how to add &ltEM&gtemphasis&lt/EM&gt to a word.<BR>
Which gives the result:<BR>
This is how to add <EM>emphasis</EM> to a word.<BR>
```

Figure 6.16 shows what this example looks like in Netscape.

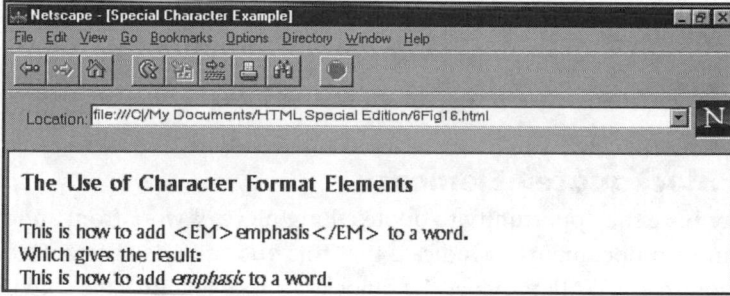

Fig. 6.16
Special characters can be added to HTML documents using the special character entities.

The Address Element

One of the most important elements for your documents is the address element. This is where you identify yourself as the author of the document and (optionally) let people know how they can get in touch with you. Any copyright information for the material in the page can be placed here as well. The address element is normally placed at either the top or bottom of a document. Figure 6.17 is an example of one such address element.

▶ See "Special Characters" in appendix A, p. 853

Note

A very important addition to the address is to indicate the date that you created the document and the last revision date. This will enable people to determine if they have already seen the most up-to-date version of the document.

II

Basic HTML Presentation

Fig. 6.17
The address element is used to identify the author or maintainer of the document.

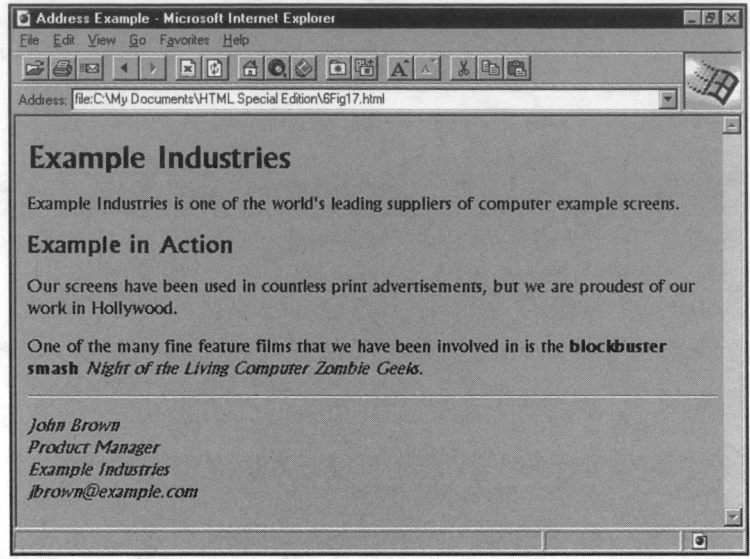

The <Blockquote> Element

You may have the opportunity to quote a long piece of work from another source in your document. To indicate that this quotation is different from the rest of your text, HTML provides the <Blockquote> element. This container functions as a body element within the body element and can contain any of the formatting or break tags. As a container, the <Blockquote> element is turned off by using the end tag.

The normal method used by most browsers to indicate a <Blockquote> element is to indent the text away from the left margin. Some text-only browsers may indicate a <Blockquote> using a character, such as the *greater than* sign, in the leftmost column on the screen. Because most browsers are now graphical in nature, the <Blockquote> element provides an additional service by enabling you to indent normal text from the left margin. This can add some visual interest to the document.

Figure 6.18 shows how a <Blockquote> is constructed, including some of the formatting available in the container. The results of this document when read into Netscape can be seen in figure 6.19.

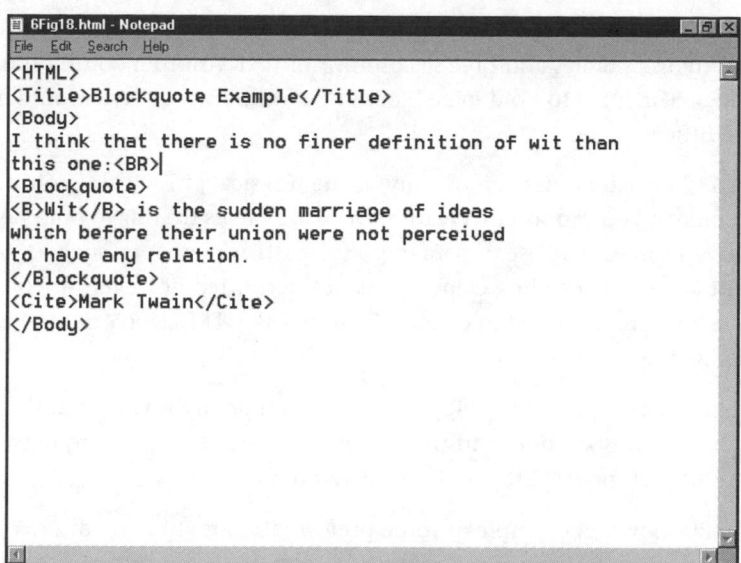

Fig. 6.18
The <Blockquote> element serves as a text container within the body.

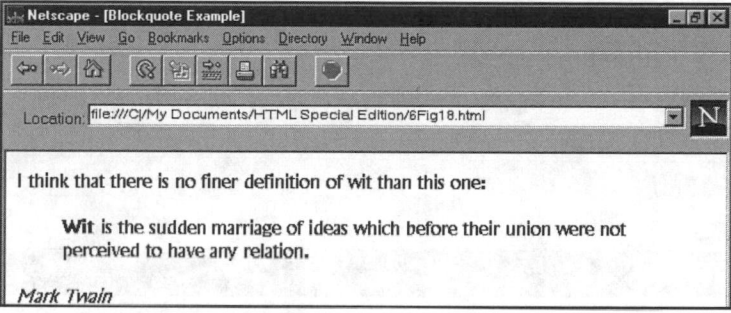

Fig. 6.19
This is the appearance of the document in Netscape.

Using Preformatted Text

Is it absolutely necessary to use paragraph and line break elements for formatting text? Well, not really; HTML provides containers that can hold preformatted text. This is text that gives you, the author, much more control over how the browser displays your document. The trade-off for this control is a loss of flexibility.

The <PRE> Container

The most useful and most common of the preformatting tags is the <PRE> container. Text in a <PRE> container is basically free-form with linefeeds causing the line to break at the beginning of the next clear line. Line break tags and paragraph tags are also supported. This versatility enables you to create such items as tables and precise columns of text. Another common use of the <PRE> element is to hold large blocks of computer code that would otherwise be difficult to read.

Text in a <PRE> container can use any of the physical or logical text formatting elements. You can use this feature to create tables that have bold headers or italicized values. The use of paragraph formatting elements, such as <Address> or any of the heading elements, is not permitted however. Anchor elements, which are described in chapter 7, "Linking HTML Documents," can be included within a <PRE> container.

The biggest drawback to the <PRE> container is that any text within it is displayed in a monospaced font in the reader's browser. This tends to make long stretches of preformatted text look clunky and out of place.

Figure 6.20 shows an example of some preformatted text in an editor. You can use the editor to line up the columns neatly before adding the character formatting tags. The result of this document is shown in figure 6.21.

Tip

HTML 3.0 introduces table elements that automatically line up text and graphic elements. If you are sure that your readers will have a proper browser, use these instead.

Caution

The definition for tab characters is that they will move the cursor to the next position, which is an integer multiple of eight. The official HTML specification recommends that tab characters not be used in preformatted text because they are not supported in the same way by all browsers. Spaces should be used for aligning columns.

The <XMP> Container

There are other preformatted container classes. The <XMP> container gives you the capability to create text that is already laid out. However, there are some disadvantages to the <XMP> container. HTML elements are not permitted inside of an <XMP> container. Browsers are not allowed to recognize any markup tags except the end tag. Unfortunately, many browsers don't comply with this standard properly, and the official specification for HTML lists <XMP> as obsolete.

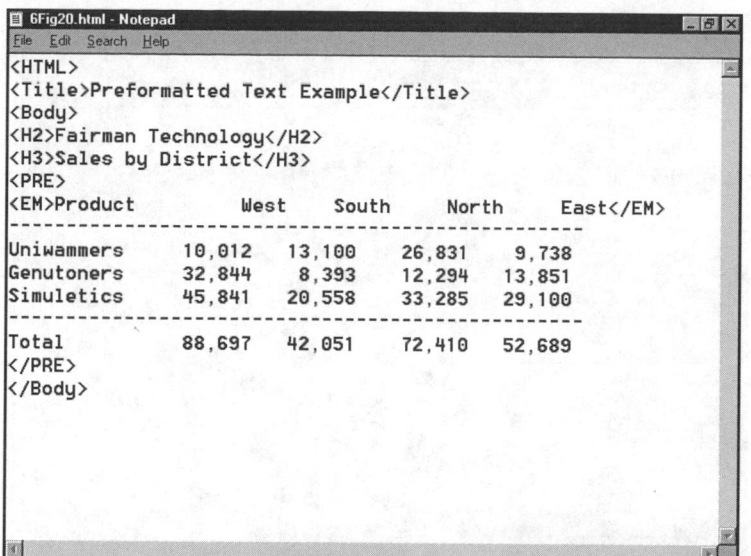

Fig. 6.20
Preformatted text
can be used to line
up columns of
numbers.

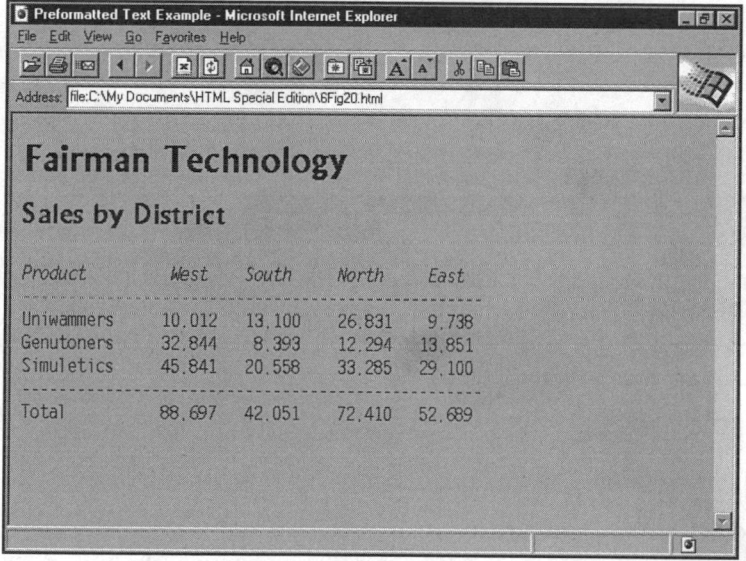

Fig. 6.21
A preformatted
table can look
professional in a
document.

Basic HTML Presentation

The <XMP> container must be rendered in a font size that permits at least
eighty characters on a line. Figure 6.22 is an example of the <XMP> container
in use.

Fig. 6.22
The <XMP>
container allows
preformatted text
in a proportional
font.

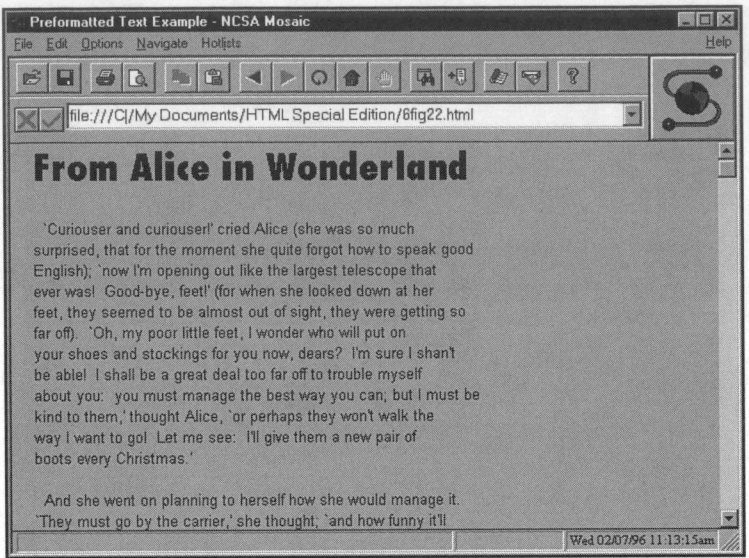

The <LISTING> Container

Another preformatted text container is the <LISTING> element. This container must display at least 132 characters on a line, but is in all other ways identical to the <XMP> container. The <LISTING> element is also obsolete as of HTML 2.0.

Caution

You should avoid using the <XMP> and <LISTING> elements unless it is absolutely necessary. Because they have been declared obsolete, browsers are not required to support them any longer. You will be more certain of what your readers are seeing if you use the <PRE> element instead.

Adding Hidden Comments

It is possible to add comments to your HTML document that won't be seen by a reader. The syntax for this is to begin your comment with the <! tag and to end it with the -> tag. Anything located between the two tags will not be displayed in the browser. This is a convenient way to leave notes for yourself or others. An example might be to add a comment when new material is added to a document that shows the date of the new addition.

> **Caution**
>
> Don't assume that your comments can't be seen by your readers. Most browsers allow the source of your document to be viewed directly, including any comments that you have added.

On the other hand, don't try to use comments to "comment out" any HTML elements. Some browsers interpret any > as the end of the comment. In any case, the chances of the browser becoming confused are pretty good, with the result that the rest of your document will be scrambled badly.

HTML 3.0 Additions

By now you may be wondering where all of these rules come from. The World Wide Web Coalition (or W3C, as it is known) is an unofficial body that publishes specifications for HTML and the Web. These specifications are prepared in draft format and then debated at great length across the Internet. At a predetermined date, a final specification is published and it becomes the standard for the Web.

Unfortunately, the W3C is an unofficial organization and can take a long time completing specifications. The problem with this process is that the developers of Web browsers and other software often introduce new features into HTML before they are approved by the W3C (and sometimes in a different form than is finally released).

The result of all of this maneuvering is that the HTML 3.0 specification (also known as HTML+) has never actually been finalized. Despite this, many of the most popular browsers already support the new proposed features. In this section, I will be referring to these features as HTML 3.0, even though such a standard doesn't actually exist yet.

> **Note**
>
> At this time, Netscape Navigator, Microsoft Internet Explorer, and NCSA Mosaic all support a significant fraction of the HTML 3.0 standard. Unfortunately, the feature sets of these three popular browsers don't completely overlap.

Text Positioning

One of the biggest additions to the standard in the HTML 3.0 specification is the ability to control the positioning of text horizontally across the page. This will give you the option of placing your headings either against the left margin, in the center of the page, or against the right margin. The flexibility to locate your headings where you want them will enable you to make your documents more appealing.

Alignment is specified for headings in the same way that it is for paragraphs, using the ALIGN attribute. The acceptable choices for heading alignment are left, right, center, and justify. Setting alignment to justify will start the heading at the left margin and add spaces to fill the entire line length, if possible. Figure 6.23 provides examples of how to specify heading alignment, and figure 6.24 shows the results of these examples.

Fig. 6.23
Alignment can be specified in the heading element.

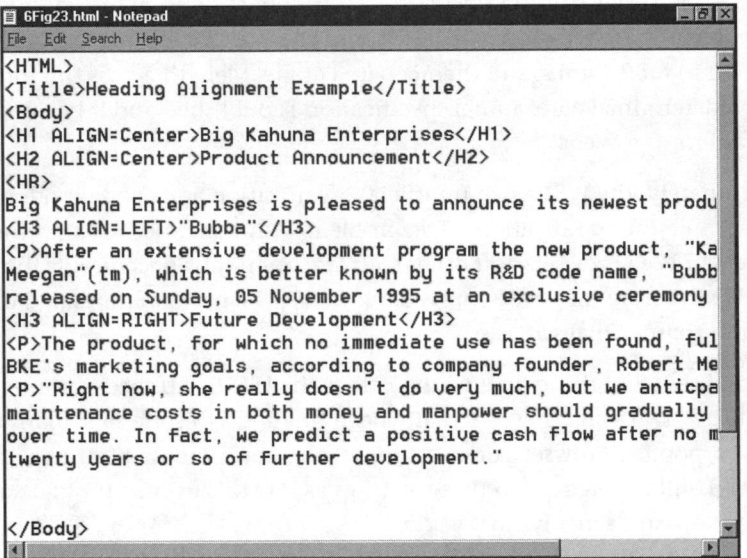

```
<HTML>
<Title>Heading Alignment Example</Title>
<Body>
<H1 ALIGN=Center>Big Kahuna Enterprises</H1>
<H2 ALIGN=Center>Product Announcement</H2>
<HR>
Big Kahuna Enterprises is pleased to announce its newest produ
<H3 ALIGN=LEFT>"Bubba"</H3>
<P>After an extensive development program the new product, "Ka
Meegan"(tm), which is better known by its R&D code name, "Bubb
released on Sunday, 05 November 1995 at an exclusive ceremony
<H3 ALIGN=RIGHT>Future Development</H3>
<P>The product, for which no immediate use has been found, ful
BKE's marketing goals, according to company founder, Robert Me
<P>"Right now, she really doesn't do very much, but we anticpa
maintenance costs in both money and manpower should gradually
over time. In fact, we predict a positive cash flow after no m
twenty years or so of further development."

</Body>
```

Additions to the
 Element

The <BR> element also has a new attribute that can be used for locating text adjacent to floating images. The CLEAR attribute can be set to LEFT, RIGHT, or ALL to break the line and start the next line of text where the left margin, right margin, or both margins are free of any images. Figure 6.25 shows an example of a <BR CLEAR=LEFT> element.

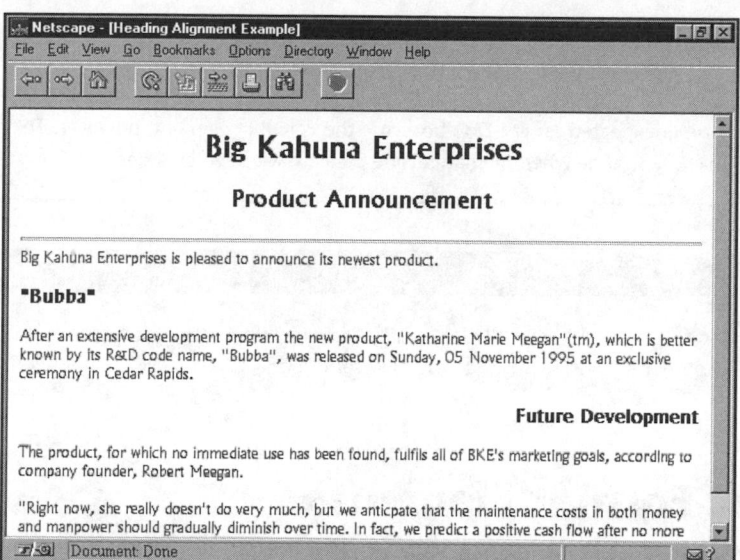

Fig. 6.24
The use of alignment can improve the appearance of headings.

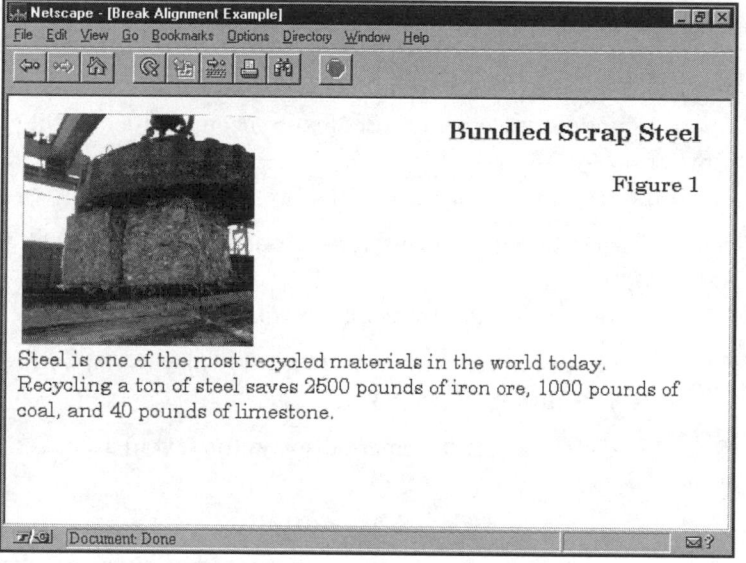

Fig. 6.25
The CLEAR attribute can be used to avoid wrapping text around images.

The <NOBR> Element

Just as there are instances in which it is convenient to break a line at a specified point, there are also times when you would like to avoid breaking a line at a certain point. Any text between a <NOBR> start tag and the associated end tag is guaranteed not to break across lines.

> **Note**
>
> This can be very useful for items, such as addresses, where an unfortunate line break can cause unexpected results. Don't overuse the <NOBR> element, however. Text can look very strange when the natural line breaks have been changed.

> **Tip**
>
> If you think you might need a break inside of an <NOBR> element, you can suggest a breaking point with a <WBR> tag. The browser will only use the <WBR> if it needs it.

Text Format Elements

The arrival of HTML 3.0 will also add a number of new physical font style elements to the ones listed above. These are used just as the older elements are, but with the caveat that if you use these elements, readers using some browsers may not see the effects that you intend.

The new elements are as follows:

- <U>—The underline element causes text to be underlined in the browser.

  ```
  This text is <U>underlined</U>.
  ```

- <S>—The strikethrough element draws a horizontal line through the middle of the text.

  ```
  This is a <S>strikethough</S> example.
  ```

- <BIG>—The big print element uses a larger font size to display the text.

  ```
  This is <BIG>big</BIG> text.
  ```

- <SMALL>—The small print element displays the text in a smaller font size.

  ```
  This is <SMALL>small</SMALL> text.
  ```

- <SUB>—The subscript element moves the text lower than the surrounding text and (if possible) displays the text in a smaller size font.

  ```
  This is a <SUB>subscript</SUB>.
  ```

- <SUP>—The superscript element moves the text higher than the surrounding text and (if possible) displays the text in a smaller size font.

  ```
  This is a <SUp>superscript</SUP>.
  ```

> **Note**
>
> Netscape Navigator uses an alternative tag, <STRIKE>, for strikethrough. Microsoft Internet Explorer and NCSA Mosaic permit both <STRIKE> and <S>.
>
> Netscape Version 2.0 does not recognize the <U> element.
>
> Internet Explorer Version 2.0 doesn't support <BIG> and <SMALL> or <SUB> and <SUP>.
>
> Is your head spinning yet?

Body Element Attributes

A number of new attributes for the <BODY> element have been added. These give the document author considerable latitude in the display of the text by adding them to the body start tag. Once any of them have been used, they are used for the remainder of the document. For example, change the text to a bright purple as follows:

```
<BODY TEXT="#ff00ff">
```

The following are the new attributes that can be used in the body element:

- TEXT changes the color of the text to the color specified. The color is set using a hexadecimal red-green-blue triplet and the format TEXT="#rrggbb", where rr, gg, and bb, are the red, green, and blue elements, respectively. Note that the color defined may not be available on the reader's browser, in which case, the browser will approximate the color the best it can. The default color for TEXT is black.

- LINK defines the color used to highlight unvisited links and uses the same format as the TEXT attribute. The default color for LINK is blue.

- ALINK defines the color used to highlight an active link and uses the same format as the TEXT attribute. The default color for ALINK is red.

- VLINK defines the color used to highlight visited links and uses the same format as the TEXT attribute. The default color for VLINK is purple.

- BGCOLOR defines the color used for the background of the text. This is not actually part of the HTML 3.0 definition, but it is supported by all of the most common browsers, so I've included it here. The background color is defined using the same format as the TEXT attribute. The default color for BGCOLOR is white.

- BACKGROUND is set to an URL that points to an image file used as the background for the document. Most browsers will tile the entire frame of the document with the image if it is smaller than the frame.

Note

If a BACKGROUND image is specified but not loaded, the browser will then attempt to use the BGCOLOR attribute. If BGCOLOR hasn't been specified, the browser will ignore the TEXT, LINK, ALINK, and VLINK attributes in order to avoid the possibility of the text disappearing against the background.

## CHAPTER 7

Linking HTML Documents

by John Jung

As you learned in chapter 4, "Building Blocks of HTML," putting a link in your home page to someone else's page is pretty easy. But now you're ready for something more advanced: linking your page to other resources on the Internet. The World Wide Web is just one of many resources on the Net; creating links to others is important. You don't always need to link your home page, but knowing how is good if you ever want to do it. Fortunately, creating links to other resources on the Net through your home page is very easy.

In this chapter, you learn about the following:

- Why you might want to link to other resources
- How to link to e-mail
- How to link to news
- How to link to FTP
- How to link to Gopher
- How to link to WAIS
- How to link to Telnet
- How these links work together

Linking to Other Net Resources

The World Wide Web is a popular part of the entire Internet, but many other resources are available. Most of them were around long before the Web was even born, and as a result, they have a lot of stuff on them. Also as a result of the Web's newness, the other resources sometimes have a much wider audience base. Whether you're designing a home page for yourself or for your company, you may want to know how to link to those resources.

These resources can take various shapes, from the peanut gallery that is Usenet news to personal e-mail to the capability to access other computers through Telnet. Although you can create your own versions of these resources using forms (see Part IV, "Forms and CGI"), most of the time you wouldn't want to do so. For example, you could easily create a page with many HTML form tags, text elements, and a submit button for e-mail, but simply creating a link to e-mail with a particular address would be easier. This way, you can more easily update the page because you don't have to worry about which forms to read. Also, sometimes browsers have built-in support for some of the other resources, giving the user faster response time.

You especially want to create links to other resources on the Net if you're already using a resource. If you already have a Gopher site with information that's updated automatically, why rebuild it to fit the Web? Just adding a hyperlink to your Gopher site makes more sense. Similarly, if you're running a BBS that's on the Internet, putting in a Telnet link to it makes more sense. There's no reason for re-creating, or even mirroring, your BBS through forms for the Web.

Creating a Link to E-Mail

The single most popular activity on the Internet is sending e-mail. More people use e-mail than any other resource on the Net. The reason is quite simple: If you're on the Internet, you have an e-mail address. The provider that gives you access to the Net often has at least one e-mail program available for your use. Most modern e-mail programs offer a friendly interface, with no complex commands to learn.

You'll most likely want to put in an e-mail link when you want people to give you feedback on a particular topic. Whatever it is you want comments on—be it your home page or your company's product—if you want to know what people think, use an e-mail link. E-mail links are also useful for reporting problems, such as a problematic or missing link. Typically, the Web master of a particular site should put these types of links to himself or herself. You really have no reason *not* to put in a link to your e-mail address.

◀ See chapter 4, "Building Blocks of HTML," p. 87, for information on the basic structure of the hyperlink.

Creating a link to an e-mail address is similar to creating a link to another home page. The only difference is the reference point for your anchor element. Normally, you put a link to a home page around some text as in the following:

```
<A HREF="http://www.mycom.com/myhome.html">Go to my home page</A>.
```

Linking to e-mail is just as simple. Instead of entering **http**, which specifies a home page, type **mailto:** to specify an e-mail address. And instead of specifying an URL, put in your full e-mail address. So the preceding example now looks like this:

```
<A HREF="mailto:me@mycom.com">Send me E-mail</A>.
```

The link created with the preceding HTML code will look like any other hypertext link. You can easily mix and match hyperlinks to different resources, and they'll all look the same (see fig. 7.1). When this link is selected, the browser opens its own e-mail interface for the user. Each interface is different, but most of them automatically get your e-mail address and real name, and prompt you for a subject.

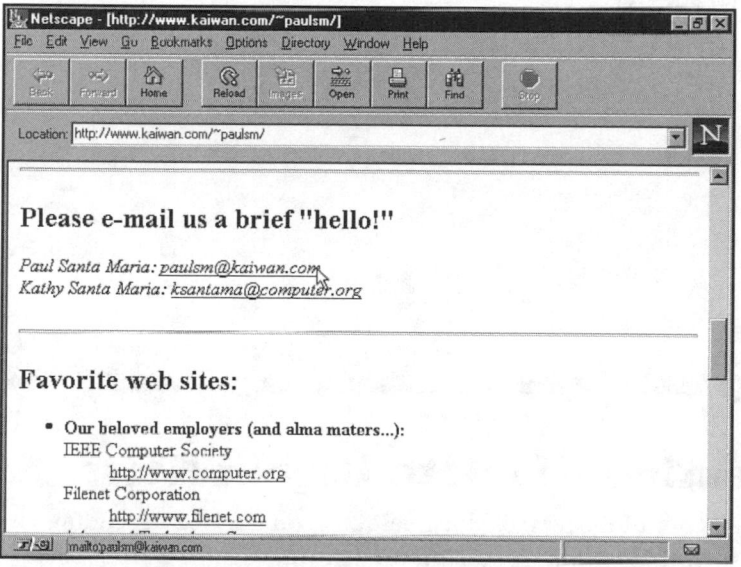

Fig. 7.1
E-mail links look just like regular hypertext links.

Tip

If you're creating a Web page of limited distribution, you don't need to put in your entire e-mail address. This often occurs in very large companies or universities, where there are internally available Web pages. Instead of putting in your complete e-mail address, just use your username. So instead of putting in:

```
<A HREF="mailto:me@mysite.com">
```

you'd use:

```
<A HREF="mailto:me">
```

Because the e-mail link is a standard URL and easily implemented, many browsers have built-in support for it. As a result, when people click an e-mail link, the Web browser will put up a primitive mail program. A few companies offer a full set of Internet applications, from an e-mail program, to a newsreader, to a Web browser. Oftentimes, these work in conjunction with each other. Consequently, when you click an e-mail link, these Internet packages will start up their own e-mail program (see fig. 7.2).

Fig. 7.2
Netscape will launch its own internal and full-featured e-mail program when you click an e-mail link.

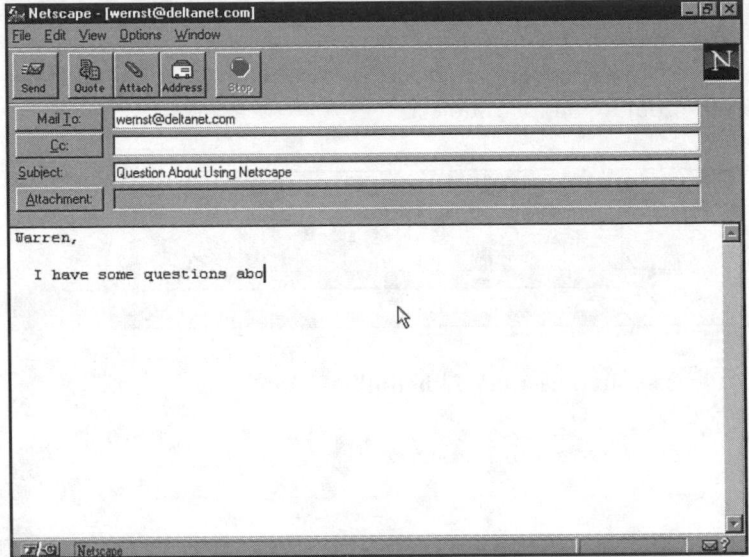

Creating a Link to Usenet News

Usenet is one of the best, or worst, resources on the Net, depending on whom you ask. Anybody with an opinion can tell you what he thinks. That person may not know what he is talking about, but he can let you know what he thinks. Usenet is the ultimate embodiment of the freedom of speech, letting everybody say anything they want.

This ability of anybody anywhere on the Net having a voice could be an asset to your home page. Often, you may want to put in a link to Usenet when you want people to read for more information. If your home page has some information about HTML authoring, for example, you might want readers to go to a particular newsgroup for more help. You can also include such a link so that people can see what differing opinions are. If you have a certain political view and want others to see what the opposition is, a Usenet news link would be helpful.

Creating a link to a Usenet newsgroup is pretty simple; this kind of link is also just a derivative of the basic hypertext link. As you did with the e-mail link, you need to modify two parts in the anchor reference. When you're creating a Usenet link, enter **news:** instead of **http:**. Likewise, instead of specifying a particular URL, you put in a specific newsgroup, as follows:

```
For more information, see <A
HREF="news:news.newusers.questions">news.newusers.questions</A>.
```

As you can see in figure 7.3, the Usenet news hyperlink looks identical to other links. When a user selects such a link, the browser tries to access the user's Usenet news server. If the news server is available to that person, the browser then goes to the specified newsgroup. The user can then read as much as he or she likes in that particular group.

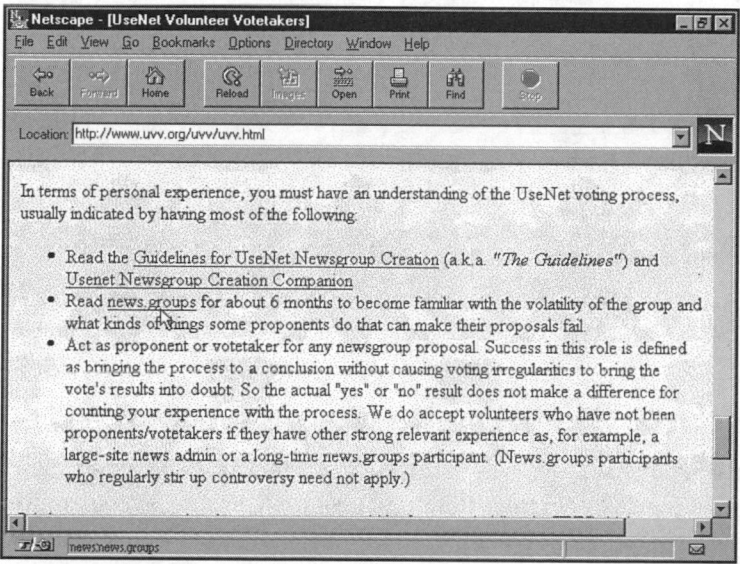

Fig. 7.3
Usenet news links allow you to make a point to people interested in your topic.

II

Basic HTML Presentation

Caution

When a user clicks a Usenet news link, his or her browser tries to access the newsgroup in question. Because it's this user's browser and environment, he or she might not have access to the group you specified. Not all Internet providers have access to the same newsgroups. When you're creating such links, be mindful that not everybody will necessarily be able to access them.

How a Usenet hyperlink is handled is left entirely up to the Web browser the person is using. Many of them treat each article in a newsgroup as an individual hyperlink. Often, there's little in the way of sophisticated newsreading features. Some companies, such as Netscape, offer an entire suite of programs, including a Usenet newsreader (see fig. 7.4). In these cases, the newsreading portion of that suite is started up.

Fig. 7.4
When a Usenet link is accessed, some sophisticated Web browsers will start up their own internal newsreader.

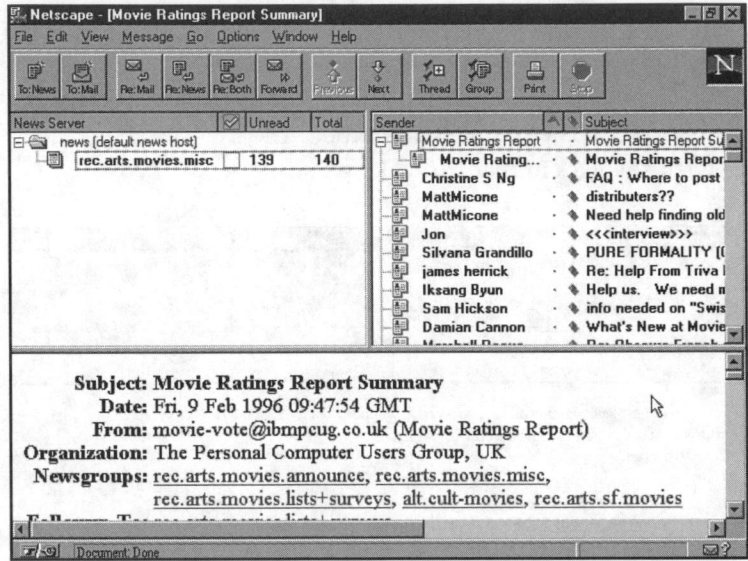

Making FTP Available on Your Site

Another popular activity is accessing an FTP site. FTP, or File Transfer Protocol, allows users to copy files from other computers (the FTP site) onto their own computers. This popular method allows companies to distribute their demo software or patches to their products.

Putting in a link to an FTP site allows users to get a specific file from a particular location. This capability is useful for companies and shareware authors in making their products available. This type of link is also great for people who review software, allowing them to let users get the files being reviewed. Also, people who have files, such as FAQs and interesting pictures that they want others to get to easily, might want to put in a link to an FTP site.

You create a link to an FTP site the same way you create other links, and they look the same, too (see fig. 7.5). You enter **ftp:** instead of the usual **http:**, and you change the URL address to **//*sitename***. Simply put, the site name looks the same as the URL address. You need to make sure that the site name you specify points to a machine that accepts FTP connections. FTP links are almost always supported by the browser natively. You can create a typical FTP link as follows:

```
You can get the FAQ <A HREF="ftp://ftp.mysite.com/pub/FAQ">here</A>.
```

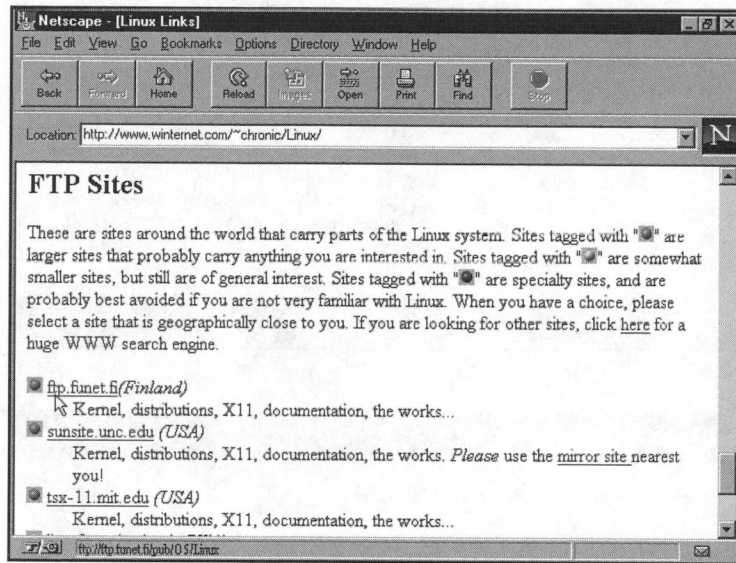

Fig. 7.5
An FTP link allows many people to access a particular file.

II

Basic HTML Presentation

Note

If you don't specify a particular file name, the browser will list the files in the directory you specified. This is particularly useful if you want the user to have access to multiple files. Programs available on multiple machines, or large files broken up into several chunks, typically fall into this category.

Technically speaking, there isn't too much of a difference between FTP and the Web. As a result, Web browsers support FTP links without needing another program. The browsers will give you a list of the files in the current directory, and indicate which ones are directories and which ones are files (see fig. 7.6). If you click a directory, it'll change into that directory. If you click a file, the browser will directly download the file.

Fig. 7.6
Web browsers will
have no problems
handling FTP links
by themselves.

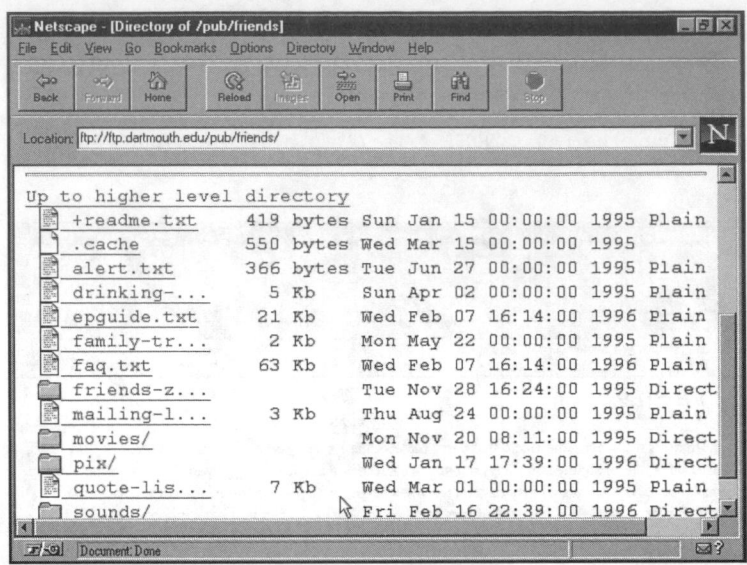

Troubleshooting

Some people can't access some of my FTP links.

If a lot of people are reporting that they can't access some of your FTP links, try finding others. This error usually comes up when you have an FTP link to a particularly busy FTP site. You should try to locate other (less busy) FTP sites that have the same file you're pointing to.

Anonymous versus Non-Anonymous FTP Links

By default, when FTP links are activated, the FTP connection that's made is known as *anonymous FTP*. This means that the FTP site the user is trying to access doesn't care who the user is. All the anonymous FTP site cares about is sending and receiving files to anybody who logs in with the username "anonymous." The password is often the e-mail address of the user, but this isn't necessary. Anonymous FTP allows software companies and the like to distribute their products to a very wide audience.

A *non-anonymous FTP* is where the FTP site is very particular about who can access it. To get access to a non-anonymous FTP site, you must have an account on the FTP site itself. Basically, you can't get into a non-anonymous FTP site unless you're already in. This is probably the most widely used FTP site around, as many companies allow employees to FTP into their own accounts.

> **Note**
>
> You can easily change an anonymous FTP link into a non-anonymous one. Simply put a **username** and the "**@**" sign before the **sitename**. This will cause most Web browsers to automatically attempt to log in as **username**. The browser will then prompt the user for the password for the login id.

Linking Your Home Page to a Gopher Site

Before there was the World Wide Web, there was something known as Gopher. It was originally designed by the University of Minnesota (the Golden Gophers) as a way of making information that's spread out easily available. Gopher has probably been the Internet resource most affected by the Web, often being superseded by it. The biggest difference between Gopher and the Web is that it is very difficult for individual people to create their own Gopher sites or holes.

Though Gopher sites are not as prevalent as they once were, they still have a strong following. You can typically find Gopher sites at places that dispense a lot of automated information. Although the site could often easily be converted to HTML, it simply hasn't bothered to. This conversion of Gopher data into usable HTML code is typically the work of a programmer, and often not worth the effort. Putting in an HTML link to a Gopher site allows people browsing your page easy access to a great deal of information.

You can create a link to a Gopher hole by modifying the same two elements of the anchor reference. Change the **http:** to **gopher:**, and change the URL to **//sitename**. The site name must be a valid Internet host name address. The link created looks like every other type of hypertext link (see fig. 7.7), and built-in support is provided by most Web browsers. A Gopher hole link usually looks something like the following:

```
For more information, go <A HREF="gopher://gopher.mysite.com">here</A>.
```

Just like FTP, Gopher is a Net resource that is built into HTML. Consequently, most Web browsers will support any links to a Gopher site internally. That is, you don't need a Gopher-specific application to go to a Gopher site; the browser will take care of it for you. But just like FTP, the built-in support for Gopher is often very bland (see fig. 7.8).

Fig. 7.7
Links to Gopher holes are great for accessing large amounts of automated information.

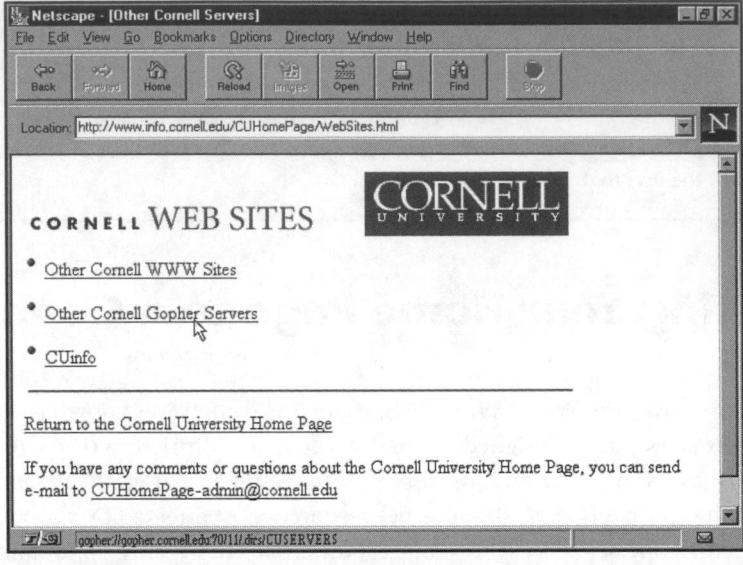

Fig. 7.8
There's only so much a Web browser can do to liven up the text-based Gopher resource.

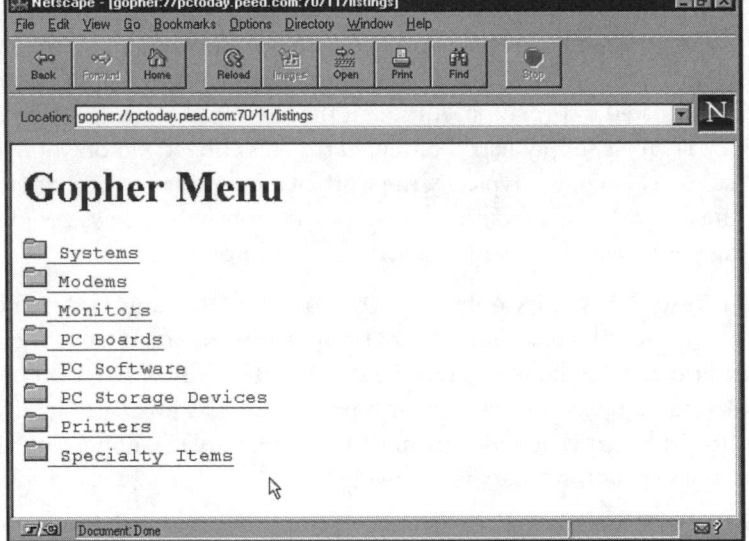

Providing Access to a Large Database with a WAIS Link

WAIS stands for Wide Area Information System, which basically means "lots of large databases that you can search through." WAIS was specially designed by WAIS Corp. as a way of accessing large amounts of information. This capability is very different from what Gopher and the Web do in that WAIS was intended to cover very large chunks of information. Typically, databases that contained several million entries were considered appropriate for WAIS.

WAIS is generally accessed through a search engine because most people don't want to plod through such large stores of information. When WAIS was first introduced, custom front ends allowed easy access to a WAIS database. With the advent of the Web, however, most WAIS databases now have HTML front ends to their databases (see fig. 7.9). Now you can simply fill out a Web form and click a button, and the WAIS search is underway.

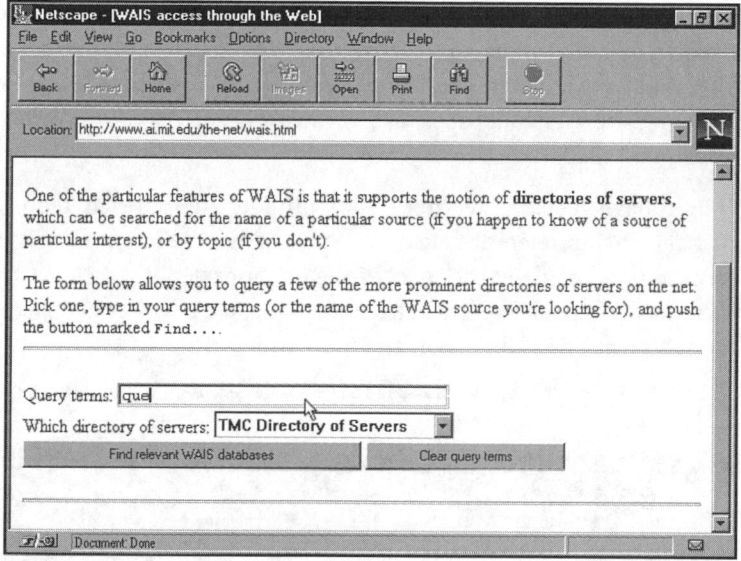

Fig. 7.9
Most WAIS databases are now searchable through HTML forms.

You can create a link in your home page to a WAIS database as easily as you do with all the other links. You have to modify the same two anchor reference elements to hold the correct information. Instead of using **http:**, enter the prefix **wais:**, and change the URL location to be the address of a WAIS database:

```
To search for a number in your area, click <A HREF="wais://wais.mysite.com">here</A>.
```

> **Note**
>
> Most browsers don't have built-in support of WAIS database searches. If you put in a link to one of these databases, be sure to include some sort of reference to where users can get a WAIS client. Of course, if the WAIS database you're pointing to has HTML forms support, you don't need to worry about including such information.

Accessing Remote Computers with Telnet Links

The capability to access other computers is not something new to the Web; it's been around for a long time. This access has always been achieved with a UNIX program called Telnet, which doesn't stand for anything in particular. Telnet allowed people to try to log in to a remote machine, much the same way some people access their Internet providers. The Web allows for support of accessing remote machines through a Telnet link to a remote computer.

Usually, people trying to get on a secure system are the people for whom you want to provide a Telnet link. People who provide access to a private, Internet-accessible BBS will most likely want to put in a Telnet link. Also, companies that offer a BBS for customer support may want to make use of a link to a Telnet site. Generally speaking, for most home pages, you have little or no reason to include a link to a remote site.

As you might have guessed, creating a Telnet link to a remote site requires modifying the anchor reference element. You change the **http:** to **telnet:**. You also need to change the URL part of the anchor reference to *hostname*. Hypertext links that refer to Telnet sites look the same as other links (see fig. 7.10). A typical Telnet link takes the following form:

```
Click <A HREF="wais://wais.mysite.com">here</A> to access our BBS.
```

Fig. 7.10
Usually, only BBSs have a need for Telnet links.

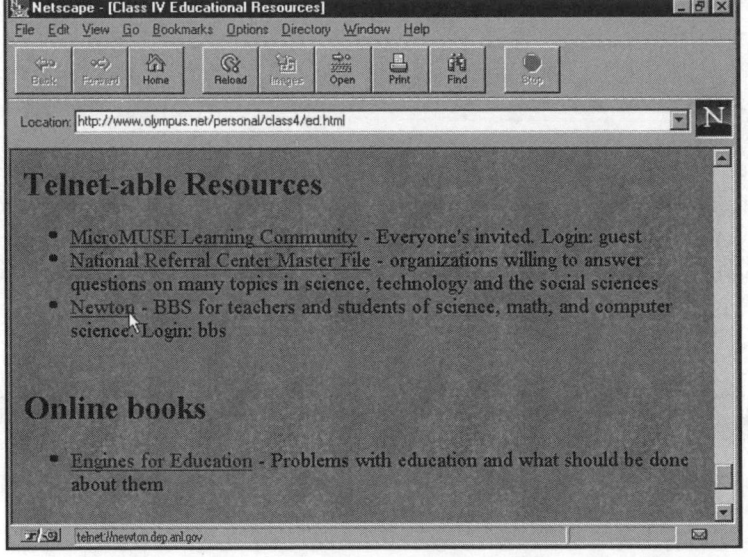

Note

Most Web browsers do not support Telnet activity natively. They typically depend on an external application to talk correctly to the remote machine. If you put in a link to Telnet to another site, be sure to also include some reference to a Telnet client.

Note

There are a few operating systems that have built-in Telnet capability. Among the OSs that have this are Windows NT and UNIX.

Even though Telnet is a rather simple Net resource, it's also a very difficult one. Among the many problem are issues of how to display the remote session and how to interpret keypresses. As simple as these problems may appear, they're hard to implement in a Web browser. For these reasons, most Web browsers don't have support for Telnet. Rather, they leave it up to the individual person to find a Telnet program and set it up (see fig. 7.11).

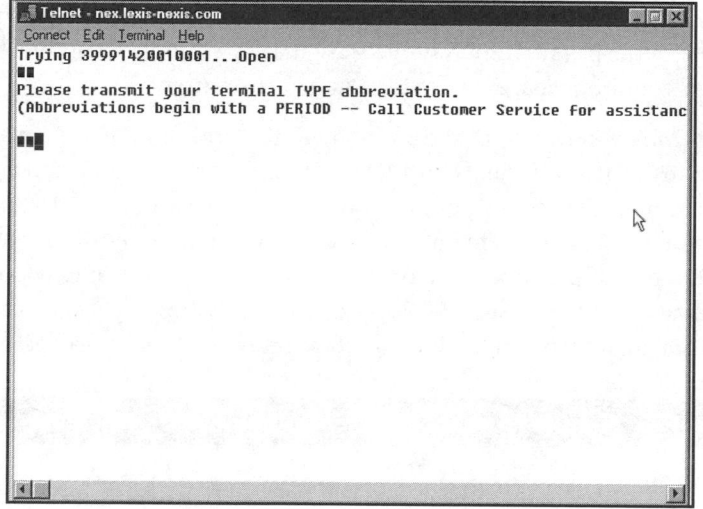

Fig. 7.11
Most Web browsers don't support the Telnet links internally, so you need another program to access these links.

Tip

Some Web browsers allow something extra in the anchor reference. Simply add the username you want the person to log in as, followed by the "@" sign, before the *sitename*. So that instead of:

```
Access my <A HREF="telnet://mysite.com/">system!</A>
```

You can have:

```
Access my <A HREF="telnet://john@mysite.com/>system</A>
```

On those browsers that support this, the Web browser will pop up a little notice. This notice tells the user what login name should be used to access the system.

How Links Work Together

You may be wondering how well these hypertext links work with each other. The answer is: very well. Even though the links are different, they all look and behave the same. This common behavior exists because of the anchor reference that all hyperlinks use. Some may need client programs not built in to a Web browser, but that's not a big deal. This identical look and feel of various hypertext links allows home pages to have a consistent feel. Consistency in a home page is important because it allows people to simply "know" they're in your home page without looking at the current URL.

The best thing you can do is to treat all hypertext links in the same manner, with slightly different formats. Just take the same basic anchors, add a reference, and put in the correct pointer to that reference (see table 7.1). As a Web author, you must always remember that each person looking at your home page could be using any browser available. No hard and fast rules about what resources all browsers will support even exist. Whatever resource you want to link to, though, try to include a link to a location where the user can get a client.

Table 7.1 Sample Formats for Creating Links

Link To...	What to Use	Sample Link
Another home page	http://*sitename*/	http://www.mysite.com/
An e-mail address	mailto:*address*	mailto:me@mysite.com
A Usenet newsgroup	news:*newsgroupname*	news:news.newusers.questions
An FTP site	ftp://*sitename*/	ftp://ftp.mysite.com/
A Gopher site	gopher://*sitename*/	gopher://gopher.mysite.com/
A WAIS database	wais://*sitename*/	wais://wais.mysite.com/
Another computer	telnet://sitename/	telnet://bbs.mysite.com/

## CHAPTER 8

Common Conventions in HTML Documents

by John Jung

After you've surfed the Web long enough, you may notice some things that appear consistently in Web pages. Obviously, no written law requires you to put these elements in your home pages. But they take up little room, and adding them is just a good idea. In some cases, these conventions are also very useful for the casual user. In this chapter, you learn about what some of the common conventions are and how to put them into your home page.

Also in this chapter, you learn about the following:

- Create alternative versions
- Specify where hyperlinks go
- Tell users how big the files are
- Sign and date your home page
- List who created the home page

Working Around Pictures

When you're designing and creating a Web page, you should always remember that not everybody is using Netscape as his or her browser. Some people are using old graphical browsers because they're accustomed to them. Others use proprietary browsers that their Internet Service Providers (ISP) give them. Some people accessing your Web site might even be using a text-only browser. Whatever they're using, however, you should try to accommodate them as much as possible.

Graphics and imagemaps are powerful tools for your Web page and can be particularly troublesome. The foremost consideration when putting images in, is letting people with nongraphical browsers see them. The second important consideration is the file format of the graphic itself. You want to try to put your image in a format that is supported natively by as many browsers as possible.

Navigating Without Imagemaps

Imagemaps are basically images that reference different URLs when different locations of the image are clicked. Unfortunately, with imagemaps, unlike images, no built-in provision exists for providing a textual alternative. Your only remedy is to provide generic hypertext links that go to the different areas in your imagemap. You can get around imagemaps in two basic ways: by putting the generic hypertext links on the same page or creating a separate page. Regardless of which method you pick, if you're going to use imagemaps, you should at least use one of these methods.

Same Page, Same Links

◀ See chapter 4 for information on creating hyperlinks.

One of the most common methods of getting around imagemaps is to put the generic links on the same page as the imagemap (see fig. 8.1). This method is useful for individuals and companies that are working with limited disk space. By using generic links with each page of an imagemap, you can easily update each page. Instead of trying to find the different versions of the same page, you just have one page to change. Creating this page is easy; you simply designate a portion of a particular page to having only regular hypertext links. You may want to use a horizontal rule to specify where the generic text-only section begins and ends.

Fig. 8.1
One way of helping people get around your site without imagemaps is to have regular hypertext links on the same page.

Horizontal rules are good ways to separate generic links and advanced HTML elements

Generic links

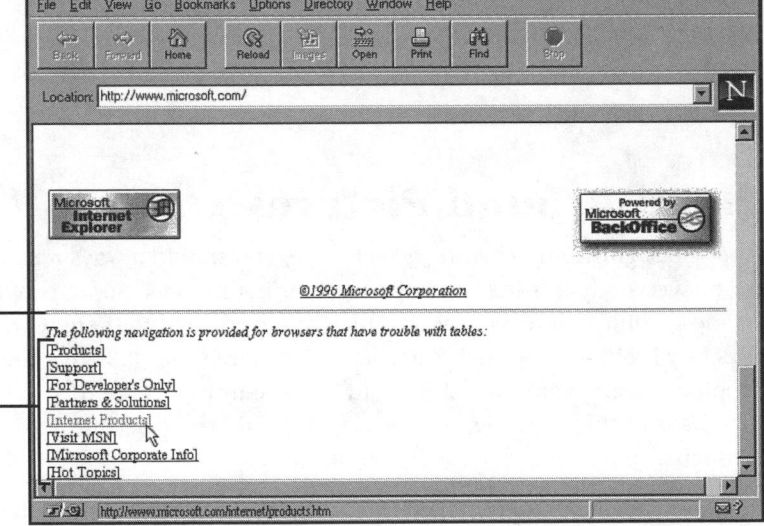

> **Caution**
>
> When you're creating the generic hypertext links section, be absolutely sure they are generic. Many Web authors put in links to generic Web pages in the middle of special HTML elements. When creating a link to a generic HTML page, make sure you're not using frames or tables. Just stick to the basics on your generic Web page link.
>
> For older and text-only browsers, these advanced HTML elements are ignored. As a result, the generic link section is completely inaccessible. So instead of trying to help people out, you're only frustrating them more. If you're still unsure whether or not your generic link is accessible, try it out yourself. Get a text-only Web browser and access your page.

Different Page, Same Links

Another method of allowing people to get to different parts of your Web site without using imagemaps is to have a separate page that has the same links. That is, you keep two versions of every page with an imagemap—one with the imagemap and one without. The advantage of this method is that it almost ensures that you will have links that are accessible to all. With this, you also can take advantage of the custom features for each browser. The obvious downside to this method is that you have to maintain all these pages. If you choose this option, put in a regular link to the generic page on the page with your imagemap (see fig. 8.2).

Fig. 8.2
Be sure to put the link to your generic Web page in an easily accessible spot.

II

Basic HTML Presentation

> **Tip**
>
> If you decide to go with the multiple Web page route, you should consider putting in links to the other pages. In other words, on your generic page, put in links to your Netscape and Internet Explorer pages. In your Netscape page, put separate links for the other two. And on the Internet Explorer page, put in links to the Netscape and generic pages.

Directing the User

HTML doesn't force you to, but as a general rule, you should consider telling people where links go in your Web page. This convention isn't always used by individuals, but most sites that deal with lots of information use them. There are two situations when you should tell the user the destination of the links: large collection of various information and widely distributed information. This need to know where links go and what they contain is the foundation of many Web page databases.

Information from Many Sources

One frequent place that you see the destination of links is in Web pages that refer to many different sources. Usually, fan-based home pages, such as for actors, actresses, models, and TV shows, use this convention. This is especially true if the object of the fan Web page is very popular (see fig. 8.3).

Fig. 8.3
Fans of the TV show "Friends" can easily access any number of resources related to it.

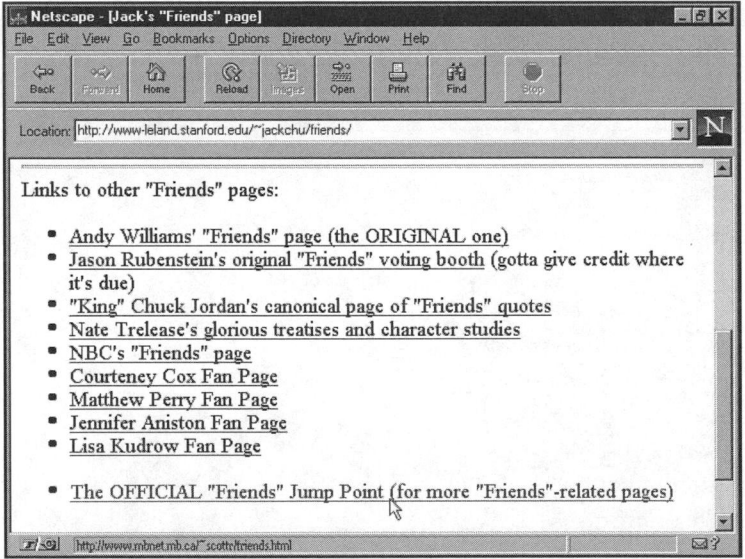

This central listing of the various Web pages, FTP sites, and mailing lists is invaluable to the fans. To add your own central listing, either before or after the link, put in some indication of the destination of that link. Refer to it by either the machine name or the name of that particular Web page author.

Distribution of Information

When you're distributing information, you also may want to tell users where links go. Typically, this situation happens when you have information that either you want many people to have or they are demanding themselves. Individuals and companies that market very popular products fall into this category. If the site has numerous customers from all over the world, telling users where links go will help reduce the load on U.S.-based FTP sites.

Also, maintainers of Frequently Asked Questions (FAQs) may want to have pages that refer to multiple locations (see fig. 8.4). This way, they can lighten the load of the constant accesses of the FAQs. By following this convention, especially popular FTP sites will become more accessible to everybody on the Net.

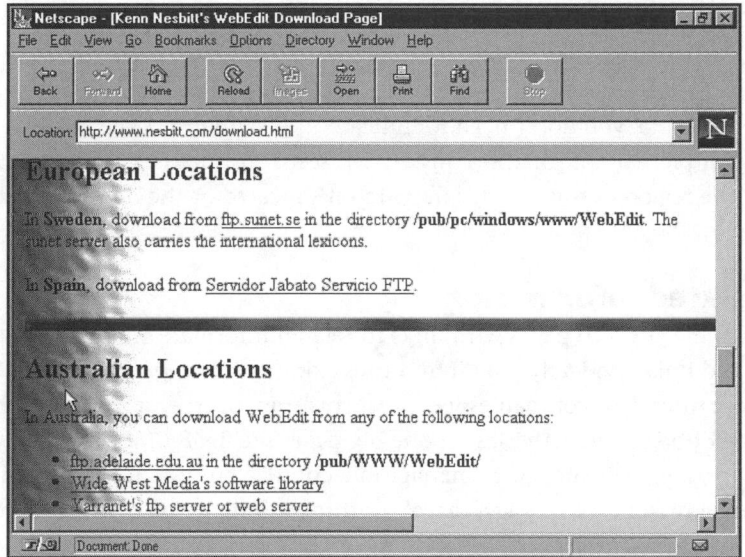

Fig. 8.4
You can get a copy of this program from whichever location is more convenient for you.

II

Basic HTML Presentation

Related Information

In some cases, you may want to specify the destination of links for related information. If you're building a Web page that is the repository for a wide range of information, you may want to indicate where links go.

Most individuals won't encounter this situation, but some companies will. For extremely large companies with many divisions spread out, a centralized page with links to the rest of the company is important (see fig. 8.5).

In this scenario, you don't need to indicate the computer name of each particular piece of information; just give it some distinctive name. Indicate either the region of the country in which it's located or the name of that facility.

Unrelated Information

Just as there are Web pages with links to related information, there are the unrelated links. Typically, you'll find these kinds of Web pages for individual people, rather than companies. People just throw together a page with their favorite hobbies and activities on one big page (see fig. 8.6). Occasionally, they'll organize the mess into manageable chunks, but not always. If you're creating a personal Web page, there's nothing wrong with putting in a page with links to your hobbies.

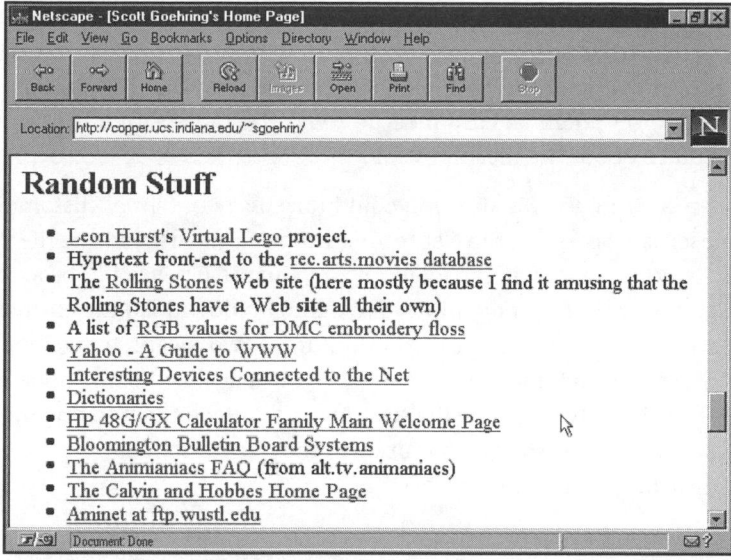

Fig. 8.6
Individuals typically have a Web page dedicated to hyperlinks that point to their interests.

Indicating File Size

One thing that you may see in many Web pages is the size specifications of files. This convention is usually used on pages from shareware and commercial software authors. Often, these people want their products to be used as much as possible. This common convention provides useful and important information that each user should know (see fig. 8.7). If you plan to make any files available on your home page, be sure to follow their suit.

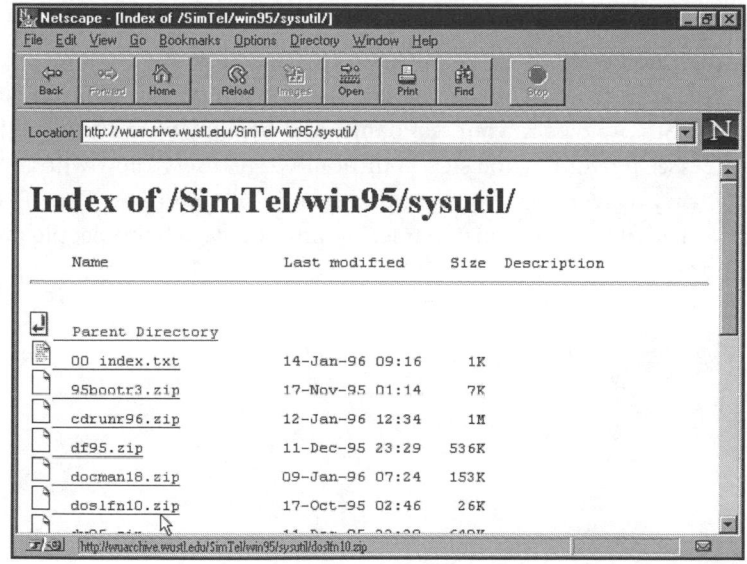

Fig. 8.7
Putting in the size of the downloadable files is an easy way to help people out.

Putting in the file size for downloadable files is just another step in helping users out. By letting people know ahead of time how big a file is, you let them know roughly how long it will take to download that file. Because you don't want to get potential customers angry at you, you want to let them know as much about the file as possible.

Without specifying the file size, you could turn away potential customers. If these users are accessing the Net through their modems, and the file is particularly large, this information would be invaluable. They could be accessing your page at any time and might not have time to download the entire file. Also, many people who access the Net do it from two means, a machine on the Net itself and their modems. If they see your page through a modem, and the file is particularly large, the file size might persuade them to download the file at a later time. They may wait until they get to school or work and then get the file from there.

Your Name and the Time

Two more common conventions you'll see used widely in Web pages are the Web author's name and the date the page was last modified. Each convention has a different reason why it should be used, but you shouldn't ignore them. Dating your Web pages allows people to see when new material has been added to it. Companies, in particular, should date almost every page on their Web sites. Signing Web pages tells people who created the Web page for any problems or praises. Everybody can find a good use of "signing" their home pages.

Stating Your Name

Putting their names on their Web sites isn't particularly useful for most people. However, you can only gain benefits by signing your name on your home page. Simply type in your real name, and possibly put in an e-mail link to yourself (see fig. 8.8). If you sign your home page, users know whom to contact if they have any questions or problems with your page. Also, if you have a particularly cryptic e-mail name, signing the page helps people properly address e-mail to you.

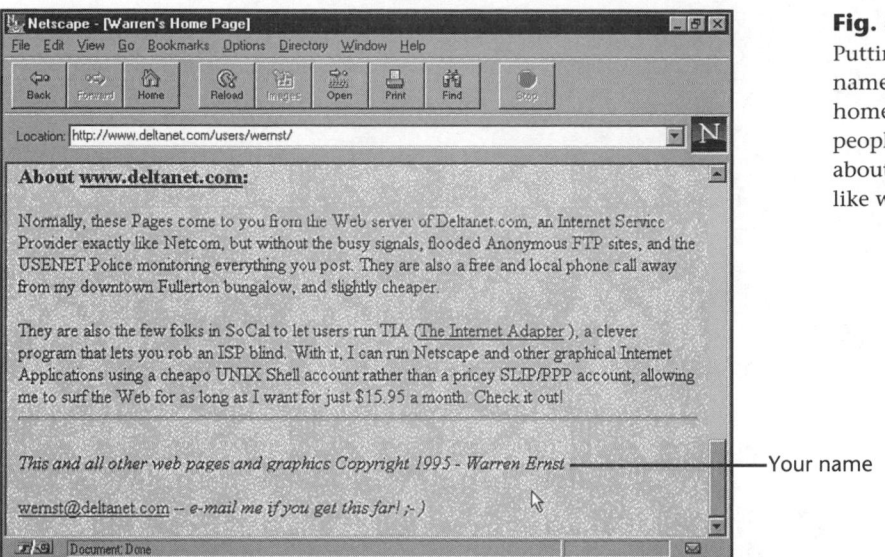

Fig. 8.8
Putting your real name on your home page tells people a little about yourself— like who you are.

Your name

Date Last Modified

People working on commercial Web sites should pay special attention to this section. An important element to put in your corporate Web page is the date you last modified that particular page (see fig. 8.9). This information is useful for almost anyone who visits your Web site. This date informs users whether new information has been added since their last visit. If they're frequent visitors, the modification date will help them budget their time. Instead of going through your site looking for new material, they can look at the date and know exactly what's new. Clearly, most individuals don't need to date their home pages, but doing so couldn't hurt. This is especially true considering that some HTML authoring programs have a provision to put in the current date.

Tip

Shareware authors who have their own home pages may want to date their HTML documents. Dating home pages that relate to a program you've written tells people when you last modified the program. This convention is an easy way for people who are interested in your program to know whether a new version is available.

II

Basic HTML Presentation

Fig. 8.9
Dating home
pages is more
important for
companies than
individuals.

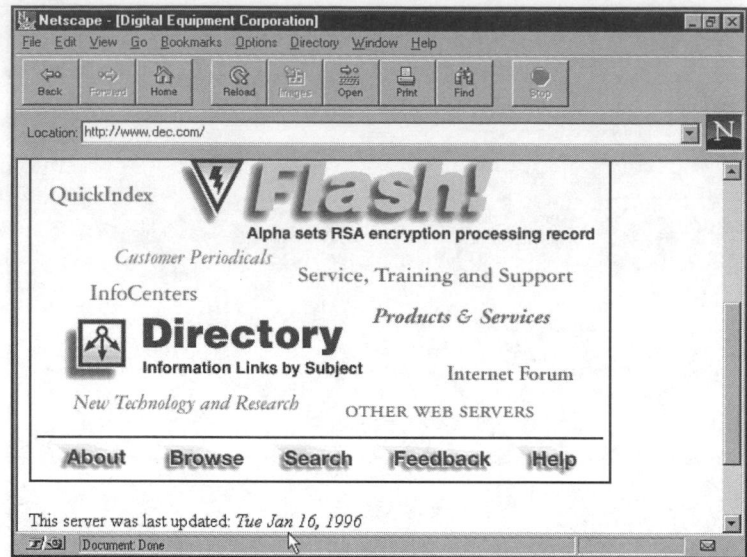

Giving Credit Where Credit Is Due

Not all people who have Web pages necessarily created them themselves. Because HTML authoring can be a pretty daunting task, professional HTML writers can keep busy. Also, most individuals who have home pages almost certainly aren't running the computer equipment that runs the Web server software. In either case, giving credit where credit is due is important. Somewhere in your Web page, put in references and links to the people who did the work for you, or tools you used.

Who Created This Page?

Professional HTML writers make part of their living by creating home pages. Most of these people write pages in their spare time, but most of them also keep current with HTML trends. They know what and when new HTML tags are available, how to create cool special effects, and other things associated with their job. Many times HTML authors charge a certain amount of money for the work they do for you. This rate can range anywhere from $50 an hour to over $200 an hour. Each writer has his or her own design and layout style for his or her Web pages, and you should look at some samples before hiring a writer.

After you've found the right person for the job, just tell him or her what you want done. Tell your writer what information you want on your home page and how you've pictured it in your head. He or she will take those ideas and try to make the Web page match your vision. You almost certainly will have to do some tweaking to clean up the page, however. After all this work is done, and you have your home page, you can make one extra addition to it. Somewhere near the bottom of the page before the </HTML> tag, you can add the following:

```
<H5>This page was created by [name].</H5>
```

Be sure to replace [name] with the name of the person who created the page. Some professional HTML writers put in this information automatically, so you may not have to do it (see fig. 8.10). The reason for putting in this information is obvious—you're giving the HTML writer free advertising. If he or she does a good job and creates an interesting page, many other people may want to seek out him or her. This name line takes up very little space on your home page, and by putting it in, you give an extra reward to the writer.

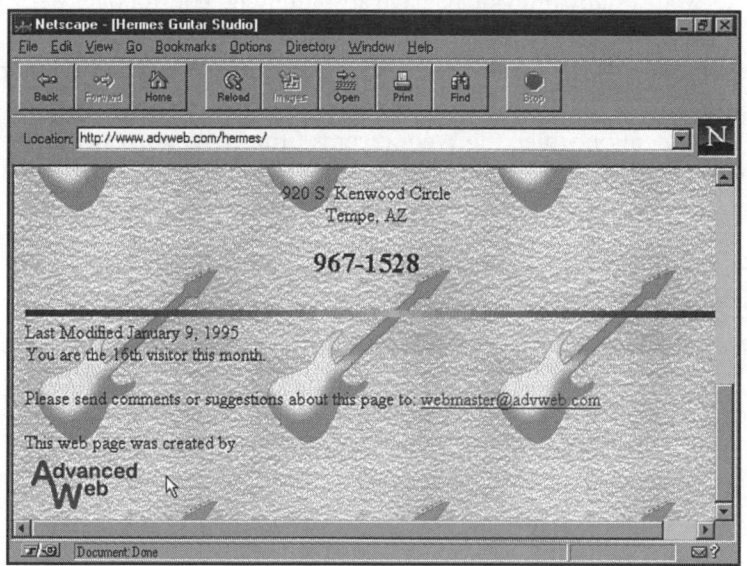

Fig. 8.10
Putting in the name of the author is an easy way of letting people know who really created your home page.

Note

If you don't want to be the middleman for the HTML author and his or her potential customers, you can get around that, too. Instead of putting in this line:

```
<H5>This page was created by [name].</H5>
```

put in this line:

```
<H5>This page was created by <A HREF="mailto:[address]">[name]
</A>.</H5>
```

Be sure to replace [address] with the e-mail address of the HTML writer. You should, of course, change [name] to the writer's name. This line of HTML code creates an e-mail link. Whenever a user clicks on that link, he or she will be sending e-mail to the creator of your home page.

Who's in Charge of This Site?

Another important aspect of Web pages is the machine that runs the Web server software. Many individuals have absolutely no control over what machine is their Web server. Also, a number of technical problems that they can't fix might arise. The only person who can really fix some of these technical problems is called the *Webmaster*. This person is in charge of the computer equipment on which the Web server is running. If you experience any computer equipment-related issues with the Web site, you should contact the Webmaster.

To make your Webmaster accessible to people viewing your home page, simply put in the following:

```
<H5>If you have any technical problems, please contact the <A
HREF="mailto:webmaster@[host]">Webmaster</A>.</H5>
```

Replace [host] with the computer name on which your home page resides. These lines create an e-mail link that, when clicked on, lets people send e-mail to the Webmaster (see fig. 8.11). Almost everybody who runs a Web site has a Webmaster e-mail address, so you don't have to worry that it doesn't exist. You want to give some sort of access to the Webmaster so that he or she can resolve any server-related issues. You don't want to spend your time forwarding e-mail to him or her, or telling people that you can't help them; that's what the Webmaster does.

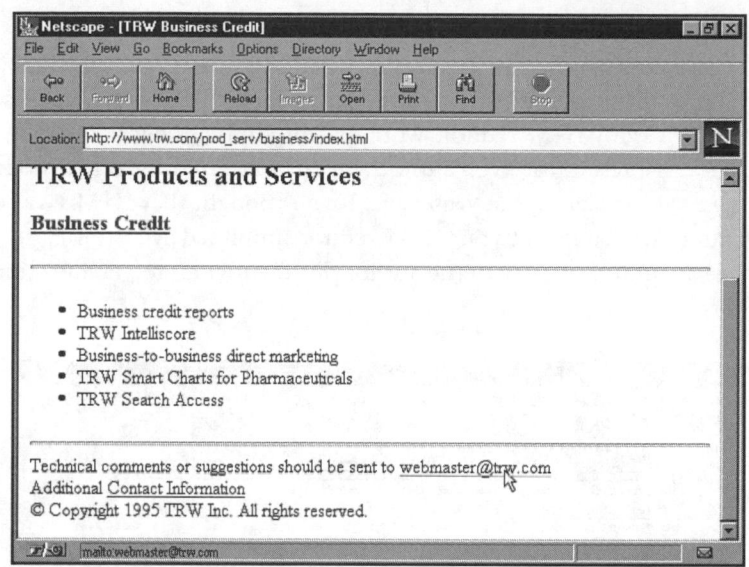

Fig. 8.11
Be sure to put in some reference to your Webmaster so that he or she can handle any Web server-related problems.

Who to Contact?

Perhaps the most difficult aspect of having a link to the Webmaster, is that it might get inappropriate e-mail. Take a look at the problem, and try to decide if it is something for the Webmaster to fix, or if it's the problem of the person whose home page you're viewing. Generally speaking, if you're having problems accessing any links or understanding the text, you should e-mail the person who runs the home page. If you're having problems establishing a secure data connection, such as for purchasing products, you should notify the Webmaster. For problems in which imagemaps don't appear to be behaving properly, deciding is a difficult call. It could be either person's problem, but your first choice should not be the Webmaster.

Most corporate-run Web sites have a handful of people taking care of their Web sites. In these situations, the Webmaster is often the person in charge of the site and also the author of the home pages. In such situations, you should e-mail the Webmaster for any problems related to the Web site or a particular home page.

The Tools You Used

Some people creating their Web pages feel that their tools were invaluable. Typically, the most commonly acknowledged tool is the HTML editor itself (see fig. 8.12). Many HTML editors work on simplifying the task of creating Web pages. As a result, the Web author will put in references to the programs he or she used in creating the Web page. If you thought that HTML was confusing and unworkable, but your HTML editor simplified everything, put in a little note about it. It may help the author of the program to get a few more customers.

Fig. 8.12
Useful programs that you use in your Web page should be acknowledged.

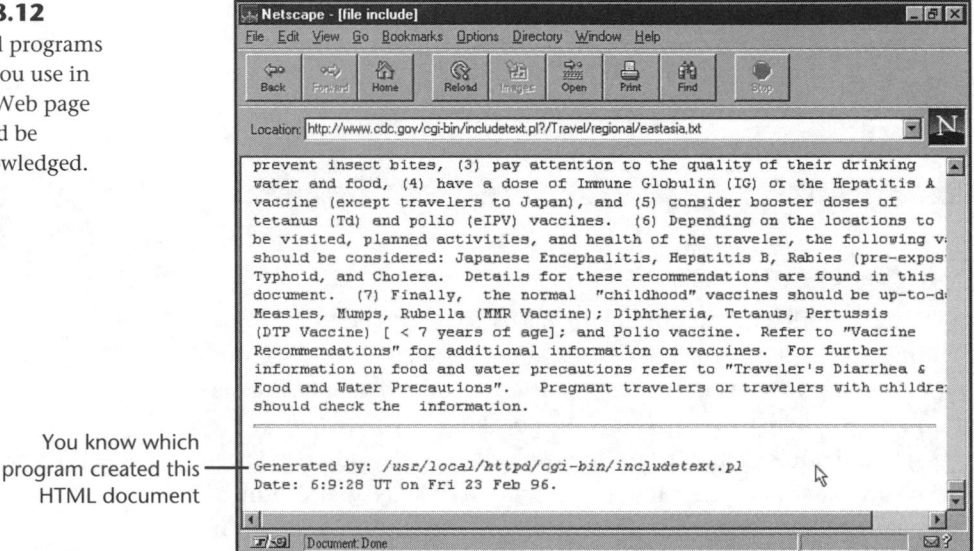

You know which program created this HTML document

Award Notices

▶ See chapter 19 for more information on common award services.

There are a number of Web sites that do nothing but look at other Web pages. These "services" typically cost nothing and are useful tools for the Web author. Sometimes they can be used to brag about how good their page is, technically. Other times, these awards can be used to verify that your Web page conforms to current standards. While these awards are certainly not required, they are certainly something to be proud of; if you have them.

Kudos and Praise

For those Web authors who are more interested in the presentation of their Web pages, they can try and get some "awards." These awards are given out by groups of people who look at the presentation of Web pages. Typically, someone will recommend a Web page to the committee, and they'll look at it. If they are impressed with the way you've made your Web page, they'll let you know. You can then put their award on your Web page and be able to show it off to others (see fig. 8.13). As you might guess, this is the sort of thing that people such as graphic artists are interested in.

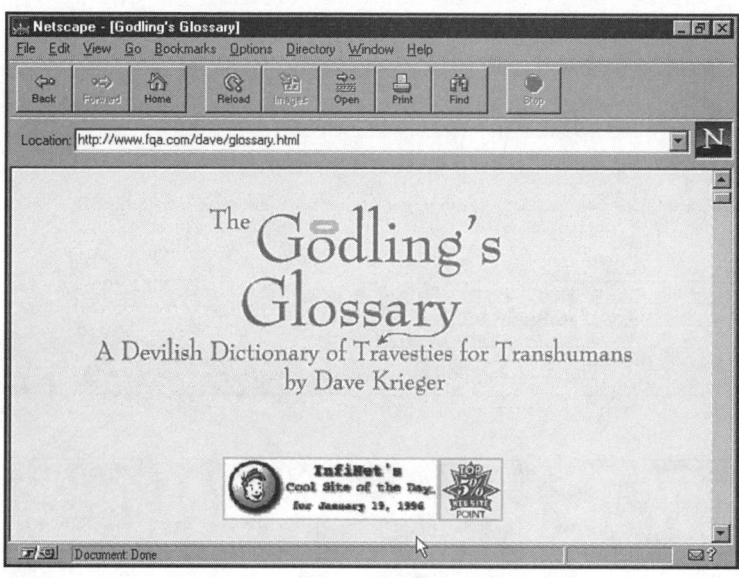

Fig. 8.13
Some people like to put up notices of the awards they've won.

II

Basic HTML Presentation

Validation

Another common convention is that some people like to get their Web pages validated. That is, they have somebody else look at their HTML source, and determine if it conforms to the HTML standards (see fig. 8.14). If it doesn't, then the Web author can always go back and revise the page, if he or she wants. If the page does conform to the HTML standards, then the Web author can reduce e-mail complaints about the page. Should the Web author get any e-mail about how a particular browser doesn't interpret the page, he or she can ignore it. After all, the Web page has been certified to conform, so it must the browser's fault.

Preferred Viewing

Though not really an award, you'll often come across Web pages that indicate their preferred browser. Typically, this is done by inserting some distinctive features (see fig. 8.15). The author went to a lot of effort to make sure the Web page looked great on the recommended browser. Oftentimes, you'll see these notices when the Web page author is exploiting certain features of the particular browser. If you're not using the specified viewer, you might not get the full effect of the Web author's intent.

Fig. 8.14
Validation services allow a Web author to be certain that his or her page will be visible by all conforming browsers.

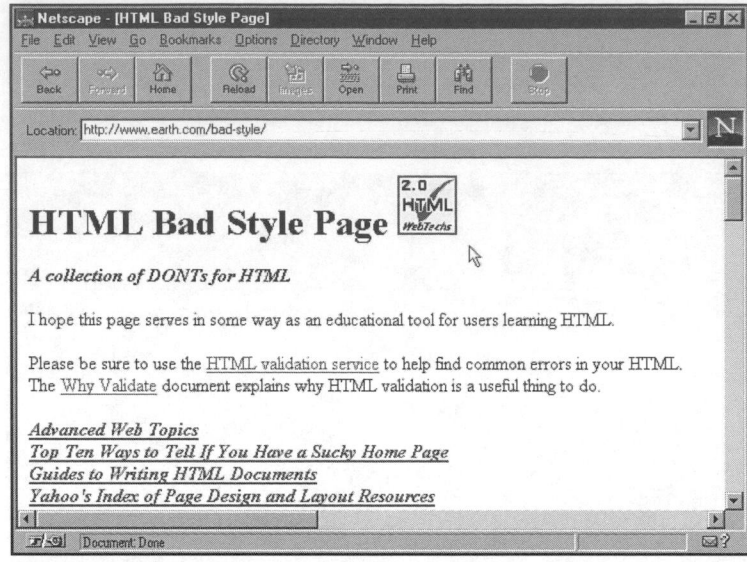

Fig. 8.15
Some HTML authors like to use some features of certain browsers, and they'll tell you which one.

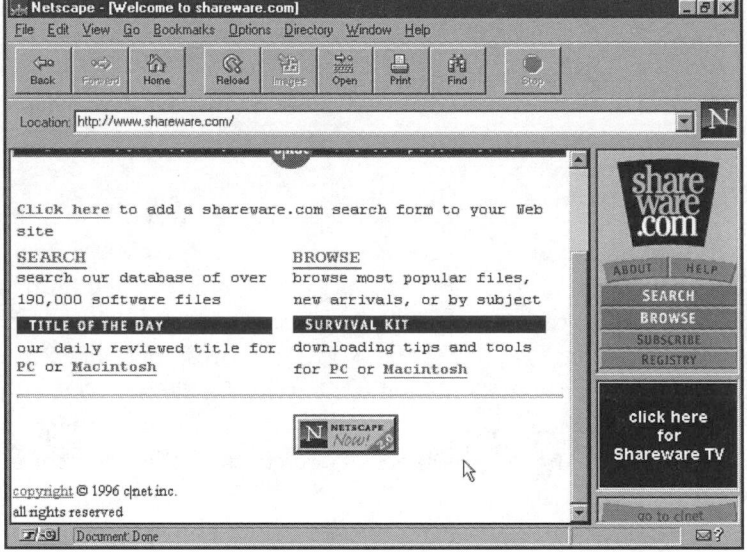

## CHAPTER 9

Displaying Text in Lists

You can organize information for presentation in many different ways. One of the most effective formats is the list. Lists are both functional and easy to read; they can define sequential procedures, relative importance, available decision options, collections of related data, and data ordering. We see lists everywhere and every day. From restaurant menus to encyclopedias to phone books, lists are a fundamental way that we organize and disseminate information.

HTML provides container elements for creating lists in HTML documents. The basic list types available are numbered, bulleted, menu, directory, and definition. You can mix these types to create a variety of display and organization effects.

In this chapter, you learn about the following:

- What types of lists are available?
- How do I create an ordered list?
- How do I develop an unordered list?
- How do I represent a menu or directory list?
- Is there a way to format a list of definitions?
- How do I create a customized list format?

Creating an Ordered List

A basic list in HTML consists of a list identifier container plus the standard list items tag. (In HTML, all list items use one tag, <LI>, and the lists are differentiated by their container tags.) An ordered list, also called a numbered list, is used to create a sequential list of items or steps. When a Web browser sees the tag for an ordered list, it sequentially numbers each list item using standard numbers, such as 1, 2, 3, and so on.

Using the <OL> Tag

Ordered (or numbered) lists begin with the <OL> tag, and each item uses the standard <LI> tag. Close the list with the </OL> tag to signal the end of the list to the browser. List containers provide both a beginning and ending line break to isolate the list from the surrounding text; it's not necessary (except for effect) to precede or follow the list with the paragraph <P> tag.

> **Note**
>
> Lists support internal HTML elements. One of the most useful elements is the paragraph tag (<P>), which enables you to separate text in a list item. Other useful tags include both logical and physical style tags (such as <EM> and <I>) and HTML entities. Headings are not appropriate for use in lists; although they're interpreted correctly, their forced line breaks make for an ugly display. SGML purists also object to them because heading tags are meant to define relationships in paragraphs, not lists.

Figure 9.1 shows how you can use the OL list container. Pay particular attention to including closing tags, especially in nested lists. You can use leading blanks and extra lines to make your list code easier to read, but Web browsers ignore them. Figure 9.2 shows how Netscape Navigator interprets this HTML code.

Fig. 9.1

Lists can include fixed data as well as links to other information sources.

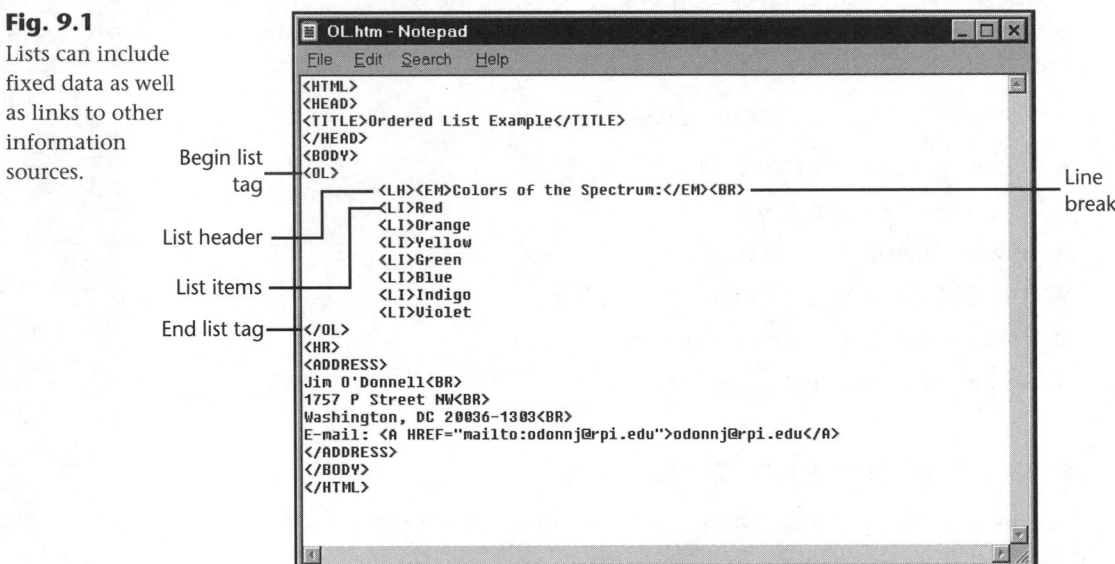

```
<HTML>
<HEAD>
<TITLE>Ordered List Example</TITLE>
</HEAD>
<BODY>
<OL>
        <LH><EM>Colors of the Spectrum:</EM><BR>
        <LI>Red
        <LI>Orange
        <LI>Yellow
        <LI>Green
        <LI>Blue
        <LI>Indigo
        <LI>Violet
</OL>
<HR>
<ADDRESS>
Jim O'Donnell<BR>
1757 P Street NW<BR>
Washington, DC 20036-1303<BR>
E-mail: <A HREF="mailto:odonnj@rpi.edu">odonnj@rpi.edu</A>
</ADDRESS>
</BODY>
</HTML>
```

Begin list tag

List header

List items

End list tag

Line break

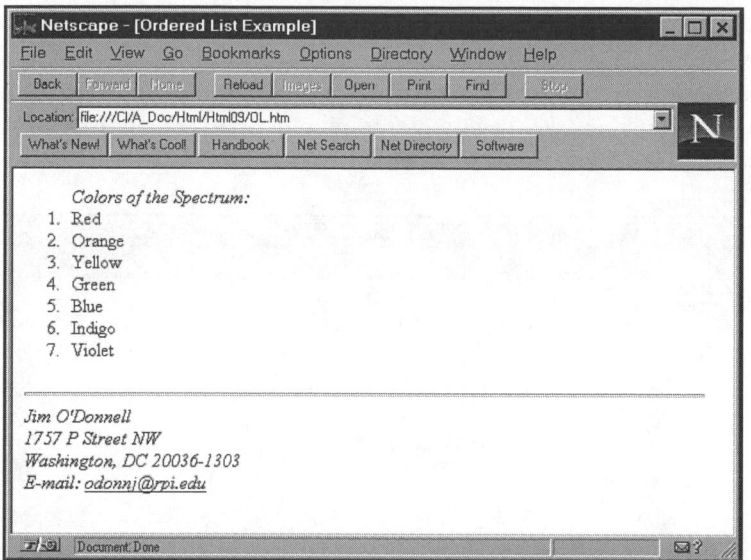

Fig. 9.2
Web browsers display internal HTML elements according to their defined usage.

Tip

The line break tag, <BR>, after the list header is not necessary for Netscape Navigator, but it is necessary for Microsoft Internet Explorer, which will otherwise put the first list item on the same line as the header.

It is also possible to nest ordered lists, creating a document that looks more like an outline. Figure 9.3 shows the HTML code for such a list, which is rendered in figure 9.4

Tip

Use indentations and blank lines to organize your data when creating HTML documents. Web browsers don't care how the text is aligned or run together, but you will appreciate the extra effort when rereading and editing the HTML code.

Users may wonder how they can create a more classical style of outline in which subheadings use different list numbers (such as Roman numerals or letters) from the primary headings. Unfortunately, standard HTML lists do not enable the author to control how a browser numbers the list items—only

▶ See "Templates for Lists," p. 301

II

Basic HTML Presentation

that the items are numbered. The draft HTML 3.0 specification does include a provision for list numbering formats to be determined by style sheets. In addition, some Web browsers, such as Netscape Navigator and Microsoft Internet Explorer, enable the end user to modify how ordered lists are displayed, as described in the next section.

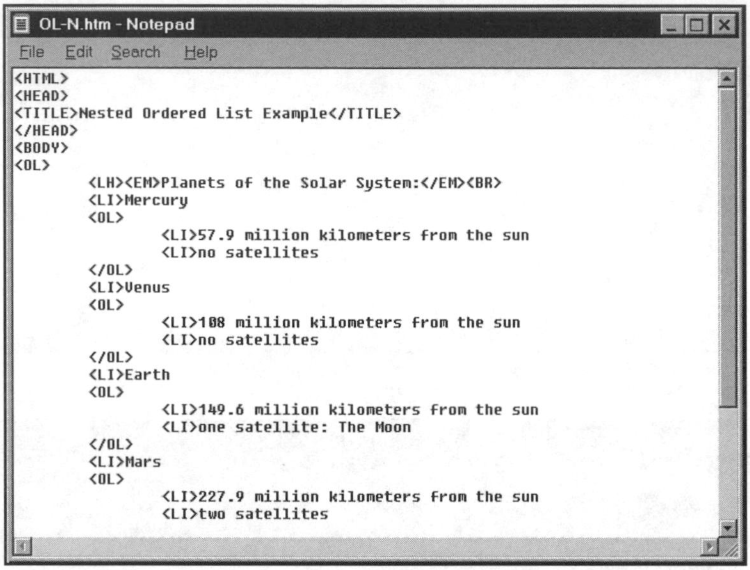

Fig. 9.3
Nested lists can be created by putting lists within other lists in HTML code.

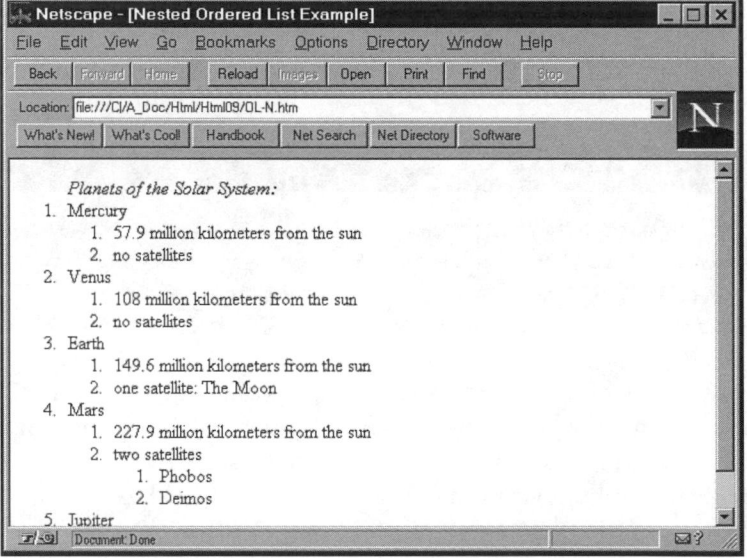

Fig. 9.4
Sublists are automatically indented to create an outline effect.

Using Netscape Extensions with the <OL> Tag

Netscape provides useful extensions to the <OL> tag supported by its own Netscape Navigator as well as Microsoft Internet Explorer. These give you control over the appearance of the item markers and the beginning marker number. Table 9.1 lists the nonstandard attributes and their functions.

Table 9.1   Netscape Extension to <OL>

Extension	Description
TYPE=A	Sets markers to uppercase letters
TYPE=a	Sets markers to lowercase letters
TYPE=I	Sets markers to uppercase Roman numerals
TYPE=i	Sets markers to lowercase Roman numerals
TYPE=1	Sets markers to numbers
START	Sets beginning value of item markers in the current list

Varying the marker style enables you to create distinctions between numbered lists in the same document. Figure 9.5 shows how an HTML document incorporates these extensions, and figure 9.6 shows how Netscape's extensions can enhance a document.

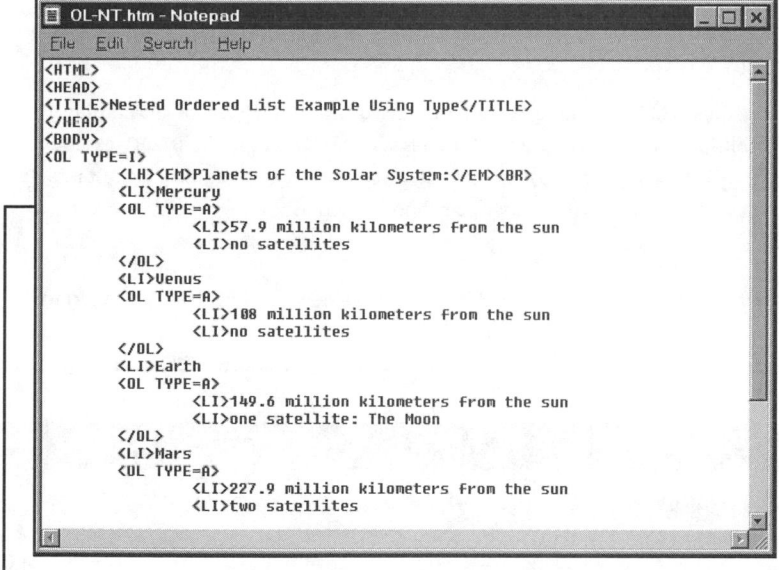

New marker type

Fig. 9.5
This TYPE attribute changes the marker to uppercase Roman numerals; browsers that don't recognize Netscape's extensions will ignore them.

II

Basic HTML Presentation

Fig. 9.6
Controlling the appearance of lists is useful for both functional and aesthetic purposes.

Ordered list uses uppercase Roman numerals

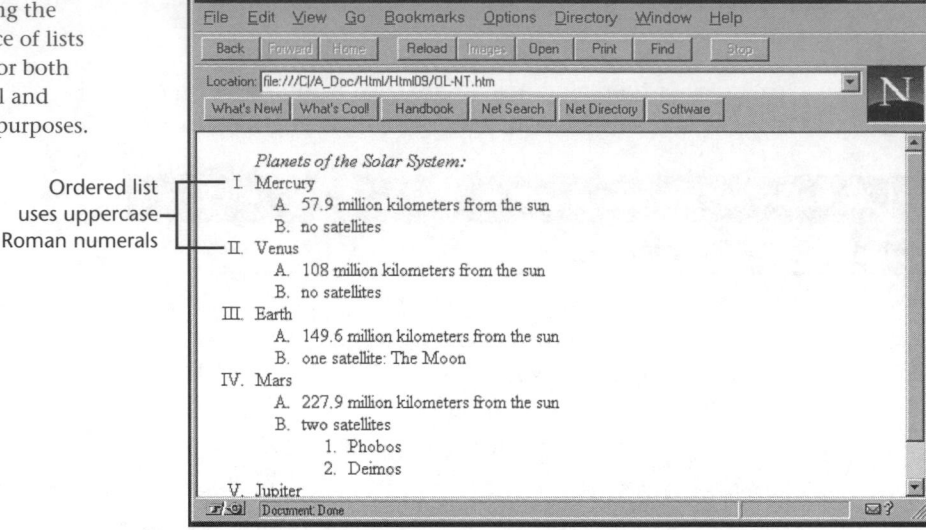

Troubleshooting

I'm creating a list of items, and I need to interrupt the list for a regular paragraph of text. How can I make the list pick up where it left off and continue numbering the items sequentially?

The draft HTML 3.0 specification included an attribute to the <OL> tag called SEQNUM. Ideally then, you could pick up, say, at item seven by specifying <OL SEQNUM=7>. Unfortunately, this attribute is not yet supported by any of the popular Web browsers.

What you can do is encourage your audience to switch to Netscape Navigator or Microsoft Internet Explorer as their Web browser, and you use the START extension to <OL>. This enables you to close the list, insert your text paragraph, and start a new list with whatever list number you choose, such as the following:

```
<OL START=7>
```

The number 7 is just an example. Put whatever value you want the numbering to start with.

Tip

This trick also works if you're being creative in Netscape and using a different list marker with the TYPE extension.

Creating an Unordered List

HTML also supports the unordered or bulleted list: a list of items that does not define a specific structure or relationship among the data.

Using the <UL> Tag

Unordered lists use the <UL> container tag. Just like ordered lists, bulleted lists provide beginning and ending line breaks and support internal HTML elements and sublists. Also, like ordered lists, they require closing tags: include the </UL> tag to signal the end of the list to the browser. Web browsers support and automatically indent sublists, and some will also vary the bullet icon based on the relative level of the list. These icons vary depending on the client software viewing the HTML document.

Figure 9.7 shows how to use the <UL> list container. Again, to make the HTML document easier to read, you can include leading blanks and extra lines, but Web browsers will ignore them. Figure 9.8 shows how Netscape Navigator will render this HTML code.

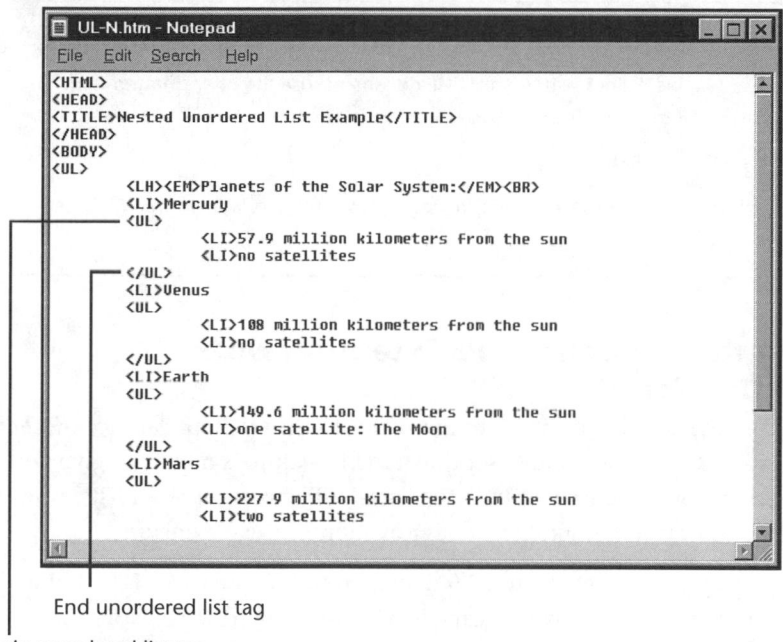

End unordered list tag

Begin unordered list tag

Fig. 9.7
Unordered lists can be used to list items where the sequence is not important.

II

Basic HTML Presentation

Fig. 9.8
Web browsers
automatically
indent sublists
and apply the
corresponding
item markers.

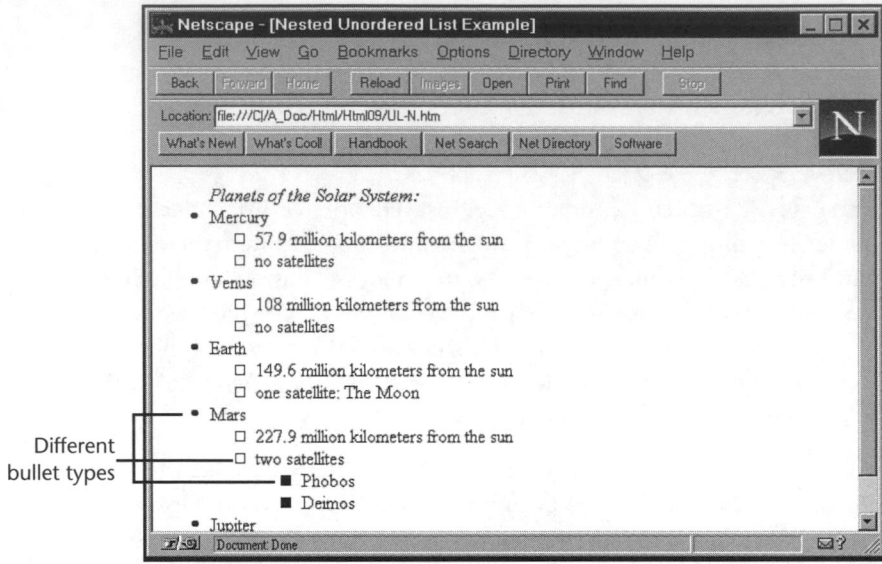

Different
bullet types

> **Note**
>
> When adding blank lines within an HTML document, use the preformatted text element <PRE> to create filler for blank lines, as follows:
>
>   <PRE>   </PRE>
>
> Remember to put two spaces inside the tags; most browsers will ignore <PRE> sections with only one.

Using the Netscape *TYPE* Extension with the <UL> Tag

Netscape Navigator enables you to manually control the appearance of item markers as either circles, squares, or discs. This feature is meant to give you more control over the look of bulleted lists. Unlike with ordered lists, however, Microsoft Internet Explorer does not support this extension

The tag extension is TYPE. Figure 9.9 demonstrates its use in an HTML document, which is rendered by Netscape Navigator in figure 9.10. Note that while the tag values shown in this case are "SQUARE" and "CIRCLE," that Netscape Navigator renders them as filled-in and empty squares, respectively.

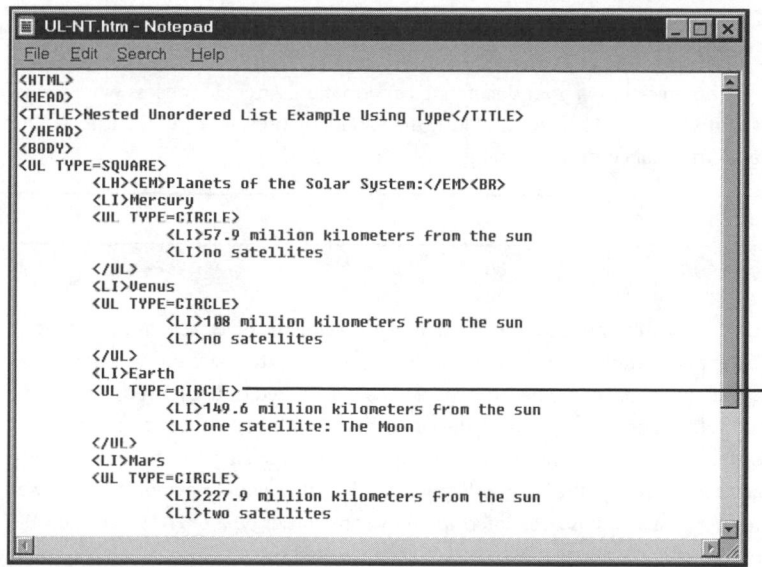

Fig. 9.9
TYPE provides control over the appearance of list bullets; browsers that don't support its use ignore the <TYPE> tag.

Author-selected bullets

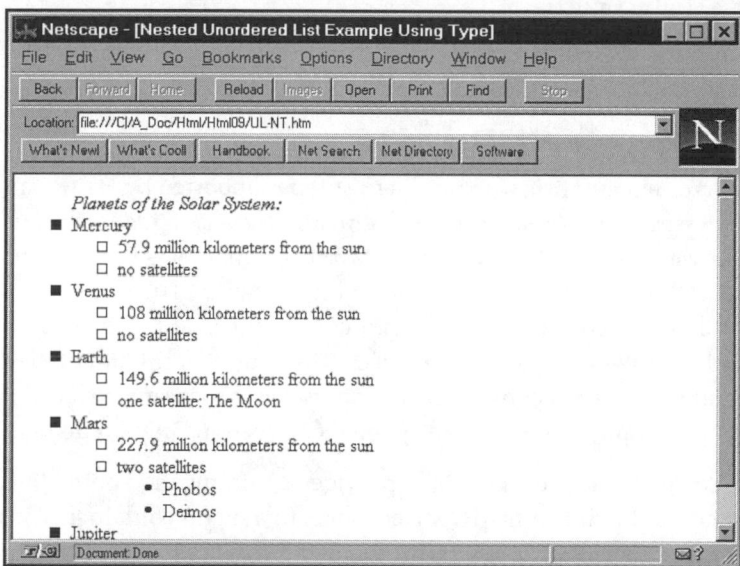

Fig. 9.10
It's easy to control the display of bullet markers for your Netscape Navigator audience.

Caution

There is a reason why HTML and its client software support multiple item markers: to provide a visual differentiation for sublists. By manually controlling the markers, however, you're working against the user's expectations and potentially weakening

(continues)

(continued)

the communication of your document's information. After all, the less work the user has to do to recognize subsets of lists, the easier any browser can read the document. Use this manual control with care!

Note

Besides the extensions to the <OL> and <UL> elements, Netscape also provides nonstandard extensions for individual list items. The extensions are based on those available to the list container that the item is in (ordered or unordered). Ordered lists pass on the capability to change the current TYPE of list items and also the VALUE they begin with—by using the VALUE tag, you can begin a list with a value other than one, or change the numbering within a list. This would be another good way to continue a list that has been interrupted by some other type of HTML object. (All subsequent items adopt the extension changes until the list closes.) You can modify unordered list items with the TYPE extension; all subsequent items in the container use the new item marker.

Creating Menu Lists

You can create menu lists with another list type supported by HTML and Web browsers. The distinction here is primarily for HTML identification; most browsers' default display for the <MENU> container is very similar to the font and style used for the unordered list container. The value of this element is enhanced if you select a distinct screen format for the menu paragraph in a Web browser's preferences. The container might also be more functional in future versions of HTML and its client software, enabling browsers and other applications to identify the menu sections in your documents.

As with the previous lists, menu lists provide beginning and ending line breaks and can include other HTML elements in a menu container. The anchor element is the most likely HTML element to use in this type of list; it is used to link the menu listings to other document resources or Internet applications. Figure 9.11 shows typical uses of the <MENU> container.

Tip

Just because HTML has specific names for these list types doesn't mean you're limited in how you can use them. Experiment to see how each list delivers your information, and use what works best.

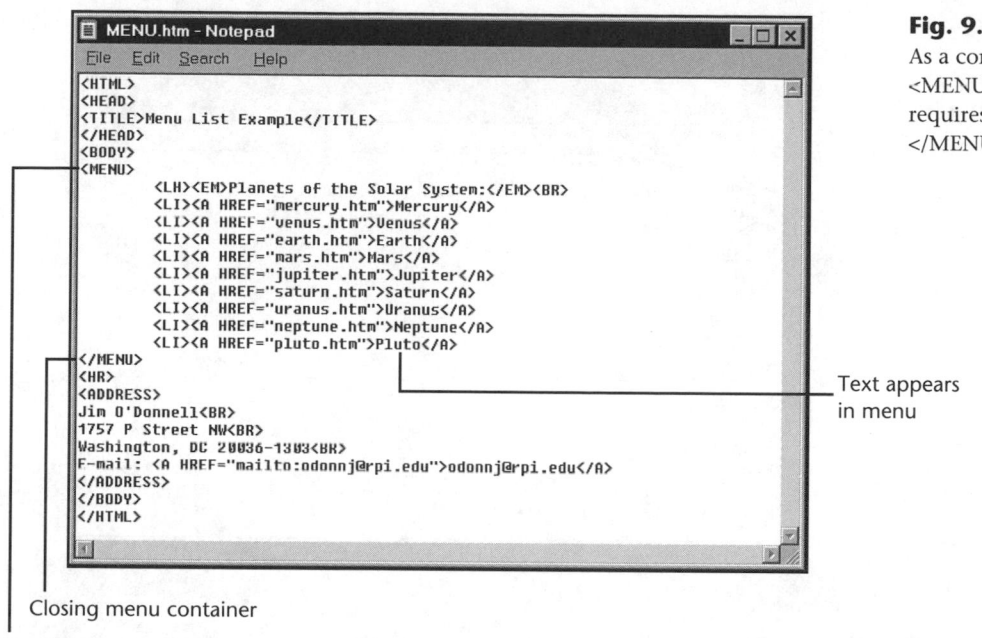

Fig. 9.11
As a container, the
<MENU> element
requires a closing
</MENU> tag.

Closing menu container

Opening menu container

Again, the current implementation of <MENU> by most Web browsers
doesn't provide a visual distinction between menu and unordered lists.
Netscape Navigator displays menu lists and unordered lists identically, while
Microsoft Internet Explorer displays them identically except it omits the bullets in the latter. NCSA Mosaic, as shown in figure 9.12, displays menu lists
slightly different than unordered lists, using a more compact format. (Note
that all types of lists can include hypertext links, as well as many other HTML
elements besides simple text.)

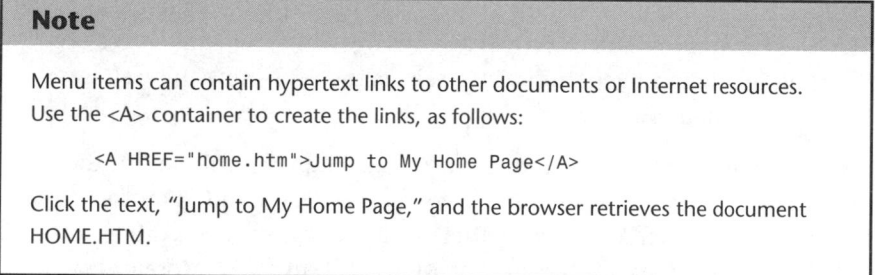

II

Basic HTML Presentation

Fig. 9.12
Unlike the tag, the
<MENU> element
doesn't support
nonstandard
extensions.

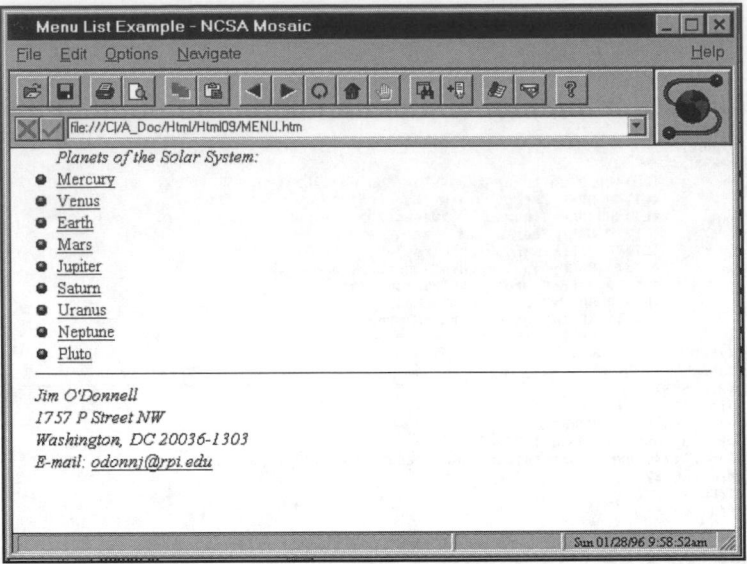

Creating Directory Lists

The <DIR> element functions much like the <MENU> element; it provides HTML identification to the section of text that has more potential usefulness than real functionality right now. Similar to <MENU>, <DIR> containers display with the same default settings as unordered lists. As browsers and other applications begin to support <DIR> as it's intended, it'll become more common.

The intended use for the <DIR> container limits items to 24 characters and displays the items in rows (like file directories in UNIX, or in DOS using the /W parameter). Current browsers don't support this interpretation. The <DIR> element also isn't intended to include other HTML elements, although browsers interpret them correctly. When using <DIR>, remember to close the container with the ending </DIR> tag. Figure 9.13 shows typical uses of the <DIR> container.

Browsers don't provide, by default, any unique display attributes for the <DIR> element. As with menu lists, Netscape Navigator and Microsoft Internet Explorer render directory lists just like unordered lists (Microsoft Internet Explorer without the bullets). My version of NCSA Mosaic also renders them as unordered lists, though in a different font and style (see fig. 9.14).

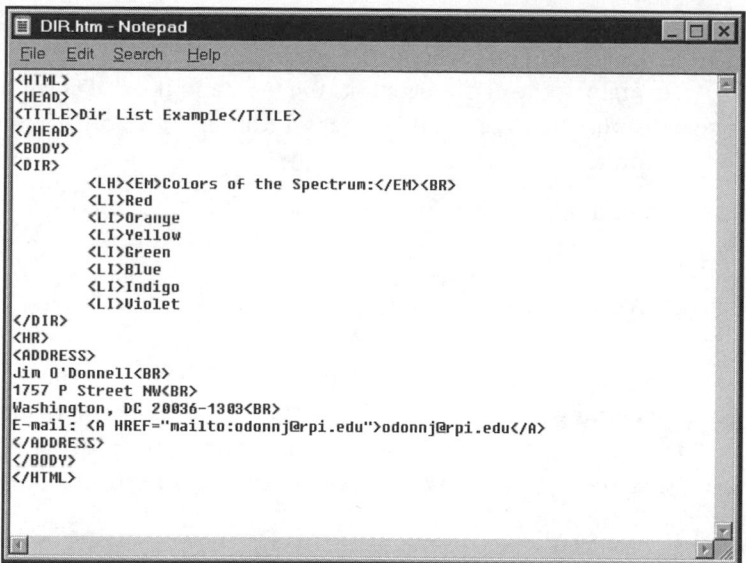

Fig. 9.13
The <DIR> element container has few frills and little browser support.

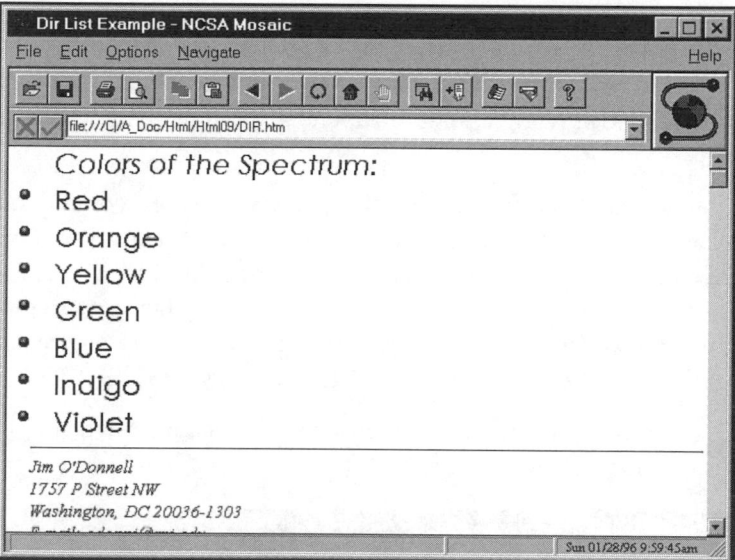

Fig. 9.14
Currently, <DIR> text displays in a single vertical column like an unordered list.

Creating Definition Lists

Definition lists, also called glossary lists, are a special type of list in HTML. They provide a format like a dictionary entry, with an identifiable term and indented definition paragraph. This format is especially useful when listing items with extensive descriptions, such as catalog items or company departments. The <DL> element provides both a beginning and ending line break. In the <DL> container, the <DT> tag marks the term and the <DD> tag defines the paragraph. These are both open tags, meaning they don't require a closing tag to contain the text.

The standard format of a definition list is as follows:

```
<DL>
<DT>Term
<DD>Definition of term
</DL>
```

The <DT> tag's text should fit on a single line, but it will wrap to the next line without indenting if it runs beyond the boundary of the browser window. The <DD> tag displays a single paragraph, continuously indented one or two spaces beneath the term element's text (depending on how the browser interprets a definition list).

The draft HTML 3.0 specification provides one important optional attribute for <DL>: COMPACT. This attribute is supposed to be interpreted as a list with a different style, presumably with a smaller font size or more compact font and character spacing. This could be useful for embedded definition lists (those inside other definition, numbered, or bulleted lists), or for graphic effect. Most browsers, however, ignore the attribute, displaying the definition list in the standard format.

Definition lists can include other HTML elements. The most common are physical and logical styles and other list containers. Although Web browsers can correctly interpret elements, such as headings, this is bad HTML; their forced line breaks are not pretty to look at, and heading tags are usually meant to define relationships in paragraphs—not within lists. Figure 9.15 shows examples of how you can create definition lists.

Figure 9.16 shows how this document displays in Netscape Navigator. Other browsers may format this text differently.

Tip

In Netscape Navigator, use a horizontal rule, <HR>, on a <DD> tagged line in a definition list. The rule indents with the rest of the <DD> lines, providing an easy-to-read separator for your definition text.

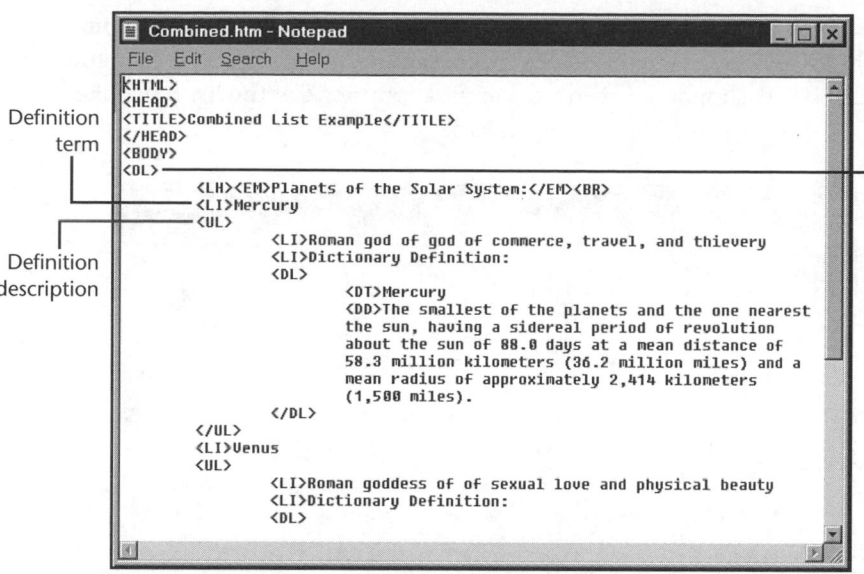

Definition term

Definition description

Fig. 9.15
You can indent definition lists for easier reading, although browsers apply their own formatting.

Begin definition list

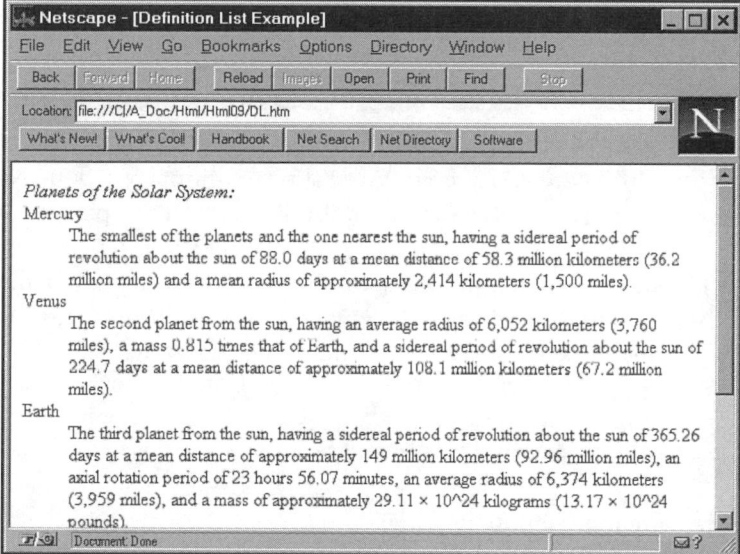

Fig. 9.16
Definition lists appear much the same as dictionary entries and enable easy reading of each term.

II

Basic HTML Presentation

Combining List Types

There are times when it's necessary to use sublists of more than one type within a single list. For instance, you may have a numbered list that includes a list as one of the numbered elements. Instead of just creating an ordered sublist, which numbers each of its items, you might prefer to display an unordered list to differentiate the sublist (while avoiding ordering the information as well). HTML supports embedded combinations of all of the list types. Figure 9.17 shows a sample of combined lists.

Fig. 9.17
Remember to use closing tags for all internal lists to avoid dropping the original list style.

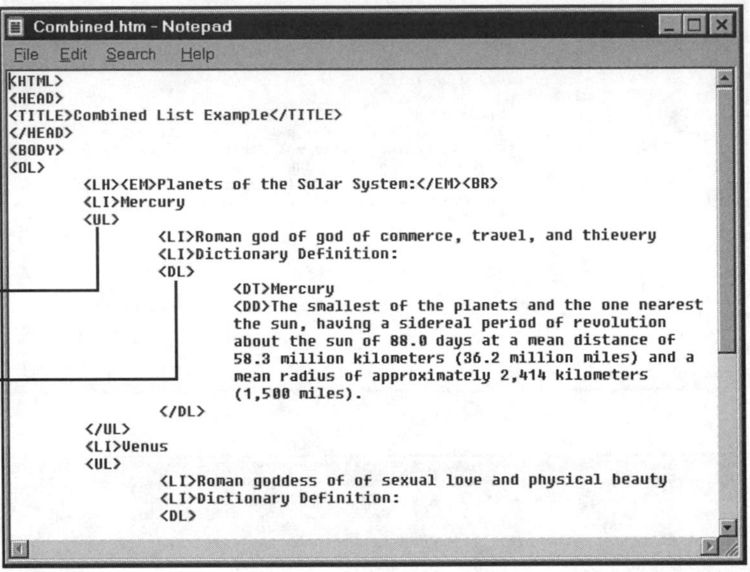

Begin ordered list

Begin unordered list

Begin definition list

```
Combined.htm - Notepad
File  Edit  Search  Help
<HTML>
<HEAD>
<TITLE>Combined List Example</TITLE>
</HEAD>
<BODY>
<OL>
        <LH><EM>Planets of the Solar System:</EM><BR>
        <LI>Mercury
        <UL>
                <LI>Roman god of god of commerce, travel, and thievery
                <LI>Dictionary Definition:
                <DL>
                        <DT>Mercury
                        <DD>The smallest of the planets and the one nearest
                        the sun, having a sidereal period of revolution
                        about the sun of 88.0 days at a mean distance of
                        58.3 million kilometers (36.2 million miles) and a
                        mean radius of approximately 2,414 kilometers
                        (1,500 miles).
                </DL>
        </UL>
        <LI>Venus
        <UL>
                <LI>Roman goddess of of sexual love and physical beauty
                <LI>Dictionary Definition:
                <DL>
```

In the example in figure 9.17, I used three list types: numbered, bulleted, and definition. The primary list is a numbered list of planets. Each planet has a bulleted sublist indicating the Roman god after whom it was named, followed by its dictionary definition. I'm relying on the users' browsers to indent embedded lists; if I want to force more indentation, I can embed the lists inside additional, empty lists. For instance, instead of the following:

```
<OL>
        <LI>Small example list
        <LI>That I want to indent more
</OL>
```

I can force more indentation by using:

```
<OL><OL>
        <LI>Small example list
        <LI>That I want to indent more
</OL></OL>
```

Because the primary difference between list types involves either the list item markers or the screen formatting of the elements and not the actual text representation itself, combined lists tend to display very well. Figure 9.18 shows how the samples in figure 9.17 display in a typical Web browser.

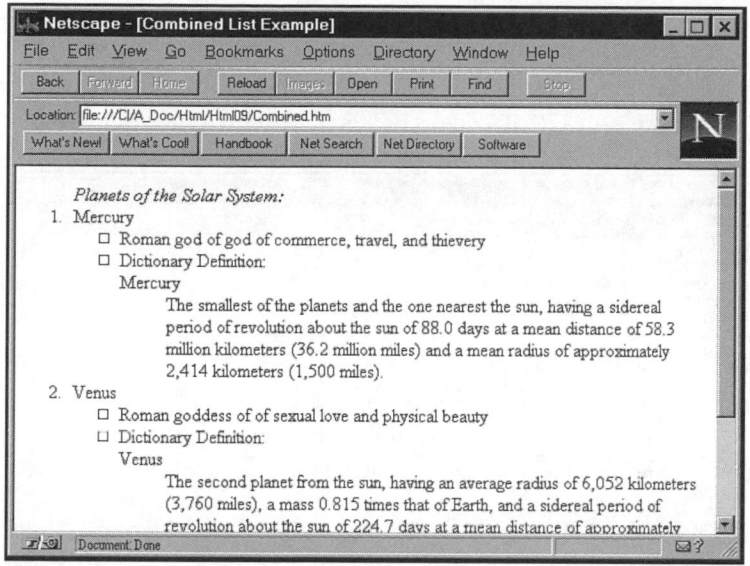

Fig. 9.18
Embedded list types inherit certain formatting characteristics from the original list styles.

Manually Formatting Lists

Beyond the types of lists and formats discussed above, there's not too much that can be done within those elements of the HTML 2.0 and draft HTML 3.0 specifications that are supported by the popular Web browsers now available. One thing in particular is the capability to specify alternative types of bullets to be used in an unordered list. This is satisfied by the HTML 3.0 SRC attribute to the <UL> tag. For instance, to use a cube image as a bullet in an unordered list, specify the following:

▶ See "Adding Graphics to Your Home Page," p. 191

```
<UL SRC="cube.gif">
```

Unfortunately, this attribute is not yet supported in any of the popular Web browsers. It is, however, possible to achieve a similar effect with a little manual effort in your HTML code. Consider the HTML code shown in figure 9.19.

The <UL> and </UL> tags are used to instruct the Web browser to set up the formatting and indentation to support an unordered list. However, no <LI> tags are used: because you don't want the standard bullets, you can't use the standard list item tag. Instead, each item in the list is specified similar to the following example:

```
<IMG SRC="cube.gif" ALIGN=TOP> Red<BR>
```

The <IMG> tag is used to specify and align the graphic you want to use as your bullet, followed by the list item. Because you're not using the standard <LI> tag to set off each item, you need to use the <BR> tag to insert a line break after each. This HTML code is rendered as shown in figure 9.20.

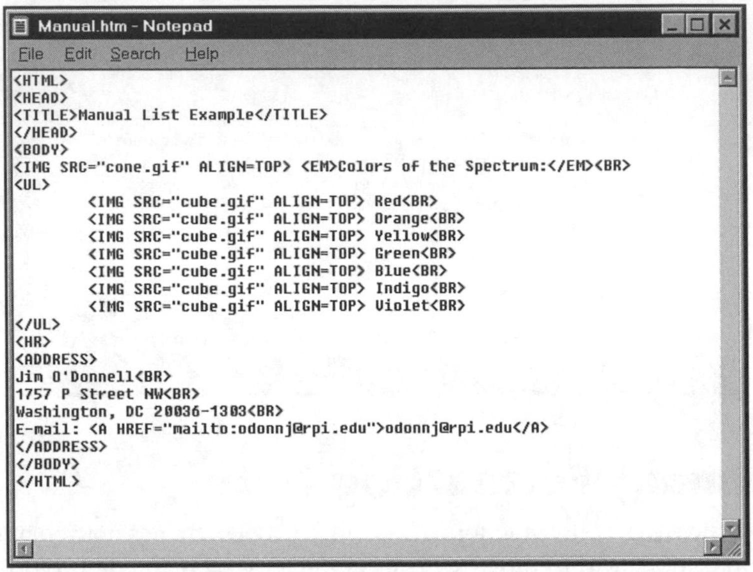

Fig. 9.19

It is possible to get alternative list formats using a little manual effort in HTML.

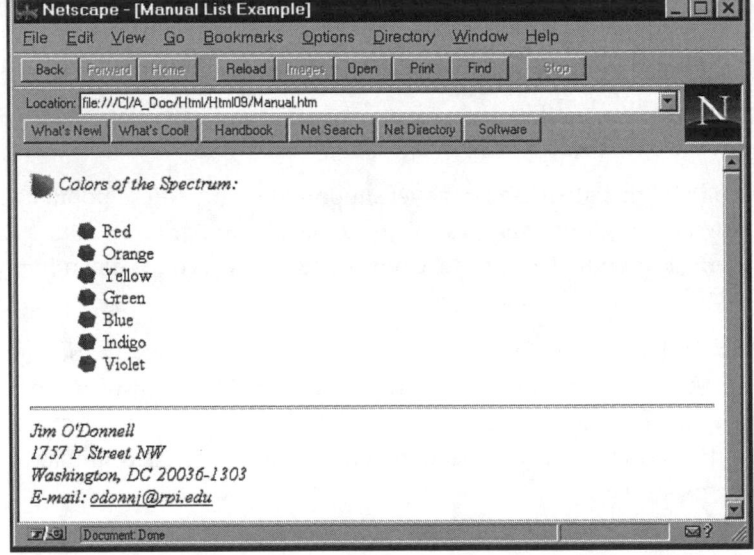

Fig. 9.20

With a little added work, nonstandard formatting and bullets can be used in your Web pages!

## CHAPTER 10

Adding Graphics to Your Home Page

by John Jung

By now, you know how to create an HTML document that simply contains hypertext links. Now you're going to learn about adding graphics to your home page to add a little spice. Images allow you to liven up your home page with more style and "eye candy." But you suffer certain intangible costs by using them. Aside from the pros and cons debate, in this chapter, you'll also learn about some of the more popular formats available to you:

- What you should avoid putting in your images
- What file format you should use
- What transparent GIFs are and when you should use them
- What progressive JPEGs are and how to use them
- How you can position images
- How to provide textual alternatives to images

When Graphics Should Be Used

Graphics are probably one of the most popular elements people put in their home pages. But going to the trouble of adding graphics to your home page entails good points and bad points. You should consider the pros and cons of putting graphics in an HTML document and decide for yourself. Chances are, though, that you'll probably make some use of images in your home page, but not too much. Using only a few images is generally a good approach, but how much is too much? Look at the following list of reasons you should and shouldn't use graphics, and decide for yourself just how much is too much.

Pros:

- Using graphics is a great way to break up large amounts of text. You won't bore (and drive off) the users with paragraph after paragraph about your company's profits last year. Instead, you can just include an image with a bar chart indicating the income.

- Using graphics is a great way to get people's attention. If you're selling goods or services on the Net, you want your specials to really stand out. Making the special offer into an image and putting it somewhere in your home page will get the attention of many people.

- Graphics that are used repeatedly, such as company logos, load faster each time they are accessed. Most modern Web browsers store frequently used data, and if you use the same graphics, they come up faster. The disk drive is much faster at getting information than the network.

Cons:

- Graphics take longer to download than text does. This is true because graphics files are almost always bigger than the typical home page. Also, most graphics are compressed, and uncompressing them takes time.

- Not everybody will be viewing your home page through a graphical Web browser. A significant number of people access the Web through generic UNIX accounts. Generally speaking, these systems have no graphical support for people logging in through a modem.

- Most images you may want to add use color, which may cause problems. Because most browsers don't support an unlimited number of colors, you have to be careful when choosing your images.

What Your Images Should and Shouldn't Have

When you're choosing the correct image (or images) to use in your home page, you need to consider what they should contain. This chapter does not tell you what types of images you should and shouldn't have. It does, however, include some general guidelines to help you make sure that the images you want to use are good ones.

Use an Appropriate Graphic

The first aspect of choosing an image for a page on your Web site is determining whether it's appropriate. You should look at the content of that particular HTML document and decide whether the image you want to use fits in. Is it appropriate to have a picture of a woman on the same page as your resume? If you're advertising one particular product, is it appropriate to have a competitor's logo on that same page? Use common sense when picking images.

Crop Your Image

A *cropped* image is one in which the unnecessary parts of the image have been removed. These parts aren't just hidden; they're completely deleted from the graphic. The *resolution*, how big the image is in terms of pixels, of the graphic is changed to fit the cropped image. This is useful in making sure that your entire image can be seen by as many people as possible. Cropping images also has the added advantage of reducing the file size. Figure 10.1 shows an uncropped image, and figure 10.2 shows the same image cropped.

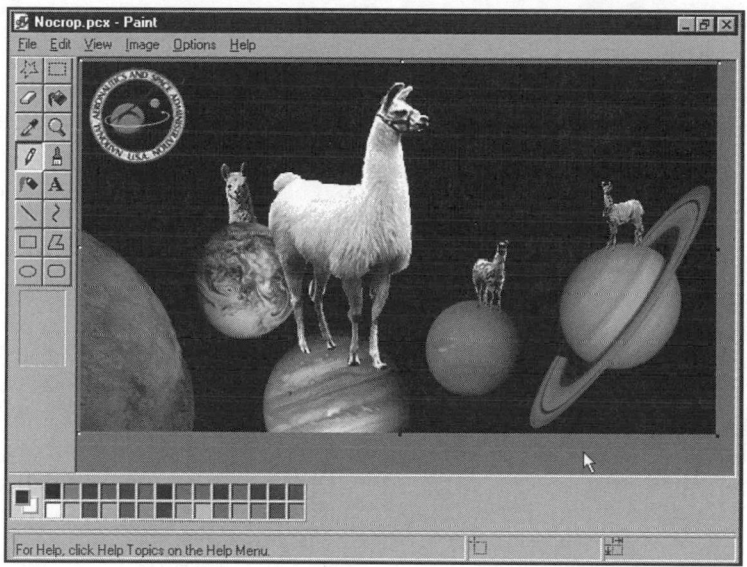

Fig. 10.1
If you want to use the NASA logo, some of the graphics on this image aren't appropriate.

II

Basic HTML Presentation

Fig. 10.2
Cropped images
not only make
smaller files, but
also they help you
focus the attention
to something
specific.

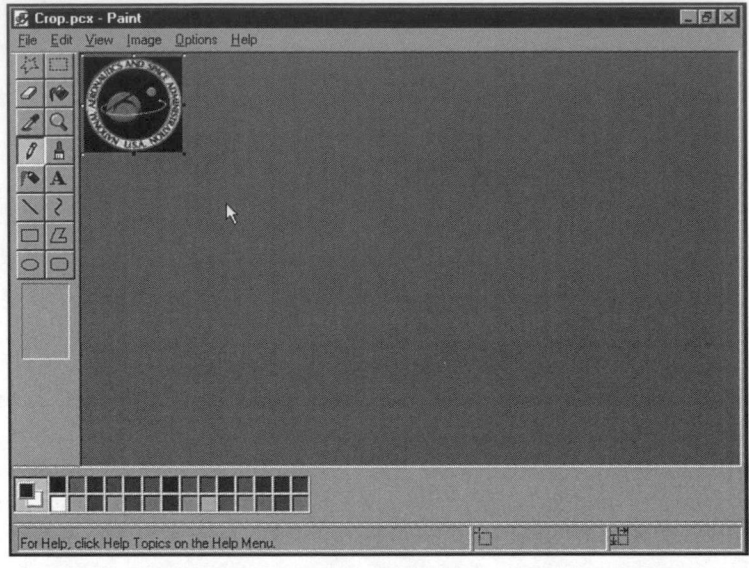

Don't Use Copyrighted Material

Pictures are just another form of expression and as a result can be copy-righted. You should use great care when using any image that is obviously from a commercial source. Pictures that generally fall into this category are images of models, actors and actresses, logos, cartoon characters, and distinc-tive images. Many people who own the copyrights to these images don't have a problem with your using them. Some copyright holders, particularly maga-zines, are much more sensitive to your use of their images, and may threaten you with a lawsuit. Others may get extremely angry and attempt to sue you and your Internet Service Provider (ISP) outright.

If you see an image you like, and it looks as though it's probably copyrighted, avoid using it. If you really want to use the image, try to contact the copy-right holder of the picture. Some of them may let you use it free of charge, whereas others may ask for a payment. If going to this trouble seems like a lot of work just for picture, good. Many pictures out there belong to someone else, and asking for permission before using the images only makes sense.

Pornographic Images

A significant minority of people with Web pages put pornographic images in their home pages. Don't. There are a lot of social and legal problems to using these images. Perhaps the most insignificant problem you'll have with using pornographic images is your personal inconvenience. Once someone interested in your graphic sees it, your Web page will be widely propogated to his or her friends. This will result in your ISP's Web server taking a heavy load, and possibly the elimination of your account.

> **Caution**
>
> The information presented about pornographic images is intended as merely common sense and reasonable suggestions. If you want the legal problems of using pornographic images, contact a lawyer in your area.

Social Aspects

A very strong reason to avoid using pornographic images is the social consequences of them. Many people, both men and women, feel that these images are harmful to society. They feel that some of the faults of society can be traced directly to these images. Whether you agree with them is not the point, they feel it's true. And should they find your Web page with its pornographic image, they will complain to you and your ISP. If your Web page is on your school's or company's machine, you can easily risk getting expelled or fired. A picture is not worth it.

Legal Aspects

You might feel that these social issues are irrelevant. You might also feel that anybody who believes in these social issues is a prude, and that your freedom of speech is being impaired. For them, there's an even better reason not to use pornographic images in your Web page: The law. By and large, the majority of pornographic images are scanned images from magazines. By using such a graphic in your Web page, you are violating the magazine's copyright. The magazine will typically warn you to remove the infringement, and failure to do so will almost guarantee a lawsuit. A picture is not worth it.

If you're still unconvinced because you think the chances of a magazine finding you are slight, there's also the possibility of a lawsuit. Different states and countries have different laws about what constitutes explicit material. Because the Internet is a world-wide network, your Web page can, potentially, be seen by anybody, anywhere, in the world. The mere act of people coming across your page, and seeing the pornographic image, can be a violation of their laws. They can rightfully seek prosecution for you to remove your graphic. A picture is not worth it.

GIFs

GIF, formally known as GIF 87a, is short for Graphics Interchange Format and was originally designed by CompuServe. It's probably one of the most widely used and supported graphic formats around. GIF is the only file format that can be viewed by almost every graphical browser around. It is, however, far from perfect.

Technical Aspects of GIF

GIF, which was created in June 1987, is technically restrictive by today's standards. Due to design restrictions, GIF can handle only up to 8-bit planes for colors. Simply put, this means that any GIF graphic can have a maximum of only 256 colors at once. Although 256 may sound like more than enough colors, it is very bad for displaying photorealistic images. Fortunately, most Web pages don't need to make use of more than 256 colors. The GIF file format does pretty straightforward compression of an image. The image is broken down into several pieces, and each piece is compressed through a particular algorithm.

How GIF Became Popular

When GIF came out, several proprietary file formats were still around. Although most programmers on their respective computers provided a way to view other file formats, the system was imperfect. The GIF file format bridged the platforms because viewers supporting it were immediately available from CompuServe. Graphics files from different computers no longer had to be converted before being viewed; GIF could be seen by everyone.

Legal Aspects of GIF

Around 1994, it was well publicized that GIF had suddenly become "illegal" in some way. When CompuServe designed GIF, they made use of a proprietary compression scheme. Unfortunately, this algorithm was copyrighted by Unisys, and CompuServe didn't obtain a license to use it. As a result, programs that supported GIF were suddenly thrown into murky waters. Unisys decided that because GIF had become so popular, it was impossible to try to stop its use. Unisys took a reasonable approach by requiring that any software that supported GIF had to get a license from them. What this all means to you, the Web author, is that you can easily use GIF images without a problem. Unisys will not, and they have said so themselves, sue anybody for using GIFs in home pages.

JPEG

In the early 1990s, a new graphics file format emerged. It was created by the Joint Photographic Experts Group. It was intended to be a new and better file format than any others available. JPEG is widely used by most people and is rapidly gaining more and more acceptance. Most older graphical browsers don't support JPEG natively, but the newer ones do.

Technical Aspects of JPEG

JPEG was designed to be a file format that used its own compression algorithm. JPEG allows for support of up to 24-bit color planes. A typical JPEG graphic therefore can have up to 16.7 million colors. JPEG's compression algorithm is far more sophisticated than GIF's. Each *pixel*, an individual dot of a picture, in the image is compared to the ones adjacent to it. A mathematical formula is generated to represent this block of pixels and is subsequently encoded.

How JPEG Became Popular

With the advent of more powerful computers, JPEG also became more and more powerful. The reason is that JPEG's algorithm is more math intensive than GIF's. Instead of basic compression/uncompression routines, JPEG used math functions. This made JPEGs unusable for all but the high-end PCs. So, with more powerful computers came faster JPEG decompression. This increase in speed led to a better appreciation for JPEG's power in displaying real-life images.

Legal Aspects of JPEG

If you're worried about any legal problems arising out of using JPEG files, don't despair. The JPEG image compression formula was derived and released into the public domain. There is no central body that has defined JPEG or would prosecute you for using it. While there *are* proprietary JPEG compression algorithms, they need the corresponding decompression program. What this means to almost everybody is that there's no problem with using JPEG images.

The File Format Debate: GIF versus JPEG

Ever since JPEG showed up on the image scene, a debate has grown about which is better, GIF or JPEG. The simple fact is that both are good for use on your home page; which is better just depends on what you want. In the following sections, you'll look at the good and bad points of each file format and learn you when it's good to use which one.

File Speed

The first and most important thing that you, as a Web author, should look at when choosing a graphic is speed. You don't want to waste people's time downloading and decoding large images. You want to inconvenience the typical user as little as possible, and choosing the right graphics file format helps (see table 10.1). GIFs are typically larger than JPEGs (slower to download) but are remarkably fast at decompression (faster to view). Conversely, JPEGs tend to be smaller than GIFs (thus faster to download), but they take longer to uncompress than GIFs (slower to display). Either file format would be fine when you consider the speed factor.

Table 10.1   GIF versus JPEG: Technical Merits

Technical Aspect	GIF	JPEG
Maximum Colors	256	16.7 million
Created By	CompuServe, Inc.	Joint Photographic Experts Group
Compression Scheme	LZW	JPEG

Browser Support

Another important consideration in choosing the correct file format is how widely supported it is—not support in terms of a particular computer type, but how much support the different formats have from browsers. The more browsers that support a particular format, the more you'll want to use it (see table 10.2). GIF has been around longer than JPEG and is supported by all but the oldest browsers. JPEG is newer than GIF and is more processor intensive. However, many newer browsers support JPEG natively along with GIF. Because of its wider support, GIF would be a better choice for your home page graphics.

Table 10.2   Graphics Format: Browser Support

Format	Extension	Browser Support
Graphics Interchange Format	GIF	Native
Joint Photographic Experts Group Bitmap	JPEG	Native or Helper Application
Device Independent Bitmap	DIB	Native or Helper Application
Tagged Image File Format	TIFF, TIF	Helper Application
PC Paintbrush	PCX	Helper Application
Truevision Targa	TGA	Helper Application
Portable Network Graphics	PNG	Helper Application

Colors

How well the image looks is another important factor in deciding the correct file format. The more colors your image has, the better and more realistic it will look to the viewer. Using fewer colors can result in warped-looking images. GIF allows a maximum of 256 colors to be displayed at once, and that's all. A JPEG graphic can have up to 16.7 million colors at once, clearly an advantage.

However, just because a file format can support many more colors doesn't mean that you really need them. If you're making a graphic of your company logo, do you really need 16.7 million colors? Also, remember that most computers can display only 256 colors at once anyway. Different computers handle this limitation in different ways, and the results are hardly ever pretty. Under certain circumstances, 16.7 million colors can be viewed on most computers, but that's not always going to be the case. You should consider using GIF for most of your graphic needs. The only exception to this rule is if you want users to be able to download your images and view them later; then you should use JPEG.

Which Looks Better?

Another aspect in deciding which graphics format to use, is how well each format will handle the image. Because of the way GIF is designed, it's a good general-purpose file format. You lose almost no information from a scanned-in image. JPEG is different in that it looks at the colors of each pixel on the image itself. It is great for scanned photographs but little else. So when it comes to showing scanned images or the like, you'll want to go with JPEG. If your graphics are line art or something similar, you'll want to use GIF.

Making Your Decision

So what do all these different points add up to? For the most part, you'll want to use the GIF file format for most of your home page graphics. They're not necessarily faster or slower to view, but they are more widely accepted. The color limitation isn't too significant because most people viewing your home page can see only 256 colors anyway.

You'll want to make use of JPEGs if you're dealing with many photographic and scanned-in images. Also, if you're making pictures of your company's products available, you'll want those images in JPEG. In both of these cases, people interested in the graphic can download it and see it at their leisure.

Improvements in GIFs and JPEGs

With all the debate over generic GIF and JPEG, some improvements have been made to each format. These improvements are exclusive to each format and can create some interesting effects. These effects are very difficult to quantify into something that you do or do not want to use. In the following sections, you look at each of the improvements and can decide for yourself if it makes that particular format more appealing for you.

Interlaced GIF

From its very inception, the GIF file format could encode images "interlaced." This means that as you get more and more of the GIF graphic, more and more details are shown to you. This capability was provided so that CompuServe users could see the image as they were downloading. This capability also is useful because it allows users who aren't interested in a particular graphic to avoid downloading the whole image. Many people use Interlaced GIFs for their imagemap graphic (see chapter 12) so that users can see the general outline of clickable regions.

The only difference between Interlaced GIFs and non-interlaced GIFs is how the images are stored. As a result, most graphics programs allow you to specify whether to save an image as interlaced or non-interlaced. On most modern image viewers, you can't see the difference. However, people who will be visiting your Web site won't be doing it from a graphics viewer; they'll be doing it from a Web browser. So even though you, while you're creating it, can't see an interlaced GIF, people visiting your site will.

Transparent GIF

Around 1989 to 1990, CompuServe revised some aspects of the GIF file format. This new format, known as GIF 89a, allowed (among other things) for the provision of having a "transparent color." That is, one particular color in the GIF image is completely ignored and not displayed. In that particular color's place, the viewer shows whatever color is in the background. As a result, the GIF image appears to "float" over the home page (see fig. 10.3).

Transparent GIFs are particularly useful for hiding the borders and backgrounds of images. To accomplish this sort of effect, you can simply specify the background color as the Transparent Index. Each graphics program that supports Transparent GIFs does so in a different manner. Some of these programs let you specify the Transparent Index when you save the file. Others let you indicate the Transparent Index while you're looking at the image itself.

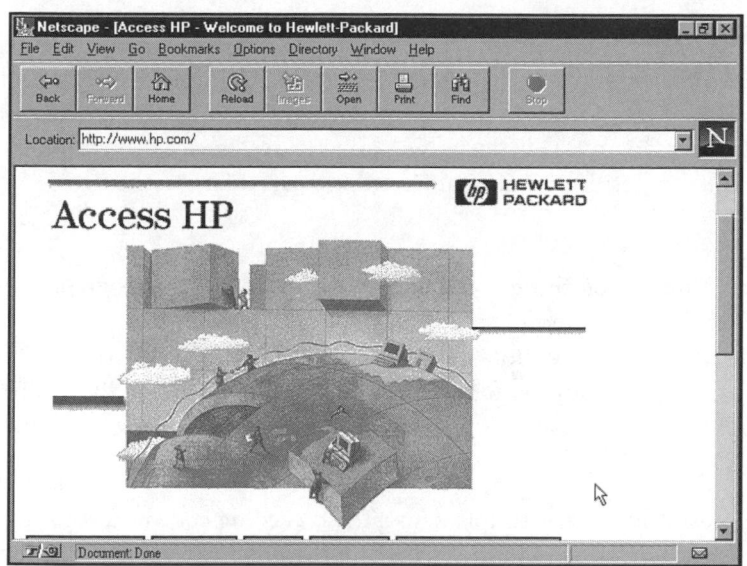

Fig. 10.3
Transparent GIFs
allow images to
blend in with the
background.

II

Basic HTML Presentation

Progressive JPEG

Netscape, a company that constantly changes the face of Web browsers, has
introduced Progressive JPEG. Visually, this new file format appears to behave
similarly to Interlaced GIF. As more of the file is downloaded, the picture becomes clearer. As of this writing, very little is known about Progressive JPEGs.
It is, however, incompatible with most JPEG viewers. The reason why very
little is known about Progressive JPEG is because it's been a long-ignored aspect of JPEG. In all likelihood, Progressive JPEGs will become more widely
supported.

JPEG images are typically stored encoded from top to bottom by using the
JPEG compression algorithm. Progressive JPEG works by storing images into
portions. Each portion improves upon the quality of the one before it. So that
the first portion of the Progressive JPEG image is very blocky and has little
detail. The next portion adds more detail to the first one, and so on until the
final image is shown.

Tip

If you have an existing graphic in either GIF or JPEG file format, don't convert it.
Because of the different methods of encoding a picture, converting between the two
formats will ruin it. The degradation may be slight, but it does occur.

Graphics and Home Pages

Now that you've decided what you want your image to show and the format to show it in, you'll want to put it in your home page. Images are just another element in an HTML document and, as a result, can be manipulated as such. You can position images and even associate a link to them.

The IMG Tag

The first, and easiest, thing you'll probably want to do is put a graphic on your home page. You don't want anything special attached to it; you simply want to have the image show up. You can do this easily using the IMG container tag and the corresponding SRC attribute. Simply assign the full path, or URL, for the desired graphic to it. The general syntax for using a graphic is

```
<IMG SRC="filename">
```

The process really is that simple. Using the preceding code results in the image ending up as close to the left side of the browser as possible. If the graphic is by itself, it will end up in the leftmost column of the browser. If text appears to its left, the image will be to the right of the text. Figure 10.4 shows some sample HTML code that makes use of graphics. Figure 10.5 shows what that sample home page looks like when viewed with Netscape.

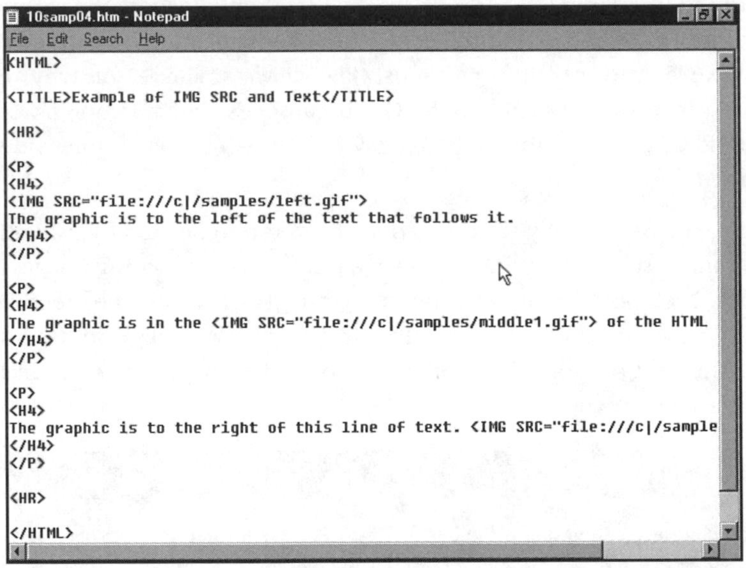

Fig. 10.4

HTML doesn't restrict where you can use the IMG SRC tag in a home page.

```
10samp04.htm - Notepad
File  Edit  Search  Help

<HTML>

<TITLE>Example of IMG SRC and Text</TITLE>

<HR>

<P>
<H4>
<IMG SRC="file:///c|/samples/left.gif">
The graphic is to the left of the text that follows it.
</H4>
</P>

<P>
<H4>
The graphic is in the <IMG SRC="file:///c|/samples/middle1.gif"> of the HTML
</H4>
</P>

<P>
<H4>
The graphic is to the right of this line of text. <IMG SRC="file:///c|/sample
</H4>
</P>

<HR>

</HTML>
```

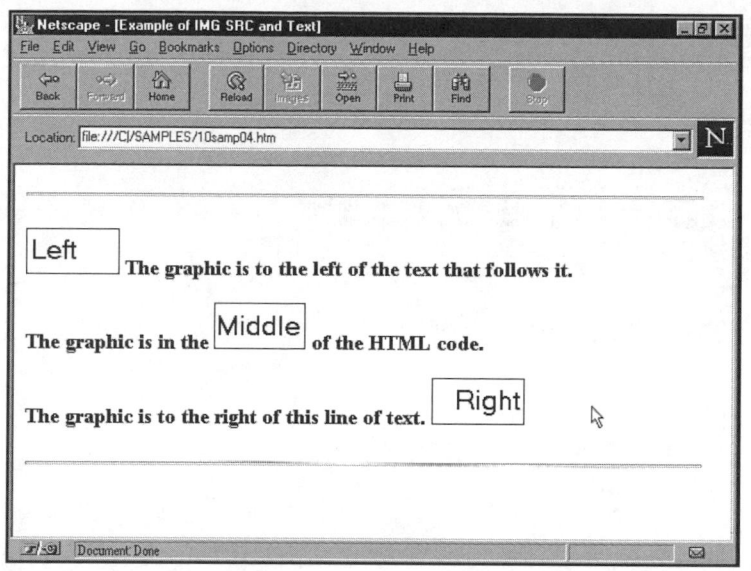

Fig. 10.5
By default, the baseline of the text is aligned to the bottom of the image, no matter where it appears on that line.

Positioning the Image

When you're placing your image, you may not like where it ended up in relation to the text. Fortunately, HTML provides a way of aligning the text with relation to the graphic. Simply add the ALIGN attribute to the IMG element. This attribute can take one of three values: TOP, MIDDLE, or BOTTOM (see fig. 10.6). If you use the TOP value for the ALIGN attribute, the browser aligns the top first line of text with the top of the graphic. The MIDDLE value puts the baseline of the current line of text even with the middle of the image. The BOTTOM value aligns the baseline of the text with the bottom of the graphic. By default, the BOTTOM value is used with the IMG element. Figure 10.7 shows all the alignment values in use on a home page.

Along with being able to position an image in relation to the text, you can also control its size. The IMG element also has the attributes HEIGHT and WIDTH. The values you can assign to both of these are values indicating the number of pixels. The image will be stretched, or shrunken, to be exactly the size you specify. For example, suppose you have an image called "test.gif" that is 300 pixels wide, by 200 pixels tall. Further, let's say that you have the following code in our Web page:

```
<IMG SRC="test.gif" HEIGHT=100 WIDTH=50>
```

The image will be resized down to 50 pixels wide by 100 pixels tall. You can use these attributes to your advantage if you're trying to create miniature samples of the picture. Instead of creating a smaller version of an image, simply scale it down. The image scaling is done by the user's Web browser, not the server.

Fig. 10.6
You can use any one of three options to align text to each image.

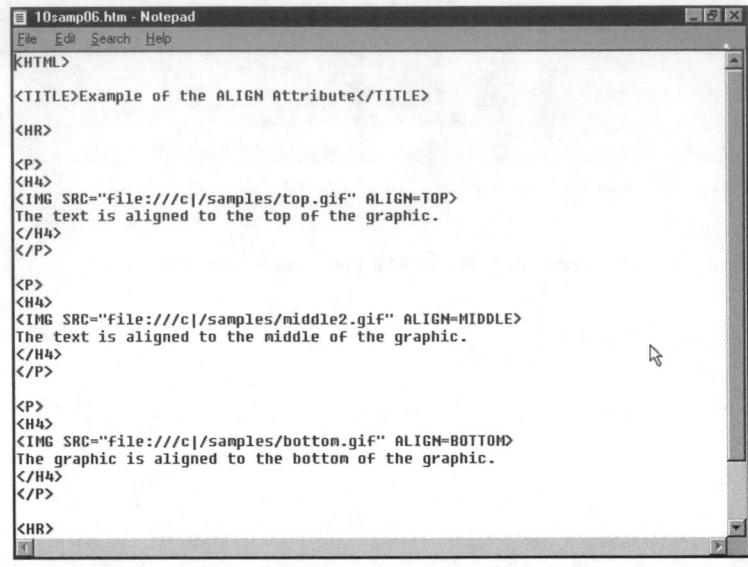

Fig. 10.7
You can see how different alignment values can help you position text better, with relation to the graphic.

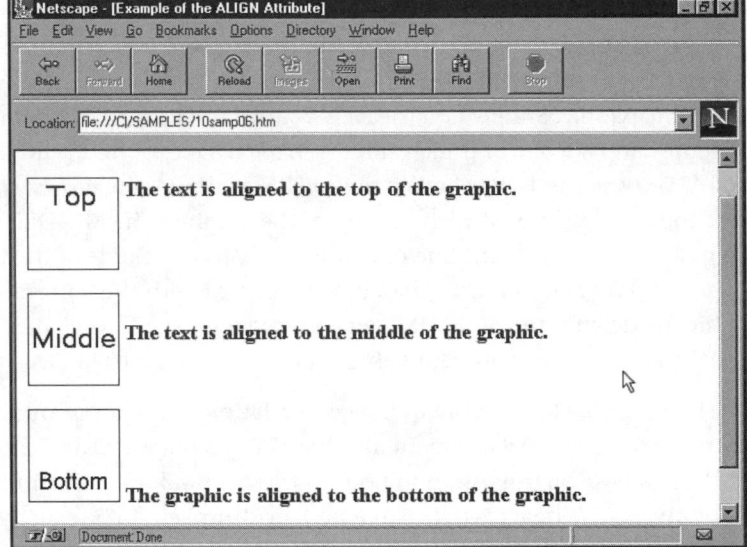

Caution

When using the HEIGHT and WIDTH attributes, the entire picture still has to be downloaded. Don't think that by scaling an image down, the page will load faster. It won't. The browser is the program that does the image scaling, not the Web server.

> **Tip**
>
> This technique is great for commercial Web sites, where you can have scaled down images of a particular product. If the user clicks on the image, they can get the full size picture of it. Since you're using the same image, you save some disk space.

Clickable Images

Many home pages on the Web contain clickable graphics. That is, you can click on some images on a home page, and you go to a new URL. You can create these images easily by building on the ideas presented in chapter 4, "Building Blocks of HTML." There, you learned how you can create a hypertext link to go to another home page. The only difference here is that, instead of using text that is clickable, you use the IMG element.

Suppose that you want to change your plain hypertext link from text that says "Click here!" to a graphic with your corporate logo. You don't want to change the URL, just the appearance of the hyperlink. Instead of using

```
<A HREF="http://www.mysite.com/">Click here!</A>
```

you use the following line:

```
<A HREF="http://www.mysite.com/"><IMG SRC="mylogo.gif"></A>
```

This results in the graphic mylogo.gif being displayed and attached to a link. If a user clicks on that image, he or she goes to the corresponding URL. You can similarly link other resources on the Net to graphics (see chapter 7, "Linking HTML Documents").

Background Images

If you don't want the background of your Web page to be a bland color, you can set it to an image. This is done not with an attribute to be used with the <IMG> tag, but is accomplished by a new Netscape and HTML 3 proposed attribute to the <BODY> tag. The new attribute is the BACKGROUND attribute, and it should point to a URL for an image. When the user's Web browser comes across this attribute, it loads the specified image. It then tiles the graphic starting from the upper-left corner of the window through the entire Web page.

Lists and Images

If you're tired of seeing the same rectangles, circles, and discs for lists, you're not trapped. You can easily spice up your list of items. Instead of creating a list with the standard unordered, numbered, or directory lists, use a definition list. As you know, you should use the <DT> and <DD> HTML tags. But what you can do is to not use the <DT> tag at all and put an <IMG> tag in the <DD> element. For example, instead of a list such as:

```
<UL>
<LI>Milk</LI>
<LI>Eggs</LI>
<LI>Cereal</LI>
</UL>
```

You can do something like:

```
<DL>
<DD><IMG SRC="mybullet.gif">Milk</DD>
<DD><IMG SRC="mybullet.gif">Eggs</DD>
<DD><IMG SRC="mybullet.gif">Cereal</DD>
</DL>
```

This will cause the graphic "mybullet.gif" to be displayed in front of each item in the grocery list (see fig. 10.8). This allows you to create snazzier looking lists for your Web page. The only hard part for you is taking out a graphics program, and drawing the bullet yourself.

Fig. 10.8
You can create lists with really fancy bullets, just don't use the conventional HTML list elements.

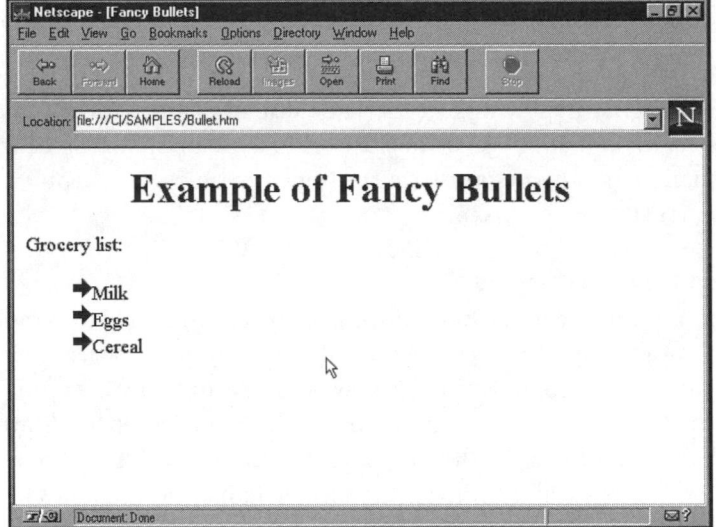

Alternatives to Graphics

After you've gone through all this work of putting graphics on your home page, you have to consider the people who cannot see them. Many people who use browsers can't see the images. A significant number of people who access the Net through UNIX machines can use only text-based Web browsers. Some people with slow modems deliberately disable automatic loading of images, so they can't see your graphics either. You must provide some way for them to be able to get the same effect of your home page without the graphics.

HTML provides for an ALT attribute for the IMG element. This attribute is basically a string that is displayed to the graphically incapable browser. No hard-set rule exists for how long the ALT string can be, but you should keep it short. Figure 10.9 shows you how to make use of the ALT attribute in the IMG SRC tag. Figure 10.10 shows what people with graphical browsers see, and figure 10.11 shows what text-only users see.

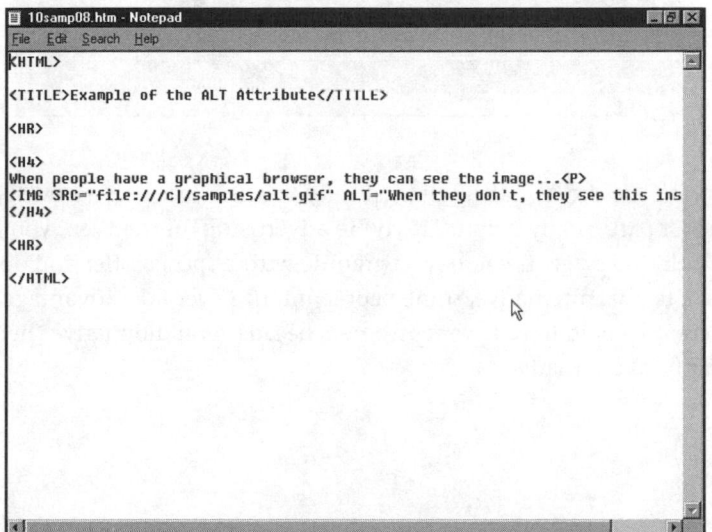

Fig. 10.9
Be sure to make use of the ALT attribute to help people without graphical browsers enjoy your home page.

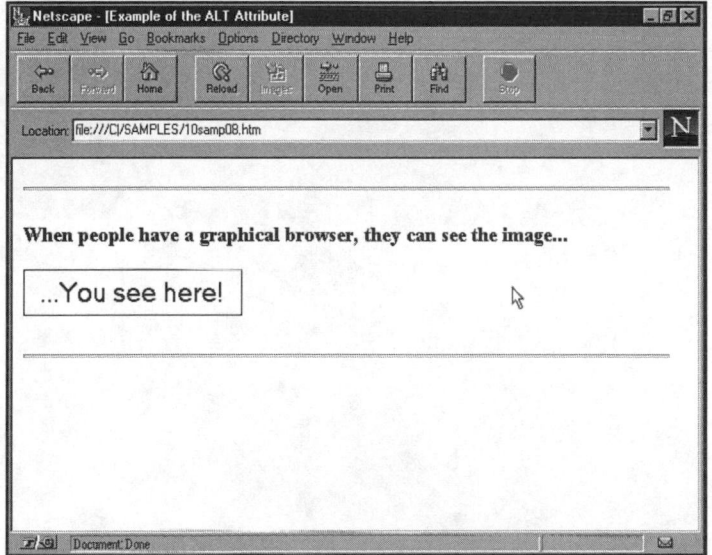

Fig. 10.10
People with graphical browsers can see all the pictures in your home page.

Fig. 10.11
People with text-only browsers can see only the ALT attributes of all the pictures in your home page.

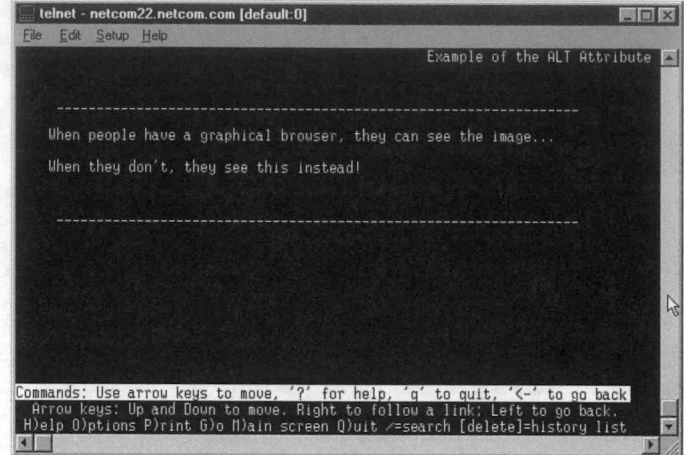

If you don't use the ALT attribute, typically the user sees only [IMAGE], which isn't particularly helpful. If you're advertising on the Web, you'll want to avoid this message. If you have a graphic with a special offer and don't provide a textual alternative, some people might never take advantage of it. You therefore could have fewer customers because you didn't give them a non-graphical alternative. ❖

## CHAPTER 11

Handling Images

by Mark Brown

There is obviously a lot more to putting an image into a Web page than merely using the <IMG> tag. You have to make sure that the graphic can be seen by as many people as possible. Not only does the picture have to be appropriate for your uses, but also it has to be well designed for the user. That is, you want the image to be downloaded as quickly as possible by the user's browser. We'll talk a lot about the more technical aspects of images and how to control them.

In this chapter, you learn about the following:

- A general overview of pictures
- Controlling a picture's file size
- Controlling a picture's image size
- Why you might want to create a custom image
- How to create a custom image
- How to modify a scanned image
- Color considerations
- Programs that you can use

The Basics of an Image

Before we can talk about creating or modifying an image, we have to know the basics of it. All graphics file formats have the same basic information. The difference between them is the way the information is stored. Because most modern Web browsers can handle both GIF and JPEG, we'll limit our discussion to these two formats.

The Color Palette

The first attribute of any picture you see is the *color palette*, which holds the colors being used by the current picture. The number of colors that can be defined is based on the image-file format used to store the image. Typically, each entry in the color palette stores the brightness of red, green, and blue. By mixing these three colors, you can get any other color. These color palette entries are sometimes referred to as *pens*.

The Image Itself

The display size of the image is known as the *resolution*, and is stored as a series of *pixels* (dots on the screen). Each pixel in the image points to an entry in the color palette. To display the graphic, you have to go through each pixel of the graphic. Then for each pixel, look at which pen it's using, and then look up the color for the pen. Based on the resolution, you'll know when you reach the end of one line of the graphic.

Compressing the Image

If you were to store an image as a color palette and a sequence of pixels, the file size would be very large. While there are file formats that store such an image, it's unworkable for a Web page. Consequently, the graphic data must be compressed to reduce the file size. To this end, GIF applies traditional compression methods to a picture. These conventional compression algorithms look for recurring patterns in the image data. The more frequent a particular pattern, the more the graphic file size will be reduced.

Due to technical restrictions of GIF, such as number of colors and file size, a new graphic file format was developed. That format was *JPEG (Joint Photographic Experts Group)*. This format differed radically from GIF in that it overcame GIF's shortcomings. Along with overcoming GIF's faults, the group used a number of studies on the human eye, and what it can actually see. As a result, instead of GIF's 256-color limit, JPEG went up to 16.7 million colors. Instead of storing an exact copy of a scanned image, JPEG offered a very good approximation of it. Because a JPEG image is an approximation, JPEG is known as a *lossy* file format.

Portable PixelMap

There is one graphic file format that stores a picture as a series of pixels with corresponding color values. This file format, developed by Jef Pozkanzer, is known as *PPM (Portable PixelMap)*. It stores images in a direct manner: the resolution of the picture and each pixel are stored as raw numbers in an ASCII file. As a result of its straightforward nature, it's found a lot of support in many programs on many platforms.

It was originally designed as an intermediate graphic file format. It provides conventional color- and image-manipulation tools that you'll find on other graphics programs. Because PPM was originally designed on a UNIX platform, the tools are actually UNIX programs. PPM tools allow you to crop, scale, and rotate PPM files. Because PPM is just a text file, you can take any image from any platform, and use PPM's tools to manipulate it.

The tradeoff between PPM's versatility and machine-independence is the file size. A typical image can easily be 10 to 20 times larger if stored in PPM format. PPM is mainly used on UNIX computers, where people don't always have easy access to a graphics-capable terminal.

An Image's File Size

Although there are a number of factors in putting images into a Web page, the most important one is the *file size* of the graphic, which is how much disk space the picture takes up. Lots of different things affect how big the file size of the graphic is. Regardless of which graphic file format you choose, either GIF or JPEG, you have to be careful about its file size.

Why Should I Care?

The reason the file size of the image is important is because it'll ultimately be seen by a user. Consequently, the file must be transferred to the user's browser to be seen, and the larger the file size of the image, the longer it'll take him to see your picture. While many browsers will show the image, large files can take a long time to view completely. Obviously, you'll want to keep the file size down to a minimum, so that it can be viewed as quickly as possible.

Size can affect you, too. Typically, individuals pay a company to store, and provide access to, their own Web pages. These companies have a limit of how much disk space the individual can use for his or her pages. People going over the limit usually have to pay for the extra disk space used. By keeping the file size of the image down, you will take up less of your allocated disk space.

What Affects File Size?

So what aspects of a graphic will directly affect the file size? All of them. The number of colors used in an image directly affect how many pens are allocated. The more pens there are, the better the odds that there'll be more patterns. For each new pattern that exists, an image's file size goes up. While more colors don't guarantee that a file size will go up, it often does.

The resolution of the image itself, as with the number of colors, will directly affect the file size. The larger the resolution of the image, the bigger the file size will be. Similarly, the smaller the picture's resolution, the smaller the file size tends to be. The bigger the picture, the more you need to encode.

What will actually be displayed on the screen is also a significant factor in a graphic's file size (more details increase the size of the file for that image). The likelihood of having a lot of detail in an image is only a factor with scanned-in images because most image scanners pick up subtle differences from pixel to pixel. With each new shade that is recognized, another pen must be allocated to represent it.

How Do I Control the File Size?

Fortunately, all the factors that can increase the file size of an image can be controlled. Most paint programs, and a few image viewing programs, will let you affect all of these factors. By using the tools at your disposal, you can easily reduce the file size of a particular graphic. Because there are so many factors that affect the file size, you can modify whichever attribute would least impact your graphic.

The number of colors used by an image can easily be modified. Most paint programs have the facility to modify an image's color depth (the maximum number of pens an image can have). If the graphic you want to use has a very large file size, you might want to decrease its color depth. For pixels that have colors that are no longer used, they are assigned a pen that closely resembles its original color. This color-matching routine is known as *dithering*.

It's also very easy to change the resolution of a particular graphic. A lot of paint programs let you resize, or *scale*, a specific image. Typically, when you scale an image, there's an option to keep the *aspect ratio,* which indicates the size relationship of pixels between the height and the width.

Types of Images

We now have a good understanding of what makes up an image, and how to control its size. Now we have to apply this knowledge to the images we want to put on a Web page. There are two types of images you can use in Web pages, a *custom image*, or a *scanned image*. A custom image is an image that you or your corporation creates from scratch. A scanned image is a picture that has been scanned into a computer-readable format. While the custom image requires more work to create, it offers the most flexibility. A scanned image is best suited for product catalogs or to put existing pictures into your Web page.

Reasons for Using Custom Images

A custom image isn't something that you get off the Net that you thought would be good to put in your Web page. It's a graphic that you took the time to create personally. Probably the biggest reason for using custom graphics is that they're extremely flexible. Instead of hunting around, looking for an image that'll fit your needs, you create what you need. Also, because they're original pictures, you don't have to worry about copyright issues.

Copying Custom Images

One of the most popular ways you can put graphics into your home page is to take someone else's. While you're surfing the Web, you may come across a home page with a cool graphic. You can use your browser's functionality to simply copy the image off the page and onto your hard drive. Copying generally isn't a problem because most people on the Net aren't very restrictive about this sort of thing. Also, some of the images you might want to copy are small, such as horizontal rules, and most people don't really care about them. Some groups even encourage you to copy their images because of some political stances (see fig. 11.1).

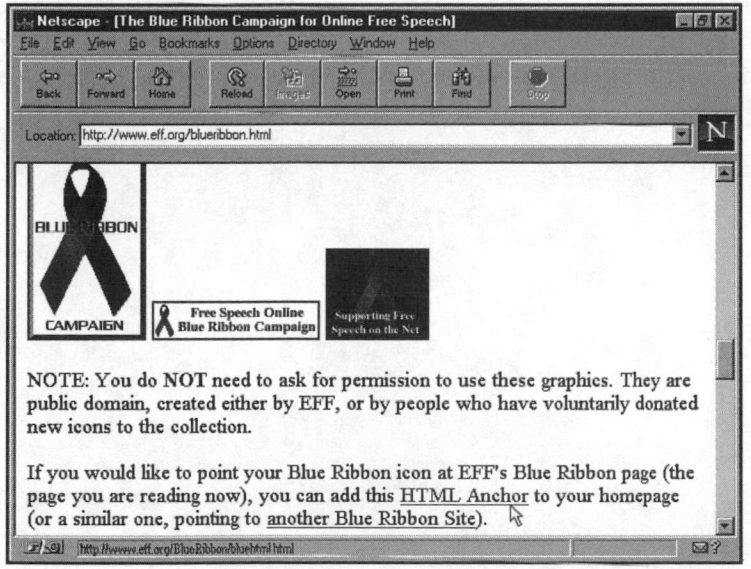

Fig. 11.1
The EFF encourages people to copy their blue ribbon, as a show of support for free speech on the Internet.

However, a number of copyrighted images appear on the Net, and copying them is illegal. Typically, these images are on the Net in the first place because of some licensing agreement between the copyright owner and the Web site. The most commonly appearing copyrighted artwork that appears on the Net includes daily comic strips. You can generally spot copyrighted work because it's indicated as such somewhere on the graphic. If that's the case, then you should contact the copyright holder and ask for permission to use that image in your home page. Sometimes, he or she may want some sort of royalty fee for the use of the image, but check to be sure. If the copyright holder decides not to let you use the image, don't do it anyway because he or she can file a lawsuit and probably win.

Controlling the Image's Contents

Another reason for going to the trouble of creating a custom graphic for your home page is to have complete control over it. Some home pages have a collection of images that the Web author wants you to copy (see fig. 11.2). As generous as this offer may be, one distinct problem is that you can't control aspects of the picture. Maybe the colors in the graphic you want to use are radically different from what you were thinking of. Maybe the resolution (the graphic's dimensions) isn't right for where you want to put it.

Certainly, you could download the image that most closely looks like something you want to use and then modify it (see fig. 11.2). But depending on what the graphic is and how it was created, going to this trouble could be a time-consuming process. Downloading and modifying an image could easily take up as much time as creating your own custom graphic. This is especially true for the home pages that make ray-traced images for anyone. You may be able to control certain aspects of the shape and lighting to be used, but you might not be able to tune everything you want.

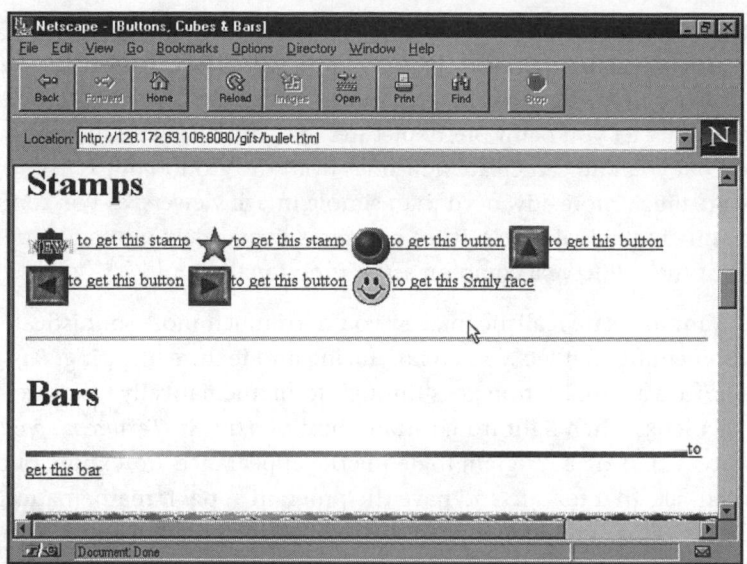

Creating the Image You Want

Probably the best reason that you have for creating custom graphics for your
home page is that the image you want simply doesn't exist. It's also possible
that the graphic you want does exist on some home page somewhere, but
there's no easy way to view all the graphics on all the home pages on the
Web. Perhaps the graphic you want to have in your HTML document is
atypical. Although a "No Llama Crossing" graphic may exist somewhere,
how hard will it be to find it?

Creating a Graphic

After you decide to create your own graphic, you want to get started right
away, right? Wrong. You need a number of things before you go about creating your custom image. Some of these items are just pieces of information
about the particular HTML document into which you want to put the
graphic. Others are questions that you can easily answer.

Basic HTML Presentation

Image Tools

For creating specialized images that may or may not look realistic, you really need only a paint program. These applications are, as their name implies, programs that let you paint pretty pictures. Not only can you modify existing images, but you also can create new ones from the ground up. These programs are much more advanced than simple image viewers, as you can actually modify individual pixels. Paint programs vary widely in the features they have, but they all have a common set of functionality.

If you want to create realistic images, you need much more sophisticated tools, something that lets you do ray tracing and texture mapping. *Ray tracing* is the process an application goes through to mathematically calculate how an object looks when light from certain locations hits it. *Texture mapping* is the process of using a program to define the appearance, or texture, of things. You then take that texture and have the program apply it mathematically to an object (see fig. 11.3). So, if you were to have the program apply a plaid texture to a sphere, the program would figure out how to twist and shape the plaid onto the sphere. Both of these processes also take up a lot of computing time for the system to do all the calculations. As a result, you may have to wait over an hour or two to generate one graphic.

Fig. 11.3
Texture-mapped graphics look great, but can you afford them?

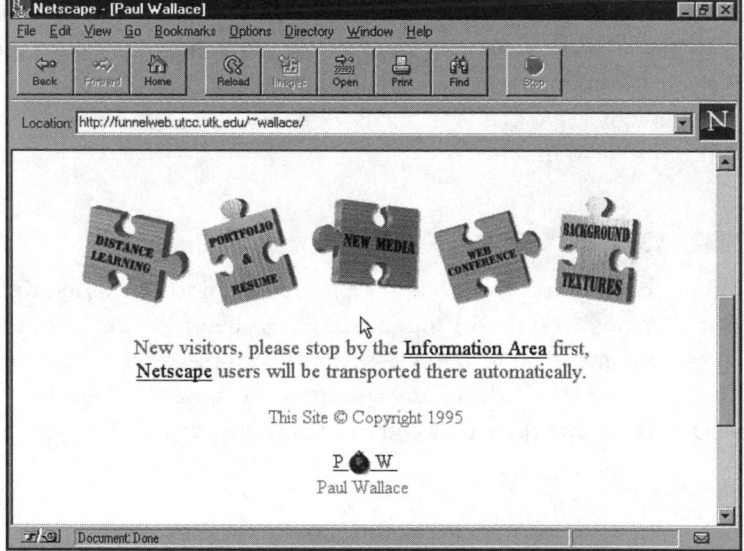

Ray Tracing

Ray-tracing programs allow the user to create definite three-dimensional objects. These objects have distinct sizes, shapes, and dimensions. You can manipulate these objects by reshaping them, or moving them behind other objects. You can also specify your viewing position in relation to the objects. But all of this is just a prelude to the power of ray tracing.

With ray-tracing programs, the user specifies light sources. These light sources are used by the program to determine how the objects on the screen will appear. A light ray is mathematically shot through each pixel in the view plane. The program traces the ray back to a point on a surface of one of the objects. The ray is then further traced back to either another point on another surface, or a light source. The ray is repeatedly traced until a light source is reached, or the ray passes outside the viewing plane.

As you might imagine, this process is rather involved and requires a lot of mathematical calculations. And remember, this is just one process for one pixel on an image. Ray tracing is repeated for as many pixels as you want an image's resolution to be. So for a ray-traced 640x480 image, you would have 307,200 rays to be processed. Once it's done, however, the resulting image looks amazingly photo-realistic.

Because of the extreme mathematical computations involved in both these processes, you need either a computer-aided design (CAD) program or a sophisticated paint program. A CAD program lets you create objects with definite characteristics such as size, shape, and position. Without physical characteristics, such as those that CAD programs use, creating ray traced images is very difficult. Similarly, texture mapping depends on physical characteristics to work properly. However, some more advanced paint programs, such as Photoshop and Fractal Design Painter, let you apply textures to regular images. Because of the high costs of these types of programs, many people don't use ray-traced or texture-mapped images on their home pages. For most home pages, a good paint program is more than adequate to create custom graphics.

HTML Document Considerations

Another consideration you should look at before designing custom graphics is the page where you want to use the graphics. Take a look at the color scheme you're either using or planning to use on that particular HTML document. You should keep the colors in the graphic from clashing with the colors in the home page. Also, avoid making the graphic colors very similar to the home page colors. You don't want to put a yellow graphic on a home page that has a white background because seeing the image is difficult.

One last thing to consider before you go about creating your own custom graphics is the resolution. See where on the page you want a custom image and decide how big it should be. This consideration is very important because it dictates how much room you have to design your graphic. The more space you want to give to the image, the less space you'll have for any supporting text. Try to keep the image resolution as small as possible for your needs. If you have a button to go to the next page, for example, it shouldn't take up half the screen.

Paint Program General Features

By and large, you probably use a paint program of some sort to design your custom graphics. Each program has different features that make it unique, but every one of them has a base of similar features (see fig. 11.4). Most paint programs have the following:

Fig. 11.4
Paint is a simple paint program that is included with Windows 95.

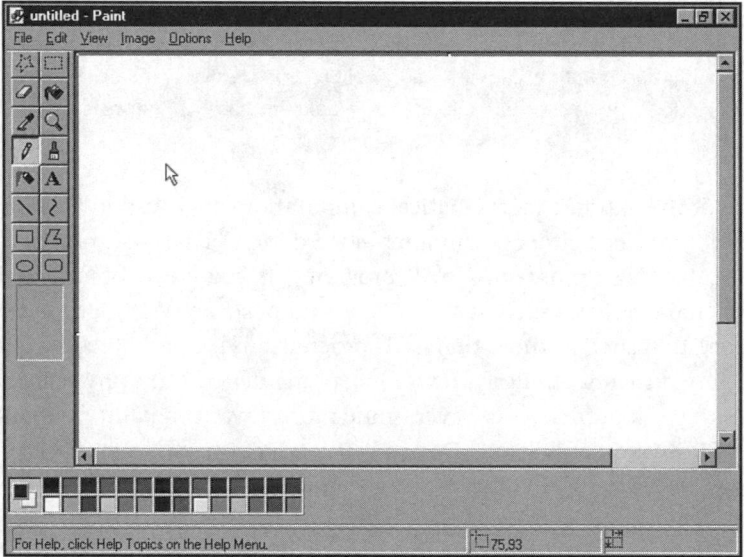

- **Brushes.** Simply select from a collection of brush types available, and you can draw. Brushes are simple geometric shapes, such as circles and lines.
- **Geometric Shapes.** Most paint programs let you create circles, lines, ellipses, squares, rectangles, and polygons. Often, you can optionally choose to have the polygon automatically filled with the specified color.

- **Freehand Drawing.** Most people are used to this type of drawing. Simply move the mouse around to draw in the foreground color.

- **Image Editing.** You can specify a region of the image and either cut or copy it into memory. You can then paste it from memory into a new location or a different graphic altogether. If you want to create a row of buttons for your imagemap graphic, simply copy and paste one button.

▶ See chapter 12 to learn about an imagemap graphic.

- **Color Palette Editing.** Each graphic has a particular palette of colors with which you can draw. You can change the colors of the palette to whatever suits your needs. If you need all grays, you can change the entire palette to be only grays.

- **Inserting Text.** If you want to add text using a particular font, you can do that with a paint program, too. Simply specify the font, size, and location you want, and type away. Typing text beats drawing each letter by hand.

- **Fill with a Color.** If you've outlined the drawing and want to fill it in, you can. Select the fill option, often pictured as a paint can, and click in the region you want to fill with the foreground color.

- **Zoom Into a Region.** For the times you want to get up close and personal, almost every paint program has a zoom feature. You can often specify the region of the graphic you want to zoom into. Sometimes you can even specify how close you want to zoom into that region. This capability is useful for tweaking minor aspects of a graphic.

Achieving the Right Look

Now that you have the tools in front of you, you can actually create the image. You can use a number of approaches to get the look you want for the image. These approaches are all dependent on what you're trying to create and what certain "look" you're going for. Generally speaking, you'll want to use the geometric shape creation features a lot. You can easily create buttons using just rectangles and circles. Geometric shapes are also great for your imagemap graphic because you can create distinct regions with them.

To make parts of the image appear to be raised above the graphic's background, just use a darker color, or black. Next, simply trace the right and bottom edges of the object you want to appear raised. To make an entire button appear raised, you can use a similar color trick. For example, if you want to make a rectangular button appear raised, color the right and bottom edges black. Then color the top and left edges white. The upper-right and lower-left corners are a little tricky because they are special cases. For these two corners, make the darker color be a diagonal line across the entire border. You can also make the shading more noticeable by simply thickening the lines of the darker color. Figure 11.5 shows a home page with buttons that use this shaded effect.

Fig. 11.5
Simple color tricks can create interesting effects for your home page.

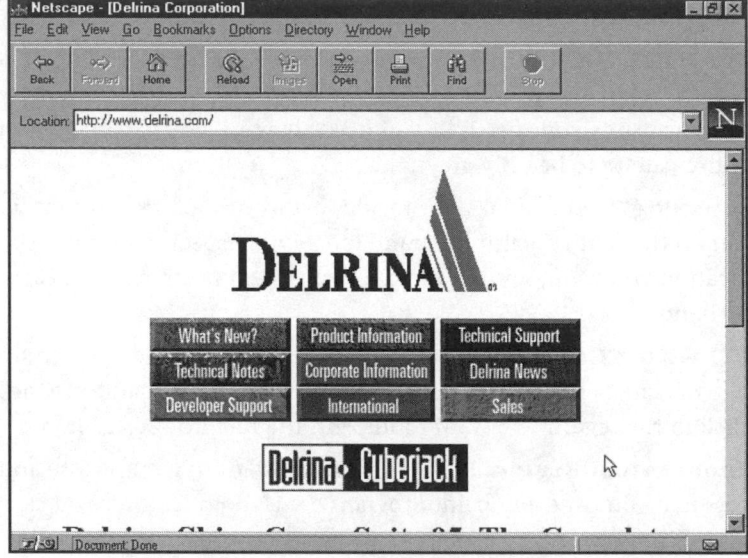

When you're designing your graphic, try not to go into too much detail. That is, if you can avoid it, don't put lots of small features into your graphic. If you're drawing a picture of the front side of a house, you don't need to draw the hinges. This desire for putting in minute touches to an image usually comes about if you've been working in zoom mode a lot. Remember that your graphic will be seen mainly by people through their browsers. The subtle things you put into an image probably won't be seen by anybody.

Tip

If you're creating two diagonal lines, and you want them to be identical, be careful. You should specify the endpoints in exactly the same manner, with both lines. In other words, if you specify the lower endpoint as your starting location for the first line, do the same with the second line. If you don't, it will almost certainly result in non-identical lines. You get this result because of a problem with the computer trying to decide exactly which pixel the line is a part of. By specifying similar endpoints as the starting location, you reduce the chances of getting different lines.

Working with Scanned Images

Just because you want to use custom graphics doesn't mean you have to create them by hand. If you want to add some fresh images not seen anywhere else, you can also use scanned images. These images differ greatly from hand-crafted drawings because they require less creation work but more touch-up work.

When to Use Scanned Images

Because you can simply create any image you want with a paint program, why would you want to use a scanned image? It saves time. If you have a graphic that isn't in a computer-readable format, you should scan it in. Company logos, signatures, and photographs are examples of images that you might want to scan. You can then put these images anywhere on your Web site for whatever reason. The main company HTML document could have the corporate logo prominently displayed, for example. A letter from the president of the company welcoming Web users could have his or her signature. Sales literature can be beefed up with scanned photos of the products (see fig. 11.6).

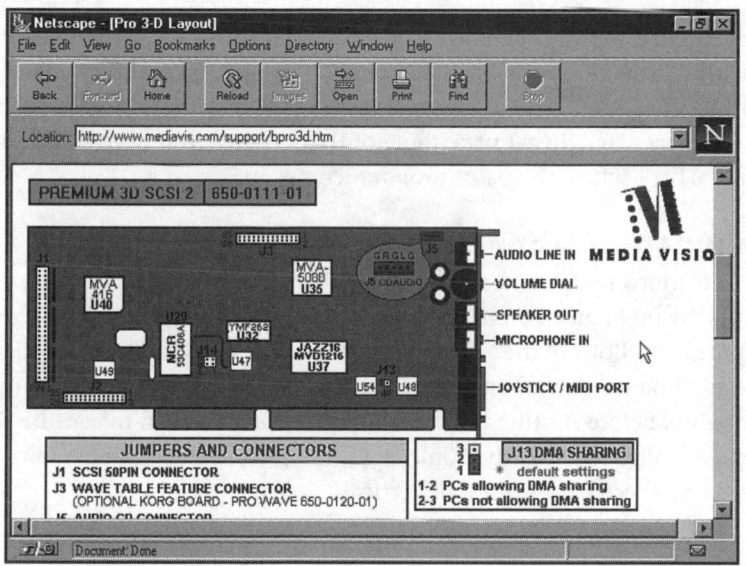

Fig. 11.6
People have a better idea of what you're selling if you use scanned images of the products.

II

Basic HTML Presentation

What's Needed for Scanned Images

You need two things before putting scanned images to use in your home page. The first thing you need is a *scanner*, a device that converts physical documents into a computer-readable format. This process isn't as complicated as it sounds; fax machines do just this task. But because you can't hook up a generic fax machine to your computer, you need to buy a dedicated scanner. If you decide to buy a scanner, the most important thing to look at is how many DPI (dots per inch) it can scan. The more DPI it can handle, the better your scanned image will look on the computer. You should also consider getting a color scanner, rather than a black-and-white one, especially for product photos.

The second thing you need for using scanned images is a paint program. Fortunately, most scanners come bundled with some sort of paint program. The quality of these programs can vary greatly between scanner makers, but they are free with the scanner. You're not going to use it to create new images but rather to touch up existing ones. Specifically, you're going to touch up the scanned images. The big trade-off with scanned images is the image size versus image quality. Because you'll want to have as small an image size as possible, you're going to have to sacrifice image quality.

In addition to a slightly degraded scan quality, scanning has inherent problems with it. You always find artifacts that show up on a scanned image that weren't in the original. These artifacts show up as dots and splotches on the scanned image. To help get back some of that quality, you need to put it in by hand. That's where the paint program comes in.

Manipulating Scanned Images

To get a scanned image into a reasonable likeness of the original, you need to clean up the problems. You have to clean up obvious graphical problems and color problems. Both of these problems are often small and hardly noticeable. As a result, you need to zoom into the scanned graphic frequently while touching up. Before starting the touch-up process, however, make sure that the image is aligned correctly. Sometimes, the physical document isn't scanned in perfectly horizontal or vertical.

One example of obvious graphical problems is straight lines appearing jagged. For this problem, you should select the background color as the foreground color. Next, use one of your drawing tools to get rid of the jagged parts. Similarly, small chunks are missing in part of a graphic, use the color of the object and fill in those areas. You should also use this method to make somewhat unreadable text readable again. For dots, smudges, and smears that weren't in the original, simply get rid of them.

You should also clean up color problems in the entire scanned-in graphic. Many times, color scanners misinterpret one color between pixels. As a result, you get two pixels, one next to the other, and one of them is slightly darker than the other. In all likelihood, the darker color is the incorrect color, so you should remove it. To do so, just specify the lighter color as the foreground color, and draw over the darker color.

All the Colors of the Rainbow

In almost all cases with graphics, you have to watch out for the colors being used. I'm not talking about choosing colors that are readable in your home page; I'm talking about how many colors you're using. Regardless of which graphic file format you choose, the more colors you use, the larger the image's file size will be. Because a larger file size translates into longer download times for the user, you should avoid using too many colors.

◀ See chapter 10, "Adding Graphics to Your Home Page," p. 191, for information on which graphic file format is right for your use.

For the images that you create from scratch, the number of colors usually isn't a problem. Typically, most paint programs default to 256 colors, which is more than enough for most people. If at all possible, try to reduce this number further by using a smaller color palette. If you don't really need all 256 colors, then try to reduce the palette to 16 colors, which should be enough for most home pages. The user can have the paint program do the color reduction automatically.

This color problem really becomes an issue when you use scanned images. Because most color scanners misinterpret two pixels of the same color as being different colors, you end up using more colors than you need. After you use the color-reduction technique specified previously (see "Manipulating Scanned Images"), try to reduce the image's color palette as well. This way, you can reduce the file size noticeably, thus helping the people viewing your home page.

Programs for You

Windows 95 has a wealth of programs that can help you with different parts of this chapter. But the ones that will help you the most are paint programs. Fortunately, some good paint programs are available as shareware and commercial software. Although commercial products are more expensive, they offer better technical support. But for most home page authors, spending a lot of money just to design custom images is not worth the price. Sadly, not many good shareware paint programs are available for the Mac.

Paint Shop Pro

A good overall paint program for Windows 95 is Paint Shop Pro (see fig. 11.7). This program offers several geometric shapes to work with, as well as some color manipulation tools. You can also resize and crop your images. Using this program, you can deform an image into a variety of shapes and perspectives. You also can define your own filters and masks and apply them to any image. Batch conversion of multiple files into a different file format and the ability to browse a directory full of pictures are also part of this shareware package.

Perhaps the most impressive feature of this program, however, is the brush support. Numerous standard brush types are available, but the ability to define your own and the functions you can perform with them are simply amazing. It is available as shareware, but if you buy it, you get extra goodies. You get Paint Shop Pro for both Windows 3.1 and Windows 95, along with some sample images.

Fig. 11.7
Paint Shop Pro is
a good, general-
purpose paint
program for
Windows 95.

Matt Paint

Matt Paint is a fairly straightforward shareware color paint program for the Macintosh. Styled somewhat after the original MacPaint program by Apple, this program offers all the basic paint program functionality. It allows for the customization of brushes and image selectors. The lasso in particular can be programmed to only pick up a chosen set of colors. Perhaps most impressive of all is that Matt Paint comes with a wide array of pre-defined color, and black and white, fill patterns. Its zoom capability is hidden under the Goodies menu heading, with the Fatbits menu item. Most of the common tools are available through floating palettes, as well as an on screen undo button.
For $25 Matt Paint is a good paint program for people on a budget. ❖

Part III
Advanced HTML Presentation

## CHAPTER 12

Graphics Navigation with Imagemaps

by John Jung

A number of advanced home pages make use of a feature commonly known as *imagemaps*. They are just pictures in which well-defined areas are marked to go to different URLs. In most cases, clicking on a picture is easier than clicking on plain text hyperlinks.

So what is involved in creating imagemaps and putting them on your home page? A lot of work. You also should consider some drawbacks to using imagemaps before including them.

In this chapter, you learn about the following:

- What imagemaps are and how they work
- How to select good imagemap graphics
- How to create the imagemap definition file
- How to incorporate imagemaps in HTML
- Guidelines for using imagemaps
- About imagemap creation programs

A Brief Introduction to Imagemaps

Because imagemaps make use of pictures, they let users navigate content-related links in a friendly fashion. The World Wide Web is the first Internet standard that allows for the easy display of graphics. This is a sharp contrast to past standards, which were all text-based, such as Gopher, WAIS, and FTP. Although these older standards couldn't transport images; I'm just saying that this capability was never designed into them (see fig. 12.1).

Fig. 12.1
Clicking on
pictures is easier
than reading text.

Simply put, imagemaps are pictures that have certain defined areas. Each of these defined areas points to different URLs to which a user can go. Because the user has to know where these clickable regions are, borders often appear around each region (see fig. 12.2). These borders are a part of the graphic itself, and not created by the Web server.

Fig. 12.2
For imagemaps to
be useful, they
should have
distinct borders
around them.

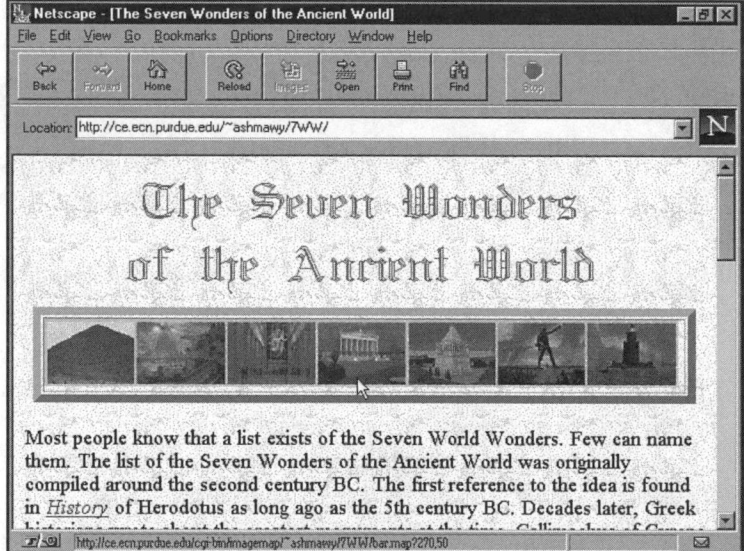

When a user clicks somewhere in the imagemap, his or her browser sends the coordinates of the mouse pointer to the Web server. The server then looks up the coordinates and determines which clickable region was accessed. The server finds the corresponding URL and goes there. Finally, the browser displays the contents of the new URL to the user.

The Pros and Cons of Imagemaps

Using imagemaps offers obvious benefits, mainly the ease of use for users. But as with almost everything else on the Net, you can always find a reason not to use imagemaps. Most of the pluses to using imagemaps are strictly for making tasks easier and friendlier for the user. The reasons not to use imagemaps are generally technical.

When to Use Imagemaps

In many situations, you should consider using imagemaps instead of hypertext links. Here's a short list of some times when using imagemaps is appropriate:

- When you want to represent links that have a physical relation to each other. For example, clicking on a map of the world is easier than picking from a list of countries.

- When you want to enable users to go to important points on your site at any time. One popular use of imagemaps is to make them a constant staple in every page on your Web site. Some sites that use imagemaps in this fashion are among the most popular sites on the Web.

- When you want to give your Web site a sense of consistency. Being consistent doesn't necessarily mean that you have the same imagemaps everywhere. You can have different imagemaps, but they have a similar look. Whenever you add new pages to your Web site, you'll probably want to add the navigation imagemap graphic to them (see fig. 12.3).

Fig. 12.3
By using imagemaps as a navigational tool for the user, you make getting around your home page easier.

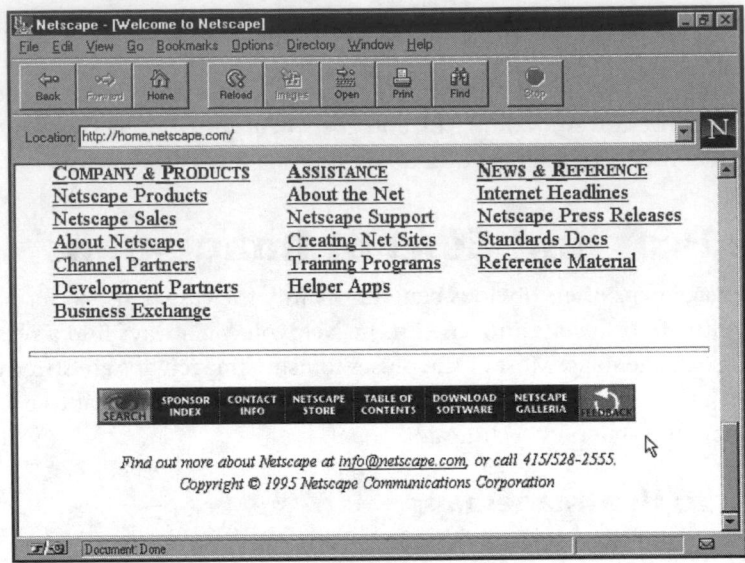

When Not to Use Imagemaps

Although imagemaps might be useful in most situations, sometimes you shouldn't use them. Here's a short list of times when you shouldn't use imagemaps:

■ Imagemaps require a Web server capable of handling them properly. Although most new Web server software is capable of correctly dealing with imagemaps, not all of them do.

■ Imagemaps can't be tested without a Web server. This means that while you're designing your imagemaps, you can't test them easily. You either have to get Web server software loaded on your own computer, or put the imagemap files on your server. Going to these extra steps can be a problem if you're creating a personal home page.

■ You must consider nongraphical browsers when designing your Web pages. Many people use text-based browsers when surfing the Web. You should provide a textual alternative to your imagemaps (see fig. 12.4). Providing a text alternative, however, can be a problem if you're designing a personal home page and are short on disk space.

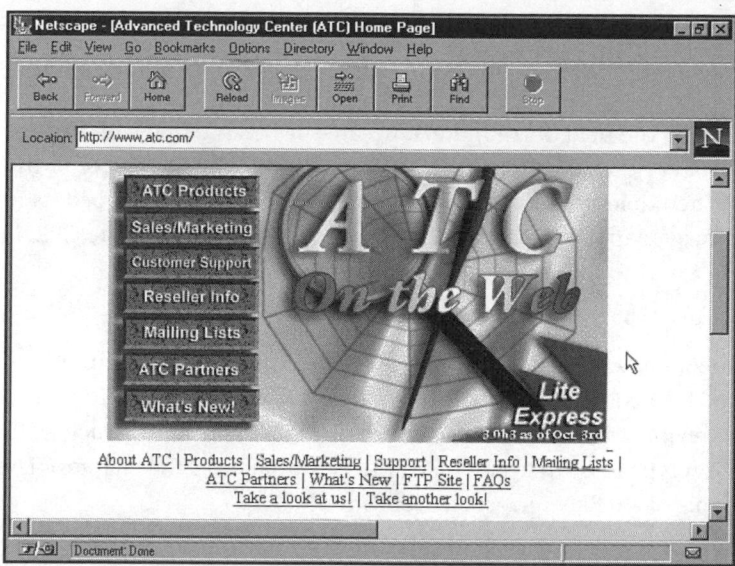

Fig. 12.4
Making textual
alternatives for
your imagemaps
is essential.

■ Because imagemaps tend to be rather large graphics, they take awhile to
download. This time factor isn't just a concern for people using slow
modems; sometimes network traffic can slow down a Web browser.
If you don't want people seeing your home page to wait, you should
avoid using imagemaps.

Imagemap Definition Files

To create an imagemap, you're going to need more than just a pretty picture
and an idea of where the regions are. You're also going to need an imagemap
definition file, which specifies where each particular region is. You also need
a CGI (Common Gateway Interface) program to build the relation between
the picture and the imagemap definition file. (You learn about CGI programs
for imagemaps later in this chapter, and more about CGI programming in
chapter 23, "All About CGI Scripts.") In this section, you focus on the
imagemap definition file, which specifies the regions.

An imagemap definition file can come in two forms: CERN and NCSA. Both
contain the same basic information for the clickable regions. Both of them
also use the same region types (see "Imagemap Region Types" later in this
chapter). The coordinates used to define the regions are also the same. The
only difference between the two is the manner that the information is presented. Because of this incompatibility, you must find out from your system
administrator which format your Web server supports.

The CERN Format

Originally, *CERN* (*Conseil Europeen pour la Recherche Nucleaire*) was founded as a research group of European physicists. The group slowly expanded its research into the field of computers. Because it was the one who first thought of the idea, it rightfully claims the honor of being "the birthplace of the Web." When imagemaps were deemed necessary, CERN developed its format for the imagemap definition file. On Web servers that follow the CERN format, you can find files that look like this:

```
region_type (x1,y1) (x2,y2) ... URL
```

The horizontal (x) and vertical (y) coordinates must be in parentheses and separated by a comma. Each pair of coordinates means something different for each region type. The ... specifies additional coordinates, such as for the *poly* region type (see "Imagemap Region Types" later in the chapter). Here's an example of a CERN imagemap definition:

```
rect (60,40) (340,280) http://www.rectangle.com/
```

The NCSA Format

The first wildly popular browser, Mosaic, came from the University of Illinois's National Center for Supercomputing Applications (NCSA). When this group heard of the demand for imagemaps, it came up with its own imagemap definition file format. A typical entry in one of its files would look like

```
region_type URL x1,y1 x2,y2 ...
```

Subtle (but significant) differences distinguish the CERN and NCSA formats. The URL for the region type comes before the coordinates with NCSA, not after, like CERN. The coordinates defining the region need to be separated by commas, but they don't need the parentheses around them. Here's an example of an NCSA imagemap definition:

```
rect http://www.rectangle.com/ 60,40 340,280
```

Client-Side Imagemaps

Netscape Navigator 2.0 introduced the concept of *client-side imagemaps*. With these new imagemaps, the HTML document being displayed has all the necessary information. The current page contains the points specifying each region along with the corresponding URLs. When the user clicks inside a client-side imagemap graphic, Netscape (not the Web server) looks up the region. The browser then fetches the appropriate home page, without ever talking to the Web server (see chapter 15, "Netscape-Specific Extensions to HTML").

Imagemap Terminology

Several terms relate to different aspects of using imagemaps. In the following sections, you learn some of the terms and what they refer to.

The Imagemap Graphic

The first thing the user sees when he or she comes across an imagemap is the image itself. This picture is typically called the *imagemap graphic*. The image can be anything, but it must be in the GIF graphics file format; whether it's interlaced or noninterlaced doesn't matter. The imagemap graphic is the main interface between the user and the imagemap itself.

The Imagemap Definition File

An imagemap depends on a file to hold the locations of hot spots. This file is known as the *imagemap definition file*. This text file, which usually has the extension .map, holds the coordinates and URLs for each hot spot region. The regions can be made from any of the standard imagemap region types (see "Imagemap Region Types" later in this chapter). This file must follow either the CERN or NCSA file format. Be sure to ask your system administrator which format your Web server supports.

Connecting Images and Regions

Most servers don't have built-in imagemap support, which means you have to add the support yourself. You have to write your own CGI program to interpret the mouse-click location and find the appropriate URL. The CGI program that does all this work is called the *imagemap program*. Also, you should ask your Web master if you can even run CGI programs on your Web server. Some Web masters, citing a security risk, disallow anybody from running CGI programs.

Putting It All Together

All the previously mentioned components make up the whole imagemap concept, which is known as *imagemap*, *image map*, *area map*, or *clickable map*. Don't let the terms fool you; they all mean the same thing: a picture that goes to different URLs. Which URL is dependent on where the user clicked his or her mouse button in the imagemap graphic.

III

Advanced HTML

Imagemap Region Types

Tip

Each imagemap depends on its own imagemap definition file to hold the information about clickable regions. This means that if your Web site has many different imagemaps, you need an imagemap definition file for each of them.

Each entry in the definition file specifies a region type. It also tells the exact points that define the region for that type. The coordinates used by each region type are an offset, in pixels, from the upper-left corner of the imagemap graphic. The available region types are mostly geometric (see fig. 12.5).

Fig. 12.5
You can use any combination of these region types, except for the default type.

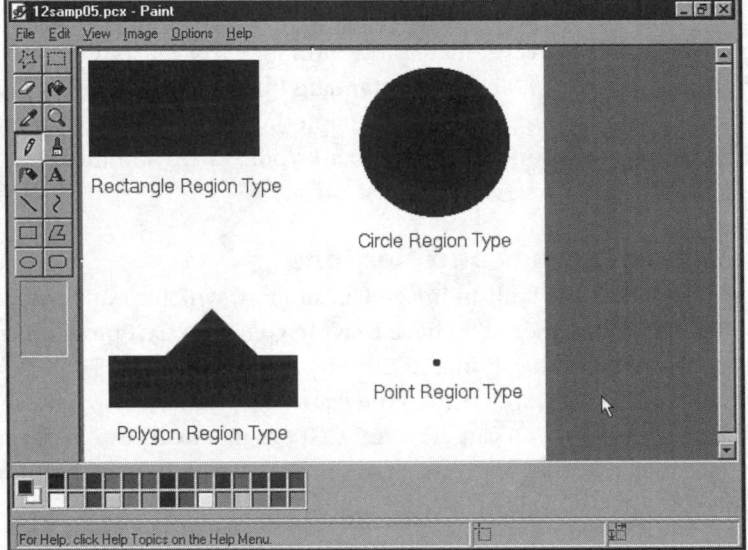

The Circle Region

To get a hot spot in the shape of a circle, you should use the *circle region type*. This element takes in two coordinates, but they are different values for different Web servers. If your Web server is an NCSA imagemap server, the two coordinates specify the coordinates for the center of the circle and a point on that circle. If your Web server is a CERN imagemap server, you really need only one coordinate and one value. The coordinates specify the center of the circle, whereas the value defines its radius. The clickable region of this type is everything enclosed within the circle.

The Polygon Region

To specify a geometric shape of an arbitrary number of sides, use the *poly region type*. This element looks for up to 100 coordinates, each referring to a vertex of the polygon. The active region is the area within the polygon.

The Rectangle Region

To get a clickable rectangle in your imagemap, use the *rect region type*. This element takes in two coordinates, the upper-left and lower-right corners of the rectangle. Any mouse-clicks inside the rectangle that are within these corners trigger this element.

The Point Region

You can easily create hot spots the size of small circles with the *point region type*. This element requires just one set of coordinates to specify the center of the circle. The area enclosed within that point is considered the active region.

The Default Region

If the user clicks in an imagemap and doesn't activate any region, the *default region type* is accessed. This element requires no coordinates.

All entries in the imagemap definition file must include the URL to be accessed (see fig. 12.6). The URL can either be an absolute path or a relative path. If you're using relative paths to specify an URL, be sure to make them relative to the directory where the imagemap definition file resides, not where the imagemap resides. Whenever multiple region types overlap, the first one with an entry in the imagemap definition file is accessed.

Caution

Whenever possible, try to avoid putting in a point alone with a default region type. Because the point region is so small, a user can easily miss it. As a result, the default region will be accessed instead. The user will be frustrated by not getting to the URL he or she wants.

Tip

You can use the point and default region types, but you have to overlap some regions. Whenever you put down a point region type, be sure to put down another (larger) region type on top of it. Try not to make the larger region too much larger than the point. Make sure that both region types refer to the same URL. This way, users can access the point region's URL more easily.

III

Advanced HTML

Fig. 12.6
An imagemap reference file must contain information specifying the region type, the coordinates that define the region, and the URL to access.

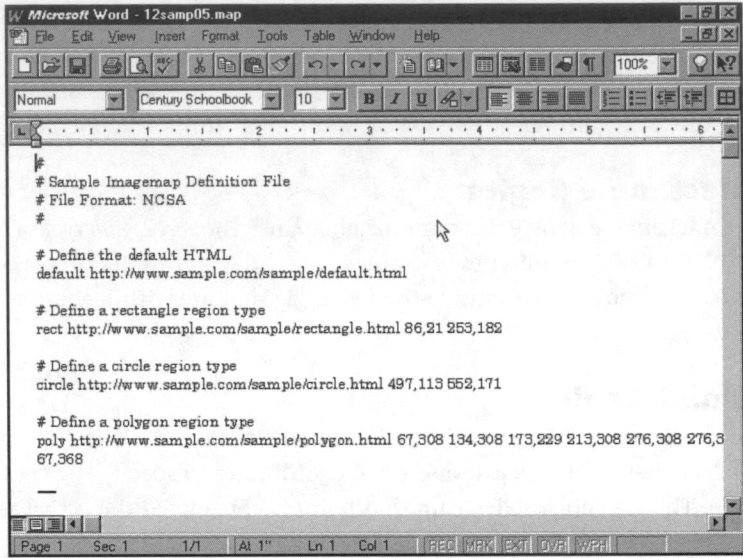

Tip

An imagemap definition file should, whenever possible, be configured with a default HTML link. The default link takes a user to an area that isn't designated as being an active link. This URL should provide the user with feedback or helpful information about using that particular imagemap.

Note

◀ See chapter 4, "Building Blocks of HTML," p. 87, for more information about internal jump points.

You can put comments to yourself in an imagemap definition file. Simply put a pound character (#) at the beginning of any line. Everything else on the same line after the pound sign will be ignored by the Web server. Comments are useful for putting in bits of information to yourself about the referenced URL, the imagemap graphic, or anything else. For corporate Web pages, comments are particularly useful for telling others when the file was last modified, who did it, and why it was changed.

The pound sign at the beginning of the line is different than the pound sign in the middle of an URL. When a pound sign is in the middle of an URL, it specifies an internal destination point.

Imagemaps: From Browser to Server and Back

Now that you understand all the parts of the imagemap, you're ready to learn how they all work together. You should now know what components contain what information and how elements relate to each other. But you may not know how everything works together. When you click your mouse anywhere in an imagemap map, the following occurs:

1. Your browser gets the coordinates of the mouse pointer, relative to the upper left-hand corner of the imagemap graphic.

2. The coordinates are sent to the Web server.

3. The server sends the coordinates of the mouse-click and the location of the imagemap definition file to the imagemap program.

4. The imagemap program uses the imagemap definition file and checks in which region type the mouse-click occurred.

5. If a clickable region was accessed, the corresponding URL is returned to the Web server. If no region was defined for the place where the user clicked, two things can happen. If a default region type was defined, that particular URL is used by the server. Otherwise an error is returned to the server.

6. The server, with the information returned from the imagemap program, sends the resulting URL to your browser. If an error was returned from the imagemap program, an error is sent to your browser.

7. Your browser either requests the returned URL or displays an error message.

Creating an Imagemap

To create an imagemap, you need tools and information; you also need to make some decisions. You need the imagemap graphic and mapping tools and some important information about the Web server.

The Imagemap Graphics

The first thing you want to look at in building an imagemap is the imagemap graphics. They are what the user will see and interact with the most. You should decide what types of graphics you want and how they should look. If you're building a company Web site, you might want to duplicate the look and feel of your corporate stationery. Chapter 11, "Handling Images," has some good information if you're planning to create fresh, new graphics or modify existing ones.

In choosing your imagemap graphic, you have many considerations. Along with general image considerations (see chapter 10, "Adding Graphics to Your Home Page"), you need to watch out for a number of specific imagemap graphic issues. Here are some things you should do when choosing an imagemap graphic:

- Get the imagemap graphic stored in the GIF graphics format. Because you want as many people as possible to see your imagemap, you should make it as basic as possible. All Web browsers support GIF, but only the more recent ones support JPEG. As popular as Netscape is, you still have to cater to those who don't use it.

- Save the imagemap graphic as Interlaced GIF. This format of storing pictures allows for an image to be displayed in stages. As each stage is downloaded, more detail is added to the image. By using this format, you let users see where the larger clickable regions are. By using interlaced GIFs as your imagemap graphic, you also help people who have slower modems.

- Keep the resolution of your imagemap graphic small. Try to keep your image from being more than 600 pixels wide by 400 pixels tall. Many different computers will be accessing your page, each with a different configuration. The lowest resolution for most modern computers is 640×480. With the 600×400 resolution recommendation, you make sure almost everybody can see your image without having to scroll.

- Try to reduce the number of colors each of your imagemap graphics uses. Using fewer colors makes the size of the file smaller. The smaller file size translates into a faster download for each user. The less time a user waits for each image, the more likely he or she will stay on your site.

Note

When you use Transparent GIFs (see chapter 10, "Adding Graphics to Your Home Page") as imagemap graphics, you could face some problems. Because Transparent GIFs can appear to have no border, users might be easily confused. Users may not know when they're in an imagemap and when they aren't (see fig. 12.7). If you do use Transparent GIFs as imagemap graphics, be sure to define a default region type.

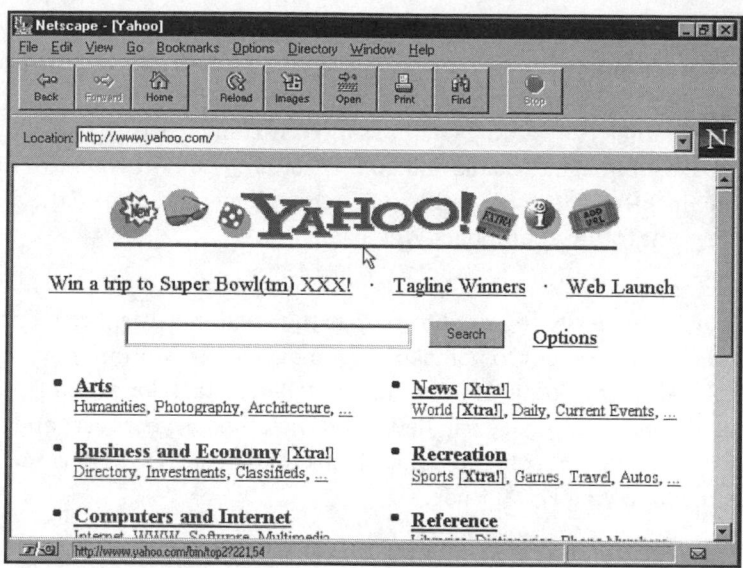

Fig. 12.7
Yahoo's main masthead is a transparent GIF and the main user navigational interface. It's not always obvious when you're in the imagemap and when you're not.

How to Create the Imagemap Definition File

The imagemap graphic is just part of the whole imagemap. You still need to create an imagemap definition file. Creating the imagemap definition file can be a tiring part of creating the imagemap for your Web site. You can create this file in two ways: the easy way and the hard way. The easy way is to use an imagemap creation program. This type of program lets you draw imagemap region types on top of an imagemap graphic of your choice and specify the appropriate URL.

The hard way of creating the file is to do it by hand. Creating the file this way really isn't as difficult as you might think, but it is dull and repetitious. You need two programs to create an imagemap definition file by hand: a graphics program and a text editor. Before you begin, decide where you want to place clickable regions. Using the graphics program, get the coordinates of the places where you want to put each point of each region type. Write down the region type, pixel coordinates, and appropriate URL using the text editor. Be careful not to actually edit the image itself using the graphics program.

> **Tip**
>
> If you choose to have multiple imagemaps using different imagemap graphics, you should organize everything. A good way to do this is to create a separate directory for each group of files for each imagemap. Another way of keeping multiple imagemap files distinct from each other is to keep the same file name for each imagemap component.

Putting Imagemaps in Your Home Page

Now that you have all the elements in place for an imagemap, you're ready to actually put it in your home page. You do so by building from what you learned in chapter 10, "Adding Graphics to Your Home Page." There, you saw how to make an image clickable and go to a certain URL. All you have to do is enclose the <IMG SRC> tag within an anchor element and have the anchor reference point to the appropriate Web page.

Two steps are needed to make an imagemap an integral part of a home page on your Web site. First, you need to change the anchor element reference from an HTML document to point to your imagemap definition file. Second, you must add the attribute ISMAP to the <IMG SRC> tag. For example, say that you've created an imagemap definition file called my_map.map, and its graphic is called my_map.gif. To put an imagemap in an HTML document, you use the following HTML code:

```
<A HREF="my_map.map">
<IMG SRC="my_map.gif" ISMAP>
</A>
```

When the imagemap is selected, the Web server runs the imagemap CGI program. The program then takes over and processes the mouse-click coordinates into a corresponding URL.

> **Note**
>
> Be sure to ask your Web master where the imagemap definition file will be stored. These file locations are determined by the configuration of your Web server.

> **Note**
>
> You can use the ISMAP attribute with any other image attributes. Just because you're specifying an imagemap doesn't restrict your ability to control the graphic. You can still use any other image controlling attributes you want.

Programs That Make Mapping Easier

As mentioned previously, you can create the imagemap definition file the easy way or the hard way. The easy way is to use one of the many programs that will create the file for you. These programs are called *mapping tools*, and they let you draw various imagemap region types on top of a specified image.

Many map-editing programs are available for both Windows 95 and the Macintosh. Generally speaking, most map-editing programs have the same basic features. They all support the three basic geometric region types, rect, poly, and circle. Some of the more advanced map-editing programs support the point and default region types. The only thing you should look for in imagemap-editing programs is how the user interface feels. Because such a wide variety is available, if one doesn't feel right to you, you don't have to use it.

Working with Mapedit

Mapedit is a shareware, no frills map-editing program for Windows 95 and UNIX. It was written by Thomas Boutell, maintainer of the FAQ (frequently asked questions) for the World Wide Web. This program allows you to create imagemap definition files in either CERN or NCSA format. Mapedit provides support for the basic geometric shapes, although the point region type isn't supported. A minor drawback is that it can load only GIF graphics files.

Navigating Mapedit is pretty straightforward. To create a new imagemap definition file for your imagemap graphic, simply choose File and then choose Open/Create. Mapedit's Open dialog box then appears. You must have an existing imagemap graphic, which you can find using the Browse button under the Image Filename heading. Mapedit supports GIF, JPEG, and the little-used PNG (Portable Network Graphics) image format for imagemap graphics.

To edit an existing imagemap definition file, you can use the Browse button under the Map or HTML File heading (see fig. 12.8). To create a new imagemap definition file, simply type in the file name you want to use. Be sure to also specify whether you want a CERN or NCSA imagemap definition file, using the appropriate radio buttons. Mapedit then asks you to confirm that you want to create a new imagemap.

After you click the OK button, the shareware notification appears. After the graphic is loaded, the shareware dialog box is dimissed, and the whole image is loaded into Mapedit. If the image is bigger than the current screen resolution, you can use the scroll bars to see different parts of the picture.

Note
If the colors on the imagemap graphic you specified look a little weird, don't worry. Mapedit isn't concerned with the way the picture looks; it's more concerned with the imagemap region types.

Fig. 12.8

When you want to create or edit an imagemap file with Mapedit, you have to fill in the information for this dialog box.

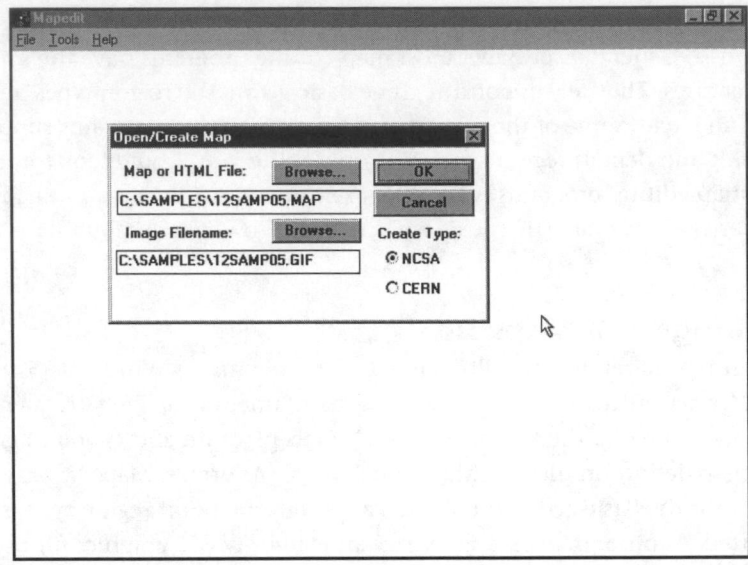

You can create any number of imagemap region types by choosing options from the Tools menu. You can create circle, polygon, or rectangle region types. For people accustomed to many paint programs, or other imagemap creation programs, the region creation interface is counterintuitive (see table 12.1). Generally speaking, you can create shapes in other programs by clicking and holding the right mouse button, dragging the shape, and then releasing the mouse button. Unfortunately, in Mapedit, it's a matter of clicking and releasing the mouse button, dragging the shape, then reclicking and re-releasing the mouse button. After you have created a region type on the imagemap graphic, you can't delete it using Mapedit.

Table 12.1   Creating Region Types Using Mapedit

Region Type	How to Create
Circle	Click on the left mouse button to specify the center of the desired circle. Use the mouse to specify the size of the circle. Click on the right mouse button when the circle is the desired size.
Rectangle	Click on the left mouse button to specify one corner of the rectangle. Use the mouse to specify the size of the rectangle. Click on the right mouse button to specify the diagonally opposite corner of the first corner.
Polygon	Click the left mouse button to specify a corner of the polygon. Move the mouse to the next corner you want to specify. Repeat these steps for each corner of the polygon. When you're back to the first corner, click the right mouse button.

After you create a region type, the Object URL window opens (see fig. 12.9). Simply type in the URL to associate with the newly created region. You can define the default URL for the entire imagemap graphic by choosing File and then Edit Default URL.

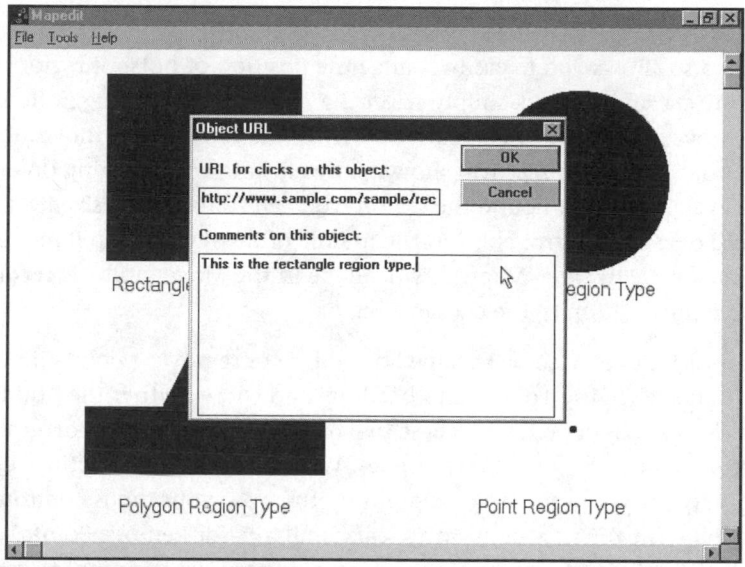

Fig. 12.9
After you create a region type, Mapedit asks for the URL to which that region should refer.

If you can't see the outline of the region type as you're creating it, don't worry. Mapedit doesn't care about the appearance of the image in its window. To change the color of the outlines for each region type, choose File and then Edit Hotspot Color.

III

Advanced HTML

Using Mapedit, you can test the regions you've created. You choose Tools and then Test+Edit. Using your mouse to move around the imagemap graphic, whenever you press the left mouse button, the URL for the corresponding region shows up. This testing capability is a function of Mapedit, and doesn't require a Web browser or server to use.

You can save your current imagemap definition file by choosing File and then either Save or Save As.

> **Note**
>
> Mapedit doesn't force any file-name extensions on you. As a result, when you're creating a new imagemap definition file, you need to specify the extension yourself. Most imagemap servers look for a file with the .map extension.

Mapedit also allows you to easily change the position of hotspot regions. To move any clickable region, simply select the Tools menu heading, followed by the Move menu item. Next, click on the region you want to move, and a number of "control points" will show up. By clicking and dragging on any of the control points that bound the region, you can reshape or resize it. If you click and drag the control point in the middle of the region, you'll move the entire region itself. Since Mapedit will still be in the Move mode, you can fine-tune the position of the clickable region.

Polygon regions can also be reshaped by adding or removing points in Mapedit. Just click the Tools menu heading, and choose either the Add Points or Remove Points menu items. These two options only work on polygon region types, and do as their name implies. With the Add Points option, click on the polygon you want to add a point to, then put your mouse on roughly where you want the new point to appear. Similarly, for Remove Points, you click on the polygon to remove a point from, then select the point to remove.

Mapedit can also be used to create client-side imagemaps. Instead of loading in a MAP file, you specify an HTML file. Mapedit will look for any HTML that mentions including a graphic. Whatever images are found, it'll present a dialog box with the pictures that were found (see fig. 12.10). Select the picture you want to create a client-side imagemap for, and click the OK button. The filename for the image is automatically filled in Mapedit's Open dialog box. Once you click the OK button, you'll be taken into Mapedit as usual. After you've created all the shapes you want, saving the changes will cause the HTML file to be updated. You can get Mapedit from **http:// www.boutell.com/mapedit/**.

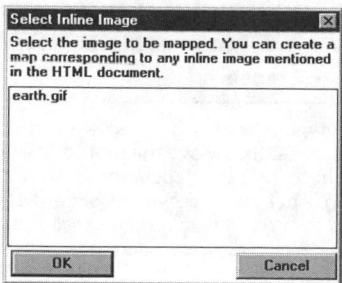

Fig. 12.10
To create client-side imagemaps, just select the picture you want to make an imagemap for.

Using WebMap

WebMap, a capable Macintosh map-editing program, is currently free, until it's released commercially. It lets you create all the geometric region types from rectangles to circles and ellipses to polygons to points. It can create imagemap definition files for CERN, NCSA, or MacHTTP Web servers. It also enables you to easily move and change regions that have already been defined.

With this user-friendly program, you can easily create imagemap definition files. Simply choose File and then New. Then, using the Mac file selector, find the location of your imagemap graphic. This picture can be in either GIF or PICT graphics formats.

You can create as many imagemap region types as you want using the floating toolbox next to the WebMap window (see fig. 12.11). The interface is similar to drawing programs (see table 12.2). The only difference between the circle and ellipse region type is that the circle has a constant radius. If you make a mistake in either the placement, size, or mere existence of a region type, you can fix it.

Table 12.2   Creating Region Types Using WebMap

Region Type	How to Create
Circle	Click and hold the mouse button to specify a corner of the square to contain the circle. Hold down the mouse button and move the mouse to specify the size of the circle. Release the mouse button when the circle is the desired size.
Ellipse	Click and hold the mouse button to indicate a corner of the square in which the ellipse will reside. While holding down the mouse button, move the mouse to size the ellipse. Let go of the mouse button when the ellipse is at the size and shape you want.
Rectangle	Click and hold the mouse button to indicate a corner of the rectangle. Release the mouse button when the rectangle is the size you want.

(continues)

III

Advanced HTML

Table 12.2 Continued	
Region Type	**How to Create**
Polygon	Click the mouse button to specify a corner of the polygon. Release the mouse button. Move the mouse pointer to the next corner you want to indicate. Repeat these steps for each corner of the polygon. After you specify the last corner, move the mouse pointer close to the first vertex and then click the mouse button.

Fig. 12.11

All the standard geometric region types are accessible through WebMap's toolbox.

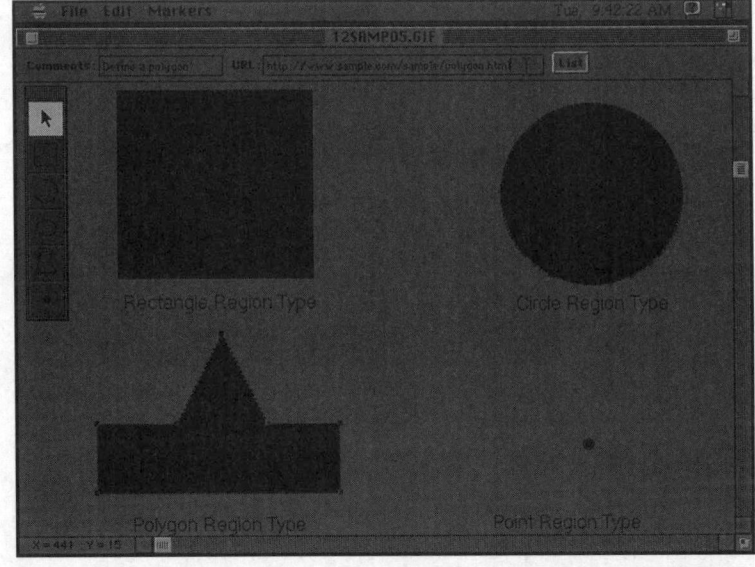

Caution

With WebMap, you can't create a smaller region on top of a larger one. However, you can easily place larger region types on top of smaller ones. As a result, you have to plan carefully which regions you place when. You should place the smaller region types first and then work your way up to the largest regions.

After you've created all the regions you want, you can save the imagemap definition file by choosing File and then Save. This saves the imagemap definition file with an .m extension, which is the default extension that MacHTTP looks for in an imagemap definition file. WebMap also automatically saves the file in MacHTTP's custom format, making it unusable for the prevalent Web servers around. To create an imagemap definition file that other Web servers can use, choose File, Export As Text. You can specify to create either a CERN- or NCSA-compatible file. You can get WebMap from **http://www.city.net/cnx/software/webmap.html**.

Caution

WebMap assumes that your imagemap definition file has the same name as the graphic. When you're editing an existing imagemap definition file, WebMap looks for an .m file based on the imagemap graphic's name. You therefore can't simply rename one of the files; you have to rename both of them. Otherwise, WebMap cannot see the other and will assume that you're creating a new imagemap definition file.

Tip

Sometimes the Undo feature doesn't work with WebMap. If you've accidentally created a region and Undo doesn't work, just clear the region. Go to the toolbox and select the Arrow icon. Then use the mouse to select the region you created by accident. Next, choose Edit and then Clear.

Putting Your Imagemap Through a Dry Run

After you've created the files for your imagemap, the only thing left to do is to test it. Even though some map-editing programs let you try the region types within the program, this built-in facility is often imperfect. The programmers have made certain assumptions with the imagemap process. The best way to test the imagemap is to put it on your Web server and act like an average user.

By testing the imagemap in this fashion, you can see different aspects that you might've overlooked. If the imagemap graphic file is too large and takes a long time to download, you'll see it. You'll also be able to see if the imagemap regions are distinct enough for the average person. Finally, you can see if the URLs for each region actually work as they should. If you're using relative links, testing the imagemap on the server is especially important.

> **Tip**
>
> Before releasing your imagemap for everyone's perusal, find someone else to try it. Get a friend with a different Internet Service Provider to access your new imagemap. He or she can give you a (somewhat) unbiased opinion of the imagemap graphic and region types.

Textual Alternatives to Imagemaps

◀ See chapter 8 for more information about imagemaps and why you should put in a textual alternative.

Imagemaps and graphics in general don't translate particularly well to text. In fact, they don't translate at all. For this reason, you should provide some alternatives for people who don't have graphical browsers. Also bear in mind that some people have configured their browsers so that they don't automatically load pictures. People who access the Web through UNIX's command-line mode and people with slow modems fall into these categories. Because they are a strong minority, you have to provide some support for them.

You can let nongraphics people access the various points on your imagemap in a number of ways. You can provide a separate home page for these people and mention it in your graphics-heavy page. You also can put in regular hypertext links at the top or bottom of all your home pages. These links can point to the same links accessible through the imagemaps. Whichever approach meets your fancy, you should take one of them. If you ignore the text-only crowd, you're alienating a large group of people. ❖

CHAPTER 13

Tables and Math Equations

by Jim O'Donnell

As a tool for government, commercial, educational, and personal Web applications, HTML has many needs and expectations to meet. It's the language for what is becoming the standard interface of the Internet, and, as such, is required to support a greater range of uses today than perhaps its original creators had first imagined. In this chapter, you learn about the following:

- What HTML 3.0 table elements are supported?
- How do I create a table in my HTML document?
- What extensions to HTML 3.0 tables are there?
- How are math equations supported by HTML?
- Can equations created with other software programs be used by Web pages?

The level of sophistication of the developing HTML 3.0 specification (currently in draft format) will far exceed the current standard, and will accommodate a wider range of user needs. Two deficiencies in HTML 2.0, the lack of support for tables and for mathematical equations, will be supported in HTML 3.0. Although none of the popular Web browsers currently support the full draft specification for either, there is support for tables (a subset of the HTML 3.0 draft specification and some extensions introduced by Netscape).

> **Note**
>
> Much of the information presented in this chapter is based on public texts and discussions regarding the development process for HTML 3.0. This new version is not a finished product (at the time of this writing), so any specific notations or expressions may change drastically before the new standard is finalized. However, most of the table elements discussed are supported by the popular Web browsers and are becoming widely used, making it unlikely that they will disappear any time soon.

HTML Tables 101

HTML 3.0 defines tables in much the same way it defines list containers. The <TABLE> element is the container for the table's data and layout. HTML tables are composed row by row: you separate the data with either the <TH> (table header) or <TD> (table data) tags and indicate a new row with the <TR> (table row) tag. Think of the <TR> tag as a line break, signaling that the following data starts a new table row. Table headers are generally shown in bold and centered by WWW browsers, and table data is shown in the standard body text format.

Basic HTML Table Elements

◄ See "Displaying Text in Lists," p. 173

The HTML for a basic table is shown in figure 13.1. All of the table elements used are supported by the latest versions of the most popular Web browsers: Netscape Navigator, Microsoft Internet Explorer, and NCSA Mosaic. This table, as rendered by Netscape Navigator, is shown in figure 13.2.

Fig. 13.1
This HTML document shows the basic table tags.

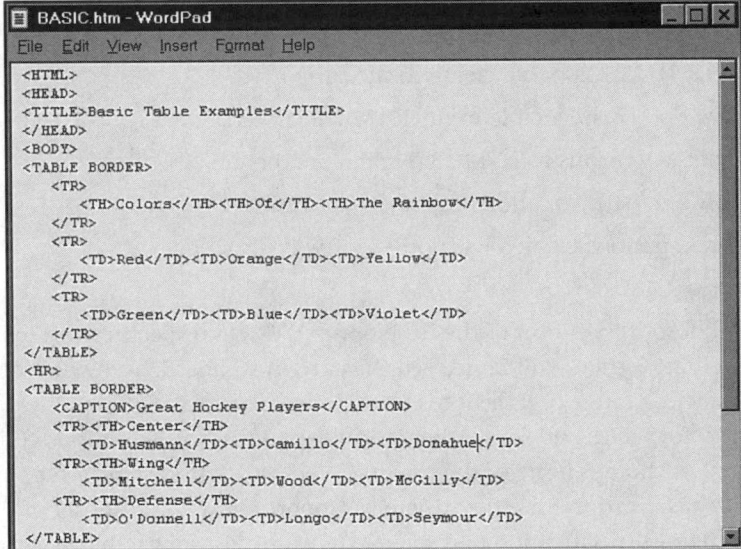

The basic HTML table tags shown in figure 13.1 and figure 13.2 are as follows:

- **<TABLE>...</TABLE>**—These HTML tags are the containers for the rest of the table data.

- **<TR>...</TR>**—Each row in the table is contained by these tags.

- **<TD>...</TD>**—Table data is contained within these tags.

- **<TH>...</TH>**—These table header tags are used to create headers, usually in the first row or column of the table.

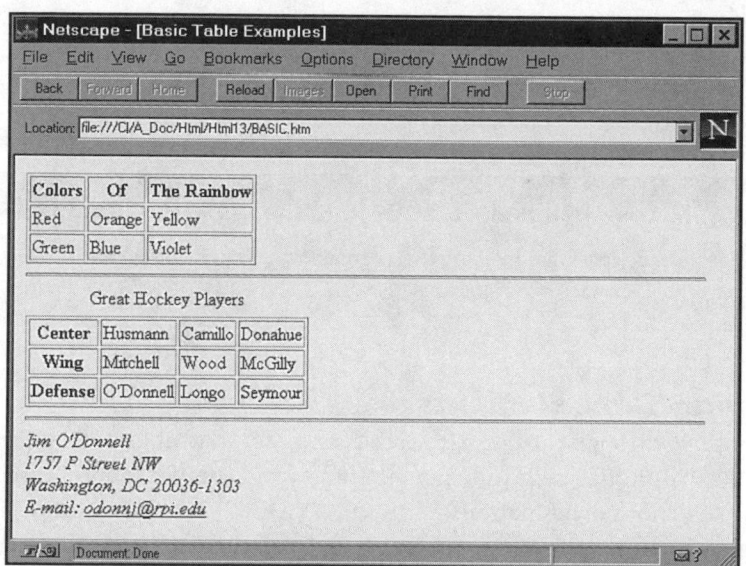

Fig. 13.2
Many of the basic
HTML 3.0 table
tags are supported
by the most
popular Web
browsers.

In addition to the basic tags shown here, some other characteristics should be noted from the example shown in figures 13.1 and 13.2:

- **BORDER attribute**—By using the BORDER attribute of the <TABLE> tag, borders are put around the table.

- **Table heads**—By default, table heads enclosed by the <TH>...</TH> tags are emphasized and centered.

- **Table data**—By default, table data enclosed by the <TD>...</TD> tags are shown in the normal font and are left-justified.

> **Note**
>
> If you're concerned about browsers displaying your header text correctly (as emphasized text, preferably in a bold font), you can use style tags to force the issue. Be careful what you wish for, though: if you want an italicized font but the browser automatically formats the text bold, you can wind up with bold italicized headers.

Cells do not necessarily have to contain data. To create a blank cell, either create an empty cell (e.g., <TD></TD>), or create a cell containing nothing visible (e.g., <TD> </TD>). Note that   is an HTML entity, or special character, for a nonbreaking space. Though you would think these two methods would produce the same result, as you will see later in this chapter, in the section "Empty Cells and Table Appearance," different browsers treat them differently.

It's not really necessary to create blank cells if the rest of the cells on the row are going to be blank; the <TR> element signals the start of a new row, so the Web browsers automatically fill in blank cells to even out the row with the rest of the table.

> **Tip**
>
> Tables are necessarily uniform with equal numbers of cells in each row and in each column. No "L-shaped" tables (or worse!) allowed.

Aligning Table Elements

It is possible, through the use of the ALIGN and VALIGN attributes, to align table elements within their cells in many different ways. These attributes can be applied in various combinations to the <CAPTION>, <TR>, <TH>, and <TD> table elements. The possible attribute values for each of these elements are as follows:

- **<CAPTION>**—The ALIGN attribute can be specified for this element with possible values of TOP and BOTTOM (the default is TOP); this places the table caption above or below the table.

- **<TR>**—The ALIGN attribute can be specified for this element with possible values of LEFT, RIGHT, and CENTER (the default is LEFT for table data elements and CENTER for table header elements), and the VALIGN attribute with possible values of TOP, BOTTOM, MIDDLE, and BASELINE (the default is MIDDLE). If specified, this will give the default alignment for all the table elements in the given row, which can be overridden in each individual element. The BASELINE element applies to all elements in the row and aligns them to a common baseline.

- **<TH>**—The ALIGN attribute can be specified for this element with possible values of LEFT, RIGHT, and CENTER (the default is CENTER), and the VALIGN attribute with possible values of TOP, BOTTOM, and MIDDLE (the default is MIDDLE).

- **<TD>**—The ALIGN attribute can be specified for this element with possible values of LEFT, RIGHT, and CENTER (the default is LEFT), and the VALIGN attribute with possible values of TOP, BOTTOM, and MIDDLE (the default is MIDDLE).

These alignments are illustrated by the HTML document shown in figure 13.3 and rendered by Netscape Navigator in figure 13.4.

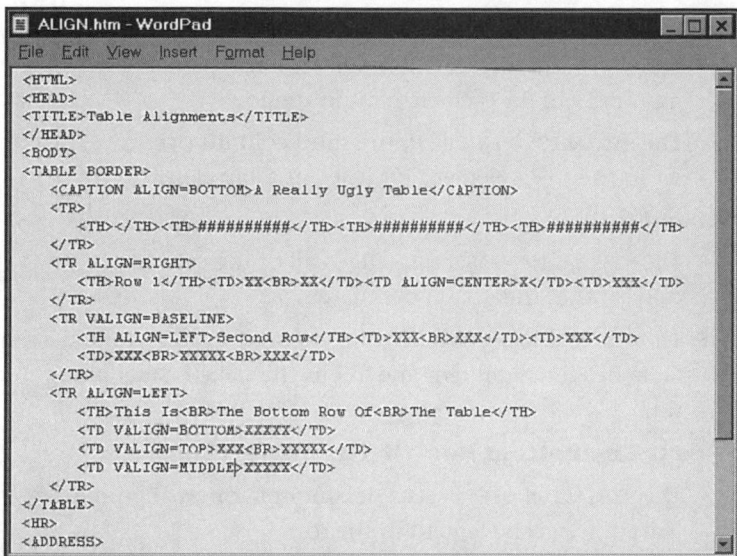

Fig. 13.3
There are many options and possibilities for aligning table elements.

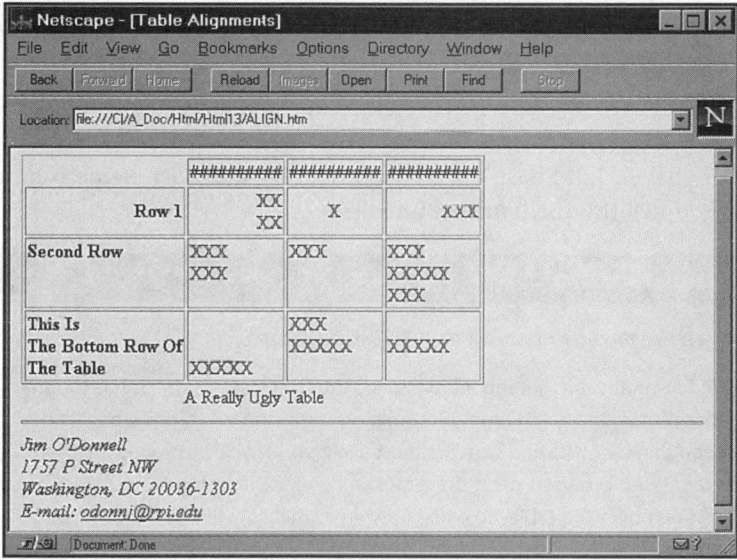

Fig. 13.4
Table element alignment can be specified row-by-row or for each individual element in the table.

Although this table is pretty ugly, it illustrates the capabilities of the different ALIGN and VALIGN attributes, as follows:

- **Table Caption:** <CAPTION ALIGN=BOTTOM> places the caption underneath the table—overriding the default value, which would put the caption on top.

- **"Row 1":**
  - The `<TR ALIGN=RIGHT>` sets a default horizontal alignment to the right margin for each element in the row.
  - The `<TD ALIGN=CENTER>` in the third column overrides the default set in the `<TR>` element for just this table element.

- **"Second Row":**
  - The `<TR VALIGN=BASELINE>` aligns all of the cells in the row vertically so that their baselines match.
  - The `<TH ALIGN=LEFT>` in the first column overrides the default table header alignment and aligns the table header along the left side.

- **"This Is The Bottom Row Of The Table":**
  - The `<TR ALIGN=LEFT>` sets a default horizontal alignment to the left margin for each element in the row.
  - The `<TR VALIGN=BOTTOM>` in the second column vertically aligns the element on the bottom of the row.
  - The `<TR VALIGN=TOP>` in the third column vertically aligns the element on the top of the row.
  - The `<TR VALIGN=MIDDLE>` in the fourth column vertically aligns the element in the middle of the row. Because this is the default behavior (and hasn't been overridden in the `<TR>` element for this row), this attribute isn't necessary.

Troubleshooting

My table doesn't look like I want it to. What am I doing wrong?

If you're having trouble getting a table to look the way you want—it has too many or not enough rows and/or columns, information is missing, or things aren't in the places you think they should be—the most likely problem is missing `</TR>`, `</TD>`, or `</TH>` tags. Web browsers need these tags to correctly determine how many rows and columns are in the table, so when they are mistakenly left out, it can lead to unpredictable results.

Intermediate Tables

There are more sophisticated things that can be done with tables, both by using additional table attributes and by different uses of some of the ones you already know about.

Borderless Tables

As mentioned previously, the BORDER attribute to the <TABLE> element is what gives the borders around the table elements. Even though this attribute is off by default, for most conventional tables—those used to organize information in a tabular format—borders are usually used to accentuate the organization of the information. Consider the HTML document shown in figure 13.5 and rendered in figure 13.6. In this case, the organization of the information is much easier to see in the version that includes borders.

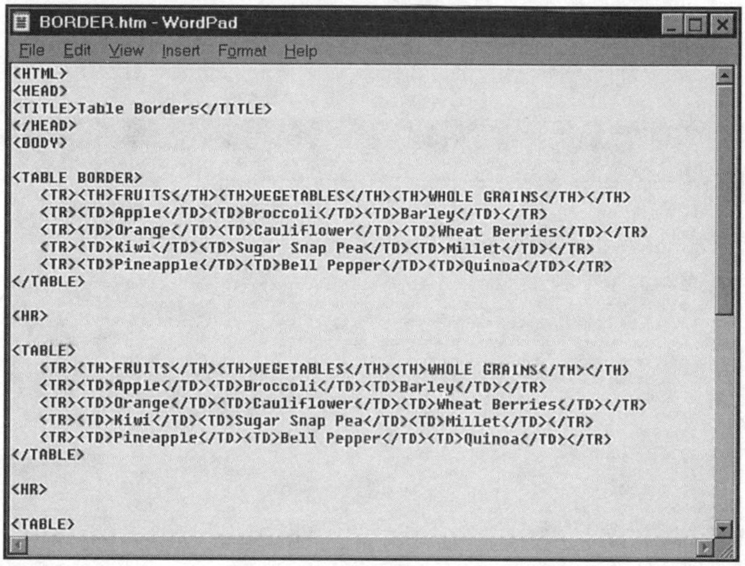


```
<HTML>
<HEAD>
<TITLE>Table Borders</TITLE>
</HEAD>
<BODY>

<TABLE BORDER>
   <TR><TH>FRUITS</TH><TH>VEGETABLES</TH><TH>WHOLE GRAINS</TH></TH>
   <TR><TD>Apple</TD><TD>Broccoli</TD><TD>Barley</TD></TR>
   <TR><TD>Orange</TD><TD>Cauliflower</TD><TD>Wheat Berries</TD></TR>
   <TR><TD>Kiwi</TD><TD>Sugar Snap Pea</TD><TD>Millet</TD></TR>
   <TR><TD>Pineapple</TD><TD>Bell Pepper</TD><TD>Quinoa</TD></TR>
</TABLE>

<HR>

<TABLE>
   <TR><TH>FRUITS</TH><TH>VEGETABLES</TH><TH>WHOLE GRAINS</TH></TH>
   <TR><TD>Apple</TD><TD>Broccoli</TD><TD>Barley</TD></TR>
   <TR><TD>Orange</TD><TD>Cauliflower</TD><TD>Wheat Berries</TD></TR>
   <TR><TD>Kiwi</TD><TD>Sugar Snap Pea</TD><TD>Millet</TD></TR>
   <TR><TD>Pineapple</TD><TD>Bell Pepper</TD><TD>Quinoa</TD></TR>
</TABLE>

<HR>

<TABLE>
```

Fig. 13.5
Tables can be displayed with or without borders.

However, HTML tables can be used in other ways, rather than for the simple tabular display of data. They give an HTML author great flexibility in presenting information, grouping it, and formatting it along with other information. Consider the HTML document shown in figure 13.7 and rendered in figure 13.8. In this case, the use of a borderless table allows the descriptive text of the image to be displayed alongside the image.

Fig. 13.6
In many cases, borders accentuate the organization of the information.

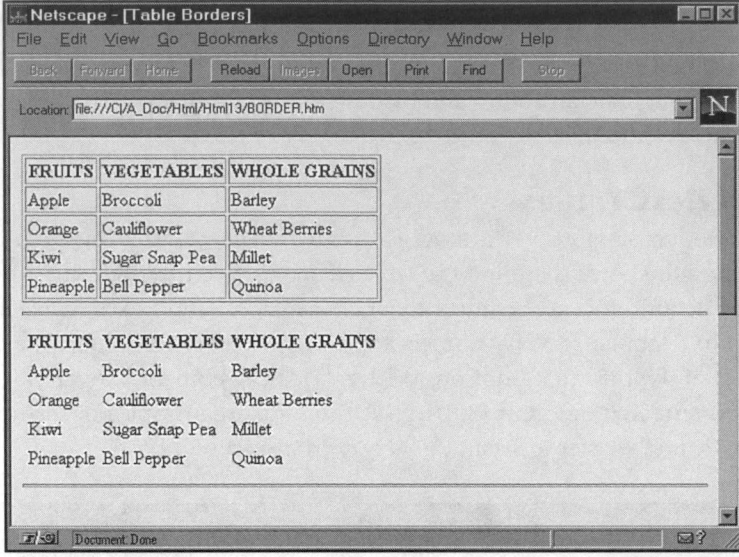

Fig. 13.7
Borderless tables can be used to present information with considerable flexibility in how that information is grouped.

```
<TABLE>
    <TR>
        <TD><IMG SRC="lion.gif"></TD>
        <TD>
The rampant lion is a symbol from Scottich heraldry. It symbolizes a duty
and willingness to defend one's ideals and values, such as aret&ecirc;. The
color of the lion, White, is for the purity of the brotherhood of PEZ, void
of the negativity associated with some fraternities. This White symbolizes
how PEZ is a practice of the pure theory of brotherhood. This brotherhood
has its roots in common ties and support rather than hazing and the like.
        </TD>
    </TR>
</TABLE>
<HR>
<ADDRESS>
Jim O'Donnell<BR>
1757 P Street NW<BR>
Washington, DC 20036-1303<BR>
E-mail: <A HREF="mailto:odonnj@rpi.edu">odonnj@rpi.edu</A>
</ADDRESS>
</BODY>
</HTML>
```

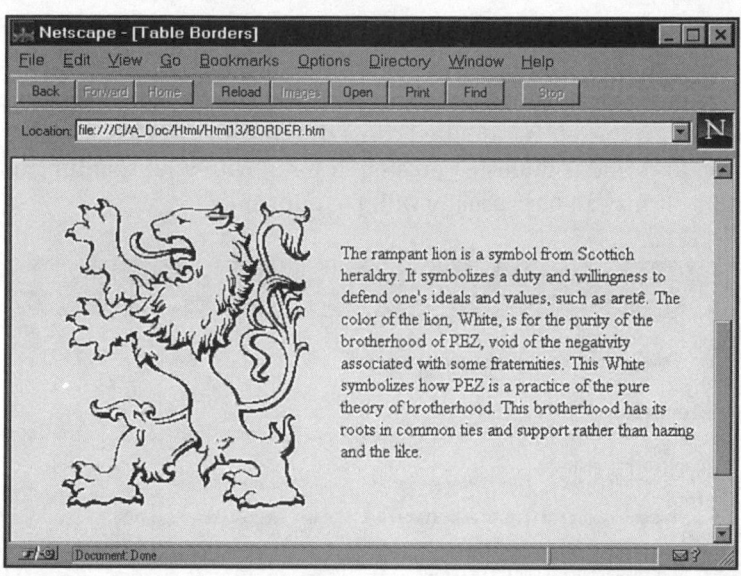

Fig. 13.8
Side-by-side
presentation of
information
elements can be
achieved using
HTML tables.

Row and Column Spanning

Rows and columns can be spanned—combined with adjacent cells to create larger cells for the data. For instance, in a table with five rows and five columns, the first row could be spanned across all five columns to create a banner header for the whole table. In the same table, each of the columns could have elements that spanned multiple rows. It would be possible, through spanning, to create rectangular table elements that span both multiple rows and columns, up to the full size of the table.

To span two adjacent cells on a row, use the ROWSPAN attribute with <TH>, as follows:

```
<UX><TH ROWSPAN=2>
```

To span two adjacent cells in a column, use the COLSPAN attribute with <TH>, as follows:

```
<UX><TH COLSPAN=2>
```

Tip

Don't forget to close your table data with the </TABLE> closing tag.

III

Advanced HTML

Figures 13.9 and 13.10 show an HTML document that makes use of row and column spanning. This example is shown in figure 13.11, which shows some of the trouble you can get yourself into with row and column spanning. The table shown on the left is formatted correctly. However, HTML will allow you to overlap rows and columns if you aren't careful with your spanning, and the results of this can (and usually will) be unfortunate.

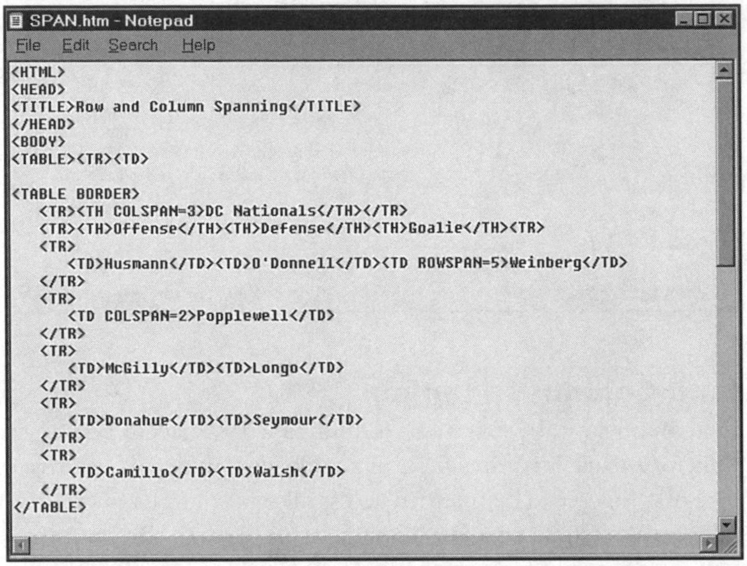


```
<HTML>
<HEAD>
<TITLE>Row and Column Spanning</TITLE>
</HEAD>
<BODY>
<TABLE><TR><TD>

<TABLE BORDER>
   <TR><TH COLSPAN=3>DC Nationals</TH></TR>
   <TR><TH>Offense</TH><TH>Defense</TH><TH>Goalie</TH><TR>
   <TR>
      <TD>Husmann</TD><TD>O'Donnell</TD><TD ROWSPAN=5>Weinberg</TD>
   </TR>
   <TR>
      <TD COLSPAN=2>Popplewell</TD>
   </TR>
   <TR>
      <TD>McGilly</TD><TD>Longo</TD>
   </TR>
   <TR>
      <TD>Donahue</TD><TD>Seymour</TD>
   </TR>
   <TR>
      <TD>Camillo</TD><TD>Walsh</TD>
   </TR>
</TABLE>
```

Fig. 13.9
Row and column spanning can be used for table banner headers and for grouping elements in more than one category.

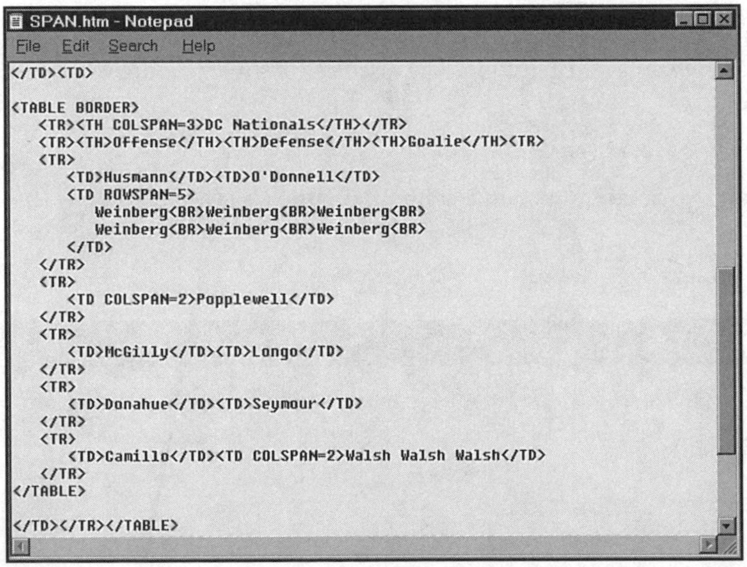


```
</TD><TD>

<TABLE BORDER>
   <TR><TH COLSPAN=3>DC Nationals</TH></TR>
   <TR><TH>Offense</TH><TH>Defense</TH><TH>Goalie</TH><TR>
   <TR>
      <TD>Husmann</TD><TD>O'Donnell</TD>
      <TD ROWSPAN=5>
         Weinberg<BR>Weinberg<BR>Weinberg<BR>
         Weinberg<BR>Weinberg<BR>Weinberg<BR>
      </TD>
   </TR>
   <TR>
      <TD COLSPAN=2>Popplewell</TD>
   </TR>
   <TR>
      <TD>McGilly</TD><TD>Longo</TD>
   </TR>
   <TR>
      <TD>Donahue</TD><TD>Seymour</TD>
   </TR>
   <TR>
      <TD>Camillo</TD><TD COLSPAN=2>Walsh Walsh Walsh</TD>
   </TR>
</TABLE>

</TD></TR></TABLE>
```

Fig. 13.10
HTML will allow you to span row and column tables in such a way that they will overlap—this is usually a bad idea.

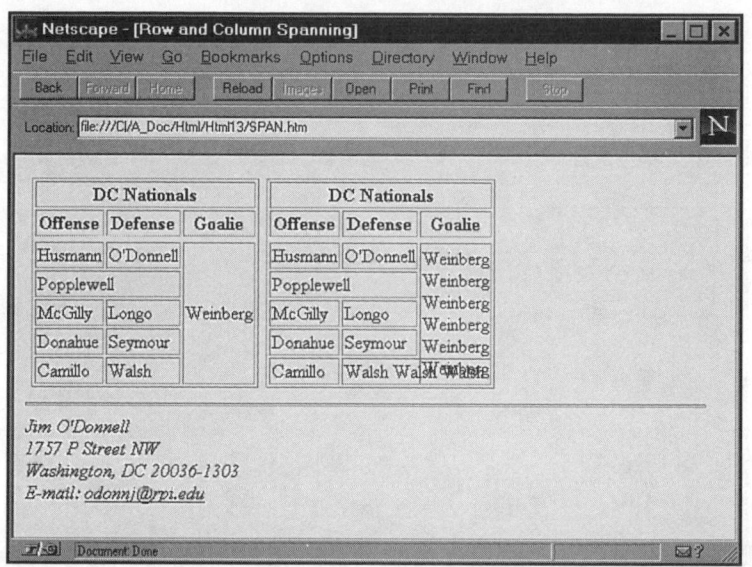

Fig. 13.11
If you aren't careful, you can overlap rows and columns when using spanning, which tends to give ugly results.

Caution

If you look closely at the code shown in figures 13.9 and 13.10, you'll see that I was able to get the two tables in figure 13.11 to appear side-by-side by nesting them in another borderless table. The nesting of tables is a Netscape enhancement to HTML and is part of the draft HTML 3.0 specification. It is also supported by Microsoft Internet Explorer. However, if you view such a file with a Web browser that does not support the nesting of tables—even if it has support for normal tables—all of the information can be lost. Figure 13.12 shows the same HTML document displayed in figure 13.11, as rendered by NCSA Mosaic. (See the "Netscape Table Enhancements" section, later in this chapter.)

Note

When you create larger cells in an HTML table, you might find that your cell data acts a bit unruly: not breaking properly, wrapping text when it shouldn't, and crowding too close to the cell divisions. Like other HTML documents, tables support internal HTML elements, such as
 (to create a line break in the data), hypertext link anchors, inline images, and even forms.

Use an HTML table in the same manner you would a spreadsheet: for data display, for creating data layouts (such as inventory lists or business invoices), and for calculation tables (when combined with a CGI script that can take your form input and generate output data that's displayed in your HTML table). The uses for tables are limited only by your data and your creativity.

III

Advanced HTML

Fig. 13.12
Trying to view
nested tables with
a Web browser
that doesn't
support them can
result in losing all
of the included
information.

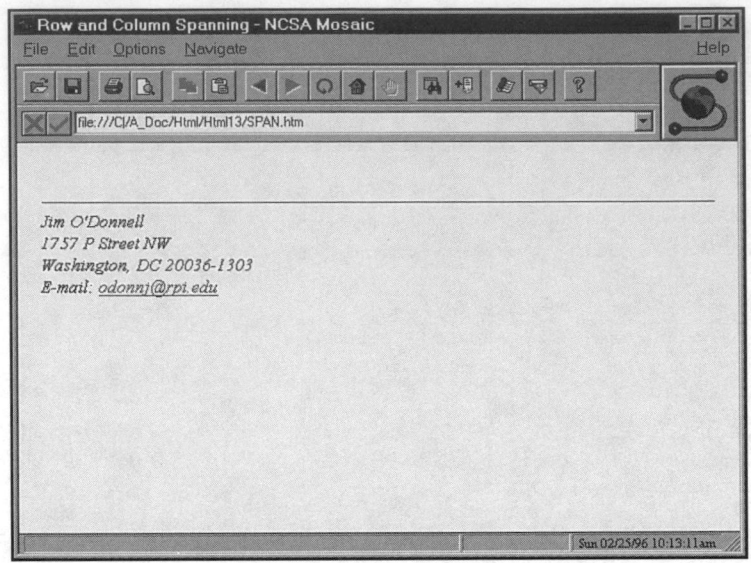

Browser Specific Table Notes

The major Web browsers—Netscape Navigator, Microsoft Internet Explorer, and NCSA Mosaic—all support tables. Tables are rendered slightly differently in each of the three browsers, and each behaves slightly differently under some circumstances. Additionally, Netscape has introduced enhancements to their table support, most of which are also supported my Microsoft Internet Explorer.

Empty Cells and Table Appearance

As mentioned earlier, there is sometimes a difference between an empty cell in a table and one with nothing visible in it. This is particularly true with Netscape Navigator, which will display the two differently. Consider the HTML document shown in figure 13.13, which shows two tables. In the top table, there are several empty table cells—cells with only white space in them, which Netscape Navigator will not treat as data. In the lower table, these same cells have something in them: the HTML entity , which is a nonbreaking space (an invisible character).

As shown in figure 13.14, Netscape Navigator will display these two tables differently. Earlier versions of Netscape's browsers displayed the table with empty cells incorrectly, and it was necessary to include some "dummy" invisible data to make the table display correctly. As you can see here, now it is mainly an aesthetic difference.

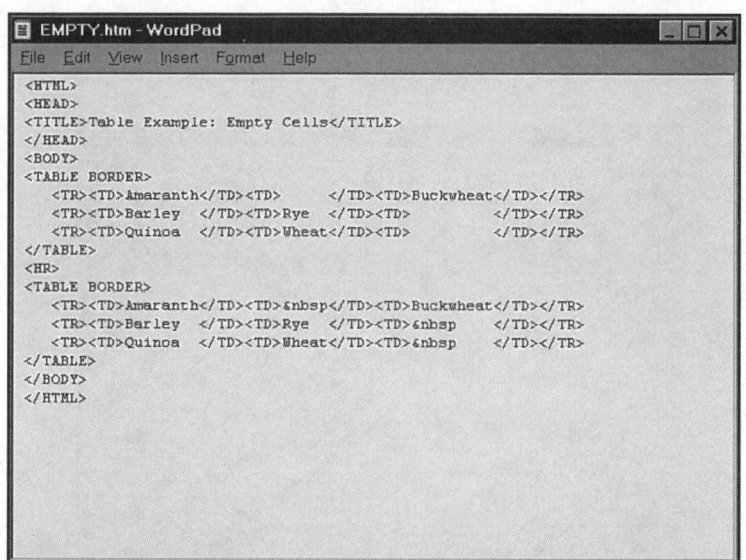

Fig. 13.13
Cells with no data in them can either be left empty or contain an invisible character; this will sometimes affect how they are displayed.

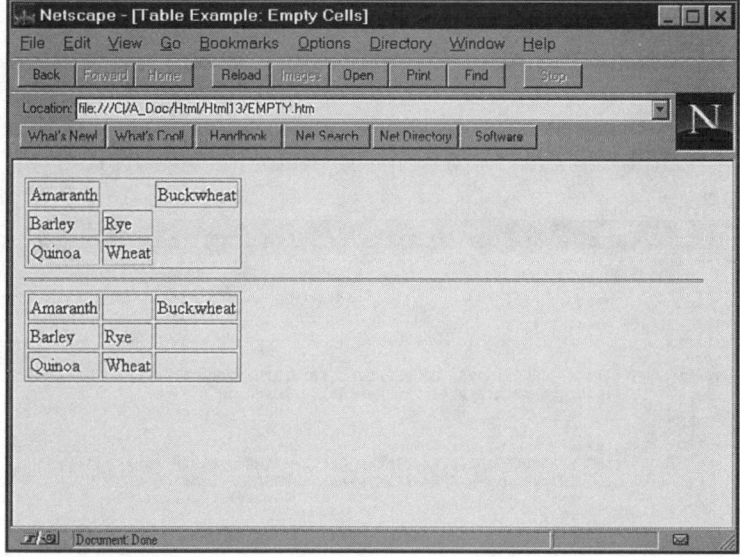

Fig. 13.14
Netscape Navigator will display tables with empty cells differently from those that contain invisible characters.

Microsoft Internet Explorer will display both of these cases the same, similar to the bottom table in figure 13.14. NCSA Mosaic, on the other hand, offers the greatest degree of control at the user end over how tables are displayed. Figure 13.15 shows the Tables tab of Mosaic's Preferences menu. This menu enables the user to decide whether empty cells are displayed (i.e., whether they appear similar to the upper table in fig. 13.14 or the lower), and whether to give the tables a 3-D and/or recessed appearance.

Fig. 13.15
NCSA Mosaic offers the user several options about how to display HTML tables.

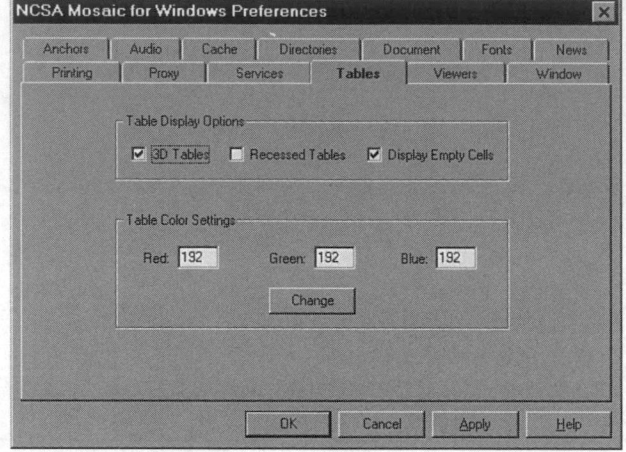

Netscape Table Enhancements

Netscape Navigator has introduced several enhancements to HTML tables to increase the degree of control HTML authors have on how their documents are displayed. Figure 13.16 shows the HTML document for these enhancements, which are rendered by Netscape Navigator in figure 13.17.

Fig. 13.16
This HTML document shows off Netscape Navigator's enhancements to HTML tables.

```
jodtab.htm - Notepad
File  Edit  Search  Help
<HTML>
<HEAD>
<TITLE>Table Demo</TITLE>
</HEAD>
<BODY>
<TABLE BORDER=10 CELLPADDING=10 CELLSPACING=10 WIDTH="100%">
        <TR><TD>Width 100%</TD><TD>Border<BR>CellPadding = 10
                                        <BR>CellSpacing</TD>
        </TR>
        <TR><TD>
            <TABLE BORDER=5 CELLPADDING=5 CELLSPACING=5 WIDTH=75%>
                <TR><TD>Width 75%</TD><TD>Border<BR>CellPadding = 5
                                        <BR>CellSpacing</TD>
                </TR>
            </TABLE>
            </TD>
            <TD>Have a nice day!</TD>
        </TR>
</TABLE>
</BODY>
</HTML>
```

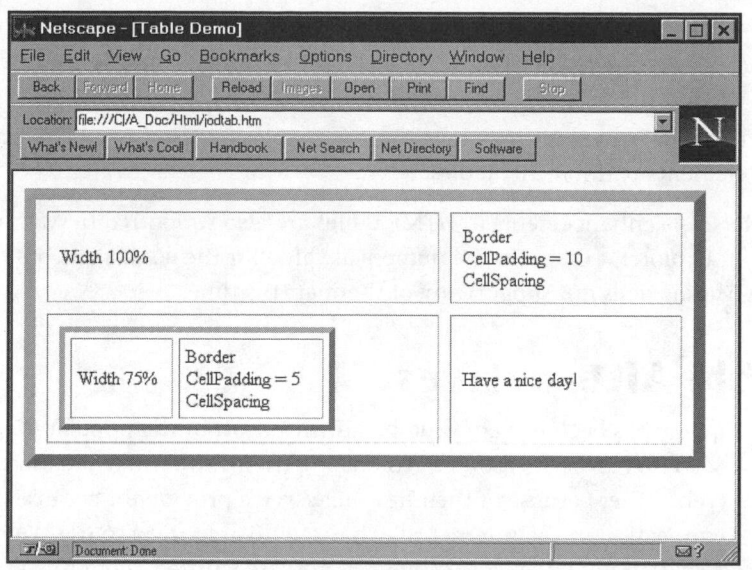

Fig. 13.17
Netscape
Navigator's table
enhancements
give the HTML
author greater
control over the
appearance of
HTML tables.

The Netscape table enhancements are as follows:

- **WIDTH attribute**—This enables the author to specify the width of the table, either in pixels or as a percentage of the width of the browser window.

- **HEIGHT attribute**—This enables the author to specify the height of the table, either in pixels or as a percentage of the height of the browser window.

- **BORDER attribute**—This attribute exists in the draft HTML 3.0 specification and puts a border around the table, and in that respect is supported by most Web browsers with table support. The enhancement also enables it to be used as a numerical attribute, BORDER=<num>, which makes the border <num> pixels wide.

> **Caution**
>
> When using the Netscape BORDER=<num> table enhancement, it is possible to specify a table with no borders by including BORDER=0 in the <TABLE> element. While this will give a borderless table when viewed with Netscape Navigator, Web browsers that do not support this enhancement will ignore the "=0" and display the table with a border. So, to use a borderless table that will work on all browsers that support tables, include the <TABLE> element without specifying a BORDER attribute.

III

Advanced HTML

- **CELLPADDING and CELLSPACING**—These numerical attributes include extra space within each cell in the table and/or within the borders of the table. If the border is not being displayed, they are equivalent.

- **Nested Tables**—Netscape Navigator enables tables to be included as elements within other tables.

The Netscape enhancements to HTML tables are also supported by Microsoft Internet Explorer, except for the numerical value for the BORDER attribute. NCSA Mosaic does not support any of them at this time.

Table Alternatives

Table support has become very widespread with most of the popular Web browsers, so there is less reason to avoid using them. Still, there are folks out on the Web, either because of their Internet service provider of because of the type of connection to the Internet they have, who are forced to use Web browsers that do not have table support. If you are worried about missing such people, there are some alternatives that you can use, either instead of or in addition to using tables themselves.

Figure 13.18 shows an HTML document for a fairly simple table shown in figure 13.19. Some other ways of displaying this information, not using tables, are as follows:

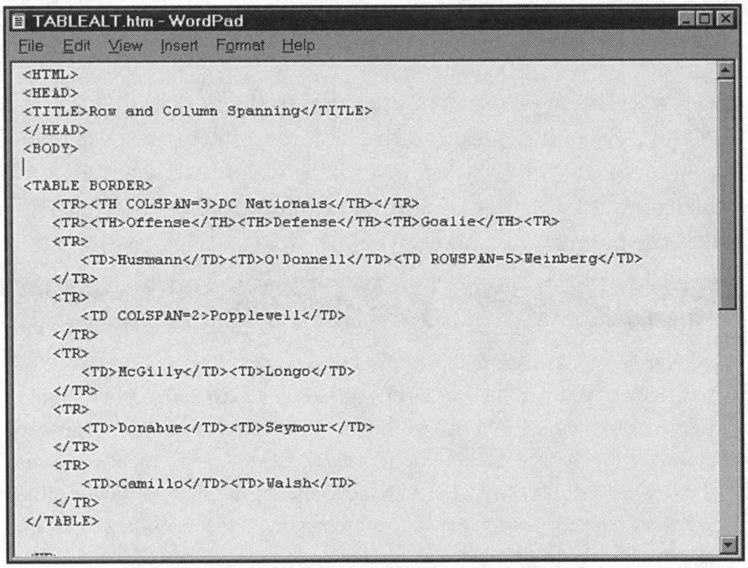

Fig. 13.18
This HTML document uses a table to display information.

```
TABLEALT.htm - WordPad
File  Edit  View  Insert  Format  Help
<HTML>
<HEAD>
<TITLE>Row and Column Spanning</TITLE>
</HEAD>
<BODY>

<TABLE BORDER>
    <TR><TH COLSPAN=3>DC Nationals</TH></TR>
    <TR><TH>Offense</TH><TH>Defense</TH><TH>Goalie</TH><TR>
    <TR>
        <TD>Husmann</TD><TD>O'Donnell</TD><TD ROWSPAN=5>Weinberg</TD>
    </TR>
    <TR>
        <TD COLSPAN=2>Popplewell</TD>
    </TR>
    <TR>
        <TD>McGilly</TD><TD>Longo</TD>
    </TR>
    <TR>
        <TD>Donahue</TD><TD>Seymour</TD>
    </TR>
    <TR>
        <TD>Camillo</TD><TD>Walsh</TD>
    </TR>
</TABLE>
```

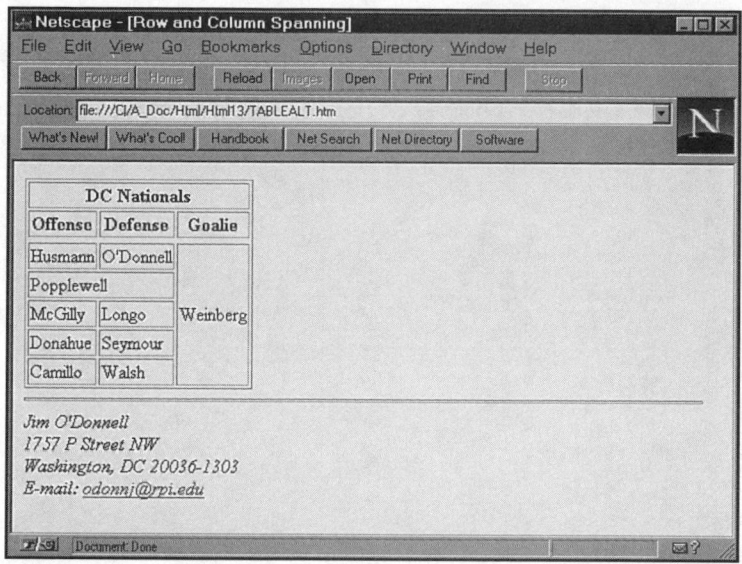

Fig. 13.19
A sample table
showing a fairly
straightforward
organization of
information.

■ Use a list. Information that is relatively straightforward can be displayed instead as a list. This information can be displayed just as well as a list, as coded in figure 13.20 and rendered by Netscape Navigator in figure 13.21.

Fig. 13.20
Simple tabular
data can also be
displayed using a
list format.

Fig. 13.21
Because support for lists is more widespread than that for tables, they can sometimes be a good alternative.

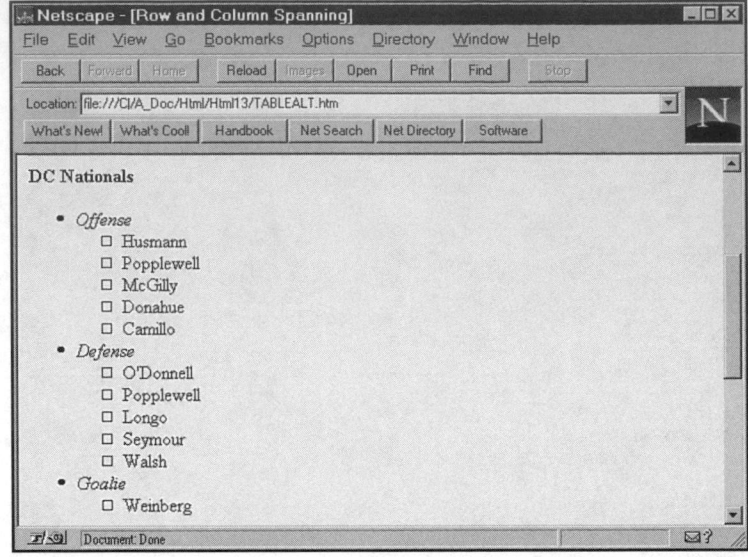

◄ See "Displaying Text in Lists," p. 173

■ Use an image instead. By creating the table in a word processor, or even in your own copy of a Web browser such as Netscape Navigator, and then taking a screen shot and cropping it down to the size of the displayed table, you can include the table in your HTML document as an image. This may not be the best alternative, however, as Web browsers that do not support tables may not support images, either.

■ Use preformatted text. This will give you a table that is pretty aesthetically unappealing, but it has the advantage of being displayed correctly in just about every Web browser, including text-only browsers such as Lynx. An example of this is shown in figures 13.22 and 13.23.

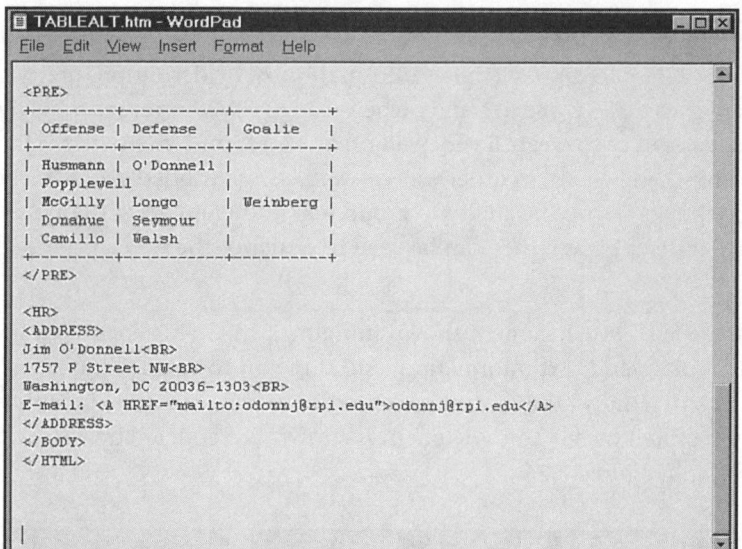

Fig. 13.22
A preformatted text block can also be used to organize information in a table.

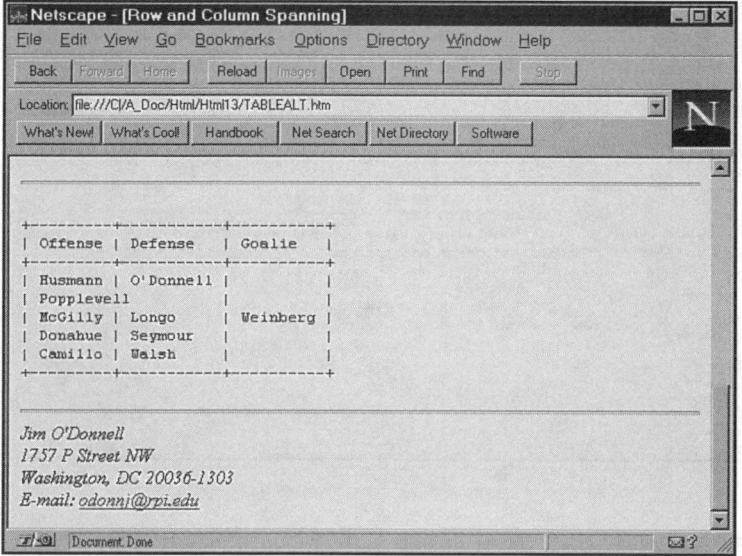

Fig. 13.23
A preformatted table isn't very pretty, but it will be displayed correctly in just about any Web browser.

III

Advanced HTML

Table Examples

The use of tables to display tabular information is, by definition, pretty obvious. Tables can also come in handy when using HTML forms, as they give you the capability to create a very well-organized form for entering information. Tables can be used in other ways as well, as mentioned briefly earlier. Because they give you the ability to group text and graphics with one another in many different ways, they can be used to enhance the way a page is displayed.

▶ See "Using HTML Tables to Line Up Forms," p. 509

Consider the HTML document shown in figure 13.24. This document includes graphics and text information, and is meant to display it as a sort-of trading card. (Forgive the shameless self-promotion, but it was the only hockey picture I have!) This document is shown, as rendered by Netscape Navigator, in figure 13.25.

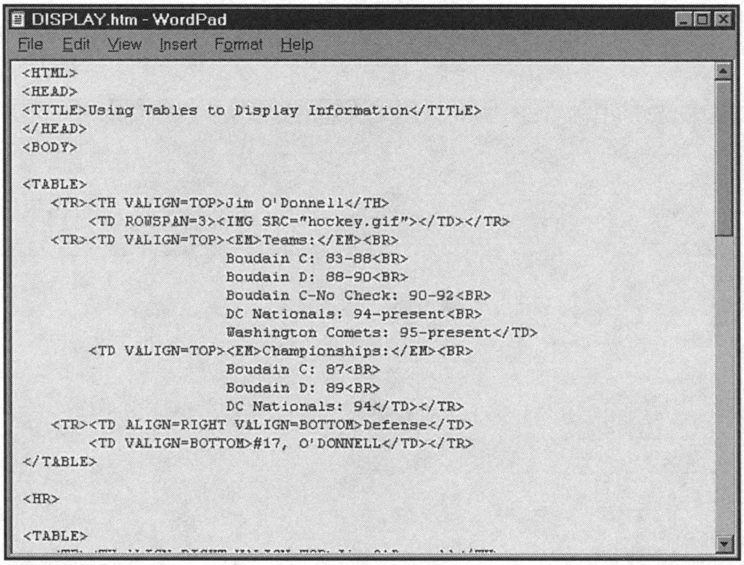


```
<HTML>
<HEAD>
<TITLE>Using Tables to Display Information</TITLE>
</HEAD>
<BODY>

<TABLE>
   <TR><TH VALIGN=TOP>Jim O'Donnell</TH>
       <TD ROWSPAN=3><IMG SRC="hockey.gif"></TD></TR>
   <TR><TD VALIGN=TOP><EM>Teams:</EM><BR>
                     Boudain C: 83-88<BR>
                     Boudain D: 88-90<BR>
                     Boudain C-No Check: 90-92<BR>
                     DC Nationals: 94-present<BR>
                     Washington Comets: 95-present</TD>
       <TD VALIGN=TOP><EM>Championships:</EM><BR>
                     Boudain C: 87<BR>
                     Boudain D: 89<BR>
                     DC Nationals: 94</TD></TR>
   <TR><TD ALIGN=RIGHT VALIGN=BOTTOM>Defense</TD>
       <TD VALIGN=BOTTOM>#17, O'DONNELL</TD></TR>
</TABLE>

<HR>

<TABLE>
```

Fig. 13.24
Tables allow you to combine text and graphics in many different ways.

Combining Text and Lists

To refine this Web page further, some of the information presented within it can be displayed differently—in this case, using an HTML list (an unordered list, but any other kind of list could be used just as easily). The HTML code for this is shown in figure 13.26—it makes sense to group lists of data using HTML list elements, and the ability to include these within a table allows the information to be conveyed more clearly. The revised Web page is shown in figure 13.27.

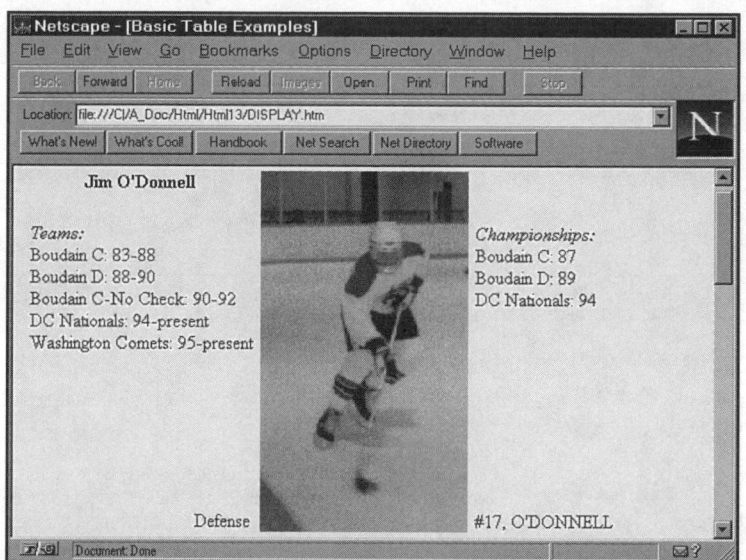

Fig. 13.25
Though at first glance this docs not look like a "table," the use of an HTML table to organize the information has made the display more effective.

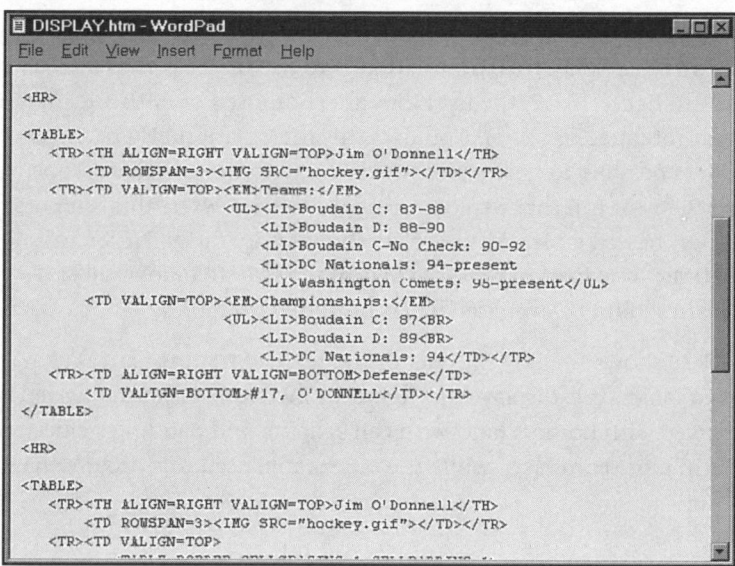

Fig. 13.26
HTML lists can be used within other HTML elements, including tables.

Fig. 13.27
Combining lists
and tables gives
you powerful
means for
organizing and
displaying
information
within your
Web pages.

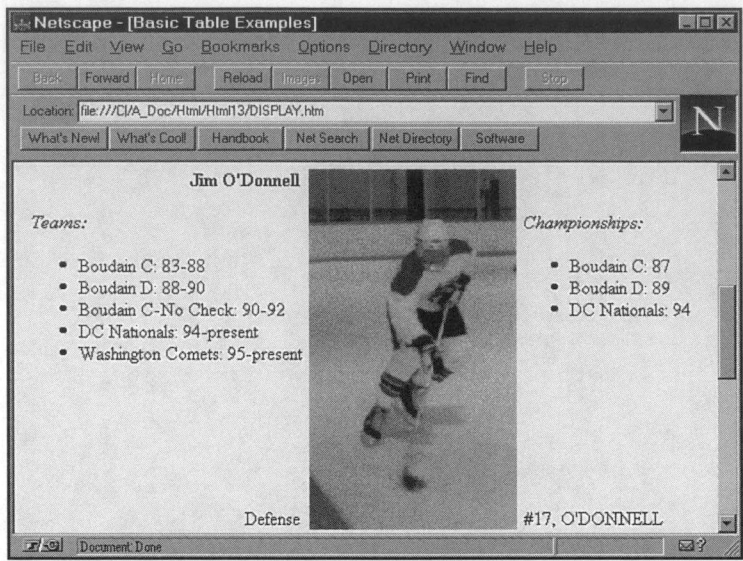

Nesting HTML Tables

Another way to display this information is to use tables within a larger table.
As shown in figure 13.27, the list items are composed of both a team name
and a year (or range of years). Couldn't this information also be displayed in
a table? It is possible to nest tables within other tables using Netscape Navigator and Microsoft Internet Explorer. Not all Web browsers that support tables
also support nested tables, however. As shown previously, NCSA Mosaic does
not, so all the information presented within the nested table is lost. For that
reason, care should be exercised when using nested tables.

Figure 13.28 shows the HTML code for the hockey trading card Web page using nested tables. It is displayed in figure 13.29. Notice that the nested tables
are displayed with borders (and with cell spacing and padding reduced to
make them more compact), while the outer table used to structure the whole
page is not.

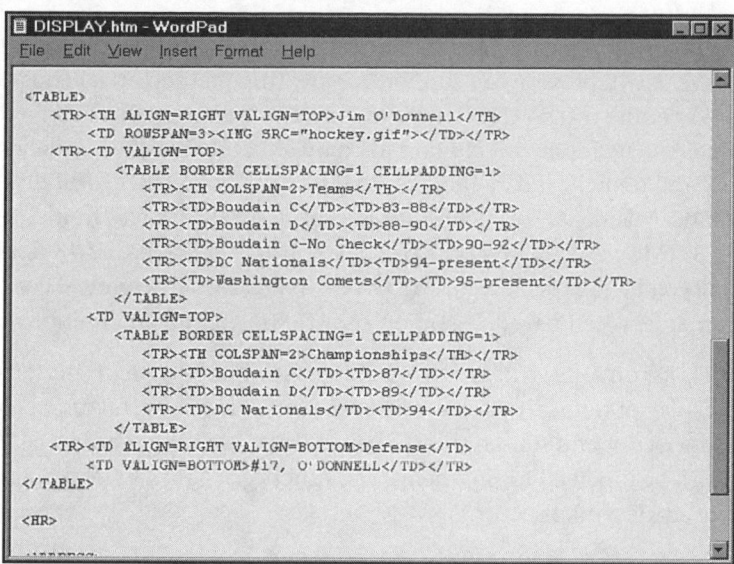

Fig. 13.28
Some Web browsers, particularly Netscape Navigator and Microsoft Internet Explorer, support nesting tables within other tables.

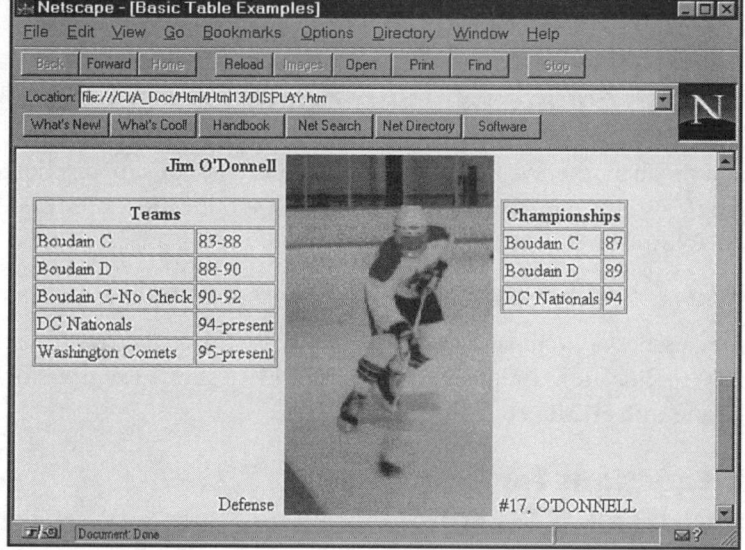

Fig. 13.29
Nested tables are another way to organize information effectively within a Web page.

Using Math Equations

HTML Level 3 will provide full support for creating mathematical equations in the body of the text in HTML documents. The basic element will be the <MATH. element, and it will contain attributes that define the formula expressions and numerical data (and variables). HTML's <MATH> will display mathematical elements in a plain font and numerical variables in italicized text. The HTML standard will borrow heavily from the LaTeX UNIX application, so if you have experience using LaTeX to create mathematical content for documents, you'll have a leg up on the HTML 3.0 implementation.

The <MATH> container will support elements for brackets, delimiters, the proper display of numerators and denominators (the former placed above the latter), superscript and subscript text, and matrices and other arrays. HTML entities will be provided for mathematical functions, Greek letters, operators, and other math symbols.

Currently, however, none of the major Web browsers support HTML math equations. Arena, a browser used as the HTML 3.0 test bed that runs under UNIX and Linux, does support them—though Arena is not a *production* Web browser.

HTML Math Equations Using Arena

As mentioned, Arena is the Web browser for the HTML 3.0 specification. It is not a production browser meant for widespread use or support, but is intended to give the developers of the HTML 3.0 specification a test bed. It is available for UNIX and Linux machines from:

http://www.w3.org/hypertext/WWW/Arena/

Arena has a series of Web pages meant to showcase the elements of the HTML 3.0 specification that it supports. Figure 13.30 shows examples of what can be done with HTML 3.0 math equations.

Math Equations for Browsers without HTML 3.0 Support

No commercial browsers offer math equation support. As mentioned in the previous section, Arena is the only browser that supports equations, and it's primarily a testing location for the HTML 3.0 development process. How then can equations be used in Web documents that anyone can access and display?

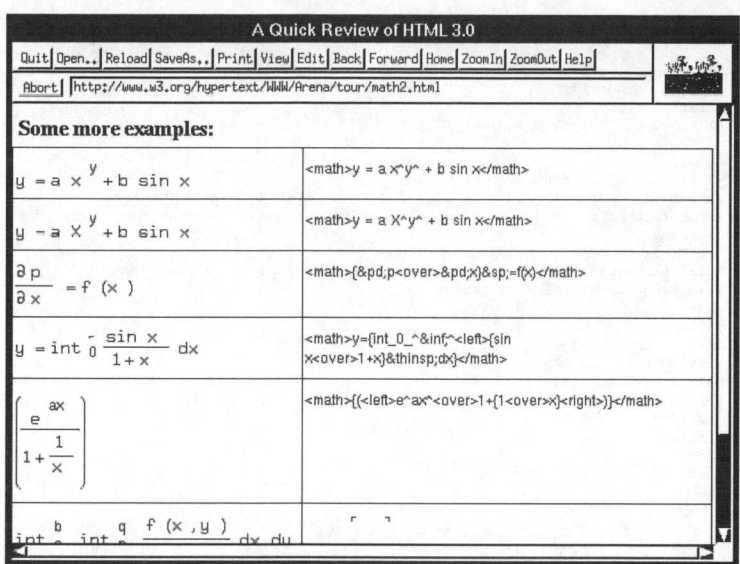

Fig. 13.30
Many different symbols and formulas can be displayed in HTML documents with the HTML 3.0 specification.

You can accomplish this through inline images. Many word processors include math equation editors. Create your math formulas in your favorite word processor or graphics program, setting the font size, style, and color to the proper size in relation to your Web document text (see fig. 13.31).

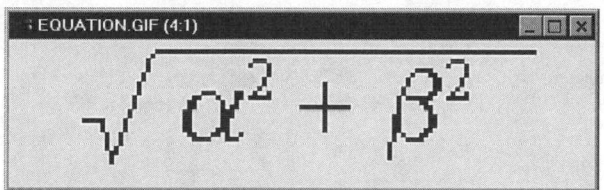

Fig. 13.31
Many word processors and graphics programs enable you to create math formulas and equations.

Once you have created the graphic and saved it as a GIF file, you can include it in your HTML documents (see fig. 13.32 and fig. 13.33).

Incorporating math equations requires a little more work than just entering text into a Web page, and it will until there is more support of the HTML 3.0 math equation specification by the popular Web browsers. If you maintain your equations in a single source file, you can always go back and edit or re-use your math "code" in future HTML documents.

III

Advanced HTML

Fig. 13.32
Equations saved in a GIF format can be included in your HTML documents.

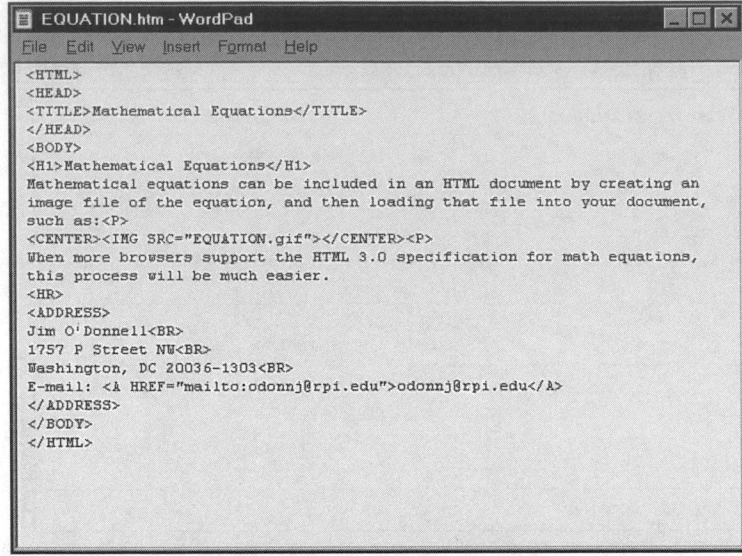

Fig. 13.33
It's a little more work getting them there than with normal text, but it is possible to include math equations in HTML documents.

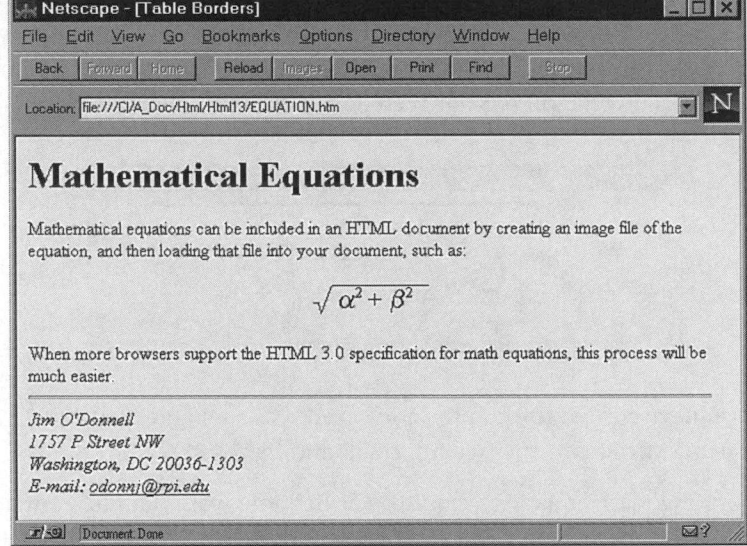

Tip

Use colors in your equations to highlight specific variables and values for your audience.

## CHAPTER 14

HTML Style Sheets

by Mark Brown

The hardest part of learning to swim is overcoming your fears and getting into the pool. That's what this chapter is for. If you're contemplating putting up your own personal or corporate Web site but aren't quite sure where to begin, in this chapter you find HTML templates for each type so that you can get into the pool.

Before you start, though, you might want to refer to chapter 3, "Distributing Information with HTML," where you learn what should appear on Web pages, and how and why. After you get your feet wet, then come back and dive right in.

You don't jump off into the deep end, though. In this chapter, you don't get in over your head. You learn how to put together some simple but attractive Web pages that you can easily modify and build up to create custom personal and professional Web pages to meet a variety of needs. You don't get into advanced HTML coding, CGI-bin programming, or anything like that.

After you've mastered the basic strokes, you might want to move on to chapters 21, "Forms and How They Work," and 22, "Form Layout and Design," which go in-depth into the design and development of two advanced Web sites with multiple pages and lots of elements. That's the place where you begin training for the Olympics.

In this chapter, you discover the following:

- How to put together an appealing and functional personal home page
- How to add functionality and class to your personal Web pages
- How to create a simple corporate home page
- How to create a Web page navigational image map without CGI programming or browser-specific HTML extensions

■ Templates for automated Web page creation on the Web and for use with your word processor

Creating Personal Web Pages

To make the process of creating personal Web pages easy, follow along with a newbie Web developer who is going through the process of putting up his first Web page. He may know more than you do; he may know less. That doesn't matter because the steps are the same no matter what your level of expertise.

Picking a Topic

Out there among you is a guy named Fred who's been reading this book at about the same pace you have and who is starting to think he might know just about enough to put his own home page on the Web.

He has read and re-read chapter 3 and has a pretty good idea of what kinds of information are appropriate (and inappropriate) for Web sites. He's been thinking about what subject he might focus on because he remembers that the number one rule for creating an appealing Web site is to focus the topic.

Fred likes golf more than about anything else in the world, but thousands of Web sites cover the topic of golf. Besides, "golf" just isn't focused enough. Putting up a golf page would be almost as bad as putting up a page for "sports" in general.

The most important corollary to the principle of focusing your topic is to pick a focal point about which you know something extra. That way, you can present new, fresh information that isn't just a rehash of what's already on the Web. If it's already there somewhere, why put up the information again? On the Web, all you have to do is provide a link to the other sites, and you're done. You don't have to re-create the same information.

After carefully considering his options, Fred has decided to build a Web site devoted to the subject of "Making Your Own Golf Clubs."

Fred started making his own clubs because he's a good player, and he thought he could get a little better if he had some really top-of-the-line clubs. Problem is, they cost a fortune. Not only that, but Fred is a bit on the diminutive side—and left-handed, to boot—so finding clubs that fit him is a problem. So he lined up some suppliers, bought a couple of tools, made a few mistakes, and eventually put together an excellent set of custom clubs for himself at a fraction of the cost of a top-quality name-brand pro set.

When Fred started playing with his custom clubs, other players began to admire them, and he started making a few for other people on the side. At first, he did this for only a few friends, but his hobby soon expanded into a garage business that is now making him a couple hundred bucks every month.

Fred knows a lot about the topic and thinks that sharing what he knows might be fun. He believes that people would show an interest because he's already found a lot of interest among his friends and acquaintances. He's searched Yahoo!, Webcrawler, and Lycos and couldn't find a thing about making golf clubs, so he knows that his site will be unique.

Fred's not concerned about drumming up business—word of mouth is giving him all the business he wants. He just wants some fame and glory and perhaps a thank you note in his e-mail box once in a while.

Planning Content

Fred's first impulse is to gather together a bunch of cool golf-related graphics and start creating his page. He's about to dive in when he remembers that the second step is not to create but to plan. So he sits down with pencil and paper and thinks about what he might want to put on-line.

After a few false starts, some whittling down, and some inspirational additions, Fred finally comes up with the following list of things he definitely wants on his Web site:

- A tasteful title graphic with a picture of some golf clubs and the words "Making Your Own Golf Clubs"
- A list of reasons that people might want to build their own clubs
- The step-by-step procedures for building golf clubs, with diagrams
- A full-motion video of himself putting together a golf club
- A list of the tools required
- A list of parts suppliers
- A few digitized photos of some of the clubs he's made
- A list of only the very best links to other golf-related sites

The video is a real inspiration. His friend Sheila runs the multimedia lab at the local university, and a quick call to her confirms that she can get studio time to videotape the whole golf club creation process and digitize it into an .avi file that can be uploaded to his site. She thinks the project is interesting and is looking forward to doing it. Problem is, her schedule is full, and she can't do anything until next month. Rather than let Sheila's schedule be a setback and just omit the video, Fred decides to make a "Coming Soon!" tag to let people know that it's on the way. That will keep them coming back.

Fred has a lot of excellent information on his list, and every element is relevant to his focus topic. This, he thinks, is going to be a great Web site!

Creating a Home Page

Fred knows that he needs to organize first, so he decides to just jump right in and create his home page. He figures it's just as easy to outline right on the HTML page as it is to come up with some artificial outline first and then try to figure out how to "HTML-ize" it. And he's right.

He knows he can use any word processor or text editor to create an HTML document, but he's checked out the CD-ROM in the back of this book and has been playing around with HTML Writer, so he decides to use it instead. Fred thinks that HTML Writer might help him remember and keep track of what all those HTML tags are for. He's right again (see fig. 14.1.)

Fig. 14.1
HTML Writer is an
excellent HTML
editor that can
provide a level
of comfort and
support during the
Web page-creation
process.

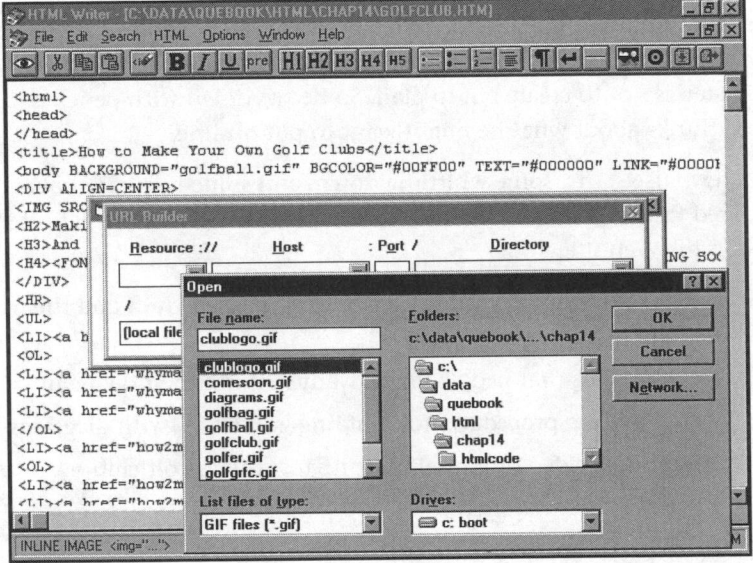

On the CD

Fred begins by laying out a generic minimum HTML document, using chapters 4, "Building Blocks of HTML," and 5, "The TITLE, HEAD, and HTML Tags," as a guide:

```
<HTML>
<HEAD>
<TITLE></TITLE>
</HEAD>
<BODY>
</BODY>
</HTML>
```

He knows that every HTML document needs to be surrounded by <HTML> </HTML> containers, and it must have a HEAD section, a TITLE section inside the HEAD, and a BODY section, in that order.

Fred decides that he wants a title and a subtitle for sure, so he adds two generic lines:

```
<H1>Title</H1>
<H2>Subtitle</H2>
```

He knows that what he puts between the <TITLE></TITLE> tags is actually just the name that will appear in the browser's window border. His Title and Subtitle lines are in the big H1 and H2 heading styles, so they'll be really *visible*.

Fred knows that the polite practice is to tell viewers when a page was last updated and to provide an easy means for them to e-mail comments. So Fred adds three more lines of HTML at the end of the document, just before the closing </BODY></HTML> tags:

```
<HR>
Last Updated DATE.<br>
Please address all questions or comments to ADDRESS
```

The <HR> adds a horizontal rule to set off these lines from the rest of the page. Fred can't quite remember how to make the last line a link to e-mail him automatically when someone clicks it, so he just puts in the word ADDRESS for now.

Fred thinks a bit about how he wants to organize his information and decides that he wants to keep his home page small (no more than two display screens tall), with links that will jump to other pages with the actual information. (Good for him!) So he makes a list of links that are enticing titles for his subject matter. He decides to put them in a list, like this:

```
<UL>
<LI>Menu
</UL>
```

The <UL></UL> container makes this list "unordered," or bulleted. Each menu item will have its own <LI> line when he is finished.

Fred then checks the list he made on paper before starting and remembers that he wants to have some links to other golf-related Web sites. Because his list of links is bigger than he wants to include on his home page, he decides to give the list its own page, too. On his home page, he can just link to the list with this line near the bottom of the page, above the bottom horizontal rule:

```
<STRONG>CLICK <A HREF="">HERE</A> FOR A LIST OF LINKS!</STRONG>
```

III

Advanced HTML

He doesn't have an URL for his links page yet, so he leaves the `HREF=""` part empty.

This is what Fred's home page looks like so far:

```
<HTML>
<HEAD>
<TITLE></TITLE>
</HEAD>
<BODY>
<H1>Title</H1>
<H2>Subtitle</H2>
<HR>
<UL>
<LI>Menu
</UL>
<STRONG>CLICK <A HREF="">HERE</A> FOR A LIST OF LINKS!</STRONG>
<HR>
Last Updated DATE.<br>
Please address all questions or comments to ADDRESS
</body>
</html>
```

Fred saves his work and clicks the big eyeball icon on the HTML Writer screen, which previews his work in Netscape, as shown in figure 14.2.

Fig. 14.2
Fred's bare-bones Web page is previewed in Netscape Navigator 2.0.

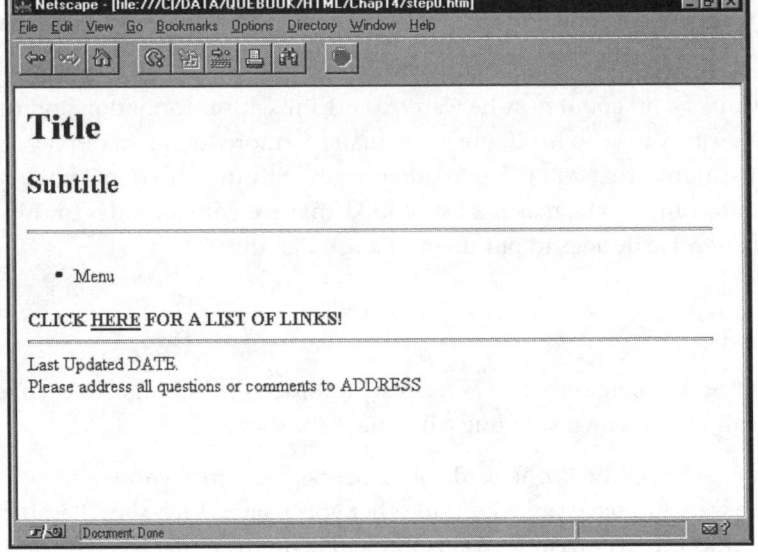

> **Note**
>
> You can use the HTML code in the preceding example as a simple template for creating any Web page. It is stored on the CD-ROM as step0.htm. The HTML code for each screen in this section is saved on the CD-ROM as step0.htm through step3.htm. The final page is saved as golfclub.htm.

Fred's pretty pumped about the fact that his first effort has actually resulted in something being displayed in Netscape. Maybe this HTML stuff isn't so tough after all!

Now he buckles down. First, he fleshes out the top of the page. Because the top is what people will see first, it's got to draw them in.

```
<HEAD>
<TITLE>How to Make Your Own Golf Clubs</TITLE>
</HEAD>
<BODY>
<H1>[How To Make Your Own Golf Clubs]</H1>
<H2>Making Your Own Clubs is Fun</H2>
<H3>And Profitable Too!</H3>
<H4>*COMING SOON!* Online Video Instructions! *COMING SOON!*</H4>
<HR>
```

Fred makes the window TITLE "How to Make Your Own Golf Clubs" to match the H1 header. As he's typing in the H1 header, though, he realizes that he doesn't really want a header. He wants a graphic logo. It's the first item on his list, and he forgot it! Oh, well. For now, he types **[How To Make Your Own Golf Clubs]** in as an H1 header. He surrounds the text with brackets [ ] to remind himself that this title is just a placeholder for a graphic he has yet to create.

He rounds out the header information with H2 and H3 headers that proclaim how fun and profitable making golf clubs can be, and he finishes up with an H4 header with the announcement about the video, surrounded by *COMING SOON* notes. He adds a horizontal rule to separate the header information from the rest of his home page.

Having learned from the title graphic mistake, he checks his list to see whether he wants to add any other graphics and sees that his site will contain both diagrams and photos. Though he knows now that they will appear on separate pages, he decides that a small graphic for each of them should go on his home page with a link to the pages that actually contain the images. So he adds this line, just to remind himself later that he has to make some "icon" graphics:

```
[DIAGRAM][PHOTO]<BR>
```

He finishes by adding the date to his update line and his e-mail address in place of ADDRESS (though he still hasn't figured out how to link it). Here's Fred's home page so far:

```
<HTML>
<HEAD>
<TITLE>How to Make Your Own Golf Clubs</TITLE>
</HEAD>
<BODY>
<H1>[How To Make Your Own Golf Clubs]</H1>
<H2>Making Your Own Clubs is Fun</H2>
<H3>And Profitable Too!</H3>
<H4>*COMING SOON!* Online Video Instructions! *COMING SOON!*</H4>
<HR>
<UL>
<LI>Menu
</UL>
[DIAGRAM][PHOTO]<BR>
<STRONG>CLICK <a href="golflink.htm">HERE</a>
FOR A LIST OF AWESOME GOLF LINKS!</STRONG>
<HR>
Last Updated February 16, 1996.
Please address all questions or comments to fred18@golf.net
</BODY>
</HTML>
```

Figure 14.3 shows what Fred's page looks like now.

Fig. 14.3

Fred's home page is coming along fine. Though still pretty generic, it has most of the elements in place.

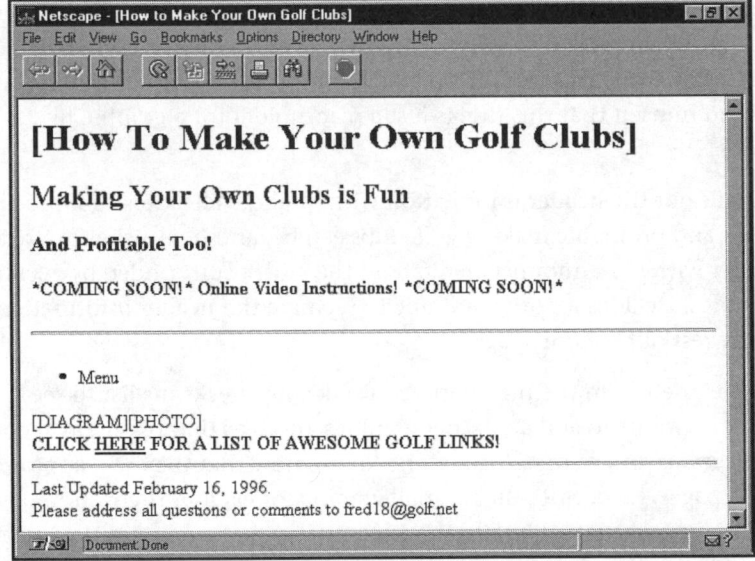

Though things are progressing nicely, the time has come for Fred to make a few decisions. He decides he's definitely going to have three documents besides his home page: one for the Why arguments, one for the How instructions, and one for his list of links. He decides to name them why2make.htm, how2make.htm, and golflink.htm. Now he can go ahead and create his menu list.

First, Fred makes a list of menu items:

```
<UL>
<LI>Why Make Your Own Clubs?
<LI>To Save Money
<LI>To Make Money
<LI>To Customize Your Clubs to You!
<LI>How To Make Your Own Clubs
<LI>Tools
<LI>Suppliers
<LI>Step-by-step Instructions
</UL>
```

Each of these lines is a link, so Fred adds an <A></A> anchor container to each line, with the URL of the appropriate page:

```
<UL>
<LI><A HREF="why2make.htm">Why Make Your Own Clubs?</A>
<LI><A HREF="why2make.htm">To Save Money</A>
<LI><A HREF="why2make.htm">To Make Money</A>
<LI><A HREF="why2make.htm">To Customize Your Clubs to You!</A>
<LI><A HREF="how2make.htm">How To Make Your Own Clubs</A>
<LI><A HREF="how2make.htm">Tools</A>
<LI><A HREF="how2make.htm">Suppliers</A>
<LI><A HREF="how2make.htm">Step-by-step Instructions</A>
</UL>
```

The list is good, but Fred thinks that something just doesn't feel right about it. He thinks for a minute and then realizes that all eight of his links go to just two destinations. That doesn't seem very helpful. A little page-turning through this book reveals that a link can lead not only to a whole Web page, but to a particular spot on that page. So Fred decides that only one link each should go to the tops of the two pages, and he adds the syntax for jumping to a named anchor for each of the rest. Because he doesn't know the names yet, he just puts in the pound sign (#) so that he knows to add the names later:

```
<UL>
<LI><A HREF="why2make.htm">Why Make Your Own Clubs?</A>
<LI><A HREF="why2make.htm#">To Save Money</A>
<LI><A HREF="why2make.htm#">To Make Money</A>
<LI><A HREF="why2make.htm#">To Customize Your Clubs to You!</A>
<LI><A HREF="how2make.htm">How To Make Your Own Clubs</A>
<LI><A HREF="how2make.htm#">Tools</A>
<LI><A HREF="how2make.htm#">Suppliers</A>
<LI><A HREF="how2make.htm#">Step-by-step Instructions</A>
</UL>
```

III

Advanced HTML

Note

Fred's named anchors will be created on the how2make.htm and why2make.htm pages using the anchor tag <A> with the NAME attribute, like this:

```
<A NAME="tools">Tools</A>
```

In this example, the preceding line would appear in the how2make.htm file in the spot where Fred wanted this link from his home page to jump to

```
<A HREF="how2make.htm#tools">Tools</A>
```

The #tools portion of the HREF attribute makes this link jump to the tools value of the NAME attribute on the how2make.htm page.

Finally, Fred has figured out that his automatic e-mail line at the bottom of the page needs a mailto: reference, and he encloses the whole line with the ADDRESS text format, as follows:

```
<ADDRESS>Please address all questions or comments to <A
HREF="mailto:fred18@golf.net">fred18@golf.net</A></ADDRESS>
```

His home page now looks like the following and appears as shown in figure 14.4.

```
<HTML>
<HEAD>
<TITLE>How to Make Your Own Golf Clubs</TITLE>
</HEAD>
<BODY>
[How To Make Your Own Golf Clubs]
<H2>Making Your Own Clubs is Fun</H2>
<H3>And Profitable Too!</H3>
<H4>*COMING SOON!* Online Video Instructions! *COMING SOON!*</H4>
<HR>
<UL>
<LI><A HREF="why2make.htm">Why Make Your Own Clubs?</A>
<LI><A HREF="why2make.htm#">To Save Money</A>
<LI><A HREF="why2make.htm#">To Make Money</A>
<LI><A HREF="why2make.htm#">To Customize Your Clubs to You!</A>
<LI><A HREF="how2make.htm">How To Make Your Own Clubs</A>
<LI><A HREF="how2make.htm#">Tools</A>
<LI><A HREF="how2make.htm#">Suppliers</A>
<LI><A HREF="how2make.htm#">Step-by-step Instructions</A>
</UL>
[Diagrams][Photos]<BR>
<STRONG>CLICK <a href="golflink.htm">HERE</a> FOR A LIST OF AWESOME
➥GOLF LINKS!</STRONG>
<HR>
<EM>Last Updated February 16, 1996.</EM>
<ADDRESS>Please address all questions or comments to <A
HREF="mailto:fred18@golf.net">fred18@golf.net</A></ADDRESS>
</BODY>
</HTML>
```

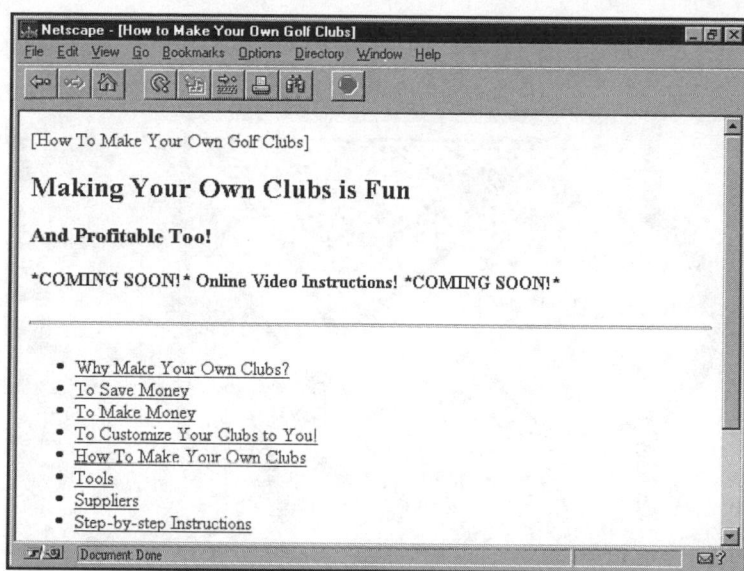

Fig. 14.4
Fred's home page is shaping up nicely. Now it's time to add some graphics!

There's no putting it off any longer—Fred knows it's time to buckle down and create some graphics. Though he's not much of an artist, he does have a CD-ROM full of clip art at hand, and he manages to find some golf-related images that should do nicely with a little modification.

> **Note**
>
> Remember not to use any copyrighted materials on your Web pages. Though Fred's CD-ROM collection of clip art is copyrighted, the end-user license agreement specifically allows him use of the images without paying royalties.

Fred fires up his copy of Paint Shop Pro and goes to work (see fig. 14.5).

Knowing that he wants his home page to look good on any graphic browser, Fred opts to keep his graphics to the 16 standard Windows colors and to format them so they'll look good on a 640×480 screen. This way, they load faster, too. He checks his list and sees he's got three images to create for his home page:

On the CD

- A title logo with a nice image of some golf clubs and the words "How To Make Your Own Golf Clubs"

- An icon-type graphic to act as a link to his diagrams

- Another icon graphic to link to his digitized photos

III

Advanced HTML

Fig. 14.5
A good graphics
program is
indispensable
for Web page
creation.
A shareware
program like Paint
Shop Pro works
fine.

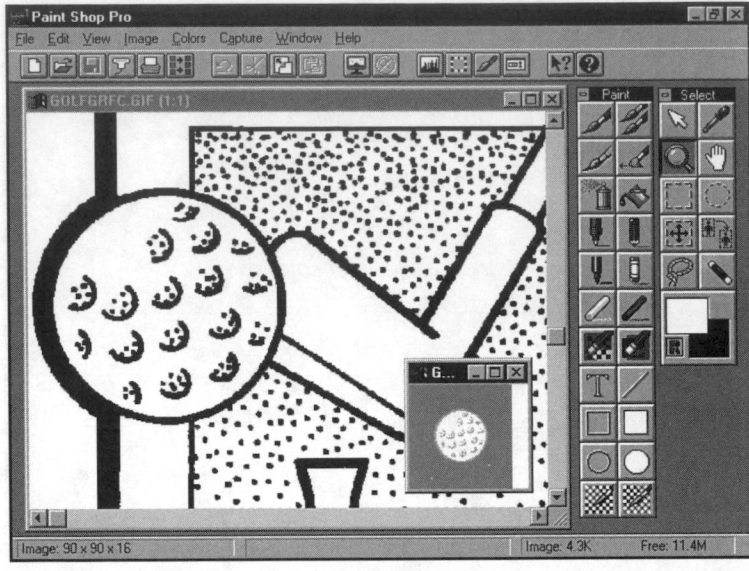

After Fred looks back at the preview of his page in Netscape, he realizes that
he'd really love to have two more graphics:

- A colorful "splash" graphic to take the place of the *COMING SOON!* text
  around the video announcement
- A background pattern

He knows he can get into big trouble if his background pattern is too gaudy,
and it's a browser-specific design, but Fred figures if he's careful, he can come
up with something tasteful that won't get in the way and that won't really be
missed on browsers that can't display it.

Figure 14.5 shows what he found—a huge golf ball that he had to trim, resize,
and recolor in subtler (not black and white) shades. He also trimmed, resized,
recolored, and generally mucked around with clip art images of a golf bag
and a set of three golf clubs to get his photo icon and logo. The diagram icon
he finally ended up drawing by hand so that it would look like a diagram. He
made the two icon images the same size so they'd look good side-by-side, and
made the logo big enough to make an eye-catching display without taking
over the entire screen.

Fred has been reading chapter 10, "Adding Graphics to Your Home Page,"
though, and wants to make the background of his logo transparent so that
the background graphic will shine through. Paint Shop Pro doesn't create
transparent GIF images, so Fred converts his logo using LView Pro (see
fig. 14.6), which is used by many Web page designers for just this purpose.

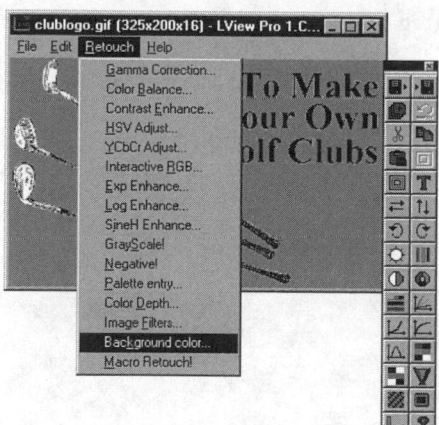

Fig. 14.6
LView Pro is an excellent Windows/Win95 tool for creating transparent GIF images for Web pages.

Fred's home page is nearly done. He adds anchor links to all the graphics he's created and keeps the placeholder names he was using as ALT definitions for non-graphical browsers. He goes back and fills in names for the named anchors in his list items. Finally, Fred adds background color and a background graphic to the BODY tag, and his home page looks like this:

On the CD

```
<HTML>
<HEAD>
<TITLE>How to Make Your Own Golf Clubs</TITLE>
</HEAD>
<BODY BGCOLOR=#00ff00 BACKGROUND="golfball.gif">
<IMG SRC="clublogo.gif" ALT="[How To Make Your Own Golf Clubs]">
<H2>Making Your Own Clubs is Fun</H2>
<H3>And Profitable Too!</H3>
<H4><IMG SRC="comesoon.gif" ALT="*COMING SOON!*"> Online
 Video Instructions! <IMG SRC="comesoon.gif" ALT="*COMING SOON!*"></H4>
<HR>
<UL>
<LI><A HREF="why2make.htm">Why Make Your Own Clubs?</A>
<LI><A HREF="why2make.htm#savemoney">To Save Money</A>
<LI><A HREF="why2make.htm#makemoney">To Make Money</A>
<LI><A HREF="why2make.htm#customize">To Customize Your Clubs to You!</A>
<LI><A HREF="how2make.htm">How To Make Your Own Clubs</A>
<LI><A HREF="how2make.htm#tools">Tools</A>
<LI><A HREF="how2make.htm#suppliers">Suppliers</A>
<LI><A HREF="how2make.htm#steps">Step-by-step Instructions</A>
</UL>
<A HREF="how2make.htm/#diagrams"><IMG SRC="diagrams.gif"
ALT="[Diagrams]"></A>
<A HREF="why2make.htm/#photos"><IMG SRC="photos.gif"
ALT="[Photos]"></A>
<BR>
<STRONG>CLICK <a href="golflink.htm">HERE</a> FOR A LIST OF AWESOME GOLF LINKS!
➥</STRONG>
<HR>
```

▶ For a short
discourse on
color names
and values, see
the sidebar
"What's in a
Color Name?"
p. 349

```
<EM>Last Updated February 16, 1996.</EM>
<ADDRESS>Please address all questions or comments to <A
HREF="mailto:fred18@golf.net">fred18@golf.net</A></ADDRESS>
</BODY>
</HTML>
```

When Fred loads his page into Netscape, he is thrilled to see all his graphics come through with flying colors. His background color is putting-green green, and everything looks great (see fig. 14.7).

Fig. 14.7

Fred's home page is almost done. He just needs to align a few things better, and he's got a home page!

Except...

Nothing is centered. He forgot about centering. And the little "Coming Soon!" graphics aren't aligned properly with the text. Then, too, his list just doesn't look right. Fred needs to break it up into two main categories, with three subcategories under each. He decides to leave bullets for the main categories but number the subcategories using the OL (ordered list) tag. Now his Web page looks like this:

```
<HTML>
<HEAD>
<TITLE>How to Make Your Own Golf Clubs</TITLE>
</HEAD>
<BODY BACKGROUND="golfball.gif" BGCOLOR="#00FF00" TEXT="#000000"
LINK="#0000FF" VLINK="#008888">
```

```
<DIV ALIGN=CENTER>
<IMG SRC="clublogo.gif" ALT="[How To Make Your Own Golf Clubs]">
<H2>Making Your Own Clubs is Fun</H2>
<H3>And <FONT COLOR=#FF0000>Profitable</FONT> Too!</H3>
<H4><IMG SRC="comesoon.gif" ALIGN=MIDDLE ALT="*COMING SOON!*">
Online Video Instructions! <IMG SRC="comesoon.gif" ALIGN=MIDDLE
ALT="*COMING SOON!*"></H4>
</DIV>
<HR>
<UL>
<LI><A HREF="why2make.htm">Why Make Your Own Clubs?</A>
<OL>
<LI><A HREF="why2make.htm#">To Save Money</A>
<LI><A HREF="why2make.htm#">To Make Money</A>
<LI><A HREF="why2make.htm#">To Customize Your Clubs to You!</A>
</OL>
<LI><A HREF="how2make.htm">How To Make Your Own Clubs</A>
<OL>
<LI><A HREF="how2make.htm#">Tools</A>
<LI><A HREF="how2make.htm#">Suppliers</A>
<LI><A HREF="how2make.htm#">Step-by-step Instructions</A>
</OL>
</UL>
<DIV ALIGN=CENTER>
<A HREF="how2make.htm/#diagrams"><IMG SRC="diagrams.gif" ALT="[Diagrams]">
<A HREF="why2make.htm/#photos"><IMG SRC="photos.gif" ALT="[Photos]">
<BR>
<STRONG>CLICK <A Href="golflink.htm">HERE</A> FOR A LIST OF
 AWESOME GOLF LINKS!</STRONG>
<HR>
<EM>Last Updated February 16, 1996.</EM>
<ADDRESS>Please address all questions or comments to <A
HREF="mailto:fred18@golf.net">fred18@golf.net</A></ADDRESS>
</DIV>
</BODY>
</HTML>
```

Rather than use Netscape's non-standard CENTER tag, Fred opts for the HTML 3.0 standard <DIV ALIGN=CENTER> option, just to be "legal." He's also added TEXT, LINK, and VLINK color attributes to the BODY tag, just to make sure that his text shows up on that green background.

A final check in Netscape (see fig. 14.8 and fig. 14.9) shows that all is well with Fred's home page. It looks great!

He's not done, of course. He still has a lot of work ahead of him preparing the content pages to which his home page links. But Fred is off to a very good start.

Fig. 14.8
Fred's home page is done, and it looks great!

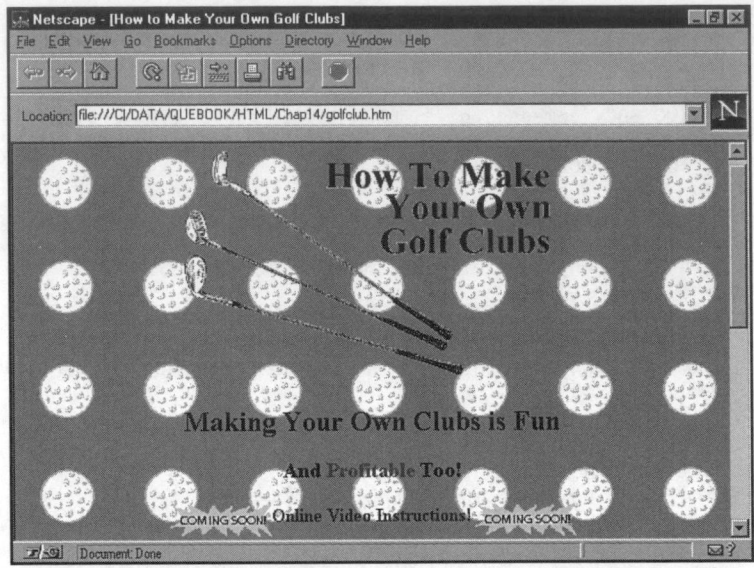

Fig. 14.9
Even the bottom half of Fred's home page looks good!

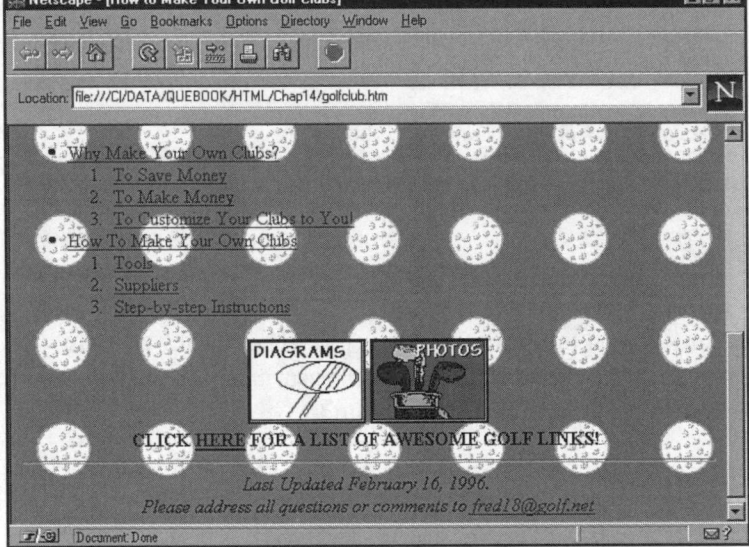

Creating Corporate Web Pages

The steps involved in developing a Web presence for your company are not much different from those for building a quality personal home page. In fact, if you're developing a business site, you have one big advantage. You already know the message you want to deliver on the Web—you want to sell something!

You have to hone that generic goal down a bit, of course, to whether you want to sell a product, a service, an image, your stock, or something else. But the bottom line is simply that whatever you put on the Web should in some way positively affect your bottom line.

For the next example, see what Honest Joe has done with his Web site for Honest Joe's Used Cars.

Focusing the Pitch

"You're putting a used car lot on the Web? Har, Har, Har!" was the reaction of Joe's main competitor when he found out what Joe had in mind. Since then, Joe has had the last laugh—all the way to the bank.

You see, even though Joe knows it's the "World Wide" Web, he also knows two other things: (1) Being on the Web is almost free, and (2) the "world" includes Milwaukee, where he sells cars. In fact, a lot of high-tech companies are located in the Milwaukee area. He knows. He's already sold cars to hundreds of their employees. In fact, thousands upon thousands of Web-browsing potential customers reside in the Milwaukee area. Joe knows that lots of them are techie-types who might not be comfortable shopping for a car on a used car lot. But they love shopping for one on the Web!

Joe introduced computers into his car showroom in the early '80s and has supervised upgrade installations a half dozen times since then. He knows computers pretty well. He studied this book until he got a pretty good handle on HTML; then he sat down and put together a set of Web pages that he felt would appeal to his potential techie customers.

Joe knew he wanted to tell them four major points:

1. He offers easy credit terms.
2. He has a wide selection of cars, from sporty models for young, single programmers to family vans for middle-management types.
3. His cars are good, quality-checked vehicles.
4. His stock turns over constantly, and viewers should check back often for new listings.

Joe knew that the convenience of car shopping on the Web would draw in customers, and the immediacy of seeing new listings daily would keep them coming back until they bought from him.

III

Advanced HTML

A Corporate Home Page

Joe decided to put a few "hot" listings up front on his home page, along with a flashy, easy-to-use clickable imagemap to send his customers off to information pages about credit, quality, and so on. Problem is, he really had no clue about how to create a clickable imagemap. He knew it involved CGI-bin programming, which sounded scary. But he thought about it, experimented a bit, and came up with a design that worked well without requiring any fancy stuff.

◀ See chapter 12, "Graphics Navigation with Image-maps," p. 229, and chapter 15, "Netscape-Specific Extensions to HTML," p. 311

Joe's solution involved putting six small graphics together on the page in two rows of three, with this HTML code:

```
<center>
<a href="quality.htm"><img src="chekmark.gif" alt="[Quality
➥Checkmark]"></a>
<a href="aboutjoe.htm"><img src="joetop.gif" alt="[Honest Joe's
➥Used Cars]"></a>
<a href="vans.htm"><img src="2doorvan.gif" alt="[Family Vans]"></a>
<br>
<a href="cars.htm"><img src="blusedan.gif" alt="[Sporty Sedans]"></a>
<a href="happycar.htm"><img src="joebottm.gif" alt="[Home of the
➥Happy Red Car!]"></a>
<a href="terms.htm"><img src="wallet.gif" alt="[Cash or
➥Credit!]"></a>
```

Each image is the same size as all the others, so the resulting grid is a symmetrical rectangular area with six clickable areas, as shown in figure 14.10.

Of course, the solution isn't perfect. It leaves a colored link rectangle around each image. But Joe figures he can live with it for now, and it looks okay. In fact, it has a kind of windowpane effect.

> **Note**
>
> Joe could get rid of the windowpane effect by adding the following attributes to the BODY tag:
>
> ```
> <BODY BGCOLOR=#ffffff TEXT=#000000 LINK=#ffffff VLINK=#ffffff>
> ```
>
> This line sets the page's background color to white, the text color to black, and the color of both followed and unfollowed links to white. Because links are the same color as the background, the windowpanes go away.

Unfortunately, so would the text of all the text links on the page, so this solution just isn't very friendly. However, Joe can use it in situations in which he doesn't have any text links to worry about.

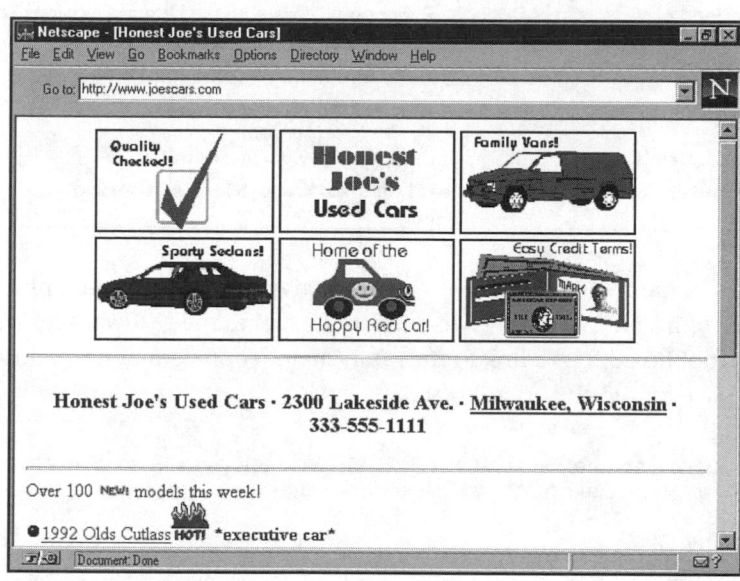

Fig. 14.10
Honest Joe's Used Car's simulates a clickable image-map by stacking six linked images. This view is in Netscape Navigator 2.0.

Two of the outside graphics link to Joe's latest (Joe updates it himself daily) list of used sedans and vans. The graphic in the upper left goes to a page that describes Joe's 12-point quality inspection and guarantee. The lower-right image leads to a page about Joe's friendly credit terms.

Joe has bowed to vanity a bit on this page—the top middle graphic jumps to a page that tells all about the dealership, complete with pictures of all the salesmen. This link is not totally for vanity's sake—Joe wants repeat customers, and the best way to get them back is to remind them who they dealt with last time and how nice they were. The bottom middle graphic goes to a page that talks about the "Happy Red Car," an Honest Joe's trademark for over 30 years. Everyone in Milwaukee knows about the Happy Red Car. It's in all of Honest Joe's TV commercials on the late news, and it's in all the parades in the Milwaukee area from St. Patrick's Day (when it's painted green, and Joe drives it dressed up like a leprechaun) to Thanksgiving. In other words, the Happy Red Car link is a good tie-in to Joe's other promotional efforts.

> **Note**
>
> Before you begin building your corporate Web pages, sit down and ask yourself just what exactly it is you are trying to do. Chapter 3 provides some guidance, and lots of good advice is also available on the Web.
>
> One good place to start is Dr. Ralph F. Wilson's "12 Web Page Design Decisions Your Business or Organization Will Need to Make." Though he'll try to sell you his services along the way, the questions he steps you through on-line are right on the money. Check it out at **http://www.wilsonweb.com/rfwilson.**
>
> Yahoo! offers a list of helpful sites at **http://www.yahoo.com/ Computers_and_Internet/Internet/World_Wide_Web/Authoring.**

Joe follows the grid of images with a tagline giving the address and phone number of his car lot. Being civic-minded, he makes the "Milwaukee, Wisconsin" part of his address a link to the local Chamber of Commerce promotional page for the city, as follows:

```
<hr>
<h3>Honest Joe's Used Cars · 2300 Lakeside Ave. · <a href="http://
➥www.milwaukee.net/">Milwaukee, Wisconsin</a> ·
333-555-1111</h3>
<hr>
</center>
```

After these lines, he's done with header stuff, so he adds a horizontal rule to divide the rest of the page and turns off centering.

> **Tip**
>
> Unlike Fred, Joe uses the non-standard <CENTER> tag rather than the HTML 3.0 <DIV ALIGN=CENTER> element. On a practical basis, using either one makes little difference.

Now come the car listings. First, Joe tells people that over 100 new cars are available; then he lists just six of them. Man, that Joe is a salesman! Only the best "featured" cars are listed on Joe's home page, and he offers an irresistible blurb and hotlink to each. Each featured car has its own page, complete with digitized picture and full sales pitch, and they're updated weekly. Finally, he provides links that lead to two separate pages for all the rest—one for sedans and one for vans. These links are the same as those for the graphic sedan and van links in the imagemap at the top of the page:

```
Over 100 <img src="new.gif" alt="NEW"> models this week!<br>
<img src="bulletbl.gif" alt="*"><a href="92cutlas.htm">1992 Olds
```

```
➡Cutlass</a><img src="hot.gif" alt="HOT!"> <b>*executive car*</b><br>
<img src="bulletbl.gif" alt="*"><a href="95carvan.htm">1995 Dodge
➡Caravan</a> <b>*loaded*</b><br>
<img src="bulletbl.gif" alt="*"><a href="94cavlir.htm">1994 Chevy
➡Cavalier</a> <b>*low mileage*</b><br>
<img src="bulletbl.gif" alt="*"><a href="96taurus.htm">1996 Ford
➡Taurus</a><img src="hand.gif" alt="<-"> <b>*the boss's wife's
➡car!*</b><br>
<img src="bulletbl.gif" alt="*"><a href="77ramchg.htm">1977 Dodge
➡Ramcharger</a> <b>*muscle car*</b><br>
<img src="bulletbl.gif" alt="*"><a href="73beetle.htm">1973 VW
➡Beetle</a> <b>*clean*</b><br>
<b>Click here for even more new <a href="cars.htm">cars</a> and <a
➡href="vans.htm">vans</a>!</b>
<p>
```

Joe could use a bulleted list for his featured autos, but he wants to use fancy graphic bullets instead.

Finally, Joe finishes up with the electronic equivalent of a hearty handshake and an invitation to come back again:

```
<center>
<hr>
<i>New cars and vans are arriving every day!<br>
<b>Bookmark</b> this page and come back often!</i><br>
<strong>Thanks for visiting Honest Joe's Used Cars.</strong>
</center>
<hr>
<strong>Page last updated April 1, 1996</strong>
<address>Email comments to: <a
href="mailto:joe@joescars.com">joe@joescars.com</a></address>
<a href="http://www.joescars.com">http://www.joescars.com</a>
```

Here's the entire home page for Honest Joe's Used Cars:

```
<html>
<head>
</head>
<title>Honest Joe's Used Cars</title>
<!-- milwaukee wisconsin used cars pre-owned autos automobiles
bargains deals easy credit terms -->
<body>
<center>
<a href="quality.htm"><img src="chekmark.gif" alt="[Quality
➡Checkmark]"></a>
<a href="aboutjoe.htm"><img src="joetop.gif" alt="[Honest Joe's
➡Used Cars]"></a>
<a href="vans.htm"><img src="2doorvan.gif" alt="[Family Vans]"></a>
<br>
<a href="cars.htm"><img src="blusedan.gif" alt="[Sporty Sedans]"></a>
<a href="happycar.htm"><img src="joebottm.gif" alt="[Home of the
➡Happy Red Car!]"></a>
<a href="terms.htm"><img src="wallet.gif" alt="[Cash or Credit!]"></a>
```

```
<hr>
<h3>Honest Joe's Used Cars · 2300 Lakeside Ave. · <a href="http://
➥www.milwaukee.net/">Milwaukee, Wisconsin</a> ·
333-555-1111</h3>
<hr>
</center>
Over 100 <img src="new.gif" alt="NEW"> models this week!<br>
<img src="bulletbl.gif" alt="*"><a href="92cutlas.htm">1992 Olds
➥Cutlass</a><img src="hot.gif" alt="HOT!"> <b>*executive car*</
b><br>
<img src="bulletbl.gif" alt="*"><a href="95carvan.htm">1995 Dodge
➥Caravan</a> <b>*loaded*</b><br>
<img src="bulletbl.gif" alt="*"><a href="94cavlir.htm">1994 Chevy
➥Cavalier</a> <b>*low mileage*</b><br>
<img src="bulletbl.gif" alt="*"><a href="96taurus.htm">1996 Ford
➥Taurus</a><img src="hand.gif" alt="<-">
<b>*the boss's wife's car!*</b><br>
<img src="bulletbl.gif" alt="*"><a href="77ramchg.htm">1977 Dodge
➥Ramcharger</a> <b>*muscle car*</b><br>
<img src="bulletbl.gif" alt="*"><a href="73beetle.htm">1973 VW
➥Beetle</a> <b>*clean*</b><br>
<b>Click here for even more new <a href="cars.htm">cars</a> and <a
➥href="vans.htm">vans</a>!</b>
<p>
<center>
<hr>
<i>New cars and vans are arriving every day!<br>
<b>Bookmark</b> this page and come back often!</i><br>
<strong>Thanks for visiting Honest Joe's Used Cars.</strong>
</center>
<hr>
<strong>Page last updated April 1, 1996</strong>
<address>Email comments to: <a href="mailto:joe@joescars.com">
➥joe@joescars.com</a></address>
<a href="http://www.joescars.com">http://www.joescars.com</a>
</body>
</html>
```

Joe doesn't bother setting any fancy background images or colors or the text colors for his page. He wants everyone to be able to see his pages. But he does make the backgrounds of all his GIF graphics (including the bullets) transparent so that whatever colors his customers pick in their browsers will shine right through.

Note

Joe has read all about how Webcrawler robot indexing programs work, so he's added this comment line near the top of his home page:

```
<!-- milwaukee wisconsin used cars pre-owned autos automobiles
bargains deals easy credit terms -->
```

He figures that the robots will pick out all these terms and add them to their index lists. That way, if a user checks for any of these keywords in an index that has "crawled" his home page, he or she will find a link to Joe's site.

Pretty sharp, that Joe.

Joe's already checked his page with Netscape (fig. 14.10), but he goes the extra mile to make sure that it looks good in Microsoft's Internet Explorer and NCSA Mosaic, too (see fig. 14.11 and fig. 14.12).

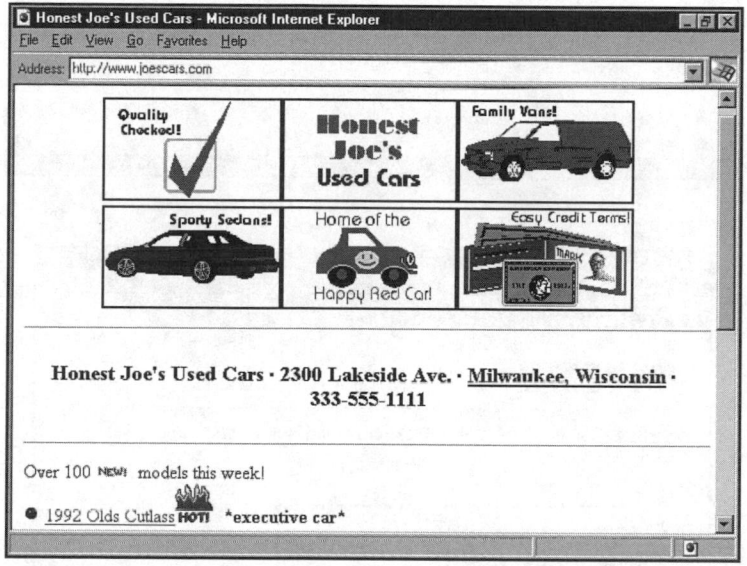

Fig. 14.11
Honest Joe's home page looks just as good in Explorer as it does in Netscape, as shown in figure 14.10.

But Joe has also sold a lot of cars to students from the University of Wisconsin and to engineers and programmers at a big UNIX-oriented research center in a Milwaukee suburb. He knows that they regularly browse the Web using an all-text Web browser called Lynx. Just to make sure, he checks out his Web page with Lynx, too (see fig. 14.13).

Joe, like Fred in the previous example, still has a lot of work to do to create pages for credit, quality, and the other issues he wants to address on his site. He's also going to have to hustle to keep his lists up-to-date. But at least his home page looks good, and he's off to an excellent start.

Fig. 14.12
Though it looks a
bit different in
NCSA Mosaic,
Joe's home page
is fine here, too.

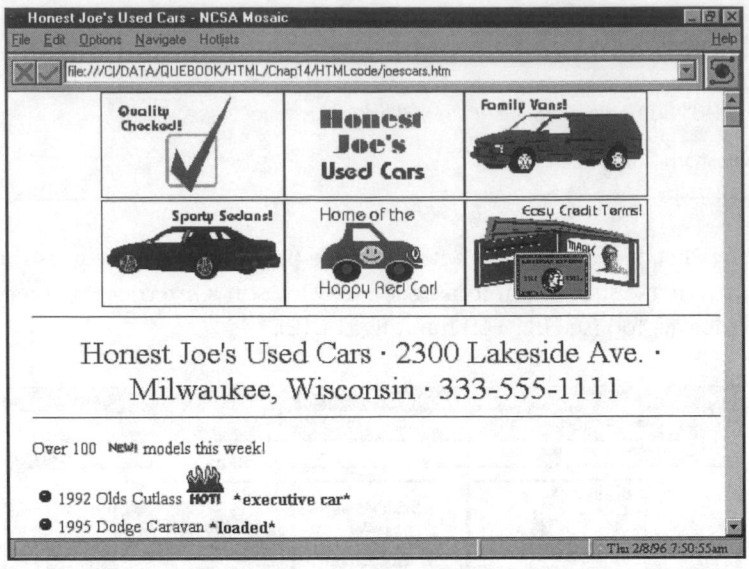

Fig. 14.13
Though not as
pretty, Joe's Web
page works fine
on the all-text
browser Lynx.

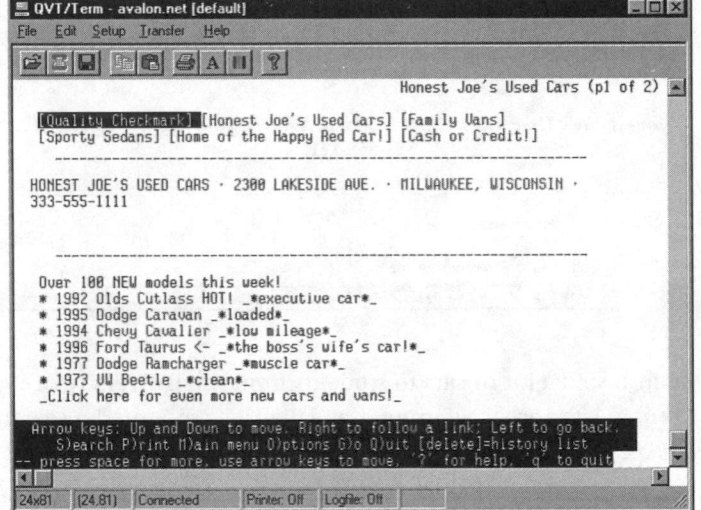

A Client-Side Imagemap

Joe easily figured out how to implement his home page using a client-side imagemap. The trouble is, if he uses an imagemap, NCSA Mosaic users can't access the
page, and he would have to make separate provisions for his Lynx customers. If Joe
decides to use a client-side imagemap, here's how he can do it:

First, he must combine all six of his image graphics into one big graphic with the same arrangement. Each individual frame is 150 pixels wide by 85 pixels high, so he would end up with a map 450 pixels wide by 170 pixels high.

Here's the HTML code that creates the same result as the "fake" map Joe is currently using:

```
<MAP NAME="joesmap">
<AREA SHAPE="RECT" COORDS="0,0,149,84" HREF="quality.htm">
<AREA SHAPE="RECT" COORDS="150,0,299,84" HREF="aboutjoe.htm">
<AREA SHAPE="RECT" COORDS="300,0,449,84" HREF="vans.htm">
<AREA SHAPE="RECT" COORDS="0,85,149,169" HREF="cars.htm">
<AREA SHAPE="RECT" COORDS="150,85,299,169" HREF="happycar.htm">
<AREA SHAPE="RECT" COORDS="300,85,449,169" HREF="terms.htm">
</MAP>
<IMG SRC="joesmap.gif" USEMAP="#joesmap">
```

This map, of course, has the advantage that the links are invisible, and it doesn't get broken up into windowpanes like Joe's current interface.

For more on the subject, see the section "Client-Side Imagemaps" in chapter 15, p. 334.

Templates for Lists

Web page lists can easily grow to unwieldy sizes, but there are no built-in provisions in HTML to create nice, neat hierarchical lists. If you are planning a site with lots of lists, this section can help you figure out how to keep things from getting out of hand.

Hierarchical Lists

The first trick of list building is to make your lists hierarchical, or nested; that is, don't list everything at one level. This example is exactly the wrong way to go:

```
<HTML>
<HEAD>
<TITLE>Magic Cards</TITLE>
<HEAD>
<BODY>
<DIV ALIGN=CENTER>
<H1>Magic: The Gathering</H1>
<H2>Card Listing</H2>
</DIV>
<HR>
<UL>
<LI>Land
<LI>Basic
```

III

Advanced HTML

```
<LI>Special
<LI>Artifacts
<LI>Creatures
<LI>Mono
<LI>Continuous
<LI>Black
<LI>Summon
<LI>Enchantment
<LI>Sorcery
<LI>Instant
<LI>Interrupt
<LI>Blue
<LI>Summon
<LI>Enchantment
<LI>Sorcery
<LI>Instant
<LI>Interrupt
<LI>Green
<LI>Summon
<LI>Enchantment
<LI>Sorcery
<LI>Instant
<LI>Interrupt
<LI>Red
<LI>Summon
<LI>Enchantment
<LI>Sorcery
<LI>Instant
<LI>Interrupt
<LI>White
<LI>Summon
<LI>Enchantment
<LI>Sorcery
<LI>Instant
<LI>Interrupt
</UL>
</BODY>
</HTML>
```

Though this page is perfectly "legal," the list is almost unusable because it has no structure (see fig. 14.14).

A better method is to move subservient portions of the list to their own sub-level, creating a hierarchical list, like this:

```
<UL>
<LI>Land
<UL>
<LI>Basic
<LI>Special
</UL>
<LI>Artifacts
<UL>
<LI>Creatures
<LI>Mono
<LI>Continuous
```

```
</UL>
<LI>Black
<UL>
<LI>Summon
<LI>Enchantment
<LI>Sorcery
<LI>Instant
<LI>Interrupt
</UL>
<LI>Blue
<UL>
<LI>Summon
<LI>Enchantment
<LI>Sorcery
<LI>Instant
<LI>Interrupt
</UL>
<LI>Green
<UL>
<LI>Summon
<LI>Enchantment
<LI>Sorcery
<LI>Instant
<LI>Interrupt
</UL>
<LI>Red
<UL>
<LI>Summon
<LI>Enchantment
<LI>Sorcery
<LI>Instant
<LI>Interrupt
</UL>
<LI>White
<UL>
<LI>Summon
<LI>Enchantment
<LI>Sorcery
<LI>Instant
<LI>Interrupt
</UL>
</UL>
```

This list is shown in figure 14.15.

The various levels of indentation and different bullets for different levels really help you track what goes where.

Each level of a hierarchical list can have its own format. For example, you could have made the second level for each secondary level in the preceding list an ordered (numbered) list by substituting <OL></OL> tags for all the second-level <UL></UL> tags.

III

Advanced HTML

Fig. 14.14
This unstructured list is confusing. It needs some hierarchies.

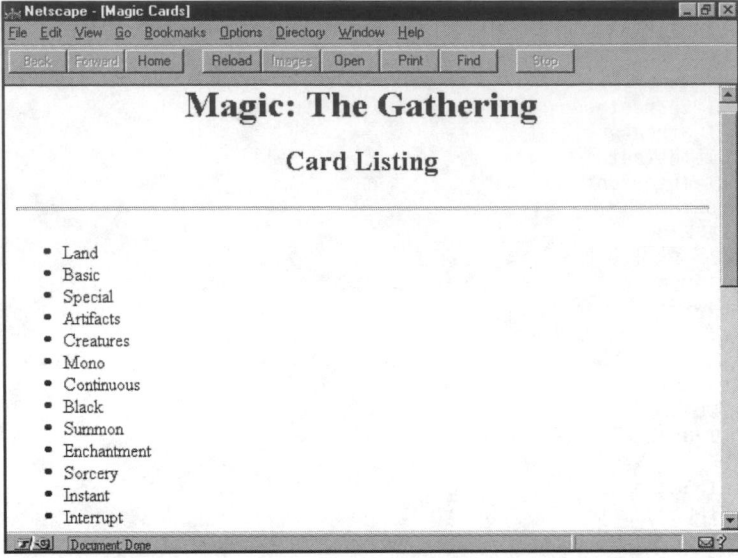

Fig. 14.15
A hierarchical list like this is much easier to comprehend.

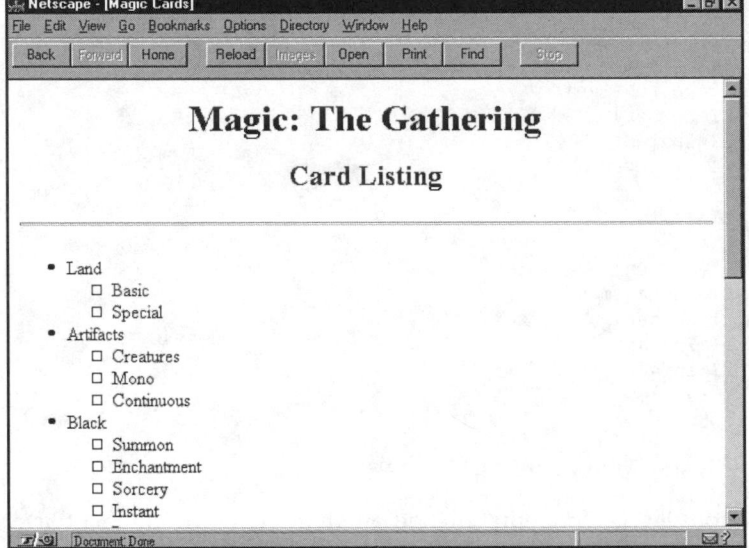

Reading through the HTML code for nested lists like these can be somewhat confusing, especially if the lists have three or four levels of depth. Mentally breaking down things helps if you consider each new level as a single element in the previous list, like this:

```
<UL>
<LI>Land
<UL><LI>Basic<LI>Special</UL>
<LI>Artifacts
<UL><LI>Creatures<LI>Mono<LI>Continuous</UL>
<LI>Black
<UL><LI>Summon<LI>Enchantment<LI>Sorcery<LI>Instant<LI>Interrupt</UL>
<LI>Blue
<UL><LI>Summon<LI>Enchantment<LI>Sorcery<LI>Instant<LI>Interrupt</UL>
<LI>Green
<UL><LI>Summon<LI>Enchantment<LI>Sorcery<LI>Instant<LI>Interrupt</UL>
<LI>Red
<UL><LI>Summon<LI>Enchantment<LI>Sorcery<LI>Instant<LI>Interrupt</UL>
<LI>White
<UL><LI>Summon<LI>Enchantment<LI>Sorcery<LI>Instant<LI>Interrupt</UL>
</UL>
```

Now you can easily see that the main list is made up of both individual list elements <LI> and sublists enclosed in <UL></UL> pairs. It's also easier to tell which </UL> tags end what lists. HTML code even works just fine when it's written this way, if that helps you to keep track of things.

Expandable Lists

The problem with the list so far is that it's still huge. Even though the nested list is organized much better than before, it scrolls off the screen and just keeps scrolling, and scrolling, and scrolling...like the Energizer Bunny of lists.

Now see if you can bring the list under better control. Start by compressing the list to just the first level, as follows:

```
<UL>
<LI>Land
<LI>Artifacts
<LI>Black
<LI>Blue
<LI>Green
<LI>Red
<LI>White
</UL>
```

This shortened list is easier to read, but you lose detail (see fig. 14.16).

Now make each list item a link to another page, like this:

```
<UL>
<LI><A HREF="land.htm">Land</A>
<LI><A HREF="artifact.htm">Artifacts</A>
<LI><A HREF="black.htm">Black</A>
<LI><A HREF="blue.htm">Blue</A>
<LI><A HREF="green.htm">Green</A>
<LI><A HREF="red.htm">Red</A>
<LI><A HREF="white.htm">White</A>
</UL>
```

Fig. 14.16
This list is easy to
read but doesn't
include as much
information.

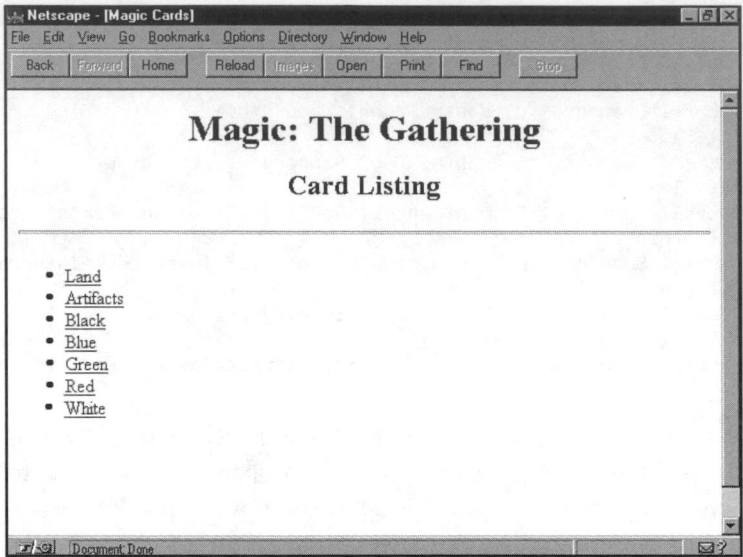

This page looks just like the previous one (refer to fig. 14.16) with the exception that every item is a link. Clicking on, say, the list item for Red makes you jump to the red.htm page. Here's the code for that page:

```
<UL>
<LI><A HREF="land.htm">Land</A>
<LI><A HREF="artifact.htm">Artifacts</A>
<LI><A HREF="black.htm">Black</A>
<LI><A HREF="blue.htm">Blue</A>
<LI><A HREF="green.htm">Green</A>
<LI>Red
<UL>
<LI>Summon
<LI>Enchantment
<LI>Sorcery
<LI>Instant
<LI>Interrupt
</UL>
<LI><A HREF="white.htm">White</A>
</UL>
```

This page is the same as the previous one, except that the Red item has no link. Instead, the sublist below Red has been expanded to show all the subitems for Red, as shown in figure 14.17.

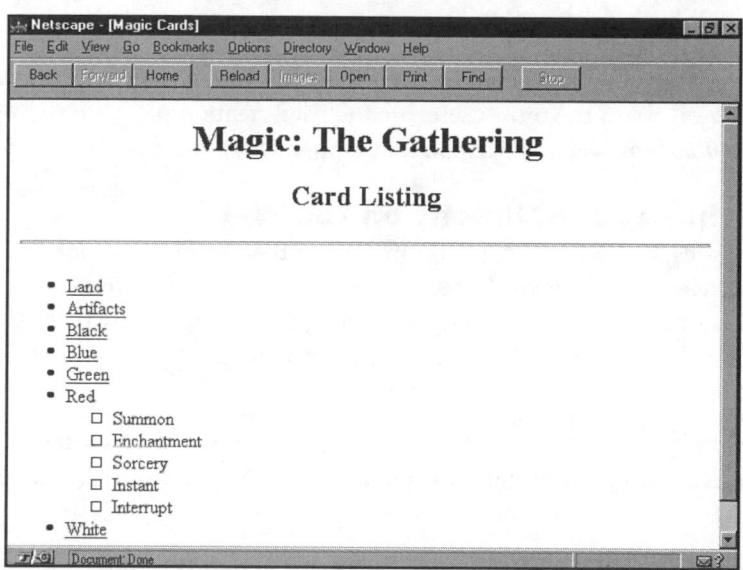

Fig. 14.17
Clicking the link
for Red in the
previous screen
expands the sublist
under it.

Though this technique demands that you create a separate page for each sublist, all are identical except for the sublist information. Because you load many pages clicking back and forth in such lists, you don't want graphic elements on these pages to slow down the load times, especially over slow modem connections.

However, this technique is excellent for making lists user-friendly—and it keeps the pages short.

> **Note**
>
> Expandable lists are so useful that the HTML 3.0 proposal includes an element for making them automatic. The <LH> (List Heading) tag lets an HTML 3.0-compliant browser choose to expand and contract the <LI> elements listed under them without having to create separate pages or special HTML code to do so.

> **Note**
>
> One final note about creating lists: Remember to pick the right kind of list for what you want to do. Besides ordered <OL> and unordered <UL> lists, you also can use menu <MENU>, directory <DIR>, and definition <DEF> list tags. Netscape and HTML 3.0 add many options to each of these elements. Check out chapter 9, "Displaying Text in Lists," for insights into the uses and format of each of these list types.

Advanced HTML

III

Template Tools

Many helpful tools are available to help get you started creating your own Web pages. Two of the most useful are the page-creation pages on the Web itself and add-on Web page templates for popular word processors.

Creating a Page Directly on the Web

Several sites on the Web feature on-line forms that, when filled out, create a Web page for you. All you need to do is fill in a few blanks and save the HTML code of the page that's created. Though pages created by these sites tend to be generic, you might use this approach to get the bare-bones HTML code that you can modify to make your own page.

Yahoo! keeps a list of such resources at **http://www.yahoo.com/ Computers_and_Internet/Internet/World_Wide_Web/Authoring/**. But here are three to get you started:

- Greg Ritter's Automatic Home Page Generator at **http:// ugweb.cs.ualberta.ca/~ritter/cgi-bin/hpg.html** (see fig. 14.18)

- Dave Hwang's Make Your Own Home Page at **http:// www.goliath.org/makepage/**

- The Internet's Create a Homepage page at **http://the-inter.net/ www/future21/create1.html**

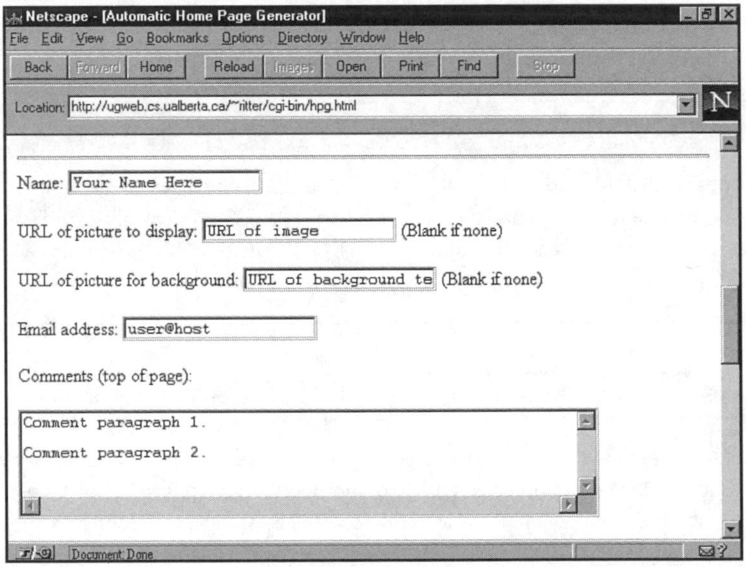

Fig. 14.18
The Home Page Generator is just one of many forms-driven HTML page-creation sites on the Web.

Templates for Word Processors

If you're the type who's married to your word processor, you might prefer creating Web pages in that old, familiar environment. Fortunately, many templates are available. They plug right into your existing word processor, effectively turning it into an HTML editing machine.

As usual, Yahoo! has an index of such templates; it's at **http:// www.yahoo.com/Computers_and_Internet/Internet/ World_Wide_Web/HTML_Converters/**.

Microsoft's free HTML editing template for Word, Internet Assistant, and Quarterdeck's Word template, WebAuthor, are so powerful that this book contains an entire chapter dedicated to each. If you're a Word user, check out chapters 29 and 30.

▶ See chapter 28, "Microsoft Internet Assistant," p. 663, and chapter 29, "Quarterdeck WebAuthor," p. 679

If you're a Microsoft Word user, download a copy of the shareware template ANT_HTML (or ANT_PLUS) from **ftp.einet.net/einet/pc**. Both are Word templates that convert Word documents to HTML or let you create HTML documents in place. ANT works on both the latest international versions of Word for Mac and Windows.

EasyHelp/Web from Eon Solutions is for all recent versions of Word. It lets you create Windows Help files as well as HTML pages. You can get more information at **http://www.u-net.com/eon/easyhelp/easyhelp.htm**.

CU_HTML.DOT is another Word for Windows 2.0 and 6.0 HTML template that you can download from **ftp://ftp.cuhk.hk/pub/www/windows/ util**.

WordPerfect users might want to check out Wp2Html, a WordPerfect template that converts DOS WP documents to HTML with tables, equations, and figures intact. You can get an evaluation copy from **http:// www.res.bbsrc.ac.uk/wp2html/**.

You might also want to check out Internet Publisher from Novell, a free HTML creation add-on to WordPerfect 6.1 for Windows, downloadable from **http://wp.novell.com/elecpub/intpub.htm**.

If AmiPro is your word processor of choice, you've got AmiWeb, an HTML add-on. You can get more information at **http://www.cs.nott.ac.uk/ ~sbx/amiweb.html**.

III

Advanced HTML

Tip

These add-ons are all well and good, you say, but what if you want to convert from HTML to something else? CERN offers a list of resources to do just that at **http://www.w3.org/hypertext/WWW/Tools/html2things.html**.

## CHAPTER 15

Netscape-Specific Extensions to HTML

by Mark Brown

The first thing you usually find out about any computing standard is that it's not really very standard at all. Programmers are an imaginative, inventive, and egotistical lot. Their usual attitude toward someone else's idea of how things should be done is "I can do it better." Then they proceed to prove that, indeed, they can. As a result, you get many computer games that bypass the computer's operating system completely, so you can get swarmed by 1,000,000 aliens per second instead of a mere 999,997. Unfortunately, these games usually don't work at all—that is, they are "busted"—on the next generation of PCs. In fact, they probably don't work on some not insignificant percentage of this generation of personal computers.

All of which brings us indirectly to HTML. The official HTML standard is up to version 2.0 now. However, when it was still at version 1.0, most of the browser programs cruising the Web supported a good portion of the "proposed" 2.0 HTML standard already. Why? Because the features were so cool and HTML 1.0 was so lame in comparison that no one could stand to wait for the 2.0 standard to become, well, standard.

Of course, even before HTML 2.0 was declared the new standard, dozens of proposals were floating around the Web for new features for HTML 3.0. Again, people could not wait to start jamming keen new features into their browser programs—and even began adding a few more of their own inventions along the way. The bright, innovative, cutting-edge programmers at Netscape were, as usual, right there leading the pack. Therefore, many extensions to HTML are built into the latest version (2.0) of Netscape Navigator.

In this chapter, you learn about the ways in which Netscape extends the HTML standard.

In this chapter, you learn about the following:

- Using Netscape's HTML extensions when creating your Web pages
- New ways to make your page presentation pop out at your viewers using frames and targeted windows
- How embedded objects and Java applets can bring Web pages alive
- How client-side imagemaps and forms enhancements make pages easier to create and easier to use
- New ways to liven up your pages with other fun Netscape-specific tags

Should You Use Browser-Specific Extensions?

Many new Web developers wonder whether they should use browser-specific tags, or whether they should stick with the HTML standard. It's a tough call.

Some could argue, "Yes, you should go ahead and use browser-specific tags because they are so flashy and cool and make your pages look and perform so much better." This argument makes a lot of sense, especially if you're talking about Netscape Navigator. After all, the most recent Web usage statistics say that over 80 percent of the people cruising through your Web site will be using Netscape anyway. If you can grab their attention by making good use of all the nifty new Netscape features such as frames and Sun's Java, maybe they'll be more likely to stick around and find out what you have to say.

Then, too, if you want to get technical, even widely used capabilities such as tables and background images are still only "proposed" HTML 3.0 features. They're not official yet. But just try to imagine how boring the Web would be if everyone avoided these features just because they don't conform to some "official" standard. And, though Netscape pioneered support for background images and tables, it didn't take long for other browsers such as Mosaic and Microsoft Internet Explorer to add them, too.

On the other hand, you could also easily answer, "No, you shouldn't use browser-specific extensions." If you write only for Netscape Navigator, what about the 20 percent who don't use it? And remember that even among Netscape users, not everyone is running the latest version of the program. In fact, as of this writing version 1.1 is still the most popular version of Netscape (although 2.0 is gaining market share rapidly). Until most everyone has made the switch, even many Netscape users may look at your fancy new pages and say "Huh?"

Perhaps the major "anti" argument is this: What are standards good for if nobody follows them? A well-established precedent exists for suggesting and approving enhancements to HTML. The IETF (Internet Engineering Task Force) handles the situation democratically through a process that allows anyone on the Web—from giants such as Microsoft and Netscape to little guys like you and me—to propose and comment on changes and additions for each iteration of the HTML standard. If you're, say, a huge publisher of Web browser software, and you just go ahead and implement your own ideas of what HTML should be like, isn't that like wresting power from everyone else?

That point of view is probably pretty cynical. In truth, Netscape and Microsoft and the other browser vendors are really trying to improve what the Web is, how it works, and what it can do. Standards committees move slowly, as do all bureaucracies. The way of the corporation has always been to throw a product into the marketplace and see if anyone buys it.

And people are buying both Netscape Navigator and the HTML enhancements that come with it. Netscape Corporation's financial reports prove the former; the proliferation of Web pages that use Netscape 2.0 extensions prove the latter (see fig. 15.1).

Fig. 15.1
You'd expect Netscape's own site to be overflowing with cool examples of Netscape 2.0's latest and greatest extensions to HTML, and it is.

Of course, there is room for compromise. Many of the Netscape HTML extensions closely match HTML 3.0 proposals. If you stick to a syntax that is supported by both, you shouldn't have any trouble keeping compatible with most of the browsers on the Web, both now and in the near future.

Do you need to be afraid of using the Netscape HTML extensions discussed in this chapter on your Web pages? Probably not. But before you do, ask yourself whether by doing so you would be alienating a good portion of your audience, or whether you would be drawing in more viewers to your site. As always, if you keep your goals in mind, the answer should be clear.

Style Sheets: the Big Difference

Many of Netscape's HTML extensions differ from the proposed HTML 3.0 standard in one big, important way. Netscape has implemented many page formatting options as custom HTML tags; HTML 3.0 proposes to handle formatting via a technique called *style sheets*. Style sheets are meant to separate presentation style from HTML structure. In other words, they are meant to keep HTML from becoming a page definition language rather than the page description language it was originally intended to be.

Style sheets will carry a Web designer's presentation preferences in a separate definition (a style sheet). The viewers could, if using browsers that support style sheets, choose to view the page using either the Web designer's preferences or their own, as defined in their browsers' setups.

Apparently, style sheets are definitely going to be in the HTML 3.0 standard, and future versions of Netscape Navigator are likely to support both types of page formatting.

▶ See chapter 16, "HTML Extensions in Internet Explorer, Mosaic, and HTML 3.0," p. 347

Tip

For more information on the topic of Netscape 2.0 versus HTML 3.0, including side-by-side comparisons of how they perform similar tasks, point your browser to the following:

http://webreference.com/html3andns/introduction.html

Netscape Version 1.1 HTML Extensions

Netscape hasn't just begun mucking around with HTML recently. Ever since version 1.1, it has included HTML extensions in Navigator. Version 1.1 included many extensions that have become widely popular on the Web. Many made it into the HTML 2.0 standard, and many more are solid for inclusion in HTML 3.0.

Table 15.1 lists some of the more important HTML innovations that Netscape included in Navigator version 1.1.

Table 15.1 Extensions to HTML Introduced in Netscape Navigator 1.1		
Tag	**Change(s)**	**Function**
BASEFONT	New	Specifies base font size
BLINK	New	Blinks text
BODY	BACKGROUND	Tiles background graphic on page
BR	CLEAR	Waits for clear margin before break
CENTER	New	Centers page elements
FONT	New	Specifies font size or +/− base size
HR	SIZE	Specifies rule thickness
	WIDTH	Specifies rule length
	ALIGN	Left, center, or right alignment
	NOSHADE	No shading
IMG	ALIGN	Left, center, or right alignment
	WIDTH	Specifies image width
	HEIGHT	Specifies image height
	BORDER	Specifies image border width
	VSPACE	Specifies space above and below image
	HSPACE	Specifies space left and right of image
ISINDEX	PROMPT	Text input field prompt
LI	TYPE	Changes type of index
	VALUE	Changes value in ordered lists
NOBR	New	Allows no breaks in marked block
OL	TYPE	Specifies counter type
	START	Specifies counter start value
UL	TYPE	Specifies bullet shape
TABLE	New	Creates tables (uses additional tags such as TD, TC, TR, and so on)
WBR	New	Allows word break in NOBR section

III

Advanced HTML

◄ See chapter 13, "Tables and Math Equations," p. 251

Of the Netscape version 1.1 additions listed in table 15.1, tables are so important and in such widespread use that this book devotes the entirety of chapter 13 to them. The changes to the BODY and HR tags, as well as the new CENTER, BASEFONT, and FONT tags, are all discussed in this chapter. The other Netscape version 1.1 HTML extensions have been around long enough and are so universally used that they are simply covered in context in the appropriate chapters of this book.

Netscape Version 2.0 HTML Extensions

In keeping with tradition, Netscape added several new ground-breaking features to HTML in version 2.0 of Navigator, and made a few changes to some of the old, familiar tags. Table 15.2 lists the major HTML extensions implemented in Netscape Navigator 2.0.

Table 15.2   Extensions to HTML Introduced in Netscape Navigator 2.0

Tag	Change	Function
A	TARGET	Opens new target display window
BASE	New	Defines a default window
DIV	ALIGN	Aligns elements left, right, or center
EMBED	New	Embeds live objects (video and so on)
FORM	ENCTYPE	HTTP file upload for forms
FRAMESET	New	Creates frames (uses additional tags FRAME and NOFRAMES)
IMG	USEMAP	Creates a client-side imagemap (uses additional tags MAP and AREA)
META	—	Implements client pull
	—	Implements international character sets
P	ALIGN	Aligns text left, right, or center
SCRIPT	New	Executes a JavaScript applet
TEXTAREA	WRAP	Specifies word wrap in forms

▶ See chapter 26, "Java and JavaScript," p. 621

All the changed and new tags listed in table 15.2 are discussed in this chapter, except Java and JavaScript.

Because frames are the biggest, newest kid on the block, I talk about them first.

Frames

Everywhere you surf on the Net these days, you find sites all gussied up with frames—at least, you do if you're using a frames-capable browser such as Netscape 2.0. Frames create independently changeable and (sometimes) scrollable windows that tile together to break up and organize a display so that it is not only more visually appealing but also easier to work with. Figure 15.1, earlier in this chapter, presented an example of the real-world use of frames at Netscape's own Web site.

Frames are similar in many ways to HTML tables. If you understand how tables work, frames will be second nature to you.

However, unlike tables, frames not only organize data, but they also organize your browser's display window. In fact, they break up the window into individual, independent panes or frames. Each frame holds its own HTML file as content, and the content of each frame can be scrolled or changed independently of the others. In a way, each frame almost becomes its own "mini-browser."

At this point, take a look at an entire block of HTML markup code that creates a frame document of medium complexity:

```
<HTML>
<HEAD>
</HEAD>
<FRAMESET ROWS="25%,50%,25%">
<FRAME SRC="header.htm">
<FRAMESET COLS="25%,75%">
<FRAME SRC="label.htm">
<FRAME SRC="info.htm">
</FRAMESET>
<FRAME SRC="footer.htm">
</FRAMESET>
<NOFRAMES>
Your browser cannot display frames.
</NOFRAMES>
</HTML>
```

This example produces the frames page shown in figure 15.2. As you can see, this HTML code produces four frames. The top frame spans the page and includes a header. The page also has two central frames, one for a label on the left, which takes up 25 percent of the screen width, and one for information on the right, which takes up the remaining space. Another frame fills the entire width of the bottom of the screen and contains a footer.

III

Advanced HTML

Fig. 15.2
The frame
document
produced by the
example HTML
code, as displayed
by Netscape
Navigator 2.0.

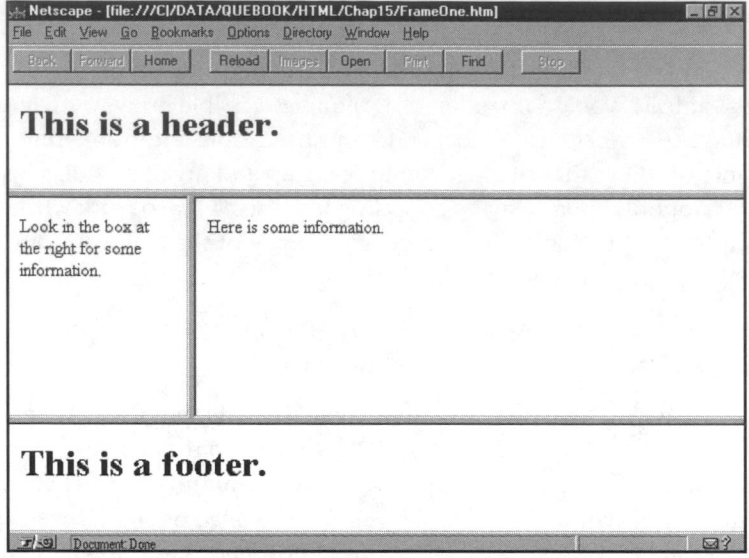

The *FRAMESET* Container

Frames are contained in a structure called a FRAMESET, which takes the place of
the BODY container on a frames-formatted Web page. A Web page composed
of frames has no BODY section in its HTML code, and a page with a BODY section cannot use frames.

> ### Caution
>
> If you define a BODY section for a page that you compose using FRAMESET and FRAME
> commands, the frame structure is completely ignored by browser programs, and
> none of the content contained in the frames is displayed.
>
> Because no BODY container exists, FRAMESET pages can't have background images
> and background colors associated with them. (They are defined by the BACKGROUND
> and BGCOLOR attributes of the BODY tag, respectively.)
>
> Make sure that you don't accidentally use BODY and FRAMESET on the same page.

The <FRAMESET></FRAMESET> container surrounds each block of frame definitions. Within the FRAMESET container, you can have only FRAME tags or nested
FRAMESET containers.

The FRAMESET tag has two attributes: ROWS and COLS (columns). Here's a fully
decked-out (but empty) generic FRAMESET container:

```
<FRAMESET ROWS="value_list" COLS="value_list">
</FRAMESET>
```

You can define any reasonable number of ROWS or COLS, or both, but you have to define something for at least one of them.

The "value list" in the generic FRAMESET line is a comma-separated list of values that can be expressed as pixels, percentages, or relative scale values. The number of rows or columns is set by the number of values in their respective value lists. For example, the following defines a frame set with three rows:

```
<FRAMESET ROWS="100,240,140">
```

These values are in absolute numbers of pixels. In other words, the first row is 100 pixels high; the second, 240 pixels high; and the last, 140 pixels high.

Setting row and column height by absolute number of pixels is bad practice, however. It doesn't allow for the fact that browsers run on all kinds of systems on all sizes of screens. Although you might want to define absolute pixel values for a few limited uses—such as displaying a small image of known dimensions—a better practice is to define your rows and columns using percentage or relative values like this:

```
<FRAMESET ROWS="25%,50%,25%">
```

This example creates three frames arranged as rows, the top row taking up 25 percent of the available screen height; the middle, row 50 percent; and the bottom row, 25 percent. If the percentages you give don't add up to 100 percent, they are scaled up or down proportionally to equal 100 percent.

Proportional values look like this:

```
<FRAMESET COLS="*, 2*, 3*">
```

The asterisk (*) defines a proportional division of space. Each asterisk represents one piece of the overall "pie." You get the denominator of the fraction by adding up all the asterisk values (if no number is specified, 1 is assumed). In this example, the first column would get $1/6$ of the total width of the window, the second column would get $2/6$ (or $1/3$), and the final column would get $3/6$ (or $1/2$).

Remember that bare numeric values assign an absolute number of pixels to a row or column, values with a % (percent sign) assign a percentage of the total width (for COLS) or height (for ROWS) of the display window, and values with an * assign a proportional amount of the remaining space.

Here's an example using all three in a single definition:

```
<FRAMESET COLS="100, 25%, *, 2*">
```

This example assigns the first column an absolute width of 100 pixels. The second column gets 25 percent of the width of the entire display window, whatever that is. The third column gets $1/3$ of what's left, and the final column gets the other $2/3$. Absolute pixel values are always assigned space first, in order from left to right. They are followed by percentage values of the total space. Finally, proportional values are divided up based on what space is left.

> **Caution**
>
> Remember, if you do use absolute pixel values in a COLS or ROWS definition, keep them small so that you are sure they'll fit in any browser window, and balance them with at least one percentage or relative definition to fill the remainder of the space gracefully.

If you use a FRAMESET with both COLS and ROWS attributes, it creates a grid of frames. Here's an example:

```
<FRAMESET ROWS="*, 2*, *" COLS="2*, *">
```

This line of HTML creates a frame grid with three rows and two columns. The first and last rows each take up $1/4$ of the screen height, and the middle row takes up half. The first column is $2/3$ as wide as the screen, and the second is $1/3$ the width.

You can nest <FRAMESET></FRAMESET> sections inside one another, as you saw in the initial example. But that's getting ahead of the game. You need to look at the FRAME tag first.

The *FRAME* Tag

The <FRAME >tag defines a single frame. It must sit inside a FRAMESET container, like this:

```
<FRAMESET ROWS="*, 2*">
<FRAME>
<FRAME>
</FRAMESET>
```

Note that the FRAME tag is not a container so, unlike FRAMESET, it has no matching end tag. An entire FRAME definition takes place within a single line of HTML code.

You should have as many FRAME tags as spaces defined for them in the FRAMESET definition. In this example, the FRAMESET established two rows, so you need two FRAME tags. However, this example is boring because neither of the frames has anything in it! (Frames like these are displayed as blank space.)

The FRAME tag has six associated attributes: SRC, NAME, MARGINWIDTH, MARGINHEIGHT, SCROLLING, and NORESIZE. Here's a complete generic FRAME:

```
<FRAME SRC="url" NAME="window_name" SCROLLING=YES¦NO¦AUTO
MARGINWIDTH="value" MARGINHEIGHT="value" NORESIZE>
```

Fortunately, frames rarely use all these options.

The most important FRAME attribute is SRC (source). You can (and quite often do) have a complete FRAME definition using nothing but the SRC attribute, like this:

```
<FRAME SRC="url">
```

SRC defines the URL of the content of your frame. It is usually an HTML format file on the same system, so it usually looks something like this:

```
<FRAME SRC="sample.htm">
```

Note that any HTML file called by a frame must be a complete HTML document, not a fragment. Therefore, it must have HTML, HEAD, and BODY containers, and so on.

Of course, the source can be any valid URL. If, for example, you want your frame to display a GIF image that is located somewhere in Timbuktu, your FRAME might look like this:

```
<FRAME SRC="http://www.timbuktu.com/budda.gif">
```

If you specify an URL that the browser can't find, the frame is created but left empty and you get a nasty error message from Navigator. Note that the effect is quite different than that produced by simply specifying a FRAME with no SRC at all. <FRAME SRC="unknown URL"> creates a frame but leaves it blank; <FRAME> is not created at all—the space is allocated and left completely empty, with no frame around it.

III

Advanced HTML

Caution

You cannot use plain text, headers, graphics, and other elements directly in a FRAME document. All the content must come from HTML files as defined by the SRC attribute of the FRAME tags. If any other content appears on a FRAMESET page, it is displayed, and the entire set of frames is ignored.

The NAME attribute assigns a name to a frame that can be used to link to the frame, usually from other frames in the same display. The following example creates a frame named Joe:

```
<FRAME NAME="Joe">
```

The Joe frame can be referenced via a hyperlink like this:

```
<A HREF="http://www.yoursite.net" TARGET="Joe">Click Here to Jump
➥to Joe</A>
```

Note the TARGET attribute that references the name of the frame.

If you don't create a name for a frame, it simply has no name. All frame names must begin with an alphanumeric character.

MARGINWIDTH and MARGINHEIGHT give you control over the width of the frame's margins. They both look like this:

```
MARGINWIDTH="value"
```

The value is always a number and always represents an absolute value in pixels. For example, the following creates a frame with top and bottom margins 5 pixels wide, and left and right margins 7 pixels wide:

```
<FRAME MARGINHEIGHT="5" MARGINWIDTH="7">
```

Remember, the topic is margins here, not borders. MARGINWIDTH and MARGINHEIGHT define a space within the frame within which content does not appear. Border widths are set automatically by the browser, not your HTML code.

Your frames automatically have scroll bars if the content you've specified for them is too big to fit the frame. Sometimes having scroll bars ruins the aesthetics of your page, so you need a way to control them. That's what the SCROLLING attribute is for. Here's the format:

```
<FRAME SCROLLING="yes¦no¦auto">
```

SCROLLING has three valid values: Yes, No, and Auto. Auto is assumed if no SCROLLING attribute appears in your FRAME definition. Yes forces the appearance of a scroll bar. No keeps them away at all costs. For example, this FRAME definition turns on scroll bars:

```
<FRAME SCROLLING=YES>
```

The user can normally resize frames. If you move the mouse cursor over a frame border, it turns into a resize gadget that lets you move the border where you want it. Doing so always mucks up the look and feel of your beautifully designed frames. You therefore always should use the NORESIZE attribute to keep users from resizing your frames. Here's how:

```
<FRAME NORESIZE>
```

That's it. No values. Of course, when you set NORESIZE for one frame, none of the adjacent frames can be resized, either. Depending on your layout, using NORESIZE in a single frame is usually enough to keep users from resizing all the frames on the screen.

NOFRAMES

"All of this is well and good," you say, "and I really want to use these keen new features on my Web pages. But I can't help feeling guilty about all those users who don't have frames-capable browsers. They won't be able to see my beautiful pages!"

Don't worry. Here's where you can provide for them, too.

The <NOFRAMES></NOFRAMES> container is what saves you. By defining a NOFRAMES section and marking it up with normal HTML tags, you can provide an alternative Web page for users without forms-capable browsers. Here's how it works:

```
<NOFRAMES>
All your HTML goes here.
</NOFRAMES>
```

You can safely think of this example as an alternative to the BODY structure of a normal Web page. Whatever you place between the <NOFRAMES> and </NOFRAMES> tags will appear on browsers without frames capability. Browsers with frames will throw away everything between these two tags.

Some Frame Examples

Frames are very flexible, which means they can get complicated fast. This section presents a few examples of real-world frame definitions.

The simplest possible frame setup is one with two frames, like this:

```
<HTML>
<HEAD>
```

```
</HEAD>
<FRAMESET ROWS="*, 2*">
<FRAME SRC="label2.htm">
<FRAME SRC="info.htm">
</FRAMESET>
</HTML>
```

This code defines a page with two frames, organized as two rows. The first row takes up $1/3$ the height of the screen and contains the HTML document label2.htm, and the second takes up the other $2/3$ and contains the document info.htm. Figure 15.3 shows how Netscape displays this page.

Fig. 15.3

Netscape displays the simple two-row FRAMESET defined by the example HTML code.

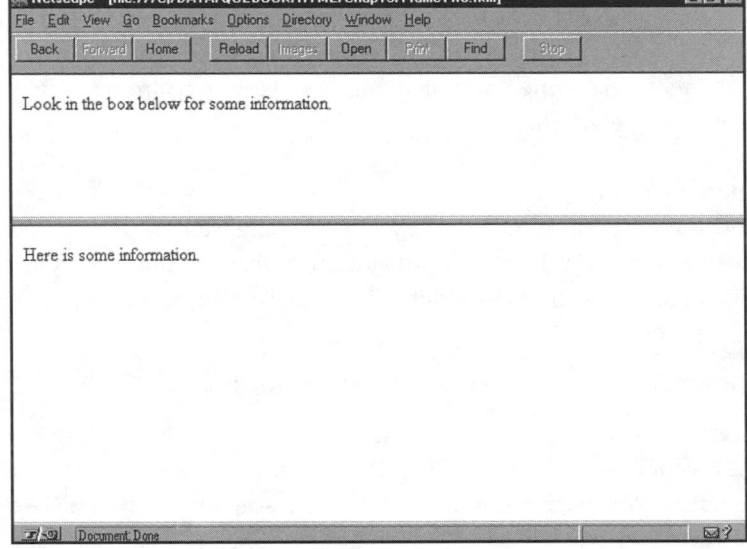

You could just as easily create ten rows, or use the same syntax substituting the COLS attribute to create two (or ten) columns. However, ten columns or rows are too many for any browser to handle gracefully. Your pages should never have more than three or four rows or columns.

Tip

If you want to display more information than three or four rows or columns, you should probably use tables rather than frames. Remember, frames are most useful when you want to add an element of control in addition to formatting the display. Tables are best if all you want to do is format data.

A regular rectangular grid of rows and columns is just about as easy to implement:

```
<HTML>
<HEAD>
</HEAD>
<FRAMESET ROWS="*, 2*" COLS="20%, 30%, 40%">
<FRAME SRC="labela.htm">
<FRAME SRC="labelb.htm">
<FRAME SRC="labelc.htm">
<FRAME SRC="info.htm">
<FRAME SRC="info.htm">
<FRAME SRC="info.htm">
</FRAMESET>
</HTML>
```

This example creates a grid with two rows and three columns (see fig. 15.4). Because you defined a set of six frames, you provide six FRAME definitions. Note that they fill in by rows. That is, the first FRAME goes in the first defined column in the first row, the second frame follows across in the second column, and the third finishes out the last column in the first row. The last three frames then fill in the columns of the second row, going across.

Also note that the math didn't work out very well, because the percentage values in the COLS definition add up to only 90 percent. No problem, as the browser has adjusted all the columns proportionally to make up the difference.

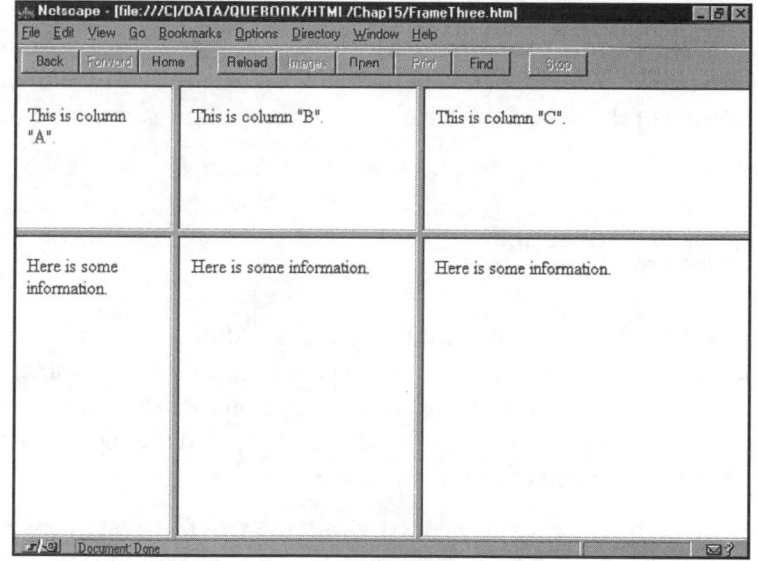

Fig. 15.4
This 2×3 grid of frames was created by the HTML example.

III

Advanced HTML

A bit tougher is the problem of creating a more complex grid of frames. For that, return to the example that opened this section:

```
<HTML>
<HEAD>
</HEAD>
<FRAMESET ROWS="25%,50%,25%">
<FRAME SRC="header.htm">
<FRAMESET COLS="25%,75%">
<FRAME SRC="label.htm">
<FRAME SRC="info.htm">
</FRAMESET>
<FRAME SRC="footer.htm">
</FRAMESET>
<NOFRAMES>
Your browser cannot display frames.
</NOFRAMES>
</HTML>
```

The output of this file was shown in figure 15.2.

This example makes use of nested FRAMESET containers. The outside set creates three ROWS, with 25 percent, 50 percent, and 25 percent of the window height, respectively:

```
<FRAMESET ROWS="25%,50%,25%">
```

Within this definition, the first and last rows are simple frames:

```
<FRAME SRC="header.htm">
...
<FRAME SRC="footer.htm">
```

Each of these rows runs the entire width of the screen. The first row at the top of the screen takes up 25 percent of the screen height, and the third row at the bottom of the screen also takes up 25 percent of the screen height.

In between, however, is this nested FRAMESET container:

```
<FRAMESET COLS="25%,75%">
<FRAME SRC="label.htm">
<FRAME SRC="info.htm">
</FRAMESET>
```

This FRAMESET defines two columns that split the middle row of the screen. The row these two columns reside in takes up 50 percent of the total screen height, as defined in the middle row value for the outside FRAMESET container. The left column uses 25 percent of the screen width, and the right column occupies the other 75 percent of the screen width.

The FRAMEs for the columns are defined within the set of FRAMESET tags, which include the column definitions, whereas the FRAME definitions for the first and last rows are outside the nested FRAMESET command but within the exterior FRAMESET in their proper order.

This code is not as confusing if you think of an entire nested FRAMESET block as a single FRAME tag. In the example, the outside FRAMESET block sets up a situation in which you have three rows. Each must be filled. In this case, they are filled by a FRAME, then a nested FRAMESET two columns wide, and then another FRAME.

By now (if you are a programming-type person) you may be asking yourself, "I wonder if it is possible for a FRAME to use as its SRC a document that is, itself, a FRAMESET?" The answer is yes. In this case, you simply use the FRAME tag to point to an HTML document that is the FRAMESET you would have otherwise used in place of the FRAME.

Let me restate the preceding example (which used nested FRAMESETs) in terms of referenced FRAME documents instead. Of course, this example takes two HTML files instead of one because you're moving the nested FRAMESET to its own document. Here's the first (outside) file:

```
<HTML>
<HEAD>
</HEAD>
<FRAMESET ROWS="25%,50%,25%">
<FRAME SRC="header.htm">
<FRAME SRC="frameset.htm">
<FRAME SRC="footer.htm">
</FRAMESET>
<NOFRAMES>
Your browser cannot display frames.
</NOFRAMES>
</HTML>
```

And here's the second file, which is called frameset.htm:

```
<HTML>
<HEAD>
</HEAD>
<FRAMESET COLS="25%,75%">
<FRAME SRC="label.htm">
<FRAME SRC="info.htm">
</FRAMESET>
</HTML>
```

In this case, the top and bottom rows behave as before. But the second row is now just a simple FRAME definition like the others. However, the file that its SRC points to is frameset.htm, which you just created with a FRAMESET all its own. When this file is inserted into the original FRAMESET, it behaves just as if it appeared there verbatim. The resulting screen is identical to the original example (see fig. 15.5).

Fig. 15.5
Though identical
to figure 15.2,
this screen was
generated by
different HTML
code.

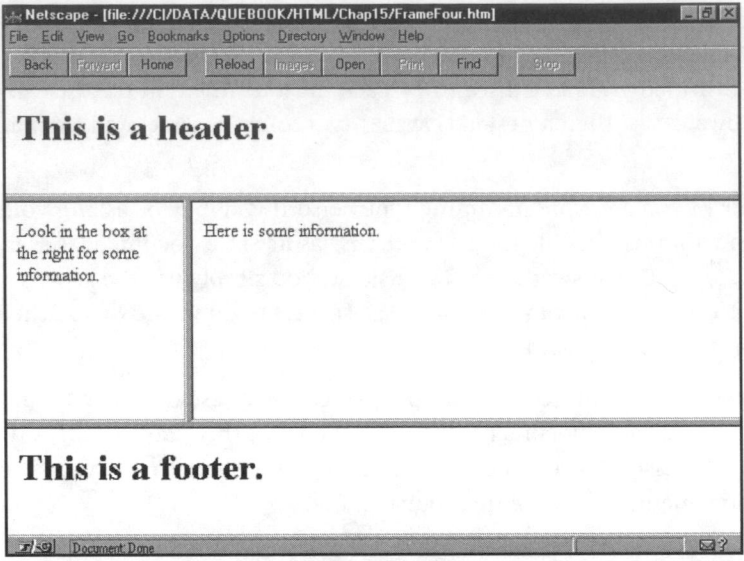

Caution

Although you can create nested FRAMESETs using FRAME tags that call the same URL, doing so certainly isn't a good idea. This process is called *infinite recursion*, and creates an infinite loop in a computer, consuming all memory and crashing the machine. Fortunately, frames-aware browsers check for this problem—if an SRC URL is the same as any of its ancestors it's ignored, just as if no SRC attribute existed at all.

By using nested FRAMESET containers in clever combinations, you can create just about any grid of frames you can dream up. But remember that you're trying to create a friendly, useful interface, not show off how clever you can be with frames.

Navigating a Site with Frames

You need to know three things about navigating through a site that uses frames.

1. The Back button doesn't back you out of a frame; it backs you out of the whole FRAMESET to the previous page. To back out of a frame, first point your mouse pointer to the frame you want to back out of. Then click the right mouse button (the Mac has only one button, so use it). You get a pop-up menu and can select Back in Frame.

2. If you're in a window with frames, and you move to one that's outside the FRAMESET, your frames disappear. They return if you use the Back button.

3. You can bookmark a frame by choosing Add Bookmark for This Link from the same pop-up menu mentioned in Point 1. If you simply choose Add Bookmark from your browser's main menu, you get a bookmark for the original FRAMESET, which may not be exactly where you are now.

Targeted Windows

Sometimes when you're browsing the Web, you want to keep a window open showing where you were while you go to someplace new. That way, you don't have to press the Back button a zillion times to return to your starting place—you just close the newer window and your old one is there waiting for you unchanged. You've always been able to open a new browser window in Netscape by choosing File, New Web Browser from the Navigator menu, or by pressing Ctrl+N.

But what if you want to keep somebody else's browser window open to your home page while a link from your site sends that user off to somewhere else? That way, when the user is done, all he or she has to do is click on the Close button in the window he or she is in, and the user then drops right back to the window displaying your page.

Before Netscape Navigator 2.0, a Web page designer couldn't do that. But with 2.0's targeted windows, it's easy. All you have to do is add a TARGET attribute to a link, like this:

```
<A HREF="URL" TARGET="window_name"> Click Here.</A>
```

TARGET names the browser window to use when jumping to the specified URL. If a window with that name doesn't already exist, the browser opens a new window and calls it by the TARGET name.

If you don't feel like adding TARGETs to every link on your site, an associated new BASE tag lets you name the default target window for all links that do not have explicit TARGETs. Its format is

```
<BASE TARGET="base_target">
```

III

Advanced HTML

> ## Allowed Names for Targeted Windows
>
> For a TARGET window, you can use any name that is alphanumeric. Anything else is ignored, except for a few reserved names. Any window name that begins with the following names is treated as though it has the reserved name (that is, _selfish is the same as _self). Note that each reserved name begins with an underscore character (_):
>
> **_blank** tells the browser to open a new untitled window in which to display the specified URL.
>
> **_self** always opens a link in the same window from which it was called.
>
> **_parent** opens a link in the previous window. If there is no previous window, it acts like _self.
>
> **_top** opens a link in the main browser window.

Embedded Objects

Multimedia is exciting, but Web browsers just aren't built for it. Since the beginning of the Web, people have had to call upon external helper applications to display video, audio, and foreign graphics files. With the advent of Netscape's new plug-in capability, however, multimedia has become integrated into the browser itself.

A *plug-in* is essentially a specially written code module that integrates seamlessly into your browser. For example, a Netscape plug-in for playing MPEG movies would, once installed, allow Netscape to display MPEG movies inline, without your having to launch an external helper application. This capability is exciting because it makes Netscape infinitely expandable and means that multimedia content may finally become commonplace on the Web.

Just to give you some idea of what's going on, here is a quick overview of a few of the plug-ins that have been announced for Netscape:

- Inline readers for several PDF (Portable Document Format) file types, including Adobe Acrobat and Envoy
- Viewers for multimedia and presentation files from WebShow and Macromedia Director (see fig. 15.6)
- Audio players for live audio in Real Audio and ToolVox formats
- Viewers for Word documents, Excel spreadsheets, and OLE objects

- Graphics and video file viewers for dozens of formats, including MPEG movies and Corel vector images
- VRML (Virtual Reality Modeling Language) display plug-ins for browsing 3-D Web sites
- New compression technologies for video and audio that promise to make real-time video conferencing on the Web a reality

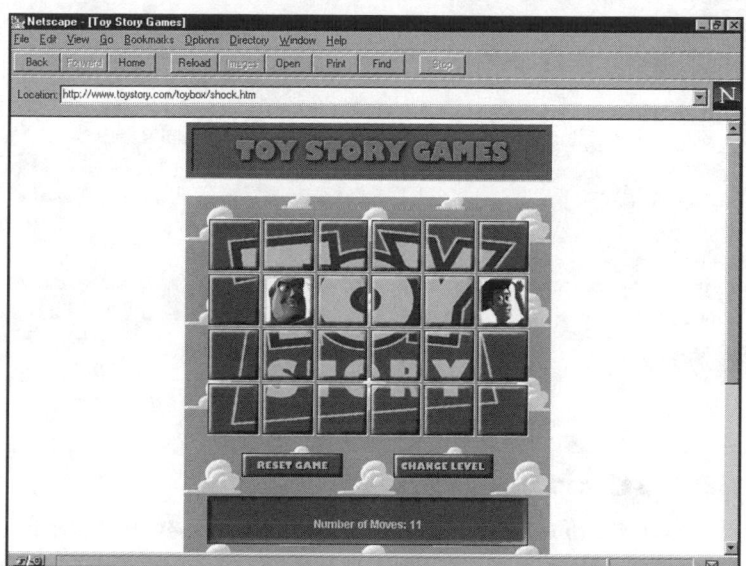

Fig. 15.6
Plug-ins allow live, interactive content to appear in the Netscape window, like this Macromedia Director concentration game on the Toy Story Web site.

For these new plug-ins, you can present live objects inline on a Web page by using the new EMBED tag. Here is a typical use:

```
<EMBED SRC="video.avi" WIDTH=100 HEIGHT=200 AUTOSTART=TRUE LOOP=TRUE>
```

This line of HTML code embeds a Video for Windows movie called video.avi in place on the Web page. When the page is displayed, the plug-in that is configured for playing .avi files launches invisibly in the background. The WIDTH and HEIGHT attributes create a playback area 100 pixels wide and 200 pixels high in the browser window. The AUTOSTART=TRUE command starts the video playing automatically, and the LOOP=TRUE attribute indicates that the video should play in a loop until stopped. These EMBED tag attributes are defined for a specific fictional plug-in. Each real plug-in has its own attribute syntax, defined by the plug-in publisher.

If you plan to support Netscape plug-ins on your Web pages, you have to find out the EMBED tag attributes for specific viewers. Netscape maintains a Web page with links to plug-in developers. You can access it by choosing Help, About Plug-ins from the Navigator 2.0 menu.

Coming Soon: LiveMedia

Plug-ins and the EMBED tag aren't Netscape's last word on inline multimedia. LiveMedia is a new framework for bringing real-time audio and video inline into Netscape. Netscape Corporation says that LiveMedia will make live audio, video-on-demand, video conferencing, Internet telephony, and other real-time on-line applications practical.

Eleven companies have initially signed on to support Netscape LiveMedia: Progressive Networks, Adobe Systems, Digital Equipment Corp., Macromedia, NetSpeak, OnLive!, Precept, Silicon Graphics, VDOnet, VocalTec, and Xing. These companies will provide inline applications based on the Internet Realtime Transport Protocol (RTP) and other open audio and video standards such as MPEG.

Netscape is publishing the LiveMedia framework on the Internet, will license key technology components of it, and hopes to get it adopted as a formal Internet standard.

Dynamic Documents

Server push and *client pull* are Netscape 2.0's innovative new techniques for automatically updating Web pages. Here are just a few uses for these "dynamic documents":

- You can create automated slide shows by loading a sequence of pages at timed intervals.

- You can automatically advance viewers to another site. This capability is especially useful if your Web site moves to a new URL.

- You can create "slippery" pages that display fine but disappear after a few seconds. You might use this feature for a "teaser" that shows users what is available at a site but that would not stay put unless the users enter passwords.

- You can create autosurf documents that advance viewers to a new random page every few seconds.

Though server push and client pull do similar things, they differ completely in how they work.

Server push is accomplished by running a CGI program on a Web server system, and is beyond the scope of this chapter. Server push differs from other CGI programs only in that server push applications keep a connection open from the server to the browser and "push" a stream of data at the browser. Server push is often used for data-driven applications such as animating icons, though it is rapidly being replaced for such purposes by Java applets.

Client pull, on the other hand, is implemented using the <META> tag and a browser capable of performing it, such as Netscape 2.0. Compared to server push, client pull is relatively easy to set up. It requires no special CGI scripts or special programming; all the work is done by Netscape. Here's how it's done.

You can use the META tag only in the HEAD section of a Web page, like this:

```
<HTML>
<HEAD>
<META HTTP-EQUIV="Refresh" CONTENT="30; URL=newpage.htm">
</HEAD>
<BODY>
Please wait 30 seconds for the next page.
</BODY>
</HTML>
```

This example displays the message Please wait for 30 seconds for the next page. Then the magic in the META tag starts. The HTTP-EQUIV="Refresh" attribute tells Netscape to load a new page. The CONTENT attribute contains two values separated by a semicolon. The first, which is numeric, tells Netscape how long to wait in seconds before performing the Refresh action. The URL=newpage.htm value tells Netscape the URL of the page to load when the time has expired.

Though simple in its implementation—and somewhat obscure in syntax—client pull is a powerful new Netscape addition to HTML.

Note

Netscape 2.0 also incorporates a second extension to the META tag. It allows MIME charset information to be contained in an HTML document. Here's the syntax:

```
<META HTTP-EQUIV="Content-Type" CONTENT="text/html;
➥charset=ISO-2022-JP">
```

This extension makes it easier to create Web pages for an international audience because the specified character set can be for any language in the world (this particular example is for Japanese).

III

Advanced HTML

Java Applets and JavaScript

Java is an exciting new cross-platform programming language from Sun Microsystems; it brings a new kind of power to the Web. Java-capable browsers such as Netscape 2.0 can run Java applet programs to create animations, automatic presentations, interactive games, and other dynamic pages.

Java and the Netscape scripting language based on Java, JavaScript, are such important new Web capabilities that this book devotes a whole chapter to the topic. Turn to chapter 26 for an in-depth examination.

Client-Side Imagemaps

With each new generation of browser programs and with each update to the HTML standard comes an increased effort to bring the exciting capabilities once reserved for CGI programmers down to humble HTML coders.

One of the prettiest and most functional features of the best pages on the Web is the clickable imagemap. Unfortunately, in the past this useful and eye-appealing tool has been reserved for those who can write server-side CGI-bin programs. Now all that has changed. Netscape 2.0 has wrested the clickable imagemap from the hands of the lofty CGI-bin programmers and given it to the people by implementing client-side imagemaps.

The great thing is that client-side imagemaps work exactly the same as server-side imagemaps. Their implementation is transparent to the user. However, you can easily create client-side imagemaps by using just a couple of new HTML tags.

> **Note**
>
> Though server-side and client-side imagemaps look and act alike, they are implemented completely differently. With server-side maps, the server does all the work. With client-side maps, the browser does it all. Chapters 11 and 12 cover in detail how server-side maps work.

Imagemaps allow users to select URLs (local or distant) by clicking on specific areas of a displayed image. Different areas are "mapped" to different URLs. Hopefully, the designer provides some sort of visual cue in the graphic to indicate to the user which areas lead to which locations.

A client-side imagemap consists of two parts: the graphic map image itself (a GIF or JPEG file) and the MAP definition that defines which areas lead to which URLs. Here's the generic usage of the MAP tag:

```
<MAP NAME="mapname">
<AREA [SHAPE="shape"] COORDS="x,y,..." [HREF="URL"] [NOHREF]>
</MAP>
```

> **Note**
>
> Note that, as with <FRAMESET> and <FRAME>, <MAP> is a container and has a corre-
> sponding </MAP> tag, and <AREA> is simply a stand-alone tag.

Here's an example of a full client-side imagemap definition:

```
<MAP NAME="menu">
<AREA SHAPE="RECT" COORDS="0,0,99,49" HREF="Item1.htm">
<AREA SHAPE="RECT" COORDS="100,0,200,49" HREF="Item2.htm">
<AREA SHAPE="RECT" COORDS="200,0,299,49" HREF="Item3.htm">
</MAP>
<IMG SRC="menu.gif" USEMAP="#menu">
```

Figure 15.7 shows the Web page created by this HTML code.

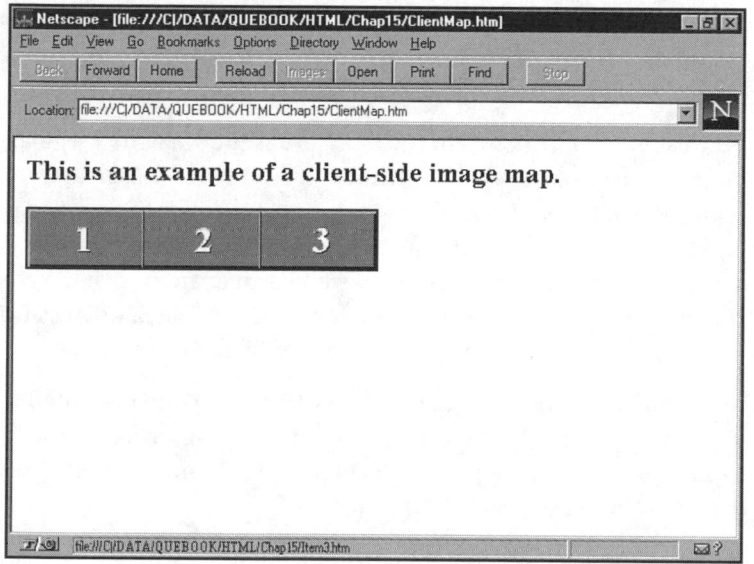

Fig. 15.7
The client-side imagemap produced by the example HTML code.

The MAP container defines and names the imagemap. In this example, the NAME attribute is set to "menu", so that is the name of the map. You reference this name later from the IMG tag.

A client-side imagemap is made up of AREA tags. Each AREA tag sets the "hot spot" for a link. For example, the first AREA tag

```
<AREA SHAPE="RECT" COORDS="0,0,99,49" HREF="Item1.htm">
```

III

Advanced HTML

defines a clickable region within the image that has 0,0 as its upper-left coordinate (in pixels) and 99,49 as its lower-right corner coordinate. This AREA tag defines the HREF link for its clickable area as the local URL Item1.htm.

The SHAPE attribute defines the shape of the clickable area. Table 15.3 lists the four currently allowed SHAPE definitions, along with the formats for entering coordinates for each.

Table 15.3 Allowable SHAPE Attributes for the AREA Tag		
Shape	**SHAPE=""**	**COORDS=""**
Rectangle	RECT	x upper left, y upper left, x lower right, y lower right
Polygon	POLY	x1, y1, x2, y2,... xn, yn
Circle	CIRCLE	x center, y center, radius
Default	DEFAULT	not specified—entire bitmap

The syntax is such that you may add other shapes to the definition when browsers support them. If the SHAPE tag is absent, SHAPE="RECT" is assumed. If two AREAs overlap, the first one defined is active for the shared area.

The HREF="URL" attribute points to the link, just as it does with a regular HTML link. In place of the HREF="" attribute, you can use NOHREF to indicate that an area is dead, or unclickable. By default, any areas not specifically designated are assumed to point nowhere anyway. But NOHREF can come in handy, especially when you're designating all leftover areas with the DEFAULT value for SHAPE, if you specifically want to exclude some area or areas from being clickable.

All relative links are considered to be relative to the document containing the MAP definition tags, not the one containing the referring USEMAP element, if different. If a BASE tag appears in the document containing the MAP description, that URL is used.

The final line of the example shows how to reference a MAP after it's built:

```
<IMG SRC="menu.gif" USEMAP="#menu">
```

This IMG tag loads the image called menu.gif, which is the image you've been reading about all along. The new USEMAP attribute is what makes client-side imagemaps work. It references the name defined for the imagemap way back in the first line of code. Remember this line?

```
<MAP NAME="menu">
```

This particular USEMAP reference is to "#menu" because the MAP definition is in the same document as the reference to it. However, the MAP definition (as well as the SRC image, of course) can be anywhere. All you need is a valid URL as the value in the USEMAP="" reference.

Surprisingly, you can define an imagemap that works as both a client-side and a server-side map. All you have to do is combine the two definitions. Here's the syntax:

```
<A HREF="/cgi-bin/binfile"> <IMG SRC="map.gif" USEMAP="#map" ISMAP></A>
```

If the browser supports client-side imagemaps, the map in the USEMAP definition is used. If not, the ISMAP attribute causes the CGI program *binfile* to be run on the server.

Note

If you want to use client-side maps but can't write CGI programs, and you're worried about non-Netscape users stumbling over your maps, here's a graceful way to take care of them: give 'em a page with an alternate menu! Here's the syntax:

```
<A HREF="textmenu.htm"> <IMG SRC="menu.gif" USEMAP="menu"> </A>
```

When the user clicks the image, this code sends a non-Netscape user to a new page, textmenu.htm, where you have thoughtfully provided a text menu.

Other Changes to the IMG (Image) Element

Though client-side imagemaps are arguably the most exciting addition to the IMG tag, Netscape 2.0 has made several other important enhancements to it.

For each of the following attributes, "n" is a dimension expressed in number of pixels.

ALIGN	This new attribute is discussed later in this chapter because it also applies to other tags.
WIDTH	Specifies the image width. WIDTH="n".
HEIGHT	Specifies the image height. HEIGHT="n".
BORDER	Specifies the image border width. BORDER="n".
VSPACE	Specifies the space above and below the image. VSPACE="n".

(continues)

(continued)

HSPACE	Specifies the space to the left and right of the image. HSPACE="n".
ISMAP	Allows the image to be used as a clickable server-side imagemap. This important feature has all of chapters 11 and 12 devoted to it.

An example of using all the attributes for the IMG tag could look something like this:

```
<A HREF="/cgi-bin/mapfile"><IMG SRC="map.gif" WIDTH="120"
HEIGHT="135" ALIGN=ABSMIDDLE BORDER=2 VSPACE=4 HSPACE=7 ISMAP></A>
```

But don't despair. Most images don't use all the allowed IMG tag attributes, just a few.

Background Graphics and Color

Two extensions to the BODY tag allow the Web page designer to define tileable background graphics and custom background colors for Web pages. Though these extensions originated in Netscape, most browsers now support them. Here's an example:

```
<BODY BACKGROUND="background.gif" BGCOLOR="#FFFFFF"
```

The BACKGROUND attribute fills the background of the browser window with the specified graphic image file. If the image is smaller than the page (hopefully!), it is tiled to fill the window.

Because graphics take a long time to transmit over the Internet (especially over modem connections), it is best to be sparing with backgrounds. Fewer colors and smaller images work best. Then, too, you often experience a problem with contrast. Because the page graphics and text are overlaid on the background image, a gaudy or non-contrasting background image can make it hard to see the page elements. Still, when done well, background graphics can add a lot of flash and eye appeal to your Web pages.

The BGCOLOR attribute lets you define a background color. This action is completely independent from specifying a BACKGROUND image. In fact, if you do both, the background color doesn't appear at all (unless your background image is a transparent GIF, in which case it shows through the "holes").

The value assigned to the BGCOLOR attribute is generally expressed as a six-digit hexadecimal value that specifies the RGB (Red, Green, Blue) values for the color you want. Unfortunately, specifying colors is a lot more like rocket science than art.

All About Hexadecimal *RGB* Values

Take a moment to learn about RGB values now because the subject pops up time after time in programming—even HTML programming.

Computer screen colors are expressed in RGB (Red, Green, Blue) values because a TV set or computer monitor builds up a color image from red, green, and blue phosphor dots. You can create all colors by mixing these three in varying intensities.

You can make over 16 million different colors by combining R, G, and B values with intensities expressed as numbers in the range from 0–255, with 0 meaning none of that color at all, and 255 meaning the maximum amount of that color possible. For example, a color value of R=128, G=128, and B=0 makes a medium yellow because red and green (without any blue) make yellow, and you are mixing each of them at about half of their possible maximum intensities.

The reason you use a range of 0–255 is that it just happens to be the range represented by 8 bits, or 1 byte. 00000000 (8 bits in computer binary) is decimal 0, and 11111111 is decimal 255. But computer people like to break up a byte into two smaller chunks called nybbles. Each contains four bits, and 1111, the maximum value for a nybble, is equal to 15 in decimal. However, computer people also like to represent a nybble as a single character. The digits 0–9 are no problem, but 10–15 take two digits to represent, so the letters A–F are substituted. This substitution is called hexadecimal notation. So A=10, B=11, and so on. This means you count 0–9, A–F, and then go into two digits.

The upshot is that, if you're numbering from 0–255 in decimal, you go from 00 to FF in hexadecimal. So a color value of #FF55DD, for example, means a Red value of FF (hexadecimal) or 255 (decimal), a Green value of 55 (hex) or 85 (decimal), and a Blue value of DD (hex) or 221 (decimal).

Many calculators can automatically convert between decimal and hexadecimal numbers. Even the lowly Windows calculator will do. Just select View, Scientific from the Windows Calculator menu. To convert from decimal to hexadecimal, first make sure the Dec button is selected, and then enter a decimal number and click the Hex button. To convert from hex to decimal, reverse the process: click the Hex button first, enter your hex number, and then click the Dec button.

Thankfully, there is an alternative to using hexadecimal color values. Netscape recognizes an exhaustive table of 140 predefined color values. You can, for example, say BGCOLOR="black", and you get a black screen. Table 15.4 lists the color values Netscape has built in. (I am not making this up, though I think someone at Netscape Corporation spent way too much time looking at the names on sample chips at the local paint store.)

III

Advanced HTML

Table 15.4   Netscape's 140 Custom Colors

aliceblue	darkslategray	lightsalmon
antiquewhite	darkturquoise	lightseagreen
*aqua	darkviolet	lightskyblue
aquamarine	deeppink	lightslategray
azure	deepskyblue	lightsteelblue
beige	dimgray	lightyellow
bisque	dodgerblue	*lime
*black	firebrick	limegreen
blanchedalmond	floralwhite	linen
*blue	forestgreen	magenta
blueviolet	*fuchsi	*maroon
brown	gainsboro	mediumaquamarine
burlywood	ghostwhite	mediumblue
cadetblue	gold	mediumorchid
chartreuse	goldenrod	mediumpurple
chocolate	*gray	mediumseagreen
coral	*green	mediumslateblue
cornflowerblue	greenyellow	mediumspringgreen
cornsilk	honeydew	mediumturquoise
crimson	hotpink	mediumvioletred
cyan	indianred	midnightblue
darkblue	indigo	mintcream
darkcyan	ivory	mistyrose
darkgoldenrod	khaki	moccasin
darkgray	lavender	navajowhite
darkgreen	lavenderblush	*navy
darkkhaki	lawngreen	oldlace
darkmagenta	lemonchiffon	*olive
darkolivegreen	lightblue	olivedrab
darkorange	lightcoral	orange
darkorchid	lightcyan	orangered
darkred	lightgoldenrodyellow	orchid
darksalmon	lightgreen	palegoldenrod
darkseagreen	lightgrey	palegreen
darkslateblue	lightpink	paleturquoise

palevioletred	salmon	tan
papayawhip	sandybrown	*teal
peachpuff	seagreen	thistle
peru	seashell	tomato
pink	sienna	turquoise
plum	*silver	violet
powderblue	skyblue	wheat
*purple	slateblue	*white
*red	slategray	whitesmoke
rosybrown	snow	*yellow
royalblue	springgreen	yellowgreen
saddlebrown	steelblue	

The 16 color names understood by Microsoft Internet Explorer 2.0 are indicated with an asterisk (*). NCSA Mosaic does not support named colors.

Caution

You can have only one background image and color set per page.

If the users have turned off Auto Load Images in their browsers, they won't see your background images. So don't count on those images being there.

Netscape 1.1 had a bug that allowed multiple changing background colors. It was widely abused, and it thankfully left this "feature" out of Netscape 2.0.

You cannot define background images or colors for individual table cells or frames. Individual frames can, however, load documents that contain their own separate background image or color, which is defined in the BODY tag of the document.

One big problem you can get into when setting your own background images and colors is that your page text is often lost in the resulting melange. Hopefully, you're putting more thought than that into your selection of backgrounds and colors, but if you really want to go with something wild—or if you just want to set a color mood—you also can use new BODY attributes to change the colors of your page text.

TEXT specifies the color of normal text; LINK defines the color for links; and VLINK modifies the color of previously visited links. With all these BODY tags in use, here's what a typical BODY element might look like:

```
<BODY BACKGROUND="wheatfield.gif" BGCOLOR="wheat" TEXT="#ddeeff"
LINK="papayawhip" VLINK="mistyrose">
```

III

Advanced HTML

Form Enhancements

Forms are ubiquitous on the Web. It seems like wherever you go, you're always filling out a form. It's almost as bad as real life.

Fortunately, Netscape has added a couple of innovations to HTML forms to make them a bit easier to use.

HTTP File Upload

You've seen them on the Web: huge forms with a zillion fields. Credit applications. Personality tests. Opinion polls. You can sit there paying for connect time for hours while you fill them out. There has to be a better way.

With HTTP file upload, there is. HTTP file upload lets a Web page creator give his or her users the option to compose a form data file offline and upload the form information all at once. This process takes only a few seconds, saving connect time and money.

This trick is accomplished through a new value for the FORM tag ENCTYPE attribute, which specifies the MIME type of a form. In the past, only one valid value existed for ENCTYPE: application/x-www-form-urlencoded. The new value defined for input files is multipart/form-data.

Here's an example of a short form that accepts file input (see fig. 15.8):

```
<FORM ENCTYPE="multipart/form-data"
ACTION="http://www.site.com/cgi-bin/getfile" METHOD=POST>
File to process? <INPUT NAME="file1" TYPE="file">
<INPUT TYPE="submit" VALUE="Send File">
</FORM>
```

Fig. 15.8
A short example of a Web form that accepts a file as input.

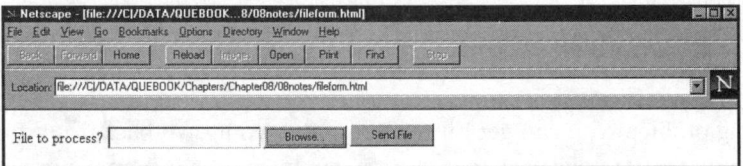

The new INPUT TYPE="file" not only lets you upload a file in response to the form request, it even adds a BROWSE button that, when clicked, brings up a standard file requester dialog box.

Of course, the FORM ACTION specifies a CGI-bin program (called "getfile" in the example) to parse the information from the file, and you need to tell people somewhere on your Web page exactly what the program expects in the way of data and formatting (or better yet, provide a template for downloading) so that your users can prepare a proper data file. Otherwise the whole process breaks down. Unfortunately, it all means that HTTP file upload is only for those who can write the CGI programs to support it. But at least it should make long forms easier to use for all.

TEXTAREA **Wrap**

The TEXTAREA tag for forms lets you specify a scrolling text box of a specified size for lengthy text fields. The problem is, if you keep typing, the box keeps scrolling sideways.

Now Netscape has added the ability to turn on word wrap in these boxes via a new WRAP attribute for the TEXTAREA tag. Here's how it looks:

```
<TEXTAREA WRAP=OFF¦VIRTUAL¦PHYSICAL>
```

WRAP=OFF turns off text wrap (this is the default, and the way it was before). WRAP=VIRTUAL turns on word wrap as far as the display is concerned but still sends the data to the server as one long line. WRAP=PHYSICAL actually splits text input into the same size chunks it displays on-screen.

Character Attributes

Once upon a time, you didn't have much control over the way text looked on your Web pages. Those days are gone. Besides the font color definitions now allowed in the BODY tag (see "Background Graphics and Colors" p. 338), Netscape has added text blink and on-the-fly font color and size changing to HTML.

BLINK

Rumors are flying that Marc Andreeson, founder of Netscape, has said that the BLINK tag was meant to be a joke. If so, it has been one of the most successful jokes in history, to judge by how much it is used on the Web.

Although huge blocks of blinking text can be annoying, the occasional judicious use of a blinking word to draw the viewer's attention to a critical item of information can be useful. The BLINK tag works just like all text markers. You surround the text you want blinking with these tags:

```
<BLINK>This blinks.</BLINK>
```

Whatever is between the tags blinks. Actually, it varies at a steady rate (on my machine about every three seconds, but your mileage may vary) between the defined text color and the defined background color or image, unless overridden by the user's browser settings.

Font Size and Color

Netscape's new FONT tag lets you specify both the font color and size for a block of text rather than for the entire page, as you must do using the various text attributes of the BODY tag.

The FONT tag works like all other text formatting tags—you surround the text you want to change. This example uses the new COLOR attribute:

```
We've got <FONT COLOR="tomato">color text</FONT> now!
```

Here the message color text appears in the Netscape predefined color called tomato. You can, of course, also specify colors in hexadecimal, as with the BODY tag attributes discussed previously in this chapter.

You can also change font size with the FONT tag using the SIZE attribute. Netscape assumes a default base font size with (what seems to be) an arbitrary numerical value of 3. The FONT SIZE tag can specify a new absolute font size, or an increment or decrement to the base size. A new tag called BASEFONT sets the base size to something other than 3. Here is an example of their use:

```
<BASEFONT=2>
<FONT SIZE=4>I'm bigger than base.</FONT>
<FONT SIZE=+3>I'm bigger yet.</FONT>
```

The BASEFONT line changes the size of the base font from its default size of 3 to a new value of 2. The first FONT SIZE line prints the message I'm bigger than base. in a font size of 4. The second FONT SIZE line increments the base font size by 3, resulting in a font size of 5 for the message I'm bigger yet. Any normal text printed after the final </FONT> appears in the new base font size of 2.

Fonts can have any size from 1 to 7. If any combination of BASEFONT or FONT SIZE elements results in numbers lower or higher than these, they are set to 1 or 7, respectively.

Of course, you can also use a single set of FONT tags to change both color and size, like this:

```
<FONT SIZE=7 COLOR="purple">I'm big and purple.</FONT>
```

You can go really crazy changing font size and color with every word or even every character, but don't. Although you might want to make these changes for occasional fun or even maybe to create an interesting logo, I'd sure hate to see a lot of "ransom note" pages where every character is a different size and color.

CENTER and *ALIGN*

Early Web pages had all the elements aligned along the left margin, with no way to arrange them nicely on the page. (And text didn't even wrap around graphics!) Fortunately, that has all changed.

The new CENTER tags let you center whatever appears between them, like this:

```
<CENTER>
This text is centered.<BR>
So is this image:<IMG SRC="centered.gif"><BR>
</CENTER>
```

That's it. You can now center just about everything quickly and easily.

The new ALIGN attribute for the IMG (image), P (paragraph), Hn (heading), HR (horizontal rule), and DIV (division) tags allows a flexible new range of alignment options for each. They all work in the same manner, though the IMG tag allows a wider range of options. Table 15.5 lists the values that you can assign to the ALIGN attribute.

Table 15.5   Valid Values for the *ALIGN* Attribute for *IMG*, *P*, *Hn*, *HR*, and *DIV* Tags

Value	Valid For	Syntax
LEFT	IMG,P,Hn,HR,DIV	Aligns with left margin
RIGHT	IMG,P,Hn,HR,DIV	Aligns with right margin
CENTER	IMG,P,Hn,HR,DIV	Centers between margins
TOP	IMG	Aligns the top of the image with the top of the tallest item in line
TEXTTOP	IMG	Aligns the top of the image with the tallest text in line
MIDDLE	IMG	Aligns the middle of the image with the baseline of the current line
ABSMIDDLE	IMG	Aligns the middle of the image with the actual middle of the current line
BOTTOM, BASELINE	IMG	Aligns the bottom of the image with the bottom of the line
ABSBOTTOM	IMG	Aligns the bottom of the image with the absolute bottom of the current line, including text descenders

Here are some real-world examples:

```
<P ALIGN=CENTER>Centered text paragraph</P>
<H1 ALIGN=RIGHT>Right Aligned Heading</H1>
<HR ALIGN=CENTER>
<IMG SRC="somepic.gif" ALIGN=ABSBOTTOM>
<DIV ALIGN=LEFT><IMG SRC="otherpic.gif">Here's a picture.</DIV>
```

The first line centers a paragraph of text consisting of the single sentence `Centered text paragraph`. The next line right-aligns the Heading 1 text `Right Aligned Heading`. Line three creates a centered horizontal rule. The fourth line of code aligns the image `somepic.gif` with the absolute bottom of the text surrounding it; that is, with the lowest point of text descenders like lowercase *g* and *p*. The final line left-aligns the image `otherpic.gif` and the accompanying text `Here's a picture`.

With all these new alignment options available, Web pages are starting to look a lot better.

Horizontal Rules

You can use horizontal rules to break up text into nice eye-sized chunks. Unfortunately, they are rather boring, which is why so many sites use long, skinny, colorful GIF images instead of HTML's `HR` tag.

Netscape has modified the `HR` tag with four attributes that help break the monotony: `SIZE`, `WIDTH`, `ALIGN`, and `NOSHADE`. `ALIGN` was discussed previously in this chapter. `SIZE` specifies a rule's thickness in pixels. `WIDTH` defines the width in pixels if the value assigned to it is an unadorned number, and a percentage of the screen width if the value is followed by a percentage sign. `ALIGN` aligns a rule to `LEFT`, `RIGHT`, or `CENTER`. (If the rule hasn't been shortened using the `WIDTH` command, all are equivalent.) Finally, `NOSHADE` creates a rule without the default shadow.

Here is an example that uses all four attributes:

```
<HR SIZE=4 WIDTH=75% ALIGN=CENTER NOSHADE>
```

This example creates a horizontal rule that is 4 pixels thick, 75 percent as wide as the browser display, centered, without shading.

That's it for Netscape extensions to HTML. The next chapter covers extensions introduced by other browser programs (mostly Microsoft Internet Explorer) as well as some proposed HTML 3.0 tags not implemented by Netscape. ❖

## CHAPTER 16

HTML Extensions in Internet Explorer, Mosaic, and HTML 3.0

by Mark Brown

Not all the popular extensions to HTML have sprung fully formed from the forehead of Netscape Communications Corporation. HTML 3.0 proposals have been the source of many so-called Netscape enhancements, and even some of the HTML extensions most closely associated with the Netscape name came originally from other vendors. Spyglass Mosaic, for example, lays claim to having implemented client-side imagemaps first, whereas HTTP file upload was originally proposed by Xerox PARC.

Netscape is the driving force behind most of the changes to HTML because it has a huge 80 percent share of the Web browser installed base. Web developers naturally follow Netscape's lead, making use of new Netscape Navigator features as they appear. Conversely, few Web sites use HTML extensions that have not yet made their way into Navigator, because they would not be visible by 80 percent of their visitors. However, that doesn't deter Microsoft from introducing new and modified HTML elements in its browser program, Internet Explorer. You may get the feeling, in fact, that Microsoft considers itself to be in a dead heat with Netscape. Each company seems determined to not only catch up with, but also outdo, the other with each new release of its software. That's good. It drives the technology.

In this chapter, you find out about HTML extensions that have not yet made their way into Netscape Navigator—at least, not as of version 2.0. Read on and you learn about the following:

- New extensions to HTML incorporated into Microsoft Internet Explorer version 2.0
- Even NCSA Mosaic holds a surprise

- Proposed HTML 3.0 elements not yet implemented by Netscape Navigator
- How VRML, browser scripting languages, live objects, and other new technologies are pushing the Web beyond HTML

Microsoft Internet Explorer

Internet Explorer, Microsoft's Web browser client, debuted as part of the initial release of the Windows 95 operating system. It was intended to serve as the built-in browser for the then brand-new Microsoft Network on-line service. Though Microsoft drew far fewer users to MSN than it intended, Internet Explorer built a following among early Win95 users, becoming the Web browser of choice (or at least, of convenience) for many of them. With the addition of a few absolutely necessary features such as tables in version 2.0—and with Microsoft's not insubstantial marketing clout behind it— Internet Explorer is shaping up as a serious challenger to Netscape Navigator. Now that it has been ported to Windows and the Macintosh, its user base is bound to expand, if for no other reason than the fact that people like to have a choice.

Version 2.0 of Internet Explorer has many features in common with Navigator 2.0. Both support tables, client pull, and client-side imagemaps, for example.

Explorer even beat Netscape to the punch with some features—named colors, for example. However, Netscape has since leapfrogged Microsoft on this feature. Where Explorer has a palette of 16 named colors, as shown in table 16.1, Navigator now has 140 (see table 15.4, p. 340).

Table 16.1 Named Colors in Microsoft Internet Explorer Version 2.0	
Black	Silver
Maroon	Red
Green	Lime
Olive	Yellow
Navy	Blue
Purple	Fuchsia
Teal	Aqua
Gray	White

What's in a Color Name?

Unfortunately, Internet Explorer and Netscape Navigator aren't very sophisticated in the way they handle color names they don't know. If they don't recognize a color name, they try—really, I am not making this up—to interpret the letters in the name as a hexadecimal number! As you might surmise, absolutely no correlation whatsoever exists between the hue of a named color and the color produced by interpreting its name as a hex number. The resulting color can be just about anything.

If, for example, you use the color named "wheat" in Netscape Navigator, it's a nice wheat-field shade of yellow because "wheat" is one of Navigator's named colors. However, Internet Explorer doesn't have a clue what color "wheat" is, so it tries to turn the letters in "wheat" into a hex number, and ends up rendering it as a sort of lime green. If you misspell the color as "what," both programs interpret it as a dark, pool-table felt kind of green. That's a long way from wheat-field yellow.

You should consider yourself lucky that both browsers misinterpret unknown color names in the same way. NCSA Mosaic—which doesn't know any color names at all—interprets "what" as a dithered dark blue, and "wheat" as a different dithered blue just a shade lighter.

I suppose this means that you really have an entire dictionary full of named colors that are presented in the same way by both Navigator and Explorer and quite differently by Mosaic. You could exploit this bug by, for example, naming colors "tuba" (medium green) or "epistemology" (medium red) or even "Grant's Tomb" (dark red), and the two most popular browser programs would faithfully represent them on the screen as un-mnemonic (but consistent) hues. If you have a twisted mind— if, for instance, you are a programmer—this scheme might appeal to you. I'd watch for Microsoft and Netscape to fix this "feature" (deep purple) in future versions, however.

Just watch your use of color names, and be aware that not all browsers know exactly what to do with them.

In the following few pages, you examine HTML extensions that are unique to Microsoft Internet Explorer 2.0.

III

Advanced HTML

Unknown Tags and Attributes

Fortunately, HTML is defined so that a browser simply throws away element tags and attributes that it doesn't recognize. This means that Netscape Navigator doesn't crash, choke, or throw up terrible, threatening error messages when it sees an Explorer-specific HTML element and vice versa. Thus, experimenting with tags and attributes that are browser-specific is easy (and fun!), as long as you remember to test your pages on both before posting them on the Net.

Make especially sure that no real information is hidden somewhere that only one browser can display.

Background Sound

Explorer's new BGSOUND tag lets you create pages with background sounds. When you load a page using a BGSOUND command, the sound plays automatically, and the LOOP attribute controls how many times it plays. Sounds can consist of .wav or .au sampled sound files or MIDI (.mid) music files. Here's an elementary example:

```
<BGSOUND SRC="carhorn.wav">
```

The SRC attribute contains the URL of the source file to be played. The sound "carhorn.wav" in the preceding example plays once when the page is loaded. Here are two examples that play more than once using the LOOP attribute:

```
<BGSOUND SRC="carhorn.wav" LOOP=5>
```

```
<BGSOUND SRC="carhorn.wav" LOOP=INFINITE>
```

The first example plays five times; the second plays until you leave the page (which will probably be soon with an infinite car horn sound playing!). LOOP can have any integer value or be INFINITE; -1 is the same as specifying INFINITE.

Explorer Additions to the *BODY* Tag

Explorer, like Netscape, adds the BACKGROUND, BGCOLOR, LINK, TEXT, and VLINK attributes to the BODY tag. But it also adds three more that Netscape doesn't have (at least, not yet): BGPROPERTIES, LEFTMARGIN, and TOPMARGIN.

BGPROPERTIES must be used in conjunction with the BACKGROUND attribute, and can have only one value, FIXED:

```
<BODY BACKGROUND="dontmove.gif" BGPROPERTIES=FIXED>
```

BGPROPERTIES=FIXED specifies a "watermark," which is a non-scrolling BACKGROUND. In other words, when you scroll up and down the page, the text, images, and other elements move, but the background image doesn't. This watermark can make users dizzy, so make sure you don't use it with a really busy background.

LEFTMARGIN and TOPMARGIN define left and top margins for the page in pixels, like this:

```
<BODY LEFTMARGIN="0" TOPMARGIN="100">
```

If either has a value of "0", the margin is set smack up against the edge of the window, as shown in figure 16.1.

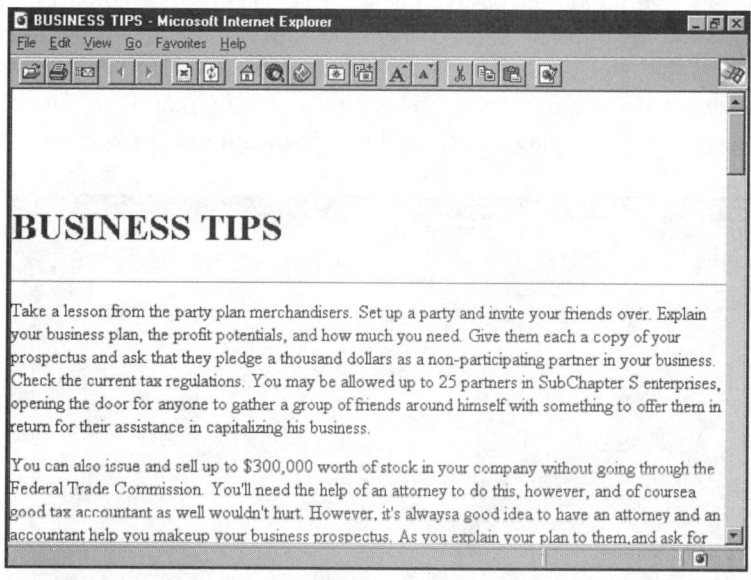

Fig. 16.1
This page uses Explorer's TOPMARGIN and LEFTMARGIN attributes to jam the page flush against the left margin and drop it down by 100 pixels from the top.

FONT Tag Enhancements

Like Netscape, Explorer adds the BASEFONT tag, as well as the FONT tag with COLOR and SIZE attributes. But it adds one more attribute to FONT: FACE, which is used to define the font, or typeface, for the tagged text. Here's the generic format:

```
<FONT FACE="name [,name2] [,name3]">Text.</FONT>
```

The FACE attribute takes a list consisting of one or more font names. If the first named font is available on the system, it is used for the tagged text. If not, the second is used, and so on. If none of the fonts are available, the text is displayed in the default font. Here's a real-world example:

```
<FONT FACE="Times New Roman", "Courier New", "Frankenstein">Welcome!</FONT>
```

III

Advanced HTML

In this example, the message `Welcome!` would be displayed in the Times New Roman font, if available. If not, Courier New would be used, or Frankenstein if Courier New didn't exist.

Inline Video with the *IMG* Tag

Explorer adds these Netscape-compatible extensions to the `IMG` tag: `ALIGN`, `HEIGHT`, `WIDTH`, `HSPACE`, `VSPACE`, `BORDER`, `ISMAP`, and `USEMAP`. (Remember, `USEMAP` is the tag that allows you to create client-side imagemaps.)

But Internet Explorer 2.0 adds an additional extremely powerful feature to the `IMG` tag, thus enabling you to embed .avi video clips in Web pages (like the little spinning cup of coffee—a brilliant lampoon of HotJava's animated steaming coffee cup!—in fig. 16.2). Navigator lets you use the separate `EMBED` tag, but `EMBED` also requires that you install a matching plug-in application. In Explorer, .avi video playback capability is built right in.

Fig 16.2
This sample page at **http:// www.microsoft. com/windows/ ie/iedemo.htm.** demos Explorer's capability to add inline .avi videos using the new DYNSRC attribute of the IMG tag.

Several new attributes have been added to `IMG` to control video playback. The one that makes it all work is `DYNSRC` (Dynamic Source), which defines the URL of the source .avi file to play:

```
<IMG DYNSRC="cartoon.avi">
```

For non-video-capable browsers, you can include a normal `SRC` command to indicate an alternate GIF or JPG image to display in its place, like this:

```
<IMG SRC="mickey.gif" DYNSRC="cartoon.avi">
```

The ultimate in Web page design politeness is to include ALT text for non-graphic browsers as well:

```
<IMG SRC="mickey.gif" DYNSRC="cartoon.avi" ALT="Mickey Mouse Cartoon">
```

Most stand-alone video players have a control bar, and you can add one under a video image by using the CONTROLS attribute:

```
<IMG DYNSRC="cartoon.avi" CONTROLS>
```

Like BGSOUND, video playback can be controlled using the LOOP attribute:

```
<IMG DYNSRC="cartoon.avi" LOOP=5>
```

The preceding example plays the video five times and then stops. As with BGSOUND, the LOOP attribute can also be set to INFINITE, which is equivalent to a numeric value of -1.

START is the final new attribute for controlling video playback. You can set it equal to values of FILEOPEN and/or MOUSEOVER, like this:

```
<IMG DYNSRC="cartoon.avi" START=MOUSEOVER,FILEOPEN>
```

This video begins playing as soon as the file is loaded (FILEOPEN) and plays again any time the user moves the mouse pointer over the video image (MOUSEOVER).

Of course, you can apply all the standard IMG attributes, such as HEIGHT, WIDTH, and so on, to videos.

Here's a real-world example that combines all Explorer's video-specific playback options:

```
<IMG SRC="mickey.gif" DYNSRC="cartoon.avi" ALT="Mickey Mouse LOOP=2 Cartoon"
START=FILEOPEN>
```

This example displays the text Mickey Mouse Cartoon on text-only browsers and the image mickey.gif on a graphic browser other than Explorer. On Explorer, it plays the video cartoon.avi as soon as it's loaded (START=FILEOPEN) twice (LOOP=2).

Scrolling *MARQUEE*s

You may get the impression that many of Explorer's extensions to HTML are meant to compete directly with the HotJava demos being shown by Sun Microsystems. They typically display small animations (which Explorer 2.0 can now re-create by playing inline .avi videos) and scrolling marquees. Explorer has added a new MARQUEE HTML tag just for creating the latter.

III

Advanced HTML

A variety of special attributes exist for controlling Explorer marquees. Here's a bare-bones MARQUEE definition:

```
<MARQUEE>Scrolling... Scrolling... Scrolling...</MARQUEE>
```

As you can see, MARQUEE is just a pair of text tags like, for example, <B></B> for bold. Any text within the <MARQUEE></MARQUEE> tags scrolls sideways.

The BEHAVIOR attribute lets you pick how the text moves. With a value of SCROLL, text scrolls in from one side and off the other. SLIDE scrolls in from one side and stops as soon as the text touches the opposite margin. ALTERNATE bounces text back and forth within the marquee.

Which way does the text move? You set that by using the DIRECTION attribute, which can have either of the values LEFT or RIGHT. (DIRECTION indicates which direction the text moves to, not the direction it comes from.) The following example uses both the BEHAVIOR and DIRECTION attributes:

```
<MARQUEE BEHAVIOR=SLIDE DIRECTION=RIGHT>Watch me slide!</MARQUEE>
```

This example slides the text "Watch me slide!" in from the left to the right, where it stops and stays. The defaults are DIRECTION=LEFT and BEHAVIOR=SCROLL, which means that

```
<MARQUEE>Scrolling text</MARQUEE>
```

creates the same effect as

```
<MARQUEE BEHAVIOR=SCROLL DIRECTION=LEFT>Scrolling text</MARQUEE>
```

Beyond these basics, MARQUEE offers an incredible amount of control over the way your marquee looks and acts. Table 16.2 lists all the attributes that affect a marquee's appearance.

Table 16.2 *MARQUEE* Attributes

Attribute & Values	Effect
BEHAVIOR=SCROLL¦SLIDE¦ALTERNATE	Defines how the text moves; SCROLL wraps, SLIDE stops, and ALTERNATE ping-pongs, as described in the preceding text
DIRECTION=LEFT¦RIGHT	Specifies the direction in which the text moves, as described previously
ALIGN=TOP¦MIDDLE¦BOTTOM	Determines whether surrounding text aligns with the TOP, MIDDLE, or BOTTOM of the marquee
BGCOLOR="color"	Defines background color as a hexadecimal value ("#FFFFFF") or color name ("blue")
HEIGHT=n¦n%	Specifies marquee height in pixels (HEIGHT=50) or as a percentage of screen height (HEIGHT=33%)

Attribute & Values	Effect
WIDTH=n¦n%	Determines marquee width in pixels or a percentage of screen height (see HEIGHT)
HSPACE=n	Defines left and right outside margins in pixels (HSPACE=35)
VSPACE=n	Specifies top and bottom outside margins in pixels (see HSPACE)
LOOP=n¦INFINITE	Determines how many times a marquee loops (as with BGSOUND and DYNSRC, LOOP=INFINITE is the same as LOOP=-1, and is the default value)
SCROLLAMOUNT=n	Defines how far the marquee moves each step, in pixels
SCROLLDELAY=n	Specifies the delay between moves in milliseconds (of course, this delay can also be affected by system speed)

MARQUEE recognizes an additional attribute that Microsoft has apparently not documented: BORDER. BORDER=n specifies an internal border, which is normally blank but which is rendered in the LINK or VLINK color if the MARQUEE is a link.

Keeping It between the Borders

Carefully note the difference between the BORDER attribute and the HSPACE and VSPACE attributes.

HEIGHT and WIDTH define the marquee size. HSPACE and VSPACE carve away the outside portions of this space to define a "no-man's land" where outside elements can't appear. Then BORDER eats away a symmetrical chunk of what's left and allocates it as a border, which is normally invisible but which will appear as a border in the LINK or VLINK color if the marquee is defined as a link (that is, is surrounded by <A HREF="URL"></A> tags). Unfortunately, if you do make a marquee into a link, the scrolling text is also colored with the LINK or VLINK color and, depending on the viewer's browser setting, may be underlined as well (see fig. 16.3).

Note, too, that the BGCOLOR fills only the space that's left over after BORDER, HSPACE, and VSPACE are done.

Think of HEIGHT and WIDTH as defining the whole space reserved for the marquee. HSPACE and VSPACE take chunks from the outside edges of this space and use it for external margins. Then BORDER takes another piece from what's left and allocates it as an outline border. Finally, BGCOLOR colors the remaining space, and that's the place where the marquee appears.

Here's a MARQUEE that uses all the options:

```
<FONT SIZE=7>
<A HREF="marquee.htm">
<MARQUEE BEHAVIOR=SCROLL DIRECTION=RIGHT LOOP=INFINITE
➥BGCOLOR="red"
HEIGHT=175 WIDTH=67% HSPACE=20 VSPACE=10 BORDER=20 SCROLLDELAY=25
SCROLLAMOUNT=3 ALIGN=MIDDLE>Welcome to the Wonderful World of
➥Scrolling
Marquees!</MARQUEE>
</A>
</FONT>
Hi there
```

The marquee text is big because you've surrounded the MARQUEE code with
<FONT SIZE=7></FONT>. This marquee scrolls (BEHAVIOR=SCROLL) the text
"Welcome to the Wonderful World of Scrolling Marquees!" in from the left
moving to the right (DIRECTION=RIGHT) forever (LOOP=INFINITE). The marquee window is red (BGCOLOR="red") and is—including borders and marginal
space—175 pixels tall (HEIGHT=175) and two-thirds as wide as the browser
window (WIDTH=67%). Outside the active marquee are horizontal margins
of 20 pixels (HSPACE=20) on each side and vertical margins of 10 pixels
(VSPACE=10) above and below. An additional 50-pixel wide border appears
around the marquee; it appears in the LINK color because you have the
whole marquee within the <A HREF="marquee.htm"></A> tags. (Note that
this has the unfortunate side effect of underlining the marquee text because
the Explorer preferences are set to underline text links.) The text moves every
25 milliseconds (SCROLLDELAY=25) and scrolls 3 pixels (SCROLLAMOUNT=3) at a
time. The following text "Hi there" is aligned with the middle (ALIGN=MIDDLE)
of the marquee, is 20 pixels away from the outside edge of the marquee border (HSPACE=20), and is in the default size because it lies outside the closing
</FONT> tag.

Figure 16.3 shows the resulting marquee (frozen in time, alas).

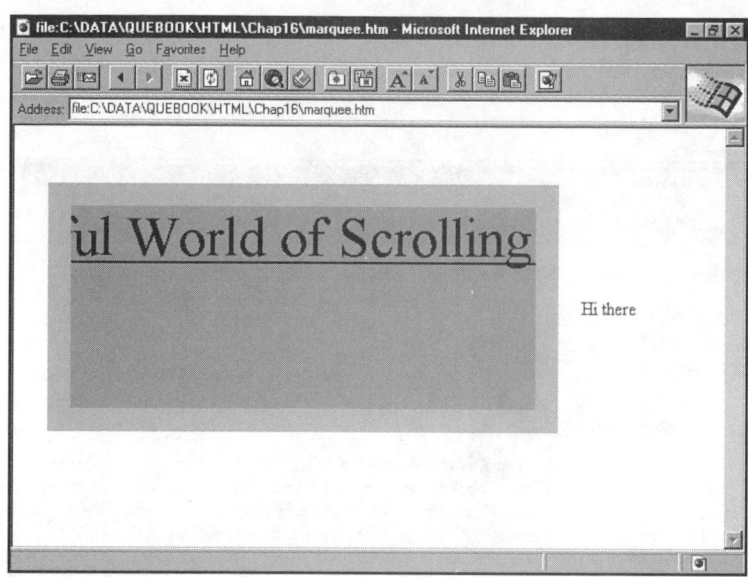

Fig. 16.3
The Internet
Explorer displays
this MARQUEE
defined by the
example HTML
code.

Explorer Tables

Internet Explorer supports the HTML 3.0 table standard, just as Netscape
does. But it adds a couple of twists of its own.

You can right-align an Explorer table by adding ALIGN=RIGHT to the TABLE tag
specification, like this:

```
<TABLE ALIGN=RIGHT>
```

Left alignment is, of course, the default.

The most interesting (and certainly the most colorful) Microsoft enhancement to tables is the addition of the BGCOLOR tag. You can use it to add color
to an entire table and to individual cells as well. The following example creates a table with the "teal" background color:

```
<TABLE BGCOLOR="teal">
```

By adding a BGCOLOR tag to each opening TD tag, you can define a unique
background color for each individual cell in a table. Here's the syntax:

```
<TD BGCOLOR=#ffdddd>Hello</TD>
```

In either command, you can use a hexadecimal color value or one of
Microsoft's 16 named colors.

Figure 16.4 shows an example of color tables from Microsoft's Web site that displays a table of all 16 named colors (shown here in glorious shades of gray).

Fig. 16.4
Internet Explorer's BGCOLOR extension to the HTML TABLE elements lets you define the background color for an entire table or for individual cells.

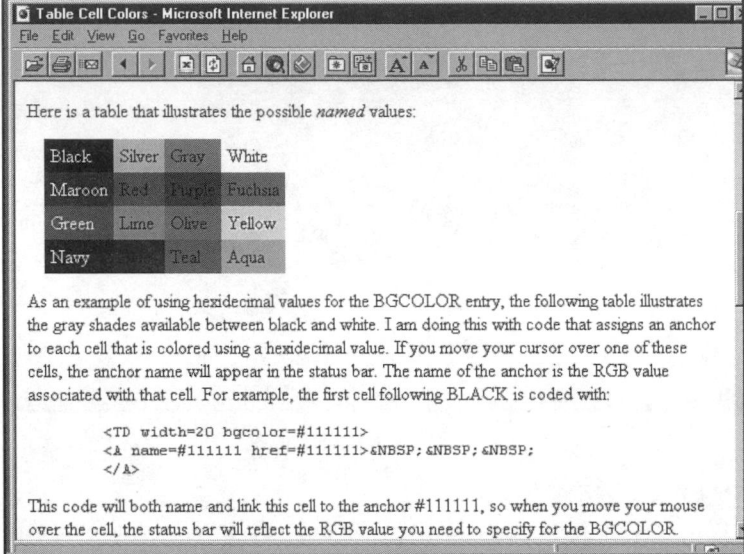

Mosaic

NCSA Mosaic was the first graphical browser for the World Wide Web; it drove the explosive early growth of the Web. In fact, it was so pervasive in the early days of the Web's development that many people mistakenly referred to the Web itself as "Mosaic."

Originally developed at the National Center for Supercomputing Applications at the Champaign campus of the University of Illinois, both the NCSA Mosaic executable and its source code were widely distributed for free. This resulted in a proliferation of browser programs, almost all of which were based to some degree on the original Mosaic code. Many even called themselves by some variant of the "Mosaic" name. As the Web matured, others developed original browsers (with their own names) not based on the Mosaic code.

◀ See additional information on the early development of the Web presented in chapter 1, "Introducing the World Wide Web," p. 9.

Eventually, Spyglass got the rights to develop Mosaic commercially and now supplies various versions of Mosaic for OEM distribution. Mosaic Communications Corporation—founded by Marc Andreesen, the originator of Mosaic at NCSA—had to change the name to Netscape Communications Corporation. And NCSA just kept right on turning out new versions of NCSA Mosaic.

Today, NCSA Mosaic is still distributed for free, and government and educational institutions can still obtain the source code for free, as well. It has evolved considerably and is now available for Win95, Windows, Macintosh, and UNIX platforms.

Development has slowed on NCSA Mosaic, however, and it is seldom the browser that introduces new features first. It keeps up pretty well, though, and the latest version sports such niceties as client pull, tables, the BODY BACKGROUND and BGCOLOR attributes, and the ALIGN attribute for P and Hn tags.

And the latest version of NCSA Mosaic does sport an HTML 3.0 feature not yet implemented by the two major players, Explorer and Navigator. NCSA Mosaic now includes integrated .wav sound file support. It is implemented in not one, but two ways. The first is the proposed HTML 3.0 SOUND tag, which has the format:

```
<SOUND SRC="audio.wav">
```

This tag supports two attributes:

```
<SOUND SRC="audio.wav" LOOP=INFINITE DELAY=5>
```

This example waits 5 seconds and then plays the file audio.wav in an infinite loop. A numeric value for LOOP tells SOUND how many times to play; a value of INFINITE loops forever.

In addition, NCSA Mosaic also supports the full syntax of Microsoft's BGSOUND tag.

Note

NCSA Mosaic doesn't support Netscape's <CENTER> tag, but it has changed the default alignment of paragraph and header tags to center. This means you add no ALIGN definition to these elements if you want them centered, and you must add ALIGN=LEFT to left-align them.

NCSA is encouraging the adoption of the <DIV ALIGN=CENTER> structure from HTML 3.0 rather than Netscape's <CENTER> element.

HTML 3.0

The evolution of Explorer and Mosaic raises the question of additions and changes to HTML that are being proposed for the upcoming HTML 3.0 standard. Some things will be in there for sure—tables, for example. Text flow around images is another sure thing. But other potential changes haven't been implemented in any browser programs—yet!

HTML 3.0 introduces, for example, a new `FIG` tag for inline figures; it will provide for implementing client-side imagemaps and text flow around figures. It will almost certainly supersede all the current additions to the `IMG` command eventually.

HTML 3.0 will also add the capability to define math equations and formulas neatly on a Web page, which will be a real boon to educational and research sites. The proposed format is highly influenced by the T_eX typesetting language.

HTML 3.0 will most likely include a static banner area for corporate logos, disclaimers, and menus; it will work in much the same way as "freezing" the header row in a spreadsheet. The page will scroll, but not the banner.

A new `LINK` element will provide standard navigational elements such as forward and back buttons. `NOTE` will add notes, cautions, and footnotes. The `LH` tag will let Web pages designers create "folding" lists.

Additions to forms will mean new controls, the ability to "scribble" on an image, and audio input fields. Client-side scripting of forms is also possible with a new script attribute for the `FORM` tag. Style sheets will add a great deal of flexibility to the appearance of Web pages, without cluttering them with a lot of superfluous markup elements.

These changes and many more are likely when HTML 3.0 is pronounced "official."

Netscape Navigator 2.0 and Microsoft Internet Explorer already implement many of the HTML 3.0 proposed changes. Indeed, in many cases, Netscape and Microsoft have been instrumental in proposing these changes. But they're not all in there yet.

What follows is a short list of proposed changes and new elements that are likely to be included in the HTML 3.0 specification. I've limited this list to elements not already discussed elsewhere in this book. In other words, everything listed here is not really being used by anyone, anywhere yet. This list is intended to be a quick overview of what is probably coming, not a reference guide to coding in HTML 3.0. That would be premature. I've listed each new element with a sample of the proposed format, though all the attributes are not necessarily explained here.

If you are interested in keeping abreast of the HTML 3.0 proposals, you can find them on the Web site of the W3 Consortium (W3C) at the following:

http://www.w3.org

ABBREV	Indicates an abbreviation.
`<ABBREV LANG="..." DIR=ltr¦rtl ID="..." CLASS="...">text... </ABBREV>`	
ACRONYM	Tags text as an acronym.
`<ACRONYM LANG="..." DIR=ltr¦rtl ID="..." CLASS="...">text... <ACRONYM>`	
AU	Represents an author name.
`<AU LANG="..." DIR=ltr¦rtl ID="..." CLASS="...">text... </AU>`	
BANNER	Creates a non-scrolling area for logos, navigation aids, disclaimers, and other information that shouldn't be scrolled with the rest of the document.
`<BANNER LANG="..." DIR=ltr¦rtl ID="..." CLASS="...">text... </BANNER>`	
BQ	Replaces BLOCKQUOTE.
CREDIT	Tags the source of a figure or block quotation.
`<CREDIT LANG="..." DIR=ltr¦rtl ID="..." CLASS="...">text... </CREDIT>`	
DEL	Tags text to be marked as deleted. (Typically rendered as strikethru.)
`<DEL LANG="..." DIR=ltr¦rtl ID="..." CLASS="...">text... </DEL>`	
DIV	To be used with the CLASS attribute, it represents different kinds of containers, such as chapter, section, abstract, or appendix. When used with the ALIGN=CENTER attribute, it is intended to replace Netscape's non-standard <CENTER> tag.
`<DIV LANG="..." DIR=ltr¦rtl ALIGN=left¦center¦right¦justify ID="..."` `CLASS="..." NOWRAP CLEAR=left¦right¦all¦"...">text... </DIV>`	
FIG	The proposed replacement for the IMG element that will allow client-side imagemaps, optional graphic overlays, a CAPTION element, a CREDIT tag, and much more.

`<FIG SRC="..." LANG="..." DIR=ltr¦rtl ID="..." CLASS="..."`
`CLEAR=left¦right¦all¦"..." NOFLOW MD="..."`
`ALIGN=left¦right¦center¦justify¦bleedleft¦bleedright WIDTH=value`
`HEIGHT=value UNITS="..." IMAGEMAP="..."></FIG>`	

FN	Identifies footnotes. The reference for a footnote will probably be an <A> tag with an HREF to the ID of the FN element. W3C recommends that graphic browsers implement footnotes as pop-up notes.
`<FN LANG="..." DIR=ltr¦rtl ID="..." CLASS="...">text... </FN>`	
INPUT	The INPUT element is enhanced with FORM-based file upload using the ACCEPT attribute. A new TYPE attribute would have the values RANGE or SCRIBBLE. RANGE would use the proposed MIN and MAX attributes to limit numeric input to a range of values. SCRIBBLE would allow the user to scribble on an image with the mouse cursor.

III

Advanced HTML

INS	Represents inserted text.

`<INS LANG="..." DIR=ltr¦rtl ID="..." CLASS="...">text... </INS>`

LANG	Changes the default LANG (language). A LANG attribute on an element overrides this default.

`<LANG ID="..." CLASS="...">text... </LANG>`

Internationalization

Note that many of the proposed HTML 3.0 tags have a LANG attribute. One of the driving forces behind the HTML 3.0 proposals is to create an environment that is universally adaptable to a truly worldwide audience.

An attempt is also made to make presentation more flexible through the use of style sheets, which will not only allow viewers to interpret Web pages in ways that are more aesthetically pleasing to them, but will also make the Web more accessible to the physically challenged.

Through the use of LANG attributes and style sheets for language localization, user specification of large fonts and high-contrast screen colors, etc., HTML 3.0 will make the Web much more accessible to those who cannot easily use it now.

LH	Stands for "List Header" and will be used in some browsers to create "folding lists," which can be expanded to full lists or contracted down to display the LH header only.

`<LH LANG="..." DIR=ltr¦rtl ID="..." CLASS="...">text... </LH>`

MATH	Defines an entire new set of elements for rendering mathematical equations. The MATH container will include a whole new family of elements for formatting equations, such as ARRAY for defining arrays, BOX for creating brackets and delimiters, SUB and SUP for super- and subscripts, ABOVE and BELOW for drawing arrows and lines; and SQRT and ROOT for square roots and roots of an expression. This example shows a very simple usage of the MATH element.

`<MATH CLASS=chem> Fe_2_^2+^Cr_2_O_4_</MATH>`

NOTE	Represents set-off notational text. The SRC attribute specifies an image to appear preceding the note, which will be indented. The CLASS value will include NOTE, CAUTION, and WARNING, with different renderings.

`<NOTE LANG="..." DIR=ltr¦rtl ID="..." CLASS="..."`
`CLEAR=left¦right¦all¦"..." SRC="..." MD="..."</NOTE>`

OVERLAY	Puts images on top of a FIG image. X and Y attributes will indicate placement.

`<OVERLAY SRC="..." MD="..." UNITS=pixels¦en X=value Y=value`
`WIDTH=value HEIGHT=value IMAGEMAP="...">`

PERSON	Tags a name for easy identification by indexing programs.
`<PERSON LANG="..." DIR=ltr¦rtl ID="..." CLASS="...">text... </ PERSON>`	
Q	Indicates a quotation. The Q tag is one of many added to HTML 3.0 for internationalization. In this case, Q will allow the proper quotation character to be picked for each language.
`<Q LANG="..." DIR=ltr¦rtl ID="..." CLASS="...">text... </Q>`	
S	Shows as strikethru font.
`<S LANG="..." DIR=ltr¦rtl ID="..." CLASS="...">text... </S>`	
TAB	Acts as a tab character, aligning the following text according to a defined horizontal position. You will define TABs by using the ID attribute. You will position text by using the TO and/or ALIGN attributes, or INDENT.
`<TAB ID="..." INDENT=ens TO="..." ALIGN=left¦center¦right¦decimal DP="...">text...`	
UL	HTML 3.0 adds CLEAR, PLAIN, SRC, MD, DINGBAT, and WRAP attributes to UL bulleted lists. SRC indicates a server-side image to use as the bullet; DINGBAT picks an image from the browser.

Note

Though no browsers support the full HTML 3.0 standard yet, the W3 Consortium has made available the source code for a "testbed" browser called Arena. This code is available to developers on the W3 Web site at **http://www.w3.org**.

Beyond HTML: VRML, Scripts, and Live Content

Though Web pages couldn't be created without HTML, other technologies are at work on the Web, too. In fact, many of the most impressive innovations on the Web in the near future are most likely to come from outside the framework of HTML.

VRML (Virtual Reality Modeling Language) for example, is already at work on the Web, allowing sites to move into a 3-D virtual reality realm that is rapidly evolving into a true cyberspace.

III

Advanced HTML

ActiveVRML

▶ For the complete story on VRML, see chapter 17, "VRML," p. 367

Internet Explorer can currently display VRML (Virtual Reality Modeling Language) 3-D worlds using an "add-in" VRML module. (The terminology is a little different, but this approach is identical to Netscape's "plug-ins.")

However, Microsoft has proposed a new standard it calls ActiveVRML, which it says will be faster and more flexible. The technology is expected to debut in mid-1996, and will be incorporated into a future version of Internet Explorer.

Compatible with current VRML worlds, ActiveVRML will, they say, make 3-D Web browsing practical at typical modem speeds. It builds on the Microsoft DirectX standard for multimedia hardware, so graphics boards that adhere to DirectX will be able to display ActiveVRML worlds quickly and efficiently.

ActiveVRML is essentially a framework for describing interactive 3-D multimedia scenes, and it also provides the ability to plug in additional software components written in Visual Basic Script, Java, and C++. It supports 2-D cel animation, 3-D geometry rendering, audio, and mouse and joystick input.

ActiveVRML has been proposed for inclusion in the VRML 2.0 standard. A beta version of the ActiveVRML specification is located on the Web at **http://www.microsoft.com/intdev/tech.htm**. Microsoft will make the source code for the reference implementation of the ActiveVRML animation engine publicly available on the Net.

Scripting languages are also changing the way the Web works. JavaScript, which is built into Netscape Navigator 2.0, lets Web page designers create animations, scrolling marquees, and interactive live content that would just not be possible using HTML alone.

▶ The lowdown on Java is in chapter 26, "Java and JavaScript," p. 621

Sun Microsystems, the developer of Java—which is the programming language on which JavaScript is based—has even introduced a Web browser program called HotJava. HotJava (free from Sun's site at **http://www.javasoft.com**) is itself written entirely in Java, and is intended as a demonstration of what the language can do. HotJava can play live Java applets inline, and Sun's site features dozens of live demonstrations of the language's capabilities, including some interactive games.

Microsoft is fighting back and promises to introduce Visual Basic Script. This scripting language will open up Web page application programming to millions of Visual Basic programmers who might not be comfortable with the C-like syntax of JavaScript.

A fast, cross-platform subset of Visual Basic, Visual Basic Script will not only be shipped as a part of future versions of Microsoft Internet Explorer, it will also be distributed for free on the Internet. It can be used to develop applications and can also link to OLE objects and Java applets.

Microsoft will propose Visual Basic Script to the W3 Consortium and the IETF as an open Internet scripting language standard. The source code will even be posted on the Internet so that third parties can implement it on other platforms.

The W3 Consortium has also worked with IBM, Microsoft, Netscape, Spyglass, and Sun Microsystems to come up with a standard way of inserting live objects like movies into Web pages. If you recall, Netscape and Microsoft currently take two different approaches to this: Navigator uses the EMBED tag, and Explorer uses a new DYNSRC attribute for the IMG element.

The new standard will allow multiple implementations of the same object as, say, a Java applet, an .avi movie, and an OLE object, with the browser able to pick content that matches its capabilities. This standard will go a long way toward making every Web site accessible to every browser program, rather than requiring pages to be set up to suit a particular brand of browser.

This standard for live content is implemented using new HTML 3.0 INSERT, PARAM, and ALIAS elements. INSERT takes the place of the IMG tag, and allows the Web designer to insert a variety of objects. PARAM and ALIAS and a full set of attributes will provide a wide range of flexibility in the presentation of multimedia content. You can find the full specification at the following:

http://www.w3.org/pub/WWW/TR/WD-insert.html

Clearly, the Web is bulging at the seams of HTML, stretching it to its limit. In the future, HTML coding will just be the first step in creating a Web page. ❖

III

Advanced HTML

CHAPTER 17
VRML

by Jim O'Donnell

The advent of the World Wide Web (WWW), the HyperText Markup Language (HTML), and Web browsers capable of viewing HTML documents including text, graphics, and sound revolutionized the Internet. Previously, the most common way of exchanging information was through e-mail and Usenet discussion groups. Because these methods could handle text only, the only way to exchange graphics, sound, or other binary information was for the sender to encode it and the receiver to decode it. HTML and the WWW changed this process by enabling you to create true multimedia information sites on the Internet, offering real-time display and exchange of text, graphics, sound, and other information.

The next big step beyond HTML for information distribution on the Internet may be the Virtual Reality Modeling Language (VRML). HTML's hypertext links and the Web browsers that make use of them create an essentially two-dimensional interface to Internet information. VRML expands this interface by allowing the creation of three-dimensional worlds on the WWW, offering a much more natural way of presenting information.

In this chapter, you learn about the following:

- The Virtual Reality Modeling Language and what it is good for
- Some basic notions of VRML programming, and how it relates to HTML
- Tools available for creating, viewing, and browsing through VRML documents and sites
- How to install and use WebFX, a Netscape plug-in module that adds VRML browsing capability

What Is VRML?

VRML, the *Virtual Reality Modeling Language*, is an authoring standard, currently defined at version 1.0, for creating three-dimensional documents on the World Wide Web. These documents create VRML worlds that a user can navigate in and around using the capabilities of a VRML-compatible browser. The current standard is file-based, involving the transfer of 3-D scenes to the local computer—VRML source files usually have a .wrl extension—after which all navigating through the scene is done there. And, like HTML documents, VRML worlds can contain links to other documents, graphics, text, HTML documents, or other VRML worlds.

Freeware, shareware, and commercial VRML tools are becoming widely available.

> **Note**
>
> Like HTML, VRML is a fast-evolving standard for conveying information over the World Wide Web. If you are going to be working with VRML a lot, you would do well to frequently consult newsgroups and other Internet and WWW resources (such as those mentioned in the "VRML Resources on the Internet" section at the end of this chapter) that deal with VRML, its tools, and its standards.

Example VRML World

Included with the Windows WebFX VRML browser, a plug-in module for Netscape Navigator 2.0 that is discussed later in this chapter, is a series of sample VRML worlds. To get a feel for what navigating around a VRML world is like and how it is different from regular HTML, you look at a simple VRML world in this chapter.

Figure 17.1 shows a sample VRML world called Netscape.wrl, which, when loaded, shows an up-close view of the familiar Netscape "N." After you install the WebFX plug-in, Netscape automatically calls WebFX when a VRML world is loaded. (You know it has been called successfully if you see the WebFX Navigation Bar at the bottom of the browser window.) At this point, this world looks like an HTML imagemap. The pointer even turns into a hand pointer when you move it over the "N," indicating the presence of a hypertext link. However, you can navigate around this three-dimensional world.

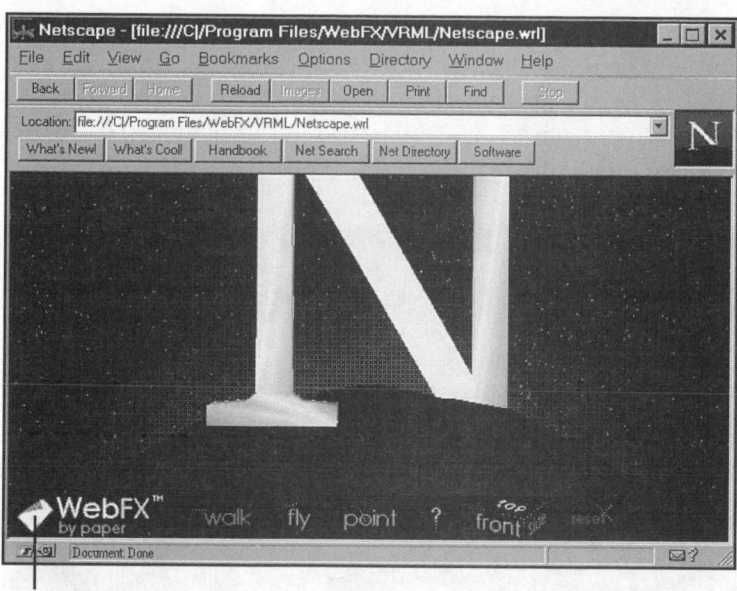

WebFX Navigation Bar

Navigating VRML Worlds

WebFX beginners can click the ? (question mark) WebFX button to turn on
the Heads up display. Then, when you click the fly button, the display shown
in figure 17.2 appears, indicating how to navigate around while you're in
WebFX fly mode.

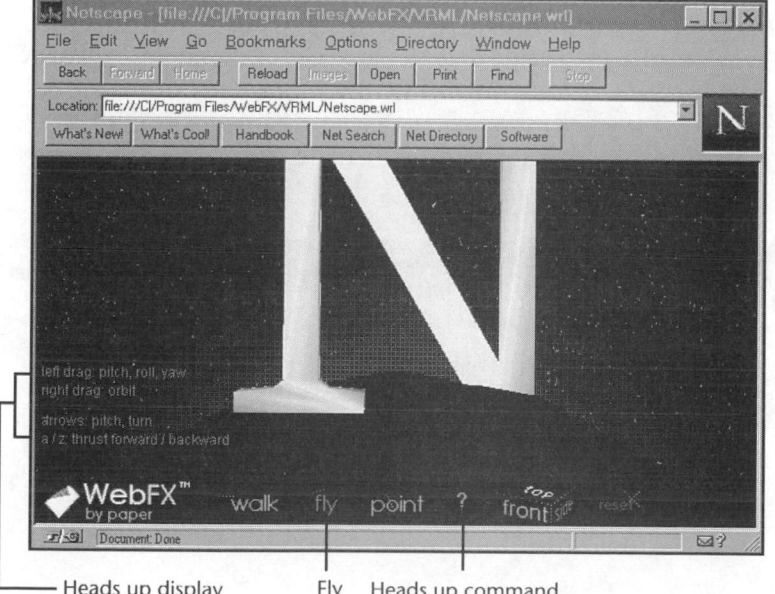

Heads up display   Fly   Heads up command

III

Advanced HTML

The quickest way to show the three-dimensional nature of the VRML world at this point is to press and hold down the Z key, which is used in fly mode to thrust backward. You quickly see the Netscape "N" world recede into the distance, as shown in figure 17.3. The star field in this figure is a background image allowed by VRML.

Fig. 17.3
By pressing Z to thrust backward, you can move away from "Netscape world."

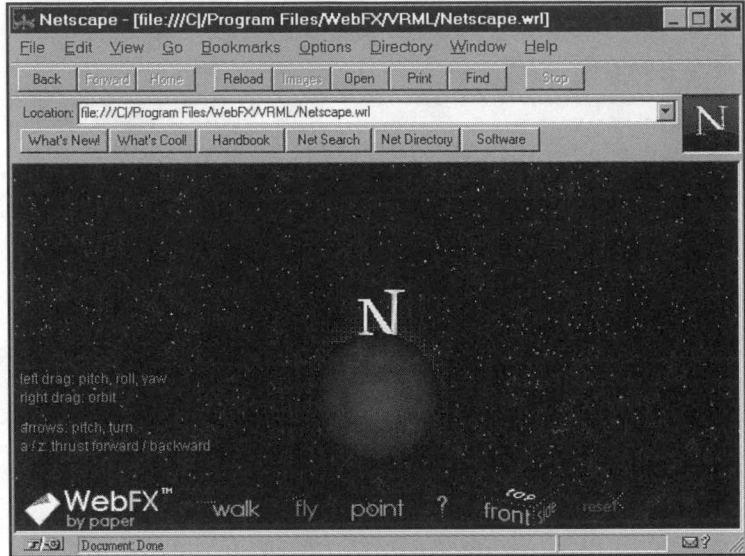

After you move some distance from the Netscape world, you can reverse course and approach it again by pressing the A key to thrust forward. Using this key, you can retrace the steps from where you began to thrust backward—you can also keep going to get a much closer view of the Netscape "N" (see fig. 17.4). You can even continue to thrust forward until you are past the "N," in which case you see only the star field background. At this point, you can turn around by pressing the right- or left-arrow key, and you actually move behind the "N" world (see fig. 17.5).

> **Tip**
>
> It's easy to get lost in a VRML world sometimes. If that happens in WebFX, right-click the screen and choose Viewpoints, Entry View to return to your starting point.

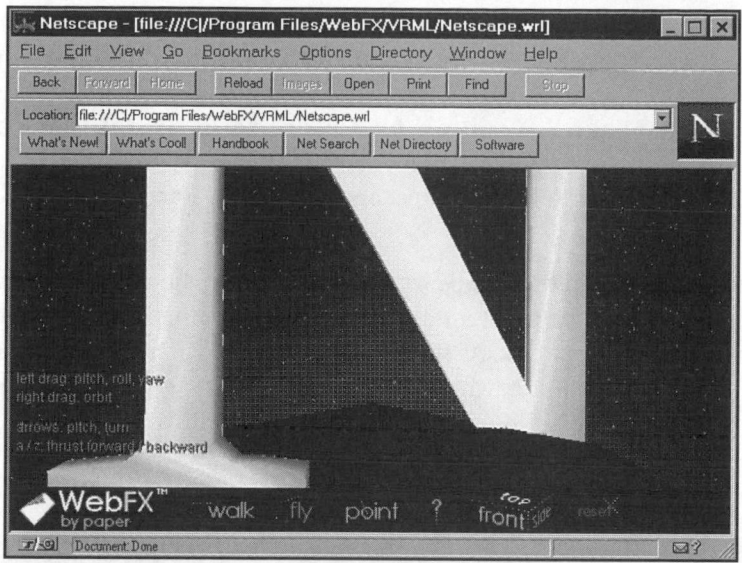

Fig. 17.4
By pressing A to
thrust forward,
you can move
right up to the
Netscape "N." You
can even move
through and
beyond it!

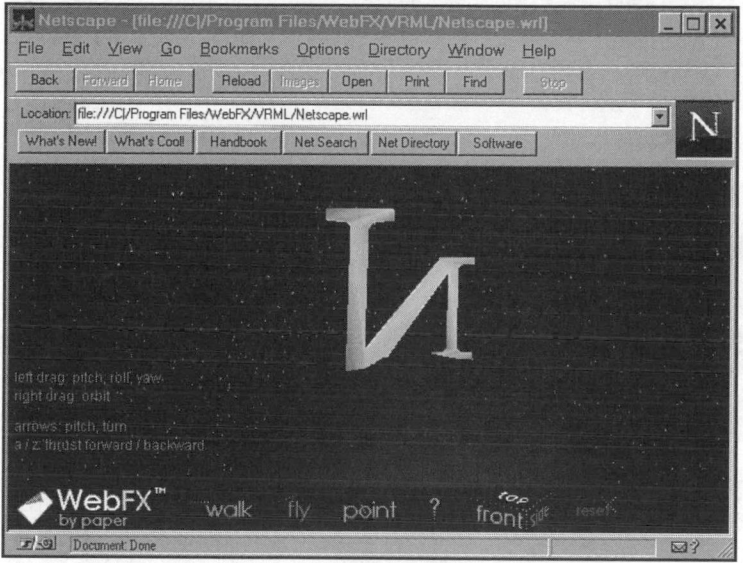

Fig. 17.5
You can even
move past the
object and turn
around to see it
from behind.

III

Advanced HTML

Hypertext Links

Because the WebFX VRML browser is a Netscape plug-in, you might suspect that, just as with an HTML document, you can link together VRML worlds using hypertext links. You can even interchangeably link VRML worlds and HTML documents! Other VRML browsers offer similar capability, whether they are Web browser plug-ins, helper applications, or stand-alone applications.

In this chapter's sample Netscape world, for instance, when you place the pointer on the "N," the pointer turns into the hand pointer, indicating the presence of a hypertext link. As shown in figure 17.6, the hand pointer and a label for the hypertext link, which appears in the upper left, indicate where the link will take you. In the case of this Netscape world, as you might expect, clicking on the link takes you to the familiar Netscape HTML home page.

Caution

Just as when using new HTML enhancements, if you would like to add VRML content to your Web pages, you should keep in mind that not everyone has the necessary software to view it. Therefore, you should also convey the information included in your VRML using conventional means.

Fig. 17.6
When you move the pointer over an object that is a hypertext link, such as an HTML anchor, it turns into the hand pointer, and an URL label for the link appears in the upper-left corner of the window.

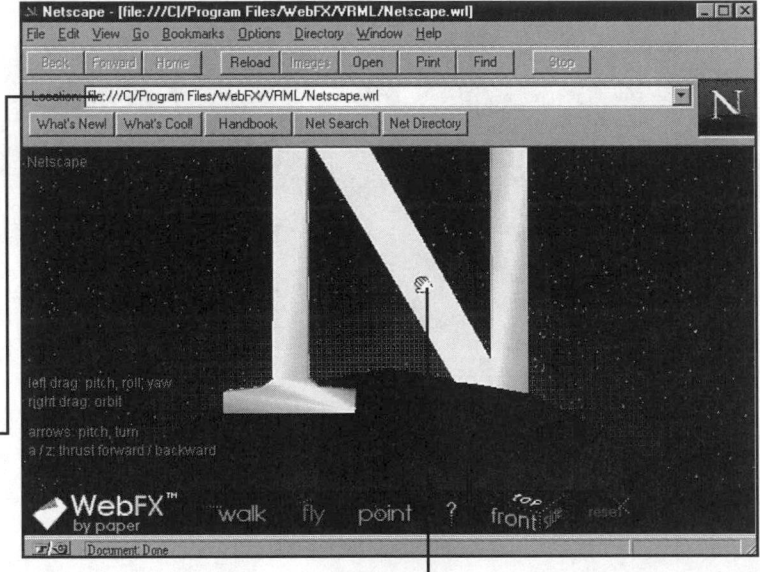

URL label ⌐

Hand pointer

VRML Basics

In many ways, VRML is an extension of HTML; the source code for HTML documents and code for VRML worlds are very different, but the concepts are similar. The differences between the two lie in the fact that HTML documents are two-dimensional, whereas VRML worlds are three-dimensional. An HTML document is like a bulletin board, where text and graphics can be displayed, and each can also represent a hypertext link to another place in the document, or another document entirely. On the other hand, a VRML world is more like a room (or world, I suppose, if it's big enough) filled with three-dimensional objects. Because of the three-dimensional nature of the VRML world, you can navigate around and see objects from all sides. In VRML, like HTML, each of these objects can also be a hypertext link.

With a VRML-compatible Web browser, users can navigate back and forth between HTML documents and VRML worlds with no additional steps. This compatibility is achieved either by means of a plug-in module such as with WebFX and Netscape Navigator, by setting up a VRML browser as a helper app for a Web browser, or by using a stand-alone VRML browser that also supports HTML. Inside an HTML document, if there is a hypertext link to a VRML world, it will be loaded and the Web browser placed into a VRML browsing mode. Conversely, HTML links from a VRML world will lead back to conventional web page viewing.

Programming in VRML

Just as with HTML documents, VRML worlds are defined by VRML source code. However, as you might imagine from the fact that VRML worlds are three-dimensional, the source code is likely to be much more complex. Figure 17.7 shows the top of the VRML source file for the Netscape world. The VRML language is much more like C/C++ than it is like HTML.

Many tools are currently being written to allow HTML authors to create Web pages and documents more easily. You can, however, create fairly sophisticated Web pages programming directly in HTML. Because of the complexity of VRML, however, it would be very difficult to do the same—to create a VRML world by directly writing VRML code. Consider the Netscape world, which consists of only a few objects—the Netscape "N," the sphere upon which it rests, and the "glow" around them. The source code to describe the Netscape "N" is partially shown in figure 17.8. Even a relatively simple object like the "N" is described by a long series of coordinates. Programming this object directly would be very difficult.

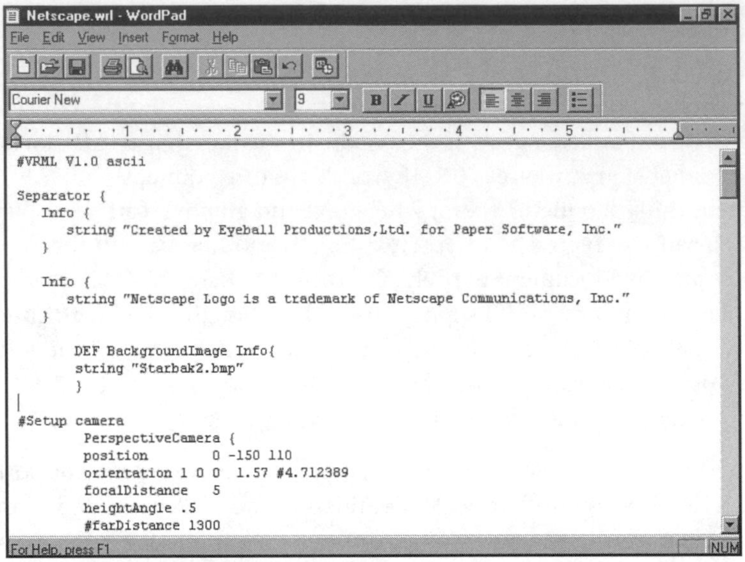
Netscape.wrl - WordPad
File Edit View Insert Format Help
Courier New
#VRML V1.0 ascii
Separator {
Info {
string "Created by Eyeball Productions,Ltd. for Paper Software, Inc."
}
Info {
string "Netscape Logo is a trademark of Netscape Communications, Inc."
}
DEF BackgroundImage Info{
string "Starbak2.bmp"
}
#Setup camera
PerspectiveCamera {
position 0 -150 110
orientation 1 0 0 1.57 #4.712389
focalDistance 5
heightAngle .5
#farDistance 1300
For Help, press F1
NUM

Fig. 17.7
VRML "worlds" are defined by VRML source code as shown here.

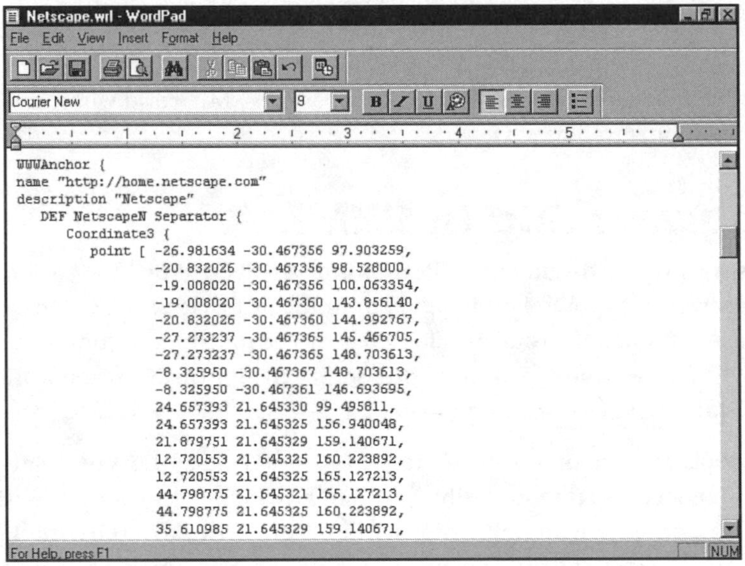
Netscape.wrl - WordPad
File Edit View Insert Format Help
Courier New
WWWAnchor {
name "http://home.netscape.com"
description "Netscape"
DEF NetscapeN Separator {
Coordinate3 {
point [-26.981634 -30.467356 97.903259,
-20.832026 -30.467356 98.528000,
-19.008020 -30.467356 100.063354,
-19.008020 -30.467360 143.856140,
-20.832026 -30.467360 144.992767,
-27.273237 -30.467365 145.466705,
-27.273237 -30.467365 148.703613,
-8.325950 -30.467367 148.703613,
-8.325950 -30.467361 146.693695,
24.657393 21.645330 99.495811,
24.657393 21.645325 156.940048,
21.879751 21.645329 159.140671,
12.720553 21.645325 160.223892,
12.720553 21.645325 165.127213,
44.798775 21.645321 165.127213,
44.798775 21.645325 160.223892,
35.610985 21.645329 159.140671,
For Help, press F1
NUM

Fig. 17.8
VRML 3-D objects, such as the Netscape "N," are defined by the coordinates of the lines that make up the object.

To be able to create VRML worlds, you need to use a VRML authoring tool for creating VRML 3-D objects and building them into a world. Libraries of VRML objects are also available on the Internet.

VRML Tools

A variety of tools for viewing and creating VRML worlds—freeware, shareware, and commercial—has begun to appear. Because of the relative infancy of the VRML version 1.0 standard, most of these products are still in the beta test stage and are available for at least trial use through the Internet. VRML tools are primarily being developed for two platforms: Windows (3.1, Windows for Workgroups, 95, and NT) and UNIX (primarily SGI and Sun) machines.

VRML Browsers

The following are some of the VRML browsers currently available, along with the platform for which they are made, and where on the WWW to look for more information:

- **WebFX**: This VRML browser is a plug-in module for Netscape Navigator that allows it to act as an integrated part of Netscape. Paper Software, the maker of WebFX, is also planning to release a product called WebFX Explorer, which will be a stand-alone VRML browser. WebFX runs under any flavor of Windows.

    http://www.paperinc.com/webfx.html

- **Microsoft VRML Plug-In for Microsoft Internet Explorer**: This is Microsoft's VRML browser, meant to act as a plug-in specifically for its own Internet Explorer.

    http://www.microsoft.com/windows/ie/vrml.htm

- **SDSC Web View**: This VRML browser is available for the SGI and Sun UNIX platforms.

    http://www.sdsc.edu/EnablingTech/Visualization /vrml/webview.html

- **VR Scout**: This stand-alone VRML browser runs under Windows 3.1 and Windows 95.

    http://www.chaco.com/vrscout/

- **WebSpace Navigator**: This commercial product (available free for beta testing) is part of SGI's VRML WebSpace suite of programs.

    http://www.chaco.com/vrscout/

- **WorldView**: This product was the first Windows VRML browser. It can act as a stand-alone program or as a helper application.

    http://www.webmaster.com/vrml

Tip

The VRML Repository, whose URL is shown at the end of this chapter, is an excellent resource for finding the latest VRML tools and examples available.

VRML Authoring Tools

VRML worlds can be considerably more complex than HTML documents, which makes sense considering that they are three-dimensional models. A full discussion of creating VRML worlds would require a book in itself, but in this chapter you go over the types of tools that you are liable to require. Later in the chapter, you find a simple example of creating a VRML world using Fountain, by Caligari Software.

- **Object Editors**: To create a three-dimensional world, you need 3-D objects naturally. You can do this in several ways. The first is to create your own using a VRML object editor, which allows you to create a 3-D VRML object to be used in one or more VRML worlds.

- **Object Libraries**: Many of the 3-D objects you are likely to need— cubes, spheres, trees, and so on—have probably already been created by someone else. Libraries of VRML objects from which you can get these objects are available on the Internet.

- **Conversion Utilities**: A third way to produce 3-D VRML objects is to convert them from other programs and other formats. You can find utilities that will convert for several different kinds of 3-D objects.

- **VRML World Building Programs**: After you have assembled the objects you need, the final step—the real act of creating a VRML world—is to assemble them to make the world you envision. To create your world, you need a program that allows you to build a VRML world from component 3-D objects, embed the hypertext links and other information that you want to include, and write out the VRML source code.

Using WebFX, a VRML Plug-In for Netscape

To get a better feel for what using a VRML browser is like, you install and try out one of them, WebFX by Paper Software, in the following sections.

Installing WebFX

The version of WebFX used herein is the WebFX plug-in for Netscape Navigator 2. To install this plug-in, follow these steps:

1. Copy the file npwfx32e.exe from the CD into a temporary directory on your hard drive.

2. Run npwfx32e.exe. Running this executable gives the following files (if you have Windows Explorer set up to hide MS-DOS file extensions for registered file types, this list might look a little different, but the files will still be there):

   Setup.exe

   _setup.dll

   Setup.ins

   _setup.lib

   Setup.pkg

   Data.z

3. Run Setup.exe. If you installed Netscape Navigator 2 in the default location and want to do the same for WebFX, you can select the defaults for each entry in the WebFX setup process.

4. You should get a message similar to the one shown in figure 17.9, indicating a successful installation. WebFX is now installed as a Netscape Navigator plug-in module, and automatically runs when you encounter a VRML source file when using Netscape.

Caution

The WebFX plug-in is usually meant for a specific version of Netscape Navigator. Make sure you have compatible versions before installing or you may have unpredictable results.

III

Advanced HTML

Fig. 17.9
When WebFX
has successfully
installed, you get a
dialog box similar
to this one.
WebFX now
automatically runs
when a VRM
source file is
encountered when
using the Netscape
Navigator.

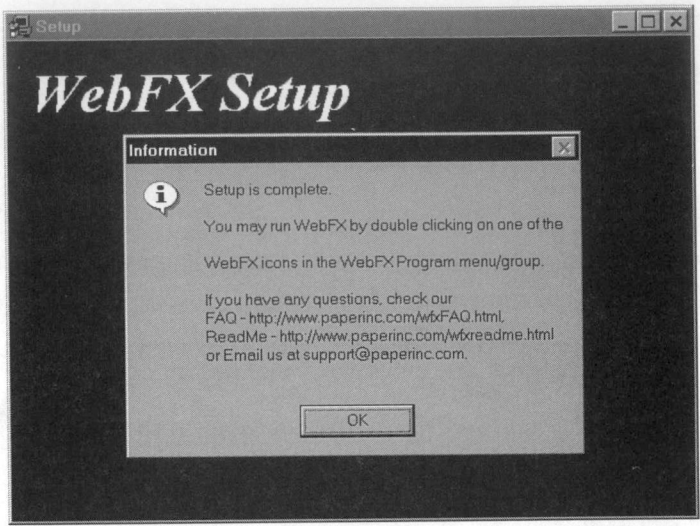

Navigating through a Virtual World Using WebFX

WebFX offers three different modes for navigating around and through a three-dimensional VRML world: *walk*, *fly*, and *point*. Other VRML browsers may have different means of navigation—the VRML source file defines the layout of the world, but the browser dictates how you travel through it.

Walk Mode

To get some help in remembering what actions work in each mode, click the ? (question mark) WebFX Navigation Bar button, which enables the Heads up display. If you then click the walk button, you have the following navigation options:

- **Left-drag** (clicking and holding the left mouse button while moving the cursor): Allows you to "walk," or move slowly, through the VRML world. The direction and speed of movement is dictated by the position of the cursor with respect to the destination point, which is set by using a double-click. When the cursor is to the left or right of the destination point, you move in that direction. When it is above or below the destination point, you move forward or backward, respectively.

- **Double-click** (rapidly clicking the left mouse button twice): Sets a destination point to go to. If the crosshairs are enabled in the Heads up display, they appear at the destination point.

- **Right-drag**: Causes the entire VRML world to "orbit" about your current position.

- **Alt**: Holding down the Alt key while using a left-drag allows you to "slide" up or down when you move the cursor above or below the destination point instead of moving forward or backward.

- **Arrows**: The keyboard arrow keys act just as a left-drag of the mouse cursor does in the appropriate direction.

Fly Mode

When you place WebFX in fly mode, the mouse and keyboard actions change to the following:

- **Left-drag**: Allows you to fly through the VRML world, traveling in all three dimensions, unlike walking, which is normally restricted to two. The placement of the cursor with respect to the destination point causes your viewpoint to *pitch*, *roll*, and *yaw*, and change your direction of travel.

- **Right-drag**: Causes the entire VRML world to "orbit" about your current position, just as in walk mode.

- **Arrows**: The keyboard arrow keys act just as a left-drag of the mouse cursor does in the appropriate direction.

- **A/Z**: Pressing and holding down the A or Z key allows you to thrust forward or backward, respectively, through the VRML world.

Point Mode

The last navigation mode of WebFX, point mode, allows you to navigate the VRML worlds as follows:

- **Left-click**: Moves you toward the VRML object upon which the cursor is positioned.

- **Left-drag**: Although this action is not defined in the Heads up display, you can use it in this mode; it performs the same function as in walk mode. The only difference is that your destination point is defined by wherever you first click the cursor, as opposed to the double-click method used in walk mode.

- **Double-click**: Moves you toward the VRML object upon which the cursor is positioned, and if that point is also a hypertext link, it causes Netscape Navigator and/or WebFX to jump to it.

- **Right-drag**: Causes the entire VRML world to "orbit" about your current position, just as in walk and fly modes.

III

Advanced HTML

- **Alt**: Holding down the Alt key while using a left-drag allows you to "slide" up or down when you move the cursor above or below the destination point instead of moving forward or backward, just as in walk mode.
- **Arrows**: The keyboard arrow keys act just as a left-drag of the mouse cursor does in the appropriate direction.

Troubleshooting

I've loaded a VRML world, and I can't see anything! What should I do?

Sometimes the initial viewpoint for a VRML world is poorly chosen, or you may have navigated yourself around until you are lost. In this case, the best way to try to find your way, in any navigation mode, is to do a right-drag, holding down the right mouse button and moving the pointer around to rotate the entire VRML world. Usually, you will be able to get the actual objects into view this way, and you can then use the navigation means discussed above to move in closer.

Configuring WebFX

WebFX allows you to customize its behavior in several different ways. This customization is achieved using a pop-up menu and submenus that first appear when you right-click. The main pop-up window shown in figure 17.10 then appears.

Fig. 17.10
Right-clicking in the VRML screen opens a pop-up menu that you can use to configure WebFX. The Entry View selection under the ViewPoints submenu returns you to where you entered the VRML world.

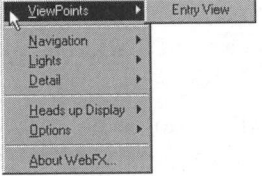

Each of the six entries shown in the main pop-up window gives you different options for customizing WebFX. The following describes the most important submenus, but you should feel free to experiment with these and the other options to get a feeling for what you can do with WebFX.

- **ViewPoints**: In a VRML world, you can easily get lost, especially when you're just learning your way around. The Entry View selection in this submenu allows you to move quickly back to the point at which you entered the VRML world (see fig. 17.10).

- **Detail**: Once a VRML world has been downloaded to your computer, the navigation through that world is handled locally. Because VRML worlds can be quite complex, this process is sometimes kind of slow, particularly on older computers. If you find this to be the case on your computer, you can adjust the level of detail by using this submenu. By switching from Solid to Wireframe or Point Cloud, you decrease the complexity of the image and may improve the response time (see fig. 17.11).

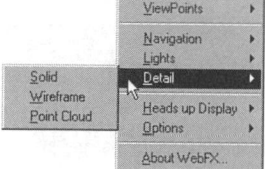

Fig. 17.11
WebFX allows you to control how much detail is shown in the three-dimensional image.

Tip

If you are using a slower computer, you can improve the performance of WebFX by changing the amount of detail that is shown.

- **Heads up Display**: The entries in this submenu dictate what information is shown on the WebFX Heads up display when it is enabled (see fig. 17.12).

III

Advanced HTML

Fig. 17.12
The Heads up
Display submenu
allows you to
control what
information is
shown in the
WebFX Heads up
display.

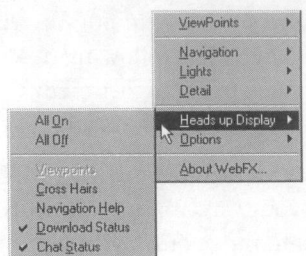

Example VRML World on the World Wide Web

In this section, you examine an example VRML world I found while surfing
the Internet. It is a good example of an achievement with VRML worlds that
might not be as effective with a standard HTML Web page. It also demonstrates how these two types of documents—representing two ways of presenting information—can be effectively used in tandem.

Using Netscape Navigator 2 with the WebFX plug-in installed, I connected to
the following URL:

http://esewww.essex.ac.uk/campus-model.wrl

Note the .wrl extension, denoting a VRML world source document. After the
connection was made by Netscape, the WebFX plug-in was called, the VRML
world source was downloaded, and the image shown in figure 17.13 appeared. Although it isn't obvious, this figure shows the University of Essex
campus, as seen from a long way off.

Fig. 17.13
The entry point to
the University of
Essex VRML
world.

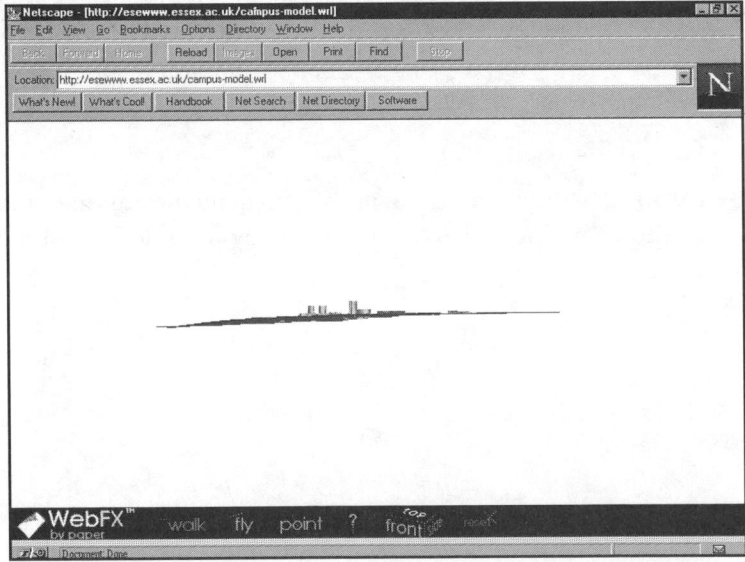

To get a closer look, put your WebFX in fly mode and fly in toward the VRML world. Give yourself a little bit of altitude to be able to see more of the campus buildings. As you get closer, you'll see the campus layout shown in figure 17.14.

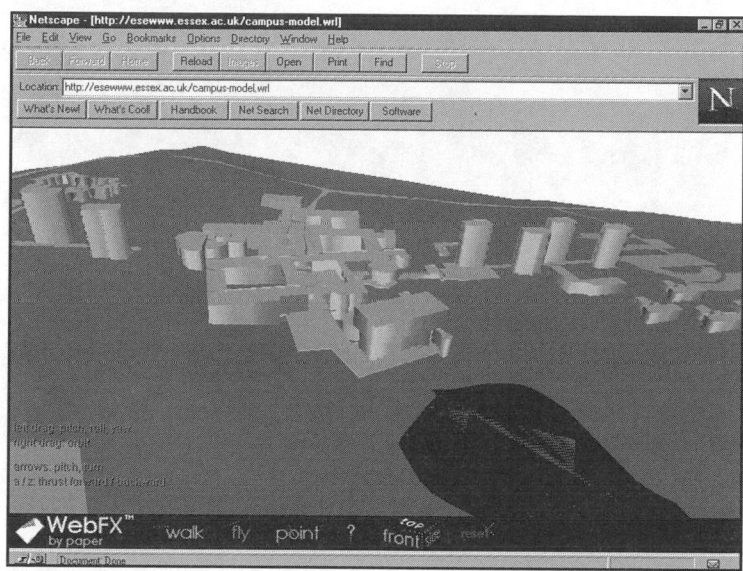

Fig. 17.14
You can fly in closer to the university and see a view of the campus.

As you learned earlier, VRML worlds and HTML documents can call one another interchangeably. The University of Essex site uses this capability to not only convey the three-dimensional layout of its campus, but also to allow visitors to learn more about the different campus facilities. Consider figure 17.15; I placed the cursor over a building that has a hypertext link, indicated by the presence of the hand pointer and the URL label in the upper-left corner of the screen. Apparently, this building is the University Library. When I double-clicked, an HTML web page was called (see fig. 17.16), giving information about the library.

Because the VRML world is a three-dimensional model, you can look at it from any angle, including from below (which isn't very helpful) and from above, as shown in figure 17.17, giving you a useful map of the University of Essex campus.

III

Advanced HTML

Fig. 17.15
By placing the pointer over a given building and clicking...

URL label

Hand pointer

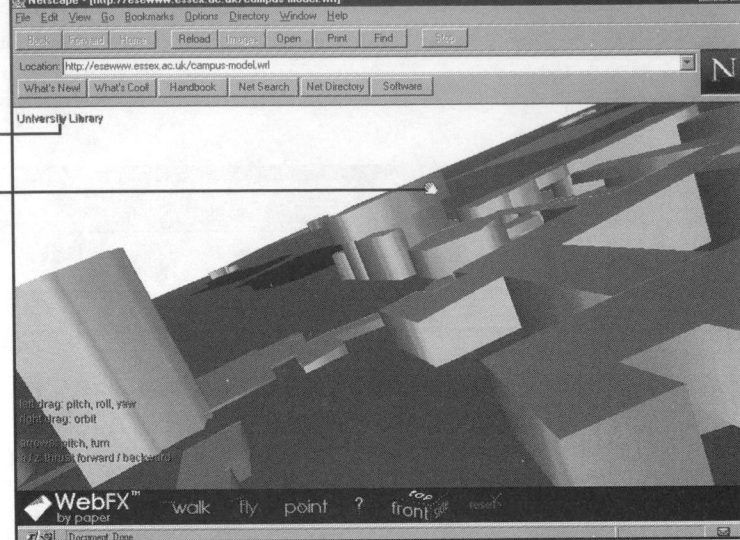

Fig. 17.16
...you can jump to an HTML document with information about it.

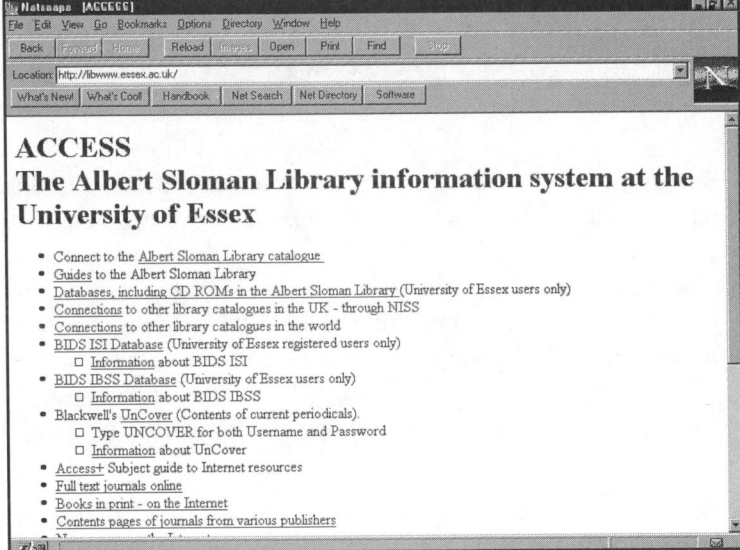

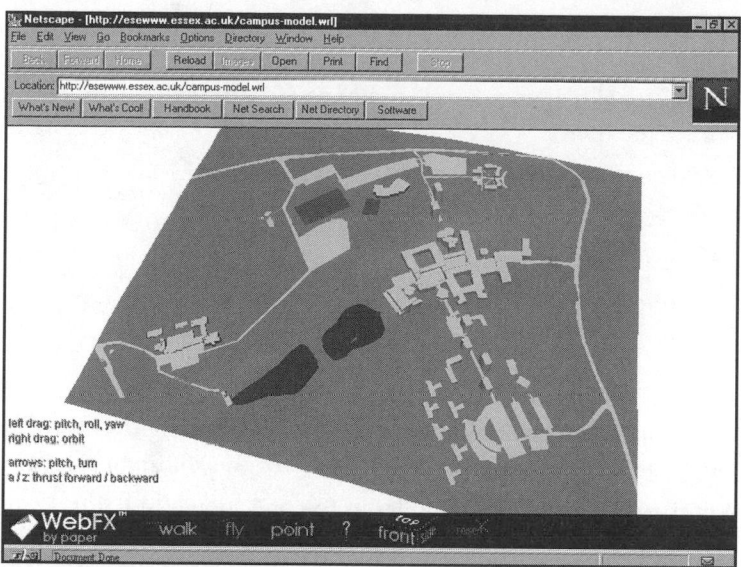

Fig. 17.17
You can even fly
up high enough
and look down to
get an aerial map
of the campus.

Authoring VRML Worlds Using Fountain

Discussing VRML authoring would take a whole book, but we'll take a quick look at what it would entail here. To do so, use Caligari Software's Fountain.

> **Note**
>
> Unless you do three-dimensional modeling for a living, you may find that creating VRML worlds is not the easiest thing in the world. To improve your productivity and the ease with which you arrive at your final product, it's probably a good idea to sketch out what you want your world to look like on paper before diving into Fountain or another VRML authoring program. See Que's *Special Edition Using VRML* book.

Installing Fountain

To install Fountain, follow these steps:

1. Copy the file Fountain.exe from the CD into a temporary directory on your hard drive.

On the CD

2. Run Fountain.exe. Running this executable gives you the following files (if you have Windows Explorer set up to hide MS-DOS file extensions for registered file types, this list might look a little different, but the files will still be there):

> Fountain.exe
>
> Setup.exe
>
> Install.ins
>
> Info.txt
>
> License.txt
>
> Fountain.z

3. Run Setup.exe. The installation process is fairly straightforward, and only requires you to decide where to install the Fountain software.

4. You should get a message similar to the one shown in figure 17.18, indicating a successful installation. Fountain is now installed on your computer. To use it, you should create a desktop shortcut icon for it, install it in the Start menu, or run it using the Run option of the Start menu.

Fig. 17.18
When Fountain has successfully installed, you get a dialog box similar to this one.

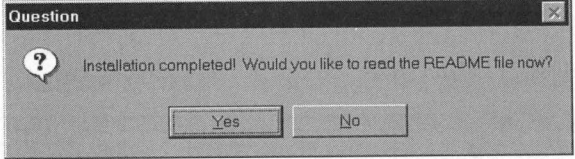

VRML Authoring Example Using Fountain

Now you're ready to create a simple VRML world using Fountain.

Simple Example with Hypertext Link

To create a simple world with one object and a hypertext link, follow these directions:

1. Start Fountain, and select File, Scene, New to create a new VRML world.

2. Select the Text Primitive button, and type some text. In figure 17.19, I typed my initials, JOD.

3. Select the Sweep button, which makes the selected object three-dimensional. By grabbing an edge of the text and dragging the cursor, you can extrude the object further, as shown in figure 17.20.

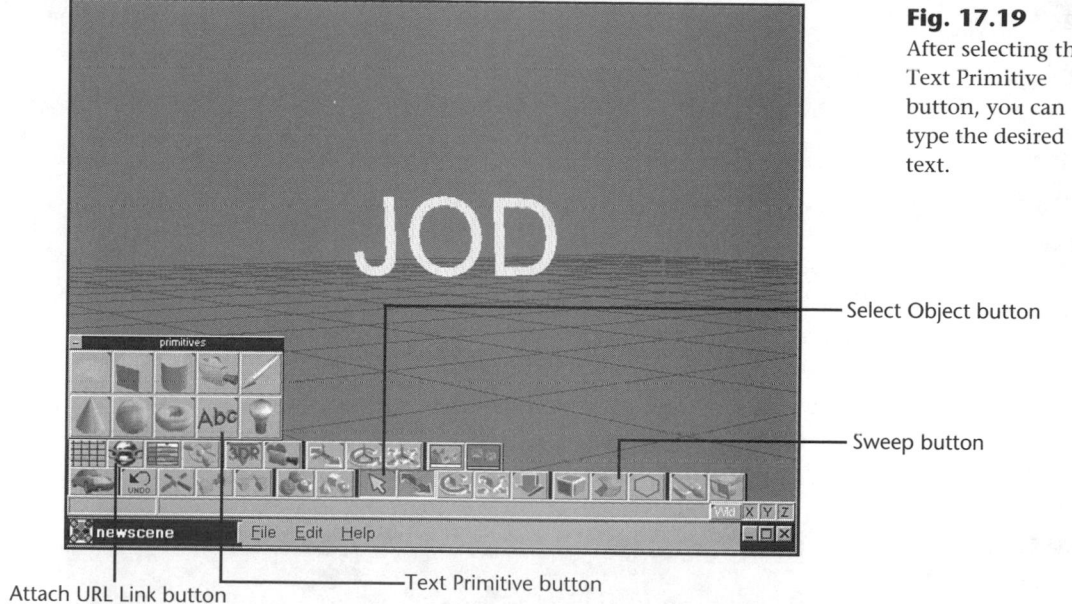

Fig. 17.19
After selecting the Text Primitive button, you can type the desired text.

— Select Object button

— Sweep button

Attach URL Link button

Text Primitive button

Fig. 17.20
With the text object selected, by selecting the Sweep button, you can make the text three-dimensional.

III

Advanced HTML

4. Select the Attach URL Link button so that you can add a hypertext link to the selected object (see fig. 17.21).

Fig. 17.21
You can attach an URL link to any VRML object. This link can point to an HTML document.

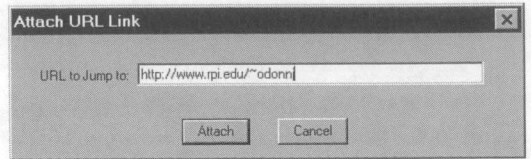

At this point, save the document by choosing File, Scene, Save. Use the file name jod.wrl. To see if you were successful, try to load this file using Netscape Navigator with the WebFX plug-in module installed. You then see the screen shown in figure 17.22. You can see that the hypertext link is there—when you move the cursor over the text object, it turns into a hand pointer and the URL label appears in the upper-left corner. Because this model is three-dimensional, you can navigate around, getting closer or farther away from the objects there, changing the viewpoint (see fig. 17.23).

Fig. 17.22
You can load my simple VRML world using Netscape Navigator and view it using the WebFX plug-in.

URL label ──

Hand pointer ──

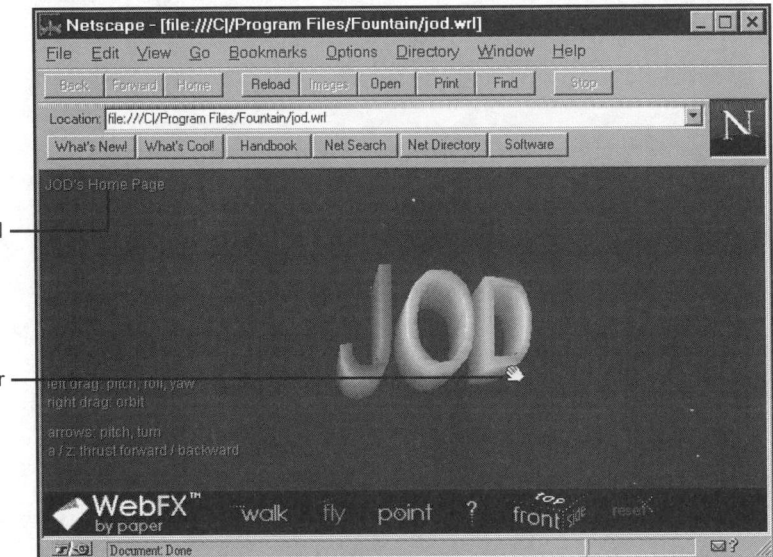

Another Example Using Multiple Objects

This example creates multiple objects and gives an idea of how to manipulate light sources and change the color of objects. In this one, we attempt to achieve a similar effect to the Netscape "N" world shown at the beginning of the chapter.

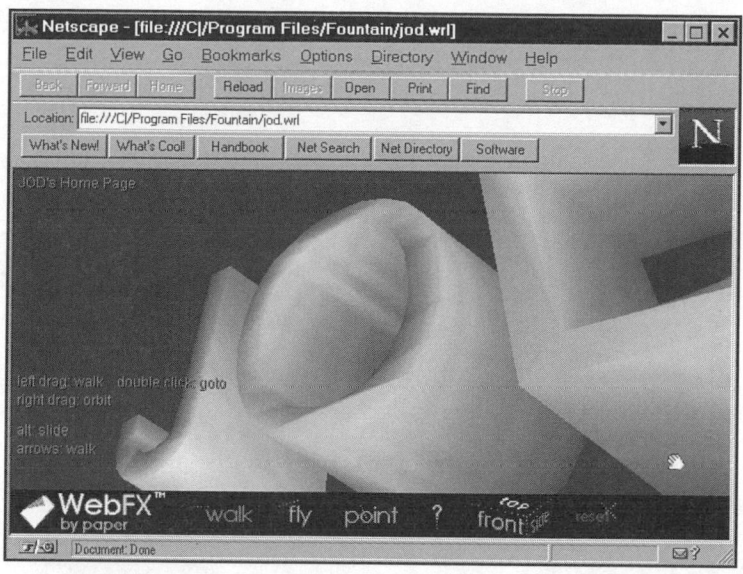

Fig. 17.23
Because this world is three-dimensional, you can move in and around the world's objects. If you click the JOD text object, the hypertext link takes you to my HTML home page.

1. Start Fountain, and select File, Scene, New to create a new VRML world. Start off by creating a sphere using the Sphere button in the Primitives panel (see fig. 17.24).

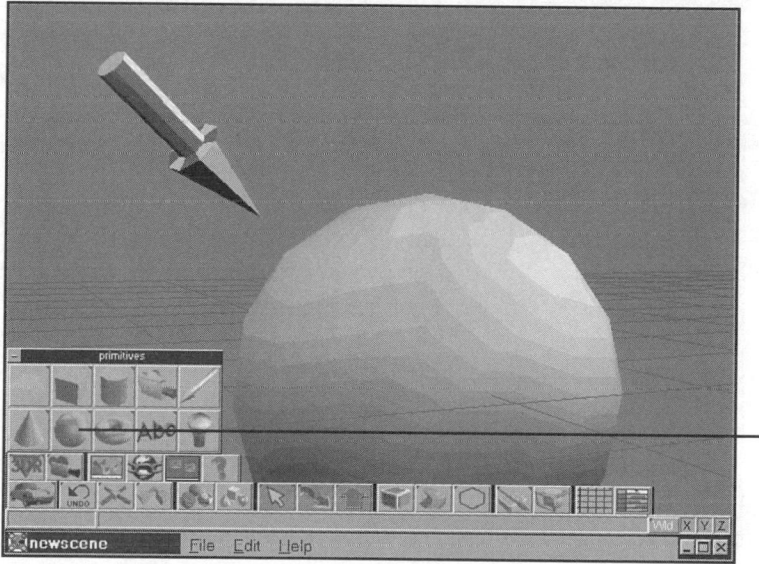

Fig. 17.24
First, you create a sphere to be your "world." The 3-D arrow points to the current object.

Sphere button

2. To create the "JOD" letters (instead of the Netscape "N"), first select the font by right-clicking the Text Primitives button, which will give you the font selection dialog box shown in figure 17.25.

Fig. 17.25
Right-clicking on the Text Primitives button allows you to pick your font and font size.

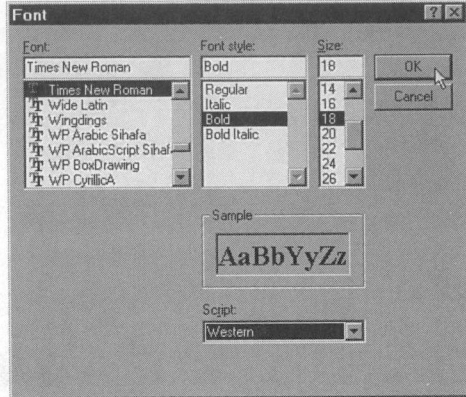

3. After selecting the font, left-click the Text Primitives button, left-click somewhere on the screen, and type the letters **JOD**. Then select the Sweep button to get three-dimensional letters (see fig. 17.26).

Fig. 17.26
After typing in the letters **JOD**, you can hit the Sweep button to create the 3-D look.

4. Now move the "JOD" on top of the sphere. To do this, select the Object
   Move button. Left-dragging moves objects right and left, or back and
   forth. Right-dragging moves them up and down. Figure 17.27 shows
   what it looks like after the "JOD" has been embedded in the top of the
   sphere.

Fig. 17.27
You can move the
JOD on top of your
"world," even
embedding it in
the top.

Object Move button

5. To change the color of an object, in this case the sphere, select the Paint
   Faces button, which gives the panels shown in figure 17.28. These panels give you the option of what color and shading to use when coloring
   an object.

6. Figure 17.29 shows the sphere after being colored blue. Now, to further
   manipulate the appearance of the world by creating and configuring a
   local light source, select the Local Light Source button from the Primitives panel. This gives the Lights panel shown in figure 17.29. The light
   source can be moved around just as any other object.

7. By moving the local light source above and in front of the letters and
   sphere, you can brighten its appearance (see fig. 17.30).

III

Advanced HTML

Fig. 17.28
The Paint Faces button brings up these panels, giving you options for what color and style to use to paint an object.

Paint Faces button

Fig. 17.29
After painting your world, you can adjust where and what color the light sources are.

Lights panel
Local Light Source button

Fig. 17.30
Moving the light
source in front of
your "world"
brightens its
appearance.

8. By selecting File, Scene, Save As, the VRML world can be saved, as
shown in figure 17.31.

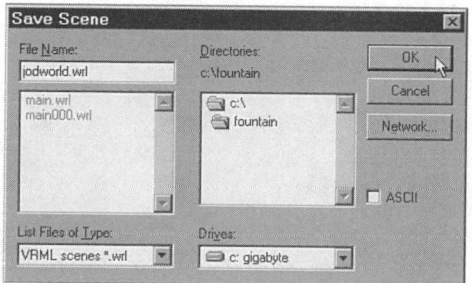

Fig. 17.31
You can save this
world as a WRL
file.

9. Your results can be viewed with any VRML-compatible browser. WebFX
displays it as shown in figure 17.32.

By navigating around this sample world, one of the hazards of working in
three dimensions becomes apparent. As shown in figure 17.33, you have to
remember to work with all sides of an object—when you are coloring objects,
for instance, be sure to get all sides!

III

Advanced HTML

Fig. 17.32
You can view this sample world using the WebFX plug-in for Netscape Navigator.

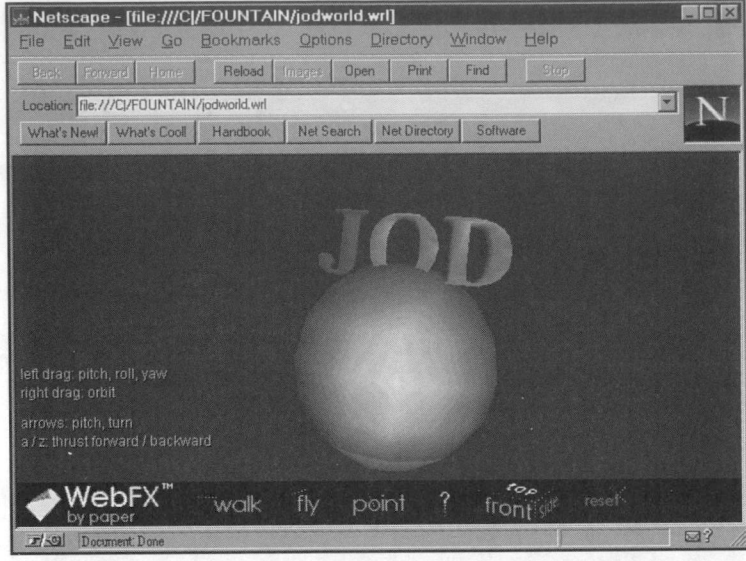

Fig. 17.33
You can see one of the effects of working in three dimensions— I didn't paint the back of my world!

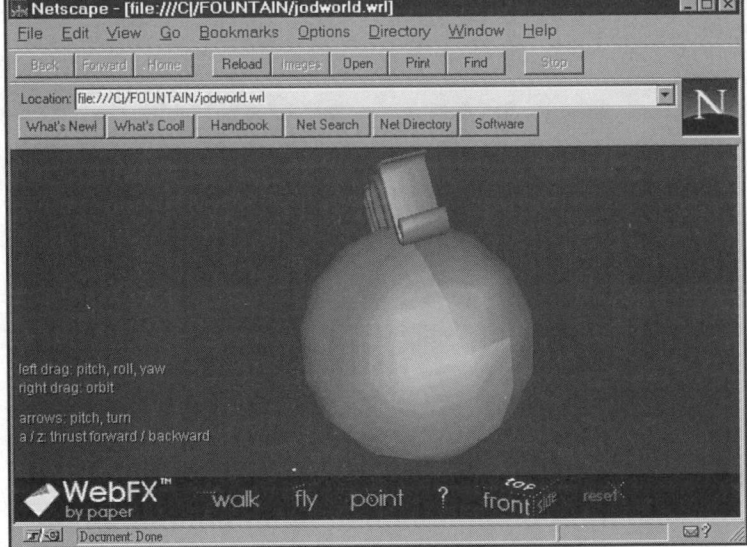

VRML Resources on the Internet

After you have your system set up to view VRML documents, you'll want to start cruising the Internet and the World Wide Web to see what VRML resources and worlds are available. The list is growing every day. Following are a few of the bigger sites that will direct you to many other VRML resources— browsers, authoring tools, worlds, and object libraries:

- The makers of WebFX maintain a directory of many VRML worlds located at

  **http://home.netscape.com/comprod/products/
  navigator/version_2.0/plugins/vrml_sites.html**

- A group called Mesh Mart also maintains a Web site of many VRML resources, including browsing and authoring tools and VRML worlds at

  http://cedar.cic.net/~rtilmann/mm/vrml.htm

- NCSA, the author of NCSA Mosaic, has a VRML Web page at

  http://www.ncsa.uiuc.edu/General/VRML/VRMLHome.html

- A repository of VRML information is maintained at

  http://rosebud.sdsc.edu/vrml/

- Wired has a VRML Forum at

  http://vrml.wired.com/

- Silicon Graphics is very active in VRML development. A site with information about its WebSpace products is located at

  http://webspace.sgi.com/

III

Advanced HTML

## CHAPTER 18

Multimedia and Animation on the Web

by John Jung

By now, you know how to create some nice-looking Web pages with some general HTML tags. But there's so much more you can do to get your point across on your Web page. Most people use pictures and lots of links, but you need something more. If you want your Web page to really stand out, you're going to need something that really gets a person's attention. You need multimedia. I'm not saying that multimedia is necessary for all Web pages; it does have its drawbacks.

If you want to know about multimedia and Web pages, you can find the answers in this chapter. You learn when you should and shouldn't use multimedia files and why multiple multimedia formats should be provided. And you also go through some of the more popular multimedia formats and learn how to view them.

In this chapter, you learn about the following:

- What multimedia is
- Informing users of multimedia files
- MPEG: The format and the players
- MOV: The format and the players
- AVI: The format and the players
- Real-time multimedia
- Embedded multimedia
- Programs to convert sound files
- Programs to convert multimedia files
- Finding sound and multimedia files

What Is Multimedia?

Multimedia is many things to many people. Unfortunately, no universally agreed upon definition of multimedia exists. Generally speaking, multimedia is a combination of sights and sounds. It can be pictures and words, words and sounds, or pictures and sounds or all three. Multimedia might not sound terribly difficult, after all, because TV and movies use it all the time. The difference is that with traditional forms of media, the images and sounds are in a physical form. When it comes to computers, multimedia can be a processor and disk- space intensive process. The results are astounding, but you get a payoff.

So what is multimedia, really? It's simply moving pictures and sounds. You don't necessarily need both components to have a multimedia file, although that would be nice. Each element of multimedia is often considered to be multimedia itself. That is, many people consider just playing sound files over the Net to be using multimedia. Similarly, they also feel that because they can see a movie using their computer, that movie is multimedia. By and large, whenever somebody mentions multimedia, he or she is talking about moving pictures, hearing sounds, or both. The fact that this process is accomplished using a computer is what's amazing to them.

The Sound Component

Computers that can play sounds are nothing new; they've been around for years. The problem was always getting a computer that had a speaker of reasonable quality. With improvements in computer technology, the sound quality has dramatically increased. Also, the fact that computer prices are now lower makes the use of sound-capable computers even more widespread.

All of this information is pretty unimpressive to many people who use computers. The truly impressive thing is that sound files can now be played over the Internet. This fact is significant because the capability to play sound overcomes a few of the shortcomings that exist on the Net. The first big obstacle was the desire to support the lowest common denominator. This always meant supporting generic text terminals with no graphics or sound. The second obstacle was the lack of demand for such features. The Net was originally made up of mainly programmers and engineers working from workstations. Workstations have little or no sound support, and what exists is not consistent across different platforms.

Sound Files

A number of sound file formats are in fairly wide use, such as Dialogic VOX, SoundBlaster VOC, and Amiga MOD. You can listen to most of them if you have the correct sound player utility. You must then use each of these players as a helper application for your browser.

Probably the most widely supported sound format is the WAV file format. This robust format allows you to encode stereo and mono sounds. You can also specify the degree with which to store the sounds. Most sound playing utilities support the WAV format without a problem.

Another popular sound format is the Audio IFF (AIFF), introduced by Apple. This was intended to be used as a means of storing high-quality sound and musical instrumentation. It's also been adopted by Silicon Graphics (SGI) in their workstations. This format has spawned the AIFF-C format, which is basically the AIFF format, except compressed. Aside from Apple and SGI, a handful of companies also support the AIFF format. Most sound players will have no problems supporting the AIFF format.

There is also the sound file format developed by Sun Microsystems and NeXT, the audio (AU) sound file. This is typically seen and supported the most in workstation environments. Also, some browsers will support the AU format without the need of getting an external program. Because of its strong workstation roots, many sound playing programs can handle AU files.

The Animation Component

Besides sound, another aspect of multimedia involves animation. Animation is, simply put, just a bunch of still pictures, one slightly different from another. This process is exactly how movies are shown, with each frame of the movie being played for a fraction of a second. When the frames are played backed at a certain rate, the frames show the animation. And in animation, just like movies, you don't necessarily need to have sounds. The silent films are still movies and considered multimedia even though they have no voices or sounds.

Animation Files

A number of attempts have been made to standardize the animation portion of multimedia. Often these formats were either too machine dependent or not robust enough, such as the GL, DL, and ANIM formats. The majority of these older animation formats basically took a bunch of pictures and strung them together. Almost none of them used any degree of sophistication to reduce the file size of the resulting movie. The most prevalent animation format in use is the MPEG format, which you learn about later in this chapter.

III

Advanced HTML

Letting People Know About Multimedia

Even though you might want to rush out and put multimedia files all over your Web page, don't. You should tell people what, when, and where certain multimedia files are located. Multimedia files should be a means of enhancing your Web pages, not replacing them. Don't include critical information that can be found only in the multimedia files.

Not Everybody Can Handle Multimedia

Multimedia files require fairly computer-intensive programs to view properly. Very few Web browsers provide support for multimedia files by themselves. As a result, most of the time you must configure your browser to run programs capable of showing multimedia files. Getting multimedia viewers is no trivial task, which means most people's computers don't automatically support multimedia files. Because of the work required for making a browser multimedia-capable, you should always warn people where you have multimedia files (see fig. 18.1).

Fig. 18.1
Letting people know where multimedia files are located is always a good idea.

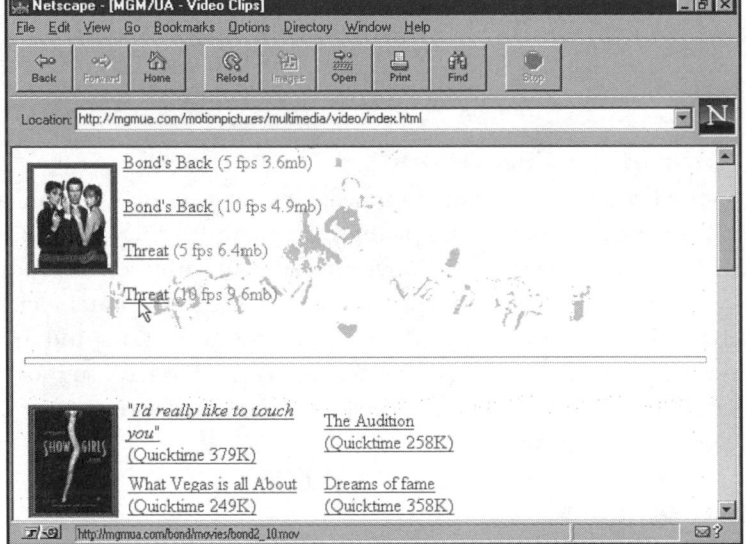

Letting the Users Decide When to See Multimedia

Another good idea is to not force multimedia files onto users. Although you can have sound files play as soon as a user accesses a page, that's not a good idea. The file has to be downloaded from the Web server to the person's computer. After that, the user has to wait for the sound player to start up and play the sound file. Although this process might be fast and unnoticeable for people with high-powered machines directly on the Net, most people don't have setups like that. Most people accessing the Net are doing it from modems, and they have to wait to get your files.

Putting in automatic multimedia files simply wastes users' time and detracts from their enjoyment of your home page.

Making Multiple Formats Available

A large number of computers can access your Web page, and most of them have their own particular brand of multimedia file formats. You should not make a multimedia file available in only one format. Cover your bases and convert (or redo) your multimedia file into multiple formats (see fig. 18.2). This way, you can make your pages more accessible to the typical users and make them more interested in coming back.

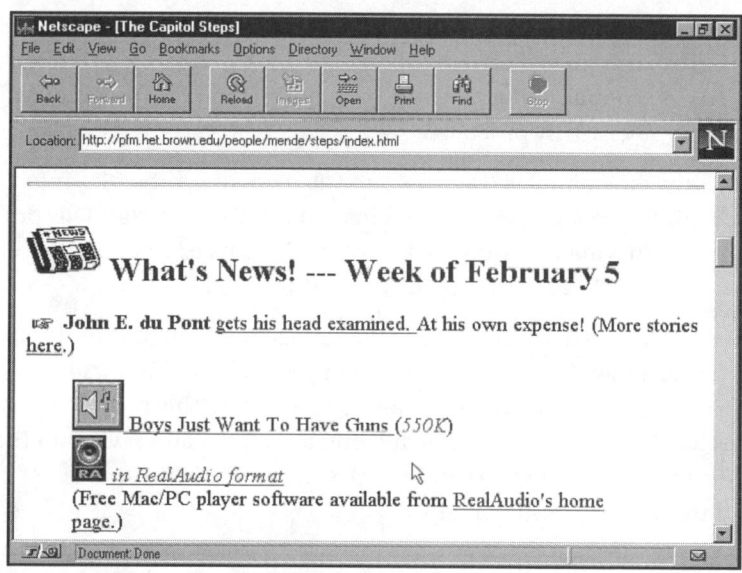

Fig. 18.2
Convert your multimedia file into as many different formats as possible. The more formats you have, the more people you attract.

Different Files, Same Content

When you're making multiple file formats available, try to make the multimedia files in the different formats show the same thing although doing so might take a lot of work. Don't leave the sound out of one of the formats just because including it is a lot of work. You can use any of a number of multimedia converters (which are covered later in this chapter) for different computers.

III

Advanced HTML

Some converters convert all aspects of a multimedia file, whereas others won't. If necessary, don't be afraid to re-record your multimedia file through a different interpreter for a different format. This process may be time-consuming, but the users will appreciate the work. Re-recording is especially important for people running commercial Web sites.

> **Note**
>
> Obviously, re-recording multimedia files into different formats is a big undertaking. As a result, only companies running commercial Web sites should do it.

Different Computers, Same File

Another aspect of making your multimedia files available to everybody is the format in which they're stored. I'm not talking about multimedia file formats, but the format in which the data is stored.

On Windows 95 and UNIX machines, files are stored in a particular fashion. On Macintosh computers, certain aspects of a file can be stored differently. Because of this format, some Mac files (of any sort) can't be properly read by Windows 95 or UNIX programs.

Typically, the programmers leave it up to the users to get the files into a format recognizable to a particular program on a certain machine. This process often involves having the users get a Mac-to-PC conversion program, putting the file on a PC disk, and reading the data off that disk.

Because the Mac has a slightly quirky file storage method, Mac multimedia people found a way around this conversion process. They allow some multimedia formats to be stored in only one manner. This process basically involves loading a Mac multimedia file into a program and saving all the data into a file that everybody else can read. Any multimedia file that goes through this process is "flattened."

> **Note**
>
> Currently, you can flatten only Apple MOV files on the Mac. Unfortunately, you must have the complete QuickTime developer's package to be able to flatten MOVs.

In contrast, the files stored on Windows 95 and UNIX machines can be read by Mac multimedia players without being flattened. Other multimedia file formats don't have this problem because they were designed with either Windows 95 or UNIX in mind.

> **Note**
>
> There are two attributes to any files stored on a Macintosh. These two attributes are known as the "resource fork" and the "data fork." Every file on a Mac disk has these attributes, but it isn't necessary to use both of them. Unfortunately, no other popular computers support the resource and data forks. As a result, when you try to copy a file from a Mac to a PC, resource and data forks are squished together. This is bad.
>
> A "flattened" MOV file is one in which all the MOV data is stored in one fork. Flattening MOVs is essential if you want your animation files to be seen by everybody. For obvious reasons, you can only flatten an MOV file while using a Mac.

Size Considerations

Another major concern in using multimedia files in your Web page is that you should look out for is the size of the multimedia file. Because multimedia formats can have animation and sound, they can be quite big. Therefore, always telling people how big your multimedia files are is a good idea. This way, you can let people know about how long they have to wait before they can see what you have on the page. Remember that the majority of people accessing Web sites are doing so from the comfort of their homes. Many large multimedia files will take well over five minutes to download on a typical system.

Just How Big Is Too Big?

Giving exact numbers on when a file becomes too big to be useful for a home page is very difficult. You should always consider your target audience before you include any multimedia files on your Web page. Most company and personal home pages try to attract everybody on the Net. Because of the different file formats, giving a good estimate for a file size is also difficult. Also, because there are so many possible system configurations, the same file won't necessarily play at the same rate on all systems.

If you're determined to have multimedia files in your home page, then make sure the file is about 300K in size. This size gives you about 10–15 seconds of animation without sound. Include sound, and you'll halve the amount of time to 5–7 seconds. Also, a typical 300K multimedia file can be transferred in 2–3 minutes. If the size seems a bit small, that's the point. You can't have large multimedia files that aren't intrusive to a significant portion of people on the Net. You need to use small multimedia files for points you really want to emphasize.

III

Advanced HTML

If you're interested in making multimedia files only for those users who are truly interested in your topic, then you have no restrictions. Because these people are already interested in seeing what you have, they'll wait for the download to complete. Just be sure to tell everybody how big your files are so that people with slow connections don't get upset at how long it takes to get the files.

File Compression

Should you compress files? This question is also tough to answer because whether you compress files depends on how much you want to emphasize multimedia. If you have large multimedia files available for users truly interested in a topic, file compression is always available.

Some file formats compress better than others, but typically you get a 1–30 percent smaller file. Compressing allows you to cram in an extra few seconds of multimedia. The trade-off here is that the users typically have to decompress the files on their end.

File compression is the single biggest reason that home pages cannot have integrated multimedia. Most browsers are smart enough to run a downloaded file automatically through a particular application. However, they aren't smart enough to run the resulting file through two applications. This means that if you have multimedia as an integral part of your home page, you can't compress the files.

If you choose to compress your multimedia file, you should use popular compression software. For Windows 95 users, that means you should use ZIP, by PKWare, to compress your files. ZIP offers good, but not the best, compression available and is the most popular format. Mac users should use StuffIt, or one of its many derivations, by Aladdin Software. Again, it's a very popular program that offers good compression rates. Both these programs are widely available on many FTP sites.

MPEG: What It Is and How to See It

One of the most popular multimedia formats is MPEG. Numerous MPEG viewers are available for Windows 95 and the Macintosh. There are also a handful of UNIX MPEG players, typically requiring you to compile it yourself. Most MPEG animation files are either silent or have an accompanying sound file. Very few MPEG files on the Net have sound embedded within the animation files themselves.

MPEG is perhaps the safest multimedia file format you can use for your home page. It has the widest support of all multimedia formats on all platforms—not just in software but in hardware as well. Most new video cards released have built-in MPEG support. And if that weren't enough, MPEG files are almost always smaller than any other multimedia format.

Overview of MPEG

MPEG got its name from its creators, the Moving Pictures Experts Group. This group defined a method of storing animation and sound files efficiently. Their first attempt at this standard resulted in what is known as MPEG 1 (more commonly called MPEG). The target audience for the MPEG 1 standard is the casual computer user playing animation files over a CD-ROM. Since that time, the group has improved MPEG by making it more efficient and improving its quality. Its next upgrade of MPEG 1 resulted in MPEG 2, which is targeted for the broadcast market. MPEG 3 was intended to be a modification of MPEG to be aimed at the HDTV (High Definition TV) market. It was abandoned when it was discovered that MPEG 2 could be slightly altered to meet that need. The latest modification to MPEG is the MPEG 4 format and is being targeted for the fiber-optics market. It is still under discussion and is expected to be completed before the turn of the century. Most MPEG players currently in use can display only MPEG 1 files because very few people are interested in making MPEG 2 files.

The MPEG 1 standard involves encoding each frame of the MPEG file through a number of mathematical gymnastic feats. The audio and video frames of an MPEG file can each be encoded by three different methods. Rather than my explaining all the math involved, just be happy to know that the process is complicated. As a result, very few MPEG players can handle all aspects of the standard.

MPEG on Windows 95

A rather large number of MPEG players is available for Windows 95. The leader of this pack is VMPEG Lite by Stefan Eckhart. VMPEG can decode all MPEG 1 video frames and a limited number of audio frames. VMPEG is a native Windows 95 application, meaning that it's a 32-bit program. VMPEG Lite is a demonstration version and limits the amount of audio that can be played to 60 seconds. The full version of VMPEG has no such time limitation and includes video CD playback. When you first run VMPEG, a window with a menu and four VCR-like buttons shows up. Underneath this window is a separate window where the MPEG animation is shown (see fig. 18.3).

Fig. 18.3
VMPEG gives you two windows; one controls the output of the other.

The menu in the main window mainly consists of configuration of VMPEG. You can go to the Configure menu to configure each component of VMPEG playback. Under the Configure menu, the Audio menu item allows you to specify the sound output of MPEG files. Most of the sound configuration options should be obvious.

The video configuration for VMPEG is similarly straightforward. The four buttons in the main window allow you to play, stop, pause, and step to the next frame of the MPEG file. You can get VMPEG Lite from the following:

> **ftp://ftp.netcom.com/cf/cfogg/vmpeg/vmpeg17.exe**

MPEG on Macintosh

Macintosh users can also view MPEG files with a very good viewer, Sparkle by Maynard Handley. This program runs under System 7.0 or later and offers you the ability to read and play back most MPEG 1 files. Simply run BinHex and StuffIt to decompress the file into its own directory, and then double-click the Sparkle icon. The result is shown as in figure 18.4.

After a file has been loaded, you can play the file by clicking the Play button in the lower-left corner. You can also drag the scroll box at the bottom to anywhere in the MPEG file. The two buttons in the lower-right corner allow you to go forward and backward one frame at a time. Sparkle offers no configuration options and no sound support.

You can get a copy of Sparkle in BinHex at the following:

> **ftp://wuarchive.wustl.edu/system/mac/info-mac/gst/mov/sparkle-25.hqx**

Fig. 18.4
Sparkle is a good
MPEG player for
the Mac.

Creating MPEGs

Since MPEG was first introduced, there haven't been a lot of MPEG creation
utilities. This is because MPEG was designed to encode broadcast television
signals. As a result, the most common place you'll find MPEG encoders is
with specialized video cards. These cards allow your computer to accept
television signals and play them on your monitor. Most of these video cards
have software that lets you save a captured sequence from the television as an
MPEG file.

QuickTime MOVies

Apple has its own standard for storing multimedia files; it is known as
QuickTime Movies. The standard was designed with the Apple Macintosh
line of computers in mind. It has since migrated to other computers, most
notably Windows 95. As mentioned before, MOV files can be correctly
viewed on computers other than the Mac if the files have been "flattened."
Apple also provides a fair amount of support for people wanting to develop
MOV applications.

Watching MOVs on the Mac

Because MOV was designed by Apple, several viewers for the Macintosh are
available. Despite this wide variety of MOV players, however, the best one is,
logically, from Apple itself. Movie Player implements all aspects of the MOV
standard.

III

Advanced HTML

To play an MOV file using Movie Player, you simply choose File, Open. The first frame of the movie shows up in a window with some control buttons (see fig. 18.5). You can adjust the volume of the playback using the lower-left button (it looks like a speaker). Next to this button is one that starts the playback process. As the movie is playing, this button turns into a pause button, which you can use to stop the animation. Also while the movie is playing, the slider moves across the play bar's region. If you paused the playback of the movie, you can drag the slider around, and the window updates to that portion of the animation. You can resize the Move Player playback window by clicking and dragging the lower-right button.

Fig. 18.5
A great QuickTime MOVie player is Movie Player by Apple.

Watching MOVs on Windows 95

Playing QuickTime MOVs using Windows 95 is just as simple as it is on the Mac because Apple has faithfully ported their MOV animation player, Movie Player. The interface, menus, and behavior are all the same with the Windows 95 version as they are with the Mac version (see fig. 18.6). Some minor features aren't present in the Windows 95 version, but most users won't notice their absence. Because this version isn't on the Mac, it can play only QuickTime movies that have been flattened. You can get the QuickTime movie player by going to **http://quicktime.apple.com/form-qt2win.html**.

Making Your Own MOVies

Because of the way QuickTime was designed, you can create your own QuickTime movie relatively easily. The first thing you need to create your own animation is to have the images of each frame in PICT format. You also need an MOV creation program for the Mac, such as MooVer. To create an MOV file, you must first have all the frames of the QuickTime movie stored in Apple PICT format. Next, you highlight all the frames you want to make into an MOV file. Now, with all the frames selected, drag all of them onto the MooVer program icon.

After you've done this, you will be presented with a dialog box asking you for some settings. Simply click the ones you want your destination MOV to have and click the OK button. Next, you'll be shown another dialog box (see fig. 18.7) to help you control the quality of the MOV. By default, MooVer will create a QuickTime file of Medium quality. The higher and better the quality, the larger your MOV file will be. You can also specify how many frames should be shown per second. The more frames you want shown each second, the smoother the QuickTime movie.

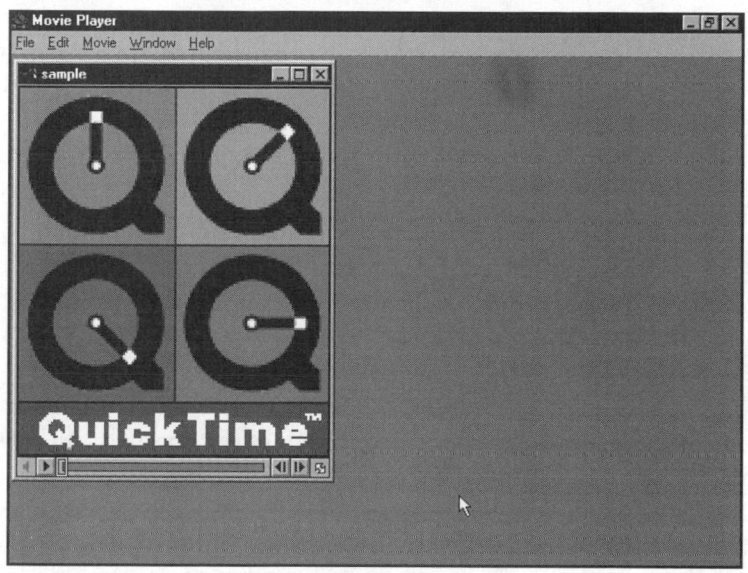

Fig. 18.6
QuickTime for Windows is a faithful port for Windows 95 of Movie Player for the Mac.

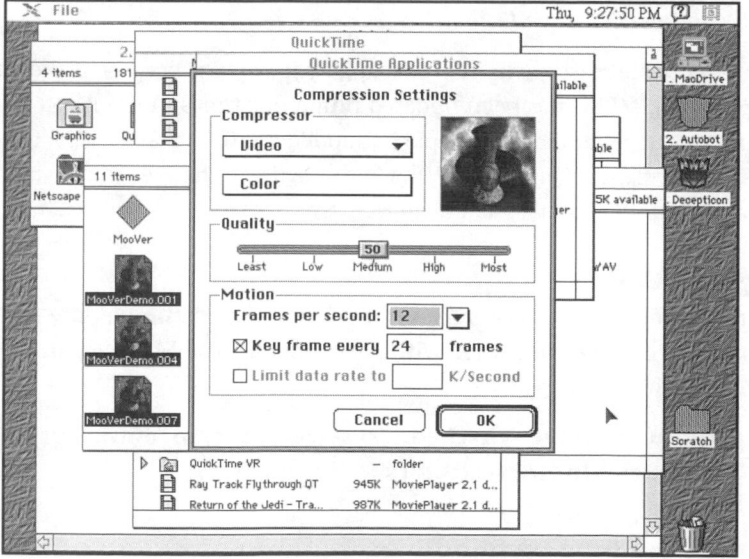

Fig. 18.7
When you create a QuickTime MOVie with MooVer, you have to specify a few attributes.

III

Advanced HTML

If you have a digital camera, you can also create MOV files. A digital camera is a hardware device that automatically digitizes whatever is in front of it. Most digital cameras come with software that enables you to use the digital camera as a digital camcorder. Simply have the software record whatever the digital camera sees and store it as an MOV file.

All About AVI

Another format for multimedia files is the Intel Indeo format, more commonly known as AVI. This format was designed by Intel, the maker of most CPUs in personal computers. The specifications for AVI files are well documented by Intel. However, Intel has left the implementation of its standard up to others. The platform that supports AVI the most is the Windows 95 operating system. In Windows 95, all you need to do is install the Media Player, and you'll have AVI support. Despite this wide userbase, AVI hasn't received as much support outside of the Windows 95 market as other platforms. You should consider using AVI multimedia files only if you expect a large number of Windows 95 users to access your home page.

What Went Wrong?

There are a number of reasons why AVI didn't take off until recently. Its distributed nature, in which one company defines the standard and others interpret it, didn't help. Instead of going to one company for questions about the format, the average developer had to go to two. Another reason for AVI's initially lukewarm reception is that the companies who were supposed to push it didn't. In the beginning, Microsoft and IBM were the two biggest supporters of AVI. However there was little mention or support for AVI in either Windows 3.1 or OS/2.

Another possible reason why AVI was largely ignored is because it didn't change much. MPEG has been updated numerous times in the last few years for different target audiences. Apple has added a virtual reality aspect to QuickTime, creating QuickTime VR. Compare these changes to the mostly unchanged, until recently, AVI format.

Playing AVIs

Because Windows 95 supports AVIs natively (see fig. 18.8), the only other major platform to be concerned with is Macintosh. The Mac version is available at the following:

> **ftp://wuarchive.wustl.edu/systems/mac/info-mac/gst/mov/ video-for-windows-11p.hqx**

Simply download the file and decompress it into its own folder using BinHex and StuffIt. No installation is required, so you can simply double-click the corresponding icon.

AVI's Comeback?

Whatever AVI's past, however, its future seems bright. It is now more heavily emphasized and supported by more companies than it has been in the past. This is partly due to Microsoft's desperate attempt to catch up in the Internet browser market. Here, Microsoft introduced their Web browser, Internet Explorer, in the largely Netscape-dominated market. Along with introducing some minor new HTML extensions, the browser also provides native multimedia support. The support is provided by allowing the browser to play AVI files without needing an external program.

Another factor that is helping AVI make a comeback is digital cameras. Most digital cameras allow the user to have real-time video capture in the computer. That is, the digital camera will automatically digitize and store an image of whatever is in front of its lens. Most digital cameras allow you to save these sequences of images as animation files. Typically you can save one of these animation files as an AVI file.

Creating Your Own AVI File

Because of AVI's long neglected past, there aren't many software-based programs to help you create them. However, if you have a digital camera, chances are very good that it will come with such software. These types of programs will continually read in the data from the digital camera and store it as an AVI file. For those people who don't have such a device, your best bet is to convert an existing file to AVI format.

III

Advanced HTML

Real-Time Sound

Generally speaking, most people make multimedia files available just like other files. That is, people browsing the Web must download the files and then use helper applications to play them. This approach, however, isn't always the best way to get your point across to people. Another method is to have the multimedia file play directly over the Net. That is, as the data is received from the remote host, it plays through an application. One such real-time multimedia application is RealAudio.

What Is RealAudio?

RealAudio is a generic Web browser helper application, created by Progressive Networks. This add-on allows you to play sound files in real time. When you click a RealAudio sound file from your browser, it starts the RealAudio program. This application takes the URL from your Web browser and retrieves the sound file over the Net. As the data is received from the remote host, it's instantly played by RealAudio.

Because RealAudio requires its own server, it's not something many people want or can use. More often than not, RealAudio is supported by sound-related companies. They typically include radio stations and music companies. Many of these entities make samples of their format or their artists available in RealAudio format.

What's So Great About RealAudio?

You may be interested in RealAudio if you're running a corporate Web site. This application takes the burden of sound playing off Netscape. Whereas Netscape has to download the file and have a helper application play it, not so with RealAudio. Netscape passes the sound-playing responsibility to RealAudio. This means that while the sound file is being played, you can continue to use Netscape.

How Can I Support RealAudio?

Unfortunately, because RealAudio delivers sound files in real time, you need to modify the server. You don't have to replace it, just add on to it. The RealAudio server works with any Web server that supports configurable MIME types. Most server software falls into this category, but a complete list is available from RealAudio at the following:

http://www.realaudio.com/products/server/software.html

Also, because the sounds are sent in real time, the sound files must be converted. The conversion program automatically converts most common sound formats into the RealAudio format. The biggest drawback is that the file conversion is slow. If you want to convert a sound file that takes 20 minutes to play, on a fast computer the file takes 20 minutes to convert. Converting sound files on slower machines can take up to twice as long.

How Do I Get RealAudio?

Because Progressive Network is so protective of its invention, they want to know who's getting it. As a result, you need to point your Web browser to the following:

http://www.realaudio.com/products/player.html

Just fill out the forms on the page, making sure to fill in all the requested information. If you don't have a particular bit of information they want, such as company name, just put anything in. After you've filled out the form, you can download the RealAudio player.

The RealAudio player that you download is a self-extracting archive file. All you have to do is double-click the file, and its installation program automatically starts up for you. You specify which components of RealAudio you want to install, as well as the destination directory.

Then, any time you're in Netscape and click a hyperlink that points to a RealAudio file, the player runs, as shown in figure 18.9. The player gets the URL from Netscape, gets the sound file itself, and plays it for you. This way, you can continue using Netscape while the sound file is being played.

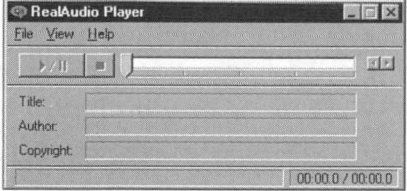

Fig. 18.9
RealAudio's sound player is automatically activated when you click a sound file from a Web page.

> **Caution**
>
> The biggest drawback to using RealAudio is that it currently works best over 28.8 kbps modems. Although RealAudio can work over 14.4 kbps modems, most RealAudio servers are going the 28.8 route. That means that people either need to have a really fast modem or a direct connection to the Net to fully appreciate RealAudio. Anything less than a 28.8 modem results in poor sound quality.

Putting RealAudio in Your Home Page

As complicated as using RealAudio may sound, putting it in your Web page is easy. All you really have to do is create a hyperlink that people can click to access the sound file. Instead of putting in an anchor reference that points to an image, for instance, just have it point to the sound file. A typical example of supporting RealAudio is

```
Hear my <A HREF="myvoice.ram">voice</A>.
```

◀ See chapter 15 for more information about "plug-ins."

This line creates a hypertext link with the word "voice" to the RealAudio sound file. When a user with the RealAudio plug-in clicks the link, the URL is passed onto the RealAudio player. The player then gets the sound file directly from your Web server and plays it back in real time.

Multimedia in Your Home Page

One of the most impressive things you can do with your home page is to access interactive multimedia files. As complicated as this process may sound, it's not really that hard. You can use a new Netscape plug-in from Macromedia; it's called Shockwave. Shockwave plays multimedia files created with Macromedia's Director program. Currently, this new plug-in is available to Macintosh and Windows 95 users. UNIX and Windows NT versions will be released soon.

What Can I Do with Shockwave?

Netscape Navigator allows for something known as plug-ins. Plug-ins can expand the capabilities of the Web browser by transparently supporting newer file formats. Although some plug-ins are essentially glorified helper applications, Shockwave takes full advantage of the power of plug-ins. You can easily have a regular home page that contains Director multimedia files.

Director allows not only for regular multimedia files but also for interactive multimedia. Putting files of this level onto your Web page may require a bit of work, but it is well worth the effort. You can have a multimedia tour of your office facilities, for example. When a user clicks your Director file, it can play some animation.

How Can I Support Shockwave?

Shockwave is really just another file type that needs to be supported by both the browser and the server. The browser is automatically supported after you install the Shockwave plug-in. Whenever you access a home page with a Shockwave multimedia file, Netscape downloads the file. After it's received on your end, the Shockwave plug-in plays the multimedia file. The really impressive aspect about Shockwave is that the multimedia file is played *within* the current home page. The browser keeps playing the multimedia file until you go to another home page.

Most Web servers can easily support Director files if you add the new MIME file type. Director has only three file extensions: DIR, DXR, and DCR. They are of the MIME type "application" and the sub-type of "x-director." After you or your administrator adds these extensions, your Web site can support Shockwave. For example, if you're using NCSA's Web server, you'll want to add the following lines to the end of the conf/mime.types file:

```
application/x-director DIR,DXR,DCR
```

How Do I Get Shockwave?

You can retrieve the Shockwave plug-in directly from Macromedia. Simply point your browser to the following:

> **http://www.macromedia.com/Tools/Shockwave/sdc/
> Plugin/index.htm**

Select the appropriate operating system that you're using. Next, specify which browser you're currently using, and then specify from where you want to download it.

A number of Internet-related programs support Director files natively and don't need the Netscape plug-in. These programs include Microsoft's Internet Studio, Silicon Graphics's WebForce, and Navisoft's NaviPress. After Shockwave is installed in your system, you can seamlessly view Director files.

Where Can I Find Director Files?

Director is a commercial program sold by Macromedia for $850. Because of its hefty price, it's unlikely that you'll find Director files in personal Web pages. Director allows you to create multimedia projects such as presentations and interactive Web pages. You can create and import two- and three-dimensional objects with Director.

For the serious multimedia developer, Macromedia also sells Director Multimedia Studio. The Studio is a collection of many Macromedia titles, including Extreme3D, xRes, and SoundEdit 16. If you get the Macintosh version, SoundEdit 16 comes with Deck II, while the Windows version comes with SoundForge XP. Director Multimedia Studio has a list price of $999. You can purchase Director and Director Multimedia Studio from Macromedia or one of their retailers.

III

Advanced HTML

Putting Director Files in Your Home Page

After you've bought Director and created some multimedia files, you can use them in your home page. Unfortunately, the current HTML standard has no provision for having multimedia files in your home page. The most widely used of the different extensions is the Netscape tag <EMBED>. This tag is basically the same as HTML's <IMG> tag, except that it refers to a multimedia file. The simplest way of making use of a Director file is by adding a line to your home page. The line looks something like the following:

```
<EMBED SRC="mymulti.dcr">
```

This puts the Director file as a separate HTML object by itself. This is fine in many cases, but you have to learn to treat the <EMBED> element as any other HTML tag. You can use the <EMBED> element as you use an <IMG> tag. You can easily put in a Director file in your Web page, as you can a graphic file. Because of <EMBED>'s flexibility, you can create interesting effects with Director files. For example, you can make Director files stand out by adding the following lines to your Web page:

```
<table border=8>
<tr>
<td>
<embed SRC="MYlogo.dcr">
</td>
</tr>
</table>
```

This creates a table with one data cell. In that cell is the Director file MYLOGO.DCR. This is great if you want to make your Director file stand out particularly well. MYLOGO.DCR appears in a table by itself, which makes it very hard to not be seen.

Another useful application of the <EMBED> tag is using it as a test of the user's browser. For example, suppose you have a Web site where you want people with Java-capable browsers and have Director files. You can do this by putting in the following lines:

```
<SCRIPT LANGUAGE="LiveScript">
<!--Beginning of LiveScript code-->
document.write('<EMBED SRC="http://www.mysite.com/mybanner.dcr">');
<!--Ending of LiveScript code-->
</SCRIPT>
<EMBED>
```

```
If you don't see my spinning logo above, you need:
<UL>
<LI>A Java-capable browser.</LI>
<LI>Shockwave installed for that browser.</LI>
</UL>
</EMBED>
```

For Java-capable browsers, this code loads the Director file. If the browser doesn't have Shockwave, the user is asked if he or she wants to get the plug-in. Those browsers that can't handle Java display the contents between the <EMBED> and </EMBED> tags.

You may optionally choose to specify the HEIGHT and WIDTH attributes of the <EMBED> tag. These values indicate the height and width, respectively, of the multimedia file you're using. After your browser comes across the <EMBED> tag, it automatically retrieves the multimedia file. The browser then hands off the file to Shockwave to display it properly in the browser window.

Converting Sounds

If you're planning on using sound files in your Web page, there's a good chance you already have a sound file. As a result, this sound file is probably in one particular format. To ensure that your file can be heard by as many people as possible, you'll probably need to convert the sound file. There are a number of applications on both the Macintosh and Windows 95 that can help you here.

Goldwave

GoldWave, by Chris Craig, is a solid Windows 95 sound editing program (see fig. 18.10). It allows you to read in .WAV, .AU, .IFF, .VOC, .SND, .AIFF, and raw sound files. You can easily convert an existing sound file by clicking the Open icon. Next, you'll be presented with a standard file open dialog box. Locate the sound file you want to convert and click the OK button. Select the File menu heading, followed by the Save As menu item. This opens a dialog box (see fig. 18.11) that lets you specify what you want to save the file as. Simply use the Save File as Type drop-down list and select the file format you want to save it as. Next, use the File Attributes drop-down list and choose the attributes you want for the sound file.

III

Advanced HTML

Fig. 18.10
GoldWave is a good editor available for Windows 95 and Windows 3.1.

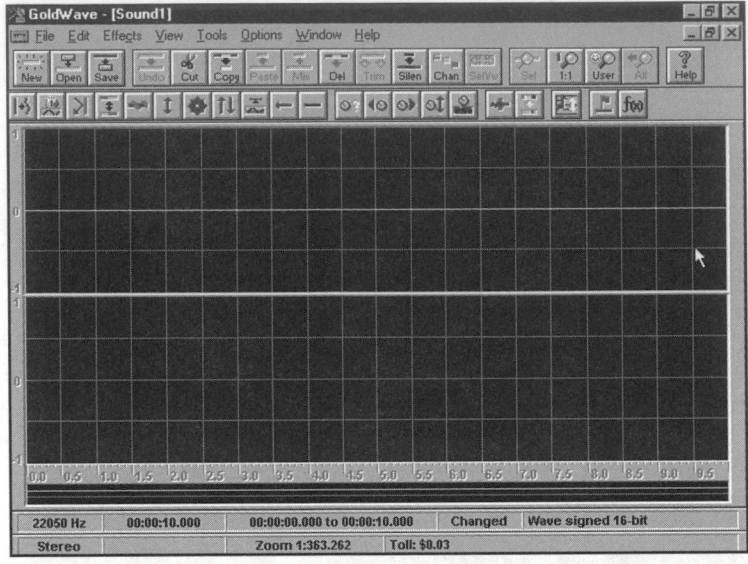

Fig. 18.11
The File Attributes drop-down list will have different options, based on the format you want to save it as.

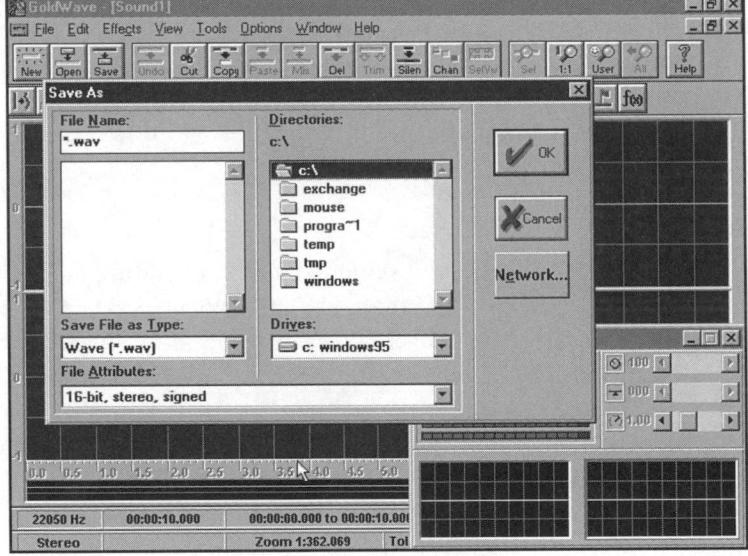

"Mono" sound files are smaller than "stereo" sound files. If your sound isn't recorded in stereo, you shouldn't convert the file as such. Also, "8-bit" sound files are smaller than "16-bit" sound files. 16-bit encoded sound files sound much better than 8-bit sound files. As a result, if you're not too concerned with the clarity of the sound, you should use 8-bit encoding. You can find out more about GoldWave at **http://web.cs.mun.ca/~chris3/ goldwave/**.

SoundApp

Mac users can also easily convert sound files to other formats with SoundApp. This program, by Norman Franke, allows you to read in AIFF, AIFF-C, AU, WAV, and VOC file formats. Unfortunately, although it can read many formats, it can only write out a handful of formats. The most prominent Windows 95 sound format that SoundApp can convert to is the WAV format. To convert a sound file, simply click the File menu heading, followed by the Convert menu item (⌘-K). You'll be presented with a file open dialog box (see fig. 18.12).

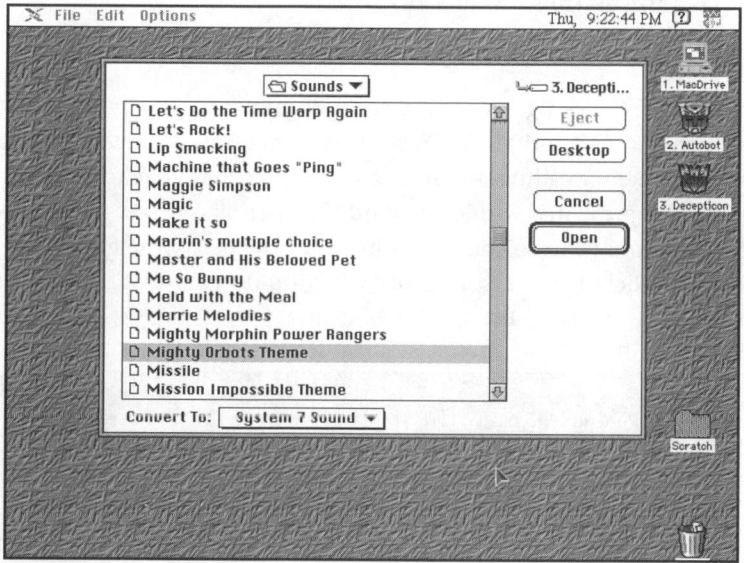

Fig. 18.12
You only use this one dialog box to convert your sound files.

Select the file you want to convert from the list of files in the dialog box. You can specify what format you want by using the Specify To drop-down list. Once you've selected the file you want to convert, click the Open button. After a little while, SoundApp returns from the conversion. A new folder in the folder of the source file is created and is called SoundApp Converted Files. In that folder, you'll find all your converted sound files from the previous directory.

> **Caution**
>
> Since SoundApp doesn't let you specify where to save the converted file, you could easily clutter up your hard drive. If you're converting sound files all over your hard drive, each conversion creates a new folder. All these folders are called SoundApp Converted Files. To reduce the number of extra folders, put all files you want to convert into one folder.

Converting Multimedia

Just as with sound files, you'll probably want to make multimedia files available in many formats. For Web authors who work for large corporations, it should be easy to re-record the data into a new format. However, many people don't have that luxury and have to convert between file formats. This has the noticable drawback that sometimes the converted file doesn't look as good as the original file. Still, for the most part, the conversions are typically very good, with little noticable quality degradation. Most of the following multimedia converters can be found at **http://www.prism.uvsq.fr/ public/wos/multimedia/medias.html**.

SmartVid

SmartVid by Intel (see fig. 18.13) is a good Windows 95 program that lets you convert between AVI and MOV. To convert from either format to the other, click the File menu heading, followed by the Open Source (Ctrl+O) menu item. You'll be presented with a standard file open dialog box, where you indicate the file you want to convert from. You can specify the format for the source file by clicking the List Files of Type drop-down list. When you've found the file you want, click the OK button.

Fig. 18.13
SmartVid by Intel
for Windows 95
lets you easily
convert MOV files
to AVI files.

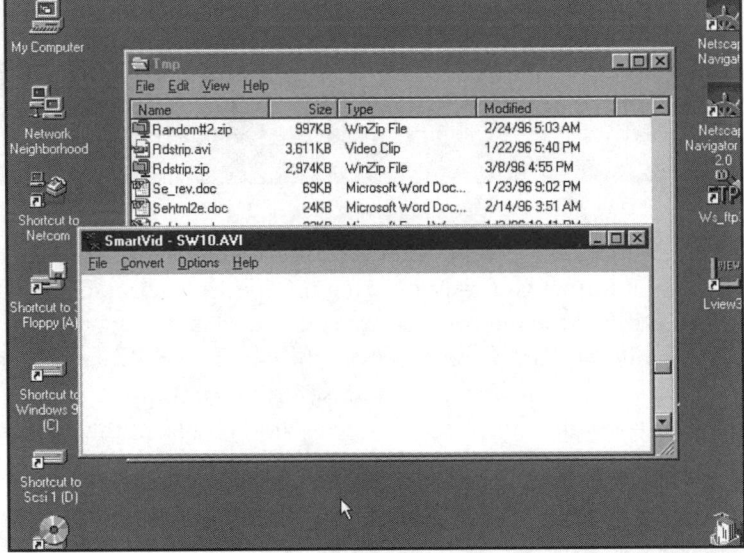

You can toggle warning messages by clicking the Options menu heading. Select either Silent or Warnings, and it controls SmartVid's behavior. Next, click the Convert menu heading, and select the Start (Ctrl+S) menu item. Once again, you'll be presented with a dialog box that lets you specify the name and type of the file you want to convert to. Clicking the OK button starts the conversion process. During the conversion process, warning messages appear, if you've enabled them. SmartVid tells you once it's done converting. You can get SmartVid at **ftp://ftp.intel.com/pub/IAL/multimedia/smartv.exe**.

Sparkle

Mac owners can easily convert between MPEG and QuickTime MOVies with Sparkle. This program is a combination of an MPEG and MOV player and converter. To convert between the file formats, load the file into Sparkle as if you wanted to play it. Next, click the File menu heading, followed by the Save As menu item. If you're converting to an MPEG file, you'll be presented with a dialog box (see fig. 18.14), which asks you for various MPEG information. The default values are usually fine, so you can click the OK button. Next, you'll be presented with a File Open dialog box. Specify where and under what name you want the converted file to be saved as, and click the OK button. Sparkle performs the conversion and notifies you when it's done.

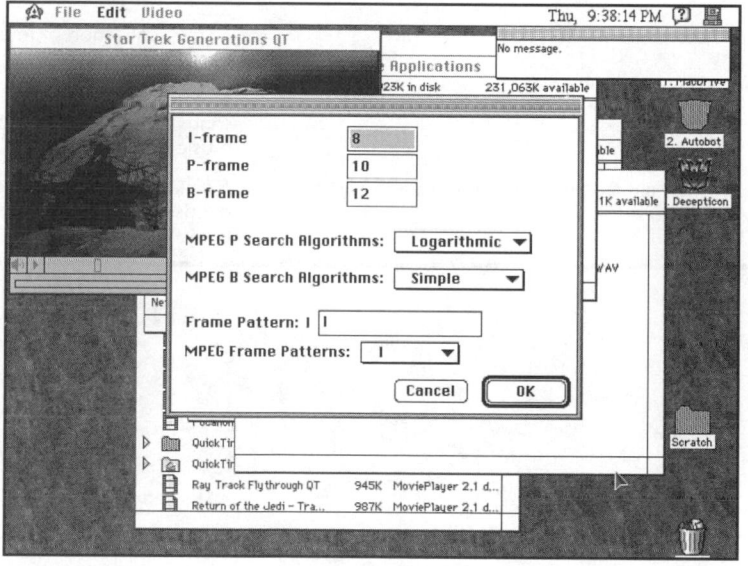

Fig. 18.14
To convert from QuickTime to MPEG, you need to specify some MPEG information.

Where to Find Files

If you're like most Web authors, you probably don't have a budget to create multimedia files. That doesn't mean you can't put in existing multimedia files into your Web page, however. The Net is filled with archives full of sound and multimedia files (see table 18.1). But since the Net is an ever-growing entity, it will undoubtedly get more large collections of sound and multimedia files.

Table 18.1   Sound and Multimedia Archives

URL	Content
http://homepages.udayton.edu/students/siefert/movies/MOVIES.HTM	A large collection of various MPEG and MOV files
http://www.ncsa.uiuc.edu/SDG/DigitalGallery/DG_science_theater.html	A large collection of science-related animation files
http://www.uslink.net/~edgerton/index.html	A collection of animation that spans various topics
http://deathstar.rutgers.edu/people/bochkay/movies.html	Various scenes from television and movies in various formats
http://tausq.resnet.cornell.edu/mmedia.htm	A collection mainly of movie clips
http://users.aol.com/ojwavs/waves.com	A small collection of movie samples in WAV format
http://www.io.org/~cme/	A small collection of music from Canadian bands
http://www.valleynet.com/~ericmort/dd.html	A directory of original songs along with links to music samples
http://www.iuma.com/IUMA/index_graphic.html	A collection of music from bands and labels around the world

## CHAPTER 19

Verifying and Checking a Web Page

by Bill Brandon

You may remember the popular line from the movie *Field of Dreams*: "If you build it, they will come." Everyone who creates a page or a site for the Web would like to communicate a message, attract attention and traffic, perhaps even win acclaim. Otherwise, there's no purpose in the effort. But you probably found out in your first few hours on the Web that not all pages are worthy of much attention, let alone acclaim. Building a great Web page takes a lot of time, attention to detail, and knowledge of your readers.

Four elements separate outstanding Web pages from the other 95 percent. First, great Web pages are always mechanically sound: the HTML is written correctly, the text and graphics display correctly, and the links all work. Second, an outstanding page is aesthetically pleasing; having a pleasant appearance is different from being cool and flashy. Third, a great page is built from the ground up to provide value to the viewers. Finally, a great Web page adheres to certain standard practices. These practices create a practical user interface and allow visitors to get the page to respond in predictable ways.

In this chapter, you learn about the following:

- HTML source code verification

  Options exist to find HTML source errors and to optimize page performance for all browsers.

- Hypertext link validation

  A variety of options exist to eliminate dead links and ensure that links in documents on the Web work correctly.

- Outstanding Web pages

  Several services on the Web will help you find examples of excellent and beautiful Web pages.

■ Recognition and awards for excellence

You can get a home page or site recognized publicly, to draw attention to your product or service.

■ Help from other authors and webmasters

You can get help with standard practices, tips and tricks of the trade.

What Is Web Page Verification?

How often have you managed to complete an entire document or program without making a single mistake? Even when I proofread and test carefully, at least one embarrassing error always seems to get past me. HTML documents are no different, except that even more things can go wrong.

Web page verification is the continuing task of making sure your HTML source code is intelligible to browsers and provides the interface you and the Web surfer expect. Web page verification also addresses the maintenance of those vital hypertext links to other pages, to images, and to files. You can think of Web page verification as a combination Quality Assurance function and continuous improvement program.

Resources are available on the Web itself to check your HTML syntax and test your links. Some of these resources run on other people's servers. Anyone on the Web can use them. These resources can go by any of several names, such as *validators* or *validation services*, but in this chapter I refer to the entire group as *verification services*.

Most of this chapter is concerned with demonstrating several of these tools on the Web. I will also show you where to download a number of these tools. You can then run them on your own server (if you have one) to perform the same functions.

The tools you will see perform at least one of the two essential verification functions: they verify HTML source code, they verify links, or they do both.

Verifying HTML Source

HTML is written to be read by Web browsers, not by human beings. Although most Web browsers are pretty forgiving, basic errors in HTML syntax prevent a page from being displayed properly. Other HTML errors cause people to have to wait longer than they like while a page loads. Such failures can destroy the effectiveness of your Web site.

Of course, you can use an SGML-aware editor such as HoTMetaL; it does syntax checking on the fly. Such a tool makes sure you use the correct tag for any given context.

But not everyone uses an SGML-aware editor. Many people use Notepad or WordPad to prepare their HTML documents. If you are using a less capable editor, you can employ any of several verification services on the Web to check out your HTML source for errors. Such services vary in their capabilities, but they have one outstanding characteristic in common: they are free. In fact, even if you use an SGML-aware editor, you should verify your source code. Why? Change.

A fact of life on the World Wide Web is the speed with which it has grown. In less than three years, the Web has acquired millions of users. At the same time, the HTML convention has gone through three standards. The browsers used to access documents on the Web have undergone a similar explosive growth. An editor that is up-to-date in its ability to parse and correct syntax today may well be obsolete in three months or less.

Some browsers now use nonstandard tags (*extensions*) in documents to deliver special effects. You may have seen pages on the Web marked "This page appears best under Netscape" or "This page appears best with Internet Explorer." To say that this presents a challenge to Web page developers is an understatement.

A developer can build a Web page to conform to the HTML 3.0 Standard, for example. The page may look wonderful when viewed with a Level 3.0 browser. But what does it look like when viewed with a Level 1.0 browser? There are also users who cruise the Web with text-only browsers like Lynx. Millions of copies of browsers that conform to standards less capable than HTML 3.0 are in use every day, all over the world. The developer wants all of them to be able to get her message, buy her products, and find her e-mail address. Meanwhile a growing percentage of the Web population worldwide uses some version of Netscape. What will they see?

◀ See "Frames," p. 317, and "Scrolling MARQUEEs Text," p. 353

One solution to this problem is for every developer to obtain a copy of every browser and check out the page under each one. This solution seems a little extreme. The on-line verification services offer a much simpler answer. And the on-line services are constantly updated as well.

Later in this chapter, you will look in detail at the three leading on-line verification services: WebTechs, Weblint, and the Kinder-Gentler Validator. You'll also be introduced to the Chicago Computer Society's Suite of Validation Suites, which provides a convenient interface for all three of these services and much more. I'll show you four excellent alternative verification services, too. Finally, you'll learn where to obtain verification tools that you can install on your own server and get a look at what it takes to do this.

Verifying Links

Simply checking the HTML source ensures only that your documents appear the way you expect them to appear on different browsers. You also need to make sure that all your links work the way they are supposed to work.

A browser tries to follow any link the user clicks. One possible source of problems is a simple typographical error. Every page designer makes these errors, and sometimes these errors happen while you're entering links. An SGML-aware editor doesn't catch this problem, and chances are you won't spot all of them either. Another source of trouble is the constant change that the Web undergoes. A link to a valid site last week may not go to anything next week. Web pages require continuous maintenance and verification to guard against these dead links.

◀ See "Using LINK," p. 108

One way to check your links is to ask all your friends to test your document periodically. This idea is good in theory, but it's a fast way to lose your friends in practice. Luckily, some verification tools and services will test your links for you.

Checking links is part of routine maintenance. Most Web browsers are very forgiving of errors in HTML. A broken link is not something that a browser can deal with, though. For this reason, you should test on a regular basis.

In the section titled, "Using Doctor HTML," you will discover an excellent on-line resource for testing your links and fine-tuning page performance. Although the Doctor is not available for installation on local servers, other link testers are; they are listed in the section titled, "Obtaining and Installing Other Verification Suites." Finally, there is a service called URL-Minder that will notify you whenever there are changes to a page to which your page is linked. This is described in the section on "Using Other Verification Services on the Web."

Examining the Options

You have a couple of ways that you can go to obtain regular verification of your pages. You can do the job yourself, or you can have someone else do it.

To do verification yourself, you install and run one or more tools on your server. These tools are CGI scripts, nearly always written in perl. Many are available from Web sites at no cost. You could also write your own CGI script.

▶ See "All About CGI Scripts," p. 525

Of course, you may not have a server of your own on which to install verification tools. In this case, you can use one of the many public tools available on the Web. This capability can be extremely convenient if you are developing pages at a client's site or in a hotel room while you're traveling.

Running verification on your own server is a good thing if you have a lot of HTML source code and Web pages to maintain. Companies that have an in-house version of the Internet (often referred to as an "intra-net") would find this an attractive option. In the sections titled, "Installing the WebTechs HTML Check Toolkit Locally," and "Obtaining and Installing Other Verification Suites," you'll learn exactly what is required to set up this capability.

Most people, however, only occasionally need to verify any source code and have just a handful of links to maintain. In these cases, even if you have a server available you may want to take advantage of the services on the Web. But where and how do you find these services?

Finding Verification Services on the Web

The first task is to find these on-line services. Fortunately, it's easy to locate a handy list of validation checkers. Using the Yahoo search engine (**http://www.yahoo.com**), search on the key `Validation Checkers` and choose the match with the label `Computers and Internet:Software:Data Formats:HTML:Validation Checkers`. Figure 19.1 gives you an idea of the results you get this way.

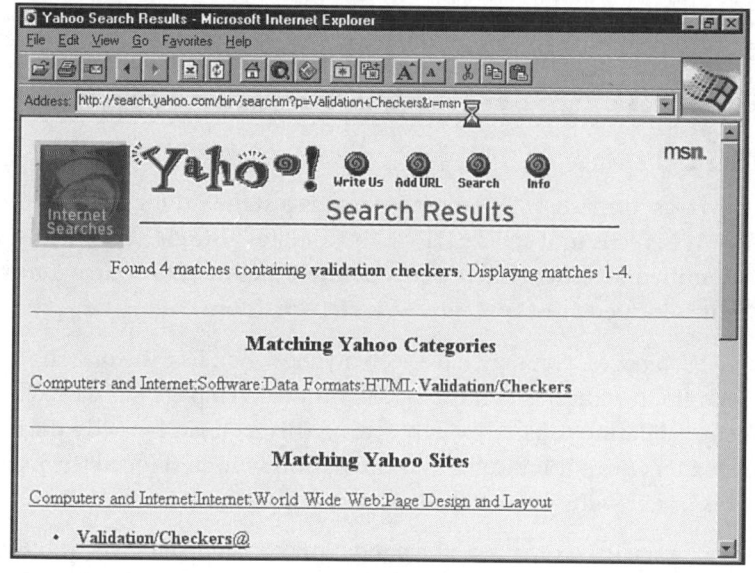

Fig. 19.1

Yahoo maintains a list of validation checkers on the Web.

III

Advanced HTML

The other search engines available on the Web can also be used to locate validation checkers. None of them provides the kind of precision the Yahoo list does, however. You should try a variety of keywords, such as *html*, *URL*, *verification*, and *service*, in addition to *validation* and *checker*. Use various combinations. From time to time, new validation or verification checkers will appear on the Web, and it is difficult to predict the keywords it will take to find them.

Table 19.1 lists four of the most popular verification services. Each of these will verify HTML source on the Web. Although all four perform similar functions, they provide subtle differences in their reports. All will be discussed in this chapter in the major sections. Other verification services available on the Web will also be described, more briefly, in the section titled, "Using Other Verification Services on the Web."

Table 19.1 Four Popular Verification Services on the Web	
Service Name	**URL**
WebTechs	**http://www.webtechs.com/html-val-svc**
Kinder-Gentler	**http://ugweb.cs.ualberta.ca/~gerald/validate.cgi**
Weblint	**http://www.khoros.unm.edu/staff/neilb/weblint.html**
Doctor HTML	**http://imageware.com/RxHTML.cgi**

Using the WebTechs Verification Service

WebTechs was formerly HALSoft, and remains a standard for on-line verification. The WebTechs tool checks HTML. It validates a single page or a list of pages submitted together, and it lets you enter lines of your source directly. WebTechs is located at **http://www.webtechs.com/html-val-svc**.

 On some Web pages, you may have seen a yellow box like the one shown in the margin. It indicates that the HTML on the Web page has passed WebTechs validation tests. Although getting this icon isn't exactly the same as winning an Oscar, it indicates that the person who developed the page knows his or her stuff.

When your page passes the test, the validation system itself gives you the graphic. It comes with some HTML code that makes the graphic link to the WebTechs site.

So how do you go about getting this bit of public recognition? The path starts with turning your Web browser to the appropriate site, as shown in table 19.2.

Table 19.2 WebTechs Validation Server Sites	
Location	**URL**
North America	**http://www.webtechs.com/html-val-svc/**
EUnet Austria	**http://www.austria.eu.net/html-val-svc/**
HENSA UK	**http://www.hensa.ac.uk/html-val-svc/**
Australia	**http://cq-pan.cqu.edu.au/validate/**

After you enter the appropriate site and start the service, you see a form similar to the one shown in figure 19.2. On this form, you can have your Web page (or bits of HTML) checked for conformance in a matter of seconds. You instantly get a report that lays out any problems with the HTML source.

> **Note**
>
> WebTechs changes the appearance and layout of this form from time to time. In particular, the last radio button in the first row is quite likely to change. For a time, it was HotJava as shown here. It has since been changed to "SQ," for SoftQuad's HoTMeTaL Pro Extensions. In the future it will probably be used to specify other sets of HTML extensions as well. These changes do not affect the use of the form.

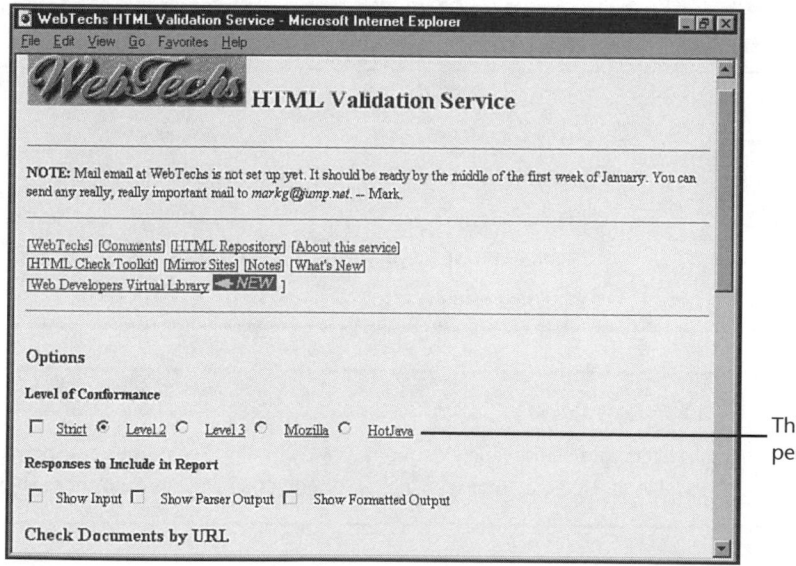

Fig. 19.2
Check your Web page by using this WebTechs HTML Validation Service form.

This option changes periodically

III

Advanced HTML

Incidentally, if you have many pages to maintain, you can add some HTML to each page to save you time and work. The code in listing 19.1 adds a button labeled "Validate this URL" to your page. Whenever you update a page, all you have to do is click on the button instead of opening up the WebTechs URL. Table 19.3 gives the possible values for each of the variables.

Listing 19.1 Add This HTML to Provide a Button That Automatically Submits Your Page for Validation

```
<FORM METHOD="POST" ACTION="http://www.webtechs.com/cgi-bin/html-
check.pl">
<INPUT NAME="recommended" VALUE="0" TYPE="hidden">
<INPUT NAME="level" VALUE="2" TYPE="hidden">
<INPUT NAME="input" VALUE="0" TYPE="hidden">
<INPUT NAME="esis" VALUE="0" TYPE="hidden">
<INPUT NAME="render" VALUE="0" TYPE="hidden">
<INPUT NAME="URLs" VALUE="http://www.foo.com/goo.html" TYPE="hidden">
<INPUT NAME="submit" VALUE="Validate this URL">
</FORM>
```

Caution

Remember to replace "http://www.foo.com/goo.html" with the proper address for the page on which this button is placed!

Table 19.3 Values for the Variables Used in Setting Up the Validate This URL Button

Variable	Meaning	Range of Settings
recommended	Type of checking	0 = standard, 1 = strict
level	Level of DTD to use	2, 3, or Mozilla
input	Echo HTML input	0 = don't echo, 1 = echo
esis	Echo output of parser	0 = don't echo, 1 = echo
render	Render HTML for preview	0 = don't render, 1 = render
URLs	Full declaration of URL	

Note

WebTechs refers to the Netscape extensions as *Mozilla*. WebTechs does not specify a "level" variable for HotJava, Internet Explorer, or any other DTD beyond those shown for HTML 2.0, HTML 3.0, and Netscape. Should they add more variables, you will find them by clicking on the hyperlink "About the HTML Validation Service," and then looking under the heading, "How do I add the 'Validate this URL' button to each of my pages?"

Selecting the Level of Conformance

When you arrive at the WebTechs HTML Validation Service, you may want to set some options. WebTechs lets you specify the level of conformance for the test. That is, you can test a document for conformance to the HTML 2.0 Specification, the HTML 3.0 Specification, the Netscape *Document Type Definition* (DTD), or some other DTD. The radio buttons marked Level 2, Level 3, and Mozilla, respectively, indicate these different specifications (see fig. 19.3.) As noted before, the identity and use of the fourth radio button on this row changes from time to time. You can select only one radio button at a time.

▶ See "Forms and How They Work," p. 489

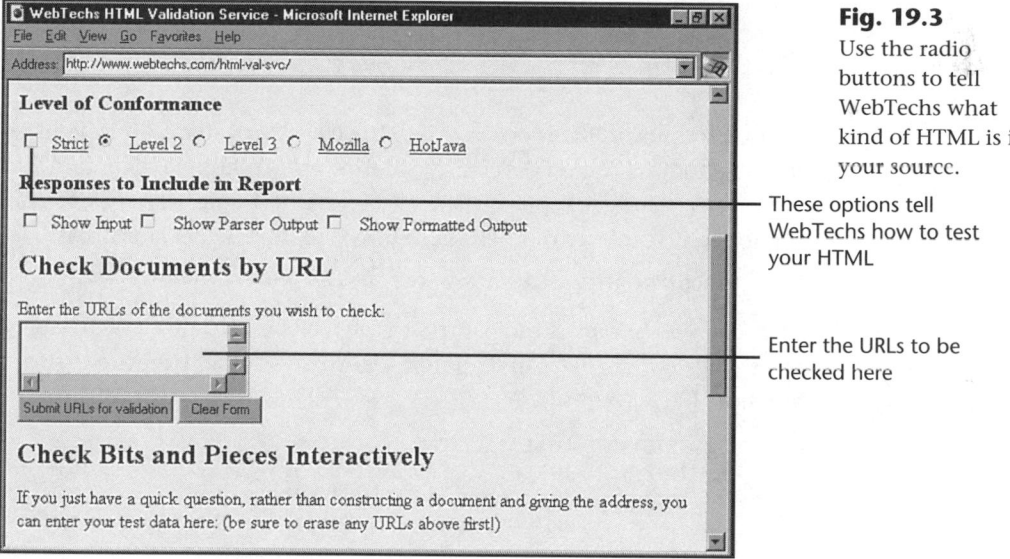

Fig. 19.3
Use the radio buttons to tell WebTechs what kind of HTML is in your source.

These options tell WebTechs how to test your HTML

Enter the URLs to be checked here

These radio buttons tell WebTechs which DTD to use in checking your page. Successful choice of DTD requires that you understand how WebTechs works, as I will explain in the next few paragraphs.

WebTechs is actually an *SGML parser*. As such, it requires a DOCTYPE declaration in the first line of any document it checks; this declaration tells it which

III

Advanced HTML

DTD to use. However, Web browsers aren't SGML parsers and ignore a DOCTYPE declaration when they find one. As a result, most Web documents do not include DOCTYPE. By selecting a radio button, you instruct WebTechs to respond as though the corresponding DOCTYPE were at the beginning of your page—if no DOCTYPE declaration is in the document when it opens.

If WebTechs finds a DOCTYPE declaration in your source when opened, it uses that declaration and ignores the radio buttons. It will also ignore the check box, provide you with the correct options settings, and (if your source passes) it will provide you with the correct validation icon.

Perhaps you don't actually know the DOCTYPE declared in your document or the species of HTML contained in it. If you select an inappropriate button, you could get a list of errors relating to a standard you perhaps didn't think applied.

> **Tip**
>
> You should look at the first line of your HTML source to see what's there before you try to validate a page.

A more serious problem occurs when the DOCTYPE declaration in your document is not one that WebTechs recognizes. WebTechs can generate an enormous number of spurious errors. Be sure that your DOCTYPE declaration is correct, if you have one. The correct syntax for the declaration is

```
<!DOCTYPE HTML PUBLIC "quoted string">
```

The `"quoted string"` is the part that WebTechs must know. WebTechs lists the strings it recognizes in its public identifier catalog. Here are the four you are most likely to need:

```
"-//IETF//DTD HTML 2.0//EN"
"-//IETF//DTD HTML 3.0//EN"
"-//Netscape Comm. Corp.//DTDHTML//EN"
"-//Sun Microsystems Corp.//DTD HotJava HTML//EN"
```

> **Tip**
>
> The WebTechs public identifier catalog is well hidden. You will find it at this URL:
> **http://www.webtechs.com/html-tk/src/lib/catalog**.

These strings must appear just as they do here, including capitalization and punctuation. The DOCTYPEs are not even necessarily the same as the "official" public identifiers for their respective DTDs.

> **Caution**
>
> Some popular HTML editors automatically insert DOCTYPE declarations into docu-
> ments. You may have to edit or remove such declarations before trying to validate
> your page. In some cases, the editor inserts a DOCTYPE that indicates the HTML
> complies with the 3.0 specification, even though this is not true. In other cases, the
> editor includes information in the DOCTYPE that confuses WebTechs about which
> DTD to use, causing your validation to fail.

Understanding Strict Mode

In the WebTechs HTML Service, a check box marked Strict appears at the beginning of the radio button row. You can use it to modify any of the radio button settings. The default is unchecked. When this item is checked, WebTechs uses a "strict" version of the DTD for the level (2.0, 3.0, Mozilla, or other choice) that you select.

◀ See "Building Blocks of HTML," p. 87

In Strict mode, WebTechs accepts only recommended idioms in your HTML. This restriction ensures that a document's structure is uncompromised. In theory, all browsers should then display your document correctly. The Strict version of the DTD for each of the four specifications tries to tidy up some parts of HTML that don't measure up to SGML standards.

Unfortunately, some browsers still in common use were written when HTML 1.0 was in effect. Under this specification, the <P> tag *separated* paragraphs. But now <P> is a *container*. Suppose that you write your HTML to pass a Strict Level 2 test. You will find that an HTML 1.0-compliant browser displays a line break between a list bullet and the text that should follow it.

> **Tip**
>
> Don't use Strict conformance to check your pages, and don't modify your pages to
> comply with Strict HTML unless you are sure of the browsers that users will employ
> to display your page.

WebTechs provides on-line copies of the formal specifications and the DTDs for both HTML versions and for Netscape and HotJava. You can find the strict DTDs here as well. All the strict DTDs enforce four recommended idioms:

- No text is used outside paragraph elements.

- No obsolete or deprecated elements (for example, <XMP>, <LISTING>) are used.

III

Advanced HTML

- Anchor elements contain only inline markup. This allows `<B>`, `<CODE>`, and `<IMG>`, but not `<H1>`-`<H6>`, `<BLOCKQUOTE>`, or `<P>`.

- Anchor names are unique and begin with a letter.

Having no text outside paragraph elements means that all document text must be part of a block container. Table 19.4 shows right and wrong according to Strict Mode. Please note that the source code on the left is different from that on the right. The difference is subtle: on the left, the paragraph containers are properly used while on the right, no paragraph containers are used at all.

Table 19.4   The Ways Strict Mode Identifies Valid Paragraph Text

Paragraphs Valid in Strict Mode	Paragraphs Not Valid in Strict Mode
<HTML>	<HTML>
<HEAD>	<HEAD>
<TITLE>Passes Strict Test</TITLE>	<TITLE>Fails Strict Test</TITLE>
</HEAD>	</HEAD>
<BODY>	<BODY>
<P>First Line</P>	First Line
<P>Veni, vidi, vici.</P>	Veni, vidi, vici.
<P>Last Line</P>	Last Line
</BODY>	</BODY>
</HTML>	</HTML>

Why is this important? Browsers that are HTML 2.0 or 3.0 compliant will display both examples in table 19.4. In the case on the left, each paragraph container of text will be shown on a separate line on the screen, with one line space before and after the text. In the case on the right, all the text will be shown on a single line.

In addition, both examples will pass a simple HTML 2.0 or 3.0 validation by WebTechs. Only the one on the left will pass a Strict Mode validation, however.

It might seem desirable to always use the Strict Mode, to ensure that browsers will always correctly interpret your source code and display your page the way you intended. However, as noted before, the container elements required to pass Strict Mode may cause HTML 1.0 compliant browsers and text browsers to display your page in ways that you never anticipated.

Even if you know that your page will not be accessed by any HTML 1.0 compliant browsers, you may still not want to use Strict Mode for checking. Table 19.5 shows the container elements for Strict HTML 2.0 and additional elements for Strict HTML 3.0. WebTechs rejects any others when the Strict level of conformance is chosen. If you are using extensions that provide container elements other than these, your source code may not pass a Strict test. This does not mean the code won't be readable to browsers, it just means it didn't pass the test. You will then spend time, maybe a lot or maybe a little, checking the error report from WebTechs line by line looking for the guilty party—without success.

Table 19.5   Container Elements under Strict HTML Rules

Valid under Strict HTML 2.0	Add These Elements for Strict HTML 3.0
`<P>[vb]<BLOCKQUOTE>[vb]<PRE>`	`<TABLE>`
`<DL>[vb]<UL>[vb]<OL>`	`<FIG>`
`<FORM>`	`<NOTE>`
`<ISINDEX>`	`<BQ>`

What rule of thumb should you draw from all this? Just one: When deciding whether to test with Strict Mode selected, be guided by the KISS Principle (Keep It Simple, Simon).

Selecting Responses to Include in Report

After you have set the level of conformance that you want to establish for your source code, WebTechs gives you some options about the report contents, as shown in figure 19.4.

The basic report that WebTechs sends to you will be either a message that says Check Complete. No errors found or an actual list of the errors found. The errors, of course, reflect the Level of Conformance you chose in the first row of check boxes. Under some circumstances, you can get an erroneous No errors found message. The options you select for the report can help you spot these errors and help you make sense out of the error listing.

The error listing that WebTechs returns refers to error locations by using line numbers. If you check the box by Show Input, your HTML source follows the error list, with line numbers added. This report can be very helpful.

Fig. 19.4
The report options
determine what
you see in the
report from
WebTechs.

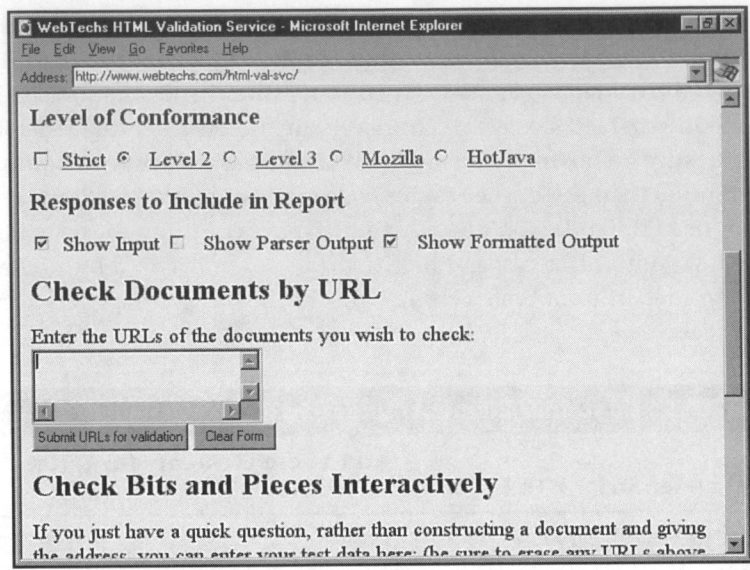

You can get additional help in interpreting the error listing by selecting Show Parser Output. This option appends a detailed list of the way WebTechs parsed your source.

Finally, by selecting Show Formatted Output, you can have WebTechs append what it tested, formatted according to the DTD you chose. This report is useful in case you enter an URL incorrectly. If you do, WebTechs gets an error message when it tries to connect to that URL. WebTechs handles some of these messages well, but not all of them. In particular, if a typo causes an `Error 302` ("Document moved") message to be returned, WebTechs parses the error message and returns the report `Check Complete. No errors found.` If you checked Show Formatted Output, you see the actual `Error` message in addition to the incorrect report and therefore avoid being tricked into thinking it was your page being validated.

Testing an Entire URL or Pieces of HTML Source

If you have an existing page on the Web that you want to test, enter the URL in the text box below the banner "Check Documents by URL." In fact, you can test several documents at the same time. Just enter the URLs, one per line, including the **http://** part.

Caution
If a file has many problems, the SGML parser stops after about 200 errors. This means the validation service stops as well and will not validate any remaining URLs.

If you want to test only a section of HTML source, you can paste it into the text box provided for this purpose. In either case, WebTechs applies the Level and gives you the Responses you specified in the preceding sections.

> **Note**
>
> WebTechs is probably the most comprehensive of the verification services on-line. Its reports can also be the most difficult to understand. For that reason, you should become familiar with the FAQ (Frequently Asked Questions) File for the service. This tool is maintained by Scott Bigham at **http://www.cs.duke.edu/~dsb/wt-faq.html**.

Using Doctor HTML

Although using WebTechs is an excellent way to verify that your HTML source is everything it should be, WebTechs does not check your links. Most of the systems designed to check links run only on your own server. If you don't have a server, fortunately, you can use Doctor HTML.

Doctor HTML is different from the other tools addressed in this chapter. To begin with, it examines only Web pages; it won't take snippets of HTML for analysis. But it also provides services not found in the other tools.

Doctor HTML performs a number of functions, as you can see in figure 19.5. Some of these functions overlap with the other HTML verifiers. But the most important reasons for using Doctor HTML are to get verification that all the hyperlinks in your document are valid and to get specific advice concerning optimization of your page performance.

Doctor HTML is located at **http://imagiware.com/RxHTML.cgi**. The Doctor performs a complete Web site analysis, according to your specifications. The strengths of the program are in the testing of the images and the hyperlinks, functions not found in other verification services. Be sure to read the test descriptions; no separate FAQ is available.

The Doctor provides you with a report that is built "on-the-fly." It contains one section for each test you specified, and a summary. You are presented with the summary first, and from it you may select the individual test report sections. As an example, the three figures that follow are individual test report sections. These were returned in response to the request in figure 19.5 for examination of the Macmillan Information Superlibrary ™ on the Web.

Fig. 19.5

You can use this form to order Doctor HTML's tests.

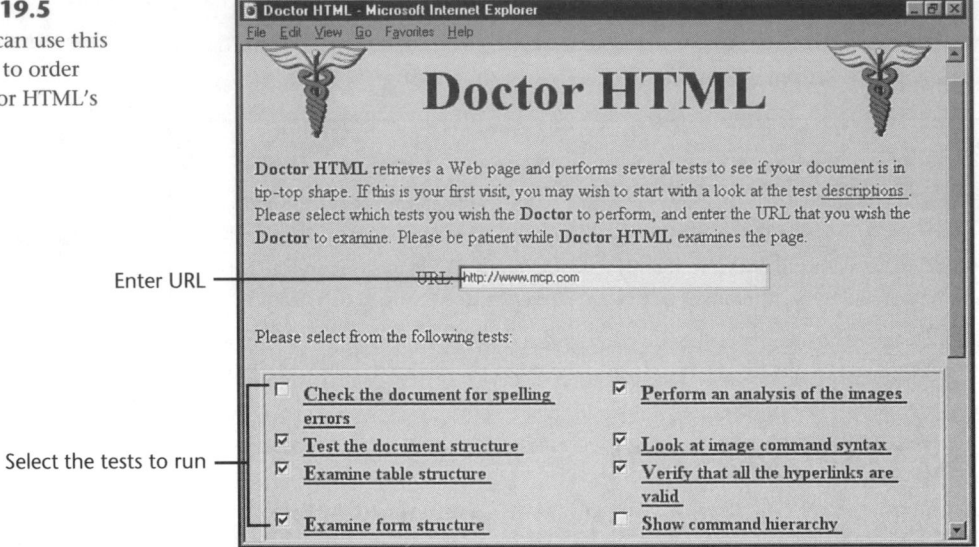

Testing Links

Testing Links

The hyperlinks test checks for "dead" hyperlinks on your page. The resulting report indicates whether the URL pointed to is still present or if the server returns an error, as shown in figure 19.6. The report also tells you how large the destination URL is; if you get a very small size for a destination, check it by hand to determine whether the server is returning an error message.

Fig. 19.6

This typical report from Doctor HTML describes the hyperlinks found in a document.

Doctor HTML's Report - Microsoft Internet Explorer

File Edit View Go Favorites Help

Address: http://imagiware.com/RxHTML/doc.cgi

Hyperlink Analysis

#	Name	Content Type	Size (bytes)	Last Modified	Comments
0	super3.map	text/html	*	**	OK
1	index.html	text/html	*	**	OK
2	imprints.map	text/html	*	**	OK
3	index.html	text/html	*	**	OK
4	index.html	text/html	*	**	OK
5	index.html	text/html	*	**	OK
6	index.html	text/html	*	**	OK
7	index.html	text/html	*	**	OK
8	index.html	text/html	*	**	OK
9	index.html	text/html	5035	Friday, 01-Mar-96 07:16:48 GMT	OK

Note that just because the report says the link is apparently valid, the page pointed to is not necessarily what it was when you set up the link. You should use the URL-Minder service described in "Using Other Verification Services on the Web" to track changes to the pages your links identify. The Doctor uses a 10-second time-out for each link test; slow links may time-out, and you will have to test them individually.

◀ See "Position-ing the Image," p. 203

Fine-Tuning Page Performance

To tweak your page performance, you get maximum results from fixing image syntax, reducing image bandwidth requirements, and making sure that your table and form structures are right. The Doctor provides a wealth of information in all these areas.

This special report identifies images that take an excessive amount of bandwidth and that load slowly, as shown in figure 19.7. It also gives the specific image command tags to set to improve overall page performance (see fig. 19.8).

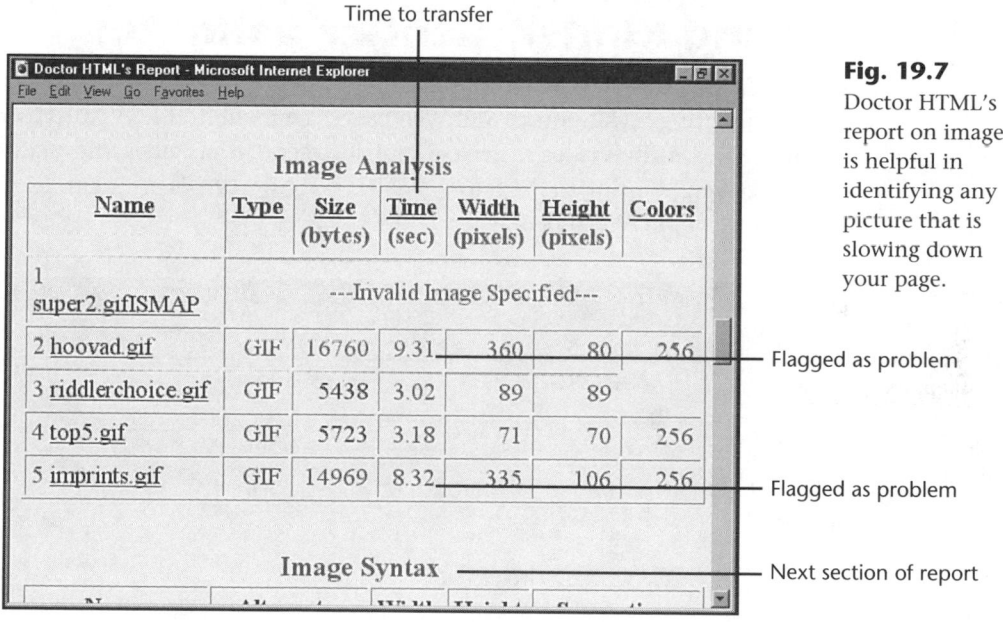

Fig. 19.7
Doctor HTML's report on images is helpful in identifying any picture that is slowing down your page.

Fig. 19.8
These image command tags require resetting, according to Doctor HTML.

No <ALT> Tag ——

These attributes should be set to improve page performance

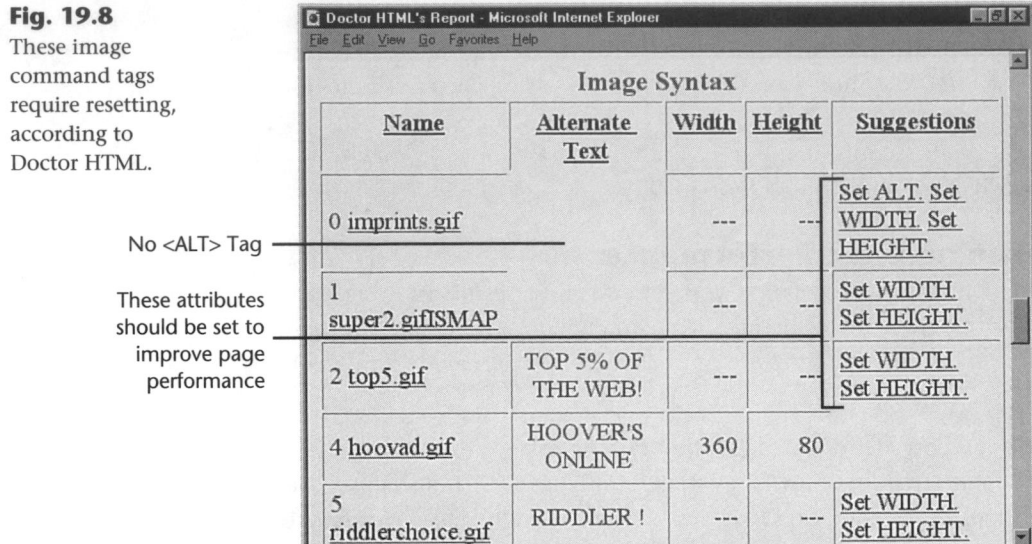

Using Kinder, Gentler Validator

The Kinder, Gentler Validator (sometimes called simply KGV) is a newer tool for validating HTML source and Web pages. You will find KGV at **http://ugweb.cs.ualberta.ca/~gerald/validate.cgi**. It provides informative reports, even pointing to the errors it detects. Figure 19.9 is an example of just how helpful KGV can be.

Fig. 19.9
This figure shows an example of the helpful reports provided by the Kinder, Gentler Validator.

KGV requires a DOCTYPE

Link to detailed explanation ——

Arrows pinpoint the problems

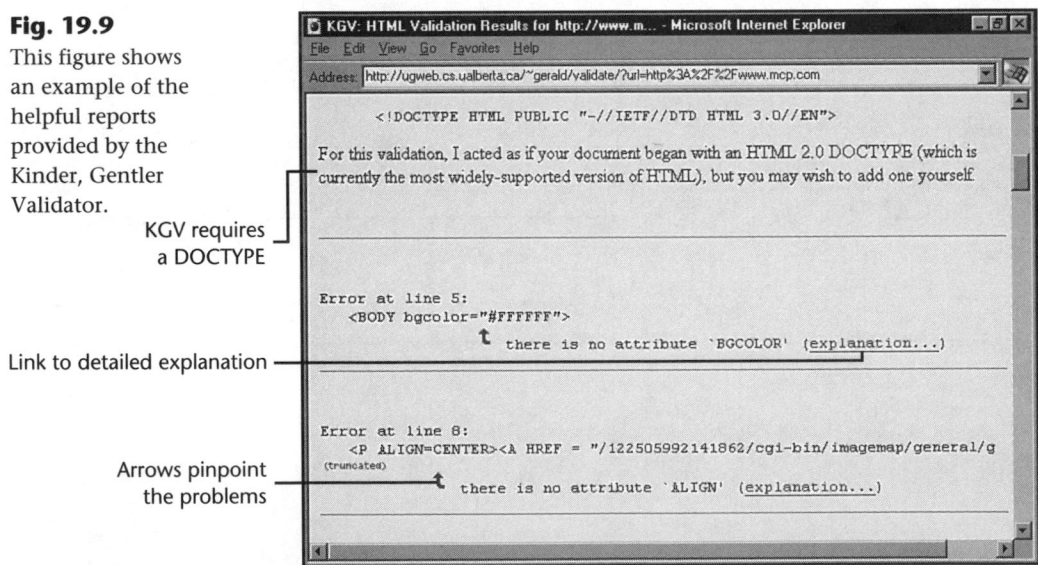

While KGV's reports are easier to interpret than WebTechs, you should obtain the KGV FAQ which explains the more impenetrable messages that still appear.

> **Note**
>
> The FAQ for Kinder, Gentler Validation by Scott Bigham is at **http://www.cs. duke.edu/~dsb/kgv-faq.html**.

KGV is very similar in some respects to WebTechs; both of them completely parse your HTML source code. Both obey the rules of the HTML language definition to the letter and both are based on James Clark's SGML parsers.

But there is at least one big difference. KGV expects that your document will either be HTML 2.0 conformant, or that it will have a DOCTYPE declaration on the first line. If KGV doesn't find a DOCTYPE, it assumes the document is supposed to be 2.0 conformant. No nice row of radio button selections here!

KGV also has a public identifier catalog, located at **http://ugweb.cs. ualberta.ca/~gerald/validate/lib/catalog**. This is a longer and more complete public identifier list than WebTechs. All the warnings given under the WebTechs description about using the correct DOCTYPE and about spelling errors apply to KGV as well.

The interface for KGV (see fig. 19.10) is a bit simpler than the one for WebTechs, as you might expect. You have the option to include an analysis by Weblint, another verification tool that is discussed in the next section of this chapter.

Notice that KGV provides two additional types of output. These may be helpful when dealing with difficult problems. Show Source Input displays the HTML text with line numbers. Show Parse Tree shows you how KGV parses your file. These are similar to WebTechs options "Show Input" and "Show Parser Output."

Finally, Kinder, Gentler Validator provides an icon when your source code passes its test, just like WebTechs. You can paste the snippet of code that KGV provides into your document so that all who view it know you build righteous HTML.

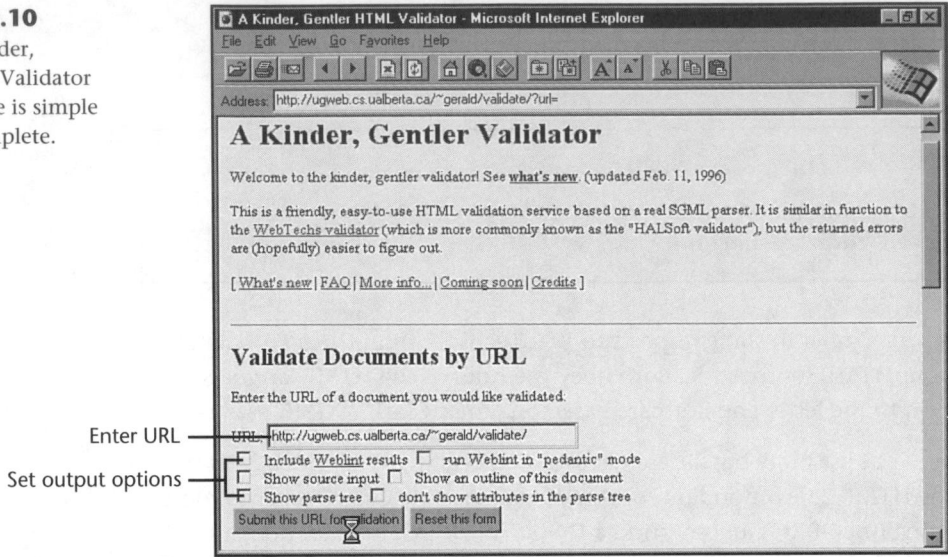

Enter URL
Set output options

Using Weblint

Weblint takes a middle ground with HTML verification. One of its strengths is that it looks for specific common errors known to cause problems for popular browsers. This makes it a *heuristic* validator, as opposed to KGV and WebTechs which are parsers. "Heuristic" simply means that it operates from a set of guidelines about HTML style.

Weblint performs 22 specific checks. It is looking for constructs that are legal HTML but bad style, as well as for mistakes in the source code. Here is the list, as shown by UniPress (Weblint's publisher) for Weblint v1.014:

- Basic structure
- Unknown elements and attributes
- Context checks to look for tags that must appear within certain elements
- Overlapped elements
- TITLE in the HEAD element
- IMG elements have ALT text
- Illegally nested elements
- Mismatched tags, such as <H1> ... <H2>
- Unclosed elements, such as <HEAD> ...

- Elements that should only appear once
- Obsolete elements
- Odd number of quotes in a tag
- Order of headings, such as <H2> followed by <H4>
- Potentially unclosed tags
- Flags markup embedded in comments (confuses browsers)
- Use of "here" as anchor text
- Tags where attributes are expected
- Existence of local anchor targets
- Flags case of tags
- Leading and trailing whitespace in some container elements
- Unclosed comments
- Checks HTML 3 elements

On the other hand it misses some outright errors from time to time. One reason that KGV offers the option of showing Weblint's findings about a Web page is to provide style feedback that WebTechs is missing. If you routinely use WebTechs, you should make it a habit to also run your page by Weblint. Or switch to KGV and always take the Weblint option. By using both a parser and a heuristic verifier, you will spot many problems that would otherwise be missed if you used only one or the other.

You can access Weblint on the Web in three places. One is **http://www.unipress.com/weblint/**; this is the publisher's site. Another is **http://www.khoros.unm.edu/staff/neilb/weblint/lintform.html**. Figure 19.11 shows the latter interface. Finally, a Weblint Gateway has recently been opened to provide a very streamlined way to obtain verification of your Web page: **http://www.cen.uiuc.edu/cgi-bin/weblint**.

With Weblint, like WebTechs, you can either submit the URL of a page to be verified, or enter HTML directly into a text box. You have the options in the reports of seeing the HTML source file (automatically line-numbered) and to view the page being checked. You also can have either Netscape or Java extensions checked.

Like KGV, Weblint reports from either Web site are easy to understand (fig. 19.12). However, the reports are not as comprehensive as those provided by WebTechs or KGV.

Fig. 19.11
The Weblint interface is another simple design; you may enter either an URL or HTML code.

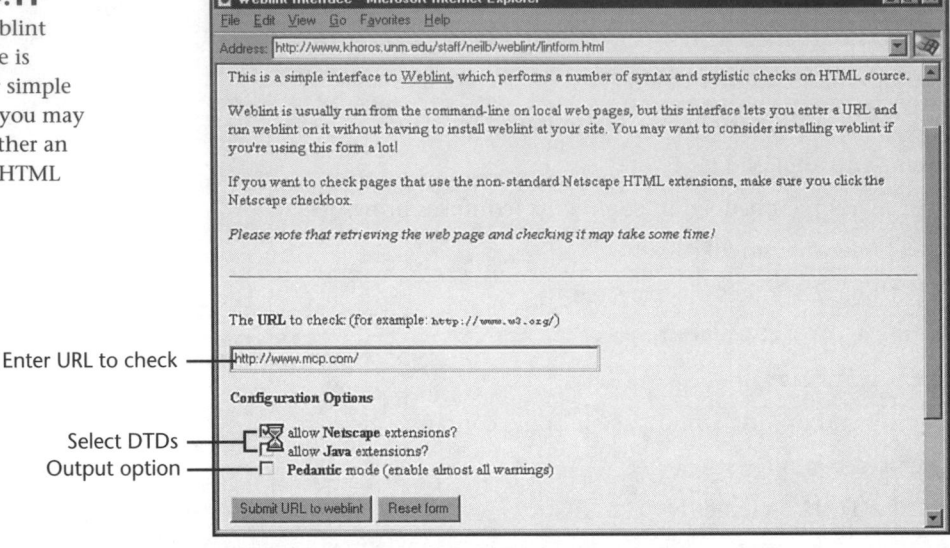

Enter URL to check ——

Select DTDs ——
Output option ——

Fig. 19.12
Weblint provides an easy-to-read, brief report.

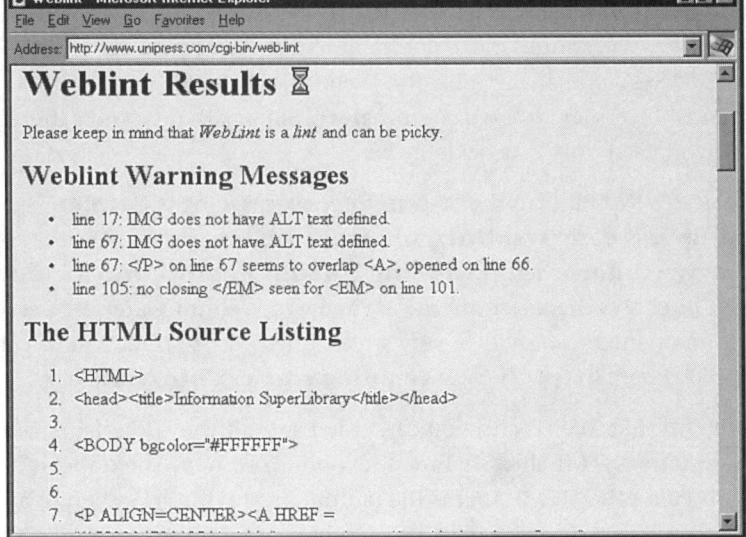

Using an All-in-One Verification Page

Wouldn't it be nice if you could do all your verification from one place, instead of having to run from one verification site to another? Well, you nearly can. Harold Driscoll, Webmaster for the Chicago Computer Society, has assembled a page at **http://www.ccs.org/validate**. This page will save you a lot of work (see fig. 19.13).

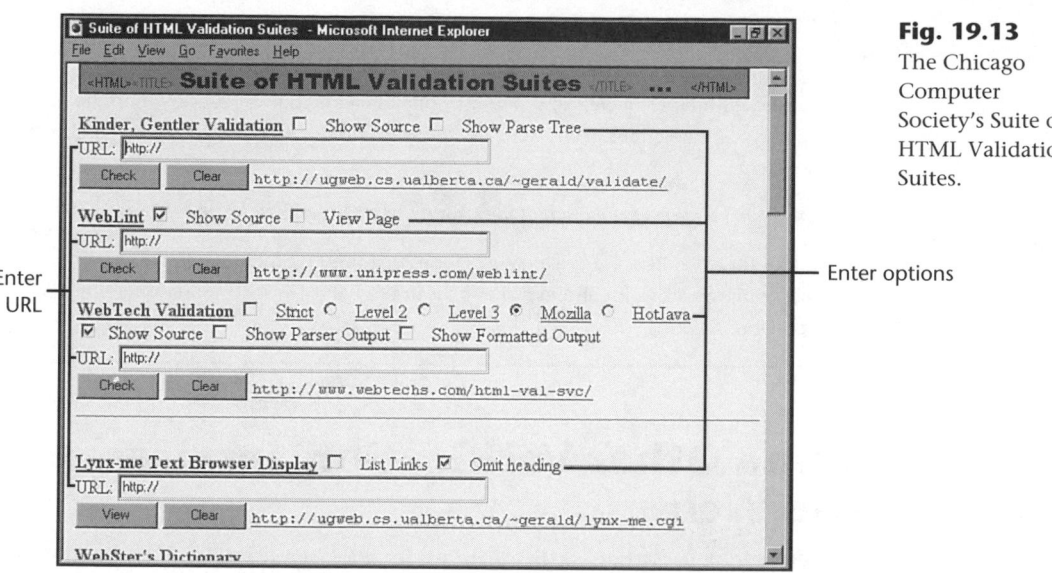

Enter
URL

Enter options

Fig. 19.13
The Chicago
Computer
Society's Suite of
HTML Validation
Suites.

The Suite of HTML Validation Suites page includes forms that check your page using the three most popular validation services (Kinder, Gentler Validation, Weblint, and WebTechs). Fill in the URL you want checked, and select the switch settings you want. The page returns all your reports in the same format.

WeblintIn addition, this one-stop service includes forms for several other tools. A spell checker (WebSter's Dictionary) returns a list of any words that it does not recognize on your page. The Lynx-Me Text Browser Display shows you what your Web page looks like to viewers using the text browser Lynx. The HTTP Head Request Form and a form titled Display Typical CGI Environment Strings can help when you are writing and debugging CGI programs and scripts. And finally, another form makes it easy to register with the URL-Minder service (see the section on URL-Minder in "Using Other Verification Services on the Web).

Troubleshooting

I notice that each verification service seems to report different problems when I submit the same URL to all of them. What can I do about this?

Always use a combination strategy when checking an URL. That is, use one of the syntax checkers (WebTechs or KGV, but not both) and one of the heuristic checkers (Weblint or its alternate at the U.S. Military Academy, described in the next section).

(continues)

III

Advanced HTML

> (continued)
>
> By using both types of checkers, and only one of each, you will cut down on the apparent contradictions. Consistency in the way you do your checks is very important.
>
> *Where can I find an explanation of the error messages in WebTechs and KGV reports?*
>
> Both of these verifiers use the error messages provided by their SGML parsers. The most comprehensive list and explanation is in the FAQs by Scott Bigham referred to in previous sections.

Using Other Verification Services on the Web

It pays to look for other verification services; a large number of them are on the Web. Perform a search on the keywords `verification service`, or use other search tools besides Yahoo. I found the services in table 19.6 this way.

I use these services mainly as a backup. The more popular services are sometimes busy, and you can't get onto them. The Slovenian site for HTMLchek, Brown University, Harbinger Net Services, and the U.S. Military Academy, all discussed in this section, are good alternatives.

Finally, the URL-Minder service can be a true blessing to the person with too many links to maintain. It provides you with a way to know when a change occurs to a page that one of your own pages references.

Table 19.6 Other Verification Services on the Web	
Service Name	**URL**
Slovenian HTMLchek	**http://www.ijs.si/cgi-bin/htmlchek**
U.S.M.A. (West Point)	**http://www.usma.edu/cgi-bin/HTMLverify**
Brown University	**http://www.stg.brown.edu/service/url_validate.html**
Harbinger	**http://www.harbinger.net/html-val-svc/**
URL-Minder	**http://www.netmind.com/URL-minder/example.html**

Using HTMLchek

HTMLchek is an interesting tool put together at the University of Texas at Austin. However, the on-Web version is offered by someone at a site in Slovenia (**http://www.ijs.si/cgi-bin/htmlchek**).

HTMLchek does syntax and semantic checking of URLs, against HTML 2.0, HTML 3.0, or Netscape DTDs. It also looks for common errors. It is another heuristic verifier and can be used as an alternative to Weblint.

HTMLchek returns reports that are not as well-formatted or easy to read as Weblint's. However, they report approximately the same kinds of problems, to the same level of detail. There is no FAQ file for the Slovenian site, but full documentation is available for download at **http://uts.cc.utexas.edu/ ~churchh/htmlchek.html**.

Using the U.S. Military Academy's Verification Service

Figure 19.14 shows the HTMLverify service offered by usma.edu (that's the U.S. Military Academy at West Point, in case you aren't an alum). The URL for the service is **http://www.usma.edu/cgi-bin/HTMLverify**. You can enter the URL of your page, or you can paste HTML source into the window. The system checks whatever you enter or paste against plain-vanilla HTML 2.0 standards alone. You can choose to have it include a check against the Netscape extensions as well.

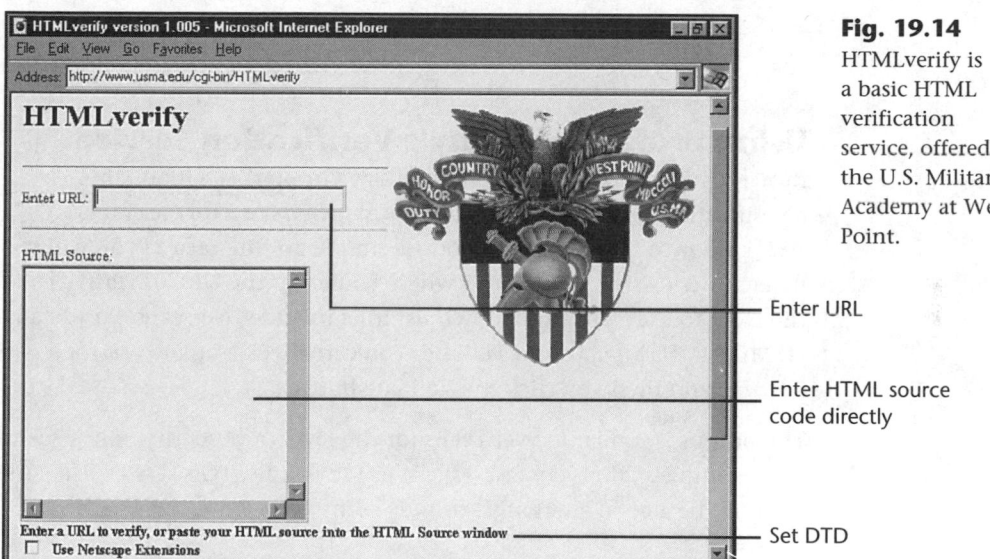

Fig. 19.14
HTMLverify is a basic HTML verification service, offered by the U.S. Military Academy at West Point.

Enter URL

Enter HTML source code directly

Set DTD

HTMLverify is actually an interface to a modified version of Weblint, so it's another heuristic checker. If you enter an URL in the first text box and then click the Verify button at the bottom of the form, you get a report of any problems Weblint found with the HTML source. This report may look something like the one shown in figure 19.15. As with any automatically generated report, not every error reported is really an error. However, the report does generate a worthwhile list of items.

Fig. 19.15
The HTML Verification Output from HTMLverify for the Web Page indicates a few problems with the source.

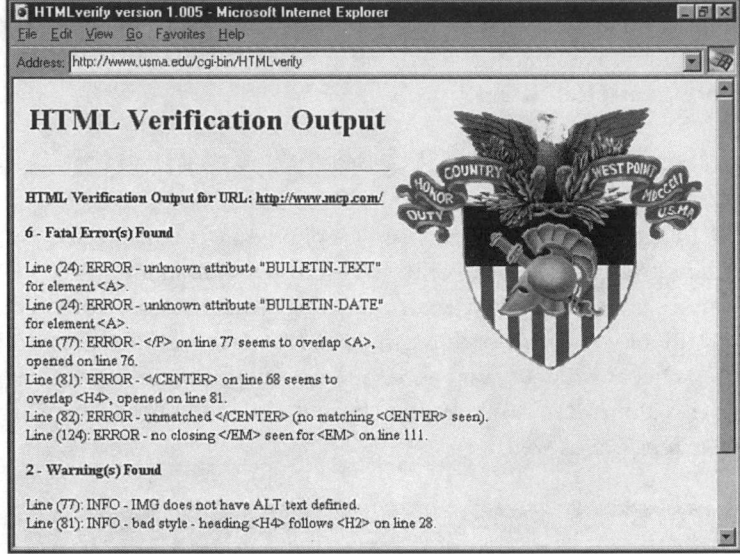

Using Brown University's Verification Service

Brown University's Scholarly Technology Group (STG) maintains a verification service at **http://www.stg.brown.edu/service/ url_validate.html**. This is about as simple an interface as you will see anywhere. It consists of a text box, where you enter the URL to verify. You select the DTD to use from a pull-down list; this includes Netscape 1.1 (default), HTML 2.0, HTML 3.0, and TEI Lite. You can check a box to ask for a parse outline, and then you click the Validate button.

The output is similar to WebTechs for the level of obscurity, but it seems to be complete. It is very fast. Like WebTechs, the STG's service is a parser. It would be a good alternative to WebTechs or to KGV. There is no FAQ.

Using Harbinger's Verification Service

This is a site where WebTechs HTML Check Toolkit has been installed and made available to the Web. The interface is an exact duplicate of the WebTechs site. The use of the tool and the reports it returns are also exactly the same in every respect.

This service was formerly located at Georgia Tech, but moved with Kipp Jones to Harbinger Net Services. You will find the verifier at **http://www.harbinger.net/html-val-svc/**.

Using URL-Minder

This isn't exactly a verification service, but it can be a great help to you in keeping your links updated and the dead links pruned. The URL-Minder service notifies you whenever there is a change to URLs to which you have embedded links on your page. You register your e-mail address and the other pages with URL-Minder at **http://www.netmind.com/URL-minder/example.html**. (This address also takes you to a complete description of the service.) The service sends you e-mail within a week of any changes to the pages you specify.

You can also embed a form on your page that readers can use to request notification from URL-Minder whenever *your* page changes. You can set this up so that customers get either a generic message or a tailored one.

Troubleshooting

I get so many errors from some of these verification services, where should I begin fixing problems?

Most of the verifiers will return more than one error statement for each actual error. In addition, if there are a lot of errors, the verifier may become confused. The best strategy is to fix the first few problems in the report, then resubmit the URL or source code for checking. This tends to very quickly reduce the number of errors reported.

I'm really having trouble understanding these terse error statements. Where can I get help?

If the verifier offers the option, try running in "pedantic" mode. This will give you longer explanations.

Installing the WebTechs HTML Check Toolkit Locally

The WebTechs Validation Service is the definitive HTML-checker on the Web. A version of the software has always been available for installation on local servers, but it wasn't always easy to obtain. It also was not easy to install successfully.

WebTechs has solved these problems with its HTML Check Toolkit.

III

Advanced HTML

WebTechs now offers an interactive on-line service whereby you specify the type of operating system you are running, the directories in which the software is to be installed, and the type of compressed tar file you require. WebTechs server will build a toolkit tailored to these specifications and download it to you. It also builds a set of installation and testing instructions tailored to your system.

To install and use the toolkit, you need about 500K of disk space, and one of the following 24 operating systems (others are being added):

- Sun OS 4.1.3
- IRIX 4.0.5 or 5.2
- Solaris 2.x
- BSD V1.1
- HP-UX 9.03
- SCO UNIX 3.2.2 and up or SCO Open Desktop 2.0 and up
- Linux 1.1.65 or 1.2.10
- AIX 3.2.5
- DEC Alpha OSF/1 2.0
- Net BSD Sparc
- DEC Ultrix 4.3
- MIPS EP/IX 1.4.3
- VAX Ultrix 4.1
- Domain/OS
- NeXTSTEP 3.3 (HPPA, Intel, NeXT, and SPARC)
- CONVEX 11.0
- X86 Solaris 2.4
- NCR 3000 (SVR4)
- Pyramid ES-Server (SVR4)
- Sequent ptx2.1.1 (SVR3.2)
- Unixware (SVR4.2)

To obtain the toolkit, go to the WebTechs home page at **http://www.webtechs.com** and choose the link "HTML Check Toolkit." From that page, after reading any updates to the information you see in this book, choose "Downloading and Configuration." You're on your way to HTML verification from the comfort and convenience of your own server. When you are finished, you will be able to type `html-check *.html` and get a complete validation of your HTML files.

Obtaining and Installing Other Verification Suites

You can download three of the other tools discussed in this chapter and install them on your own server. There are a number of others tools available as well. Several of these are listed in table 19.7.

Table 19.7 Verification Tools Available from Web Sites to be Run on Your Server		
Tool	**Function**	**Source**
Weblint	Checks syntax and style	**http://www.khoros.unm.edu/staff/ neilb/weblint.html**
HTMLChek	Syntax checker	**http://uts.cc.utexas.edu/~churchh/ htmlchek.html**
HTMLverify	Weblint interface	**http://www.usma.edu/cgi-bin/ HTMLverify**
MOMspider	Robot link maintainer	**http://www.ics.uci.edu/WebSoft/ MOMspider**
Webxref	Cross-references links	**http://www.sara.nl/cgi-bin/ rick_acc_webxref**
Verify Web Links	Checks validity of links	**http://wsk.eit.com/wsk/dist/doc/ admin/webtest/verify_links.html**
lvrfy	HTML link verifier	**http://www.cs.dartmouth.edu/ ~crow/lvrfy.html**

Tip

In most cases, Frequently Asked Questions (FAQ) or README files accompany the scripts for these programs.

Nearly all of these are perl scripts but not all require that your server be running under UNIX. For example, HTMLchek will run on any platform for which perl and awk are available, including the Mac and MS-DOS.

After you download and install the script for the program of your choice, your server can run your maintenance program for you. Most of programs run from the command line and report directly back. Some of the tools will e-mail the reports to you or to whomever you designate.

III

Advanced HTML

Obtaining and Using Weblint

Weblint is available at no charge via anonymous ftp from **ftp://ftp.khoral.com/pub/weblint/**, as a gzip tar file or a ZIP archive for PC users. The tar file (weblint-1.014.tar.gz) is 46K, the ZIP file (weblint.zip) is 53K. Neil Bowers **<neilb@khoral.com>** is the owner of the program and welcomes your comments, suggestions, and bug reports.

The program is also supported by two e-mail lists. Announcements for new versions are made via **weblint-announce@khoral.com**. Discussions related to Weblint and prerelease testing are carried on via **weblint-victims@khoral.com**. E-mail Neil Bowers to be added to either list, or to obtain details of system requirements for Weblint.

Obtaining and Using HTMLchek

HTMLchek, when run on your own server, will perform more functions than the version available over the Web. Specifically, it will check the syntax of HTML 2.0 or 3.0 files for errors, do local link cross-reference checking, and generate a basic reference-dependency map. It also includes utilities to process HTML files; examples include an HTML-aware search-and-replace program, a program to remove HTML so that a file can be spell-checked, and a program that makes menus and tables of contents within HTML files.

HTMLchek runs under perl and awk but is not UNIX-dependent; it can be run under any operating system for which awk and perl are available. This would include MS-DOS, Macintosh, Windows NT, VMS, Amiga, OS/2, Atari, and MVS platforms.

HTMLchek is available at no charge via anonymous ftp (use your e-mail address as password) from **ftp://ftp.cs.buffalo.edu/pub/htmlchek/**. The files are available as **htmlchek.tar.Z, htmlchek.tar.gz,** or **htmlchek.zip**. Download the one that suits your platform. The documentation can be browsed on line over the Web from **http://uts.cc.utexas.edu/~churchh/htmlchek.html.** Other ftp sites from which the program can be obtained are listed in the documentation, under the heading, "Obtaining HTMLchek." These alternatives include the Usenet (**comp.sources.misc** archives), Uunet, and one site in Germany.

HTMLchek is supported by the author, H. Churchyard, at **<churchh@uts.cc.utexas.edu>.**

Obtaining and Using HTMLverify

Erich Markert, the webmaster at the Academy, has authorized downloading of the perl CGI script for HTMLverify. All you need do is click the button marked "Source" at the bottom of the HTMLverify form (**http://www.usma.edu/cgi-bin/HTMLverify**) to obtain the perl script. Clicking the "About" button will bring you the details of installation.

In addition to the source code for HTMLverify, you will need perl 5, Lynx version 2.3.7, Weblint (Markert offers his modified version), Lincoln Stein's CGI Module, and Markert's HTML module. All of these except for Lynx are available from the USMA site.

HTMLverify may be the easiest of all the verification checkers to obtain and install.

Obtaining and Using MOMspider

MOMspider is a freeware robot designed to assist in the maintenance of distributed hypertext infostructures. When installed, MOMspider will periodically search a list of webs provided by you. It looks for four types of document change: moved documents, broken links, recently modified documents, and documents about to expire. MOMspider builds a special index document that lists these problems when found, plus other information you requested. MOMspider will report directly to you or by e-mail to any address you provide.

MOMspider requires perl 4.036 and runs on UNIX-based systems. You will need to customize the perl script for your site. You obtain MOMspider, with installation notes, configuration options, and instruction files, from **http://www.ics.uci.edu/WebSoft/MOMspider**. You can also obtain it via anonymous ftp from **ftp://ftp.liege.ics.uci.edu**, in the directory **/pub/arcadia/MOMspider**. A paper describing the MOMspider and its use can be obtained from **http://www.ics.uci.edu/WebSoft/MOMspider/www94/paper.html**.

Obtaining and Using Webxref

Webxref is a perl program that makes cross-references from an HTML document and the HTML documents linked from it. It is designed to provide a quick and easy check of a local set of HTML documents. It will also check the first level of external URLs referenced by the original document.

When the program has run, it prints a list, with direct and indirect references, of items it found in the file in 17 different categories, including:

- All HTML files and their associated directories, images, and mail-tos
- All News, FTP, telnet, and gophers
- All external URLs

- Cgi-bin forms and scripts
- Named anchors
- Files and images that could not be found or that are not world readable
- Directories and named anchors that could not be found
- http:// URLs that failed and those that tested OK

You can download Webxref directly from the author at **http://www.sara.nl/cgi-bin/ric_acc_webxref**. The author is Rick Jansen and you can contact him by e-mail at **<rick@sara.nl>**.

Obtaining and Using Ivrfy

Ivrfy is a freeware shell script that verifies all the internal links in HTML pages on your server. It also checks the inline images in the documents. Ivrfy is slow; the author reports that it can process 10,000 links to 4,000 pages in an hour and a half on a Sparc 1000 with dual 75MHz CPUs.

Ivrfy assumes that you have five programs in your path: sed, awk, chs, touch, and rm. Obviously this means this is a UNIX-only program. Ivrfy is not secure and should not be run as root. The script requires customization, to specify the name of the server in use, the server's root directory, and three other variables. These are all identified in the README found on the Ivrfy Web page.

Ivrfy is executed from the command line. It reports back the links for which pages were successfully found, those for which the links are broken, and those for which the link was an HTTP link to another server. Broken links include nonexistent pages, unreadable pages, and server-generated index pages. There are a few known bugs and these are all listed in the README.

Download the Ivrfy script from **http://www.cs.dartmouth.edu/~crow/Ivrfy.html**. The author, Preston Crow, can be reached by e-mail at **<crow@cs.dartmouth.edu>**.

Obtaining and Using Verify Web Links

Enterprise Integration Technologies Corporation is in the process of developing a Webtest tool suite for its Web Starter Kit. One part of this suite is a link verifier for use by server administrators. It will aid in maintaining links within documents managed at a site. The link verifier tool starts from a given URL and traverses links outward to a specified limit. The verifier then produces a report on the state of the discovered links.

In its present form, the link verifier verifies only http: HREFs in SRC, A, FORM, LINK and BASE tags. It does not verify non-HTTP links (gopher, ftp, file, and so on). This is planned for the future. The verifier will exercise links to remote servers, but it does not attempt to examine the contents of the documents on those servers. Among other interesting features, the verifier can send reports to the administrator by e-mail, and will verify form POST actions. The tool does try to use bandwidth well; it uses HEAD requests on image data and remote documents.

The link verifier tool can be downloaded by anonymous ftp from **ftp:// ftp.eit.com/pub/wsk/<OS_TYPE>/webtest/verify_links.tar**. The <OS_TYPE must be one of the following: **sunos** (for 4.1.3), **solaris** (for 2.3), **irix**, **aix**, or **osfi**. No other platforms are supported at this time. A description of the tool is available at **http://wsk.eit.com/wsk/dist/doc/ admin/webtest/verify_links.html**.

▶ For assistance with scripts, refer to "All About CGI Scripts," p. 525

▶ If you would like to know more about perl and awk, see "Which Language Should You Use?" p. 546

Public Recognition for Quality Web Pages

All the verification services discussed to this point in this chapter ensure that your Web page makes sense to the Web browsers. Using valid HTML is only one of several factors in creating a quality Web page. What makes a great page is valid HTML plus outstanding content, attractive presentation, elegant layout and style, and a certain *je ne suis quoi*. To master these elements, considering what other Webmasters have done to create exemplary Web pages is very useful. The various recognition services can be of great use in this area.

Several recognition services appear on the Web. Many of them seem to focus on identifying the "cool" sites. Some of the "cool" sites have so many awards, plaques, badges, and other meritorious graphics displayed that they appear to have had a plate of fruit salad spilled on them.

Being cool is fine, but not necessarily a sign of quality that endures and attracts customers with money to spend (if that is your aim). Being cool is a fashion statement for the day, and perhaps you are looking for something a little more enduring. Finally, being cool and being worth a second read may be different concepts.

So how does a Web author who aspires to quality, like yourself, find the paragons of taste and utility? Two awards have distinguished themselves for their ability to pick enduring winners. They are High Five and Point Top Five. You can and should study sites that have received these honors, with the confidence that such sites had to meet extraordinarily stringent standards.

III

Advanced HTML

High Five

You may have seen this icon on a few especially elegant pages on the Web. The High Five Awards Committee gives this plaque to one well-designed site a week. Any site that displays this icon has been selected on the basis of design, conception, execution, and content, with an emphasis on clear information design and aesthetics. High Five (**http://www.highfive.com**) is sponsored by David Siegel and sustained by the efforts of his six interns. They reside in Palo Alto, California.

No matter who the other person or persons on the High Five Awards Committee may be, the guiding light is David Siegel. David is a type designer, typographer, writer, and Web site designer. He has some very definite ideas about what is good in Web site design and what is not.

Because David is a graphic designer, you will find that his ideas about quality are different from what many HTML mavens define as quality. For example, many SGML and HTML purists don't much care for Netscape. David believes that Netscape lets him do more of the things he wants to do. He does not feel obligated to make pages that are optimized for all browsers.

As a technical person who has also been a calligrapher for many years, I like what David Siegel does in his page designs. Before you make up your mind about Siegel's philosophy, take a look at the pages that receive the High Five. Let your eyes tell you what they like instead of being guided solely by what the HTML rulebook says.

Spending some time on David Siegel's Web site, the Casbah at **http://www.dsiegel.com/**, would be well worth your while. David provides an informative set of Tips for Writers and Designers, which includes some invaluable help with layout via the "single-pixel GIF trick." You will also like his tip on using images well.

Understanding High Five's Criteria

If you look through David Siegel's gallery of past winners, you are going to see some beautiful, effective Web pages. To understand why they work and how to make yours look like them, consider the three High Five criteria. High Five awards a perfect page five points in each of the following categories: Degree of Difficulty, Execution, and Aesthetics.

These three criteria have equal weight (in theory), and they are all subjective. You may want to read the critiques of past winners to get a handle on the meaning of each term and what each one contributes to the final appearance of a page. Reading Siegel's essays, "Severe Tire Damage," and "The Balkanization of the Web," may also help.

The High Five page itself also provides some further hints. It is pretty clear that four things will rule out a page from consideration: table borders, Netscape backgrounds, GIFs that interfere with the message, and general ugliness.

The whole point to High Five and Siegel's Web site is that you, as a designer, should not just accept the way HTML tries to get you to make your pages look. You are designing pages to be read by human beings, not by Web browsers. What a human being sees and how a human being responds to what is seen is informed by thousands of years of culture and individual experience with books and art. You aren't going to change or get past that human bias with one more example of default layout. To be successful and rise above the gray mass of most cyber-publishing, appeal to the aesthetics and culture of your reader.

Obtaining Recognition by High Five

You can submit your Web page to the High Five Awards Committee for consideration. The instructions are in David Siegel's Frequently Asked Questions file, and guidelines appear on the High Five page. Read them thoroughly, along with the rest of the information on the Casbah and High Five sites.

As Siegel reminds you several times, High Five is the Carnegie Hall of Web page awards. You won't get there overnight. But when you think your site is ready, submit it by sending e-mail to **submissions@highfive.com.** David's interns will review your site first, and if it passes their scrutiny, they will bring it to David's attention. If it also passes David's scrutiny, he will work with you to polish your page to meet his standards.

Siegel also responds to e-mail questions about page design. Read the FAQ to find out what will catch his attention.

Another, more difficult, way to be recognized is to send up to three URLs to **interns@highfive.com**, along with a message about yourself. If one of the sites you submit is good enough to qualify as a High Five, Siegel will also take a look at your site.

Point Top Five

You've probably seen this icon also, but on a larger number of Web sites. This icon indicates the Point Top Five Survey award. Point also maintains a set of lists of "top tens" in a number of fields.

The HTML verification services and High Five measure Web pages against particular set standards of perfection. Point takes a different approach and tries to measure Web sites with a utilitarian scale: how good is a site from the user's point of view?

Point is a fairly large Internet communications company located in New York. ("Fairly large" is a relative term; in this case it means large enough to maintain a staff of up to 24 Web site reviewers.) Point's Web Reviews give descriptions and ratings of the top five percent of all World Wide Web sites. They consider it their mission to be a guide to the "good stuff."

The home page for Point is at **http://www.pointcom.com/**; from there you can get to its Top Ten list and other features. One of the first things you should grab is the FAQ file, which gives all the details about Point's award system.

Unlike High Five, Point never offers a critique of your page and does not work with award winners to help improve their products. You submit your page and wait. If the page isn't reviewed and awarded, wait a few months and notify the editors when you have added new material on your page.

Understanding Point's Criteria

Although High Five looks for aesthetic perfection, Point works hard at identifying "the best, smartest, and most entertaining sites around." In addition to the large staff of reviewers, Point considers self-nominations and nominations that it receives from Web surfers to locate sites for review.

Web sites are rated on 50-point scales against three criteria: Content, Presentation, and Experience. To be more specific, here are the official descriptions:

- **Content:** How broad, deep, and amazingly accurate is the information? Are the links good? Good clips? Is the page accurate? Complete? Up-to-date?

- **Presentation:** Is the page beautiful? Colorful? Easy to use? Does it lead visitors through the information nicely? Does it use video, audio, and original graphics? Does it break new ground?

- **Experience:** This is the key rating. Is this page fun? Is it worth the time? Will viewers recommend it to friends? All things considered, does this site deliver the goods?

Point reviews each page at least four times a year, and it removes sites that have fallen to lower standards. The reviewers give the Top Five award to any page that meets the excellence criteria, whether the page is commercial, private, or student-run.

Obtaining Recognition by Point

You can submit your own page for review by using the Write Us form on the home page, or you can e-mail the URL and a description of the site to

submit@pointcom.com. You are notified only if you are awarded a Top Five. If you don't hear from Point, resubmit your page at a later time.

Once a page is recognized, Point places it among the other winners in its category. Newly reviewed sites also appear in "New & Noteworthy," a daily feature on Point's home page. Finally, the best of the best are added to the Top Ten lists; they are the top ten sites in each category in the Point review catalog.

Learning Standard Web Practices from Other Developers

One of the best resources you could ever hope for comes in the form of other Web developers. Many other people have been through the process of developing a Web site into a thing of beauty, value, or usefulness. When you see a Web site or a page that you really like, drop the Webmaster or the page owner a note to say how much you enjoy the creation. If you ask a polite question or two about how that author did something, you'll most likely get an answer.

You can find other Web developers in many Usenet newsgroups and mailing lists. Here are some of the best:

Newsgroups

alt.fan.mozilla

alt.hypertext

comp.infosystems.www.authoring.cgi

comp.infosystems.www.authoring.html

comp.infosystems.www.authoring.images

comp.text.sgml

Mailing Lists

HTML Authoring Mailing List (see **http://www.netcentral.net/lists/html-list.html**)

NETTRAIN Mailing List

You can also find plenty of pages and other features that give you good advice about page design. Here are three of the best:

- The HTML Bad-Style Page (**http://www.earth.com/bad-style/**)
- Top Ten Ways to Tell If You Have a Sucky Home Page (**http://www.winternet.com/~jmg/topten.html**)
- Yahoo's Index of Page Design and Layout Resources

CHAPTER 20
Make Yourself Known

by Robert Meegan

Current estimates indicate that the Web has more than 20 million pages. Even using the fastest connection and taking just seconds to glance at each page would take a reader the better part of a decade to see them all, by which time perhaps 10 times as many new pages would have appeared. Because of the scale of the Web, it is very unlikely that many people will find your page by pure chance. In fact, if your page has no links leading to it from other pages, it is very likely that no one will ever find it!

Because the reason to create a Web page in the first place is to exchange information, you probably want to encourage other people to visit your page. The best way to bring people to your page is to make the job of finding it as easy as possible.

In this chapter, you will learn about the following:

- **Types of advertising**

  Advertising on the Web comes in many forms, including sponsorships, indexes, and links from other home pages.

- **Search Servers**

  There are many different search tools on the Web that can be used to advertise a Web page.

- **Web Crawlers**

  By knowing how these programs comb the Web, you can increase your site's visibility.

- **Attracting Links from Other Pages**

  The nature of the Web encourages the connection of pages by links. The number of connections that a page has linked to it can greatly influence the success of the page.

■ **Advertising Off-line**

A successful advertising campaign should include listing your URL in many different locations.

What Kind of Advertising Do You Need?

The type of the advertising that you do depends greatly on the nature of your page. If you are doing a page as a hobby, paying a thousand dollars to get a week's worth of exposure on one of the popular sites probably isn't worth the cost to you. On the other hand, if your site is the home page of a major multinational corporation, the attention that a professionally designed advertisement can bring more than justifies the expense.

Note

Although I use the term *advertising* extensively in this chapter, most of the methods listed here are free. A better term might be *Web page promotion*.

With this point in mind, you should take the first step to advertising on the Web, which is to answer the following questions about your site:

- How much traffic do I want at my site?
- Does my site have a broad appeal, or is it for a more specialized audience?
- How much of a budget do I have to advertise my site?
- How much time can I devote to advertising my site?
- How important is it to the success of my business (or hobby or organization) that my site become well known?

If your page is just a hobby, where you share information with others who share your interests, you can mount a low-key advertising campaign. Most of the people who find your page will do so through links with other pages that cover the same topics. Think hard about the sites that you like to visit, and you'll probably find that most of your visitors like the same sites.

Note

Even if you are starting a page just as a hobby, it doesn't need to end there. Many of the most successful aspects of the Web began as part-time activities.

Non-profit organizations can achieve tremendous exposure on the Web, far out of proportion to the amount of money invested. These organizations often have enough manpower to find a large number of free locations to advertise the site.

For a small business, the Web can be an excellent place to advertise. On the Web, unlike most other forms of advertising, even a small company can produce a presence as impressive as that of a huge conglomerate. Unlike the print world, the Web allows anyone access to full-color images regardless of budget. In the democratic world of the Web, all addresses are equally impressive, giving your company real estate that is just as valuable as that of your larger competitors.

If your company is a mail-order or service business that can support customers around the country, or even the world, investing a greater proportion of money and energy in Web advertising may well be worthwhile. If you work at one of these companies, you may want to consider using a commercial marketing service.

Registering with WWW Search Servers

Most people find what they're looking for on the Web by using one of the many available search tools. These systems are huge databases containing as many as 20 million Web pages, coupled with powerful indexing software that allows for quick searches. Many of the searchers are run on mainframe computers or large parallel processors that can handle hundreds of searches simultaneously.

In the beginning of the Web, the first search servers were run by universities, but now most of these early efforts have been taken over by private companies. What benefit do these companies find in providing free searches on these expensive computers? Advertising! The index sites are some of the most frequently visited on the Web, and the maintainers of these sites can charge high rates to the companies that advertise on these pages.

> **Note**
>
> In WebTrack's study of Web advertising, they discovered that five of the top ten sites in terms of revenues from advertising were search tools.

In addition to the older sites, more than a hundred newer indexes are available. Some of them are restricted to a specific topic, and others are still very small, but all offer the opportunity to get your site noticed.

As you explore the Web, you soon discover that it possesses its own collection of fauna. The wildlife of the Web consists of autonomous programs that work their way across the millions of links that connect the sites, gathering information along the way.

These programs are known by such colorful names as *robots*, *crawlers*, *walkers*, *spiders*, *worms*, and (in the case of one Australian program) *wombats*. What do these wanderers do? Almost without exception, they arrive at a page and search it for any links to other pages. These new links are recorded and followed in turn. When all the links on a particular chain have been followed, the next path is restored from the database, and the process continues. Examples of these searchers are Lycos and Webcrawler. A large number of special-purpose wanderers are also used to generate statistics regarding the Web. These programs do not generate databases that can be used for text searching.

The alternatives to these crawlers are the structured systems. They store Web pages indexed against a series of categories and subcategories. The hierarchical nature of these systems appeals to many people who are more comfortable using an index where they can see all the categories.

The type of system on which you perform your searches is entirely up to your personal preferences. From the standpoint of advertising your site, you need to be aware of the differences. Some of the structured systems restrict you to a limited number of index entries. This limitation can mean that people who are looking for just the things that you offer may not find you because they are looking in the wrong place.

Major Search Servers

A complete listing of indexes would be out of date as soon as it was finished. New sites are added monthly, and even sites that are maintained by large corporations have disappeared. I have listed a few of the main sites in this section, but you should take the time to do some of your own searching when you decide to publish your pages.

In the big league is a handful of sites that can claim to have indexed a sizable portion of the Web. These sites are the most popular systems used by the majority of Web surfers. You need to register with these servers first to maximize your exposure. The following sites are the cream of the index crop at this time:

- *Alta Vista*—A new and very fast site run by Digital. This system will become much more popular as people become aware of it. It is located at **http://www.altavista.digital.com/**.

- *Infoseek*—A popular site with a good general-purpose index. The URL for Infoseek is **http://www.infoseek.com/**.

- *Inktomi*—A new site at the University of California at Berkeley. It is very fast and complete but with an emphasis toward academic sites. You can find Inktomi at **http://inktomi.berkeley.edu/**.

- *Lycos*—One of the granddaddies of the indexing world. Lycos started at Carnegie Mellon University. This huge site has a broad international database. It is located at **http://www.lycos.com/**.

- *Nerd World*—A category-based system that has a dedicated following. Nerd World's main page is at **http://www.nerdworld.com/**.

- *Webcrawler*—The biggest of the Web spiders, Webcrawler was started in 1994 at the University of Washington, but it is now owned by America Online (see fig. 20.1). This system is one of the fastest available. You can find Webcrawler at **http://webcrawler.com/**.

- *Yahoo*—The largest of the category-based systems, Yahoo started out as a hobby but has grown into a major provider of search services (see fig. 20.2). It is located at **http://www.yahoo.com/**.

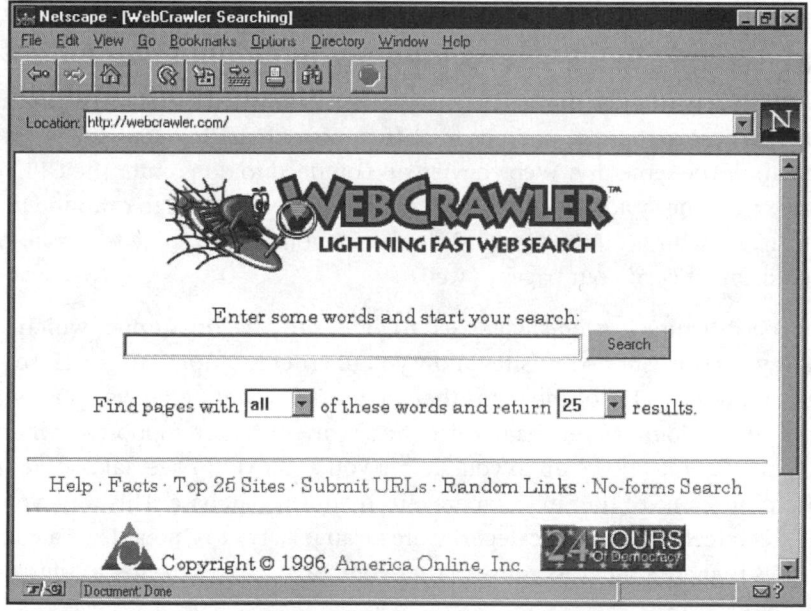

Fig. 20.1
Webcrawler is a Web spider that searches the Web for links to pages not in its index.

Fig. 20.2
On the other hand, Yahoo is a database that organizes sites based on a structure of categories.

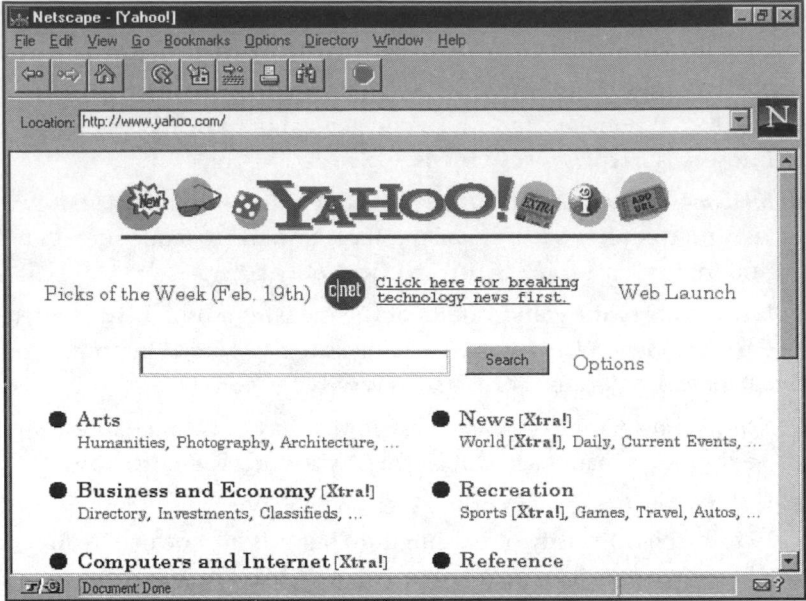

Just below this first tier is a larger group of very good sites. These sites don't have the traffic that the bigger sites do, but that can change quickly. These sites tend to have loyal audiences who use them instead of the primary sites, often because of their indexing categories.

Registering with the Search Servers

Registering with most of these servers is easy. Almost all sites have a page that you can access from the main page, with a form for adding your site to the system. If the server is a Web crawler, all you need to do is enter the URL for your page. The system then dispatches a robot to your page to examine it. This robot returns all the keywords found on your pages. Some servers also record the titles of your pages as well.

For the structured systems, you need to enter the categories under which you want your site listed. Most sites allow you to enter multiple categories, so you should prepare a list of the items that are most relevant before you start your submission. Some servers have a list of categories that are supported, whereas others leave the choice up to you. Before you enter your page, take some time to explore some of the sites that are already in the database. This way, you can get a feel for how the categories are arranged. Try to find at least a couple of sites that are similar to yours so that your page will not be lost in the wrong sections.

In this example, I walk you through the registration of a Web page on Yahoo! This example is a Web page that lists the naval battles in the American Civil War located at **www.civilwar.org/pub/html/naval/home.html**.

1. Because Yahoo! is a structured system, the first step toward registering a page is to determine which category the page belongs to. Go to the Yahoo! home page and pick the category that most closely fits the page. In this case, it is Social Science.

2. Continue to select subcategories until you reach the level that best describes your page. For you, it would be the category **Arts:Humanities:History:American History:19th Century: Civil War**.

3. Click on the Add URL menu item at the top of the page. The Add URL form then appears with the Category field already filled out (see fig. 20.3).

4. Now you fill in the rest of the blanks. Under additional categories, you can enter any other categories that you find to be applicable. In this case, every other path that you take from the Yahoo! home page brings you back to the same subcategory, so you can leave this blank. If the location of the site were relevant, you could add the information to the correct fields.

5. You need to write a brief description of the site for the Comments section. You should write a short sentence or two that lets users of Yahoo! know what your page is about (see fig. 20.4).

6. You then need to give your name and e-mail address. The form also asks if the name that you used is also the contact person for the site. Because you are submitting your own site, the answer is yes.

7. Click on the Submit button.

8. Yahoo! attempts to locate the page that you submitted and verify that URL is valid. If it is, you're informed that the submission was successful. Yahoo! then reviews the site and the category and, if everything is correct, lists your site in about two weeks.

Maybe this process seems like a lot of work to you. After all, you just spent the last three months huddled over your keyboard perfecting the last details on the perfect Web page, and now you want to take it easy for a while. Why worry about advertising your page when a handy little Web crawler is bound to wander by and index the whole thing for you?

The first problem with this approach is that a Web robot can't find your site unless it's linked to a page that the robot already knows about and is traversing.

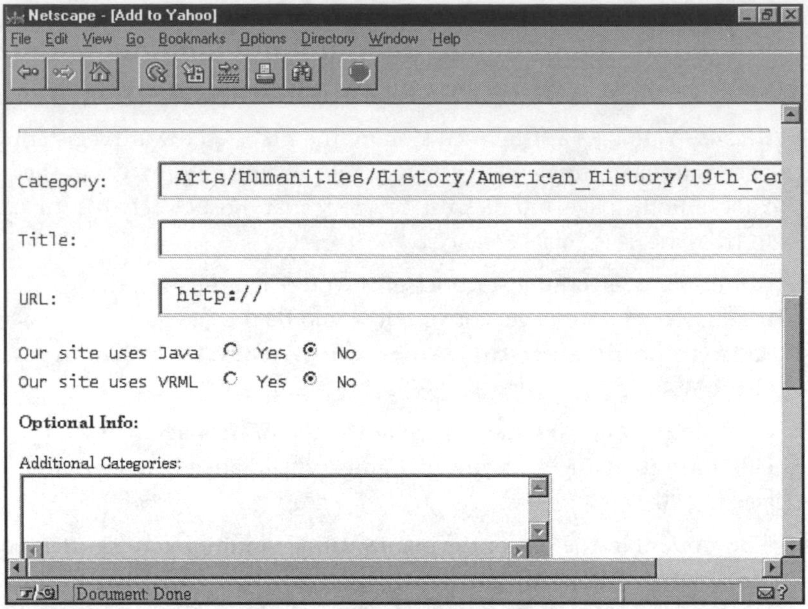

Fig. 20.3
You add URLs
to the Yahoo
database using a
forms-based
interface.

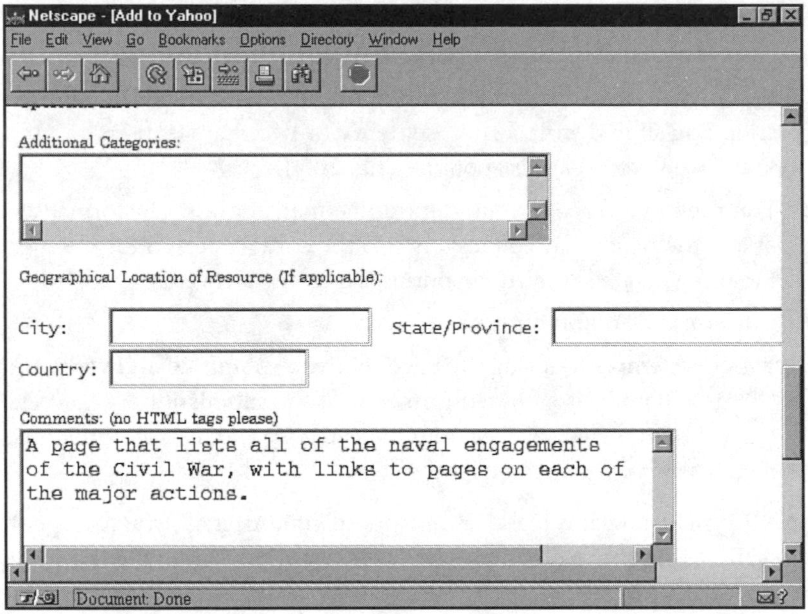

Fig. 20.4
After you select
the categories, you
need to write a
brief description
of your page.

The second problem is more subtle. When a Web crawler explores your page, it can get the information used in the index from many sources. Some servers use the page titles, others use the headings, still others actually scan the entire body and attempt to make sense of it. The problem with all these methods is that they may not find all the categories that can refer to your site. Often, the words that are used in headings or titles are not in their simplest form. It would be a shame not to be listed because the title of your page uses an irregular verb.

The location problem can be worked around in one of several ways, depending on the nature of the crawler. Some systems scan the newsgroups looking for new URLs to add to their search list. Others accept URLs that are e-mailed to them. Finally, you can just go to the searcher's home page and submit your page. Any or all of these methods invite the robots to pay a visit to your site. Of these methods, the most reliable by far is to drop in on the Web page of one or two of the more popular servers and submit your URL. Most of the Web crawlers are far easier to register with than are the structured systems.

Caution

Some of the earliest robots were poorly written and could swamp a server with hundreds of requests within seconds of each other. Fortunately, most recent robots are courteous enough not to overload their hosts. If your server does crash, check the logs for a single site that retrieved many documents within a short period of time. If such a site exists, try to contact the postmaster at the site that made the requests and let him or her know about the problems that you saw.

The problem with misindexing is a little more difficult to solve. Fortunately, most of the crawlers search the HTML source for a Web page looking for the META tag. If a keyword list is assigned to a META field, the crawler parses the keywords and uses them for the index.

Troubleshooting

I don't really want to have little autonomous programs wandering around in my system. How can I keep Web robots away?

You really cannot keep a robot out of a Web page that's visible to the rest of the Internet. However, many of the robot writers follow an unofficial standard. If you include the file /robots.txt on your server with the proper information in it, many robots read the file and follow your wishes.

The syntax for robots.txt is as follows: Create a line that begins with the field name User-agent:. This field must then contain the name of the robot that you want to restrain. You can have multiple User-agent fields, or if you want to exclude all agents not specifically mentioned in a User-agent field, you can use a field value of *. The line following each User-agent field should begin with the field name Disallow:.

(continues)

III

Advanced HTML

(continued)

This field should contain a URL path. Any URL that begins with the path specified in the Disallow field should be ignored by the robot named in the User-agent field.

Some examples of this file are

Any text that begins with a pound-sign is treated as a comment

User-agent: Webcrawler # This restriction will only apply to the robot named Webcrawler

Disallow: /webpages/data/ # Any URLs that begin with the path shown here will be skipped by Webcrawler

This example is the universal "do not disturb" sign

User-agent: * # All robots

Disallow: / # Every URL begins with a / in the path

Using Submission Services

You do not always have to do all the work yourself. Several good services submit your pages to the major search systems for you. Many of these services have a charge for this function, but a few services are available for free.

> **Note**
>
> *Submit-it* is a nice forms-based system that allows you to enter all the relevant data for your page, after which it registers you with your choices of more than a dozen popular search tools (see fig. 20.5). This service is provided for free and can help you to hit most of the major search sites. You can found it at **<http://www.submit.com>**.

Just as with the search tools, any list of services on the Web is obsolete almost as fast as it is generated. Your best bet is to do a little checking on your own to see what else is out there. A good place to start looking is at the Web Announcements topic on Yahoo.

The big advantage of a submission server is that it cuts down on the amount of work that you have to do. The disadvantage is that your submissions are made automatically, using the same categories and keywords for each database. This is probably sufficient if your page is personal or is intended for a specific audience.

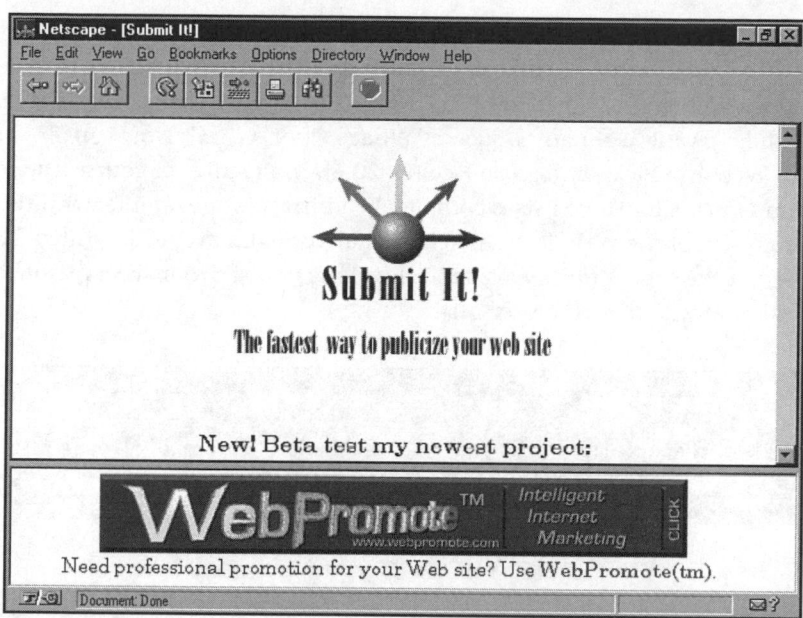

Fig. 20.5
Submit-it! is a powerful tool for registering with multiple search engines quickly.

If your page is the Web presence for your company or your organization, spending the time learning each of the databases yourself is probably better, so that you can ensure that your listing ends up under the right headings. After all, the time required to submit your page is nothing compared to the hard work that you've put into making it as good as it is.

What's New Servers

Many servers are dedicated to posting new listings. These systems may display a new site for many weeks or for just a few hours, depending on the nature of the server and the number of new submissions that it receives. Some of these servers have strict rules regarding acceptability, so be sure to check them out thoroughly before submitting your site.

The advantage of these "what's new" services is that many people visit them on a regular basis, so getting listed can bring visitors to your site who might not have found it otherwise. The disadvantages are that your stay on the server is for a limited time, the traffic tends to be casual browsers rather than people with a strong interest, and some of the servers have an annoying habit of listing sites in alphabetical order. This last disadvantage may seem unimportant, but the *Aardvarks Anonymous* site is much more likely to get noticed than is the *Zoological Society of Aardvark Fanciers*.

III

Advanced HTML

Best of the Web Listings

One of the more amazing things to come out of the Web has been the tremendous proliferation of "Best of the Web" sites. These systems generate listings under a variety of names, such as What's Cool, What's Hot, Top 5%, Best of the Web, Hot Picks, and so on (see fig. 20.6). In practice, of course, the selection of pages for these lists is completely arbitrary. For example, with the rapid growth of the Web, it is unlikely that anyone has ever even visited five percent of the sites currently available, let alone enough to make a reasonable judgment of which are the very best.

Fig. 20.6

Several organizations present "Best of the Web" awards.

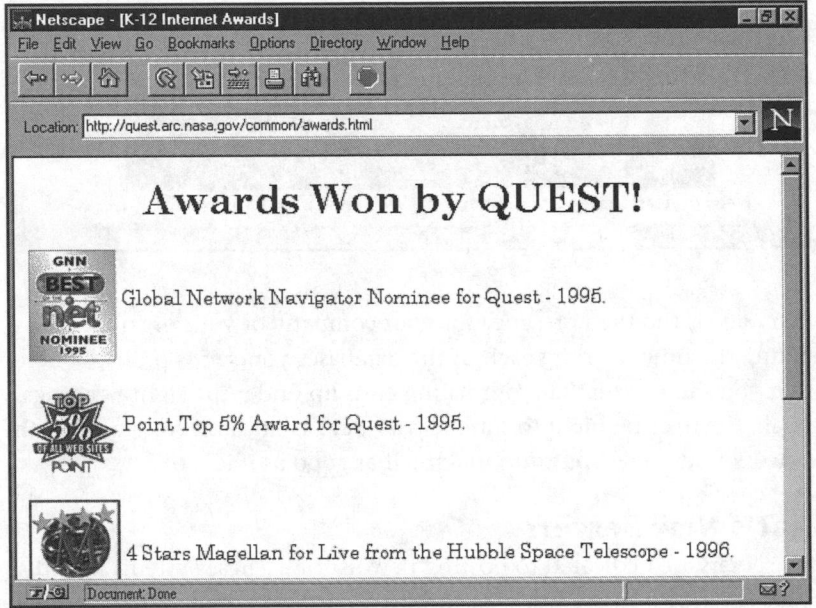

So how are these lists maintained? In most cases, you can submit the URL of your site to the administrator of the list, and he or she visits your site and reviews it. If your site meets whatever selection criteria the list is based on, you get added to the list.

Some of these lists provide you with a small graphic that you can display on your page to indicate that you have been awarded the honor, and virtually all the lists include links to your page after you have been accepted.

What is the real value of these lists? In the cosmic scheme of things, very little. But some of these lists are well known, and many people use them as launching points for random surfing. If you have a general interest site, getting it listed on a couple of these pages can really boost your traffic.

Some examples of these sites are

- *Cool Site of the Day*—A strange and quirky site located at **http://cool.infi.net/**.

- *Macmillan Winner's Circle*—A site that recognizes excellence in personal home pages at **http://www.mcp.com/general/workshop/winner/**.

- *What's Cool*—If you can manage to get yourself onto Netscape's What's Cool Page, you'll have to beat back the visitors with a stick. You can find this page of pages at **http://home.netscape.com/home/whats-cool.html**.

Links from Other Web Sites

Even more than the Web crawlers and structured systems, the primary method for traversing the Web is by using links found on other pages (see fig. 20.7). To expose your page to the maximum number of potential visitors, you should make an effort to get as many sites as possible to include links to your site.

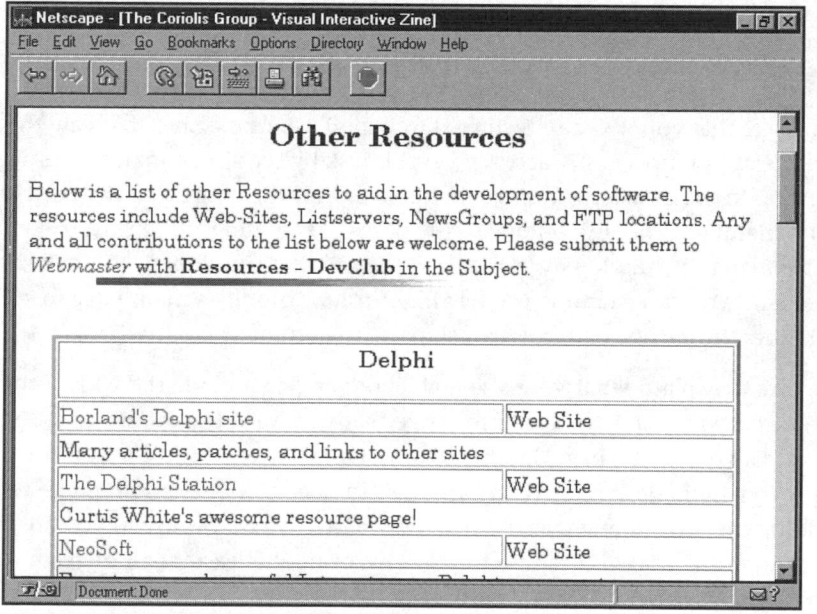

Fig. 20.7
Many sites have long lists of links to other related sites.

Most sites that cover a specific topic are more than pleased to include links to other sites that cover the same topic. By including as many links as possible,

III

Advanced HTML

they make themselves more useful and, hence, more popular. To encourage people to link to your page, you need to identify sites that might be interested in linking to yours and then contact the site administrator.

The best way to find sites to contact about linking to your site is to surf the Web. Find sites that are of interest to you, and you'll probably find the sites that are of interest to people who would visit your site. Where should you start surfing? The same places that your visitors would.

Start with the indexes and see what's out there. Try several of the more popular ones, and be sure to try both structured systems and Web crawlers. If one of indexes is particularly useful, you know that it is a good place to register your site. The ones that aren't useful can wait before you submit to them.

After you find some sites, visit them and see what they have to offer. You're looking for sites that have a theme that is similar to yours, without being identical. For example, if your page contains links to everything that a person might ever want to know about hog farming, pages that might make good links to your page include general farming pages, pages that cover animal husbandry, and pages for companies that do business with hog farmers, including both suppliers and consumers. Other pages that also cover aspects of hog farming but that are not duplicates of yours would also be worth linking to.

The best way to get a link to your Web page is to simply contact the owner of the page that you'd like to be linked from and ask him or her to create the link. You can most easily accomplish this task by sending e-mail to the page author. In most cases, you should be able to find the address of the person who maintains the link on one of the pages at the site. Failing this, try sending e-mail to the address *Webmaster* at the site that interests you. Finally, if all else fails, you can examine the HTML source for the site's main page to see whether the author's address is included in a comment field.

Be sure to explain what your site is all about and to include the URL of the home page in your message. If the page that you want the other site to link to is not your home page, let the Webmaster know what the correct URL is. A brief (one-line) description of your page can save him or her some time when adding the link. Remember that the Webmaster is just as busy as you are and that anything that you can do to make his or her life easier will increase the chance that he or she links to your page.

Of course, you can expect that the person in charge of the other site will check out your page before adding a link. He or she will want to make sure that your page actually is what you say it is and that the quality is such that it will improve his or her site to be linked to yours.

To make your site more worthwhile for others to link to, the first step is to ensure that it is free of HTML errors and that it loads correctly. Have your site examined by other people from outside your site to check that all the images are available and that all the tags display in the proper format. No one wants to be associated with a site that is filled with sloppy work.

Second, include useful, current, and interesting information and images. No one wants to spend time downloading a site just to find that it contains a mess of outdated or boring gibberish. Links to shareware programs can also make your page more popular.

Caution

Before adding a link to download any program, be sure that the program explicitly states that it is for freeware or shareware distribution, particularly if it is not stored on your server.

Finally, make it attractive. Ask yourself if the page makes you want to read it; then get the opinions of some people you can trust.

An important step toward making your site successful is to include a number of links to other sites that might be of interest to visitors to your site. The entire concept of the Web revolves around the interconnection of millions of sites. Don't make your page a dead end.

Tip

Check occasionally that all the links on your page still lead somewhere. Pages maintained by other people may disappear, often without notice.

If your site is a personal page, include connections to pages of your friends and colleagues. A hobby site should include as many links to other sites with similar interests as you can find. Check the links to make sure that they point to pages that you want to be associated to; then include them.

Note

Although you can certainly add a link to a page without the prior consent of the owner of the page, contacting the maintainer of the page to let him or her know of the new link is courteous. He or she may also have a preference as to which page you establish the link to.

Business and organization pages can include links to other sources of information related to your site. Including links to your competitors is not necessary, but having links that point to your suppliers and customers might be very effective. Encourage them to include reciprocal links back to your page. Remember that the most effective form of advertising is networking and that a link to your page is an implicit recommendation.

Specialized Index Pages

If your pages are focused on a specific topic, registering with any specialized index pages that cover your area of interest is well worth the time.

At present, you can find many sites for business-related topics. This fact isn't surprising, but what is amazing is the incredible variety of index pages available for other interests as well. A search of the Web turns up many specialized pages that contain dozens of links. The following are a few examples of these pages:

■ *Art Planet*—A professionally run site that allows searches based on companies, keywords, or artists (see fig. 20.8). It is located at **http://www.artplanet.com/index.html**.

Fig. 20.8

You can use specialized search tools such as Art Planet to locate your page successfully.

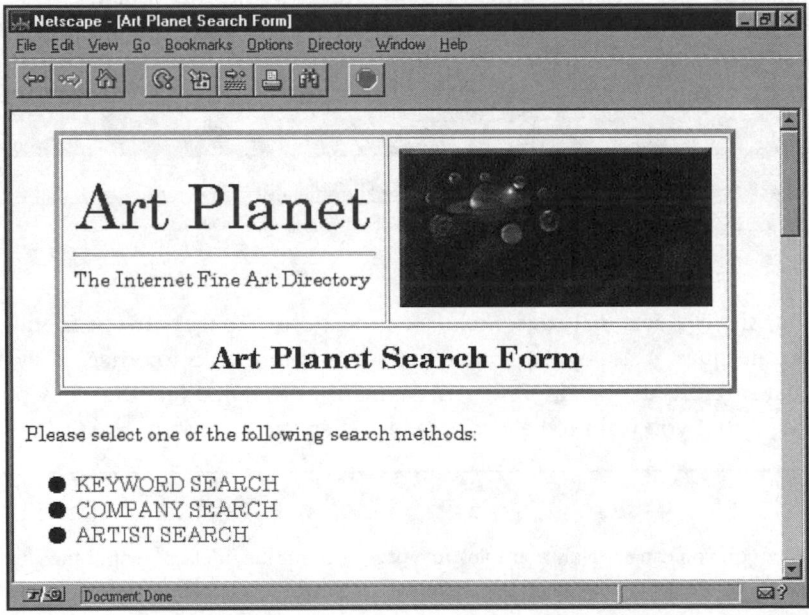

■ The *Hamster Page*—This is the *definitive* hamster resource page, and you can find it at **http://www.tela.bc.ca/hamster/**.

- *Special Needs Education Network*—A site that provides a number of links to resources for people with special needs and parents of children with special needs. You can find it at **http://schoolnet2.carleton.ca/ ~kwellar/snewww.html**.

- *Chess Space*—A comprehensive index to everything in the chess world. It is located at **http://www.redweb.com/chess**.

- *Points of Pediatric Interest*—More than 650 links dedicated to pediatric medicine and child care. You can find it at **http:// www.med.jhu.edu/peds/neonatology/poi.html**.

- *Church Online*—A worldwide list of Christian churches. It is located at **http://www.churchonline.com/index.html**.

In the business world, pages exist for many different types of companies. You can see some of the tremendous variety in the following pages:

- *TruckNet*—A site specializing in just about everything that you might ever want to know about the trucking industry. It is located at **http:// www.truck.net**.

- *Petro-Links*—This site has links to oil companies, suppliers, petroleum industry magazines, and applicable government agencies. It is located at **http://www.findlinks.com/petrolinks.html**.

- *Fashion Net*—A service with hundreds of links to companies that are involved in the fashion and clothing industries. Not all these companies have Web sites, but many do. You can find Fashion Net at **http:// www.fashion.net**.

- *Thomas Register*—A site run by the company that publishes the famous Thomas Register of Manufacturers. If you work for a manufacturing company or if you supply manufacturing companies, you really should submit your site at **http://www.thomasregister.com**.

Using the Newsgroups Effectively

A Web site is very difficult to find in the vast reaches of the Internet. Fortunately, you can use public bulletin boards to broadcast information to a number of people at the same time. These public areas are known as *newsgroups*, and they serve as public forums for communications and debate.

Much like everything else on the Internet, these groups have their own rules and customs. Very broadly, they fall into two categories: *open* and *moderated* groups. Open groups are pretty much what they sound like, in that anyone can post a message. Unfortunately, this freedom often leads to a very low signal-to-noise ratio. Moderated groups require that all postings are passed through a moderator (or group of moderators) who screens the messages and removes off-topic messages. This process greatly improves the proportion of postings that are relevant to the subject of the newsgroup.

Regardless of the type of newsgroup, proper use can greatly increase the traffic at your Web site. By the same token, however, improper use can cause ill feelings and will not attract the visitors that you are looking for.

The Announcement Groups

The first newsgroups to use when spreading the word about your new Web site are the *announcement* groups. These groups are dedicated to the purpose of broadcasting messages dealing with new sites and services (see fig. 20.9). Most of these groups are moderated and do an excellent job of keeping messages on topic.

Fig. 20.9
Comp.infosystems.
www.announce is
the number one site
for posting new sites.

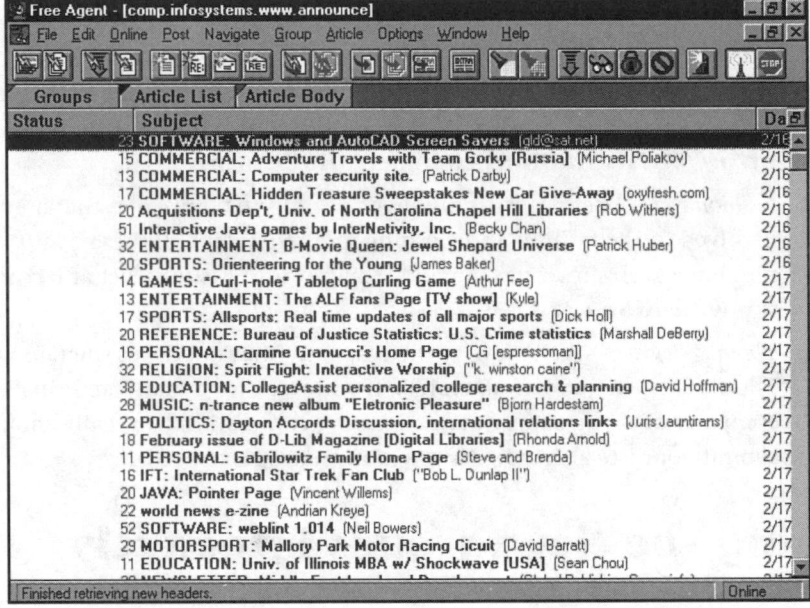

The number one group for new Web page announcements is **comp.infosystems.www.announce**, which lists virtually every site that is submitted to it. The rules of this group are standard for many of the announcement groups. Postings should be relevant to the purpose of the group and should not have a commercial purpose other than the announcement of a Web site that provides further information about a commercial product or service. The message announcing the site should have the URL of the page clearly listed in the message, preferably on a separate line. The message should also include a clear but brief description of the nature of the site. Finally, the subject of the message should be clear and precise. It is recommended that the subject begin with a word or two that clearly defines your site. See the example shown in figure 20.10.

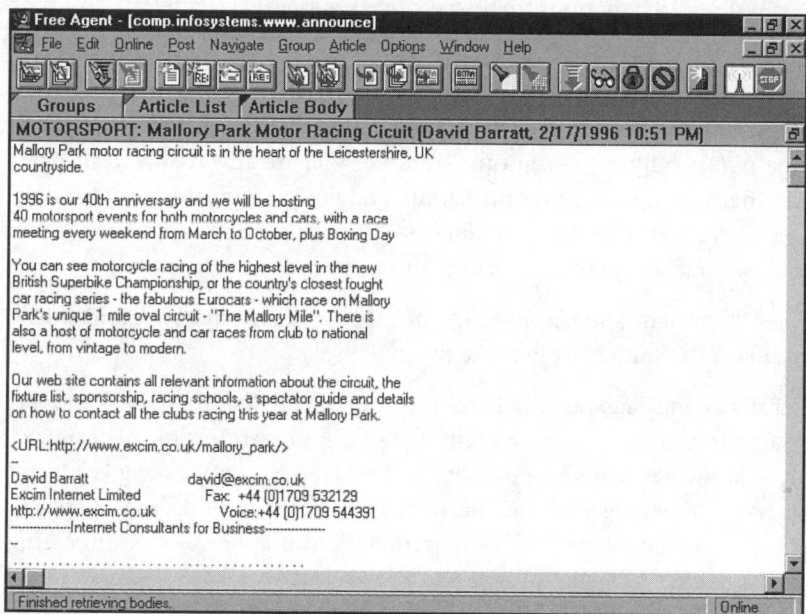

Fig. 20.10
This announcement is clear and concise, and it lets potential visitors know what they can expect.

Other good groups to announce in are **comp.internet.net-happenings** and **misc.entrepreneurs** (for business sites).

Other Newsgroups

After you have posted on the announcement newsgroups, you should take some time to find any other groups that may involve topics covered in your Web site. Far more than 20 thousand newsgroups are operating right now, although your Internet provider may cache only a fraction of this number. With this kind of diversity present, finding the groups that most closely match your interests is normally not difficult.

After you narrow down the field to a small handful of groups, the next step is to read the various messages that are posted. Try to identify people who are regular posters, and look for threads that have a long life. This practice of reading messages on a group without posting is known as *lurking*. You lurk in a group to become more familiar with it before you post.

III

Advanced HTML

One of the features of many groups is the occasional posting of what is called a *FAQ*. This message is a list of *Frequently Asked Questions*, and reading it carefully can help you avoid asking any questions that might have been answered repeatedly in the past.

The primary benefit to lurking is that when you are ready to post messages, you can do so in a manner that is perceived as highly competent and professional.

After you do start posting, you should make a special effort to ensure that your posts are well written and on topic. Remember that you are not just carrying on a friendly conversation, but rather you are advertising your page. Avoid mentioning your Web site in the body of your posting, but include your signature at the end of the message. If your postings are worth reading, people will make an effort to visit your pages, too.

On the other hand, *flames*, messages that are rude or offensive, and those that are off the subject only make people upset.

One form of message posting is *not* recommended: Sending large numbers of messages to post on many different newsgroups regardless of the group's topic is known as *spamming* (see fig. 20.11). This kind of posting is a tremendous waste of bandwidth, and many people, particularly those who pay for their access based on time spent logged in, do not appreciate your postings.

Fig. 20.11
The message about saving on long-distance charges is off-topic for this group and is an example of spamming.

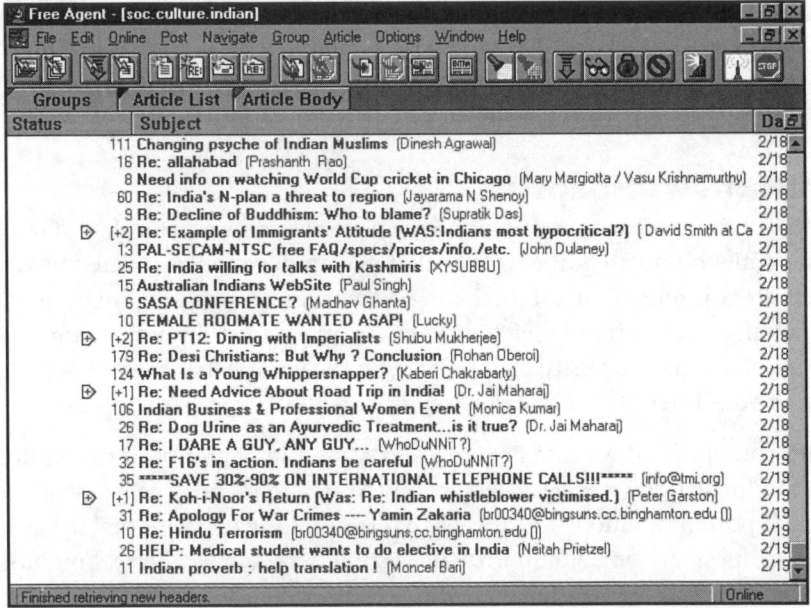

An unfortunate side effect of spamming is that it tends to attract retaliation from residents of the Internet. This retaliation can begin at the annoyance level and rapidly escalate. To avoid any unpleasantness, you should follow the rules and act in a responsible manner.

> **Note**
>
> The primary offense caused by spamming is the waste of huge amounts of storage space on computers around the world. To help curb the problem, many newsgroups have programs that can excise spamming messages automatically from the group, often before most people even see the message. One side effect of spamming is that you may become blacklisted, which can expose you to remarkable levels of harassment from cybervigilantes.

Purchasing Advertising Space

Although the idea of advertising on the Web is just starting to become popular, the potential is tremendous. A recent survey by WebTrack identified more than $12.4 million of spending in the fourth quarter of 1995. More than 250 active advertisers were found, some of whom had Web advertising budgets of over a half million dollars.

Although competing against a budget many times larger than yours may seem impossible, remember that in no other major media is the amount of money needed to reach thousands of potential customers so small. For a small- to medium-sized company, the Web can be an outstanding advertising bargain—if it is used carefully.

Many sites have more than one million visitors per day. This represents more potential customers than any method of advertising other than major magazines and newspapers. Most of these heavily visited sites recognize the value that their pages represent and have started to lease space on the pages. This space can vary from $250 per month up to $50,000 or more depending on the traffic at the site.

Although advertising at a site like one of the major search tools or on Netscape's home page might seem to be most effective, the most cost-effective sites may be those that have lower traffic counts. Look for sites that have traffic of at least a couple of thousand hits per day (see fig. 20.12). A number of services audit the number of visits (hits) that a site receives in a given period. Sites that subscribe to these services may be more expensive up front, but at least you'll know what you are paying for.

Fig. 20.12
Advertising on a busy site can bring many visitors to your site.

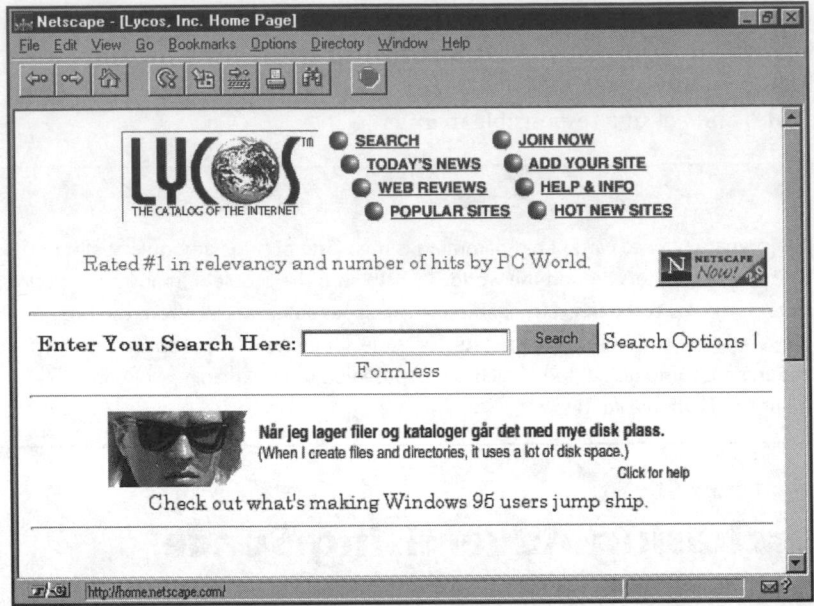

Tip

When you sponsor a site, make certain that your ad falls within a part of the page that people will spend most of their time looking at. For the most part, this is the top of the screen, but if the primary feature of the page is a form field that needs to be filled out, this could be the best area. Also check that a text anchor to your site is visible if the graphic image is not loaded. Many people working on slower connections regularly turn off automatic loading of images. Finally, if a text-only version of the page exists, have the site put an anchor on that page as well.

Internet Malls

A recent phenomena on the Web is the growth of the malls. These sites maintain links or pages for up to a couple of dozen different retail companies. The primary difference between these sites and the specialized directories is that the directories provide links to non-commercial sites as well.

At this time, the traffic on these sites has not yet reached the high levels that would command the top advertising rates. If your company deals primarily in mail-order retail or in services that can be performed remotely, exploring the possibility of opening a store front in one of these malls may be worthwhile (see fig. 20.13).

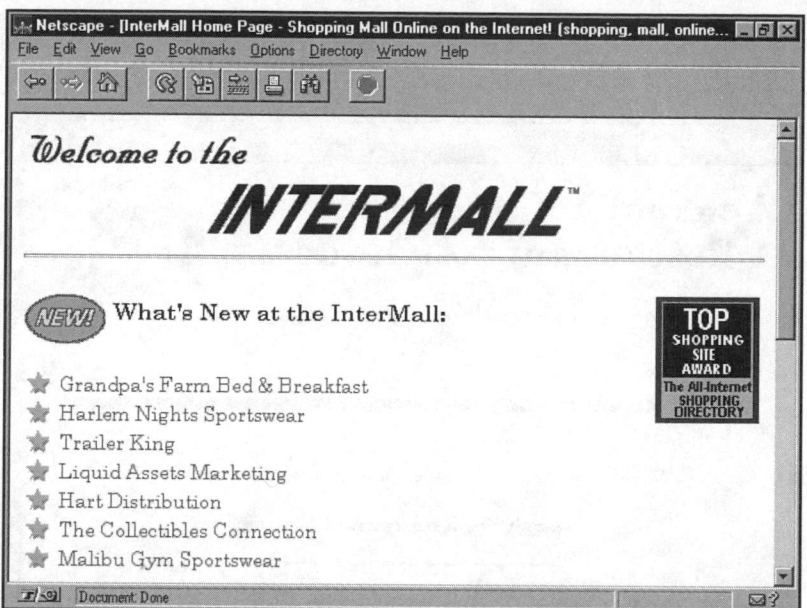

Fig. 20.13
A storefront in an Internet mall can be a good way to raise the visibility of your site.

Here are some examples of Internet malls:

- *DealerOnline*—A service that provides links for new and used car dealers and sellers of specialty and exotic automobiles. It is located at **http://www.dealeronline.com/**.

- *The Internet Mall*—This site lists over 8,000 different sites. Listings are free and include a paragraph of text. You can find The Internet Mall at **http://www.internet-mall.com/**.

- *fashionmall*—A site with a large number of connections to men's and women's clothing stores. A nice touch is the question and answer columns. You can find it at **http://www.fashionmall.com/**.

- *A Restaurant Netguide*—A mall filled with restaurants from around the world (see fig. 20.14). It may sound a little strange, but think about how many people travel to cities that they're not familiar with. It is located at **http://www.restaurant-guide.com/**.

III

Advanced HTML

Fig. 20.14
A Restaurant Netguide is a chance to show your menu to people before they even arrive in your city.

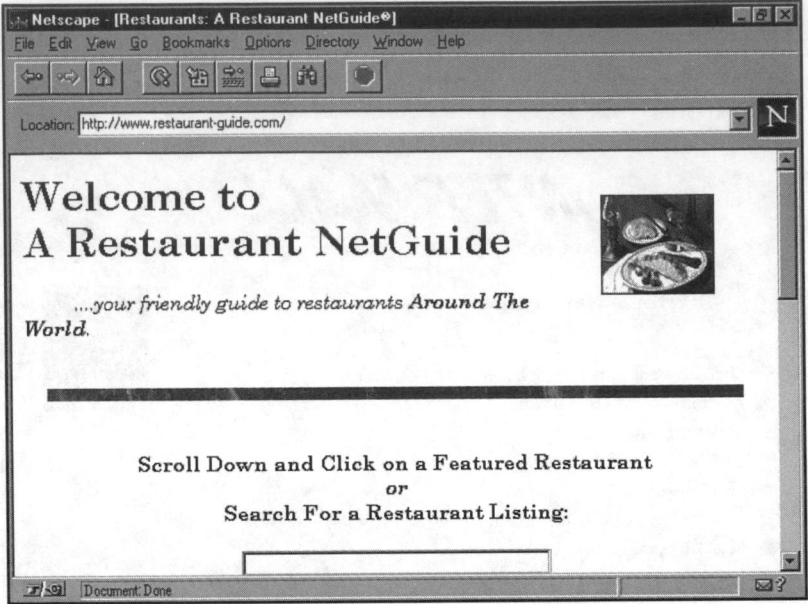

Using a Publicity Consultant

As you may have noticed, developing an effective Web advertising campaign can be a lot of work. For someone working on a page for a hobby, all this work might not matter much, but for a busy professional who is trying to build up business through the Web, the time required may be more than he or she can afford. One solution to this problem is to use a *publicity consultant*. This person is an agent who handles the details necessary for getting your site noticed.

Some of the functions that a publicity consultant should perform are as follows:

- Submitting your site to all the major search engines and to any others that may be appropriate. This submission should be followed up to make certain that the database actually added your site and that it can be located under the correct headings.

- Locating appropriate newsgroups. Some agents also identify threads that are relevant to your site and then post messages that subtly promote your site. This task is rather delicate, so you should ask to see examples of the agent's work before hiring him or her for this job.

- Identifying pages for reciprocal links. An agent should also take care of contacting the other sites and arranging for the links.

- Locating and purchasing advertising space on commercial Web pages. An agent with many contacts and clients may be able to arrange lower rates than you could by yourself.

- Developing and editing your Web site. Most agencies also do Web site development work. This can be useful if you are too busy to develop your own site or if you have no artistic capabilities. Even if you are a skilled artist or writer, having a professional critique your work and make suggestions may be productive.

Tip

Before you enter into a contract with anyone, you should ask for references from previous clients. Contact the references and ask if the agent was aggressive in promoting their sites and prompt in communicating with the clients. Also take the time to look at the client sites themselves. Are they professional in appearance? Well-designed pages indicate that the client's recommendation should carry a solid weight.

The cost of consultant services can range from a few hundred dollars to tens of thousands, depending on the scope of the work. When you do contract with one of these consultants, consider the possibility of basing his or her fee on the amount of traffic that is received at your site. This approach requires that the agent put his or her money on the line and increases the incentive to provide good service. Be aware that this tactic may increase the cost of services to you because the consultant is now sharing some of the risk.

Other Ways to Advertise Your Site

In this chapter, you've examined a number of ways that you can advertise your site on the Internet. This certainly does not mean that you can't increase your exposure through other methods. Indeed, if you don't use these other techniques, you may miss out on many opportunities.

The simplest of all of these methods is to include your site's URL in the signature on all your e-mail. Including your URL costs nothing and has the advantage of appearing before an audience that is (or at least should be) receptive to your message already.

You should also add your Web site URL to your business cards and stationery. In effect, your Web site is your office in cyberspace, and you should include its address alongside your physical office. Before you do so, however, remember to walk through your site carefully to check for a professional and

III

Advanced HTML

finished appearance. You wouldn't invite potential clients into a half-finished office covered with graffiti, and you shouldn't show them your work in progress on the Web either.

Finally, include your URL on any ads that you might place in magazines, newspapers, or trade journals. For many people, the discovery of a Web site in an advertisement is an illicit thrill. It's a way of letting people with access to the Web feel that they're an exclusive group and that you're catering especially to them. Take advantage of the cachet that comes with being on the Web whenever you can. ❖

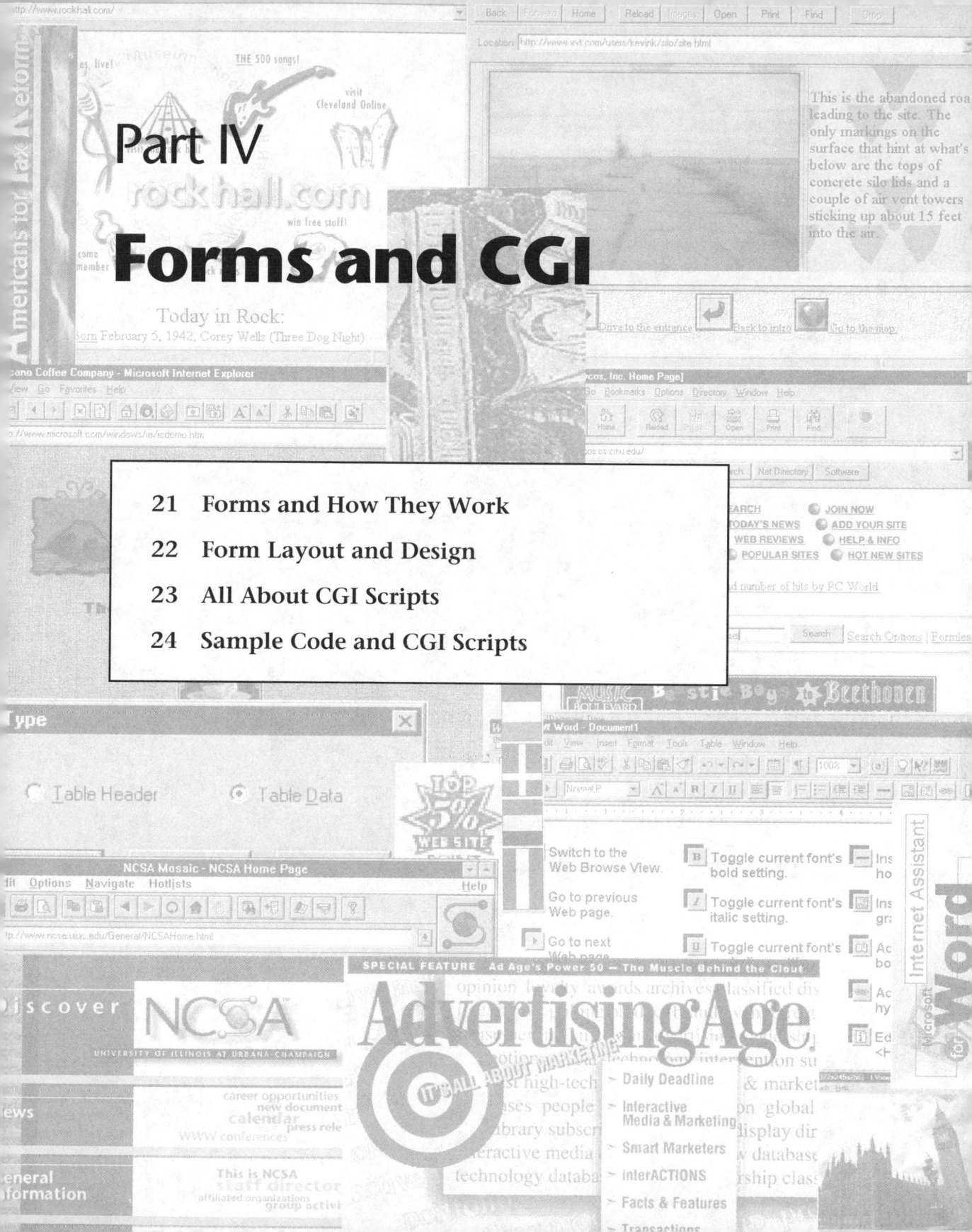

Part IV

Forms and CGI

## CHAPTER 21

Forms and How They Work

by Jim O'Donnell

Forms are one of the most popular features on the World Wide Web. They enable users to interact with the text and graphics that are displayed on your machine. You can make forms with simple *yes* or *no* questions, you can make highly complex order forms, or you can make a form for people to send you comments.

You create forms by providing a number of fields in which a user can enter information or choose an option. Then, when the user submits the form, the information is returned to a script. A script is a short program that is written specifically for each form. You can create them to do any number of things.

In this chapter, you learn about the following:

- What an HTML form is
- How to create a form
- How to use lists, check boxes, and radio buttons to present a list of options
- How to allow for the entry of text, secret text (such as passwords), and arbitrary length text
- How to allow the user to reset and submit completed forms

HTML Forms

HTML forms give the Web author the opportunity to solicit input from people reading his Web pages. Just as HTML provides many mechanisms for outputting information, the use of HTML forms enables information input. These forms can be used to solicit free-form text information, get answers to *yes* or *no* questions, and get answers from a set of options.

Forms can be used in Web pages for many different reasons. They can be used for something as simple as allowing visitors to your home page to sign a guest

▶ See "Adding
Live Chat Pages
to Your Site,"
p. 599

book or comment about your pages. Forms input can be used to create and maintain a discussion group over the Web. When combined with a secure method of transmission, forms can be used to conduct business over the Web. These, and many other uses can be achieved with HTML forms.

An Overview of HTML Forms Tags

The HTML tags you use to display forms are straightforward. There are three types of tags for creating fields: <TEXTAREA>, <SELECT>, and <INPUT>. You can put any number of these tags between the <FORM> and </FORM> container tags. The following is a brief description of each tag:

- **<TEXTAREA>**—This tag defines a field in which the end user can type multiple lines of text.

- **<SELECT>**—This tag enables the end user to choose among a number of options in either a scroll box or pop-up menu.

- **<INPUT>**—This tag provides all of the other types of input: single lines of text, radio buttons, check boxes, and the buttons to submit or clear the form.

<FORM>

The <FORM> element comes at the beginning of any form. When you create a <FORM> element, you also define the script it uses and how it sends data, using the ACTION and METHOD attributes:

- **ACTION**—This attribute points the form to a URL that will accept the form's information and do something with it. If you don't specify an ACTION, it sends the information back to the same URL the page came from.

- **METHOD**—This attribute tells the form how to send its information back to the script. The most common method is POST, which sends all the information from the form separately from the URL. The other option for METHOD is GET, which tacks the information from the form to the end of the URL.

Tip

Use POST for all of your forms unless it's a very simple query, especially because URLs have a definite length that they can't exceed.

The following is an example of a <FORM> tag:

```
<FORM METHOD="POST" ACTION="/cgi-bin/comment_script">
...
</FORM>
```

This example says that I want the form to send the completed form to the script `comment_script` in the `cgi bin` directory on my server and to use the `POST` method to send it.

▶ See "All About CGI Scripts," p. 525

IV

Caution

You can put any number of forms on the same HTML page, but be careful not to nest one form inside another. If you put in a <FORM> tag before finishing that last one, that line is ignored and all the inputs for your second form are assumed to go with the first one.

<TEXTAREA>

With <TEXTAREA>, you can provide a field for someone to enter multiple lines of information. By default, a <TEXTAREA> form shows a blank field four rows long and 40 characters wide. You can make it any size you want by using the ROWS and COLS attributes in the tag. You can also specify some default text by simply entering it between the <TEXTAREA> and </TEXTAREA> tags.

Tip

<TEXTAREA> fields are ideal for having users enter comments or lengthy information because they can type as much as they want in the field.

The options for the <TEXTAREA> tag are as follows:

- **NAME**—This is required. It defines the name for the data.
- **ROWS**—This sets the number of rows in the field.
- **COLS**—This sets the width of the field in characters.
- **Default text**—Any text between the <TEXTAREA> and </TEXTAREA> tags is used as default text and shows up inside the field.

While the ROWS and COLS attributes are not required, there is no default value for these that you will be guaranteed to get on every Web browser, so it's always a good idea to set them.

Tip

All input fields in a form—<TEXTAREA>, <SELECT>, and <INPUT>—must each have a NAME defined for its information.

Caution

Browsers can't interpret any HTML coding inside <TEXTAREA> tags (see listing 21.1).

Listing 21.1 TEXTAREA.HTM—<TEXTAREA> Default Text

```
<HTML>
<HEAD>
<TITLE>TEXTAREA.HTM</TITLE>
</HEAD>
<BODY>
<FORM>
<TEXTAREA NAME="comments" ROWS=4 COLS=40>Default text
1  2  3  ...
</TEXTAREA>
</FORM>
</BODY>
</HTML>
```

The result of listing 21.1 is shown in figure 21.1.

Fig. 21.1
The default text is shown as preformatted text in the <TEXTAREA> element.

<SELECT>

The <SELECT> element shows a list of choices in either a pop-up menu or a scrolling list. It's set up as an opening and closing tag with a number of choices listed in between. Just like the <TEXTAREA> element, the <SELECT> tag requires you to define a name. You can specify how many choices to show at once, using the SIZE attribute.

The options for the <SELECT> element are as follows:

- **NAME**—This is required. It defines the name for the data.

- **SIZE**—This attribute determines how many choices to show. If you omit SIZE or set it to 1, the choices are shown as a pop-up menu. If you set it to 2 or higher, it shows the choices in a scroll box. If you set SIZE larger than the number of choices you have within <SELECT>, a "nothing" choice is added. When the end user chooses this, it's returned as an empty field.

- **MULTIPLE**—This allows multiple selections. If you specify multiple, a scrolling window displays—regardless of the number of choices or the setting of SIZE.

Tip

Some WWW browsers won't properly display a scrolling window if the SIZE is 2 or 3. In that case, leave it as a pop-up menu or think about using the <INPUT> field's radio buttons.

You present the choices the end user will make within the <SELECT> and </SELECT> tags. The choices are listed inside the <OPTION> tag and don't allow any other HTML markup.

The options for the <OPTION> tag are the following:

- **VALUE**—This is the value to be assigned for the choice, which is what is sent back to the script and doesn't have to be the same as what is presented to the end user.

- **SELECTED**—If you want one of the choices to be a default, use the SELECTED option in the <OPTION> tag.

Consider listing 21.2, the result of which is shown in figure 21.2 and figure 21.3.

Listing 21.2   SELECT1.HTM—Selection via Pop-up Menu

```
<HTML>
<HEAD>
<TITLE>SELECT1.HTM</TITLE>
</HEAD>
<BODY>
What type of connection:
<FORM>
<SELECT NAME="network">
<OPTION SELECTED VALUE="ethernet"> Ethernet
<OPTION VALUE="token16"> Token Ring - 16MB
```

On the CD

(continues)

Listing 21.2   Continued

```
<OPTION VALUE="token4"> Token Ring - 4MB
<OPTION VALUE="localtalk"> LocalTalk
</SELECT>
</FORM>
</BODY>
</HTML>
```

Fig. 21.2
The <SELECT>
element will use
the default of a
pop-up menu
(size=1).

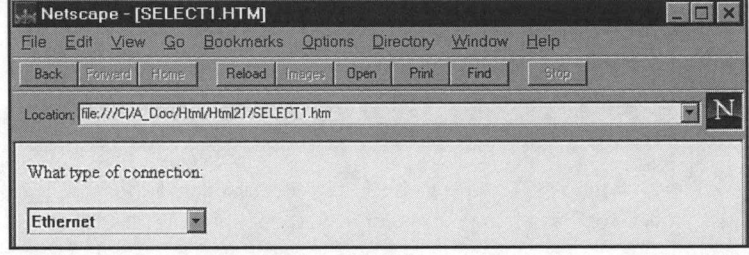

Fig. 21.3
The width of the
pop-up menu is
determined by the
size of the entries
listed with the
<OPTION>
elements.

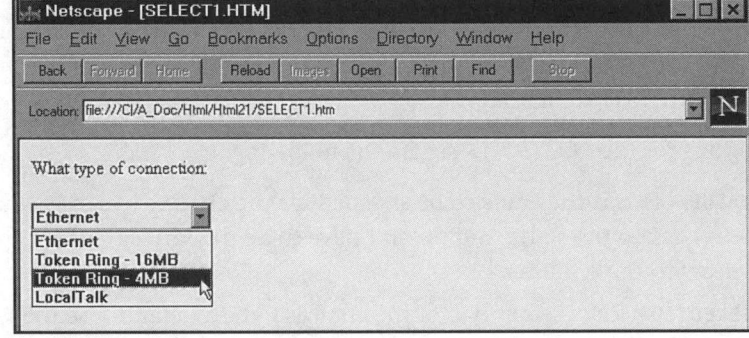

Suppose that you set the tag as shown in listing 21.3.

Listing 21.3   SELECT2.HTM—Selection via Scrollable List

On the CD

```
<HTML>
<HEAD>
<TITLE>SELECT2.HTM</TITLE>
</HEAD>
<BODY>
<FORM>
What type of Connection:
<SELECT MULTIPLE NAME="network">
<OPTION SELECTED VALUE="ethernet"> Ethernet
<OPTION VALUE="token16"> Token Ring - 16MB
<OPTION VALUE="token4"> Token Ring - 4MB
<OPTION VALUE="localtalk"> LocalTalk
</SELECT>
```

```
</FORM>
</BODY>
</HTML>
```

The result of listing 21.3 is shown in figure 21.4.

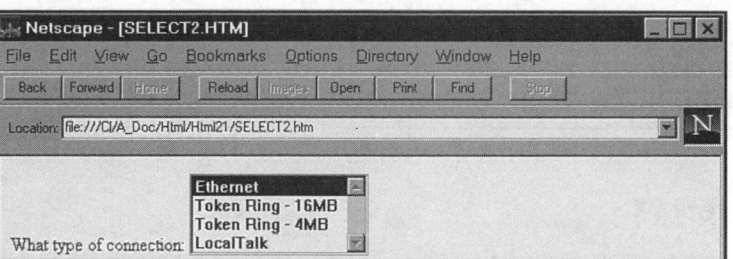

Fig. 21.4
If you use MULTIPLE within the <SELECT> tag, then the field becomes a list of choices.

IV

Troubleshooting

I know the most common choices I want to present, but I want to allow people to enter their own value if they want to. How can I do that?

Your best bet is to display the common choices in a <SELECT> box or pop-up menu, with one of the options set to Other. Then include an <INPUT> text field or a <TEXTAREA> field right after the list of choices (see listing 21.4).

Listing 21.4   SELECT3.HTM—Selection with "Other" Option

```
<HTML>
<HEAD>
<TITLE>SELECT3.HTM</TITLE>
</HEAD>
<BODY>
<FORM>
What type of Connection:
<SELECT MULTIPLE NAME="network">
<OPTION SELECTED VALUE="ethernet"> Ethernet
<OPTION VALUE="token16"> Token Ring - 16MB
<OPTION VALUE="token4"> Token Ring - 4MB
<OPTION VALUE="localtalk"> LocalTalk
<OPTION VALUE="other"> Other...
</SELECT>
<BR>
If other, please specify:<INPUT TYPE="text" NAME="network_other">
</FORM>
</BODY>
</HTML>
```

The result of listing 21.4 is shown in figure 21.5.

On the CD

Fig. 21.5
This type of form layout provides both a common list and a place for exceptions.

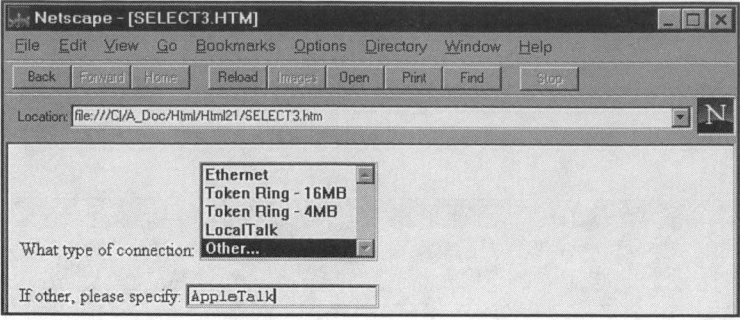

<INPUT>

<INPUT>, unlike <TEXTAREA> and <SELECT>, is a single tag option for gathering information. <INPUT> contains all of the other options for acquiring information, including simple text fields, password fields, radio buttons, check boxes, and the buttons to submit and reset the form.

The attributes for the <INPUT> tag are the following:

- **NAME**—This defines the name for the data. This field is required for all the types of input except SUBMIT and CLEAR.

- **SIZE**—This is the size of the input field in number of characters for text or password.

- **MAXLENGTH**—This specifies the maximum number of characters to be allowed for a text or password field.

- **VALUE**—For a text or password field, it defines the default text displayed. For a check box or radio button, it specifies the value that will be returned to the server if the box or button is selected. For the SUBMIT and RESET buttons, it defines the text inside the button.

- **CHECKED**—This sets a check box or radio button *on*. It has no meaning for any other type of <INPUT> tag.

- **TYPE**—This sets the type of input field you want to display. (See the types in the following section.)

INPUT TYPE

This section describes the possible values for the INPUT TYPE attribute.

TEXT

TEXT, the default input type, displays a simple line of text. You can use the attributes NAME (this is required), SIZE, MAXLENGTH, and VALUE with TEXT. For example, consider listing 21.5, the result of which is shown in figure 21.6.

Listing 21.5   INPUT1.HTM—Text Input Box

On the CD

```
<HTML>
<HEAD>
<TITLE>INPUT1.HTM</TITLE>
</HEAD>
<BODY>
<FORM>
A Phone Number: <INPUT TYPE="text" NAME="Phone" SIZE="15"
➥MAXLENGTH="12">
</FORM>
</BODY>
</HTML>
```

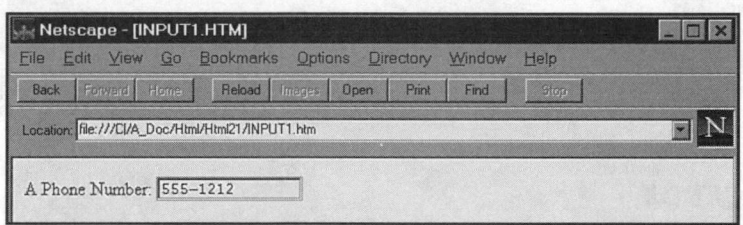

Fig. 21.6
The INPUT TEXT element provides a very flexible input field.

Troubleshooting

I want to let someone put in a very long URL, but the screen is not wide enough. How do I do that?

A good way to enable someone to put in an extremely long text line is to simply set the size to 60 or 80 characters and not set a maximum length. This will allow someone to put in a very long string, even if you can't see it all at once.

PASSWORD

PASSWORD, a modified TEXT field, displays typed characters as bullets instead of the characters actually typed. Possible attributes to include with the type PASSWORD include NAME (this is required), SIZE, MAXLENGTH, and VALUE. Consider listing 21.6, the result of which is shown in figure 21.7.

On the CD

Listing 21.6   INPUT2.HTM—Text Input Box with No Echo

```
<HTML>
<HEAD>
<TITLE>INPUT2.HTM</TITLE>
</HEAD>
<BODY>
<FORM>
Enter the secret word: <INPUT TYPE="password" NAME="secret_word"
➥Size="30" MAXLENGTH="30">
</FORM>
</BODY>
</HTML>
```

Fig. 21.7
Although it will look different in different browsers, the PASSWORD element hides the text that is typed.

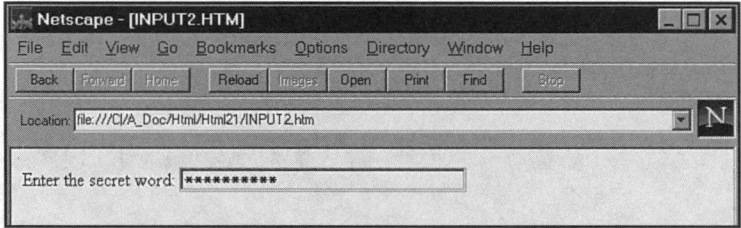

CHECKBOX

CHECKBOX displays a simple check box that can be checked or empty; use a check box when the choice is *yes* or *no* and doesn't depend on anything else. Possible attributes to include with the TYPE text include NAME (this is required), VALUE, and CHECKED (which defaults the check box as checked). Consider listing 21.7, the result of which is shown in figure 21.8.

Listing 21.7   CHECKBOX.HTM—Checkbox Form Input

On the CD

```
<HTML>
<HEAD>
<TITLE>CHECKBOX.HTM</TITLE>
</HEAD>
<BODY>
<FORM>
<INPUT TYPE="checkbox" NAME="checkbox1" VALUE="checkbox_value1">A
➥checkbox
<INPUT TYPE="checkbox" NAME="checkbox2" VALUE="checkbox_value2"
➥CHECKED>A preselected checkbox
</FORM>
</BODY>
</HTML>
```

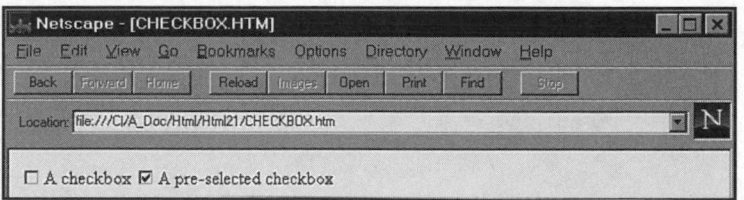

Fig. 21.8
Select the check boxes that are commonly checked to make the form easier to use.

Caution

You want to be especially careful when using check boxes and radio buttons in HTML documents with custom backgrounds or background colors. Depending on the Web browser used, check boxes and radio buttons will sometimes not show up with dark backgrounds.

RADIO

RADIO is a more complex version of a check box, allowing only one of a set to be chosen. You can group radio buttons together using the NAME attribute; keep all buttons in the same group under one NAME. Possible attributes to include with the TYPE text include NAME (this is required), VALUE, and CHECKED. Consider listing 21.8, the result of which is shown in figure 21.9.

Listing 21.8   RADIO1.HTM—Radio Button Form Input

```
<HTML>
<HEAD>
<TITLE>RADIO1.HTM</TITLE>
</HEAD>
<BODY>
Form #1:
<FORM>
<INPUT TYPE="radio" NAME="choice" VALUE="choice1"> Yes.
<INPUT TYPE="radio" NAME="choice" VALUE="choice2"> No.
</FORM>
<HR>
Form #2:
<FORM>
<INPUT TYPE="radio" NAME="choice" VALUE="choice1" CHECKED> Yes.
<INPUT TYPE="radio" NAME="choice" VALUE="choice2"> No.
</FORM>
</BODY>
</HTML>
```

On the CD

Fig. 21.9

In the top form, without selecting *yes* or *no*, the end user can send back a "blank" value for this selection.

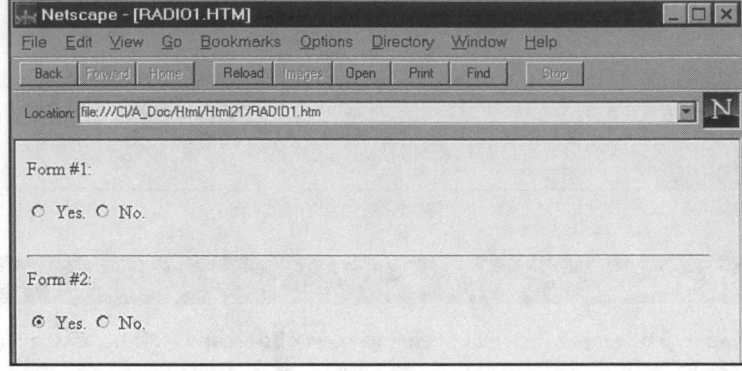

Listing 21.9 is a variation on listing 21.8. The result is shown in figure 21.10.

Listing 21.9 RADIO2.HTM—Radio Button Form Input with More Choices

```
<HTML>
<HEAD>
<TITLE>RADIO2.HTM</TITLE>
</HEAD>
<BODY>
<FORM>
One Choice:<BR>
<INPUT TYPE="radio" NAME="choice1" VALUE="choice1" CHECKED>(1)
<INPUT TYPE="radio" NAME="choice1" VALUE="choice2">(2)
<INPUT TYPE="radio" NAME="choice1" VALUE="choice3">(3)
<BR>
One Choice:<BR>
<INPUT TYPE="radio" NAME="choice2" VALUE="choice1" CHECKED>(1)
<INPUT TYPE="radio" NAME="choice2" VALUE="choice2">(2)
<INPUT TYPE="radio" NAME="choice2" VALUE="choice3">(3)
<INPUT TYPE="radio" NAME="choice2" VALUE="choice4">(4)
<INPUT TYPE="radio" NAME="choice2" VALUE="choice5">(5)
</FORM>
</BODY>
</HTML>
```

Fig. 21.10

The end user has more choices in this variation. The first choice was the default in each list—this choice has been overridden in the second list.

> **Tip**
>
> If you want to provide a long list of choices, use the <SELECT> tag so the choice doesn't take up as much space on the page.

> **Caution**
>
> If you don't specify a set of radio buttons or check boxes with one of the values as SELECTED, then you could receive an empty field for that <INPUT> name.

RESET

RESET displays a push button with the preset function of clearing all the data in the form to its original value. You can use the VALUE attribute with the RE-SET tag to provide text other than "Reset" (the default) for the button. For example, consider listing 21.10. The result is shown in figure 21.11.

Listing 21.10   RESET.HTM—Form Reset Button

```
<HTML>
<HEAD>
<TITLE>RESET.HTM</TITLE>
</HEAD>
<BODY>
<FORM>
<INPUT TYPE="reset">
<BR>
<INPUT TYPE="reset" VALUE="Clear that form!">
</FORM>
</BODY>
</HTML>
```

On the CD

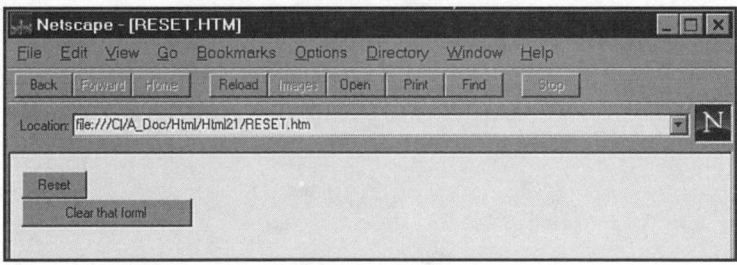

Fig. 21.11
The top button shows the default text for the RESET element.

SUBMIT

▶ See "All About CGI Scripts," p. 525

SUBMIT displays a push button with the preset function of sending the data in the form to the server to be processed, typically by a CGI script. You can use the VALUE attribute with RESET to provide text other than "Submit Query" (the default) for the button. Consider, for example, listing 21.11. The result is shown in figure 21.12.

On the CD

Listing 21.11   SUBMIT.HTM—Form Submit Button

```
<HTML>
<HEAD>
<TITLE>SUBMIT.HTM</TITLE>
</HEAD>
<BODY>
<FORM>
<INPUT TYPE="submit">
<BR>
<INPUT TYPE="submit" VALUE="Send in the data!">
</FORM>
</BODY>
</HTML>
```

Fig. 21.12
The top button shows the default text for the SUBMIT element.

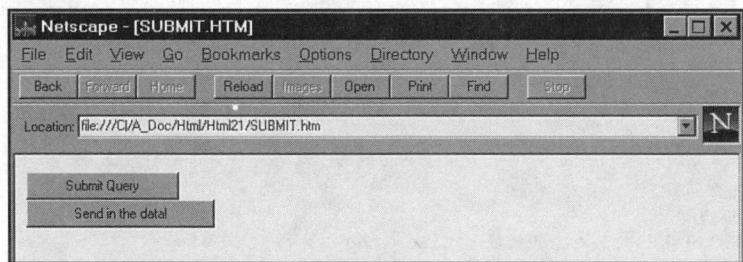

## CHAPTER 22

Form Layout and Design

Forms can be easy-to-read, simple one- or two-entry affairs with little to display; they can also be terrifically complex devices. As your forms get more complex, you need to carefully consider their layout. Think about how to make it obvious that certain titles are connected to certain fields, and think about how to make your forms easy for anyone to use. People are often put off by complex forms that are hard to understand, so it's in your best interest to make them easy and fun to use—regardless of their complexity.

In this chapter, you learn how to do the following:

- Use line breaks to make a form easier to read
- Mix forms and lists
- Mix forms and tables
- Create logical layouts for check boxes and radio buttons
- Put multiple forms in one HTML document

Using Line Break Tags

When you mark up HTML documents, you usually just let the words wrap across the screen. Although this flexibility is wonderful to have for segments of text, it can make reading a form incredibly difficult. A quick and simple solution is to include the line break tag, <BR>, to move something to the next line.

Forcing Fields onto Separate Lines

If you want to have two fields, Name and E-Mail Address, for example, you can simply mark them up as shown in listing 22.1.

On the CD

Listing 22.1   LB1.HTM—Forms without Line Breaks

```
<HTML>
<HEAD>
<TITLE>Form Layout and Design</TITLE>
</HEAD>
<BODY>
<H1>Line Break Tags</H1>
<FORM>
Name: <INPUT NAME="name" SIZE="30">
E-Mail Address: <INPUT NAME="email" SIZE="40">
</FORM>
</BODY>
</HTML>
```

Although this might look great now, it can wrap strangely on some WWW browsers and look shabby when displayed (see fig. 22.1).

Fig. 22.1
Without some types of organization, your forms can be very hard to read.

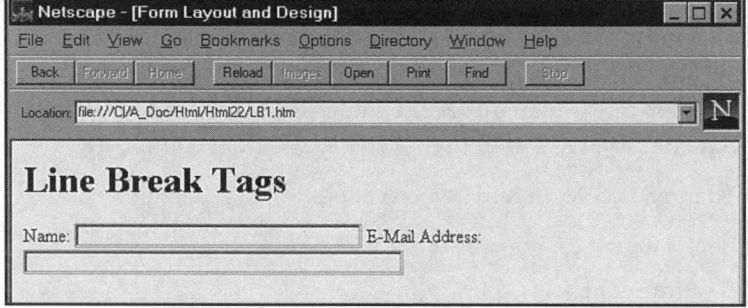

To split these lines and make them more readable, you need to include the line break tag <BR> between them, as shown in listing 22.2.

On the CD

Listing 22.2   LB2.HTM—Line Breaks within Forms

```
<HTML>
<HEAD>
<TITLE>Form Layout and Design</TITLE>
</HEAD>
<BODY>
<H1>Line Break Tags</H1>
<FORM>
Name: <INPUT NAME="name" SIZE="30"><BR>
E-Mail Address: <INPUT NAME="email" SIZE="40">
</FORM>
</BODY>
</HTML>
```

Adding the <BR> tag between the two fields forces the browser to wrap the field to the next line, regardless of the width of the screen. The result of listing 22.2 is shown in figure 22.2.

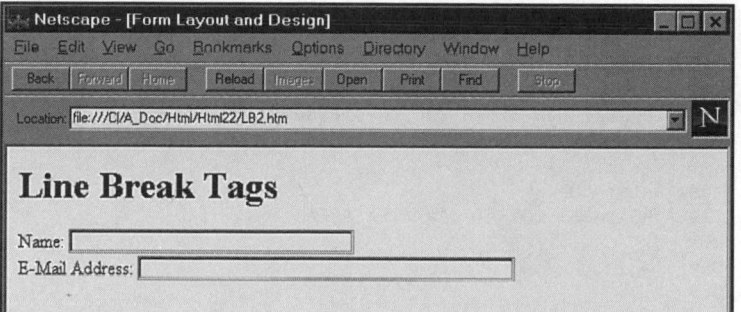

Fig. 22.2
The <BR> tag enables you to control the placement of form text.

> **Note**
>
> The wrapping feature of HTML can work for you to help keep a form small in size. If you have several multiple-choice items that could take up huge amounts of space on your form, you can try to keep them small and let them wrap closely together on the page.
>
> If you're using the <SELECT> tag, the width of the popup menu on the screen is directly related to the words in the options to be selected. If you keep it all small, you can provide a relatively large number of choices in a small area.

Working with Large Entry Fields

If you're working with long text entry fields or perhaps with a <TEXTAREA> field, it's often easier to put the text just above the field and then separate the different areas with paragraph breaks.

For example, if you have a text input line that is very long, or a long field description, it doesn't work well to put them side by side. Also, if you want to leave a space for comments, it's easier—and looks nicer—to have the field description just above the comment area. This makes it appear that there's more space to write in. Listing 22.3 is an example of this sort of design. The result of this code is shown in figure 22.3.

On the CD

Listing 22.3   LARGE.HTM—Large Fields for Text Input

```
<HTML>
<HEAD>
<TITLE>Form Layout and Design</TITLE>
</HEAD>
<BODY>
<H1>Line Break Tags</H1>
<FORM>
Please enter the new title for the message:<BR>
<INPUT NAME="name" SIZE="40">
<HR>
Your comments:<BR>
<TEXTAREA ROWS="6" COLS="70"></TEXTAREA>
</FORM>
</BODY>
</HTML>
```

Fig. 22.3

Using the line break tags enables you to put a label just above the field.

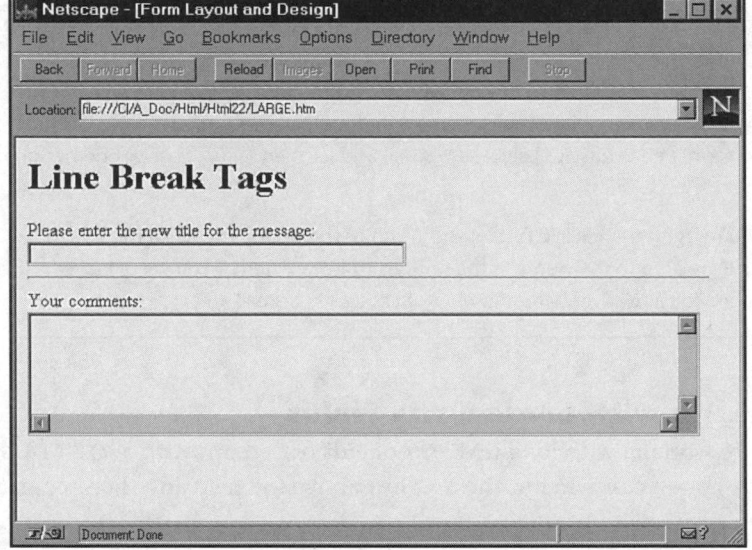

Note

Most browsers automatically wrap a large field to the next line, treating it like an image. Because you don't know how wide (or narrow!) the client screen is, take steps to ensure that the form will look as you want. If, for example, you want the field to be on the next line, put in a <BR> tag to make sure it will be!

Using the Preformatted Text Tag to Line Up Forms

A very common sight on many forms is simple text entry fields aligned haphazardly. A great trick for aligning text fields is to use the <PRE> tag. This ensures that some spaces appear before the field.

> **Caution**
>
> If you're using the <PRE> tags to line up fields, don't use any other HTML tags inside that area. Although the tags won't show up, they'll ruin the effect of lining everything up perfectly.

Listing 22.4 is an example of an entry form that only uses line breaks. The result of this code is displayed in figure 22.4.

Listing 22.4   PRE1.HTM—Form Fields Are Not Aligned by Default

On the CD

```
<HTML>
<HEAD>
<TITLE>Form Layout and Design</TITLE>
</HEAD>
<BODY>
<H1>Using PRE tags</H1>
<FORM>
Name: <INPUT TYPE="text" NAME="name" SIZE="50"><BR>
E-Mail: <INPUT TYPE="text" NAME="email" SIZE="50"><BR>
Street Address: <INPUT TYPE="text" NAME="street1" SIZE="30"><BR>
<INPUT TYPE="text" NAME="street2" SIZE="30"><BR>
City: <INPUT TYPE="text" NAME="city" SIZE="50"><BR>
State: <INPUT TYPE="text" NAME="state" SIZE="2"><BR>
Zip: <INPUT TYPE="text" NAME="zip" SIZE="10">
</FORM>
</BODY>
</HTML>
```

If you space things out and use the tags for preformatted text, you can create a very nice looking form. Listing 22.5 is an example of aligning fields using the <PRE> tag, which produces the layout shown in figure 22.5.

Listing 22.5   PRE2.HTM—Aligning Forms Fields with Preformatted Text

On the CD

```
<HTML>
<HEAD>
<TITLE>Form Layout and Design</TITLE>
</HEAD>
<BODY>
```

(continues)

Listing 22.5   Continued

```
<H1>Using PRE tags</H1>
<FORM>
<PRE>
Name:             <INPUT TYPE="text" NAME="name" SIZE="50">
E-Mail:           <INPUT TYPE="text" NAME="email" SIZE="50">
Street Address: <INPUT TYPE="text" NAME="street1" SIZE="30">
                  <INPUT TYPE="text" NAME="street2" SIZE="30">
City:             <INPUT TYPE="text" NAME="city" SIZE="50">
State:            <INPUT TYPE="text" NAME="state" SIZE="2">
Zip:              <INPUT TYPE="text" NAME="zip" SIZE="10">
</PRE>
</FORM>
</BODY>
</HTML>
```

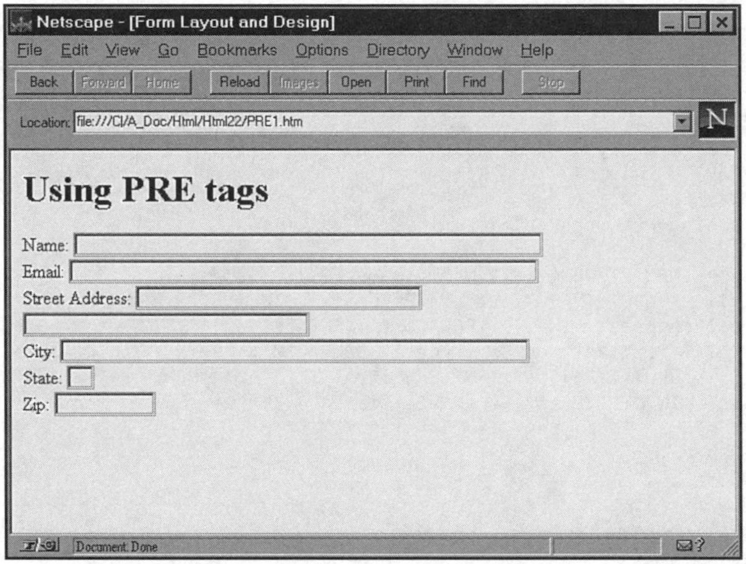

Fig. 22.4

These fields were organized only with line breaks, so they align haphazardly.

Caution

Make sure you keep the size of the fields smaller than the general browser, or your lines will wrap off the screen. If the input fields have to be large, you can use a line break to put it on its own line.

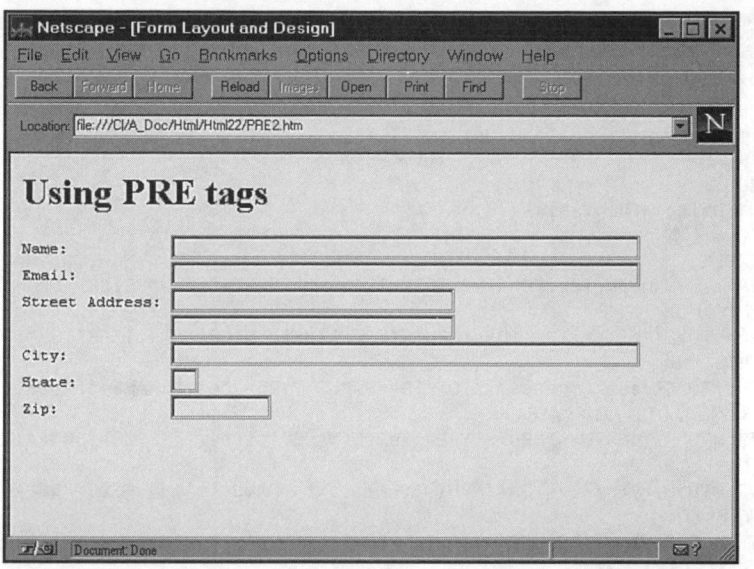

IV

Forms and CGI

Fig. 22.5
The layout of the
preformatted text
is organized and
easy to follow.

Troubleshooting

When I set up the preformatted text, it doesn't come out aligned in my HTML document! Why doesn't it match up?

In some text editors, the width of each letter on the screen isn't the same. If you're creating HTML documents with a text editor or word processor, make sure you use a monospaced font (each character, including spaces, takes up exactly the same amount of space). That should solve the problem.

Using HTML Tables to Line Up Forms

Another way to line up form fields is to place them in an HTML table. This can produce an effect similar to using preformatted text but, because you are using regular HTML rather than preformatted text, you can also include other HTML constructs within the form. So, by using a table rather than preformatted text to align your form, you're also able to include images, hypertext links, or other HTML elements as part of the form.

Listing 22.6 is an example of the entry form shown in figure 22.4 and figure 22.5, formatted using an HTML table. The result of this code is displayed in figure 22.6.

On the CD

Listing 22.6   TABLE.HTM—Aligning Forms Fields with Tables

```
<HTML>
<HEAD>
<TITLE>Form Layout and Design</TITLE>
</HEAD>
<BODY>
<H1>Using HTML Tables</H1>
<FORM>
<TABLE>
<TR><TD>Name:</TD><TD><INPUT TYPE="text" NAME="name" SIZE="50"></
➥TD></TR>
<TR><TD>E-Mail:</TD><TD><INPUT TYPE="text" NAME="email" SIZE="50"></
➥TD></TR>
<TR><TD>Street Address:</TD><TD><INPUT TYPE="text" NAME="street1"
➥SIZE="30"></TD></TR>
<TR><TD></TD><TD><INPUT TYPE="text" NAME="street2" SIZE="30"></TD></
➥TR>
<TR><TD>City:</TD><TD><INPUT TYPE="text" NAME="city" SIZE="50"></
➥TD></TR>
<TR><TD>State:</TD><TD><INPUT TYPE="text" NAME="state" SIZE="2"></
➥TD></TR>
<TR><TD>Zip:</TD><TD><INPUT TYPE="text" NAME="zip" SIZE="10"></TD></
➥TR>
</TABLE>
</FORM>
</BODY>
</HTML>\
```

Fig. 22.6
HTML tables text can be combined with forms to enable the aligning of different form fields.

Netscape - [Form Layout and Design]

File Edit View Go Bookmarks Options Directory Window Help

Back Forward Home   Reload Images Open Print Find   Stop

Location: file:///C|/A_Doc/Html/Html22/TABLE.htm

Using HTML Tables

Name:

E-Mail:

Street Address:

City:

State:

Zip:

Document: Done

Tip

Some people use browsers, particularly text-only ones, that do not support tables. If you use tables with your forms, consider including an alternate page without tables for these folks.

Using Paragraph Marks to Separate Form Sections

If you have a large form with different sections, it's handy to separate those sections. The paragraph container tag, <P>...</P>, provides a way of adding some space without making the delineation so hard that it appears to be another form. Note that Web browsers also allow you to use the <P> opening tag without the </P> closing tag to give identical results.

For example, a simple comment form might have places for a name and an e-mail address, but these might not be a required part of the form. In this case, separate the "comment" part of the form from the area that's optional. It's also possible to make it more obvious by simply making some comments in the form, such as a small heading titled Optional. A simple comment form with optional Name and E-Mail fields can have the code shown in listing 22.7.

On the CD

Listing 22.7   P.HTM—Using Paragraphs to Improve Spacing

```
<HTML>
<HEAD>
<TITLE>Form Layout and Design</TITLE>
</HEAD>
<BODY>
<H1>Using &lt;P&gt; tags</H1>
<FORM>
<PRE>
<I><B>Optional:</B></I>
Name:   <INPUT TYPE="text" NAME="name" SIZE="50">
E-Mail: <INPUT TYPE="text" NAME="email" SIZE="50">
</PRE><P>
Your comments:<BR>
<TEXTAREA ROWS="6" COLS="70"></TEXTAREA>
</FORM>
</BODY>
</HTML>
```

Listing 22.7, using both <PRE> tags and line break tags, produces the layout shown in figure 22.7. A similar effect can be achieved using a table instead of preformatted text.

Fig. 22.7
Combining
preformatted and
wrapped areas can
make your form
very easy to use.

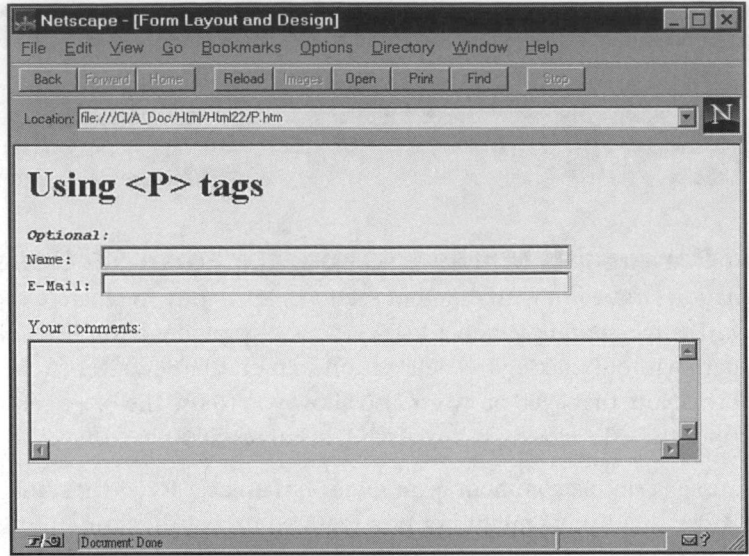

Using List Tags

There are a few occasions when line breaks and paragraph tags can't set up the form exactly as you'd like. At these times, list tags can provide just the right look! The best use of list tags is for the indenting and numbering of text.

Indenting Form Entries with Descriptive Lists

On the WWW, it's common to see order forms for merchandise. Finding out the method of payment is a perfect use for descriptive list tags to lay out the choices. Indenting some items more than others makes the options obvious and easy to read.

> **Note**
>
> When I lay out lists, I indent the areas in my HTML documents that will be indented on-screen. This makes it easier to remember to finish with the descriptive list tag, </DL>.

For example, listing 22.8 shows how to separate a section of credit cards from the rest of the payment methods. The result of this code is shown in figure 22.8.

Listing 22.8   LIST1.HTM—Organizing Forms Using a Descriptive List

```
<HTML>
<HEAD>
<TITLE>Form Layout and Design</TITLE>
</HEAD>
<BODY>
<H1>Descriptive List Tags</H1>
<FORM>
<DL>
<DT>How would you like to pay for this?
<DD><INPUT NAME="pay" TYPE="radio" VALUE="cash" CHECKED>Cash
<DD><INPUT NAME="pay" TYPE="radio" VALUE="check">Check
<DD><INPUT NAME="pay" TYPE="radio" VALUE="debit">Debit Card
    <DL>
    <DT>Credit Card
    <DD><INPUT NAME="pay" TYPE="radio" VALUE="mc">Mastercard
    <DD><INPUT NAME="pay" TYPE="radio" VALUE="visa">Visa
    <DD><INPUT NAME="pay" TYPE="radio" VALUE="disc">Discover
    <DD><INPUT NAME="pay" TYPE="radio" VALUE="ae">American Express
    </DL>
</DL>
</FORM>
</BODY>
</HTML>
```

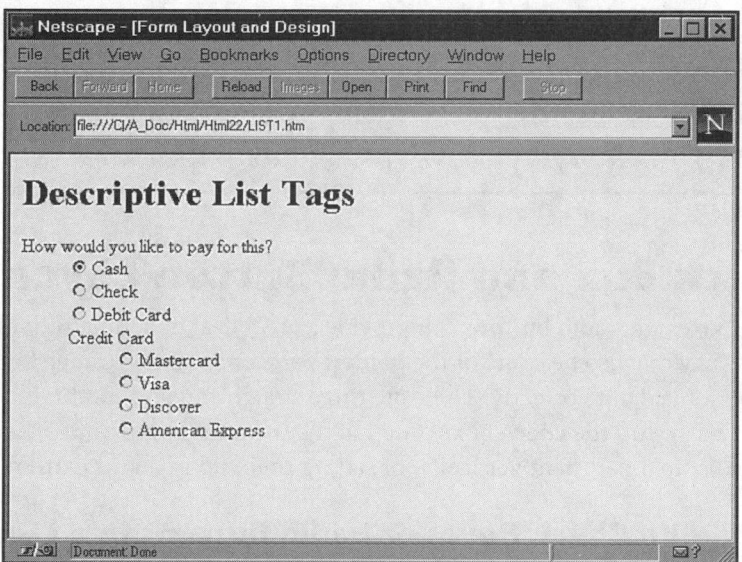

Fig. 22.8
Descriptive lists make the break-down of choices obvious.

Using Ordered Lists to Number Fields

It's easy to display a numbered list if you use the ordered list tag, <OL>. Listing 22.9 uses the <OL> tag to automatically number the fields. The result of this code is shown in figure 22.9.

On the CD

Listing 22.9   LIST2.HTM—Organizing Forms Using an Ordered List

```
<HTML>
<HEAD>
<TITLE>Form Layout and Design</TITLE>
</HEAD>
<BODY>
<H1>Ordered List Tags</H1>
<FORM>
What are your three favorite books?
<OL>
<LI><INPUT NAME="1st" SIZE="20">
<LI><INPUT NAME="2nd" SIZE="20">
<LI><INPUT NAME="3nd" SIZE="20">
</OL>
</FORM>
</BODY>
</HTML>
```

Fig. 22.9
Using ordered lists, you can reorder fields without retyping all those numbers!

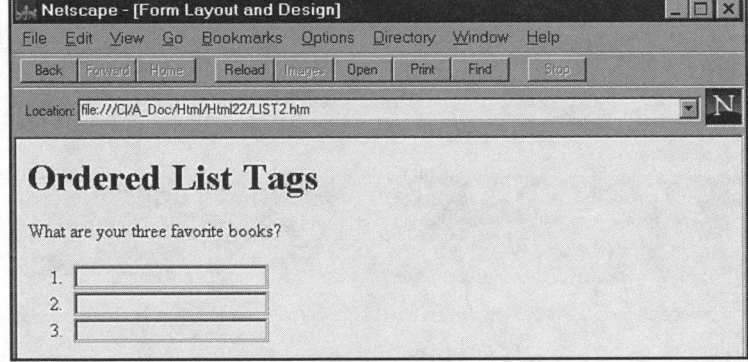

Check Box and Radio Button Layouts

Check boxes and radio buttons can provide a great deal of simple *yes* or *no* input. They can also be some of the hardest parts of a form to understand if they're not laid out correctly. There are three straightforward methods of layout: setting up the check boxes and radio buttons in a line horizontally, using a list to order them vertically, or setting them up in a grid pattern.

Setting Up Check Boxes or Radio Buttons in a Line

Probably the easiest method is listing the check boxes in a line horizontally (see listing 22.10). It has the benefits of being very simple to set up, relatively compact on the browser, and easy to understand. The only caution is to make sure there aren't too many items for one line. The intent of the form might not be obvious if you let check boxes wrap unintentionally. The result of listing 22.10, which specifies a horizontal line of radio buttons, is shown in figure 22.10.

Listing 22.10   BUTTON1.HTM—Organizing Forms Checkboxes and Radio Buttons

On the CD

```
<HTML>
<HEAD>
<TITLE>Form Layout and Design</TITLE>
</HEAD>
<BODY>
<H1>Checkboxes and Radio Buttons</H1>
<FORM>
What size would you like?<BR>
<INPUT NAME="size" TYPE="radio" VALUE="sm">Small
<INPUT NAME="size" TYPE="radio" VALUE="md">Medium
<INPUT NAME="size" TYPE="radio" VALUE="lg">Large
<INPUT NAME="size" TYPE="radio" VALUE="x">X-Large
<INPUT NAME="size" TYPE="radio" VALUE="xx">XX-Large
</FORM>
</BODY>
</HTML>
```

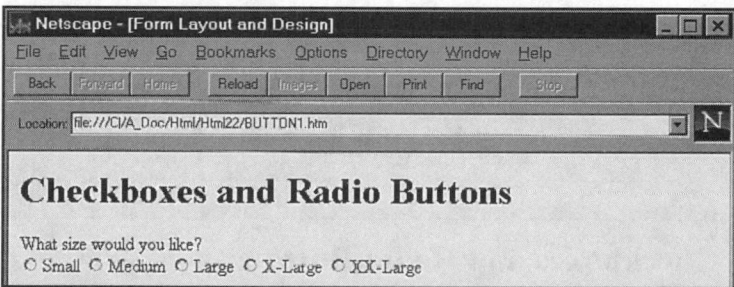

Fig. 22.10
This method works well for check boxes too!

Tip

When creating a web page with a line of buttons, check it with your Web browser set to the width of a 640x480 screen, to make sure your line won't be wrapped.

Lists of Check Boxes

When the choices get more complex than a simple line selection, it's best to forgo compactness and spread out the choices in a list, as specified in listing 22.11. The result of using a descriptive list in this code is shown in figure 22.11.

On the CD

> **Listing 22.11 BUTTON2.HTM—Organizing Forms Buttons Using Lists**

```
<HTML>
<HEAD>
<TITLE>Form Layout and Design</TITLE>
</HEAD>
<BODY>
<H1>Checkboxes and Radio Buttons</H1>
<FORM>
<DL>
<DT>What machines do you work on?
<DD><INPUT NAME="mac" TYPE="checkbox">Macintosh
<DD><INPUT NAME="pc" TYPE="checkbox">IBM Compatible PC
    <DL>
    <DT>UNIX Workstation
    <DD><INPUT NAME="sun" TYPE="checkbox">Sun
    <DD><INPUT NAME="sgi" TYPE="checkbox">SGI
    <DD><INPUT NAME="next" TYPE="checkbox">NeXT
    <DD><INPUT NAME="aix" TYPE="checkbox">AIX
    <DD><INPUT NAME="lin" TYPE="checkbox">Linux
    <DD><INPUT NAME="other" TYPE="checkbox">Other...
    </DL>
</DL>
</FORM>
</BODY>
</HTML>
```

Fig. 22.11
Complex choices are often easier to understand in a list format.

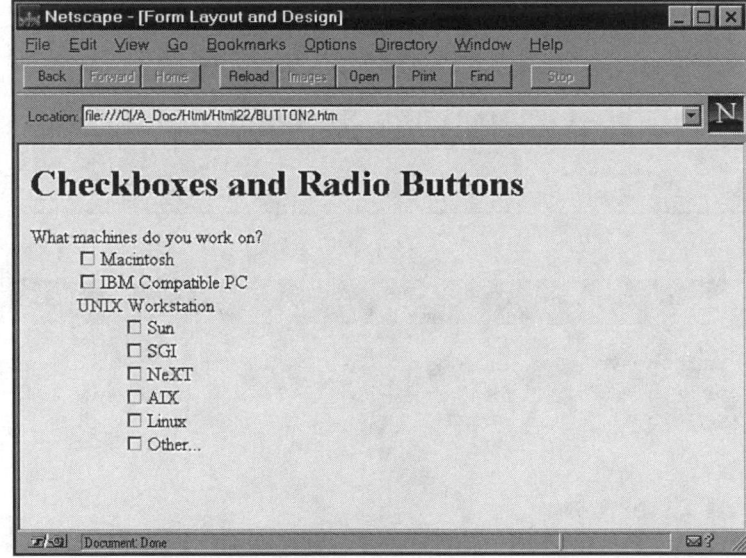

Making a Grid

The most complex method for displaying check boxes is in a grid. Using tables, you can space out the display to create a grid effect (see listing 22.12). You can also create a grid of radio buttons by substituting radio for check box in the <INPUT> tags. The result of setting up the grid in listing 22.12 is shown in figure 22.12.

On the CD

Listing 22.12   GRID.HTM—Creating a Grid of Buttons Using Tables

```
<HTML>
<HEAD>
<TITLE>Form Layout and Design</TITLE>
</HEAD>
<BODY>
<H1>Checkboxes and Radio Buttons</H1>
<FORM>
What combinations?
<TABLE>
<TR><TD></TD><TD>Red</TD><TD>Blue</TD></TR>
<TR><TD>Small</TD><TD><INPUT NAME="sr" TYPE="checkbox"></TD>
                <TD><INPUT NAME="sb" TYPE="checkbox"></TD></TR>
<TR><TD>Medium</TD><TD><INPUT NAME="mr" TYPE="checkbox"></TD>
                <TD><INPUT NAME="mb" TYPE="checkbox"></TD></TR>
<TR><TD>Large</TD><TD><INPUT NAME="lr" TYPE="checkbox"></TD>
                <TD><INPUT NAME="lb" TYPE="checkbox"></TD></TR>
</TABLE>
</FORM>
</BODY>
</HTML>
```

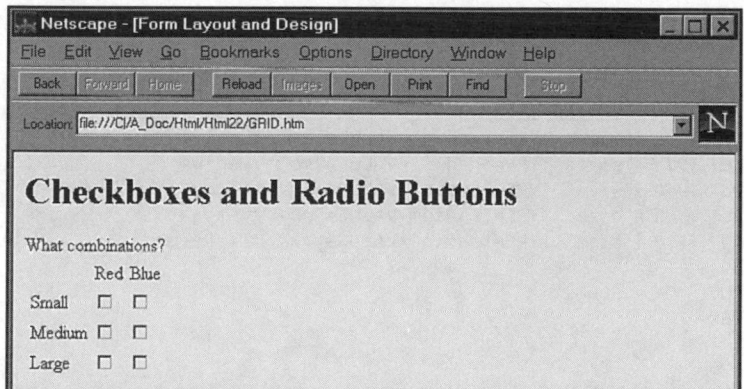

Fig. 22.12
Grids provide a very intuitive method of making a choice.

Multiple Forms in a Document

It's quite possible to put multiple forms in a single document; it often makes the document more concise and easier to understand. An example of using multiple forms is a document with a number of different methods for searching. From one form, you can choose to do a search from any of a number of locations by having each <FORM> point to a different search method.

Tip

Also consider using multiple forms when your form would be too large to fit on one or two screens, to make it easier for your readers to use the form.

When including multiple forms in a document, visibly separate them to make them easier to understand. A common way to break up a form is to use the horizontal rule tag, <HR>, or a wide image in an <IMG> tag. Put line breaks before and after the tags. For example, listing 22.13 shows how to separate three forms by using <HR> tags to break them up. The result of this code is shown in figure 22.13.

On the CD

Listing 22.13   MULTIPLE.HTM—Using Multiple Forms in a Single HTML Document

```
<HTML>
<HEAD>
<TITLE>Form Layout and Design</TITLE>
</HEAD>
<BODY>
<H1>Multiple Forms in a Document</H1>
<FORM>
What size would you like?<BR>
<INPUT NAME="size" TYPE="radio" VALUE="sm">:Small
<INPUT NAME="size" TYPE="radio" VALUE="md">:Medium
<INPUT NAME="size" TYPE="radio" VALUE="lg">:Large
<INPUT NAME="size" TYPE="radio" VALUE="x">:X-Large
<INPUT NAME="size" TYPE="radio" VALUE="xx">:XX-Large
<P>
<INPUT TYPE="submit">
</FORM>
<HR>
<FORM>
<TABLE>
```

```
<TR><TD>Name:</TD><TD><INPUT TYPE="text" NAME="name" SIZE="50"></TD></TR>
<TR><TD>E-Mail:</TD><TD><INPUT TYPE="text" NAME="email" SIZE="50"></TD></TR>
<TR><TD>Street Address:</TD><TD><INPUT TYPE="text" NAME="street1" SIZE="30">
➥</TD></TR>
<TR><TD></TD><TD><INPUT TYPE="text" NAME="street2" SIZE="30"></TD></TR>
<TR><TD>City:</TD><TD><INPUT TYPE="text" NAME="city" SIZE="50"></TD></TR>
<TR><TD>State:</TD><TD><INPUT TYPE="text" NAME="state" SIZE="2"></TD></TR>
<TR><TD>Zip:</TD><TD><INPUT TYPE="text" NAME="zip" SIZE="10"></TD></TR>
</TABLE>
<P>
<INPUT TYPE="submit">
</FORM>
<HR>
<FORM>
<DL>
<DT>How would you like to pay for this?
<DD><INPUT NAME="pay" TYPE="radio" VALUE="cash" CHECKED>Cash
<DD><INPUT NAME="pay" TYPE="radio" VALUE="check">Check
<DD><INPUT NAME="pay" TYPE="radio" VALUE="debit">Debit Card
    <DL>
    <DT>Credit Card
    <DD><INPUT NAME="pay" TYPE="radio" VALUE="mc">Mastercard
    <DD><INPUT NAME="pay" TYPE="radio" VALUE="visa">Visa
    <DD><INPUT NAME="pay" TYPE="radio" VALUE="disc">Discover
    <DD><INPUT NAME="pay" TYPE="radio" VALUE="ae">American Express
    </DL>
</DL>
<P>
<INPUT TYPE="submit">
</FORM>
</BODY>
</HTML>
```

Troubleshooting

I put multiple forms in one document, but I only see one. Why aren't both showing up?

Check to make sure you finished one form before beginning another. If you didn't include the </FORM> tag to stop the first form, the second <FORM> tag will just be ignored.

Fig. 22.13
By using horizontal rules to break up the multiple forms in this document, the intent of the form is easily apparent.

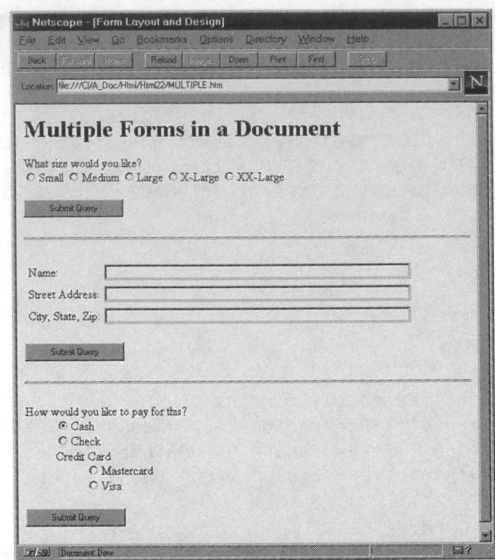

Combining Forms with Tables

As discussed earlier in this section, forms can be used very effectively with HTML tables, allowing more control of the positioning of different fields. Listing 22.14 shows an address entry form that uses a table to align the different fields. The resulting web page is shown in figure 22.14.

On the CD

Listing 22.14 TABLE2.HTM—Combining Forms and Tables

```
<HTML>
<HEAD>
<TITLE>Form Layout and Design</TITLE>
</HEAD>
<BODY>
<H1>More HTML Tables and Forms</H1>
<FORM>
<TABLE>
<TR><TD ALIGN=RIGHT>Name:</TD>
    <TD COLSPAN=4><INPUT TYPE="text" NAME="name" SIZE="40"></TD></TR>
<TR><TD ALIGN=RIGHT>Street Address:</TD>
    <TD COLSPAN=4><INPUT TYPE="text" NAME="street1" SIZE="40"></TD></TR>
<TR><TD ALIGN=RIGHT>City, State, Zip:</TD>
    <TD><INPUT TYPE="text" NAME="city" SIZE="30"></TD><TD>,</TD>
    <TD><INPUT TYPE="text" NAME="state" SIZE="2"></TD>
    <TD><INPUT TYPE="text" NAME="zip" SIZE="15"></TD></TR>
</TABLE>
</FORM>
</BODY>
</HTML>
```

Fig. 22.14
The ability of
tables to position
items side by side
and align them in
many different
ways makes them
a natural for use
with forms.

This idea can be taken even further, including other form elements such as
checkboxes or radio buttons to allow the user more input options. A further
refinement of the address entry form, allowing the user to input both a home
and business address, and to specify which is preferred, is shown in listing
22.15—the corresponding web page is shown in figure 22.15.

Listing 22.15 TABLE3.HTM—More on Combining Forms and Tables

On the CD

```
<HTML>
<HEAD>
<TITLE>Form Layout and Design</TITLE>
</HEAD>
<BODY>
<H1>More HTML Tables and Forms</H1>
<FORM>
<TABLE>
<TR><TH ALIGN=LEFT COLSPAN=5>HOME ADDRESS</TH><TD><EM>Preferred?</EM></TD></TR>
<TR><TD ALIGN=RIGHT>Name:</TD>
    <TD COLSPAN=4><INPUT TYPE="text" NAME="name" SIZE="40"></TD>
    <TD ALIGN=CENTER><INPUT TYPE="radio" NAME="pref" VALUE="home"></TD></TR>
<TR><TD ALIGN=RIGHT>Street Address:</TD>
    <TD COLSPAN=4><INPUT TYPE="text" NAME="street1" SIZE="40"></TD></TR>
<TR><TD ALIGN=RIGHT>City, State, Zip:</TD>
    <TD><INPUT TYPE="text" NAME="city" SIZE="25"></TD><TD>,</TD>
    <TD><INPUT TYPE="text" NAME="state" SIZE="2"></TD>
    <TD><INPUT TYPE="text" NAME="zip" SIZE="15"></TD></TR>
<TR><TD COLSPAN=6><HR></TD></TR>
<TR><TH ALIGN=LEFT COLSPAN=5>BUSINESS ADDRESS</TH><TD><EM>Preferred?</EM></TD></TR>
<TR><TD ALIGN=RIGHT>Name:</TD>
    <TD COLSPAN=4><INPUT TYPE="text" NAME="name" SIZE="40"></TD>
    <TD ALIGN=CENTER><INPUT TYPE="radio" NAME="pref" VALUE="bus"></TD></TR>
<TR><TD ALIGN=RIGHT>Street Address:</TD>
    <TD COLSPAN=4><INPUT TYPE="text" NAME="street1" SIZE="40"></TD></TR>
<TR><TD ALIGN=RIGHT>City, State, Zip:</TD>
    <TD><INPUT TYPE="text" NAME="city" SIZE="25"></TD><TD>,</TD>
```

(continues)

Listing 22.15 Continued

```
        <TD><INPUT TYPE="text" NAME="state" SIZE="2"></TD>
        <TD><INPUT TYPE="text" NAME="zip" SIZE="15"></TD></TR>
</TABLE>
</FORM>
</BODY>
</HTML>
```

One final refinement of the address entry form substitutes different submit buttons for the radio buttons shown in figures 22.14 and 22.15. This allows the users to enter the information on the form, and then specify which is the preferred address by their choice of submit button. Specifying a NAME attribute for the submit button enables the choice of button to be determined.

Fig. 22.15
HTML tables allow you to combine many different form fields and position them logically.

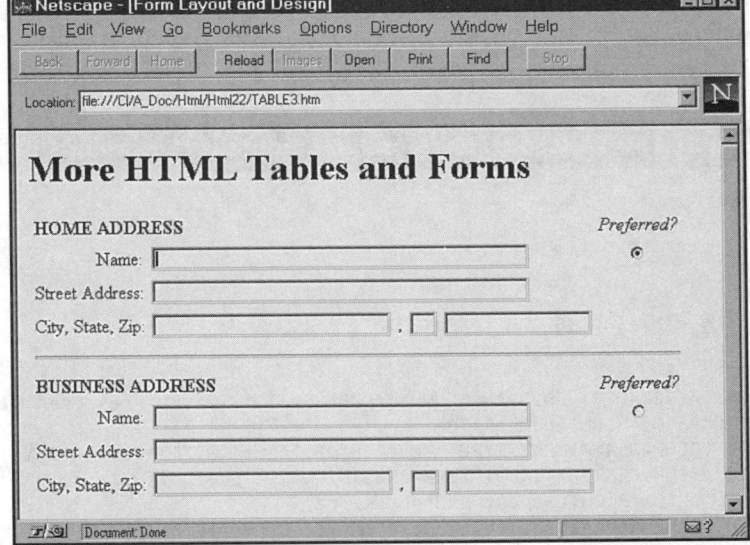

On the CD

Listing 22.16 TABLE4.HTM—Another Example of Forms and Tables

```
<HTML>
<HEAD>
<TITLE>Form Layout and Design</TITLE>
</HEAD>
<BODY>
<H1>More HTML Tables and Forms</H1>
<FORM>
<TABLE>
<TR><TH ALIGN=LEFT COLSPAN=5>HOME ADDRESS</TH>
    <TD ALIGN=CENTER><EM>Preferred?</EM></TR>
<TR><TD ALIGN=RIGHT>Name:</TD>
```

```
  <TD COLSPAN=4><INPUT TYPE="text" NAME="name" SIZE="40"></TD>
  <TD ALIGN=CENTER><INPUT TYPE="submit" NAME="home" VALUE="Home"></TD></TR>
<TR><TD ALIGN=RIGHT>Street Address:</TD>
  <TD COLSPAN=4><INPUT TYPE="text" NAME="street1" SIZE="40"></TD></TR>
<TR><TD ALIGN=RIGHT>City, State, Zip:</TD>
  <TD><INPUT TYPE="text" NAME="city" SIZE="25"></TD><TD>,</TD>
  <TD><INPUT TYPE="text" NAME="state" SIZE="2"></TD>
  <TD><INPUT TYPE="text" NAME="zip" SIZE="15"></TD></TR>
<TR><TD COLSPAN=6><HR></TD></TR>
<TR><TH ALIGN=LEFT COLSPAN=5>BUSINESS ADDRESS</TH>
  <TD ALIGN=CENTER><EM>Preferred?</EM></TR>
<TR><TD ALIGN=RIGHT>Name:</TD>
  <TD COLSPAN=4><INPUT TYPE="text" NAME="name" SIZE="40"></TD>
  <TD ALIGN=CENTER><INPUT TYPE="submit" NAME="bus" VALUE="Business"></TD></TR>
<TR><TD ALIGN=RIGHT>Street Address:</TD>
  <TD COLSPAN=4><INPUT TYPE="text" NAME="street1" SIZE="40"></TD></TR>
<TR><TD ALIGN=RIGHT>City, State, Zip:</TD>
  <TD><INPUT TYPE="text" NAME="city" SIZE="25"></TD><TD>,</TD>
  <TD><INPUT TYPE="text" NAME="state" SIZE="2"></TD>
  <TD><INPUT TYPE="text" NAME="zip" SIZE="15"></TD></TR>
</TABLE>
</FORM>
</BODY>
</HTML>
```

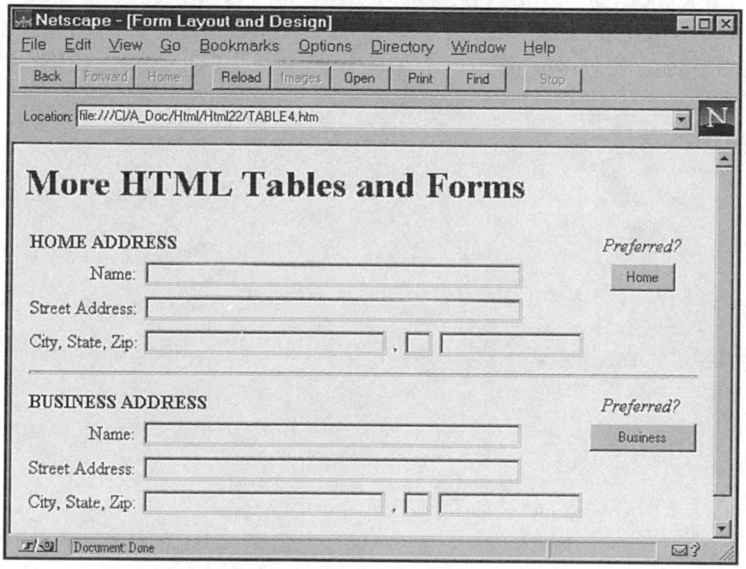

Fig. 22.16
The options available for using forms with HTML tables are limited only by your imagination.

Final Notes on Form Layouts

When you're creating forms, it's always a good idea to keep the form on a single page. Further, because you can't control what browser someone uses to look at your pages, you need to observe some general guidelines, as follows:

- If your form is very short, keep it under 14 lines. This ensures that it will fit on one page in most browsers. It won't always work, but it does create a compact page that's easy for most people to see. A good trick for keeping the pages compact is using <SELECT> tags with the size set to one (to show a popup menu) or set to three or four (for a small scrolling window for multiple choices) instead of large numbers of check boxes and radio buttons.

- If your form is large (more than two pages on any browser), don't put the <SUBMIT> or <RESET> buttons in the middle of the form. If you do, someone reading the form might not continue beyond those buttons and might miss an important part of the form.

- Put the fields on your form in a logical order. This sounds obvious, but it's easy to forget.

- Think about your forms well before you start creating them. If you know what choices you want to provide, it'll make your final layout much easier.

## CHAPTER 23

All About CGI Scripts

In previous chapters you have learned how to mark up content for your Web site using the HTML standard. Now, we will begin our exploration of the CGI (Common Gateway Interface), which will greatly enhance the level of interactivity on your site. With the use of CGI scripts, you can make your Web presentations more responsive to your users' needs by allowing them to have a more powerful means of interaction with your material.

In this chapter, you will learn about the following:

- How the CGI works
- Uses for CGI scripts
- Seeing if you can write CGI scripts
- Common CGI scripting languages
- How to find CGI Resources

What Is CGI?

Here is the answer to the hundred dollar question. What is the CGI anyway? Well, in order to answer that, you are going to need a little background information first.

Each time you sit down in your favorite chair (I *hope* it is anyway) and start surfing the WWW, you are a client from the Internet's point of view. Each time you click on a link to request a new Web document, you are sending a request to the document's server. The server then receives the request, gets the document, and sends it back to your browser for you to view.

The client/server relationship that is set up between your browser and a Web server works very well for serving up HTML and image files from the server's

Web directories. Unfortunately, there is a large flaw with this simple system. The Web server is still not equipped to handle information from your favorite database program or from other applications that require more work than simply transmitting a static document.

One option the designers of the first Web server could have chosen was to build in an interface for each external application from which a client may want to get information. It is hard to imagine trying to program a server to interact with every known application and then trying to keep the server current on each new application as it is developed. Needless to say, it would be impossible. So they developed a better way.

These wizened developers anticipated this problem and solved it by designing the Common Gateway Interface or CGI. This gateway provides a common environment and a set of protocols for external applications to use while interfacing with the Web server. Thus, any application engineer (including yourself) can use the CGI to allow an application to interface with the server. This extends the range of functions the Web server has to include the features provided by a potentially limitless number of external applications.

How the CGI Works

Now that you have read a little background, you should have a basic idea of what the CGI is, and why it is needed. The next step in furthering your understanding of the CGI is to learn the basics of how it works. To help you achieve this goal, I will break down this material into the following sections:

- The Process
- Characteristics
- The output Header and MIME Types
- Environment Variables

The Process

The CGI is the common gateway or door that is used by the server to interface—or communicate—with applications other than the browser. Thus, CGI scripts act as a link between whatever application is needed and the server while the server is responsible for receiving information from, and sending data back to, the browser.

Note

As a technical note, you should be aware that some people like to use the term program to refer to longer, usually compiled, code and applications written in

---

languages like C and C++. When this is the case, the term `script` is then used to indicate shorter, noncompiled code written with languages like SH and PERL. However, for the purpose of this and the following chapter, the terms *program* and *script* will be used interchangeably as the divisions between them are being rapidly broken down.

For example, when you enter a search request at your favorite search engine, a request is made by the browser to the server to execute a CGI script. At this time, the browser passes the information that was contained in the online form plus the current environment to the server. From here, the server passes the information to the script. This script provides an interface with the database archive and finds the information that you have requested. Once this information is retrieved, the script sends it to the server which feeds it back to your browser as a list of matches to your query.

Tip

There is a very nice online description of the CGI at The Common Gateway Interface:

URL address: http://hoohoo.ncsa.uiuc.edu/cgi/

Characteristics of the CGI

Another way of looking at the CGI is to see it as a socket that attaches an extra arm on your server. This new arm, the CGI script, adds new features and abilities to the server that it was previously lacking.

The most common use for these new features is to give the server the ability to dynamically respond to the client. One of the most often seen examples of this is allowing the client to send a search query to a CGI script which then queries a database and returns a list of matching topics from the database. Besides information retrieval, another common theme for using CGI scripts is to customize the user interface on the Web site. This commonly takes the form of counters and animations.

Tip

If you see bin or cgi-bin in the pathnames of images or links, it is a good indication that the given effect was produced by a CGI script.

These and some of the other common uses for CGI scripts will be discussed in more detail later in this chapter, so stay tuned.

The MIME Content-type Output Header

It won't be long into your CGI programming career when you will want to write a script that sends information to the server for it to process. Each file that is sent to the server must contain an output header. This header contains the information the server and other applications need to transmit and handle the file properly.

The use of output headers in CGI scripts is an expansion of a system of protocols called MIME (Multipurpose Internet Mail Extensions). Its use for e-mail began in 1992 when the Network Working Group published RFC (Request For Comments) 1341, which defined this new type of e-mail system. This system greatly expanded the ability of Internet e-mail to send and receive various non-text file formats.

> **Note**
>
> Since the release of RFC 1341, a series of improvements has been made to the MIME conventions. You can find some additional information about this by looking at RFC 1521 and RFC 1522. A list of all the RFC documents can be found online at **http://ds0.internic.net/rfc/**. These documents contain a lot of useful information published by the Network Working Group relating to the function and structure of the Internet backbone.

Each time you, as a client, send a request to the server, it is sent in the form of a MIME message with a specially formatted header. Most of the information in the header is part of the client's protocol for interfacing with the browser. This includes the request method, a URI (Universal Resource Identifier), the protocol version, and then a MIME message. The server then responds to this request with its own message which usually includes the server's protocol version, a status code, and a different MIME message.

The bulk of this client/server communication process is handled automatically by the WWW client application—usually your Web browser—and the server. This makes it easier for everyone, since you don't have to know how to format each message in order to access the server and get information. You just need a WWW client. However, to write your own CGI scripts, you will need to know how to format the Content-type line of the MIME header in order for the server to know what type of document your script is sending. Also, you will need to know how to access the server's environment variables so you can use that information in your CGI scripts. In the following sections, you will learn everything necessary to accomplish both of these tasks.

Note

If you decide to write your own WWW client, then you will need to understand the client/server communication process before you can begin. A good place to start your search for more information about this is the W3C Reference Library at **http://www.w3.org/hypertext/WWW/Library/Status.html**.

Using a Content-type Output Header

Each document that is sent via a CGI script to the server, whether it was created "on-the-fly" or is simply being opened by the script, must contain a Content-type output header as the first part of the document so the server can process it accordingly. In table 23.1 you will see examples of some of the more commonly used MIME Content-types and their associated extensions.

Table 23.1   Examples of MIME Types and Extensions

Content-type:	Extensions
application/octet-stream	bin exe
application/postscript	ai eps ps
application/pdf	pdf
application/x-csh	csh
application/x-sh	sh
application/x-wais-source	src
application/x-gtar	gtar
application/x-gzip	gz
application/x-tar	tar
application/zip	zip
audio/x-wav	wav
image/gif	gif
image/jpeg	jpeg jpg jpe
text/HTML	HTML htm
text/plain	txt
text/richtext	rtx
video/mpeg	mpeg mpg mpe
video/quicktime	qt mov
video/x-msvideo	avi
video/x-sgi-movie	movie
x-world/x-vrml	wrl

To help you better understand how to properly use Content-types within a CGI script, let's work through an example. Suppose you have decided to write a CGI script that will display a GIF each time it is executed by a browser.

The first line of code you need is a special comment that contains the path to the scripting language that you are using to write the program. In this case it is PERL 4. The comment symbol **#** must be followed by an exclamation point **!** then the path. This special combination of **#!** on the first line of the file is the standard format for letting the server know which interpreter to use to execute the script. The reason that this special comment is used is that while UNIX servers use this line of code to locate the script's interpreter, other types of server systems have alternate methods of specifying the interpreter's location. However, since this line of code starts with a **#** symbol, it is still a valid PERL comment and does not cause problems on non-UNIX servers.

> **Tip**
>
> You should double-check to make sure you include the correct pathname to your language's interpreter.

```
#!/usr/local/bin/perl
```

The next line you will need simply sets the variable **$gif** to the full path name of the image you wish to display.

```
$gif = "/file/path/your.gif";
```

Now it is time to let the server know that it will be receiving an image file from this script to display on the client's browser. This is done using the MIME Content-type line. The print statement prints the information between the quotation marks to the server. Each set of **\n** characters that you see on this line adds a carriage return with a line feed. This gives you the required blank line that must occur after the Content-type information. A blank line lets the server know where the MIME header stops and where the body of information, in this case the gif, starts.

```
print "Content-type: image/gif\n\n";
```

The next line creates a file handle named IMAGE that forms a link from this script to the file contained in the variable **$gif** which we set earlier.

```
open(IMAGE,$gif);
```

Now, we create a loop that sends the entire contents of the gif to the server as the body of the MIME message we began with the Content-type line.

```
while(<IMAGE>) { print $_; }
```

To avoid being sloppy, we will close the file handle to the gif now that we are done sending the image.

```
close(IMAGE);
```

Finally, we let the PERL interpreter know that the CGI script is finished running and can be stopped.

```
exit;
```

This type of script can be modified into something a little more useful. For example, you could turn it into a random image viewer. Each time someone clicks on the link to the script, it executes and feeds a random gif to the client's browser.

Environment Variables

Hopefully, you now have a little better understanding of what is involved as the client and server communicate with each other. Along with the information that I discussed earlier, a host of environment variables are sent during the client/server communications. Although each server can have its own set of environment variables, for the most part, they are all subsets of a large set of standard variables described by the Internet community to help promote uniform standards.

If you have bin access on a UNIX server, then you can use the following script to easily determine which environment variables your server supports. In addition, this script should also work on other server types such as Microsoft Windows NT server if you properly configure the server to recognize and execute PERL scripts.

Once again, this is the magic line that lets the server know which type of CGI script this is so it can launch the appropriate interpreter.

```
#!/usr/local/bin/perl
```

This next line, as was described above, is the MIME output header that lets the server know to expect an HTML document to follow.

```
print "Content-type: text/html\n\n";
```

Now that the server is expecting to receive an HTML document, we will send it a list of each environment variable's name and current value by using a **foreach** loop.

```
foreach $key (keys(%ENV)){
        print "\$ENV{$key} = \"$ENV{$key}\"<br>\n";
}
```

Finally, we need to tell the interpreter that the script is finished.

```
exit;
```

> **Tip**
>
> If the browser you use doesn't support an environment variable, the value of the variable is set to null and is left empty.

As you can see from the example, most of the variables contain protocol version information, and location information such as the client's IP address and the server's domain. However, if you are creative, you can put some of these variables to good use in your CGI scripts.

The best example I have seen so far is the use of the environment variable **HTTP_USER_AGENT**. This contains the name and version number of the client application, which is usually a Web browser. As you can see from figure 23.1, the Netscape 2.0 browser that I used when running this script has an HTTP_USER_AGENT value of Mozilla/2.0 (Win95; I).

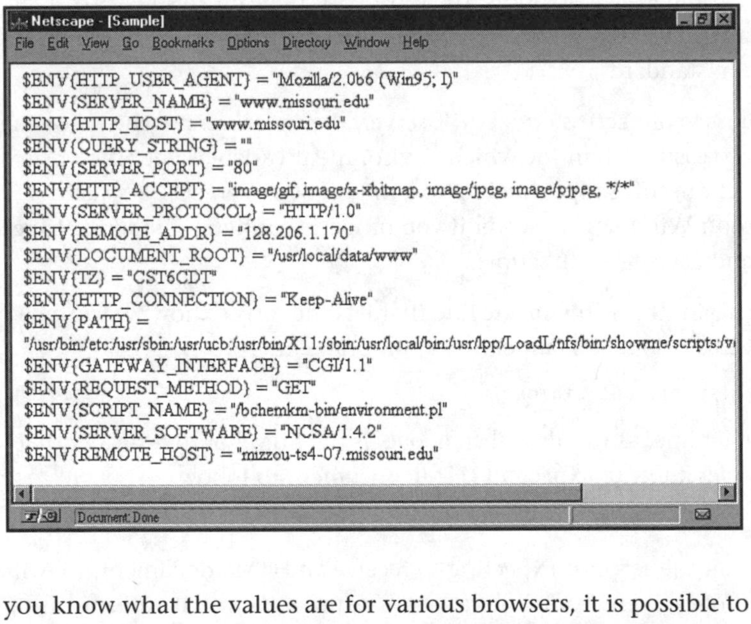

Fig. 23.1
Using the CGI script environment.pl from a browser will generate a screen similar to this one.

```
Netscape - [Sample]
File  Edit  View  Go  Bookmarks  Options  Directory  Window  Help

$ENV{HTTP_USER_AGENT} = "Mozilla/2.0b6 (Win95; I)"
$ENV{SERVER_NAME} = "www.missouri.edu"
$ENV{HTTP_HOST} = "www.missouri.edu"
$ENV{QUERY_STRING} = ""
$ENV{SERVER_PORT} = "80"
$ENV{HTTP_ACCEPT} = "image/gif, image/x-xbitmap, image/jpeg, image/pjpeg, */*"
$ENV{SERVER_PROTOCOL} = "HTTP/1.0"
$ENV{REMOTE_ADDR} = "128.206.1.170"
$ENV{DOCUMENT_ROOT} = "/usr/local/data/www"
$ENV{TZ} = "CST6CDT"
$ENV{HTTP_CONNECTION} = "Keep-Alive"
$ENV{PATH} =
"/usr/bin:/etc:/usr/sbin:/usr/ucb:/usr/bin/X11:/sbin:/usr/local/bin:/usr/lpp/LoadL/nfs/bin:/showme/scripts:/v
$ENV{GATEWAY_INTERFACE} = "CGI/1.1"
$ENV{REQUEST_METHOD} = "GET"
$ENV{SCRIPT_NAME} = "/bchemkm-bin/environment.pl"
$ENV{SERVER_SOFTWARE} = "NCSA/1.4.2"
$ENV{REMOTE_HOST} = "mizzou-ts4-07.missouri.edu"

Document: Done
```

Once you know what the values are for various browsers, it is possible to write a CGI script to serve different Web documents based on browser type. Thus, a text-only browser might receive a text version of your Web page, while image-capable browsers will receive the full version.

Uses for CGI Scripts

Web sites are interactive by their very nature. Every time you click on a hyper link, you are actively involved in the site, rather than passively reading information. Most users enjoy this added level of interactivity and the feeling of participation it brings. However, hyper links are just the beginning. With CGI scripts, you have access to a whole new set of tools to make your Web site more interactive and dynamic.

The list of uses for CGI scripts is always growing. Here are but a few of the more common ones.

- Processing forms
- Image maps
- Animations
- HTML "on the fly"
- Counters
- Search Engines
- WAIS servers
- Spiders, Robots, & WebCrawlers

As you can see, you probably have already interacted with many CGI scripts, possibly without even realizing it.

Processing Forms

Processing the information entered into a form is by far the most common use of CGI scripts. These scripts are activated when you press the submit/send button on the form, that is usually found near the bottom. Once the script is executed the server sends the script the information that was entered. Then, the script processes this information and, if appropriate, sends some information back to the browser via the server. This information is then displayed on your monitor.

Tip

If you execute a script that sends nothing back to the browser, let it know this by using the following line in place of the Content-type line with a blank line.

```
Status: 204 No response
```

You can take a look at the following URL to see an example of a simple form on the Web for adding a response to a guestbook.

URL Address: http://www.missouri.edu/~bchemkm/ guestbook.htm

Note

If you use the browser's **View Source** command (with Netscape, pull down the View menu and select the View Source option), you should be able to find a line in the HTML document that looks something like this.

```
<FORM ACTION="http://absolute_path_name/CGI-bin/scriptname.type"
➥METHOD="POST or GET">
```

The **ACTION** tag tells the browser which script to execute each time the information from the form is sent to the Web server. By using the absolute pathname for the script, you provide a means for the Web server to find the desired script. It is important to remember that you should always use the absolute pathname when indicating the location of scripts on a server.

The **METHOD** tag lets the script know what format the form's information is sent in (either GET or POST). This allows the script to process the form's data correctly. For more information on the METHOD tag, you can look in chapter 21 on forms.

◀ See "Form Layout and Design," p. 503

Fig. 23.2
Notice that you can create a nice looking form by inserting the form fields within table tags.

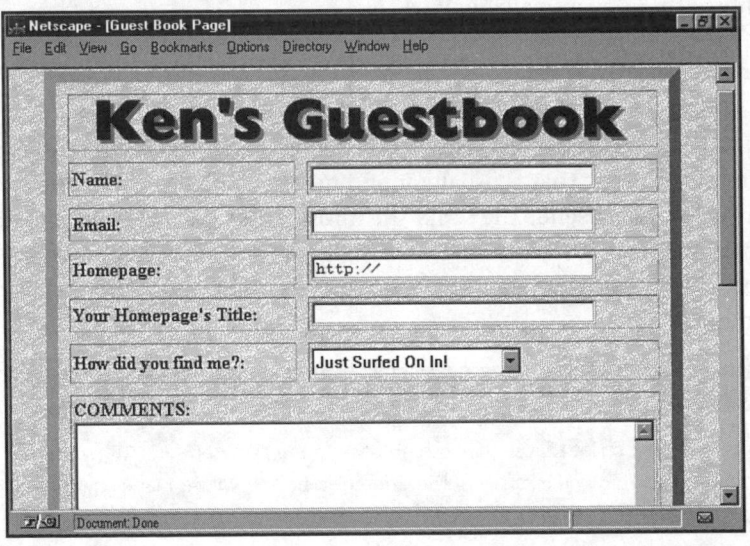

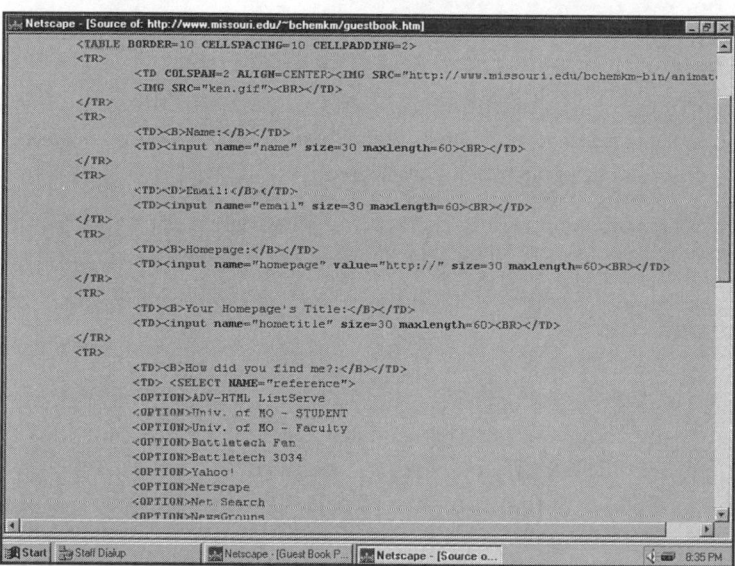

Fig. 23.3
Here is a sample of the source code that is used to produce the table in figure 23.2.

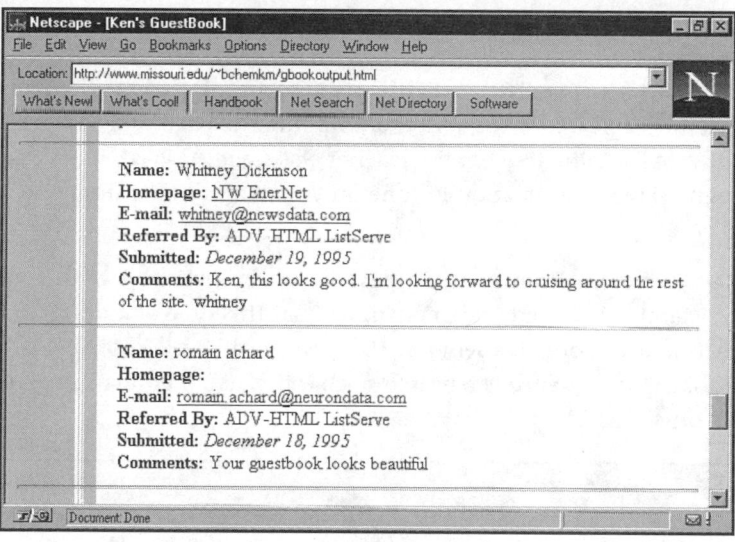

Fig. 23.4
You can use borderless tables, as with this response page, to nicely lay out the script's output.

The script that processes this form has several common features that you can find in other forms as you explore the Web.

- Contains one or more levels of error checking to insure that the form is filled out properly.

- Provides an opportunity for the users to double-check the information they have entered.

- Notifies you that the information was sent correctly, with a brief thank-you and then points out what you should do next.

- Processes the form's information. In this case, the information is added to a response page and the owner of the guestbook—me—is notified via e-mail that the guestbook was signed.

CGI scripts are also commonly used to collect survey information, or update the contents of a database. Later, in chapter 24, you will learn exactly how each of these features works as you write your own guestbook script, much like this one.

Imagemaps

◀ See "Image-maps: From Browser to Server and Back," p. 239

CGI scripts are commonly used, as is discussed in detail in chapter 12, for running imagemaps. Each time you use one of these clickable images, you are executing a CGI script that comes packaged with the Web server. This script compares the coordinates of your "click" with those in the imagemap's configuration file to determine which URL to send to the server. The server then transmits the information to the browser.

Animations

Think back to when you were a kid in grade school. Do you remember drawing stick men, one on a page, and then flipping the pages quickly to animate it (instead of listening to what the teacher was saying)? Well, this same kind of sequential image animation is done on Web sites using a simple CGI script.

At **http://www.missouri.edu/~bchemkm/guestbook.htm** you will find an example I created to demonstrate what this type of animation looks like. Each image is one in a series of 10 gifs from the well-known Duke JAVA animation. This sequence is repeated so that the actual animation plays several times.

Note

The Duke animation that is described above was originally designed by Sun MicroSystems for use with its JAVA animation applet called ImageLoop. You can see the original version of this animation at **http://java.sun.com/applets/applets/ImageLoop/index.html** if you have a browser that supports Hot Java, such as a version of Netscape 2.0.

By using JAVA to perform the animation instead of a different CGI language, they are able to add several key features. First, the JAVA applet downloads onto the client's system and runs using that system's resources. This removes some of the processing

---

overhead from the remote server. Also, since the animation applet runs locally, there is no delay in the animation while each image is downloaded to the client's system. Thus, the animation is a lot smoother.

To give you a better feel for how an animation script works, you will need to have a basic understanding of the concept of a boundary. When the script runs, it happily creates the HTML document until it comes to the boundary—another way of saying an artificial divider. Then, the script inserts the graphic for the first animation. Once the first image is accounted for, the script generates the rest of the HTML document. However, the script remembers where the boundary is in the document and overlays each new image on top of the previous one, creating the animation. This is done using the MIME Content-type for multipart documents.

Would you like to have this type of simple CGI animation on your own Web site? If so, all you need to do is keep reading. I have provided a very simple PERL animation script to produce these for your own pages in the next chapter. Along with this script is a more detailed discussion of how animation scripts work.

▶ See "CGI Animation Script," p. 569

HTML "on the fly"

Another nifty trick using simple CGI scripts is to generate customized HTML pages. These pages produced "on the fly" by the script can include such things as the current time and date, the name and version of the user's browser, or even the user's name.

You can use a simple SH shell script, for example, to generate a little clock (with the date) and indicate which browser the client is using to view your site. To make everything look better, the output can be displayed using table formatting.

◀ See "HTML Tables 101," p. 252

Now, I will walk you through this short SH CGI script.

The first line of code is the special comment line that lets the server know what language interpreter to use as it tries to execute the script. In this case, it is the SH shell scripting language usually located in the bin directory on the server.

```
#!/bin/sh
```

The SH command **cat << top** appears in the next line. The cat (which stands for concatenation) command tells the server to echo or print to the browser everything between two identical parameters. In this case **top** is used.

```
cat << top
```

Now, we tell the server what type of document it is receiving so that it can notify the browser. This is done using an output header with the appropriate MIME Content-type output header discussed earlier in this chapter.

```
Content-type: text/HTML
```

> **Caution**
>
> As a reminder, you must leave at least one blank line below the Content-type line for the command to work properly. Basically, the blank line lets the server know that the header information is finished and that the rest of the information is the message body.

These are standard HTML structural tags.

```
<HTML>
<HEAD>
```

The next line is a META tag. As you learned in chapter 5, this tag can be used to reload a page after an indicated amount of time, in this case one minute. Thus, after each minute elapses, the script is executed again and the page is rebuilt on the fly. This way, the clock maintains the current time.

> **Tip**
>
> If the browser you use does not support META tags, then you will need to reload the page each time you wish to update the time.

```
<META HTTP-EQUIV="refresh" CONTENT="60";
URL=http://www.missouri.edu/bchemkm-bin/timescript.sh">
Some more vanilla HTML.
<TITLE>Sample Time Script</TITLE>
</HEAD>
<BODY TEXT="#000000" BGCOLOR="#FFFFFF">
<HR><P>
<CENTER>
<TABLE BORDER=5 CELLSPACING=10 CELLPADDING=2>
<TR>
<TD>
top
```

Here, we execute the built in UNIX command **date** and pass it several formatting options. The **+** command is used to send formatting information to the date command. The **%** symbol followed by a character represents a format code to tell the date command what to include in the output.

```
/bin/date "+ %I:%M %p %Z
```

Note

You can get a full list of formatting switches for the date command using the UNIX command **man**. This will display the manual pages for the requested command. For the date command just type the following on a UNIX command line.

```
$ man date
```

The echo commands used here print the information contained within the quotation marks to the browser. Also, we see another use of the **date** command with a different formatted request.

```
echo "<BR></TD>"
echo "<TD>"
/bin/date "+%A %B %d, %Y"
echo "<BR></TD>"
echo "</TR><TR>"
echo "<TD COLSPAN=2>"
```

Now, here is an example of incorporating an environment variable to tell the client which browser he is using to view your page.

```
echo $HTTP_USER_AGENT
```

Now that you have created the clock and let the user know which browser she is using, it is time to finish off the HTML page. This is done with the **cat** command again, sandwiching the desired HTML between two identical parameters, this time **bottom**.

```
cat << bottom
<BR></TD>
</TR>
</TABLE>
</CENTER><P>
<HR>
<P>The rest of your page's content goes here.<P>
<HR>
</BODY>
</HTML>
bottom
```

If you have copied everything correctly, and are using a browser that supports META tags, you should see something that looks like figure 23.5.

Fig. 23.5
This is an example of a simple clock produced by using a CGI script.

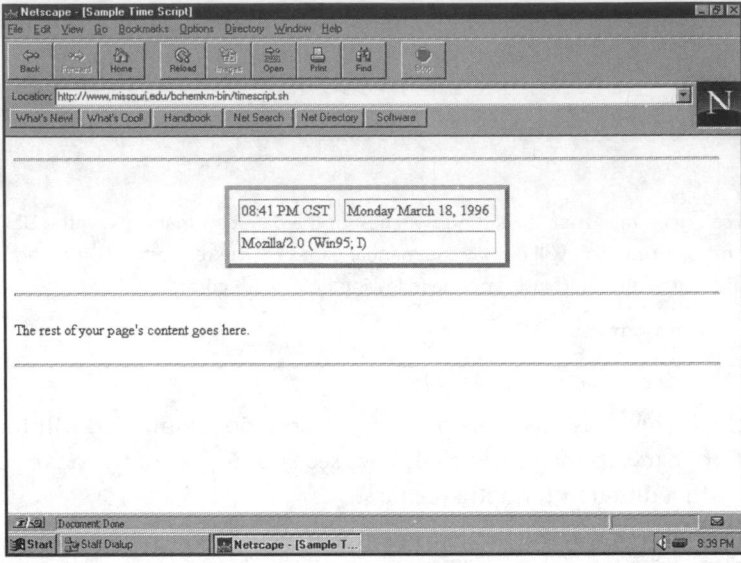

Counters

If you surf the Web much, you have probably seen several pages that tell you what number visitor you are to the site. The way these sites keep track of the number of visitors is by using a counter. This is a CGI script that increments an internal counter each time the page is requested by the server and then displays the appropriate series of graphics to indicate the current "count."

If you would like to have a counter on your Web site, there are several ways you can go about setting one up. If you have root access to your server, you can install a counter that is accessible by any user on the server. With this option, you will use fewer system resources than if everyone on the system has his own counter script. A nice choice for this type of script is WWW Homepage Access Counter [Counter Release 2.2] which can be found at **http://www.semcor.com/~muquit/Count.html**.

If you have a working CGI-bin directory, there are several counter scripts you can install for your use. By placing the script in your bin directory, you will be the only user on the system who will have access to it, but if you don't have root access on the server, then this is your best bet. One such script is HTML Access Counter - Counter 4.0 located at **http://www.webtools.org/counter/**.

Unfortunately, your site may be hosted on a server that is not configured for CGI use. If you find yourself in this situation, you can still have an access counter, but you will need to use one that is hosted by a remote site. Each time someone visits your site, a CGI script is executed on the remote server that exports the count information back to the client's browser. One of the most popular hosted access counters for Web sites is The Web Counter at **http://www.digits.com/Web_counter/**.

There is a lot of information available about access counters on the Internet already. The FAQ - How do I set up an HTML Counter at **http://pantheon.cis.yale.edu/~nakamura/counterfaq.html** is an excellent source for further information. Also, if you are running a WinNT server, you can take a look at ED Counters, counters... at **http://charon.assert.ee/counters.htm**. If you're operating a Mac server then you can try Simple Counters at **http://cy-mac.welc.cam.ac.uk/CGI-simplecounter.html** for more information.

Once you have your counter set up on your site, you should take a look at Counter Digits at **http://www.issi.com/people/russ/digits/digits.html**. Here you will find a nice collection of images for use with counter scripts.

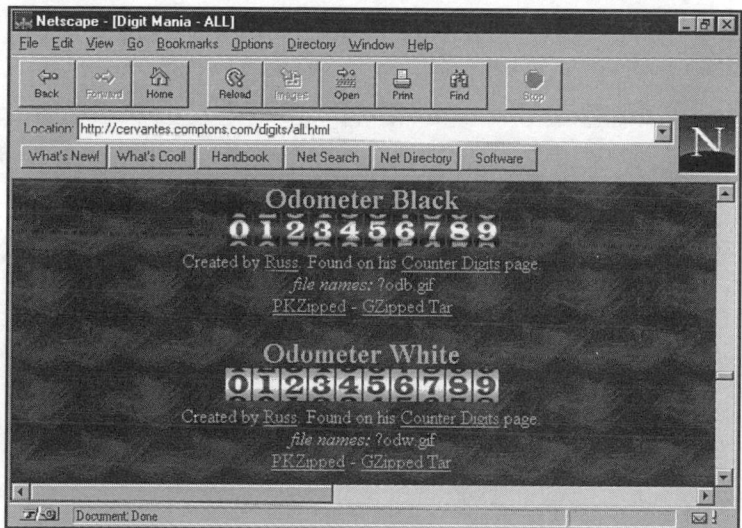

Fig. 23.6
Two of my favorite image sets from Digit Mania's counter archive.

Search Engines

A common stopping point on the Web is the search engine. These massive information repositories are easily searched thanks to CGI scripts that allow you to interface with them.

Some of the most well-known search engines include:

- Yahoo at **http://www.yahoo.com/**
- Lycos at **http://www.lycos.com/**

- WebCrawler at **http://webcrawler.com/**
- WWW Yellow Pages at **http://www.mcp.com/nrp/wwwyp/**

For example, if you enter "search engine" into the Lycos search engine, as in Fig. 23.7, you should get back a list of hits. Each hit in the list is formatted as in figure 23.8.

Fig. 23.7

The Lycos search engine's front page.

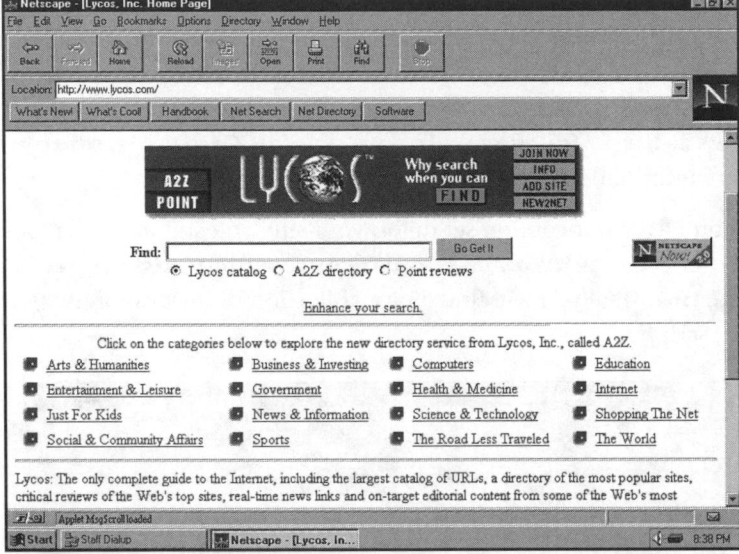

Fig. 23.8

The first match of the search query "search engine."

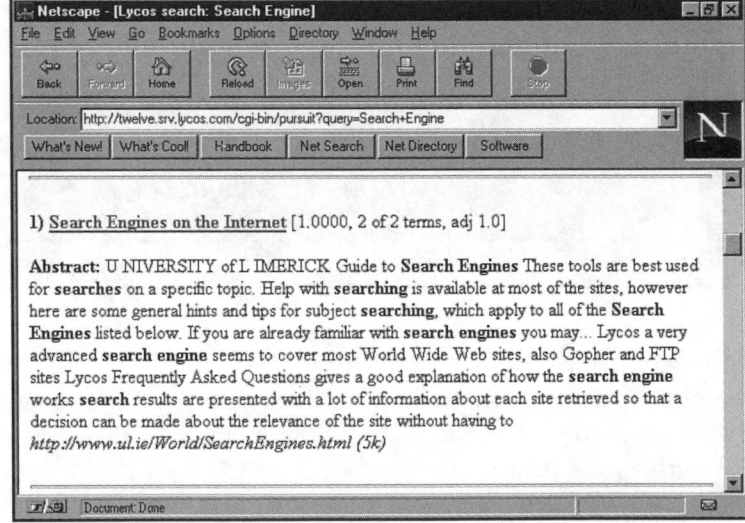

Some of the more advanced search engines, like Lycos, will allow you to use the logical operators **and** and **or** to help widen or narrow your search. You can even control the amount of information listed for each site in the search results and the number of matches that are returned.

> **Tip**
>
> If one search engine fails to meet your needs, try another. No one search engine can keep a complete list of all web sites.

If your site has a large amount of information to present, then you might want to look into getting your own search engine. This allows people using your site to quickly and efficiently locate the information they need. If you feel that a search engine is what your site needs to improve its presentation of information, then you should consider the following options:

- If you are a confident programmer, you can write your own search engine CGI script.
- If programming is not your strong point at the moment, you can always port an existing search engine to your site from the Web. Here is a list of links to more information about some of the better freeware and shareware packages:
  1. WILLO at **http://www.washington.edu:1180/willow/home.html**
  2. GLIMPSE at **http://glimpse.cs.arizona.edu:1994/glimpsehelp.html**
  3. HIDX at **http://mall.turnpike.net/~jc/hidxq.html**
  4. SWISH 1.1.1 at **http://www.eit.com/software/swish/swish.html**
- Finally, if the previous options fail to meet your needs, you can always buy a commercially available search engine.

Interface with WAIS Servers

If these search engines are not enough to satisfy your site's information distribution needs, you might want to consider implementing a version of WAIS (Wide Area Information Server, pronounced "ways") like freeWAIS on your site. One of the best features of this system is that it catalogues many more types of information than the standard HTML documents that are collected by the web wanderers for use with the standard search engines. A WAIS server keeps track of gifs and other image documents as well as several types of audio and video files. If you have a lot of information in formats other than HTML, then this is a great means of allowing clients to search your site for the information they need.

The WAIS server was originally designed to allow multinational corporations and other organizations the ability to search their internal databases. Each WAIS server forwards incoming queries to the next server on a list. As the request passes along the chain of servers the amount of collected information grows until all the server locations are searched and one large summary document is sent back to the client.

Recently, the WAIS server has been successfully put to use on stand-alone systems. So, you shouldn't feel the need to have multiple server and database locations before you start considering a WAIS server as a means of allowing clients quick and easy access to your site's information.

If you are interested in having these search capabilities on your site, consider getting a current version of freeWAIS (a version of WAIS in the public domain). For more information, you can consult the online FAQ at **http:// www.cis.ohio-state.edu/hypertext/faq/usenet/wais-faq/freeWAIS- sf/faq.html**. Also, you should definitely take a look at the information on the WAIS homepage at **http://kaos.erin.gov.au/technical/retrieval/ wais/wais.html**. Finally, if you would rather have a proprietary version of WAIS software, you should visit WAIS Inc.'s homepage at **http:// www.wais.com/** for more information. WAIS Inc. is now a part of AOL Productions, Inc.

Spiders, Robots, & WebCrawlers

As you have seen earlier, search engines are used to search vast archives of information on the Web. But how does all that information get compiled? The answer is with CGI scripts called Web wanderers, Web robots, spiders, or webcrawlers. These robots are constantly moving from server to server, site to site, methodically searching for links and pages to process.

You can think of a robot as an automated Web browser. In fact, these programs use the same protocols to access servers and retrieve Web documents that browsers do. They just do it much faster. Each time a robot moves to a new server, it proceeds to systematically archive each Web document's title and URL, directory by directory. It may even note the outgoing links and use them to hunt down the next server to visit.

These programs are usually written for one of three major purposes. The most obvious one is to attempt to maintain a single archive that contains information on every document on the Web. However, it is currently taking the fastest robots more than half a year to travel the entire Web. So, it appears that a complete, up-to-date archive of Web documents will become increasingly difficult to maintain. For this reason most newer robots are only looking for information on a specific topic. This helps these archives stay more current than the larger global search sites. Finally, some robots are built to synchronize mirrored sites.

For a well-kept listing of all the currently known (more than 50) robots on the Internet and a nice starting point for finding more information, see Martijn Koster's site on web wanderers at:

> URL Address: **http://info.webcrawler.com/mak/projects/ robots/robots.html**

Writing CGI Scripts

Hopefully, you now have a good idea of some of the more common uses for CGI scripts. As you can see, many of them provide helpful tools that you can incorporate into your personal Web site. If you would like to use some of these tools to make your site more dynamic, then you will need to consider a few things before you start.

- Can you write CGI scripts?
- Choosing a CGI scripting language

Can You Write CGI Scripts?

Before you can get started writing your own CGI scripts, you need to find out if your server is specially configured to allow you to use them. The best thing to do is contact your system administrator and find out if you are allowed to run CGI scripts on the server. If you can, you also need to ask what you need to do to use them, and where you should put the scripts once they are written.

In some cases, system administrators do not allow clients to use CGI scripts because they feel they cannot afford the added security risks. In that case, you will have to find another means of making your site more interactive.

If you find that you can use CGI scripts and are using a UNIX server, then you will probably have to put your scripts into a specially configured directory which is usually called cgibin or cgi-bin. If you are using Microsoft's Internet Server, then you will probably put your CGI programs in a directory called `scripts`. This allows the system administrator to configure the server to recognize that the files placed in that directory are executable. If you are using an NCSA version of HTTPD on a UNIX system then this is done by adding a ScriptAlias line to the conf/srm.conf file on the server.

Four Steps to Better Script Writing

It is important to remember that although CGI scripts are not necessarily complex, you need to have some basic understanding of the programming language you wish to use and the server you plan to run the scripts on. Poorly written scripts can easily become more trouble than they are worth. For example, you could delete entire directories of information or shut down your server if your script were to start forking off new processes in a geometric fashion.

Before starting down the road to becoming a CGI scripter, you should do the following:

- Get a programming book on the scripting language you plan to learn.

- Notify the network administrator of your local server to find out how to run scripts on your system and what security features she wants you to implement in them.

- Subscribe to a listserve and read the appropriate news groups on the language you plan to use. These are wonderful resources for programming information and good places to ask for help if you are stuck.

- Find a friend who has experience programming in your scripting language and who can help you smoothly overcome some of the early hurdles you will face.

Which Language Should You Use?

Now that you know what a CGI script is, how it works, and what it can do, the next thing you need to consider is which language you should use. You can write a CGI script in almost any language. So, if you can program in a language already, there is a good chance you can use it to write your scripts. This is usually the best way to start learning how to write CGI scripts, since you are already familiar with the basic syntax of the language. However, you still need to know which languages your Web server is configured to support.

UNIX-based NCSA and CERN Web servers are by far the most common. These platforms are easily configured to support most of the major scripting languages including C, C++, JAVA, PERL, and the basic shell scripting languages like SH. On the other hand, if your Web server is using the Mac server then you might be limited to using AppleScript as your scripting language.

Likewise, if you are using Windows NT server, then you might need to use Visual Basic as your scripting language. However, it is possible to configure both these systems to support other scripting languages like C and PERL, or even Pascal.

Note

If you are interested in finding out which scripting languages your server is configured to support, you should ask your system administrator to give you a listing of what is available on your server.

Also, if you have access to a UNIX-based server and can log into a shell account, then you can find out which languages your system supports by using the UNIX command **which**.

If you are using the SH shell, you should see the following:

```
$ which sh
/usr/bin/sh
$ which perl5
/usr/local/bin/perl5
```

Many scripting languages are freely distributable and fairly easy for an experienced administrator to install. As a last resort, you can always request that a new language be considered for addition to your local system.

If you are lucky, you may find that your server is already configured to support several CGI scripting languages. In this case, you just need to compare the strengths and weaknesses of each language you have available with the programming tasks you anticipate writing the scripts for. Once you do this, you should have a good idea of which programming language is best suited to your specific needs.

Common CGI Scripting Languages

When it comes to the CGI, anything goes. Of the vast numbers of programming languages out there, many more than you could possibly learn in a lifetime, most can work with the CGI. So, you will have to spend a little time sifting through the long list to find the one that will work best for you.

Even though there are a lot of different languages available, they tend to fall into several categories based on the way they are processed—compiled, interpreted, and compiled/interpreted—and on the logic behind how the source is written—procedural and object-oriented.

> **Note**
>
> This chapter will discuss the most common scripting languages that are available for use on a UNIX server. All of the major languages presented here will be available for both MacHTTPD and WinHTTPD if they are not available at this time. You should note that MacHTTPD comes with AppleScript as its built-in scripting language, while WinHTTPD comes with Visual Basic.
>
> If you would like some more information on either AppleScript or Visual Basic, you can consult the following:
>
> ■ For information of AppleScript books, see **http://www.ultranet.com/ ~mfenner/books.html**. Also, for additional information see **http:// www.mtt.com/theSource/mtt/appleScript.html**.
>
> ■ For a fairly comprehensive listing of Visual Basic Resources on the Web you should take a look at **http://www.gns.com/~robinson/vb/vb.html**.

> **Tip**
>
> Shell languages are easier to learn than robust scripting languages like C or PERL. Likewise, object-oriented languages like C++, PERL 5, and JAVA are the hardest to get used to.

Compiled Languages

Some of the available programming languages are compiled rather than being interpreted. The two most commonly used are C and C++. When using a compiled language, the program as it appears when you write it is referred to as the source code. This source code is then processed by the language's compiler into a much smaller version that is in the machine's native language and is usually referred to as object code. Once the source code is successfully compiled, the object code can be run by the server without fear of syntax errors. In this more compact form, the object code usually executes much faster than code from scripting languages that are compiled at runtime. Unfortunately, this does mean that you have to recompile the source code each time a change is made in the script.

C

One of the most popular CGI scripting languages is C. It was developed by Brian Kernighan and Dennis Ritchie in 1972 at Bell Labs. This procedural language is already familiar to a large number of programmers, and thus, is their scripting language of choice. As such, there are many large archives of existing C source code that you can adapt to fit your specific programming needs.

Since C is a compiled language, it must be processed into a small binary object code before it can be executed. As was mentioned earlier, this allows these scripts to execute very quickly. So, if a quick response from the script is your primary consideration for picking a scripting language, you should stick with a compiled language like C. The best use for CGI scripts coded in C is for processing large amounts of numeric information quickly and efficiently.

Unfortunately, most of the CGI scripts written today focus on complex regular expressions and string data. These types of programs can be very awkward to write in C. This is one major reason why many CGI programmers are using PERL instead.

> **Tip**
>
> All UNIX-based servers come equipped with C, C++, and at least one shell language such as SH.

C++

Like its predecessor C, C++ (developed by Bjarne Stroustrup at AT&T) is a compiled language that executes small binary object code very quickly. However, C++ is not as similar to C as you might anticipate from the name. While C is a procedural language, C++ is part of the object-oriented paradigm. What this means is that as an object-oriented language, C++, is much more concerned with the function, interaction, and reusability of its objects than it is with the actual steps it takes to get the job done.

> **Note**
>
> Since C++ is object-oriented, it will take quite an adjustment if you aren't already familiar with this type of programming. So, expect a large learning curve if you will be writing your first object-oriented source. However, if you do take the time to learn it, you will find that C++ objects are much easier to reuse and to expand their functionality than other procedural language's source.

The only other major drawback for using C++ for your CGI scripting is that there is not a lot of public domain source. Only recently have software engineers started to program object-oriented solutions for CGI scripting needs. Thus, you might have to wait awhile before you start to see large archives of code for public use. However, as time goes on, this will become much less of an issue.

A good source for more information on C++ is the Usenet group **comp.lang.c++.moderated**.

Interpreted Languages

Unlike C and C++, some languages are not compiled into tight binary code before they are executed. Some, like the shell language SH, are interpreted during execution. This means that any syntax errors in the script will not be detected until the program has already started to run. This, coupled with the limited power of the shell languages, means that they are not as useful for larger scripting jobs as some of the other languages dealt with in this chapter.

PERL, along with several other interpreted languages, avoids this problem by being compiled at runtime. What this means is that the PERL interpreter checks each line of code for proper syntax before the code is compiled. Then, the code is compiled and executed. However, unlike C, this doesn't result in a truly compiled object that can then be reused. PERL scripts are interpreted and compiled each time they are executed. Thus, there is no need to keep track of separate source and object files for the same script.

SH and C Shell

There are several commonly available shell scripting languages, or command interpreters as they are sometimes called. The most common ones are SH and C shell. Although these are among the most important user interfaces for the UNIX environment, they are not the best choice for a CGI scripting language.

These shell languages are designed as UNIX tools and thus lack much of the power and features of true programming languages. However, they can be put to good use when writing simple, rather disposable CGI scripts or when you need a little job done in a hurry.

Caution

If you do decide to write a script using one of these languages, you should remember that they are not compiled. Rather, they are interpreted line by line, each line of code being executed before the next is read into the command interpreter. Thus, if you have any syntax errors in your script, you won't find them until the script has already executed part way. At that time, your application will crash and could cause serious problems with your system.

PERL 4.036

One of the most commonly used languages for CGI scripting is PERL 4.036. PERL, which stands for "Practical Extraction and Report Language," was developed by Larry Wall, who still maintains it. All the versions of PERL except the newest one, are procedural. The newest release, version 5, is object-oriented and represents a major restructuring of the PERL language. However, most PERL 4 programs should run fine using PERL 5. This latest version will be discussed briefly later in this chapter.

A key feature of PERL is that it is very open ended. It doesn't confine the user to a certain rigorous set of syntax. Instead, PERL usually provides several methods of doing each task, which makes it easier to program using your own personal style. Also, PERL supports almost all the common features of C, so a C programmer can write PERL code that looks very much like the C he or she is used to.

Another key feature of PERL is its powerful handling of strings and regular expressions. Using the built-in string manipulation functions of PERL, many scripts are easily written that would be much harder to program in C. Since the overwhelming majority of all CGI scripts handle string data, it is no wonder that so many CGI scripts are written in PERL.

Another thing to keep in mind is that PERL is completely interpreted and compiled at runtime. This means that you won't get a syntax error after the program is already running like you might programming in a shell language. At the same time, it means that you can simply make a change in your source code and it will take effect. You don't have to precompile your source into object code each time you make a change like you do using C.

Since PERL 4 is currently the most widely used CGI scripting language on the Web, and as it can be run on a wide variety of server types, I have chosen to use it for the majority of the CGI scripting examples used in both this and the following chapter. If you would like more information about this scripting language you should take a look at the PERL Language Home Page at **http://www.perl.com/perl/index.html**.

PERL 5.000

At this point, you may be asking yourself why this guy is telling me about PERL 5 when he just got finished making PERL 4 seem like the perfect CGI scripting language? Well, the answer, my friend, is simple. PERL 5 is to PERL 4 what C++ is to C. What this means is that while PERL 4 is procedural, PERL 5 is object-oriented. Also, while PERL 4 is forced mostly to go it alone, PERL 5 comes equipped to handle reusable modules along with a lot of other new features.

> **Note**
>
> PACKAGE - A package is a programming context in which local variables are defined and used, as in a subroutine.
>
> This description of the PERL 5 modules comes directly from the hypertext version of the PERL 5 manual, which can be found at **http://www.phlab.missouri.edu/perl/perl5man/**.
>
> PERL Modules
>
> In PERL 5, the notion of packages has been extended into the notion of modules. A module is a package that is defined in a library file of the same name, and is designed to be reusable. It may do this by providing a mechanism for exporting some of its symbols into the symbol table of any package using it. Or it may function as a class definition and make its semantics available implicitly through method calls on the class and its objects, without explicit exportation of any symbols. Or it can do a little of both.
>
> For a very up-to-date list of all the PERL 5 modules, see the PERL 5 Module List at **ftp://rtfm.mit.edu/pub/usenet/news.answers/perl-faq/module-list**.

As it stands, PERL 5 represents a total renovation of this language. Almost every line in the original code has been redone. This, coupled with the transition from a procedural to an object-oriented language with a lot of new bells and whistles, will make PERL 5 a very popular CGI scripting language for a long time to come.

For more information on this new version of PERL, see the PERL 5 WWW Page at **http://www.metronet.com/1h/perlinfo/perl5.html**. Or, you can subscribe to the PERL Usenet group at **comp.lang.perl**.

Compiled/Interpreted Languages

So far you have been given some examples of compiled and interpreted languages. Recently, though, a language has been developed that is both compiled and interpreted. This programming language is JAVA, which is first compiled into a platform independent binary bytecode. Then, when the script is executed, the precompiled bytecode is interpreted by the local platform into a platform-specific machine code. Thus, as long as there is a JAVA interpreter for the platform you are using, you can use any JAVA bytecode regardless of the platform it was written for. This design allows these programs to become truly platform-independent. Thus, programmers will no longer have to grapple with porting their software across platforms.

IV

JAVA

The JAVA language is being hailed on the Internet as the scripting language of the future and a possible replacement for the CGI. When Sun MicroSystems first started developing JAVA, it intended to write it entirely in C++. However, as time went on, it decided that there were too many limitations within the language for it to be optimally suited for Internet programming. So, it struck out on its own. However, it has endeavored to stick closely to C++ while designing the language. As a result, JAVA is a member of the object-oriented programming paradigm and should be fairly easy for experienced C++ programmers to pick up.

The object-oriented structure of JAVA is what makes its applications modular while its platform independence makes it very portable. JAVA was defined by Sun MicroSystems in its first white paper as follows:

JAVA: *A simple, object-oriented, distributed, interpreted, robust, secure, architecture-neutral, portable, high-performance, multi-threaded, and dynamic language.*

If JAVA can actually live up to this description, then it might very well become the dominant scripting language on the Internet.

▶ See "Java and Javascript," p. 621

Finding CGI Resources

As you advance down the path to mastery (or at least proficiency) in your favorite CGI scripting language, you need to know where to look for help and the latest online information.

Listserves

My personal favorite is using listserves. These are groups of people who share a common interest. Each time someone posts a message to the list, everyone who is subscribed will get a copy. Then, any of the hundreds or even thousands of people who received your post may choose to answer your mail and give you the information you requested. The fastest way to find a news group that is right for you is to check out L-Soft's search engine for its listserves at **http://www.lsoft.com/lists/LIST_Q.html**. Just pick a topic like HTML, CGI, or JAVA and you will get a series of mailing lists with information on how to subscribe to each one.

Newsgroups

If you like the idea of a listserve, but don't want your mailbox filled with mail every day, then a newsgroup may be for you. These are similar to a listserve except that you read the posts off of a news spool rather than out of your inbox. Also, many newsgroup applications allow you to search the posts by subject, author, or keyword. Here is a list of some of my favorite newgroups on CGI programming.

- comp.infosystems.www.authoring.cgi
- comp.lang.perl
- comp.lang.c++
- comp.lang.java
- comp.lang.javascript

> **Tip**
>
> You will avoid upsetting others on listserves and newsgroups if you remember to always try to figure out problems on your own before asking for help.

Individual Archives

Another great source of online CGI information is personal Web sites. Many individuals have amassed a mountain of links to key information archives on the net for their favorite scripting language. Finding a couple of these gems can save hours of surfing the Web for information.

Beyond the CGI

As is inevitable with most technology, the CGI for all it's worth, is already becoming outdated. With the explosive growth of technology in this day and age, the CGI is starting to show its age as new and exciting alternatives to CGI scripting are being developed. In this, the final section of this chapter, I will discuss a few of these alternatives including SSI (Server Side Includes), as well as JavaScript and Visual Basic Script.

SSI (Server Side Includes)

If you are using an NCSA server on a UNIX system, then you have access to a special feature of this server commonly referred to as Server Side Includes (SSI). If you turn on this feature of the server, the server will recognize .shtml files as html documents that need to be treated specially. When the server sends a .shtml file it doesn't passively send the requested document to the browser, but rather actively parses it. This means that the server looks at the HTML document line by line as it is sending it to see if the HTML page includes any special instructions that the server should carry out while it is sending the page. Usually these instructions take one of the following forms.

- Adding the current date or time
- Adding a file like a standard header or footer
- Adding the output from a script

For example, if you have a standard footer that you need to place on every page of your Web site, with SSI you can simply place the following line of code at the bottom of each document where you want the footer to appear.

```
<!--#include file="footer.html"-->
```

or

```
<!--#include virtual="http://www.blah.com/footer.html"-->
```

Just remember that if you use `file`, then you must include the relative path for the file to be included, and that the file must be in the same directory or a subdirectory of the main document. Also, if you want you can use `virtual` and specify the complete URL for the file you wish to include. Or, if you have a script that generates a custom footer for each page, then you can include the output from that script by placing the following line where you would like the script's output to appear within the document.

```
<!--#exec cgi="/cgibin/footer.pl"-->
```

The main advantage for using SSIs within your Web pages is that it can allow your documents to display current information like the date and time without the use of a CGI script. Also, it can allow you to maintain only a single version of information you would have to repeat on many pages under normal circumstances.

However, there is one drawback of using SSIs that you should be aware of. By forcing the server to parse each document it sends to the browser, line by line, a lot of processing time is required which both slows down the server and makes the Web pages take longer to load. If a high-traffic site were to parse every page that it sent out to check for SSIs, the server would very likely experience a very marked decrease in efficiency.

For a more detailed discussion of SSIs you should refer to NCSA's online SSI tutorial at **http://hoohoo.ncsa.uiuc.edu/docs/tutorials/includes.html**.

JavaScript

Along with the development of the new programming language JAVA that was briefly introduced earlier, JavaScript is providing Web authors with alternatives to more traditional CGI programming. By embedding the JavaScript code directly into the Web page, newer browsers like Netscape 2.0 are able to execute these scripts directly on the client's machine without the need to make a call to the server. This can greatly increase the speed at which the clients get feedback from their actions and reduce the load on the Web server at the same time. It is hoped my many that this new scripting language will reduce the heavy server load imposed my many traditional CGI programs by moving much of the processing overhead to the client's machine.

JavaScript is a simpler version of the object-based JAVA language that is interpreted at runtime much like PERL, rather than having to be compiled before it can be executed. Although JavaScript is a simpler version of the JAVA language, it still retains much of its power. Also, JavaScripts can be written to recognize and react to such things as mouse clicks, form field data, and the use of page navigation.

The complete JavaScript Authoring Guide by Netscape can be found at **http://cgi.netscape.com/eng/mozilla/Gold/handbook/javascript/index.html** and is an excellent place to start your exploration of this alternative to CGI programming.

Visual Basic (VB) Scripting

Another very promising alternative to CGI will be Visual Basic Script or VBScript, which is a cross-platform subset of Visual Basic 4.0 by Microsoft. This scripting language will be in direct competition with JavaScript and will provide much the same functionality as a similar scripting language embedded within the HTML pages themselves.

Like JavaScript, VBScript's major function will be to reduce server overhead by moving the processing load to the client's machine and, in the process, greatly speed up the response to clients' actions. VBScripts will be able to link and automate many types of objects including OLE objects and JAVA applets. Currently, Microsoft plans for its VBScripting language to be fully implemented in the 3.0 release of Microsoft Internet Explorer.

You can find the latest information on VBScript from the Visual Basic Microsoft Web site at **http://www.microsoft.com/VBASIC/vbscript/vbscript.htm**. ❖

## CHAPTER 24

Sample Code and CGI Scripts

by Ken Murphy

Nestled snugly out of sight on most Web sites are CGI scripts busily giving the site its dynamic look and feel. Scripts allow you to include, for example, on-line forms, animations, search engines, and customized Web pages on your Web site.

By far, form processing is the most common use of CGI scripts on the Web today. Whether you have your own business and would like an on-line order form or you just want to give people stopping by a cool way to leave you a message, you need forms on your Web site. Luckily, processing forms with CGI scripts is fairly easy.

In this chapter, you do the following:

- Learn standard forum output format
- Set up an e-mail form
- Set up a color conversion form
- Set up your own animation
- Discover a find-replace utility
- Set up your own guestbook

Form Output

Every time you send information via a form on a Web site, you must first package that information into a special standardized format for CGI scripts to process. In this section, you learn how the form output is formatted and where you can get a simple PERL script to take this formatted information and change it into a form that is easy to work with.

The Output Format

Each time you fill out a form and send the information, the CGI script specified in the form's ACTION attribute is executed to process the information.

When the browser sends this information to the Web server for processing by a CGI script, it is sent in a standard format. This format is basically a long string of name/value pairs. The NAME portion of each pair comes from the NAME attribute within the form field designations, and the VALUE half of the pair is the information that is entered into the form for that field. The browser then uses an = (equal sign) to separate these two halves of the pair. Any blank spaces between words in the form are replaced with + (plus signs). Finally, an & (ampersand symbol) is placed between each set of name/value pairs.

Note

When a special, non-7-bit ASCII character is entered into a form, the character is sent as a percent sign followed by its hexadecimal equivalent. The same occurs for such common symbols as +, =, %, and & if they appear as form input.

For example, if you visit my guestbook at **http://www.missouri.edu/ ~bchemkm/guestbook.htm** and take a peek at the source code, you see a line similar to the following:

```
<FORM METHOD="POST" ACTION="http://www.missouri.edu/bchemkm-bin/
framebook.pl">
```

As mentioned previously, the ACTION attribute indicates the location of the CGI script that is executed by the server and given the information in the form. If you enter your name and a comment in the form and click on the submit button, the PERL CGI script framebook.pl is executed by the Web server. At this time, your browser passes your name and the comment to the CGI script in the following format:

```
?name=your+name&comments=your+comment+goes+here
```

Luckily, you normally don't need to remember how this works. As you learn later in this chapter, a freely available PERL program can decode the form's information for you.

Using cgi-lib.pl for Form Processing

Thanks to the standard format that forms use to send information to CGI scripts, you can easily write a CGI script to handle this information. In fact, this task is so simple that you don't even have to write a script. Just go to

Steven Brenner's Web site at **http://www.bio.cam.ac.uk/cgi-lib/**, and ftp a copy of cgi-lib.pl. This library is a collection of several short subroutines that you can use to make processing forms easier. The most important subroutine in this library is called ReadParse. This subroutine actually processes the form's information into a format that you can work with by turning the name/value pairs into the keys and values of an associative array.

Once you have cgi-lib.pl downloaded, remember to place it in a directory that is set up for CGI scripts. After doing so, make sure that the file permissions have been set correctly. To do so, make sure that the Web server has permission to read and execute the file. If you are using a UNIX server, one method is to go to the script's directory and type the following command at the UNIX prompt:

```
$ chmod 755 cgi-lib.pl
```

This command sets the file's permissions to the following:

```
rwxr-xr-x
```

The permission value used indicates that all users have permission to read and execute this file, but only the owner can write to it.

◀ See "Can You Write CGI Scripts?" p. 545

Sample E-Mail Form

The first form that you learn about in this chapter is a simple e-mail form called mail.htm that your visitors can use to send you e-mail (see listing 24.1) if you are using a server that has the sendmail utility installed. The simple CGI script used to process this form contains many features that carry over into the more complex scripts that are discussed later in this chapter.

Listing 24.1   Sample E-Mail Form

```
<HTML>
<HEAD>
<TITLE>E-Mail Form</TITLE>
</HEAD>
<BODY TEXT="#000000" BGCOLOR="#FFFFFF">
<CENTER>
<!--The action attribute below must be set to the correct URL-->
<!--for the place you put the email.pl file on your server.-->
<FORM METHOD="POST" ACTION="http://www.missouri.edu/bchemkm-bin/email.pl">
<TABLE BORDER=10 CELLSPACING=10 CELLPADDING=2>
<TR>
<TH COLSPAN=2>E-Mail Form<BR></TH>
</TR><TR>
<TD ALIGN=RIGHT><B>Name of Sender:</B></TD>
```

(continues)

Listing 24.1 Continued

```
<TD><INPUT SIZE=40 TYPE="text" NAME="from"><BR></TD>
</TR><TR>
<TD ALIGN=RIGHT><B>Subject:</B></TD>
<TD><INPUT SIZE=40 NAME="subject"><BR></TD>
</TR><TR>
<TD COLSPAN=2 ALIGN=CENTER><B>Body of Mail:</B><BR>
<TEXTAREA WRAP=VIRTUAL NAME="message" COLS=50 ROWS=10></textarea><BR></TD>
</TR><TR>
<TD ALIGN=CENTER><INPUT TYPE="submit" VALUE="Send Mail"></TD>
<TD ALIGN=CENTER><INPUT TYPE="reset" VALUE="Clear"><BR></TD>
</TR>
</TABLE>
</FORM>
</CENTER>
</BODY>
</HTML>
```

How the Script Works

The first thing you should notice when looking at this CGI script in listing 24.1 is that, in PERL, all variables begin with a $ (dollar symbol), making them easy to spot. PERL also uses a @ symbol to indicate a standard array and a % symbol to indicate an associative array. Likewise, each subroutine that is called is indicated by an & before its name. This script uses the ReadParse subroutine from the cgi-lib.pl library, which was discussed in the preceding section. This subroutine takes the form's output and puts it into an associative array that allows the CGI script to handle it easily.

One common practice when writing PERL CGI scripts is to initialize the script's variables near the beginning. This way, it is easier to go back in later and make minor changes to the values of these variables. The assignment of the major variables is usually followed by the body of the program. The body of this script is designed to send the information from the e-mail form to you as a formatted e-mail message letting you know someone has dropped by your site, and to send a brief thank-you message to the visitor letting him or her know that everything went smoothly.

For this script to function properly on your system, you must be using a UNIX server with the sendmail utility installed and then properly set several variable's values within this script. The $myname variable should contain your name as you want it to appear on the To: line of your e-mail. Likewise, the $myemail should contain your full e-mail address. Finally, you need to set the path for the $sendmail variable to indicate the location of this program on your server.

If you are using a different type of server or your server doesn't have the sendmail utility installed, you will need to determine what e-mail utility is provided by your system. Once you have that information, you will then need to look at that utility's documentation to determine how to send an e-mail from a file via the comand line and substitute that information for the call to the sendmail utility in this program.

Tip

If you are using a UNIX server, you can find a complete listing of all the sendmail command-line flags by typing **man sendmail** at a UNIX prompt.

You should understand two main features in the body of the script. First, the script opens a *filehandle* called MAIL to the sendmail program on your server. Filehandles allow the PERL program to interact with something other than a browser, which is considered the standard output device for the server during Web surfing. After the filehandle to the sendmail program is opened, the script prints the e-mail to the sendmail program using the filehandle to redirect the information away from your visitor's browser. Second, after the e-mail portion of the script is finished, the script proceeds to send a brief HTML document to their browser to let them know that everything went smoothly after he or she submitted the form. The easiest way for the script to generate this HTML document is to include normal HTML code as the body of a concatenated print statement.

Note

Remember that when using the sendmail utility, the To: line must be the first line in the mail message. Also, you must left-justify the line so that the *T* is the first character in this line. If you tab it over or put any blank spaces before the To:, the sendmail program will not send the e-mail.

Caution

Consider this friendly advice when you're writing e-mail subroutines for your CGI scripts. First, avoid writing a CGI script that allows users to input the To: address for an e-mail subroutine. If you do so, anyone can send hate or threatening e-mail using your server, leaving you partly responsible. Also, note that sending unsolicited e-mail is considered a breach of Internet etiquette.

The HTML E-Mail Form's CGI Script

By careful examination of the email.pl CGI scirpt in listing 24.2, you will soon find that e-mail scripts are quite easy to write. Once you become more familiar with PERL scripting, you should be able to take this small script, modify it, and use it as a subroutine in other scripts to give them similiar e-mail capabilities.

Listing 24.2   E-Mail Form's CGI Script

On the CD

```perl
#!/usr/local/bin/perl
require "cgi-lib.pl";
&ReadParse;
print "Content-type: text/html\n\n";
# Sendmail options
#  -n no aliasing
#  -t read message for "To:"
#  -oi don't terminate message on line containing '.' alone
#  -f this is to be used when you need to specify who is sending it for
#     security reasons or for a listsrv
$sendmail = "/usr/lib/sendmail -t -oi -n";
$from = $in{'from'};
$subject = $in{'subject'};
$message = $in{'message'};
$myemail = 'bchemkm@showme.missouri.edu';
$myname = "Kenneth E. Murphy";
open (MAIL,"¦$sendmail") ¦¦ die "<HTML><BODY>Failed in opening
➥sendmail</BODY></HTML>\n";
print MAIL <<SOM;
To: $myname <$myemail>
From: $from
Subject: $subject

$message
SOM
print <<BROWSER;
<HTML>
<HEAD><TITLE>Mail Results</TITLE></HEAD>
<BODY BGCOLOR="#FFFFFF">
Thank You!<P>
I will answer your letter ASAP.
</BODY>
</HTML>
BROWSER
```

Input/Output Look

If you get the e-mail form mail.htm up and running, it should look like figure 24.1. Each time someone uses this form at your site, you will get an e-mail that will look like figure 24.2 if viewed using Netscape 2.0's e-mail utility. After you have everything working correctly, you can modify the form's look to match the style for the rest of your Web site.

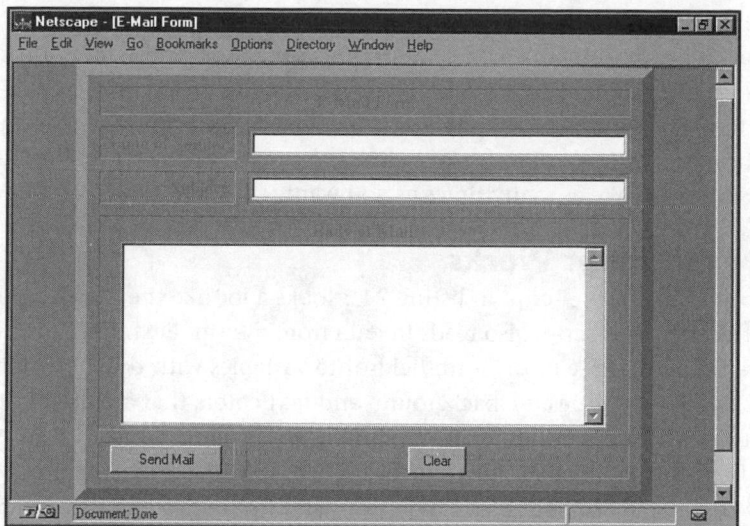

Fig. 24.1
The e-mail form.

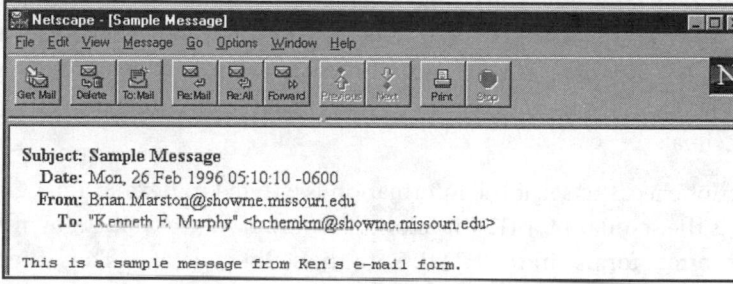

Fig. 24.2
Here is what the
e-mail looks like
viewed with
Netscape Mail.

> **Note**
>
> As a general rule, you must use complete URLs in hyperlinks that are on pages loaded
> to the browser by one of your CGI scripts. When the server tries to follow one of
> these hyperlinks, it does so from your script's directory, not your HTML page direc-
> tory as it usually does. So, if you use a relative URL, the server will not be able to find
> the desired file.

A Color Conversion CGI Script

Hopefully, now you know how to place a working e-mail form on your Web
site. Next, you learn how a different type of CGI form processing script
works. The script in listing 24.3 allows you to input color values in either

hexadecimal or decimal and then displays the resulting conversion between the two types of units in a table. So that this process is a little more fun, the script uses the entered color codes as the background and text colors for the page that it generates. Each time the script runs, it generates a new form using the color settings from the form. Thus, you can change the colors and see what they look like as many times as you want.

How the Script Works

The beginning of the script in listing 24.3 looks a lot like the e-mail form's script because this script also reads in data from a form. First, the script stores the values from three of the form fields into variables with the same name. Then the script defines the background and text colors that are used in the event that the script is run for the first time. Because this script generates its own form, the first time it is executed, it needs to display a background color and text color even though you have not had a chance to enter their values into the form yet.

The hex() operator used with some variables takes a hexadecimal value and returns the corresponding decimal value, which is stored in the variable for later use. The sprintf("%lx, $variable_name) portion of some statements takes the specified variable containing a decimal number and converts it into hexadecimal.

This script checks to see if the information is entered in hexadecimal format, which is the standard for HTML color attributes. If so, the values are in the correct format for use in the HTML form the script generates. Thus, the script only needs to convert these values to their decimal equivalents for display in the conversion table that appears under the form. However, if the background and text colors are entered in decimal format, they need to be converted into hexadecimal for the HTML tags and for the hexadecimal portion of the conversion table.

Tip

When you define a variable in PERL, you can use the . (period) to concatenate two string arguments into a single string.

After all the color variables are set properly for use, the script creates the form and sends it to the browser. Most of this form is just standard HTML. However, variables are needed to indicate the background and text colors correctly. Also, remember to change the file path in the ACTION attribute of the form tag to the complete file path of this script. This script also uses table tags to format the form fields. The input field's VALUE attributes are specified using the appropriately defined variable.

Also the script needs to set a flag within the form to let the script know if it is receiving input from the form, or if the script is being executed for the first time and the form has not been sent yet. If the script is being executed for the first time, the script needs to use its own values for the background and text colors.

After the new form is generated, a second table is created; this table displays the inputted hexadecimal or decimal color codes and displays their values. As an extra feature, the script generates a <BODY> tag line that is viewable on the screen. The attributes indicate the values used to generate the current version of the form and can be pasted into other HTML documents to give them the same color settings that are on the form.

The CGI Script

The colorex.pl script may seem a little intimidating at first glance, but with a closer look at listing 24.3 you should notice that the bulk of this script is very uniform and highly repetative. Thus, the length of a script is not a good indicator of it's overall complexity.

Listing 24.3   Color Conversion CGI Script

```perl
#!/usr/local/bin/perl
require "cgi-lib.pl";
&ReadParse(*in);

print "Content-type: text/html\n\n";
#######################################################
$dec          =       "$in{'dec'}";
$hex          =       "$in{'hex'}";
$hidden       =       "$in{'hidden'}";
#######################################################
if ($hidden ne "1") {
$bgcolor_red = "EE";
$bgcolor_green = "EE";
$bgcolor_blue = "EE";
$text_red = "00";
$text_green = "00";
$text_blue = "AA";
$dec_bgcolor_red = hex($bgcolor_red);
$dec_bgcolor_green = hex($bgcolor_green);
$dec_bgcolor_blue = hex($bgcolor_blue);
$dec_text_red = hex($text_red);
$dec_text_green = hex($text_green);
$dec_text_blue = hex($text_blue);
```

On the CD

(continues)

Listing 24.3 Continued

```
}
if ($hex eq "hex") {
$bgcolor_red = $in{'bgcolor_red'};
$bgcolor_green = $in{'bgcolor_green'};
$bgcolor_blue = $in{'bgcolor_blue'};
$text_red = $in{'text_red'};
$text_green = $in{'text_green'};
$text_blue = $in{'text_blue'};
$dec_bgcolor_red = hex($bgcolor_red);
$dec_bgcolor_green = hex($bgcolor_green);
$dec_bgcolor_blue = hex($bgcolor_blue);
$dec_text_red = hex($text_red);
$dec_text_green = hex($text_green);
$dec_text_blue = hex($text_blue);
}
if ($dec eq "dec") {
$dec_bgcolor_red = $in{'bgcolor_red'};
$dec_bgcolor_green = $in{'bgcolor_green'};
$dec_bgcolor_blue = $in{'bgcolor_blue'};
$dec_text_red = $in{'text_red'};
$dec_text_green = $in{'text_green'};
$dec_text_blue = $in{'text_blue'};
$bgcolor_red = sprintf("%lx", $dec_bgcolor_red);
$bgcolor_green = sprintf("%lx", $dec_bgcolor_green);
$bgcolor_blue = sprintf("%lx", $dec_bgcolor_blue);
$text_red = sprintf("%lx", $dec_text_red);
$text_green = sprintf("%lx", $dec_text_green);
$text_blue = sprintf("%lx", $dec_text_blue);
}
$bgcolor = "$bgcolor_red" . "$bgcolor_green" . "$bgcolor_blue";
print <<formpage;
<HTML>
<HEAD>
<TITLE>The Color Converter</TITLE>
</HEAD>
<BODY TEXT="#$text_red$text_green$text_blue"
BGCOLOR="#$bgcolor">
<CENTER>
<H2>The Color Converter</H2>
<FORM METHOD="POST" ACTION="http://www.missouri.edu/bchemkm-bin/colorex.pl">
<TABLE BORDER=5 CELLSPACING=10>
<TR>
<TH COLSPAN=4>COLOR TEST SUITE<BR></TH>
</TR><TR>
<TD WIDTH=130 ALIGN=CENTER></TD>
<TH WIDTH=50 ALIGN="CENTER">RED</TH>
<TH WIDTH=50 ALIGN=CENTER>GREEN</TH>
<TH WIDTH=50 ALIGN=CENTER>BLUE<BR></TH>
</TR><TR>
<TD WIDTH=130 ALIGN=CENTER><B>BGCOLOR: </B></TD>
<TD WIDTH=50 ALIGN=CENTER>
<INPUT TYPE=TEXT SIZE=5 MAXLENGTH=3
```

```
NAME="bgcolor_red" VALUE="$bgcolor_red"></TD>
<TD WIDTH=50 ALIGN=CENTER>
<INPUT TYPE=TEXT SIZE=5 MAXLENGTH=3
NAME="bgcolor_green" VALUE="$bgcolor_green"></TD>
<TD WIDTH=50 ALIGN=CENTER>
<INPUT TYPE=TEXT SIZE=5 MAXLENGTH=3
NAME="bgcolor_blue" VALUE="$bgcolor_blue"><BR></TD>
</TR><TR>
<TD WIDTH=130 ALIGN=CENTER><B>TEXT: </B></TD>
<TD WIDTH=50 ALIGN=CENTER>
<INPUT TYPE=TEXT SIZE=5 MAXLENGTH=3
NAME="text_red" VALUE="$text_red"></TD>
<TD WIDTH=50 ALIGN=CENTER>
<INPUT TYPE=TEXT SIZE=5 MAXLENGTH=3
NAME="text_green" VALUE="$text_green"></TD>
<TD WIDTH=50 ALIGN=CENTER>
<INPUT TYPE=TEXT SIZE=5 MAXLENGTH=3
NAME="text_blue" VALUE="$text_blue"><BR></TD>
</TR><TR>
<TD WIDTH=130 ALIGN=CENTER><B>HEX:</B></TD>
<TD WIDTH=50 ALIGN=CENTER>
<INPUT TYPE=CHECKBOX NAME="hex" VALUE="hex"></TD>
<TD WIDTH=50 ALIGN=CENTER><B>DEC:</B></TD>
<TD WIDTH=50 ALIGN=CENTER>
<INPUT TYPE=CHECKBOX NAME="dec" VALUE="dec"><BR></TD>
</TR><TR>
<TD COLSPAN=2><INPUT TYPE=SUBMIT VALUE="SUBMIT COLORS"></TD>
<TD COLSPAN=2><INPUT TYPE=RESET VALUE="RESET COLORS"><BR></TD>
</TR>
</TABLE>
<INPUT TYPE=HIDDEN NAME="hidden" VALUE="1">
</FORM>
</CENTER>
<CENTER>
<TABLE BORDER=5 CELLSPACING=5>
<TR>
<TH COLSPAN=7>Your Color Information</TH>
</TR><TR>
<TH></TH>
<TH COLSPAN=3>HEX</TH>
<TH COLSPAN=3>DEC<BR></TH>
</TR><TR>
<TH></TH>
<TH WIDTH=60>RED</TH>
<TH WIDTH=60>GREEN</TH>
<TH WIDTH=60>BLUE</TH>
<TH WIDTH=60>RED</TH>
<TH WIDTH=60>GREEN</TH>
<TH WIDTH=60>BLUE<BR></TH>
</TR><TR>
<TH>BGCOLOR:</TH>
<TD>$bgcolor_red</TD>
<TD>$bgcolor_green</TD>
<TD>$bgcolor_blue</TD>
<TD>$dec_bgcolor_red</TD>
<TD>$dec_bgcolor_green</TD>
```

(continues)

Listing 24.3   Continued

```
<TD>$dec_bgcolor_blue<BR></TD>
</TR><TR>
<TH>TEXT:</TH>
<TD>$text_red</TD>
<TD>$text_green</TD>
<TD>$text_blue</TD>
<TD>$dec_text_red</TD>
<TD>$dec_text_green</TD>
<TD>$dec_text_blue<BR></TD>
</TR>
</TABLE>
</CENTER>
<P>
\&lt;BODY TEXT=\&quot;\&#35;$text_red$text_green$text_blue\&quot;
  BGCOLOR=\&quot;\&#35;$bgcolor\&quot;
\&gt;
<P>
<HR>
</BODY>
</HTML>
formpage
```

Input/Output Look

If everything has gone smoothly, you should see a form similar to figure 24.3 appear on your screen when you run the colorex.pl script using your Web browser. If you want, you should be able to expand the script to include the rest of the link types without much trouble.

Fig. 24.3
The form generated by the color conversion script colorex.pl.

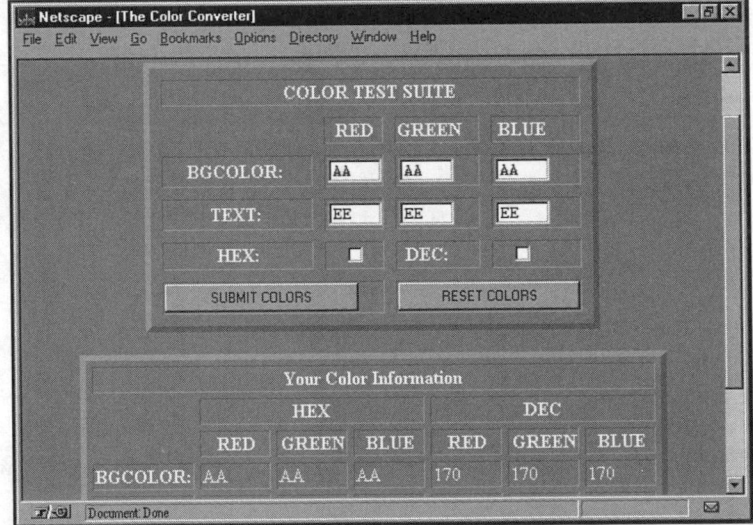

> **Note**
>
> Every time you write a script, you should try to think of ways to reuse code from CGI scripts you already have. This way, you can save a lot of time that you would otherwise spend rewriting existing code.
>
> To give you a better idea of how to do this, the color conversion script you just saw is a good example of a script that generates its own form. So, when you need a second script that also generates its own form, you should refer to this one to see how it works.

CGI Animation Script

Although most of the CGI scripts you use are probably going to be designed to process forms or send mail messages, sometimes you may want to do something a little more exciting on your Web site. One easy script you can write is an animation script that works with Netscape's 2.0 browser if your server has been configured to understand the `multipart/x-mixed-replace` MIME type.

How the Script Works

The CGI script in listing 24.4 uses the MIME Content-type `multipart/x-mixed-replace` to create a boundary that is used to keep track of a portion of the document that can be replaced with new information. In this case, the script replaces an image with a new one, repeating the process several times. If you create your images properly, the process of replacing images creates a simple animation.

The main body of this script contains two subroutines. The first subroutine consists of all the variables that need to be defined. As mentioned previously, placing all the variables together in one place is a good habit to practice. By doing so, you can keep track of your variables more efficiently.

> **Tip**
>
> Initialize all your variables at the beginning of each script. Doing so makes editing variables' file paths a lot easier if you ever have to move your scripts.

The `$animateDir` variable indicates the name of the directory that contains the images for the animation. This directory should be a subdirectory created off the directory where you place the animate.pl script. The remaining variables that are defined are used to properly indicate the MIME types for the various sections of the output created by the `Animate` subroutine. Also, the subroutine defines the `AnimateImages` array, which contains the list of images to be animated.

The second subroutine for this script does the actual animation. Basically, the animation occurs as follows:

1. The MIME Content-type is sent to the browser.

2. The upper boundary is sent.

3. An image file is opened and sent to the browser.

4. Steps 2 and 3 are repeated until all the images are sent.

5. Finally, the lower boundary is sent.

After you have the script set up correctly, you need to place a reference to it in your HTML document where you want the animation to appear. The easiest way to do this is to place the following code in the image tag:

```
<IMG SRC="URL for the script">
```

If you view the source file for the example, you should see a line on the page as follows:

```
<IMG SRC="http://www.missouri.edu/bchemkm-bin/animate.pl">
```

> **Note**
>
> When you begin to write new scripts, you should do so in a safe environment off your Web site. This way, you can protect yourself from the security risks involved with giving outside visitors access to scripts that you are still developing.

The CGI Script

◀ See "Using a Content-type Output Header," p. 529

The animate.pl CGI script, as you can see in listing 24.4 is quite short. This is a good example of a short script that is more complex than many longer CGI scripts. Learning how this script works should help you develop a solid foundation in understanding MIME types.

Listing 24.4   CGI Animation Script

On the CD

```perl
#!/usr/bin/perl
# Animation CGI script.
# Written by Paul Saab 1-12-96
&Init;
&Animate;
sub Init {
```

```
$AnimateDir = "animation";
$MainContent = "Content-Type: multipart/x-mixed-replace;boundary=BOUNDRY\n";
$Boundry = "\n--BOUNDRY\n";
$EndBoundry = "\n--BOUNDRY--\n";
$ImageType = "Content-type: image/gif\n\n";
@AnimateImages = ("1.gif","2.gif","3.gif","4.gif",
                  "5.gif","6.gif","7.gif","8.gif");
}
sub Animate {
printf("%s",$MainContent);
foreach $file (@AnimateImages) {
open(IMAGE,"$AnimateDir/$file");
printf("%s",$Boundry);
printf("%s",$ImageType);
print <IMAGE>;
close(IMAGE);
}
printf("%s",$EndBoundry);
}
```

Input/Output Look

You can find an example of this animation script on the Web at **http:// www.missouri.edu/~bchemkm/guestbook.htm**. Because this type of animation runs as fast as the browser can download the images, you will notice a change in speed based on the amount of your local bandwidth. One way to make the animation last longer for viewers on a LAN is to repeat the images multiple times in the @AnimateImages array. Or you can make the animation loop again by repeating the whole list in the same order.

A Utility Script

If you already have your own Web site, then you are well aware of the amount of time it takes to make minor corrections repeatedly across your entire site. For example, changing every instance of a blue dot graphic used for bullet lists to green ones may take a few hours. Or you may find that you need to go into every HTML file and change part of the footer, the date on the page, or part of a URL. Listing 24.5 is a little PERL script—not a CGI script—that you can run on the command line of a UNIX machine to automate this kind of task. This script performs find-and-replace string searches on multiple HTML documents in a given directory.

How the Script Works

The find-and-replace utility script works by opening every .htm or .html file in your working directory and then looking for the search string. If the script finds the string, it gives you the option of replacing the search string with the replacement string. However, before the script makes any changes in a file, it saves the file as file_name.save in case you need to undo the changes later. This script's main limitation is that it can find and replace strings only within a single line of the document. Thus, you can't find and replace large multi-line segments within a document. However, this script should save you hours of changing dates and hyperlink URLs on your site.

The Script

Once you feel comfortable with how find-replace.pl in listing 24.5 works, you can expand it to deal with other types of documents or to work with more than one line at a time. You can use utility scripts like this one to help speed up many types of routine file maintainence.

On the CD

Listing 24.5   Find-and-Replace Utility Script

```perl
#!/usr/local/bin/perl
print "What do you want to find?\n";
$findthis = <STDIN>;
chop($findthis);
print "What do you want to replace it with?\n";
$replacewith = <STDIN>;
chop($replacewith);
while($filename = <*.ht*>) {
print "Do you want to check in $filename? (y)\n";
$response = <STDIN>;
chop($response);
$check = $response;
&testyes;
if ($check eq "y") {
open(HTMLDOC, $filename);
open(HTMLDOCSAVE,">$filename.save");
while($line = <HTMLDOC>) {
chop($line);
print HTMLDOCSAVE $line,"\n" if $line ne "";
}
print "$filename was saved to $filename.save\n";
close(HTMLDOCSAVE);
close(HTMLDOC);
open(HTMLDOCSAVE,"$filename.save");
open(HTMLDOC,">$filename");
$changes = 0;
while($line = <HTMLDOCSAVE>) {
chop($line);
$_ = $line;
s#$findthis#$replacewith#g;
$newline = $_;
if ($line ne $newline){
print "Do you want\n$line\nreplaced with\n$newline? (y)\n";
$validate = <STDIN>;
```

```
chop($validate);
$check = $validate;
&testyes;
if ($check eq "y") {
print HTMLDOC $newline,"\n" if $line ne "";
print "The replacement was made.\n";
$changes = ++$changes;
}
else {
print HTMLDOC $line,"\n" if $line ne "";
print "The replacement was not made.\n";
}
}
else {
print HTMLDOC $newline,"\n" if $line ne "";
}
}
print "$filename was written with $changes changes.\n";
print "\n";
close(HTMLDOC);
close(HTMLDOCSAVE);
}
else {
print "$filename was not inspected for a match.\n";
}
}
sub testyes {
$num = 0;
while ($num == 0) {
if ($check eq "y") {
$num = 1;
}
elsif ($check eq "n") {
$num = 1;
}
else {
print "Please enter y or n.\n";
$check = <STDIN>;
chop($check);
}
}
}
```

Input/Output Look

In hopes of giving you a clearer idea of how to use the find-replace.pl script,
figure 24.4 shows the output produced by this script while I was using it with
an example file. Hopefully, you will save many hours of making routine
changes by using this script.

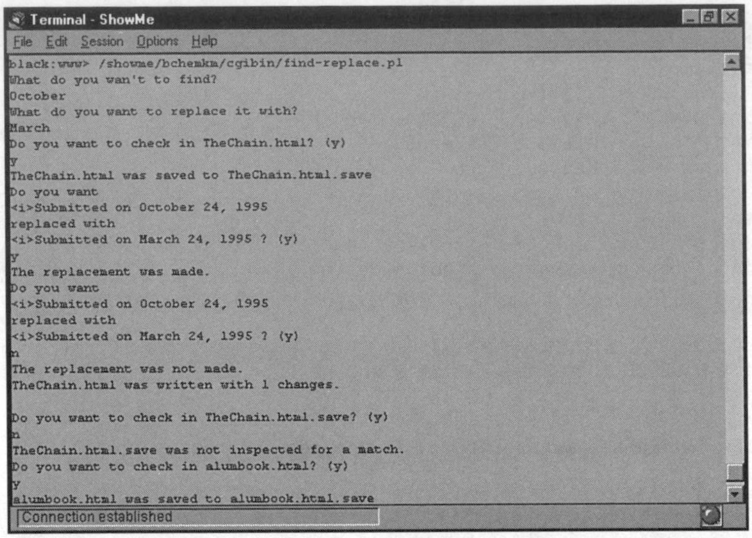

Fig. 24.4

An example
session using find-
replace.pl.

> **Caution**
>
> As you begin your adventure in writing CGI scripts, you should always be security
> conscious while you're planning what to write. You can greatly reduce the security
> risk a script imposes by not allowing command-line operators to be passed to the
> script via a form or other means. Someone may take advantage of this security hole
> and send other types of commands to the server through the script.

Creating a Guestbook

In this section, you learn how to write a CGI script for your very own
guestbook. Basically, a guestbook script is a CGI script that takes the information visitors enter into a form and adds it to a second HTML page that everyone can read.

The Guestbook's Form

To get started, you need to have a form that your visitors can use to let you
know how much they like your site. Listing 24.6 is a basic guestbook form
called gbform.html that you can use to get started. If you want, you can
change the background color to one of your favorite colors. Also, you need to
change the path in the ACTION attribute of the <FORM> tag to the location of
your CGI scripts.

Finally, so that you can keep track of where your visitors are coming from, your visitors can select a choice from a pop-up menu letting you know how they found out about your Web site. If you think of a choice that is more appropriate for your site, you should add it by modifying the option attributes of the <SELECT> tag in the form to meet your needs.

◀ See "HTML Tables 101," p. 252

On the CD

Forms and CGI

IV

Listing 24.6   Guestbook Form

```html
<HTML>
<HEAD>
<TITLE>Bare Guest Book Page</TITLE>
</HEAD>
<BODY>
<BODY BGCOLOR="#FFFFFF">
<FORM ACTION="http://your_path/gbookbare.pl" method="POST">
<H2>GuestBook</H2><P>
<B>Name:</B>
<input name="name" size=30 maxlength=60><BR>
<B>Email:</B>
<input name="email" size=30 maxlength=60><BR>
<B>Homepage:</B>
<input name="homepage" value="http://" size=30 maxlength=60><BR>
<B>Your Homepage's Title:</B>
<input name="hometitle" size=30 maxlength=60><BR>
<B>How did you find me?:</B>
<SELECT NAME="reference">
<OPTION>ListServe
<OPTION>Student
<OPTION>Search Engine
<OPTION>NewsGroup
<OPTION>Word of Mouth
<OPTION>Advertisment/Brochure
<OPTION>Personal Friend
<OPTION selected>Just Surfed On In!</SELECT><BR>
<B>COMMENTS:</B><BR>
<TEXTAREA WRAP=PHYSICAL NAME="comments" COLS=50 ROWS=8></textarea><P>
<input type="submit" value="Sign GuestBook">
<input type="reset" value="Clear">
</form>
<BR>
<A HREF="gbookbare.html">¦ View GuestBook ¦</A>
</BODY>
</HTML>
```

Caution

You should feel free to customize the look of your guestbook form to match your site's look and feel. For example, you can add your own header, footer, and other graphics without affecting the CGI script that processes this form.

(continues)

(continued)

However, you need to remember that the script uses the values in the NAME attribute of the <INPUT> and <TEXTAREA> tags to keep track of the information that is entered into the form. If you change these values without changing them in the script, they won't match and the script will not process the form correctly.

After you have set up the form correctly, it should look like figure 24.5. Later in this chapter, you learn how to use table formatting to make your guestbook form look even better.

Fig. 24.5
A simple guestbook form.

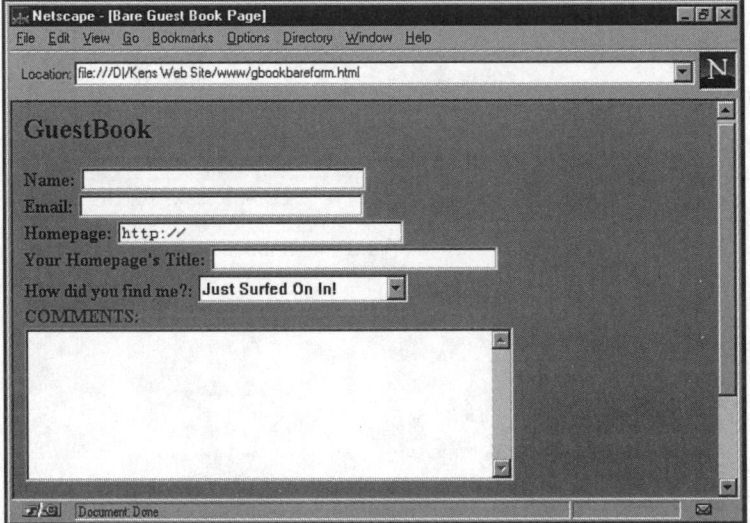

CGI Subroutines

At this point, you should have your guestbook form up and running on your Web server. Also, you should have the subroutine library cgi-lib.pl copied into your cgi-bin directory with the read and execute permissions turned on. This may require you to check the permissions for the file, the directory it is in, or both, depending on the type of server you are using. Here, I am assuming that you are using a UNIX server. After you have these tasks completed, you are ready to start writing the CGI script that processes the guestbook form's output and adds it to the response page.

Most larger scripts contain subroutines that are called from the main body of the script or even from within the subroutines themselves. By placing commonly repeated code into subroutines, you don't have to repeat the code each time it is used. Another common use for subroutines is for breaking a script down into its logical functions or tasks. If you write your scripts this way, you can easily copy subroutines, modify them slightly, and place them into different scripts.

The guestbook CGI script uses several subroutines to make the process easier to follow. Each of these subroutines is discussed later, followed by an overall description of the guestbook script to wrap up.

> **Note**
>
> A standard programming practice is to put all your subroutines either at the top or bottom of the script. This way, you make the logical flow of the main body of the program easier to follow. I prefer to put the subroutines at the bottom of the script, below the main body of the program.

> **Tip**
>
> If you find yourself repeating a subroutine in several scripts, turn it into a library by placing that subroutine in a separate file and including it in each script with the require function.

Performing Error Correction

Every CGI script that you write to process a form should contain some level of error checking. By using some simple error-checking methods in your scripts, you can reduce the number of improperly filled out forms that you receive. The first subroutine used in the script in listing 24.7 is called redo; it represents a simple level of error checking. The subroutine's function is to make sure that a value is entered into the form for both the name and comments fields of the guestbook form. If either of these fields is left blank, the if condition in the subroutine will evaluate true and its contents will be executed. This causes an HTML page to be sent to the visitor's browser letting him or her know that the form was not filled out properly. Some of your visitors may be unable to fill out the remaining fields on the form, so the script allows those fields to be empty.

If your guest has entered something into both the name and comments fields on the form, then the form's information is acceptable. In this case, the if statement is skipped, the subroutine is exited, and the interpreter moves on to the addbook and writefile subroutines, which are discussed next. The first one loads an HTML page to the visitor's browser, letting him or her know that his or her information has been added to the guestbook. This page also provides the visitor with a link to the guestbook responses. The second subroutine actually adds the information from the form to the HTML response page.

Outputting a Static Document

The second subroutine in the script in listing 24.7 is called addbook. As mentioned previously, it creates a link to the HTML page specified in the $thankyoupage variable, which is initialized near the beginning of the script. The link is called a filehandle, and is named THANKYOUPAGE in this instance. You use the open function to create this filehandle to the HTML page that contains information showing the visitor the location of the response page after he or she has signed the guestbook.

You use a while function to create a loop that repeats everything inside it as long as its test condition is true. In this case, it checks the value of <THANKYOUPAGE>. The <> part is called the *diamond operator,* and it acts on the filehandle THANKYOUPAGE. The diamond operator reads one line of the file, which is linked to the filehandle, each time it is called. The while function evaluates true until the filehandle reads in the last line of the file. The information in the current line of the file is automatically assigned to the $_ variable. Thus, as long as another line in the file remains to be read, the while loop continues to read one line at a time from the file, and it immediately prints that line to the browser. When the last line of the file is read and printed, the loop exits.

The if statement block of the redo subroutine does exactly the same thing as the addbook subroutine, except that it prints a different HTML file to the browser.

Creating a Response Page

The writefile subroutine is the last one needed for the script in listing 24.7, and it does most of the work. The first part of this subroutine takes the already-existing HTML response page and stores a copy of it in a second file specified in the $outputstore variable defined earlier in the script. Then the original file specified in the $outputfile variable is re-created, so the script can construct the new response page.

To construct the new response page, the script uses a concatenated print command to print out an HTML header for the new response page. With this type of print function, the script prints out each line until it comes to the parameter specified with the print function. In this case, the script prints each line until it comes to the word stuff. Thus, if you want to print out a paragraph, you can do start with the following line of code.

```
print <<STUFF;
```

When the script gets to this line of code, it will print out each new line of code that it comes to until it sees the word STUFF on a line by itself. So, the following code will print a three sentence paragraph.

```
Print <<STUFF;
sentence one
sentence two
sentence three
STUFF
```

By using this type of print structure, you can avoid using a print statement for every line of output.

Next, the script adds the guest's information to the top of the response list. Everything being printed is standard HTML except that each time the PERL interpreter prints out a line, it substitutes each variable's value in place of that variable's name.

So far, the script has rebuilt the header of the response page and has added the new visitor's information below. Next, it takes the old responses from the stored copy of the response page, appends them to the bottom of the new response page, and deletes the stored version. This process is straightforward, except for one detail. The stored copy of the response page contains the original page's header. Therefore, if the script appends this file (as is) to the bottom of the new response page, it will have two headers. The solution to this problem is to count the number of lines in the header and skip that many lines of the old response page before the script starts appending to the bottom of the new version. In this way, the script can chop off the old header and only add the responses and footer from the previous version of the response page to the new version.

How the Script Works

If you are using a UNIX server, you may remember from the preceding chapter that the first line of a PERL CGI script always contains the special comment line that lets the server know where to locate the PERL interpreter.

When writing the script, you use the `require` command to tell the PERL interpreter that it's going to be using subroutines from the cgi-lib.pl library. Without this line, the interpreter will be unable to find the `ReadParse` subroutine when looking for it. Also at some point, the server must know that the output from this script will be an HTML file. This is done by printing out a MIME Content-type line.

◀ See "Using a Content-Type Output Header," p. 529

> **Note**
>
> Commonly, when you use a script from an archive on the Web, you have to make several changes to the variables within the script. Most of these changes require you to enter the correct directory paths for the various input and output files that the script uses. If you forget to make these changes, the script will be unable to locate the information that it needs to execute correctly. If you are lucky, all these variables will have been gathered into an initialization section at the beginning of the script making them easier to find.

> ## More on the ReadParse Subroutine
>
> When the ReadParse subroutine receives the information that is entered into the guestbook form, it digests it and places the resulting information into a special type of list called an associative array. Each field name from the form can then be used as a key to access the value that was entered into that field from the list. The name of this array is called *in*.
>
> To retrieve this information, you need to indicate the name of the array and the key for which you want to retrieve the value. Commonly, this information is then assigned to a variable with the same name as the key for the array.
>
> For example, if the form you are processing contains a field named comments, then you can assign the information that is placed in the comments field on the form to a variable named $comments as follows:
>
> ```
> $comments = $in{'comments'};
> ```
>
> Then you can refer to the $comments variable throughout the script to retrieve the information from the comments field.

Most of the variables initialized near the beginning of the script in listing 24.7 contain the information that is entered into the guestbook form. You should not modify them unless you have changed the corresponding NAME attribute within the guestbook form. However, you do need to modify four variables in this script for the script to execute properly on your site. These four variables contain the location and file names for the four HTML pages that are used with this CGI script. You need to set each variable to a specific value based on your site. To do so, you have to replace the complete/file/path portion of each variable's value with the correct path to the directory in which you store your HTML pages.

> **Tip**
>
> If you are using a UNIX server and don't know the complete path name for your HTML file's directory, try typing **pwd** (print working directory) on the UNIX command line while in that directory.

After the script finishes initializing the variables at the beginning of the script, the interpreter executes the three subroutines discussed previously. The first subroutine makes sure that the form is filled out correctly. If the form is correct, the second subroutine sends a thank you page to the visitor's browser, and the final subroutine takes the form's information and creates the new response page.

Guestbook Script with Subroutines

As you examine the code for the gbbare.pl script in listing 24.7, you will soon see the logic behind each section of code. Once you become more familiar with how all the pieces fit together, you will be well on your way to writing CGI scripts to process any form you may wish to create.

Listing 24.7   Guestbook's CGI Script

On the CD

```perl
#!/usr/local/bin/perl
require "cgi-lib.pl";
&ReadParse(*in);
print "Content-type: text/html\n\n";
$thismonth = (January, February, March,
April, May, June, July, August,
September, October, November, December)[(localtime)[4]];
$thisday = (localtime)[3];
$thisyear = (localtime)[5];
$name = $in{'name'};
$email = $in{'email'};
$homepage = $in{'homepage'};
$hometitle = $in{'hometitle'};
$reference = $in{'reference'};
$comments = $in{'comments'};
$outputfile = "/complete/file/path/gbookbare.html";
$outputstore = "/complete/file/path/gbooksave.html";
$redopage = "/complete/file/path/redopage.html";
$thankyoupage = "/complete/file/path/thankyoupage.html";
&redo;
&addbook;
&writefile;
sub redo {
if ($name eq "" || $comments eq "") {
open(REDOPAGE,$redopage);
while (<REDOPAGE>) {
print $_;
```

(continues)

Listing 24.7   Continued

```
}
close(REDOPAGE);
exit;
}
}
sub addbook {
open(THANKYOUPAGE,$thankyoupage);
while (<THANKYOUPAGE>) {
print $_;
}
close(THANKYOUPAGE);
}
sub writefile {
open(STOREFILE,">$outputstore");
open(OLDFILE,$outputfile);
while (<OLDFILE>) {
print STOREFILE $_;
}
close(OLDFILE);
close(STOREFILE);
open(NEWFILE,">$outputfile");
print NEWFILE<<stuff;
<HTML>
<HEAD>
<TITLE>Ken's GuestBook</TITLE>
</HEAD>
<BODY BGCOLOR="#FFFFFF">
<H1>My Guestbook!</H1>
<P>
<HR>
<B>Name: </B>$name<BR>
<B>Homepage: </B><A HREF=\"$homepage\">$hometitle</A><BR>
<B>E-mail: </B><A HREF=\"mailto:$email\">$email</A><BR>
<B>Referred By: </B>$reference<BR>
<B>Submitted: </B><I>$thismonth $thisday, 19$thisyear</I><BR>
<B>Comments: </B>$comments
stuff
open(SAVEFILE,$outputstore);
$num = 0;
while (<SAVEFILE>) {
if ($num >= 7) {
print NEWFILE $_;
}
++$num;
}
close(SAVEFILE);
close(NEWFILE);
unlink($outputstore);
}
```

Input/Output Look

After you have set up this script on your server, the hard part is over. Now, you need to wrap up by creating several HTML pages that the script needs. Because they are standard HTML pages, you can modify them to suit your needs without fear of damaging the script. For example, you can add your own customized header graphic and footer to each page.

The Guestbook's Redo Page

The first page the script needs is the redo page that the script sends to the visitor if he or she leaves the name or comments field in the form blank. Listing 24.8 of redopage.html provides this page.

Listing 24.8   Sample Redo Page for Guestbook

```
<HTML>
<HEAD><TITLE>Guestbook Form's Redo Page</TITLE></HEAD>
<BODY>
<BODY BGCOLOR"#FFFFFF">
<CENTER><H2>Please  Note!</H2>
You have left some important information
out of the Guestbook's form.<BR>
Please use the back button on your browser to go back<BR>
and make sure you have entered at least your name and a comment.
<P>
<H2>Thank You!</H2>
</CENTER>
<HR>
</BODY>
</HTML>
```

On the CD

The result is shown in figure 24.6.

Fig. 24.6

A sample redo
page for the
guestbook.

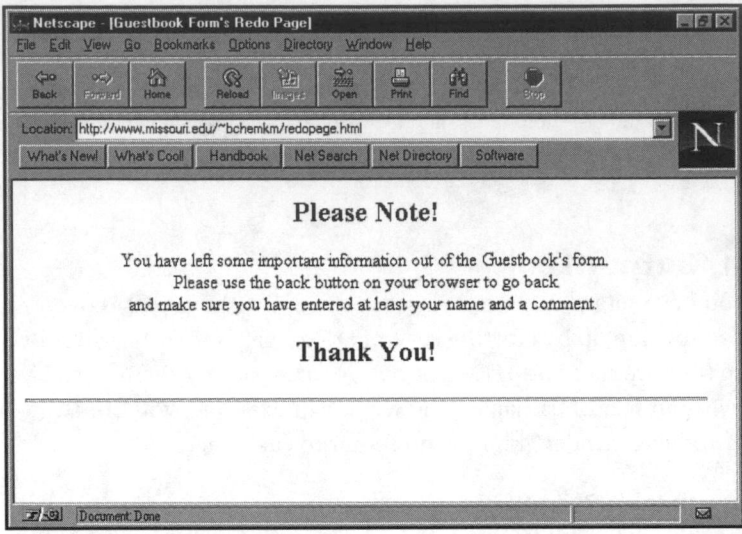

The Guestbook's Thank You Page

Likewise, the script sends a different HTML page called thankyou.html to the
guest if the proper fields in the form have been filled in (see listing 24.9). This
page thanks the guest for filling out the form and gives him or her a link to
the newly updated response page.

> **Caution**
>
> You must include the full URL to the response page, not the relative URL, in the
> hyperlink when using the HTML page shown in listing 24.9. When the server goes for
> this page, it does so from your script's directory, not your HTML page directory as it
> usually does. So, if you use a relative URL, the server will not be able to find the
> desired file.
>
> As a general rule, you must use complete URLs in HTML pages that are loaded to the
> browser by one of your CGI scripts.

Listing 24.9   Thank You Page for Guestbook

On the CD

```
<HTML>
<HEAD><TITLE>Thank you for signing my Guestbook</TITLE></HEAD>
<BODY>
<BODY BGCOLOR="#FFFFFF">
<CENTER><H2>Thank You For Signing!</H2>
¦<A HREF="http://complete/url/gbookfancy.html">View GuestBook</A>¦
```

```
  </CENTER>
  <HR>
  </BODY>
  </HTML>
```

The thank you page is shown in figure 24.7.

Fig. 24.7
The thank you
page for the
guestbook.

The Guestbook's Response Page

Finally, the last HTML page that this script needs is an empty response page.
You should modify listing 24.10 of gbbare.html to meet your needs. However, you need to make sure that the number of lines in the header matches
the number of lines that the CGI script skips when it appends the old response page to the bottom of the newly created version. Currently, the script
is set to skip the first seven lines of this response page, which is everything up
to, but not including, the <HR> line.

Listing 24.10   Response Page for Guestbook

```
<HTML>
<HEAD>
<TITLE>Ken's GuestBook</TITLE>
</HEAD>
<BODY BGCOLOR="#FFFFFF">
<H1>My Guestbook!</H1>
<P>
<HR>
</BODY>
</HTML>
```

On the CD

The result of running listing 24.10 is shown in figure 24.8.

Fig. 24.8
The guestbook's response page.

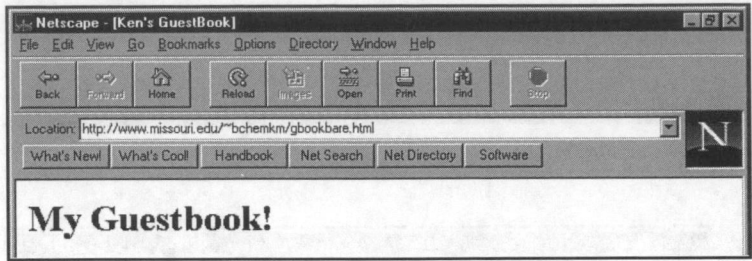

After you have set up the response page, it looks something like figure 24.9 when it is signed for the first time.

Fig. 24.9
The guestbook's response page with a signature.

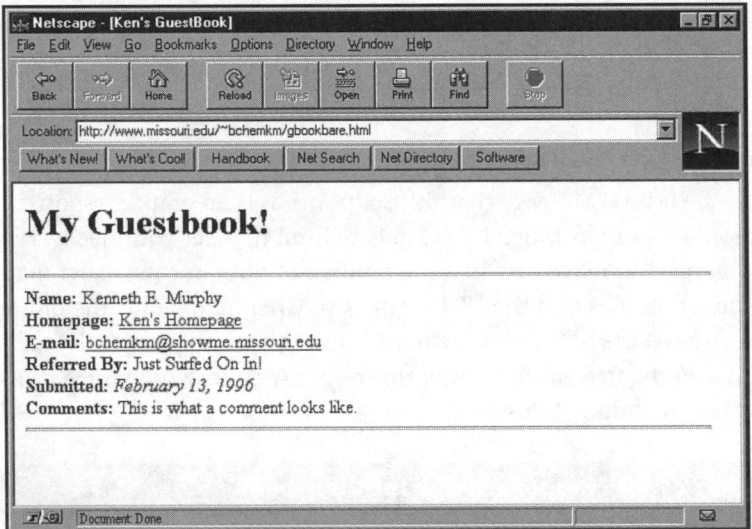

If everything goes well, you should now have the guestbook up and running on your Web site. If you're having problems, you should hang in there and check out the troubleshooting section in this chapter for some help with common problems.

Troubleshooting

When I submit the guestbook information using the form, the information is not added to the response page.

You should make sure that the script has permission to write the information to the file. For the script to do so, the write permissions must be on for both the file and the directory in which it is located. You can set these permissions correctly by going to the UNIX command line and entering **chmod 766 filename.** This command gives everyone read and write privileges for that file or directory. Because it is not a good idea to give everyone write permissions in your main document directory, you might want to create a subdirectory that contains only those files that need to be written to by a script.

Improving the Guestbook's Form and CGI Script

Because form processing is the most common use of CGI scripts on the Web at this time, you should learn how to format your form so your visitors can easily follow it and thus fill it out. By far, the easiest way to do this is by placing the entire form into a well-designed table. That way, your form looks like the forms you fill out on paper.

Table-Formatting the Guestbook Form

Using the HTML form gbform2.html in listing 24.11, you can see what your guestbook form can look like if you use a table to format it. Here is the HTML source for this new version of the form. As a reminder, don't forget to modify the action attribute of the <FORM> tag to include the location of the file gbfancy.pl and to include the correct URL for the response page in the anchor for viewing the guestbook responses.

◀ See "Form Layout and Design," p. 503

Listing 24.11   Table Formatted Guestbook Form

```
<HTML>
<HEAD>
<TITLE>Fancy Guest Book Page</TITLE>
</HEAD>
<BODY>
<BODY BGCOLOR="#FFFFFF">
<CENTER>
<form action="http://complete/file/path/gbookfancy.pl" method="POST">
<TABLE BORDER=10 CELLSPACING=10 CELLPADDING=2>
<TR>
<TH COLSPAN=2 ALIGN=CENTER>GuestBook<BR></TH>
</TR><TR>
<TD><B>Name:</B></TD>
<TD><input name="name" size=30 maxlength=60><BR></TD>
</TR><TR>
<TD><B>Email:</B></TD>
<TD><input name="email" size=30 maxlength=60><BR></TD>
</TR><TR>
<TD><B>Homepage:</B></TD>
```

On the CD

(continues)

Listing 24.11 Continued

```
<TD><input name="homepage" value="http://" size=30 maxlength=60><BR></TD>
</TR><TR>
<TD><B>Your Homepage's Title:</B></TD>
<TD><input name="hometitle" size=30 maxlength=60><BR></TD>
</TR><TR>
<TD><B>How did you find me?:</B></TD>
<TD> <SELECT NAME="reference">
<OPTION>ListServe
<OPTION>Student
<OPTION>Search Engine
<OPTION>NewsGroup
<OPTION>Word of Mouth
<OPTION>Advertisment/Brochure
<OPTION>Personal Friend
<OPTION selected>Just Surfed On In!</SELECT><BR></TD>
</TR><TR>
<TD COLSPAN=2>
<B>COMMENTS:</B><BR>
<TEXTAREA WRAP=VIRTUAL NAME="comments" COLS=50 ROWS=8></textarea><BR></TD>
</TR><TR>
<TD ALIGN=CENTER>
<input type="submit" value="Sign GuestBook"></TD>
<TD ALIGN=CENTER>
<input type="reset" value="Clear"></TD>
</TR>
</TABLE>
</form>
<BR>
<A HREF="gbookfancy.html">¦ View GuestBook ¦</A>
</CENTER>
</BODY>
</HTML>
```

You can see from figure 24.10 that this version of the form is easier to read and looks nicer than the previous version shown in figure 24.5.

Note

Some browsers that are currently in use don't support the tags for tables. One way to help make your tables easier to read for these users is to place a <BR> tag at the end of each row of the table, right before the row's <TD> tag.

Next, you learn how to add an extra subroutine to your guestbook script to improve its error-checking properties.

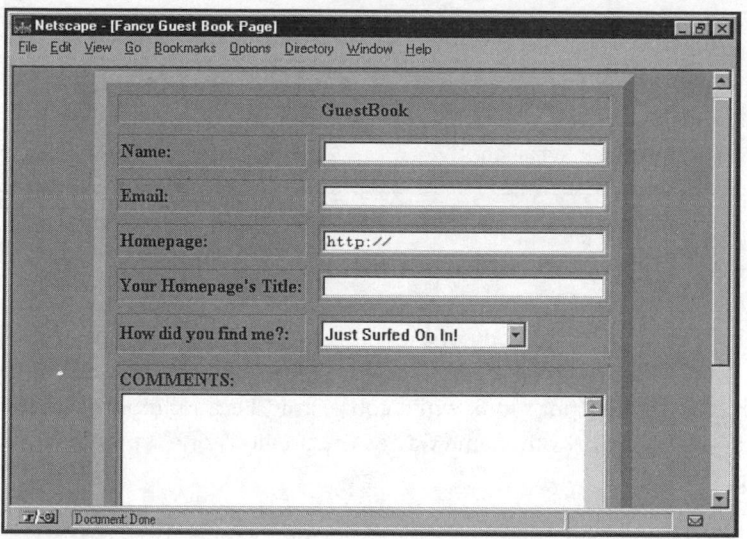

Fig. 24.10
A table formatted
guestbook form.

Creating a Better Error-Checking Subroutine

The makesure subroutine provides an additional level of error checking that is very useful in a wide variety of forms. After you add it to your script, visitors can see what their responses look like before the responses are added to the response page. This way, they have a second chance to make sure all the information is correct, and even test the link to their homepage to make sure it works.

To accomplish this, the subroutine generates a hidden form that contains the values for the fields that are in the original form's input fields. This way, the information is not lost. In addition, the script sets the $test variable to act as a flag so that the script can tell the difference between the information from this form and the original one. The page that the subroutine creates, as you can see later in figure 24.11, includes a standard submit button for the visitors to click after they have double-checked their information and want it added to the response page.

Troubleshooting

When I submit the guestbook information using the form, I receive a file contains no data *error.*

The most common cause for this type of problem is that the script is accessing a variable that contains the wrong file path for the desired output page. You should go into the script and make sure that all the variables for the output pages contain the

(continues)

> (continued)
>
> correct file path information. Another possible cause for the error is that the MIME Content-type line has an error in it, or the necessary blank line is not being sent to the server with this information.

How the Script Works

In addition to adding the makesure subroutine, you need to make some minor changes in the main body of the script to call the subroutine at the right time. Also, because you gave the form a face-lift using table formatting, you can improve the output's look while you're at it. Because most of this guestbook script works the same way as the previous one, I point out the changes only.

First, this script needs a new variable—called $test—for the makesure error-checking subroutine. Just as in the previous version, this script checks to see if the visitor has entered his or her name and a comment into the form. If he or she didn't, the visitor is shown a page letting him or her know what to add. This is the first level of error checking in this script. Now, assuming that the visitor has correctly entered information into the form, the script shows what the response is going to look like and gives him or her a second chance to make sure that everything is okay. If it is, the visitor can click on the new submit button to send the information for addition. The new page that is generated by the script is considered the second level of error checking because it takes effect only if the first level is passed.

Unfortunately, the script has no way of knowing if the information that it is receiving is from the original posting of the form or from the next page showing what the output will look like. This happens because the information that the visitor has filled out has not changed between submissions. So, to solve this problem, the script uses the $test variable.

The $test variable acts as a flag that indicates that the information the script is receiving is from the second submission of the form. If the flag is set, the script knows that the information in the form has been checked by the visitor and that the script can add it to the current response list and thank him or her for visiting your site. If the flag is not set, the script executes the makesure subroutine. This way, the visitor gets a chance to double-check and make sure the information he or she submits is correct.

IV

Forms and CGI

> **Note**
>
> Just as a reminder, the redo and addbook subroutines don't require modification from the previous version of the guestbook.

Two changes have been made to the writefile subroutine from the previous version. First, a background graphic is used to create a vertical gray stripe down the left side of the screen. Second, table formatting is used to force the response information to appear just to the right of this stripe, making for a nice-looking response page.

Advanced Guestbook CGI Script

If you examine gbfancy.pl in listing 24.12 closely, you will find that most of the changes to this version from listing 24.7 are contained neatly in their own subroutines. By using subroutines in this way, it is easy to add new features into existing scripts.

Listing 24.12   Advanced Guestbook's CGI Script

On the CD

```
#!/usr/local/bin/perl
require "cgi-lib.pl";
&ReadParse(*in);
Print "Content-type: text/html\n\n";

$thismonth = (January, February, March,
April, May, June, July, August, September,
October, November, December)[(localtime)[4]];
$thisday = (localtime)[3];
$thisyear = (localtime)[5];
$test = $in{'test'};
$name = $in{'name'};
$email = $in{'email'};
$homepage = $in{'homepage'};
$hometitle = $in{'hometitle'};
$reference = $in{'reference'};
$comments = $in{'comments'};
$outputfile = "/showme/bchemkm/www/gbookfancy.html";
$outputstore = "/showme/bchemkm/www/gbooksave.html";
$redopage = "/showme/bchemkm/www/redopage.html";
$thankyoupage = "/showme/bchemkm/www/thankyoupage.html";
&redo;
if ($test eq "makesure") {
&addbook;
&writefile;
exit;
}
&makesure;
sub redo {
```

(continues)

Listing 24.12   Continued

```perl
if ($name eq "" || $comments eq "") {
open(REDOPAGE,$redopage);
while (<REDOPAGE>) {
print $_;
}
close(REDOPAGE);
exit;
}
}
sub addbook {
open(THANKYOUPAGE,$thankyoupage);
while (<THANKYOUPAGE>) {
print $_;
}
close(THANKYOUPAGE);
}
sub makesure {
print <<OUTPUT;
<HTML>
<HEAD>
<TITLE>Guest Book Checking Page</TITLE>
</HEAD>
<BODY>
<BODY BGCOLOR="#AAAAAA">
<CENTER>
<H2>Hello $name !</H2>
Please make sure the following is correct.<P>
If you find you need to make a change,<BR>
use the back feature on your browser to return to the original form.<P>
</CENTER>
<HR>
<TABLE BORDER=0>
<TR>
<TD WIDTH=80 NOWRAP><BR></TD>
<TD><B>Name: </B>$name<BR>
<B>Homepage: </B><A HREF=\"$homepage\">$hometitle</A><BR>
<B>E-mail: </B><A HREF=\"mailto:$email\">$email</A><BR>
<B>Referred By: </B>$reference<BR>
<B>Submitted: </B><I>$thismonth $thisday, 19$thisyear</I><BR>
<B>Comments: </B>$comments
</TD>
</TR>
</TABLE>
<CENTER>
<form action="http://www.missouri.edu/bchemkm-bin/gbookfancy.pl"
➥method="POST">
<input type="hidden" name="test" value="makesure">
<input type="hidden" name="name" value="$name">
<input type="hidden" name="email" value="$email">
<input type="hidden" name="homepage" value="$homepage">
<input type="hidden" name="hometitle" value="$hometitle">
<input type="hidden" NAME="reference" value="$reference">
```

```
<input type="hidden" NAME="comments" value="$comments">
<HR>
<TABLE CELLSPACING=10 CELLPADDING=2 BORDER=5>
<TR>
<TD><input type="submit" value="Sign GuestBook"></TD>
</TR>
</TABLE>
</FORM>
</CENTER>
<HR>
</BODY>
</HTML>
OUTPUT
}
sub writefile {
open(STOREFILE,">$outputstore");
open(OLDFILE,$outputfile);
while (<OLDFILE>) {
print STOREFILE $_;
}
close(OLDFILE);
close(STOREFILE);
open(NEWFILE,">$outputfile");
print NEWFILE<<stuff;
<HTML>
<HEAD>
<TITLE>The Fancy Guestbook</TITLE>
</HEAD>
<BODY BACKGROUND="http://www.missouri.edu/~bchemkm/greybar.gif">
<CENTER><H2>Guestbook</H2>
</CENTER>
<HR>
<TABLE BORDER=0>
<TR>
<TD WIDTH=80 NOWRAP><BR></TD>
<TD><B>Name: </B>$name<BR>
<B>Homepage: </B><A HREF=\"$homepage\">$hometitle</A><BR>
<B>E-mail:</B><A HREF=\"mailto:$email\">$email</A><BR>
<B>Referred By: </B>$reference<BR>
<B>Submitted: </B><I>$thismonth $thisday, 19$thisyear</I><BR>
<B>Comments: </B>$comments </TD>
</TR>
</TABLE>
stuff
open(SAVEFILE,$outputstore);
$num = 0;
while (<SAVEFILE>) {
if ($num >= 7) {
print NEWFILE $_;
}
++$num;
}
close(SAVEFILE);
close(NEWFILE);
unlink($outputstore);
}
```

Troubleshooting

When I submit the guestbook information using the form, the hyperlinks don't work properly.

This problem is caused by using a relative URL on a page that is loaded to the browser by a script. When a script loads a Web document, the server uses the script's directory as its starting place for finding the new document. Because the hyperlink is usually relative to the HTML document's directory and not the script's directory, the link does not work. The best way to avoid this problem is to use Absolute URLs in those files that are loaded to the browser by a script.

Figure 24.11 shows the response page generated by the subroutine in listing 24.12.

Fig. 24.11
The HTML page generated by the makesure subroutine.

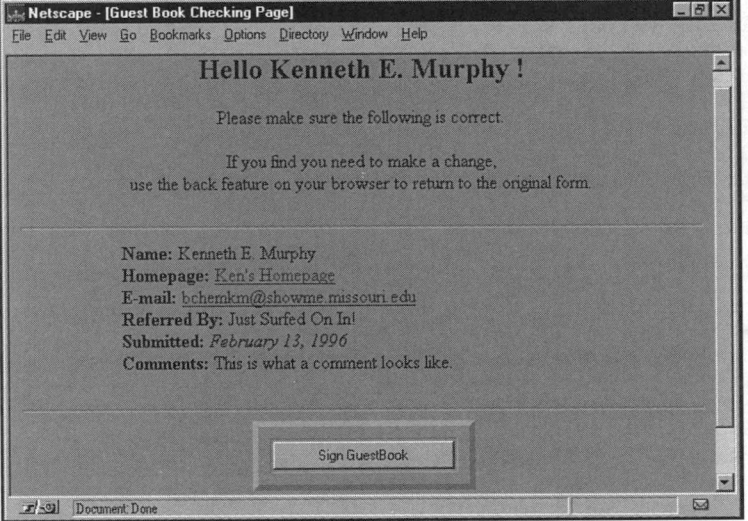

An Improved Guestbook Response Page

On the CD

The HTML page gbfancy.html found in listing 24.13 is the copy of the HTML response page that you should use with this new version of your guestbook.

Listing 24.13   New Guestbook Response Page

```
<HTML>
<HEAD>
<TITLE>The Fancy Guestbook</TITLE>
</HEAD>
<BODY BACKGROUND="Http://www.missouri.edu/~bchemkm/greybar.gif">
```

```
<CENTER><H2>Guestbook</H2>
</CENTER>
</TR>
</TABLE>
<HR>
</BODY>
</HTML>
```

The resulting page is shown in figure 24.12, and figure 24.13 shows the guestbook response page containing a signature.

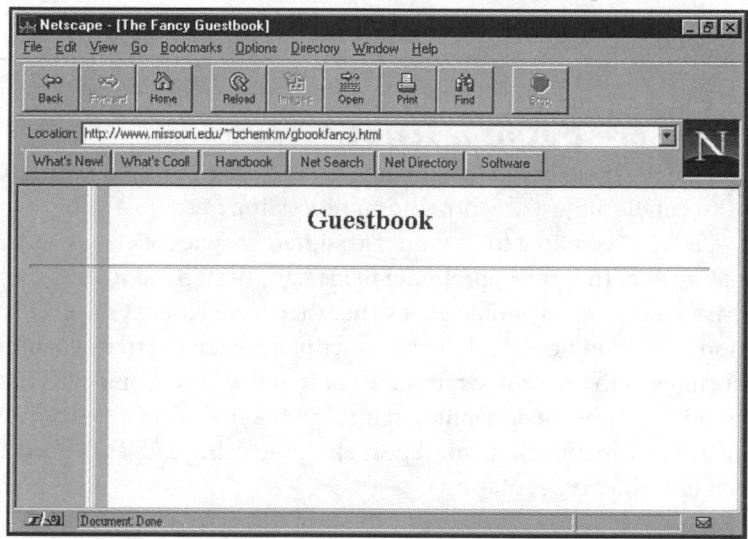

Fig. 24.12
The guestbook's new response page.

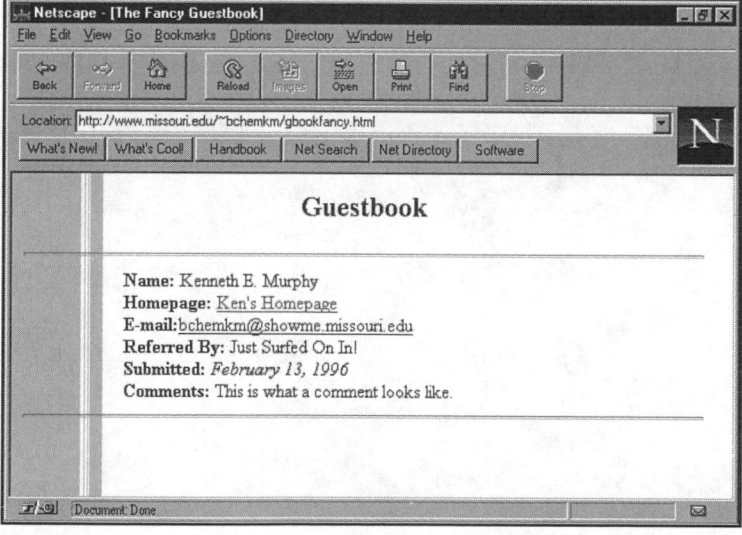

Fig. 24.13
The guestbook's new response page with a signature.

> **Note**
>
> So far, you have seen how a standard guestbook script takes the guest's form input and appends it to a response page. Now, imagine that you are the guest, and that you have just signed the guestbook. The next thing you will probably do is go and look at your response on the page. If other people were also looking at the same guestbook, and they signed it too, then when you reload the page, you see their responses on the page also. With a little modification of the guestbook's format, these responses easily become live chat. Each guest simply refreshes the response page, reads the current reply, and then sends in his or her own comments to be added to the page.

Getting More Out of a Script

After you get the hang of how your guestbook CGI script works, you can adapt it to handle almost any other form processing need. Just with this example, you have seen how to perform two different types of error checking—both making sure that the appropriate fields have been filled in and giving your visitors a chance to double-check that they have entered the correct information. Also, don't overlook that this script also demonstrates loading static documents to the browser and file reads and writes, along with the more complex process of appending output to the middle of an existing document. You can recombine or repeat all these techniques as needed to process many other types of forms. ❖

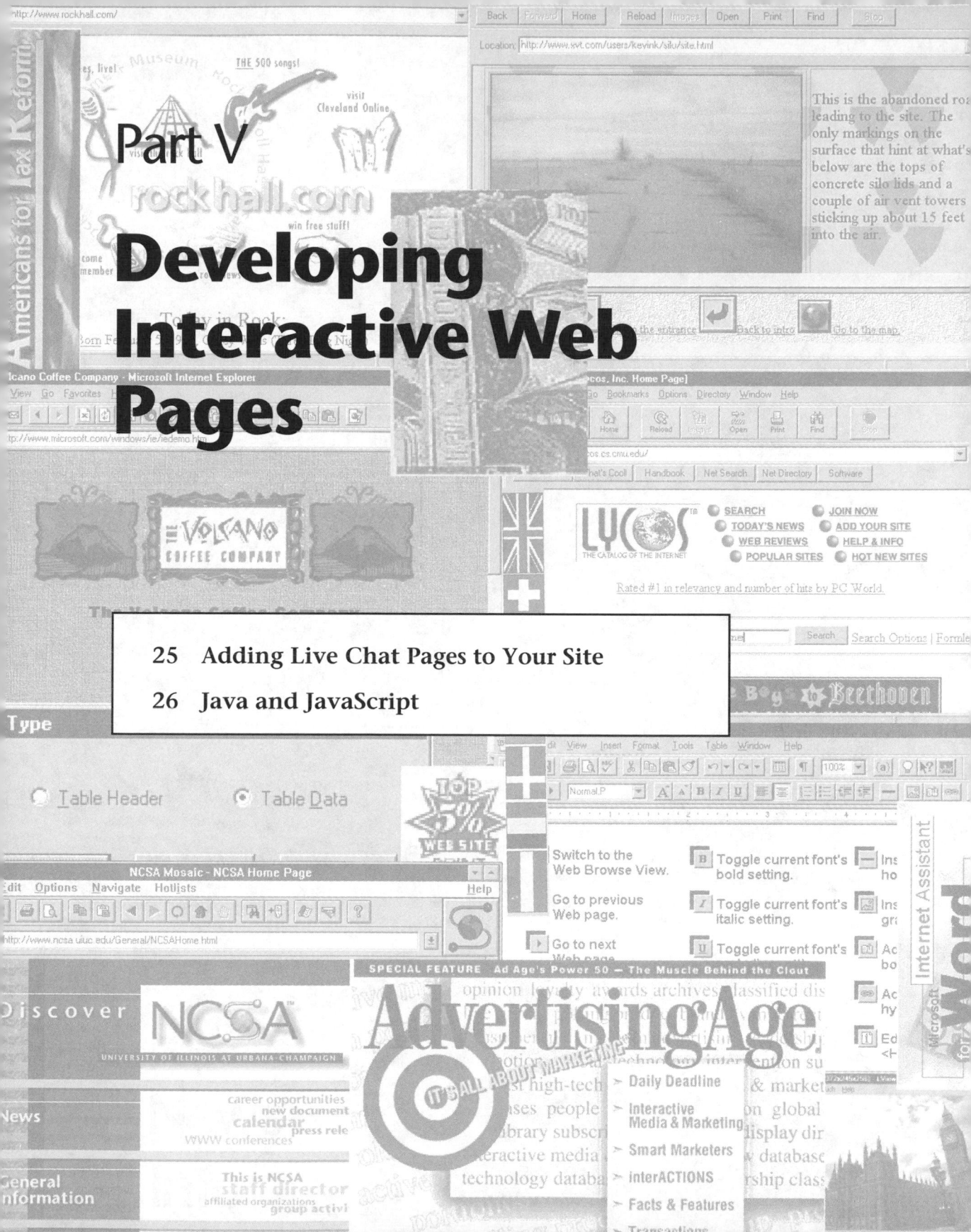

Part V

Developing Interactive Web Pages

## CHAPTER 25

Adding Live Chat Pages to Your Site

by Bill Brandon

Many people are accustomed to thinking of the Internet and the World Wide Web as a kind of reference library. If you need information, you do a search for it, download it, and log off. At any point you may never be aware of the many other people who may be viewing the same pages at the same time along with you.

This experience is somewhat contrary to the rest of your experience of life. If you go to a diner and sit at the counter, the interaction with the other people there is a key part of the experience. Just because the person next to you is reading a book doesn't make your outing into a trip to the library.

The vision of the citizens of the World Wide Web is being expanded by new opportunities for interactivity. Not only interactivity between each individual user and the system, but interactivity between users is here and growing. Increasingly, people go on-line to meet other people.

In this chapter, you learn about the following:

- **Chat Page Concept**

  What makes a "chat page" different from IRC, conferencing, and the like is immediacy and ease of use.

- **Chat Page Demonstration**

  There are many places on the Web where you can go to see and use a chat page.

- **Chat Page Installation**

  It's easy to understand how a chat page works, and easy to put one on your site.

Surveying Chat and Chat Pages

Chat, in one form or another, has been a feature of computer networks for decades. On the earliest systems with remote terminals for access, users could send messages to each other and to the system operator. In the early 1980s, CompuServe added the CB Simulator feature, enabling worldwide chat between hundreds of people at a time. Other commercial on-line services soon followed with similar features. Internet Relay Chat has also been around for several years.

You can easily forget that chat features developed early in the history of distributed computing. However, in the immediate future you won't be able to overlook the fact that they are an important part of the services people expect from their networked systems. At first, of course, the tendency in computing was to emphasize information and data, calculation and rules. People adapted to the system and the rules, not the other way around. Over time the systems matured, users became more sophisticated, and each adapted to the other. Now users have become much more interested in the capacity of systems to build and support relationships and interaction between people.

A natural outcome of this change is that the Internet is becoming more interactive in nature. The World Wide Web itself is a response to this trend. You see the rapid addition of interactive features to the Web, but it has a price. Bandwidth becomes a critical resource, and all features compete for it. As in any other situation, features that offer more value are rewarded with a bigger share of that bandwidth. At this point, chat appears to offer a great deal of value to many Web users, so much so that they seek out this facility for communicating directly and immediately with their fellow explorers.

For these reasons, you may want to consider adding a chat page to your Web site. As you will see, some serious business outcomes can be attained by doing so. Far from being just a way for idlers to pass the time, chat is a simple tool that can support major strategies.

Caution

Bandwidth is a major concern when considering the options you may wish to add to your Web pages. Users with 14.4 modems may become discouraged and give up trying to use an interactive Web page when there are many users accessing it. This is especially true if you are using a chat page system that allows users to send in-line images and audio along with their conversational entries. These can slow a server down considerably in addition to increasing transmission time for each entry.

Defining Chat and Its Uses

What is "chat"? For the purposes of this chapter, chat is a system feature that enables Web users to do two things:

- Know who else is connected to the same Web page or server as themselves *at any given moment*

- Communicate (at their own election) with those other users directly and immediately, whether by typing; by sending graphics, animation, or images; by speaking; or by some combination of these forms

Other Web services and interactive system features are similar to chat, but they are generally implemented separately. Such features include conferencing (bulletin board) systems, for example. The chief difference is immediacy. In chat, all users participating in the discussion are on-line at the same time and their comments (graphics, voices, typed comments) are shown to the other participants right away (allowing for server delays, of course). In other interactive Web features, user comments are stored for later, repeated display to other users.

Another difference is that, in chat, you are communicating with other people, not with a system or program. You can create a program that seems to respond to typed comments in much the same way that a person would respond. Such a program is often called a *robot* or *'bot*. This program is not the same thing as chat.

Bring on the 'bots

What's a 'bot? Early Internet Relay Chat administrators used simple scripts to deliver preconstructed messages to users ("Thank you for visiting Carol's Cat Chat Channel"). This evolved over time into scripts that could make decisions and carry on a limited conversation with users. These simple scripts have evolved further into self-sustaining automatic processes called "'bots" (for "robots").

A 'bot performs whatever function its creator intended. A helpful bot can engage in a little light conversation, respond to specific words typed into the channel, and moderate topics. Some tend bar, some are card dealers, and some enforce rules. There are also malevolent bots that try to annoy, confuse, or harrass users. Many servers ban 'bots totally, while others will allow trusted users to bring their 'bots in with them. If this reminds you of the bar scene in *Star Wars*, it should. Actually, a lot of IRC seems to be based on that scene.

In the beginning on the Internet, chat was supported through IRC (Internet Relay Chat). This way to chat is relatively crude and is based on the client-server model. (See fig. 25.1.) To connect to other Internet users in real-time chat, using IRC, you have to do the following:

1. You must have a direct Internet connection, such as a dial-up PPP connection.

2. You must have an Internet Dialer program or Winsock software stack.

3. You must have an Internet Relay Chat program that runs on your computer.

4. You must have an Internet Relay Chat Host to connect to.

5. If you want to chat with a specific person or group, you must coordinate the specific time and date at which all the chat parties will connect to a specified IRC Host, and you must all agree on the room name you will use. The first one onto the IRC Host types the command **/join #<channel>** to create a virtual space for the conversation; each other party joins in by typing the same **/join #<channel>** command.

Fig. 25.1
Internet Relay Chat is a client-server arrangement that connects users to each other in channels.

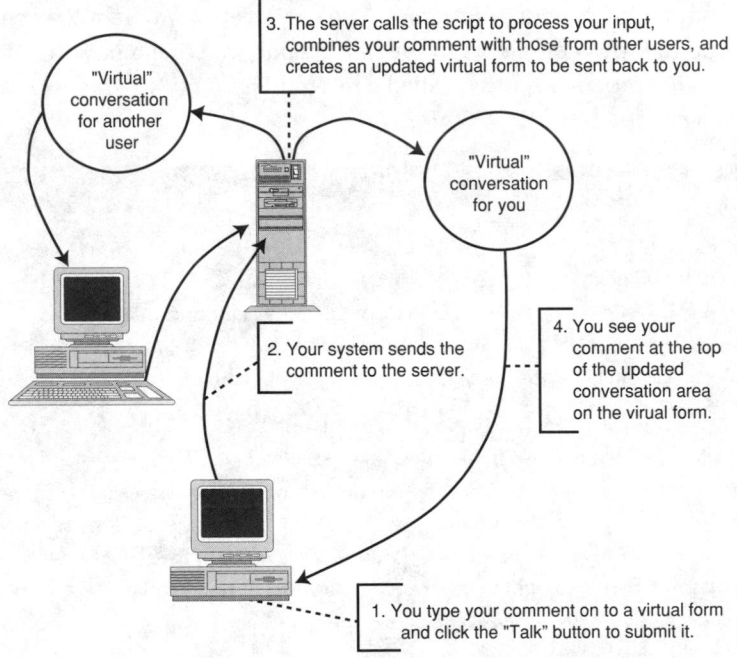

3. The server calls the script to process your input, combines your comment with those from other users, and creates an updated virtual form to be sent back to you.

"Virtual" conversation for another user

"Virtual" conversation for you

2. Your system sends the comment to the server.

4. You see your comment at the top of the updated conversation area on the virual form.

1. You type your comment on to a virtual form and click the "Talk" button to submit it.

If you are content to chat with anyone who may be available on the IRC Host, you don't have to do the coordination part in step 5. However, you have to remember (or have written down) the commands to enter to find out who else is present, how to send a message, and so on.

The point is that this process takes effort and knowledge of out-of-the-way information. And yet thousands of people make the effort every day, testifying to the power and attraction of chat in an otherwise anonymous medium. Now consider the newer alternative.

With a chat page, you type in the URL of the page. After you're on the page, you probably have to enter an alias (which can be your real name), but that's all. You and your colleagues (or newfound friends) are ready to chat.

On most chat pages, you find out who else is present by clicking a button or by scrolling to the bottom of the page where a current roster is kept. You click another button to send a message that you have typed into a text box on the chat page. If you want to send others a picture of yourself with your messages, you enter the URL where your picture can be found. No wonder chat pages are an instant success any place they are added!

Of what possible use is chat? As it turns out, the chat feature can be an important part of building an excellent Web site and even a part of your business strategy. Chat is being used today to do the following:

- Attract people to Web sites
- Develop "communities" around products and services
- Support branding
- Deliver services
- Support distance learning
- Support help desks
- Provide easy global conferencing

Expect to see these uses increase in variety and importance over time.

Finding Chat Pages

Finding chat pages is very easy. Do a Yahoo search on the word "chat." You will get dozens of hits. Some of them are IRC servers or hosts, but many are interactive chat pages. Table 25.1 lists four of these choices. The list of large companies that have included chat facilities in their Web sites is very impressive.

This whole area is one of great ferment, with companies springing up, being bought, and merging on a weekly basis. For example, Ubique, which has a 3-D chat product called Virtual Places, was bought by America Online; AOL will incorporate this technology into future offerings. The software could at one time be downloaded for use by Webmasters under license, but it is no longer available. The Global Chat experiment, sponsored by Digital Equipment Corp., is now operated by AcmeWeb Services, Inc. You can still obtain the Global Chat software for use on your system, however.

Table 25.1 Choices for Chat on the Web	
Name	**URL**
WebChat	**http://www.irsociety.com/webchat/webchat.html**
ESPNET SportsZone	**http://espnet.sportszone.com/editors/talk/index.html**
Intercontinental Conferencing Services (was DEC Global Chat)	**http://chat.acmeweb.com**
Cybersight	**http://cybersight.com/cgi-bin/cs/ch/chat**

Try the pages shown in table 25.1 to get a better idea of the way chat pages work. All of them are based on forms (your browser must support forms to use them) and work approximately the same way.

Caution
Chat is addictive! (Don't say I didn't warn you.)

Chatting Live Using Forms

The most common form of live chat page uses forms. (An alternative is described in the section "Linking Live Chat to Browsers.")

By using forms, you make chat available to most of the browsers in use today. Your guests or customers do not need additional software because the action takes place on the server side.

The following sections give you an overview of the principles involved in chat pages and present an example of their implementation. Finally, I outline a general procedure that you can use to create your own implementation of chat. This process is really much easier than you would think!

Basic Principles

All form-based chat systems have two things in common. First, they are client/server-type applications. Second, the server part of the application is always a CGI script; the browser is the client side. The script handles all input from chat participants and also returns updated chat pages to the participants.

Figure 25.2 shows an overview of the process. Each user accessing the page is presented with a form that provides a text area into which comments can be typed. Other information (the user's name or an alias, for example) may also be entered. When the form is submitted (by clicking on a Talk or Chat button), the chat script running on the server processes the input. This processing consists of parsing the information on the form, adding the user's comments to those made by other people who are also using the same page at the same time, and generating a new form that is sent back to the user. Each user at any given moment may be looking at a unique screen, depending on when he or she last clicked on the Talk button.

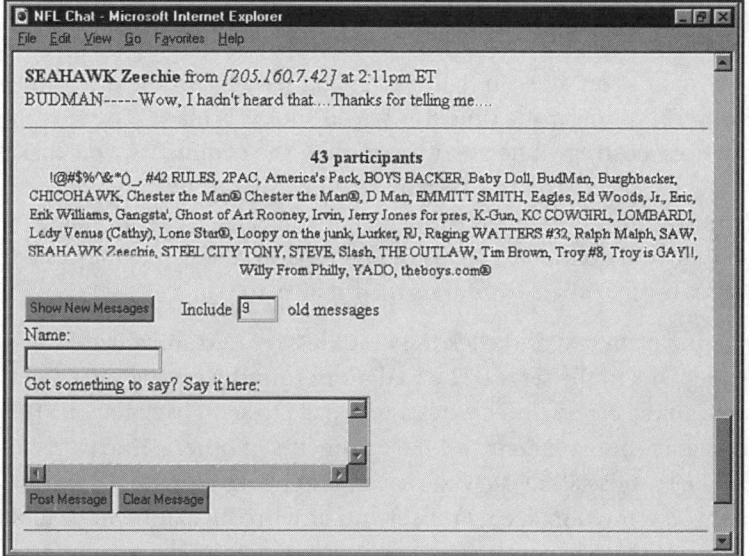

Fig. 25.2
The overall process behind the operation of a Web chat page.

Figure 25.3 is an example of such a chat page. In this case, it is a screen shot taken while I was using the ESPNET SportsTalk page. As you can see, the browser is looking at the bottom of the form. One participant's comment is visible at the top of the window; you view the other comments by scrolling up.

Fig. 25.3

A typical chat page arrangement with output and input areas.

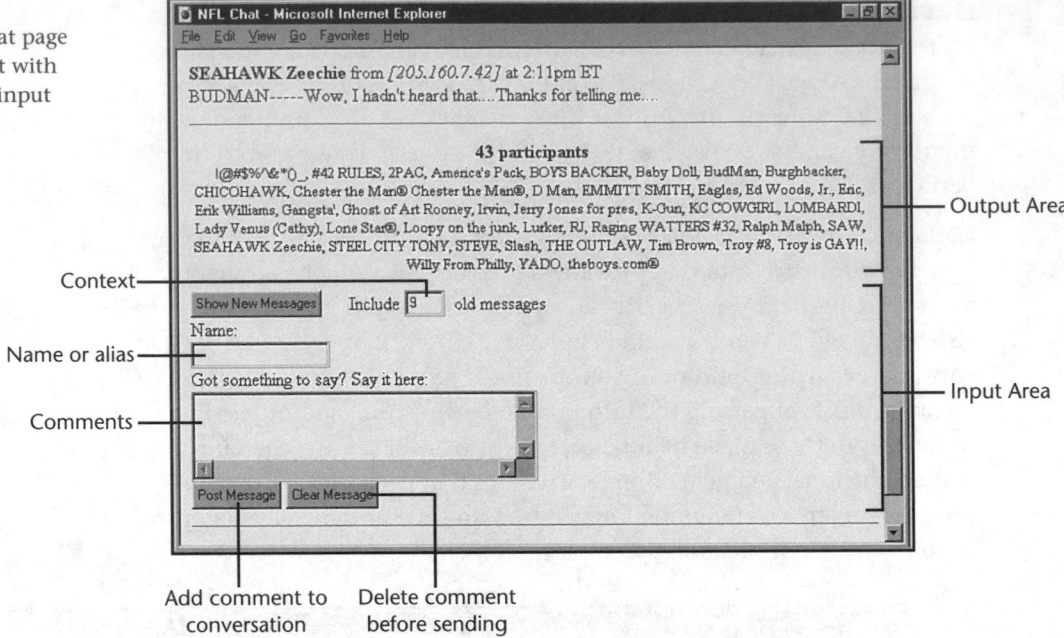

Below the user's comment in figure 25.3, you see a list of the other individuals who were on-line at the time this screen shot was made. To see what others have been posting while you were reading the comments, you click on Show New Messages. You can keep any number of old messages at the top of the form to help maintain context. Finally, you can enter your name or an alias so that your comments are attributed to you. Using a name or alias makes it easier for others to address their replies to you.

When you type in text and click the Post Message button, you are submitting your comments to the server. The CGI script running on the server adds your comment to the others and creates a new page to send back to you. This new page contains your comment, all the comments of other participants added since you last chose Show New Messages, and however many old messages you said you wanted to keep. Probably no other participant will be looking at exactly the same page you are at any given moment.

The chat page in figure 25.3 has the same structure as many other chat pages. The conversation transcript comes first. Some chat pages add new comments to the top of the list; others, to the bottom. In the middle of the page is a set of user options, including a way to enter your name or alias, and to specify the number of old comments you want to keep on the page when you post a message or show new ones. Finally, at the bottom of the page is the input area, where you enter your comments and submit the form to the server.

The script takes the input from the user and extracts the various parts to various files on the server. For example, the alias is added to a list of the people currently taking part in the chat. The comments are filed as a single numbered paragraph, in sequence with all the other comments.

Normally a well-behaved script will acknowledge form input from a user, with a message such as `Your input has been received, thanks for stopping by`. A chat script, however, creates a new version of the form *on the fly* and sends it back to the user. That is, the entire form, including the conversation area, the user options area, and the input area, is generated instantly (or very quickly, at least) and sent back to the user.

Just how you accomplish this task is the subject of "How to Set Up Chat with Forms on Your Site." For now, take a look at another example.

Example: WebChat

WebChat is one of the more successful chat systems. It is unusual for two reasons. First, it offers full multimedia capability (including live video feed). Second, it is the product of an open collaborative project, sponsored by the Internet Roundtable Society. The software is free and may be copied and modified under the terms of the GNU Public License. You can buy a commercial version as well. The free version supports a single channel, whereas the commercial version supports multiple channels and other features.

Because WebChat is forms based, you need only a standard browser to use it. The Netscape, Microsoft Internet Explorer, AOL, Prodigy, and CompuServe browsers all work equally well. To try WebChat, point your browser to the Web Broadcasting System (WBS1) at **http://www.irsociety.com/ webchat/webchat.html**.

Figure 25.4 shows the lower part of a WebChat form. It is similar to what you saw with ESPNET in the "Basic Principles" section of this chapter. The most apparent difference is that some capabilities have been added.

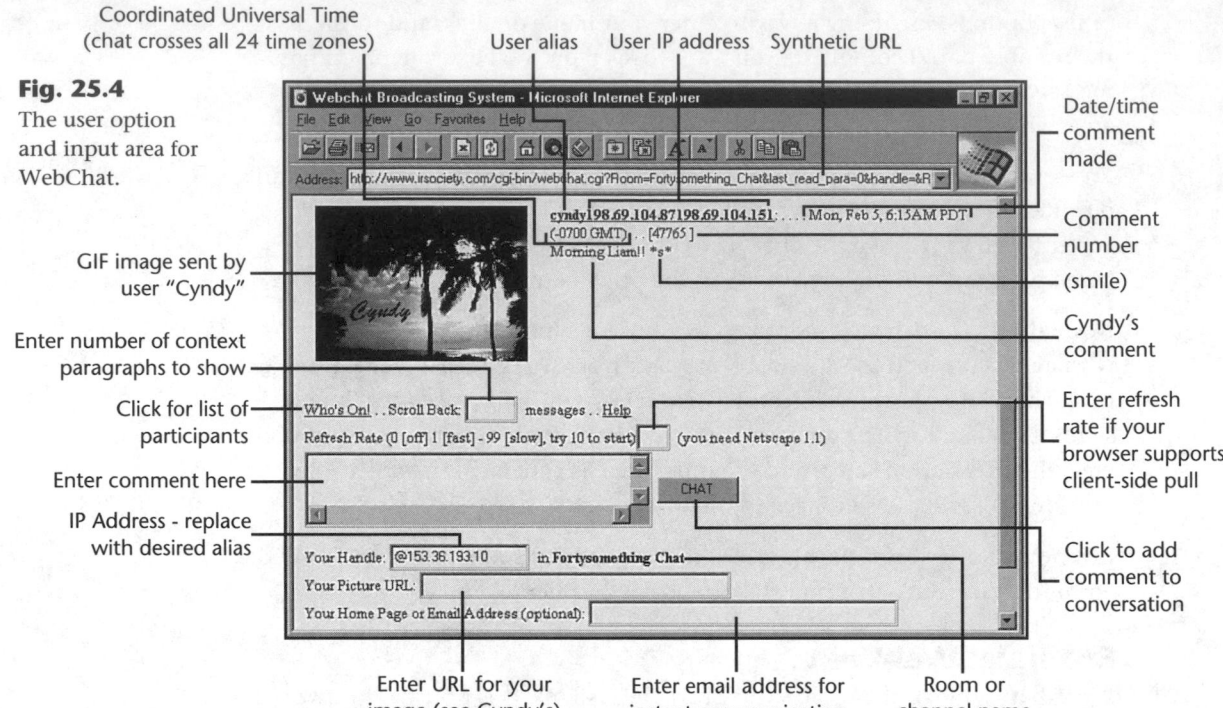

Coordinated Universal Time
(chat crosses all 24 time zones)

User alias   User IP address   Synthetic URL

Fig. 25.4

The user option
and input area for
WebChat.

Date/time
comment
made

GIF image sent by
user "Cyndy"

Comment
number

(smile)

Cyndy's
comment

Enter number of context
paragraphs to show

Click for list of
participants

Enter refresh
rate if your
browser supports
client-side pull

Enter comment here

IP Address - replace
with desired alias

Click to add
comment to
conversation

Enter URL for your
image (see Cyndy's)

Enter email address for
instant communication

Room or
channel name

For example, WebChat can use client pull to refresh your screen automatically if you are using the Microsoft Internet Explorer or Netscape. You do not need to keep clicking a button to update the conversation. You set the refresh rate in the user options area. WebChat allows you to select the number of *context paragraphs* that will be displayed when you update the conversation. A context paragraph is one that you have already seen prior to the update. Having several context paragraphs on your screen helps you keep track of the multiple simultaneous conversations that tend to take place on the typical chat page. Other chat page programs may not give you any context paragraphs, or they may use a fixed number that you cannot change.

Tip

Keep the refresh rate in WebChat set to the recommended number or slower. If you increase the number of context paragraphs, slow the refresh rate further. Four to five context paragraphs should be plenty.

Another difference is that you can send a picture with any or all of your WebChat messages. If you have a *GIF* or *JPEG* image of yourself, your house, or anything else, as long as the image is available at a URL, you can enter the location in the space provided, and it is then placed to the left of your entry. You can also embed images within any of your entries by simply typing the URL into the body of the message. The image then appears in-line.

The WebChat site offers an extensive library of small images that you can insert into your conversation. To reach this library, click on `PICS Library` at the bottom of the form. The images in the library have their URLs listed next to them. If your browser supports copying and pasting, highlight the URL of the image you want, copy it, return to your message, and paste the locator into the text.

In a similar fashion, you can insert a link into any entry. Just enter the URL. Readers then see a highlighted link. If they click the link, they will go to that URL. If you have a video or audio clip somewhere on the Internet, insert the URL, and readers will see or hear it when they click the resulting link.

You can also add your home page or e-mail address to your messages by entering them in the text boxes provided. They show up as highlighted links.

Because all the activity on WebChat pages is handled by the server, you might experience a performance penalty. When a large number of people are using the same Web page for chat, WebChat may run slow or skip messages. This is especially true if many of the users have entered an address for a graphic to be displayed next to their input.

> **Caution**
>
> If you are using a WebChat page and want to help the system's performance, either use no graphics or use very small ones.

WebChat does not show the current users on the same screen with the conversation. You click the `Who's On?` link to get this information (see fig. 25.5). WBS1 also tells you how many people are in channels other than the one where you are. WBS1 offers a large number of channels, all available through a unique "Tune" feature.

> **Tip**
>
> If there are more than about 12 users in a WebChat channel, pick another channel for your conversation to minimize lag problems.

Fig. 25.5
WebChat shows
you the names of
other users via
the Who's On?
feature.

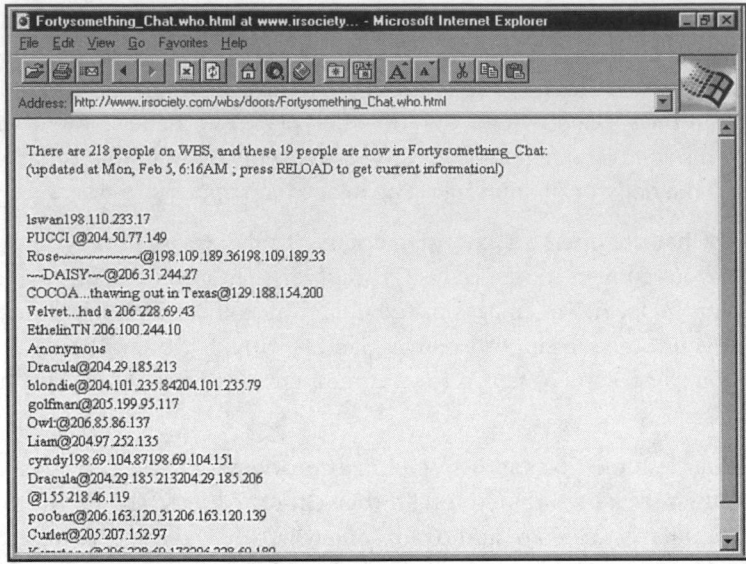

You can download all the software needed to set up and run a single channel WebChat right from the WebChat Home Page. The necessary scripts, forms, and other materials are provided in a single TAR file. This method is probably the single easiest way to add chat to your own home page, not to mention the cheapest. You can also easily modify the user interface to suit your requirements.

How to Set Up Chat with Forms on Your Site

Chat done with forms is created entirely by a CGI script running on a server. In this section, you look at the HTML created by the script and sent to the user's browser. Everything the user sees, with the exception of what he or she inputs onto the form, is created by the script *for that user alone*.

Listing 25.1 shows typical HTML source built by the server to create a basic chat input area. An annotated copy of this source code is on the CD-ROM as CHATIN.HTM.

Listing 25.1   This Source Code Could Be Generated by Script to Provide a Basic Chat Input Area

```
<HTML>
<HEAD>
<TITLE>Chat Input Area Example</TITLE>
</HEAD>
<BODY>
<FORM ACTION="http://www.someplace.com/" METHOD="POST">
```

```
</FORM>
<A HREF="\relative\who.html"> Who's here? </A>
<BR>
<HR>
<FORM>
<P> What's your alias?
<BR>
<INPUT NAME="alias" VALUE="anonymous" >
<P>What do you have to say?
<TEXTAREA NAME="UserInput" ROWS=5 COLS=75>
</TEXTAREA>
<BR>
<BR>
<CENTER> <INPUT TYPE="submit" NAME="Talk" VALUE="TALK"> </CENTER><BR>
</FORM>
</BODY>
</HTML>
```

This listing places the words "Chat Input Area Example" in the title bar of the browser. You can make your own personalized script insert something more apropos, such as "Chuck's Chat Center for Chiropractors."

Next, the browser is told where to send the information entered on the page when the submit button ("TALK") is selected:

```
<FORM ACTION="http://www.someplace.com/" METHOD="POST">
```

"POST" tells the browser to send the data to the processing program rather than wait for the program to retrieve the data from the current document.

"Who's here?" is actually a user option, not an input. Accessing who.html causes the script to output the current list of users on the fly.

Tip

Many users prefer to keep the updated list of users visible at all times, rather than having to constantly refresh the list. The ESPNET SportsZone is a good example of a system that does this.

The user input form area begins just after the horizontal rule under the user option. It consists of two parts: one to capture the user's alias and the other to capture the user's comments.

```
<P> What's your alias?
<INPUT NAME="alias" VALUE="anonymous" >
<P>What do you have to say?
<TEXTAREA NAME="UserInput" ROWS=5 COLS=75> </TEXTAREA>
<INPUT TYPE="submit" NAME="Talk" VALUE="TALK">
```

The input area can appear at the top or bottom of the chat page (that is, before or after the conversation transcript). When the user clicks on TALK, the alias and the text in the input area are submitted to the server to be processed.

As you can see in figure 25.6, this code produces a very basic kind of input area. This form has no frills at all. It submits a user name and a comment to the server. The chat script breaks them apart. The user name is added to a list of current users, and the comment is added to a file of user comments.

Fig. 25.6

The type of input area generated by a Web chat page script.

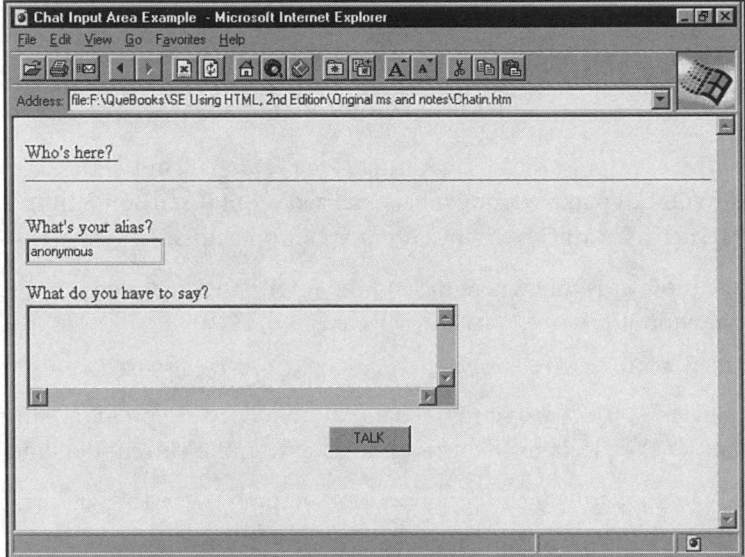

To return the names or aliases of others on-line, the script sets up a list of individuals currently accessing the page. At first, the script merely detects the user at the time of connection to the page. The server can then add an alias for an individual when he or she provides one, use a default alias (such as "anonymous") until an individual alias is entered, or not include individuals on the list until they enter actual comments. This action depends on the way you write the script. The script also needs to detect when someone leaves the page and then remove his or her alias from the list.

When someone clicks the Who's Here? link, the server returns the names on the list at that moment. The user may believe he or she is viewing a Web page containing this list. In fact, what the user sees only a virtual page created on the fly in response to his or her request. Other users on-line at the same time may see a different list. Some servers (such as WebChat) update the list when the user clicks the Refresh button on his or her browser.

Returning an updated chat transcript is a bit more complicated. How much more complicated depends on the features you decide to implement. For example, if you want to provide some context paragraphs, as WebChat does, all comments submitted must be tracked with a unique identification number. (Not all chat pages provide context paragraphs.) This number is assigned by the script as each comment is received. The script could begin numbering comments with "1" (say, at noon GMT), or it could use the time the comment was received.

This identification number is used to select the comments that are returned when the user enters the chat channel or clicks the Chat or Update buttons. The system knows the number of the last paragraph seen by the user. It knows the number of the latest comment submitted, and it knows how many comments to repeat for context. A little math identifies the comments that must be shown.

> **Tip**
>
> Give the user about five context paragraphs on entering a channel, to help get things started.

You might want to make it possible for users to enter live links as part of their comments. These links could be to images, sounds, or pages. This setup requires your CGI script to parse the user's input, identify URLs, and output the links in a way that browsers will recognize, display, and treat as links.

The next task for the script is to format the entire page. Listing 25.2 shows the HTML source that might be generated and sent to the user's browser during a chat session. (This source code will be found on the CD-ROM as CHATPAGE.HTM). Notice that much of this source is the same as shown in listing 25.1. The difference is that the conversation transcript has been added. Each individual paragraph of the transcript has the same formatting applied:

```
<B>Paladin@123.456.78.90</B>: 20:52 GMT <BR>
Mike: I'm back<BR CLEAR=left><P>
```

The preceding is the paragraph (or comment) submitted by a user who calls himself "Paladin." The CGI script has taken his input and pulled out the alias. To the alias, the script appended the Host IP address that it captured when Paladin accessed the chat page. These elements were dropped into a bold format and the time at which Paladin's input was received was appended to them. A line break was added. Then Paladin's comment was added to the next line, followed by another line break. Incidentally, the Mike: that begins Paladin's comment is something that Paladin typed himself. On a busy chat page, most users provide some kind of reference that helps other users keep track of the conversations.

Listing 25.2   HTML Source Generated by the Web Chat Script, to Return an Updated Conversation to the User

```
<HTML>
<HEAD>
<TITLE>My Chat Page on the Web</TITLE>
</HEAD>
<BODY>
<H1>Welcome to My Chat Page!</H1>
<HR>
<FORM ACTION="http://www.someplace.com/" METHOD="POST">
</FORM>
<B>Paladin@123.456.78.90</B>: 20:52 GMT <BR>
Mike: I'm back<BR CLEAR=left><P>
<B>Joker@098.765.43.21</B>: 20:52 GMT <BR>
Indy: It would seem you have some competition for your name.<BR
➥CLEAR=left><P>
<B>Megan@135.792.46.80</B>: 20:53 GMT <BR>
MARIE — Guess what! I had an argument with them (BUT IT WAS NOT MY
➥FAULT!) <BR CLEAR=left><P>
<B>My Name Is Mike@246.801.35.79</B>: 20:53 GMT <BR>
PALADIN: Where did you go?<BR CLEAR=left><P>
<BR>
<HR>
<A HREF="\relative\who.html"> Who's here? </A>
<BR>
<HR>
<FORM>
<P> What's your alias?
<BR>
<INPUT NAME="alias" VALUE="">
<P> What do you have to say?
<BR>
<TEXTAREA NAME="UserInput" ROWS=5 COLS=75>
</TEXTAREA>
<BR>
<BR>
<CENTER><INPUT TYPE="submit" NAME="Talk" VALUE="TALK"></CENTER><BR>
</FORM>
</BODY>
</HTML>
```

The server script simply keeps adding comments and formatting them until all the user inputs down to the very last one are in this format and strung together. Then the whole chunk of HTML source is sent back to the individual user, who sees something like figure 25.7 on his or her browser.

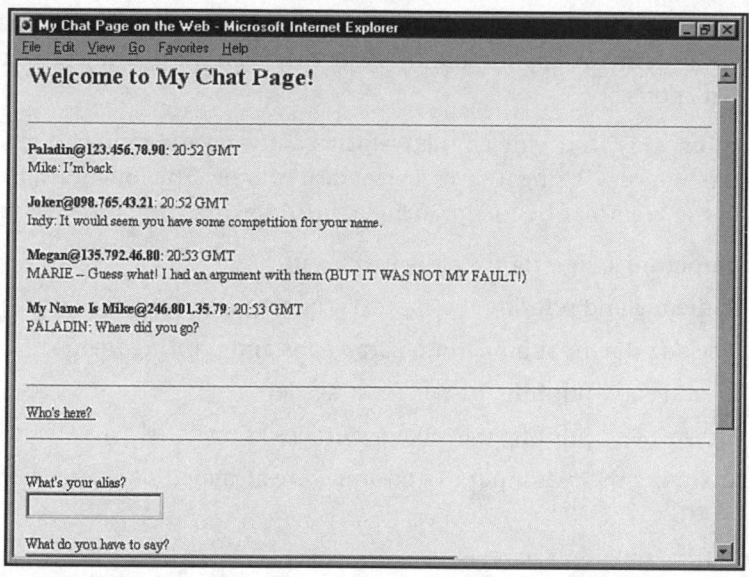

Fig. 25.7
The way the user sees the updated conversation provided by the HTML source in listing 25.2.

Figure 25.8 depicts the way that the server script parses input and generates output.

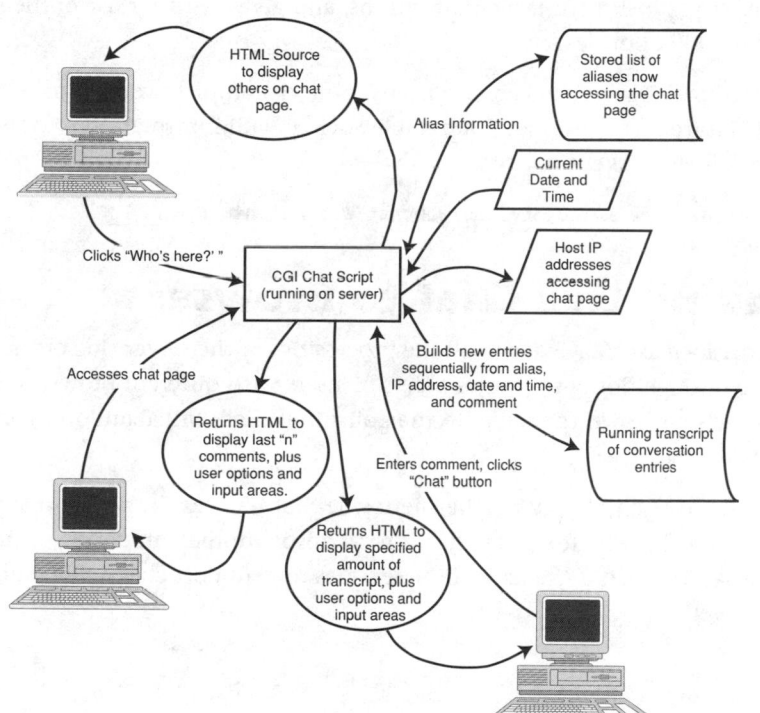

Fig. 25.8
The Web chat script parses input from all users and assembles output that is returned to users individually.

V

Interactive Web Pages

◄ For more information on setting up a form on a Web page, see "Forms and How They Work," p. 489

You can find the basic elements of a script that performs these tasks in chapter 24. The guestbook application in that chapter can serve as the start for your own efforts.

In addition, you can download the WebChat software and modify it to suit your own purposes. Using it saves a great deal of time. The functions provided in the WebChat CGI script include the following:

- Outputting a new form for the user
- Gathering and printing the context paragraphs
- Breaking the input buffer into paragraphs and printing them
- Creating and printing the talk form header
- Creating and printing the talk form trailer
- Analyzing the user input to find and convert hyperlink references to HTML
- Getting the user's handle
- Converting the user's head URL to HTML form

◄ To learn how to do the posting of new comments onto a Web chat page, see "Form Layout and Design," p. 503

◄ You can find out more about writing CGI scripts to support chat features in "All about CGI Scripts," p. 525

Note that you can adapt the WebChat script in whatever way is required for your application. However, you must retain the copyright notice that appears in the script, document the modifications, and give credit for use of the library of PERL routines.

As noted previously, you can also license a more complete version of WebChat from the Internet Roundtable Society. Full information is available at the following WebChat site:

`http://www.irsociety.com/webchat/webchat.html`.

Linking Live Chat to Browsers

Systems such as WebChat put all the processing on the server side of the Web. Although doing so assures access by users with different browsers, it also may slow down the server to the point that users will abandon their efforts to chat.

You can create a program for the client side that relieves the server of some of the burden. The client-side application can also automate updating of the conversation, even if the user's browser does not support client-side pull.

In these programs, the application runs concurrently with the user's browser. The user goes to a page that is enabled for this type of chat and clicks a Connect button (or something similar) on that page. The client-side application is called and links to the page. At this point, the user can chat.

UgaliChat is an example of this approach. In this commercial system, the server manager sets up UgaliChat-enabled pages or makes it possible for users to create their own chat pages. This is done by installing the UgaliChat Server on the host computer. The server can be modified by the manager (it's another simple script), and server access can be limited.

The UgaliChat Server performs various housekeeping functions automatically. These functions include removing inactive clients, providing new users with several minutes of past conversation, and presenting an information page on use of UgaliChat to the users' Web browsers. The Server also tracks user counts. The Server advises the server manager of chat-enabled pages that have been set up on the system. The manager can disable chat functionality on individual pages, and can also set the Server up so that the manager's approval is required in order to chat-enable a page.

From the user's perspective, the UgaliChat page automatically displays a list of users on-line, with a notice indicating that UgaliChat is available. The client-side application (the Ugali Communicator) is a MIME reader that automatically updates the reader's display at intervals determined by the user. The user types a message and presses Enter when ready to send it to the other users.

The UgaliChat server is provided and supported for a fee that varies by the type of service provider. The Communicator is free to those who use it in their private homes or in certain educational institutions. For all others, a fee is required for each copy of the Communicator program.

Although the use of a client-side application makes chat run faster, there are some drawbacks. First, you have no guarantee that the application will work with all browsers. Second, although the server manager can change the server code at any time, the code for the client side may not be modified directly. Third, the client-side application requires installing a proprietary reader on the user's system. This is not always desirable and may limit the number of people who can use the Chat system. Finally, the practice of charging a fee for use of the client-side application may make these systems less attractive to businesses.

Planning for the Future

The evolution of interactivity on the World Wide Web has been the subject of a great deal of discussion. An influential project was done between 1994 and 1995 at the Massachusetts Institute of Technology (MIT). This project, called the Sociable Web, is no longer available. However, you can still read the white paper on the project by pointing your browser to the following:

`http://judith.www.media.mit.edu/SocialWeb/`

Although this paper is brief, it is worth study for its definition of a number of key concepts that are likely to be influential in future Web chat page systems. The Web is a social environment, so the important features are the ones that enhance interaction. The authors of the Sociable Web placed their focus on four of these features:

- Seeing who else is present
- Having a virtual location
- Providing privacy
- Participating in "WebTalk," or discussions that occur in the context of the Web and that use its rich hypermedia capabilities

Much of the functionality described by Judith Donath, Niel Robertson, and their colleagues at the MIT Media Lab has already been or is being realized in WebChat. However, the notion of a "virtual location" has yet to be implemented. A virtual location is a "place" at which contact with an individual user can usually be made, even though that user may be off wandering the Web most of the time.

Web chat pages as now implemented require all the users to be simultaneously accessing the same page and no others. A virtual location would permit users to carry on conversations even if they were not all accessing the same page. This process is a little like monitoring a certain channel on a CB radio while driving your car across country. Your friends would know that they could contact you on that channel no matter where you were.

And the idea of social uses of the Web is growing beyond what was foreseen in the Sociable Web. You now see applications that allow a group of individuals to tour around the Web together, for example. Other developments under way make it possible to converse with a Web page, and for Web pages to make small talk, respond to questions, and carry out searches. A good Web page would be able to do searches while serving as the virtual host for a group conference, for example. Finally, you can also expect to see pages that can support simultaneous public and private conversations.

Tip

You can implement some of these ideas now as 'bots if you write your own chat page script.

In this chapter, you have wandered far from the concept of the Internet as a reference library. Consider the ways in which the Web is like a diner, instead. With a great menu and interesting conversation, you can make your Web site a destination, not just another way station on the road to somewhere else. ❖

## CHAPTER 26

Java™ and JavaScript™

by Stephen R. Pietrowicz

Sun Microsystems's object-oriented programming language Java™ and the jointly developed JavaScript are both creating a lot of interest on the Web. You can use Java and JavaScript to create dynamic, interactive Web pages. This chapter gives you a brief introduction to both Java and JavaScript and explains how you can use both of these technologies in your own Web pages.

In this chapter, you learn about the following:

- Why Java was created
- How to add Java applets into your own HTML pages
- What JavaScript is
- How to add JavaScript programs to your own HTML pages
- How Java protects your system
- Where to find Java applets and other Java resources

How Java Got Started

In 1991, Sun started the "Green" project to create intelligent consumer electronics devices. James Gosling, an engineer at Sun, created a new object-oriented language, called Oak, to support the project. He intended to create a language that could be used to write programs for devices like cellular phones and television remote controls. Instead of pre-programming the devices before they left the factory, Oak programs could be downloaded as they were needed. When new features were added, the customer would be able to take advantage of them right away without having to send the device back to the factory. In 1993, Sun built prototypes of remote controls using this technology, and although it was promising, they were having problems gathering support from other vendors. On top of everything else, they found that "Oak" was already in use as a trademark.

In 1994, the Internet and the World Wide Web experienced explosive growth. The Oak team began to realize their downloadable technology could be applied to the Web. They decided to begin work on a new Web browser that would showcase their work. They also renamed the language "Java," a slang word for coffee, a beverage that many engineers drink every day.

Up until that point, Web pages consisted of static images and text. A few interesting examples of complex server-side imagemaps and CGI scripts did show up on the Web to create simple paint programs, for instance, but they weren't really interactive. Requests still had to be sent back to the server, and these requests created additional load on the machine serving the documents.

A browser with the ability to download programs and run them on the client machine would offload the server, allowing it to serve more documents. That's exactly the sort of browser the Java team decided to build.

The Java team's browser, HotJava, was the first program capable of automatically loading and running Java programs. HotJava created quite a bit of interest in Java on the Web, and many companies have licensed Java from Sun so that they can incorporate the technology into their own products. Some of the same consumer electronics companies Sun tried to interest with the Green project are now contacting them to license Java.

Java has proven to be so popular that on Jan. 9, 1996, Sun spun off a new business unit called Javasoft that will concentrate on Java development.

Getting Started with Java

The Java language is object oriented and very similar to C++. It was designed to take many of the best features of C++ while simplifying it to make writing programs easier.

Programs are normally created to run on only one type of operating system. Windows 95 programs have been specifically created to run on systems running the Windows 95 operating system, and will not run on the Macintosh or on a UNIX system. Java programs, however, are intended to be platform independent. Java programs are compiled into a series of bytecodes that are interpreted by a Java interpreter. After a Java program has been compiled, it can run on any system with a Java interpreter. You do not need to recompile it.

This capability makes Java an ideal language for programs on the Web. With so many different systems on the Web, creating programs that will work with all of them is very difficult. Because Java programs are platform independent, programs are no longer restricted to running on one platform. They can run on any platform to which Java has been ported.

Java has been ported to many different platforms. Sun has ported Java to Solaris, Windows NT, Windows 95, and the Macintosh. Other companies have ported Java to Silicon Graphics IRIX, IBM OS/2, IBM AIX, and Linux.

Using Java Applets in Web Pages

Java programs that can be embedded into WWW pages are called *Java applets*. To run applets from Web pages, you must have a browser that supports Java, such as HotJava or Netscape 2.0.

If you want to write your own Java applets, you should download the Java Development Kit from Javasoft. It's available for free on the Web. You can download it from the Javasoft Home page:

http://www.javasoft.com

Now take a look at a few examples. Listing 26.1 shows the code for a simple Java applet. This listing is called HelloWorld.java on the CD-ROM.

On the CD

Listing 26.1   A "Hello World" Java Applet

```
import java.applet.*;
import java.awt.*;

class HelloWorld extends Applet {

    public void paint(Graphics g) {
        g.drawString("Hello World!",20,20);
    }
}
```

When you place this applet into a page and run it, it prints `Hello World!`. But before you can use it in a page, you must compile the applet by using *Javac*, the Java compiler. The files that Javac creates are called *Java class files*. A class file is the platform-independent object file that the browser retrieves when downloading a Java applet.

To use this applet on an HTML page, you have to describe it by using the APPLET element. Figure 26.1 shows an HTML page that loads this example applet.

Fig. 26.1
An HTML page
with an applet
definition.

CODE attribute
APPLET container tags
HEIGHT attribute
WIDTH attribute

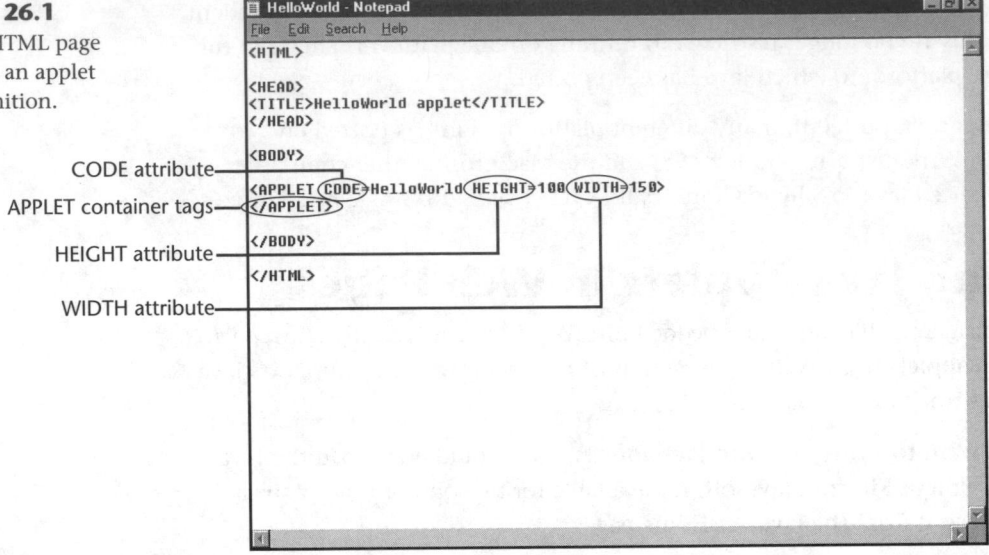

The <APPLET> and </APPLET> tags act as a container for the Java applet definition. They indicate to the browser that a Java applet should be loaded. The CODE attribute tells the browser which Java applet should be downloaded. The browser reserves space in the page using the WIDTH and HEIGHT attributes, just as it reserves space for the IMG element. Then the browser downloads the Java class specified in the CODE attribute and begins running the applet.

In this case, the applet being downloaded is HelloWorld, and it reserves a space 150 pixels high and 200 pixels wide in the page. Figure 26.2 shows what the page looks like when the browser loads it.

Browsers that can't display Java applets don't display anything when this page is loaded. To prevent this situation from happening, you can place HTML markup or text between the <APPLET> and </APPLET> tags. Browsers that can't display Java applets display the HTML markup instead. You can use this approach to tell visitors to your pages what they would have seen if the applet had loaded.

Browsers that can display applets don't display any of this HTML markup. Figure 26.3 shows an HTML page with alternative HTML markup. This HTML page is called HelloWorld.html on the CD-ROM.

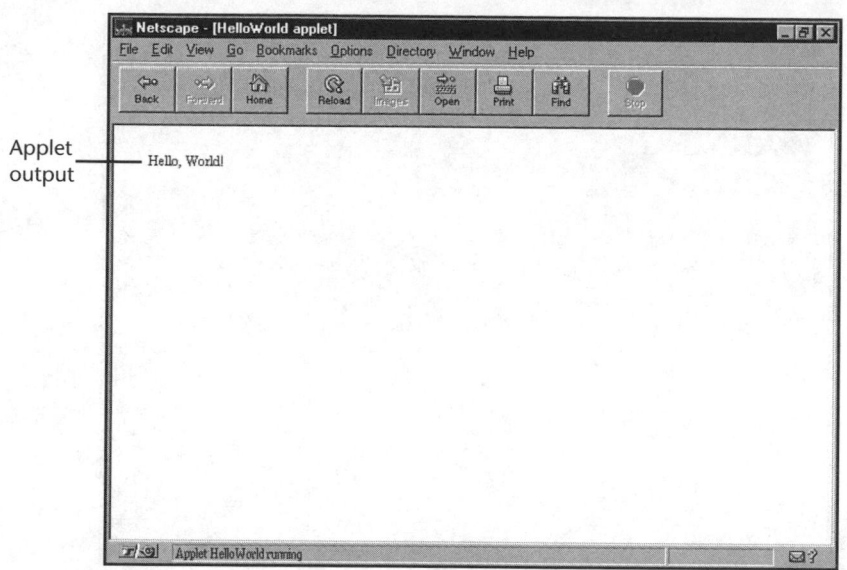

Applet output

Fig. 26.2
A simple Java applet.

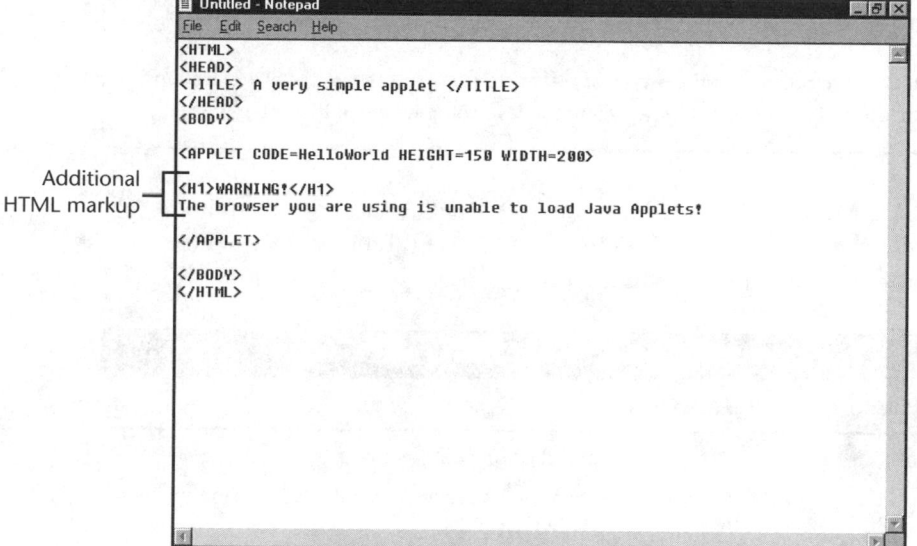

Additional HTML markup

Fig. 26.3
The HTML markup in the APPLET container is shown by browsers that cannot display Java applets.

V

Interactive Web Pages

Figure 26.4 shows how this page looks in a browser that doesn't support Java applets.

Fig. 26.4
Instead of showing
the Java applet,
the HTML text is
displayed. This
way, you can alert
visitors to your
page about what
they're missing.

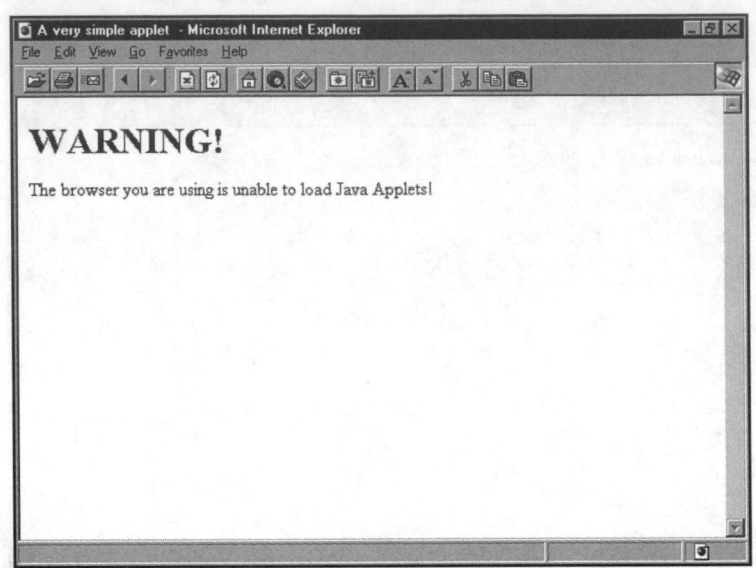

> **Note**
>
> You aren't restricted to writing Web applets with Java. You can write full applications
> with it as well. The HotJava browser and the Java compiler are both written in Java.

The CODE, WIDTH, and HEIGHT attributes of the APPLET tag are all required.
You also can use other attributes in the APPLET tag. Table 26.1 shows the
attributes available and their functions.

Table 26.1   APPLET Attributes and Their Functions

Attribute	Function
CODE	Defines the applet class to load. (*required*)
WIDTH	Defines the width in pixels of the area in the HTML page to reserve for the applet. (*required*)
HEIGHT	Defines the height in pixels of the area in the HTML page to reserve for the applet. (*required*)
ALT	Defines the alternate text to display if the applet tag is understood, but applet loading is turned off or not supported.
CODEBASE	Defines the directory where the classes for the applet are stored. If this attribute is not specified, the directory of the HTML page is searched.

Attribute	Function
NAME	Defines the name of this instance of an applet. This attribute can be used by an applet to find another applet on the same page.
ALIGN	Defines how this applet is aligned in the HTML page. Any of the ALIGN options discussed in previous chapters are legal here.
VSPACE	Defines how many pixels of space are reserved above and below the applet.
HSPACE	Defines how many pixels of space are reserved on either side of the applet.

Listing 26.2 shows a more complex applet called URLsound. (This applet is called URLsound.java on the CD-ROM.) It displays an image with which a user can interact. When the user moves the mouse pointer over the image, this applet changes to another image and plays a sound. When the user clicks on the image, the applet causes the Web browser to go to a new URL.

On the CD

Caution

If you have loaded a background image or changed the background color and used an applet, the area reserved for the applet will be drawn with the browser's default grey color.

Listing 26.2   The URLsound Java Applet

```java
import java.awt.*;
import java.applet.*;
import java.net.*;

/**
 * URLSound - This applet displays an image in a page. If the mouse
cursor
 * moves over the image, it changes to an alternative image, and
 *      a sound is played. If the image is clicked, the browser
 * changes to another page. The images, sound and new page are
 * all user definable.
 */
public class URLsound extends Applet {
    String sound;
    String href;
    Image image1, image2, current;

    public void init() {
        /*
         * retrieve parameters given to the applet on the HTML page
         */
```

(continues)

V

Interactive Web Pages

Listing 26.2   Continued

```java
        String pic1 = getParameter("picture1");
        String pic2 = getParameter("picture2");
        sound = getParameter("sound");
        href = getParameter("href");

        /*
         * The MediaTracker class is used to ensure the images
         * have been loaded before we attempt to use them.
         */
        MediaTracker tracker = new MediaTracker(this);

        try {
            image1 = getImage(getDocumentBase(), pic1);
            tracker.addImage(image1, 0);

            image2 = getImage(getDocumentBase(), pic2);
            tracker.addImage(image2, 0);
        } catch (Exception e) {
        }

        try {
            tracker.waitForID(0);
        } catch (Exception e) {
        }

        current = image1;

    }

    /*
     * This routine is called each time the mouse enters the
     * applet area. It plays a sound and changes the displayed
     * image.
     */
    public boolean mouseEnter(Event evt, int x, int y) {

        /*
         * Try to play the sound
         */
        try {
            play(getDocumentBase(), sound);
        } catch (Exception e) {
            System.out.println("Unable to play Sound");
        }

        /*
         * Change "current" to the alternate image and force a
         *   ➥repaint
         */
        current = image2;
        repaint();
        return true;
    }
```

```
/*
 * This routine is called each time the mouse leaves the
 * applet area. It restores the initial image and forces
 * a repaint.
 */
public boolean mouseExit(Event evt, int x, int y) {
    current = image1;
    repaint();
    return true;
}

/*
 * This routine is called each time the mouse is clicked in the
 * applet area. It causes the browser to jump to the specified
 * URL.
 */
public boolean mouseDown(Event evt, int x, int y) {
    URL hrefURL = null;

    try {
        hrefURL = new URL(href);
        getAppletContext().showDocument(hrefURL);

    } catch (Exception e) {
        System.out.println("Couldn't go to URL");
    }

    return true;
}

/*
 * The paint method is what actually displays the image.
 */
public void paint(Graphics g) {
    g.drawImage(current, 0, 0, this);
}

}
```

You can customize URLsound to allow you to specify which images to display, which sound to play, and which URL to jump to. You do so by using the PARAM element inside the APPLET container.

On the CD

Figure 26.5 shows an HTML page that uses URLsound twice, with different parameters. This HTML page is called URLsound.html on the CD-ROM.

Fig. 26.5
You can change parameters in the URLsound applet to customize it.

NAME attribute

PARAM tag

VALUE attribute

```
url_example - Notepad
File  Edit  Search  Help
<HTML>
<HEAD>
<TITLE>
Examples of URLsound
</TITLE>
</HEAD>
<BODY>

<APPLET CODE=URLsound.class HEIGHT=100 WIDTH=100>
<PARAM NAME="picture1" VALUE="stop.gif">
<PARAM NAME="picture2" VALUE="go.gif">
<PARAM NAME="sound" VALUE="goahead.au">
<PARAM NAME="href" VALUE="http://www.yahoo.com/">
</APPLET>

<APPLET CODE=URLsound.class HEIGHT=100 WIDTH=100>
<PARAM NAME="picture1" VALUE="calm.gif">
<PARAM NAME="picture2" VALUE="surprised.gif">
<PARAM NAME="sound" VALUE="ohoh.au">
<PARAM NAME="href" VALUE="http://www.lycos.com/">
</APPLET>

</BODY>
</HTML>
```

The <PARAM> tag has two required attributes: NAME and VALUE. When an applet initializes, it requests the parameters it's expecting by using the specified NAME, and it receives the VALUE. More than one parameter can be passed to an applet if you put more than one <PARAM> tag in the APPLET container. Parameters that the applet does not recognize are ignored.

In figure 26.5, the URLsound applet takes four parameters: picture1, picture2, sound, and href. picture1 names the picture in its inactive state. picture2 is revealed when the mouse pointer moves over the picture area, and the audio file specified by sound is played. When the user clicks the mouse on the picture, the browser jumps to the URL specified by href. In figure 26.6, a browser shows this page.

Note

Special server software is not needed to serve Java applets. You can use your Internet server provider's current Web server to serve Java applets.

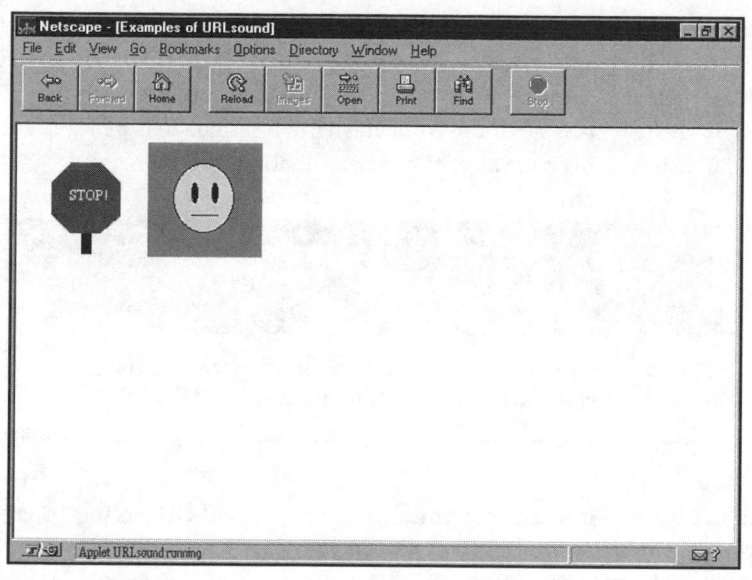

Fig. 26.6
Two copies of
URLsound in one
page.

JavaScript

JavaScript is a scripting language that was jointly created by Netscape and
Sun. JavaScript programs are not compiled like Java applets. JavaScript programs are embedded in the HTML markup of a page. After the page is loaded,
the browser interprets the JavaScript program and runs it.

Figure 26.7 shows an example of a JavaScript program. The HTML page for
this example is called simple.html on the CD-ROM.

On the CD

Fig. 26.7
A simple JavaScript
program in an
HTML page.

SCRIPT tag ⟶

LANGUAGE attribute

JavaScript code ⟶

Ending
SCRIPT tag ⟶

```
<HTML>
<HEAD>
<TITLE>A very simple JavaScript Program</TITLE>
</HEAD>
<BODY>
<SCRIPT LANGUAGE="JavaScript">

document.writeln("<H2>");
document.writeln("This is a very simple example of a JavaScript program.");
document.writeln("<br>");
document.writeln("Now we'll count from one to ten: ");

for (i = 1; i <= 10 ; i++)
        document.writeln(i);

document.writeln("</H2>");

</SCRIPT>
<BODY>
</HTML>
```

V

Interactive Web Pages

The <SCRIPT> and </SCRIPT> tags enclose JavaScript programs. The required LANGUAGE attribute tells the browser what type of scripting language to use. In this case, it uses "JavaScript". If the browser supports more than one language, the LANGUAGE attribute indicates which language is being used. Figure 26.8 shows this page after it has been loaded into a browser.

Fig. 26.8
The results of the simple JavaScript program.

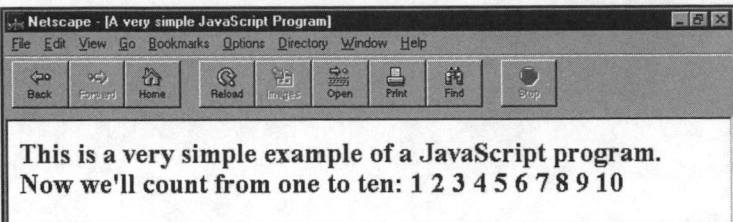

In chapter 24, you learned that you can use forms and CGI scripts to create interesting programs with which a visitor to a page can interact. One of the problems with CGI scripts is that they require the Web server to execute the script. The additional workload on the server causes it to slow down, especially on a busy server with many CGI scripts. You might have noticed this slowdown when trying to connect to a site that takes awhile to transmit a document. Every time a CGI script runs, it uses valuable resources that could be used to serve more documents.

JavaScript solves the problem of overburdened Web servers. Instead of writing a CGI program that must be executed by the server, you can write and transmit a JavaScript program with the HTML page. The client browser, instead of the server, then executes the JavaScript program.

The HTML page in listing 26.3 contains a JavaScript program to convert between the Celsius and Fahrenheit temperature scales. The result of loading this page is shown in figure 26.9.

Listing 26.3   A JavaScript Program That Converts Temperature Scales

```
<HTML>
<HEAD>
<TITLE>Temperature Converter</TITLE>
<SCRIPT LANGUAGE="JavaScript">

function c2f(form) {
    celsius = form.celsius.value;
    form.fahrenheit.value = (celsius*1.8)+32;
}
```

```
function f2c(form) {
    fahrenheit = form.fahrenheit.value;
    form.celsius.value = (fahrenheit-32)/1.8;
}

</SCRIPT>
</HEAD>
<BODY>
<FORM>
Celsius value
<INPUT TYPE="text" NAME="celsius" SIZE=15>
is
<INPUT TYPE="text" NAME="fahrenheit" SIZE=15>
degrees Fahrenheit.
<br>
<INPUT TYPE="button" VALUE="Calculate" ONCLICK="c2f(this.form)">
<br>
</FORM>
<FORM>
Fahrenheit value
<INPUT TYPE="text" NAME="fahrenheit" SIZE=15>
is
<INPUT TYPE="text" NAME="celsius" SIZE=15>
degrees Celsius.
<br>
<INPUT TYPE="button" VALUE="Calculate" ONCLICK="f2c(this.form)">
<br>
</FORM>
</BODY>
</HTML>
```

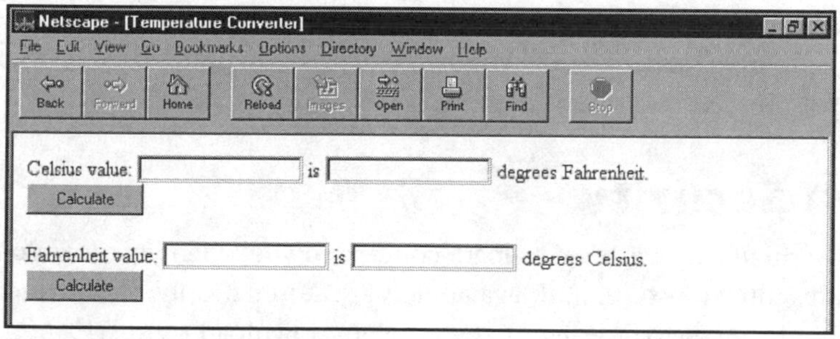

Fig. 26.9
The JavaScript program is loaded, and the fields have no initial values.

The code between the <SCRIPT> and </SCRIPT> elements defines two functions, c2f and f2c, which are used to calculate temperatures. Notice that neither of the functions produces any output. How are these functions used?

The answer is farther down in the document. The ONCLICK attribute of the <INPUT> element is used to execute a JavaScript function, or series of JavaScript statements. In the first form, the function c2f is called. In the second form, the function f2c is called. The parameter to the function call in each of these forms is this.form. All the values in the form are passed to the functions, which interpret the values that the user types into the forms and perform the calculations.

Another thing you may have already noticed about this page is that the JavaScript code is loaded in the HEAD container of the document. Loading the code this way is important so that you can assure the JavaScript functions are loaded before the rest of the page is loaded. This way, you can prevent a user from accidentally trying to interact with a JavaScript program before it is fully loaded. If the user were to press a button before all the functions were loaded, he or she would receive an error.

Figure 26.10 shows the results of typing values in each of the temperature fields and pressing the Calculate button of each form.

Fig. 26.10
The JavaScript program computes the temperature values after the values 25 and 32 are entered and the Calculate buttons are both pressed.

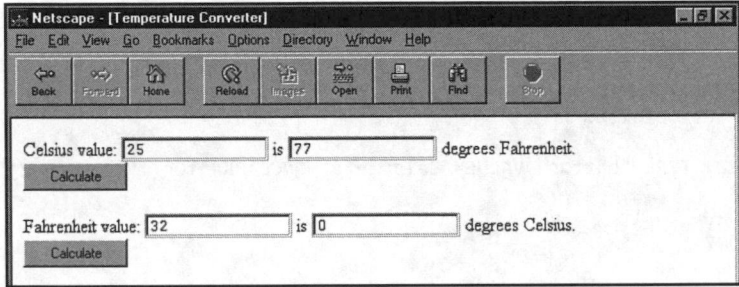

This section gives you only a brief introduction to JavaScript. See the "Web Resources" section at the end of this chapter for additional JavaScript information.

Java Security

Security should always be of primary concern to you when you download programs into your system. If Java applets are automatically downloaded and run, should you be concerned that you might download a virus?

Fortunately, the answer is no. Security mechanisms built into the Java class structure allow browsers to prevent Java applets from doing anything malicious to your system.

You don't have to worry about having viruses installed or having your private financial files stolen through Java because Java applets that your browser loads from the Web can't read or write files on your hard drive. The security policy in the browser prevents it.

Because files can't be read, Java applets can't start other programs you may already have installed on your system. No need to worry about a rogue applet coming in and wiping out your hard disk.

Java applets can create their own windows outside the browser, however. This could be a problem. What if the applet you download looks exactly like another program you already have on your system? What's to prevent you from entering data, like a password, into the applet that you're trying to protect?

Java takes care of this situation, too. To prevent you from thinking that these windows were created by your own system, an applet's window is labeled so that you know a Java applet has created the window. This label cannot be overridden by the Java applet, so you know it is always displayed. Figure 26.11 shows a labeled applet window.

Fig. 26.11
Windows outside the browser contain the words `Untrusted Java Applet Window` at the bottom of the window.

Caution

If you ever see an unexpected window on your screen with the words "`Untrusted Java Applet Window`, asking for your password, **DO NOT** type your password. It's likely that someone is trying to use a Java applet to get your password to break into your system. Report the break-in attempt to your local system administrator or your Internet service provider.

Java applets are also incapable of searching through your system's memory to obtain information. The Java language itself doesn't have access to random memory locations in your system, which is a method some criminals use to steal passwords and other confidential information.

Notable Java Applets

The following are just a couple of the most notable Java applets on the Web. They're both great examples of what is possible with Java.

The Impressionist, by Paul Haeberli of Silicon Graphics, is one of the most remarkable applets available (see fig. 26.12). It applies Haeberli's patented computer painting techniques to allow you to draw in the style of an impressionist painter. You select one of the nine pictures available on the page or use one of your own, and start with a blank canvas. As you move your mouse pointer over the canvas, the picture is drawn in the impressionist style.

V

Interactive Web Pages

The Impressionist is available from **http://reality.sgi.com/grafica/ impression/**.

Fig. 26.12
The Impressionist.

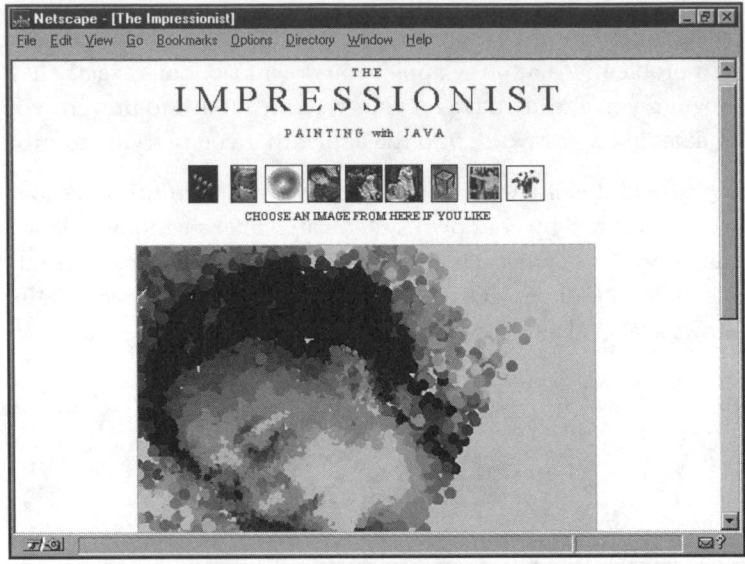

BulletProof has created the first site on the Internet that uses Java to display stock quotes and stock histories (see fig. 26.13). This subscription service allows you to keep your stock portfolio up to date and to search thousands of different securities. Look for it at **http://www.bulletproof.com/ WallStreetWeb/**.

Fig. 26.13
The WallStreetWeb Java applet by BulletProof.

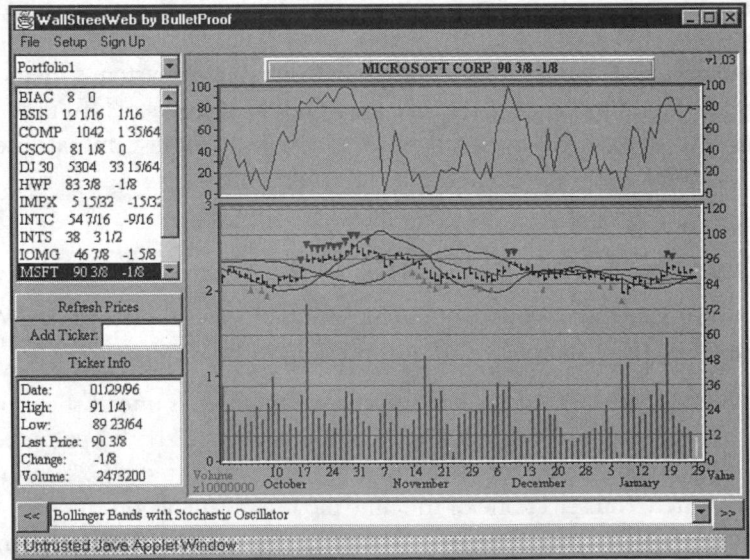

Java and JavaScript Resources

Creating Java applets and JavaScript programs can be a bit difficult, especially for the novice programmer. If you're interested in writing Java applets or JavaScript programs, there are a number of development tools and informational resources available to you.

Development Tools

Since Sun's announcement, many companies have licensed Java and have created Java development tools. Some free development tools are also available. Here are a few:

Symantec (**http://www.symantec.com/**) has created an integrated development environment (IDE) for Java called Symantec Cafe. Symantec Cafe is available for Windows 95, Windows NT, and Power Macintosh. You can read more about it at **http://www.symantec.com/lit/dev/javaindex.html**.

Borland International (**http://www.borland.com/**) has a new debugger for Java. This graphical debugger is available on the Windows 95, Windows NT, and Solaris platforms.

Silicon Graphics (**http://www.sgi.com**) has ported Java to their IRIX operating system and has created a development environment called Cosmo Code. Cosmo Code provides an extensive set of utilities for Java programming, including a source-level debugger. It is available only for Silicon Graphics machines.

Javamaker is a free IDE from Korea. It contains an editor and has buttons to compile your Java programs automatically. It's simple but very effective. Javamaker is available from **http://net.info.samsung.co.kr/~hcchoi/javamaker.html**.

Diva, another IDE available on the Internet is a more sophisticated utility than Javamaker. It provides graphical class representations, the ability to write HTML documents, an integrated editor and more. It is available from **http://www.inch.com/~friskel/**.

Web Resources

Javasoft has a special WWW site set up especially for Java (see fig. 26.14). You can reach it at **http://www.javasoft.com/**. You can find the latest version of the HotJava browser and the Java Development Kit (JDK) at **http://www.javasoft.com/download.html**.

> ### Tip
>
> The Java web site has a "What's New" page that's updated frequently with news from Sun. It can be accessed from the Java home page or from: **http://www.javasoft.com/new.html**

The Gamelan home page (**http://www.gamelan.com**) keeps an extensive list of Java applets and other Java resources.

Fig. 26.14
The Java Home
page.

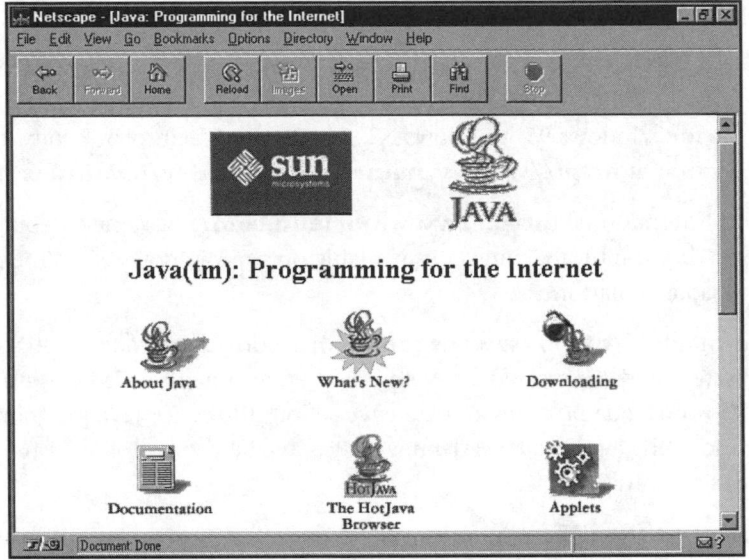

You can learn more about JavaScript by going to Netscape's Authoring Guide page: **http://home.netscape.com/comprod/products/navigator/version_2.0/script/script_info/index.html**.

The JavaScript Index (**http://www.c2.org/~andreww/javascript/**) contains a list of JavaScript links with many examples.

Internet Newsgroups and Mailing Lists

The Internet newsgroups for Java are shown in table 26.2.

Table 26.2 Internet Java Newsgroups	
Group	**Purpose**
comp.lang.java	General Java language discussions
comp.lang.javascript	General JavaScript discussions
alt.www.hotjava	HotJava browser discussions

Reading these newsgroups is a great way to keep up to date with the most current Java information, and a great way to meet other people who are also interested in Java.

Many mailing lists also support Java. Sun maintains several of these Java mailing lists. You should be aware that some of these mailing lists have a tremendous amount of traffic, so be prepared to receive a lot of e-mail if you subscribe to them.

The **java-announce** list, a moderated mailing list, distributes press releases and announces new software releases. Subscribe to this mailing list by sending e-mail with the word **Subscribe** in the message to **java-announce-request@java.sun.com**.

The **java-porting** list discusses porting Java to different platforms. If you're interested in porting Java to a new architecture, this is the list for you. Subscribe to this mailing list by sending e-mail with the word **Subscribe** in the message to **java-porting-request@java.sun.com**.

The **java-interest** list is an unmoderated forum for discussing Java programming issues that aren't covered by the other lists. The traffic on this list is also sent to **comp.lang.java**. If you already read that newsgroup, you don't need to subscribe to this list. Subscribe to this mailing list by sending e-mail with the word **Subscribe** in the message to **java-interest-request@java.sun.com**.

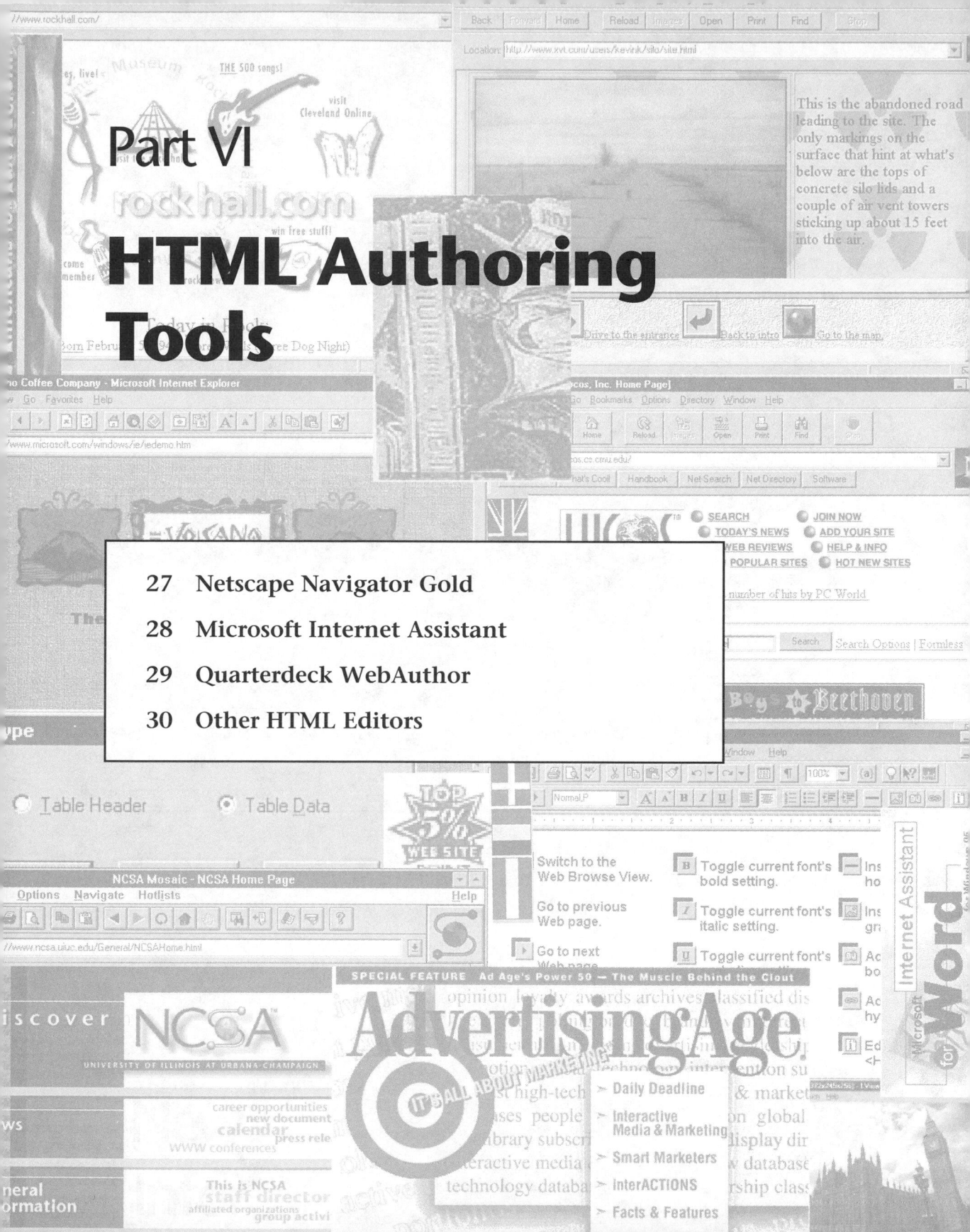

Part VI

HTML Authoring Tools

## CHAPTER 27

Netscape Navigator Gold

Most people surfing the Web typically do so with Netscape Navigator. The people who make this program, Netscape Communications, have created a souped-up version of their browser. That program, known as Netscape Navigator Gold 2.0, is significantly different from the regular browser in that it includes an HTML editor. This program, like the new e-mail and Usenet news programs, makes Netscape the front-runner among Web programs. No other company offers a more complete package to accessing the Web, and various Internet resources, than Netscape. Instead of needing an e-mail program, a newsreader, a Web browser, and an HTML editor, Netscape Gold has it all.

In this chapter, you learn about the following:

- What Netscape Gold can do
- Getting around Netscape Gold
- Putting text in your Web page with Netscape Gold
- Adding graphics in Netscape Gold
- Putting links in your Web page using Netscape Gold
- How to define your HTML Documents
- How to install Netscape Gold

What Is Netscape Gold?

Because Netscape Gold is a different program from the regular browser, you're going to have to decide if it's worth it. For general Web browsing, there's really no reason to get Netscape Gold. Netscape Navigator does a magnificent job. However, for people who want to create their own Web pages, Netscape Gold is well worth investigating.

The most obvious difference in using Netscape Gold is its built-in HTML editor. It's a stand-alone WYSIWYG (**W**hat **Y**ou **S**ee **I**s **W**hat **Y**ou **G**et) editor, and unlike others of its kind, it's *fast*. Netscape Editor currently provides support for HTML 2.0 tags and some HTML 3.0 tags. No doubt Netscape plans to add more features in the near future to this powerful HTML editor.

> **Note**
>
> Netscape Gold currently doesn't allow you to create forms. However, if you load an existing Web page with a form, it'll work fine.

Installing and Running Netscape Gold

Netscape Gold is currently in wide release, and anybody can get a copy of it. Simply FTP to any Netscape computer, go to the /2.0gold directory, and download the file g32e20.exe. This is a self-extracting archive that's about 3.4 megabytes in size. Once it's on your system, use Windows 95 to find the file you just received. Double-click the icon, and you'll be asked if you want to install Netscape Gold. Click OK, and you'll be prompted for the directory where you want it installed. After it's done copying all the files, you can go ahead and use Netscape Gold.

When you first start up Netscape Gold, you'll notice that the Netscape logo is now in gold. This is in indication of the things that are different with Netscape Gold. It's basically the same Web browser you know and love, but it has been improved. It's still fully integrated with the other Netscape programs, such as Netscape Mail and Netscape News. The most notable change to the Web browser that you'll see is the addition of a new button on the toolbar (see fig. 27.1). The Edit button will invoke a new session of Netscape Editor. You can also start the editor by selecting File, Edit Document.

Fig. 27.1
Netscape Navigator Gold 2.0 enables you to edit HTML documents by clicking the Edit button.

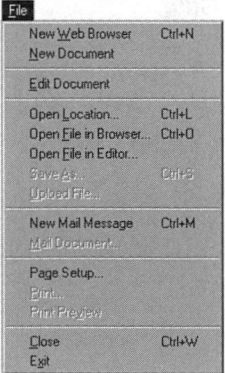

Using Netscape Gold

Netscape Editor looks a lot like the Netscape browser except that it's really an HTML editor (see fig. 27.2). It sports three new toolbars that contain the most commonly accessed HTML tags. Also, because it's WYSIWYG, HTML authoring will be more approachable for those new to the language. Netscape Editor will give the author a good idea of what the Web page will look like. You won't have to know the different HTML tags; you can see how the different tags behave.

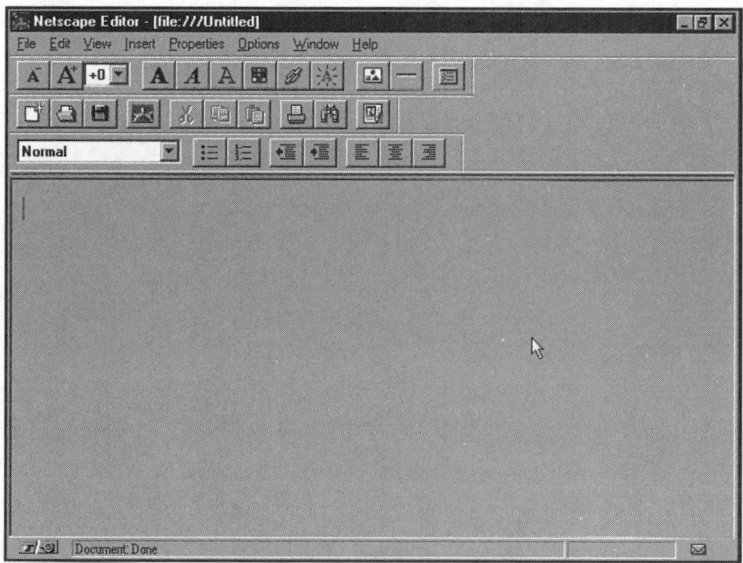

Fig. 27.2
Netscape Editor is like other Netscape applications, except you can modify HTML documents.

Moving Around Netscape Editor

Because it's WYSIWYG, the HTML portion of Netscape Gold makes maneuvering through an HTML document easy. Anybody who's ever used a text editor or word processor will find Netscape Editor very easy to work with. The arrow keys move the cursor in the corresponding directions. You can also go to the next or previous screen of your Web page with the Page Up and Page Down keys, respectively.

The Home key takes you to the beginning of the line, while the End key takes you to the end. Holding down Control while pressing the Home key will take you to the very top of the document. If you hold down Control and press the End key, you'll be taken to the very bottom of the document. You can also use the mouse to move the cursor to a certain point in your Web page.

Navigating Through Netscape Windows

You can only start up Netscape Editor through Netscape Navigator. It is currently not possible to edit an HTML document from either the e-mail or Usenet reading programs of Netscape. No doubt this is just a slight oversight on Netscape's part that will be corrected soon.

If you've already started the HTML editor, you can jump into it from any other Netscape program. To accomplish this, simply click Window, and you'll be presented with a list of Netscape windows (see fig. 27.3). Find the entry that has the title of your HTML document and click it. You'll find yourself in Netscape Editor with the appropriate HTML document. If the Web page you're working on doesn't have a title, you'll see Untitled in the list.

Fig. 27.3

You can easily switch to Netscape Editor by choosing it in the Window menu.

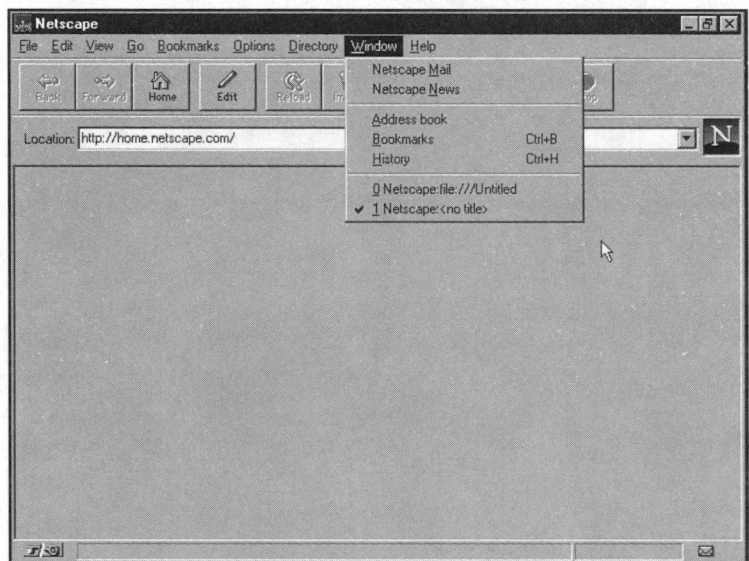

Creating a Web Page with Netscape Gold

Because Web pages are made up of many elements—text, images, and lists—Netscape Gold must provide for all of these. Fortunately, the basic HTML tags are admirably supported by Netscape Editor. Currently, the most commonly used HTML tags are easily accessible through the three toolbars. The less common elements can be found under the menu headings of the editor.

Currently, there is no way of putting in advanced HTML elements such as forms, tables, and frames. No doubt that Netscape has plans on incorporating these elements into future releases of Netscape Gold.

> **Caution**
>
> Be careful when you click the Open File to Edit button in Netscape Editor. After you've specified the Web page to load, a new Netscape Editor session will be started.

> **Tip**
>
> You can test any Web page you have by first loading it into Netscape Editor. Next, just click the Open Browser button. Netscape Navigator will start up and automatically load in the HTML document.

Text and Fonts

Probably the most common element you'll find in Web pages is descriptive text. Whether it's text that describes what's on the Web site or text that describes a link, a Web page is mostly text. You can easily add text to any HTML document you're working on by simply typing. The characters you type will appear right where your cursor is located.

You can easily specify the style of element type that you want the text to have by selecting the Paragraph Style drop-down list. This box brings down a list of available tags that you can use. The different headings are intended for the Web author's use as, well, headings. The smaller the heading number, the larger the heading will appear. If you've selected a block of text when you select the drop-down list, the highlighted text will be changed. If, however, no text has been highlighted, the new paragraph style will take affect when you start typing.

A feature you'll see in some of the more advanced Web pages is the use of different font sizes. This is also easily accomplished by using the Font Size drop-down list. This controls how much larger or smaller the current font will be in relation to its default size. By selecting some text and changing the font size, you'll make the text that much bigger or smaller. Netscape Editor allows for seven different font sizes, –2, –1, 0 (the default size), and +1 through +4. You can step through this list of font sizes with the Increase Font Size and Decrease Font Size buttons.

A new feature of HTML, introduced by Netscape, is the capability to specify font colors. Not surprisingly, the HTML editor built into Netscape Gold also provides support for this. You can change the color of the text you're typing by choosing Properties, Font Color. You'll be presented with the dialog box shown in figure 27.4, where you simply pick the color you want for the text.

After you've picked the font color, any text that you type will appear in the selected color. If you've highlighted some text when you chose the font color option, the selected text will change. The Color dialog box is also accessible by clicking the Font Color button.

Fig. 27.4
Pick the color you want to use, or define your own.

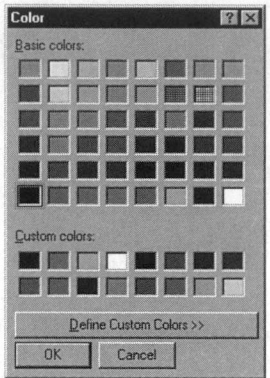

Putting Graphics into Your Documents

Another popular element you'll find in many Web pages is some sort of image. Typically, the graphic is a picture of the Web author, a product being advertised, or a company logo. Suppose you wanted to add an image to your Web page. All you have to do is position your cursor where you want the graphic to appear at (see fig. 27.5). You can easily insert a graphic into your Web page with Netscape Editor by clicking the Insert Image button. You'll be presented with a dialog box with a lot of parameters that enable you to control the image (see fig. 27.6). Type the full path of the image you want to use in the Image File Name field. If you're not sure where the graphic is located, simply click the Browse button. You can also access the Insert Image dialog box by selecting Insert, Image.

Once you've specified the graphic you want to use, be sure to type some descriptive text in the Text field (see fig. 27.7). This text is what will be seen by people visiting your Web page with a non-graphical browser. Some people with graphical browsers also turn off the capability to see images because they have a slow connection to the Net. Because there are a lot of people who fall into both of those categories, you really should type *something* into the Text field.

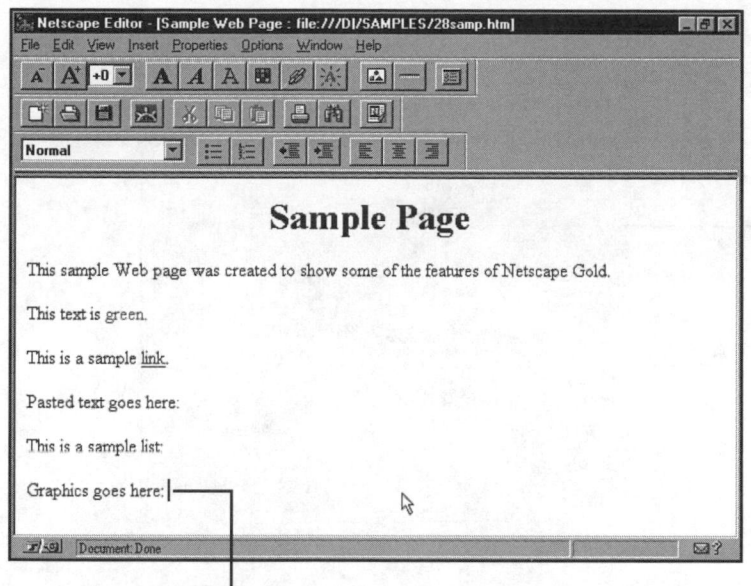

Fig. 27.5
Let's spice up this
Web page with a
picture.

We want to put a picture here

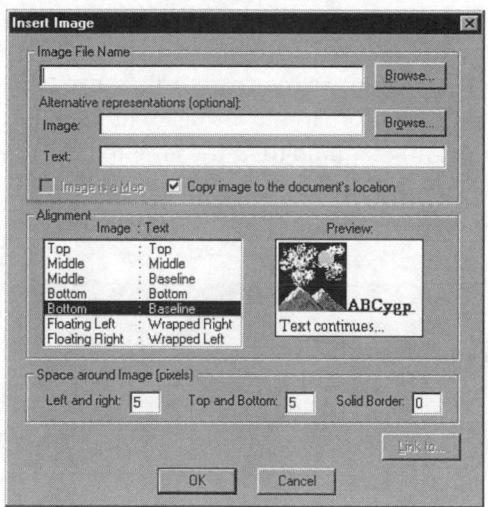

Fig. 27.6
Putting a picture
into your Web
page is a simple
matter of typing
its file name.

When you insert a graphic, you can also determine how text will behave
around it. By default, the text's baseline is aligned with the bottom of the
image. You can change this behavior by selecting any of the options in the
Alignment section. As you click an option, you'll see how the text will wrap
in relation to the image in the Preview area.

VI

HTML Authoring Tools

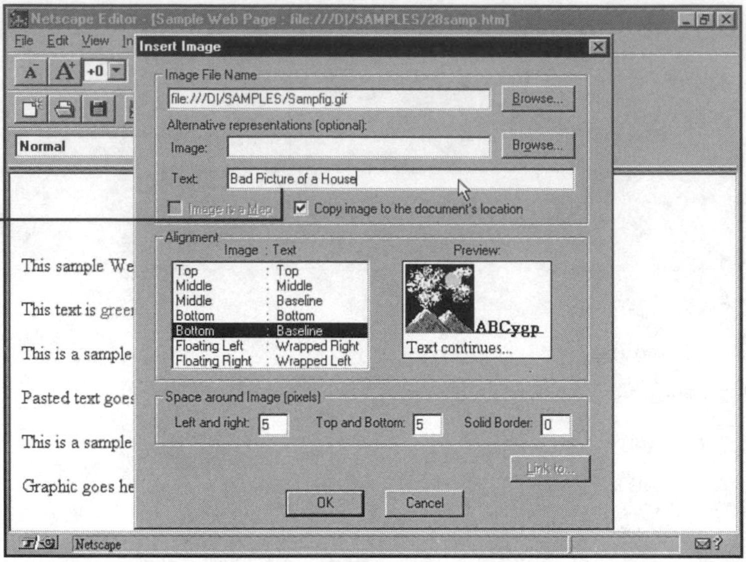

Fig. 27.7
Whenever possible, try to describe the picture you're using.

Type in something for people who'll be seeing your page with a text browser

Creating Links

The underlying component of the World Wide Web is the hyperlink. This enables you to take people who are visiting your site to other places of interest. To make some existing text into a hypertext link, simply highlight the text and click the Make Link button. In the dialog box that appears, simply type the URL you want the link to jump to in the Link to field (see fig. 27.8). If you click the Make Link button without highlighting any text, you can enter your desired text in the Type text to display for new link field (see fig. 27.9).

Fig. 27.8
When you make existing text into a hypertext link, the highlighted text will be filled in for you.

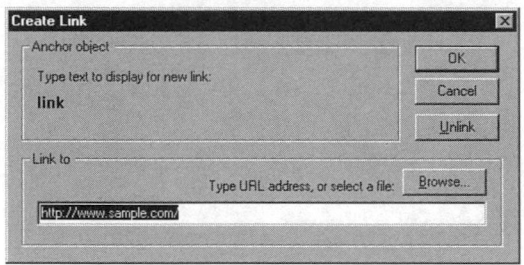

Creating a hyperlink for an image is similar to putting in a hyperlink for text. Simply click anywhere in the image and then click the Make Link button. As with creating a hypertext link, just type the URL for the document you want that image to go to. You'll notice that the Anchor Object field tells you the path of the graphic you've selected.

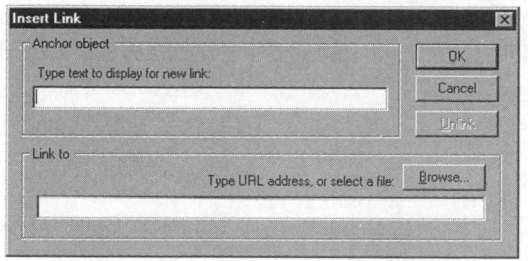

Fig. 27.9
Simply type the URL, or the path to a local file, that you want to link to.

You can also create a combined graphical and textual hyperlink very easily with Netscape Editor. To do this, highlight the text and the image you want to go to the same URL. Next, click the Make Link button to bring up the Make Link dialog box. Simply type the URL for the HTML document you want the graphic and text to jump to in the Link to field. Even though the Anchor Object doesn't show the image's file name, it'll still get the link.

Making a List

There will be times as you're creating your Web page when you'll need to make a list: either a list of instructions or a list for showing a large number of items in an orderly fashion. Whatever the case may be, you'll need to use the HTML list element. The two most common list types are the bulleted list and the numbered list. You can access more list types by clicking Properties Paragraph and Lists (see fig. 27.10).

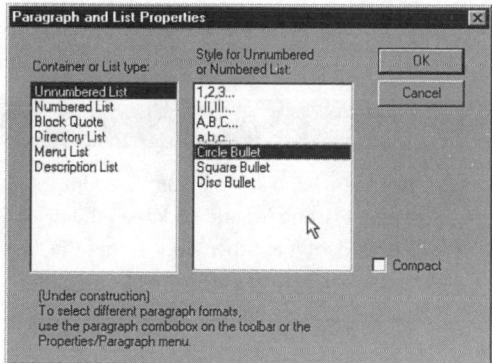

Fig. 27.10
You can create something other than numbered and bulleted lists with this dialog box.

VI

HTML Authoring Tools

You can create a list by clicking either the Bulleted List button or the Numbered List button and then typing in the elements. When you press one of the list buttons, you will be in "list mode" (see fig. 27.11); that is, whatever you type in will be part of the list. A list prefix will appear and you can just enter one element. When you're done with that list entry, press return, and a list prefix will appear on the next line (see fig. 27.12). If you're creating a bulleted list, a bullet will appear. If you're creating a numbered list, the next number in the sequence will appear. Keep doing this until you've typed all the elements for your list. After you've typed in the last element in your list, press Enter one last time. Now click on the list button that you used to start this list, this will take you out of "list mode" (see fig. 27.13). If you're creating a bulleted list, click the Bulleted List button again. If you've created a numbered list, just click the Numbered List button.

Fig. 27.11

When you press one of the list buttons, you'll go into list mode.

You have two ways of telling if you're in list mode

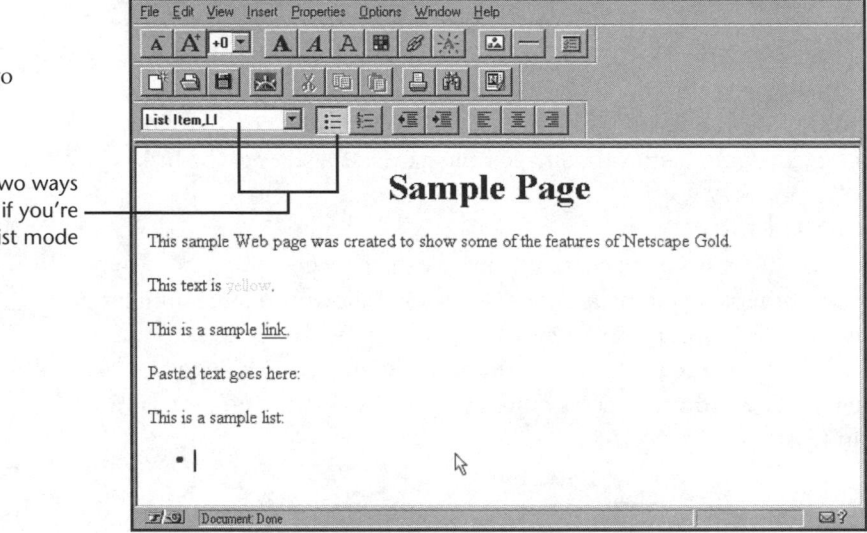

> **Caution**
>
> When you're trying to convert a bulleted list to a numbered list, or vice versa, be careful. When you highlight the existing list and click the other list button. This will convert the list, but it will also indent it another level. To get the list back to the proper indentation level, simply click the Remove Indent.

If you have already typed in a list without the list element, don't worry. Converting an existing list into an HTML list is also easily accomplished. Highlight the text in your Web page that you want to make into a list, and click the appropriate list button. Netscape will automatically enter list mode, update the elements to the proper list type, and then exit list mode.

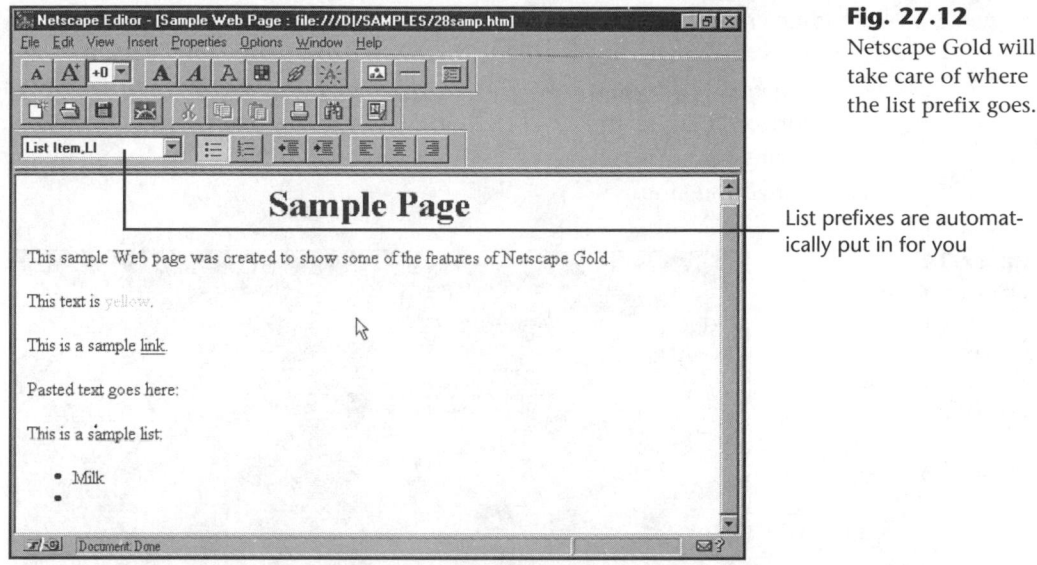

Fig. 27.12
Netscape Gold will take care of where the list prefix goes.

List prefixes are automatically put in for you

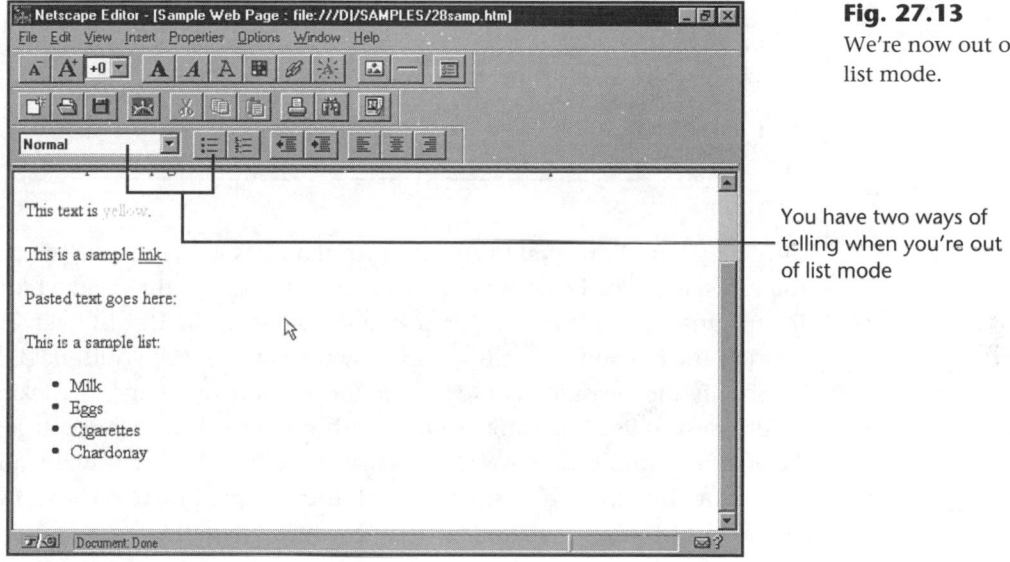

Fig. 27.13
We're now out of list mode.

You have two ways of telling when you're out of list mode

VI

HTML Authoring Tools

Horizontal Rules

You can also easily create a horizontal rule, or a horizontal line, in your Web page. Position your cursor where you want the line to appear. Next, click the Insert Horiz. Line and a line will be created where your cursor is. If the cursor is on a line with some text, it'll put the horizontal rule on the next line. The line created will have a height of 2 pixels and have a 3-D appearance. If you want to change this, simply select the horizontal rule, and click the Object Properties button. This will bring up a dialog box that lets you modify the horizontal line's attributes (see fig. 27.14). You can also access this dialog box by selecting the menu heading Properties, followed by the menu item Horizontal Line.

Fig. 27.14
You can't create a horizontal rule with certain specifications; you have to create a generic one first, then modify it with this dialog box.

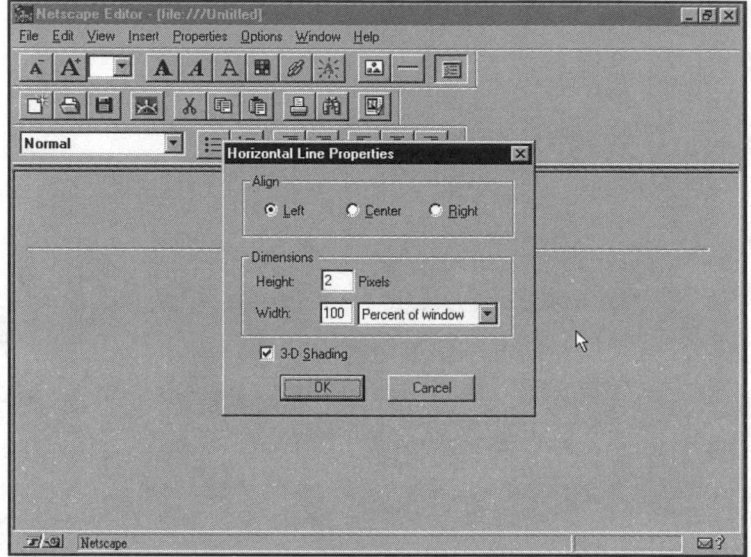

The dialog box allows you to create horizontal rules with different effects. You can specify the horizontal rule's alignment with the three radio buttons. The height of the line is configured with the value in the Height field. The width of the horizontal line is specified by the value in the Width field. You can specify the measurement to be used for the horizontal line by clicking the drop-down list. You can have the width value be either a percentage of the browser's window, or exactly how many pixels wide. The way the horizontal line will look can be specified with the 3-D Shading checkbox. If you disable the 3-D effect, the horizontal rule will be one solid line.

Modifying HTML Elements

What most WYSIWYG HTML editors do in the case of many elements is to treat the elements as objects. That is, certain HTML elements are treated as separate entities. You can't affect part of the element, you have to make changes to the whole thing. Netscape Gold's built-in HTML editor is different from similar editors in that it doesn't do this. Netscape Gold allows you to easily affect both the element itself, as well as its attributes. You don't need to fumble around with one function that allows you to modify all aspects of the element. You can simply modify whichever aspect you want, independently of all other aspects.

Changing Links

Because Netscape Editor lets you change the attributes of HTML elements, without looking at the whole thing, you can easily change hypertext links. Other WYSIWYG editors require you to select the link and use buttons to modify a link. Netscape Gold doesn't need that: simply modify the visible text of the hypertext link. That is, put your cursor somewhere in the middle of the hypertext link, and add or remove text as you see fit. As long as there's some text from the original hypertext link, you don't need to worry about losing the destination URL.

You can also modify the destination URL for a particular link without needing to highlight the entire link. For images that have an associated link, click somewhere in the image and then click the Make Link button. Simply modify the destination URL listed under the Link To field in the dialog box that appears. Modifying hypertext links is even easier: just put the cursor somewhere in the middle of the visible text (see fig. 27.15), and click the Make Link button. Even though you won't see the visible text for the link, you'll be able to change the destination URL for the entire link (see fig. 27.16).

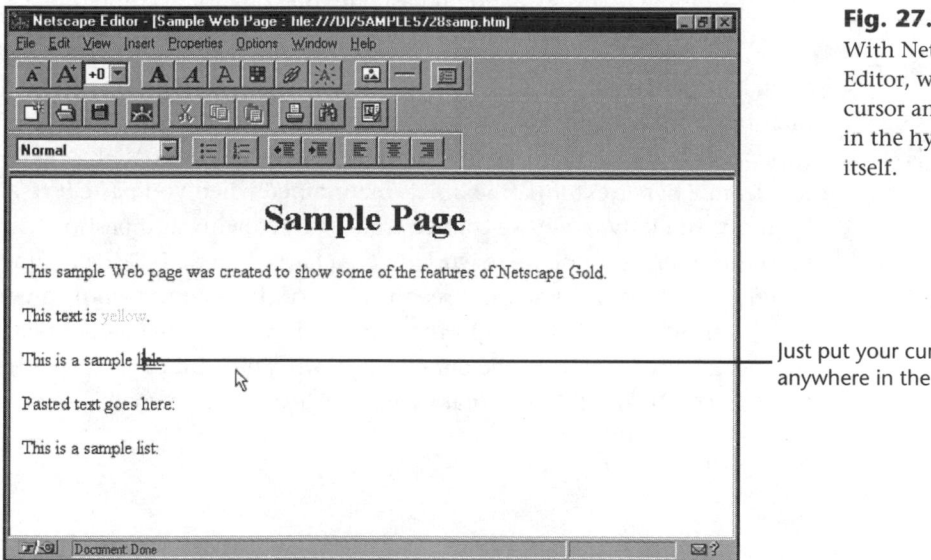

Fig. 27.15
With Netscape Editor, we put our cursor anywhere in the hyperlink itself.

Just put your cursor anywhere in the link

Fig. 27.16
Clicking the Make
Link button will
let us change the
destination URL
without affecting
the visible text.

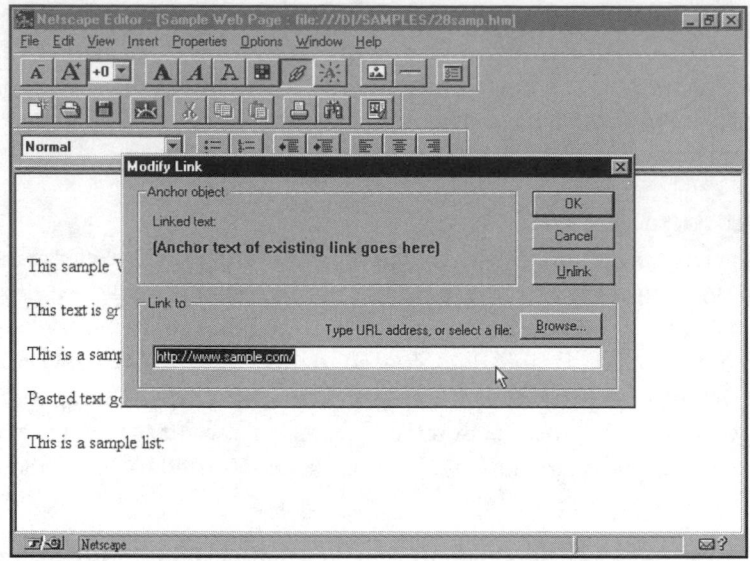

Cut, Copy, and Paste

So Netscape Editor has built-in cut, copy, and paste facility? So what? This is
an impressive feature with Netscape because it treats text as more than just
text. This makes the cut, copy, and paste features much more powerful than
with other HTML editors. In other editors, whenever you cut, copy, or paste
text, just the visible text is carried over, so that if you cut out a hypertext
link, the visible text is what you'll paste. If you copy some colored text, the
pasted text won't be colored.

With Netscape Gold, the text that you've cut or copied into the Clipboard
maintains its attributes. What this means is that any text you place into the
clipboard will be pasted with the same features. If you've copied some visible
text from a hypertext link, the link is maintained when you paste it to a new
location. Similarly, if you've colored some text, copying and pasting it will
keep the color. Suppose we're working on a fairly generic HTML document
(see fig. 27.17). While you can't see the color of the text, the word "green"
is in green. We simply highlight the "green" portion of the colored text
(see fig. 27.18). Now we move our cursor down a bit, and paste somewhere
(see fig. 27.19). You'll notice that the pasted text is still in green.

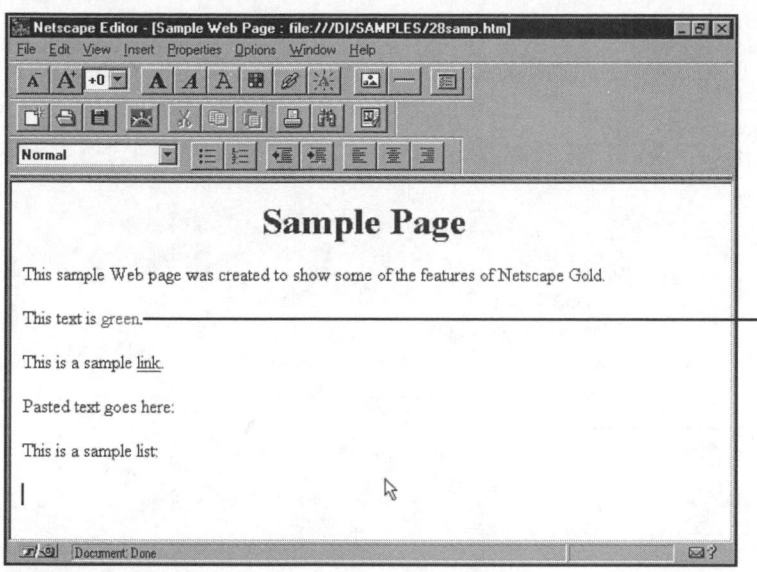

Fig. 27.17
A fairly generic
Web page that
we're updating and
we want to keep
part of the green
text.

We want to copy some
of this text as well as its
color

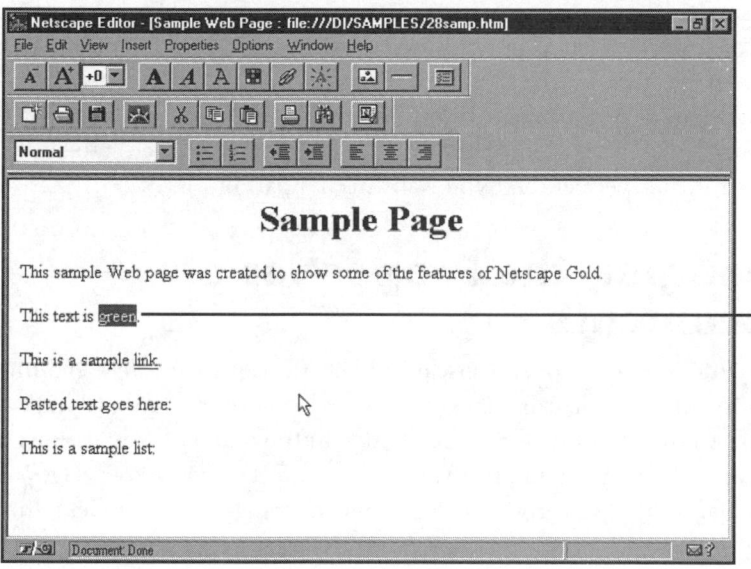

Fig. 27.18
Just select the
portion of the text
that you want to
use.

We highlight the text
we want to copy

Fig. 27.19
The pasted text not only keeps its contents, but its colored attribute as well.

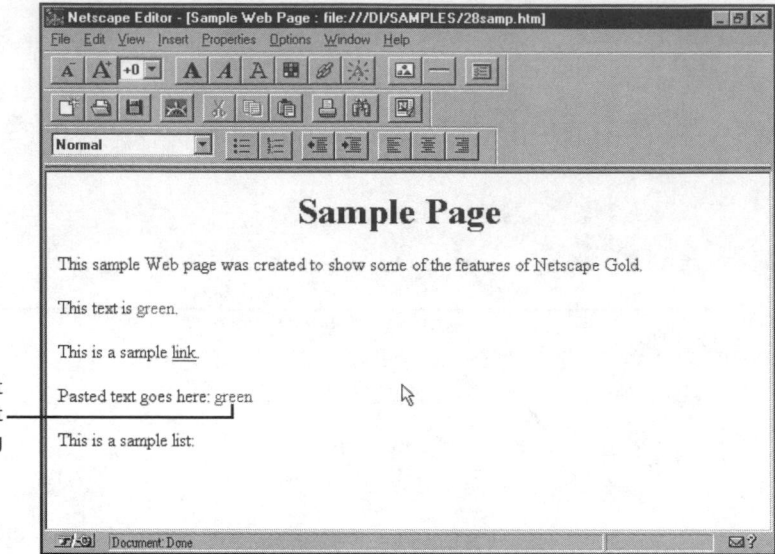

We paste the copied text where we want to use part of its text and coloring

This smarter cut, copy, and paste facility of Netscape Gold is great for software companies' Web pages. This makes it easier for you to repeat certain links, such as to your FTP site. Also, when color is used to highlight some text, you can take advantage of this new capability. Simply copy the text that you want to use the color for and paste it in a new area; then, replace the old text with whatever new text you want in that part of the Web page.

Changing the Properties of Documents

A very nice capability of all Netscape applications is their level of configurability. That is, you can change the behavior of the various Netscape programs. All the things that you can change in the different applications make Netscape a better program. Instead of being forced to view Web pages in a particular font or background color, you can change it. Fortunately, this tradition continues with Netscape Gold's HTML editor.

Defining Your Current HTML Document

Probably the first thing you'll want to do when creating your Web page is give it a title. You can easily accomplish this by selecting Properties, Document. This will bring up a dialog box that enables you to specify various pieces of information about your HTML document. In the Document Information tab (see fig. 27.20), you can indicate the title of the document by typing it in the Title field. You can also put your name in the Author field.

Currently, the Netscape System Variables are not accessible. In the future this region will allow for the creation and editing of special Netscape extensions. The User Variables field is used for people who want to specify META elements. To create a META element, click an existing variable, and click the New button. To edit an existing variable, just highlight the META variable, and the variable name and value will appear at the bottom. Change the value to whatever you want, and click the Set button. To delete a META variable, select it, and click the Delete button.

▶ See Chapter 5 for information on what META elements are and how they're used.

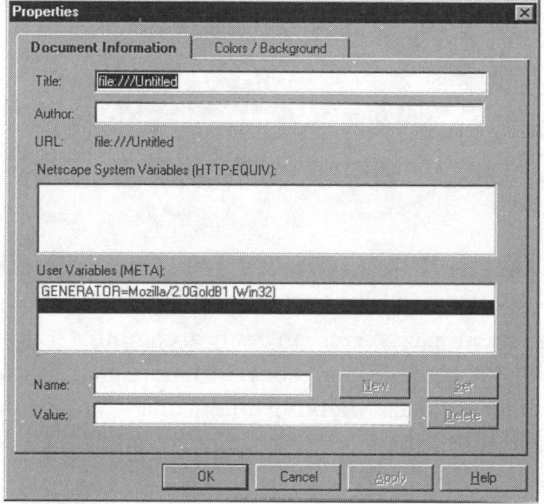

Fig. 27.20
You can specify different attributes for the current HTML document you're editing.

The Colors/Background tab enables you to define the general look and feel of your Web page (see fig. 27.21). By default the current HTML document will use the browser's colors. You can, of course, define your own color scheme by clicking Use Custom Colors. This will enable you to change the different colors that appear on your HTML document. You can modify the colors for Normal Text, Link Text, Active Link Text, and Followed Link Text. Simply click the appropriate button, and you'll be presented with a color palette. Select the new color you want to use, and click OK. You'll see an example of what the color will look like next to the button.

The Background section enables you to define a background color or image. Click Choose Color to pick the color you want as the background. An image tiled in the background is also possible by typing the full path to the image in the Image File field. If you're not sure where the graphic is located, click the Browse button to help you find it. When you're satisfied with your configuration, click the Apply button, followed by the Close button.

VI

HTML Authoring Tools

Fig. 27.21
Use this dialog box to change the general appearance of the current HTML document.

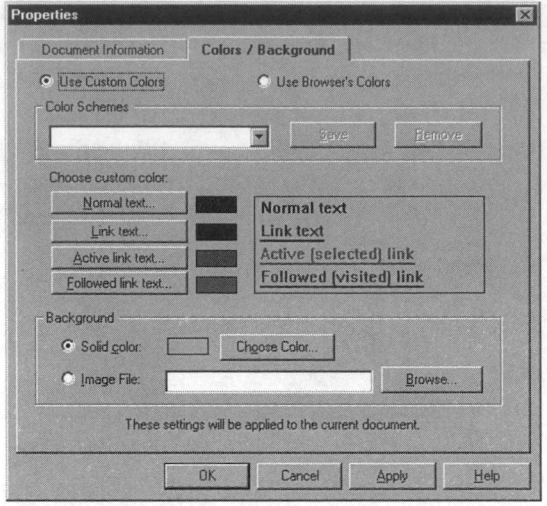

Specifying Default Attributes for Your Documents

If you're in charge of an entire Web site, you'll want to have a consistent look and feel to each of your pages. You can easily accomplish most of this by specifying the default attributes for your HTML document. Simply select Options, Editor Preferences. This will bring up the dialog box shown in figure 27.22, which is similar to the one that enables you to define document-specific attributes.

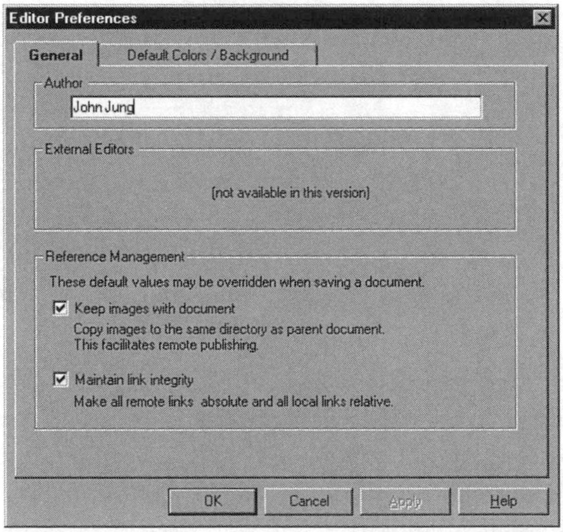

Fig. 27.22
You can make all the HTML documents you create have a standard look and feel.

The Default Colors/Background tab enables you to control the colors and images for all your pages. This is done by using the same dialog box you used to control the look of the current document (see fig. 27.8). The only difference is that this time you'll be modifying all future HTML documents. In the current version of Netscape Gold, the General tab is very limited. You can type your name in the Author field and decide how links and images are to be stored in the HTML document.

Note

If you already have an HTML document open, changing the default colors will not affect it. To change the colors or background for the current HTML document, see "Defining Your Current HTML Document," earlier in this chapter.

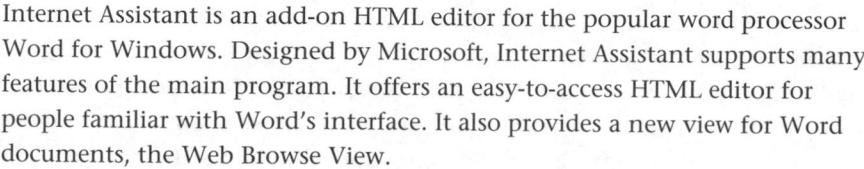

## CHAPTER 28

Microsoft Internet Assistant

Internet Assistant is an add-on HTML editor for the popular word processor Word for Windows. Designed by Microsoft, Internet Assistant supports many features of the main program. It offers an easy-to-access HTML editor for people familiar with Word's interface. It also provides a new view for Word documents, the Web Browse View.

In this chapter, you learn about the following:

- Different versions of Internet Assistant
- Installing Internet Assistant
- How to get around Internet Assistant
- Special features of Internet Assistant
- The Web Browse View

Getting Internet Assistant

Internet Assistant is currently available in two versions 1.0z and 2.0z. Both are directly available for download from Microsoft's home page (**http://www.microsoft.com**). Version 1.0 is the first release of Internet Assistant that has some useful HTML functionality. The 2.0 version adds much more functionality and more HTML tags support.

Internet Assistant 1.0

The first limitation of Internet Assistant 1.0 is that it works only on the English, German, and French versions of Word for Windows 6.0a and 6.0c. All other versions of Word do not work properly with version 1.0 of Internet Assistant. I do not want to imply that the first version is limited in scope; it's still a useful product. The only noticeable limitation that veteran Web authors may notice is that it supports only HTML Level 2. Netscape's and Microsoft's extensions, as well as HTML Level 3, are not supported.

Internet Assistant 2.0

Like any good product, Internet Assistant 2.0 is an improvement on its pre-decessor. This new version provides support for commonly used extensions, Microsoft's Internet Explorer's extensions, as well as strict HTML Level 2 support. Internet Explorer is Microsoft's own Web browser; along with supporting many extensions to HTML Level 2, it defines its own. This version runs only on Word for Windows 95 and Word for NT in English, Italian, German, and French.

Installing Internet Assistant

On the CD

Installing Internet Assistant on your computer is very easy. Just point your favorite browser to **http://www.microsoft.com/msoffice/freestuf/ msword/download/ia/ia95/default.htm**. This site gives a brief overview of Internet Assistant, and lets you download it. Internet Assistant requires four megabytes of disk space and Word for Windows 95. After you download the self-extracting executable, simply double-click it. You are then prompted with Microsoft's installation program, which basically lets you choose whether or not to install Internet Assistant.

Using Internet Assistant

Internet Assistant is a seamless integration of providing HTML support for an exceptional word processor. You don't need to be in a distinct view, as with other add-ons, to use the HTML functionality. This capability makes for a better overall application because it doesn't get in the way of restricting your work. Word with Internet Assistant does have a new view, HTML Source, but you don't need to be in this view to work with HTML documents. You simply start up Word, and you can create your home page, if you want. If you don't, you won't notice a difference because Internet Assistant is so transparent. Internet Assistant basically just adds a Web browser to Word and a new file format in which you can save your documents.

HTML View

Word works in distinct "views," in that some options are only available in a particular view. One of the new views that Internet Assistant gives you is the HTML View. What HTML View offers you is better and easier access to the HTML tools of Internet Assistant. The HTML view merely adds or modifies toolbars and changes the menus (see fig. 28.1). You can only get into this mode by loading in an HTML file with Word. The toolbars in this view give you shortcuts to the most commonly accessed HTML features. A few things you can do only in HTML view, such as give the title of your home page, but by and large, most of the things you can do in HTML view can be done outside of it as well.

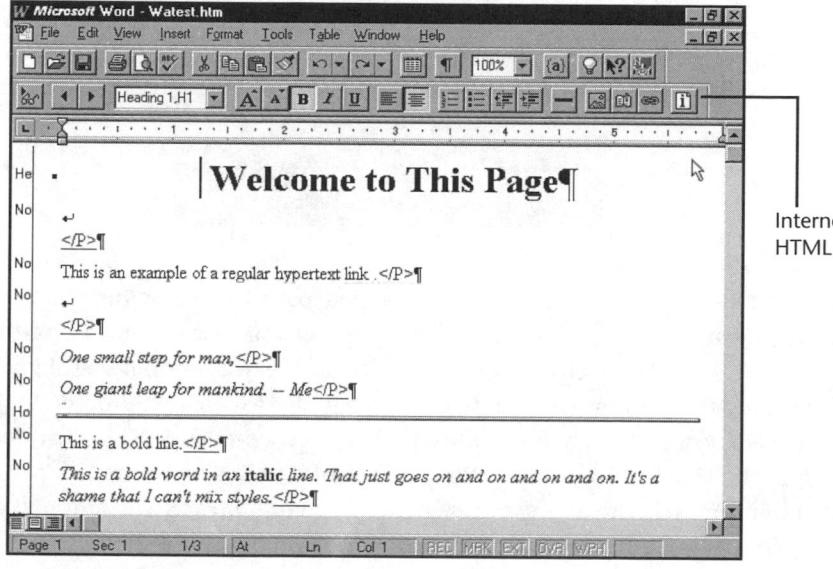

Fig. 28.1
Internet Assistant's HTML view offers a small, new toolbar.

Internet Assistant's HTML toolbar

Managing Text

Because Internet Assistant isn't always in use with Word, you manage text through Word. That is, you use Word like you always do—same keystrokes, same performance, same everything. There is no difference between the way Internet Assistant deals with text and the way Word deals with text. The only problem comes when you're dealing with links of any sort. Whenever you select a link, the whole link becomes highlighted, and you can't easily modify it.

Even in HTML view mode, the text manipulation is the same as using Word by itself. You will notice, however, that you don't have font size control, but that's because HTML doesn't recognize fonts and point sizes. You can change the font size by using the Increase Font Size and Decrease Font size buttons.

Adding Graphics

You can easily weave any GIF or JPEG file into your home page by using Internet Assistant. Simply choose Insert, Picture. If you're not in HTML view, you are then presented with Word's file selector dialog box. Simply locate the graphic you want to insert, and Internet Assistant makes sure that it becomes part of the HTML document. If you're in HTML view, however, you are presented with Internet Assistant's Picture dialog box (see fig. 28.2).

Fig. 28.2
If you want to add
any sort of graphic
to your home
page, you'll have
to use this dialog
box.

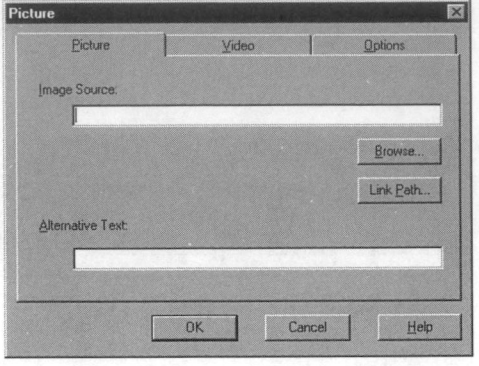

◄ See chapter
10, "Adding
Graphics to
Your Home
Page," p. 191,
for information
on what scaling
an image
will do.

In the Image Source field, type the complete path to the graphic you want to
use. In the Alternative Text field, type some sort of descriptive text for the
picture. You can specify how the text around the image should be aligned by
clicking the Options tab and using the Alignment with Text drop-down list.
If you know the height and width of the image, enter these specifications
into the Height and Width fields. If you want to scale an image to a particular
resolution, you can also use these fields. The Web browser will automatically
scale the image to your specified size.

> **Tip**
>
> If you're not sure about the exact path to the image, use the Browse button. Clicking
> this button opens Word's file selection dialog box in which you can locate the
> graphic.

Working with Links

While you're designing your home page, you may need to put in a link. You
can easily do so by choosing Insert, Hyperlink. The Hyperlink dialog box
pops up (see fig. 28.3), and if you've highlighted some text, it appears in
the Text to Display field. If you didn't highlight anything, that field will be
empty, and you can put in whatever visible text you want. In the File or URL
field, type the name of the URL or the absolute path for the local file. If
you're in the HTML view, you can easily access the Hyperlink dialog box by
clicking the Hyperlink button.

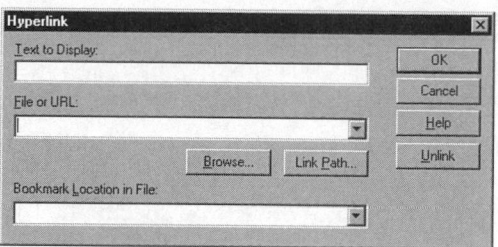

Fig. 28.3
The Hyperlink
dialog box gives
you an easy
interface to
create a link.

Because the Hyperlink dialog box has no provision for creating a link associated to an image, what do you do? You simply can't create a new graphical link with Internet Assistant; you must have a graphic in place first. After you have a graphic, you can create the link.

To create a graphical link, follow these steps:

1. Determine where you want the graphical link, and put the image at that location.

2. Highlight the picture.

3. Choose the menu heading Insert, followed by the menu item Hyperlink to open the Hyperlink dialog box. Notice that the Text to Display field is disabled, for obvious reasons.

4. Type the URL to which you want to link the graphic.

◀ See the earlier
section, "Adding Graphics,"
p. 665, on how
to add an image
to your home
page.

Similarly, if you want to create a text and graphic link, put the graphic where you want in relation to the text. Next, highlight both the text and the graphic that you want to make into a link. Finally, open the Hyperlink dialog box to specify the URL to which you want to point.

For most HTML editors that try to show you what the home page will look like beforehand, links are always tricky for programmers. You can't treat them as individual HTML tags, to give the user flexibility to change the visible text. You must treat the links as an entire entity all its own and give some means of altering it. The same is true with Internet Assistant.

To alter a hyperlink, simply select the link, and open the Hyperlink dialog box again. The values for the particular fields will already be filled in, so simply change them to suit your needs.

To remove a hyperlink associated with some text, simply highlight the text, open the Hyperlink dialog box, and click the Unlink button.

Jumps and Destinations

As with any other good HTML editor, internal links and the ability to jump to them are supported. An *internal link* is one in which a certain location in an HTML document is specified as a destination point. This destination must have a specific name attached to it so that URLs can refer to it. Other Web pages can jump into that specific point if you specify the URL for the Web page and append a # and then the destination name. When jumped to, the line where the destination is specified is displayed at the top of the browser. With Internet Assistant, Word's bookmarking feature is the main point of working with internal jumps.

Defining a Destination

You can easily create a destination by putting your cursor where you want the destination to be. Next, choose Edit, Bookmark, or if you're in HTML view, click the Bookmark icon. The Bookmark dialog box then appears with a list of existing bookmarks (see fig. 28.4). Under the Bookmark Name text box, type the name you want to give the internal link, and then click the Add button.

Fig. 28.4
Use Word's bookmarking features to help you create internal jumps.

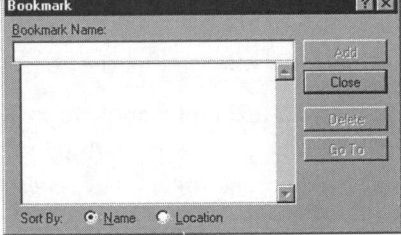

If you want to remove a bookmark, simply open the Bookmark dialog box, select the bookmark to be removed, and click the Delete button.

> **Note**
>
> The bookmarks created by Word are invisible. If you're not sure where a bookmark goes, open the Bookmark dialog box, select the bookmark, and click the Go To button.

Going to a Destination

After a while, you'll have defined a few bookmarks that you want to get to. Internet Assistant only lets you jump to a destination point within the same

Web page. You can do this with the help of Word's built-in bookmark facility. When you want to create an internal jump, open the Hyperlink dialog box. Next, use the Bookmark Location File drop-down list to select the destination point you want.

Advanced HTML Tags

Internet Assistant also offers good support for the more advanced HTML tags. You can easily create forms, tables, and lists by using the menus or toolbars. You don't have to be in HTML view to create tables, lists, or forms. Some of the more advanced features of forms are available only in HTML view. But considering that you'll probably have saved your HTML document by this point, this isn't too unreasonable. (If you haven't, then save your file as an HTML file, and get into HTML view.)

Tables

You go about creating tables in Internet Assistant the same way you do in Word. Put your cursor somewhere in the document, and choose Table, Insert Table. You then are prompted with Word's own Table Creation dialog box. Indicate how many rows and columns you want as well as the width of the columns. Word creates the empty table cells for you to fill in. Then type in the data for each cell in the table. If you have an existing set of data you want to put into a table, Internet Assistant also lets you use it. Highlight the values you want to put into a table, and choose Table, Convert Text to Table.

You can specify which cells are the table headings and which ones are the data cells. Simply highlight the cells for which you want to define the attributes, and choose Table, Cell Type. The Cell Type dialog box then appears (see fig. 28.5). You can also add a caption to the table by highlighting the table, selecting the Table menu heading, and then choosing the Caption menu item. Simply type in the text you want to appear as the caption of the table. You can also specify where you want the caption to appear by clicking the appropriate button.

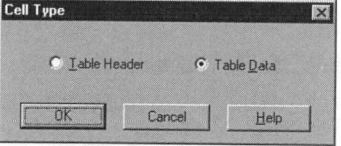

Fig. 28.5

Internet Assistant lets you define which cells are headings and which are data.

Creating Forms

You can create forms only when you're in HTML view, and you can get in that view only by loading in an HTML file. You can't load in a Word document and simply go into HTML view. To create some common forms quickly, bring in the Form toolbar (see fig. 28.6). This is done by selecting the <u>V</u>iew menu heading, followed by the <u>T</u>oolbars menu item. You'll be presented with a dialog box which lists the available toolbars. Simply click the "Forms" entry. With this toolbar, unlike other HTML editors, you can't create a group of check boxes. The icons on the toolbar create only one button, check box, text form, whatever.

Fig. 28.6
The Form toolbar lets you quickly create common form fields.

The Form toolbar

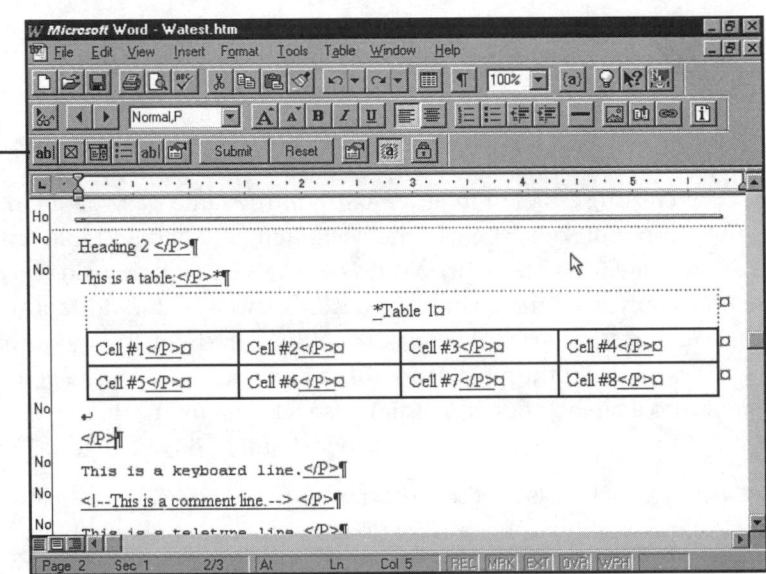

You can create a form control field by putting your cursor where you want the control field to appear. Then click the button on the Forms toolbar, that represents the form control field you want to create. If you don't want to use the toolbar, just choose <u>I</u>nsert, For<u>m</u> Field. The Form Field dialog box then appears (see fig. 28.7).

Fig. 28.7
You can use this dialog box, instead of the Form toolbar, to create forms.

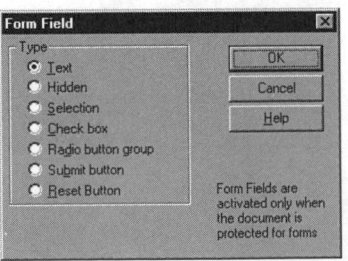

Depending on the type of form control field you want to create, you are prompted for different information. Check boxes are available by clicking the Check Box Form Field button, second from the left on the Forms toolbar. This will bring up a dialog box, where you are prompted for the Name and Value of the new item you want to create. By clicking the leftmost button on the Forms toolbar, you'll be creating a text control field. Another dialog box will show up (see fig. 28.8) and you are prompted for the name of the form as well as attributes for it. If you want to create more control fields of any sort, put your cursor where you want the control to go, between the start and end form regions. Next, simply click the button that represents the form field you want to create.

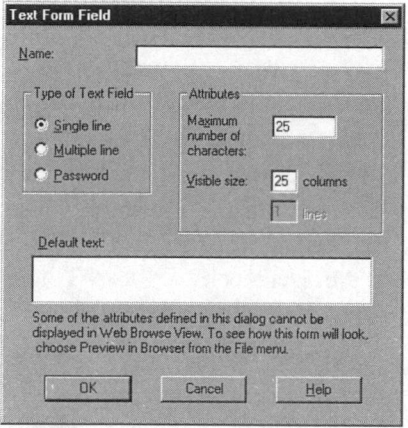

Fig. 28.8
You have to specify the names and attributes for each text form field you want to make.

Note

Internet Assistant doesn't put in any captions for any forms. It leaves this task to you. To create a caption, simply put your cursor where you want the caption, and then type it in.

List boxes are a bit more difficult to create than other forms because each entry in the list box must have a name and a value. Unlike the other forms, these entries must all be known when you're creating the list. You can't create a list box piecemeal, as you can with button and check box forms.

To create a list box, follow these steps:

1. Click the List Form Field button, the third button from the left on the Forms toolbar.

2. Under the <u>N</u>ame text field at the top, type the name you want to give the entire list box.

3. Type the string you want the user to see under the <u>O</u>ption Name field, under the Name text field.

4. Under the <u>V</u>alue when selected field, found under the <u>O</u>ption Name text field, type the value you want to be returned by the form when that particular item is selected.

5. Click the <u>A</u>dd button, underneath the <u>V</u>alue when selected text field.

6. Repeat steps 3–5 for each entry you want in the list box.

7. When you're finished, click the OK button, located at the top of the dialog box.

To remove entries from the list box, select the item you want deleted and click the <u>R</u>emove button. To move entries up and down, first select the entry you want moved. Next, click the up or down arrow, depending on where you want that entry to go. When you click the A<u>d</u>vanced button, the dialog box is extended somewhat. The dialog will now have some more options that allow you to create a list box that accepts multiple entries, as well as defining a default entry (see fig. 28.9). You can similarly create a group of radio buttons by using the Radio Button Form Field icon.

Fig. 28.9
The Advanced button extends the Selection Form Field dialog box to let you do more sophisticated things.

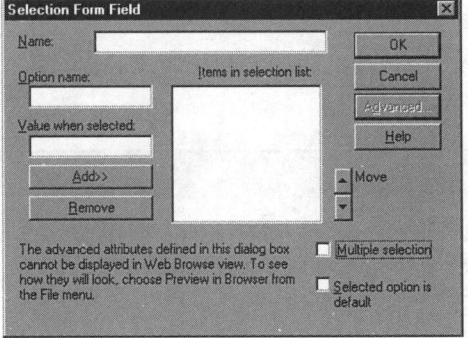

Finally, you may want to have some CGI program that can interpret the interaction with the forms. Typically, only the Submit button actually needs to access a CGI script. When you click the Submit icon on the Internet Assistant toolbar, the Submit Button Form Field dialog box appears (see fig. 28.10). Type the name you want to assign the Submit button in the <u>N</u>ame field. In the Action field, type the name of the URL for the CGI script, and then click the OK button.

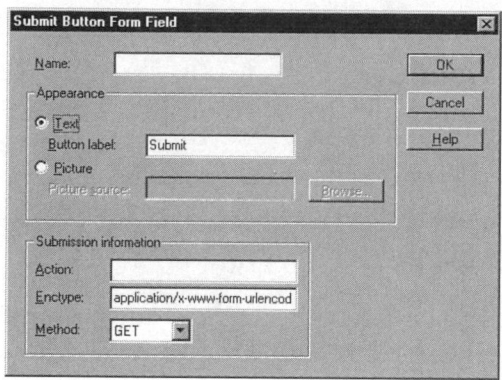

Fig. 28.10
The only time you can define a CGI script for the Submit button is when you first create it.

Creating Lists

Internet Assistant almost makes creating bulleted and numbered lists easy. For bulleted lists, you can click the Bulleted Lists icon and create a new entry. Type the text for that line of the bulleted list, and then press Enter. After you finish the list, just press the Enter key one last xtime. Now click the button you used to create the list to begin with. If you clicked the Bulleted List icon to create the list, click it again to stop the list. Similarly, just click the Numbered List icon to stop the numbered list you're creating. If the toolbar isn't available, you can choose Format, Bullets to do the same procedure.

Numbered lists are just as easy to create. You can use either the Numbered List icon, or you can choose Format, Numbering. As soon as you select either one, 1. appears on the line with the cursor. Type whatever text you want for that particular line, and press Enter. The numbering continues until you move the cursor off the line.

> **Tip**
>
> Internet Assistant automatically renumbers the list for you. If you want to add a new item after a particular line, that's no problem. Just move your cursor to the end of that line, press Enter, and type.

If you already have a list of items, you can easily convert it into either list type. Simply highlight the list of items you want to convert, and select the type of list you want. The entries are automatically bulleted or numbered, depending on which option you pick.

VI

HTML Authoring Tools

Special Features of Internet Assistant

As with many other HTML editors trying to be distinctive, Internet Assistant has some unique features, right? Sort of. One special Internet Assistant feature is its extensive support for Microsoft's extensions to HTML. Unfortunately, enough other HTML editors already provide support for these extensions. Sadly, some of them do it better than Internet Assistant does.

Marquee

One of Microsoft's extensions to HTML is the Marquee element. This element allows the Web author to create a window with scrolling text. This text can scroll either left to right, or vice versa, and is supported at the browser level. That means that you don't have to write any CGI scripts to accomplish this feat.

You can insert a marquee at the current line by choosing Insert, Marquee. The Marquee dialog box then appears (see fig. 28.11). In the Text field, type the string you want to have scroll across the screen, and select the direction you want. The Movement Speed and Delay fields both control the speed at which the marquee scrolls by. The Amount field indicates how many pixels you want the marquee to shift each time it's redrawn. The smaller the Amount value, the smoother the text will move across the screen.

Fig. 28.11
The Marquee dialog box lets you set various attributes for the marquee element.

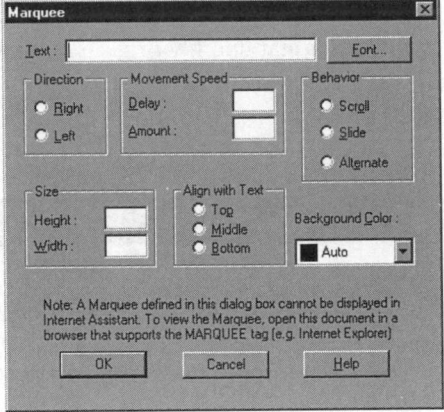

The Behavior radio buttons dictate how the marquee text moves. If none is specified, the Scroll behavior is used. This behavior has the text starting completely off the marquee. The text then moves across the marquee, and then completely off the marquee itself. The Slide behavior scrolls the text horizontally across the marquee. After the text gets to the opposite side, it stops. The

Alternate behavior works by having the text start in the marquee and then scroll across to one side. After the text reaches this location, it scrolls back to the other side.

The size of the marquee itself is defined by the value in the Size field. The Height and Width fields indicate the height and width of the marquee, in pixels. You can align text around the marquee using the Align with Text options, and you can define the background color of the marquee using the Background Color drop-down list.

Background Sounds

You can easily specify the background sound for the current home page with Internet Assistant. Choose Format, Background Sound. The Background Sound dialog box then appears (see fig. 28.12). Type the full path to the sound file in the Sound field, or use the Browse button. Enter the number of times you want the sound to be played back in the Playback loop field. To get the sound to play an infinite amount of time, press the down arrow as soon as the dialog box shows up.

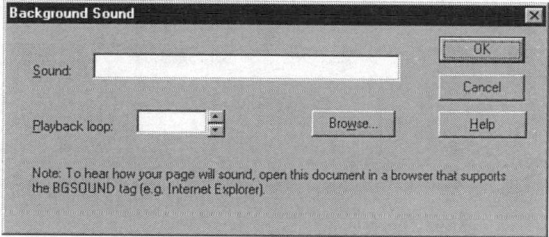

Fig. 28.12
Microsoft's extensions to HTML let you have a sound play in the background when your page is accessed.

Multimedia Files

The Microsoft HTML extensions also provide for more multimedia file support. Most browsers support the GIF and JPEG graphic file formats, but Microsoft's HTML extensions allow for more file formats. You can insert a multimedia file the same way you insert an inline image. The only difference is that you should select the Video tab in the Picture dialog box (see fig. 28.13).

Inside the Video Source field of the Video tab, enter the full path for the Video for Windows AVI file you want to play. If you don't know the path, you can click the Browse button to find it. The Start Play drop-down list indicates when the browser should start the AVI file. You can specify how often the multimedia file is played back in the Loop field. If you press the down arrow as soon as this dialog box shows up, you can have the file played an infinite number of times. If you enable the Show Controls option, the browser lets the user control the multimedia playback with a set of buttons.

◀ See the earlier section, "Adding Graphics," p. 665, on how to bring up the Picture dialog box.

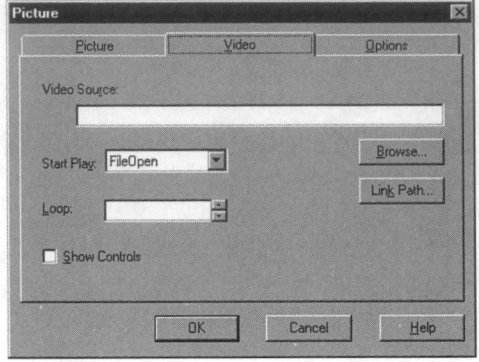

Web Browse

Perhaps the most impressive feature of Internet Assistant is the Web Browse
view, which basically turns Word into a World Wide Web browser. You can
go into the Web Browse view by clicking the Switch to Web Browse icon. The
Web Browse view presents you with two new toolbars to help you navigate
through the Web (see fig. 28.14).

Fig. 28.14
The Web Browse
view gives you a
small number of
controls to help
you get around
the Web using
Word.

The Web Browse
view gives you
these new controls.

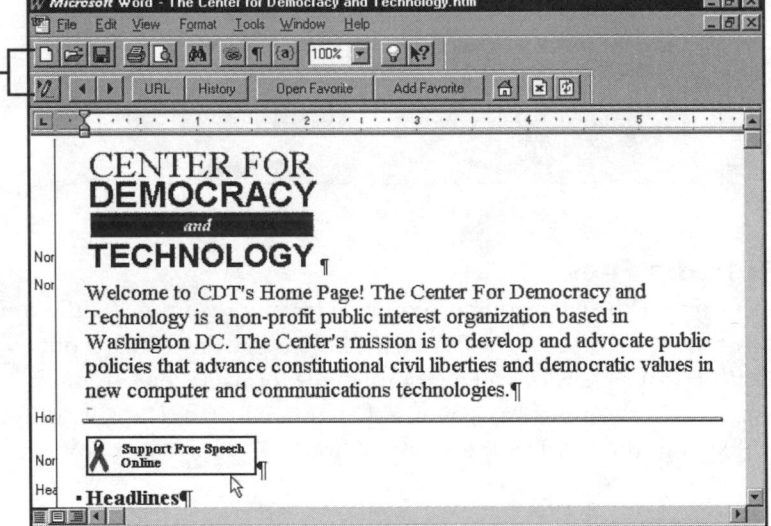

Tip

You can also access the Web Browse view by opening up an URL. Just click the File menu heading, followed by the Open URL menu item.

The left and right arrow icons on the toolbar move you forward and back through the list of URLs visited. When you click the URL button, you are prompted for an URL. After you enter an URL, the Web Browse view tries to open it up for display, just like a regular Web browser. The History button shows a list of previously visited links and lets you jump back to a selected one.

The toolbar even provides support for a collection of your frequently visited links. Simply click the Add Favorite button to put the current URL in that list. The Open Favorite button shows you your current list of frequently visited sites. The Home, Stop, and Reload buttons behave as they would in any other Web browser. ❖

## CHAPTER 29

Quarterdeck WebAuthor

QuarterDeck, Inc., makers of the QEMM memory management product, has also thrown its hat into the ring of HTML authoring tools. WebAuthor 2.0 isn't really a program; it's an add-on module for Microsoft Word 6.0 for Windows. Word for Windows works in distinct "views"—not all features are available at all times. Sometimes you need to use a specific view to use some of the features. WebAuthor merely adds another view in which you can work in Word. While in the WebAuthor view, you can access numerous HTML functions that are unavailable to other Word documents.

In this chapter, you learn about the following:

- How to install WebAuthor
- General navigation of WebAuthor
- Creating Tables with WebAuthor
- Creating Forms with WebAuthor
- Configurable options of WebAuthor

Installing and Starting WebAuthor

WebAuthor 2.0 is available from QuarterDeck (**http://www.qdeck.com/**) for 30 days for evaluation purposes. It comes as a self-extracting executable file. To install WebAuthor, you first need to run the executable from a temporary directory. Next, when you're using Windows 95's install program option, find the full path to that temporary directory and use the file INSTALL.EXE. Finally, follow WebAuthor's installation wizard for your name, company name, address, and the directory to which you want WebAuthor installed. Don't worry about any privacy issues because none of this information is transmitted to QuarterDeck or anybody else.

If you want to use the product longer than 30 days, you have to purchase the full version directly from QuarterDeck. The trial version of WebAuthor does work after that time, but it cannot convert and save files into HTML. It also doesn't come with an uninstall feature, so to remove WebAuthor, you have to delete a specific list of files. Fortunately, QuarterDeck provides the list of files to be deleted if you don't like WebAuthor.

The price of the full version of WebAuthor is $49.95. By the time you read this chapter, the 32-bit version of WebAuthor, which works with Word for Windows 7.0, should be released.

After you've installed WebAuthor, you can easily access it from within Word for Windows 6.0. To get to WebAuthor, start up Word, and then select the Tools menu heading. In this menu, you'll see a new menu option, WebAuthor. When you start up WebAuthor, you are presented with a dialog box (see fig. 29.1). If you accidentally chose WebAuthor, you can click the Cancel button and return to Word.

Fig. 29.1
The first thing you see when you access WebAuthor is this dialog box.

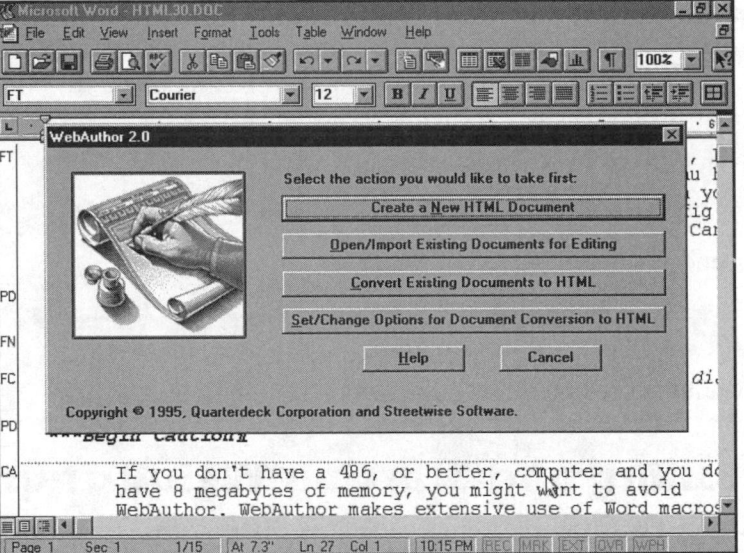

Caution

If you don't have a 486, or better, computer and you don't have 8 megabytes of memory, you might want to avoid using WebAuthor. WebAuthor makes extensive use of Word macros, which can cause the Windows swap file to be accessed frequently. Also, on such slower machines, the response times to what you type and select can be somewhat sluggish.

Creating and Editing Web Pages

To get started on making your new Web page, you should click the Create A New HTML Document button on the initial WebAuthor dialog box. Clicking this button opens a blank document into Word and puts it into WebAuthor view. This view offers multiple toolbars, each with a different area of specialization. The menu headings and items also get changed when you're in WebAuthor view.

It's unlikely that you'll finish your Web page in one sitting, because you'll probably want to decorate it a little. If you click Open/Import Existing Documents for Editing on the initial WebAuthor dialog box, you can open up your existing Web page, or open a file to edit as your Web page. Use the Windows 95 file selector and choose either an HTML, Word for Windows, or Rich Text Format (RTF) file. While you can load an HTML document directly into Word, it will be treated as a regular text file. If you want to use WebAuthor's HTML functionality while in Word, you must go through WebAuthor. WebAuthor automatically converts the specified document into a format readable by Word for Windows. It then loads the specified file into a new window and goes into the WebAuthor view.

> **Tip**
>
> WebAuthor actually keeps track of two documents for your Web page: the Word document and the HTML document. To load your Web page faster, simply use Word to open the Word document that represents your Web page. Word then loads the file and puts you into the WebAuthor view immediately.

Converting Existing Documents

You can also automatically convert large Word for Windows or RTF files. Simply click the Convert Existing Documents option in the initial WebAuthor dialog box. Clicking this button opens the file selector where you can specify the file to convert. You can convert either a Word for Windows document or an RTF file. Using this option is different from loading the Open/Import option in that the conversion is more interactive.

With this option, you're prompted for how you want the different paragraphs in your document to be converted. After you go through the whole document, you're given the option to load the file into Word (see fig. 29.2). The conversion isn't perfect, particularly failing on oddly formatted documents.

But for people who have lots of existing documents that are internal memos or press releases, using this option is an easy way to put them into HTML format.

Fig. 29.2
After WebAuthor converts a document, you can do a variety of things with the HTML file.

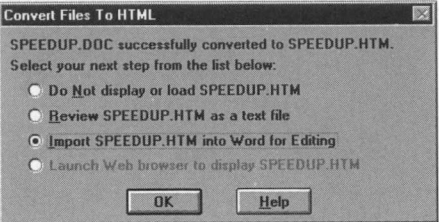

You can also configure WebAuthor's conversion behavior by using the Set/ Change Options for Document Conversion to HTML option. This choice takes you to the WebAuthor configuration program. Of the handful of menu headings, the only one of interest is Options. Under this menu heading, you can find options to configure the styles, the behavior of tables, and general HTML output format. These options affect WebAuthor's conversion of Word documents into HTML only. You learn more about the configuration of WebAuthor later in this chapter.

> **Tip**
>
> You can easily access WebAuthor's configuration program without starting Word. Click the Windows 95 Start button and select the Programs menu item. There you'll see a new menu heading, "Quarterdeck WebAuthor 2.0." Selecting that will bring up a window with a few items in it. Double-click the Conversion Options icon, and you can configure WebAuthor.

Key Elements of WebAuthor

After you get into WebAuthor, you see many changes to Word. If you're creating a new Web page, you are asked to enter its title, which is required for working in WebAuthor. The first change you'll notice is an entirely new toolbar (see fig. 29.3). But that's not the only thing that changes with Word. The entire menu bar changes, with new options under almost every menu heading. The most commonly accessed HTML tags are available through the buttons, but some of the more advanced HTML elements are under the menu headings.

You notice another subtle modification to Word by WebAuthor when you save a Word file. WebAuthor asks whether you want to update the HTML document. If you tell it to generate a new HTML file, you are asked for certain characteristics for some parts of the file, mainly tables. After the conversion to HTML, you have the option of having WebAuthor verify the HTML file. It also lets you start up the default browser (see "Configuring WebAuthor" later in this chapter) and load the new HTML file directly. This capability is particularly useful if you're creating a Web page that makes use of Netscape extensions. Simply define your default Web browser to be Netscape and have WebAuthor pass the HTML file to it.

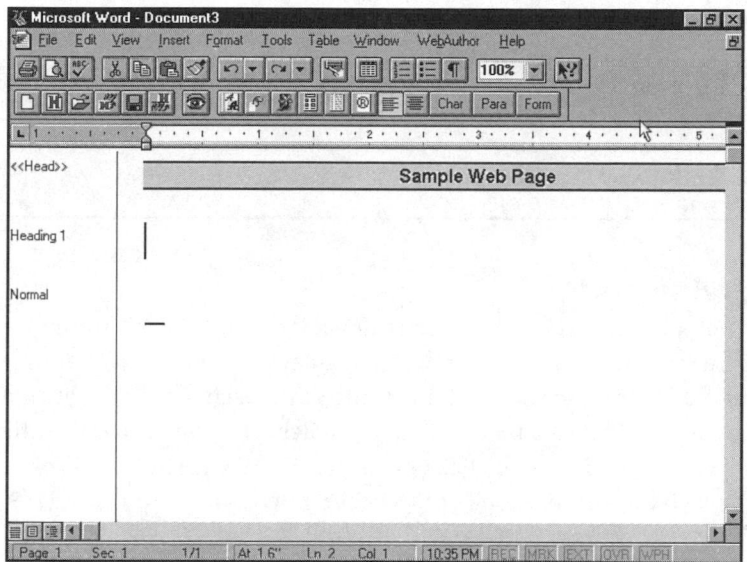

Fig. 29.3
WebAuthor adds a new toolbar to help you create your Web pages.

General Work with WebAuthor

In WebAuthor view, the tasks you'll most want to do are to enter and delete text for your Web page. You can do so seamlessly with WebAuthor because it basically just takes Word documents and converts them into HTML code. For some HTML-specific tags, WebAuthor uses macros to do the HTML conversion.

Working with Text

If you're creating a new HTML document, after you enter the title for it, you can start typing away. Because Word is reading all the keyboard input, you don't have to learn any new commands. Simply use Word like you always do, and forget that you're in the WebAuthor view. You can even use Word's spell checker and thesaurus when creating your Web page.

Because WebAuthor basically sits on top of Word, you can delete text just as if you were modifying a regular document. The only keyboard-related difference you have to watch out for is that some of the shortcut keys have been changed. Aside from that, you really don't have to learn special keystrokes with WebAuthor.

You do have to be careful when trying to modify the text of hyperlinks because you can't do it directly. When you select a link, you must work with it as an entire object. So if you have a bit of text linked to something else, you must deal with both objects. You learn how to edit links later in this chapter.

> **Caution**
>
> WebAuthor is exceedingly slow when deleting a single character. As a result, try to avoid deleting words a letter at a time.

Specifying Styles

You can modify the HTML style of any line at any time. WebAuthor gives you a generous left-hand column, which displays the HTML style of the current line. Changing the style of a line is the same as changing the attribute of text in Word: you select a block of text and click a button. The only difference here is that you have to click one of the HTML style buttons. You can open the styles as another toolbar by clicking the Char button (see fig. 29.4).

Fig. 29.4
You can easily modify the styles of any text by using this toolbar.

 If you have a small monitor and want to use as few toolbars as possible, you can also modify the HTML style. Simply click the Format Character button in the WebAuthor main toolbar.

Clicking this button opens the Character Formatting Selector dialog box, which lets you choose the specific style you want to apply (see fig. 29.5). You can also access this dialog box by choosing Format, Character. A notable shortcoming of WebAuthor is that you can't apply multiple styles to text.

This means that a word can either be bold or italic, but not both. If you try to mix different styles together, WebAuthor will warn you ahead of time before it overwrites the other style.

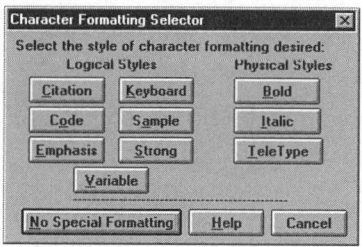

Adding Graphics

You can easily insert graphics at any point in your HTML document by choosing Insert, Image. The New Graphic Image dialog box then appears (see fig. 29.6). You can also get to this dialog box by clicking the Image Manager button.

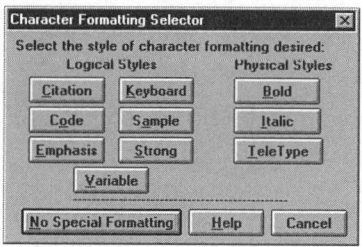

> **Tip**
>
> WebAuthor uses relative references whenever you add graphics to your Web page. Be sure to save your document before you insert a graphic. That will allow WebAuthor to work out all the references correctly.

In this dialog box, specify the attributes of the graphic you want to use. In the Image Path, type in the full path of the graphic you want to use, or click the Select Graphic Image button to find it. You can also indicate the height and width of the image if you know it, but these fields are optional. Specify how you want the text around the graphic to be aligned by using the Alignment drop-down list. Be sure to type in a description of the graphic you're using in the Alternate Text field.

Adding Links

Probably the second most important thing you will want in your Web page is hypertext links (see chapter 4). Links basically let you put a pointer to another document on the Web that people can access. You can do so easily by using the Anchor Manager dialog box (see fig. 29.7), which you access by choosing the Anchor Manager button. You can also access this dialog box through the Insert menu heading, followed by the HyperText Link menu item.

Fig. 29.7
If you want to create any type of hyperlink, you need to use this dialog box.

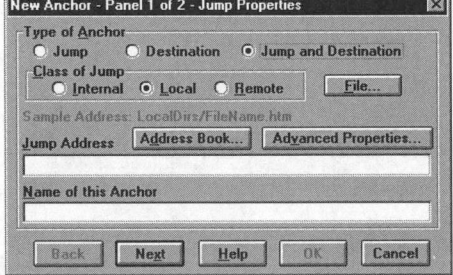

Creating Links

Creating simple hypertext links is easy using WebAuthor, especially when you use the Anchor Manager dialog box. Because most of the time you'll want to jump to other Web pages or Net resources, you'll first learn about creating those links. You'll learn about creating destinations and jumping to them later in this chapter.

If you want to turn some existing text into an anchor, simply highlight the text you want to be the text of the anchor. Next, click the Anchor Manager button, and the corresponding dialog box shows up. Only the Class of Jump and Jump Address fields are accessible to you. To create a link to an URL, follow these steps:

1. Specify that you want a Remote jump class.

2. Type in the URL path of the destination link in the Jump Address field.

3. Click the OK button.

If your computer is the Web server, and you want to create a link to a file on your hard drive, you can do that, too. Instead of choosing the Remote jump class, choose the Local jump class. As for the Jump Address field, type in the full path of the file to which you want to link. If you don't remember the complete path to the file, you can click the File button and use Word's file selector to find it.

You can use the Return for Visible Display field of the URL Address Book dialog box to alter the text of the hypertext link itself. If you specify Nothing, whatever text is highlighted will stay the same. The URL option replaces the highlighted text with the name of the URL. The URL Description option replaces the highlighted text with whatever description you've previously typed in for that entry.

WebAuthor also allows you to keep frequently accessed URLs in a central location. When you're creating a Remote jump, simply click the Address Book button in the Anchor Manager dialog box. The Address Book is a simple list of commonly accessed URLs that you enter yourself (see fig. 29.8). In the URL Address Book dialog box, use the Add, Edit, and Delete buttons to manipulate the entries. Find the entry you want to use, and click the Select button.

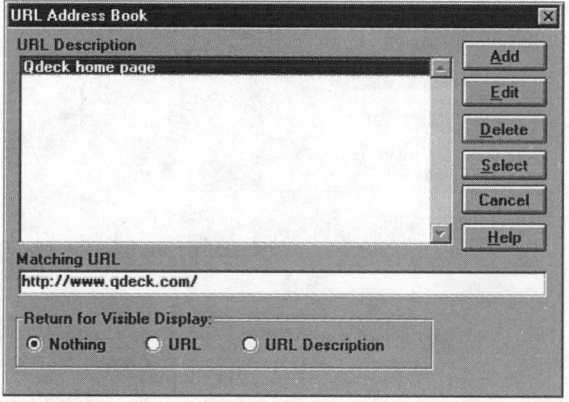

Fig. 29.8
Using the Address Book is a handy way to not have to type in commonly accessed URLs.

Graphics and Links

WebAuthor lets you put in graphics with your hypertext links. After you type in all the information for the link, click the Next button in the Anchor Manager dialog box. Doing so lets you modify the display properties of the hypertext link you're creating (see fig. 29.9). By default, the Type of Display is set to Text Only, which means you're creating a regular text link.

Fig. 29.9

You can control what type of link you'll create by using the Display Properties dialog box.

To create a graphics-only link, click the Image Only radio button, and you are presented with the Image Properties fields. Click the Choose Image Properties button to specify the attributes of the graphic you want to use (see fig. 29.10). You'll notice that this is simply a modified New Graphic Image dialog box. Fill in the fields for the graphical link as you would for inserting a regular graphic. You can determine how big a border you want around the image by typing a value into the Border Size field.

Fig. 29.10

You can specify various attributes about the graphic you want to use as a link.

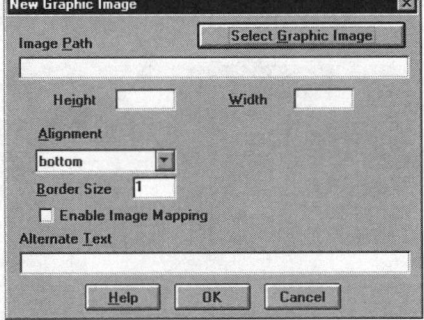

> **Note**
>
> The Enable Image Mapping field toggles the creation of the ISMAP attribute for the graphic (see chapter 12). It does not, however, help you create the imagemap definition file or create a client-side imagemap.

To create a text and graphics link, click the Text and Image radio button in the Anchor Manager dialog box. Fill in the image attributes as you would for an image-only link. Notice that the text in the Visible Text with Image field now has <IMAGE> at the end of it. This string is basically a placeholder for where the graphic will appear in relation to the text of the link. So if you want your graphic on the left of the text, move the `<IMAGE>` string to appear before the text of the link. You can even move the `<IMAGE>` string somewhere in the middle of the text of the link.

Jumps and Destinations

One nice feature of HTML links is that you can have them jump to other points in your documents. These links are typically known as *internal links* because they are internal to the current HTML document. To create such a link, you need to define a destination point somewhere in the document. You can define a destination point with WebAuthor by specifying a Destination anchor type in the Anchor Manager dialog box. Type in a name you want to assign to the current cursor position in the Name of this Anchor, and click the OK button.

You can go directly to that destination point by choosing to create an Internal jump class. You can also jump directly to that point from another Web page. All you have to do is specify the URL for the current document and add # followed by the name of the destination. This capability is useful if you have a Web page on your site that has a list of services (see fig. 29.11). Just create destinations for each definition, and put in links to the appropriate destination. Jumps to an internal point put the line of that destination at the top of the browser.

> **Tip**
>
> Internal jumps are also useful for very long pages. You can simply have the top part of your page list the contents on your Web page. Each entry can have a link that makes an internal jump somewhere further down the Web page.

The Jump and Destination anchor type lets you combine the capability for something to be a reference point and refer to something else. With this anchor type, you can make URLs be reference points. When another person's Web page refers to your destination point, the user will see the link you've created. You'll want to use this feature when you're creating links to other Net resources in the middle of your Web page. Because the line with the link is at the top of the browser, you can put some text before the link. This text will allow you to explain either what the link points to, or why you're pointing to it.

Fig. 29.11
Internal destination points are useful for putting all your services in one Web page.

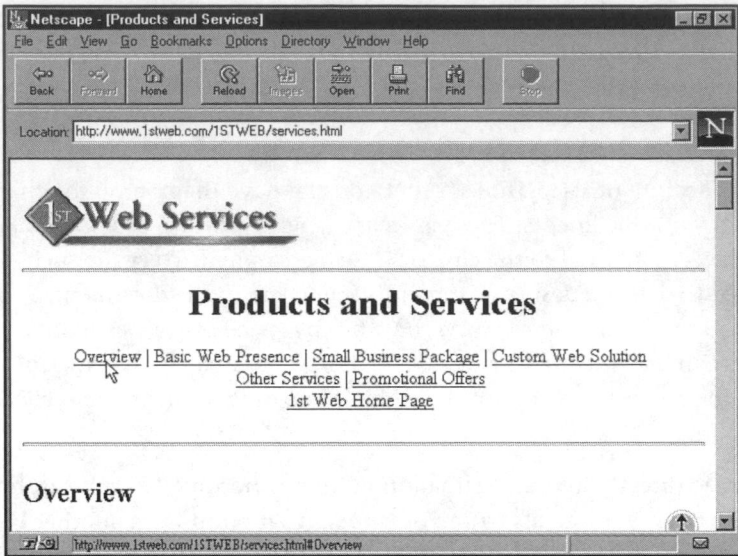

Editing Links

For the most part, WebAuthor treats HTML text the same way as Word does, as individual characters. The only major difference is that WebAuthor treats links as entire objects. That means that if you want to change the visible text of the link, you can't simply change it using WebAuthor. To modify an existing link, select the link and open the Anchor Manager dialog box. Notice that all the fields that have been specified are already filled in. Simply modify any of the link's attributes to suit your taste. If you want to change the visible text, go to the Display Properties dialog box for the link, and edit the text. To change the graphic of a link, change the path of the image to be used.

Tables and Forms with WebAuthor

You can also use WebAuthor to create sophisticated HTML elements, such as tables and forms. These HTML tags can create interesting and useful effects for your Web page. You can use tables to display a great deal of information in an ordered fashion (see chapter 13). Forms are useful for creating Web pages that are accessible via password only or for getting user feedback (see chapter 21). These HTML elements are also very easy to create using WebAuthor's new toolbars and menus.

Creating Tables

One of the few Word menus that hasn't changed when in WebAuthor view is the Table menu. This menu still behaves as it does with Word in any of its default modes. You can easily create a table at the current cursor location by choosing Table, Insert. You then are prompted with Word's own Table Creation dialog box. Specify how many rows and columns you want as well as the size of the width of the columns. Next, type in the values for each cell of the table.

You can add a caption to the table by selecting the table to which you want to add a caption. Then choose Table, Caption, and you are presented with Word's Caption dialog box. Simply type in the name of the caption you want to assign to that table under the Caption heading (see fig. 29.12). The Label drop-down list automatically puts in the corresponding label string, followed by the next available value. You can also specify the location of the caption by using the Position drop-down list.

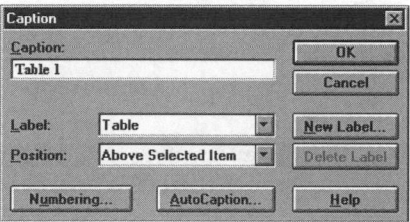

Fig. 29.12
You can add all sorts of captions by using Word's own dialog box.

You can change the borders of the table by choosing the Table menu heading, followed by the Border menu item. The Table Borders dialog box then appears, with the default value set to None (see fig. 29.13). To change the border thickness, simply click the appropriate value you want. When you're finished, click the OK button.

Fig. 29.13
You can control the thickness of the border for your tables.

If you have an existing set of values that you want to put into a table, choose Table, Convert Text to Table. You are prompted for the number of rows and columns to create, as well as how to interpret the text.

VI

HTML Authoring Tools

Creating Forms

One of the more difficult tasks in working with HTML is the creation of forms. WebAuthor simplifies this task by giving you the Forms toolbar, which you can access by clicking the Form button on the main WebAuthor toolbar. You can access the dialog box version of the toolbar by clicking the Form Manager button. You can also access the dialog box by choosing Insert, Form.

To create a text-based form, follow these steps:

◀ See chapter 22, "Form Layout and Design," p. 503, for more information about CGI scripts.

1. In the dialog box, be sure to fill out something for the Uniform Resource Locator (URL) of Server. Here, you should type in the name for the URL of the CGI script that will handle the form.

2. Specify the type of interaction you want to be performed with that form under the Method drop-down list. GET gets information from the Web server, whereas POST sends information.

3. If you didn't click one of the buttons in the Forms toolbar, you are prompted to choose the type of form you want to create (see fig. 29.14).

Fig. 29.14
You can choose to create a wide assortment of forms.

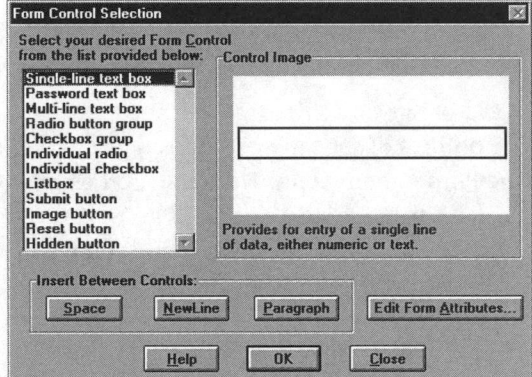

4. Type in the name you want to assign to that control field and text attributes for it.

5. Click the OK button, and select the type of the text control field you want to create.

6. You can optionally create a label above, to the left, or to the right of the field.

After the control field is created, WebAuthor takes you back to the list of fields that you can create. This way, you can make multiple fields all at once. This capability is useful for creating user-feedback Web pages.

Radio buttons and checkboxes are more complicated to create than regular text fields, because text fields simply take input from the user and relay it to the CGI script. Radio buttons and checkboxes require a definite set of items to be created and names for each entry. As a result, you have more work to do and more things to keep track of. Here, too, WebAuthor simplifies the work of writing out the HTML code.

After you select the radio button or checkbox group that you want to create, you are presented with the New CheckBox Button Group dialog box (see fig. 29.15).

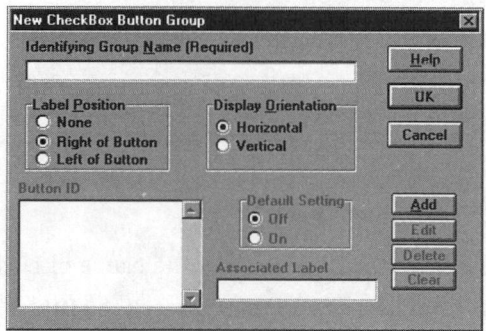

Fig. 29.15
You have to enter several variables when creating new button and checkbox groups.

To create a new radio button or checkbox group, follow these steps:

1. Type in the name of the radio button group under the Identifying Group Name field.

2. Use the Label Position section of the dialog box to specify where the text of the label will appear in relation to the radio button or checkbox.

3. Choose whether you want the radio buttons or checkboxes to appear horizontally or vertically with the Display Orientation buttons.

4. Click the Add button to add a new radio button or checkbox to the group.

5. Type in the string you want to be sent to the CGI script under the New Button ID field.

6. Type in the text you want the user to see in the Associated Label field.

7. Click the Add button again.

8. Repeat steps 4–7 for as many radio buttons or checkboxes as you want to create.

Creating a listbox is similar to creating a checkbox or radio button group. The only real difference is the dialog box; see the ListBox Definition dialog box in figure 29.16. You also don't have nearly as many fields to fill in as with the radio button group.

Fig. 29.16
The ListBox Definition dialog box is similar to the radio button and checkbox dialog box.

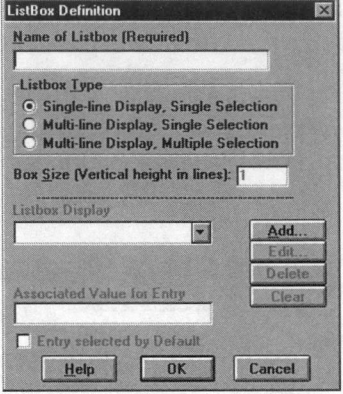

To create a listbox, follow these steps:

1. Type in the name of the listbox under the Name of Listbox.

2. Select what type of listbox you want under the Listbox Type.

3. Enter a number in the Box Size to indicate how many lines the browser should give to the listbox.

4. Click the Add button to add a new entry to the listbox.

5. Type in the string you want to be sent to the CGI script under the List Display field.

6. Type in the text you want the user to see in the Associated Label field.

7. Click the Add button again.

8. Repeat steps 4–7 to create as many entries as you like for the listbox.

Configuring WebAuthor

You can actually configure two different aspects of WebAuthor. You can change the regular WebAuthor options, which apply only when you're in WebAuthor itself. You also can change the WebAuthor conversion options, which you use only when you're trying to load HTML or RTF files.

WebAuthor Program Options

You can access the WebAuthor program options by choosing Tools, WebAuthor Options. Because WebAuthor is an add-on module to Word for Windows, it doesn't have many options of its own; see the WebAuthor

Options dialog box shown in figure 29.17. You can control the general display of Word while in WebAuthor view by using the View options. The Width Settings specify how much of a left-hand margin is given to show the HTML style names. By default, WebAuthor sets the margin width to one inch so that all style names are visible.

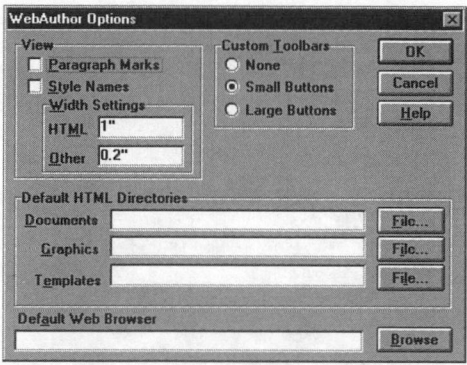

Fig. 29.17
WebAuthor doesn't have many of its own configurable options because it runs on top of Word.

The Custom Toolbar options control the size of WebAuthor's toolbars. Choosing None actually gets rid of the toolbars that WebAuthor comes with. You use the Default HTML Directories section to specify where you keep HTML-related documents. WebAuthor uses the directory specified by the Documents field under the File Locations tab of Word's configurable options, by default.

Under the Default Web Browser field, you can specify the browser you want to start up whenever you have WebAuthor build a new HTML document.

WebAuthor Conversion Options

The bulk of the configurable options for WebAuthor comes with its conversion facility. You can change these options by choosing Tools, Conversion Options. Doing so actually launches another application to let you change the conversion behavior of WebAuthor. Of the available menus, the one that you'll want to use is the Options menu (see fig. 29.18).

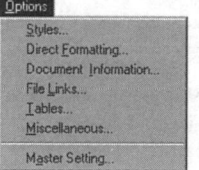

Fig. 29.18
WebAuthor's conversion behavior is controlled by this drop-down menu.

VI

HTML Authoring Tools

By default, WebAuthor comes with a predefined set of conversion rules defining how Word attributes should be converted into HTML styles. You can add or remove conversion rules by choosing Options, Styles. The Style Options dialog box then appears (see fig. 29.19). This dialog box shows all the currently defined rules. You can alter the list of rules by using the Add, Edit, and Delete buttons.

Fig. 29.19
The Style Options dialog box lets you decide what HTML tags will be assigned to what Word styles.

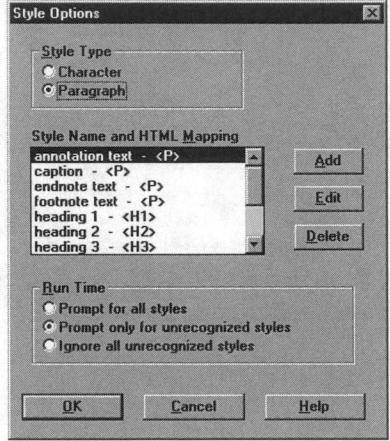

Similarly, you can configure the way text with certain fonts gets converted into HTML by using the Direct Formatting item under the Options menu. You can either assign entire fonts to a particular style or general attributes of the font, such as bold or italics.

You can also specify whether some information in Word is exported to the HTML file. You control whether this information gets exported by using the Document Information menu item.

The File Links menu item lets you decide when WebAuthor will prompt you for file information. You can also configure how WebAuthor processes default links, both for text and graphics, with the Linked Files dialog box (see fig. 29.20).

Because of the way tables can be created in WebAuthor, they have their own menu item under the Options menu heading. The Tables menu option lets you decide what type of HTML output to create, either Netscape or formatted with <PRE>. You can also define what fonts and their attributes are to be used for both table headings and cells.

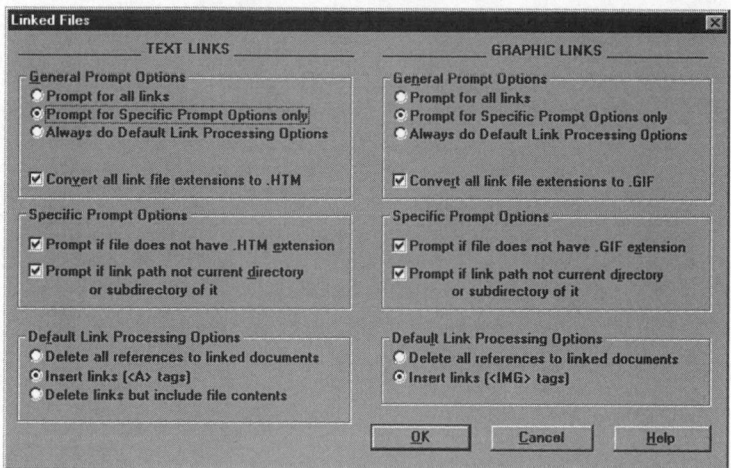

Fig. 29.20
The Linked Files
dialog box lets you
determine how
often WebAuthor
prompts you for
link formation.

The Miscellaneous menu option of the Options menu lets you configure, as you might have guessed, a hodgepodge of options. You can determine whether WebAuthor provides Netscape support or HTML Level 2 support. You can also decide when bidirectional links should be created between foot-notes, endnotes, and others. ❖

VI

HTML Authoring Tools

## CHAPTER 30

Other HTML Editors

As you might've guessed, there are literally scores of HTML editors around. Netscape Gold, Microsoft Internet Assistant, and Quarterdeck WebAuthor— covered in chapters 27, 28, and 29, respectively— are just the big names. Because the World Wide Web is so popular nowadays, a lot of people have taken a shot at making HTML programs. These programs range from being barely functional to feature-laden.

In this chapter, you'll learn about the following:

- Stand-alone editors versus add-on editors
- HTML tags editors versus visual editors
- The HotDog HTML Editor
- Kenn Nesbitt's WebEdit
- LiveMarkup
- The Arachnid Editor
- World Wide Web Weaver
- HTML.edit
- UNIX and X Windows HTML editors

HTML editors can take the form of either a stand-alone program or an add-on program. They can also just show you HTML codes or give you a rough idea of what the page will look like. Whatever shape they take, however, HTML editors all fulfill the same basic function: they help you make a home page. How well they help you is another matter.

Because there's such a tremendous number of editors available, you can take your time deciding which one is best for you. If an editor doesn't meet your needs or just plain doesn't feel right, then throw it out. When choosing an HTML editor, consider the following questions:

- Is the editor a stand-alone program (an application that runs on its own)?
- Is the editor an add-on module for an existing program?
- Does the editor show your soon-to-be home page as HTML tags?
- Does the editor try to give you an idea of what your page will look like?

Ultimately the decision is yours, but I'll cover some of the good and bad points of each editor to help you choose the right one.

Stand-Alone Editors

A stand-alone HTML editor is a separate program that doesn't depend upon another program. Put another way, a stand-alone program is a complete HTML editing package. You don't need to have a program already installed on your system to use a stand-alone editor. These are probably the most prevalent types of editors around. All it takes to make such a program is a little HTML knowledge and a little programming experience. The programmers who create these stand-alone editors must decide on their look and feel: the button layout, which menu bar items go where, and so forth. Stand-alone editors are typically shareware and written in the author's spare time.

Stand-Alone Editors' Strengths

A particularly strong reason for using a stand-alone editor is that it's shareware. This is good because most shareware registration costs are under $50. Also, they are generally the first ones to undergo changes, which is a benefit for you because the HTML standard is constantly evolving.

Shareware authors are typically one-man operations and can give you an updated editor usually within a week. As soon as they hear about a new HTML tag, they put it in, recompile the program, and make it available to everybody. All you have to do is check in regularly for the latest update. On the other hand, it takes a lot of time for a company to learn about the new standard, update its editor, update the manual, and inform you. As a general rule, therefore, most shareware stand-alone editors will be more up-to-date than anything else.

Another good reason to use stand-alone editors is that you don't need another program to use it. This makes it easier if you really like an editor and want your friends to use it. You don't need to make sure they have a particular program; you just point them to an FTP site. Stand-alone editors are also useful if you want to uninstall the HTML editor. Although some uninstall programs will watch for installation of program executables, they might not catch the installation of new libraries for an existing program.

Stand-Alone Editors' Weaknesses

Of course, there's got to be some drawbacks to using stand-alone editors or else that's all that would be available. Because they are self-contained programs, the user interface might be weird to you. Although you can overcome this after using the program for a while, you might not have that time if you want to jump right in and start writing HTML code. An unfamiliar user interface for a stand-alone editor might slow you down.

Another reason not to use a stand-alone editor is that it could take up a substantial amount of disk space. Because stand-alone programs are self-contained packages, they might need to install their own custom runtime libraries. Although you might already have some of these on your system, there's no guarantee that you will. Further, you're going to need disk space for any help files or related text files for showing you how to use the program. Although you'll still need some disk space for add-on modules, there is less overhead. The libraries needed for a program are already loaded on your system, as are the useful text and help files.

Add-On Editors

An add-on editor is a module or program that connects to an existing piece of software. Typically, the only people who can create extensive add-on modules are the authors themselves. Because most shareware programmers would just write a new program for new functionality, add-ons aren't usually done by the average person. Typically, the software companies with large user bases write add-on modules. But just because an established program has added HTML functionality doesn't mean you should go out and use it.

Add-On Editors' Strengths

Because most add-on modules or programs are provided by companies, they typically provide some form of support for their add-ons. Although they might not necessarily provide technical support, you can at least give them feedback. You also know that the add-on product will probably be upgraded in the future. The fact that it's a company backing the add-on—and not an individual—is a strong reason for using an add-on editor.

A very good reason to use an add-on HTML editor is that it's an extension of existing software. Because it's extending the functionality of a program you already have, it'll be easier to use immediately—you won't have to learn new buttons or menu bars with an add-on module.

Add-On Editors' Weaknesses

Add-on modules aren't the panacea of HTML editors, and there's a number of good reasons for it. If you have an old or underpowered machine, avoid add-on modules. You may already be waiting a while for some programs to start up. With an add-on editor, you're going to lengthen that wait. For example, if you find yourself waiting for a word processor to launch, avoid getting an HTML add-on for that word processor.

Another reason to avoid an HTML editor that is an extension to an existing program is the user interface. Although the buttons and menus may be familiar, the add-on module's behavior may not be what you expect. Just because it's an extension to a program doesn't mean the program will know about its interface. You might not be able to control the way text is displayed or other subtle nuances that may annoy you.

Tags-Only Editors

There's more to an HTML editor than just whether it's a separate program or not. You have to decide how that editor enables you to modify your home page. An HTML editor that is a tags-only editor is one that shows you the actual HTML tags. That is, it doesn't show you what your home page will look like, just the codes being used. You're essentially *programming* your home page on the HTML-source level with a tags-only editor. Because you're dealing with a home page in its raw form, most HTML editors are similar to text editors. The majority of HTML editors available are tags-only editors.

Strengths of Tags-Only Editors

There are a number of good reasons that favor the use of tags-only HTML editors. For one thing, tags-only HTML editors are usually the first programs for which new tags are supported. Because most tags-only editors simply dump out the start and end elements for HTML tags, it's easy to accommodate new HTML tags. When new HTML start and end tags are finalized, tags-only editors can be quickly updated. They don't have to worry about what the new tags look like; they just need to know what they are.

Another good reason to use HTML tags-only editors is because they're generally faster for navigation. This is especially important if you're on a slow machine or you have a large home page. Because most tags-only editors do no HTML interpretation, they're mainly concerned with getting keyboard input and displaying text. This makes scrolling through a home page and text manipulation tasks much faster on tags-only editors.

Weaknesses of Tags-Only Editors

For all the good reasons you can find for using tags-only editors, there's an equal number of reasons not to. HTML editors that are tags-only are very bad for newcomers to HTML coding. People new to HTML have no concept of what the tags do, how they look, and how they behave. Because tags-only editors do nothing to get around any of these issues, they're not good vehicles for learning how to write HTML code. Very few people unfamiliar with HTML would be willing to fire up a tags-only editor and a browser just to see what each tag does. Tags-only editors are typically for people who already know HTML and don't want to keep typing tags.

Another reason to avoid tags-only editors is that most of them have no form of syntax checking. Because tags-only editors are only concerned with the tags, they really don't care how they look. Those tags-only editors that do syntax checking are mixed bags; the majority of them start up a browser with the current HTML document. This is little better than having you start up the browser yourself, saving the current HTML document, and loading it in the browser.

WYSIWYG Editors

WYSIWYG (What You See Is What You Get) editors are a good alternative to tags-only HTML editors. These HTML editors are programs that show you what the page will actually look like. The interpretation for the HTML code is left up to the programmers, but frequently the tags are correctly rendered. Often, these editors shield the Web author from the raw HTML tags. There are many reasons for using these editors.

Strengths of WYSIWYG Editors

If you're a person new to HTML tags, page layout design, and the like, WYSIWYG editors should be your first choice. Because they show you what the rendered page will look like, you can get an idea of how to design your home page. Instead of worrying about missing starting or ending tags, WYSIWYG editors take that responsibility away from you. Just select an HTML tag to use, type the text for that style, and move on. You don't need to make guesses on how the different HTML tags will look—you'll see it right there.

Another reason for using WYSIWYG HTML editors is because they're self-contained packages. What I mean by this is that you don't necessarily need a browser when making your home page. Granted, if you know your HTML code, you won't need a browser anyway, but most people new to HTML aren't so fortunate. Because WYSIWYG HTML editors show you what the page will look like, you don't need to start a browser to see it. If you're running an underpowered machine, this is a great alternative for you. You won't need to start another application and use up more of the system's resources.

Weaknesses of WYSIWYG Editors

As a beginner, you might be thinking that WYSIWYG editors are great for learning. This is true, but there are a number of things wrong with them. Most of these faults lie with the inherent nature of WYSIWYG editors doing HTML interpretation. For one thing, these types of editors tend to be rather slow and sluggish. The program has to spend a lot of processor time interpreting HTML code and then displaying it correctly on the screen.

For people with underpowered computers, WYSIWYG editors can be exceedingly slow. If you're not using at least a 486-level computer and 8 megs of RAM, you're not using a reasonably powerful computer. Rather than spending time creating your home page, you could be spending a lot of time listening to your hard drive crunching away. Not only is this bad if you're impatient, but all that activity adds to the wear and tear of your equipment.

Another problem with HTML editors that are WYSIWYG is that they won't always have the latest tags. Because the editor must do the correct interpretation and displaying of HTML tags, the programmer must know what they look like and how they behave with other tags. This research process could take a programmer more than a few weeks to accomplish in his spare time.

HotDog

HotDog by Sausage Software is a much ballyhooed, stand-alone, tags-only editor for Windows 95 (see fig. 30.1). Like most anything with so much hype, the big question is, does it deserve all the praise? In HotDog's case, sadly, no. That's not to say it's a bad editor, just that it's not an exceptional editor. HotDog is a capable HTML editor trapped in a muddled user interface. It provides support for HTML 2, HTML 3, Netscape's extensions, and even Microsoft's extensions.

> **Tip**
>
> HotDog is useful for converting existing HTML documents into plain text. Simply load the HTML file into HotDog and save it as a text file. This will preserve all the document formatting of the home page without the HTML code. This is useful if you want to convert a large batch of HTML documents into plain text.

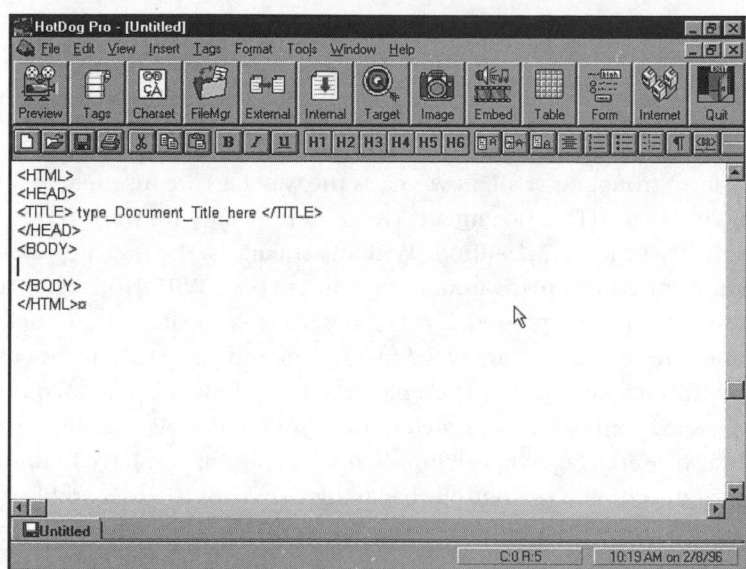

Fig. 30.1
HotDog is a very popular and well regarded stand-alone HTML editor.

Getting and Installing HotDog

HotDog is available in two versions, the Standard version and the Pro version, from **http://www.sausage.com/**. The Pro version offers a pseudo-WYSIWYG viewer, spell checking, and extra configurability. Also, when you run the Pro version under Windows 3.1, it uses buttons similar to those in Windows 95. Unfortunately, this slows the whole program tremendously, and it is uneven in its attempt to simulate Windows 95. The Standard version is a much better buy at $29.99 than the Pro version, which goes for $99.99. HotDog's sleek and polished look makes it a good editor for most people new to HTML tags.

Once you get the version of HotDog you want, installing it is a simple matter. Using Windows 95's Explorer, simply find the program you just downloaded. Double-click its icon, and you'll be presented with Sausage Software's installation utility. It allows you to specify where you want to install the program. Also, you'll be asked if you want to make a backup copy of files that it will modify. This is a good idea if you're evaluating HotDog, as it'll let you restore your system to the way it was before installing it. After it's done copying the files into the necessary locations, you can start HotDog.

Moving Around

The general navigation of HotDog is intuitive as it follows general cursor conventions. The arrow keys move the cursor in the appropriate directions. Unfortunately, there's almost no good thing you could say about HotDog's user interface. There are a number of ways to insert tags, but they won't necessarily behave the same way. Some buttons appear to recede when pressed while others don't. Some buttons that insert HTML tags are controlled by user preferences, while other methods of inserting the same tags aren't.

Perhaps most troubling of all, however, is the way tags are inserted by HotDog into your HTML document. The built-in facility for most HTML tags isn't quite like other HTML editors. With other editors, the tags are automatically put in the correct place around the selected text. With HotDog, when a button to insert a tag is pressed, it acts more like a keyboard macro: cursor commands are issued, keys are typed in, and cut and paste features are used. Although this may not seem to be a big deal, the problem is that all of these HotDog-issued commands are stored in the Undo buffer. As a result, if you accidentally insert a tag, you can't undo one operation; you have to undo a number of operations. The buttons behaving as macros is also a problem when you change your mind in creating an HTML element. There are some buttons in HotDog, that when you cancel out of them, will dislocate the object you had selected.

One bright spot in HotDog's favor is its versatility. It has many home page elements that are mere mouse clicks away. You can have a floating window with a complete list of HTML tags (see fig. 30.2). When you double-click one of the tags, it's automatically inserted into the document for you. You can similarly have floating windows for specific groups of HTML tags, such as heading, document, and body tags.

Fig. 30.2
You can easily insert HTML elements by double-clicking in this floating window.

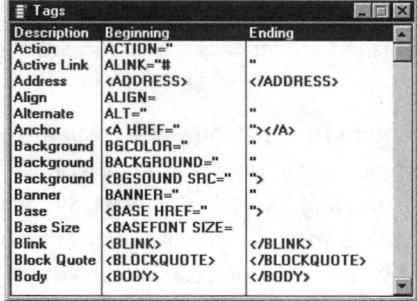

Working with Links

The most common element you'll want to put into your home page, aside from regular text, is a hyperlink. You can easily create hyperlinks by highlighting the text you want as a link and then clicking the button labeled External (Ctrl+H). This will bring up a dialog box in which you just fill out the information. If you're unsure of the syntax of URLs, you can also create a link through friendlier means. Instead of clicking the External button, click the Internet button. This will bring up a dialog box (see fig. 30.3), where you can select the resource you want to link to. You'll then be asked for the necessary information for that resource.

Fig. 30.3
You can easily link the selected text to other Internet Resources. Just pick the resource you want to link to.

If you want jumps to go to another location in your home page, you can do that too. Internal links are easily created. First, define your destination spot: put your cursor where you want the destination point to be, click Target, and type the name of the destination when you're prompted for it. Next, high-light the text that you want to jump *to* the destination and click Internal (Ctrl+K). You'll get a dialog box with a list of existing destinations (see fig. 30.4). Just choose the one you want, and the internal jump is automatically done for you.

Caution

HotDog's linking facility seems to have problems when you're running more than one program. Sometimes, when you're cancelling out from creating a link, HotDog will switch over to another program. This happens even when HotDog is fully maximized.

Caution

You cannot create an internal jump until after you've defined the destination. There is no provision in HotDog for jumping to an unspecified destination. This will cause problems for those people who lay out their home pages ahead of time.

VI

HTML Authoring Tools

Fig. 30.4
Find the internal
destination point
you want, and
select it.

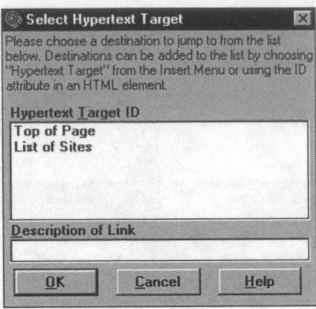

Forms and Tables

Eventually, you'll want to put more sophisticated elements in your Web page.
You can easily put in forms and tables with HotDog, although support is uneven. <FORM> is probably the weaker of the two advanced HTML tags to be
supported. When you click the Form button, you'll be presented with a list of
forms you can create (see fig. 30.5). Each form brings up a different set of required attributes to be filled out. For whichever form you choose, enter as
much information as you can for each field.

Fig. 30.5
HotDog enables
you to put in
many different
forms.

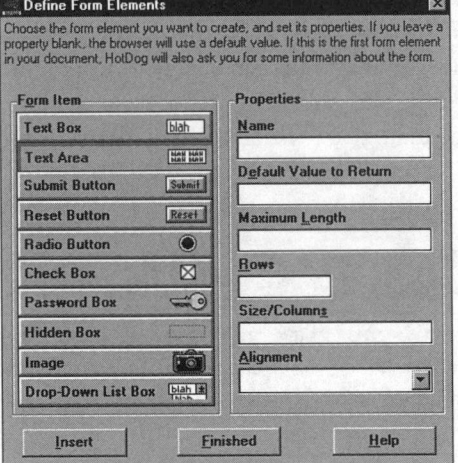

Caution

HotDog's Forms support is extremely unstable. Too many times while telling HotDog
to create the form, it will crash.

Tables, on the other hand, are incredibly well done and supported. HotDog provides possibly the most impressive interface for creating tables. Simply click the Table button (Ctrl+T) and you'll be given a dialog box (see fig. 30.6). You can change the Caption, the Columns, and the Rows just by typing the appropriate value. As you change the column and row values, the table at the bottom of the dialog box changes to match the new values. Not only do you see exactly what the dialog box will look like, you can also type the values for it. Just click the table cell you want to put data into, and type away.

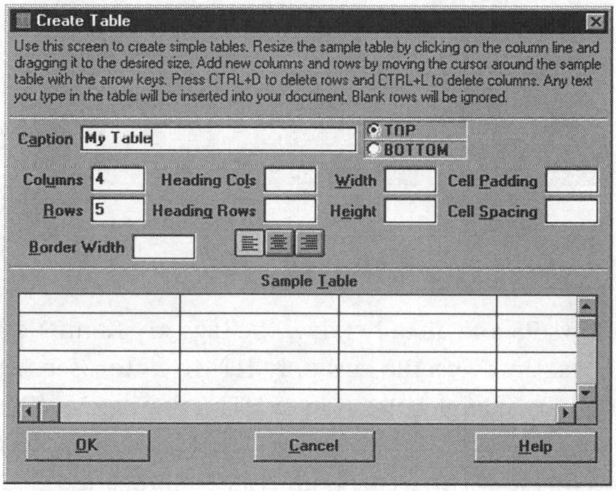

Fig. 30.6
You can create tables and the data they'll hold with this dialog box.

Advanced Elements

Various other advanced HTML elements are also supported by HotDog. Creating drop caps is very easy for new HTML authors: simply highlight the letter you want enlarged, choose Format, Big First Letter. You can define the colors for the foreground font or link by selecting Format, Document. Click the Graphics/Colors tab, and you'll see a list of fonts and links and their current colors (see fig. 30.7). Click one of those entries, and change the color by using the Red, Green, and Blue sliders.

> **Note**
>
> Creating lists in HotDog requires a bit of HTML knowledge. When you tell HotDog to create a list, it'll generate the start and end markers for the list tag. It will also make the appropriate code for the first list item. It's up to you to keep typing the other list items.

Fig. 30.7
Link and text
colors are changed
through this
dialog box.

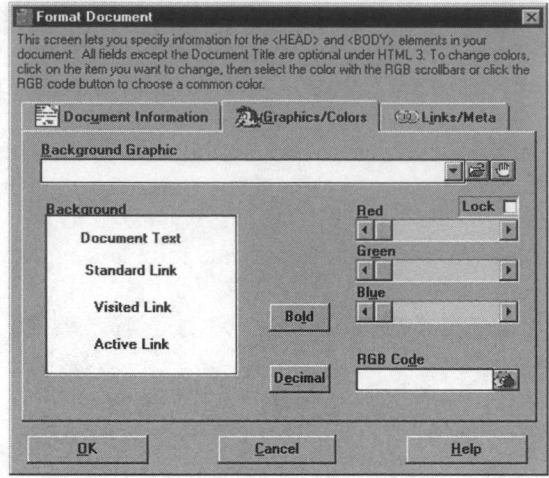

Kenn Nesbitt's WebEdit

If you use Windows 95 and already know the tags, try Kenn Nesbitt's
WebEdit. It's a great and versatile tags-only HTML editor (see fig. 30.8).
Sporting two toolbars, a large collection of HTML tags are available for your
use. This program supports HTML 2 and HTML 3, as well as Netscape and
Microsoft extensions to HTML. This is an HTML editor intended for the pro-
fessional and people very well versed in HTML tags. This is probably the best
HTML editor around for Windows 95.

Fig. 30.8
Kenn Nesbitt's
WebEdit is a
feature-loaded,
tags-only HTML
editor.

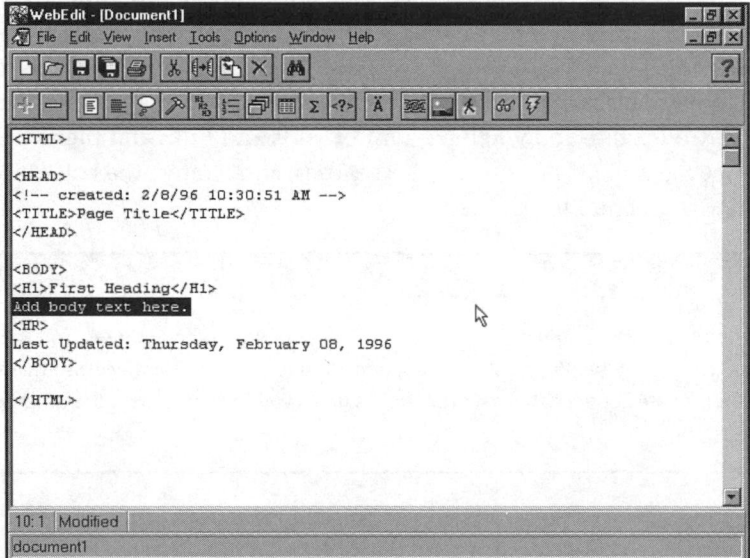

Getting and Installing WebEdit

You can get Kenn Nesbitt's WebEdit from **http://www.nesbitt.com/** for a free 30-day evaluation. If you like it, you can buy it for $39.95 for educational users or $79.95 for business use. It comes on two disks and takes approximately five megabytes of disk space for a full installation. This is easily the best HTML editor available.

Installing WebEdit is a simple matter of double-clicking the installation program. You'll be prompted for the directory that you want to install WebEdit to. Once it's done copying all the files, you'll be asked which language lexicons you want. These lexicons are basically dictionaries to be used by WebEdit's spell-checker. The full version of WebEdit comes with dictionaries for American English, British English, French, German, Italian, Spanish, and HTML Tags.

The WebEdit Toolbars

Of the two toolbars, the top one is used for all file-related tasks. The icons are pretty self-evident, enabling you to start a new home page, open an existing HTML document, and save the current or all loaded files. The print, cut, copy, paste, and delete icons are obviously visible. The binoculars represent not just the find capability, but also the ability to search and replace.

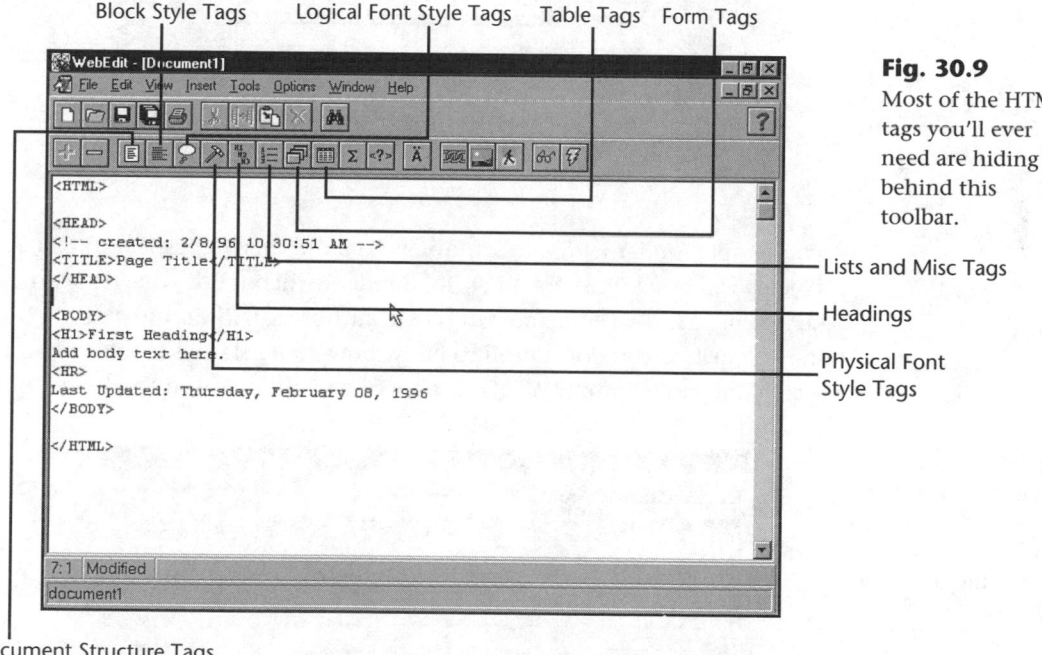

Fig. 30.9
Most of the HTML tags you'll ever need are hiding behind this toolbar.

For most people, however, the bottom toolbar is the one they'll use the most (see fig. 30.9). This is the toolbar where the HTML tags are most accessible. Whenever you select any of the buttons in the bottom toolbar, you're given a list of choices to select from. The server side includes (SSI) tags are the few HTML elements that aren't available through this toolbar, but are available through the menus. Simply choose Insert, and the selecting SSI+.

Creating Links

Everything in WebEdit is represented in text at the raw HTML code level. This makes everything, from text to images, easy to create hyperlinks for. It's a simple matter of highlighting the text or image tag, or both, and clicking the Anchor/Link button (Ctrl+L). This will bring up the Anchor/Link dialog box where you can specify any link-related attributes you want (see fig. 30.10). The drop-down list in some of the fields holds a list of recently accessed values. Creating destination points for internal hyperlink jumps is a simple matter of filling out the Name field.

Fig. 30.10
Links of any sort are easy to create with WebEdit; use this dialog box.

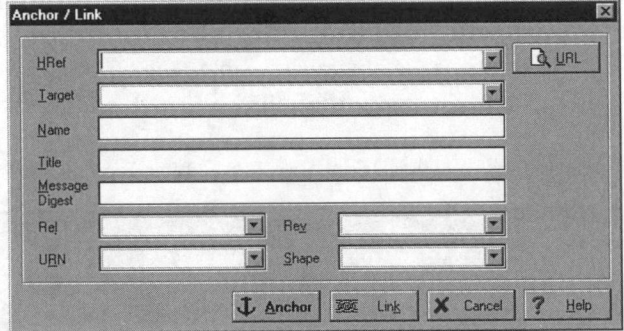

If you're not familiar with URLs and how to build them, click the URL button. This will bring up WebEdit's URL Builder, which helps you create an URL (see fig. 30.11). People new to HTML authoring will find this dialog box to be invaluable. You don't need to know how many slashes to add, when to use a colon, and whatnot. WebEdit takes care of all of that in this dialog box.

Fig. 30.11
The URL Builder is a great feature for new Web authors to learn the URL structure.

HTML Tags

All other tags available in WebEdit—for tables, font styles, or whatever—behave the same. You can insert them into the document by one of two ways. The first way is to highlight the text that you want to apply a particular tag to and then select the appropriate tag. The text will be positioned correctly within the starting and ending markers of that particular element. The second method is to simply select the appropriate tags. For HTML containers, WebEdit will put out the start and end markers for the tag and then position the cursor in between. For other HTML elements that don't contain anything, it'll bring up a dialog box. Simply fill out whatever fields you want and proceed; if you're not sure what a particular field does, don't put anything there.

Special Features

This program is already jam-packed with all the HTML support you'd ever want. It provides support for Microsoft's proposed extensions to HTML, including Banner, Marquee (see fig. 30.12), and Background Sound. Netscape's extensions are also impressively supported with built-in tags for Frames, Font Colors, and Client-Side Imagemaps. All the proposed HTML 3 tags are also included in this program. To add to all of this, there is a pseudo-WYSIWYG previewer that shows you roughly what your Web page will look like. Although the previewer doesn't show images and can't really jump to links, it's still better than many other tags-only previewers.

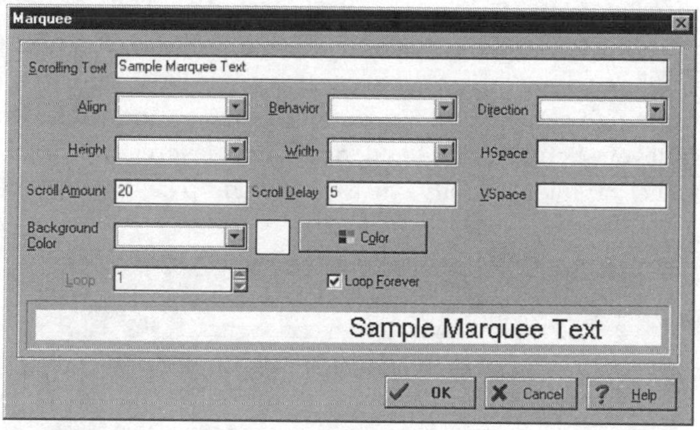

Fig. 30.12
You can see roughly what your marquee will look like at the bottom of the dialog box.

Getting Help

Probably the best thing about WebEdit is its built-in help facility. To help you learn about HTML, you can find out which elements are supported by which browsers. Bring up the online help file, and search for a particular HTML tag. In the upper-left corner, you'll either see a Netscape icon or a Microsoft icon (see fig. 30.13). This tells you right away which browsers will be most likely to view your home page. For those people creating browser-specific Web pages, this is invaluable.

Fig. 30.13
Even WebEdit's Help file will assist your learning about HTML.

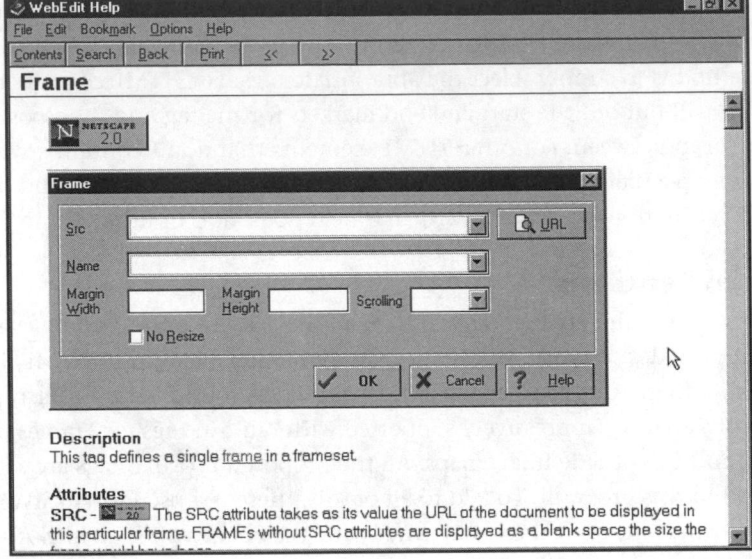

Whenever you add almost any HTML tag to your home page, you're presented with a dialog box. This is useful because all the HTML-related buttons and fields have button tips. Just leave your mouse cursor over any of the fields or buttons and you'll find out what it's for (see fig. 30.14). You don't need to dig through a manual to find out what each attribute does; the dialog boxes will tell you. Kenn Nesbitt has done a fantastic job in making HTML writing so much simpler with his extensive button tip facility.

Fig. 30.14
All of WebEdit's dialog boxes have button tips for HTML attributes.

Configuring WebEdit

WebEdit doesn't come with many configurable options, but that's because it does everything. Its few configurable options are under the Option menu. If you have a local directory where you keep other URLs you plan to use, you should choose the Select URL File Path. With WebEdit, you can have a browser load the HTML document you're currently working on. You can specify the location of the browser you want by Choosing the Select HTML Viewer. For those of you who don't want the toolbars to use tags, you can have floating toolbars as well. Choose Tools, Toolbars, and select the toolbars you want; they'll become floating toolbars.

Live Markup

Live Markup (see fig. 30.15) by MediaTech (**http://www.mediatec.com/**) is a well-intentioned WYSIWYG HTML editor for Windows 95. It provides support for HTML 2, some Netscape extensions, and popular HTML 3 elements. It's handicapped by a cumbersome user interface, but is workable for people new to Web authoring. Even though its WYSIWYG facility isn't perfect, it does give a great idea of what your Web page will look like, without needing a browser.

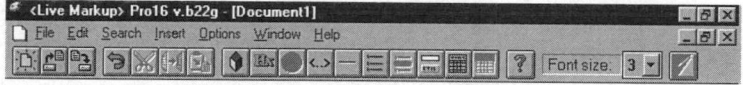

Fig. 30.15
Live Markup is a good HTML editor for people who aren't familiar with HTML.

Getting and Installing

Getting Live Markup is a simple matter of pointing your favorite Web browser to **ftp://ftp.mediatec.com/pub/mediatech/lv16b22g.exe**. It's about 1.1 megabytes to download the entire package, which will work on Windows 3.1 as well as Windows 95. Once you get it, simply locate the file and double-click on its icon. The self-extracting archive will pop up a dialog box, asking you where you want to uncompress the files to. Once it's done uncompressing files, the installation program will begin. All you have to do is specify where you want to install the entire program, and Live Markup will be installed. The entire distribution takes about three megabytes of disk space.

The version that MediaTech makes available to everybody is its evaluation version. It's a 16-bit application, meaning it's not optimized for Windows 95. After the 14-day evaluation, you may purchase the complete version for $49.

General Navigation

Probably the worst part about Live Markup is its user interface. All objects in Live Markup are treated as objects, which while not inherently bad, is poorly implemented. Most HTML elements that you create will have a default set of attributes used. To change these attributes, you must first select the object, then click on the right mouse button. This allows you to edit the attributes for that particular element (see fig. 30.16).

Tip

Be sure to use the right mouse button a lot with Live Markup. Many HTML elements and attributes alike are hidden under it.

Caution

Some of the options for a particular element aren't available through the right mouse click menu. What isn't available might be available under editable attributes.

Fig. 30.16
Most of the options you want to use for text elements are available with the right mouse click button.

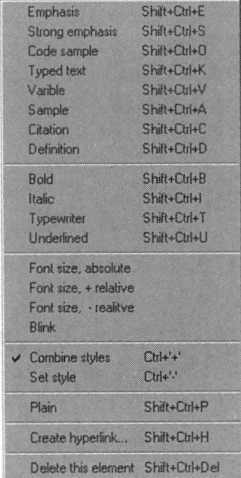

Emphasis	Shift+Ctrl+E
Strong emphasis	Shift+Ctrl+S
Code sample	Shift+Ctrl+O
Typed text	Shift+Ctrl+K
Varible	Shift+Ctrl+V
Sample	Shift+Ctrl+A
Citation	Shift+Ctrl+C
Definition	Shift+Ctrl+D
Bold	Shift+Ctrl+B
Italic	Shift+Ctrl+I
Typewriter	Shift+Ctrl+T
Underlined	Shift+Ctrl+U
Font size, absolute	
Font size, + relative	
Font size, - realitve	
Blink	
✓ Combine styles	Ctrl+'+'
Set style	Ctrl+'-'
Plain	Shift+Ctrl+P
Create hyperlink...	Shift+Ctrl+H
Delete this element	Shift+Ctrl+Del

Inserting an HTML element of any sort is also problematical with Live Markup. Whatever HTML tag you want to create will depend on which element is currently selected. If no elements are selected, the newly created tag will appear at the **top** of the Web page. If you already selected an element, the new tag will be below it. While this may not appear too unfriendly or unworkable, the fact that you can't move objects around is a tremendous problem.

Caution

So confusing is Live Markup's interface, that most of the help file is goal-oriented. Rather than explaining what particular HTML tags do, or are used for, Live Markup focuses on how to get around its interface.

Caution

Live Markup's help files are poorly written.

Another problem with Live Markup relates with how it displays your Web page. On the whole, its HTML interpretation is fairly good, but there are obvious holes in it. Its interpretation ability breaks down when you do advanced HTML tricks. Colored backgrounds and the like can easily confuse the HTML interpreter. Also, when you interact with any HTML tag, Live Markup will completely refresh the Web page. Sometimes it'll update objects that aren't visible in the window.

Working with Elements

By and large, the general method of inserting any HTML element is done by clicking on its icon. You can also access the same elements as the icons, by selecting the Insert menu heading. What elements you don't see, are probably available by selecting an existing element, and clicking the right mouse button. Some elements, when selected, will bring up a dialog box, prompting you for more information (see fig. 30.17).

Perhaps Live Markup's one saving grace is that it allows you to put in images almost anywhere. In particular, Live Markup supports the little-known ability to put images into table cells. While this may not sound terribly impressive, the fact that few other HTML editors do the same thing is impressive. Where some HTML editors restrict you to mere text for table cell data, Live Markup will let you put in pictures. This allows you to create sophisticated Web pages easily.

VI

HTML Authoring Tools

Fig. 30.17
Once you specify
the size and
appearance of a
table, you can
enter data into
each cell.

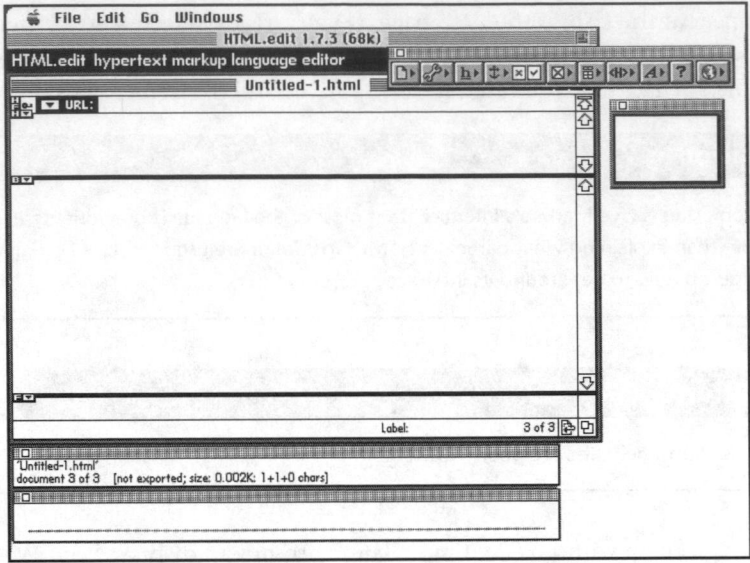

Arachnid

Arachnid by Second Look software at the University of Iowa is a well-regarded
HTML editor for the Mac. It provides support for HTML 2, HTML 3, and some
Netscape extensions. This WYSIWYG HTML editor is a respectable program
that is good for new Web authors. It shields the HTML code from the new
HTML writer while providing adequate support for tags. For people who are
still learning the HTML ropes, this is a good starting program.

Getting Around

When you first start Arachnid, you'll see the main window with two floating
windows (see fig. 30.18). This is a bit cramped on a 14-inch monitor, but fortunately, you can get rid of the extra windows if you want. Arachnid works
from a *project* concept: you don't design individual home pages; you design
a Web site. As a result, the more Web pages you work on at once, the more
useful some of Arachnid's features become. Also, the files that are created by
Arachnid are not standard HTML documents. You must convert these project
files into Web pages by choosing File, Export to HTML.

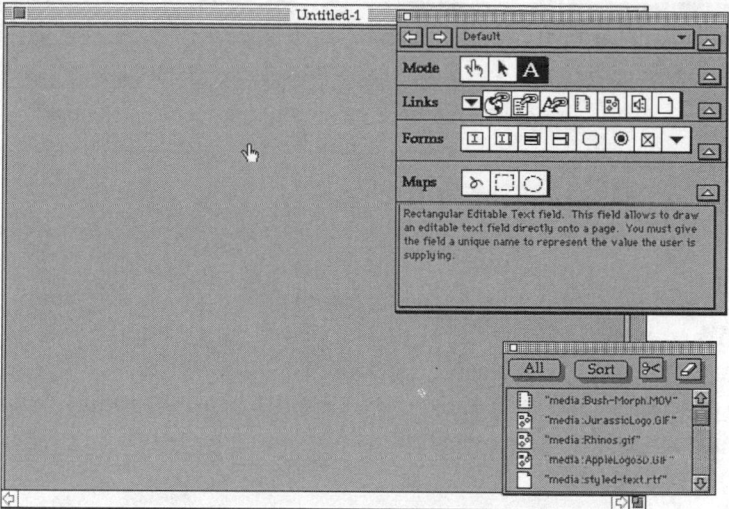

Fig. 30.18
Arachnid comes
with a main
WYSIWYG
window and two
floating windows.

This editor also has three distinct modes: the *Text* mode, the *Pointer* mode, and the *Preview* mode. The Text mode is where you enter actual text into the current Web document. The Pointer mode enables you to move the different Arachnid objects around. Finally, the Preview mode shows you Arachnid's interpretation of how the current HTML document will behave in a real Web browser.

Objects and Arachnid

Almost everything you put into a Web document will become an Arachnid object. An object is first created when you leave the Pointer or Preview modes and begin adding HTML elements. When you've finished adding to the object by not being in Text mode, you stop adding to that object. What this means is that when you want a horizontal rule or a graphic after a body of text, you'll create a new object. Also, Arachnid will prevent you from having overlapping objects. In addition, you can control the size of the objects while Arachnid automatically arranges the objects in its own particular fashion.

Adding Text

You can add text to your home page by going into Text mode. Once you've clicked an area that doesn't have an object, the entire line becomes highlighted. Now, you can start typing whatever you want on that line. You can easily change the style of text by highlighting it in Text mode and choosing Format. Choose the appropriate style or element from the cascading menu. Most of the different text elements will only affect the highlighted text.

> **Caution**
>
> Choosing Format, Text Alignment will affect all the text in the current object. If you don't want this to happen, go into Pointer mode and create a new text object.

Managing Links

The most important attribute in any home page is the hyperlink. Unfortunately, Arachnid's support of links—although extensive—is very cumbersome. You can create links in Arachnid by first highlighting the text or graphic that you want linked. Next, choose the appropriate link type from the floating menu and then drag it to the main Arachnid window. You can create links to other home pages, another page in your project, or a line in a page in your project.

When creating links to multimedia files, it's a simple matter of finding the file. However, when you're creating a link to anything specified by an URL, you must select from a list of existing URLs (see fig. 30.19). If the URL you want to link to isn't on the Arachnid list, you have to add it. Adding a new URL is a simple matter of clicking the New button (Command+N). You'll be prompted for the URL you want to add along with the name you want to assign it. This might not seem to be a problem, but when you're using Arachnid for the first time, it's tedious adding your favorite URLs.

Fig. 30.19
To link something to an URL, you must select the URL from a list of existing URLs.

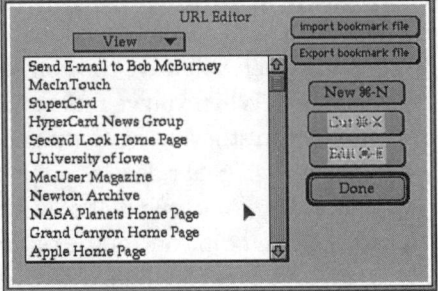

Working with Rules and Graphics

You can easily add a horizontal rule by choosing File, Insert Ruler (Command+R). It will create a horizontal line that spans across the entire width of the window. If you want to change the appearance of this line, simply go into Pointer mode and click the line. Next, choose Format, followed by Ruler Alignment, and choosing either Left, Center, or Right. The width of the rule can be changed to any value from one percent to 100 percent of the window width by choosing Format, Ruler Width. The Ruler Thickness can be set to any value from one through 10 as well as a user-defined value. Additionally, you can set the Ruler Shade to either Black or No Shade.

Adding graphics is even easier; simply choose File, Import Picture (Command+I). You'll be presented with the standard Macintosh file selector, which you use to locate the graphic you want (see fig. 30.20). After you've clicked OK, the image will appear in the next open space on your home page. Once loaded, this picture is an Arachnid object by itself. You can change the border width by selecting the graphic and choosing Format, Image Border Size.

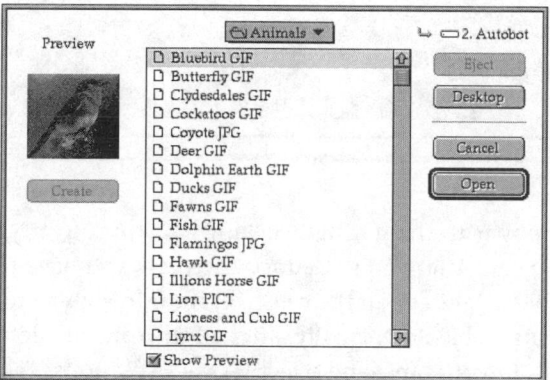

Fig. 30.20
Inserting a graphic is a simple matter of finding the picture you want.

> **Tip**
>
> Arachnid only enables you to load images that are in the same folder as your project file.

Putting Tables

<TABLE> is a newly supported HTML element with Arachnid, and it shows. The interface for creating tables is still a bit uneven and counter-intuitive. To create a table, you must first type in the data for the table itself. Next, go into Text mode and highlight the text that you want to be in one cell. Now choose Format, HTML Extensions and select Table Data. A dialog box will be displayed that enables you to define the appearance of the table row (see fig. 30.21).

VI

HTML Authoring Tools

Fig. 30.21
Arachnid enables
you to define the
appearance of
each cell in your
table.

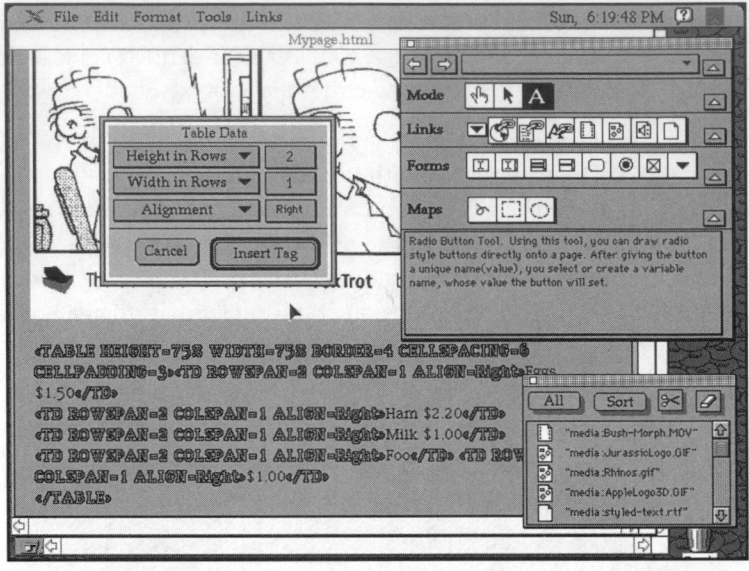

Once you're happy with the settings, clicking OK will convert the existing data into a table cell. After you've defined each cell, you have to define the rows for the table. Highlight all the cells you want in a given row and choose HTML Extensions, Table Row. Finally, after all the rows are defined, highlight all the cells in your table and select HTML Extensions, Table. You'll be prompted with another dialog box that will enable you to control the overall appearance of the table (see fig. 30.22). You can add a table header or caption before or after you've created the table.

Fig. 30.22
The appearance of
an entire table can
be controlled with
this dialog box.

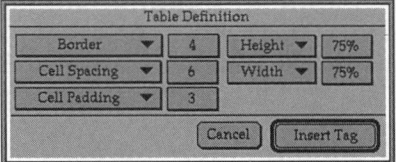

Working with Forms

Working with the complex HTML element, <FORM>, is made easy with Arachnid. Creating a form is a simple matter of clicking the appropriate form you want to create and using the mouse pointer to define the size and shape of the form. The form will instantly appear in the region you define, and you'll be prompted for its variable name.

Tip

After you've created any selection form, you can enter the data into the form directly. Simply go into Text mode, and click somewhere in that form. You can start typing the values you want for each line in that selection form.

Buttons, check boxes, and radio buttons are also very easy to create with Arachnid. Simply select the appropriate form to create from the floating window. Next, use the mouse to specify the size and shape of the item. You'll be prompted to give the button or check box a distinct name (see fig. 30.23). For Submit and Reset buttons, you'll be asked which button you want to create (see fig. 30.24).

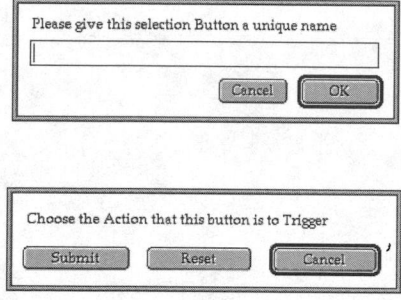

Fig. 30.23
You must give a distinct name to every button form.

Fig. 30.24
You can add either a Submit button or a Reset button to your Web page.

HTML Extensions

There are a number of new HTML extensions that Arachnid adequately supports. The capability to specify colors for various home page elements, such as visited link color and background color, is possible. Whenever you want to change a color of your home page, you'll be given a color wheel (see fig. 30.25). Simply find the color you want to use and click it. You can fine-tune the color until you're happy with it, then click OK.

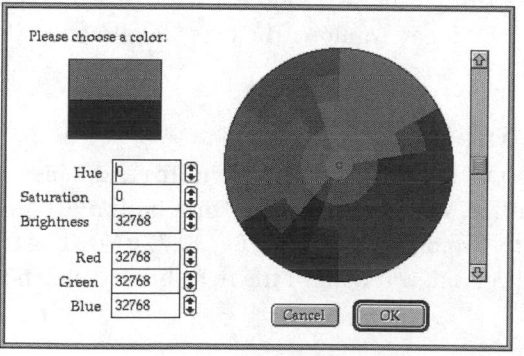

Fig. 30.25
Specifying colors is easy with Arachnid.

World Wide Web Weaver

World Wide Web Weaver by Miracle Software (**http://www.northnet.org/ best/**) is a solid, tags-only HTML editor for the Macintosh (see fig. 30.26). It supports HTML 2, some HTML 3, and some of the Netscape extensions to HTML. It makes use of floating windows and a toolbar to provide access to HTML tags. The Netscape-specific tags are provided along with the standard set of HTML tags. So, as a Web author, this means you'll have to know HTML tags fairly well to create a generic home page.

Fig. 30.26
World Wide Web Weaver makes all of its supported HTML tags available through multiple windows.

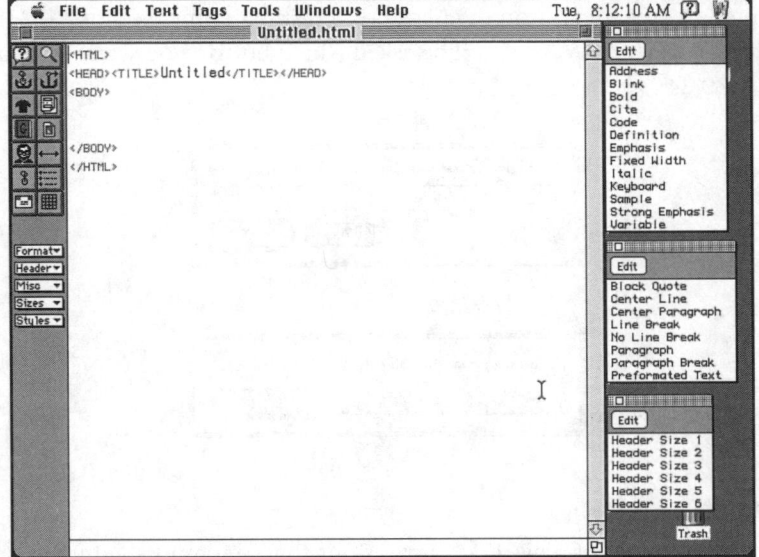

Putting in HTML Elements

The floating windows, although a little cumbersome at first, become a very workable user interface. Unlike other editors that embed the tags within menus or complex dialog boxes, World Wide Web Weaver makes the tags available in the floating windows. So to make use of any HTML tag, simply click one of the tags in any window. The tag will automatically be used by World Wide Web Weaver.

Forms and Tables

World Wide Web Weaver makes putting in forms and tables very easy for the casual HTML author. When you click the Form button (Command+;), you'll be presented with two dialog boxes (see fig. 30.27). You create forms by selecting whichever one you want in the right-hand dialog box. You'll be prompted for information for that particular form. Once you're done, the form and its name will appear in the left-hand dialog box. You can modify the attributes for any forms in the dialog box by simply clicking it.

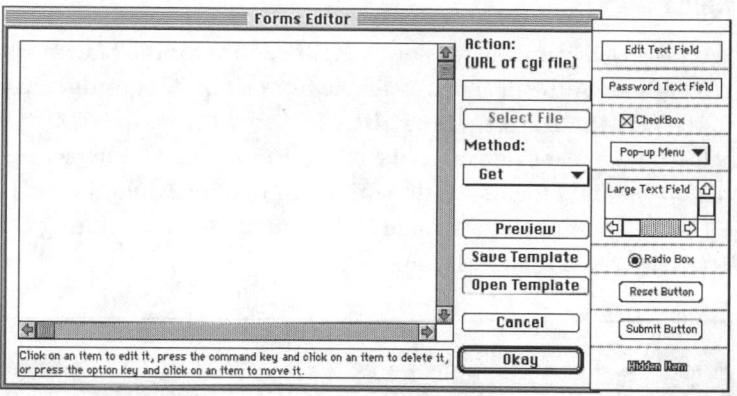

Fig. 30.27
Click the form you want to create on the right, and it will appear on the left.

Tables are also similarly easy to create in World Wide Web Weaver. By clicking the Simple Table button (Command+T), you'll be presented with a dialog box (see fig. 30.28). You can change the table's size and dimension on the right, and the preview of the table will be updated on the left. You can manually add the elements for each table cell just by clicking it. You'll be presented with a dialog box in which you can enter whatever information you want.

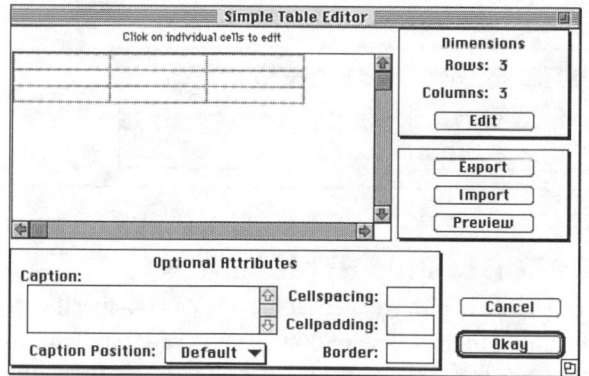

Fig. 30.28
You can see what your table will look like in this dialog box.

Text Tags

The various HTML text elements are also supported with World Wide Web Weaver. You can change the style and point size of the font from the Tags menu. Simply choose the appropriate menu item, and pick the value you want. The Text menu is only intended to help you create your home page.

This can be misleading to new HTML authors who think that they're setting the font's color and typeface.

HTML.edit

HTML.edit is a well-rounded, tags-only, HTML editor for the Macintosh. It's written by Murray Altheim and is available from **http://ogopogo.nttc. edu/tools/HTMLedit/HTMLedit.html**. It provides up to HTML 2 support including popular extensions like tables and forms. All interaction between HTML.edit and the user is done through floating windows (see fig. 30.29). The few menu items available all have to do with navigating through the Web pages stored by HTML.edit.

Fig. 30.29
Although HTML.edit has many floating windows, you only need to concern yourself with the floating toolbar.

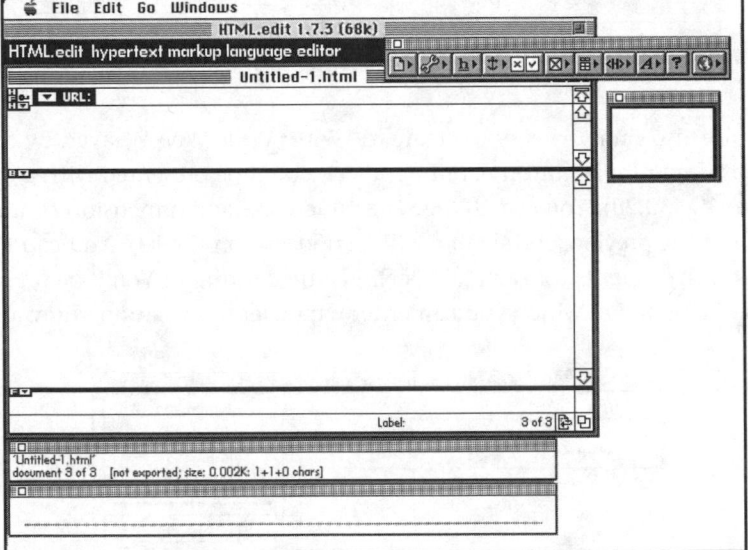

Getting and Installing HTML.edit

HTML.edit is available in three executables: the 68000-specific, the PowerPC-specific, or the "fat" binaries. The 68000-specific program will only work on most older Macs, while the PowerPC file only works on PowerPC Macs. If you're unsure which computer you have, get the fat binaries, as they will run on any Mac. You'll typically need about four megabytes of disk space to hold the entire HTML.edit distribution.

Navigating HTML.edit

HTML.edit works off the idea that you don't want to design just one Web page, you want to design a lot of them. To that end, HTML.edit doesn't allow you to open up individual HTML documents. There is one master index of

HTML documents that you add your Web pages to (see fig. 30.30). You can create new, and import existing, HTML documents into the index, as well as exporting individual pages. This allows you to easily see all your Web pages at a glance.

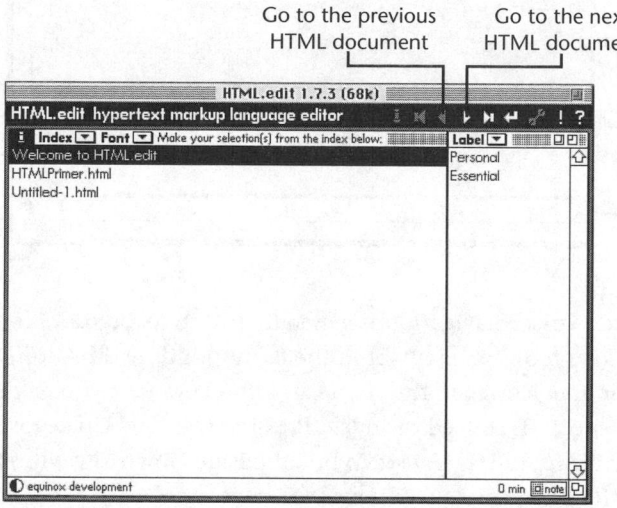

Fig. 30.30
HTML.edit allows you to easily jump to the next, and previous Web pages in the master index of your Web pages.

When you're ready to add a new page to the master index of HTML documents, you'll have to give it a title (see fig. 30.31). After that, you'll be presented with HTML.edit's main window (see fig. 30.32). Here, your Web page is broken up into three distinct regions, the header, the body, and the footer. You can only go into each region by moving your mouse into that region, and clicking the button.

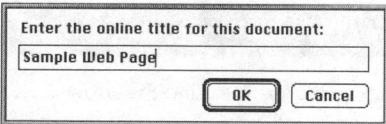

Fig. 30.31
Before you can start creating a new Web page, you have to give it a title.

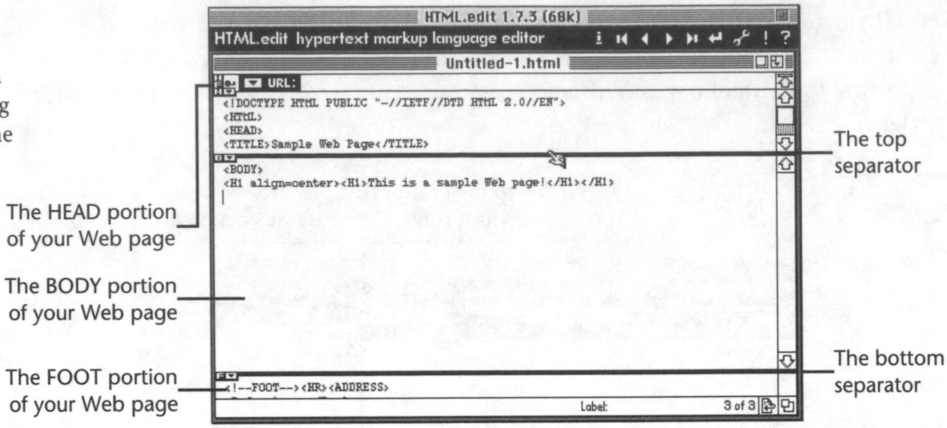

Fig. 30.32
You can resize
each region of a
page, by clicking
and dragging the
separator.

The HEAD portion
of your Web page

The BODY portion
of your Web page

The FOOT portion
of your Web page

The top
separator

The bottom
separator

The keyboard cursor navigation is generally intuitive, but does have its faults.
The arrow keys move your cursor in the corresponding direction, by one
character or line. However, the Home and End keys take you to the first and
last documents in HTML.edit's index. Pressing the Page Up key will show the
previous screenful of HTML text. While the Page Down key will similarly
show you the next screenful of your Web page.

Tip

Don't ignore the little tabs on the separators, near the left side of the window. They
are used to create and save global headers and footers. This is particularly useful if
you're trying to keep your Web pages consistent. It even comes with three predefined headers and footers for your use.

Caution

Make sure you see the text cursor before using the arrow keys. Some commands in
HTML.edit will actually get rid of the cursor. When this happens, the cursor keys will
act like some of the buttons in the main window. The left arrow will show you the
document previous to the current Web page, while the right arrow will bring up the
next HTML document.

The Toolbar

Almost everything you want to put in your Web page is accessible through
the floating toolbar (see fig. 30.33). This toolbar can be clicked and dragged
by its title bar to anywhere on the screen you want. Simply put your mouse

cursor over a particular button on the toolbar. Next, click and hold the mouse button. You'll be presented with a drop-down menu list of available options and HTML tags. These drop-down menus behave as normal menus on the menu bar, complete with cascading menu options.

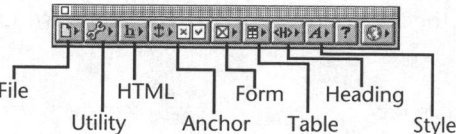

File Utility HTML Anchor Form Table Heading Style

Fig. 30.33
While you can get rid of the floating toolbar, there's really no reason to do so.

Tags and Styles

As with most Web pages, you'll probably want to put in some sort of text. This is done by simply putting your text cursor where you want to add text, and start typing. You can assign an HTML tag to that particular text by first highlighting it. Then, depending on which HTML attribute you want to give it, choose a particular button.

The HTML button allows you to use the less-often used HTML tags. That is, elements such as as <TITLE>, <HEAD>, and <BODY> can be found here. All of the HTML tags that relate with creating lists can also be found here. The Heading button will insert, obviously, any of the six HTML headings. Finally, the Style button hides the majority of HTML text tags that you can use. Physical and semantic HTML elements can be found under here. In particular, any user-defined HTML tags can also be accessed with the Style button.

> **Tip**
>
> Special characters, such as the less than, greater than, and ampersand are available under the HTML button. They are grouped under the general menu heading of "Entities."

The HTML, Heading, and Style buttons all have Index and Highlight options. The Index option, when selected will generate a list of all of a particular tag used in the current HTML document. This is useful if you're checking to make sure that certain words are of a particular style. The Highlight option emphasizes the text enclosed within a particular style. Any text that HTML.edit finds that meets the criteria, will be displayed in bold.

Creating Links

Probably the most common HTML element you want to put in your Web page is a link. This can be a link of text or an image, to anything else on the Net. Links don't necessarily have to go to other Web pages, they can also go

VI

HTML Authoring Tools

to other Internet resources. You can easily link in text or images to any URL you want. Simply use the mouse to highlight the block of HTML code that you want to create a hyperlink to. Next, click on the Anchor button on the floating toolbar. Select HyperText Link to make the highlighted text into a link. You'll be presented with a dialog box (see fig. 30.34) asking you for some details about the link. Simply fill out as much as you know, and click the OK button.

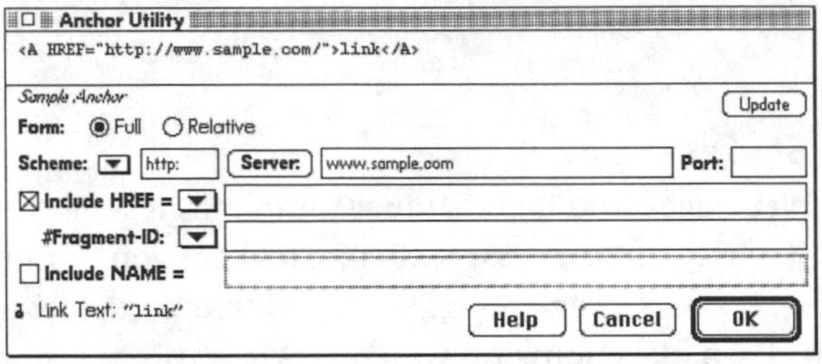

Fig. 30.34
The Anchor Utility dialog box is used to specify attributes for hyperlinks.

Adding Images

▶ See chapter 7 for information on how to link to other Internet resources.

Images can easily be inserted into your Web page with HTML.edit. Simply click and hold the mouse button on the HTML button, and you'll see an option for inserting an image (Command+I). You'll be presented with a dialog box where you can enter various attributes for the image (see fig. 30.35). Clicking on the Source SRC tab, followed by the External File option, will take you to a file locator dialog box. The Alternate Text field is displayed when people are viewing your Web page without a text browser.

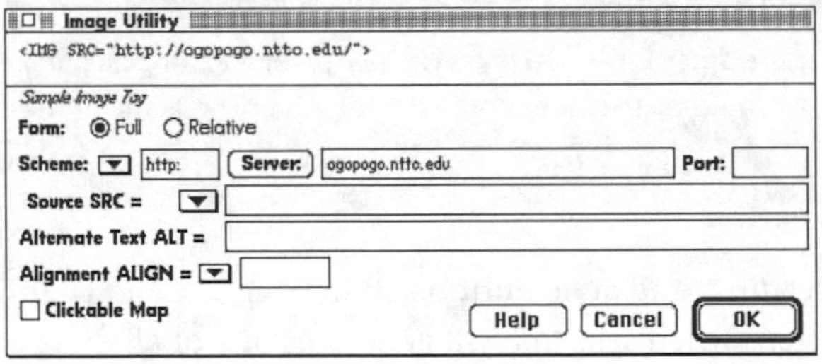

Fig. 30.35
You specify which file on your hard drive to use as an image by clicking in the SRC field.

Creating Tables

Tables are sophisticated HTML elements that HTML.edit also allows you to create. You can create a table from one of two basic ways, a cell at a time, or convert existing text. The more cumbersome of the two is to define your table one cell at a time. Simply click and hold the mouse button over the Table button on the toolbar. Select Table Cell and enter in the data you want for that cell. Repeat this process for as many cells as you want. You next have to define each row in your table, then the rows, headers, and finally the caption.

> **Tip**
>
> If you choose to create a table one cell at a time, you can make things easier on yourself. At the bottom of the Table button is the Table Palette option. This will bring up a floating window with all the table-related HTML tags (see fig. 30.36).

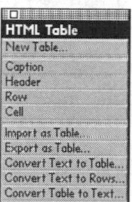

Fig. 30.36
The Table Palette floating window is a great way to easily access table-related tags.

The easier way of creating tables is to type in the data for the table itself. Next, click and hold down the mouse button over the Table button. Select the Convert menu item, followed by the Text to Table menu option. This will bring up a dialog box (see fig. 30.37), asking you how many pixels should be used for padding for the table. Next, you'll be asked for the character to be used to separate entries in the table (see fig. 30.38). Finally, you have to decide whether you want the columns or rows as table headings (see fig. 30.39).

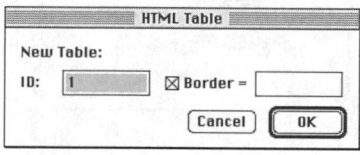

Fig. 30.37
During the text to table conversion process, you have to indicate some display attributes of it.

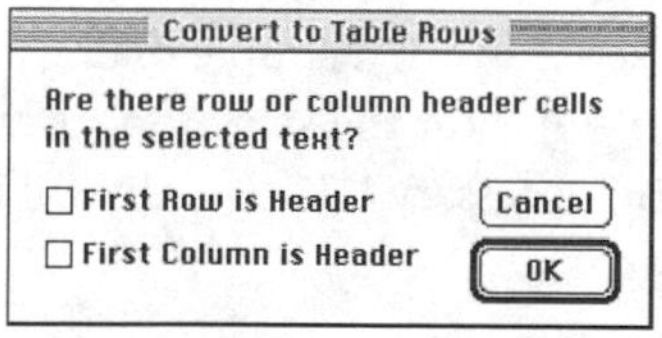

Fig. 30.38
Next, you have to tell HTML.edit what type of headings you want for the table.

VI

HTML Authoring Tools

Fig. 30.39
Finally, you have to define when one cell data ends, and another begins.

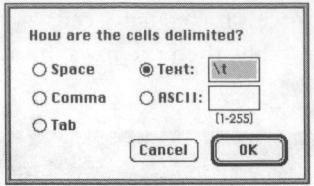

Creating Forms

Forms are another advanced element that you'll see in many Web pages. Here too, HTML.edit provides an easy way of creating them. Simply position your screen cursor where you want the form to appear, and use the Form button on the toolbar. If you're creating a form for the first time, you'll be asked for some general information (see fig. 30.40). Most of the time, such as for a text text-input form (see fig. 30.41), you'll just be asked for some information.

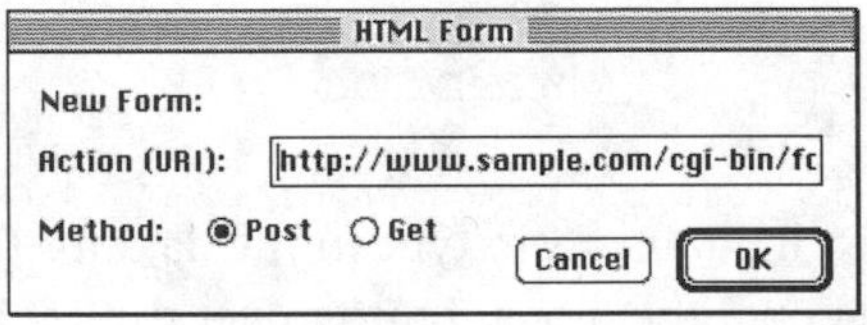

Fig. 30.40
All new forms must be given some critical information that controls its behavior.

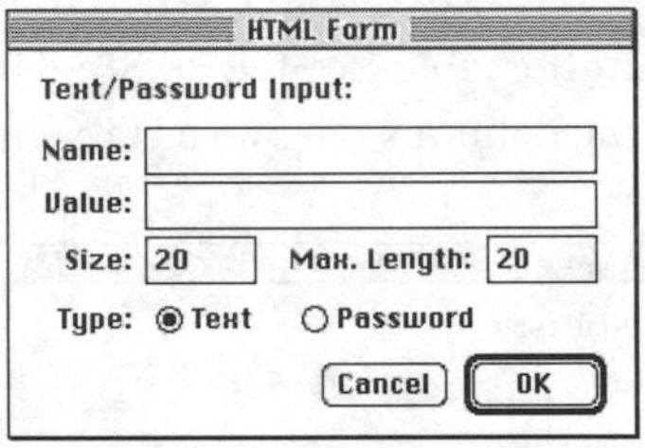

Fig. 30.41
With most forms, HTML.edit just asks you for some basic parameters.

The only exception to this rule is the selection list form. Here, you must select existing text that you want as the items in the selection list. Next, specify that you want to create a list selection form field, with the Form button on the toolbar. You'll be presented with a simple dialog box (see fig. 30.42), where you specify the attributes for the selection form field. Once you've clicked the OK button, the necessary HTML code will be wrapped around the selected text.

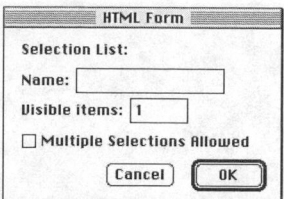

Fig. 30.42
Use this dialog box
to specify the
behavior of your
list selection form
field.

Tip

If you want to create a series of forms, you can bring up the Form Palette. At the
bottom of the Form button is the Form Palette menu item. This will bring up a floating window with all the table-related HTML tags (see fig. 30.43).

Fig. 30.43
The Form Palette
floating window
is a great way to
create lots of
forms.

asWedit

For those HTML authors who mainly use UNIX and X Windows/Motif,
asWedit by AdvaSoft (**http://www.advasoft.com/**) is a good package to
look at. This X Windows/Motif program gives you all the power and functionality you'd want from a good HTML editor. It supports HTML 2, HTML 3,
and Netscape extensions. This product is free for students and nonprofit organizations. Individuals and corporations can try it out for 30 days free of
charge.

Perhaps the most striking thing about asWedit is its user interface (see fig.
30.44). It looks more like a Windows application than an X Windows application. There are button tips, context-sensitive help, and familiar keyboard
shortcuts. The program comes with two toolbars that have the most commonly accessed features available. All the menu bars can be "torn off" the
program and left as floating windows. People who might be afraid of the un-
friendliness of UNIX and X Windows/Motif will feel at home with asWedit's
interface.

VI

HTML Authoring Tools

Fig. 30.44
Although it has the look and feel of a Windows program, asWedit is an X Windows/Motif HTML editor.

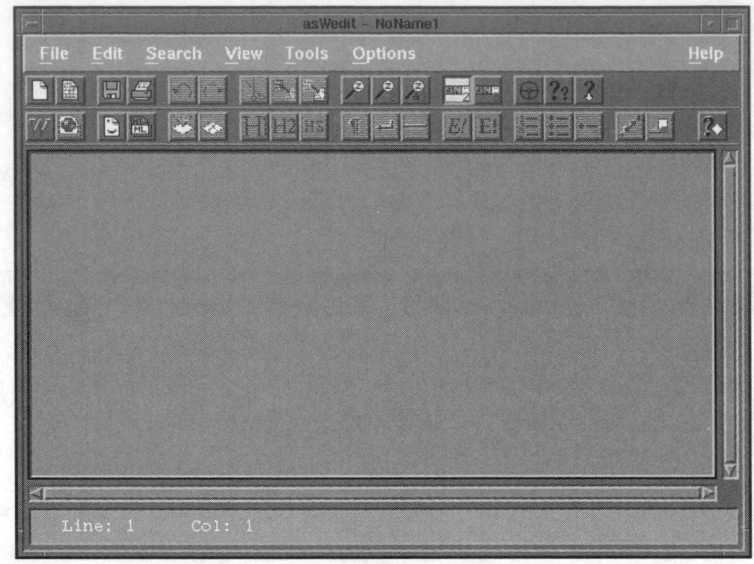

Getting and Installing asWedit

Getting asWedit is a simple matter of downloading a pre-built binary. Simply download the executable that matches your UNIX box from **ftp://sunsite.doc.ic.ac.uk/packages/www/asWedit/**. Available platforms include Sun Sparc, DEC Alpha, AIX, NeXT, and HPUX. The file size varies greatly depending on which platform you're getting, ranging from half a megabyte to three megabytes. Once you get the distribution that matches your system, uncompress and un-tar the file. asWedit will be installed into its own directory which has all the necessary files.

> **Tip**
>
> If you're low on disk space, use the following command to extract the asWedit distribution:
>
>   zcat [asWedit filename] | tar xvf -

If, for some reason, you find that asWedit is a limited or unfriendly package, don't despair. There's ASWedit (note the capitalization), which is the commercial version of asWedit. This version has some extra functionality, enables greater user customization, and has an even friendlier user interface. It retails for $149 and, like its cheaper counterpart, is available on all major UNIX platforms.

General Look and Feel

Entering text with asWedit is a simple matter of putting your cursor somewhere, and typing. It also helps that asWedit follows the typical cursor movement conventions of many other programs. Consequently, if you've used
almost any other word processor, or HTML editor, you'll have no problems
with asWedit. It also comes with a full help file system, including context-
sensitive help. If you're not sure what a particular field is for a dialog box,
simply hit F1.

asWedit also features "tear-off" menus, which allow you to have all the menu
lists in floating windows (see fig. 30.45). At the top of each of the menu lists
is a dashed line which is selectable. Simply select that dashed line, and the
menu will become floating. You can still access the menu through the regular
menu bar, but its floating aspect makes it more accessible.

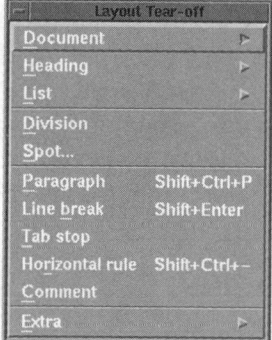

Fig. 30.45
Tear-off menus are
great if you access
particular menu
items a lot.

Working with Tags

Unlike many other tags-only HTML editors, this program doesn't give you
any attributes up front. That is, you select a particular tag, and it's inserted
into your Web page. If you want to activate certain attributes, you often can't
do it when you first create the tag. Most of the time, the only way to get an
attribute is to put it after you've created the tag. Simply put your text cursor
somewhere in an HTML element marker, and click the Edit Tag button.
A dialog box pops up, depending on which HTML element the cursor is
in, and allows you to activate whatever attributes you want (see fig. 30.46).

Note

When your cursor is in an HTML tag, some menu and toolbar options will become
enabled.

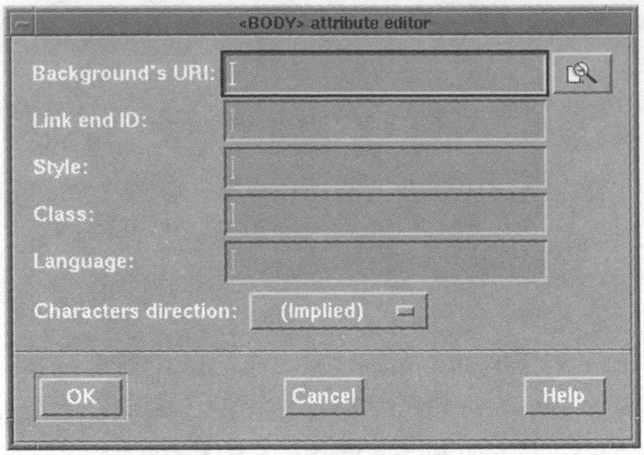

Fig. 30.46
Most of the time, you can only put in HTML attributes by modifying an HTML tag itself.

Creating Links

Probably one of the most common HTML elements you'll want to utilize is the hyperlink. This is done by simply clicking the Hyperlink button on the toolbar. Once you've done that, you'll be presented with a dialog box (see fig. 30.47). Most of the time, you simply enter an URL for the Link Destination field and click the OK button. You can specify the values for as many attributes as you want, and they will all be incorporated into the link. If you want to access some more anchor attributes, just click the More button.

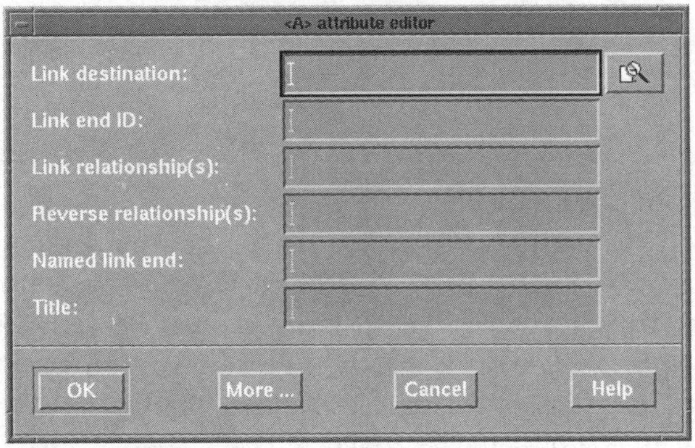

Fig. 30.47
You can make basic or advanced links with this dialog box

Special Features

Perhaps asWedit's strong suit is that it's just jam-packed with features. It has three distinct editing modes: text, HTML 2, and HTML 3. The text mode is equivalent to a tags-only editor in which all of the HTML elements are visible. In either HTML 2 or HTML 3 mode, only tags that are defined for that HTML level of specification are shown. When in one of these modes, the tags are color coordinated so you always know which tags belong together. Almost everything you'd ever want to put into a home page—tables, colored text, forms, and client-side imagemaps—are *all* in this impressive program. In addition to all of this, asWedit also provides support for inserting JAVA Applets into a home page (see fig. 30.48).

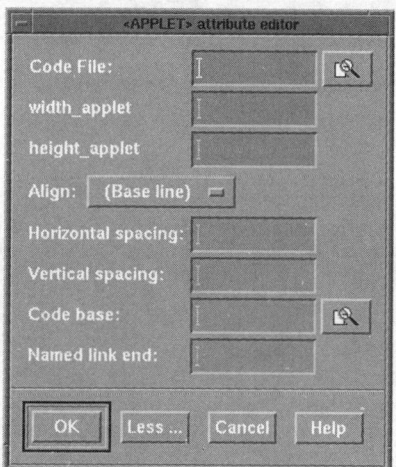

Fig. 30.48
Putting in JAVA Applets is a simple matter of filling out this dialog box.

Emacs HTML Mode

Emacs is an incredibly powerful text editor for UNIX, VMS, and Windows machines. This free text editor goes beyond the breadth and scope of most others. It has features that are often the domain of word processors, including spell checking, text justification, and multiple file support. Emacs works in very distinct modes: some features are only available in certain modes. It was just a matter of time before someone would take this text editor and create an HTML add-on module for it. Nelson Minar has created such a facility.

> **Note**
>
> Emacs is a keyboard-intensive, powerful text editor. A lot of the keystrokes here may seem strange to those unfamiliar with Emacs.

HTML Tags Support

This free Emacs add-on module, written in the Emacs flavor of LISP, adds a new mode (see fig. 30.49). The new HTML helper mode provides easy access to the most common HTML codes. It provides support for most HTML 2 tags, but not HTML 3 or any of Microsoft's or Netscape's extensions. Consequently, this makes HTML helper mode a bit limited in the sophistication of your home page.

Tip

LISP is a programming language used mainly for artificial intelligence.

Fig. 30.49
Emacs users can also write HTML code by getting HTML helper mode.

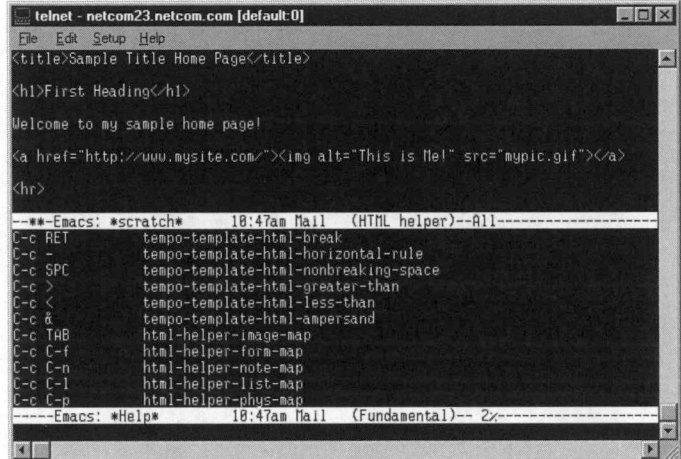

Also, the tag support is very basic. When you insert a tag, you're given just the bare minimum for that particular tag. Link tags don't have extra fields to fill in the extra attributes. The different attributes are only available through other Emacs keystrokes. This makes it difficult for new HTML authors, who might be familiar with Emacs, to create a Web page. The tag support also doesn't work on marked Emacs regions.

Entering Text

To start writing in HTML helper mode, simply have Emacs switch over to it. Traditionally, this is done by hitting the Esc and X keys and then typing **html-helper-mode**. As with some other Emacs modes, most **html-helper-mode** commands are accessible by first pressing Ctrl+C. After that, you can generally just hit the key that corresponds to the first letter of the HTML tag you want to use. For example, if you want to specify the title for your home page, hit Ctrl+C and then Ctrl+B followed by the T key. The cursor is placed in between the start and end markers, so you can type in the title.

Creating Lists

Lists of all sorts are adequately supported with HTML helper mode. When you choose to create a list, Emacs will automatically create the start and end markers of that list. It will also put in the starting marker for the appropriate HTML tag for the list element you want to create. It won't create the ending marker for that tag, nor will it keep adding markers as you add more elements. ❖

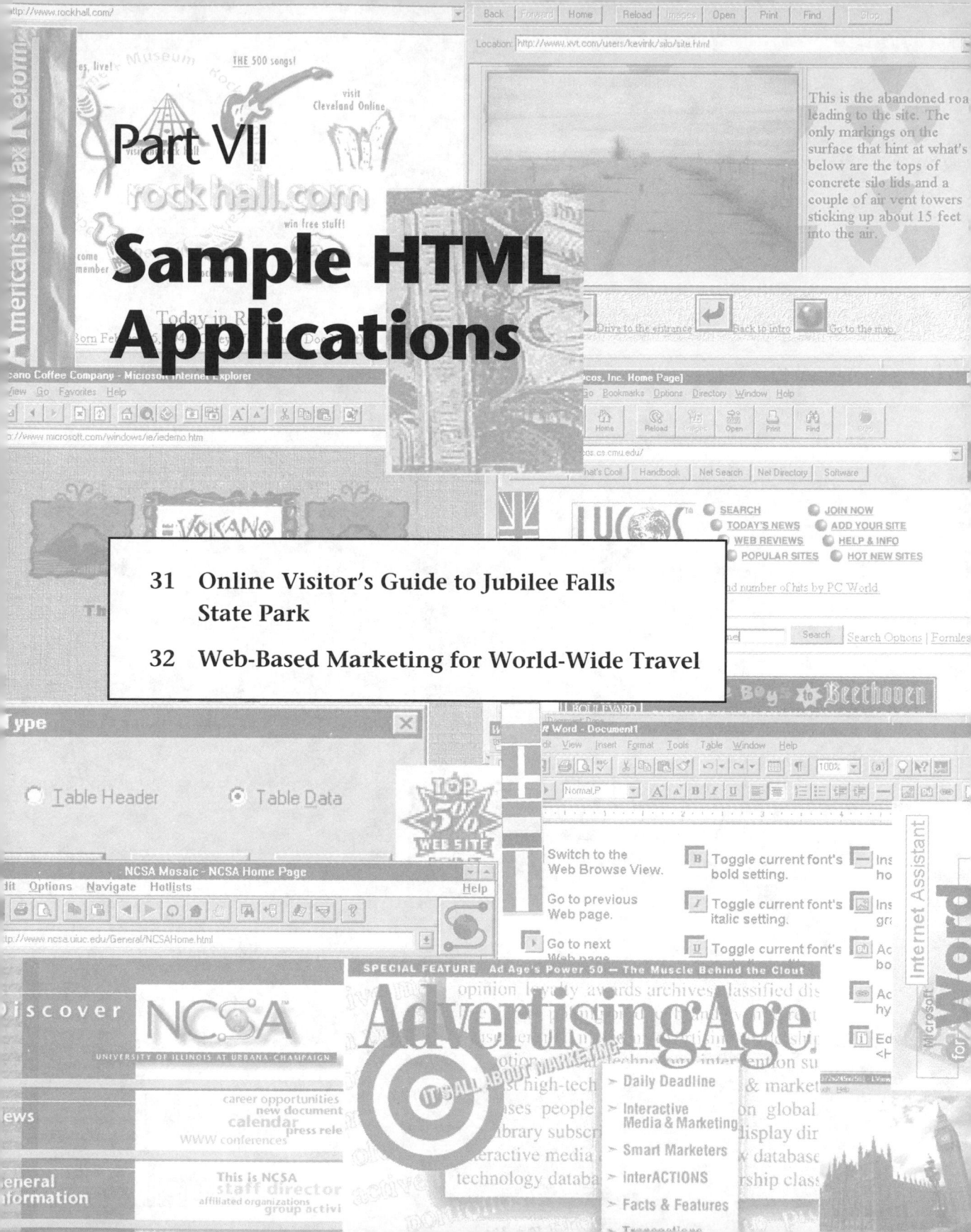

Part VII

Sample HTML Applications

Online Visitor's Guide to Jubilee Falls State Park

by Robert Meegan

The Web is a powerful tool for communications. Unlike most other media, it is both graphical and interactive. These capabilities make it an excellent tool for providing information about tourist attractions and scenic areas.

In this chapter, I'll walk you through the construction of a Web-based guidebook and travel reference for a fictitious Pacific Northwest state park.

The steps we'll undertake are:

- **Defining the goals of the site**

  A clear set of goals is required to create a functional site.

- **Outlining the structure of the site**

  Designing the site before beginning construction helps to ensure that it meets the goals.

- **Creating the guidebook's body text**

  Writing and formatting the text is a fundamental part of a web site project.

- **Designing the guide's graphics and images**

  Graphic design contributes to the overall integrity of the site.

- **Creating the response forms**

  Most sites that provide information should include a form for feedback.

- **Putting the information into HTML documents**

  Assembling the site into documents is the step that converts the plan into an actual site.

- **Adding action with JavaScript**

  Adding Java elements make the site more dynamic and involve the reader in the pages.

Defining Goals

Jubilee State Park is a scenic getaway in the Pacific Northwest, encompassing parts of a mountain range, lakes, waterfalls, and broad forests. For this example, assume that the state park administration has hired you to produce a guidebook for the park.

After interviewing the park staff, you find that their goals include the following:

- To provide an electronic guide complete with seasonal information and park maps
- To broadcast the guidebook over the WWW in an effort to attract tourists
- To display the guidebook on the park's visitor information kiosks
- To provide current information without incurring the costs of reprinting literature
- To increase the park's attendance while managing budget costs

As one of many local and federal facilities trying to increase its seasonal business, and in on-line competition with larger "name" locations such as the Grand Canyon and the Napa Valley region, Jubilee Falls needs to make a concerted effort to promote and advertise its presence on the Internet. As you learned in chapter 20, "Make Yourself Known," you can publicize a Web site in many ways.

First, the Guidebook will be listed on the Web's popular new site references, including the NCSA "What's New on the WWW" page and by post in the UseNet newsgroup **comp.infosystems.www.announce**. Second, the park's designated Webmaster (the person who will manage the site when you are finished) will maintain an on-line presence in UseNet discussion groups that might be interested to know about the park's facilities, such as **alt.rec.camping**, **rec.outdoors.fishing**, **rec.travel.usa-canada**, **rec.climbing**, **misc.kids.vacation**, and **rec.animals.wildlife**.

Outlining the Application

The park rangers have identified four sections for their Web application: the introduction, with a list of services and a history of the park; the park's seasonal schedules and fee and reservation information; a "what's there to do" section, with a list of activities indexed to the park location and when the activity is recommended; and a scenic tour of park images to give users a glimpse of the park's highlights.

The first task is to create a flow chart for each section to lay out the basic structure of the site. These charts show only the individual pages or subgroup of pages, not the intuitive links users will expect when the pages are distributed on-line. Figure 31.1 shows how the main sections of the site interact, figure 31.2 shows the seasonal schedules and fees section, figure 31.3 shows the index of activities, and figure 31.4 shows the scenic tour.

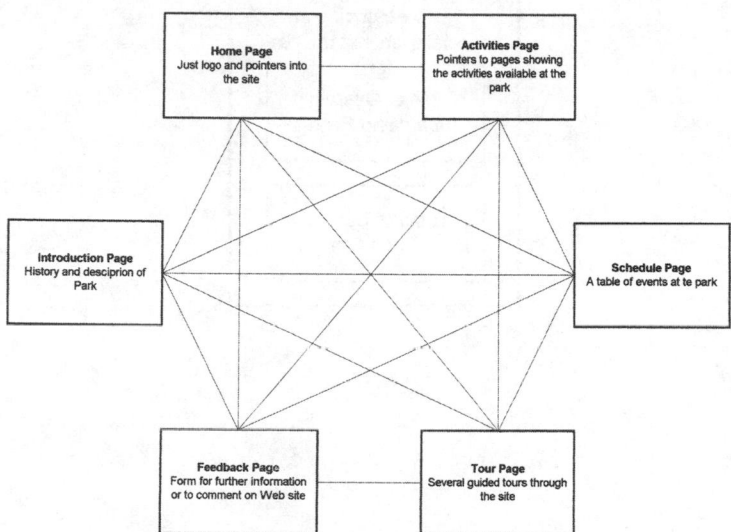

Fig. 31.1
Laying out the structure of the site is the first step

Fig. 31.2
The tables on the schedule and fees pages are also laid out before starting development.

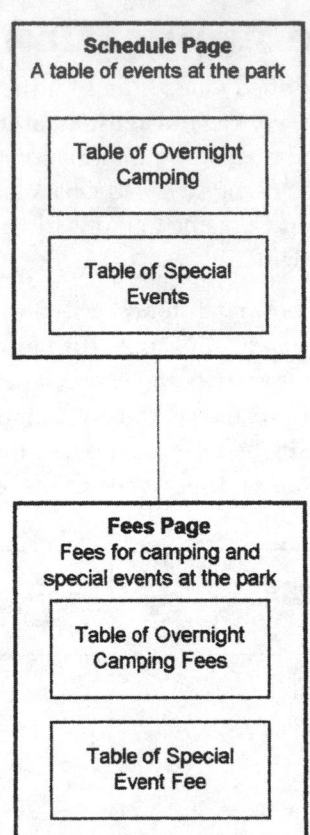

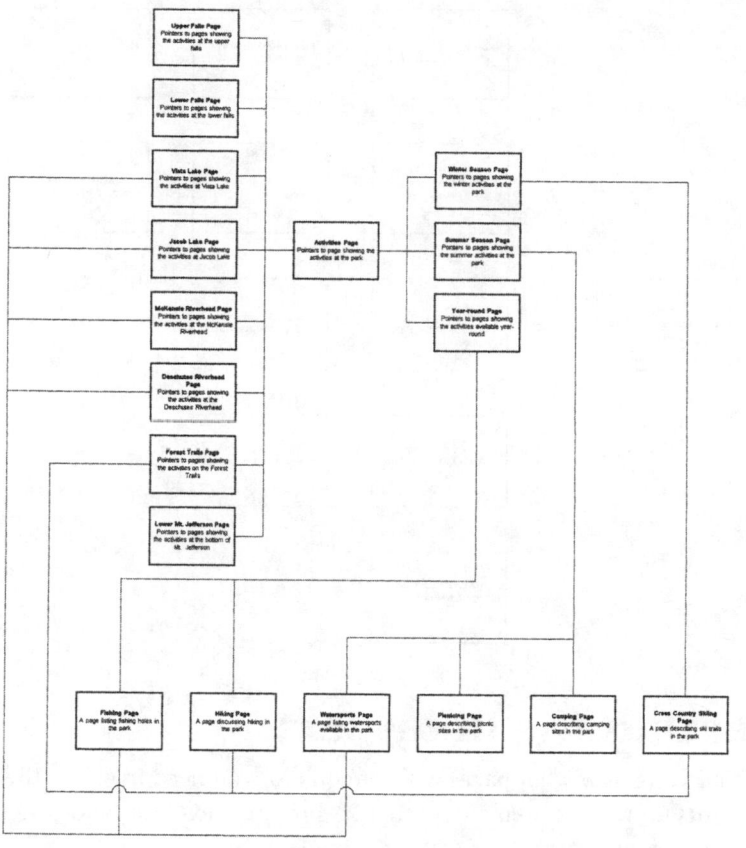

Fig. 31.3
By showing the nature of the connections between the activities, seasons, and locations we can see what links will be needed.

Fig. 31.4
Again, by showing the nature of the connections between the activities, seasons, and locations we can see what links will be needed.

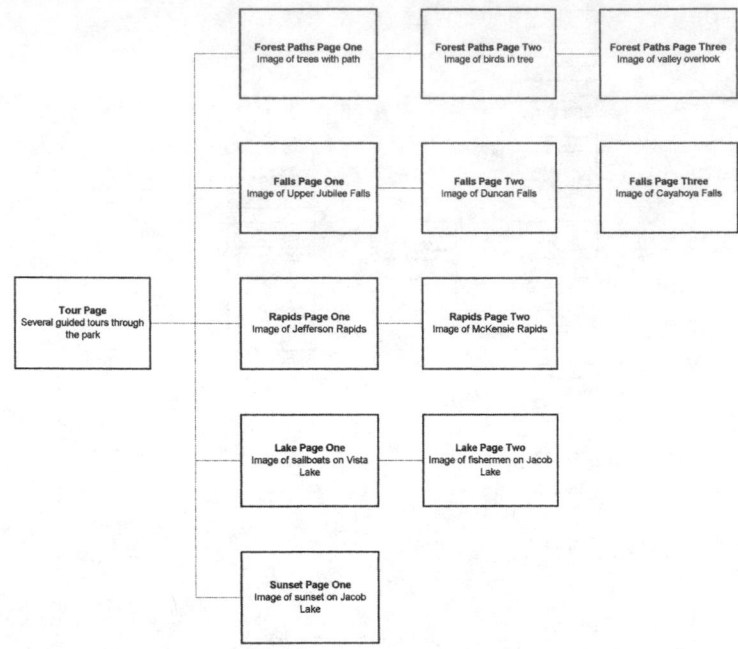

Creating the Body Text

Now that you know what pages will be required, you need to create the text documents for the site. Remember that keeping the text clear and concise on these pages is important.

After the paragraph text is complete, you can add formatting such as headings, lists, and emphasis to the pages. Formatting makes the text more interesting and easier to scan quickly for the desired information. It's important that the pages contain accurate information because visitors will be planning their trips around what is listed here.

◀ See "Creating an HTML Document," p. 115, to find out how to create and format the text.

To help clarify complex information such as the activity schedule listing the overnight camping schedule and the special events for 1996, you can use a couple of tables.

◀ See "Tables and Math Equations," p. 251, for information on table creation.

Creating the Graphics and Images

The park has an official logo, so you can use it on each of the pages. The logo won't create a burden for visitors with slow connections because their systems will cache it after they load it the first time. The logo was created in CorelDRAW! and is stored as a CDR file. Because it is not a standard Web graphic format, you can open CorelDRAW! and export the logo as a GIF file). This way, you also get a chance to resize it so that it fits nicely on the page.

Because you're running CorelDRAW! already, you also can take the time to make some icons that are similar to the signs used at the park to direct visitors (see fig. 31.5). These icons help give your site a visual consistency that's just a little different than other sites. You need to export each of these icons into GIF format as well.

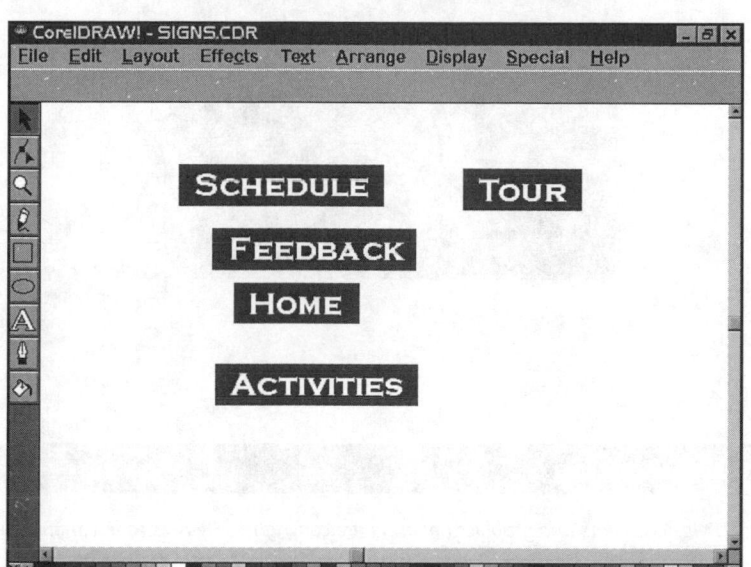

Fig. 31.5
Special icons created just for your site make it more interesting for the visitor.

> **Note**
>
> Graphic design is more than just making pictures; it entails choosing an overall organizing purpose and graphical "feel." Mixing unrelated graphic types, mismatched color schemes, and inconsistent elements indicates a novice approach to graphic design.

Many of the Web pages will display color photo images of scenic sights and activities. The park hired a photographer last summer to document the park's natural beauty. When the photographs arrived, they were converted to a CD-ROM disc in the Kodak PhotoCD format. You can use an excellent shareware program, LView Pro, to manipulate the photos, as shown in figure 31.6.

A couple of the images need some cropping, to reduce the image size, but LView handles that chore easily. If the color balance or contrast is out of line, you can adjust that as well. Finally, reduce the color depth to 256 colors and resize the images to make thumbnail-sized pictures. Using smaller pictures reduces the amount of time needed to download the pictures. You can put a link to the full-sized true-color images so viewers can download them if they want to.

Fig. 31.6
A graphics file conversion program is a must for building a web site.

Troubleshooting

The HTML documents and graphics I'm using are copyrighted by my organization. How do we protect our intellectual property over the Web?

Truthfully, you can't. If people want to steal from you badly enough, they will. What's prudent, though, is to protect the accidental misuse of your work. This happens when users include links from their Web pages to pages on your server that are "inside" the application, away from the main page that usually contains the author's information and company affiliation. For the best protection, include copyright statements on each page (using the smallest heading size, H6, to keep them unobtrusive) and LINK statements in the documents' head sections to identify the author and the originating organization. You can also add copyright statements in fine print to graphics if necessary.

Creating the Input Forms

The Jubilee Falls Guidebook is primarily intended to deliver information; an on-site kiosk is less complicated if users aren't asked to input information (and a keyboard isn't necessary). But, for the on-line audience, using a form that can be filled out to receive additional park information by mail is a great idea. The people who use it are most likely not from the local area and probably don't have access to the Park Service's printed materials.

In chapter 21, "Forms and How They Work," you learned that a response form is the perfect way to get feedback from site visitors, so create one to give people a way to get in touch with you. The form is written in HTML as follows (LOG.HTM):

Listing 31.1   The Log Page

```
<HTML>
<HEAD>
<TITLE>Jubilee Falls Visitor's Log</TITLE>
</HEAD>

<BODY>
<IMG ALIGN=middle SRC="../ logo.gif">
<H1>Jubilee Falls State Park</H1>
<H2>Visitor's Log </H2>
<P>
As a public facility, we exist to serve you.
 Tell us how we are doing, or let us know if you would
 like more information mailed to you.
<P>
If you would like to be on our electronic mailing list
 choose the "Yes" button below — we will keep you informed
 of special park schedules, special holiday rates and
 regional activities that might interest you to visit
 our neck of the woods.
<P>
<HR>
<FORM METHOD=POST ACTION="http://www.jubilee.org/cgi-bin/log_script">
<H3>Visitor's Log</H3>
<P>
First Name: <INPUT TYPE="text" NAME="fname" SIZE=25 VALUE=""><BR>
Last Name: <INPUT TYPE="text" NAME="lame" SIZE=25 VALUE=""><BR>
Mailing address: <BR><TEXTAREA NAME="message" ROWS="4" COLS="30">
 </TEXTAREA>
<P>
E-mail address (for responses and mailing list):
<BR>
<INPUT NAME="email" SIZE=25 VALUE="">
<P>
I would like to receive <SELECT NAME="mailer">
<OPTION SELECTED VALUE="nothing"> Nothing
<OPTION VALUE="brochure"> Jubilee Falls brochure
<OPTION VALUE="calendar"> Jubilee Falls Calendar
<OPTION VALUE="activities"> Jubilee Falls Activities Schedule
<OPTION VALUE="stateparks"> Oregon State Parks catalog
<OPTION VALUE="everything"> All information
</SELECT>
```

(continues)

Listing 31.1   Continued

```
<P>
Enter a message if you wish:
<P>
<TEXTAREA NAME="message" ROWS="10" COLS="60"></TEXTAREA>
<P>
I would like to be on your Internet mailing list.
<INPUT TYPE="radio" NAME="list" VALUE="yes">Yes
<INPUT TYPE="radio" NAME="list" VALUE="no">No
</FORM>
<HR>
<P>
Thank you for visiting the Jubilee Falls Guidebook and for taking
 a few minutes to send us a message. We appreciate your patronage!
<P>
<A HREF="http://www.jubilee.org/cgi-bin/menu">
<IMG SRC="../graphics/menubar.gif" ISMAP></A>
<H6>&copy 1996 Jubilee Falls State Park</H6>
</BODY>
</HTML>
```

You can check how your form looks by opening it in Netscape Navigator, as shown in figure 31.7.

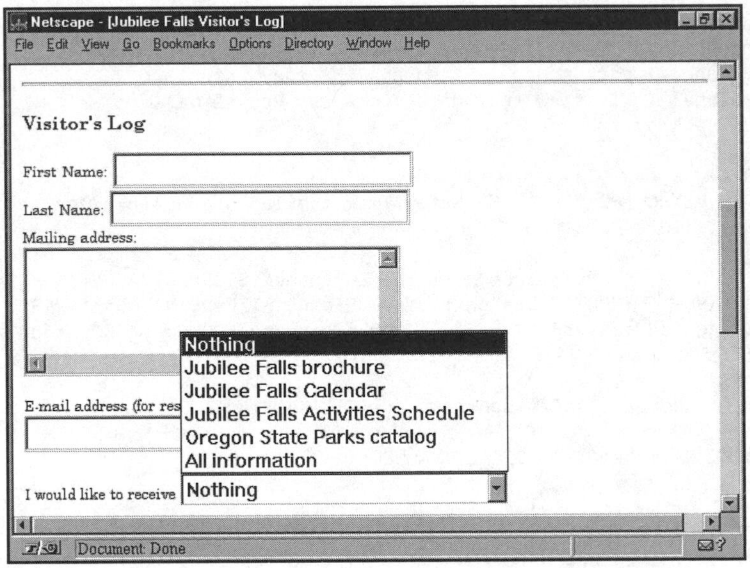

Fig. 31.7
The log page is ready for entry by site visitors

Writing the Pages

You know that the majority of visitors to your site will probably run Netscape Navigator or Microsoft Internet Explorer, but some will use a Mosaic-based browser. To avoid limiting your site to visitors with a specific browser, stick to HTML 2.0, with the exception of the form and some tables. Most browsers support these HTML 3.0 extensions now, and they add a lot to the site.

The Home Page

The following code is the Jubilee Falls State Park home page in HTML (HOME.HTM). This page is intentionally simple so that it will load quickly. If anyone contacts you about adding a link to the site, you want them to point to this spot.

Listing 31.2   The Main Page

```
<HTML>
<HEAD>
<TITLE>Jubilee State Park Guidebook</TITLE>
</HEAD>
<BODY>
<IMG SRC="..\logo.gif" ALT="Welcome to the Jubilee Falls State Park Guidebook">
<P>
<H3>Select a menu option:</H3>
<P>    <A HREF="intro.htm">[Introduction]</A>    <A HREF="schedule.htm">
 [Schedules and Fees]</A>
<P>   <A HREF="activity.htm">[Park activities]</A> <A HREF="tour.htm">
 [Scenic walking tour]</A>
<P>
<HR>
<P>
<A HREF="schedule.htm"><IMG ALIGN=bottom SRC="../schedule_sign.gif"></A>
<A HREF="activity.htm"><IMG ALIGN=bottom SRC="../activities_sign.gif"></A>
<A HREF="tour.htm"><IMG ALIGN=bottom SRC="../tour_sign.gif"></A>
<A HREF="feedback.htm"><IMG ALIGN=bottom SRC="../feedback_sign.gif"></A>
<P>
<H6>&copy1996 Jubilee Falls State Park</H6>
</BODY>
</HTML>
```

The result is shown in figure 31.8.

Fig. 31.8
The Jubilee Falls
State Park home
page is designed to
load quickly.

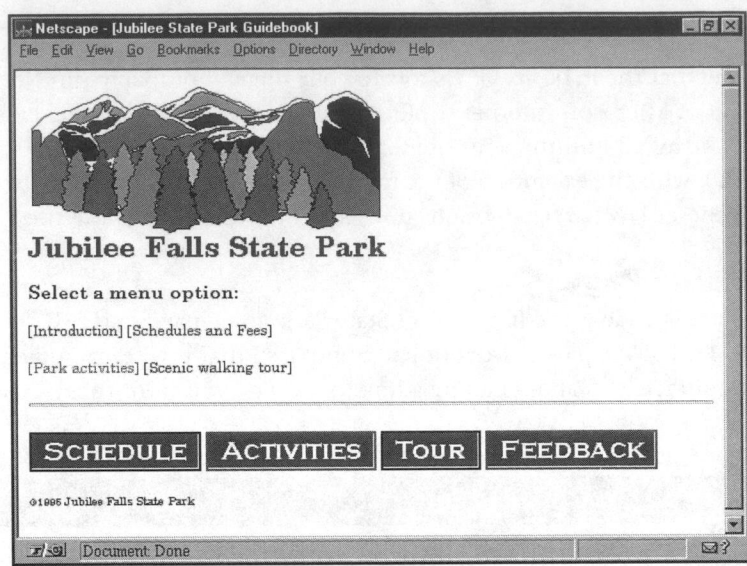

The Introduction Page

The following code is the Jubilee Falls State Park welcome page in HTML
(INTRO.HTM).

Listing 31.3   The Introduction Page

```
<HTML>
<HEAD>
<TITLE>Jubilee Falls Guidebook</TITLE>
</HEAD>
<BODY>
<IMG ALIGN=bottom SRC="..\logo.gif">
<H1>Jubilee Falls Guidebook</H1>
Welcome to Jubilee Falls State Park, the crown jewel of the Cascades.
 A day's drive from five northwestern U.S. states and Canada's
 British Columbia, Jubilee Falls is a frequent destination for
 families and outdoors enthusiasts.
<P>
Jubilee Falls State Park provides year-round facilities for such
 popular activities as fly cast fishing and hiking. Our overnight
 facilities are open nine months a year, including two winter months
 for snow activities.
<P>
Covering an area of 1151 square miles, Jubilee Falls is roughly the
 same size as Yosemite National Park, and boasts as wide and
 spectacular assortment of natural wonders. The Jubilee Falls are
 among the most spectacular in the world, many with a vertical drop
 of over 900 feet. Jubilee Falls was commissioned by Governor Robert
 MacKensey in 1937, and is proud to have served over eight million
 visitors from countries worldwide.
```

```
<P>
You are invited to <A HREF="facility.htm">check out our facilities</A>,
 discover the natural beauty of the Cascades in our
<A HREF="tour.htm">walking scenic tour</A>, and learn about the
<A HREF="activity.htm">rich experience</A> awaiting you at Jubilee
 Falls State Park.
<HR>
<P>
<A HREF="jubilee.htm"><IMG ALIGN=bottom SRC="../home_sign.gif"></A>
<A HREF="schedule.htm"><IMG ALIGN=bottom SRC="../schedule_sign.gif"></A>
<A HREF="activity.htm"><IMG ALIGN=bottom SRC="../activities_sign.gif"></A>
<A HREF="tour.htm"><IMG ALIGN=bottom SRC="../tour_sign.gif"></A>
<A HREF="feedback.htm"><IMG ALIGN=bottom SRC="../feedback_sign.gif"></A>
<P>
<H6>&copy1996 Jubilee Falls State Park</H6>
</BODY>
</HTML>
```

The result is shown in figure 31.9.

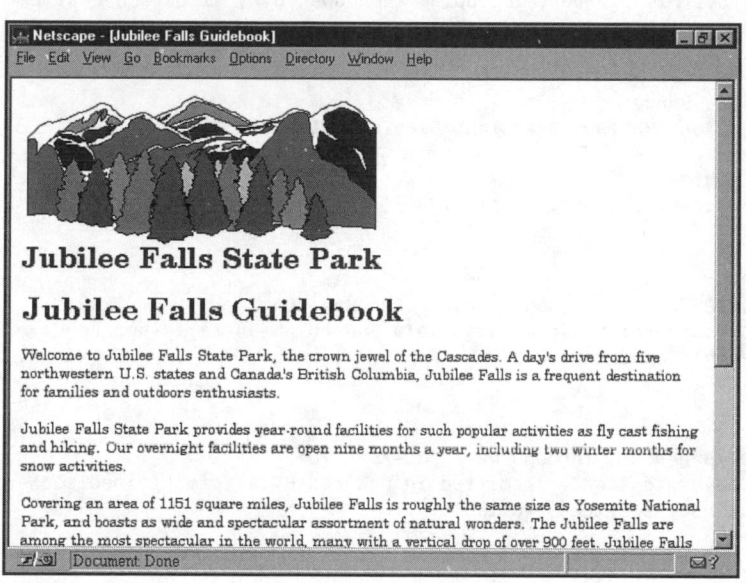

Fig. 31.9
The introduction page gives a detailed description of the park.

The Schedule Page

The following code is the Jubilee Falls State Park Schedules and Fees page in HTML (SCHEDULE.HTM).

Listing 31.4   The Schedule Page

```
<HTML>
<HEAD>
<TITLE>Jubilee Falls State Park Schedules and Fees</TITLE>
</HEAD>
<BODY>
<IMG ALIGN=middle SRC="..\logo.gif">
<H1>Schedules and Fees</H1>
<P>
<H2 ALIGN = CENTER>Jubilee Falls Day Areas</H2>
<P>
<EM>Open 365 days a year, including major holidays.</EM>
<P>These areas include the hiking trails and boat slips on the
 McKensie riverhead. A <A HREF="fees.htm">list of fees</A> for entry
 and activities is available.
<P>
<P>
<H2 ALIGN = CENTER>Jubilee Falls Overnight Areas</H2>
<P>
The overnight areas, including the powered RV slips and rustic
 camping sites, are available on a seasonal basis.
<P>

<Table Border>
<Caption><H3>1996 Overnight Camping Calendar<H3></Caption>
<TR>
<TH>Date</TH>
<TH>Acceptable Activities</TH>
</TR>

<TR>
<TD><B>Jan. 1 through February 29</B></TD>
<TD>No overnight areas available due to potentially hazardous winter
 weather conditions.</TD>
</TR>

<TR>
<TD><B>March 1 through March 31</B></TD>
<TD>Overnight only permitted in powered RV slips. Limited shower and
 bathroom services available.</TD>
</TR>

<TR>
<TD><B>April 1 through October 31</B></TD>
<TD>Overnight available in all areas. Full shower and bathroom
 services available. Weather advisories may close the camping sites,
 so check with the local weather information before planning your
 stay.</TD>
</TR>

<TR>
<TD><B>November 1 through November 30</B></TD>
<TD>Overnight only permitted in powered RV slips. Limited shower and
 bathroom services available.</TD>
</TR>
```

```
<TR>
<TD><B>December 1 through December 31</B></TD>
<TD>No overnight areas available due to potentially hazardous winter
  weather conditions.</TD>
</TR>
</Table>

<P>
<H2 ALIGN = CENTER>1996 Activities Calendar</H2>
Jubilee Falls hosts many events year-round for outdoors enthusiasts.
  The following activities have been scheduled. Please
<A HREF="feedback.htm"> contact us</A> for late-breaking events and
  calendar changes.
<P>

<Table Border>
<Caption><H3>Schedule of Events for 1996<H3></Caption>
<TR>
<TH>Date</TH>
<TH>Event</TH>
<TH>Description</TH>
</TR>

<TR>
<TD><B>May 11-12</B></TD>
<TD><B>Couples Caravan Weekend</B></TD>
<TD>Jubilee Falls throws a party for adult couples, including our
  nightly chuckwagon banquet and music under the stars. Midnight
  walking tours are held and all water activities are included in the
  registration fees.</TD>
</TR>

<TR>
<TD><B>June 22</B></TD>
<TD><B>Lightning Bug Races</B></TD>
<TD>Overnighters can participate in Jubilee Falls' renowned Lightning
  Bug Races. This evening activity is open to children of all ages and
  features prizes galore.</TD>
</TR>

<TR>
<TD><B>July 6</B></TD>
<TD><B>Falls Jubilee</B></TD>
<TD>The holiday weekend features the Falls Jubilee, a celebration of
  the natural landmarks that make our park special. Walking tours and
  public swimming are available in the high pools, underneath the
  Widow Falls, the tallest waterfalls in the park.</TD>
</TR>

<TR>
<TD><B>August 17-18</B></TD>
<TD><B>Kids Camp Jubilee</B></TD>
<TD>A weekend for pre-teens, Jubilee Falls hosts over a dozen local
  teen groups for fun in the sun. The weekend's highlight is the
```

(continues)

Listing 31.4 Continued

```
McKensie Olympics, pitting teams of water-logged kids in seven
competitive events.</TD>
</TR>
</TABLE>
<HR>
<P>
<A HREF="home.htm"><IMG ALIGN=bottom SRC="../home_sign.gif"></A>
<A HREF="activity.htm"><IMG ALIGN=bottom SRC="../
➥activities_sign.gif"></A>
<A HREF="tour.htm"><IMG ALIGN=bottom SRC="../tour_sign.gif"></A>
<A HREF="feedback.htm"><IMG ALIGN=bottom SRC="../
➥feedback_sign.gif"></A>
<P>
<H6>&copy1996 Jubilee Falls State Park</H6>
</BODY>
</HTML>
```

The Schedules and Fees page is shown in figure 31.10.

Fig. 31.10
The schedules page shows how tables can be used for an attractive layout.

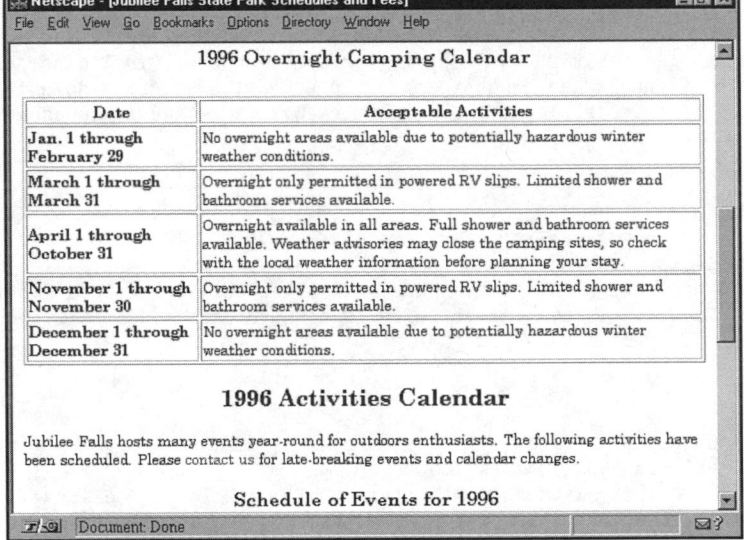

The Activities Page

The following code is the Jubilee Falls State Park Activities Index page in HTML (ACTIVITY.HTM).

Listing 31.5   The Activity Page

```
<HTML>
<HEAD>
<TITLE>Jubilee Falls State Park Activities Index</TITLE>

</HEAD>
<BODY>
<IMG ALIGN=middle SRC="..\logo.gif"><H1>Activities Index</H1>
<P>
Jubilee Falls offers a wide variety of activities for everyone from
 the avid outdoorsman to the weekend nature lover. This index
 provides the following for park activities:
<UL>
<LI>Location
<LI>Seasonal availability
<LI>Available park resources
<LI>Fees required
<LI>Recommended experience
</UL></DL>
<P>
<A HREF="file://../activity.qtw"><IMG ALIGN=bottom
 SRC="../movie_button.gif"></A>A short QuickTime video shows many of
 our most popular activities.
<P><PRE> </PRE>
<P>
<H2>Index Starting Point</H2>
Choose a category to begin your search from. You can return to this
 menu at any time by clicking the activities button: <IMG
ALIGN=middle
 SRC="../activities_sign.gif">
<P>
<DL>
<DT><B>By Season</B>
<DD><A HREF="winter.htm">Winter Season</A>
<DD><A HREF="summer.htm">Summer Season</A>
<DD><A HREF="yearly.htm">Year-round</A>
</DL>
<DL>
<DT><B>By Location</B>
<DD><A HREF="mckensie.htm">McKensie Riverhead</A>
<DD><A HREF="deschute.htm">Deschutes Riverhead</A>
<DD><A HREF="mt_jef.htm">Lower Mt. Jefferson</A>
<DD><A HREF="up_falls.htm">Upper Falls</A>
<DD><A HREF="low_falls.htm">Lower Falls</A>
<DD><A HREF="vista.htm">Vista Lake</A>
<DD><A HREF="jacob.htm">Jacob Lake</A>
<DD><A HREF="trail.htm">Forest Trails</A>
</DL>
<HR>
<P>
<A HREF="jubilee.htm"><IMG ALIGN=bottom SRC="../home_sign.gif"></A>
<A HREF="schedule.htm"><IMG ALIGN=bottom SRC="../
➥schedule_sign.gif"></A>
```

(continues)

Listing 31.5   Continued

```
<A HREF="tour.htm"><IMG ALIGN=bottom SRC="../tour_sign.gif"></A>
<A HREF="feedback.htm"><IMG ALIGN=bottom SRC="../
➥feedback_sign.gif"></A>
<P>
<H6>&copy1996 Jubilee Falls State Park</H6>
</BODY>
</HTML>
```

The resulting page is shown in figure 31.11.

Fig. 31.11
The activity page
includes a link to
a downloadable
Quicktime movie.

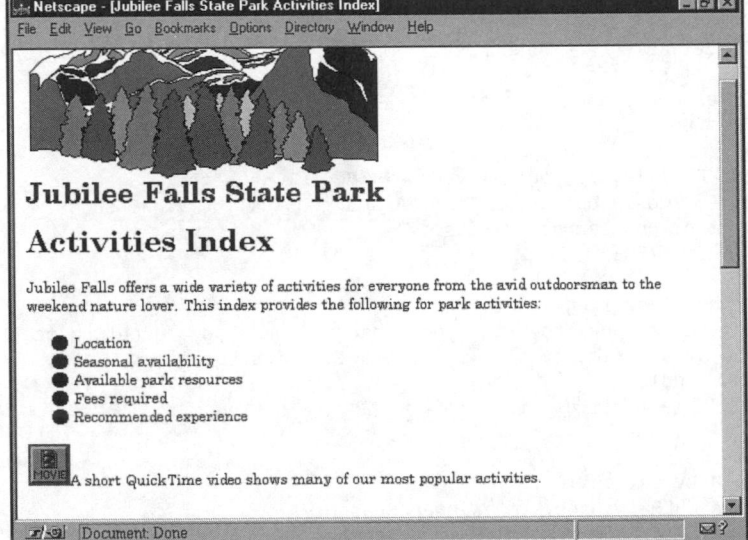

The Tour Page

The following code is the Jubilee Falls State Park Scenic Walking Tour page in
HTML (TOUR.HTM).

Listing 31.6   The Tour Page

```
<HTML>
<HEAD>
<TITLE>Jubilee Falls State Park Scenic Walking Tour</TITLE>
</HEAD>
<BODY>
<IMG ALIGN=middle SRC="..\logo.gif">
<H1>Scenic Walking Tour</H1>
<P>
Jubilee Falls is a place of great natural beauty. Don't believe us,
 or want to see more? Then join us on a walking tour of the park. You
```

```
 can let us lead the way or choose your own path to explore the
 wonders of Jubilee Falls State Park.
<P>
<A HREF="path1.htm"><IMG ALIGN=middle SRC="../tour_sign.gif">Follow
 the park's guide down the wooded path.</A>
<P>
or choose a path for yourself:
<P><A HREF="path1.htm"><IMG ALIGN=middle SRC="../tour_sign.gif">
 Walk the forest paths</A>
<P><A HREF="falls1.htm"><IMG ALIGN=middle SRC="../tour_sign.gif">
 Do you hear falling water?</A>
<P><A HREF="river1.htm"><IMG ALIGN=middle SRC="../tour_sign.gif">
 Water rushing into rivers</A>
<P><A HREF="lake1.htm"><IMG ALIGN=middle SRC="../tour_sign.gif">
 Alone on a lakeshore</A>
<P><A HREF="sunset.htm"><IMG ALIGN=middle SRC="../tour_sign.gif">
 Until tomorrow . . .</A>
<P>
<HR>
<P>
<A HREF="home.htm"><IMG ALIGN=bottom SRC="../home_sign.gif"></A>
<A HREF="activity.htm"><IMG ALIGN=bottom SRC="../ activities_sign.gif"></A>
<A HREF="schedule.htm"><IMG ALIGN=bottom SRC="../ schedule_sign.gif"></A>
<A HREF="feedback.htm"><IMG ALIGN=bottom SRC="../ feedback_sign.gif"></A>
<P>
<H6>&copy1996 Jubilee Falls State Park</H6>
</BODY>
</HTML>
```

The Scenic Walking Tour page is shown in figure 31.12.

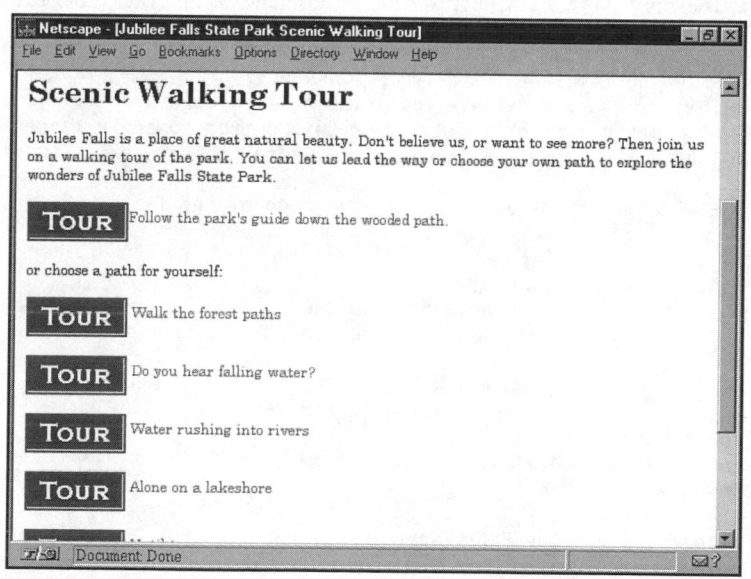

Fig. 31.12
The walking tour page provides links to a series of guided tours through the park.

The Falls Tour Page One

The following code is the Jubilee Falls State Park Walking Tour: The Falls page in HTML (FALLS1.HTM).

Listing 31.7   The Falls Page One

```
<HTML>
<HEAD>
<TITLE>Walking Tour: The Falls</TITLE>
</HEAD>
<BODY>
<H1>Scenic Walking Tour</H1>
<P>
<H2>Jubilee Falls</H2>
<P>
The highlight of Jubilee Falls State Park is its namesake, the
 Jubilee Falls. This series of water drops begins in the Upper Falls,
 where the park's tallest waterfall is located, and continues with
 the Lower Falls, where the series of small drops creates a chain of
 swimming holes with dense forest undergrowth.
<P>
The park's namesake can be seen from many vantage points, but this
 rest stop is one of the most dramatic.
<P>
<IMG ALIGN=bottom SRC="../falls1.gif"><BR>
<A HREF="../graphics/falls1a.jpg"><IMG ALIGN=middle
 SRC= "../grn_bullet.gif"></A> Click this button to see a larger
 version of the Jubilee Falls (<I>note: this file is 370K</I>).
<P>
The Lower Falls is filled with the sound of falling water. These
 small drops are a main outflow of snow-bound water from the local
 segment of the Cascade mountain range.
<P>
<IMG ALIGN=bottom SRC="../falls2.gif"><BR>
<A HREF="../graphics/falls1a.jpg"><IMG ALIGN=middle
 SRC= "../grn_bullet.gif"></A> Click this button to see a larger
 version of the lower Jubilee Falls (<I>note: this file is 370K</I>).
<P>
<A HREF="falls2.htm">Continue</A> your tour of the falls.
<P>
<HR>
<P>
<A HREF="home.htm"><IMG ALIGN=bottom SRC="../home_sign.gif"></A>
<A HREF="activity.htm"><IMG ALIGN=bottom SRC="..
activities_sign.gif"></A>
<A HREF="tour.htm"><IMG ALIGN=bottom SRC="../tour_sign.gif"></A>
<A HREF="schedule.htm"><IMG ALIGN=bottom SRC="../
schedule_sign.gif"></A>
<A HREF="feedback.htm"><IMG ALIGN=bottom SRC="../
feedback_sign.gif"></A>
<P>
<H6>&copy1996 Jubilee Falls State Park</H6>
</BODY>
</HTML>
</BODY>
</HTML>
```

The result is shown in figure 31.13.

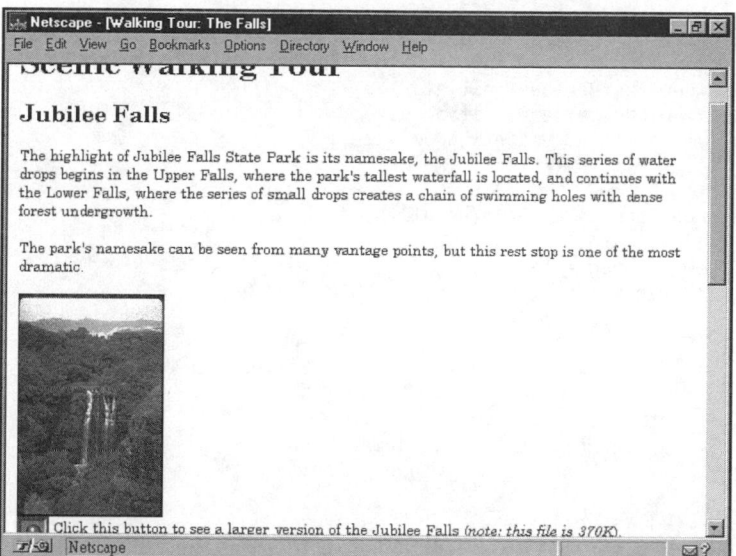

Fig. 31.13
A small graphic
can be included in
a web page, with a
link to the much
larger original
version.

Adding a JavaScript Marquee

In chapter 26, "Java and JavaScript," you learned how you can add Java
applets and JavaScript programs to an HTML page to make it dynamic. One
very popular type of Java applet is a marquee that scrolls a message. You can
use such a marquee on the example site to scroll information about special
events and the weather.

To simplify your work, write the marquee in JavaScript. Following is the code
that scrolls a message in the status bar of the browser. You add this code to
the <HEAD> section of any page on which you want to have the information
appear.

Listing 31.8   The JavaScript Code for Adding a Scrolling Marquee

```
<SCRIPT LANGUAGE="JavaScript">

<!-- Comments hide this program for browsers that don't understand JavaScript

var window_size = 0;

// These two lines are the message that is scrolled in the status
// window
```

(continues)

Listing 31.8 Continued

```
var Status1="Overnight camping begins on March 1st.";
var Status2="The weather will be sunny and 65F this weekend.";

function StartMarquee(initial_size) {
        window_size = initial_size;
        ScrolledMessage(window_size);
}

function ScrolledMessage(scrollto) {
        var StatusLine;
        var msg = " ";
        var i = 0;
        var speed = 50;

        StatusLine = Status1+"......"+Status2;

        scrollto--;
        if (scrollto == -StatusLine.length)
                scrollto = window_size;

        if (scrollto > 0) {
                for (i = 0; i < scrollto; i++)
                        msg = " "+msg;
                msg = msg + StatusLine;
        } else
                msg = StatusLine.substring(-scrollto,
StatusLine.length);

        msg = msg.substring(0,window_size);
        window.status= msg;
        window.setTimeout('ScrolledMessage('+scrollto+')',speed);
}
// end of comment that hides the JavaScript code -->

</SCRIPT>
</HEAD>
<BODY onload="StartMarquee(200)">
</BODY>
```

Figure 31.14 shows what the Activities page looks like with the marquee scrolling across the status bar.

Now, take a look at what this script does. The JavaScript functions StartMarquee and ScrolledMessage are contained entirely within the HEAD container to ensure that the browser loads the program before it is called. The BODY container's attribute onload causes the browser to run the program when the page has been loaded.

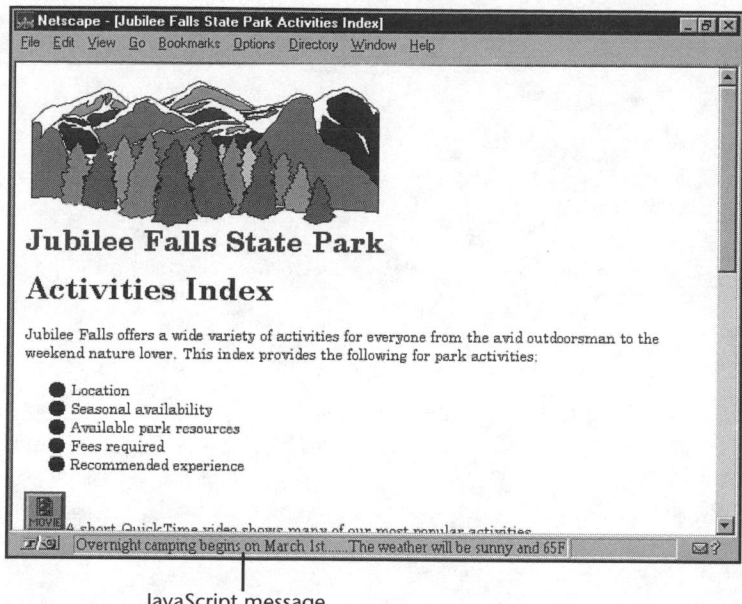

Fig. 31.14
By adding a
JavaScript message
to the scrollbar,
we can make a
page much more
dynamic.

JavaScript message

When the browser calls the `StartMarquee` function, it initializes the window size for the marquee. The initial value is 200, but you can use a smaller value to make the marquee window smaller. `StartMarquee`, in turn, calls `ScrolledMessage`. After `ScrolledMessage` is called, the message continues to run for as long as the page is displayed.

The actual message that scrolls in the status window is in `ScrolledMessage`, where it is split into two parts: `Status1` and `Status2`. You can change to a new message if you want. On this page, remind your visitors that the camping season starts on March first and let them know that the weather should be nice this weekend.

The speed at which the message scrolls is controlled by the variable `speed`. The lower the value of `speed`, the faster it scrolls. It's set to 50 in this case.

After this program starts, it begins scrolling the marquee message within the status bar of the browser. The great advantage to having the message in the status bar is that it will always remain on the screen, even if the user scrolls the document window.

The next chapter will take many of the techniques that we developed here and use them in an entirely different environment. ❖

## CHAPTER 32

Web-Based Marketing for World-Wide Travel

by Robert Meegan

The Web provides many opportunities for a business to greatly increase its exposure to potential customers. If a company's business is a retail outlet or a service that can be performed remotely, it can use a Web site to provide an online catalog of goods or services.

In this chapter, you will create a Web-based brochure for a travel agency.

The steps needed to complete this task are:

- **Defining the goals of the site**

  In order to make the site an effective business tool, the goals must be clear and well defined.

- **Outlining the structure of the site**

  To meet the goals that we defined, the site must be completely designed before construction begins.

- **Designing the guide's graphics and images**

  A commercial site should make use of a strong graphic presence on the Web to attract customers.

- **Creating the response forms**

  Once customers have been drawn into the site, the next step is to provide a location for feedback and requests.

- **Reusing previously written elements**

  One of the principles of cost effective computer development is that code and other elements should be designed to be flexible enough for reuse.

- **Adding action with JavaScript**

  A commercial site can make excellent use of a short JavaScript.

Defining Goals

For this example, assume that the owner of World-Wide Travel (WWT) was exploring the Web, looking at potential destinations for his services when he came across the Jubilee Falls State Park site that you created in the preceding chapter. He was impressed enough with the quality of the site to contact the park's Webmaster and inquire as to who developed it. He then contacted you and asked if you would be interested in building a site for his company.

After you accepted the contract, you met with him and his staff and found out that they are a medium-sized travel agency that is not affiliated with any of the major chains. Several members of the staff were familiar enough with the Web to realize that it represented the opportunity to develop a nation-wide customer base for relatively little expense.

Their goals for the site included the following:

- Developing a corporate presence on the Net that could serve to attract customers
- Showcasing the tours and travel packages that the agency represented
- Showing a listing of current travel specials that could change daily
- Providing an online information request form for visitors to request literature
- Improving the agency's market size without greatly increasing advertising costs

Creating a Corporate Presence Online

To get as much exposure as possible for their site, the people at WWT have decided to use many of the methods discussed in chapter 20, "Make Yourself Known," for advertising a Web site.

After the site is complete, the site's Webmaster (the person in charge of maintaining the site) will register the site with as many search tools as he or she can. This includes registering with all the major databases and Webcrawlers, and trying to locate any specialized travel, business, and vacation sites that might be willing to list the WWT site. At this time, the management at WWT doesn't think that it would be cost effective to sponsor one of the popular Web sites, but they might be willing to rent a storefront on one of the Internet malls, if the site begins to bring some new business.

> **Note**
>
> This strategy is probably good for a small- to medium-sized company—building a Web presence using inexpensive methods first and gradually increasing the expenditure as justified by the returns.

Laying Out the Structure of the Site

After your interviews, you can identify three primary areas on which the company would like to focus the site: the travel packages developed by the company, bargains available on travel, and a form for ordering additional materials.

To give the site a proper structure, plan it out completely before you begin to build it. You can create a set of flow charts to show how the pages interconnect. Figure 32.1 shows how the main sections of the site interact, figure 32.2 shows the travel package section, figure 32.3 lays out the travel specials section, and figure 32.4 is a depiction of how you can expect the information request form to look when it is complete.

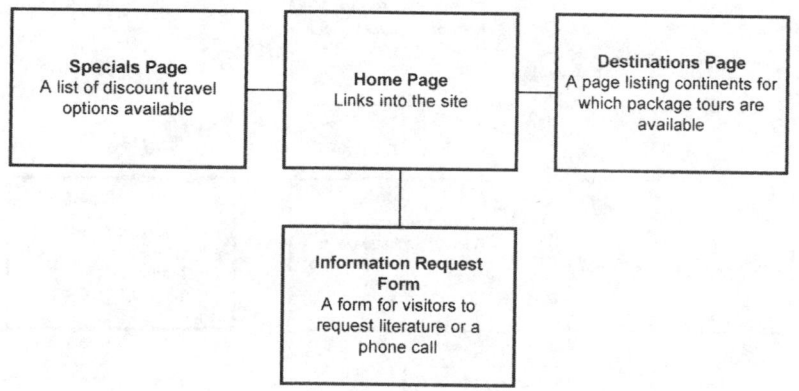

Fig. 32.1
The three sections of this site spread out from the main page.

Fig. 32.2
The travel package section shows the packages available by destination.

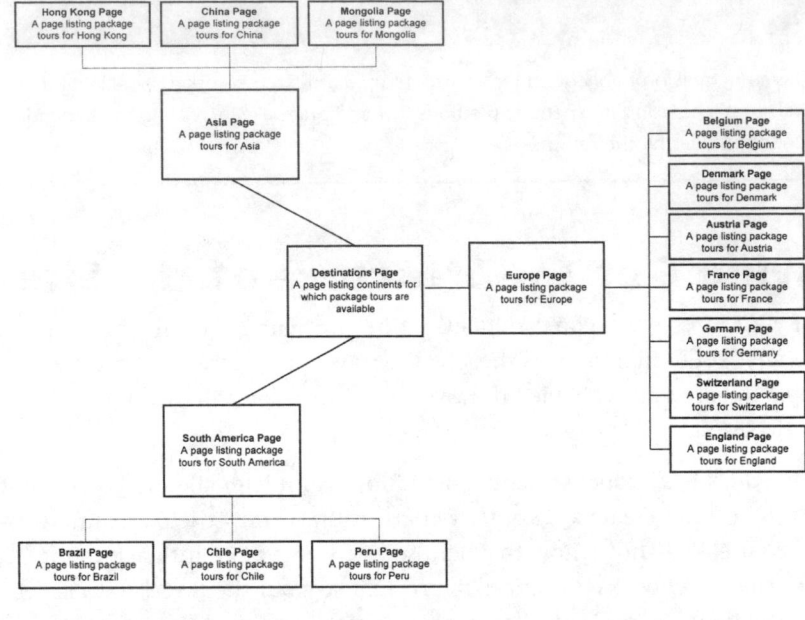

Fig. 32.3
The specials section lists bargain rates that are available.

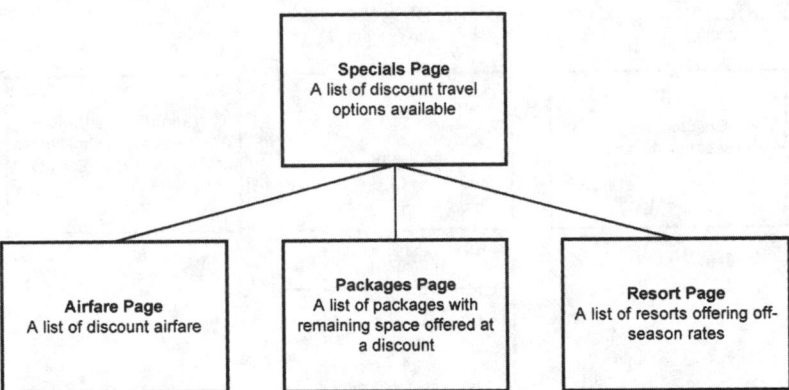

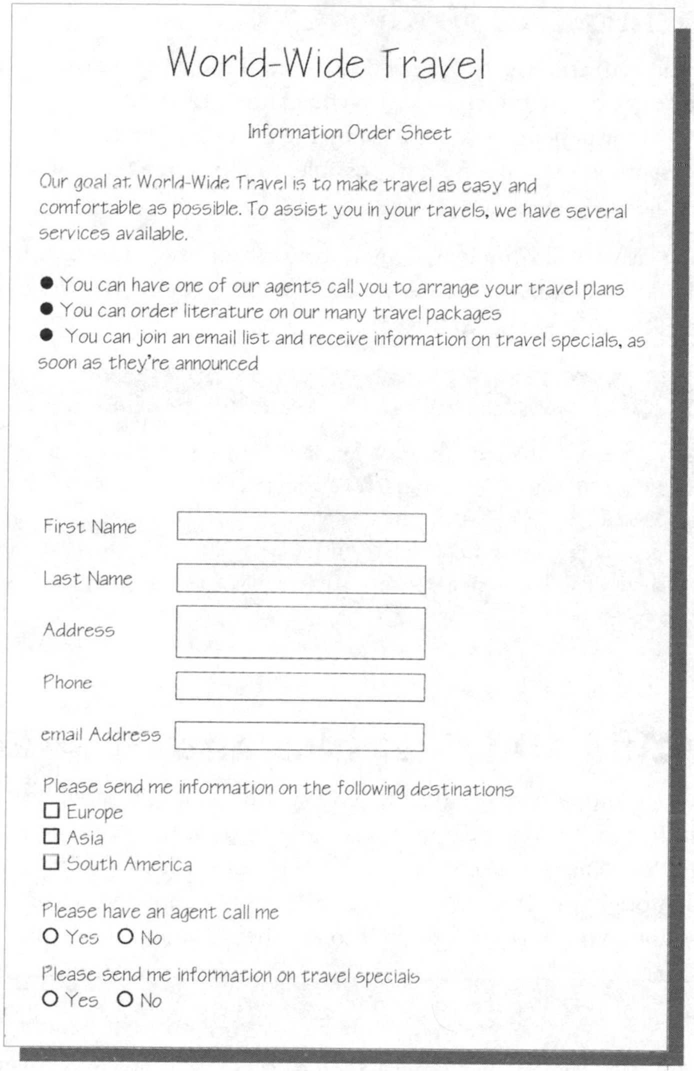

World-Wide Travel

Information Order Sheet

Our goal at World-Wide Travel is to make travel as easy and comfortable as possible. To assist you in your travels, we have several services available.

- You can have one of our agents call you to arrange your travel plans
- You can order literature on our many travel packages
- You can join an email list and receive information on travel specials, as soon as they're announced

First Name

Last Name

Address

Phone

email Address

Please send me information on the following destinations
☐ Europe
☐ Asia
☐ South America

Please have an agent call me
○ Yes   ○ No

Please send me information on travel specials
○ Yes   ○ No

Fig. 32.4
This figure shows what the finished response form will look like.

Creating the Body Text

After you lay out the pages, you need to develop the body text to be used in them. For most of the travel packages, you can use the text that has already been created for paper brochures used by the agency. Whenever this type of text is present, you should use it, if possible, to minimize the amount of writing that is required.

To make it easy to edit the text, copy it from a Word file and paste it into an HTML file using Notepad as the editor. The next step is to identify headings and to add the proper tags to the page.

> **Tip**
>
> Microsoft provides a free add-in to its Microsoft Word program that can greatly assist in the production of web pages from existing Word documents. The Microsoft Internet Assistant provides the formating and mark-up macros necessary to convert a Word document into a usable HTML document. Even with the Internet Assistant, you should carefully check your pages to make certain that everything converted as you expected.

Creating the Graphics and Images

WWT uses a company logo on its letterhead and on all its paper brochures, so to maintain a uniform appearance, you can use it for the Web site also. This logo is provided as an encapsulated PostScript (EPS) file by the graphic design house that originally created it. Because EPS is not generally supported by Web browsers, you have to convert it to another format.

> **Note**
>
> The most commonly supported graphics formats are the Graphical Interchange Format (GIF) and the JPG format. Of these, the JPG format generally produces smaller image sizes, albeit with some loss in quality. For our images, the JPG images are quite suitable.

CorelDRAW! can read EPS files, and because you're already familiar with it, that's what you can use here. Figure 32.5 shows the logo in CorelDRAW!. Export it as a GIF file and convert it to JPG later. You also can use CorelDRAW! to create banners for the top of each page. Creating banners takes a lot of time, but the effect should be worth the extra effort. One of the banners is shown in figure 32.6.

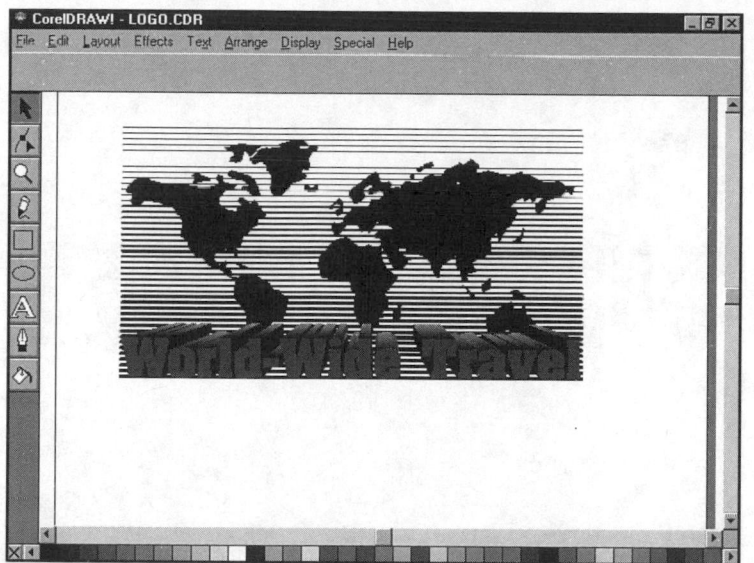

Fig. 32.5
You can use CorelDRAW! to modify image formats.

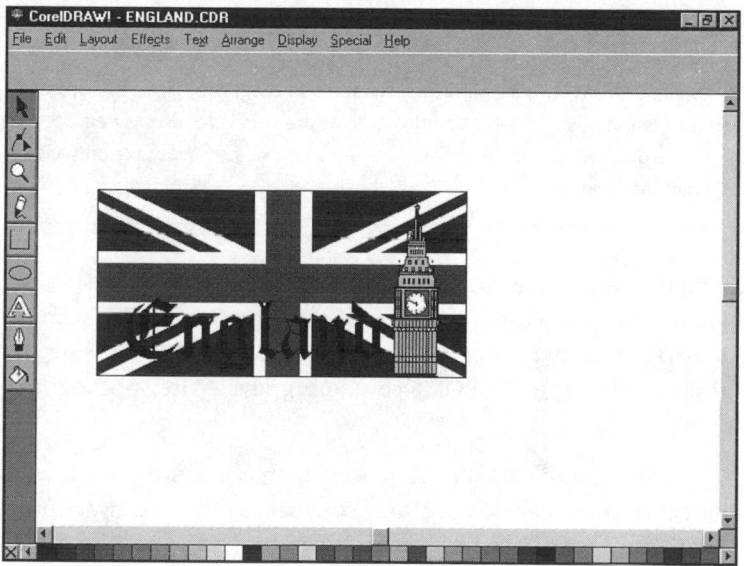

Fig. 32.6
By creating a banner that shows the flag and an image from the country, you can create a feeling of adventure and excitement.

Another nice element is to use graphic maps to allow visitors to move around the site. On the screens that list travel by continent, you can build a map of the flags of each country. By clicking the flag for the country they want, visitors can jump to the correct page. Figure 32.7 shows what one of these maps looks like.

Fig. 32.7

An image map
with the flags of
several countries
serves as a guide
into the site.

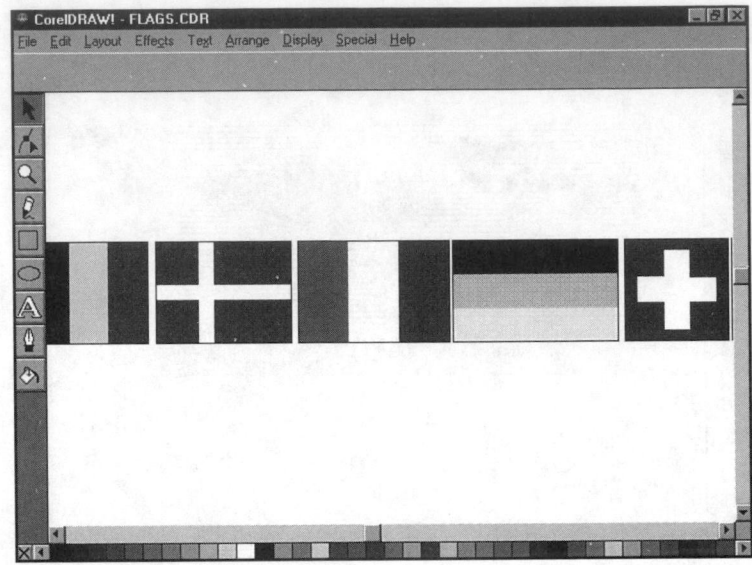

> **Note**
>
> Remember that the Web is a graphical interface and that crisp, clean images can
> make your site more attractive. The other side of the coin is to also remember that
> many people don't load images for every page, so make sure that text-only viewers
> can still navigate your site.

Your customers would like you to add some pictures to the pages. Each destination should have a picture that captures the local flavor. Unfortunately,
WWT doesn't have any photographs. On a trip to the local software store,
you find several low-cost CD-ROMS containing royalty-free photographs that
you can use.

On the disk the files are stored as TIF files, which is a common format for files
that can be used on either PCs or Macs. You can use the shareware program
LView Pro to manipulate the photos, as shown in figure 32.8.

Finding enough images that meet your needs may take awhile. Some of the
images need cropping because of black edges in the photos. Using LView,
you can resize the images and convert them to JPG format. On this site, you
won't have the original high-color, large images available for downloading.

Fig. 32.8
LView Pro is
an example of
the excellent
shareware
programs that are
available to help
you construct Web
sites.

> **Caution**
>
> Carefully read the license agreement that comes with the images. In most cases,
> you can use the images, but you should not distribute them. In other words, you
> shouldn't make downloading the images an option at your site.

Creating the Input Forms

The World-Wide Travel on-line brochure will have a page for visitors to the
site to request more information. Some of the options that your clients want
to have available are the ability to order literature, to request that an agent
contact them by telephone, and to be notified by e-mail when new specials
are announced.

You can create a form similar to the one you used for the park in chapter 31,
but with more options for the visitor to set. The form is written in HTML as
follows:

Listing 32.1   The Log Page

```
<HTML>
<HEAD>
<TITLE>World-Wide Travel Response Form</TITLE>
</HEAD>

<BODY>
<IMG ALIGN=middle SRC="logo.gif">
<H1>World-Wide Travel</H1>
<H2 ALIGN=Center>Information Order Sheet</H2>
```

(continues)

Listing 32.1   Continued

```
<P>
Our goal at World-Wide Travel is to make traveling as easy and
 comfortable as possible. To assist you in your travels, we have
 several services available.
<UL>
<LI> You can have one of our agents call you to arrange your travel
➥plans
<LI> You can order literature on our many travel packages
<LI> You can join an email list and receive information on travel
 specials, as soon as they're announced
<P>
<HR>
<FORM METHOD=POST ACTION="http://www.wwt.com/cgi-bin/
➥response_script">
First Name: <INPUT TYPE="text" NAME="fname" SIZE=25 VALUE=""><BR>
Last Name: <INPUT TYPE="text" NAME="lname" SIZE=25 VALUE=""><BR>
Telephone: <INPUT TYPE="text" NAME="phone" SIZE=25 VALUE=""><BR>
Mailing address: <BR><TEXTAREA NAME="message" ROWS="4" COLS="40">
 </TEXTAREA>
<P>
E-mail address (for responses and mailing list):
<BR>
<INPUT NAME="email" SIZE=25 VALUE="">
<P>
<HR>
Please send me information on the following destinations:<P>
<input type=checkbox name=destination value=europe>Europe<br>
<input type=checkbox name=destination value=asia>Asia<br>
<input type=checkbox name=destination value=samer>South America<br>
<HR>
Please have an agent call me:
<INPUT TYPE="radio" NAME="list" VALUE="yes">Yes
<INPUT TYPE="radio" NAME="list" VALUE="no" checked>No
<HR>
Send me information on travel specials:
<INPUT TYPE="radio" NAME="list" VALUE="yes" checked>Yes
<INPUT TYPE="radio" NAME="list" VALUE="no">No
<HR>
Send a message to us:
<P>
<TEXTAREA NAME="message" ROWS="10" COLS="60"></TEXTAREA>
<P>
</FORM>
<HR>
<P>
Thank you for visiting us at World-Wide Travel!
<P>
<H6>&copy1996 World-Wide Travel</H6>
</BODY>
</HTML>
```

You can check how your form looks by opening it in Netscape Navigator, as shown in figure 32.9.

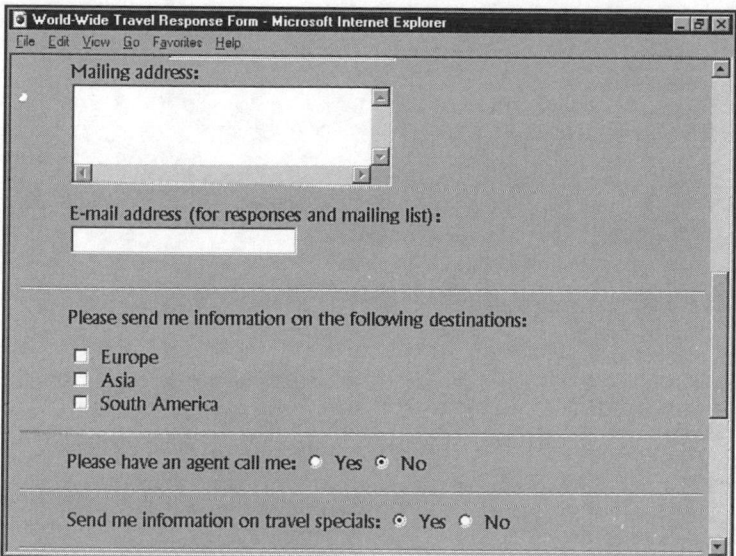

VII

Sample HTML Applications

Fig. 32.9
Visitors to the
site can request
additional infor-
mation from WWT
using this page on
their browsers.

Writing the Pages

When you talk to the owner of WWT, you find out that he is more interested
in having a visually exciting site than he is in having one that can be read using every browser available. With this fact in mind, you can use HTML extensions that are supported by both Netscape Navigator and Microsoft Internet
Explorer.

This way, you can use variable font sizes, background colors, and (most importantly) client-side maps. Client-side image maps have a number of advantages, but the two that are most relevant for you are that the number of hits
on the server is greatly reduced and that the users can get their links somewhat quicker. These advantages are important because WWT can't afford a
high-powered server yet, so anything you can do to improve performance
will be welcome.

The Home Page

The following code is the World-Wide Travel home page in HTML
(HOME.HTM).

Listing 32.2   The Home Page

```
<HTML>
<HEAD>
<TITLE>Welcome to World-Wide Travel</TITLE>
```

(continues)

Listing 32.2   Continued

```
</HEAD>
<BODY>
<IMG SRC="logo.jpg" ALT="World-Wide Travel">
<P>
World-Wide Travel is proud to offer the finest in travel packages.
 Please take the time to tour our site and we think that you'll be
 ↪glad that you did.
<P>
<HR>
<H3>Click on a page</H3>
<IMG SRC="menumap.gif" USEMAP="menumap">
<MAP Name="MENUMAP">
<AREA SHAPE="RECT" COORDS="0,0,75,90" HREF="destination.html">
<AREA SHAPE="RECT" COORDS="80,0,170,90" HREF="specials.html">
<AREA SHAPE="RECT" COORDS="171,0,135,90" HREF="moreinfo.html">
</MAP>
<H3>Or select a menu option</H3>
<P>    <A HREF="Destination.htm">[Destinations]</A>   <A
HREF="specials.htm">
 [Specials]</A>
<A HREF="moreinfo.htm">[More information]
<P>
<HR>
<H6>&copy1996 World-Wide Travel</H6>
</BODY>
</HTML>
```

See the result shown in figure 32.10.

Fig. 32.10
The home page is intentionally simple. Later you can add some JavaScripts to spice it up somewhat.

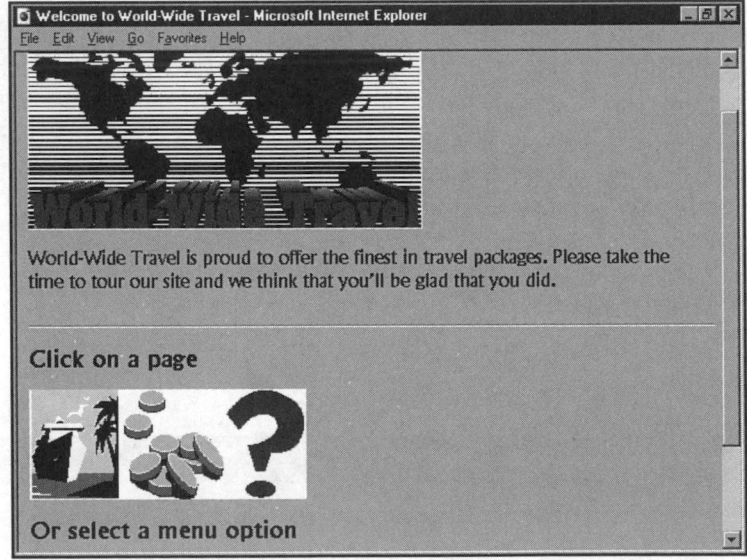

The Destinations Page

The following code is the WWT destinations page in HTML (DESTINATION.HTM).

Listing 32.3   The Destinations Page

```
<HTML>
<HEAD>
<TITLE>World-Wide Travel Destinations</TITLE>
</HEAD>
<BODY>
<IMG ALIGN=bottom SRC="logo.gif">
<H1>Circling the world, World-Wide Travel is Your Travel Connection</
H1>
World-Wide Travel has over twenty years of experience in the travel
 business. Don't trust your travel to a fly-by-night operator.
<P>Instead, contact us for all your international travel needs.
<HR>
<H2>Select a destination continent</H2>
<A HREF="europe.htm"> [Europe] </A>
<A HREF="asia.htm"> [Asia] </A>
<A HREF="samer.htm"> [South America]</A>
<HR>
<P>
<H6>&copy1996 World-Wide Travel</H6>
</BODY>
</HTML>
```

The resulting page is shown in figure 32.11.

Fig. 32.11
The destination page is something of a placeholder at this point. You need to add graphics of the continents before you're done.

The Europe Page

The following code is the European Destinations page in HTML (EUROPE.HTM).

Listing 32.4   The Europe Page

```
<HTML>
<HEAD>
<TITLE>World-Wide Travel European Destinations</TITLE>
</HEAD>
<BODY>
<IMG ALIGN=middle SRC="logo.jpg">
<H1>European Destinations</H1>
<P>World-Wide Travel has been sending travelers to Europe for more
than twenty years now. We are specialists in package vacations in
many European countries. Leave your troubles behind and let us handle
all of your needs.
<HR>
<H2 ALIGN = CENTER>Select a country</H2>
<IMG SRC="euroflags.gif" USEMAP="euroflagmap">
<MAP Name=" euroflagmap">
<AREA SHAPE="RECT" COORDS="0,0,78,50" HREF="austria.html">
<AREA SHAPE="RECT" COORDS="86,0,141,50" HREF="belgium.html">
<AREA SHAPE="RECT" COORDS="150,0,218,50" HREF="denmark.html">
<AREA SHAPE="RECT" COORDS="227,0,302,50" HREF="france.html">
<AREA SHAPE="RECT" COORDS="310,0,395,50" HREF="germany.html">
<AREA SHAPE="RECT" COORDS="444,0,494,50" HREF="switzerland.html">
<AREA SHAPE="RECT" COORDS="455,0,560,50" HREF="england.html">
</MAP>
<P>
<A HREF="austria.htm"> [Austria] </A>
<A HREF="belgium.htm"> [Belgium] </A>
<A HREF="denmark.htm"> [Denmark]</A><BR>
<A HREF="france.htm"> [France] </A>
<A HREF="germany.htm"> [Germany] </A>
<A HREF="switzerland.htm"> [Switzerland] </A>
<A HREF="england.htm"> [England]</A>
<HR>
<H6>&copy1996 World-Wide Travel/H6>
</BODY>
</HTML>
```

The European Destinations page is shown in figure 32.12.

The England Page

The following code is the English Destinations page. It is an example of what the other countries' pages would look like (ENGLAND.HTM).

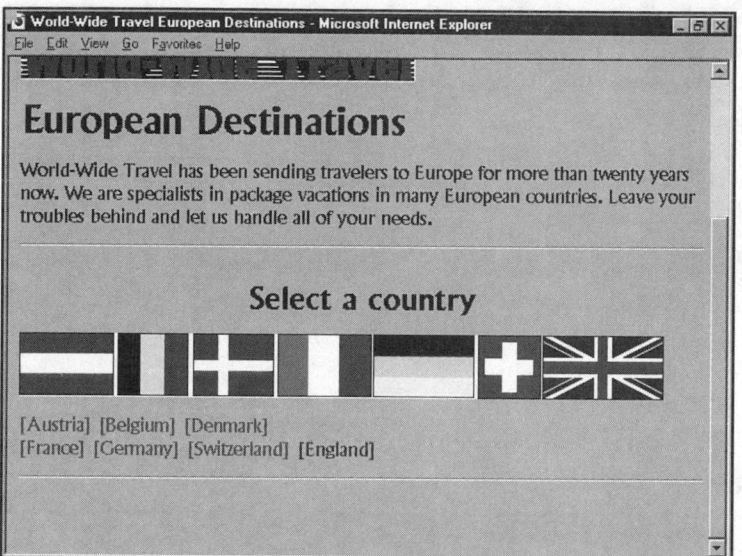

Fig. 32.12
The European destinations screen has plenty of room for additional countries as new packages are developed.

Listing 33.5   The England Page

```
<HEAD>
<TITLE>World-Wide Travel English Destinations</TITLE>
</HEAD>
<BODY>
<IMG ALIGN=left SRC="england.jpg">
<H1>English Destinations</H1>
<P>
<IMG ALIGN=right SRC="london.jpg">
Of all the many countries that World-Wide Travel sends people to, England
 remains the most popular. With its pleasant summers and mild winters,
 England remains a prime year-round vacation spot.
We offer a number of trips to England, with plans to suit almost any
 interest and budget. Some of our more popular trips are listed here.
<P Align = right>
<Table Border>
<Caption><H3>Spring 1996 English Travel Packages<H3></Caption>
<TR>
<TH>Length Days/Nights</TH>
<TH>Cities</TH>
<TH>Sights</TH>
<TH>Price</TH>
</TR>

<TR>
<TD>3/4</TD>
<TD>London</TD>
```

(continues)

Listing 32.5   Continued

```
<TD>The Tower, the British Museum, 221B Baker Street</TD>
<TD>$1,750</TD>
</TR>

<TR>
<TD>5/6</TD>
<TD>Oxford</TD>
<TD>Stratford upon Avon, Stonehenge, Rollright Stones, Oxford
 University</TD>
<TD>$2,250</TD>
</TR>
</Table>

<HR>
<H6>&copy1996 World-Wide Travel</H6>
</BODY>
</HTML>
```

The English Destinations page is shown in figure 32.13.

Fig. 32.13
A stock photo
really adds drama
to the page,
especially when
added to the
custom banner.

Adding a JavaScript Marquee

Just as you added a scrolling marquee to the park pages in the preceding
chapter, you can add the same tool to the main page at the travel agency.
This is an example of how you can reuse Java code, after you have it working
and bug free.

The following is the same code that you used in chapter 32, with the variables Status1 and Status2 changed to show their new use. You add this code to the <HEAD> section of any page on which you want to have the information appear.

Listing 32.6   The Response Script

```
<SCRIPT LANGUAGE="JavaScript">

<!-- Comments hide this program for browsers that don't understand
 JavaScript

var window_size = 0;

// These two lines are the message that is scrolled in the status
// window

var Status1="Our hours are 8:00am to 6:00pm Central Time M-F";
var Status2="Call us at 1-800-555-2921";

function StartMarquee(initial_size) {
        window_size = initial_size;
        ScrolledMessage(window_size);
}

function ScrolledMessage(scrollto) {
        var StatusLine;
        var msg = " ";
        var i = 0;
        var speed = 50;

        StatusLine = Status1+"......"+Status2;

        scrollto--;
        if (scrollto == -StatusLine.length)
                scrollto = window_size;

        if (scrollto > 0) {
                for (i = 0; i < scrollto; i++)
                        msg = " "+msg;
                msg = msg + StatusLine;
        } else
                msg = StatusLine.substring(-scrollto, StatusLine.length);

        msg = msg.substring(0,window_size);
        window.status= msg;
        window.setTimeout('ScrolledMessage('+scrollto+')',speed);
}
// end of comment that hides the JavaScript code -->

</SCRIPT>
</HEAD>
<BODY onload="StartMarquee(200)">
</BODY>
```

After this program starts, it begins scrolling the marquee message within the status bar of the browser. Figure 32.14 shows how the main page looks with a marquee scrolling across the status bar.

Fig. 32.14
The main page now shows the scrolling marquee running in the status bar.

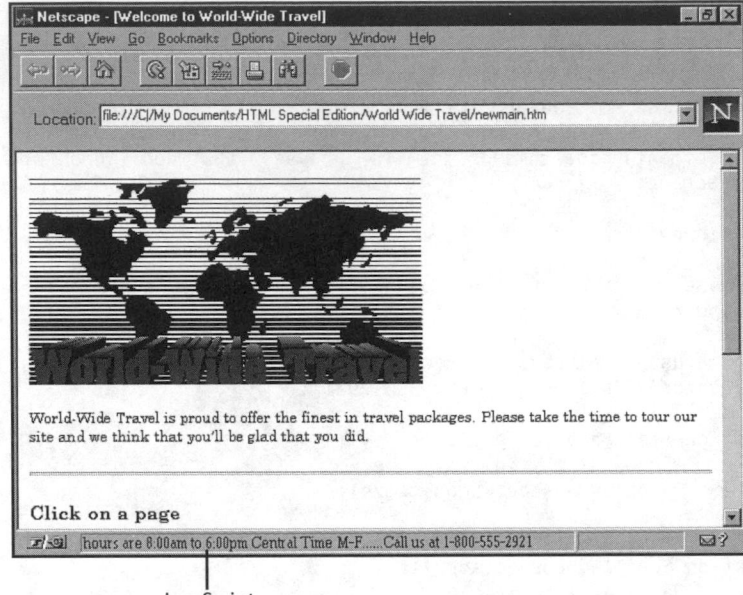

JavaScript

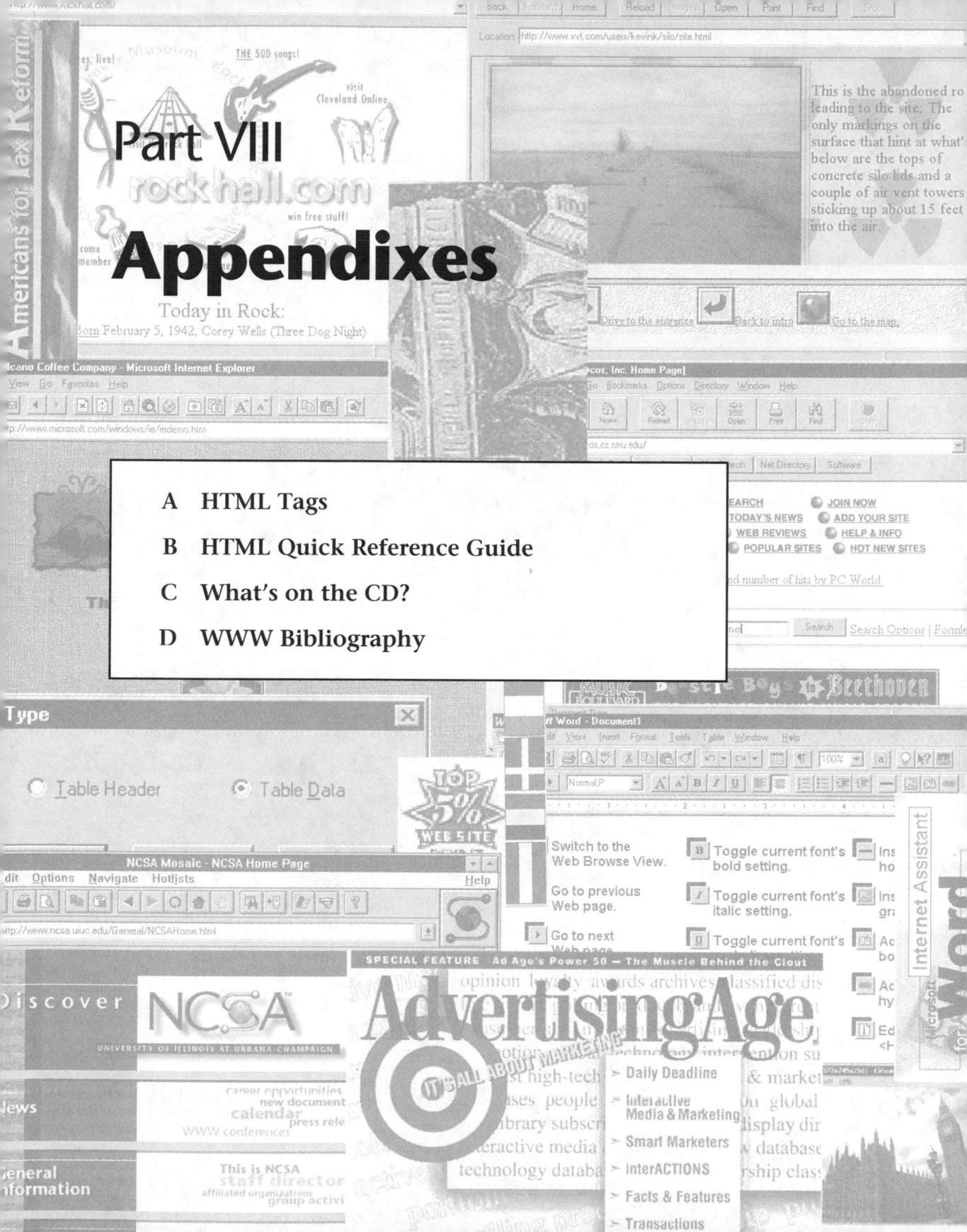

Part VIII

Appendixes

APPENDIX A
HTML Tags

by John Jung

There are many HTML elements, and each has its own set of attributes that it can use. This is a complete list of HTML tags, their corresponding attributes, and a description of what they do.

<!--> and --> Comment

You can put in a comment in your Web document by enclosing it between the <!-- beginning marker, and the --> ending marker. Some browsers will not properly handle HTML-related characters within the comments. Also, not all browsers correctly recognize the double dashes as being needed for the start of the comment. This HTML tag has no attributes.

The following is an example of <!-- -->:

```
<!-- This line of text will only be seen by people who look at the
➥HTML source. -->
```

<A>: Anchor

The Anchor HTML tag is an important element for hypertext links of any sort. The Anchor element type can have the following attributes:

- CHARSET—This is a proposed attribute to HTML for internationalization. It indicates what type of character set is used by the hypertext link.

- CLASS—This is a proposed attribute to HTML 3 as part of a style sheet proposal. This is a list of calls and subclasses separated by spaces. Acceptable values that you can use have not been defined by HTML 3.

- DIR—This is a proposed attribute to HTML for internationalization. It's used to indicate which direction to display the text. It can either have the value ltr (left to right) or rtl (right to left).

- HREF—This indicates the destination URL.

■ ID—This is a proposed attribute to HTML 3 as part of a style sheet proposal. This is intended to supercede the NAME attribute.

■ LANG—This is a proposed attribute to HTML for internationalization. This attribute is composed from the two-letter language code from ISO 639. You can optionally add a period, followed by a two-letter country code from ISO 3166. This attribute can be used by parsers to select language-specific choices for quotation marks, ligatures, and hyphenation rules.

■ MD—This is a proposed attribute to HTML 3 as part of a style sheet proposal. This attribute is used to specify a message digest or checksum. This is used when you want to be sure that a linked object is the one the Web author specified.

■ METHODS—This indicates a list of HTTP METHODS supported by the object. This is a little used and little supported attribute.

■ NAME—This defines the current line as a destination point. These points are used for internal jumps or jumps to a specific line.

■ REL—When used with the HREF attribute, this indicates a particular relationship with the destination. This is a little used and little supported attribute and will probably be superseded in the future.

■ REV—When used with the HREF attribute, this is the inverse of the REL attribute. This establishes a backwards relationship between the current Web page and the URL that brought up this HTML document. This is a little used and little supported attribute and will probably be superseded in the future.

■ SHAPE—This proposed attribute is supposed to indicate the corresponding clickable region in a FIG element. This was originally intended as a substitute for imagemaps.

■ TARGET—This indicates the name of the window to be used when going to the hypertext link. If the window doesn't exist, the browser will open up a new window, and assign it that name. This attribute is an extension introduced by Netscape.

■ TITLE—When used with the HREF attribute, this attribute indicates the title of the destination URL. This is a little used and little supported attribute.

■ URN—The Universal Resource Number was originally intended as a better method of referring to destination links, instead of URLs. It is currently not used or supported.

The following is an example of <A>:

```
<A HREF="http://www.mysite.com/" NAME="destination1"> Sample anchor element.</A>
```

<ABBREV>: Abbreviations

The proposed Abbreviations tag will change some of the enclosed text into abbreviations. This does not change the actual text, just how it's displayed by the browser. This is a work in progress. The Abbreviations tag can have the following attributes:

- CLASS—This is a proposed attribute to HTML 3 as part of a style sheet proposal. This is a list of calls and subclasses separated by spaces. Acceptable values that you can use have not been defined by HTML 3.

- DIR—This is a proposed attribute to HTML for internationalization. It's used to indicate which direction to display the text. It can either have the value ltr (left to right) or rtl (right to left).

- ID—This is a proposed attribute to HTML 3 as part of a style sheet proposal. This defines the current line as a destination point. These points are used for internal jumps or jumps to a specific line.

- LANG—This is a proposed attribute to HTML for internationalization. This attribute is composed from the two-letter language code from ISO 639. You can optionally add a period, followed by a two-letter country code from ISO 3166. This attribute can be used by parsers to select language-specific choices for quotation marks, ligatures, and hyphenation rules.

The following is an example of <ABBREV>:

```
<ABBREV>Some of these words will be abbreviated when displayed.</ABBREV>
```

<ACRONYM>: Acronym

The proposed HTML 3 tag, <ACRONYM>, will display the enclosed text with acronyms. This does not change the actual text, just how it's displayed by the browser. This is a work in progress. The Acronym tag can have the following attributes:

- CLASS—This is a proposed attribute to HTML 3 as part of a style sheet proposal. This is a list of calls and subclasses separated by spaces. Acceptable values that you can use have not been defined by HTML 3.

- DIR—This is a proposed attribute to HTML for internationalization. It's used to indicate which direction to display the text. It can either have the value ltr (left to right) or rtl (right to left).

- ID—This is a proposed attribute to HTML 3 as part of a style sheet proposal. This defines the current line as a destination point. These points are used for internal jumps or jumps to a specific line.

- LANG—This is a proposed attribute to HTML for internationalization. This attribute is composed from the two-letter language code from ISO 639. You can optionally add a period, followed by a two-letter country code from ISO 3166. This attribute can be used by parsers to select language-specific choices for quotation marks, ligatures, and hyphenation rules.

The following is an example of <ACRONYM>:

```
<ACRONYM>Some of these words will be reduced to acronyms when
➥displayed.</ACRONYM>
```

<ADDRESS>: Address

The <ADDRESS> tag is used to indicate an address, typically the e-mail address of the Web author. The Address element can have the following attributes:

- ALIGN—This is a proposed attribute to HTML for internationalization. It's used to indicate the alignment of the text in the address. It can have the value of center, justify, left, or right.

- CLEAR—This is a proposed attribute to HTML 3. It can have the value of left, right, or all. These values indicate which margin is to be clear of images so that text can appear on it.

- DIR—This is a proposed attribute to HTML for internationalization. It's used to indicate which direction to display the text. It can either have the value ltr (left to right) or rtl (right to left).

- LANG—This is a proposed attribute to HTML for internationalization. This attribute is composed from the two-letter language code from ISO 639. You can optionally add a period, followed by a two-letter country code from ISO 3166. This attribute can be used by parsers to select language-specific choices for quotation marks, ligatures, and hyphenation rules.

- NOWRAP—This is a proposed attribute to HTML 3 to indicate that the address should not be word wrapped.

The following is an example of <ADDRESS>:

```
<ADDRESS>This page was created by me.</ADDRESS>
```

<APPLET>: JAVA Applet

This proposed HTML extension was introduced in Netscape Navigator. When used, browsers that can run JAVA applications will run the specified JAVA applet. Parameters that you want to pass to a particular JAVA application can be done with the <PARAM> tag. <APPLET> can have the following attributes:

- ALT—This attribute indicates to browsers that recognize the <APPLET> tag an alternate text string to be displayed. This behaves the same as the ALT attribute for the <IMG> tag.

- ALIGN—This attribute indicates the display alignment of the JAVA applet. It can have the following values: absbottom, absmiddle, baseline, bottom, left, middle, right, texttop, and top.

- CODE—This indicates the file that contains the JAVA applet program. The file name indicated cannot point to an absolute URL.

- CODEBASE—You specify the base URL for the JAVA application with this attribute. This is used in conjunction with the CODE attribute.

- HEIGHT—This indicates the initial height of the display for the JAVA applet. The value must be specified as the number of pixels.

- HSPACE—This indicates how many pixels to reserve for the JAVA applet, horizontally.

- NAME—This attribute gives a name to the JAVA applet that is about to be executed. This is useful when you want different applets on the same Web page to talk to each other.

- VSPACE—This indicates how many pixels to reserve for the JAVA applet, horizontally.

- WIDTH—This indicates the initial width of the display for the JAVA applet. The value must be specified as the number of pixels.

The following is an example of <APPLET>:

```
<APPLET CODE="myprogram" WIDTH=200 HEIGHT=200>My first JAVA applet.</APPLET>
```

<AREA>: Area for a Clickable Map

This proposed extension to HTML by Netscape is used to create client-side imagemaps. This tag is intended to specify one clickable region on a graphic. <AREA> has the following attributes:

- ALT—This provides a text-based alternative to non-graphical Web browsers. Currently, this has not been defined.

VIII

Appendixes

- COORDS—This indicates the position of the specified area on the image. The coordinates are put in quotation marks, and the coordinates are separated by commas. The upper left-hand corner of the image is "0,0".

- HREF—This specifies the destination URL if this area is accessed.

- NOHREF—This is used to indicate that a region isn't linked to anything.

- SHAPE—This is used to indicate the shape of the clickable region. If this attribute is rect, then COORDS must indicate the coordinates for the upper-left corner followed by the lower-right corner. For the circle value, COORD indicates the coordinates of the center followed by the radius. As for the polygon value, COORD indicates a successive set of coordinates. Each pair of coordinates indicates a vertex of the polygon.

The following is an example of <AREA>:

```
<AREAD COORD="0,0","100,100" SHAPE=rect HREF="http://
➥www.mysite.com/" ALT="Go to my site!">
```

<AU>: Author

This proposed HTML 3 tag is used to indicate the name of an author. <AU> can have the following attributes:

- CLASS—This is a proposed attribute to HTML 3 as part of a style sheet proposal.

- DIR—This is a proposed attribute to HTML for internationalization. It's used to indicate which direction to display the text. It can either have the value ltr (left to right) or rtl (right to left).

- ID—This is a proposed attribute to HTML 3 as part of a style sheet proposal. This defines the current line as a destination point. These points are used for internal jumps or jumps to a specific line.

- LANG—This is a proposed attribute to HTML for internationalization. This attribute is composed from the two-letter language code from ISO 639. You can optionally add a period, followed by a two-letter country code from ISO 3166. This attribute can be used by parsers to select language-specific choices for quotation marks, ligatures, and hyphenation rules.

The following is an example of <AU>:

```
The authors of this book are <AU>Mark Brown and John Jung</AU>.
```

<B>: Bold

This tag will make whatever text is enclosed within it display in a bold font. The <B> tag can have the following attributes:

- CLASS—This is a proposed attribute to HTML 3 as part of a style sheet proposal.

- DIR—This is a proposed attribute to HTML for internationalization. It's used to indicate which direction to display the text. It can either have the value ltr (left to right) or rtl (right to left).

- ID—This is a proposed attribute to HTML 3 as part of a style sheet proposal. This defines the current line as a destination point. These points are used for internal jumps or jumps to a specific line.

- LANG—This is a proposed attribute to HTML for internationalization. This attribute is composed from the two-letter language code from ISO 639. You can optionally add a period, followed by a two-letter country code from ISO 3166. This attribute can be used by parsers to select language-specific choices for quotation marks, ligatures, and hyphenation rules.

The following is an example of <B>:

```
This word is in <B>bold</B>.
```

<BANNER>: Banner

This is a proposed HTML 3 tag that will display something as a banner. The text in this tag will not scroll with the rest of the HTML document. It's mainly intended to be used for company logos or navigational aids. You can use the following attributes:

- CLASS—This is a proposed attribute to HTML 3 as part of a style sheet proposal. This is a list of calls and subclasses separated by spaces. Acceptable values that you can use have not been defined by HTML 3.

- DIR—This is a proposed attribute to HTML for internationalization. It's used to indicate which direction to display the text. It can either have the value ltr (left to right) or rtl (right to left).

- ID—This is a proposed attribute to HTML 3 as part of a style sheet proposal. This defines the current line as a destination point. These points are used for internal jumps or jumps to a specific line.

- LANG—This is a proposed attribute to HTML for internationalization. This attribute is composed from the two-letter language code from ISO 639. You can optionally add a period, followed by a two-letter country code from ISO 3166. This attribute can be used by parsers to select language-specific choices for quotation marks, ligatures, and hyphenation rules.

VIII

Appendixes

The following is an example of <BANNER>:

```
<BANNER>This home page was created by MeSoft.</BANNER>
```

<BASE>: Base URL

The <BASE> HTML element is used to indicate the default location of relative URL links. This is useful in the event that you move your home page to another computer. If this happens, all relative links on that page will not have to be updated. This tag can have the following attributes:

- HREF—This indicates the baseline URL that relative links will be based upon.

- TARGET—This indicates the name of the window to be used when going to the hypertext link. If the window doesn't exist, the browser will open up a new window and assign it that name. This attribute is an extension introduced by Netscape.

The following is an example of <BASE>:

```
<BASE HREF="http://www.mycomputer.com/homepage/mystuff/">
```

<BASEFONT>: Default Font Size

This HTML element is used to indicate the default font size for the current HTML document. <BASEFONT> was originally introduced as an extension by Netscape. It has only one attribute: SIZE. This attribute indicates which default font value to use. By default, the font value used is 3. There are seven possible values for this attribute: 1, 2, 3, 4, 5, 6, and 7. These do not indicate point sizes, but rather a predetermined font size.

The following is an example of <BASEFONT>:

```
<BASEFONT SIZE=4>
```

<BDO>: Directional Override

This proposed tag is intended for the internationalization of HTML. The <BDO> tag is used to indicate how text should be displayed by the browser. It has the following attributes:

- DIR—This is a proposed attribute to HTML for internationalization. It's used to indicate which direction to display the text. It can either have the value ltr (left to right) or rtl (right to left).

- LANG—This is a proposed attribute to HTML for internationalization. This attribute is composed from the two-letter language code from ISO 639. You can optionally add a period, followed by a two-letter country code from ISO 3166. This attribute can be used by parsers to select language-specific choices for quotation marks, ligatures, and hyphenation rules.

The following is an example of <BDO>:

```
<BDO DIR=ltr>This will cause text to flow from the left to the right.</BDO>
```

<BGSOUND>: Background Sound

Microsoft introduced this proposed extension to HTML for adding more flair to home pages. This will cause a sound file to be played in the background while the user is looking at the home page. This tag can have the following attributes:

- LOOP—This indicates how many times the sound file should be played. This can either be a numerical value or the word infinite. If no value is specified, the sound file is played once.

- SRC—This attribute indicates the URL for the sound file to be played. Available sound file formats are .WAV, .AU, and .MID.

The following is an example of <BGSOUND>:

```
<BGSOUND SRC=http://www.mysite.com/intro.wav>
```

<BIG>: Big

This is a proposed HTML 3 tag that instructs the browser to make the enclosed text big. This can have the following attributes:

- CLASS—This is a proposed attribute to HTML 3 as part of a style sheet proposal. This is a list of calls and subclasses separated by spaces. Acceptable values that you can use have not been defined by HTML 3.

- DIR—This is a proposed attribute to HTML for internationalization. It's used to indicate which direction to display the text. It can either have the value ltr (left to right) or rtl (right to left).

- ID—This is a proposed attribute to HTML 3 as part of a style sheet proposal. This defines the current line as a destination point. These points are used for internal jumps or jumps to a specific line.

- LANG—This is a proposed attribute to HTML for internationalization. This attribute is composed from the two-letter language code from ISO 639. You can optionally add a period, followed by a two-letter country code from ISO 3166. This attribute can be used by parsers to select language-specific choices for quotation marks, ligatures, and hyphenation rules.

The following is an example of <BIG>:

```
This word will come out <BIG>BIG</BIG>
```

VIII

Appendixes

<BLINK>: Blink

This HTML tag will cause the enclosed text to blink. This tag was introduced by Netscape as a proposed extension. Some people find the <BLINK> tag to be quite annoying.

The following is an example of <BLINK>:

```
See what's <BLINK>NEW</BLINK> at this page!
```

<BLOCKQUOTE>: Blockquote

When a browser comes across this HTML tag, it will show the text as quoted text. This typically means that the text will be indented on both the left and right. <BLOCKQUOTE> can have the following attributes:

- ALIGN—This is a proposed attribute to HTML for internationalization. It's used to indicate the alignment of the text in the address. It can have the value of center, justify, left, or right.

- DIR—This is a proposed attribute to HTML for internationalization. It's used to indicate which direction to display the text. It can either have the value ltr (left to right) or rtl (right to left).

- LANG—This is a proposed attribute to HTML for internationalization. This attribute is composed from the two-letter language code from ISO 639. You can optionally add a period, followed by a two-letter country code from ISO 3166. This attribute can be used by parsers to select language-specific choices for quotation marks, ligatures, and hyphenation rules.

The following is an example of <BLOCKQUOTE>:

```
<BLOCKQUOTE>To be or not to be, that is the question.</BLOCKQUOTE>
```

<BODY>: Body

This HTML tag encloses the body of the Web page. Everything you want users to see is enclosed within the <BODY> tag. This element can have the following attributes:

- ALINK—This Netscape extension indicates the color to be used when a link is clicked. This color is represented by three pairs of hexadecimal numbers. The pairs represent the red, green, and blue color values.

- BACKGROUND—This Netscape extension provides for a background image. This extension has also been proposed for HTML 3. The value you set for this must be the URL for the graphic you want displayed in the background.

- BGCOLOR—This Netscape extension indicates the color of the background for this page. This color is represented by three pairs of hexadecimal numbers. The pairs represent the red, green, and blue color values.

- BGPROPERTIES—This is a Microsoft extension and can currently only be set to fixed. It provides for a background watermark image.

- CLASS—This is a proposed attribute to HTML 3 as part of a style sheet proposal. This is a list of calls and subclasses separated by spaces. Acceptable values that you can use have not been defined by HTML 3.

- DIR—This is a proposed attribute to HTML for internationalization. It's used to indicate which direction to display the text. It can either have the value ltr (left to right) or rtl (right to left).

- LANG—This is a proposed attribute to HTML for internationalization. This attribute is composed from the two-letter language code from ISO 639. You can optionally add a period, followed by a two-letter country code from ISO 3166. This attribute can be used by parsers to select language-specific choices for quotation marks, ligatures, and hyphenation rules.

- LINK—This Netscape extension indicates the color to be used when there is a hypertext link that hasn't been visited. This color is represented by three pairs of hexadecimal numbers. The pairs represent the red, green, and blue color values.

- TEXT—This Netscape extension indicates the color to be used to display the text of your home page. This color is represented by three pairs of hexadecimal numbers. The pairs represent the red, green, and blue color values.

- VLINK—This Netscape extension indicates the color to be used when a link has already been visited. This color is represented by three pairs of hexadecimal numbers. The pairs represent the red, green, and blue color values.

The following is an example of <BODY>:

```
<BODY BACKGROUND="http://www.mysite.com/backdrop.gif">[Web page]</BODY>
```

<BQ>: BlockQuote

This is a proposed HTML 3 element that is intended to replace the <BLOCKQUOTE> tag. <BQ> is different from <BLOCKQUOTE> in that it does not imply word wrapping. This tag has the following attributes:

- CLASS—This is a proposed attribute to HTML 3 as part of a style sheet proposal.

- CLEAR—This is a proposed attribute to HTML 3. It can have the value of left, right, or all. These values indicate which margin is to be clear of images so that text can appear on it.

- DIR—This is a proposed attribute to HTML for internationalization. It's used to indicate which direction to display the text. It can either have the value ltr (left to right) or rtl (right to left).

- ID—This is a proposed attribute to HTML 3 as part of a style sheet proposal. This defines the current line as a destination point. These points are used for internal jumps or jumps to a specific line.

- LANG—This is a proposed attribute to HTML for internationalization. This attribute is composed from the two-letter language code from ISO 639. You can optionally add a period, followed by a two-letter country code from ISO 3166. This attribute can be used by parsers to select language-specific choices for quotation marks, ligatures, and hyphenation rules.

The following is an example of <BQ>:

```
<BQ>We hold these truths to be self-evident</BQ>
```


: Line Break

This HTML tag forces a new line to be created at that point. This means that whether or not word wrap will take effect, the line break will occur. This element has the following attributes:

- CLASS—This is a proposed attribute to HTML 3 as part of a style sheet proposal. This is a list of calls and subclasses separated by spaces. Acceptable values that you can use have not been defined by HTML 3.

- CLEAR—This is a proposed attribute to HTML 3. It can have the value of left, right, or all. These values indicate which margin is to be clear of images so that text can appear on it.

- ID—This is a proposed attribute to HTML 3 as part of a style sheet proposal. This defines the current line as a destination point. These points are used for internal jumps or jumps to a specific line.

The following is an example of <BR>:

```
Even though this line may word wrap on your browser, it'll still
↪have a line break at the end.<BR>
```

<CAPTION>: Caption

This HTML 3 proposed tag was originally a Netscape proposed extension. This element is used to attach a label to a table or a figure. <CAPTION> has the following attributes:

- ALIGN—This attribute will determine where the caption is placed. Acceptable values are top, bottom, left, and right.

- CLASS—This is a proposed attribute to HTML 3 as part of a style sheet proposal. This is a list of calls and subclasses separated by spaces. Acceptable values that you can use have not been defined by HTML 3.

- CLEAR—This is a proposed attribute to HTML 3. It can have the value of left, right, or all. These values indicate which margin is to be clear of images so that text can appear on it.

- DIR—This is a proposed attribute to HTML for internationalization. It's used to indicate which direction to display the text. It can either have the value ltr (left to right) or rtl (right to left).

- ID—This is a proposed attribute to HTML 3 as part of a style sheet proposal. This defines the current line as a destination point. These points are used for internal jumps or jumps to a specific line.

- LANG—This is a proposed attribute to HTML for internationalization. This attribute is composed from the two-letter language code from ISO 639. You can optionally add a period, followed by a two-letter country code from ISO 3166. This attribute can be used by parsers to select language-specific choices for quotation marks, ligatures, and hyphenation rules.

The following is an example of <CAPTION>:

```
<CAPTION>Table 1.1</CAPTION>
```

<CENTER>: Center

This Netscape-specific extension to HTML will center all enclosed text. This has since been superseded by the HTML 3 proposals. Now, all text elements have an ALIGN attribute that can be set to center.

Example:

```
<CENTER>This text is centered on the browser.</CENTER>
```

<CITE>: Citation

The CITE element is used when you want to indicate a citation of some sort. It has the following attributes:

■ DIR—This is a proposed attribute to HTML for internationalization. It's used to indicate which direction to display the text. It can either have the value ltr (left to right) or rtl (right to left).

■ LANG—This is a proposed attribute to HTML for internationalization. This attribute is composed from the two-letter language code from ISO 639. You can optionally add a period, followed by a two-letter country code from ISO 3166. This attribute can be used by parsers to select language-specific choices for quotation marks, ligatures, and hyphenation rules.

Example:

```
<CITE>Hamlet, ACT V, Scene I</CITE>
```

<CODE>: Source Code

The <CODE> element should be used when you want to indicate source code. If you're giving people instructions on how to do something with a computer, use this tag. You can use the following attributes:

■ CLASS—This is a proposed attribute to HTML 3 as part of a style sheet proposal. This is a list of calls and subclasses separated by spaces. Acceptable values that you can use have not been defined by HTML 3.

■ DIR—This is a proposed attribute to HTML for internationalization. It's used to indicate which direction to display the text. It can either have the value ltr (left to right) or rtl (right to left).

■ ID—This is a proposed attribute to HTML 3 as part of a style sheet proposal. This defines the current line as a destination point. These points are used for internal jumps or jumps to a specific line.

■ LANG—This is a proposed attribute to HTML for internationalization. This attribute is composed from the two-letter language code from ISO 639. You can optionally add a period, followed by a two-letter country code from ISO 3166. This attribute can be used by parsers to select language-specific choices for quotation marks, ligatures, and hyphenation rules.

The following is an example of <CODE>:

```
At the UNIX prompt, type in <CODE>ls -al</CODE>
```

<COL>: Column Defaults

There is a new proposed HTML 3 standard for table creation. One of the new tags included in that proposal is the <COL> element. You can use this element to define some standard behavior for table columns. This tag has the following attributes:

- ■ ALIGN—This attribute indicates the alignment of the text within the column. It can have the value of char, center, justify, left, or right.

- ■ CHAR—This is used to indicate which character the column is to be aligned with. This is only interpreted when the ALIGN attribute has been set to char.

- ■ CHAROFF—This number is used to indicate the offset of the alignment character from the table cell.

- ■ CLASS—This is a proposed attribute to HTML 3 as part of a style sheet proposal. This is a list of calls and subclasses separated by spaces. Acceptable values that you can use have not been defined by HTML 3.

- ■ DIR—This is a proposed attribute to HTML for internationalization. It's used to indicate which direction to display the text. It can either have the value ltr (left to right) or rtl (right to left).

- ■ ID—This is a proposed attribute to HTML 3 as part of a style sheet proposal. This defines the current line as a destination point. These points are used for internal jumps or jumps to a specific line.

- ■ LANG—This is a proposed attribute to HTML for internationalization. This attribute is composed from the two-letter language code from ISO 639. You can optionally add a period, followed by a two-letter country code from ISO 3166. This attribute can be used by parsers to select language-specific choices for quotation marks, ligatures, and hyphenation rules.

- ■ SPAN—This number is used to indicate how many table cells the cell value applies to. If you set SPAN=0, it will apply the current value to all cells. The default value is 1.

- ■ VALIGN—This indicates the vertical alignment of the text of the table cell. Acceptable values for this attribute are baseline, bottom, middle, and top.

- ■ WIDTH—This value indicates the width of each column. You can also specify the unit of measurement for the width. The standard units are pt (point size), pi (picas), in (inches), cm (centimeters), mm (millimeters), em (em units), and px (screen pixels). Instead of a unit, you can put an asterisk (*) to specify a relative width.

The following is an example of <COL>:

```
<COL ALIGN=char CHAR="." WIDTH="100mm">
```

<COLGROUP>: Column Group

The <COLGROUP> element is a container for a group of columns. It also enables you to set the defaults for all of these columns. This element has the following attributes:

- ALIGN—This attribute indicates the alignment of the text within the column. It can have the value of char, center, justify, left, or right.

- CHAR—This is used to indicate which character the column is to be aligned with. This is only interpreted when the ALIGN attribute has been set to char.

- CHAROFF—This number is used to indicate the offset of the alignment character from the table cell.

- CLASS—This is a proposed attribute to HTML 3 as part of a style sheet proposal. This is a list of calls and subclasses separated by spaces. Acceptable values that you can use have not been defined by HTML 3.

- DIR—This is a proposed attribute to HTML for internationalization. It's used to indicate which direction to display the text. It can either have the value ltr (left to right) or rtl (right to left).

- ID—This is a proposed attribute to HTML 3 as part of a style sheet proposal. This defines the current line as a destination point. These points are used for internal jumps or jumps to a specific line.

- LANG—This is a proposed attribute to HTML for internationalization. This attribute is composed from the two-letter language code from ISO 639. You can optionally add a period, followed by a two-letter country code from ISO 3166. This attribute can be used by parsers to select language-specific choices for quotation marks, ligatures, and hyphenation rules.

- VALIGN—This indicates the vertical alignment of the text of the table cell. Acceptable values for this attribute are baseline, bottom, middle, and top.

- WIDTH—This indicates the default width of grouped columns. You can specify relative size by appending an asterisk (*) at the end.

The following is an example of <COLGROUP>:

```
<COLGROUP ALIGN=char CHAR=".">10.0</COLGROUP>
```

<CREDIT>: Credit

This HTML 3 proposed tag should be used to name the source of information. The following attributes are available:

- CLASS—This is a proposed attribute to HTML 3 as part of a style sheet proposal. This is a list of calls and subclasses separated by spaces. Acceptable values that you can use have not been defined by HTML 3.

- DIR—This is a proposed attribute to HTML for internationalization. It's used to indicate which direction to display the text. It can either have the value ltr (left to right) or rtl (right to left).

- ■ ID—This is a proposed attribute to HTML 3 as part of a style sheet proposal. This defines the current line as a destination point. These points are used for internal jumps or jumps to a specific line.

- ■ LANG—This is a proposed attribute to HTML for internationalization. This attribute is composed from the two-letter language code from ISO 639. You can optionally add a period, followed by a two-letter country code from ISO 3166. This attribute can be used by parsers to select language-specific choices for quotation marks, ligatures, and hyphenation rules.

The following is an example of <CREDIT>:

```
<CREDIT>By William Shakespeare</CREDIT>
```

<DD>: Definition List Data

If you choose to make use of a definition list in your home page, you'll need <DD>. This HTML tag is used to indicate a definition for the definition list. A <DD> tag should always be preceded by a <DT> tag. The <DD> element has the following attributes:

- ■ DIR—This is a proposed attribute to HTML for internationalization. It's used to indicate which direction to display the text. It can either have the value ltr (left to right) or rtl (right to left).

- ■ LANG—This is a proposed attribute to HTML for internationalization. This attribute is composed from the two-letter language code from ISO 639. You can optionally add a period, followed by a two-letter country code from ISO 3166. This attribute can be used by parsers to select language-specific choices for quotation marks, ligatures, and hyphenation rules.

The following is an example of <DD>:

```
<DD>Sample Definition</DD>
```

<DEL>: Delete

This HTML 3 tag is meant to supersede the <S> or <STRIKE> elements. Text enclosed within a <DEL> tag will be shown as strikethrough. You have the following attributes available:

- ■ CLASS—This is a proposed attribute to HTML 3 as part of a style sheet proposal. This is a list of calls and subclasses separated by spaces. Acceptable values that you can use have not been defined by HTML 3.

- ■ DIR—This is a proposed attribute to HTML for internationalization. It's used to indicate which direction to display the text. It can either have the value ltr (left to right) or rtl (right to left).

- ID—This is a proposed attribute to HTML 3 as part of a style sheet proposal. This defines the current line as a destination point. These points are used for internal jumps or jumps to a specific line.

- LANG—This is a proposed attribute to HTML for internationalization. This attribute is composed from the two-letter language code from ISO 639. You can optionally add a period, followed by a two-letter country code from ISO 3166. This attribute can be used by parsers to select language-specific choices for quotation marks, ligatures, and hyphenation rules.

The following is an example of <DEL>:

```
This is a <DEL>mistake<DEL>.
```

<DFN>: Definition

This HTML 3 tag will have the browser display the enclosed text as a description. If the current Web page makes use of a lot of definitions, you should use this tag. This element has the following attribute:

- CLASS—This is a proposed attribute to HTML 3 as part of a style sheet proposal. This is a list of calls and subclasses separated by spaces. Acceptable values that you can use have not been defined by HTML 3.

- DIR—This is a proposed attribute to HTML for internationalization. It's used to indicate which direction to display the text. It can either have the value ltr (left to right) or rtl (right to left).

- ID—This is a proposed attribute to HTML 3 as part of a style sheet proposal. This defines the current line as a destination point. These points are used for internal jumps or jumps to a specific line.

- LANG—This is a proposed attribute to HTML for internationalization. This attribute is composed from the two-letter language code from ISO 639. You can optionally add a period, followed by a two-letter country code from ISO 3166. This attribute can be used by parsers to select language-specific choices for quotation marks, ligatures, and hyphenation rules.

The following is an example of <DFN>:

```
<DFN>HTML—HyperText Markup Language</DFN>
```

<DIR>: Directory List

The <DIR> element is used when you want to create an unordered list of single-line elements. Each line in the <DIR> list is defined by the <LI> tag. You can apply the following attributes to the <DIR> tag:

- ALIGN—This attribute indicates the alignment of the text on the line. It can have the value of center, justify, left, or right.

- CLASS—This is a proposed attribute to HTML 3 as part of a style sheet proposal. This is a list of calls and subclasses separated by spaces. Acceptable values that you can use have not been defined by HTML 3.

- COMPACT—This attribute tells the browser to display the list in a compact manner. It is not, however, supported by many browsers.

- DIR—This is a proposed attribute to HTML for internationalization. It's used to indicate which direction to display the text. It can either have the value ltr (left to right) or rtl (right to left).

- LANG—This is a proposed attribute to HTML for internationalization. This attribute is composed from the two-letter language code from ISO 639. You can optionally add a period, followed by a two-letter country code from ISO 3166. This attribute can be used by parsers to select language-specific choices for quotation marks, ligatures, and hyphenation rules.

The following is an example of <DIR>:

```
<DIR ALIGN=center><LI>MYFILE.EXE</LI><LI>MYFILE.TXT</LI></DIR>
```

<DIV>: General Text Division

This proposed HTML 3 tag is intended to be used to replace the Netscape-specific <CENTER> tag. It has the following attributes:

- ALIGN—This attribute indicates the alignment of the text on the line. It can have the value of center, justify, left, or right.

- CLASS—This is a proposed attribute to HTML 3 as part of a style sheet proposal. This is a list of calls and subclasses separated by spaces. Acceptable values that you can use have not been defined by HTML 3.

- DIR—This is a proposed attribute to HTML for internationalization. It's used to indicate which direction to display the text. It can either have the value ltr (left to right) or rtl (right to left).

- ID—This is a proposed attribute to HTML 3 as part of a style sheet proposal. This defines the current line as a destination point. These points are used for internal jumps or jumps to a specific line.

- LANG—This is a proposed attribute to HTML for internationalization. This attribute is composed from the two-letter language code from ISO 639. You can optionally add a period, followed by a two-letter country code from ISO 3166. This attribute can be used by parsers to select language-specific choices for quotation marks, ligatures, and hyphenation rules.

VIII

Appendixes

The following is an example of <DIV>:

```
<DIV ALIGN=center>This line is centered.</DIV>
```

<DL>: Definition List

If you're going to use a lot of definitions or have a page of definitions, you need this tag. Each entry in the definition list is made up of <DT> and <DD> tags. You can use the following attributes:

- ALIGN—This attribute indicates the alignment of the text on the line. It can have the value of center, justify, left, or right.

- CLASS—This is a proposed attribute to HTML 3 as part of a style sheet proposal. This is a list of calls and subclasses separated by spaces. Acceptable values that you can use have not been defined by HTML 3.

- COMPACT—This attribute tells the browser to display the list in a compact manner. It is not, however, supported by many browsers.

- DIR—This is a proposed attribute to HTML for internationalization. It's used to indicate which direction to display the text. It can either have the value ltr (left to right) or rtl (right to left).

- ID—This is a proposed attribute to HTML 3 as part of a style sheet proposal. This defines the current line as a destination point. These points are used for internal jumps or jumps to a specific line.

- LANG—This is a proposed attribute to HTML for internationalization. This attribute is composed from the two-letter language code from ISO 639. You can optionally add a period, followed by a two-letter country code from ISO 3166. This attribute can be used by parsers to select language-specific choices for quotation marks, ligatures, and hyphenation rules.

The following is an example of <DL>:

```
<DL><DT>Internet</DT><DD>A distributed collection of computers
➥spread worldwide.</DD></DL>
```

<DT>: Definition List Title

This is one of the three HTML elements you need to use when creating a definition list. You create headings for your definitions with the <DT> tag. This HTML element comes with the following attributes:

- DIR—This is a proposed attribute to HTML for internationalization. It's used to indicate which direction to display the text. It can either have the value ltr (left to right) or rtl (right to left).

- LANG—This is a proposed attribute to HTML for internationalization. This attribute is composed from the two-letter language code from ISO

639. You can optionally add a period, followed by a two-letter country code from ISO 3166. This attribute can be used by parsers to select language-specific choices for quotation marks, ligatures, and hyphenation rules.

The following is an example of <DT>:

```
<DT>Definiton Heading</DT>
```

<EM>: Emphasis

There are a number of ways of making text stand out. Place this HTML tag around the text that you want to emphasize. It has the following attributes:

- CLASS—This is a proposed attribute to HTML 3 as part of a style sheet proposal. This is a list of calls and subclasses separated by spaces. Acceptable values that you can use have not been defined by HTML 3.

- DIR—This is a proposed attribute to HTML for internationalization. It's used to indicate which direction to display the text. It can either have the value ltr (left to right) or rtl (right to left).

- ID—This is a proposed attribute to HTML 3 as part of a style sheet proposal. This defines the current line as a destination point. These points are used for internal jumps or jumps to a specific line.

- LANG—This is a proposed attribute to HTML for internationalization. This attribute is composed from the two-letter language code from ISO 639. You can optionally add a period, followed by a two-letter country code from ISO 3166. This attribute can be used by parsers to select language-specific choices for quotation marks, ligatures, and hyphenation rules.

The following is an example of <EM>:

```
I repeat, you're <EM>WRONG</EM>!
```

<EMBED>: Embed Netscape Plugin

Netscape Navigator 2.0 provides for the capability to insert arbitrary objects. This is done with the newly created Netscape-specific tag, <EMBED>. You have a number of attributes you can use:

- Attributes—The <EMBED> element enables arbitrary and undefined attributes. These attributes are supposed to be application-specific, which makes documentation difficult.

- HEIGHT—This indicates the initial height of the display for the embedded object. The value must be specified as a number of pixels.

- SRC—This points to an URL for the object you want to embed.
- WIDTH—This indicates the initial width of the display for the embedded object. The value must be specified as a number of pixels.

The following is an example of <EMBED>:

```
<EMBED SRC="mymovie.dcr">
```

<FIG>: Figure

A new element in the HTML 3 proposal is the <FIG> tag, an improved <IMG> tag. You can include text elements as well as specify hotspots with other tags. You can also use the <OVERLAY> element to put overlays on top of figures. <FIG> has the following attributes:

- ALIGN—This attribute indicates the alignment of the text on the line. It can have the value of bleedleft, bleedright, center, justify, left, or right.
- CLASS—This is a proposed attribute to HTML 3 as part of a style sheet proposal. This is a list of calls and subclasses separated by spaces. Acceptable values that you can use have not been defined by HTML 3.
- CLEAR—This is a proposed attribute to HTML 3. It can have the value of left, right, or all. These values indicate which margin is to be clear of images so that text can appear on it.
- DIR—This is a proposed attribute to HTML for internationalization. It's used to indicate which direction to display the text. It can either have the value ltr (left to right) or rtl (right to left).
- HEIGHT—This indicates the initial height of the display for the embedded object. The value must be specified as a number of pixels.
- ID—This is a proposed attribute to HTML 3 as part of a style sheet proposal. This defines the current line as a destination point. These points are used for internal jumps or jumps to a specific line.
- LANG—This is a proposed attribute to HTML for internationalization. This attribute is composed from the two-letter language code from ISO 639. You can optionally add a period, followed by a two-letter country code from ISO 3166. This attribute can be used by parsers to select language-specific choices for quotation marks, ligatures, and hyphenation rules.
- MD—This is a proposed attribute to HTML 3 as part of a style sheet proposal. This attribute is used in conjunction with the SRC attribute, to specify a message digest or checksum. This is used when you want to be sure that a linked object is the one the Web author specified.

- SRC—This points to an URL for the image you want to use.

- UNITS—This attribute enables the HEIGHT and WIDTH attributes to use units other than screen pixels.

- WIDTH—This indicates the initial width of the display for the embedded object. The value must be specified as a number of pixels.

The following is an example of <FIG>:

```
<FIG SRC="http://www.mysite.com/mygraphic.gif"></FIG>
```

<FN>: Footnote

A new proposed HTML 3 tag is the footnote element. Currently, very few browsers support this tag. You have the following attributes available:

- CLASS—This is a proposed attribute to HTML 3 as part of a style sheet proposal. This is a list of calls and subclasses separated by spaces. Acceptable values that you can use have not been defined by HTML 3.

- DIR—This is a proposed attribute to HTML for internationalization. It's used to indicate which direction to display the text. It can either have the value ltr (left to right) or rtl (right to left).

- ID—This is a proposed attribute to HTML 3 as part of a style sheet proposal. This defines the current line as a destination point. These points are used for internal jumps or jumps to a specific line.

- LANG—This is a proposed attribute to HTML for internationalization. This attribute is composed from the two-letter language code from ISO 639. You can optionally add a period, followed by a two-letter country code from ISO 3166. This attribute can be used by parsers to select language-specific choices for quotation marks, ligatures, and hyphenation rules.

The following is an example of <FN>:

```
<FN>This is a footnote.</FN>
```

<FONT>: Font Size

The <FONT> element, first introduced by Netscape, enables various font manipulations. It has not been adopted as part of the new HTML 3 proposal. <FONT> has the following attributes:

- COLOR—This attribute enables the font to be drawn in a particular color. This color is represented by three pairs of hexadecimal numbers. The pairs represent the red, green, and blue color values.

- FACE—This attribute was introduced by Microsoft as a means of specifying a font style. There are currently no defined values.

VIII

Appendixes

- SIZE—This attribute indicates how much to increase or decrease the <BASEFONT> size. An acceptable value is anything between –7 and +7. You can also specify an absolute font size, with acceptables values between 1–7.

The following is an example of <FONT>:

```
<FONT SIZE=+2>
```

<FORM>: Fill Out Forms

The fill-out form is one of the best ways to get user input. The biggest drawback to using <FORM> is that you must have a CGI script to retrieve the information. Here is a list of attributes for this tag:

- ACCEPT-CHARSET—This attribute was introduced in the HTML internationalization attempt. This indicates the character sets that the receiving URL can handle.

- ACTION—This indicates the URL to send the information to.

- ENCTYPE—This attribute specifies the behavior of the form. Currently, there are only two defined: application/x-www-form-urlencoded and multipart/form-data.

- DIR—This is a proposed attribute to HTML for internationalization. It's used to indicate which direction to display the text. It can either have the value ltr (left to right) or rtl (right to left).

- LANG—This is a proposed attribute to HTML for internationalization. This attribute is composed from the two-letter language code from ISO 639. You can optionally add a period, followed by a two-letter country code from ISO 3166. This attribute can be used by parsers to select language-specific choices for quotation marks, ligatures, and hyphenation rules.

- METHOD—This attribute describes what should be done with the form. There are currently only two acceptable values: GET, which sends the information to the URL specified by ACTION; and POST, which enables you to do an HTTP upload.

- SCRIPT—This is an HTML 3 proposed attribute. The file specified by SCRIPT is sent to the browser's computer for execution. This program is intended to do some data manipulation before sending it to the URL in ACTION.

The following is an example of <FORM>:

```
<FORM ACTION="http://www.mysite.com/cgi-big/get.cgi"
➥METHOD="GET"></FORM>
```

<FRAME>: Frame

This is a new Netscape-specific HTML extension, which provides better handling of the browser's window. Netscape enables URLs to update certain frames or for some frames to remain on the browser. The <FRAME> tag has a number of attributes:

- MARGINHEIGHT—This indicates the height of the frame, specified in pixels.

- MARGINWIDTH—This indicates the width of the frame, specified in pixels.

- NAME—This attribute assigns a name to the frame to be used as a target for hypertext link updates. There are four reserved names: _blank, _self, _parent, and _top. These values must begin with the underbar character and each have different meanings. The _blank name indicates a new, unnamed window. The _self name indicates the same window as the calling URL. The _parent name indicates that the destination is the parent frame of the destination URL. Finally, the _top indicates that the top window should be used.

- NORESIZE—When this attribute is used, the user cannot resize the frame.

- SCROLLING—This attribute is used to determine if there is a scroll bar. You can use either YES, NO, or AUTO. By default, AUTO is used.

- SRC—This indicates the URL for the HTML document to be shown in the frame.

The following is an example of <FRAME>:

```
<FRAME SRC="http://www.mysite.com/myframe.html" SCROLLING="YES" NORESIZE>
```

<FRAMESET>: Frame Setup

The <FRAMESET> tag is another proposed extension from Netscape to be used instead of the <BODY> element. This tag is used only to set up other frames that will be the actual page. You must use the <FRAME> element if you use this tag. You have a number of attributes available:

- COLS—This list of widths of the frame is separated by commas. By default, you specify the frame widths in pixels. Alternatively, you can add the percent sign (%) after a number to make the frame width a percentage of the browser's width.

- ROWS—This attribute is similar to the COLS attribute, except that it applies to the frames' heights. These values for each consecutive frame are separated by commas. By default, the height specifications are expressed in screen pixels. Alternatively, you can add the percent sign (%) after a number to make the frame height a percentage of the browser's height.

The following is an example of <FRAMESET>:

```
<FRAMESET COLS="50%,50%" ROWS="600, 400"></FRAMESET>
```

<H1>: Heading, Level 1

This HTML tag displays text as the most prominent header. It has the following attributes:

- ALIGN—This attribute indicates the alignment of the text on the line. It can have the value of center, justify, left, or right.

- CLASS—This is a proposed attribute to HTML 3 as part of a style sheet proposal. This is a list of calls and subclasses separated by spaces. Acceptable values that you can use have not been defined by HTML 3.

- CLEAR—This is a proposed attribute to HTML 3. It can have the value of left, right, or all. These values indicate which margin is to be clear of images so that text can appear on it.

- DIR—This is a proposed attribute to HTML for internationalization. It's used to indicate which direction to display the text. It can either have the value ltr (left to right) or rtl (right to left).

- ID—This is a proposed attribute to HTML 3 as part of a style sheet proposal. This defines the current line as a destination point. These points are used for internal jumps or jumps to a specific line.

- LANG—This is a proposed attribute to HTML for internationalization. This attribute is composed from the two-letter language code from ISO 639. You can optionally add a period, followed by a two-letter country code from ISO 3166. This attribute can be used by parsers to select language-specific choices for quotation marks, ligatures, and hyphenation rules.

- MD—This is a proposed attribute to HTML 3 as part of a style sheet proposal. This attribute is used to specify a message digest or checksum. This is used when you want to be sure that a linked object is the one the Web author specified.

- NOWRAP—When used, this attribute will prevent the browser from word wrapping the heading.

The following is an example of <H1>:

```
<H1>This is the largest heading.</H1>
```

<H2>: Heading, Level 2

This HTML tag displays text as the second most prominent header. It has the following attributes:

- ALIGN—This attribute indicates the alignment of the text on the line. It can have the value of center, justify, left, right.

- CLASS—This is a proposed attribute to HTML 3 as part of a style sheet proposal. This is a list of calls and subclasses separated by spaces. Acceptable values that you can use have not been defined by HTML 3.

- CLEAR—This is a proposed attribute to HTML 3. It can have the value of left, right, or all. These values indicate which margin is to be clear of images so that text can appear on it.

- DIR—This is a proposed attribute to HTML for internationalization. It's used to indicate which direction to display the text. It can either have the value ltr (left to right) or rtl (right to left).

- ID—This is a proposed attribute to HTML 3 as part of a style sheet proposal. This defines the current line as a destination point. These points are used for internal jumps or jumps to a specific line.

- LANG—This is a proposed attribute to HTML for internationalization. This attribute is composed from the two-letter language code from ISO 639. You can optionally add a period, followed by a two-letter country code from ISO 3166. This attribute can be used by parsers to select language-specific choices for quotation marks, ligatures, and hyphenation rules.

- MD—This is a proposed attribute to HTML 3 as part of a style sheet proposal. This attribute is used to specify a message digest or checksum. This is used when you want to be sure that a linked object is the one the Web author specified.

- NOWRAP—When used, this attribute will prevent the browser from word wrapping the heading.

The following is an example of <H2>:

```
<H2>This is the second largest heading.</H2>
```

<H3>: Heading, Level 3

This HTML tag displays text as the third most prominent header. It has the following attributes:

- ALIGN—This attribute indicates the alignment of the text on the line. It can have the value of center, justify, left, or right.

- CLASS—This is a proposed attribute to HTML 3 as part of a style sheet proposal. This is a list of calls and subclasses separated by spaces. Acceptable values that you can use have not been defined by HTML 3.

- CLEAR—This is a proposed attribute to HTML 3. It can have the value of `left`, `right`, or `all`. These values indicate which margin is to be clear of images so that text can appear on it.

- DIR—This is a proposed attribute to HTML for internationalization. It's used to indicate which direction to display the text. It can either have the value `ltr` (left to right) or `rtl` (right to left).

- ID—This is a proposed attribute to HTML 3 as part of a style sheet proposal. This defines the current line as a destination point. These points are used for internal jumps or jumps to a specific line.

- LANG—This is a proposed attribute to HTML for internationalization. This attribute is composed from the two-letter language code from ISO 639. You can optionally add a period, followed by a two-letter country code from ISO 3166. This attribute can be used by parsers to select language-specific choices for quotation marks, ligatures, and hyphenation rules.

- MD—This is a proposed attribute to HTML 3 as part of a style sheet proposal. This attribute is used to specify a message digest or checksum. This is used when you want to be sure that a linked object is the one the Web author specified.

- NOWRAP—When used, this attribute will prevent the browser from word wrapping the heading.

The following is an example of <H3>:

```
<H3>This is the third largest heading.</H3>
```

<H4>: Heading, Level 4

This HTML tag displays text as the fourth most prominent header. It has the following attributes:

- ALIGN—This attribute indicates the alignment of the text on the line. It can have the value of `center`, `justify`, `left`, or `right`.

- CLASS—This is a proposed attribute to HTML 3 as part of a style sheet proposal. This is a list of calls and subclasses separated by spaces. Acceptable values that you can use have not been defined by HTML 3.

- CLEAR—This is a proposed attribute to HTML 3. It can have the value of `left`, `right`, or `all`. These values indicate which margin is to be clear of images so that text can appear on it.

- DIR—This is a proposed attribute to HTML for internationalization. It's used to indicate which direction to display the text. It can either have the value `ltr` (left to right) or `rtl` (right to left).

- ID—This is a proposed attribute to HTML 3 as part of a style sheet proposal. This defines the current line as a destination point. These points are used for internal jumps or jumps to a specific line.

- LANG—This is a proposed attribute to HTML for internationalization. This attribute is composed from the two-letter language code from ISO 639. You can optionally add a period, followed by a two-letter country code from ISO 3166. This attribute can be used by parsers to select language-specific choices for quotation marks, ligatures, and hyphenation rules.

- MD—This is a proposed attribute to HTML 3 as part of a style sheet proposal. This attribute is used to specify a message digest or checksum. This is used when you want to be sure that a linked object is the one the Web author specified.

- NOWRAP—When used, this attribute will prevent the browser from word wrapping the heading.

The following is an example of <H4>:

```
<H4>This is the fourth largest heading.</H4>
```

<H5>: Heading, Level 5

This HTML tag displays text as the fifth most prominent header. It has the following attributes:

- ALIGN—This attribute indicates the alignment of the text on the line. It can have the value of center, left, right, or justify.

- CLASS—This is a proposed attribute to HTML 3 as part of a style sheet proposal. This is a list of calls and subclasses separated by spaces. Acceptable values that you can use have not been defined by HTML 3.

- CLEAR—This is a proposed attribute to HTML 3. It can have the value of left, right, or all. These values indicate which margin is to be clear of images so that text can appear on it.

- DIR—This is a proposed attribute to HTML for internationalization. It's used to indicate which direction to display the text. It can either have the value ltr (left to right) or rtl (right to left).

- ID—This is a proposed attribute to HTML 3 as part of a style sheet proposal. This defines the current line as a destination point. These points are used for internal jumps or jumps to a specific line.

- LANG—This is a proposed attribute to HTML for internationalization. This attribute is composed from the two-letter language code from ISO 639. You can optionally add a period, followed by a two-letter country

VIII

Appendixes

code from ISO 3166. This attribute can be used by parsers to select language-specific choices for quotation marks, ligatures, and hyphenation rules.

- ■ MD—This is a proposed attribute to HTML 3 as part of a style sheet proposal. This attribute is used to specify a message digest or checksum. This is used when you want to be sure that a linked object is the one the Web author specified.

- ■ NOWRAP—When used, this attribute will prevent the browser from word wrapping the heading.

The following is an example of <H5>:

```
<H5>This is the fifth largest heading.</H5>
```

<H6>: Heading, Level 6

This HTML tag displays text as the least prominent header. It has the following attributes:

- ■ ALIGN—This attribute indicates the alignment of the text on the line. It can have the value of center, left, right, or justify.

- ■ CLASS—This is a proposed attribute to HTML 3 as part of a style sheet proposal. This is a list of calls and subclasses separated by spaces. Acceptable values that you can use have not been defined by HTML 3.

- ■ CLEAR—This is a proposed attribute to HTML 3. It can have the value of left, right, or all. These values indicate which margin is to be clear of images so that text can appear on it.

- ■ DIR—This is a proposed attribute to HTML for internationalization. It's used to indicate which direction to display the text. It can either have the value ltr (left to right) or rtl (right to left).

- ■ ID—This is a proposed attribute to HTML 3 as part of a style sheet proposal. This defines the current line as a destination point. These points are used for internal jumps or jumps to a specific line.

- ■ LANG—This is a proposed attribute to HTML for internationalization. This attribute is composed from the two-letter language code from ISO 639. You can optionally add a period, followed by a two-letter country code from ISO 3166. This attribute can be used by parsers to select language-specific choices for quotation marks, ligatures, and hyphenation rules.

- ■ MD—This is a proposed attribute to HTML 3 as part of a style sheet proposal. This attribute is used to specify a message digest or checksum. This is used when you want to be sure that a linked object is the one the Web author specified.

- NOWRAP—When used, this attribute will prevent the browser from word wrapping the heading.

The following is an example of <H6>:

```
<H6>This is the smallest heading.</H6>
```

<HEAD>: Head

This element is intended to hold information about the HTML document. Although you can put other HTML elements within the <HEAD>, none of them will be displayed in the browser's window. This tag has the following attributes:

- DIR—This is a proposed attribute to HTML for internationalization. It's used to indicate which direction to display the text. It can either have the value ltr (left to right) or rtl (right to left).

- LANG—This is a proposed attribute to HTML for internationalization. This attribute is composed from the two-letter language code from ISO 639. You can optionally add a period, followed by a two-letter country code from ISO 3166. This attribute can be used by parsers to select language-specific choices for quotation marks, ligatures, and hyphenation rules.

The following is an example of <HEAD>:

```
<HEAD><TITLE>This Is My Home Page</TITLE></HEAD>
```

<HR>: Horizontal Rule

When used, the <HR> tag creates a horizontal line. It has the following attributes:

- ALIGN—This proposed extended attribute indicates the positioning of the rule. It can have the value of left, right, center, or justify.

- CLASS—This is a proposed attribute to HTML 3 as part of a style sheet proposal. This is a list of calls and subclasses separated by spaces. Acceptable values that you can use have not been defined by HTML 3.

- CLEAR—This is a proposed attribute to HTML 3. It can have the value of left, right, or all. These values indicate which margin is to be clear of images so that text can appear on it.

- DIR—This is a proposed attribute to HTML for internationalization. It's used to indicate which direction to display the text. It can either have the value ltr (left to right) or rtl (right to left).

- ID—This is a proposed attribute to HTML 3 as part of a style sheet proposal. This defines the current line as a destination point. These points are used for internal jumps or jumps to a specific line.

- **LANG**—This is a proposed attribute to HTML for internationalization. This attribute is composed from the two-letter language code from ISO 639. You can optionally add a period, followed by a two-letter country code from ISO 3166. This attribute can be used by parsers to select language-specific choices for quotation marks, ligatures, and hyphenation rules.

- **MD**—This is a proposed attribute to HTML 3 as part of a style sheet proposal. This attribute is used in conjunction with the SRC attribute, to specify a message digest or checksum. This is used when you want to be sure that a linked object is the one the Web author specified.

- **SRC**—This proposed HTML 3 attribute is intended to specify a custom image. Traditionally, the horizontal rule was a browser-specific graphic. This attribute enables the Web author to determine the image.

- **SIZE**—This Netscape extension to HTML specifies the thickness of the horizontal line in pixels.

- **WIDTH**—By default, the horizontal rule is drawn as wide as the page. This Netscape extension attribute enables the Web author to define the horizontal length of the rule in pixels. Alternatively, if you add the percent sign (%) after a number, the horizontal rule will be a percent of the width of the document.

- **NOSHADE**—For those times when you want a solid horizontal line, use NOSHADE. This will prevent the browser from doing any shading of the horizontal line.

The following is an example of <HR>:

```
<HR SIZE=5 NOSHADE>
```

<HTML>: HTML

This is the main container for a home page. All other HTML tags contained within this element are shown in the browser window. This tag has the following attributes:

- **DIR**—This is a proposed attribute to HTML for internationalization. It's used to indicate which direction to display the text. It can either have the value ltr (left to right) or rtl (right to left).

- **LANG**—This is a proposed attribute to HTML for internationalization. This attribute is composed from the two-letter language code from ISO 639. You can optionally add a period, followed by a two-letter country code from ISO 3166. This attribute can be used by parsers to select language-specific choices for quotation marks, ligatures, and hyphenation rules.

The following is an example of <HTML>:

```
<HTML>[Your home page]</HTML>
```

<I>: Italic

This tag will italicize the text that is enclosed within it. The <I> tag can have the following attributes:

- CLASS—This is a proposed attribute to HTML 3 as part of a style sheet proposal. This is a list of calls and subclasses separated by spaces. Acceptable values that you can use have not been defined by HTML 3.

- DIR—This is a proposed attribute to HTML for internationalization. It's used to indicate which direction to display the text. It can either have the value ltr (left to right) or rtl (right to left).

- ID—This is a proposed attribute to HTML 3 as part of a style sheet proposal. This defines the current line as a destination point. These points are used for internal jumps or jumps to a specific line.

- LANG—This is a proposed attribute to HTML for internationalization. This attribute is composed from the two-letter language code from ISO 639. You can optionally add a period, followed by a two-letter country code from ISO 3166. This attribute can be used by parsers to select language-specific choices for quotation marks, ligatures, and hyphenation rules.

The following is an example of <I>:

```
This word is in <I>italics</I>.
```

<IMG>: Image

Currently, any time you want to make use of graphics on your home page, you have to employ the <IMG> tag. This element enables you to specify imagemap information, hypertext link information, and positioning information. It has the following attributes

- ALIGN—This attribute indicates the alignment of the text on the line. It can have the value of absbottom, absmiddle, baseline, bottom, left, middle, right, texttop, or top.

- ALT—This attribute contains a text string that will be displayed by people who aren't using graphical browsers.

- BORDER—This attribute indicates the thickness of the border around the image. The unit of measurement for the thickness is determined by the UNITS attribute.

- CLASS—This is a proposed attribute to HTML 3 as part of a style sheet proposal. This is a list of calls and subclasses separated by spaces. Acceptable values that you can use have not been defined by HTML 3.

- CONTROLS—This is a Microsoft proposed attribute extension. If a video file is specified by the SRC attribute, a set of controls is displayed under the video clip.

- DIR—This is a proposed attribute to HTML for internationalization. It's used to indicate which direction to display the text. It can either have the value ltr (left to right) or rtl (right to left).

- DYNSRC—This is a Microsoft proposed attribute extension that points to an URL. The URL is a video clip or VRML world to be displayed.

- HEIGHT—This indicates the initial height of the display for the embedded object. The value must be specified as a number of pixels.

- HSPACE—This Netscape proposed extension controls the amount of horizontal space around the image. The value specified is expressed as a number of pixels.

- ID—This is a proposed attribute to HTML 3 as part of a style sheet proposal. This defines the current line as a destination point. These points are used for internal jumps or jumps to a specific line.

- ISMAP—When using imagemaps, you must use this attribute. This indicates that the graphic specified in the SRC attribute, is an imagemap.

- LANG—This is a proposed attribute to HTML for internationalization. This attribute is composed from the two-letter language code from ISO 639. You can optionally add a period, followed by a two-letter country code from ISO 3166. This attribute can be used by parsers to select language-specific choices for quotation marks, ligatures, and hyphenation rules.

- LOOP—This is a Microsoft proposed attribute extension. The value indicates how many times the video clip is played. If you put in the string INFINITE or use the value of -1, the video clip will play continually.

- LOOPDELAY—This is a Microsoft proposed attribute extension. The value specified with this attribute, indicates the number of seconds to wait before a video clip is replayed.

- LOWSRC—This a Netscape 1.1 extension. The file specified with this attribute will be loaded before the file indicated in the SRC attribute. This is intended for Web authors to use low resolution image, which has all the important information of the higher resolution image.

■ MD—This is a proposed attribute to HTML 3 as part of a style sheet proposal. This attribute is used in conjunction with the SRC attribute, to specify a message digest or checksum. This is used when you want to be sure that a linked object is the one the Web author specified.

■ SRC—This indicates the URL for the HTML document to be displayed.

■ START—This is a Microsoft proposed attribute extension for video clips. This attribute indicates when the video file will start playing. Supported values for this attribute are FILEOPEN and MOUSEOVER. The FILEOPEN value indicates that as soon as the browser loads in the file, it will play it. The MOUSEOVER value indicates that the video clip will play when the user moves the mouse over the clip.

■ UNITS—This attribute enables the HEIGHT and WIDTH attributes to use units other than screen pixels.

■ USEMAP—This is a Netscape proposed attribute extension for implementing client-side imagemaps. This attribute should point to an URL with a #NAME suffix. The MAP element is used in conjunction with this attribute.

■ VSPACE—This Netscape proposed extension controls the amount of vertical space around the image. The value specified is expressed as a number of pixels.

■ WIDTH—This indicates the initial width of the display for the embedded object. The value must be specified as a number of pixels.

The following is an example of <IMG>:

```
<IMG SRC="mymap.gif" WIDTH=5 HEIGHT=5 BORDER=2 ISMAP>
```

<INPUT>: Input

This HTML 3 proposed element works with the FORM element. The <INPUT> tag enables the user to upload a file through the Web server. It has the following attributes:

■ ACCEPT—This attribute indicates a list of media types that the server will accept.

■ ALIGN—This attribute indicates the alignment of the <INPUT> form. Acceptable values for this attribute are bottom, left, middle, right, and top.

■ CHECKED—This indicates that the specific form will be a check box. If this is not specified, it will default to a radio button.

■ CLASS—This is a proposed attribute to HTML 3 as part of a style sheet proposal. This is a list of calls and subclasses separated by spaces. Acceptable values that you can use have not been defined by HTML 3.

VIII

Appendixes

- DIR—This is a proposed attribute to HTML for internationalization. It's used to indicate which direction to display the text. It can either have the value ltr (left to right) or rtl (right to left).

- DISABLED—This proposed HTML 3 attribute will display the form, but prevent the user from modifying it.

- ERROR—This proposed HTML 3 attribute is used when an incorrect value is entered. The text specified in this attribute is displayed on invalid input.

- ID—This is a proposed attribute to HTML 3 as part of a style sheet proposal. This defines the current line as a destination point. These points are used for internal jumps or jumps to a specific line.

- LANG—This is a proposed attribute to HTML for internationalization. This attribute is composed from the two-letter language code from ISO 639. You can optionally add a period, followed by a two-letter country code from ISO 3166. This attribute can be used by parsers to select language-specific choices for quotation marks, ligatures, and hyphenation rules.

- MAX—This value is only used when the TYPE attribute is set to RANGE. This indicates the acceptable maximum numeric value.

- MAXLENGTH—This proposed HTML 3 attribute specifies the maximum number of characters acceptable for input.

- MD—This is a proposed attribute to HTML 3 as part of a style sheet proposal. This attribute is used in conjunction with the SRC attribute, to specify a message digest or checksum. This is used when you want to be sure that a linked object is the one the Web author specified.

- MIN—This value is only used when the TYPE attribute is set to RANGE. This indicates the acceptable minimum numeric value.

- NAME—The string in this attribute is the name for the input form.

- SIZE—This attribute specifies the physical size of the input form. This value is specified in number of characters.

- SRC—When the TYPE attribute is set to IMAGE, this points to an URL. When the user clicks the image and the form is submitted, the mouse coordinates are sent over as well. This is similar to having a form-based imagemap.

- TYPE—This attribute indicates the behavior of the INPUT form. Acceptable values are CHECKBOX, FILE, HIDDEN, IMAGE, JOT, PASSWORD, RADIO, RANGE, RESET, SCRIBBLE, SUBMIT, or TEXT.

■ VALUE—This attribute changes based on the TYPE attribute. Generally speaking, the VALUE attribute will contain the value returned by the user.

The following is an example of <INPUT>:

```
<INPUT TYPE="SUBMIT" NAME="submit1" ALIGN="left">
```

<INS>: Insert

This proposed HTML 3 element will display the enclosed text as inserted text. The text embedded by the starting and ending markers of this element, will be shown in a strikethrough font. This tag is mainly intended for legal documents and has the following attributes:

■ CLASS—This is a proposed attribute to HTML 3 as part of a style sheet proposal. This is a list of calls and subclasses separated by spaces. Acceptable values that you can use have not been defined by HTML 3.

■ DIR—This is a proposed attribute to HTML for internationalization. It's used to indicate which direction to display the text. It can either have the value ltr (left to right) or rtl (right to left).

■ ID—This is a proposed attribute to HTML 3 as part of a style sheet proposal. This defines the current line as a destination point. These points are used for internal jumps or jumps to a specific line.

■ LANG—This is a proposed attribute to HTML for internationalization. This attribute is composed from the two-letter language code from ISO 639. You can optionally add a period, followed by a two-letter country code from ISO 3166. This attribute can be used by parsers to select language-specific choices for quotation marks, ligatures, and hyphenation rules.

The following is an example of <INS>:

```
This is <INS>inserted text.</INS>
```

<ISINDEX>: Searchable Index

This HTML element is used before the <FORM> tag to indicate a searchable index. When this tag is put in the HEAD section of the HTML document, the entire document can be examined using a keyword search. <ISINDEX> has the following attributes:

■ ACTION—When <ISINDEX> is used in the <BODY> portion of the Web document, this points to a CGI script. The script is the program on the server that can handle the search.

- DIR—This is a proposed attribute to HTML for internationalization. It's used to indicate which direction to display the text. It can either have the value ltr (left to right) or rtl (right to left).

- LANG—This is a proposed attribute to HTML for internationalization. This attribute is composed from the two-letter language code from ISO 639. You can optionally add a period, followed by a two-letter country code from ISO 3166. This attribute can be used by parsers to select language-specific choices for quotation marks, ligatures, and hyphenation rules.

- PROMPT—This is a proposed HTML 3 attribute that enables the Web author to specify a prompt. The string assigned to this attribute will be displayed as the prompt, for the searchable index.

The following is an example of <ISINDEX>:

```
<ISINDEX>
```

<KBD>: Keyboard

This HTML element will cause the enclosed text to be displayed as keyboard input. This is typically done when you want to give users instructions on what to type into the computer. This tag has the following attributes:

- CLASS—This is a proposed attribute to HTML 3 as part of a style sheet proposal. This is a list of calls and subclasses separated by spaces. Acceptable values that you can use have not been defined by HTML 3.

- DIR—This is a proposed attribute to HTML for internationalization. It's used to indicate which direction to display the text. It can either have the value ltr (left to right) or rtl (right to left).

- ID—This is a proposed attribute to HTML 3 as part of a style sheet proposal. This defines the current line as a destination point. These points are used for internal jumps or jumps to a specific line.

- LANG—This is a proposed attribute to HTML for internationalization. This attribute is composed from the two-letter language code from ISO 639. You can optionally add a period, followed by a two-letter country code from ISO 3166. This attribute can be used by parsers to select language-specific choices for quotation marks, ligatures and hyphenation rules.

The following is an example of <KBD>:

```
Type in <KBD>ls</KBD> at the UNIX command prompt.
```

<LANG>: Default Language

This is a proposed HTML 3 attribute that changes the LANG context. The text enclosed within this tag will have its LANG context changed, as well as all subsequent LANGs. This tag has the following attributes:

- CLASS—This is a proposed attribute to HTML 3 as part of a style sheet proposal. This is a list of calls and subclasses separated by spaces. Acceptable values that you can use have not been defined by HTML 3.

- ID—This is a proposed attribute to HTML 3 as part of a style sheet proposal. This defines the current line as a destination point. These points are used for internal jumps or jumps to a specific line.

The following is an example of <LANG>:

```
The LANG context will <LANG>change.</LANG>
```

<LH>: List Header

This proposed HTML 3 element enables you to define the header for a list. This tag has the following attributes:

- CLASS—This is a proposed attribute to HTML 3 as part of a style sheet proposal. This is a list of calls and subclasses separated by spaces. Acceptable values that you can use have not been defined by HTML 3.

- DIR—This is a proposed attribute to HTML for internationalization. It's used to indicate which direction to display the text. It can either have the value ltr (left to right) or rtl (right to left).

- ID—This is a proposed attribute to HTML 3 as part of a style sheet proposal.

- LANG—This is a proposed attribute to HTML for internationalization. This attribute is composed from the two-letter language code from ISO 639. You can optionally add a period, followed by a two-letter country code from ISO 3166. This attribute can be used by parsers to select language-specific choices for quotation marks, ligatures, and hyphenation rules.

The following is an example of <LH>:

```
<LH>A Heading</LH>
```

<LI>: List Item

This attribute takes the enclosed text and makes it part of the list. This element has the following attributes:

- ALIGN—This attribute specifies the alignment of the list item. You can set it to the value of center, justify, left, or right.

- DIR—This is a proposed attribute to HTML for internationalization. It's used to indicate which direction to display the text. It can either have the value ltr (left to right) or rtl (right to left).

- LANG—This is a proposed attribute to HTML for internationalization. This attribute is composed from the two-letter language code from ISO 639. You can optionally add a period, followed by a two-letter country code from ISO 3166. This attribute can be used by parsers to select language-specific choices for quotation marks, ligatures, and hyphenation rules.

- TYPE—This Netscape extension enables you to specify the prefix for this particular item. If you're using a <UL> list type, TYPE can be circle, disc, or square. If the list is an <OL> list type, TYPE can be A, a, I, i, or 1.

- VALUE—This Netscape extension works with the TYPE attribute. When you specify an <OL> list type, this attribute indicates the starting number of the list. By default, this value is 1.

The following is an example of <LI>:

```
<LI>A list item</LI>
```

<LINK>: Link

This HTML tag is used to specify a relationship between the current Web page and other HTML documents. This element is used along with the Anchor attribute REL. This element has the following attributes:

- CHARSET—This is a proposed attribute to HTML for internationalization. It's used to indicate what type of character set is used by the hypertext link.

- DIR—This is a proposed attribute to HTML for internationalization. It's used to indicate which direction to display the text. It can either have the value ltr (left to right) or rtl (right to left).

- HREF—This indicates the destination URL you want to establish the relationship with.

- LANG—This is a proposed attribute to HTML for internationalization. This attribute is composed from the two-letter language code from ISO 639. You can optionally add a period, followed by a two-letter country code from ISO 3166. This attribute can be used by parsers to select language-specific choices for quotation marks, ligatures, and hyphenation rules.

- METHODS—This indicates a list of HTTP METHODS supported by the object. Currently, the only acceptable values are GET and TEXTSEARCH. This is a little used and little supported attribute.

- REL—When used with the HREF attribute, this indicates a particular relationship with the destination. This is a little used and little supported attribute, and will probably be superseded in the future.

- REV—When used with the HREF attribute, this is the inverse of the REL attribute. This establishes a backwards relationship between the current Web page and the URL that brought up this HTML document. This is a little used and little supported attribute and will probably be superseded in the future.

- TITLE—When used with HREF, this attribute indicates the title of the destination URL. This is a little used and little supported attribute.

- URN—The Universal Resource Number was originally intended as a better method of referring to destination links, than URLs. It is currently not used or supported.

The following is an example of <LINK>:

```
<LINK HREF="http://www.mysite.com/destination1.html">
```

<MAP>: Client-Side Imagemap

This Netscape proposed HTML element describes imagemap regions. The one attribute allowed is NAME, which points to a file with the imagemap regions defined.

The following is an example of <MAP>:

```
<MAP NAME="myregions.map"></MAP>
```

<MARQUEE>: Marquee

This HTML element proposed by Microsoft will create an area with scrolling text inside of it. The text to be scrolled is contained within the start and end markers of this element. This tag has the following attributes:

- ALIGN—This attribute specifies how the text will be displayed in the marquee. You can set it to the value of bottom, middle, or top.

- BEHAVIOR—This attribute determines whether the text will scroll completely off the marquee. You can set this attribute to alternate, scroll, or slide. The alternate value will cause the text to move back and forth from side to side. The text will scroll completely off the marquee when the value is scroll. The text in the marquee will enter the marquee and stay there with the slide value. The default is scroll.

- BGCOLOR—The background color of the marquee can be specified with this attribute. The color is represented by three pairs of hexadecimal numbers. The pairs represent the red, green, and blue color values.

- DIRECTION—This attribute indicates how the text will scroll in the marquee. You can either set this to left or right.

- HEIGHT—The height of the marquee is controlled with this attribute. You can specify the size in either pixels or as a percentage of the window height. If you're specifying a percentage of the window, you'll need to add a percent sign (%) after the number.

- HSPACE—This attribute defines how many pixels separate the marquee from surrounding text. This controls the amount of pixels to use as a buffer horizontally.

- LOOP—This number specifies how many times the marquee text will loop. A value of -1 or the string INFINITE will cause the text to loop forever.

- SCROLLAMOUNT—This number determines the number of pixels to scroll the marquee text.

- SCROLLDELAY—You can specify the number of milliseconds between marquee updates with this value.

- VSPACE—This attribute defines how many pixels separate the marquee from the surrounding text. This controls the number of pixels to use as a buffer vertically.

The following is an example of <MARQUEE>:

```
<MARQUEE BEHAVIOR="scroll" DIRECTION="left">This is a marquee.
➥</MARQUEE>
```

<MENU>: Menu

This HTML element will display any <LI> enclosed within it in a menu list. HTML 3 proposed to remove this element. This tag has the following attributes:

- ALIGN—This attribute specifies the alignment of the list item. You can set it to be the value of center, justify, left, or right.

- COMPACT—This attribute causes the menu list to be displayed in a physically compact form.

- DIR—This is a proposed attribute to HTML for internationalization. It's used to indicate which direction to display the text. It can either have the value ltr (left to right) or rtl (right to left).

- LANG—This is a proposed attribute to HTML for internationalization. This attribute is composed from the two-letter language code from ISO 639. You can optionally add a period, followed by a two-letter country code from ISO 3166. This attribute can be used by parsers to select language-specific choices for quotation marks, ligatures, and hyphenation rules.

The following is an example of <MENU>:

```
<MENU><LI>Milk $1.00</LI><LI>Eggs $2.00</LI></MENU>
```

<META>: Meta Information

This HTML tag is intended to specify document information not available with other HTML elements. The information contained in this element may be extracted by the server or the browser. This tag has the following attributes:

- CONTENT—This attribute specifies the meta-information to be associated with the value in the NAME attribute. You can also use this attribute to indicate the information to be associated with an HTTP response header. If the HTTP-EQUIV attribute is set to the Netscape-specific REFRESH, Then CONTENT will indicate the number of seconds to update the current Web page.

- HTTP-EQUIV—You specify which attribute to associate the <META> element with. Netscape introduced the value of REFRESH to enable home pages to be updated.

- NAME—If the HTTP-EQUIV attribute is not defined, this attribute is used to identify the information.

- URL—This Netscape attribute extension is used to indicate which home page is to be updated. After the number of seconds specified in CONTENT, this URL will be reloaded.

The following is an example of <META>:

```
<META URL="http://www.mysite.com/anim.html" CONTENT=5 HTTP-EQUIV-REFRESH>
```

<NOBR>: No Line Break

This element is used to control line breaks on certain lines. The text enclosed within the beginning and ending markers will not word wrap based on the width of the browser.

The following is an example of <NOBR>:

```
<NOBR>This line of text will always be one line, regardless of how
➥wide the browser window.</NOBR>
```

<NOEMED>: Non-Embedded Text

This Netscape HTML extension element is intended to be used for browsers that understand, but don't implement, the <EMBED>/<NOEMBED> tags. If one of these browsers comes across the <NOEMBED> element, the enclosed text will be displayed. This is basically equivalent to the ALT attribute for the <IMG> element.

The following is an example of <NOEMBED>:

```
<NOEMBED>You'll only see this if your browser doesn't support the
➡EMBED tag.</NOEMBED>
```

<NOFRAMES>: Non-Frames Text

This Netscape HTML extension element is intended to be used for browsers that understand, but don't implement, the <FRAMESET>/<NOFRAMES> tags. If one of these browsers comes across the <NOFRAMES> element, the enclosed text will be displayed. This is basically equivalent to the ALT attribute for the <IMG> element.

The following is an example of <NOFRAMES>:

```
<NOFRAMES>You'll only see this if your browser doesn't support the
➡FRAMESET tag.</NOFRAMES>
```

<NOTE>: Note

This proposed HTML 3 element will cause the enclosed text to be displayed as a note. The <NOTE> tag has the following attributes:

- CLASS—This is a proposed attribute to HTML 3 as part of a style sheet proposal. This is a list of calls and subclasses separated by spaces. Acceptable values that you can use have not been defined by HTML 3.

- CLEAR—This is a proposed attribute to HTML 3. It can have the value of left, right, or all. These values indicate which margin is to be clear of images so that text can appear on it.

- DIR—This is a proposed attribute to HTML for internationalization. It's used to indicate which direction to display the text. It can either have the value ltr (left to right) or rtl (right to left).

- ID—This is a proposed attribute to HTML 3 as part of a style sheet proposal. This defines the current line as a destination point. These points are used for internal jumps or jumps to a specific line.

- LANG—This is a proposed attribute to HTML for internationalization. This attribute is composed from the two-letter language code from ISO 639. You can optionally add a period, followed by a two-letter country code from ISO 3166. This attribute can be used by parsers to select language-specific choices for quotation marks, ligatures, and hyphenation rules.

- MD—This is a proposed attribute to HTML 3 as part of a style sheet proposal. This attribute is used in conjunction with the SRC attribute, to specify a message digest or checksum. This is used when you want to be sure that a linked object is the one the Web author specified.

- SRC—This points to an URL for an image to be displayed before the <NOTE>.

The following is an example of <NOTE>:

```
<NOTE>This is a note.</NOTE>
```

<OL>: Ordered List

This HTML element will display any enclosed <LI> elements as an ordered list. The order is listed numerically. It has the following attributes:

- ALIGN—This attribute specifies the alignment of the list item. You can set it to be the value of center, justify, left, or right.

- CLASS—This is a proposed attribute to HTML 3 as part of a style sheet proposal. In the ordered list, this indicates what type of numerical sequence to use.

- CLEAR—This is a proposed attribute to HTML 3. It can have the value of left, right, or all. These values indicate which margin is to be clear of images so that text can appear on it.

- COMPACT—This attribute causes the menu list to be displayed in a physically compact form.

- CONTINUE—This proposed HTML 3 attribute will continue the numbering sequence. If you've already started another <OL> list, the numbering will continue with this attribute.

- DIR—This is a proposed attribute to HTML for internationalization. It's used to indicate which direction to display the text. It can either have the value ltr (left to right) or rtl (right to left).

- ID—This is a proposed attribute to HTML 3 as part of a style sheet proposal. This defines the current line as a destination point. These points are used for internal jumps or jumps to a specific line.

- LANG—This is a proposed attribute to HTML for internationalization. This attribute is composed from the two-letter language code from ISO 639. You can optionally add a period, followed by a two-letter country code from ISO 3166. This attribute can be used by parsers to select language-specific choices for quotation marks, ligatures, and hyphenation rules.

- SEQNUM—This proposed HTML 3 attribute will define the starting number for the ordered list.

- START—This Netscape extension is the equivalent of the SEQNUM attribute.

- TYPE—This Netscape extension is used to indicate the numbering option. You can set this attribute to A, a, I, i, or 1.

The following is an example of <OL>:

```
<OL ALIGN=LEFT SEQNUM=5>This is an item in an ordered lists.</OL>
```

<OPTION>: Option Form

This HTML element identifies a particular selection in the SELECT element. You can set the following attributes:

- CLASS—This is a proposed attribute to HTML 3 as part of a style sheet proposal. This is a list of calls and subclasses separated by spaces. Acceptable values that you can use have not been defined by HTML 3.

- DIR—This is a proposed attribute to HTML for internationalization. It's used to indicate which direction to display the text. It can either have the value ltr (left to right) or rtl (right to left).

- DISABLED—When this attribute is used, the form is displayed, but the user can't select it.

- ERROR—This proposed HTML 3 attribute takes on a string of characters as a value. This string is displayed if the user enters an invalid value.

- ID—This is a proposed attribute to HTML 3 as part of a style sheet proposal. This defines the current line as a destination point. These points are used for internal jumps or jumps to a specific line.

- LANG—This is a proposed attribute to HTML for internationalization. This attribute is composed from the two-letter language code from ISO 639. You can optionally add a period, followed by a two-letter country code from ISO 3166. This attribute can be used by parsers to select language-specific choices for quotation marks, ligatures, and hyphenation rules.

- SHAPE—This proposed HTML 3 attribute defines the shape of the form.

- SELECTED—This attribute determines the default option.

- VALUE—This attribute, when defined, holds the value to be returned.

The following is an example of <OPTION>:

```
<OPTION VALUE="line1"></OPTION>
```

<OVERLAY>: Overlay a Graphic

This proposed HTML 3 tag is intended to be used along with the <FIG> element. The <OVERLAY> tag enables you to overlay an image on top of a <FIG> image. It has the following attributes:

- HEIGHT—This indicates the initial height of the display for the overlaid image. The value must be specified as a number of pixels.

- IMAGEMAP—When using imagemaps, you must use this attribute. This indicates that the overlay is to be treated as imagemap.

- MD—This is a proposed attribute to HTML 3 as part of a style sheet proposal. This attribute is used in conjunction with the SRC attribute, to specify a message digest or checksum. This is used when you want to be sure that a linked object is the one the Web author specified.

- SRC—This points to the image to be overlaid on top of a <FIG>.

- UNITS—This attribute enables the HEIGHT and WIDTH attributes to use units other than screen pixels.

- WIDTH—This indicates the initial width of the display for the overlaid image. The value must be specified as a number of pixels.

- X—This value indicates the number of units horizontally offset from the upper-left corner of the <FIG> graphic. The units used is determined by the UNITS attribute. If UNITS isn't specified, then the default value for the X attribute is pixels.

- Y—This value indicates the number of units horizontally offset from the upper-left corner of the <FIG> graphic. The units used is determined by the UNITS attribute. If UNITS isn't specified, then the default value for the Y attribute is pixels.

The following is an example of <OVERLAY>:

```
<OVERLAY SRC="overlay.gif" HEIGHT=200 WIDTH=150 X=50 Y=50>
```

<P>: Paragraph Break

This HTML tag will prevent the enclosed text from being word wrapped. The browser will not attempt to word wrap the text contained in this element. You can set the following attributes:

- ALIGN—This attribute specifies the alignment of the list item. You can set it to the value of center, justify, left, or right.

- CLASS—This is a proposed attribute to HTML 3 as part of a style sheet proposal. This is a list of calls and subclasses separated by spaces. Acceptable values that you can use have not been defined by HTML 3.

- CLEAR—This is a proposed attribute to HTML 3. It can have the value of left, right, or all. These values indicate which margin is to be clear of images so that text can appear on it.

- DIR—This is a proposed attribute to HTML for internationalization. It's used to indicate which direction to display the text. It can either have the value ltr (left to right) or rtl (right to left).

- ID—This is a proposed attribute to HTML 3 as part of a style sheet proposal. This defines the current line as a destination point. These points are used for internal jumps or jumps to a specific line.

- LANG—This is a proposed attribute to HTML for internationalization. This attribute is composed from the two-letter language code from ISO 639. You can optionally add a period, followed by a two-letter country code from ISO 3166. This attribute can be used by parsers to select language-specific choices for quotation marks, ligatures, and hyphenation rules.

- NOWRAP—This proposed HTML 3 attribute replaces the NOWRAP attribute. Acceptable values for this attribute are on or off.

- WRAP—This proposed HTML+ attribute will enable or disable word wrap. If this attribute is present, the browser will word wrap the enclosed text.

The following is an example of <P>:

```
<P>This line of text will always be this long, regardless of the
➥size of the browser.</P>
```

<PARAM>: JAVA Parameter

This HTML element is proposed to support JAVA applets. It enables the Web author to specify parameters to be passed to the <APPLET> application. This tag has the following attributes:

- NAME—This attribute defines the name of the parameter to be given a value.

- VALUE—This attribute defines the value to be assigned to the NAME attribute.

The following is an example of <PARAM>:

```
<PARAM NAME="myvar" VALUE="true">
```

<PERSON>: Person

This proposed HTML 3 tag will cause the enclosed text to be displayed as the name of a person. This element is used for indexing programs to automatically extract these names. It has the following attributes:

- CLASS—This is a proposed attribute to HTML 3 as part of a style sheet proposal. This is a list of calls and subclasses separated by spaces. Acceptable values that you can use have not been defined by HTML 3.

- DIR—This is a proposed attribute to HTML for internationalization. It's used to indicate which direction to display the text. It can either have the value ltr (left to right) or rtl (right to left).

- ID—This is a proposed attribute to HTML 3 as part of a style sheet proposal. This defines the current line as a destination point. These points are used for internal jumps or jumps to a specific line.

- LANG—This is a proposed attribute to HTML for internationalization. This attribute is composed from the two-letter language code from ISO 639. You can optionally add a period, followed by a two-letter country code from ISO 3166. This attribute can be used by parsers to select language-specific choices for quotation marks, ligatures, and hyphenation rules.

The following is an example of <PERSON>:

```
<PERSON>John Doe</PERSON>
```

<PRE>: Preformatted Text

This HTML tag will display the enclosed text as is and in monospaced characters. Normally, text elements will remove multiple spaces and line breaks to clean up the output. The use of <PRE> will prevent this. This element has the following attributes:

- CLASS—This is a proposed attribute to HTML 3 as part of a style sheet proposal. This is a list of calls and subclasses separated by spaces. Acceptable values that you can use have not been defined by HTML 3.

- CLEAR—This is a proposed attribute to HTML 3. It can have the value of left, right, or all. These values indicate which margin is to be clear of images so that text can appear on it.

- ID—This is a proposed attribute to HTML 3 as part of a style sheet proposal. This defines the current line as a destination point. These points are used for internal jumps or jumps to a specific line.

- LANG—This is a proposed attribute to HTML for internationalization. This attribute is composed from the two-letter language code from ISO 639. You can optionally add a period, followed by a two-letter country code from ISO 3166. This attribute can be used by parsers to select language-specific choices for quotation marks, ligatures, and hyphenation rules.

- WIDTH—This attribute indicates the maximum number of characters per line. Most browsers ignore this attribute.

The following is an example of <PRE>:

```
<PRE>I can put as many        spaces        as I want, and they'll
➥all show up!</PRE>
```

VIII

Appendixes

<Q>: Quotation

This proposed HTML 3 element will display the enclosed text as a quotation. The LANG context defines the appropriate quotation marks. There are a number of attributes you can set:

- CLASS—This is a proposed attribute to HTML 3 as part of a style sheet proposal. This is a list of calls and subclasses separated by spaces. Acceptable values that you can use have not been defined by HTML 3.

- DIR—This is a proposed attribute to HTML for internationalization. It's used to indicate which direction to display the text. It can either have the value ltr (left to right) or rtl (right to left).

- ID—This is a proposed attribute to HTML 3 as part of a style sheet proposal. This defines the current line as a destination point. These points are used for internal jumps or jumps to a specific line.

- LANG—This is a proposed attribute to HTML for internationalization. This attribute is composed from the two-letter language code from ISO 639. You can optionally add a period, followed by a two-letter country code from ISO 3166. This attribute can be used by parsers to select language-specific choices for quotation marks, ligatures, and hyphenation rules.

The following is an example of <Q>:

```
<Q>Ask not what your country can do for you.</Q>
```

<S>: Strikethrough

This proposed HTML 3 element replaces the <STRIKE> tag. This will display a strikeout line through the enclosed text. This tag has the following attributes:

- CLASS—This is a proposed attribute to HTML 3 as part of a style sheet proposal. This is a list of calls and subclasses separated by spaces. Acceptable values that you can use have not been defined by HTML 3.

- DIR—This is a proposed attribute to HTML for internationalization. It's used to indicate which direction to display the text. It can either have the value ltr (left to right) or rtl (right to left).

- ID—This is a proposed attribute to HTML 3 as part of a style sheet proposal. This defines the current line as a destination point. These points are used for internal jumps or jumps to a specific line.

- LANG—This is a proposed attribute to HTML for internationalization. This attribute is composed from the two-letter language code from ISO 639. You can optionally add a period, followed by a two-letter country

code from ISO 3166. This attribute can be used by parsers to select language-specific choices for quotation marks, ligatures, and hyphenation rules.

The following is an example of <S>:

```
This word appears as a <S>strikethrough</S>.
```

<SAMP>: Sample

This element displays the enclosed text as a sampling of text. You have the following attributes available:

- CLASS—This is a proposed attribute to HTML 3 as part of a style sheet proposal. This is a list of calls and subclasses separated by spaces. Acceptable values that you can use have not been defined by HTML 3.

- DIR—This is a proposed attribute to HTML for internationalization. It's used to indicate which direction to display the text. It can either have the value ltr (left to right) or rtl (right to left).

- ID—This is a proposed attribute to HTML 3 as part of a style sheet proposal. This defines the current line as a destination point. These points are used for internal jumps or jumps to a specific line.

- LANG—This is a proposed attribute to HTML for internationalization. This attribute is composed from the two-letter language code from ISO 639. You can optionally add a period, followed by a two-letter country code from ISO 3166. This attribute can be used by parsers to select language-specific choices for quotation marks, ligatures, and hyphenation rules.

The following is an example of <SAMP>:

```
This word is a <SAMP>sample</SAMP>
```

<SELECT>: Select Menu

This form element creates a menu of selectable entries. The selectable entries are defined by the <OPTION> element. The <SELECT> tag has the following attributes:

- ALIGN—This attribute specifies the alignment of the entries. You can set it to the value of bottom, left, middle, right, or top.

- CLASS—This is a proposed attribute to HTML 3 as part of a style sheet proposal. This is a list of calls and subclasses separated by spaces. Acceptable values that you can use have not been defined by HTML 3.

- DIR—This is a proposed attribute to HTML for internationalization. It's used to indicate which direction to display the text. It can either have the value ltr (left to right) or rtl (right to left).

VIII

Appendixes

- DISABLED—When this attribute is used, the form will be displayed, but the user won't be able to select it.

- ERROR—This proposed HTML 3 attribute takes on a string of characters as a value. This string is displayed if the user enters an invalid value.

- HEIGHT—The height of the list of entries is controlled with this attribute. You can specify the size in either pixels or as a percentage of the window height.

- ID—This is a proposed attribute to HTML 3 as part of a style sheet proposal. This defines the current line as a destination point. These points are used for internal jumps or jumps to a specific line.

- LANG—This is a proposed attribute to HTML for internationalization. This attribute is composed from the two-letter language code from ISO 639. You can optionally add a period, followed by a two-letter country code from ISO 3166. This attribute can be used by parsers to select language-specific choices for quotation marks, ligatures, and hyphenation rules.

- MD—This is a proposed attribute to HTML 3 as part of a style sheet proposal. This attribute is used in conjunction with the SRC attribute, to specify a message digest or checksum. This is used when you want to be sure that a linked object is the one the Web author specified.

- MULTIPLE—When this attribute is used, multiple selections may be made.

- NAME—The string in this attribute is the name for the selection form.

- SIZE—This attribute specifies how many options are visible.

- SRC—When this attribute is defined, it points to an URL for an image. That image will be displayed instead of the text defined by the <OPTION> elements.

- UNITS—This attribute enables the HEIGHT and WIDTH attributes to use units other than screen pixels.

- WIDTH—This indicates the width of the selection window. The value must be specified as a number of pixels.

The following is an example of <SELECT>:

```
<SELECT NAME="list1"></SELECT>
```

<SMALL>: Small

This proposed HTML 3 and Netscape element will cause the enclosed text to be displayed in a smaller font. This tag has the following attributes:

- CLASS—This is a proposed attribute to HTML 3 as part of a style sheet proposal. This is a list of calls and subclasses separated by spaces. Acceptable values that you can use have not been defined by HTML 3.

- DIR—This is a proposed attribute to HTML for internationalization. It's used to indicate which direction to display the text. It can either have the value ltr (left to right) or rtl (right to left).

- ID—This is a proposed attribute to HTML 3 as part of a style sheet proposal. This defines the current line as a destination point. These points are used for internal jumps or jumps to a specific line.

- LANG—This is a proposed attribute to HTML for internationalization. This attribute is composed from the two-letter language code from ISO 639. You can optionally add a period, followed by a two-letter country code from ISO 3166. This attribute can be used by parsers to select language-specific choices for quotation marks, ligatures, and hyphenation rules.

The following is an example of <SMALL>:

```
This text is a lot <SMALL>smaller</SMALL>.
```

<SPAN>: Span Languages

This internationalization proposed element is used to set language characteristics. Whatever text is enclosed within the markers for this element, will have the specified language characteristics. It has the following attributes:

- DIR—This is a proposed attribute to HTML for internationalization. It's used to indicate which direction to display the text. It can either have the value ltr (left to right) or rtl (right to left).

- LANG—This is a proposed attribute to HTML for internationalization. This attribute is composed from the two-letter language code from ISO 639. You can optionally add a period, followed by a two-letter country code from ISO 3166. This attribute can be used by parsers to select language-specific choices for quotation marks, ligatures, and hyphenation rules.

The following is an example of <SPAN>:

```
Many languages are supported by<SPAN>this</SPAN> element.
```

<STRONG>: Strong Emphasis

This element is intended to display the enclosed text with a stronger emphasis than when the <EM> tag is used. This tag has the following attributes:

VIII

Appendixes

- CLASS—This is a proposed attribute to HTML 3 as part of a style sheet proposal. This is a list of calls and subclasses separated by spaces. Acceptable values that you can use have not been defined by HTML 3.

- DIR—This is a proposed attribute to HTML for internationalization. It's used to indicate which direction to display the text. It can either have the value ltr (left to right) or rtl (right to left).

- ID—This is a proposed attribute to HTML 3 as part of a style sheet proposal. This defines the current line as a destination point. These points are used for internal jumps or jumps to a specific line.

- LANG—This is a proposed attribute to HTML for internationalization. This attribute is composed from the two-letter language code from ISO 639. You can optionally add a period, followed by a two-letter country code from ISO 3166. This attribute can be used by parsers to select language-specific choices for quotation marks, ligatures, and hyphenation rules.

The following is an example of <STRONG>:

```
This is something I want you to pay <STRONG>attention</STRONG> to.
```

<SUB>: Subscript

This Netscape proposed extension will force the browser to display the enclosed text as subscripts. It has the following attributes:

- CLASS—This is a proposed attribute to HTML 3 as part of a style sheet proposal. This is a list of calls and subclasses separated by spaces. Acceptable values that you can use have not been defined by HTML 3.

- DIR—This is a proposed attribute to HTML for internationalization. It's used to indicate which direction to display the text. It can either have the value ltr (left to right) or rtl (right to left).

- ID—This is a proposed attribute to HTML 3 as part of a style sheet proposal. This defines the current line as a destination point. These points are used for internal jumps or jumps to a specific line.

- LANG—This is a proposed attribute to HTML for internationalization. This attribute is composed from the two-letter language code from ISO 639. You can optionally add a period, followed by a two-letter country code from ISO 3166. This attribute can be used by parsers to select language-specific choices for quotation marks, ligatures, and hyphenation rules.

The following is an example of <SUB>:

```
This word is a <SUB>subscript</SUB> of the other words.
```

<SUP>: Superscript

This Netscape proposed extension will force the browser to display the enclosed text as superscripts. It has the following attributes:

- CLASS—This is a proposed attribute to HTML 3 as part of a style sheet proposal. This is a list of calls and subclasses separated by spaces. Acceptable values that you can use have not been defined by HTML 3.

- DIR—This is a proposed attribute to HTML for internationalization. It's used to indicate which direction to display the text. It can either have the value ltr (left to right) or rtl (right to left).

- ID—This is a proposed attribute to HTML 3 as part of a style sheet proposal. This defines the current line as a destination point. These points are used for internal jumps or jumps to a specific line.

- LANG—This is a proposed attribute to HTML for internationalization. This attribute is composed from the two-letter language code from ISO 639. You can optionally add a period, followed by a two-letter country code from ISO 3166. This attribute can be used by parsers to select language-specific choices for quotation marks, ligatures, and hyphenation rules.

The following is an example of <SUP>:

```
This word is a <SUP>superscript</SUP> of the other words.
```

<TAB>: Tab Alignment

This proposed HTML 3 element will force the enclosed text to be aligned by defined horizontal positions. This tag has the following attributes:

- ALIGN—This attribute specifies the alignment of the entries. You can set it to the value of center, decimal, left, or right.

- ID—You can define tab positions with this attribute.

- INDENT—This attribute will indicate where the indents will be.

- TO—This attribute will help you line up the text.

The following is an example of <TAB>:

```
<TAB ALIGN="center">This text will be aligned by a tab stop.
```

<TABLE>: Table

This element is used to define a series of rows as table cells. Table elements are defined by <TR> elements. This element has the following attributes:

- ALIGN—This attribute indicates the alignment of the text on the line. It can have the value of bleedleft, bleedright, center, left, right, or justify.

- BORDER—This attribute indicates the thickness of the border around the table.

- CELLPADDING—This attribute specifies the spacing inside the cells.

- CELLSPACING—This attribute determines the spacing between the cells.

- CLEAR—This is a proposed attribute to HTML 3. It can have the value of left, right, or all. These values indicate which margin is to be clear of images so that text can appear on it.

- COLS—This attribute defines the total number of columns in the table. This is used to help the browser determine how the table is shown.

- FRAME—This attribute determines which parts of the table are affected by the BORDER attribute. This can have the value of above, below, border, box, hsides, lhs, rhs, void, or vsides.

- ID—This is a proposed attribute to HTML 3 as part of a style sheet proposal. This defines the current line as a destination point. These points are used for internal jumps or jumps to a specific line.

- LANG—This is a proposed attribute to HTML for internationalization. This attribute is composed from the two-letter language code from ISO 639. You can optionally add a period, followed by a two-letter country code from ISO 3166. This attribute can be used by parsers to select language-specific choices for quotation marks, ligatures, and hyphenation rules.

- NOFLOW—This attribute prevents text from flowing around the table.

- NOWRAP—This prevents the cell data from being word wrapped.

- RULES—This attribute determines whether or not there are rules between rows and columns inside the table. This attribute can take on the value of all, basic, cols, none, or rows.

- UNITS—This attribute defines the number of units to be used by the other attributes. This attribute supports the following attributes: en, pixels, or relative.

- WIDTH—This indicates the width of the table cells. The value must be specified as a number of pixels.

The following is an example of <TABLE>:

```
<TABLE ALIGN="center" COLS=5 WIDTH=20 CELLPADDING=5>[Table
➥definition]</TABLE>
```

<TBODY>: Table Body

This proposed HTML element is used to enclose a series of table rows. This tag is not widely supported. There are a number of attributes available for this element:

- ALIGN—This attribute indicates the alignment of text within the column. It can have the value of char, center, left, right, or justify.

- CHAR—This is used to indicate which character to align the column with. This is only interpreted when the ALIGN attribute has been set to char.

- CHAROFF—This number is used to indicate the offset of the alignment character from the table cell.

- CLASS—This is a proposed attribute to HTML 3 as part of a style sheet proposal. This is a list of calls and subclasses separated by spaces. Acceptable values that you can use have not been defined by HTML 3.

- DIR—This is a proposed attribute to HTML for internationalization. It's used to indicate which direction to display the text. It can either have the value ltr (left to right) or rtl (right to left).

- ID—This is a proposed attribute to HTML 3 as part of a style sheet proposal. This defines the current line as a destination point. These points are used for internal jumps or jumps to a specific line.

- LANG—This is a proposed attribute to HTML for internationalization. This attribute is composed from the two-letter language code from ISO 639. You can optionally add a period, followed by a two-letter country code from ISO 3166. This attribute can be used by parsers to select language-specific choices for quotation marks, ligatures, and hyphenation rules.

- VALIGN—This attribute indicates the vertical alignment of the table cells. You can set this attribute to baseline, bottom, middle, or top.

The following is an example of <TBODY>:

```
<TBODY>[Table row information.]</TBODY>
```

<TD>: Table Data

This element is used to define a particular cell in a table. This tag has the following attributes:

- ALIGN—This attribute indicates the alignment of the text within the column. It can have the value of char, center, left, right, or justify.

- AXES—This attribute is a list of names to be displayed for the axes. The names are separated by a comma.

- AXIS—This attribute is used to define the name for a particular axis of a cell.

- BGCOLOR—This Microsoft proposed extension enables you to specify the background color for the particular cell. This color is represented by three pairs of hexadecimal numbers. The pairs represent the red, green, and blue color values.

- CHAR—This is used to indicate which character to align the column with. This is only interpreted when the ALIGN attribute has been set to char.

- CHAROFF—This number is used to indicate the offset of the alignment character from the table cell.

- CLASS—This is a proposed attribute to HTML 3 as part of a style sheet proposal. This is a list of calls and subclasses separated by spaces. Acceptable values that you can use have not been defined by HTML 3.

- COLSPAN—This value indicates how many columns this table cell occupies. A value of 0 indicates that the cell will span all columns.

- DIR—This is a proposed attribute to HTML for internationalization. It's used to indicate which direction to display the text. It can either have the value ltr (left to right) or rtl (right to left).

- ID—This is a proposed attribute to HTML 3 as part of a style sheet proposal. This defines the current line as a destination point. These points are used for internal jumps or jumps to a specific line.

- LANG—This is a proposed attribute to HTML for internationalization. This attribute is composed from the two-letter language code from ISO 639. You can optionally add a period, followed by a two-letter country code from ISO 3166. This attribute can be used by parsers to select language-specific choices for quotation marks, ligatures, and hyphenation rules.

- NOWRAP—This attribute will prevent word wrapping from occurring in the table cell.

- ROWSPAN—This value indicates how many rows this table cell occupies. A value of 0 indicates that the cell will span all rows.

- VALIGN—This attribute indicates the vertical alignment of the table cells. You can set this attribute to baseline, bottom, middle, or top.

- WIDTH—This proposed Netscape extension enables you to specify the width of the table cell in pixels.

The following is an example of <TD>:

```
<TD ALIGN="center" WIDTH=20>A table cell</TD>
```

\<TEXTAREA>: Text Area Form

This element is used to create a form input that takes up multiple lines.
This HTML tag has the following attributes:

- ALIGN—This proposed HTML 3 attribute determines where the caption is placed. Acceptable values are top, bottom, left, middle, and right.

- CLASS—This is a proposed attribute to HTML 3 as part of a style sheet proposal. This is a list of calls and subclasses separated by spaces. Acceptable values that you can use have not been defined by HTML 3.

- COLS—This attribute defines the total number of columns in the form. This is used to help the browser determine how the table should be shown.

- DIR—This is a proposed attribute to HTML for internationalization. It's used to indicate which direction to display the text. It can either have the value ltr (left to right) or rtl (right to left).

- DISABLED—This proposed HTML attribute shows the contents of the tag, but prevents its modification.

- ERROR—This proposed HTML 3 attribute is used when an incorrect value is entered. The text specified in this attribute is displayed on invalid input.

- ID—This is a proposed attribute to HTML 3 as part of a style sheet proposal. This defines the current line as a destination point. These points are used for internal jumps or jumps to a specific line.

- LANG—This is a proposed attribute to HTML for internationalization. This attribute is composed from the two-letter language code from ISO 639. You can optionally add a period, followed by a two-letter country code from ISO 3166. This attribute can be used by parsers to select language-specific choices for quotation marks, ligatures, and hyphenation rules.

- NAME—The string in this attribute is the name for the input form.

- ROWS—This attribute defines the total number of columns in the form. This is used to help the browser determine how the table should be shown.

- WRAP—This proposed Netscape extension provides for control of the text inside this element. You can use the values of off, physical, and virtual.

The following is an example of \<TEXTAREA>:

```
<TEXTAREA NAME="mytext" COLS=60 ROWS=20></TEXTAREA>
```

<TFOOT>: Table Footer

This proposed HTML 3 element will enable you to specify the attributes for a group of table rows. Depending on the browser, these attributes will be applied across multiple browser pages, as table footers. That is, separate HTML documents will not be affected by the TFOOT element; rather, the way it is displayed is affected. The browser will display the table as it breaks across browser page boundaries. The table rows to be defined are enclosed within the start and end markers for the tag. This element has the following attributes:

- ALIGN—This attribute indicates the alignment of the text within the column. It can have the value of char, center, left, right, or justify.

- CHAR—This is used to indicate which character to align the column with. This is only interpreted when the ALIGN attribute has been set to char.

- CHAROFF—This number is used to indicate the offset of the alignment character from the table cell.

- CLASS—This is a proposed attribute to HTML 3 as part of a style sheet proposal. This is a list of calls and subclasses separated by spaces. Acceptable values that you can use have not been defined by HTML 3.

- DIR—This is a proposed attribute to HTML for internationalization. It's used to indicate which direction to display the text. It can either have the value ltr (left to right) or rtl (right to left).

- ID—This is a proposed attribute to HTML 3 as part of a style sheet proposal. This defines the current line as a destination point. These points are used for internal jumps or jumps to a specific line.

- LANG—This is a proposed attribute to HTML for internationalization. This attribute is composed from the two-letter language code from ISO 639. You can optionally add a period, followed by a two-letter country code from ISO 3166. This attribute can be used by parsers to select language-specific choices for quotation marks, ligatures, and hyphenation rules.

- VALIGN—This indicates the vertical alignment of the text of the table cell. Acceptable values for this attribute are baseline, bottom, middle, and top.

The following is an example of <TFOOT>:

```
<TFOOT>This is a table footer.</TFOOT>
```

<TH>: Table Header

The text enclosed within this HTML tag, becomes a table header. This element has the following attributes:

- ALIGN—This attribute indicates the alignment of the text within the column. It can have the value of char, center, decimal, left, right, or justify.

- AXES—This attribute is a list of names to be displayed for the axes. The names are separated by a comma.

- AXIS—This attribute is used to define the name for a particular axis of a cell.

- BGCOLOR—This Microsoft proposed extension enables you to specify the background color for the particular cell. This color is represented by three pairs of hexadecimal numbers. The pairs represent the red, green, and blue color values.

- CHAR—This is used to indicate which character to align the column with. This is only interpreted when the ALIGN attribute has been set to char.

- CHAROFF—This number is used to indicate the offset of the alignment character from the table cell.

- CLASS—This is a proposed attribute to HTML 3 as part of a style sheet proposal. This is a list of calls and subclasses separated by spaces. Acceptable values that you can use have not been defined by HTML 3.

- COLSPAN—This value indicates how many columns this table cell occupies. A value of 0 indicates that the cell will span all columns.

- DIR—This is a proposed attribute to HTML for internationalization. It's used to indicate which direction to display the text. It can either have the value ltr (left to right) or rtl (right to left).

- ID—This is a proposed attribute to HTML 3 as part of a style sheet proposal. This defines the current line as a destination point. These points are used for internal jumps or jumps to a specific line.

- LANG—This is a proposed attribute to HTML for internationalization. This attribute is composed from the two-letter language code from ISO 639. You can optionally add a period, followed by a two-letter country code from ISO 3166. This attribute can be used by parsers to select language-specific choices for quotation marks, ligatures, and hyphenation rules.

VIII

Appendixes

- NOWRAP—This attribute will prevent word wrapping from occurring in the table cell.

- ROWSPAN—This value indicates how many rows this table cell occupies. A value of 0 indicates that the cell will span all rows.

- VALIGN—This attribute indicates the vertical alignment of the table cells. You can set this attribute to baseline, bottom, middle, or top.

- WIDTH—This proposed Netscape extension enables you to specify the width of the table cell in pixels.

The following is an example of <TH>:

```
<TH VALIGN="middle" WIDTH=50>Table Header</TH>
```

<THEAD>: Table Header

This proposed HTML 3 element enables you to specify the attributes for a group of table rows. Depending on the browser, these attributes will be applied across multiple browser pages, as table headers. That is, separate HTML documents will not be affected by the TFOOT element; rather, the way it is displayed is affected. The browser will display the table as its breaks across browser page boundaries. The table rows to be defined are enclosed within the start and end markers for the tag. This element has the following attributes:

- ALIGN—This attribute indicates the alignment of the text within the column. It can have the value of char, center, left, right, or justify.

- CHAR—This is used to indicate which character to align the column with. This is only interpreted when the ALIGN attribute has been set to char.

- CHAROFF—This number is used to indicate the offset of the alignment character from the table cell.

- CLASS—This is a proposed attribute to HTML 3 as part of a style sheet proposal. This is a list of calls and subclasses separated by spaces. Acceptable values that you can use have not been defined by HTML 3.

- DIR—This is a proposed attribute to HTML for internationalization. It's used to indicate which direction to display the text. It can either have the value ltr (left to right) or rtl (right to left).

- ID—This is a proposed attribute to HTML 3 as part of a style sheet proposal. This defines the current line as a destination point. These points are used for internal jumps or jumps to a specific line.

- LANG—This is a proposed attribute to HTML for internationalization. This attribute is composed from the two-letter language code from ISO 639. You can optionally add a period, followed by a two-letter country code from ISO 3166. This attribute can be used by parsers to select language-specific choices for quotation marks, ligatures, and hyphenation rules.

- VALIGN—This indicates the vertical alignment of the text of the table cell. Acceptable values for this attribute are baseline, bottom, middle, and top.

The following is an example of <THEAD>:

```
<THEAD>This is a table header.</THEAD>
```

<TITLE>: Title

This HTML element defines the enclosed text as the title for the current Web page.

- DIR—This is a proposed attribute to HTML for internationalization. It's used to indicate which direction to display the text. It can either have the value ltr (left to right) or rtl (right to left).

- LANG—This is a proposed attribute to HTML for internationalization. This attribute is composed from the two-letter language code from ISO 639. You can optionally add a period, followed by a two-letter country code from ISO 3166. This attribute can be used by parsers to select language-specific choices for quotation marks, ligatures, and hyphenation rules.

The following is an example of <TITLE>:

```
<TITLE>My Home Page</TITLE>
```

<TR>: Table Row

This HTML tag defines a table row for a <TBODY>, <TFOOT>, or <THEAD>. This element has the following attributes:

- ALIGN—This attribute indicates the alignment of the text within the column. It can have the value of char, decimal, center, left, right, or justify.

- CHAR—This is used to indicate which character to align the column with. This is only interpreted when the ALIGN attribute has been set to char.

- CHAROFF—This number is used to indicate the offset of the alignment character from the table cell.

- CLASS—This is a proposed attribute to HTML 3 as part of a style sheet proposal. This is a list of calls and subclasses separated by spaces. Acceptable values that you can use have not been defined by HTML 3.

- DIR—This is a proposed attribute to HTML for internationalization. It's used to indicate which direction to display the text. It can either have the value ltr (left to right) or rtl (right to left).

- ID—This is a proposed attribute to HTML 3 as part of a style sheet proposal. This defines the current line as a destination point. These points are used for internal jumps or jumps to a specific line.

- LANG—This is a proposed attribute to HTML for internationalization. This attribute is composed from the two-letter language code from ISO 639. You can optionally add a period, followed by a two-letter country code from ISO 3166. This attribute can be used by parsers to select language-specific choices for quotation marks, ligatures, and hyphenation rules.

- VALIGN—This indicates the vertical alignment of the text of the table cell. Acceptable values for this attribute are baseline, bottom, middle, and top.

The following is an example of <TR>:

```
<TR><TD>Table Data</TD>
```

<TT>: Teletype

This HTML element displays all of the enclosed text as a teletype. Typically, the width of each of the characters will be exactly the same. You can set the following attributes:

- CLASS—This is a proposed attribute to HTML 3 as part of a style sheet proposal. This is a list of calls and subclasses separated by spaces. Acceptable values that you can use have not been defined by HTML 3.

- DIR—This is a proposed attribute to HTML for internationalization. It's used to indicate which direction to display the text. It can either have the value ltr (left to right) or rtl (right to left).

- ID—This is a proposed attribute to HTML 3 as part of a style sheet proposal. This defines the current line as a destination point. These points are used for internal jumps or jumps to a specific line.

- LANG—This is a proposed attribute to HTML for internationalization. This attribute is composed from the two-letter language code from ISO 639. You can optionally add a period, followed by a two-letter country

code from ISO 3166. This attribute can be used by parsers to select language-specific choices for quotation marks, ligatures, and hyphenation rules.

The following is an example of <TT>:

```
This text will be displayed as <TT>teletype characters</TT>.
```

<UL>: Unordered List

This element shows enclosed <LI> elements as a bulleted (unordered) list. This HTML tag has the following attributes:

- ALIGN—This attribute indicates the alignment of the text on the line. It can have the value of center, left, right, or justify.

- CLASS—This is a proposed attribute to HTML 3 as part of a style sheet proposal. This is a list of calls and subclasses separated by spaces. Acceptable values that you can use have not been defined by HTML 3.

- CLEAR—This is a proposed attribute to HTML 3. It can have the value of left, right, or all. These values indicate which margin is to be clear of images so that text can appear on it.

- COMPACT—This attribute tells the browser to display the list in a compact manner. It is not, however, supported by many browsers.

- DIR—This is a proposed attribute to HTML for internationalization. It's used to indicate which direction to display the text. It can either have the value ltr (left to right) or rtl (right to left).

- ID—This is a proposed attribute to HTML 3 as part of a style sheet proposal. This defines the current line as a destination point. These points are used for internal jumps or jumps to a specific line.

- LANG—This is a proposed attribute to HTML for internationalization. This attribute is composed from the two-letter language code from ISO 639. You can optionally add a period, followed by a two-letter country code from ISO 3166. This attribute can be used by parsers to select language-specific choices for quotation marks, ligatures, and hyphenation rules.

- MD—This is a proposed attribute to HTML 3 as part of a style sheet proposal. This attribute is used to specify a message digest or checksum. This is used when you want to be sure that a linked object is the one the Web author specified.

- TYPE—This Netscape proposed HTML attribute enables you to specify the type of bullets to be used. You can use the value of circle, disc, or square.

■ WRAP—If this proposed HTML 3 attribute is present, the browser will word wrap the enclosed text.

The following is an example of <UL>:

```
<UL><LI>A list item.</LI></UL>
```

<VAR>: Variable

This HTML element displays the enclosed text as a variable. This tag has the following attributes:

■ CLASS—This is a proposed attribute to HTML 3 as part of a style sheet proposal. This is a list of calls and subclasses separated by spaces. Acceptable values that you can use have not been defined by HTML 3.

■ DIR—This is a proposed attribute to HTML for internationalization. It's used to indicate which direction to display the text. It can either have the value ltr (left to right) or rtl (right to left).

■ ID—This is a proposed attribute to HTML 3 as part of a style sheet proposal. This defines the current line as a destination point. These points are used for internal jumps or jumps to a specific line.

■ LANG—This is a proposed attribute to HTML for internationalization. This attribute is composed from the two-letter language code from ISO 639. You can optionally add a period, followed by a two-letter country code from ISO 3166. This attribute can be used by parsers to select language-specific choices for quotation marks, ligatures, and hyphenation rules.

The following is an example of <VAR>:

```
Set <VAR>myvar</VAR> equal to 0.
```

<WBR>: Word Break

This Netscape proposed extension forces a word break to occur. This is mainly used if you want to force a word break in the middle of a non-breaking HTML element. It has no attributes.

The following is an example of <WBR>:

```
A line break will occur now.<WBR>
```

<XMP>: Multi-Line Text

This HTML element displays the enclosed text as is. No text formatting by the browser will be done to the enclosed text. This tag has the following attributes:

- DIR—This is a proposed attribute to HTML for internationalization. It's used to indicate which direction to display the text. It can either have the value ltr (left to right) or rtl (right to left).

- LANG—This is a proposed attribute to HTML for internationalization. This attribute is composed from the two-letter language code from ISO 639. You can optionally add a period, followed by a two-letter country code from ISO 3166. This attribute can be used by parsers to select language-specific choices for quotation marks, ligatures, and hyphenation rules.

- WIDTH—This proposed Netscape extension enables you to specify the width of the multiple lines..

The following is an example of <XMP>:

```
<XMP>
This text will appear as you see it.
There are no special HTML elements to create
the line breaks you see.
</XMP>
```

Special Characters

HTML allows for the insertion of any character defined in the ISO 8859-1 character set, into Web pages. These characters may not always be visible to all browsers, but they are defined as available entities. Table A lists all the special characters with their corresponding HTML code. If you want to put a particular character in your Web page, simply type in the entire string under the "HTML Code" heading. Some of the characters have two possible HTML codes, so simply use one of them. Be sure to include the ampersand (&) before the code, and the semicolon (;) after the code.

Table A.1   HTML Codes for ISO 8859-1 Characters

Description of Character	HTML Code	Example of Character
Quotation mark	&quot;	"
Ampersand	&amp;	&
Less-than sign	&lt;	<
Greater-than sign	&gt;	>
Non-breaking space		
Inverted exclamation mark	&iexcl;	¡
Cent sign	&cent;	¢

(continues)

VIII

Appendixes

Table A.1 Continued

Description of Character	HTML Code	Example of Character
Pound sterling	&pound;	£
General currency sign	&curren;	¤
Yen sign	&yen;	¥
Broken vertical bar	¦ or &brkbar;	¦
Section sign	&sect;	§
Umlaut (dieresis)	¨ or ¨	¨
Copyright	&copy;	©
Feminine ordinal	&ordf;	ª
Left angle quote (guillemotleft)	&laquo;	«
Not sign	&not;	¬
Soft hyphen	&shy;	−
Registered trademark	&reg;	®
Macron accent	¯ or &hibar;	¯
Degree sign	&deg;	°
Plus or minus	&plusmn;	±
Superscript two	&sup2;	²
superscript three	&sup3;	³
Acute accent	&acute;	´
Micro sign	&micro;	µ
Paragraph sign	&para;	¶
Middle dot	&middot;	·
Cedilla	&cedil;	¸
Superscript one	&sup1;	¹
Masculine ordinal	&ordm;	º
Right angle quote (guillemotright)	&raquo;	»
Fraction one-fourth	&frac14;	¼
Fraction one-half	&frac12;	½
Fraction three-fourths	&frac34;	¾
Inverted question mark	&iquest;	¿
capital A, grave accent	&Agrave;	À
Capital A, acute accent	&Aacute;	Á
Capital A, circumflex accent	&Acirc;	Â

Description of Character	HTML Code	Example of Character
Capital A, tilde	&Atilde;	Ã
Capital A, umlaut (dieresis)	&Auml;	Ä
Capital A, ring	&Aring;	Å
Capital AE, diphthong (ligature)	&Aelig;	Æ
Capital C, cedilla	&Ccedil;	Ç
Capital E, grave accent	&Egrave;	È
Capital E, acute accent	&Eacute;	É
Capital E, circumflex accent	&Ecirc;	Ê
Capital E, umlaut (dieresis)	&Euml;	Ë
Capital I, grave accent	&Igrave;	Ì
Capital I, acute accent	&Iacute;	Í
Capital I, circumflex accent	&Icirc;	Î
Capital I, umlaut (dieresis)	&Iuml;	Ï
Capital Eth, Icelandic	Ð or Đ	Ð
Capital N, tilde	&Ntilde;	Ñ
Capital O, grave accent	&Ograve;	Ò
Capital O, acute accent	&Oacute;	Ó
Capital O, circumflex accent	&Ocirc;	Ô
Capital O, tilde	&Otilde;	Õ
Capital O, umlaut (dieresis)	&Ouml;	Ö
Multiply sign	&times;	x
Capital O, slash	&Oslash;	Ø
Capital U, grave accent	&Ugrave;	Ù
Capital U, acute accent	&Uacute;	Ú
Capital U, circumflex accent	&Ucirc;	Û
Capital U, umlaut (dieresis)	&Uuml;	Ü
Capital Y, acute accent	&Yacute;	Y
Capital THORN, Icelandic	&THORN;	Þ
Small sharp s, German (sz ligature)	&szlig;	ß
Small a, grave accent	&agrave;	à
Small a, acute accent	&aacute;	á
Small a, circumflex accent	&acirc;	â
Small a, tilde	&atilde;	ã
Small a, umlaut (dieresis)	&auml;	ä

VIII

Appendixes

(continues)

Table A.1 Continued

Description of Character	HTML Code	Example of Character
Small a, ring	&aring;	å
Small ae diphthong (ligature)	&aelig;	æ
Small c, cedilla	&ccedil;	ç
Small e, grave accent	&egrave;	è
Small e, acute accent	&eacute;	é
Small e, circumflex accent	&ecirc;	ê
Small e, umlaut (dieresis)	&euml;	'
Small i, grave accent	&igrave;	"
Small i, acute accent	&iacute;	'
Small i, circumflex accent	&icirc;	"
Small i, umlaut (dieresis)	&iuml;	•
Small eth, Icelandic	&eth;	
Small n, tilde	&ntilde;	ñ
Small o, grave accent	&ograve;	ò
Small o, acute accent	&oacute;	ó
Small o, circumflex accent	&ocirc;	ô
Small o, tilde	&otilde;	õ
Small o, umlaut (dieresis)	&ouml;	ö
Division sign	&divide;	÷
Small o, slash	&oslash;	ø
Small u, grave accent	&ugrave;	ù
Small u, acute accent	&uacute;	ú
Small u, circumflex accent	&ucirc;	û
Small u, umlaut (dieresis)	&uuml;	ü
Small y, acute accent	&yacute;	y
Small thorn, Icelandic	&thorn;	þ
Small y, umlaut (dieresis)	&yuml;	ÿ

HTML Quick Reference Guide

by John Jung

HTML is made up of a lot of different elements. Each element behaves differently from all the other HTML tags. Some of them are so straightforward that you only need to invoke them and they'll be used. Others require beginning and ending markers for the element's behavior to be applied to the enclosed text.

For those tags that do have attributes, most of them are optional. To use a specific attribute, you must include the attribute name, the equal sign (=), and the value to set it to. Invalid values are automatically ignored by most Web browsers. The assignment of attributes is done inside the starting marker of the particular HTML element that you want to use.

Every HTML document must be enclosed within the <HTML> starting marker and the </HTML> ending marker. Between these two markers is the actual Web page. The content of a particular HTML document is made up of head and body portions. The information for the head portion is enclosed within the <HEAD> and </HEAD> markers. The information for the body portion is enclosed within the <BODY> and </BODY> markers.

The following list is not intended to be a complete list of every HTML tag and its attributes (see Appendix A, "HTML Tags"). This is meant as a list of commonly used elements and their commonly used attributes.

Elements in the HEAD

- <BASE>—This is used to indicate the default location of relative URL links. Common attributes:

    HREF—Baseline URL for relative links.

    TARGET—Indicates in which window to display the destination hypertext link.

- <ISINDEX>—This is used to indicate that the entire home page can be searched by keywords.

- <LINK>—This is used to specify relationships to other HTML documents. Commonly used attributes:

    HREF—Destination URL to establish a relationship with.

    REL—Indicates relationship with destination document.

    REV—Used to verify a reversed relationship with destination document.

    TITLE—The title for the destination URL.

- <TITLE></TITLE>—You can specify the document's title with this element.

Elements in the BODY

The majority of tags are specified in within the BODY elements. Typically, anything contained inside the start and end markers will be displayed. The following sets of related elements are all available:

Text Elements

This group of tags is used to apply general attributes to a group of text. Typically, these elements are word wrapped by the browser.

- <BLOCKQUOTE>[Text]</BLOCKQUOTE>—This will cause [Text] to be displayed as quoted text.

- <P>[Text]</P>—The [Text] is treated as if it were an entire paragraph by itself. The [Text] will be word wrapped.

- <PRE>[Text]</PRE>—The [Text] will be displayed as it is, but not in a proportional font. Use this if you've already had some text lined up in ASCII, such as in tables and grids. Commonly used attribute:

    WIDTH—Maximum number of characters per line.

Hypertext Links

Hyperlinks are the underlying component of the Web.

- <A>[Text]</A>—This defines that [Text] is a hypertext link. If the <IMG> element is used in place of [Text], the image will be hyperlinked. Common attributes:

    HREF—URL to link to.

    NAME—Defines the current line as a destination point. Destination points are accessed by specifying the pound sign (#) followed by the desired NAME.

TARGET—This indicates the name of the window to display the destination URL.

TITLE—The title of the destination URL.

Headers

Header elements are used to provide a consistent look for your document. There are no commonly used attributes for these elements.

- <H1>[Text]</H1>—[Text] is displayed in the most prominent header.

- <H2>[Text]</H2>—[Text] is displayed in the second most prominent header.

- <H3>[Text]</H3>—[Text] is displayed in the third most prominent header.

- <H4>[Text]</H4>—[Text] is displayed in the third least prominent header.

- <H5>[Text]</H5>—[Text] is displayed in the second least prominent header.

- <H6>[Text]</H6>—[Text] is displayed in the least prominent header.

Logical Text

Logical style elements define attributes for a group of text. The text is automatically word wrapped by the browser.

- <CITE>[Text]</CITE>—This tag is used to indicate that the [Text] is a citation.

- <CODE>[Text]</CODE>—The [Text] is displayed as being computer source code.

- <DFN>[Text]</DFN>—[Text] will be displayed as if it were a definition. There are no commonly used attributes.

- <EM>[Text]</EM>—The [Text] is emphasized in some way. There are no commonly used attributes.

- <KBD>[Text]</KBD>—This tag is used to display [Text] as something to be typed on the keyboard. There are no commonly used attributes.

- <SAMP>[Text]</SAMP>—To display [Text] as a sampling of something, such as from an article, use this element. There are no commonly used attributes.

- <STRONG>[Text]</STRONG>—This element displays the [Text] as more emphasized than <EM>. There are no commonly used attributes.

- <VAR>[Text]</VAR>—This displays [Text] as some sort of variable, such as for formulas. There are no commonly used attributes.

Physical Styles

This group of HTML elements is used to affect the visual display of text. There are no commonly used attributes for these elements.

- <B>[Text]</B>—[Text] will be made boldface.
- <I>[Text]</I>—[Text] will be set in italics.
- <TT>[Text]</TT>—[Text] will be made to look as though it came from a teletype.
- <U>[Text]</U>—[Text] will be underlined.

Definition List

This list type allows you to present a dictionary-type presentation of a definition. The left-hand side has the word, <DD>, and the right-hand side has the definition, <DT>.

- <DL>[Definitions]</DL>—This is the main container for a definition list. It has the following commonly used attribute:

   ALIGN—Specifies that the text for the definitions is to be aligned centered, justified, left, or right.

- <DD>[Text]</DD>—This element is used to specify that [Text] is the definition portion of the definition list. It will be displayed on the right-hand side of the screen. There are no commonly used attributes.
- <DT>[Text]</DT>—This element is used to specify that [Text] is the term portion of the definition list. It will be on the left-hand side of the screen. There are no commonly used attributes.

Unordered (Bulleted) List

You can create a list with a bullet in front of each item.

- <UL>[List of items]</UL>—This presents [List of items] as an unordered (bulleted) list.
- <LI>[Text]</LI>—[Text] will be an item in the list. There are no commonly used attributes.

Ordered (Numbered) List

You can create a list with a number in front of each item. The number is automatically added.

- <OL>[List of items]</OL>—This presents [List of items] as an ordered (numbered) list.
- <LI>[Text]</LI>—[Text] will be an item in the list. There are no commonly used attributes.

Directory List

You can create a list so that items appear to be a list of files from a directory.

- <DIR>[List of items]</DIR>—This presents [List of items] that appears to be a list of files from a directory.

- <LI>[Text]</LI>—[Text] will be an item in the list. There are no commonly used attributes.

Graphics

Graphics can be inserted into your home page very easily.

- <FIG></FIG>—This element is intended to replace the <IMG> tag. Commonly used attributes:

    ALIGN—This attribute indicates how the picture will be aligned. It has a number of acceptable values: bleedleft, blecdright, center, justify, left, or right.

    HEIGHT—This value indicates the height of the image.

    SRC—This points to an URL that contains the graphic to use.

    WIDTH—This value indicates the width of the image.

- <IMG></IMG>—This element is used to put a GIF or JPEG graphic into your home page. It has the following commonly used attributes:

    ALIGN—This attribute indicates how the picture will be aligned. It has a number of acceptable values: bleedleft, bleedright, center, justify, left, or right.

    ALT—This string will be shown if the user doesn't have a graphical browser.

    HEIGHT—This value indicates the height of the image.

    ISMAP—This tells the Web browser that this graphic is an imagemap.

    SRC—This points to an URL that contains the graphic to use.

    WIDTH—This value indicates the width of the image.

Miscellaneous Tags

There are several unclassifiable, commonly used HTML tags.

- <![Text]>—This element is completely ignored by the Web browser. The [Text] is treated as comments from the HTML author.

- <ADDRESS>[Text]</ADDRESS>—This tag shows [Text] as an address of some sort. There are no commonly used attributes.

What's on the CD?

by Oran J. Sands

The CD-ROM found in the back of this book has been carefully prepared and researched so you'll have a variety of tools and examples to assist you in enhancing your web pages. The entire CD has been linked with HTML web pages so that it can be accessed via your favorite browser (there's even a browser included, in case you need one). You'll find that the web pages have links to the software programs on the disk, the graphics files and examples, and actual web sites on the World Wide Web (you'll need an Internet connection to use these).

Starting Up

Starting up the CD is simple. From within your browser, load the file LOADME.htm. The first page will lead you to the next pages; there, you can choose what you'd like to see next. There is a "back" button at the bottom of every page that returns you to the selections page.

Many of the programs you'll see on the CD are *beta versions* (they are works in progress; functional, but not all of the bugs are worked out or all the features active yet). We offer them so you can sample what their technology has to offer; if you're still interested, you can download the latest version from the Web. But first, cut your Internet connect charges by using the version on our CD.

> **Note**
>
> Many of the programs on the CD are *shareware* (offered free for a period of time so that you can evaluate them). If you want to use a program further, you can register with the software company, pay a fee, and receive a fully working version (and possibly other perks). Please respect the efforts of the software authors who have toiled over a hot monitor late into the night to bring you quality programs at a reasonable price.

Some of the Best Tools

The following sections describe a few of the excellent programs that you may be interested in.

Hotdog HTML Editor

We've included Hotdog for one simple reason: it's one of the best and easiest tools for creating and managing web pages. The program you'll find on the CD is the standard version, which is upgradable to the professional version (click the link to Sausage Software for more information). It's solid and reliable, and will serve you for years to come. If you upgrade to the professional version, you'll not need another HTML editor for quite a while.

PaintShop Pro

There are a lot of shareware programs available for manipulating graphics, but there are few for creating them from scratch. PaintShop Pro is a fully featured paint program that also excels at image manipulation, making it the program of choice for creating your web page graphics. Registering the shareware version will get you even more capability.

MapThis!

Those lovely image maps you see on other web pages are quite difficult to control unless you have a program such as MapThis! It's an excellent utility for setting up the links from different areas of your image.

WebForms

The creation of a web-page form can be a daunting task without a program such as WebForms, which makes it simple and easy.

Java Development Kit

This is a must-have if you decide to get involved with Java programming. It includes the Java applet viewer. Both Mac and Windows versions can be found on the CD.

Netscape Plugins

You'll find a directory full of the latest Netscape plugins, many of which are mentioned throughout this book. If you're going to set up your pages to use plugin features, you'll need these to see whether your page works for your visitors!

Movies, Buttons, Bars, and Other Pretty Things

We have plenty of sample graphics for you to add to your web pages and several links where you can find even more. Check out the great collection of digital movie clips we've licensed exclusively for this CD.

But Wait, That's Not All!

For those of you who want to know what else is available, we've put a lot of other software on the CD:

World Wide Web Browsers and Utilities

- Microsoft Internet Explorer
- Microsoft Virtual Explorer
- Hot Java
- I-Comm
- Indexer
- Fountain
- HomeSpace Builder
- WebWatch

HTML Editors and Utilities

- Color Wizard
- Color Manipulator
- EasyHelp
- HotDog
- HTML Assistant for Windows
- HTML Author
- HTML Easy Pro
- HTML Notepad
- HTML Writer
- HTMLed
- Kenn Nesbitt's WebEdit
- Live MarkUp
- Microsoft Internet Assistant
- Web Spinner
- Web Wizard: The Duke of URL

- Webber
- WebEdit
- WebForms
- WebWebMania

Multimedia Editors and Viewers

- Adobe's Acrobat Reader
- ACDSee
- CoolEdit
- Drag and View
- GraphX Viewer
- LView Pro for Windows 95
- MapThis
- MidiGate
- Mod4Win
- MPEGPLAY
- PaintShop Pro
- PolyView
- Quicktime Player
- QuickTime VR Player
- Real Audio
- Streamworks
- VuePrint
- Web Image
- Wham
- WinJPEG
- WinECJ
- WPLANY

WWW Bibliography

by John Jung

Because the World Wide Web came from the Internet, many people have had a chance to look at and comment on it. There are a lot of documents about HTML, the Web, and Web authoring, and much of it is available on the Web itself. This is just a partial listing of some of the more useful sources. Because the Internet and the World Wide Web are evolving entities, they will probably move sometime in the future. You'll generally be informed of any such moves by the Web site itself. But if you have problems finding one of these documents, feel free to use one of the Web's many search engines.

The quality of these documents varies greatly with each author's flavor and research. Be sure to take a look at who wrote each document to determine how much weight you should give it. Some of these documents are just one person's opinion or perception about a particular topic. Also, many of these pages have hypertext links to related documents.

RFC 1866—Hypertext Markup Language 2.0

http://www.cis.ohio-state.edu/htbin/rfc/rfc1866.html

This is the official specification for HTML 2.

Netscape's Extensions to HTML 2

**http://home.netscape.com/assist/net_sites/
html_extensions.html**

A list of Netscape extensions to the HTML 2 specifications, by Netscape.

Netscape's Extensions to HTML 3

**http://home.netscape.com/assist/net_sites/
html_extensions_3.html**

A list of Netscape extensions to the HTML 3 specifications, by Netscape.

HTML 3.0 and Netscape 2.0
http://webreference.com/html3andns/

This is a page that shows the HTML 3 and Netscape extensions that are in common use. It also provides ways to get around Netscape's extensions with HTML 3 tags.

Microsoft Internet Explorer Extensions
http://www.microsoft.com/windows/ie/IE20HTML.htm

This is a list of all of Microsoft's proposed extensions to HTML. It has links relating to its extensions.

ISO8859-1 (Latin-1) Table
http://www.uni-passau.de/~ramsch/iso8859-1.html

This is the official list of special characters and the HTML codes that represent them.

FAQ: The Ten Commandments of HTML
http://www.visdesigns.com/design/commandments.html

This is a good list of ten things you should do or watch out for when creating your home page.

A CGI Programmer's Reference
http://www.best.com/~hedlund/cgi-faq/

This is a good reference for up-and-coming CGI programmers.

FAQ—World Wide Web
http://www.boutell.com/faq/

A good overview of the Web with a special section on Web authoring.

A Beginner's Guide to HTML
http://www.ncsa.uiuc.edu/General/Internet/WWW/
HTMLPrimer.html

One of the many introductory guides to HTML for new Web authors. It comes from the creators of Mosaic.

HTML Bad Style Page
http://www.earth.com/bad-style/

Here you will find some things you shouldn't do in a Web page.

Composing Good HTML

http://www.cs.cmu.edu/~tilt/cgh/

This home page shows ways to make your home page look good with any browser.

Crash Course in HTML

http://www.nashville.net/~templedf/crash/
CrashCourse.html

For the absolute HTML beginner, this is a good place to start.

Style Guide for Online Hypertext

http://www.w3.org/hypertext/WWW/Provider/Style/
Overview.html

An online guide for how to create Web pages that deliver your message effectively.

How Do They Do That with HTML?

http://www.nashville.net/~carl/htmlguide/index.html

This is a page that shows you some of the neat tips and tricks you can do with HTML.

HTML Authors Toolkit

http://www.obscure.org/~jaws/htmltoolkit.html

This page has a collection of programs that HTML authors should have.

Macmillan's HTML Workshop

http://www.mcp.com/general/workshop/

This is a great online guide for HTML authors of all skill levels.

Index: HTML Tags

http://www.willcam.com/cmat/html/crossref.html

This provides a fairly comprehensive list of HTML tags.

Background of the Day

http://web-star.com/botd/botd.html

A Web site that provides a different background image every day.

Background Colors

http://www.infi.net/wwwimages/colorindex.html

A page that has a collection of color names, and corresponding values. You can plug the values for any color you might want to use into the appropriate field.

Imagemap Help Page (IHiP)

http://www.hway.net/ihip/

A page dedicated to helping people create imagemaps.

Letting Users Search Your Web Pages

http://www-rlg.stanford.edu/home/jpl/websearch.html

This page discusses ways of setting up search engines for your Web pages.

High Five Award Page

http://www.highfive.com/

This is a home page dedicated to looking (and showing) great Web pages.

Point: It's What You're Searching For

http://www.pointcom.com/

Here's another home page appreciation page.

Submit It!

http://www.submit-it.com/

A Web page that will submit your URL into a variety of Web search engines. Free!

Accessing a Database Server via the World Wide Web

http://cscsun1.larc.nasa.gov/~beowulf/db/web_access.html

This page discusses methods of creating an interface between the Web and databases.

Mag's Big List of HTML Editors

http://union.ncsa.uiuc.edu/HyperNews/get/www/html/editors.html

A collection of reviews and overviews of many HTML editors for various platforms.

Yahoo!

http://www.yahoo.com/

This is a great database of home pages.

The WWW Virtual Library

http://www.w3.org/hypertext/DataSources/bySubject/
Overview2.html

The Virtual Library is a collection of distributed links that cover a broad set of topics.

The Common Gateway Interface

http://hoohoo.ncsa.uiuc.edu/cgi/

This page has discussions on writing CGI scripts, as well as an archive of submitted ones.

An Introduction to SGML

http://www.brainlink.com/~ben/sgml/

A good introduction to SGML, the predecessor to HTML.

PERL: Practical Extraction and Report Language

http://www-cgi.cs.cmu.edu/cgi-bin/perl-man

This Web page provides a good overview of programming in Perl, a popular CGI scripting language. ❖

VIII

Appendixes

Index

Symbols

* (asterisk) frameset definitions, 319
@ (at symbol)
  standard arrays, 560
  non-anonymous FTP sites, 151
$ (dollar symbol) PERL variables, 560
<!-> HTML tag, 787
% (percent symbol)
  frameset definitions, 320
  PERL associative arrays, 560
(pound symbol) imagemap definition files, comment delineator, 238
 , HTML entity, 253
$test variable, CGI scripts, 590
8-bit sound files, 418
16-bit sound files, 418
28.8 kbps modems, RealAudio sound playback, 413

A

<A> HTML tag, 316, 787
  attributes
    CHARSET, 787
    CLASS, 787
    DIR, 787
    HREF, 787
    ID, 788

    LANG, 788
    MD, 788
    METHODS, 788
    NAME, 286, 788
    REL, 788
    REV, 788
    SHAPE, 788
    TARGET, 788
    TITLE, 788
    URN, 788
<ABBREV> HTML tag, 789
  attributes
    CLASS, 789
    DIR, 789
    ID, 789
    LANG, 789
ACCEPT attribute (<INPUT> HTML tag), 821
ACCEPT-CHARSET attribute (<FORM> HTML tag), 810
access counters, Web pages, 540-541
accessing Webmasters on home pages, 168
<ACRONYM> HTML tag, 789
  attributes
    CLASS, 789
    DIR, 789
    ID, 790
    LANG, 790
ACTION attribute
  <FORM> HTML tag, 490, 810

  forms output format, CGI scripts, 558
  <ISINDEX> HTML tag, 823
add-on HTML editors, 701-702
adding horizontal lines to HTML documents, 125-127
<ADDRESS> HTML tag, 790
  attributes
    ALIGN, 790
    CLEAR, 790
    DIR, 790
    LANG, 790
    NOWRAP, 790
addresses
  domain names, 13, 24-25, 33
  e-mail, 13-14
    specifying for document links, 145
  FTP sites, 20
  Gopher sites, 22
  HTML elements, 131
  IP, 34
    Web server requirements, 40
  see also URLs
Adobe Web site, 55
Adobe Acrobat Web site, 55
advanced guestbook CGI script, code listing, 591-594

H

Complete and Return this Card
for a *FREE* Computer Book Catalog

Thank you for purchasing this book! You have purchased a superior computer book written expressly for your needs. To continue to provide the kind of up-to-date, pertinent coverage you've come to expect from us, we need to hear from you. Please take a minute to complete and return this self-addressed, postage-paid form. In return, we'll send you a free catalog of all our computer books on topics ranging from word processing to programming and the internet.

Mr. ☐   Mrs. ☐   Ms. ☐   Dr. ☐

Name (first) ☐☐☐☐☐☐☐☐☐☐☐☐   (M.I.) ☐   (last) ☐☐☐☐☐☐☐☐☐☐☐☐☐☐☐☐☐☐☐

Address ☐☐☐☐☐☐☐☐☐☐☐☐☐☐☐☐☐☐☐☐☐☐☐☐☐☐☐☐☐☐☐☐☐☐☐

☐☐☐☐☐☐☐☐☐☐☐☐☐☐☐☐☐☐☐☐☐☐☐☐☐☐☐☐☐☐☐☐☐☐☐

City ☐☐☐☐☐☐☐☐☐☐☐☐☐☐☐   State ☐☐   Zip ☐☐☐☐☐ ☐☐☐☐

Phone ☐☐☐ ☐☐☐ ☐☐☐☐   Fax ☐☐☐ ☐☐☐ ☐☐☐☐

Company Name ☐☐☐☐☐☐☐☐☐☐☐☐☐☐☐☐☐☐☐☐☐☐☐☐☐☐☐☐☐☐☐☐

E-mail address ☐☐☐☐☐☐☐☐☐☐☐☐☐☐☐☐☐☐☐☐☐☐☐☐☐☐☐☐☐☐☐☐

1. Please check at least (3) influencing factors for purchasing this book.

Front or back cover information on book .... ☐
Special approach to the content .... ☐
Completeness of content .... ☐
Author's reputation .... ☐
Publisher's reputation .... ☐
Book cover design or layout .... ☐
Index or table of contents of book .... ☐
Price of book .... ☐
Special effects, graphics, illustrations .... ☐
Other (Please specify): _____ ☐

2. How did you first learn about this book?

Saw in Macmillan Computer Publishing catalog .... ☐
Recommended by store personnel .... ☐
Saw the book on bookshelf at store .... ☐
Recommended by a friend .... ☐
Received advertisement in the mail .... ☐
Saw an advertisement in: _____ ☐
Read book review in: _____ ☐
Other (Please specify): _____ ☐

3. How many computer books have you purchased in the last six months?

This book only .... ☐   3 to 5 books .... ☐
2 books .... ☐   More than 5 .... ☐

4. Where did you purchase this book?

Bookstore .... ☐
Computer Store .... ☐
Consumer Electronics Store .... ☐
Department Store .... ☐
Office Club .... ☐
Warehouse Club .... ☐
Mail Order .... ☐
Direct from Publisher .... ☐
Internet site .... ☐
Other (Please specify): _____ ☐

5. How long have you been using a computer?

☐ Less than 6 months   ☐ 6 months to a year
☐ 1 to 3 years   ☐ More than 3 years

6. What is your level of experience with personal computers and with the subject of this book?

	With PCs	With subject of book
New	☐	.... ☐
Casual	☐	.... ☐
Accomplished	☐	.... ☐
Expert	☐	.... ☐

Source Code ISBN: 0-7897-0758-6

7. Which of the following best describes your job title?

Administrative Assistant .... ☐
Coordinator .... ☐
Manager/Supervisor .... ☐
Director .... ☐
Vice President .... ☐
President/CEO/COO .... ☐
Lawyer/Doctor/Medical Professional .... ☐
Teacher/Educator/Trainer .... ☐
Engineer/Technician .... ☐
Consultant .... ☐
Not employed/Student/Retired .... ☐
Other (Please specify): _____ ☐

8. Which of the following best describes the area of the company your job title falls under?

Accounting .... ☐
Engineering .... ☐
Manufacturing .... ☐
Operations .... ☐
Marketing .... ☐
Sales .... ☐
Other (Please specify): _____ ☐

9. What is your age?

Under 20 .... ☐
21-29 .... ☐
30-39 .... ☐
40-49 .... ☐
50-59 .... ☐
60-over .... ☐

10. Are you:

Male .... ☐
Female .... ☐

11. Which computer publications do you read regularly? (Please list)

_____
_____
_____
_____
_____
_____
_____
_____
_____
_____

Comments: _____
_____
_____

Fold here and scotch-tape to mail.

Before using any of the software on the disc, you need to install the software you plan to use. If you have problems with the NETCD95, please contact Macmillan Technical Support at (317)581-3833. We can be reached by e-mail at **support@mcp.com** or by Compuserve at **GO QUEBOOKS**.

Read This Before Opening Software

By opening this package, you are agreeing to be bound by the following:

This software is copyrighted and all rights are reserved by the publisher and its licensors. You are licensed to use this software on a single computer. You may copy the software for backup or archival purposes only. Making copies of the software for any other purpose is a violation of United States copyright laws. THIS SOFTWARE IS SOLD AS IS, WITHOUT WARRANTY OF ANY KIND, EITHER EXPRESS OR IMPLIED, INCLUDING BUT NOT LIMITED TO THE IMPLIED WARRANTIES OF MERCHANTABILITY AND FITNESS FOR A PARTICULAR PURPOSE. Neither the publisher, nor its dealers and distributors, nor its licensors assume any liability for any alleged or actual damages arising from the use of this software. (Some states do not allow exclusion of implied warranties, so the exclusion may not apply to you.)

The entire contents of this disc and the compilation of the software are copyrighted and protected by United States copyright laws. The individual programs on the disc are copyrighted by the authors or owners of each program. Each program has its own use permissions and limitations. To use each program, you must follow the individual requirements and restrictions detailed for each. Do not use a program if you do not agree to follow its licensing agreement.